Political Theologies

Political Theologies

PUBLIC RELIGIONS IN A POST-SECULAR WORLD

Edited by HENT DE VRIES

and LAWRENCE E. SULLIVAN

FORDHAM UNIVERSITY PRESS   NEW YORK   2006

"On the Prepolitical Moral Foundations of a Free Republic," by Pope Benedict XVI ©
2006 Libraria Editrice Vaticana

Copyright © 2006 Fordham University Press

Library of Congress Cataloging-in-Publication Data

Political theologies : public religions in a post-secular world / edited by Hent de Vries
    and Lawrence E. Sullivan.
        p.   cm.
    Includes bibliographical references.
    ISBN-13: 978-0-8232-2644-3 (cloth : alk. paper)
    ISBN-10: 0-8232-2644-1 (cloth : alk. paper)
    ISBN-13: 978-0-8232-2645-0 (pbk. : alk. paper)
    ISBN-10: 0-8232-2645-X (pbk. : alk. paper)
    1. Political theology.   I. Vries, Hent de.   II. Sullivan, Lawrence Eugene, 1949–
BT83.59.P65   2006
201'.72—dc22
                                2006032059

Printed in the United States of America
08 07   5 4 3 2
First edition

Contents

CONTENTS

Preface

Hent de Vries and Lawrence E. Sullivan

The age of globalization, as we seem destined to regard it, confronts us with more ironies than sources of clarity. The apparent triumph of Enlightenment secularization, manifest in the global spread of political and economic structures that pretended to relegate the sacred to a strictly circumscribed private sphere, seems to have foundered on an unexpected realization of its own parochialism and a belated acknowledgment of the continuing presence and force of "public religions" (the term is José Casanova's).

As Nobel laureate for economics Joseph Stiglitz notes, "A particular view of the role of government and markets has come to prevail—a view which is not universally accepted within the developed countries, but which is being forced upon the developing countries and the economies in transition."[1] Even in the Western world, the prevailing model for the organization of political and economic life, representative or parliamentary democracy, and the capitalist enterprise have come under increasing pressure from a variety of social and cultural movements whose religious origins and overtones are more and more difficult to ignore. Both the model of limited governance in political liberalism, with its corollary conception of civil society (implying religious freedom and tolerance), and the unstoppable engine of globalization find their match in spreading expressions of discontentment and resistance, which are often articulated in *theologico-political* terms. But does this make them necessarily "religious"? Or were the pillars of sovereign power not from the outset theologico-political, if not mythico-religious, at core, just as the engines that continue to drive the forces and interests of economic exchange, their real and virtual monetary flows, have, as Max Weber was the first to realize, affinities with mental dispositions fostered by certain conceptions of faith and belief? Should we (still or again) study current tendencies in society and politics with reference to the tradition called "the religious"? Or is that tradition merely an epiphenomenon of larger empirical processes, which need no reference to transcendent-transcendental motifs and motivations in order responsibly to be explained and engaged?

The rigid boundaries, once imagined to be universal, with which the Enlightenment sought to separate the public sphere of political processes from private commitments to the values inculcated by religious and spiritual traditions have come to be a focus of mounting opposition. In the most poignant cases, expressions of "religion" inform or orient resistance by the supposed beneficiaries of globalization to pressures from without to modernize, rationalize, democratize, liberalize, individualize, and (hence?) secularize, integrate culturally and politically, and ultimately assimilate. A renewed and ever more desperate appeal to the separation of church and state and the neutrality of the public domain, with its institutionalized agnosticism, seems unlikely to be a successful counter to such resistance. After all, the resistance is often benign enough, de facto enrichment of our understanding and experience of the common good, despite the widely, indeed excessively, mediatized cases in which it becomes dangerous and a threat to the security of all. Against this, to raise the chant of secular humanism, resolute atheism, the religion of secularism, or the sacredness of *laïcité* seems no more than whistling in the dark, vainly hoping that the specter of "religion," roaming like a zombie, dead-alive, through the political landscapes of the modern world, will go away (again). A different form of political, legal, cultural, and even psychological accommodation may need to be envisioned.

The modern critique of religious conviction—focused on theological truth- and normative claims by churches, councils, or charismatic leaders, which sought to speak about the ordering of society with unanswerable authority and in universal terms—now appears utterly misplaced. It seems to have missed the point or, perhaps, just to have done too little too late. Religious authority and power seem, in what has, rightly or wrongly, been called the "information age" or "network society" (Manuel Castells) to be manifest (revealed?) and effective in increasingly diffuse and globally mediatized and marketed, some would say commodified, ways, for good and for ill. The legal barriers of separation, once the salutary and defining characteristic of modern democracies, seem to be contested both de jure and de facto in hitherto unimaginable and, indeed, undesirable ways. Even policymakers in the West have come, if only recently, to understand this. "It is clear," aver Harlan Cleveland and Mark Luyckx, in a recent policy study prepared for the European Commission, "that the wall between religion and government is now so porous as to be an unreliable guide to attitudes and actions."[2]

It is time to take stock of this development, which has its chances as well as its perils. But that complex task can only be undertaken in a collective effort, aided by intellectual tools and interdisciplinary methods and inquiries that historically, culturally, conceptually, analytically, even ontologically and metaphysically reach beyond the equally urgent interrogation of pragmatic issues in the politics of the everyday, governments and nongovernmental bodies, national and international law, social policy and diplomacy, or social critique and cultural exchange. Yet such an ambitious assertion poses more questions than it answers. In what precise ways do the claims of religious belief—concerning words and gestures, powers and things—exert pressure on structures of governance? What implications do theologically imbued justifications of substate and interstate violence—that is, of terror and "just war"—have for the credibility of religious traditions in much-needed attempts to reshape patterns of representation and structures of authority, social cohesion and cultural integration? Do the teachings of the world's faith traditions a priori support or undermine the political institutions and economic markets that arise through globalization (or that enabled it to take on massive proportions)?[3] Can the resurgent interest in "political theologies" offer any insights to the scholarly approaches now being employed to examine globalization's historical and contemporary effects?

These questions, and others following from them, were debated during a three-day conference entitled Political Theologies: Globalization and Post-Secular Reason, in Amsterdam in June 2004. This gathering was the culmination of a collaboration between the Center for the Study of World Religions (CSWR) at the Divinity School of Harvard University and the Amsterdam School of Cultural Analysis (ASCA) at the University of Amsterdam. Lawrence E. Sullivan (at the time Director of CSWR) and Hent de Vries (at the time Director of ASCA) headed the project, and it was jointly funded by the Netherlands Organization for Scientific Research (NWO), the CSWR, and ASCA. The 2004 gathering built upon two preceding conferences from the same project—in Amsterdam in June 2001 and at Harvard in May 2003. The present volume offers a selection from the papers read and discussed during the three conferences, as well as essays solicited afterward in order to strengthen its overall historical and analytical breath and the depth of its combined perspectives.

When this collaborative effort was first discussed, in 1997–98, *political theology* was a term seldom heard in the wider academic debate, beyond historical references to the writings of Ernst Kantorowicz, Carl Schmitt, and "theologies of liberation." In the years since September 11, 2001, however, the concept has become so relevant a focus of interest that similar conferences have blossomed at other universities. The present volume will, we hope, widen the number of people who can benefit from the research and ideas debated during the conferences. Given the range of the questions brought up and left open, it should both resonate with other collective interdisciplinary endeavors that have long been underway and offer correctives and directions to the wave of more recent interest in the domains of religion and the political.[4]

We would like to thank our host institutions, the University of Amsterdam and Harvard University, as well as NWO, for their generous support. We would like to extend a special word of gratitude to Dr. Eloe Kingma, Managing Director of ASCA, Mark D. W. Edington, at the time Senior Administrator at the CSWR, who drafted a memo on whose wording we have freely drawn for this preface, and Rebecca E. Kline, the CSWR's Events Coordinator. We would also like to acknowledge the financial support of the Johns Hopkins University's Zanvyl Krieger School of Arts and Sciences and its Dean of Research and Graduate Education, Professor Eaton E. Lattman, and of the University of Notre Dame.

Our grateful thanks go to Jeff Fort, Eduardo Mendieta, and Fr. Joseph T. Lienhard, S.J., for vetting translations of the essays by Jean-Luc Nancy, Jürgen Habermas, and Pope Benedict XVI, respectively. Thanks, too, to Neil Hertz, who has allowed us to use his remarkable photographs of Baltimore on our display pages.

Without the indefatigable energy, sustained support, and editorial skills of Helen Tartar, Editorial Director of Fordham University Press, the publication of this volume could not have succeeded. We are immensely grateful for her wise counsel and persistent effort in bringing this project to a good end.

HdV & LS, Baltimore-Amsterdam-South Bend May 2006

Political Theologies

Introduction

Before, Around, and Beyond the Theologico-Political

Hent de Vries

What has happened to "religion" in its present and increasingly public manifestation, propelled by global media, economic markets, and foreign policies as much as by resistance to them? How should we understand the worldwide tendencies toward the simultaneous homogenization *and* pluralization of our social and cultural practices, that is to say, of our individual and shared forms and ways of life? To answer these questions, we must interrogate a complex and shifting semantic, axiological, and imaginative archive, whose historical origins and modern disseminations have pragmatic ramifications for burning contemporary issues of the political (*le politique*) and politics (*la politique*), of commerce and exchange, of economics and law. In doing so, we will touch upon the legal separation and accommodation between church and state, the freedom of religion, and the professed confessional-ideological neutrality of government and the public sphere. But our questions also concern issues of pluralism and social cohesion, the quest for identity and the need for integration, respect for others (that is to say, for their beliefs and values), as well as the liberty in principle to express oneself (albeit in ways that others may perceive as idolatrous, blasphemous, or offensive in nature).

Religion's reassigned place and renewed function in the public domain may owe their contours to the very theological traditions and practices, the systems of thought and sensibilities, whose authority they seek to curb or hold in check and whose explicit or subterranean workings—in words, things, gestures, and powers—we have hardly begun to comprehend. To open or, rather, reopen an inquiry concerning religion's engagement with the political (i.e., with its very concept and its conceptual analogues, such as sovereignty, democracy, etc.), as well as with politics (i.e., in its juridical, administrative or policy-oriented, national, and international aspects), is the aim of this volume.

1

Before investigating the term *political theology* and the reasons for its pluralization, we should begin by asking: What in fact, in its very definition, is this phenomenon we so easily call "religion"? With that generic term, we not only invoke monotheisms but suppose that we identify cultic and cultural objects, together with accompanying individual and collective dispositions.[1] How should we conceptualize "religion"—realizing that, in order to avoid abstraction, we ought perhaps to begin by saying "religion*s*," in the plural, given the notional, ethical, figurative, and rhetorical complexity, including the different ideational systems, corporeal senses, and overall affects, expressed by the religious idiom and by religious imagery? To this equation we should also add "religion's" irreducible, if often ignored, materiality, as well as its increasingly mediatized performance, that is to say, its now troubling, then promising forms of authority, sovereignty, and empowerment. In other words, how should we approach such basic analytical and descriptive categories as its words, things, gestures, and powers, which offer points of entry into this elusive yet stunningly manifest phenomenon, which at once inspires and terrifies—even terrorizes—civil society, that is to say, the domain of public life, as it traverses the political, politics, and policies, whether we like it or not, for good and for ill?

More specifically, what *pre-*, *para-*, and *post-*political forms do religion and its functional equivalents and successor beliefs or rituals assume in a world where the global extension of economic markets, technological media, and informational networks have contributed to loosening or largely suspending the link that once tied theologico-political authority to a social body determined by a certain geographic territory and national sovereignty? Is a disembodied—virtual, call it transcendental—substitute for the theologico-political body politic thinkable, possible, viable, or even desirable? A *corpus mysticum*, as it were, in a new, post-secular guise? Or might we eventually dispense with reference to the theologico-political and the religious archive on which, in all its transformations (including secularist ones), it continues to rely for genealogical, conceptual no less than rhetorical-strategic, reasons? And what forms—in Emmanuel Levinas's idiom, what "curvatures"—would its functional equivalents or structural analogues impose upon the limits and enabling conditions of our "social space," that is to say, upon the unique and singularly experienced as well as the shared times of our lives, if not in community or even friendship, then at least by way of a "living together," whose contours are less fixed than ever (as Jacques Derrida taught us in his last writings)?[2]

These questions are relevant when discussing contemporary religion in the public domain or "public religions in a post-secular world" (echoing José Casanova's *Public Religions in the Modern World*), especially if one understands the term *post-secular* not as an attempt at historical periodization (following upon equally unfortunate designations such as the "post-modern," the "post-historical," or the "post-human") but merely as a topical indicator for—well, a problem. In the words of Hans Joas: "'Post-secular' . . . doesn't express a sudden increase in religiosity, after its epochal decrease, but rather a change in mindset of those who, previously, felt justified in considering religions to be moribund."[3] Joas analyses the term in a critical discussion of Jürgen Habermas's work, where it designates the situation in which a nation-state, paradoxically, "counts on the continuous presence of religious communities in a continually secularizing society."[4] A society is "post-secular" if it reckons with the diminishing but enduring—and hence, perhaps, ever more resistant or recalcitrant—existence of the religious. In this view, a second interpretation of the term *post-secular* is possible, one that stresses less a change in the societal role of religion than a different governmental or public perception of it: "'Post-secular' doesn't mean, then, an increase in the meaningfulness of religion or a renewed attention to it, but a changed attitude by the secular state or in the public domain with respect to the continued existence of religious communities and the impulses that emerge from them."[5] In such a reading, what undergoes transformation is less the nature of the secular state, let alone its constitutional arrangements guaranteeing, say, a separation between church and state, but rather the state's "secularist self-understanding."[6] Needless to say, it is far from clear what kind of "self-understanding" might come to substitute for the secularism (or "secular fundamentalism") of old, not least because the phenomenon on which the post-secular condition reflects—namely, religion's persistent role—is increasingly difficult to grasp conceptually and to situate empirically. Strictly speaking, neither the locus of "self" (often implying self-identity and self-determination) nor that of "understanding" (with its now cognitivist, then historicist, culturalist, and hermeneutic overtones) can be of much help where religion and the theologico-political are concerned.

Here, let it suffice to mention just one reason for this predicament. Religion and the theologico-political (like so many historical, social, cultural, and political words, things, gestures, and powers) tend to show a Janus face. Religion, at least in its present-day public manifestations, reveals a dual possibility, for better and for worse. Moreover, it does so at once intelligibly (for reasons that we can make perfectly transparent) and obscurely, miraculously (that is to say, inexplicably, driven by causes, forces, or affects that escape us, whether in principle or just for now). A potential source of inspiration and democratic openness, it simultaneously—inevitably?—presents a danger of dogmatism and hence of closed societies and mentalities. As Derrida suggests, its striving toward perfection (or perfectibility) and its tendency toward perversion (or, more precisely, "pervertibility") go hand in hand. Religious orthodoxies of all stripes seek to interpret the latter possibility or virtuality as external to themselves—and, by extension, as inessential to their theologico-political project. They portray these aberrations as idolatry, blasphemy, apostasy, heresy, scandal, or offense.

But what if one belongs to the other and does so necessarily, as a standing possibility, a danger that must—indeed, ought to—be risked? Then it is important to ask how this double, potentially duplicitous, and often deeply contradictory or even treacherous— terrorist or rogue—tendency emerged in the first place. What historical articulations and interpretations has it received? What chances and perils does it (still or yet again) hold in store? Finally, what new possibilities might it set free, create, or open up, for us or for others, known and unknown? Could one address such questions concretely, with existing and alternative national, inter- and non-governmental policy orientations in mind?

Timely Considerations?

The conference that provided the core papers of this volume examined interrelationships between the political, economic, and cultural characteristics of the "age of globalization," on the one hand, and the vision of society and structures of governance developed over millennia by major faith traditions, as well as by supposedly less systematized indigenous traditions, on the other. That such an undertaking has about it an element of urgency cannot be doubted, in view not only of 9/11 and subsequent attacks in Madrid and London but also—more broadly and perhaps, in a longer view, more importantly—of religiously informed resistances and responses to pressures to secularize and to assimilate in cultural and political terms. These resistances and responses are implicit in the continuing sources of tension and conflict between the self-proclaimed secularism of the West and its allies, on the one hand, and the self-perception of developing, often postcolonial, societies with their state-sponsored, popular, or alienated fringe political movements, on the other.

The West still imagines developing societies and underprivileged communities and individuals to be inevitable beneficiaries of globalization, of its markets no less than its cultural goods, its constitutional democracy as well as its interpretation of human rights. In the end, if somewhat indirectly, they very well may be. But these societies' present place in a hegemonic world ruled by imbalances in power, news, money, and markets is a source of permanent frustration, indeed, of humiliation and contention. This has repercussions for internal relationships in Western nations, with their significant immigrant communities, no less than for the establishment and maintenance of international law. The recent dramatic difficulties with policies of integration and accommodation in European countries (for example, in France and the Netherlands, whose respective political troubles are extensively discussed in this volume), as well as the recent escalation in the Middle East of hostilities between Israel and the Palestinian authority (Hamas) and Hezbollah in Lebanon. So is the immobility, not to say paralysis, of European governance in dealing with its internal affairs, to say nothing of the inability or unwillingness of the international community to enforce an immediate end to reiterated acts and crimes of war or to guarantee minimal assurances for security, justice, and peace for all.

To illustrate that, sadly, the studies of political theologies collected here are all too timely, let me refer to the example of "political Islam," especially the much-debated danger represented by dispersed militant movements. Having emerged in the wake of globalization, after the failure of so many of its state-based and "secular" nationalist projects, these groups are at times merely virtual, then again all too real in their operation as "cells" and informal, ad hoc "networks." What has emerged in some of the more careful scholarly and journalistic analyses of this phenomenon is the need for a theoretical matrix that also has relevance for engagements of religion with the political and politics (or vice versa) in major religions other than Islam, such as Christianity, Judaism, Hinduism, and Buddhism. Since many of the current troubles have little to do with Islam per se—other major and minor religious and nonreligious traditions and sensibilities are potentially just as entangled with the question of the political and of politics as it presents itself globally today—we might expect such a theoretical matrix also to illuminate some of the developments and prospects of secularism. The phenomenon of secularism constitutes more than a modern public religion in disguise, which some have accused it of being, but its implication in our conception of the political and in our formulation of policies follows a logic similar to that of political, public religions in the modern world. The theoretical matrix we are seeking should thus be able to encompass religious and nonreligious or secular systems of thought, practices, and other modes of expression. Its central concepts and insights should hold for religious communities or groups that are numerically smaller than the major religions, just as it should offer indirect lessons, if not for the policies of governments and international institutions or nongovernmental organizations as such, then at least for the intellectual and affective dispositions with which their representatives approach religions in a post-secular world. This being said, let me now turn to our example and discuss some of its implications.

The Western fixation on political Islam is unfortunate but consequential, not least since it is echoed and amplified in the United States, where in some influential circles a caricature has taken hold, that of an emerging "Eurabia" or "Londonistan," the mirage of an "ever-growing Muslim-Europe-within-Europe—poor, unassimilated, and hostile to the United States."[7] In this hyperbolic view—which in the words of a respected European journal, *The Economist*, looks very like "scaremongering"—a fatal process would seem to be unfolding: "Stagnant Europe, goes the argument, cannot offer immigrants jobs; appeasing Europe will not clamp down on Islamo-fascist extremism; secular Europe cannot deal with religiosity (in some cities more people go to mosques than to churches). Europe needs to study America's melting pot, where Muslims fare better."[8] Just as it downplayed the Soviet threat during the Cold War and let ethnic cleansing rage in the Balkans, Europe this time around lacks both the socio-political flexibility and the moral stamina to "either give the newcomers a decent economic life or to confront extremism successfully."[9] In the final analysis, so the narrative concludes, this political-cultural weakness runs aground not only in "a godless continent's failure to understand the depth of other people's faith" but in an apparent inability or unwillingness to give quite the same public space to the culture of free speech as is characteristic of the United States.[10]

Demographically, economically, and culturally these negative and slightly resentful assessments may soon prove false. The Muslim inhabitants of the European Union constitute an estimated 15 million, or 4 percent of the total population, a figure that is expected to rise to 30 million, or 10 percent, by 2025, not taking into account Turkey's eventually joining the E.U. By contrast, the current estimated figures for the U.S. and Canada are 1.7 percent and 2.3 percent, respectively. Moreover, the fear of an emerging "Eurabia" ignores the vast economic and cultural differences between immigrant populations in the different European countries—and between these and the U.S. Moreover, references to "Eurabia" simultaneously overestimate and underestimate the present force of the political elements and forms of Islam—and other major and minor religions. The fact that religions constitute both an integrative and a potentially disintegrating or even violent aspect of modern societies has to do less with persistent or newly emerging ties to nation and traditional doctrine and law than with a novel configuration of post-secular identities, whose volatile dynamics contain as much promise as potential for political havoc. To begin to acknowledge and then interpret this built-in ambivalence of religion in relation to the very definition of the political, as well as to concrete politics or policies, may well be a key to the understanding and mitigation, if not anticipation or prevention, of religion's most pernicious effects.

If there is any lesson to be drawn from the more extreme—and heavily mediatized— phenomena of violence inspired or framed by religion, it is that the relationship between the theological and the political is no longer obvious, let alone direct. Previously limited to problems of national sovereignty (pitting the Holy Roman Empire against the princes, stipulating religious allegiance based upon one's belonging to a given territory) or of constitutional law (the separation of church and state, the ban on "conspicuous religious signs" in public schools in France and Turkey), the most interesting and troubling cases of religion's continuing and renewed role at present are more elusive, more delocalized and hence difficult to grasp, both conceptually and empirically. We are left with blanks and dots (that is to say, words, things, gestures, and powers)—the very stuff of utterances and affects (both passive and active, destructive and salutary)—which we continue to attribute to "religion," as if we knew what that means. The ways these disarticulate and reconstellate themselves as the elementary forms of political life in the twenty-first century are no longer transparent, nor can they be reduced to simple empirical (naturalistic or, philosophically speaking, immanent) terms. Rather, for all their this-worldly, indeed, down-to-earth impact, they place great demand on our theoretical skill, even our speculative imagination and sensibilities, in reading not so much the transcendent as the absolute: that which tends to loosen its ties to existing contexts (including the context or text of "existence," hence of ontology, onto-theology, and its substitutes). New concepts need to be coined, novel practices of research attempted, even though they may turn out to be—may even need to be—out of sync with the phenomena in question (and hence untimely in their intended timeliness). Such is the life of the mind. At least for now.

. . .

To return to our example, the contemporary political and public presence of "religion" seems no longer dependent upon—or especially effective through—broad popular, let alone democratic support (although such is, of course, not excluded either, as is witnessed by the victory of Hamas in the January 2006 Palestinian elections, just as it is further illustrated by the success of ideological-nationalist, left- and right-wing populist movements in Venezuela, Poland, and elsewhere). The journalistic and scholarly debate concerning the exact meaning and impact of public religions in the post-secular world (of the theologico-political, that is) has remained fragmentary and disoriented. The reasons for this impasse are not difficult to determine. For one thing, it seems as if the more challenging issues raised by these public religions address a multidimensional space and time *before*, *around*, and *beyond* the "theologico-political," at least in its ancient, medieval, and modern definition, even though no plausible account of current transformations can ignore the historical archive for which this term, with its many semantic connotations, visual associations, rhetoric, and affects, still stands. That the most burning political issues are not so much directly but indirectly—some would say, tangentially or negatively— related to the "theological" can already be glimpsed in the unforeseen ways in which the subject of "religion" has entered the contemporary public domain and debate, nationally and internationally.

"Religion," in its more concrete and abstract, local and global determinations is perceived as a "problem" to which policy- and opinion-makers, social and political scientists, cultural critics and philosophers, media theorists and economists tend to direct their attention with either increasing fascination or barely veiled irritation. Yet the phenomenon manifests itself in more and more ethereal ways—elusive and ab-solute, but then also quite visceral. It is upon this paradox, if not aporia, that the contemporary presence and often virulence of "religion" (of its words, things, gestures, and powers) is premised. No longer a given, it cannot simply be given up, either, not even by the most persistent—and supposedly enlightened—of its detractors. The post-secular condition and its corresponding intellectual stance consist precisely in acknowledging this "living-on" of religion beyond its prematurely announced and celebrated deaths. While it increasingly escapes pre-established contexts and concepts, horizons and expectations, it nonetheless takes on an ever more ghostly appearance. In order to track its movements, new methodological tools and sensibilities are needed.

For this "retreat" yet "permanence" of "religion" and the theologico-political (to echo titles coined by Jean-Luc Nancy, Philippe Lacoue-Labarthe, and Claude Lefort[11]), several complementary explanations could be given. They include the fate of metaphysics in the philosophical and cultural discourse of modernity, especially the critical onslaughts on *metaphysica specialis* or *theologia naturalis*, the overcoming of "onto-theology" on which Heidegger mused, and the symbolic interpretation of the "popular metaphysics" with which Schopenhauer, not unlike Spinoza, equated historical and revealed or positive religion (that is to say, superstition). More material trends, having to do with the development of markets and the fortune or failure of nation-states, have contributed to the deterritorialization, delocalization, mediatization, and even virtualization of religion, together with the invention of new forms of agency and community. No unified theory is currently available to hold these trends together in a compelling explanatory account or historical narrative. No political theology, in the singular, ever will. But several building blocks can be discerned along the road leading up to the post-secular condition, as the contributions to this volume testify.

· · ·

The geographical and demographic-sociological base of physical struggle inspired or at least verbally legitimated by religion—*no religion without (at least some) violence, no violence without (at least some) religion*[12]—is characterized by an increasingly delocalized, deterritorialized, and volatile mobility. The beliefs and theological rationalizations that motivate spectacular forms of violence against states and civilians need no longer take hold in the minds and hearts of whole groups and generations—and general stoicism, if not resignation, may well be the dominant public response. Yet the elusive effects of such militant religious manifestations and the terror associated with them have come to permeate the life of all institutions and to affect the substance of legal systems, political hopes, and cultural sensibilities, well beyond the borders in which they are committed and out of all proportion. How should we explain this discrepancy? And how can citizens, nongovernmental organizations, and nations respond to it in a responsible and effective way? Is there a policy of and for the unpredictable and the disproportional?

Clearly, the "war on terror"—or any other version of military preemption and judiciary, let alone para- or extra-legal, repression—cannot be it. Sweeping gestures invoking labels such as "global terrorism" (or "terrorists of global reach") and a "global war on terror" are no more helpful, since they cling to an outdated concept, "war," and fail to specify the—often "local"—conditions and special effects to which the adjective *global* refers.[13] Other approaches are required, ones that can engage local issues of legal, political, economic, and cultural integration or dialogue, though *without any certainty*, whatever other ills they may undo, that they can identify a single, now moving, now immobile—in any case, invisible, inaudible, ungraspable, and often unintelligible—target. Can such approaches be learned and taught, let alone be planned or institutionalized? Where the proclaimed "enemy" has no clear strategy other than inflicting terror and provoking wrath, can one develop strategies? And without them, what would the political be? Where the perceived threat turns out to elude the state apparatus's horizon of expectation, is there anything left *to do*? Or is acting and reacting no longer the proper modality of response? Where diplomacy is not an option, is one condemned to respond either too little, too late, or in a disproportionate way? A whole new art of conducting war and establishing peace—something other than war and warfare, peace and peacefulness in their traditional definitions, based upon the existence of and dealings among states and sovereigns—seems needed, together with a different attunement to nonstate actors and actions whose sensibilities, passions, and affects obey a logic and rhythm that eludes the modern understanding of data, numbers, cause, and effect.

Has the theologico-political tradition prepared us for that task? Has the time come for it to release its critical potential? Or is its legacy part of the problem, merely symptomatic of the present difficulty in thinking about the political, politics, and policies in altogether different terms, perhaps by turning toward what lies beyond, before, and around them? This task may be more challenging than the appeal to what recent "progressive realists," in search of an alternative to the impasses of American liberalism, on the one hand, and neoconservatism, on the other, have called "moral imagination," putting oneself in the shoes of the other political actor.[14]

More often than not, we now realize, minimal, seemingly negligible differences and differentiations, whether ideational, sociological, or organizational, can cause maximal effects (whether enormous havoc, countless blessings, or both), whereas, conversely, maximal investments in, say, lofty ideas or excessive economic or military power too often result in minimal or virtually no effects at all. Indeed, these maximal investments may very well, in their expansion and promulgation, revive or provoke the minimal differences whose larger—but structurally elusive—effects unsettle the distribution of forces and resources that state-regulated social and cultural policies, market-inspired measures, or high-tech military strategies had sought to bring about in a comprehensive and controlled manner, whether by piecemeal engineering or in a single stroke.

This paradoxical tendency obeys a logic that one may be tempted to analyze as a "dialectic of Enlightenment" (as Theodor W. Adorno and Max Horkheimer argued), as the paradox of Western rationalization (as Jürgen Habermas, following Max Weber, added), or as the performative contradiction of universalism (as Judith Butler, Ernesto Laclau, and Slavoj Žižek have insisted in more psychoanalytically informed ways). The difference matters little for present purposes. What remains important is to rethink and, as it were, reframe these paradoxes and aporetics in terms that are suitable for the novel problems and challenges that face us at present. How is one to ponder the imponderable, manage the unmanageable? And what experiences or sensibilities are most likely to prepare us for this increasingly difficult—and, we might add, eminently political, perhaps quintessentially theologico-political—task?

This question has become all the more difficult to answer because in the present, post-secular domain the inspiration, motivation, and effectuation of political theologies no longer lie within the cultural and institutional, ecclesial or communal heritage of the major religions or within the modern forms of political sovereignty with which their theologically (or cynically) driven politics were, historically, geographically, empirically, and conceptually linked. Instead, their authority (to the extent that it still, or once again exists) resides in infinitely mediated and refracted forms of "make believe" (call them special effects), which are in many ways elements of "belief in the making." Indeed, they, more than anything else, are the wonders and miracles—sometimes the "shock and awe"—of the contemporary world.

The very shrinkage and evaporation of the doctrinal substance of historical religion may propel the remainder of its believers into rhetorical overdrive—a whistling in the dark that becomes shriller as fewer and fewer give heed—just as the staunch defense of self-proclaimed Western Enlightenment values (whether in the name of a "clash of civilizations," *laïcité*, tolerance, militant humanism, or political liberalism; the difference matters little) may find itself adopting a no less troublingly devout and often even "apocalyptic tone" (irrespective of its professed atheism, humanism, materialism, naturalism, skepticism, or immanentism).[15] In a latest twist of the dialectic of Enlightenment, of the paradox of universalism, secularism might find itself to have become sacral—and, as "secular fundamentalism," even parochial—while the so-called religious fundamentalisms of the world continue to express and further the very disenchantment of the modern world against whose vehicles (global markets, media, hegemonic political models, economic liberalization, and cultural liberties) they believe they protest. Religion, in its most dramatic and terrifying, even terrorist forms could thus be seen as the flipside of modernity, not just in the "age of extremes," but, in this century, in the hyperbolic effects of exponential growth, the expansion and displacement of populations, the movement of capital and ideas, the spread of democratic ideals—in short, of openings and closures alike.

Olivier Roy sees one consequence of "deterritorialization" as being a paradoxical "congruence between contemporary Islam and Christianity," which lose nothing of their potential for conflict and confrontation even as they disarticulate and reconstellate themselves in the same geographical spaces, becoming contemporaries and cohabitants in a increasingly global realm.[16] On the contrary, he writes, even as they "become closer" they "become more antagonistic, precisely because they are no longer separated by linguistic and territorial borders."[17] In other words, "globalization does not necessarily imply moderation."[18] Where we are all more or less the same, the need to manufacture differences, to create and stigmatize "others," may become a temptation, one easily susceptible to political exploitation. The psycho-sociological, possibly even biological mechanisms of mimetic rivalry, aggression, and a death drive, visible in larger groups and nations, may well first emerge in small disaffected factions and cells that can seem to constitute themselves out of the blue, parting ways with the familial, parental, and religious-cultural environments into which they had heretofore blended, gray on gray.

A case in point is violent jihadism, which, as international investigations and polls repeatedly demonstrate,[19] finds little overall support among Muslim populations in predominantly Muslim countries and entertains a complicated relationship with the internal colonies of immigrant communities in the West. The special report "Muslim Extremism in Europe," published in the aftermath of the July 7, 2005, London attacks, which killed fifty-two victims (and the four bombers) and which, while not unexpected, struck the intelligence community, political elites, and the general public because of their home-grown, suburban origins,[20] gives important indications of how jihadism is a product of globalization and its vehicles (markets, modern secularism, and media).[21] The report makes two related claims, both of which illustrate the changing meaning of national sovereignty and the redefinition—one is tempted to say the virtualization and perhaps even profanization—of the theologico-political. First, it suggests that "in an age of globalized communication and porous borders, there is no real distinction between domestic and foreign threats." Indeed, it continues: "Even if everyone involved in terrorizing London turns out to have been British-born [as turned out to be the case], it is clear that the bombers had access to sophisticated explosives, not easily available in suburban Yorkshire; and, more important, that they were influenced by ideas, images, and interpretations of Islam that would continue to circulate electronically, even if every extremist who tried to enter Britain were intercepted." Second, profiling the suspects of the London attacks revealed a pattern: disaffection with the home country, familial authority, local community, and mosque often preceded petty criminalization, conversion, and reterritorialization, as it were, in what is often a merely *virtual* group of like-minded, radicalized individuals, which establishes itself through the Internet and which—when effective guidance by experienced veterans from actual battlegrounds is finally found—may or may not coalesce into an ad hoc death squad that dissolves (through suicide, arrest, or flight) after the fateful action has been undertaken.

In "The Ideology of Terror," Roy observes that what inspires this religious violence has, in the end, little to do with circumscribed local conflicts, often of a postcolonial nature (say, Israel/Palestine, Bosnia, Chechnya, Kashmir, Afghanistan, Iraq, Indonesia, or Somalia).[22] Rather, it is characterized by a process he calls the "delinking of Islam as a religion from a given culture—from any given culture."[23] He stresses the striking modernity—including the increasing irreality—of the ideological outlook of Islamic militancy. It cannot, he suggests, be adequately captured in terms of "fundamentalism," "Islamism"—that is, the "movement that conceives of Islam as a political ideology"[24]—or *intégrisme*, but instead acquires near-phantasmatic features, which are increasingly difficult to read, let alone respond to. Not mechanistically linked to such causes as geopolitics in the Middle East or the publication, on September 30, 2005, of cartoons of the Prophet Muhammad by the conservative Danish journal *Jyllands Posten*,[25] these relatively spontaneous acts of violent rebellion lack a political aim that could merit the title of a strategy, an agenda, or a concerted effort to change or reform anything in and of this world. If there is any communitarian aspiration in militant jihadism or Islamism, it is, Roy suggests, one of virtual belonging, a belonging without belonging, an identitarianism without identity, a communality without community.

Pointing out that the 9/11, Madrid, and London bombers were not from regions directly affected by the conflict in the Middle East and were often "Western-born converts to Islam," Roy makes a further observation: "What was true for the first generation of Al

Qaeda is also relevant for the present generation: even if these young men are from Middle Eastern or South Asian families, they are for the most part Westernized Muslims living in or even born in Europe who turn to radical Islam."[26] Their imagination of belonging to a worldwide community of believers finds its ground not in deeply ingrained participation in the daily life of traditional families, groups, or mosques in the West, let alone in their countries and cultures of origin, but in their increasing alienation from both.

Roy compares their "dream of a virtual, universal ummah" not with Muslim history in general (as historians such as Bernard Lewis had somewhat ominously suggested) but rather with the fantasies of a "world proletariat" and "Revolution" that inspired the terrorist movement of the ultra-left in the 1970s, notably the Baader-Meinhof Group in the Federal Republic of Germany, the Red Brigades in Italy, and the Japanese Red Army.[27] Like the jihadists, these groups had no clear (or particularly effective) strategy other than acting out what they perceived to be a universal—a global and near-cosmic—conflict, to which their response was one of theatrical or almost ritual behavior (acting out or "performance violence"). As Roy notes: "The real genesis of Al Qaeda violence has more to do with a Western tradition of individual and pessimistic revolt for an elusive ideal world than with the Koranic conception of martyrdom."[28] It is not even the case, he adds, that "most present-day conflicts involve Muslims"; rather, it would be more appropriate to say that "most conflicts that are of interest to the West involve Muslims. . . . But clearly few of these conflicts involve Islam as such, even if the reference to Islam contributes in the aftermath to reshaping these conflicts in ideological terms."[29]

Roy's position is ultimately based upon the assumption that "politics" prevails over the religious—as well as over its metaphysical understanding and inflection of "the political"—so that political Islam must necessarily fail. Roy calls this its "becoming commonplace," "being integrated into politics," and suggests that political Islam has "'social-democratized' itself." Indeed, in its very appeal to Muslim law or *sharia*, it does not invent "new political forms" but is "condemned to serving as a mere cover for a political logic that eludes it—a logic in which we ultimately find the traditional ethnic, tribal, or communal divisions, ever ready to change their discourse of legitimization, hidden beneath the new social categories and regimes."[30] Roy goes so far as to claim that political Islam or Islamism "is no longer a geostratic factor; it is at most a societal phenomenon."[31] The "illusion" of its supposed fundamentalism, that of a "return" to a purer origin, is, like such movements in all religions, above all a reaction to the failure of other models. Roy singles out three: secularism, Marxism, and nationalism, all of which reflect a broader spectrum of "symptoms of state crises": "Islam is not a 'cause.'"[32] With the revolutionary moment gone, Roy draws a sober conclusion: "Only the rhetoric remains."[33] Yet this *diminished* role of religion in its ontological—or onto-theological—weight does not exclude its *continued* appeal as a semantic, axiological, figural, and, indeed, theologico-political archive and resource. Roy sees in this circumstance the reduction of political Islam to a culturalized and individualized—a marketed and mediatized—notion of religiosity. But other interpretations might be possible. Might religion, precisely in its minimal remainder—despite or thanks to being elusive, erratic, volatile, and virulent—be all the more able to produce maximal effect? And to do so for good and for ill, as historical circumstance, fate, and luck allow?

Political Islam shares its "failure"—in a sense, due to the success of its accommodation—with other claims to political authority, indeed, with the theologico-political concept of sovereignty as such. Wherever it engages in down-to-earth concerns of governance and policy, law and order, it cannot but secularize—that is to say, ultimately render profane—its ways. The ways of politics are the ways of the world. One cannot but be *of this world*, that is, come to belong *to this world*, as soon or as long as one is *in this world*, in other words, as soon or as long as history and human finitude follow their course. *The Economist*'s special report gives a concrete example:

> In the municipal politics of Britain and the Netherlands, some radical Muslims quite often find themselves doing political business with other anti-establishment groups on the secular left, to the dismay of older immigrants. During a recent contest in east London, the candidate for the new Respect party—a young Muslim lawyer—was chided by his co-religionists for sharing a platform with homosexuals. But Abdurahman Jafar held his ground: "We want equality for Muslims and we would seem insincere if we didn't stand together with other minorities who face discrimination." The rhetoric that emerges from this sort of politics in a variety of European countries is not always attractive to American ears, since one of the few common denominators between angry Muslims and secular leftists is hostility to America. But, given a choice between pious self-segregation and plunging into public affairs, many European Muslims are choosing the latter. . . . A process of political assimilation is, hesitantly but visibly, taking place. This will change the politics of Europe. It may affect Europe's relations with the outside world. But, in the process, Muslims also change—and perhaps settle into their homelands as comfortably as most American Muslims have done.[34]

In also assuming this general trend, Roy approaches Gauchet, who, in *The Disenchantment of the World*, albeit from a different genealogical and a more philosophically based perspective, claims that the role played by religion proper (in Roy's formulation, "Islam as such") is, in the modern world, basically over.[35] While Christianity, for Gauchet, is instrumental in its own demise—being "the religion of the end of religion"—Islam, or at least political Islam, undermines its own stature the more successful, that is to say, the more globalized and mediatized, it becomes.

Roy draws another conclusion, which seems at once to exculpate *and* to implicate religion (and hence the theologico-political) as a determining factor. He takes his observation to imply that "the key to understanding the contemporary 'territorial' struggle is nationalism and ethnicity, not religion. Two factors give Islam a *post hoc* importance: the reciprocal rationalization of some conflicts in religious or civilizational terms, and the growing deterritorialization of Islam, which leads to the political reformulation of an imaginary *ummah*."[36]

In this view, radical jihadism is merely the contemporary successor form of an internationalist struggle, taken up by marginalized youths from Muslim immigrant communities (or, in a few cases, by converts) for whom the old leftist movement—or, for that matter, present-day antiglobalization movements—are no longer available options. We are thus dealing with "a 'modern' coalition of 'negative' and radical forces whose roots are not in the Koran but in a Western tradition of a 'red-brown' confusion, which has recently been given some green brushstrokes by Islamic radicals."[37] This conjunction has everything to do with the influence of popular culture and the role of media:

> the fault-line between Europe and the Third World goes through Muslim countries, and former spaces of social exclusion in Western Europe are partly inhabited by Muslims at a time when the radical Marxist Left has disappeared from them. But a closer look shows that these antagonistic identities are less entrenched in the actors than "played" by them. The Islamization of the French suburbs is largely a myth: youngsters are fascinated by Western urban youth subculture (baseball caps, hamburgers, rap or hip hop, fashionable dress, consumerism).[38]

Indeed, he notes, we should understand that in the outburst of rioting in fall 2005 in destitute neighborhoods and slum-suburbs (*cités* or *banlieus*) of Paris and other French cities there was "nothing particularly Muslim or even French," and that the phenomenon was merely "the temporary rising up of one small part of a Western underclass culture that reaches from Paris to London to Los Angeles and beyond."[39] The insight that those involved were second-generation immigrant (and male) youth of French citizenship, who were burning property (cars, schools, gymnasiums, etc.) belonging to their own communities in a self-destructive response to unemployment and racism, economic and social exclusion, with a counter- or subcultural gusto whose model stems from Western urban centers rather than from the rioters' Arab or African countries and communities of origin, inspired *New York Times* columnist David Brooks to see in it a tragic paradox of global hegemony: the fact that the pop- or counterculture of gangsta rap and hip hop, with its accompanying "poses of exaggerated manhood," by now defines "how to be anti-American."[40]

This being said, the local detail of the events in France and their context in the everyday lifeworld were barely reported by the media (an exception being the work done by the blogger-reporters on location in Bondy for the Swiss journal *L'Hebdo* and by a new generation of scholars in France who align themselves under the ambitious title "La Nouvelle Critique Sociale").[41] What apparently stuck in viewers' and readers' minds was yet another instance of a seemingly inevitable clash of religions (or, rather, of religion, notably Islam, on the one hand, and the "religion of secularism, or *laïcité*," on the other). This perception, however, is largely a media-induced effect.[42]

If deterritorialization and deculturalization are keys to understanding urban unrest, well-intended appeals to multiculturalism are not of much use in addressing contemporary religious violence. In Roy's words: "In the end, we are dealing here with problems found in any culture in which inequities and cultural differences come in conflict with high ideals . . .—the struggle to integrate an angry underclass is one shared across the Western world."[43] This is not to say that jihadists are not recruited under such conditions. But other forms of violent destructiveness—aptly documented, long before the events of 2005, in Mathieu Kassovitz's 1995 film *La Haine*—may be more prominent (not least of them sexual violence against women within the suburban communities themselves).

As in the case of the Bondy blog, the role of new media, notably the Internet, in this constitution of contemporary identities is not exclusively that of social and psychological isolation, compensated by a merely virtual, phantasmatic, and disembodied community of likeminded souls. Another and more surprising tendency can be observed.

Shortly after the beginning, on July 12, 2006, of new hostilities between Hezbollah and Israel, which soon involved missile launches into Israeli cities and relentless bombardments by Tsahal on southern Lebanon and Beirut, it was widely reported that Israeli and Lebanese bloggers established or kept open lines of communication with personal observations and video images concerning events and developments on the ground that largely escaped the official media of television and the printed press, to say nothing of official channels of diplomatic exchange and military propaganda. Not for the first time, though in a significant international conflict—and for worldwide Internet users to witness directly—citizens refused to play by the rules laid down by states and semipolitical factions, armies, and ideological movements. They are helped by an informational network (the Internet) that is decentralized and allows no (simple or direct) control. Israelis consulted Lebanese blogs and vice versa, and both sides expressed themselves—for example, on the blog of a certain Ramzi ("Ramzi blah blah")—thus maintaining a dialogue, finding mutual sympathy otherwise frustrated, and preventing the war and its victims (most of them civilians) from being anonymous. But would attempts to personalize or singularize the effects of war—rendering them visible, audible, palpable through media that are no longer simple instruments of propaganda in the hands of governments and organizations (as happened during the Balkan wars, as well)—make it easier one day to interrupt or mitigate its violence?[44] It is clear that in affluent societies and emerging economies (China, India, and several countries in Southeast Asia and Latin America) new technological media—the Internet and the relatively recent phenomenon of personal participatory media such as blogging, text and instant mobile phone messaging—are already dramatically transforming the mass media industry, as well as the socio-cultural and political landscape as a whole, albeit not everywhere with the same intensity, pace, and consequences.[45] Time will tell whether and how this process will shape third-world regions. Could cheap and easily maintainable computers, laptops with instant access to the Internet—which are currently being designed by MIT's Media Lab under the direction of Nicholas Negroponte (the brother of John Negroponte, former ambassador to the U.N. and at present the national director of U.S. intelligence)—change the face of the earth, with its inequalities in income, health, education, and democratic powers?[46] Or can this dream—some twenty-five years after the invention of the personal computer (of which approximately one billion are currently in use around the world, albeit unequally distributed)—be fully realized only with newer, cheaper, and more easily accessible digital technologies, such as "pocket computers" in the form of, say, mobile phones or "handsets with simple web-browsers, calculators, and other computing functions"?[47]

We might be witnessing a transition paralleling that from the technology of movable type introduced in 1448 by Gutenberg, via mass media production, through the Internet and beyond (the blogs, etc.), whose general features will be those of generalization, intensification, and trivialization: a transition from undivided sovereignty (one nation, under God[48]) to a multiplication and diversification of the theologico-political that simultaneously echoes, produces, and expresses not only transformations in the so-called first, second, and third worlds but also the remarkably swift shift from the bipolar world of the second half of the twentieth century, through the unipolar episode of American supremacy after the fall of the Berlin Wall in 1989, to a more complicated and volatile twenty-first-century multipolar world, characterized by the rise of non-Western nations, international corporations, nongovernmental organizations, regional and ethnic movements, the emergence and multiplication of new countries, and, increasingly, nonstate actors, networks, and so on—most if not all of them invoking "religion" as a referent. The undeniable promises of this development, given the unprecedented sharing of power and information, communication tools and publicly heard opinions, it implies, are overshadowed only by its perils:

> Developments in technologies with violent potential mean that very small groups of people can challenge powerful established states, whether by piloting an aeroplane into the World Trade Center in New York, targeting a missile at Haifa, taking on the military in Iraq, bombing the London underground, or squirting sarin gas into the Tokyo subway. Developments in information technology and globalized media mean that the most powerful military in the history of the world can lose a war, not on the battlefield of dust and blood, but on the battlefield of world opinion. . . . The net effect of these very disparate trends is to reduce the relative power of established Western states, above all the U.S.[49]

The British journal *The Economist*, in its yearly outlook, predicts changes in the multipolar world in these terms:

By 2026, China's economy will be bigger than America's, and India's will be much larger than that of any individual European country (Russia, Brazil, and Indonesia will not be far behind). The press will be full of articles about "Asian values" and the "Beijing consensus." As these countries develop, so will their voracious appetite for natural resources and human capital. . . . But even the biggest powers will be vulnerable. The privatization of destruction—with computer nerds able to wreak havoc from the bedroom and terrorists able to buy weapons of mass destruction in a global market—will allow groups of individuals to take on nation-states. This vulnerability may encourage "defensive imperialism": powerful countries taking over states to prevent them from serving as bases or breeding grounds for hostile groups. As economic might shifts from the north and west to the south and east, so will cultural power. The rise of al-Jazeera and Bollywood already means that the world no longer looks at things overwhelmingly through American eyes. Ancient civilizations like China and India will become more self-confident and will project their own ideas onto concepts such as democracy, freedom, and the rule of law.[50]

The introduction of more and more actors on the geopolitical stage seems to clash with an international order whose ideals and institutions, forms of cooperation and conflict, dreams of peace and declarations of war, were for at least a century premised upon the primacy of nation-states and the explicit formulation and official guaranteeing of their bi- or multilateral agreements. In short, the rules of the game have dramatically changed, and all drawn into it make up the rules as they go along.

Recent surveys suggest that identities online succeed in reaching out to members of different faith-based or ethnic groups more often and more easily than was previously assumed. So-called allochthonous and autochthonous youth, a Dutch report claims, overcome social and cultural segregation in virtual forums, in which religion, the relation between the sexes, and homosexuality—all subjects on which they are likely to disagree with their parents or educators—are the topics of the day. "The Internet is good for integration," a Dutch newspaper quipped on its front page, noting that more than 80 percent of Turkish, Moroccan, Antillean, and Surinam youths communicate—albeit it virtually—with peers from different ethnic backgrounds, whereas only 20 percent limit themselves to their own groups, shunning *kaaskoppen* ("cheese heads," as Dutch autochthonous people are unflatteringly called).[51]

The reports in question also find that more than half those interviewed present themselves as someone different on the Internet from who they are in "real" life. And one might argue that integrating verbally, perhaps even visually (through webscams, etc.) is not quite the same—or at least not as demanding and promising—as integrating as bodies in space that do or do not "get along." Is virtual coexistence, being mindful of others who may be other still than one thinks (and not necessarily present themselves in their true identity) a way of coming to terms with the otherness of others, a way of learning to live with the skepticism concerning "other minds," as Stanley Cavell might say? But it should not be forgotten that the medium in question also gives rise to more disturbing phenomena, such as mob "Internet hunting" and "Internet wars."[52]

In his recent *Market Islam*, Patrick Haenni claims that, since the second half of the 1990s, political Islam and radical jihadism are slowly but steadily being overcome by strategies of engagement and accommodation centered less on the state (the nation, the *ummah*), let alone on violence and terror, than on more subtle promises of economic achievement. The ensuing "'theology of prosperity' announces a new *Muslim pride*, which no longer passes through armed confrontation or affirmation of an ostentatious piety, but via performance and competitiveness."[53] Haenni observes that a management- and bourgeoislike individualistic culture of "*free riders*" of islamization, an emphasis on the powers of "*positive thinking*," is emerging, to be substituted for past disappointments concerning the restitution of the Caliphate and the general introduction of *sharia*—in short, a "neo-liberal politicization of Islam," which, ironically, resembles the agenda of "faith-based initiatives" and "compassionate conversation" of the American Republican Party more than anything else.[54] No longer focused on acquiring power in the nation-state and shunning the Jacobin (but also Marxist and Keynesian) models of intervention-ist policies in state-sponsored socialist and welfare states, the new practice of "market Islam" puts its money on reforming mores in "civil society."

This development goes hand in hand with tendencies in recent Islamic global invest-ment and private banking in the Middle East and in Malaysia, Singapore, and Indonesia, operating in compliance with the requirements of *sharia* (which bans usury, the charging of interest on loans, and all commercial transactions having to do with alcohol, tobacco, and gambling), while attempting to provide competitive returns (such as *sukuk*, or nonin-terest rent on revenue). Since February 2006, the Singapore stock exchange lists a "Shariah 100 Index," which covers Asian banking and trading indexes that comply with traditional law.[55]

Tracking the disillusionment of former Muslim Brotherhood militants, notably in Egypt, both in conversation and on the Web site islamonline, Haenni sees an aspiration to turn away from pyramidical hierarchies toward "operating in networks."[56] Its result will be a "multipositioned" engagement, which no longer aspires to a global political agenda for Islam but opts instead for a variety of managerial (antiglobalist, ecological, feminist, cybercultural, etc.) local interventions, whose overall effect will be that of a "new mental universe," based upon "bricolage."[57] Again, this new agenda would seem to be carried out by individuals rather than movements, brotherhoods, or small groups and cells. They are typically well integrated, oriented toward self-realization, and weary of great global causes. Its guiding concepts are that of a nonviolent "civil jihad" or even an "electronic jihad" (or "hacktivism," also meaning, it should be added, taking out anti-Islamist sites).[58]

While this process takes shape, other tendencies and potentialities may emerge, presenting threats that must be assessed and politically addressed. Jihadists, in Roy's view, share a tendency with other religious terrorists (such as the Hindu Tamil Tigers) and also some Third-Worldist movements to engage in what Mark Juergensmeyer, in his seminal *Terror in the Mind of God*, calls "performance violence," an acting out in which political calculation is less prominent than the desire to make a statement in the eyes of the world and to draw perceived enemies into a conflict of "cosmic" proportions. As Roy aptly notes: "Osama bin Laden has no strategy in the true sense of the word. . . . His aim is simply to destroy Babylon."[59]

Rather than being merely retrograde or reactive, the jihadists' expressions of religious extremism are thus, Roy concludes, ways of mimicking and superlatively outbidding—and, in that sense, directly getting back at—what are perceived to be hegemonic Western economic, political, and cultural principles and trends: "The Western-based terrorists are not the militant vanguard of the Muslim community; they are a lost generation, unmoored from traditional societies and cultures, frustrated by a Western society that does not need their expectations. And their vision of a global ummah is both a mirror of and a form of revenge against the globalization that has made them what they are."[60]

It has been suggested that—fueled by repeated and nightmarish Western lapses, which can be indicated by such proper names as Guantánamo Bay, Abu Ghraib, Hadhita, and now Qana)—jihad is becoming a "global fad," which, like other counter-cultural expressions, "feeds" on the lurid images readily provided by the Western media (as well as al-Jazeerah, the Internet, etc.), shaping a generation whose fascination seems increasingly that of "making war, not love."[61] Jessica Stern argues that "among many Muslim youth, especially in Europe, jihad is a cool way of expressing dissatisfaction with a power elite that is real or imagined; whether power is held by totalitarian monarchs or by liberal parliamentarians."[62] In other words, jihad is in the process of becoming "a millenarian movement with mass appeal," whose narratively constructed "identity of victimhood" is constantly being reinforced by damaging images, that is to say, by "facts, or at least pictures that appear to be facts."[63] Beyond real-life issues in Europe and the Middle East (i.e., immigration, occupation, and terror), the conflicts in question express—and require—a battle for an "idea, not a state": "Military action minimally visible and carefully planned and implemented may be necessary to win today's battles. But the tools required in the long run to win the war are neither bombs nor torture chambers. They are ideas and stories that counter the terrorist narrative—and draw potential recruits away from the lure of jihad."[64]

After the dismantling of its traditional geographical bases in Afghanistan and Pakistan through U.S.–led military intervention, Al Qaeda has virtually regrouped in the intractable realm of the Internet. Its members are dispersed in some four thousand different Web sites, leaving Western intelligence communities with the dilemma of either targeting and, where possible, destroying them or leaving them intact in order to monitor them and so pick up possible announcements of things to come or learn to discern nuances of "disagreement" and "inner cleavages" (e.g., concerning the legitimacy, from the viewpoint of Islam, of violence against Muslims or "noncombatant non-Muslims") that might help efforts to "broaden gaps" within these Internet communities.[65] As with all technological monitoring, there are structural—logical-mathematical—difficulties in doing so, even beyond the question of allocating financial and other resources.[66]

Whereas the U.S. seeks to contain the war on terror by localizing it abroad in specific territories (first Afghanistan, then Iraq)—thereby, paradoxically, producing the very territorial base for terror that, in the case of Iraq, was previously lacking—the online jihadists dream of unleashing or at least staging a global, indeed, cosmic conflict, which would have no geographical boundaries or concretely envisioned terms of political (let alone diplomatic) resolution. In fact, it now seems just as unlikely that the Bush administration will stop identifying, taking on, and thereby unintentionally creating potential geopolitical threats against its perceived economic interests, democratic ideals, and cultural values as it is unrealistic to assume that militant jihadhism would tone down its rhetoric (and put down its arms) the moment that Western forces were to withdraw from Islamic holy grounds. In the meantime, inflammatory and inflated words and gestures, along with a brandishing of things and powers, continues unabated. There is no end to conflicts that one does not—and, for identitarian reasons cannot—want to end or whose possible victor one cannot realistically imagine oneself to be one day.[67]

These processes, in which on all sides the "masters of war" (Bob Dylan) get the upper hand, obey a relentless logic of "escalation," which *Le Monde*, in a telling editorial concerning the most recent war in Lebanon, summarized as follows: "It is tempting to believe that military logic, when it reaches a certain level of escalation, has become a fatality. Nonetheless, nothing in this conflict is uncontrollable. Israel, like Hezbollah, acts in a considered and determined manner, even though both might have been surprised by the amplitude of the enemy's reaction."[68] Political theology might well become the discipline of studying and eventually mastering such "escalation," that is, the excesses of sovereignty and their violence, as well as the rhetorical overdrive with which they are accompanied, ideologically justified, and irresponsibly spiced up.

. . .

One could be tempted to follow Spinoza, who in the *Ethics* supplements his earlier views, developed in the *Theologico-Political Treatise*, with a theory of the passions, more precisely, of the imitation of affects—of reciprocal, near-specular affect-effects (or effect-affects)—in which individual (and, by extension, also socio-political) bodies, all of which are composite, mimic, rival, and seek to outbid each other quasi-mechanically, quasi-machinally, quasi-automatically. He writes: "If we image a thing like us, toward which we have had no affect, to be affected with some affect, we are thereby affected with a like affect. . . . This imitation of the affects . . . is nothing but the desire for a thing which is generated in us from the fact that we imagine others like us to have the same desire" (*Ethics* III, Prop. 27 and Scholium).

According to this conception of a comparative "differential genesis of affects," these bodies mirror each other *necessarily* or *constitutively*, hence their necessary mutual dependency, even sociality. But, just as inevitably, they do so *to their own detriment*, hence their strife, antisociality, and perpetual relapse into the state from which they had only just emerged, with great difficulty—and by the same mechanism—the state of nature, that is to say, of the war of all against all.[69] Spinoza's view, we are reminded by several commentators, finds its radical modernity in precisely this relentless exposure of the composition and decomposition of bodies in the body politic, of subjects and citizens, which breaks with the traditional Aristotelian-Thomist assumption of an intrinsic possibility of spontaneous sociability that enables humans to take leave of nature and to turn—by way of a pact—to a civil state.

If much of modern philosophy consists in demolishing the foundations of natural theology, Spinoza adds an extra twist by deconstructing the *natural political theology* upon which both traditional-hierarchical and modern-contractual theories of natural right (such as Hobbes's) remained built. The risk of relapsing into the state of nature—widely acknowledged by the theoreticians of the social contract—does not depend, in this view, on specific individuals who are, as it were, "rotten apples." For Spinoza, on the contrary, entry into a pact (and a peace) is *from the outset* compromised, tainted, indeed, poisoned, because it is necessarily feigned, that is to say, an act not so much of promise as of pretense. As Pierre-François Moreau writes, for Spinoza:

> It matters little whether people are good or bad; by the simple game of their everyday life, by the functioning of their bodies and of the passions of the soul that are their corollary, they become enemies of the state. Civil war and the destruction of the state are not a *risk*, but *the necessary horizon* of the appearance of society. . . . Spinoza is the only one [of the seventeenth-century theoreticians] who explains why it is *necessary* that it not function. He therefore completely inverts the theoretical landscape of the theoreticians of the pact. For him, the question is not what are the hindrances to sociability laid down by the pact, but to push anti-Aristotelianism to the point of saying that not only is there no originary sociability but, moreover, there is no derived sociability, either. The antipolitical character of individuals exists in their nature before the pact and persists in their nature after the pact: the reasons that explain why there was a state of nature remain the same once civil society is instituted. . . . The Spinozistic problem, properly speaking, will consist in asking how to set backfires in the passions [*contre-feux passionels*] to the apocalypse that perpetually menaces the state. If the ruin of the state is not the exception but the norm, how does it come to be that there are states that subsist?[70]

The imitative expression of the affects anticipates some of Spinoza's later views in the unfinished *Tractatus Politicus*, which seeks a solution for the perpetuation—even the "eternity," that is to say, the internal causation—of the state's stability in a "play" of "counter-balance" and "counterweights."[71] Spinoza's problem is thus less that of the "constitution" (foundation, institution) of the state than of its "victory over the forces of destruction, once it is constituted."[72]

What emerges in Spinoza is a deeply paradoxical—indeed, aporetic—account of the structural nature of opposition, which, in political life (in and between states or federations of states) can take the form of antagonism and agonism, competition and commerce, the dogmatic suppression or the free expression of ideas, just as in social life it can lead to envy, contempt, and allergy, according to a self-destructive tendency that Derrida terms "auto-immunity," by which he means the disturbing biological possibility that "a living organism destroys the conditions of its own protection," in other words, that the body "destroys its proper defenses or organizes in itself . . . the destructive forces that will attack its immunitary reactions."[73]

Spinoza conceives of destructive forces and affects on the basis of a "universal model of poisoning": "internal, immunal affections are the forms by means of which we become conscious of ourselves, of other things, and of God, from within and eternally, essentially." The reverse tendency can also be discerned: "what is bad should be conceived of as an intoxication, a poisoning, an indigestion—or even, taking account of individuating factors, as an intolerance or an allergy."[74] The latter process, Deleuze explains, can have dire consequences:

> the modification can be such that the modified part of ourselves behaves like a poison that disintegrates the other parts and turns against them (in certain diseases and, in the extreme case, suicide). The model of poisoning is valid for all these cases in their complexity. It applies not only to the harm that we suffer, but to the harm that we do. We are not only poisoned, we are also poisoners; we act as toxins and poisons.[75]

Since in Spinoza this dynamic between two or more individual and social bodies is quasi-automatic and quasi-mechanical (as if billiard balls were hitting each other, with the same amount of energy maintained), one wonders whether and how novelty, that is to say, creativity and innovation, difference and repetition (plus change), can ever arise. How, in this perspective, is asymmetry produced, let alone maintained (as clearly it is, for good and for ill)? Is this because energy (appetite, desire, *conatus*) transfers from one body to the next (and, although sometimes only partially, back)? Perhaps, but it would seem that excess, gift, the event—again, difference and repetition—have no place here. Or is the dynamism, indeed, the automaticity, also quasi-spiritual, meaning that what appears, under one aspect of Nature (or God), to be merely mechanical exchange of force reveals itself, under another aspect, to be an expression of something else—concerning thought, the life of the mind, and ultimately a *scientia intuitiva*, a third kind of knowledge that is an *amor Dei intellectualis*, as well? But, then, are affect-effects new merely to the extent that *no* expression of Nature or God is simply identical with any other, that is to say, with what immediately precedes or eternally coexists with it?

Furthermore, does Spinoza's model manage to regulate the meaning and dynamics of the theologico-political in its "differential genesis of affects"? Or does the theologico-political elude and resist—that is to say, absolve itself from—this quasi-automaticity and quasi-mechanicity? Does the theologico-political allow and create, reveal and evoke some multidimensional space and time before, around, and beyond the imitation of affects and its logic by which all composite bodies are determined? Is there a minimal room for resistance to the order of things, whose "effects"—again, without intrinsic, sufficient causes—may nonetheless have maximal consequences of an altogether different nature, testifying to an altogether other God: a god, perhaps, no longer "contaminated" by but "otherwise than Being and Essence" (as Levinas would say)?

This being said, Spinoza's account of the imitation of affects may help explain why attempts by the state and, nowadays, increasingly by nonstate actors to generate ideological (and often theologico-political) counterforces—through press conferences, media releases, deliberate leaks, and horrific Internet video (of beheadings, etc.), all special effects, of sorts—are all too easily interiorized as affect-effects without intrinsic, sufficient causes that would enable them to harmonize with us and be of objective, reasonable interest. In other words, these effects infuse—indeed, poison—us with a subjective mindset that once (Spinoza claims) informed superstition, namely, the belief in miracles.

Even (or especially) the most cynical, down-to-earth engineers of "make-believe" seek to transform ideas into articles of faith, or at least belief in the making, and hence aspire to produce what traditionally was perceived to be a wondrous event. Miracle workers and believers, on the one hand, and newsmakers or spinmasters, together with their audiences, on the other, thus seem to operate in nearly identical ways.[76] Such is the fate of the post-secular world, where political conflict has become a perpetual, self-generated "battle of perceptions," enabled—indeed, produced—by omnipresent media that echo in the streets of capitals worldwide.[77]

A graffito, found in an unremarkable Parisian street in July 2006, seems to say it all. Perhaps because of the origin of the word *assassin*,[78] the anonymous writer may call to mind the newly unleashed violence in the world, in the midst of the fighting between Israel and Hezbollah in Lebanon—if this is indeed the reference. No one can know, not least because the words may be ascribed to the joker or clown beneath whose face they have been written. At least one other anonymous author, presuming to see what the graffito speaks of, has glossed: "So you love Bush?"

Why is the praised assassin paired or identified with some triad of events or persons, being the latest in a series of "III"? If the repeated vertical lines are not to be taken as incomplete exclamation marks, is the allusion to, say, Lebanon, coming after Afghanistan

23

FIGURE 1   Parisian graffito: "I love the assassin.
He who kills us and he who makes us dream." "So you love Bush?"

and Iraq? Or to Ehud Olmert, coming after George W. Bush and Tony Blair? Or, supposing that the anonymous author sympathizes with the West or with Israel, is the indirect name-calling that of Sheik Hassan Nasrallah, the leader of Hezbollah, coming after Osama bin Laden, and Abou Moussab Al-Zarkawi, one of his self-appointed deputies, assassinated by American troops in Iraq?[79] Or is the reference to an adult movie or an interactive video game, given that both exist under the title "Assassin III"? There is no way to tell. The anonymous gloss "So you love Bush?" may have gotten things wrong, just as we may have overinterpreted (or not interpreted well enough).

Indeed, we may be eagerly anticipating meaning and message where there is none: here, a call to arms or—by acting out such a call in front of our eyes—its indirect, as it were negative-dialectical denunciation. *Omnis determinatio negatio est*: every determination, to vary Spinoza freely, allows, implies, and requires (its) negation. To state things as clearly as this writing on the wall does—that is to say, perversely, given that most people don't tend to love killers, while keeping ambiguity intact—might already dispel their worst potential, and do so miraculously, as a special effect in its own right.

To articulate all this with the help of Spinoza means rewriting a certain idea of transcendence (the notions, dimensions, or experiences with which "religion" and the "theologico-political" are most often identified) in the language of immanence, associated with the history of atomism, materialism, naturalism, and pantheism. The latter traverses the history of thought as a heretical countercurrent, of sorts. Yet this rewriting also implies interrogating the historical and systematic pertinence of the very distinction and opposition between transcendence and immanence, as well.

Beyond this ontological—and, ultimately, metaphysical—hypothesis, one could return to the original theologico-political question and ask: Where and how did this fatal dualism, if not manicheism, of two supposedly separate and antagonistic realms—an opposition that contains the seeds of its better alternative—first enter the historical world in its theologico-political guise? In antiquity, the Middle Ages, or modernity, including today's uni- and multipolar worlds? And what are its perils and chances for contemporary and future democracy, for an openness associated with tolerance and hospitality, with the flourishing of human rights as well as with novel possibilities for the living together of bodies and minds, peoples and cultures, animals and things? The four consecutive parts of this volume are devoted to shedding light on these questions.

What, Then, Are Political Theologies?

Systematically and traditionally, the concept of "political theology" connotes, as Jan Assmann suggests in *Authority and Salvation: Political Theology in Ancient Egypt, Israel, and Europe*, the "ever-changing relationships between political community and religious order, in short, between power [or authority: *Herrschaft*] and salvation [*Heil*]."[80] Yet its contemporary range and implications reach further and encroach upon the central questions of political philosophy and political theory, in its comparative anthropological, sociological, economic, and juridical varieties, from which its original metaphysical impetus must also be distinguished. In addition to theorizing "the political," "political theology" also enters into relationship with urgent questions of daily "politics," without, of course, being immediately (or fully) rendered (or contradicted) by them. Precisely this irreducible tension will interest us throughout; it signals this tradition's continued recalcitrance—as if, so far, nothing could really substitute for it.

Historically, the term *political theology* dates to Marcus Terentius Varro (116–27 B.C., who is discussed by St. Augustine in *The City of God* (cf. 4.27 and 31). Varro speaks of the Stoic tripartition of theology (*theologia tripertita*), in which a political theology (*theologia politikē*) is juxtaposed with mythical (*mythikē*) and cosmological (*kosmikē*) theologies. In Varro's Latin, the distinction is between *theologia civilis*, *fabularis*, and *naturalis*, each of which applies to a different sociological or cultural group: namely, the priests, the poets, and the philosophers.[81]

After Varro, the term *political theology* disappears, even though its idea continues to work subterraneanly throughout a long history of political thinking, as reconstructed by Ernst H. Kantorowicz in his classic *The King's Two Bodies: A Study in Medieval Political Theology*.[82] Between Varro and the medieval jurists studied by Kantorowicz lies an influential scholastic tradition inspired by Francisco Suárez and others.[83] The term resurfaces in the title of a treatise by Daniel Georg Morhof, *Theologiae gentium politicae dissertatio prima de Divinitate Principium*, published in Rostock in 1662, in the title of Simon van Heenvliedt's *Theologico-politica Dissertatio*, of the same year, and in Spinoza's *Tractatus Theologico-Politicus*, published anonymously in 1670. In Spinoza's oeuvre the term is a *hapax legomenon*, however, and his unfinished *Tractatus Politicus* avoids the term.[84]

As Jacqueline Lagrée suggestively notes in her discussion of the historical context and reception of the *Tractatus Theologico-Politicus*, the precise meaning of the composite expression *the theologico-political* remains a matter of debate. Referring to the tradition leading up to Spinoza, she asks:

> how should one understand the coordination of the two adjectives *theological* and *political*? As a conjunction or as a distinction? As a subordination—and in which sense—or as interdependence? Five positions are logically possible, without taking into account the nature of the possible link—analytical or synthetic, contingent or necessary:
>
> 1. conjunction by simple juxtaposition (Plato?)
> 2. strict separation (epicureanism)
> 3. subordination of the political to the theological (Jewish theocracy or strict Calvinism)
> 4. subordination of the theological to the political (Hobbes)
> 5. interdependence (between natural religion and a democracy favorable to the freedom of thought).[85]

But the complexity of the relationship between the two terms goes deeper. Are they distinct, interchangeable, alternative, parallel, polar, complementary, or supplementary? The genealogical and structural correspondences between these apparently at least conceptually or terminologically separable domains requires extended analysis, to which the essays in this volume, as well as this introduction, are merely modest contributions, scratching the surface of a vast but far from homogeneous "social space," open on all sides yet characterized by multidimensional "curvatures" where the question of "religion" as a relation to the other/Other but also to all other others opens up before all knowledge and freedom, initiative and deliberation (as Levinas suggestively showed).

Apart from the singular occurrence of the term in Spinoza, another modern articulation of the theologico-political can be discerned in the motif of the "omnipotence of God" and its Hobbesian translation.[86] Since the "radical Enlightenment" (to use Jonathan Israel's provocative ascription of Spinoza's influential role throughout Europe at the time) there have been still other ways to trace to religious sources the concepts of the political, authority, the law, and sovereignty, including the state's prerogative of violence, in particular, war. Even where these political concepts tended to be defined in down-to-earth terms, in the wake of a seemingly irreversible "disenchantment of the world" (to use Max Weber's expression), their formal features and fundamentally ontological weight continued to be invested in—indeed, produced by—the very religious tradition whose historical privilege they sought to overcome or at least to hold in check.[87]

In the following, I will draw out the most important elements of these traditions in order to provide some relevant historical and systematic background to the diverse studies collected in this volume. This will require, as the title of this introduction suggests, shedding light on what has preceded or escaped (or might yet come to exceed) the theoretical matrix and practical delimitations of "political theology." I will ask what constitutes the origin and dissemination as well as the *homogenization* and possible *pluralization* of this concept, no less than its (now desirable, then deplorable) effects on key issues in contemporary policy. Is there a future for its past and present meaning? Does its role exhaust itself where traditional and modern notions of sovereignty (of "nation-states" and their relations, of peoples and their geographical boundaries, which convey seemingly obvious modes of belonging, hence of *jus sanguinis* and *jus solis*) have been rendered virtually obsolete or are at least steadily undermined by the flows of capital and information, immigration and migration, bodies and ideas? And how, exactly, do we counter those progressivists, whether market liberals and technocrats or left-leaning communitarians and secular pragmatists (to say nothing of Muslim humanists and atheists), who, without being reductionist naturalists, and often with the best intentions, urge us to see (at last) that "religion has absolutely nothing to do with it" and that we would do better to focus on economic and socio-cultural deprivations and inequalities instead of speculating about a turn, let alone a return, to religion? Why and in what way does—or should—"religion" matter at all in discussing the question of the political, of politics? But then, why is the disengagement of church and state still considered to be the primary event in the "order of separations" that constitutes the modern concepts of democracy and political liberalism? Why consider the theologico-political problem as a peculiar "vector," of sorts?[88]

Can we not also envision societies that open onto the beyond of the theologico-political (assuming, for a moment, that a return to its antecedents would be impossible, undesirable, or in any case regressive)? Or will the theologico-political, as Lefort suggests in a famous essay, reproduced in this volume, have a certain "permanence," so that it will continue to cast its shadow on—and beyond—its functional equivalents and eventual substitutes, hence even on some of the most challenging ideas concerning the end of sovereignty, or of a democracy yet and forever to come (*à venir*), which no longer fits the ancient or modern understanding of geo- or bio-political dictates?

With this in mind, we can see how Assmann's work on political theology in the ancient world inspires two further sets of related questions. First, is it true that "the further one goes back in time, the more difficult it becomes to distinguish between religious and political institutions"?[89] Might the same indistinction not be plausible as we progress toward an as yet undetermined future? Indeed, does the distinction between the theological and the political not crumble when we analyze its unstable arrangement in the present? In other words, is there a "permanence of the theologico-political," however conceived (Lefort's view being one possible articulation), or does the mutual imbrication of "salvation" and "power" reveal complexities—and potentialities or, should we say, virtualities—we have not even begun to address or to realize?

Second, can one plausibly argue, as Assmann does, that political theology emerges *only* "where such problems [of salvation and power] are treated in forms that implicate the gods or God,"[90] although he immediately adds "that concepts and models of a 'horizontal' order of living together also belong to political theology wherever they draw in the divine"?[91] Or does the theologico-political also have relevance—and thus some permanence—beyond the literal or implicit invocation of gods or God, that is to say, of the divine, salvation, and the sacred? Should we entertain the possibility that its significance reveals itself with even more consequence under the reign of the secular, where it works its wonders in more oblique—and hence intractable—ways? And, if this is so, can one still claim that a "theology is political, and a state doctrine theological, only when it postulates a nonsecular foundation, for example, in the form of the holy and hence, in the final analysis, imperative *status* of a political association [*Verbandes*], . . . in the form of a regime of divine grace [*Gottesgnadentum*], or in the form of the political assignment [*Auftrag*] of the Church"?[92] Or, by contrast, is *any* reference to some transcendence, whether vertical or horizontal, that is to say, to some empty signifier, absolute performative, or conditionless condition by itself already sufficient to conjure up the explicitly or implicitly religious motif and motivation documented in the tradition of "political theology"? Is it crucial to decide this, or would the mere distinction between, say, "static" and "dynamic," "closed" and open" societies (but also moralities and religions) inaugurate the theologico-political questioning that interests us here?

In short, is there any relevance or permanence of the theologico-political *before* and *beyond* the dual perspectives of (or on) what Assmann terms "the implicit theology of the political" and "the implicit politology, sociology, or anthropology of theological or, more generally, religious discourses"?[93] That is to say, is there a political theology that is *not yet* or *no longer* strictly or simply theological or even political, in the traditional and modern definitions of these terms?

Assmann recalls that political theology has, at least historically, counted as "a specific notion [*ein Spezifikum*] of Western history and hence of Christendom,"[94] despite the latter's borrowings from other traditions of political reflection: paganism (beginning with Varro), Judaism, Islam, or even Hinduism and Buddhism. In his view, we had to wait for an elaboration of the "comparative" concept of "the religious"—indeed, for the concept of "world religions"—before the fundamentally Christian designation *political theology* could be significantly broadened, extended, and retroactively projected into the historically and culturally different contexts of ancient Egypt, Mesopotamia, India, China, and the pre-Columbian empires of the Americas. We might add that, mutatis mutandis, the same argument could be made for the so-called primitive, nonscriptural cultures that formed a central object of study in the emerging discipline of anthropology.[95]

But if the expansive use—indeed, the pluralization—of the term *political theology* is permitted, what might be the intrinsic or external limits of its concept, of its governing idea and, perhaps, ideal? Does everything *turn around* the theologico-political? Or could we just make it *turn around*, make it *turn around itself* by speaking of what, in its very genesis and meaning, it unwittingly involves, what obscurely revolves around it, again, what lies before and beyond it, that is to say, what orients—and troubles—it from a distance? Is there, in light of this (spatial or temporal, transcendental or virtual?) distance not also a certain intrinsic limit that our Greco-Latin Christianity—including its concept of the theologico-political—must encounter, without thereby being negated, sublated, rendered obsolete, or reduced to a mere historical curiosity? If not everything has a theologico-political significance, what, exactly, remains exterior to its concept and the very diversity of its reception?

The question, if not the explicit concept, of the theologico-political and everything for which it stands—the contested nonseparation and irremovable imbrication of religion and the *polis*, the disputed consubstantiality of the two orders of the *ecclesia* and the imperial state, but also of an emphatic understanding of love (*agapē*) as the normative source and affective life of the *communitas*—already makes its appearance in the ancient world of pre-Christian Greece and the arrangement of the Roman empire before, in the year 325, the Emperor Constantine declared Christianity to be its official religion. From two different angles, Marcel Detienne and Jean-Luc Nancy, in their opening contributions to this volume, suggest that the theologico-political problem is perceived and lived well before being theorized and named as such. Starting out either from an original nonseparation of the theological and the political (Detienne) or from their inaugural separation (Nancy), both the historical-anthropological-comparative and the philosophical-deconstructive approaches of their respective essays uncover a remarkable mélange, whose distinctive threads, though they can be identified analytically and conceptually, cannot be disentangled or disengaged *in fact*.

Detienne, in his suggestive essay "The Gods of Politics in Early Greek Cities," makes clear that the question of the political (captured since Herodotus by the neuter term *to politikōn*) hardly originated with the Greek city-state, the *polis*, with Athenean democracy, nor did it make its first appearance with the definition of "power" or even the distinction—central to Schmitt's work—between friend and foe. Detienne starts out from the observation of concrete practices that, in the geographical, linguistic, historical, and ethnic diversity of ancient Greece and its legacy constitute what he calls the "political domain." He distinguishes, for example, the phenomenon of the assembly or, rather, "the practices of people deliberately assembling in order to debate affairs of common interest" (p. 92) as one such constituent, whose basic features have been either ignored or shunned by modern reflection on the question of politics. Analyzing the political domain within such a "framework" or "notional field"—for example, by taking the Greek conception or "microconfigurations" of discursive deliberation of the common good as one's point of departure or reference—would allow one, Detienne claims, to adopt a view of the political that is somewhat less "heavy-handed" than, say, the insistence on the "paradigm of civic humanism" introduced by John Pocock in his studies of the "Machiavellian Moment." The latter characterization, Detienne acknowledges, might indeed fit the basic tenets of a "post-sixteenth-century Anglo-Saxon world," but, like the concept of "empire," it does not adequately describe the actual constitution of the political, not just in the smaller Greek cities, but also in Buddhist communities in Japan, or African, Amerindian, and Cossack societies, to mention just a few of the historical instances in which assemblies have taken on their singular forms (p. 93).

Other points of entry into the comparative experiment might be such notions as "public matters," "citizen-citizenship," "sameness-equality"—all of which, Detienne asserts, would likewise allow one to take a certain distance from facile associations of the political with the "religious" or "religion," whose semantic link to the Latin *religio-religere*, as well as its "ritualistic scruples," tends to block the historical and comparative importance of "cults" (and hence of "gods"). It was partly through the Roman legacy, Detienne claims, that in the academic study of religion "there was pressure, already in the Christian Augustine, to consider polytheisms as vast *terrae incognitae* that were destined eventually to receive True Religion, whether from Christianity or from Islam." The favor, Detienne muses with irony, is promptly returned: "Polytheistic societies revel in their ignorance of churches and episcopal authorities, whether pastoral or papal. They mock these upstart monotheists for their insistence on 'having to believe' and their proselytizing efforts." Yet this "vast continent," he continues, represents a whole "world of the possible relations that link divine powers." As the gods are virtually everywhere, they also inhabit the places for politics and do so in multifarious ways, since in the polytheistic system "a god is always plural, constituted by the intersection of a variety of attributes. In this sense, a god is conjectural, a figure with many angles and many facets" (pp. 94–95).

Gods, or at least their altars, Detienne illustrates with reference to the *Iliad*, make their appearance in the *agora*, a term referring to a space that the Achaeans created on the way to their siege of Troy as they gathered among the ships on the beach. It connotes at once the "physical place of the assembly, the men who came there to deliberate, and the words that they exchanged there" (p. 96). The beginning of the consultation and veneration of gods such as Apollo and Hestia in the emergence and territorial organization of cities, including their sanctuaries, lies here. They bestow foundation and authority upon the political or public (*demosion*) space, the *agora*, which, Detienne notes, thereby "functions as a deity of effective publicity," to "make known to all," by way of decisions and their decrees, the "words solidly established" (as Solon reportedly called them; p. 98).

These first experimentations, in the early Greek cities, with the independence of the political, while drawing upon references to the divine, extended their deliberations even to the affairs of the gods, if only by deciding on the calendar of their honoring. While the gods had their place in politics, politics was seen as originally and ultimately a matter of human autonomy, that is to say, of "law unto itself." What the comparativist approach would invite us to see, Detienne concludes, is, first of all, the elementary forms of a concrete "politico-religious configuration," before taking, in all too abstract ways, "the combination of politics and religion, or that of theology and politics, or even that of politics and ritual as some kind of universal standard" (p. 101). As with religion's words, things, gestures, and powers, the elementary forms of political life can enter into a variety of possible combinations, depending on spatiotemporal determinants whose arrangement is never settled once and for all, defying the dream—or, rather, nightmare—of the autochthonous.

Jean-Luc Nancy insists on a persistence of the Greco-Latin-Christian model, which, in a sense (as has been argued by Gauchet in *The Disenchantment of the World*), provides the reasons and means of its own deconstruction. Following up on his seminal "The Deconstruction of Christianity,"[96] Nancy argues that the relationship between church and state must be rethought in light of the fact that religion, while "not a 'private' preference" but rather "a mode of representing and organizing both personal and collective existence," is the original and polar opposite of the political. Being "nothing more or less than the collective or communitarian possibility other than that constituted by politics," the separation of *ecclesia* and *imperium*, of church and state, should be seen as "the one true birth of politics" (p. 103).

Indeed, *ekklēsia*, Nancy reminds us, is "a term taken from the institutions of the Greek city, which now designates an 'assembly' and a specific mode of being together, distinct from the social and political mode" (p. 106). We find this distinction echoed in the differentiation and at times separation between the Kingdom of God and the Kingdom of Caesar, in the Old Testament's "law of sin" and the New Testament's "law of love," in St. Augustine's evocation of the heavenly and earthly cities, and even in Kant's distinction between the phenomenal and noumenal realms, the domain of freedom and of spatio-temporal necessity.

Christianity, in this reading, echoes and amplifies a primary act of separation and subsequent mediation that forms the paradigm for the establishment and maintenance of the political—indeed, of politics—as such. Paradoxically, it is as if the Greeks and Romans were *already* Christian and as if the modern conception of the political—until its "re-treat"—had been *still* Christian: "The political . . . is autonomy by definition and by structure. Theocracy, . . . as the other of politics, represents heteronomy by definition and by structure. Manifestly, autonomy cannot but resist heteronomy, and vice versa" (p. 103). Nancy, who refers in this context to messianism, thus seems to echo Benjamin's claim, in the "Theologico-Political Fragment," that there is and must be an unbridgeable cleavage between "theocracy" and the political—or, more broadly, historical—realm.

But Nancy's point is more nuanced. No simple dichotomy is observed, let alone advocated, here. Not only does the religious form itself, in its very act of separation, on a political model (the Kingdom of Heaven and the City of God are cases in point), what interests Nancy even more are the concrete ways in which the question of politics is already a reaction against the polarity expressed by the analytical distinction between church and state. In consequence, politics—conceived as a "form of political or moral resistance" (p. 103)—can be seen to imply a relation between autonomy and heteronomy, that is to say, between the political and the ecclesial (and hence, we may suspect, ulti-mately between democracy and theocracy).

This argument develops ideas Nancy began to explore in the days he co-founded, with Lacoue-Labarthe and Lefort, the Center for Philosophical Research on the Political, in Strasbourg. As in his contributions to the collective volume *The Retreat of the Political*, Nancy insists that whenever the "relation" between civil autonomy and religious heteron-omy dissipates, that is to say, wherever recourse to the "image, idea, or scheme of a 'civil religion' more or less consciously underlies our principal representations of the political. . . . it seems that the political is destined to withdraw [*retirer*] the essence we assumed it to have, leaving this essence to dissolve into 'administration' and the 'police,' which henceforth appear before us as the miserable remnants of what politics could or should have done" (p. 105).

Before it does so, however, a different tendency can be observed, which grants reli-gion, to the extent that it continues or emerges in the city-state, a "double aspect" of appearing now as a "remnant of" and "substitute for" heteronomous, theocratic religion, then as a "specific religion, distinct from the 'religion of the priests.'" This specific reli-gion, Nancy explains, reminds us of a religion "within the limits of reason alone," as Kant said, which constitutes the *polis* in principle and does so in spite (or on the very basis?) of the latter's foundation as an autonomous intervention. Religious "insofar as it is politi-cal, and not the other way around," this second aspect expresses the consubstantiality of cult and culture, of *religio*—etymologically understood, this time—as a "scrupulous observance" and "establishing a bond." The civic, civil, or political religions of Athens and especially of ancient Rome are cases in point. But what does it mean for religion to be more than just a remnant? For one thing, Nancy claims, it "signifies the inclusion of autonomy in a heteronomy that, without subverting this autonomy, gives it the double dimension of a transcendence and a fervor" (p. 104). This projected image of a (theological?) transcendence or self-transcendence of the immanent principle of the political is the legacy invoked by the self-appointed heirs of the Roman model. Nancy mentions the French Revolution and Italian fascism, each invested in a different mode of civil religion, whether based on the "residual minimum of political affect," namely, fraternity (as in the French Revolution and Italian fascism), or on a celebration of community, reverting to dictatorship (as in what Nancy calls "'real' communisms"; pp. 108–9). In genuine and perverse ways, these modern political formations sought to supplement the rational deduction of the social contract with affects that rendered it "perceptible to the hearts of citizens" by appealing to fervor and desire and hence by bringing about a regime of assembly other than on the basis of interest.

Next to "fraternity," the appeals to "friendship," "solidarity," "responsibility," and "justice" are so many recent examples of affects resisting the autonomy upon which the political remains nonetheless premised. The typically French articulation of "secularism [laïcité]" is characterized by the same motif and motivation, namely, "the necessity of conceiving and practicing something like the observance and celebration of the values, symbols, and signs of recognition that attest to everyone's adherence to the community as such." This affective significance of laïcité is more important than its formal indication of a juridical arrangement concerning the precise modalities of the constitutional separation of church and state. Indeed, the Christian concept of "love" all along expressed a similar exigency or concern, as is clear from the texts of the Gospels and St. Paul all the way up to Hegel's philosophy of right and, Nancy suggests, Jürgen Habermas's idea of "constitutional patriotism."

Nancy thus postulates a more fundamental and effective/affective modality of relation (here called "love"), which precedes or supersedes the distinction between autonomy and heteronomy and exerts itself in—and beyond—the very resistance between the two poles that has constituted the essence of the political since Greece, Rome, and the earliest beginnings of Judaism, Christianity, and Islam. Religion and faith, its doctrine and ritual, its words, places, and commonplaces can no longer be had and lived they way we (think) we did.[97] What remains is the need to "invent a new way to play the political institution," *without* the theological backup of any of the historically exhausted civil religions, and premised on nothing more (and nothing less) than a "Being in common, or being together—or even more simply, and in the barest form, being several" (p. 111).[98]

In the end, from the beginning the question of the political thus refers to a fundamental ontological problem, not least because, as Nancy writes, "the general idea of tolerance, and of the state as a space of tolerance, remains inferior or even foreign to what is rightfully expected of the political: namely, to take charge of a force of affect inherent in being-with" (p. 109). This intrinsic resistance is no longer necessarily or even primarily that between church and state but rather the resistance of (our) "being-with" to itself: that is to say, of a "being-with" that, for this very reason, "refuses to be fulfilled under any form of hypostasis, configuration, institution, or legislation" (p. 112), but, on the contrary, expresses its *anomaly* in the very interruption of its gathering (or *rassemblement*) as such. Only thus, Nancy concludes, can we circumvent the pernicious extremes of either swallowing or annihilating the other (and all other others), that is to say, of sacrifice,[99] or of imposing cosmic, organico-political totality—extremes that both deny human finitude. A "deconstruction of Christianity" prepares the ground for an assessment of emerging forms of "being-with," the experience and experiment of freedom and community, of which the political—especially in its very retreat—is, perhaps, not even the most significant instance. And the fact of globalization contributes to no small extent, Nancy suggests in the opening essay of *La Déclosion*, to the dis-closure that may or may not help us rethink these matters in a sharper light than ever before. For one thing, it forces us to recognize the continuous presence of Christianity—of the Judeo-Christian, and whatever it touched upon and was touched by—in the seemingly secular West, which may or may not emerge out of the self-deconstruction of that same Christianity.[100]

As M. B. Pranger and Antónia Szabari demonstrate in their contributions to the volume, a subtle counter-paradigm to the Greco-Roman city-state–imperium is developed from St. Augustine through the early Reformation. What stands out in their respective readings is an analysis of the theological articulation of the aspiration toward conjoining the political and the religious (as in the Augustinian motif of the *civitas permixta*), on the one hand, and the Reformation's concern with modulating and moderating divisive speech acts), on the other. Whereas Pranger brings out the intrinsic instability and fragility, that is to say, the temporality or finitude, of Augustine's sense of the individual self and the communal body (i.e., the Church), suggesting that they remain premised upon creation and contingency, authority and grace, at least so long as history runs its course, Szabari, by contrast, emphasizes a different instability in the theological dealing with self and other, faith and the visible Church, by analyzing the nature of Luther's conception of "public speech" as it intermingles praise (or prayer) and insult (or cursing) and thereby creates—or, rather, stages—a whole new world, reversing the former hierarchical order.

Referring to the historical studies of Janet Coleman, Pranger recalls that Augustine contributed to the modern understanding of the state as the guarantor against chaos and hence to the conception of the secular as premised upon the curtailment of sin. Augustine, in this view, could even be seen as a precursor of Thomas Hobbes in that he portrays the whole spectrum of the political—absolute terrestrial sovereignty and the state's down-to-earth politics (including war)—as the sole solution to the tragedy of the human condition. In a different reading of Augustine's conception of the *saeculum*, there is a tradition of medieval political thinking that counterbalances the unstable temporality of the terrestrial *civitas* with the motif of the *corpus mysticum*, the mystical body of Christ. This line of thought is explored by Henri de Lubac, and it is the historical basis for the understanding of the temporal continuity of the state—in particular, of the monarchy—that Kantorowicz, in *The King's Two Bodies*, develops against the backdrop of the doctrine that the church "cannot not be" or "never dies" (*ecclesia nulla esse non potest, ecclesia numquam moritur*).

The exclamation "Le roi est mort, vive le roi" echoes the insight that sovereignty is not primarily tied to the individual king's body (which may die, fall ill, etc.), but to the political body, the body politic (which cannot die, even though it relies on serial incarnation in one person at a time)—a situation, we might add, that has reversed itself in modern parliamentary democracy, where all too often the individual functionary (e.g., the president) outlives the demise of his auratic authority and hence credibility well before his mandate is officially over. Examples abound.[101] Then again, former presidents may acquire universal admiration as elder statesmen, towering above all parties, after their de facto tenure has expired.[102]

Pranger takes up the Augustinian model, which, in a sense, extends to Shakespeare,[103] by focusing on its temporal dimension, thus relating (as Nancy does) the question of the political, of politics, to that of "finitude." Noting that autobiography and historiography assume that "inside historical sources and throughout the succession of events and experiences can be construed identities, both personal and corporate, that are capable of resisting the disintegration of time," Pranger zooms in on the specific ways in which the *Confessions* and *The City of God* address transience, both as a theme and in their very mode of presentation (p. 113). In both works, he notes, the individual self and its voice, as well as the body politic and its institutions, depend for their shaky existence— characterized by personal sin and skepticism concerning communal forms—on the sustenance of their Creator, that is to say, on grace and authority. In a nutshell, we find here a disenchanted view of the foundations of the modern state, even of secularism, 'in that the institutions of the civil community are seen as infected with sin and merely as means to overcome the state of nature and to ward off chaos.

Pranger suggests that it seems as if "the ghosts of the unresolved aporias of time, discussed in book 11 of the *Confessions*, have come back to haunt Augustine's attempts at 'making history'" (p. 118). More succinctly, the relationship between the earthly and heavenly cities is far from obvious. The latter is not simply the Platonic idea of which the former is but a shadowy image: "It is time that prevents the city of God from materializing as a lesser copy of a fuller original" (p. 119). History, including the history of political institutions, is thus not so much ambiguous as it is fathomless. As Pranger rightly concludes: "inside the *saeculum*, we have no reason to expect the durability of a mystical body" (p. 120). And yet the heavenly city, far from being a mere idea, may insinuate its presence anywhere, anytime, as a "voice exorcising the invading, alien night" (pp. 120–21).

We would thus be dealing with an internal division of—a principle of contestation within—the political-juridical realm, which allows sovereignty to come into its own, to exert its power, precisely by withholding itself at an a priori indeterminable but nonetheless decisive point in time and space. The lofty essence of the political and the mundane struggle of the politics of the everyday likewise draw their meaning and function from this dual aspect of ideality and practicality, that is to say, of "two bodies," whose mutual exclusion *and* accommodation is *theologico*-political, since no strictly humanly finite or naturalist reasoning, let alone any mechanistic principle or rule-governed pattern, can account for the paradoxical logic of its operation.

Insight into the fragility and contestability of the theologico-political is amplified during the period of the Reformation and the emerging modern world that it expresses as much as announces. Its implications can now be methodically studied *and* enacted at the linguistic level, where a specific speech act—namely, that of insult—comes to exemplify and dramatize the earlier paradox, as the ontological or ontico-theological difficulty discussed by Kantorowicz becomes the predicament of public speech. Drawing on a 1531 pamphlet of Martin Luther's in which, with typical vehemence, he states: " 'Hallowed be Thy name' . . . Cursed, damned, and outraged be the papacy together with all earthly kingdoms that are against your kingdom,' " Szabari elaborates a remarkable theology of offense and scandal that, she demonstrates, at once presupposes and contests existing ecclesial traditions, canons, and procedures regarding blasphemy and anathema. Luther is stretching the limits of blame set by these conventions, and, in so doing, he inaugurates a different way of symbolic world making.

Paradoxically, Szabari observes, Luther's "extreme rudeness," based on a decidedly biblical war cry, reveals a significant feature of the role that religious speech, during the Reformation and thereafter, acquires in the emerging modern public sphere. She argues that Luther's masterly move is that of satire and a strategic turning of tables. Indeed, Luther's cunning reasoning implies "that what was conventionally accepted as pious language is in fact blasphemy and that what appeared to be blasphemy is in fact true piety." This move not only redirects theological discourse and expands the customary boundaries of rhetorical language but, more significantly, subverts political hegemonies by way of social exclusion or ostracism.

Szabari demonstrates that, unlike his contemporary, the Humanist Desiderius Erasmus, in his invective Luther exploits the limits of classical rhetoric as it stylizes language and thus achieves a distinctively modern form of its public impact. Luther's "theology of the performative," Szabari maintains, does not primarily reform the propositions of scholastic theology but is much more dynamic in that it takes words (the *modus loquendi*, as Michel de Certeau said) to be agents (and hence speaking as a *modus agendi*), "not as magic words that produce static substances but as essentially social and intersubjective events" (p. 127). As such, Szabari adds, it is also attuned to a modern articulation of the insight that divine speech is essentially iterable, especially in the "reproducibility and variability of printed type" (p. 127).

In a preliminary way, we might assess the results of our inquiry so far by saying that the ancient, medieval, and modern concept of political sovereignty and authority in city, state, empire, and nation, whatever the discursive and rhetorical modes of its immanent, earthly, and lay theoretical justification—which may well include a magical-mythological imaginary of sacredness, even in the most secular of its articulations—has more often than not been presented as inherently "theological" or "theologico-political," premised upon a "mystical foundation," as Derrida, following Montaigne and Pascal, reminds us in his "Force of Law: The 'Mystical Foundations of Authority.'" One need not share Schmitt's appeal to the state of exception and its theological presuppositions to discern the systematic—at once structural and hence more than merely metaphorical or analogical—relevance of the divine and the transcendent for the terrestrial and the profane, that is to say, for immanence.

From Augustine's *City of God*, whose distinction between the heavenly and earthly cities, if not their interpenetration, their being set in parallel, sets an intellectual standard for as recent and dialectical a thinker as Theodor W. Adorno, in his pivotal essay "Progress," beyond the early modern contractarian theories of natural right analyzed by Patrick Riley in his *The General Will Before Rousseau*, to Michael Theunissen's characterization of Hegel's doctrine of absolute Spirit as a "theologico-political treatise," it seems that some version of political theology has always played a determining, if often oblique, historical and conceptual role.[104] This is made clear by Hans Kelsen's co-implication of "God and State," by Leo Strauss's studies of the motif of the *theos nomos* and its transformation into revealed positive law, all the way up to the critical reexaminations of the theologico-political, community, and bio-politics in the writings of such authors as Roberto Esposito, Giorgio Agamben, and Myriam Revault d'Allonnes.[105]

The systematic point that interests us here is made nowhere more poignantly than in the theoretical studies of Ernesto Laclau concerning the "empty signifier" of sovereignty and investigating its unexpected precursors in the negative-theological tradition of divine names. Laclau gives the clearest possible formal analysis of the parallel sense in which the tradition of theological thinking—here, in its heterodox, negative, apophatic, or, in his words, mystic current—may well have constituted (and, indeed, still form) the basis of the most concrete and everyday forms of political engagement and disengagement, of militancy, revolution, and populist action.

Beginning with his rediscovery and reformulation of the theory of hegemony and radical democracy, in the wake of Antonio Gramsci and in close collaboration with Chantal Mouffe,[106] Laclau has worked toward elaborating a "grammar of emancipation" that culminates in the reconceptualization of a notion of universality that is "not a static presumption, not an a priori given" but that "ought instead to be understood as a process or condition irreducible to any of its determinate modes of appearance."[107] The political, as it were, does not let itself be absorbed into various elements and movements—words, things, gestures, and powers—of "politics," even though (like the Saussurian system of *langue* in relation to any *parole*) it is has no existence and relevance elsewhere, that is, before or beyond them. These are important implications for an innovative theory of human rights, emancipation, and international law. Central elements in this program can be found in such seminal works as Laclau's *New Reflections on the Revolution of Our*

Time, his *Emancipation(s)*, and his illuminating contributions to the collective volume *Contingency, Hegemony, Universality: Contemporary Dialogues on the Left*, co-authored by Judith Butler and Slavoj Žižek.[108] His recent *The Populist Reason* pursues this agenda further.[109] These studies, as indicated in the programmatic description of the book series Phronesis, edited by Laclau since 1989, are all motivated by the philosophical critique of "essentialism" and based on the assumption that "the most important trends in contemporary theory—deconstruction, psychoanalysis, the philosophy of language initiated by the later Wittgenstein and post-Heideggerian hermeneutics—are the necessary conditions for understanding the widening of social struggles characteristic of the present stage of democratic politics, and for formulating a new vision for the Left in terms of radical and plural democracy."[110]

In the present volume, we reproduce Laclau's seminal essay "On the Divine Names of God," which, in a concise and elegant tour de force, formalizes the irreducibility of difference in the constitution of the political with a central insight of mysticism (whether dualist, monist, pantheist, Jewish, Christian, or even Buddhist and, more indirectly, Hindu, and perhaps—although Laclau doesn't say so—Islamic). By way of a powerful rereading of Pseudo-Dionysius and Meister Eckart, the essay elaborates the systematic parallel between Laclau's own assessment of the meaning of "empty signifiers" for a theory of hegemony and the tradition of the divine names. The observed formal, rather than historical, analogies can be seen as "the expression, in mystical garb, of something belonging to the general structure of all possible experience." With their oblique and indirect gesturing toward some "*transcendens*," they signal an ontological predicament, which Laclau formulates as follows: "Finitude involves the experience of fullness, of the sublime, as that which is radically lacking—and is, in that sense, a necessary beyond." Historically and systematically speaking, the significance of mystical discourse is the fact that, "by radicalizing that 'beyond,' it has shown the essential finitude that is constitutive of all experience." This, however, is not all, for Laclau goes on to point out that "its historical limit has been, in most cases, its having surrendered to the temptation of giving a positive content to the 'beyond'—the positive content being dictated not by mystical experience itself but by the religious persuasion of the mystic" (pp. 143–44).

These heterodox traditions enable our attempts to understand the political in its ontological dimensions and the concrete-material politics of present-day engagement and ethics (or militancy). Just as mysticism, in Laclau's reconstruction, indefatigably insists that "the name of God, if we are not going to soil His sublime reality (and our experience of it), has to be an empty signifier, a signifier to which no signified can be attached" (p. 142), so also an ontology of the political and of politics, here of the collective-revolutionary will, must realize that it aims at "hegemony." This means that any particular claim, any "content," must be seen against the foil of deprivation, finitude, and facticity, and hence as the positive reverse of a lack, that is to say, as assuming merely the function of incarnating an absent fullness (and, therefore, not being that elusive presence itself).

In all of this Laclau is above all interested in how the mystic *modus loquendi* and *modus agendi* (to use de Certeau's terminology) is governed by a remarkable paradox: "mystical experience does not lead to an actual *separation* from things and daily pursuits but, on the contrary, to a special way of joining them, so that we can see in any of them a manifestation of God's presence" (p. 141). Laclau simply asks how this can done. The answer refers to a formal logic of (nontautological, nonsynonymous) equivalences and substitutions—as, in the logic of divine names, God is neither this nor that nor yet something else in particular—that forms the backbone of "hegemony" and the universal and that Laclau has sought indefatigably to systematize and refine in a host of publications. Concretely, it means something both dauntingly complex and surprisingly simple, that "Essential detachment and actual involvement are the two sides of the same coin. . . . Paradoxically, it is the detached nature of what is invested in a particular action, its purely contingent link to it, that guarantees that involvement in that action will be a serious one" (pp. 141–42).

In politics, Laclau takes the perspective of finitude, contingency, and facticity. He demarcates it from a specifically Spinozist view, that is to say, from the perspective *sub specie aeternitatis* (no longer a perspective really, but a "view from nowhere," as Thomas Nagel called it—or a view from "everywhere," to vary the same 'position'). To this, Laclau opposes a seeming obvious insight, echoing Kantorowicz, though at a certain distance: "historical life takes place in a terrain that is less than eternity. If the experience of . . . the dual movement 'materialization of God' and a 'deification of the concrete' is to live up to its two sides, neither the absolute nor the particular can find a final peace with each other" (p. 147).

In our understanding of the political and of politics—indeed, of the politics of the everyday—this implies the necessity of "keeping open the two sides of this paradox: an absolute that can only be actualized by being something less than itself, and a particularity whose only destiny is to be the incarnation of a 'sublimity' that transcends its own body" (p. 147). The very evocation of "Oneness," that is to say, of "unity" and "simplicity," is therefore no more than a necessary illusion. And so, we must assume, are its political equivalents. No positive present fullness is to be had or hoped and strived for. Every claim requires (and ipso facto is) its (own) disclaimer, and yet it is only the series of fundamentally "equivalent" claims and counter-claims, together with their disclaimers, that makes the political—in its process no less than its idea, not to mention ideal—possible and necessary as such.

The parallel with apophatic discourse suggests itself once more: "while the mystical experience underlies an ineffable fullness that we call 'God,' that name—*God*—is part of a discursive network that cannot be reduced to this experience" (or to which that experience cannot be reduced; p. 142). Mutatis mutandis, the same would hold true for the political and its general concepts (democracy, but also the revolutionary, the people). Both would be doomed—and blessed—by their inevitable "irreverences." Political idolatry (hence, in a sense, blasphemy, scandal, and conflict) would be the order of the day; indeed, only thus can we avoid the totalitarian "collapse into simple identity." The polar opposition of radical finitude and absolute fullness is de facto and de jure tainted—and enabled—by what Laclau, in Derridian terminology, calls "contamination," because of the fact that "differential remainders"—and the "complex language games" to which they give rise—are the very "condition of possibility" of the discourses of mysticism, ethics, and politics alike (p. 145).

In consequence, democratic politics can only consist in keeping nominations and terms (and, by extension, principles and rights, norms and rules, customs and causes) open for revisions that can have no determinable end, just as in negative theologies there has always been "an alternative way of naming God, which is through the self-destruction of the particularized contents" that theological language can come up with. But does that not mean that (the strife for) political hegemony must be held in check by an apophatic critique of all political idolatry (whether that of party and parliamentary politics as usual, or of states of exception, popular revolutions, etc.)? Amidst the unstoppable flight toward fullness, it might, indeed, help to plant empty (translucent, plastic) flags here and there.

Claude Lefort, in a by now classic essay, circles in a different way around the question of the emptiness of the signifier of sovereignty and suggests that the denunciation of religion and its constitutive role in the political are of little help in capturing its contemporary function. Lefort provocatively suggests that the religious "survives in the guise of new beliefs and new representations," and that such beliefs can at any moment "return to the surface, in either traditional or novel forms, when conflicts become so acute as to produce cracks in the edifice of the state." To say this undercuts the presupposition of a teleological development of Western intellectual and political history (read: Hegel), of seemingly irreversible learning processes (read: Habermas), and the like. Yet more than the well-known paradoxes of modernity or the dialectic of Enlightenment is at stake here. The "permanence of the theologico-political" is more abrupt, instantaneous, undecidable—out there, but only virtually. The "permanence" in question is not an indubitable presence but rather a permanent possibility, for good and for ill. It is never given once and for all, in its purity, as such, or intact.

Lefort further suggests that "the 'modern' notion of politics" has become "an index of our ignorance or disavowal of a hidden part of social life, namely the processes that make people consent to a given regime—or, to put it more forcefully, that determine *their manner of being in society*." Exploring such attachments requires rethinking one's terms, to begin with, *the religious* and *the political*. Lefort writes: "We can define *the religious* in broader or narrower terms, and the threshold beyond which the word loses all pertinence is a matter for debate; it would, however, seem that we can readily agree that certain beliefs, attitudes, and representations reveal a religious sensibility." Taking a genealogical approach, he argues that the "expression 'religious sensibility' retains a fairly precise content if we relate it to historically and culturally determined phenomena; in other words, not to religion in general but to the Christian religion, whose various manifestations we can identify without any risk of error" (pp. 150–51).

The same, Lefort cautions, cannot be said of "the political," as distinguished from "politics." Already the mere fact that this terminological distinction is possible and that we can thus "choose to say either *the political* or *politics*" is, Lefort suggests, "an index of this ambiguity" (p. 151), which is conceptual and has analytical consequences. Of course, one could ask whether the distinction between *the political* and *politics* does not merely parallel that between *religion* and *religion(s)* (or between *messianicity* and *messianism* or between *Christianicity* and *Christendom*).[111] Lefort, however, argues that "We arrive at a very different idea of *the political*" from what results simply by opposing it to the *nonpolitical* "if we remain true to philosophy's oldest and most constant inspiration, if we use the term to refer to the principles that generate society or, more accurately, different forms of society" (p. 152).

In Lefort's characterization of the "theologico-political labyrinth," its very "schema" stipulates that "any move toward immanence is also a move toward transcendence; that any attempt to explain the contours of social relations implies an internalization of unity; that any attempt to define objective, impersonal entities implies a personification of those entities"; to which he adds: "The workings of the mechanisms of incarnation ensure the imbrication of religion and politics, even in areas where we thought we were dealing simply with purely religious or purely profane practices or representations" (p. 187).

Far from clear, however, is Lefort's answer to the question that gives the title to his essay, namely, whether this very schema is also permanent. He ends his essay:

> should we not conclude . . . that a new experience of the institution of the social began to take shape, that the religious is reactivated at the weak points of the social, that its efficacy is no longer symbolic but imaginary, and that, ultimately, it is an expression of the unavoidable—and no doubt ontological—difficulty democracy has in reading its own story, as well as of the difficulty political or philosophical thought has in assuming, without making it a travesty, the tragedy of the modern condition? (p. 187)

The theologico-political finds its "permanence" in what seems an *irrevocable latency,* that is to say, in the reactivation of the religious—a transcendence in immanence—but only "at the weak points of the social," whose "institution" can, in modernity, be experienced in a novel way, one that is disincorporated. The theologico-political erupts as the difficulty this novel experience has in making sense of itself, a difficulty Lefort calls both "unavoidable" and "ontological." The religious can no longer claim to have a "symbolic" working, only an "imaginary" one, meaning that it has no further force in structuring the political and can no longer occupy the center—the empty place—of what was once an embodied, incarnate power. Wherever it tries to do so, it turns the "tragedy" of the human condition into a farce.

The permanence of the religious, thus defined, is the transcendental illusion of the political: the "move toward immanence" being seemingly one "toward transcendence," the insistence on social relations that reintroduces "unity," and the "disincorporation" of the body politic, which seems unthinkable without renewed "personification." But its permanence has other features as well.

At this point, a second preliminary result might suggest itself. Political theology seems a intellectual discipline not of the general or universal (which, traditionally, would be metaphysics, including general metaphysics or ontology but also special metaphysics, within which one counts natural theology), nor of the individual or singular (of which, traditionally, there can be no scientific knowledge at all), but of the elusive, that is to say, of that which absolves itself (the ab-solute), the spiritually and motivationally recalcitrant, the invisible, imperceptible, intangible, and imponderable. These give themselves to be read through words, things, gestures, and powers, without being reducible to them. But then, political theology could also be seen as the analysis and phenomenological description of the wide spectrum of all too literal, material, and figurative fixations of this theologico-political difference within dogmatic forms of thought, rigid and ritualized codes of conduct, and idolatrous images of aesthetic representation, all of which reduce the theologico-political to partial—and inevitably exclusive—incarnations and sedimentations all built upon a principle of exaggeration whose necessary effect is that of escalation. Perhaps a final, no less crucial, task for political theology—in the singular and the plural—would be that of a search-engine, locating and exposing theologico-political noise, often in the form of babble and sophistry.

In his contribution, Marc de Wilde seeks to determine the status of theologico-political motifs in the work of Benjamin and Schmitt. He argues that these authors' intellectual affinity, to which important references in their work testify, can be adequately understood only in light of their shared theologico-political convictions. In their work, he shows, the concept of political theology stands neither for an explicitly theological discourse in politics nor for some kind of hidden theological agenda. Rather, it marks the continuous resurfacing of theological figures of thought in what seems an otherwise relentlessly secularized world. The theological, in their view, resurfaces not only in fundamental political beliefs, ideologies, and myths but also, more obliquely, in theories of sovereignty, in theories and practices demonstrating the force of law, and, last but not least, in the state of exception (a term critically redeployed by Giorgio Agamben, with whose work de Wilde takes issue in this context).

The second part of de Wilde's essay consists in a close reading of Benjamin's 1921 essay "Critique of Violence" and Schmitt's 1922 study *Political Theology*. These texts, he argues, mark a new sensibility in the transformations of sovereignty, bearing witness to the reappearance of the theologico-political in political discourse. Although it is uncertain whether Schmitt was familiar with Benjamin's essay, for both the concept of political theology implies the task of inventing or reinventing a politics that bears witness to divine violence, albeit without being able to understand itself as a direct representation of that violence. They suggest that the relation between secular politics and divine violence can only be an *indirect* one, mediated by solitary struggles before the law. What is at stake in their political theologies, therefore, is the attempt to articulate a certain kind of responsibility, whose essential traits elude the traditional and modern contours of practical and moral philosophy.

In the third part of his essay, de Wilde examines whether the political theologies of Benjamin and Schmitt can provide a clarification of the violence inherent in "contemporary states of exception," that is, in the border zones between positive law and bare life, for example, within the United States as well as outside its territory, in camps such as the ones at Guantánamo Bay or Abu-Ghraib, and their lesser-known doubles in Europe and elsewhere. De Wilde argues, with Benjamin and in a certain sense against Schmitt, that, in the most notorious among the known cases, it is not the *absence* of law that characterizes the state of exception but the deliberately created para-legal possibility of a depersonalizing juridical violence, without recourse to due process, that tends to escalate in the presence of ideologically invoked political theologies, as in the Bush administration's "justifications" of the use of physical and psychological abuse. As soon as a sovereign power starts to think of its lawmaking violence as an instrument of salvation, even with the most inspired democratic ideals in mind, it is bound to cause and provoke the worst, namely, a senseless sacrifice of "mere life" to myth.

In late June 2006, the U.S. Supreme Court reversed some of the rulings in question, declaring the military tribunals concerning ten foreign suspects at Guantánamo Bay to constitute a violation both of statutes of American military law and of the Geneva Conventions (and hence ruled the applicability of its Common Article 3, which prohibits "outrages upon personal dignity, in particular humiliating and degrading treatment" of prisoners): a decision to which the Bush administration responded by drafting new rulings that would keep much of its earlier policy in these matters in place.[112]

The important thing, de Wilde concludes, is that sovereign democracies should become aware that—within the state of exception—with the emergence of unlimited authority (whether existing constitutional, state, and federal, not to mention international, laws remain intact or are suspended altogether), responsibility is likewise without limits. Yet few powers are willing or able to limit their tendency to expand the horizon of their interest and control. Extending their authority, they thus inevitably undermine—or, in any case, delegitimate and invalidate—that very authority, overstepping bounds into a void that the theologico-political once sought to mark. The question remains whether such theologico-political marking invites or obstructs reflection and action, that is to say, whether it construes necessities where there are none or whether it frees up possibilities, indeed, radical novelties, together with all the responsibilities they entail.

Judith Butler, in her contribution, amplifies her profound and longstanding philosophical inquiry into the critical work done by norms in the contemporary domains of the political, jurisprudence, and international law, as well as into the forms of individual and shared lives. In her study *Precarious Life: The Powers of Mourning and Violence*, she had addressed the impossibility, in contemporary post 9/11 American public life, for certain groups and individual voices to be heard, let alone be mourned. Butler takes up the question of the distinction in Benjamin's "Critique of Violence" between "law-instating" and "law-preserving" violence, as well as the relationship between them, and addresses the difficult question of what it is that he counterposes to these conceptions. She thereby prepares the ground for a reassessment of the political and politics at a moment—in Benjamin's time and, not so differently, our own—of a redefining of the rulings and jurisdiction of legal courts, an increase in the intermediary role of "the police," and an increasing role of the military in matters of national and international security and intelligence (with the checks and balances between them rapidly—and disturbingly—fading). While not blurring important historical and moral-political distinctions, Butler makes it explicit that Benjamin's "opposition to the binding, even coercive character of law seems less savory once we consider the rise of fascism, as well as the flouting of both constitutional and international law that characterizes U.S. foreign policy in its practices of war, torture, and illegal detention" (p. 206).

Recalling that Benjamin provides a critique of "*legal* violence, the kind of violence that the state wields through instating and maintaining the binding status that law exercises on its subjects" (p. 201), Butler raises the question of what alternative trajectory might possibly also be opened here, albeit in an idiom and argumentation that remains in need of translation into our own historical context. The answer, she suggests, lies in a further unfolding of a now seemingly theological, then again political perspective, epitomized by what Benjamin calls "divine intervention" and "the general strike," terms and figures that are formally almost interchangeable. Benjamin takes one from the tradition mediated by his friend Gershom Scholem, the other from the anarcho-syndicalist theorist Georges Sorel. This dual influence leads us to the heart of the problem, for Benjamin, Butler notes, is "elaborating, on the one hand, the conditions for a general strike that would result in the paralysis and dissolution of an entire legal system, and, on the other, the notion of a divine god whose commandment *offers a kind of injunction that is irreducible to coercive law*" (p. 204).

Not the least interesting motivation behind Benjamin's view may be the fact that his essay, as Butler explains, should be understood as intervening in an intellectual context in which such intellectuals as Hermann Cohen, Franz Rosenzweig, and Martin Buber took critical issue with Zionism as a an attempt to establish a legal and political territoriality for Judaism, which, they felt, could only result in compromising its spiritual mission. Benjamin's essay should thus be seen as exploring the possibility of another form of violence or authoritative force that would be noncoercive or, as Butler puts it, "a violence that can be invoked and waged against the coercive force of law," and that hence, in a sense, would be fundamentally nonviolent (p. 201). Benjamin's term for this alternative, nonviolent violence is that of a messianic-Judaic "divine violence." In Butler's summary: "Divine violence is unleashed against the *coercive force* of that legal framework, against the accountability that binds a subject to a specific legal system and stops that very subject from developing a critical, if not a revolutionary point of view on that legal system" (p. 203).

As in *Precarious Life* and *Giving an Account of Oneself*,[113] the argument and sensibility Butler distills from Benjamin's engagement with the Marxist and anarchist, Zionist and Judaic-messianic debates of his day—all of which are recast in light of his own earlier metaphysical investigations—comes down to a subtle attempt to envision "the release from legal accountability and guilt as a way of apprehending the suffering and the transience in life, of life, as something that cannot always be explained through the framework of moral or legal accountability." What can be gathered from Benjamin's text, with its theologico-political overtones, then, is an important lesson regarding the structure of "ethical address," now seen as a "commandment" that "delivers an imperative precisely without the capacity to enforce in any way the imperative it communicates. . . . an imperative that does *not* dictate, but *leaves open* the modes of its applicability, the possibilities of its interpretation, including the conditions under which it may be refused" (pp. 203–5).

Close to Benjamin, in his critique of Hegelian dialectics, is the view of Franz Rosenzweig, whose "antisystem" deeply influenced Levinas in what resulted in a genuinely demystifying and sobering "philosophy of war" and the violence of history. Stéphane Mosès, in his contribution, makes it clear that Rosenzweig, in the opening pages of *The Star of Redemption*, and Levinas, in the preface to *Totality and Infinity*, take stock of the political, ontological, and metaphysical-religious repercussions of the two world wars, albeit it with different emphasis. Mosès tracks the fateful consequence of the disintegration of the identity, presupposed in Western thought "from Ionia to Jena," between the rational and the real, being and totality, from Rosenzweig's meditation on death and the human individual against the backdrop of "total war" to Levinas's reflection upon the totalitarian and systematic annihilation of peoples—and hence of a certain idea of humanity. In Levinas's conception of "absolute forsakenness, there is for the self no beyond war" (p. 222). Whereas Rosenzweig seeks to postulate a "space of peace"—namely, that of the subjective "I"—outside the negative totality, the system of Spirit, "entirely governed by war," Levinas sees such recourse as being no longer available under present historical and more broadly ontological conditions. He thus envisions war as "the permanent state of humanity," revealing the "agonistic essence of the real," indeed, of "reason itself," against whose backdrop the appeal to individuality or even morality seems illusory, a "naïveté" (pp. 228–29). The Hegelian conception of mediating consciousnesses and states reduces them, Levinas writes, to "bearers of forces that command them unbeknownst to themselves"—and hence commits them to war (p. 229). To this Levinas contrasts an "ethical optics," which consist in considering man "outside all context." In so doing, Moses suggests, Levinas does not refute Rosenzweig's appeal to singularity (here, the "extra-territoriality" of the ego) but rather radicalizes Hegel's conception of totality, which comes to express reason, indeed, the reasonableness of the real—but not intelligibility and a more emphatic sense of giving reasons (to the Other)—as such. Exteriority to the system can be found in the idea of the Infinite alone. Yet this idea, Moses concludes, precisely because it "surpasses all thought," can give itself "only indirectly, in a roundabout way or a displacement, in which it shows itself, as if by metonymy, through a lived experience: that of the revelation of the exteriority of others" (p. 230).

Drawing upon many of the premises of Mosès's interpretation, Hent de Vries's contribution asks what are the theologico-political stakes in two of the most challenging engagements that have accompanied Levinas's life-long philosophical project: the interpretation of Scripture, in *Difficult Freedom* and the Talmudic lectures, and his elliptical and often indirect confrontation with Spinoza, the thinker who at first glance would seem to epitomize the metaphysical counterposition to Levinas's thought by giving perhaps the most consistent expression of the philosophy of the same.

· · ·

At this point, let me attempt to formulate a third preliminary conclusion, closely related to the first—which distinguished "political theology," on the one hand, as the *scientia* of the elusive and absolute that governs and often unconsciously drives and inspires, or destabilizes and terrorizes, the public domain (the "theologico-political"), and, on the other hand, especially in its plural dimension, as the name and description of the many diverse forms in which this "empty" notion or open dimension can become dogmatically fixated, socially reified, and aesthetically fetishized. On both counts, descriptive and normative aspects of the analysis should be differentiated in principle, even though they inevitably interfere with—indeed, mutually presuppose and solicit—each other.

Two extreme positions in a distinctively ancient and modern tradition can be discerned along a broad spectrum. From the "implicit theology of the political" discussed, for example, by Schmitt in *Political Theology* to the "politology, sociology, and anthropology implicit in the theological and in religious discourse in general" of which Jakob Taubes speaks in his interpretation of St. Paul's Letter to the Romans, in *The Political Theology of Paul*, political theology assumes a now descriptive, then normative content and orientation.[114] Both perspectives, however, often also respond to profoundly metaphysical—both messianic and historical materialist—intuitions, such as, for example, those expressed in Benjamin's "Theologico-Political Fragment" and his "Theses on the Concept of History."[115]

Schmitt states that all decisive concepts of the modern doctrine of the state are "secularized theological concepts," a formulation that implies a claim concerning the genesis of the political and the "neutralization" of the religious. Theological concepts, in this view, have been, whether slowly or suddenly, transposed into the realm of the body politic: for example, the concept of the omnipotence of God has been translated into the idea of an all-powerful lawgiver, just as the miracle prefigures the decisive event.

But historical derivation is not the only possible consequence of Schmitt's position. He seems equally interested in the descriptive value of the systematic and formal resemblance between the domains of the theological and the political. Only by taking into account the conjunction between two elements—two poles or two sources, each of which is constitutive of human finitude—can one arrive at a sociology of legal concepts. As Jean-François Courtine and others have noted, Schmitt hesitates between these two analytically distinct positions. According to the first, politics finds its origin in the theological, which it seeks to suppress and forget, albeit it in vain and to its peril; according to the second, there is merely a structural analogy between the two.[116] Courtine attributes this oscillation to a change in intellectual position in Schmitt's thinking between the publication, in 1922, of *Political Theology* and the appearance, in 1970, of its sequel, *Political Theology II: The Legend of the Demise of All Political Theology*.[117] In the later text, Schmitt revised certain of his earlier views, mainly in response to criticism from two authors: Erik Peterson, in his *Monotheism as a Political Problem*, had sought to establish "theological impossibilities" and insisted on the ultimate liquidation of political theology, and Hans Blumenberg, in his *The Legitimacy of the Modern Age*, had claimed that Schmitt's political theology could be taken only as "a metaphorical theology."[118] Whereas in his 1922 study Schmitt seems to imply a relationship of foundation—and nothing else would authorize one to speak of historical processes of "secularization" or "neutralization" of antecedent theological tropes—his later position is more cautious. In *Political Theology II*, Schmitt merely insists on the structural similarity in outward features between the political and the theological. Indeed, the hypothesis of a simple homology seems less vulnerable to historical and systematic objection than the earlier, stronger, genealogical claim. Yet the weaker hypothesis still allows him to think the "transposition," the "translation," or the "redistribution [*Umbesetzung*]" of fundamental concepts and doctrinal schemes from one domain to the next.

On closer scrutiny, however, the oscillation between the earlier and later reading is already present in the first volume of *Political Theology*. Here, Courtine argues, Schmitt likewise hesitates between the historicist reduction of the theological to the political (the more metaphysical genealogical view) and a mode of reasoning reminiscent of Max Weber's insistence on the elective affinity between one domain and the other (the more modest analogical view). In other words, Schmitt from the outset attempts to avoid the alternatives of either transcribing the theological into the political (by way of "secularization" and "neutralization") or *strategically re-theologizing* the political, binding its central concepts backward to their supposedly religious origins. The contributions to the present volume illuminate these alternative (descriptive-reductive or normative-strategic) ways of assessing and using the theologico-political across a broad spectrum of historical and analytic positions.[119]

Beyond Tolerance: Pluralism and Agonistic Reason

One should not yield too quickly to the temptation to associate the descriptive-recon-structive (that is to say, the institutional-juridical, or, as Assmann says, *beschreibende*) and the normative-constructive (that is, the political, or *betreibende*) uses of the concept of the theologico-political with the more explicitly confessional (or "appellative") adoption of the term. The last can be found in twentieth-century Catholic and Protestant theologies of revolutionary hope (Johann Baptist Metz, Jürgen Moltmann, Dorothee Sölle, and others), especially in the Latin American and Third World liberation theologies of the 1960s and 1970s (in the writings of South American authors such as Gustavo Gutiérrrez, Leonardo Boff, and, more indirectly, Enrique Dussel[120]). In a different tone, a confessional use of the theologico-political appears in the writings of the British Radical Orthodoxy group (John Milbank, Catherine Pickstock, Graham Ward, Philip Goodchild, and others). These *normative* investments—which are also visible in recent antiglobalization protests[121]—are but the latest expression of a longer and richer tradition of articulating the connection between religion and the socio-juridical, public realm in ways that, even if they do not challenge the strict legal separation of church and state, question the latter's ideological neutrality and supposed liberality, just as they caution the Church to give up its illusory and somewhat deceptive apolitical stance.[122]

That things are more complex here is clear from Pope Benedict XVI's first encyclical, *Deus Caritas Est* (*God Is Love*), published in January 2006: "The church cannot and must not take upon herself the political battle to bring about the most just society possible. She cannot and must not replace the state. Yet at the same time she cannot and must not remain on the sidelines in the fight for justice."[123] That this does not allow the Vatican to absent itself from straightforward confrontation with the powers that be, precisely in its insistence on the intra-ecclesial and pastoral role of its mission, is clear from its recent clash with the Chinese authorities over the state's imposed appointment (and the Church's subsequent excommunication) of bishops on the mainland. The episode, which played itself out in May 2006, had an ironic sequel. When the highest official of the Roman Catholic Church in China, Cardinal Joseph Zen, also bishop of Hong Kong and elevated to Cardinal by Pope Benedict XVI in February 2006, commemorated the seventeenth anniversary of the Tiananmen Square massacre, he criticized the Communist regime on several counts. He was contradicted by Liu Bainian, Secretary General of the government-approved Chinese Catholic Patriotic Association, who expressed his surprise at Zen's comments, saying: "According to God's holy teachings, what belongs to Caesar should be left with Caesar, and what belongs to God should be left with God."[124]

In a remarkable conversation with Jürgen Habermas at the invitation of the Catholic Academy of Bavaria in January 2004,[125] then Cardinal Joseph Ratzinger, who was elected Pope Benedict XVI in April 2005, reiterates the Roman Catholic Church's view that science and modern democratic institutions cannot as such—or drawing on their own intellectual and cultural resources—"generate a renewed ethical consciousness," which is ever more needed in a time when "the acceleration of the tempo of historical developments" confronts us with "the formation of a world society" in which different "individual political, economic, and cultural powers depend, more and more, on each other," and in which human technological possibilities exceed "everything to which we have previously been accustomed," thus requiring unanticipated political intervention and legal regulation. Stressing the "shattering" of "old moral certainties," as an (unintended) result of the increasing permeation, if not necessarily clash, of different cultures, Benedict XVI calls on "philosophy's responsibility to separate the nonscientific element from scientific results with which it is so often intermingled, and in this way to remain attentive to the whole, to the further dimensions of the reality of human existence, only some aspects of which can reveal themselves in science" (pp. 261–62). The claim is consistent with his overall theological outlook, which has been characterized as more "traditionalist" than that of his predecessor.[126] Influenced by *la nouvelle théologie* (represented notably by Henri de Lubac), with its critique of abstract neo-scholasticism and its strong emphasis on ecclesial authority, especially on patristic tradition, in the interpretation of Scripture, he is said to hold a "vision of Christianity as a community with a distinctive culture,"[127] rather than a set of doctrines, from which secular society and other communities of faith should be engaged in a pluralistic spirit (which, from the historical and present standpoint of Catholic doctrine is, of course, not to be confused with the adoption of metaphysical, ontological pluralism—and hence the affirmation of many truths or truth-events—per se).

In this unlikely dialogue between the strict Catholic theologian who from 1981 until his election as the 265th Pope was the head (or Prefect) of the Holy Congregation for the Doctrine of the Faith (Sacra Congregatio pro Doctrina Fidei, the successor to the Inquisition) and the liberal philosopher of the discourse of modernity, intellectual heir of the Frankfurt School Critical Theory of Western Marxism, Habermas starts out from a question raised in the mid-sixties by Ernst Wolfgang Böckenförde, a "doubt that the democratic constitutional state can renew the normative preconditions of its existence out of its own resources." This question seems to express a modern predicament, for if the state is "dependent upon autochthonous conceptual or religious traditions" (p. 251), how can it assert its "neutrality" in matters of "comprehensive doctrines," which, as John Rawls argued, must be seen as an essential requirement for "political liberalism" (or for Kantian republicanism, Habermas adds), and which Rawls associates with religion in the most public of its manifestations? In his contribution, Habermas rearticulates his long-held view that the distinctively modern conception and legitimacy of constitutional law, the legal process, and its core statutes and principles (such as human rights) are self-sufficient and hence independent of religious and metaphysical traditions. He nonetheless holds that there remains an open question from the viewpoint of motivation as to how the public good will be upheld by citizens if they perceive themselves not as the law's authors but as merely its addressees and subjects. The former requires "a greater motivational outlay, one that cannot be legally commanded" (p. 253). While this need for political virtues does not necessarily imply that only religion can generate this motivational force, let alone that it provides "an argumentative 'surplus'" (p. 251), its traditions may still—or again—provide a reservoir whose potential "the secular forces of communicative reason" cannot fully exhaust or for which rational discourse cannot fully substitute.[128] "Political virtues," according to Habermas, "are a matter of socialization and of acclimating oneself to the practices of modes of thinking within a liberal political culture. The status of citizen is, in a certain sense, embedded in civil society, which derives sustenance from spontaneous and, if you like, 'prepolitical' sources" (p. 254). He concedes that this is not merely an empirical matter. If critical reflection, especially philosophy, needs to take "the phenomenon of the continued existence of religion in a continually secularizing environment" as more than a "mere social fact," this is because this phenomenon also constitutes a "cognitive challenge from within" (p. 256). This is not to deny the generic distinction between "a secular mode of speaking, which requires itself to be generally accessible, and a religious mode of speaking, which depends upon the truths of revelation" (p. 257), nor does this insight exhaust itself in an attitude of respect toward the expressiveness with which individuals and collectives often exemplify a religious way of life. Rather, if something remains intact in religious traditions, "so long as they avoid dogmatism and moral constraint," it is, Habermas claims, their "sufficiently differentiated possibilities of expression and sensibilities for misspent life, for societal pathologies, for the failure of individual life plans and the deformation to be seen in distorted life contexts." Part of the content of religious traditions that Habermas considers worth saving is the "translation of the notion of man's likeness to God into the notion of human dignity, in which all men partake equally and which is to be respected unconditionally" (pp. 257–58). More broadly, against the backdrop of his famous diagnosis of the paradoxes of modernity, of the "colonization" of the life-world by the systems and media of increasingly global economic markets (i.e., money), on the one hand, and bureaucratic and juridified forms of national and international administration (i.e., power), on the other, Habermas states that it is "in the constitutional state's own interest to treat with care all cultural sources upon which the consciousness of norms and the solidarity of citizens draw" (p. 258). It is in this context that he wishes to situate the discussion concerning "post-secular society." He concludes: "The ideological neutrality of the state authority, which guarantees the same ethical freedoms for every citizen, is incompatible with the political generalization of a secularistic worldview" (p. 260).

It would seem that Habermas's latest views on the relationship between "faith and knowledge" (the title of one of his most recent writings) and their mutual and complementary learning processes come within a hair's breadth of Pope Benedict XVI's more decidedly theological view of the "necessary correlativity," "polyphonic correlation," and "essential complementarity of reason and faith" (p. 268). For him this implies fundamentally a reflection on the modern phenomenon of "interculturality" (p. 266), whose implications he draws out even more fully than Habermas by insisting on the "de facto nonuniversality of both major cultures of the West—the culture of Christian faith as well as that of secular rationality" and by critical appraisal of Hans Küng's appeal for a "world ethos" as being a mere "abstraction." The reason for this assessment is simple enough: "there is no rational or ethical or religious universal formula about which everyone could agree and which could then support everyone," a claim that is hardly an affirmation of ontological pluralism, since it is immediately followed by the statement: "In any case, such a formula is presently beyond our reach" (p. 267). Pluralism, then, as a concept and practice, has a political and theological use that is at once essential and limited.[129] As if echoing Habermas's well-known metaphor of the unity of reason amid the plurality of its voices, Benedict XVI claims that, both socially and ecclesially, genuine pluralism is based upon a "*symphonia*," premised upon the prevalence of a whole, since it is:

> the fundamental form of the expression of truth in the Church, resting as this truth does on a complex *ensemble*, rich in tensions. The voice of the faith is not heard as mono-phony, but as symphony; not as a monophonic chant but as a composition in polyphony, with many notes which seem dissonant. . . . To lay aside one of the themes of this symphony is to impoverish the whole. The Fathers called this attitude "heresy": that is, a simplificatory choice, for only in the totality with its tensions is the truth to be found.[130]

Or again: "Only that pluralism is great which is directed toward unity." Such "fruitful pluralism" or "true catholicity" should be distinguished from "ruinous pluralism," which Benedict XVI defines as the "lost . . . ability to re-unite the great tensions internal to the totality of the faith." To forgo "unity" and "totality" amounts to reducing the subjective and ecclesial elements of faith to mere "contradictory and disordered linguistic fragments," substituting for its "symphony" the "dislocated pluralism of a home-made Christianity."[131]

Pope Benedict XVI's position differs in many ways from the at times "sophisticated theology of history" of the administration of George W. Bush, analyzed rhetorically by Bruce Lincoln on the eve of the November 2004 American presidential contest. In Lincoln's subtle reading, Bush's theology reveals itself to be a composite and multiply coded doctrine that strategically blends "an evangelical theology of 'born again' conversion" and a "Calvinist theology of vocation" with a "theology of American exceptionalism" and "a Manichaean dualism of good and evil" (p. 275).

Speaking in California in April 2006, Bush claimed that he bases "a lot of foreign policy decisions on things that I think are true. One, I believe there's an almighty. . . . Secondly, I believe that one of great gifts of the Almighty is the desire in everybody's soul . . . to be free."[132] These words and the difference between the sensibility they reflect and that of most European and of American policy makers prompted one American commentator to state the obvious: "The next American president will undoubtedly invoke God's blessing on America, as American presidents have always done. But it is one thing to ask God for blessing and guidance. It is an entirely other to believe the Almighty blesses everything that we do."[133]

Lincoln had already argued in his *Holy Terrors: Thinking about Religion after September 11* that only a careful textual and rhetorical analysis of the discourses of both the perpetrators and the president could unveil the presuppositions and contradictions of reinvigorated ideologies on either side of the divide made up by the "war on terror."[134] In an example of the usefulness of historical religious concepts for such analysis, Lincoln demonstrates in his present contribution that Bush and his speechwriters create a tense compromise between Pauline and Hegelian perspectives on salvation, based on uncertain individual election and on "an impersonal and inevitable process of gradual world-perfection," respectively (p. 275). As Philip Blond and Adrian Pabst have suggested, this compromise may well subscribe to a profoundly secular logic, according to which the original tension that early Judaism, Islam, and Christianity maintained between communal forms of faith and worldly power—that is, between prophets and kings, imams and caliphs, the heavenly and the earthly city—is dissolved in favor of the modern "liberal" relegation of beliefs to the uncontrollable private sphere of individual conscience, while delivering the political realm over to a blatant, cynical strife to establish Western hegemony (economically and in the imposition of its democratic model). Blair's words "The only way you can take a decision like that is to do the right thing according to your conscience" merely confirm the extent to which a certain liberalized (interiorized, Evangelical, Protestant?) religion has become, if not a ploy or an ideological justification, then at least a welcome vacuum for the (external) powers that be.[135] This, these authors argue, provoked the fundamentalist response, turning what seemed two opposite sides in the "war on terror"—the American neocons and the leadership of Al Qaeda—into mirror images of one another.[136]

International relations and geopolitics have come to be fatefully determined by a group of thinkers identified with the legacy of Leo Strauss (one thinks of the intellectual agenda extensively reported in recent years in *The New York Times, The New Yorker,* and *The New York Review of Books,* and associated with such names as Paul Wolfowitz, William Kristol, Richard Perle, and Robert Kagan, but also with certain subtle dissenters, such as Francis Fukuyama, who in his earlier writings did not always steer clear of a certain neo-evangelical streak). In his contribution, William E. Connolly takes a reflective step back to reassess one of the central themes and more "subtle elements" of Strauss's work, not to depoliticize, let alone justify or exculpate, Strauss's oeuvre, but to use it to think and engage the political—and hence also to politicize—otherwise. It is, Connolly notes, "the only professorial movement in the United States that has attained the standing of a public philosophy" (p. 278).[137]

Connolly's analysis resonates with one proposed by Heinrich Meier, general editor of Strauss's *Collected Writings* and the author of several erudite and provocative studies of the work of Schmitt and Strauss, and of their intellectual relationship. In his *Leo Strauss and the Theologico-Political Problem*,[138] Meier amplifies and systematizes one of the two central questions obliquely guiding Strauss's earlier works, namely: What constitutes the political, and how does its classical and modern regime moderate or mitigate the age-old relationship between reason and revelation, which, in the history of Western thought, has been variably characterized by antagonism, analogy, co-dependence, and multiple attempts at reconciliation and amalgamation? Meier recalls Strauss's claim, in *What Is Political Philosophy?*, that we are "compelled to distinguish political philosophy from political theology" and cites his seemingly simple and unambiguous attempt to define their difference: "By political theology we understand political teachings that are based on divine revelation. Political philosophy is limited to what is accessible to the unassisted human mind."[139]

Connolly highlights precisely what is contestable in such a view, which associates cultural diversity with the abandonment of standards, rootlessness, perversion, or "absolute tolerance," and he formulates his own position as one that allows contestability—and hence an emphatic conception of "deep" or "multidimensional" pluralism—as a matter of principle, practical politics, and "existential faith" alike. The last, he notes, "consists in a creed or philosophy plus the sensibility that infuses it" (p. 285).

Pluralism, even or especially "deep" pluralism, is not the same (as Straussians would seem to believe) as "cultural relativism." The latter tends merely to "support the culture that is dominant in a particular place": "for relativism is most at home with itself when it is situated in a concentric image of territorial culture. Here culture is said to radiate from the family to larger circles such as neighborhood, locality, and nation. . . . Given such an understanding of culture, a relativist is one who supports whatever practices and norms prevail in each concentrically ordered 'place.' " By contrast, pluralism opposes such segmented unitarianism and is "ec-centric" by nature and temperament: it emphasizes "ec-centric connections that cut across the circles of family, neighborhood, and nation" (p. 280).

Such a pluralistic view would agree with Strauss that "absolute tolerance is altogether impossible," but it would espouse different—antiunitarian—civic virtues, which set limits differently. Moreover, it would not think of these virtues and limits as attributable to a single source, written in stone or fixed in eternally "unchangeable standards founded in the nature of man and the nature of things." Perhaps, Connolly suggests, Strauss himself never believed they were, but thought of these claims as "politically necessary but philosophically unanchored" (p. 282). This would put Strauss's harsh criticisms of certain liberal educators—such as Eric Havelock, whom he discusses in *Liberalism: Ancient and Modern*—in a radically new light: "The virulence of Strauss's attack on Havelock, then, might express a desire to identify the single, universal basis of virtue *or* a desire to veil his own skepticism about the ability to provide the ground that civilization needs" (p. 282). Ultimately, Strauss might be right, Connolly surmises, in claiming that—as in the conflict between the heterodoxy of a Spinoza and the orthodoxy of revealed religion—the difference is not of a cognitive but of a moral nature. Connolly agrees, therefore, with Strauss's postulation of a "ubiquity of faith," but he conceives of this faith—and, one might add, of its spatial or public distribution—as being open in principle and hence contestable. Indeed, he adds, "it is the relational sensibility attached to faith that needs work, not the admission that faith plays an important role in life," in other words, the insight that "faith commitments vary in intensity, content, and imperiousness" (pp. 285–86).

Here, in nourishing pluralist sensibility, more than in any formal or procedural decision concerning reason and revelation, immanence or transcendence—whose ontological distinction and existential weight (for different religious and secular "faiths") nonetheless remain a matter of fact and of principle—would reside the chances for democracy's renewal (or, more pessimistically, its very survival). So would a certain acknowledgment that secular republicanism and political liberalism, although indebted to Western Enlightenment, remain shot through with embedded and embodied practices as well as modes of ritual enactment that are often ignored by defenders of the neutrality of its public sphere (whether theorists of rational choice, deliberative consensus, legal proceduralism, etc.). These tend to "pretend to identify *a forum above faith through which to regulate diverse faiths*," forgetting that this gesture is a theologico-political move in its own right. The pluralist response to such curtailment is that of an "ethics of engagement," resulting in "a healthy politics of creedal ventilation within and between faiths" (pp. 292–93). The principal possibility of such exchange and negotiation draws on resources in each tradition, not least on the fact that all faiths—whether in transcendence (as in the religions of the Book) or in immanence (as in Spinoza, Bergson, Deleuze, and the many paganisms and atheisms throughout history)—find a "disruptive moment," which is also a moment of "mystery," within themselves (p. 295). The prospects for its practical and political realization, however, depend upon the cultivation of sensibilities and civic virtues as well as institutional practices, whose fragile nature implies that "pluralism emerges as a possibility to pursue rather than as the certain effect of determinate conditions" (p. 295).

At this point, a further question imposes itself: What, if anything, would be the principle of interruption within the perspective of openness, that is to say, within deep pluralism itself? Wouldn't an internal rupture of any philosophy of (or faith in) immanence—and hence also of any immanence of abundance, creativity, and so on—need to be accounted for as well? And could such an interruption be produced immanently, in turn? What could that interruption be but, once again, a moment of lack, passivity, or heteronomy— call it transcendence, in short—everything that philosophies of immanence, with their presumed lack of lack, argue against? Can reference to "time," albeit a "time out of joint," fulfill that function? Should one not also invoke an irreducible moment of "no-time," that is to say, a foil against which creation and novelty become perceptible, if not, strictly speaking, possible, in the first place? Belonging to time, it seems, requires its polar opposite, if not ontologically then at least analytically. But what would this entail? A nonbelonging, a sense of "eternity" (perhaps as analyzed by Spinoza, in Deleuze's reading, but also as introduced by Adorno and developed by Lefort)? Finally, what resources would the theologico-political tradition(s) offer for tackling these questions?

Along lines both like and unlike Connolly's, Wendy Brown develops a critique of political liberalism's ideal of tolerance, and Chantal Mouffe sets forth a conception of agonistic pluralism in which benign or productive forms of cultural and political disagreement supplant rigid—and fatally antagonistic—fixations of sovereignty and democracy. Brown starts out with the troubling observation that recent years have seen a "culturalization of conflict" (p. 299), in which (following public intellectuals such as Bernard Lewis and Samuel Huntington in "The Roots of Muslim Rage" and *The Clash of Civilizations*, respectively) an opposition has been drawn between liberal culture, premised upon moral autonomy, neutrality, and tolerance, on the one hand, and nonliberal, intolerant, and ultimately barbaric cultures, on the other. The transposition of conflict from questions of the market, the state, capitalism, or democracy to "culture" rests, Brown argues, on an "overt premise of liberal tolerance," namely, that "religious, cultural, or ethnic differences are sites of natural or native hostility" (p. 299). Given this association, she asks two sets of related questions, which reflect several of the governing concerns of this volume: first, "What is the relation between the binding force of the social contract and the binding force of culture or religion? Why isn't the social contract sufficient for reducing the significance of subnational group hostilities?" (p. 300); and second, "If national 'civic religion' was featured by the classic social contract theorists—Hobbes, Locke, and Rousseau—as a necessary *supplement* to the social contract, where did the contents of what was deposited in that supplement go and what is the relationship of this loss to the rise of subnational identities requiring civic tolerance?" (p. 729n.4).

Brown shows that an answer to these questions can be prepared only by revisiting the assumptions that pit a formal concept of subjectivity, with its understanding of culture as an "option" or "background" to be espoused or rejected at will, against a supposedly "organicist" individuality that has stayed within—or, as Freud says, can always regress again into—a primordial understanding of "culture as religion" and "religion as culture." In the liberal view, religion is a freely chosen—or freely accepted—source of inspiration, whereas in the organicist view, it affectively predetermines a given course of action or suffering. Thus, she writes: "Bush's religiosity is figured as a source of strength and moral guidance for his deliberations and decisions, while the devotee of Allah is assumed to be without the individual will and conscience necessary to such rationation" (p. 301). She uses Freud to deconstruct that opposition by teasing out the assumptions underlying his conviction that "individuation" constitutes the "agent," "sign," and "telos" of civilization, whereas groups, being based first on "primary mutual hostility" and "sexual rivalry" and second on mechanisms of projection and the idealization of externalized love objects (such as the leader or some collective ideal) represent "a condition—whether temporary or enduring—of barbarism" (p. 304). Brown analyzes this conception of group identification as regression less in light of its considerable explanatory value for nationalism and facism than as it continues to inform "liberal figurations of the inherent intolerance and dangerousness of organicist societies" (p. 308). With liberalism and the Kantian conception of individual autonomy and reason on which it is based, Freud's pathologization of groups shares the conviction that cultural beliefs are more volatile if they are "public" rather than "private" or "familial," an assumption that immediately slips into the claim that "to be without liberalism is not simply to be oppressed but to be exceptionally dangerous" (p. 310). In sum, liberalism is structurally incapable of appreciating culture and collective identities—in their group-related and, strictly speaking, public dimension—as a potentially, let alone intrinsically common good. Culture, in the liberal view, can be judged and justified only as "optional" and from a "noncultural"—indeed, a moral or formal and deliberative—point of view. Political liberalism, by contrast, aspires toward "a public rationality that overcomes cultural particularism in favor of putatively acultural concerns with justice as fairness." But this alleged "solution," Brown concludes, "involves a set of interrelated ideological moves in which religion and culture are privatized and the cultural and religious dimensions of liberalism itself are disavowed." This presupposes an analytical move in which culture is defined as "extrinsic to the individual, as forming the background of the individual, as that which the individual 'chooses' or has a right to" (pp. 312–13).

Following the itinerary set out in her earlier *The Return of the Political* and *The Democratic Paradox*,[140] Mouffe develops a model of pluralism that she terms "agonistic." She argues that it would provide a better framework than contemporary theories of political liberalism and deliberative democracy for accommodating the continuing and renewed role played by religion in the formation of personal and collective identities, and in the symbolic ordering of social relations. The concept of "agonistic pluralism" would allow one to articulate an understanding of democracy—indeed, of "the political"—no longer based on the assumption of an eventual and consensual, that is to say, argumentative or procedural, resolution of conflicts. The assumption of procedural resolution ignores the perpetual need to resort to nonformalizable and "substantial ethical commitments" or, more broadly, "normative concerns" (pp. 321, 320), whose genesis and structure Mouffe analyzes with the help of the late Wittgenstein's invocation of the ensemble of practices called "language games" and the agreement in judgments grounded in shared "forms of life."

This, Mouffe concludes, suggests that "a specific type of ethos" or, more precisely, "comprehensive doctrines" cannot in principle be kept out of the realm that Rawls defines as "political liberalism," just as they cannot be separated from his procedural and deliberative conception of "justice as fairness." In consequence, there can be no strict neutrality of the state, even though (or precisely because) it is premised upon specific values associated with the common good, such as the separation between the church's and its own jurisdictions. In Mouffe's words: "Those separations make possible the emergence of civil society as a distinct realm" (p. 321). Indeed, she goes on to claim, "the liberal notion of a secular state implies not only the distinction between church and state, but also the conception of the church as a voluntary association" (p. 321).

Yet the legal separation of church and state does not take place within a neutral space or starting out from a supposedly impartial (call it secular) point of view, nor does it imply that religion and politics do not jointly constitute the public realm at different levels. To deny this is to confuse politics and the political with the question of state power and to identify the latter with things public. On the contrary, Mouffe goes on to claim, the separation between church and state does "not require that religion should be relegated to the private sphere and that religious symbols should be excluded from the public sphere" (p. 325). Within constitutional limits, which will be differently interpreted depending on historical context and cultural tradition, religious motifs and causes can inform democratic struggles in the public arena, and hence contribute to the definition or readjustment of the common good.

This being said, the "social imaginary," or the constituted "we" implied in the common good, is conceived here, not as a natural or historical given, but as a "vanishing point," a "horizon of meaning" whose empirical referent is impossible to represent fully under modern conditions, precisely because it must always remain an object of contestation in view of temporary hegemonies. The nature or dimension of the political requires that politics—especially democratic politics or agonistic pluralism—steer clear of the antagonism whose intrinsic and destabilizing hostility is a standing possibility and, indeed, risk of the social and public realm. The Greek and modern understanding of *polis* and *polemos*, for essential reasons, never lie far apart. An agonistic and pluralistic democratic ethos or practice would not prevent the possibility or risk of exclusion—of the very distinction between "us" and "them"—nor, to be sure, should it have the illusion that disagreements will eventually be resolvable through rational agreement brought about by certain formal procedures. Yet it makes sure that in the cultivation, expression, and confrontation of impassioned utterances or divisive affects (that is to say, all the values, beliefs, and motivations that are irreducible to self-declared interests and reasons, let alone moral judgments, but that bring people into the political process in the first place) "the opponent is not seen as an enemy to be destroyed but as an adversary whose existence is legitimate and must be tolerated. We will fight against his/her ideas, but we will not put into question his/her right to defend them" (p. 323).

That alternative conceptions of pluralist democracy might require further questioning, both of the very concept of tolerance and of elusive notions of transcendence, is aptly argued by Lars Tønder and Matthew Scherer. Tønder's succinct analyses build upon a thorough investigation of the historical and intellectual underpinnings—and limitation—of the fundamentally Christian idea of tolerance, showing it to be in need of further articulation. Scherer's contribution inscribes itself into the broader project of retracing a "politics of persuasion" that, against the historical background of the tradition of spiritual exercises and moral perfectionism—constructs itself via prophetic, saintly, and creative forms of (and, indeed, appeals to) "conversion."

Little attention has been paid to the fact that the long tradition of tolerance—whose central concern has accompanied classical modern political theory and concepts of political liberalism up to the present day—has a deeply ambiguous genealogy (a nuance that Tønder seeks to capture in the terminological distinction between *toleration* and *tolerance*). Tønder asks what religious and moral sensibilities and normative claims underlie the concept, the function, and the practice of "tolerance" or are solicited by it. He aims to think through the concept's *sui generis* character—that is to say, its irreducibility to other constitutive concepts of the political, such as "freedom," "justice," and "truth"—by drawing on an unorthodox canon of eighteenth-century Enlightenment and twentieth-century phenomenological thinkers, including Locke, Kant, Voltaire, and Merleau-Ponty, whose writings have not often been studied in conjunction. These thinkers allow him to explore the hypothesis that in early modern political thought the concept of tolerance finds its most significant articulation less in classical discussions concerning the institutional separation between church and state than in shifting contrasts between religious vocabularies expressive of philosophies of immanence and transcendence. The concept of tolerance thus emerges as a critical and privileged category for modern democratic thought, which comes into its own when analyzed in terms of human embodiment and the accompanying emotion—or "affect"—that it presupposes. In the larger project of which this is part, Tønder goes on to ask what it means to experience tolerance phenomenologically and spells out the premises of a political theory of the sensibilities.

Scherer reads the icon of modern liberal thinking against the backdrop of what Rawls would have called a "comprehensive doctrine," namely, that of saintliness. Ironically, the political liberalism that prides itself on a certain neutrality in matters of faith requires for its understanding and the propagation of its central claims the very structure of valuation whose historical premises and existential thickness it brackets out for the sake of the intellectual integrity—and modernity—of its philosophical project. Scherer's contribution is distilled from a larger project concerning the public role of motifs of prophetic, saintly, and creative conversion and the forms of persuasion and loyalty they inspire. In it, he devotes careful attention to the rhetorical underpinnings of political discourse, construing a conversation between philosophical authors and political theorists who have usually been studied in separate disciplinary realms, in unrelated methodological registers, and with different normative aims. He thus opens a whole new area of inquiry, which brings out surprising comparisons and unexpected alliances in twentieth-century and early-twenty-first-century approaches to political and democratic processes in relation to the broader horizon of motivational, affective, and, last but not least, religious orientations.

Scherer uses the motif of saintliness, a term that must first be historically and contextually situated, then analyzed and formalized in rigorous ways, to highlight aspects of the "religious" elements and dynamics in post-Enlightenment or post-secular thought. Drawing on the tradition of spiritual exercises (as theorized by Pierre Hadot and Arnold Davidson) and on the ideal of moral perfectionism (a term coined by Stanley Cavell), he focuses on how ways of life, modes of acknowledgment, and forms of loyalty enable and structure the experience of the political in a fashion that interpretations of utilitarianism, political liberalism, communicative rationality, and rational choice cannot, for conceptual reasons, appreciate. He compellingly argues that motifs such as saintliness—and, in addition, the miraculous, faith in shared concepts, and belief in the world—form the very heart and fabric of political experience.

Democratic Republicanism, Secularism, and Beyond

Can the concept of political theology be retrieved within the wider tradition of "moral perfectionism," of imagining philosophy as a way of life? In his contribution, Bhrigupati Singh examines this strand of thought, which runs from Emerson and Thoreau not only to Stanley Cavell, but via Emerson's influence on Nietzsche to Deleuze, and also to Gandhi, who invokes Emerson and Thoreau as intellectual sources of inspiration. Stating the case against persistent cynicism and intellectual despair, Singh claims that the current international scene, determined by 9/11 and ongoing globalization, requires philosophy to speak otherwise than with wholesale condemnations of the Enlightenment or a "belligerent, stupid, and white America." He asks, "what would it be like to demand intelligence, to show that there is evidence of it in this milieu, that thinking has been possible here?" Or, again: "In what ways has America expressed itself philosophically?" (p. 367). Cavell and via him Emerson suggest an alternative route in which the "distrust of the present or actual state within which one finds oneself," that is to say, of culture and its institutions, is less cause for exhaustion, let alone "withdrawal," than for "a turning toward the eventual, in the task of attempting to sense the new, to create a philosophy of the future" (p. 369).

Singh recognizes this disposition in Gandhi's "anticolonial manifesto" *Hind Swaraj* (*Home Rule for India*), as well as in his autobiography *My Experiments with Truth*. Here, he notes, Gandhi establishes an intrinsic link between the Emersonian "impulse to the perfectibility of the self" and "a call for the transformation of the world as a whole, not a lament for a world gone by but a summons to one still to be borne." Such hopes, mediated for Gandhi by Thoreau's "Civil Disobedience," circumvent simple oppositions, such as that between individualism and communitarianism. Singh finds their echo in the meetings of the World Social Forum, which has followed in the footsteps of the antiglobalization movement. Gandhi's way of "reinhabiting," more than simply reformulating or resituating, Thoreau's concept of "civil disobedience" was based, Singh claims, on a positive "relation to desire," on "a form of attraction," irreducible to any Kantian sense of obligation, ought, or pure duty, but rather an experimentation with a "further self" that is one with "another world, the eventual, struggling to emerge from the actual." This reactualized version of Emersonian "aversive thinking," Singh concludes, has as its opposite less the imperative- or rule-oriented fear of "disorder or lawlessness" than "the complete impoverishment of desire and of capabilities," in other words, "the impossibility of the emergence of newness (of becoming)" (p. 373). Such a view, Singh suggests, invokes the Spinozist conception of relations between individual bodies (and of these making up the "body politic"), which can be seen in the background of Gandhi's problematization of the distinction between the private and the public, as well as between the religious and the political. This is epitomized in his famous statement "Anyone who thinks that religion and politics can be kept apart, understands neither religion nor politics." A more complex thought, premised less on a "libertarian" philosophy than on cultivated "sensibilities," is a legacy of Romanticism and its refusal either to hypostatize and deify or to reify and materialize the "soul," a legacy that, Singh argues, should not too quickly be reduced to a naturalized or secularized theology. Not only is this legacy pagan as much as Christian; its referent, if one can still say so, is not personal but a "specific form of life," as it expresses itself in "interrelations of nature, culture, and individuation" (p. 374).

In his latest writings, especially the "trilogy" consisting of *Specters of Marx*, "Faith and Knowledge," and *Rogues*, discussed by Samuel Weber in his contribution, Derrida argues that the place and function of the body politic is taken by the *demos*, now no longer seen as the fuller and universal expression of humanity but as something—some "thing"—that precedes, exceeds, surrounds, and traverses the conceptions and instances of sovereignty and nationhood, freedom and community (all premised upon necessarily exclusionary assumptions of oneness and indivisibility, sameness and selfhood, identity and value, and structurally allergic, if ultimately not immune, to repetition and diffusion, that is to say, to language and media).[141] Instead, he explains in his dialogue with Habermas, the concept of *demos* should be viewed as:

> *at once* the incalculable singularity of anyone, before any "subject," the possible undoing of the social bond by a secret to be respected, beyond all citizenship, beyond every "state," indeed every "people," indeed even beyond the current state of the definition of a living being as living "human" being, *and* the universality of rational calculation, of the equality of citizens before the law, the social bond of being together, with or without contract, and so on.[142]

The body politic is thus tied to a notion of force and power (a "-cracy," Derrida writes) that is no longer identified with instinctual "social pressure," as, say, in Henri Bergson's understanding of "moral obligation" and "static religion" (discussed below by Paola

Marrati) or with law. Rather, it is linked to a concept of "justice" that exceeds the Kantian (or, for that matter, Rawlsian and Habermasian) regulative idea, while stopping short of more emphatic ideals of salvation, both religious and this worldly.

In its full consequence, such a notion of a never-present—and, in a sense, nonpresentable and no longer simply representational—"democracy to come" cannot "ultimately" be designated a "political regime,"[143] as "democracy" had been in the Greco-Christian and Latin world, with its theologico-political overdetermination of republican sovereignty (and its monarchical, aristocratic, or otherwise oligarchical analogues). The spread of this model across the world was from the outset a *mondialatinization* or "globalatinization" (to use Samuel Weber's felicitous translation), that is to say, a becoming progressively Latin (or Greco-Roman-Christian) of the West and its spheres of domination. Indeed, as if conjuring up—and radically inverting—the early medieval theologico-political construct of the "king's two bodies," Derrida reminds us that "the democratic, having become consubstantially political in this Greco-Christian and globalatinizing tradition, appears inseparable in the modernity following the Enlightenment from an ambiguous secularization (and secularization is always ambiguous in that it frees itself from the religious, all the while remaining marked in its very concept by it, by the theological, indeed, the onto-theological)."[144] Not even a democracy always already still "to come" could fully escape that logic. It remains tied back to a legacy that it may not want to call its own but that it cannot but somehow affirm and reaffirm, at least for some time still to come. The preparation—*ex negativo*, as it were—for a democracy to come would involve deconstructing the very pillar of the political, the concept of sovereignty, whose necessary unsettling and no less inevitable reaffirmation form the poles between which deconstructive analysis and practice should oscillate, with ever-heightened vigilance.

Weber cites a telling passage from Derrida's account of the "logic" of sovereignty, of its internal constitution and demise, which argues that the present excesses of the Bush administration—its disregard for international law,[145] its reserving for itself the privilege of declaring other states to be "rogues" ("outlaws," "evil empires," "renegade regimes," etc.), and the lack of shame with which its high-level officials adopt a "double-speak" that would make Orwell cringe[146]—reveal a general political, perhaps, a theologico-political problem rather than just ineptitude on the part of one particular nation or current administration:

> a priori, the states that are able or are in a state to make war on rogue states are themselves, in their most legitimate sovereignty, rogue states abusing their power. As soon as there is sovereignty, there is abuse of power and a rogue state. Abuse is the law of use; it is the law itself, the "logic" of a sovereignty that can reign only by not sharing. More precisely, since it never succeeds in doing this except in a critical, precarious, and unstable fashion, sovereignty can only *tend*, for a limited time, to reign without sharing. It can only tend toward imperial hegemony.[147]

In other words, no geopolitical dominance can last; it is unstable for structural reasons, internal to the very concept and practice of sovereignty. As Weber writes, "Sovereignty," in its purported universality and indivisibility—its near apophatic or mystically postulated "silence," as Derrida says, or its "empty signifier," as Laclau would add—"seeks to transcend time, as well as language, insofar as both require it to partition and share, to divide and compromise its unity and integrity—in short, to *compose* with alterity, rather than simply *impose* itself upon it" (p. 387). Where sovereignty is defined, as in the Charter of the United Nations (a "super-sovereign," in Schmittian terms), as the "exception to the recommendation made to all states not to resort to force," namely, to resort to the suspension of law only for the sake of self-defense in international conflict, that is, where a threat to the nation-state's survival that could not otherwise be eliminated is perceived (or construed), a similar logic of self-deconstruction takes place. A price is inevitably paid for the transition from legitimacy to sheer power—not just de facto, because of the resistance of things and peoples, but for reasons based on the aporetic nature of the concept of sovereignty—and ultimately of democracy—itself. In Derrida's words: "The paradox—always the same—is that sovereignty is incompatible with universality, even as it is appealed to by every concept of international, and thus universal or universalizable—and thus democratic—law."[148]

Such a conception of sovereignty, Derrida and Weber recall, has deep theological and monotheistic roots, as indicated by Alexis de Tocqueville's statement, in *Democracy in America*, that the people "reign over the American political world as God rules over the universe. It is the cause and the end of all things; everything rises out of it and is absorbed back into it" (p. 392). Could one imagine an auto-deconstruction of the theologico-political parallel to the one just observed in the concept and practice of sovereignty? Are these notions—and hence also God, the people, and their structural analogues—aporetic, plural, no longer coinciding with themselves, no longer what they claimed or seemed, namely, one, simple, and indivisible?

Building on his recent *Targets of Opportunity: On the Militarization of Thinking* and the final chapters of *Theatricality as Medium*,[149] Weber discusses the ways in which Derrida, drawing on Aristotle, invents a vocabulary to prepare for an alternative view of democracy, positing a concept of "life" and "living together" that is irreducible to common understandings of bio-politics, while "exceeding the juridico-political sphere," "beyond government and democratic sovereignty." Furthermore, returning to Rousseau, Derrida invokes this author's reference to a "people of gods," which, if it existed, "would govern itself democratically," by contrast to Tocqueville's metaphor of the "people-as-God," in the singular (pp. 393–94). Democracy would thus have to be reconceived in light of a "plural divinity," thereby breaking away from a long monopolar theologico-political tradition resting upon an impossible—a silent, mystical, apophatic, empty—postulation of sovereignty in terms of unity and indivisibility. Weber concludes his essay by considering that this would imply a reorientation of a certain culture of visibility and invisibility, of media coverage and secrecy, on the one hand, and a reimagining, with the help of Benjamin, of "capitalism"—yet another medium, vehicle, and refraction of democracy—as itself already a "religion" or "cult," indeed, a theatrical parading of "banknotes" with their "effigies," on the other.

That the theatricalization of the theologico-political—designating others as "rogues" and inciting religious violence for near-cosmic causes—together with the deterritorialization or becoming more and more "global" and virtual of the forms and elements of faith, may produce all too real and, indeed, visceral effects can be illustrated in many ways. A further poignant example from the Americas is discussed by Rafael Sánchez, who, in his essay on Latin American populism—specifically, on the fate of the political and of politics in contemporary Venezuela—demonstrates in what sense certain mediatic effects can produce an instant deflation of, indeed, blow "a gaping hole" in, what Sánchez provocatively characterizes as a "theologico-political balloon," the Bolivarian republic of the Hugo Chávez regime, in power since December 1998. Sánchez evokes the hilarious media event that epitomized—or triggered—the regime's loss of auratic authority, shifting the overall tone of public debate from deference to ridicule, as the military was put on the spot for its alleged impotence via the (first anonymous, then televised) sending of women's colored lingerie: a fateful provocation, Sánchez explains, whose violence is more symbolic than physical, threatening "to blow the regime's transcendental claims and illusions to smithereens" (p. 404). Yet another sample of an effective politics of scandal and insult, just as it is one of sexual politics (or, rather, of using the sexual politically), the "panties episode" intervened in the public domain of a state whose "gendered identity and auratic authority . . . are largely contingent upon its being demarcated from the domain of privacy and feminine sexuality" (p. 408). The laughter thus provoked put all such demarcations, together with the collective and individual identities they vainly seek to establish, under erasure or, at least, on the defensive.

As in an earlier essay, "Channel-Surfing: Media, Mediumship, and State Authority in the María Lionza Possession Cult (Venezuela),"[150] and a forthcoming book, *Dancing Jacobins: A Genealogy of Latin American Populism (Venezuela)*, Sánchez queries the usefulness of the concept of the theologico-political for our understanding of historical and contemporary trends in Latin American politics. Turning our gaze from "the placid heavens of philosophy" to the "hells of history," Sánchez proposes deploying sophisticated theoretical concepts and modes of reasoning that underpin (accompany, and are in turn enriched by) erudite historical and ethnographic analyses. What the recent tumultuous event in Venezuela illustrates is how the theatricality or theatrical machinery of representation has something of the "religious" about it, or at least something that allows a "presumption of secrecy" in a seemingly "invisible chamber of power" to be suddenly undone in a "serialized exposure."

Sánchez offers a conceptual matrix that draws on the writings of Lacoue-Labarthe, Nancy, and Laclau, even though it modifies, that is to say, concretizes and historicizes their premises. In the theatricality, as well as in the structure of "monumental governmentality," that inspires the nationalist and populist imagination to aim at "healing the nation's fractures by once again uniting the nation in an inclusive totality" via appeal to its founding father, the "Rousseauean Great Legislator and People's Delegate," Simón Bolívar, Sánchez discerns the characteristics of the theologico-political, in the precise sense that Schmitt and then Kantorowicz have given to this term (p. 413).

In particular, he invites us to raise the question of whether this link between the religious and the political or theologico-political is structural or accidental, that is to say, revelatory of a general law—or ontology—of the political or explainable in terms of the historical effect of "the Spanish King's awesome disappearance some two hundred years ago and the catastrophic consequences that followed. Among these were the collapse of the entire colonial order, with its articulated orders and estates, now bereft of the kingly 'thing' that had glued it together." What follows is an avalanche of repetitions and re-enactments, each outstripping its predecessor, a "lateral mimetic flight" in which "the new subalterns sought to fill the postcolonial spaces now made vacant and flattened," to which one tribune after the next (Chávez being only the last in a long series) sought to put a halt by "arresting through reflection" this movement of flight and by staging a radical and fundamentally Jacobin constitutionalism, in which the law would mirror the general will of the people (p. 414). But then, following a more fundamental logic, which dictates the ultimate irreconcilability of the universal (the law) and the particular (the audiences that make up the people), Latin America's tribunes do inevitably lose their constituencies and hence legitimacy. For all their "hyperbolic frenzy," they remain behind, "gesticulating in an empty theater," signaling once more the "retreat" of the political—here, the theologico-political—in that the "withdrawal of any communal figure of identification" becomes increasingly palpable the more it is fantasized in one hyperbolic invocation after another (e.g., in the moves and countermoves of the regime and its opposition). Its only answer would seem to be yet another—and, Sánchez leaves no doubt, ultimately vain—appeal to a "power from the outside," to the "reservoir of transcendence" for which Bolívar is the proper name and stand-in, conjuring up the "vertical prosthesis" of a general will that is all too inclined to disperse itself into a "horizontal transcendence" of "tribunal prosthesis" and its myriad singular cases. Insight into this logic, rather than into that of, say, bio-politics, offers us a key to understanding what happens to the political, at least on this continent (p. 416).

The more force is invoked, the less presence it has. What is intriguing in Sánchez's analysis of the internal logic of the "politics of exemplarity" and the "aporetic nature of the 'general will'" (p. 415) is that no ontico-empirical origin or end of the series of iterations that punctuate political history seems presupposed, conjured up, or called for, not even as a transcendental illusion of sorts. The reference to singularity, representation, and incarnation should be seen instead as a fall into conflicted, fragmenting interests and desires, which are portrayed as necessarily at odds with the unified, totalizing, vertical transcendence of the "general will." In this, he parts ways with a central assumption of thinkers who insist on the historically a priori status, that is to say, the ontico-empirical conditionality, of even the most ideal or idealized concepts, and hence deconstructs the possible grounds for distinguishing between horizontal and vertical supplementarity or prostheses at all. Sánchez suggests that, whereas the theatricality inherent in representation thrives on absence and transcendence, the religious plays a far more complicated role in the constitution of such "monumental governmentality."

Far from claiming a simple "permanence of the theologico-political," as Lefort had surmised and as Laclau sometimes seems to echo, Sánchez thus indicates that the historical and ethnographic study of groups, and especially crowds, peoples, and states, contributes to a more grounded anthropology of religion, in a radically new guise. The task of this type of inquiry, he demonstrates, poses itself differently in the postcolonial nineteenth and twentieth centuries and in a present-day modernity gone haywire—but a modernity nonetheless.

That the theatricalization of the political and of politics has effects that are unequally distributed and affect some citizens more than others—even or especially where the violence is in an almost calculated way indiscriminate—is hard to deny. But where, how, and why is this so? Veena Das's contribution, concerning the figure of the abducted woman during the 1947 Partition of India and Pakistan, analyzes not only the impact of communal violence on citizens as gendered but also the ways in which turmoil and horror allowed the nation-state to imagine and to portray itself as the protector of a more rational, fundamentally purified, and by implication masculine social order. In this particular essay, Das puts less emphasis on the silencing of women's voices in the official and professional historiographical renderings of the Partition, which has been an important issue in the work of feminist historians on trauma and testimony. Rather, she focuses on how hearsay and rumor tainted subsequent government fact-finding commissions and search-and-recovery operations, and highlights the ways in which elements of myth (dating back to epic depictions in the *Ramayana* and *Mahabharata*) and popular narrative or film circulated in an imaginary of social and sexual disorders that "created the conditions of possibility in which the state could be instituted as essentially a social contract between *men* charged with keeping male violence against women in abeyance" (p. 429). This insight importantly alters a central tenet in Western contractual theories of natural right, notably Hobbes, even as it reinstates an insight present already in Rousseau: "The figure of the abducted woman acquires salience because it posits the origin of the state not in the mythic state of nature but in 'correct' relations between communities. Indeed, the *mise-en-scène* of nature itself is that of heads of households at war with other heads of households over control of the sexual and reproductive powers of women, rather than unattached 'natural' men at war with each other" (p. 440).

Das suggests that the very demand for and mutual insistence on legislation intended to restore women to their families of origin "sanctified a sexual contract as the counterpart of the social contract" (p. 433). In other words, norms of kinship and the purity or honor of the national population—expressed in the state's nonrecognition and undoing of forced marriages and conversions (of children and women, that is)—were rigidified by being turned into the rule of law, thus producing a "disciplining of sentiment according to the demands of the state," while, conversely, "sovereignty continues to draw life from the family." Indeed, Das, concludes: "Does this story, located at the juncture of the inauguration of the nation-state in India, tell us something about the nature of sovereignty itself?" (pp. 436 and 440). Such analysis reminds us of the stakes involved, even or especially in scholarly inquiry into what might seem the most abstract and ethereal of concepts—for example, that of the theologico-political.

Markha G. Valenta's incisive discussion of European responses to the veil or headscarf and the politics of gender clarifies how the confrontation between ideologies of secularism and the multifarious strategies of conversion fails to register what should have been clear all along: namely, that anxious contemporary Western responses to Islam exemplify a collective amnesia concerning a long history of mutual imbrication and interaction, obfuscated by colonialism and orientalism alike. Drawing on the pioneering work of Edward Said, Leila Ahmed, Lila Abu-Lughod, and others, Valenta suggests that only "with the arrival of the northern Mediterranean powers—the Greek conquest of 333 B.C. (by soldiers bearing under their arms learned Aristotle's treatise on women's natural inferiority to men), followed by the Romans and the spread of Christianity—did the practice of veiling and, more broadly, of women's enclosure, devaluation, and repression spread. In this sense, veiling was the material measure of ancient Egypt's Hellenization and Romanization, its 'Europeanization'" (pp. 450–51). In consequence, the current debates surrounding the veil—conceived by both its detractors and its proponents as a "primary site of attack and counterattack" (p. 445)—does not constitute a problem in and of itself, but rather "dramatizes Europe's encounter not just with the Islamic world but with its very own foundations" (p. 451). This paradox explains why in the nineteenth century, when Egypt was under British rule, those who vehemently opposed Muslim veiling often agitated against women's suffrage and feminism "at home." Perhaps it also helps explain why present-day Western feminism has hardly been more successful in addressing the issue posed by the marker of the veil.

Valenta's anamnestic recovery treats the genealogy of the problem dramatized by the veil as one that has at least as much to do with Europe's insecurities about itself as with its exterior and interior "others." More importantly, she argues that the problem "is not a matter of lacking adequate knowledge of Europe's actual Islamic history and heritage, which is well documented if not well known. Rather, it is that that history cannot be told within the logic of a History that allows for only one trajectory through space and time, one reality per territory" (p. 461). Europe cannot narrate, let alone conceptualize, its identity, fate, and future in its own terms alone. Acknowledging this fact would mean engaging in "rigorous" rather than merely "easy tolerance," recognizing that minorities are not "allochthonous" but "vitally constitutive of the nation and its future," and giving them, "whoever they may be, a say not just over themselves, but over us" (p. 462). Such a tolerance, Valenta notes, quoting Thomas Scanlon, is necessarily a "risky matter, a practice with high stakes" (p. 462). Some of the most compelling pages in Valenta's contribution deal with Europe's resistance to a new phase of (its) history, its lack of creativity and imagination in envisioning a future that would be more than a fortification of its postwar recovery after its "bestial implosion half a century ago." Neither the hope of further secularization or secularism—whether as a bulwark against or an enabler of religious diversity—nor, to be sure, a simple return to forgotten religious values can fill this void. If any post-secular thought and political theology of Europe and the West there may be, we do not yet know what it is.

This analysis sets the stage for the analyses of the doctrine—one is tempted to say the religion, sacrality, or "existential belief" (to use Connolly's term)—of *laïcité* by Yolande Jansen and Talal Asad, who from different angles discuss the modern intellectual and cultural history behind the intricate French debates in the report of the commission chaired by Bernard Stasi (whose members included public figures and scholars such as Régis Debray, Alain Touraine, Mohammed Arkoun, and Gilles Kepel), leading up to the 2004 legal ban in state-run schools on headscarfs or, more precisely, on "conspicuous religious signs," such as Muslim veils, Jewish yarmulkes, and outsized Christian crucifixes.[151] The *New York Times* responded to this measure with an editorial under the provocative heading "Secular Fundamentalism," stating its criticism in no uncertain terms, ones echoed by the State Department, and voicing a difference in sensibilities concerning free speech and behavior in American and European political cultures, epitomized by the fact that the European Court of Human Rights, in November 2005, upheld Turkey's even more severe—and severely contested—curbing of the headscarf on college campuses and in state offices, a ban effective since 1986:

> Speaking before a gathering that included religious leaders from all major faiths, [French President] Chirac cast his decision [to support the ban] as a reaffirmation of France's commitment to a rigorous separation of church and state. But it is not that at all. Banning believers from following the discipline of their religion is, in fact, state-imposed secular fundamentalism. One fallacy is that for a Christian to wear a cross is not analogous to a Sikh wearing a turban, a Muslim wearing a scarf, or a Jew wearing a yarmulke. To hang a crucifix around your neck is a personal display of faith. To observant Muslims, Jews, and Sikhs, however, head coverings are obligations. Their observance therefore falls under the rubric of freedom of expression and conscience, not proselytism.[152]

The point goes to the heart of French *Républicanisme*—the belief that "a universal citizen, abstracted from social and economic conditions (whether residential, religious, or racial), engages in a direct relationship with the state," which "reciprocates by playing down the role of such identities in the political process," rejecting "balkanization" and "identity politics," but also sectarianism and communitarianism, as "incompatible with the realization of the common good."[153] Jansen examines this perspective by revisiting the historical context of the concept of *laïcité* in the conflict between secular republicans and the Catholic Church in the French Third Republic. She recalls that republicans, in this struggle, "required more than just a juridically defined secularity," as would be provided by the 1905 law ratifying the official separation of church and state—they "needed a pedagogy to institutionalize a culture of Republicanism." Rather than a merely formally defined "freedom of conscience" and the "disestablishment" of religion in its public aspect, they sensed they had to provide a "communitarian concern for civic unity," whose aim was to "substitute democratic civil loyalty for religious and traditional allegiances," and whose vehicle would be public education (p. 477).

In particular, Jansen scrutinizes the political and cultural imagery invoked in this debate by analyzing political cartoons. She draws two important conclusions from her consideration of this material. First, she notes that a "revolution-based conception of history," implied in its schematic antithesis of before and after, blocks our view of the interweaving of tradition and modernity, belonging and freedom. Second, she spells out important differences between the nineteenth-century conflict and the state's present dealing with a religious minority that, at least in France, "has no history of political domination, as Catholicism did" (p. 480). In other words, what the older controversy reveals is that we should not "transpose the imaginary structure of the struggle between church and state into an abstract opposition between politics and religion, then translate it into a concern about the role of 'political religion' in contemporary society" (p. 480). That abstract opposition, she suggests, was already overcome theoretically by Durkheim, but his lessons seem largely forgotten in the recent debate. Taking issue with Roy, Jansen opts for a richer understanding of "culture" so as to accommodate—philosophically and politically—the multifarious ways in which all individuals and groups (and not just immigrant populations) negotiate agency (or lack thereof) in the contemporary domain.[154]

Asad starts out from an anthropologist's concern, which, he claims, consists in "trying to see a particular public event—or series of interlinked events—as the articulation of a number of organizing categories typical of a particular (in this case political) culture" (p. 497). In other words, what Asad presents, in his discussion of the Islamic veil affair, is less a critical rejoinder to that debate or a juridico-political solution to the "crisis of *laïcité*" than a description of the implicit "grammar of concepts" that governs the ideological positions taken, the affects expressed or suppressed, the pains inflicted or suffered.

This analysis amplifies a line of inquiry begun in such important studies as his *Genealogies of Religion* and *Formations of the Secular*.[155] The latter work sets itself the seemingly simple but in fact truly daunting task of understanding the concept, the existential forms, the practical instantiations, and the political formations of the "secular" and "secularism" by no longer reducing them to an offshoot or by-product of the Western concept of "religion," while nonetheless stressing the intrinsic relationship between these phenomena. Asad's "anthropology of the secular"—in the present essay called the "political theology of *laïcisme*"—is informed by a host of historical, philosophical, empirical, and political analyses. It studies the often-ignored complexity of the concept of the secular by viewing it as something other than the mere successor to religion, with whose concept and doctrinal elaborations it entertains an indirect and paradoxical relationship. Like Detienne and Nancy, Asad asserts: "Contrary to what is popularly believed, it was not the modern world that introduced a separation between the religious and the political. A separation was recognized in medieval Christendom, although of course it meant something very different from what it means today" (p. 498). Its "complementary organizing principles," Asad continues, were those of "temporal power" versus "spiritual power," the "body natural" and the "body politic," which together covered—and personalized—the whole spectrum of social and juridical relations in partly physical, partly metaphysical terms. The modern state "transfigured" these pairs of principles by depersonalizing and de-Christianizing them: "political status (a new abstraction) could be separated from religious belonging, although that doesn't mean it was totally unconnected with religion. The dominance of 'the political' meant that 'religion' could be excluded from its domain or absorbed by it. . . . The reading of uncontrolled religion as dangerous passion, dissident identity, or foreign power became part of the nation-state's performance of sovereignty" (p. 498). The headscarf affair dramatized this fairly recent transition: "The state's inviolable personality was expressed in and through particular images, including those signifying the abstract individuals whom it represented and to which they in turn owed unconditional obedience. The headscarf worn by Muslim women was held to be a religious sign conflicting with the secular personality of the French Republic" (p. 500).

Neither merely religious nor simply on the side of the rational and the profane, the secular is treated as a category with a multilayered history and internal logic of its own, one that sheds an indirect—and surprising—light on the major premises of modernity, democracy, minority representation, and the concept of human rights, hence also on agency, cruelty, and the like. But, here as elsewhere, Asad's interest and method is less hermeneutic than that of the anthropologist-grammarian. He follows Wittgenstein's recommendation to look for "use," not for "meaning," steering clear of all attempts to essentialize either "religion" or its supposed counterpart, "the secular," and insisting instead on seeing both as something "processual" rather than, say, a "fixed ideology" (even less that of a "particular class").[156] In so doing, in rethinking the powers of a certain "authoritative discourse" that does not simply come from "outside" but stems at least equally from an "*inner binding*," as the "internal shaping of the self by the self," he circumvents the simple opposition created by "lingualism" and "sociologism."[157]

In his recent writing, Asad thus propels the concepts of the secular, secularism, and *laïcité* into a privileged subject of study over and against the constructs that have formed the preferred object of historical and theoretical anthropology (such as myth, magic, witchcraft, and shamanism). What results is a succinct analysis of the "epistemological assumptions" and (to cite Foucault's term) the very *episteme* of the secular ("the secular as a social ontology" or, more precisely, "the shifting web of concepts making up the secular") in relation to "secularism as a political doctrine." The emergence of the secular in nineteenth-century liberal society is, Asad acknowledges, somewhat less elusive than its predecessor concept, the religious. But neither religion nor the secular was ever historically, let alone "essentially," a "fixed category." In consequence, it will not do to "see Christianity as being at the root either of capitalism or of the modern drive for world domination. Nor at the root of modern intolerance, something now being attributed not merely to Christianity but to all monotheism."[158] Rather, a Wittgensteinian attention to the "grammar of concepts" enables one to perceive in what ways "Christian discourse is not being played out as it was earlier."[159]

And yet, in accordance with another Wittgensteinian insight, Asad also asks what the forces and needs behind essentializing definitions and simple dichotomies have been and continue to be. In his recent work, he aims at "something seemingly paradoxical—to problematize 'the religious' and 'the secular' as clear-cut categories but also to search for the conditions in which *they were* clear-cut and were sustained as such. In other words, . . . 'how can people make these distinctions when they aren't sustainable?' but also 'what are the conditions in which these dichotomies, these binaries, *do* seem to make some sense?'"[160]

In Asad's suggestive reading of the secular and of secularism, it will not do to correct naïve views of modernization in terms of Enlightenment rationality, differentiation, and secularization by appealing to the "myth of the state" in order to locate its foundation in attachment to belief in the supernatural force of, say, sovereignty. In that respect, his perspective differs from the projects of the older political theology (from, say, Schmitt to Kantorowicz, as well from Benjamin to Agamben), but also from attempts to revise—and save—at least some elements of the secularization thesis at the heart of modern sociology (as in the work of Habermas and Casanova).

The originality of Asad's anthropology of the secular, of his "political theology of *laïcisme*," is that it establishes the indissoluble link between the secular and religion along radically different lines, insisting, for example, in *Formations of the Secular*, on the fact that "the word 'myth' that moderns have inherited from antiquity feeds into a number of familiar oppositions—*belief* and *knowledge*, *reason* and *imagination*, *history* and *fiction*, *symbol* and *allegory*, *natural* and *supranatural*, *sacred* and *profane*—binaries that pervade modern secular discourse, especially in its polemical mode."[161] Yet unlike some radical anthropologists (such as Michael Taussig), who have sought to denounce such binaries, or unlike most critical theorists (notably the representatives of the first and second generation of the Frankfurt School), who tend to insist on their functional equivalents and supposedly formal pragmatic transformation, Asad's questioning is first of all genealogical, in that he asks how these binaries "have come to be constituted rigidly as such." His primary concern is, therefore, less with historical narrative, let alone a social history of secularization, than with a series of inquiries, all of which establish the secular and secularism in their analytical, systematic, political, and juridical specificity, while granting that there has been neither a "single line of filiation in the formation of the secular" nor a singular origin, and hence a stable historical identity, of the concept and construct in question.

This circumstance, Asad stresses, does not condemn us to silence. There have been significant breaks in the relationship between the secular and the religious in which "words and practices were rearranged, and new discursive grammars replaced previous ones." These breaks can be studied and evaluated in critical ways. In fact, only such an approach allows one to take a distance from all too reductive accounts, for the secular is not simply "a mask for religion," even though the former may "simulate" the latter. And there is no such thing as "the apparently secular" parading for "the truly religious"; in other words, "signs are a part of reality and not a way of pointing to it."[162] And the rearrangement of the symbols and narratives that make up history lead to unexpected effects, which finally determine the perception of concrete issues such as the controversy surrounding the veil.[163]

In his contribution, Peter van der Veer documents and analyzes another widely reported incident, this time in the Netherlands, namely, the murder of Theo van Gogh, preceded by but not unrelated to the assassination of Pim Fortuyn, both of which have haunted Dutch politics ever since. Van der Veer sketches the historical and socio-cultural context against whose foil we should place the murders of Fortuyn and van Gogh and especially the devastating impact they have had on the political and intellectual climate in the Netherlands, bruising its longstanding reputation for tolerance and diversity. He suggests that the recent upheavals exposed the fragility of this much-cultivated and somewhat self-congratulatory self-image of liberalism and the apparent inability of Dutch society so far to deal with the fact that its newcomers are there to stay or, rather, have already become part and parcel of a radically changed political landscape, one that will not necessarily correspond to a unilaterally imposed model of integration, with its expectation of cultural (or often even linguistic) adaptation. In other words, van der Veer claims that van Gogh's murder was more revelatory of Dutch culture at the crossroads than of Islam and its perceived global militancy. An unwillingness or incapacity to come to terms with this fact helps explain why the responses of the political and cultural elites to this event were (with a few exceptions) so unhelpful. And no easy solution seems in sight.[164]

That more constructive approaches than those of artistic and mediatic provocation, counter-reaction, and repression by the state apparatus are thinkable, desirable, and possible, not just theoretically but at the level of municipal governmental policy in modern democracies, is demonstrated by the contribution of Job Cohen, since 2001 the mayor of Amsterdam (in 2003 he was also the Dutch Labor Party's candidate for prime minister during the national elections). Over the years, Cohen has gained enormous popularity and respect, especially in the wake of the murder of van Gogh (a relentless critic of Cohen),[165] when he immediately called upon the city population to "kick up a ruckus and make yourself heard," a call to which some twenty thousand demonstrators, including the Muslim community, responded by gathering at the central Dam Square, in an outlet for outrage that defused tension and undercut subsequent acts of reprisal (of which there were, sadly, many in the rest of the country), setting a counterexample to some of the more irresponsible, inflammatory comments by Dutch politicians in the heat of the moment. After a career as a professor of law and *rector magnificus* of the University of Maastricht, Cohen has played a prominent role in national politics, in which, as an undersecretary of state (or junior minister) for *Vreemdelingenbeleid* from 1998 to 2000, during the government of Wim Kok, he was not only the architect of some of the Netherlands' new and tougher asylum procedures and immigration policies but was also responsible for the introduction and legalization of same-sex marriages. The Netherlands was the first country in the world to do this.

Cohen's leadership has contributed to a sound policy that pairs a soft-spoken personal style and calm modesty with courageous statesmanship, in a city in which almost half of the population is now of non-Dutch descent—and this in a society that does not typically see itself as a nation of immigrants. Social and cultural tensions, until recently simply ignored or glossed over, have been legion. Yet Cohen declared to *Time Europe Magazine*: "Immigrants have always been part of our city and Amsterdam is, and remains, tolerant. Jews should not be afraid to walk the streets wearing their skullcaps, Moroccans must be able to find jobs, and homosexuals must not be insulted. The only 'us and them' that exist are the citizens who want to live together in peace and those who don't."[166]

While being a popular mayor, Cohen plays the role of an intellectual, issuing a steady stream of theoretically and juridically ambitious policy papers, the most recent of which—his 2005 "Multatuli Lecture"—we reproduce below. The lecture follows on a series of earlier public presentations in which Cohen has outlined a consistent and daring approach to the question of the relationship between Enlightenment tolerance and civil, multicultural society, church and state, national identity and the integration of "strangers."[167] Cohen argues that, historically and in more recent times, the Netherlands has been a nation of minority groups (cities, provinces, pillars, and parties), each in need of pragmatically compromising their interests with regard to those of the changing—and partitioned—majority from which they demarcate themselves economically, geographically, religiously, culturally, and politically. To this general pattern, which runs from the Golden Age through the nineteenth century, the twentieth century added gradual recognition of the dignity of others (workers, women, homosexuals, etc.) and equal treatment for them, followed in the 1960s and 1970s by a wave of migration of "guestworkers." Cohen uses the term *minority* as a descriptive category, while acknowledging that it has come to designate "newcomers" or, worse, "allochthons," that is to say, newly immigrated ethnic groups, which happen to be mostly Muslim. At the same time, for the first time in Dutch history a majority culture has emerged, which identifies itself as secular, liberal, and white. Since the members of this larger group no longer perceive themselves as a minority with a "mono-identity" (as they would have in the past), they are less inclined to perceive and respect others as others. Cohen argues further that the process of democratization and individualization prepared the Dutch poorly for the need to acknowledge—and deal with—"strangers" and their "difference." Mounting international conflict and tension, as well as a rise in petty crime and hostility in the streets of major cities, have created a widespread sense of uncertainty and threat. With shared group values lost, mutual expectations become opaque, and suspicion and the pursuit of mere self- or minority interests prevail. The result is self-centeredness, retreat from other minority-majorities, and, almost inevitably, intolerance and radicalization.[168]

Cohen focuses on the juridical checks and balances—for example, between the constitutional freedom of expression and its limits—that allow citizens (individually and as members of a group) to make and defend their claims, to articulate their grievances, and to seek that justice be done. He concludes that the most important problems are not of a legal but of a social or societal nature; they concern not matters of politics or policy but a confrontation of "styles" or "ways of life," in neighborhoods and on the street. Daily practices seem more relevant than the appeal—however legitimate, strategic, or appropriate—to the judgment of the courts. Not unlike Habermas, Cohen thus warns against a relentless "juridification" of society as the path to greater equality, integration, and inclusiveness. Fear, he claims, is "bad counsel" and to avoid (further) "polarization" requires effort—the "mobilization of positive forces"—and, especially, time invested by minorities and majorities alike. Examples of such processes might be the creation of sites for encounter in the public domain and in the popular media, the moderation of insults, and the cultivation of more informed perspectives on others and, thereby, on oneself.[169]

A different approach to the questions of living together among strangers and of human rights, in an even more difficult and volatile political and cultural context, is described by Bettina Prato, who in her contribution analyzes the peace activism of a group of some ninety Israeli rabbis, Rabbis for Human Rights, founded in 1988 in reaction to the military repression of the Palestinian Intifadah. Although in the Israeli-Palestinian conflict all sides seem entrenched in unmovable positions founded in two different histories and perceptions of collective trauma (the Shoah, on the one hand, and the *Nakbah*, the Arabic term for "catastrophe," referring to the creation of Israel and the expulsion of Palestinian inhabitants, on the other), Prato argues that the practical and ad hoc solutions proposed by this group succeed in negotiating the more abstract and ultimately universalist intent of the general declaration of human rights with the concrete and particular ethnico-identitarian concerns that govern the every politics of exclusion-inclusion on the contested ground of Israel/Palestine.[170]

Drawing on Rabbis for Human Rights's miscellaneous intellectual resources in different strands of Jewish law and philosophical thinking, as well as in human rights literature and a general humanist philosophical outlook, Prato also spells out the specific theological motifs behind the legal and humanitarian activities of this group, which cuts across the left-right political spectrum of contemporary Israeli politics and even across the historical secular-religious divide. These motifs range from *tikkun ha olam*, or "repair/care of the world," to the biblical notion of the creation of humans *b'tselem Elohim*, "in the image of God," in the writings of Maimonides and Saadiah Gaon, and to the Levinasian idea of responsibility as an immediate responsiveness to "the presence and needs of others/strangers rather than delegating that response to the institutions of formal politics" (p. 561), a responsiveness expressed, for example, in his notion of "dwelling" (a concept forcefully interpreted in Derrida's *Adieu to Emmanuel Levinas*[171]).

Against this backdrop, Prato raises the question of "whether the religious appropriation of human rights discourse may generate opportunities for transgressing the exclusionary loyalties that trauma-laden identity narratives seem to encourage in today's Israel" (p. 560). The group under consideration does so, she explains, by establishing "a viable niche for its pursuit of justice on behalf of Palestinians and marginalized Israelis," while it refrains from advocating a non-Jewish Israeli state (p. 561). The rabbis' group thus does not seek to "replace Zionist narratives," but rather "works in counterpoint to these narratives" and "actually exists only thanks to these narratives and the state of Israel as a Jewish state" (p. 561). Prato interprets this strategy as one of "limited, practical resistance to the 'ontological closures' of political Zionism," which sterner opponents have characterized in explicitly theologico-political terms as "Constantinian Judaism," thereby suggesting a "'state of emergency' Judaism," which compromises itself to "justify rights violations for the sake of a pure Jewish space, where state and citizens may bear witness in isolation to their exceptional fate of trauma and redemption" (p. 569).

The question remains what the alternative view, explored by Prato, might entail, especially when it is formulated in somewhat abstract terms, namely, those of "a Zionism respectful of the rights of Palestinians" (p. 572). Prato goes on to tease out and evaluate the subtle discrepancies between this neither right-wing religious nor left-wing secularist conception and the equally ambiguous practices of solidarity that the group demonstrates in its engagement with the Palestinian population (by defending homes targeted for demolition and rebuilding them, replanting uprooted orchards, harvesting and selling products, protesting the wall of separation, etc.). She suggests that it may articulate a viable, albeit "imperfect," possibility, for the time being. "The result is a multiplicity of small acts that engage people as bearers of relative power 'to do,' pushing the limits of ethno-national, trauma-laden identity from *within*, rather than from *beyond* the discourse and institutions of ethno-national ontology, toward a politics neither of recognition nor of love, but rather of cautious togetherness, occasional friendship, and respectful distance" (p. 562). Interestingly, she concludes that a reciprocal initiative concerning forms of togetherness between strangers/enemies from the Palestine side could reasonably be expected only once certain conditions had been fulfilled, not least the acquisition of a "thematized ontology," a collective "dwelling," a state of their own.

Opening Societies and the Rights of the Human

The political, we have said, regardless of ideological justification and representation, has often been seen as *inherently theological*, premised upon a "mystical foundation," that is to say, on some reference to an "empty signifier," whose historical and systematic connection to the tradition of religion, in particular, to the divine names, seems evident. Conversely, both historical religions—"primitive" religions as well as the monotheistic religions of the Book—and those that haunt the contemporary imagination, including alternative religions associated with New Age forms of spirituality, have always supplemented their beliefs, rituals, and institutions with a practical politics in addition to a more abstract interpretation of the political.

In order to understand the relationship between the domains of the religious and the theological, on the one hand, and the political and politics, on the other—as well as the violence and horrors they might each separately and in relation provoke (or allow)—we must interrogate the historically fairly recent assumption of the autonomy, neutrality, and homogeneity of the public realm, just as we must rethink the origin and range of the state's sovereignty in light of its more elusive constituents. This assumption should not only be understood against the background of an age-old tradition, whose metaphysical premises and religious elements have, in modernity, often been ignored or played down, and whose very idea and structure is captured by the term *political theology*. We should simultaneously recast it in light of the new dimensions opened up by the late-twentieth-century revolution in and exponential development of modes of communication and the newest technological media, as well as in view of global processes, economic markets, and the ideas that they have accompanied, enabled, indeed, expressed and propelled. An even greater challenge, broached in some of the contributions discussed above, remains the task of rethinking the theologico-political in view of the twentieth- and twenty-first-century revolutions in the "technologies of life," both organic and artificial, and the ontological and existential, not to mention ethical and juridical, consequences they entail. These questions are more complex than current references to Foucauldian bio-politics or reductionist neuroscientific explorations of artificial intelligence, gene technology, and so on suggest. The final part of this book discusses some of these issues and their repercussions for our understanding of life and living together, experience and perception, agency and human rights.

Paola Marrati's lucid opening essay raises the question of what light the evolutionary perspective set out by Henri Bergson in his late *The Two Sources of Morality and Religion* might shed on the question of the theologico-political. Or should we leave the answer to this question open, as she will suggest?

A succinct analysis of the philosophical problem of "the possible" in its (impossible) relation to "the real"—more specifically, the nature of "future events" and the creation of "novelty"—opens the way to addressing this issue. As Marrati demonstrates, this analysis brings out Bergson's conception of philosophy's necessary *conversion*—to a different understanding of the power of time, together with its implications for "invention" in religion, ethics, art, and the political. Indeed, the "assumption that the possibility of things precedes their existence comes down to denying the reality of the new, to speaking of time without thinking it, to erasing the only feature that defines time, its power of creation." This is what Marrati calls Bergson's "ontological pragmatism," recalling that, for this thinker, "if time *does* nothing, it *is* nothing" (p. 593).

A philosophical testament of sorts, *The Two Sources of Morality and Religion* should perhaps be seen less as the epilogue to an oeuvre whose metaphysical and scientific conception rested upon the repeated affirmation of a metaphysics of process than as the diagnosis of a blind spot in Western reason, which makes it susceptible to and productive of the worst no less than the best—in particular, closure and the static, on the one hand, and opening and dynamism, on the other. In fact, Bergson's final work, as Marrati brings out, can be seen as a (desperate?) attempt to counter the pernicious effects of reason's inevitable—Kant would have said transcendental—illusions as well as technology's (in Bergson's parlance: "mechanicism's") tendency toward a closed society of exploitation, domination, and stagnation. It is around this ambiguity—the challenge and chance of the "absence of any determinate object" (p. 600)—that Marrati's rigorous interpretation of Bergson revolves. Bergson's work, she claims, should be interpreted as an endeavor to understand the age-old mystical impulse, which is not only the sole instance capable of keeping dynamic and open the emergence and formation of our concepts, images, practices, and democracies but also a movement that tends to close off this creatively evolutionary perspective.

The whole difficulty of understanding Bergson on the question of the "retrospective illusion of the possible" (p. 601), implied in historical (read: Hegelian) teleology, finalism, and doctrines of progress (read: Kant) is to situate it properly within its original context, which is, for Bergson, primarily that of psychology and biology, regardless of its further illustrations in references to art (especially music), literature, politics, and democracy. This brings Marrati to her central question: "How is one to think the origin of morality, the history and future of human societies, or the function of religion once one situates oneself—as Bergson does—outside any historicist perspective, as well as outside any abstract rationalism?" (p. 594). In other words, how is one to situate Bergson's central intuition by demarcating it from the long shadows cast by the work of Hegel and Kant, that is to say, by the "philosophy of history" and the "universalism of pure reason"?

Negatively speaking, Bergson's *Two Sources* seemed simply to amplify and clarify his original break with the Greek Parmenidean-Eleatic conception of a static, atemporal being, which subconsciously continued to govern philosophical thinking "since our intelligence secretes it naturally,"[172] as well as with the Cartesian privileging of mathematical reasoning. Positively speaking, it deepened the alternative view of a processual and dynamic metaphysics, inspired by the nineteenth-century emergence of "sciences of life" (notably evolutionary biology, but also sociology and psychology).[173] Like Descartes, as Henri Gouhier notes in his introduction to the Centennial Edition of the published works, Bergson conceived of philosophy as a science, but, Gouhier goes on to explain, the critique of Cartesian rationalism and Kantian criticism, central to Bergson's overall project, is no simple return to the metaphysical thought their projects had set out to overcome.[174] Kant was right, Bergson argues, to suppose that to apprehend "the absolute" one must invoke "intuition," *intellektuelle Anschauung*—which, Kant claims, is no option for us finite rational beings—but he understands neither the concept of the absolute or substance nor the method of intuition in these restrictive Kantian terms. In Bergson's words: "If one reads the *Critique of Pure Reason* closely, one realizes that Kant has made a critique, not of reason in general, but of a Cartesian mechanism or of Newtonian physics."[175]

As the conclusion of *Time and Free Will* explains, taking mechanism as directive of natural science and as the model for positive knowledge in general, Kant was forced, like Descartes, to remove all "acts of freedom" from the realm of the empirical, where experience is governed by laws of causal connection. By contrast, taking one's lead from a methodic intuition rigorously defined and, more broadly, from the nascent insights of the sciences of life would, Bergson suggests, open up a completely different perspective and allow one to touch upon "the 'noumena' immanent in 'phenomena.'"[176] In consequence, our knowledge need no longer be relative to a world of appearances cut out in causally linked—indeed, strictly mechanically determined—spatial instances and temporal instants. Instead, it may turn out to be expansive and limited in surprisingly different ways: "Relative, it [our knowledge] would be struck by complete metaphysical impotence, it would leave us outside the *thing in itself*, that is to say, reality. On the contrary, being limited, it keeps us within the real [*le réel*], even though it shows us naturally only a part. It is up to us to make an effort to complete it."[177]

The motif of making the necessary extra "effort" reveals a broader conviction, namely, that, for all we know, we may not yet have exhausted—and, indeed, may never fully know, let alone know in advance—what our minds, our bodies, our spirit, can do. Kept within "the real," we may very well end up making (producing, inventing, creating) "gods," which is to say, "everything or nothing," in any case, a necessary indeterminacy, as Marrati clearly explains. Precisely this process, Bergson suggests, constitutes the very fabric of "life."

But if the model for reason—for philosophy, with its scientific, intuitive method—should be "life," another question immediately imposes itself: "According to what model should we think life?"[178] Gouhier—unlike Marrati and Deleuze, on whom she draws in her essay—seems to think it must be art (and several of Bergson's formulations point in that direction). But could it be technology, mysticism, technology as mysticism, mysticism as technology, as Bergson—and not only in *The Two Sources*, which reflects on these matters in the most explicit of terms—seems to allow as well? What, if anything, do the internal propulsion of life and the quasi-automaticity of habit and the intellect—that is to say, of closed morality and religion, but of spiritual or dynamic religion as well—have to do with each other? Why bring together "mechanicism and mysticism" (the title of the final part of the book) at all? Marrati's essay sets the stage for such questions and provides the central elements that allow us to answer them. For one thing, she notes: "That which can communicate open morality, propagate it, cannot be a corpus of doctrines or an institution." On the contrary, the "feeling" with which the open soul goes hand in hand will be "triggered" by examples alone, "the exemplary figure among these being the Christ of the Gospels." Such exemplarity, she immediately adds, does not fill "the void of the open: if imitation is necessary, it is also, strictly speaking, the imitation of nothing. There is no set of rules, norms, or conduct to follow: what must be imitated is an attitude, a tendency of the mind, and a capacity to act" (p. 600).

Bergson illustrates this "attitude" or "tendency," which is that of the "open soul," open onto everything or nothing, via the mystics. Echoing a motif we found in Laclau's essay, but with a different resonance, he stresses that they are not in retreat from the world but, on the contrary, are "men and women of action" (p. 599). Such openness, Marrati further explains, is not acquired through "progressive broadening" of one's horizon of inclusion and solidarity (from one's family and kin to groups, nations, and humanity). It is based on a tendency of life itself toward creative change. With a helpful analogy, Marrati reminds us that, "in non-Bergsonian terms," the emerging idea of "the universal" has thus "no figure," that is to say, "the universal is empty" (p. 600).

What, then, would it mean to translate the principal presuppositions and terms of Bergson's intellectual and political engagement into the terms of the present century? Marrati urges that any extrapolation of Bergson's views, let alone the politics implied, should proceed with caution. In her words: "Bergson's political theology—if he has one, which is not certain—is an act of belief in the moving and in change; an appeal to act in order to open up societies and institutions, which by their very essence seek to freeze" (p. 601). She proposes that it is Bergson's novel exploration of the notion of novelty, well beyond the common possibilisms that make up the bulk of Western metaphysics in its ancient, Christian, and modern guises, that gives us most to ponder and that—who knows?—might unlock his thought's timely untimeliness for the present day. Marrati leaves no doubt that this discussion, let alone its repercussions for the problem of the theologico-political, has only just begun.

The contributions of Jane Bennett and Kate Khatib explore whether the concept of political theology can be extended in the direction of material, mechanical-technological theologies. They draw upon two different models—Deleuze's theory of assemblages and the surrealist understanding of automaticity—to explicate how the question of religion can no longer be kept apart from the increasingly complex and multilayered realm of the technological and of technologies, which had been viewed as its antipodes.

Bennett argues that one of the consequences of globalization has been the expansion of the categories with whose help we situate (human) agency. References to "earth," "empire," and "networks" are legion, but Bennett proposes the Deleuzian term *assemblage* as a better way of analyzing the present "whole and its style of structuration." The advantage of introducing this ad hoc and living grouping, a decentralized web, of sorts, is that it allows us to conceptualize the ways in which, at present, there are increasing interactions between the human and the nonhuman, animal and vegetal life, material nature and technology. In other words, reference to the assemblage enables one to understand the theoretical and empirical "inadequacy of human-centered notions of agency" (p. 602).

Her key example is the electric power grid and the ways in which, in almost anthropomorphic and sociological terms, analysts described the 2003 U.S. East Coast power blackout. Hence Bennett's central question: "How does the agency of assemblages compare to more familiar notions, such as the willed intentionality of persons, the disciplinary power of society, or the automatism of natural processes? How does recognition of the nonhuman and nonindividuated dimensions of agency alter established notions of moral responsibility and political accountability? . . . Is not the ability to make a difference, to produce effects, or even to initiate action, distributed across an ontologically diverse range of actors?" At the basis of these questions lies the hypothesis, Bennett writes, of a "materialist ontology," more precisely, a "vitalism" or "enchanted materialism," according to which "the world is figured as neither mechanistic nor teleological but rather as alive with movement and with a certain power of expression" (p. 603). With this last, Deleuzian term (*expression*), and drawing on her earlier studies of Thoreau's understanding of "the nature of the wild" and her *The Enchantment of Modern Life*,[179] as well as with reference to Lucretius and Spinoza, Bennett refers to "the ability of bodies to become otherwise than they are, to press out of their current configuration and enter into new compositions of self, as well as into new alliances and rivalries with others" (p. 603).

These characterizations allow for a dual reading or "dual-aspect-theory" (Stuart Hampshire) not unlike Spinoza's system itself. Relentlessly immanent in its pursuit of a multitude of causes and effects/affects, Bennett's perspective is nonetheless presented as a "faith," a "profession of faith," one that, ironically, resembles the structure of the Nicene Creed: "I believe in one Nature, vibrant and overflowing, material and energetic, maker of all that is, seen and unseen." Nature is seen as a "pluriverse," in particular, as a "generative mobility" that escapes our full conceptual and experiential grasp, even though with each subsequent move or reconfiguration it enhances the "prospects for an intelligent way of life" (p. 604). A common misunderstanding is that only "human exceptionalism"—and its related notions such as "time," "culture," "event," "life," and "kinship"—can warrant a rich concept of responsibility and accountability. In a critical discussion of Kant and the phenomenological tradition, Bennett counters that view, suggesting that "figurations of agency centered around the rational, intentional human subject—even considered as an aspirational ideal—understate the ontological diversity of actants" (p. 607). Reversing the transcendental argument of both traditions, she states that "even what has been considered the purest locus of agency—reflective, intentional human consciousness—is from the first moment of its emergence constituted by the interplay of human and nonhuman materialities" (p. 608).

What are the consequences of this view for the problem that interests us here—the fate and potential of political theologies? Is it the "pantheist" view, now elaborated for the age of mechanical reproduction? Or does it merely spell out the ecological claim that "all things are interconnected," with the added insight that there "was never a time when human agency was anything other than an interfolding network of humanity and nonhumanity," and that the present, with its "higher degree of infrastructural and technological complexity" has, for us, only "rendered this harder to deny" (p. 614)?

For one thing, Bennett's materialist monism complicates the naïve conception of agency, human and other, that has dominated debates in philosophy and the social sciences: "persons are always engaged in an intricate dance with nonhumans, with the urgings, tendencies, and pressures of other bodies, including air masses, minerals, microorganisms, and, for some people, the forces of fate, divine will, or karma." Invoking the figure of the assemblage, Bennett suspects, might help us to spell out the forms and dynamics of agency in more plausible ways than has been done so far: "The active power of assemblages is concealed under the rubric of (social) structures, (cultural) contexts, (religious) settings, (economic) climates, or (environmental) conditions—terms that denote passive backgrounds or, at most, states of affairs whose sole power is the negative one of constraint or resistance." Again, analyzing them (and also, e.g., governmental institutions, public spaces, collective practices, architectural products, artifacts, and viruses) with a different conceptual approach reveals "spirited actants." Doing so, she suggests, is not necessarily to fall back into the "mortal sins of anthropomorphism, vitalism, or fetishism" (pp. 608–9). Drawing on the work of Bruno Latour, Bennett thinks of materiality as having a vitality distinct from the "passivity of an object," and, with reference to Adorno, she invokes *constellation* as a way of describing the "sticky web" (p. 609) through which moving elements of agency produce, no, create forms of life-matter that in turn spirit ever newer elements into existence, without preconceived plan and hence without predictable outcome: a "cascade of becomings," to cite a further Deleuzian theme, one Bennett creatively relates to Derrida's conception of "messianicity," that is to say, "the *promissory* quality of a claim, image, or object." These motifs, she concludes, enable us to rethink the implications of "an open-ended kind of directionality, a directionality delinked from the strict logic of purpose or intentionality" (pp. 610–11). Other witnesses of this alternative register, Bennett notes, would be Bergson, with his vision of the universe as "a nontotalizable sum, a 'whole that is not given,' because its evolution produces *new* members and thus an ever-changing array of effects" (p. 781n.5), and Hannah Arendt, who entertains a notion of nonlinear patterns of agency, for example, by distinguishing between "causes," which "entail singular, stable, and masterful initiators of effects," and "sources," which "invoke a complex, mobile, and heteronomous enjoiner of forces" (p. 611).

In sum, Bennett insists on a certain ineliminable "mystery" in human agency, which fully justifies our inquiry into possible "family resemblances" or "isomorphical operations" in the comparison with nonhuman agents. Moreover, such inquiry would have to extend to conceptualizing the total movement of agents as well. Bennett introduces the Chinese concept of *shi* to capture "the style, energy, propensity, trajectory, or élan inherent to a specific arrangement of things. Originally a word used in military strategy . . . *shi* names the dynamic force emanating from a spatiotemporal configuration rather from any particular element within it." The assemblage in question, Bennett continues, is "vibratory," as *shi* characterizes "an open whole where both the membership changes over time and the members themselves undergo internal alteration" (p. 613).

If philosophers, cultural critics, social scientists, and policy makers were more aware of these intangible aspects of agency and agencies, they might realize that they characterize the mood and style of individual actants and collective milieus in ways that can be either "obvious or subtle." As Bennett concludes, *shi* might "at one time consist in the mild and ephemeral effluence of good vibes, and at another in a more dramatic force capable of engendering a philosophical or political movement—as it did in the cafes of Sartre and Beauvoir's Paris and in the Islamist schools in Pakistan" (pp. 613–14). What such insight might yield is what Bennett calls "a cultivated discernment of the web of agentic capacities" (p. 615). The latter would enable a far more "hesitant attitude" when the question of "blame" is at issue, detaching ethics from moralism, even though it will not necessarily still the need for moral outrage, where and when appropriate. And this, ultimately, would be a matter of political judgment.

Khatib finds yet another entry into to the question of whether there is a place for theology in the post-secular age. Her essay examines one of the most influential examples of the antireligious critique of theological concepts by analyzing twentieth-century surrealism in the context of Mircea Eliade's notion of the hierophany—the manifestation of the sacred in everyday reality—in an attempt to resituate surrealist thought within a new, post-secular narrative of redemption. Taking the surrealist interest in the reenchantment of everyday life as its starting point, her essay investigates the movement's central theoretical preoccupations not from the standpoint of art but from the standpoint of interpretation, recasting surrealism as a philosophy of immanence, in which surreality appears as a redemptive potential found in the objects of the everyday world.

Benjamin's 1929 essay "Surrealism" provides the guiding framework for this argument, which seeks to elucidate the political-theological dimensions of both Benjaminian and surrealist thought through an investigation of the temporality of Benjamin's "profane illumination" and to demonstrate why surrealism's central concept of automatism might best be seen as a strategy for engendering mystical encounters with objects in the everyday world. With its emphasis on the commingling of reality and imagination and its insistence on the potential of everyday objects to make manifest a chance encounter with something magical, surrealism seems not too distantly related to profane illumination, in addition to Mircea Eliade's hierophany, a point unwittingly underscored by Paul Ricoeur when he suggests that the objects imbued with a special significance in the hierophany are "transformed into something supernatural—or, to avoid using a theological term, we may say that [they are] transformed into something superreal [*suréel*], in the sense of being super-efficacious while still remaining a part of common reality" (p. 625). It might not be going too far to suggest that what one finds in the practice of automatism is so many hierophanies—manifestations of, if not the numinous element of the sacred, then at least its secular counterpart. Yet far from simply equating surrealism's irreligious approach and Eliade's and, to a lesser extent, Benjamin's deeply theological philosophies, this essay also underscores an important point of divergence between these epistemologies, in the form of the different notions of presence implied by each. The Eliadian hierophany suggests that the sacred may manifest itself in any object, at any time, without warning. But surrealism's central theory seems to be a step ahead: the numinous element—not God, but at least the potential for earthly redemption—already exists in every object; what is at stake is finding a way to experience what is already present.

Beyond investigating the lines of resonance between surrealism and the theological preoccupations of Benjamin and Eliade, the essay thus pays close attention to surrealism's insistence on the disavowal of the sacred in favor of a radically egalitarian immanence. Looking at the horizontal experience of secular revelation, one is able to recast surrealist automatism as something of a spiritual exercise, proceeding through the depths of Benjaminian antireferential linguistic meaning toward a communicative "politics of equality," in which the experience of the everyday is recast as a site of revolutionary praxis.

What is at stake, then, in attempting to discuss this tenuous relationship between surrealism and theology—and to do so in a *positive* sense—is something of a post-secular *via negativa*: in seeking to represent "whole races deprived of life and liberty for the 'crime' of not believing man unfit for heaven on earth" (p. 619), surrealism's critical theory unwittingly provides exactly the negation of religious tropes that is necessary if we are to begin the process of reaffirming post-secular theology.

Stefanos Geroulanos and Thierry de Duve address two different modalities of interrelating the theological with the visual, the mediatic, and the aesthetic. By taking up the motif of a "theoscopic" regime, Geroulanos connects the religious and theological tradition in which God's omniscient gaze is a central if not constitutive characteristic of His omnipotence to two recent theories of power and society: the analysis of panopticism in Foucault and that of the spectacle in Debord. He shows how, even though both thinkers shared a fundamental mistrust of theological interpretations of modernity, their analyses of the use of power and vision to organize and oppress deploy a series of similar theologico-political operations and themes. In both, humans are defined by the limitations of a finite individual's gaze, and consequently are mired in social structures and power relations that exploit this limitation. For these thinkers, human entanglement in visually encoded interpersonal relations results in submission to social structures that enforce the metaphor of theoscopy, that is to say, the projection of a perfect, divine gaze on the very form of modern society. By pursuing the seemingly theological dimensions of these theories of power, Geroulanos seeks to understand the role of tropes, traditions, metaphors, and practices normally attributed to religious thought in a post–"death of God" conception of the political and the social. He suggests that what replaces God and Man is in fact an emptiness that calls out to be called "God" anew.

Thierry de Duve essays a "translation" of central Christian and theological virtues (faith, hope, and love) into the republican triad of "liberty, equality, and fraternity." To remind us of the transcription of the New Testament "maxims" into a decidedly political register, de Duve asserts, would mean, first of all, "to demystify the modern claim to secularism and state its failure, to provide a (hasty and partial) explanation for the stubborn persistence or the vengeful return of the religious in the public sphere" (p. 654). Thus, he writes, when the French Revolution "translated the Christian maxim of love as 'fraternity,' it merely took cognizance of a virtuality contained from the very start in the doctrine of Christ. . . . The only love that saves is universal love: this is the point that articulates the political and the religious, and it applies identically to St. Paul and to Marat" (p. 656). But something more paradoxical is at work. A more important claim to make, in de Duve's view, is that "the motto of the French Revolution takes charge of the three Christian maxims and that it is only by doing so that it opposes superstitious, unenlightened religiosity" (p. 654). De Duve takes this last idea from Gauchet's *The Disenchantment of the World*, which defines Christianity as the "religion of the exit from religion." But he takes Gauchet's argument one step further, suggesting that the "signs pointing to the exit from religion already contained in the Christian maxims" do their work "even more so" in these traditional virtues than in their presumed "lay translation" (p. 655). In consequence, there is a longer way to go with the maxims faith, hope, and love before one can see how their translation by liberty, equality, and fraternity really does point to a possible exit from religion, a telos that de Duve, with Gauchet, considers both historically and empirically inevitable, as well as politically and ideologically desirable. This is their shared "optimism."

De Duve considers non-Christian possible exits from religiosity, as well. One way of walking this path would be "to 'gender' the postreligious virtualities of Christianity left unattended by the Revolution," rethinking the way in which, in Christianity, women have been "condemned to being the medium and the vehicle of incarnation, receiving their own incarnation only as feedback from this Word made flesh through their agency" (something that can be countered by artistic and conceptual counterimages, such as "an incarnate image not born from the breath of a God and the womb of a Virgin," as prepared by some contemporary artworks; p. 661). Another would be to consider some central tenets of post-Holocaust Judaism, as differently articulated by Hans Jonas and Levinas, which dismantle the Christian doctrine of incarnation from a different vantage point.

Rather than pursuing this line of thought, de Duve reexamines how Mary's virginity-maternity has historically been privileged over Joseph's "virginity-paternity"—which, in accord with Jacques Lacan's "Christian translation of Freud," he takes to symbolize the patriarchal fear concerning uncertain paternity *tout court*—and insists that the phallus, not unlike political sovereignty and its equivalents, is thus "a sign without any signified." Rereading the Gospels thus, against the grain, yields a psychoanalytically conceived religious exit from religion, or, as de Duve says, a "post-Christian utopia" that resembles the modern predicament of skepticism, as theorized by Stanley Cavell: "when it has been understood that paternity consists in acquiescing in a basic uncertainty through an act of faith, and faith in the faith of the other—which is to say, that the man who gives his name to a child relies blindly on the trust he puts in the faithfulness of his woman—the power of the fathers evaporates. Obviously, this has been understood from the outset, but one doesn't wish to admit it because it calls for too much love. Foolish are those who think that a DNA test can be a substitute" (p. 663).

A further inquiry addresses, via a reading of Alain Badiou's suggestive interpretation of St. Paul, what de Duve calls "the political meaning of the resurrection of Christ," which as "laicized grace" (Badiou) and a pluralization of the event and eventhood of incarnation, "proceeds by way of humankind's becoming the son—humankind transfixed by an event, like Paul on the road to Damascus." In this view, "Revolutions, including the French one, may be such events" (p. 664). This is another way of breaking away from the doctrine of incarnation, conceived in terms of "mediation," albeit this time not by exiting religion (for which Badiou seems to have no further use or concern) from within (as de Duve himself, following Gauchet, attempts). Incarnation becomes the event of God's renouncing His transcendent separation, which de Duve takes as His renouncing His patriarchal omnipotence. This brings us back to the earlier point: "The abandonment of the Son by the Father is neither the negative moment in a dialectical process nor simply the 'site' of the resurrection [as Badiou asserts]. It refers back to Christ's birth, and every birth is the particular resurrection of the life that is transmitted through it—there is absolutely no need to believe in the Christian fable to be in awe of this" (p. 666). In the end, it also refers to a further scene of abandonment, which exceeds the one that left Adam his freedom to sin further (and still allowed men to "wait for the Messiah who will deliver them"; p. 669). Now, as the Father abandons the Son at the cross, this situation changes and the true exit from the religious has occurred: "He came, nothing has changed, so it's up to you from here on out." God leaves humans their freedom for good: "He henceforth relies on them to disentangle the political from the religious, while He withdraws" (p. 669).

The contemporary "excess of visibility" of Christian iconography (p. 670), a typical manifestation of the increased spectacularization of the public sphere, has the paradoxical result of creating a certain blindness on our part. In their simulation of religiosity, icons and idols lead us to forget that the exit from the religious took place long ago, and in the heart of religion—or, at least, Christianity—itself. De Duve's and Gauchet's paradoxical formulation of this (irrevocable?) trend is revealing in its own terms. Speaking of "the religion of the exit from religion" (p. 653), it leaves open the possibility that the exit from religion is still or yet again religious (religious in an alternative, perhaps superlative sense of the term). The exit from religion would thus signal the—true or genuine—entry into it. The "antireligious virtualities" of Christianity would, in this view, be merely its "other-religious" or "otherwise-religious" potentialities, its affirmation rather than its negation, its continuation much more than its discontinuation.[180] In de Duve's definition, the society of the spectacle is "the form taken by religion when society has exited from the religious. It starts with Golgotha, and with what luster!" (p. 670). But then, it is also clear that the fact that it shrouds itself is hardly "a smokescreen that can be dispersed." Religiousness, the desire for mediation with the invisible, is all the more defended the more it seems overcome. Paradoxically, de Duve concludes, the contemporary form of society, with its "blinding, dazzling excess of visibility of the spectacle is there to conceal that there are things that remain invisible and that between the visible and the invisible there is no mediation" (p. 670).

In his concluding contribution, Werner Hamacher engages the historical and philosophical debates surrounding the concept and articulation of human rights, from the Declaration of the Rights of Man and of the Citizen in 1789 and the Universal Declaration of Human Rights in 1948 up to present-day concerns, and teases out their conceptual and political consequences for our dealings with sovereignty and democracy, with the internal and external other or stranger, with generations gone and to come, with the natural and the technical. Starting with a consideration of the strict meaning of "rights" and the "human" in their declarative-performative (their "impredicable" and hence "afformative") and metaphysical-ontological-phenomenological form—suggesting that they refer "neither to the empirical totality of a bio- or zoological species nor to any individuals as the privileged (because exemplary) instances of such a species" but rather to the human "as such" or "in truth" (p. 671)—Hamacher follows the lead of Plato, Aristotle, Locke, Marx, Kant, Arendt, Benjamin, and Levinas to suggest that there is a structural openness and promissory character to the law, just as there is—before, beyond, and around law—a possible-impossible pre-, post-, and para-juridical reserve for the beings that we and others are.

A further thesis propounded by Hamacher is that, whereas human rights and their declaration are essentially "a judgment," indeed, a judgment "about man," this seemingly trivial observation is in fact revelatory of a much larger linguistico-ontological truth, which is not without a historical index, giving it unique articulation. The universal declaration of the rights of man, Hamacher asserts, "establishes the paradigm for every predicative judgment that men can make about men, and defines the human being as the one who is essentially judging, equally essentially judged and inescapably condemned to judge himself. The era of human rights is the era of judgment" (pp. 674–75).

Hamacher analyzes the fact that the classic texts codifying human rights "do not define man in his historically contingent appearance, but rather provide an explication of human essence as it presents itself in and of itself after all external attributes have been subtracted" (p. 671). This is not a modern formalism—as Hamacher will demonstrate, one can lead it back historically to a myth in Plato's *Gorgias*—nor is it an abstract philosopheme; indeed, he concludes with a telling literary narrative that encapsulates this essence. What interests him is the insight that, according to the classic declarations of human rights, the essence of man is not so much invented as rediscovered as "natural, unalienable, and sacred," and placed "under the auspices of the Supreme Being." This means, he writes, that "they only need to be made accessible to reason, to be recovered from the obscurity of oblivion, and to be restored to universal respect. The declaration of human rights, by codifying and making public these rights, becomes at the same time an elucidation of human essence as it has always existed. It proclaims nothing new, but only makes explicit and public what implicitly has determined human nature for as long as the being called man has existed" (pp. 671–72).

Precisely the openness of rights to the meta-juridical before and beyond of law—its central historicity, eventhood, and futurity—is crucial here, not least in its striking resemblance to (as well as distinction from) any notion of messianic expectation, inherited from traditional religion and transformed in modern literary expressions or philosophical parables, as in Kafka and Benjamin. Yet openness, Hamacher explains, although it draws upon and contrasts with the messianic—if only by lamenting that the Messiah has not come—is not therefore messianic (or even theologico-political) itself. It is *ammessianic*, which is to say, "both amessianic (without a messianic referent) and admessianic (relating to the possibility of a messianic event)" (p. 689). In other words, in the speech acts of juridical judgment we can discern the contours of an "advocatorial language" whose "testimony" is characterized by "grief," "complaint," "outrage," and "revolt," and which therefore remains "impracticable."

Hamacher makes much of the auto-proclamatory nature and hence, as he calls it, the onto-tautology of the existing declarations of human rights. These concern both their form and their content. In their form, they reveal themselves "*in actu*: as speech acts and actualizations of concepts that do what they say and politically realize what they claim—even though at first only in the mode of an explication, publication, and instruction.

They assert themselves as the performance of a grounding and install themselves—and stall—through this very assertion" (p. 674). In their content, they claim nothing but this: the right to proclaim rights, the right to have rights, which, for Hamacher, also implies the right to refrain from (either having or using) rights: a "stoppage" of all appeal to "judicial power" whose foundation is ultimately given with the linguistico-ontological fact that language "*is its own stoppage.*"

Not only do declarations of human rights abstract from "race, color, sex, language, religion, political or other opinion, national or social origin, property, birth, or other status," they also gesture in the direction of possibilities that exceed the very concept and order of law. But more important than any speculation concerning what these might one day be is the insight that the very implication of judgment and rights is that the latter are best served where "political, anthropological, and theological authorities who claim to be the advocates of human rights would serve the justice, freedom, and dignity of man best by expanding the zones of their indecision and by bringing about circumstances in which none of their rights need ever be appealed to—circumstances in which the right not to need and not to use rights could be exercised without any limits" (p. 690). Yet such a perspective on the law's stoppage or suspension comes into view only after the notion of rights has taken hold and is, as Hamacher says, "internally developed to be as just as possible." Until then, there is no other responsible (if not yet "just") politics other than to operate negatively, by removing "degrading, incapacitating and impoverishing elements from human rights or to render them harmless by transforming them" (p. 690). Not a critique of "juridification" (as in Habermas), of relegating laws to their proper sphere, is at issue, then, but an at once negative and affirmative Benjaminian-Adornian strategy of paradoxically overcoming law *in toto*, not in a single stroke, but in the logic of its own consequence and by, as it were, playing its own tune. Such is the fate of the theologico-political and the key concepts that cement—and undermine—it. Where it defines and codifies the "form of the human" (albeit in humanistic and otherwise human terms), it betrays the human whose rights, it says, it protects.

In Conclusion

Perhaps there is no better way to sum up this all too lengthy introduction than to return briefly to the guiding question from which we set out. Can we say that the contributions to this volume, in painting a rich panorama of concepts that govern the theologico-political in all its diversity and, as we have said, *pluralization*, point to a certain "return" or "permanence" of its guiding idea(s)? Moreover, do the historical legacy and contemporary formations of political theologies have practical and juridical relevance for quotidian aspects of policies and decision making,[181] as well as for public cultures and private lives?

And what, exactly, is the religious echo that colors or burdens such a politics (including a "politics of life," rather than a bio-politics)?

Or will this archive and resource, whose richness we have, perhaps, not fully realized, one day exhaust itself, having nothing more to add, nothing left to teach or inspire? With that possibility in mind—and who would wish to exclude it?—should we not rather begin by observing and interpreting the relentless process of fragmentation then inflation that the concept of the theologico-political—and everything for which it stands—has undergone and continues to undergo? Indeed, do the real questions not situate themselves *before*, *around*, and *beyond* this notion, to the point where a different vocabulary—different words, gestures, things, and powers—needs to be invoked or invented? Or has the theologico-political—as a concept and term—drifted away from its historical legacies, its dense and multilayered vocabularies, its varied argumentative archives, its suggestive imaginary, its hopes and nightmares, while nonetheless staying on in mere obsolescence? But then, how are we to explain the recurrent—and now and again virulent—investments in this notion? In other words, how are we to understand the diminishing yet abiding intelligibility of its concept, practice, and imaginary?

Would an ontology, indeed, a metaphysics, of the political or a pragmatic, skeptical-agnostic turn to the politics of the everyday provide more promising solutions to contemporary predicaments that allow no concrete answer so long as they remain phrased in a language reminiscent of "religion," albeit of its disconnected and dislocated words, things, gestures, and powers? Perhaps. But if any plausible meaning can be given to the designation of the present time as the "post-secular," it is precisely that an answer to our questions must be left in suspension, though they call for our utmost vigilance nonetheless. There is no more urgent project, therefore, than to ask in what sense the legacies of "religion" disarticulate and reconstellate themselves as the elementary forms of life in the twenty-first century. The dissemination of political theologies—in the plural—is an important terrain (sometimes, a military "theater") on which this ambivalent process plays itself out. To interpret its historical background and to analyze its present potential—again, for good and for ill—is the purpose of this volume.

PART I

What Are Political Theologies?

The Gods of Politics in Early Greek Cities

Marcel Detienne

I have decided to speak of "the gods" rather than "religion," and of the "political domain [*le politique*]" to identify the specific domain that has been recognized as such (as *tō politikōn*) ever since Aristotle. As for the earliest Greek cities, they constitute the area of my present fieldwork.

No doubt you thought "Presumably, he's a Hellenist" . . . and there is surely nothing shameful about being a Hellenist. All the same, I should like to make it clear that, very early on, I was lucky enough to embark upon comparative studies. What kind of comparative studies? The kind in which historians work with anthropologists, and vice versa. But to work as an anthropologist concerned with the comparativist approaches of ethnologists and historians is more complex than it might appear.[1]

When Hellenists hear of someone "doing anthropology with the ancient Greeks," they manifest irritation. Historians too—and I am thinking of mainstream historians, those of our "major" nations of both today and yesterday—are usually less than enthusiastic, particularly if one is embarking upon comparativism of a wide-ranging nature.

Let me explain. The comparativism that I have been practicing for the past twenty years or so is *experimental* and *constructive* and—yes—it involves both anthropologists and historians. First, *experimental*: in what sense?

Between us historians and ethnologists, we have amassed a rich fund of knowledge about several thousand different cultures and societies, spanning both space and time. It is my deep conviction that we need to analyze human societies and understand as many of their cultural products as possible. So why not "experiment" (that is, test hypotheses), given that it is not only possible to do so but also an excellent form of intellectual activity? It involves working freely together, for years, moving from one society to another, always—indispensably—in the company of experts and specialists in the field in question.

For roughly ten years I have been engaged in comparative inquiry in a field that may be described as consisting of "places for politics."[2] That will be the subject of the first part of this essay.

People often like to believe that "the political domain," or "politics," fell from the skies one fine day in Pericles' Athens, in the miraculous form of democracy. Needless to say, its subsequent history is superbly linear. It leads us ineluctably from a predestined American Revolution, by way of the so-called French Revolution, straight to our own dear Western societies, which are so happily convinced that their divine mission is to convert other peoples to the true religion of democracy.

I have always shown the greatest filial respect for the *gent helléniste*, that is, the tribe of Hellenists, and in that spirit I have been determined to learn more about certain early beginnings in the hundreds of small cities that made their appearance between the eighth and seventh centuries B.C. I should, however, acknowledge, confidentially, that across the globe—for Hellenism is universal—eminent historians, such as the French "Immortals of the Académie Française," and many German scholars of weighty authority have long been arguing, sometimes courteously, sometimes pugnaciously, about the invention in Greece of the domain of politics. What was its date, day, hour, and place of birth, the color of its eyes, and the nature of its sex (a matter of major interest in the American universities of today: in French, *le politique*, the domain of politics, differs from *la politique*, political practice; the Greek *tō politikōn* is a neuter, which seems to have been introduced by a certain lecturer who came from Halicarnassus to Athens, by name Herodotus).

As soon as I had taken stock of the state of the question in Greek studies, I made good my escape from "the Greek city," wasting neither time nor ink in drawing up an inventory of the modish guises in which it has been presented in Munich, in the Quartier Latin, and in Cambridge, to mention only the most prestigious houses of intellectual fashion. I would not venture to pass judgment on the sentiments of those Hellenists, but the Greek city gods are grateful to me (as they have recently assured me) for having tried to find out how such a thing as the domain of politics can be fabricated. I have come across people who insist that every society is political, that politics means power, or that it all began with drawing a distinction between friend and foe. But I found nothing to deter me from starting out anew, more or less from scratch.

The comparative study that I have mentioned—which is now published[3]—begins by observing a number of concrete practices that seemed to me to be constitutive of the political domain. By this I mean the practices of assembly, or, rather, the ways in which people assembled. It seems to me that it is possible to study these even in situations involving very early beginnings, that is to say, in very simple forms.

People assembling: I shall focus on the practices of people deliberately assembling in order to debate affairs of common interest. I am not concerned with a whole series of other kinds of assemblies: for instance, people getting together in order to go fishing or in order to barter one commodity for another, although perhaps in another study I shall return to those different kinds of assembly.

Anyone who decides to observe and compare needs to delimit his or her field, choose a particular "framework," a notional domain. In my case, this, for better or for worse, has been the field constituted by "the procedures for expressing in words a particular idea of what is in the common interest of all those who have deliberately assembled to discuss this." It will no doubt be pointed out that the assumptions underlying that formula are more Greek than African. Maybe. But at any rate, my starting point is "the wish to meet together in an assembly, to discuss matters of common interest." I have called this a "framework" or "notional field." It might, at a pinch, be called a paradigm. But this point of departure of mine is different from the, to my mind, somewhat heavy-handed paradigm of civic humanism introduced by my colleague at The Johns Hopkins University, John Pocock: his is a construction in which the Prince acts as a political agent, surrounded by associates tailor-made for a Florentine society, in the shape of citizens, rhetoricians, and inspired legislators. It is, to be sure, an excellent paradigm for the post-sixteenth-century Anglo-Saxon world. It is as inappropriate for the Amerindian world, Cossack societies, or the tiny Greek cities, however, as is, for example, the category of "empire" and others of that kind commonly found in encyclopedias. I would say that "the wish to assemble around the Common Good" constitutes a paradigm that is neither too local nor too general. It seemed to me to open up a set of questions, many of them very concrete, that would be helpful to an observer of practices seen in perspective. Who initiates the process of assembling a group? Can it be anyone in the group, or should it be an elder, a man with authority, an individual endowed with supernatural powers, or an elected leader? Where is the assembly held? Each time in a different place? In a space that is marked off? In a fixed, specially arranged, even built-up venue? In a place that has been ritually designated? Ritually designated secretly? Or solemnly? Who opens such an assembly? How is it brought to a close? Who presides over it, and how? Is it preceded by a more select committee? If so, of what kind? Is there a formal agenda? How does one gain permission to speak? Using what gestures? If there is an argument or a debate, what form does it take? Do speakers contradict one another? Do they adhere to a model created by the assembly? What is its tempo? Does it reach a formal decision? If so, does it do so by consensus? By a vote? What kind of vote? A show of hands? A written vote? A secret vote? A majority vote? What constitutes a quorum? And how does a quorum relate to the total membership of the assembly?

As you can see, we need to devote considerable thought to the early processes that created something that might have turned into a "political domain." Historians and ethnologists exchange questions and subquestions like these for a particular purpose, namely, to set up an experiment: by means of precise mechanisms, to acquire a perspectival view on a whole series of societies as widely different as the Italian communes of the Middle Ages, the Buddhist communities of Japan, the French *Constituants*, the Cossacks who were the contemporaries of Machiavelli, the Ochollos of Southern Ethiopia of both today and yesterday—not to mention the secular canons of the ninth to the fourteenth centuries, or the Senoufos of the Ivory Coast.

We are concerned with twenty or so societies observed as *microconfigurations*, which are elaborated for common use by the historians and ethnologists who study them. I use the term *microconfigurations*, for it is not a matter of global comparativism. It is not my intention to set up a "typology" or a "morphology" of "the wish to assemble together to speak of matters of common interest" that is valid *urbi et orbi*. I must repeat: this comparativism aims to be *experimental* and *constructive*. It needs these microconfigurations, for they allow wide-ranging, free *experimentation*. We can go see what is happening in Japan, for example, in the company of Japanese specialists who are already analyzing assembly practices there; or we can launch an expedition into deepest Africa, to discover egalitarian settings for initiation assemblies; or we can discover what "political settings" await us in Kabylia or the forests of Amazonia.

The aim is to be both experimental and constructive. I should warn historians who continue to cultivate homologies that we need to shun these like the plague. And I would earnestly advise against "term by term" comparisons between societies that keep a jealous eye on one another. Our kind of wide-ranging comparativism must be determinedly constructive. It needs to fabricate or fashion *elements that are comparable*, and this is done in the laboratory of a "workshop," where historians and anthropologists work and experiment together, adopting a long-term view. In order to discover elements suitable for comparison in an inquiry devoted to assembly practices, I have tried to make the most of a series of notions that seemed potentially fruitful in our field of investigation as we progressively narrow it down. Let me cite just a few. First is the notion of "public matters" or affairs of common interest. This becomes increasingly complex as soon as it is applied to different societies. Next is the category of "citizen-citizenship," along with its subcategories, and then there is the fascinating "sameness-equality" pair. Are these the best objects of comparison? Maybe not, but I believe we could do worse, and that they may prove to be of some use as we begin to try to see what the domain of politics might be in this context. The political domain in general? Well, why not? In the wake of the first great anthropologists, such as Lewis Morgan and Edward Burnett Tylor, are we not all generalists? I, for my part, am happy to salute them, as one who hails from what used to be called the Continent, or, rather, the part of it that is France, a country where the creation, in 1986, of the first department of anthropology at the University of Nanterre constituted the first anthropological clearing in the dense forest of history peopled with hordes of national and nationalist historians.

Those are some of my reasons for mentioning "politics" in the title of this lecture. Meanwhile, the gods have been waiting patiently for our attention. They know why I have rejected a modern reference to "religion." I confess that I have never held the terms *religious* and *religion* in high esteem. And that is not solely because those terms, with their associations with *religio-religere* and the idea of ritualistic scruples, conjure up certain scruples with regard to cults. No sooner had I won the freedom to embark upon research at the École des Hautes Études than I began to plot how to escape from the protected territory known as *Sciences religieuses* (religious studies). My first collaborative seminar set out to explore the limits of the field of religion. Where did it begin? And how was it changing before our very eyes? The specialists of that protected territory, a good fifty or so of them, shared a stubborn reluctance to ask fundamental questions about what was conventionally called the "religion" of the ancient Babylonians, the Old Testament, or the Aztecs. Among the topmost ten or twelve professorial chairs in Paris, there was even one for Greek Religion, the one that I persistently endeavored to shake up in order to develop its full potential during the period when it served as the basis for my comparativist operations. Although the Roman legacy cannot be held entirely to blame, it was through it, its language, and its culture that there was pressure, already in the Christian Augustine, to consider polytheisms as vast *terrae incognitae* that were destined eventually to receive True Religion, whether from Christianity or from Islam. As our experts have established, over three-quarters of the world is naturally polytheistic. Consider for a moment the eight hundred myriad deities in Japan, the countless metamorphoses of the deities of Hinduism, the thousands of genies and powers of Black Africa. Likewise, the forests and mountain ranges of Oceania, the Indian subcontinent, and South America are teeming with pantheons with great clusters of deities.

It is probably fair to say, without fear of contradiction, that, in the limitless horizon of polytheisms, monotheism appears as a kind of religious mistake—for these do occur, just as sentimental mistakes do, although the latter fortunately tend to be more short-lived. Polytheistic societies revel in their ignorance of churches and episcopal authorities, whether pastoral or papal. They mock these upstart monotheists for their insistence on "having to believe" and their proselytizing efforts.

As we all know, the field of polytheisms constitutes a vast continent, one that awaits all those wishing to experiment in the world of the possible relations that link divine powers.[4] I will venture into it solely to seek out the gods who speak Greek, who, however, are delighted to be translated and interpreted into other languages. Just as in Japan there are *kami* for ovens, for food, for costumes, and for domestic altars, so, too, in Greece the gods are everywhere. So why should they not be there in the political domain?

To uncover the network of these Greek-speaking gods, it was necessary to concentrate less on their individual features and to resist the attraction of their fine appearances, and instead to identify all the different ways in which deities are associated on altars and in sanctuaries. In a polytheistic system, a god is always plural, constituted by the intersection of a variety of attributes. In this sense, a god is conjectural, a figure with many angles and many facets.

Greek culture presents observers with well-established arrangements and organized relations between two or more powers, relations of explicit partnership and complementarity between deities. As Georges Dumézil has stressed, any attentive observer cannot fail to note the "structural" aspect of Greek culture. Moreover, it is possible to analyze these networks of relations between the same sets of deities over a full twelve centuries, from Homer right down to Porphyry. This is a wonderful field for experimentation, and I have recently begun to explore it in a work on Apollo. It is a very rich seam, crying out to be exploited.

There may be gods everywhere, but which are the gods of the political domain? What is so particular about them? Is it not rather surprising that there should be any need for gods in a space defined by assembly practices whose major object seems to be the affairs of the human group? What are the gods doing in a space that seems principally concerned with human matters and is devoted to a Common Good (xunōn) that is the business of all the group members?

We can study the beginnings of such phenomena in many different societies. Those that came about in dozens of communities in Italy between the eleventh and the thirteenth centuries owe nothing to those that arose among the Cossacks of Zaporojie, in quite a different history, or to all the "places for politics" that can be detected in the soil of Graecia Magna or on the shores of the Black Sea. But I believe that the beginnings of the tiny, first Greek cities deserve the full attention of a comparativist-cum-Hellenist, fascinated by the ever-changing colors of their "places for politics," that shimmering quality which the Greeks called poikilōs.

Let me concentrate on three examples of beginnings in the Greek terrain: the precarious city of the Achaeans who came to besiege the town of Priam, the imaginary city of the Phaeacians; and the early archaeological and material evidence found at Megara Hyblaea, in Sicily, dating from about 730 B.C.

First, the Iliad. The Greeks who sailed to Troy hailed from many different places. In the midst of the ships hauled up onto the beach, they created a space where the Achaeans assembled to deliberate together. The spot was known as an agora: the word referred at once to the physical place of the assembly, the men who came there to deliberate, and the words that they exchanged there. We also know that this space marked out by the warriors who gathered to speak there contained an "agora, themis, and the altars of the gods." Let us, for the moment, leave aside themis and all that the word evokes in the way of decisions debated and taken. The most significant point is that altars for the gods were here—for the gods of all the Greeks? Maybe, maybe not. At any rate, there are gods in this place, which, by virtue of the series of practices of sharing between the warriors there, may be called a place of "equality."

Next, the Phaeacians. The name of Nausicaa's grandfather was Nausithoos. In the past, he had lived in the neighborhood of the rowdy and violent Cyclops, who despised the gods and their altars and had no conception of what an assembly, an agora, was. They exasperated Nausithoos, who decided to move away and eventually came to found the city of the Phaeacians. He did so as a proto-founder of what we, using a Latin word, came to call the "colonies" of Sicily and elsewhere. To be on the safe side, Nausithoos built great ramparts of stone around his city; he shared out parcels of land, for which lots were drawn; and he designed a magnificent *agora*, made of well-hewn stone, flanked by a temple for Poseidon. It was as if this god had an unquestionable right to the rank of *poliad* (or city) deity. Athena, who arrived to guide Odysseus as he made his way to the city of Nausicaa, was careful to go no further than a small sacred grove, situated well outside the precinct of Poseidon's realm.

The town laid out on the Phaeacian shore was strangely like the city of Megara Hyblaea in Sicily, whose foundations archaeologists have patiently reconstructed. The future city was plotted on virgin soil by its founder around 730 B.C. In its center, a space was immediately marked out for the *agora*, the public area that would be completed one century later. Another site, close to the *agora*, seems to have been chosen to accommodate several sanctuaries, which were then gradually built. The land of the city founded by Megara was initially divided up into more or less regular allotments, according to the method followed by Nausicaa's grandfather.

Meetings in assembly, for the purpose of deliberation according to the rule of "debating *pro* and *contra*," such as those described in the *Iliad*, followed practices with an easily observable ceremonial that makes it possible for us to determine the role and place of the gods within the space of the *agora*. As the great work by Françoise Ruzé (*Délibération et pouvoir dans les cités grecques*, Paris, 1997) describes, from Nestor down to Socrates, the space of deliberative speech took the form of a circle or a semicircle. Whoever wished to speak for "the common good" would advance to the middle, *es mesōn*, where he would be handed the scepter that conferred authority upon his words so long as his *agora* (in the sense of speech) concerned what the *Odyssey* calls "a public matter" (*ti demiōn*). It all thus began amid a gathering of warriors, men who set as much store by the art of speech as by the martial arts (which is not the case in all warrior societies). The altar, with its gods, set up by the Achaeans at the center of their semicircle of ships, was to be longer-lasting than the siege of Troy, for the Greek-speaking gods were to continue to be involved in the founding practices of cities and of these special places devoted to "the political domain." Two divine powers were always directly involved in the planning of a new city. First, Apollo, known as a founder, an *Archēgetēs*. Hard on his heels came Hestia, the Greek Vesta, with her sacrificial fire. Apollo was the god of Delphi. Any would-be founder had to go to consult him. Apollo was revered as a god of paths and of reliable plans, and he liked to accompany human founders, keeping an eye on them. Being an architect and a geometrician, Apollo the Founder was the patron of the art of city planning, dividing the territory into allotments of land, building roads and sanctuaries (*temēne*), and marking out the space for the *agora*.

There could be no city without an *agora*, no city without altars and sacrificial fire. In many cases, immediately upon disembarking the founder would consecrate an altar to his own Apollo. But an altar was not enough to make a city. There was also a need for sacrificial fire that had been brought from the central altar of the founder's native city.

So Hestia, the deity of fire in general and sacrificial fire in particular, always came along too on the voyage, bringing a seed of fire kept in a cooking pot. Very early on, Hestia, the virgin deity of the fire that was never extinguished, was set up to preside over a very public edifice known as the *Prytanēion*, what some might call a town hall, the center of the executive department for Communal Affairs. Hestia represented what you might call "a particular idea of the city." Symbolically, she embodied the unity of the multiplicity of individual domestic hearths and altars. She was a figure at once concrete and abstract. With her central altar in the Prytanēion, she presided over the sacrificial commensality that was officially practiced by the magistrates, the *prytanēis*, who received their powers as magistrates from her altar, the altar of Hestia. "Political" authority thus came from Hestia; not from Apollo the Founder nor from any god known as a god "of the city," a poliad god, *polias-polieus*. In this eminently "public" place, Hestia reigned over the complex interplay of what I earlier called "sameness and equality." This was the place where the multiple configurations of "citizenship" were constructed, all the rights and obligations of those who came forward to speak.

When one observes the assembly practices of these early cities, it is not hard to see that they take place in a space in the shape of a circle, or a semicircle, and that they are peculiar to a space called an *agora*, a fixed space that is common to the greatest possible number of citizens. It is a space that is both common and *public*, *demosion*, as the Greek puts it. The *agora*, which in Crete is sometimes called the *agora* of the assembled citizens, functions as a deity of effective publicity. Here charges were proclaimed in cases of homicide, and certain benefactions were publicly accepted. These were public applications of speech of a legal nature, and they helped to create something that seems to become essential in the constitution of a "place for politics" in Greece, namely publicity. It was necessary to publicize—make known to all—the decisions taken by a majority of those who set out to deliberate on what we may now call "public affairs" and who aimed to have these decisions observed and applied by others in their city. To this end, these little cities of between two hundred and five hundred men, with territories of no more than between five and ten square kilometers, at about the same time invented the art of writing on bronze tablets and stone *stelae*. These were sometimes affixed to walls, sometimes displayed in what were considered to be public places. The intention, sometimes explicitly spelled out in these inscriptions, was to place on view, for all to see, the decrees that had been passed and the decisions that had been taken—"words solidly established [*thesmoi*]," as Solon puts it. In Chios, for example, a narrow island roughly level with Smyrna, an early-sixth-century *stele* urges the elected magistrates, *in the name of Hestia*, to observe the decisions of the people, the *demos* of Chios. Inscribing words on *stelae* and writing on walls were the constitutive practices of "the political domain" in the village-cities that engaged in various forms of assembly. But what with all this talk of public space, publicity, and public opinion, I am perhaps moving too fast, as the gods are now reminding me. Long before the printing press and the wide diffusion of debates in our eighteenth-century Europe of only yesterday, in every village-city there were temples with walls and sanctuaries with space: it was there, in the temples of Apollo, Artemis, Hera, Poseidon, and others, that public documents such as the rules of sacrifice and the decisions of the assembly were *published*, that is to say, exhibited, posted. Temples and sanctuaries were public places, open to all. There was no Holy of Holies, and the "priests" were annually elected magistrates who were expected to give an account of the spending of public money. The sanctuaries of the *agora*, the temples on the Acropolis, and the altars scattered through the countryside were all public places, places of publicity by decision of the council and the assembly, which could thus make known to all and sundry what they ought to do.

Just as there were gods on the *agora*, on the acropolis, in the Prytanēion, and in the council chamber, there were gods for becoming a citizen, for all males born from parents who lived in the city territory. Such youths had to be presented to the altars and members of their phratry, and then be accepted into a *dēme*, which was a city in miniature, with its own assemblies, its own sacrifices, its own particular gods, and its own sanctuaries, which were used to publicize the decrees passed by the *dēme* members, the *dēmotes*.[5]

In a polytheistic society, the gods are everywhere. But not in a random manner. There are certain domains in which they seem to be concentrated, certain types of experience in which they are organized in unusual or improbable ways. The multiplicity of gods seems to make it possible to think through and form an image of a large number of the activities and problems that people encountered in their social lives. I think we should try to discover whether or not gods, particular gods, were directly involved in what I shall—if I may—call "the autonomy of the political domain in itself."

Let me spell this out. I have described the practices of the deliberative assembly and the repeated and regulated exercises performed by a decision-taking group that progressively comes to think of itself as a unity made from a plurality and that creates for itself this new public space. All these practices sooner or later, depending on the circumstances, played their part in forging the by no means ordinary idea of *the group's sovereignty over itself*. Yes, sovereignty, and I am of course thinking of those first Greek cities, which never needed to behead a sovereign or to abolish an ancien régime. But now, as a careful comparativist, my thoughts also turn to the whole of "traditional" West Africa, which does not appear to have any "public places." Indeed, you could even say that there is no space at all there between the power of the king or royal chieftain and society, which is organized into clans. The king accumulates in his person all the powers that are disseminated among the clans and lineages. As the Africanist Alfred Adler puts it, in many cases the sacralized power that is vested in him leaves no separating gap between his person, which is set about with prohibitions, and the society, made up of clans and lineages. This society seems to base its idea of itself on its recognition that the king assumes the (often weighty) privilege of ensuring the society's union with the whole collection of the forces of nature, both visible and invisible. On the one hand, we thus find a society that forms an image of itself through a sacred king; on the other, one in which a certain idea of the city, *Hestia*, is formed by a group that, for its part, comes to believe that the sovereignty of this new unit, the city, resides in itself.

It is possible to observe how this "sovereignty of the group over itself" operates in practice. And the gods are directly involved. Let us consider a concrete case. At the end of the sixth century, somewhere in the mountains of Crete, a little city engaged a scribe, for a large fee. His name was Spensithios, and he was an expert in purple letters, that is to say, Phoenician writing. His contract specified that he should set down in writing all public matters (*dēmosia*), or, to be more precise, both the affairs of the gods and the affairs of men. The two were kept clearly separate, as is attested by scores of epigraphical documents. The contract also stated that Spensithios of Crete should be responsible for the management of public sacrifices, those known as "common" or "ancestral," which were an essential part of the communal affairs of any city. As all Hellenists know, the ritual calendar, with all its information, relayed about fifty percent of the "laws" of Solon. But the essential point for me is that "the affairs of the gods," the first section of "public matters," were debated, discussed, and decided in the assembly and—moreover—in the first part of the assembly. The assembly decided by a majority vote how the new calendar should be organized and the order in which the various gods would be honored. So the sovereignty of the group over itself clearly also covered its gods and their affairs. I should perhaps interject, in passing, that there was a hierarchy in the way that things were ordered: the affairs of the gods were dealt with first, and by this select circle of citizens from long-established families. But why and how did mortals, human beings, gain such a hold over "the affairs of the gods"? It turns out that among these people, "our" Greeks, the gods, the gods of Olympus and the whole world, never thought of inventing such a thing as a "city." Cities were an invention of men, of mortals, and one fine day the gods woke up to this fact. In no time, they were jostling at the gate, clamoring for the privileges of a so-called poliad deity—as it were, a better paid "chair" than an ordinary seat in the pantheon.

Of all the human activities, politics was thus the one that was specifically constructed by human beings: politics, the government of men by men, a government with full sovereignty that, what is more, sought to affirm that autonomy, in other words, was "a law unto itself."

The autonomy of the political domain did not simply fall from the sky. It was problematic, fragile, had to be invented by whatever available means. To come back to this field in which so much still remains to be done, I would like, finally, to suggest that a number of important aspects of action, decision, and the strategies of politics took shape and were analyzed with reference to the divine powers. Hestia, who represented such a complex category, is certainly one of them. I also believe that the Aphrodite-Ares pair, which is of major importance and represents the relationship between the rituals of warfare, on the one hand, and harmony and concord, on the other, introduces a set of major tensions that must be taken into account in any analysis of the political field.

The so-called Aphrodite of Magistrates is no zoological curiosity but is, on the contrary, central to thought about the nature of the council and about the concept of decision and the power to deliberate upon communal matters. The all too Greek aspects of those concepts, which may well try your patience, lead us to a whole micropantheon that spoke solely of the political domain.

Let me return to the subject of comparativism and the question of what it is possible to compare. It would be mistaken to take either the combination of politics and religion, or that of theology and politics, or even that of politics and ritual as some kind of universal standard. "Politics" and "religion" are no more than dry encyclopedia entries. The modernity of the Shintō of the Meiji was invented using the deification and cult of a top-hatted emperor who opened electric-power stations and new railway networks. The "minister of divine affairs" collaborated with the department of "National Studies" to redefine the relations between Buddhists, Confucians, and Shintoists of a variety of persuasions. This was in the early twentieth century. It was an extraordinary politico-religious configuration, which it was impossible to view in perspective until an attempt was made to analyze its components and the formation of its successive strata. Shintō was reason enough, at the time. No doubt, but what kind of reason? And on the basis of what practices was it constructed? And what about the Christian West? Does it justify liberated minds declaring that politics was invented in the religious domain—and besides, which religious domain? Similarly, even if, as a hasty and preliminary hypothesis, in ancient Rome religious power legitimated political power, is it not advisable to work with historians who can analyze the extremely complex system of assemblies and the interaction of what the Romans called *auctoritas* and *inauguratio*? Rome may have introduced citizen gods and various kinds of contracts between men and the gods, but how and in the course of what parallel or successive experiences did the domain of politics take shape there?

What I wish to suggest is that this kind of experimental and constructive comparativism, practiced by historians in collaboration with anthropologists, may provide a useful way to probe the complexity of societies such as present-day Israel (which is but one of many) that draw attention to the extreme fragility of what we call the "political domain." It was much the same in the past. Nothing much has changed.[6]

—Translated by Janet Lloyd

Church, State, Resistance

Jean-Luc Nancy

1

The separation of church and state is the French expression, linked to the dominant Catholic Church in that country, used to signify the complete differentiation between the laws [*droits*] and powers of the religious order (whether ecclesiatical or constituted in another way) and the political order. In any civil or public matter, the political order is understood to prevail; whereas in any religious matter—henceforth considered to be private or having to do with an intimacy of conscience—the authority exercised is defined by a religious instance to which anyone is free to adhere.

Today this separation is recognized as a given of democracy, whatever the precise form in which it is enunciated in public law (even where, as in England, there exists a very particular situation that may seem to be, but is not really, one of nonseparation). The constitutional and/or institutional affirmation and imposition of a consubstantiality of religion and state contravenes the general rules of democracy and the rule of law—law being charged precisely with assuring, among other things, the independence of religions and the appropriate conditions to be placed upon this independence, in the same way that it is charged with assuring the conditions for freedom of thought and of expression.

We are accustomed to consider this separation between church and state to be an achievement of modern democracy. This is not wrong, insofar as the juridical inscription of this separation is historically recent (notwithstanding certain details that we will consider later). But it is no less necessary to recall that such a separation, or at least its principle and condition of possibility, appears at the very beginning of politics: in Greece. It is necessary to recall this because, to go straight to the point, it means that the separation of church and state is not one political possibility among others, but a constitutive element of politics as such—if we agree to give this term the sense derived from its Greek origin, rather than a vague and rarefied sense that would encompass any possible way of organizing the collectivity.

2

Though the *polis*, the city, has its own religion, celebrates its own rites, and also makes room for other less public or less "civic [*citoyens*]" forms of worship [*cultes*], it nonetheless presupposes, in its principle, its very being as *polis*, a fundamental rupture with any kind of theocracy, whether direct or indirect. Starting with Aristotle and even Plato, up to Machiavelli and Jean Bodin, even before the more official and modern "separations," this principle is borne out: politics encompasses any kind of "cracy" except theocracy. Reciprocally, theocracy encompasses any kind of societal organization that rests on a religious principle, except for politics—even where the latter seems to call for a religious dimension. The stakes are considerable: in principle, religion and freedom of thought have very different implications. Religion is not a "private" preference; it is a mode of representing and organizing both personal and collective existence. Therefore, religion is nothing more or less than the collective or communitarian possibility other than that constituted by politics. The separation of church and state should be considered as the one true birth of politics.

The *polis* rests, first, on the fact that it gives itself its own law [*loi*]. It can invoke a prescription or a divine guarantee for this law, but it is nonetheless to the *polis* itself that the determinate establishment, the formulation, the observation, and the implementation of law belongs. In this respect, nothing is more instructive than, on the one hand, the displacement and progressive abandonment of various forms of trial by ordeal and, on the other, the development, predating the *polis* (in Babylon in particular), of codes of property and exchange (trade, inheritance, etc.), which themselves anticipate part of the general *auto-nomy* upon which the city will be based.

The political [*le politique*]—if we can use this term to designate an essence or principle—is autonomy by definition and by structure. Theocracy, in the sense we have just given it as the other of politics, represents heteronomy by definition and by structure. Manifestly, autonomy cannot but resist heteronomy, and vice versa. In general, we can even say that any form of political or moral resistance implies a relation between an autonomy and a heteronomy; for us its most authentic form (perhaps even its only authentic form) is the resistance of autonomy—individual as well as collective—to any kind of heteronomy.

3

Under these conditions, the religion proper to the city—where there is one—has a double aspect. On the one hand, it appears as a remnant of and a substitute for theocratic religion. Everything takes place as if the *polis* did not yet know very well how to regulate its relationship to the very principle of its institution—let us say, to its founding authority—without giving it the customary form, which in reality is not political, of a recourse to the divine. From this perspective, and whatever its precise form, one might consider the separation of church and state to be the logical outcome—however remote in time it is or might seem to be—of the invention of politics. Civil autonomy here is separated without ambiguity from religious heteronomy.

On the other hand, the religion of the *polis* tends to constitute itself as a specific religion, distinct from the "religion of the priests," to use the expression by which Kant seeks to distinguish religion in the ordinary sense from the sense he puts in play "within the limits of reason alone." This religion purports to be political *and* religious, but religious insofar as it is political, and not the other way around.

In some respects, at least, this is already the case with the religion of Athens, a city that does not by chance bear the name of its tutelary goddess. It is even more visibly the case with Rome, which probably provides the most fully realized example in Western history of a religion that is somehow consubstantial with the city and the state—to the point that the Latin word *religio*, which we inherit to name a phenomenon that only Rome named as such, offers a sense that is consubstantially juridico-political and religious, whether we understand this according to the etymology of scrupulous observance or according to the more uncertain etymology of establishing a bond.

What does the Roman religion signify as a political, civic, or civil religion? It signifies the inclusion of autonomy in a heteronomy that, without subverting this autonomy, gives it the double dimension of a transcendence and a fervor. "Rome" transcends its own autonomous immanence; the Roman body politic (*Senatus Populus que Romanus*) is something more and other than the effective existence of the assembled Romans, of their laws and their institutions. Thus, for example, the Roman Republic is able to take up the legendary heritage of the kings who preceded it: it is by virtue of the same truth—that of "Rome," precisely—that the Republic prides itself on having supplanted royalty and that the kings are venerated as ancestors and precursors of republican law.

Rome has at its disposal a heteronomy *of* its own autonomy, or a transcendence of its own immanent principle. Whether this Roman model does or does not strictly conform to the reality of history matters less here than the fact that Rome was able to create this image of itself and to leave its effigy to posterity as an exemplary figure: Roman civic virtue, a close combination of juridical observance and the cult of patriotism, the representation of the Senate as an "assembly of kings" (Friedrich Schlegel), together with an urban administration that was both social and economic, an army more national than ever before in antiquity, and finally, in a general manner, the *exemplum* par excellence, that of the magistrate-priest whose name, *pontifex*, carries a double meaning, a dual sacral and civil genius—this exemplary figure has been regularly invoked, as much by the French Revolution as by Italian fascism, to mention only the most famous and representative cases.

4

The importance of the Roman example reveals how much we have wanted to associate the image of Greek democracy—essentially represented by the agora and the free discussion concerning justice that, for Aristotle, constitutes the *politikōn* character of the human *zōon*—with the image of a religious reality of the public thing or *res publica*, anterior to any space and any articulation of a relation. What does it mean that we have "wanted" this? Have we desired it, and why? Have we felt it as a need inherent to the public thing itself from the moment that it makes itself autonomous—and where does this need come from? It is probably not possible—at least not now—to answer all these questions. But to broach the political question in all its breadth—as it is revealed to us today—it is necessary to underline the extent to which the image, idea, or scheme of a "civil religion" more or less consciously underlies our principal representations of the political.

This is how one should understand the Schmittian motif of a "political theology." Even if Carl Schmitt himself does not ask the question of civil religion—irrespective of the fact that he felt entitled to find some suitable equivalent of his "theological" model in Nazism—or perhaps precisely because he does not ask this question as such, his rigorous thought of sovereignty shows that recourse of a religious sort remains or obscurely returns on the horizon of modern politics. Failing such recourse, which the idea of a "Republic," in its French form in particular, will have kept alive until only recently (to say nothing of the model of the United States, of Habermas's "constitutional patriotism," or of everything that could be analyzed in Japanese and Chinese actualities, in the constitutional monarchies of Europe, etc.), it seems that the political is destined to withdraw [*retirer*] the essence we assumed it to have, leaving this essence to dissolve into "administration" and the "police," which henceforth appear before us as the miserable remnants of what politics could or should have done.

Marx was thus right to link the critique of religion to that of politics. The point for him, at least according to his first and founding inspiration, was to undo the specificity of politics and suppress its separate existence ("the state"), much as the critique of religion was supposed to eliminate the separation of heaven and earth: but this was in order to arrive at a world that would no longer be a world "devoid of spirit and heart." In other words, the true spirit and heart, the spirit and heart of the true human community at work in the production of man himself, were to substitute their immanent authenticity for the false transcendences of the political spirit and the religious heart.

As we can see, politics and religion were to be sublated (*aufgehoben*) together, in the same unique movement, itself arche-political and—in consequence—arche-religious, the movement of real social being, beneath and beyond its politico-religious representations.

Thus everything happens as if the great alternative of modernity had been either definitively to emancipate politics, so that it is entirely separate from religion, or to expel them both from the effectivity and seriousness of the autoproduction of humanity. Either politics is conceived as the effectivity of autonomy (personal as well as collective); or politics and religion together are represented as heteronomous, and autonomy consists in freeing oneself from them. Either resistance of the political to the religious, or resistance to the politico-religious. (In the latter case, resistance of what, of whom? Let us leave this question in suspense.)

5

This alternative had its condition of possibility in the second Roman event, the one that was the successor to the republic and the empire insofar as the latter retained something *republican* about it. This event is none other than Christianity, and Christianity brings with it nothing other, from the point of view that interests us here, than an essential separation between church and state. In fact, this separation is so fundamental that it is even foundational: for it is in Christianity that the conceptual couple "church/state" is properly formulated. It is formulated with the constitution of the *ekklēsia*, a term taken from the institutions of the Greek city, which now designates an "assembly" and a specific mode of being together, distinct from the social and political mode.

Before the creation of the Church, or even the local churches, Christianity already presented two major features: the distinction between two kingdoms and the correlative distinction between two laws. The Kingdom of God and the kingdom of Caesar, the law of Moses ("the law of sin," according to Paul) and the law of Jesus or the law of love ("the law of freedom," according to James). Heir to a dehiscence that appeared within Judaism, Christianity constitutes a major political event, as I indicated above—or an event in relation to the political. In a single operation, it rigorously, ontologically separates the political from the religious, on the one hand (since there are two "worlds," and this division has great religious consequences), and, on the other, in a paradoxical gesture, it constitutes the religious itself on the political model of the kingdom or the city ("kingdom" in the Gospels, "city" for Augustine).

The origin of this entirely new formation in the religious order is to be found in what messianism signified: the Messiah had been expected as the one who would restore the kingdom of Israel, but he becomes instead the instaurator of an entirely different King-dom, one that totally escapes nature and the laws of the human kingdom. Or rather: only in this way is the political unveiled as a human order, only human and "all too human" . . .

From then on, civil religion becomes impossible. All manner of alliances will become possible between church and state—and as we know, it is by way of the conversion of the empire to the new religion that a new age begins, an age that will recognize the double destiny of the empire between the Orient and the Occident, according to a double articu-lation of the relation between the two kingdoms—yet the fundamental principle of the heterogeneity of the two orders will never be fundamentally called into question.

(In passing, this is also why an important aspect of the tradition or diverse traditions of Islam concerns, as we know, the relation between temporal and spiritual authorities—a formulation that is not possible, *stricto sensu*, save in a Christian terminology.)

The separation of church and state that democracy eventually produced is more or less the direct consequence of the double regime inaugurated by Christianity, a double regime that displaced the order of the city and the order of religion at the same time. This displacement came about as the consequence—here, too, more or less direct—of the precarious and always newly destabilized situation of the city endowed with civil religion in the ancient world.

6

It is not surprising, under these conditions, that the modern thought of the political should have passed through two decisive stages with regard to the relationship between the state and religion.

The first stage is the invention of sovereignty. From Machiavelli to Bodin—though we should not place too much emphasis on the motif of a certain continuity from one to the other—it is clear that the center of gravity of the problem of the political has cease-lessly shifted toward a profane, temporal (even atheist, to use Pierre Bayle's word about Bodin) condition of the state. The very notion of the "state," with its value of establish-ment and stability, testifies to the need to find a principle of grounding and solidity where an absolute foundation is definitively lacking. The expression *absolute monarchy*, although it is applied to regimes encompassed with ecclesiastical and theological guarantees, speaks for itself: the sovereignty of the monarch, that is to say, of the state, cannot by definition depend upon any authority other than itself, and, notwithstanding appearances, its reli-gious consecration does not constitute its political legitimacy.

The sovereign state is the state that must derive its legitimation from itself. Without emphasizing the essential character, in this context, of the right to decide the state of exception from law (by which Schmitt defines sovereignty), we must acknowledge that *autonomy*, as the principle of the political, makes its major demand here: the state must or should, in one way or another, found, authorize, and guarantee its own law by its own means. Is this possible in any other way than by invoking the need for security born of the weakness and hostility of men? But can such necessity found more than an expedient—even, in some cases, an authority usurped for the sole good of some? Thus we see delineated the general scheme of the political problematic from the classical age on.

The second stage is none other than the demand for a civil religion, as formulated by Rousseau. What is this about? Rendering "perceptible to the hearts of citizens" all the rules and conditions deduced from the transcendental deduction of the social contract. Why this need for a specific affectivity? Why, if not because affect was excluded from the contract—whose very notion implies rationality, but not fervor, desire, or sentiment?

Appearances notwithstanding, Rousseau's civil religion is not something added, in the manner of a more or less gratuitous ornament, onto the edifice constructed by the contract. On the contrary, it seeks to repair the intrinsic flaw of the contract, which does not know how to bring about a regime of assembly except on the basis of interest—even though this contract forms man himself in forming the citizen. (The Protestant filiation or provenance of this civil religion obviously deserves further development, but there is no room for that here.)

7

As we know, Rousseau's civil religion remained a dead letter. At any rate, it remained a dead letter, or very nearly so, as far as the execution of Rousseau's program is concerned. It nevertheless left two traces at once enduring and problematic, under the double guises of "fraternity" and "secularism [*laïcité*]."

Like the "separation of church and state," *fraternity* and *secularism* have political senses that are specifically French. Yet, like *separation*, one must interpret them broadly and as designating notions of general value for the current representation of democracy. (I leave the task of justifying this affirmation in more detail for another time.)

With "fraternity"—added, as we know, as an afterthought to the motto of the French Republic—one might say that we are dealing with the residual minimum of political affect. Which is to say that we are also dealing with the minimal form of a latent question, more or less clearly resurgent, concerning the force of affect supposed by the simplest being-with. It is not that the idea of "fraternity" necessarily accounts for this very well— that is another debate, one Derrida reopened several times in opposition to Blanchot and myself. What matters to me here is that, even if we disagree about the term, this only leads us to substitute for it other terms with an affective denotation or connotation: *friendship* for Derrida, or elsewhere *solidarity* or even *responsibility*, terms that cannot be entirely divested of an affective tonality—and, in the final analysis, this also applies to the term *justice*, if we think about it. To say it as briefly as possible, what resists in *fraternity* is affect, and something of affect thus resists, under one term or another, at the heart of the political order considered as an order of integral autonomy—supposing the latter to be thinkable without affect (or thinkable at all, which perhaps amounts to the same thing).

With "secularism," another aspect of the same resistance manifests itself: namely, not the mere possibility of holding the politico-social order exempt from any religious interference, nor that of charging this order with organizing the free practice of worship according to necessary conditions, but beyond this—and somewhat contradicting the two preceding propositions—the necessity of conceiving and practicing something like the observance and celebration of the values, symbols, and signs of recognition that attest to everyone's adherence to the community as such.

To be sure, the previous sentence cannot fail to arouse the suspicion that what is being defined here is a kind of vague fascism . . . But I would like to point out that fascisms, and with them "real" communisms, as well as some types of dictatorship, have well and truly seized upon an unutilized desire to celebrate community, and that if this desire has remained unutilized—and remains so today—that is because politics has not been able to put it to work. That is to say, because politics has not known how or was unable to fulfill the intentions or expectations that the words *fraternity* and *secularism* designate as best they can. Or, to put this in an inverted form, because the general idea of tolerance, and of the state as a space of tolerance, remains inferior or even foreign to what is rightfully expected of the political: namely, to take charge of a force of affect inherent in being-with.

8

If autonomy resists heteronomy throughout all representations of democracy, heteronomy resists autonomy in the force of affect. Affect is essentially heteronomous, and perhaps we should even say that affect *is* heteronomy.

Christianity put into effect a division [*partage*] that was implied in the Greek foundation of the political: the dividing of two orders and two cities: on the one side, the order and the city of the useful and the rational (in the restricted sense that we most often give to this word) and, on the other side, the order and the city of a law that does not call itself the "law of love" by accident.

Throughout the duration of what has been called Christian civilization, love has not failed to return, at least as a question, an exigency, or a concern—which is to say, also and fundamentally as a resistance—in connection with the political. Thus the subjects of kings were supposed to love their sovereigns, and thus Hegel thinks love as the very principle of the state; thus have fraternity, patriotism (including Habermas's "constitutional patriotism"), national liberations, democracy itself—or else the Republic (European style) or the Nation (American style)—thus have all these, along with a number of generous representations of Europe, amounted to so many efforts to employ and reactivate something of this love. The inventors of democracy have always known, like Rousseau and along with him, that democracy cannot abandon love to the other kingdom and that it should perhaps even recapture love for itself without remainder, because, failing that, it will be merely . . . a democracy, that is to say, a simple order of the useful and rational management of a world in itself devoid of affect, which is also to say of transcendence.

Democracy is thus by birth (we could even say by its double birth, Greek and modern) too Christian, and not Christian enough. Too Christian because it fully assumes the separation between the two kingdoms; not Christian enough because it fails to rediscover in its kingdom the force of affect, which the other kingdom has reserved for itself. At the same time, Christianity, deprived of the public positions through which it recuperated with one hand the material power it had abandoned with the other—and through which it also continued to instill a little bit of love or the semblance of love into the political order—this Christianity has dissolved itself as a social religion, and because of that has tended to dissolve itself as a religion *tout court*, taking with it—again, as a tendency—all religions.

Neither of the two kingdoms resists the other any more—except under the brutal form of fanaticisms, whether they be of church or of state. In reality, this is not a relation of resistance, it is a relation between wills to dominate and to absorb one kingdom within the other, a relation of a conquering and destructive hostility, pure and simple.

9

We no longer live in a time of resistance, but in one of confrontation. We no longer live in a time of difference in nature between two kingdoms, but in a time of difference in force between empires. If it is certain that we will return neither to a Christian civilization, nor to the Roman republic, nor to the Athenian city, and if it is certain that it is not in any way desirable that we return to any of these forms, it is just as certain that we must now invent a new way to replay the political institution itself, by henceforth clearly formulating its exigency as that of *the impossibility of civil religion*. If civil religion is impossible—and if we know only too well where its realizations lead, by default (republican celebrations . . .) or by excess (fascist celebrations), while its "just measure" is precisely the impossible itself—then we must rethink, from top to bottom, the whole question of the affect according to which we co-exist. After that, we will have to ask ourselves how we should truly separate church and state—or, rather, how we should henceforth give up not only the seizure of politics by any given religion but also the desire for a politics that could put to work this affect and its heteronomy. It seems too much to ask for the two things together. Yet this is what we must give ourselves at least as an exploratory and heuristic rule.

We could start (again) as follows:

Being in common, or being together—or even more simply, and in the barest form, being several—is being in affect: being affected and affecting. It is being touched and touching. "Contact"—contiguity, brushing together, encountering, and clashing—is the fundamental modality of affect. What touch touches is the limit: the limit of the other—of the other body, because the other is the other body, that is to say, what is impenetrable (penetrable only by a wound, not penetrable in the sexual relation, where "penetration" is only a touch that pushes the limit to its farthest point). What is at stake above all in being-with is the relation to the limit: How can we touch and be touched there without violating it? And we desire to violate the limit, for the limit exposes finitude. The desire to merge and the desire to murder constitute the double modality of an essential trouble that agitates us in our finitude. Wanting to swallow or to annihilate others—and yet at the same time wanting to maintain them as others, because we also sense the horror of solitude (which is properly the exit from sense, if sense is essentially exchanged or shared). That being said, humanity regulates or has regulated the relation to the limit in two ways: either by some modality of sacrifice, which consists in crossing the limit and thus establishing a link with totality (more generally still, I would say, a modality of consecration, since bloody sacrifice is not the only one at stake); or by means that lie outside of consecration—and that is the West, that is politics and the law, in other words, and essentially the recourse to an autonomy of finitude. The city may want to be regulated according to some cosmic, physical, or organic model, but the very fact of this will and this representation indicates that it is totality, "consecration to the whole," that is felt to be lacking.

Thus the city establishes itself, if I may put it this way, in a problematic situation with respect to affect: the relation to limits, the relation of limits among themselves, is no longer taken charge of by a virtually total "consecration." From the outset, the political is born as a regulation of affects. It is not by chance that Christianity appears in a context in which the city that will soon be called the "human city" finds itself at an impasse with regard to personal relations and in which the empire testifies to a check or a halting of the *polis* and of *autonomia* for the benefit of a model of domination (the *imperium*) that, despite its efforts, will not succeed in capturing affect (because it is no longer truly sacred: it itself issues from civil law, from "dictatorship" in the Roman sense). And it is not by chance that Christianity—that is to say, prophetic Judaism and the Judaism of the diaspora (I mean the two figures of a certain separation between the kingdom of Israel and Israel as the people of God), having arrived at a decisive point of transformation in the midst of and in the face of empire (in the same way as, in a convergent mode, Stoic and Epicurean philosophy were seeking to regulate affect)—should respond with both the "law of love" and the "kingdom of God." At the same time, Christianity proposes the distinction between two kingdoms or two cities, and the distinction between the legal law and the law of love, that is also to say, the other of law or its reverse. Christian love signifies above all the reverse of law: its inversion or its subversion, its hidden side also—that is to say, that from which the law comes from without being able to recognize it, namely, the very sense of being-with.

Under these conditions, it is no more a question of the church resisting the state than of the state resisting the church—rather, it is being-with itself that resists *itself* and refuses to be fulfilled under any form of hypostasis, configuration, institution, or legislation. What resists is being-with in its resistance to its own gathering [*rassemblement*]. This resistance touches the truth of being's "with," of this proximity of the *with* that is forever impossible to effectuate as a being and is always resistant. Neither autonomous nor heteronomous: but rather anomic in the mutual resistance of the autonomous and the heteronomous.

—*Translated by Véronique Voruz*

Politics and Finitude

The Temporal Status of Augustine's *Civitas Permixta*

M. B. Pranger

If, generally speaking, readers' and writers' attitudes toward the auto-biographical genre can be characterized as naïve in that they take for granted the sincerity of the author, it is even harder for historians to be professionally effective without taking their products to be authentic reflections of time. There is a sense, however, in which histories of the state, histories of the church, and, indeed, histories of great institutions at large are so many contradictions in terms, at least if state and church are taken—as they are bound to be—to be bodies whose temporal existence transcends the moment, to say the least, or are believed to be continuous to the point of sempiternity, to say the most. Even a title such as Gibbon's *Decline and Fall of the Roman Empire*, though recording the inevitability of history's downward course, is set against the backdrop of what, in the author's view, should have gone on forever. It was not his ambition to look time and transience straight in the face. Thus the writing of both autobiography and history proceed on the assumption that inside historical sources and throughout the succession of events and experiences can be construed identities, both personal and corporate, that are capable of resisting the disintegration of time.

It is one of the ironies of history that, although via his two major works, *The Confessions* and *The City of God*, Augustine can be seen as the founder of both Western subjectivity and Western historiography, in retrospect the Western tradition has seemed bent on undermining the very concept of Augustinian temporality.[1] The shaky subject of the self in the *Confessions* is forced to cry out for the gift of grace ("give what you command and command what you will"[2]) in order to sustain its voice and, by implication, its existence, and the body politic, as evoked in *The City of God*, is no less dependent on the creator of time and history.[3] In other words, there is no moment at which history is not intrinsically temporal.

This seems less a truism if the razor of time is recognized as cutting through any attempt to lend either the self or the community duration beyond the dynamics of time as a relentless drive from the future, through the present, to the past. If there is any thread to be detected throughout Augustine's work, it is this prominence of time and creation, not surprisingly so, since the created and temporal status of the world had been his great discovery in his search for wisdom. Regrettably, too much emphasis on the fact of Augustine's conversion to Christianity as a logical step away from skepticism toward the certainty of faith has tended to distract attention from the implications of this "conversion" for life inside creation and time. Instead, that conversion has itself been seen as an almost atemporal event. Yet for Augustine, being a converted Christian turned out to be a far from stable affair. Being the divine response to the *da quod iubes*, grace and grace alone is able to sustain life, whether personal or communal, as it is given, here and now. And though Augustine's later works on grace and predestination are often judged to be a deflection from his early acceptance of faith, as well as from his captivating and playful ruminations on time, memory, and the soul—a matter of interest even to the non-committed intellectual—they should rather be seen as consistent with this primordial discovery of temporality, their increasingly repetitive and monomaniac wording notwithstanding.

As if the fragility of temporal and created existence as such were not troublesome enough, Augustine tirelessly draws attention to the fact that existence is tainted with sin. As a result, the distance between creator and creation, which before Adam's fall was bridged by the natural access of man to the divine light, has become quite problematic. In order to bridge that gap, the notion of authority—and, therefore, of grace—becomes tantamount. It has often been pointed out that, obsolete though the Augustinian concept of sin may have become, it resulted in the skepticism concerning the status of political institutions, as well as the emphasis on the necessity of authority (both negative and positive), that laid the foundations of the modern state.

> By stressing the need for curbing violence and the sins that men will commit . . . Augustine unwittingly erected the signposts to what would emerge as the much later theory of the modern state, despite his intention, in his own times, to liberate the church from its dependence on the secular framework. This liberation would itself lead, much further down the road, to a kind of secularization of history and politics. The civil community, for the Christian, is to be used in its maintenance of peace and order, serving simply to protect men from the invasion of chaos. But in this view, the sphere of politics still belongs irrevocably to the realm infected with sin. It is for this reason that absolute authority alone can constrain the psychology of the state of nature and, even with man's reason somewhat weakened, he can still at least agree to go this far and transfer to an absolute sovereign authority his free will to do as he

wishes. Such a man sees politics as the only solution to the tragedy of his human condition. Hobbes took over this insight.[4]

I shall return to the secularizing tendencies in Augustine's thought when discussing the proliferation and contraction of historical time within the different *civitates*. Admittedly, out of the shifting movements of the city of God, the city of the devil, the image of the city of God, and the image of the city of the devil—and the possible images of those images—one concrete city emerges, the *civitas permixta*, which, as Janet Coleman, following Robert Markus's seminal study *Saeculum*, argues, rightly lays claim to being secular, historical, and temporal.[5] Branding the *civitas permixta* temporal, secular, and historical, however, is only part of the truth, since there is more to time and history than the state of *saeculum* would seem to suggest. The fact that time itself simultaneously contains more flux and more stability than the *civitas permixta* allows for reminds one of the fact that time and history, in their "secular" guise, are part of a problem rather than a solution.

In order better to see the complexity of this problem, I now turn to the way in which the medieval church and political institutions developed an alternative to the fragile fabric of Augustine's *civitas permixta*. On the one hand, Augustine can be seen as the precursor of the (Hobbesian) model of the modern state in its intrinsically temporal guise. On the other hand, one can detect, in the course of medieval political thought, a trend to counterbalance the temporality of Augustine's *saeculum* with the "mystical body," the *corpus mysticum*, which was to become an equally important precursor of the modern state in the guise of a claim to permanence. Although not central to the development of the *corpus mysticum*, Augustine's concept of *civitas* did play a role in its establishment as a body political. Once one of the many *civitates*, the *civitas caelestis*, could be isolated from the complex of occurrences intertwined in this *saeculum*, it could be identified with the *ecclesia militans*, the church on earth in its temporal state. Thus a kind of permanence was taken away, so to speak, from the *ecclesia triumphans* in heaven and bestowed on its earthly shadow.

In his *The King's Two Bodies*, Ernst Kantorowicz has traced early modern ideas of the perpetuity of the state (the king never dies) back to the construct of the church as a mystical body, which in turn could never die: "the church is incapable of non-existence: the church never dies."[6] The way in which the *corpus mysticum* developed into a body politic, as well as the final result, is quite extraordinary and abounds with paradoxes. In accounting for the origins of the church as the mystical body of Christ, Kantorowicz leans heavily on the groundbreaking study of Henri de Lubac, *Corpus mysticum*.[7] The long and short of that story is that, although the church is called the body of Christ by Paul, there was nothing mystical about that. For over a thousand years, the term *mystical body* was the exclusive denomination of the Eucharist, without any ecclesiastical connotation.

When, in the eleventh and twelfth centuries, the Eucharist became at once more and less mystical—less so because of the increasingly real and realistic presence of Christ (being called *corpus verum* rather than *corpus mysticum*), and more so because of the increasingly miraculous nature of real presence, culminating in the doctrine of "transubstantiation"—the mystical part was transferred to the sole possessor and executor of this mysterious sacrament, the church. A second extraordinary feature of this story is the fact that *corpus mysticum* as designation of the church, in spite of its mystical ring, came to symbolize the church in its longitudinal, organizational shape (the pope as the head), without any mystical connotation other than the perpetuity of the institution guaranteed by its head. Kantorowicz sums up these developments succinctly: "Whereas the *corpus verum*, through the agency of the dogma of the transubstantiation and the institution of the feast of *Corpus Christi*, developed a life and mysticism of its own, the *corpus mysticum* proper came to be less and less mystical as time passed on, and came to mean simply the Church as a body politic or, by transference, any body politic of the secular world."[8]

One may wonder whether it is this empty "mystical"/"nonmystical," organizational preeminence of the church as keeper of eternity's mysteries that has guaranteed its survival up to the present day. If so, that would shed light on the image of the church as *ecclesia triumphans*, so popular in the Baroque period, in a seamless—and, it should be added, bizarre—embrace of heaven and earth. Transferred and applied to the state, the notion of the *corpus mysticum* could also shed light on the equally dubious nature of the triumphant "king who never dies."

Unsurprisingly, Kantorowicz, in order to underpin the longevity of institutions, tries to detect a category of temporality that would do justice to both the temporal and the supra-temporal nature of the mystical body. Having found such a notion in the scholastic concept of *aevum* as the go-between between eternity and time proper, he attempts to supplement Augustine's "forcefully simplifying dualism" between time and eternity with "a kind of infiniteness and duration which had motion and therefore past and future, a sempiternity which according to all authorities was endless."[9] The introduction of *aevum* does not show Kantorowicz at his strongest, if only because there is no shred of evidence for any relation between an ongoing discussion about time and eternity, in particular the eternity of the world, by the scholastic left, on the one hand, and reflections about institutional and political time, on the other. Yet even if the clever though fanciful notion of angelic time (*aevum* being associated with the time of the angels) is taken out of the description of institutions, it testifies to our embarrassment with regard to the problem of time as such, an embarrassment once so eloquently phrased by Augustine in his famous exclamation that we know what time is so long as no one asks us about it, whereas we must admit to being utterly ignorant the moment we try to answer that question.

What we have so far is twofold. On the one hand, *saeculum* as the state in which "those two cities are interwoven and intermixed" may offer real temporality, albeit at the cost of fixity.[10] On the other hand, we have seen the institutions of both church and state emerge out of this entanglement as hypostatized into a continuity of sorts. Roughly speaking, longevity was granted to the *personae* of church and state through a kind of idealization (although Aristotle should be taken into account also), with the big difference that, in the *corpus mysticum*, it was the organization that was hypostatized into durability, rather than any real body of flesh and blood or even of bread and wine (such as, e.g., Christ in the sacrament). In that respect, one might say that we witness here the birth of the modern *Western* state, which, unlike alternatives from the Byzantine Empire up to the communist corporate ideals of Stalin's Soviet Union, identified itself in terms of the (ambiguous) formal structure of *aevum* rather than of the (simple) fullness of eternity.

Let us now return to Augustine. Considering the growing stability—and atemporality—of church and state outlined above, what exactly does it mean to say that for Augustine time contains both more flux and more stability than the *civitas permixta* would seem to allow? With regard to flux as the expression of historicity, the problem seems relatively simple. As Markus has pointed out, "the realities of the *saeculum* must be spoken of in historical or political, not in theological terms." In other words, they are basically temporal, part of the flux of time. Indeed, in book 5 of *The City of God* Augustine assesses the merits of the Roman Empire from a realistic and secular point of view. Taking as his point of departure the words of Jesus about the Pharisees, "I tell you in truth, they have received their reward in full" (Matthew 6:1), he assesses the undeniable merits of the Romans. True, underlying all their activities is a fundamental *insignifiance des choses*— "Take away national complacency, and what are all men but simply men? If the perverse standards of the world would allow men to receive honours proportional to their deserts, even so the honor of men should not be accounted an important matter; smoke has no weight."[11] Yet the Romans have, in a sense, rightly received their reward. "Let us consider all the hardships these conquerors made light of, all the sufferings they endured, and the desires they suppressed to gain the glory of men. They deserved to receive that glory as a reward for such virtues."[12] "If we do not display, in the service of the most glorious City of God, the qualities of which the Romans, after their fashion, gave us something as a model, in their pursuit of the glory of their earthly city, then we ought to feel the prick of shame."[13]

It is clear, then, that Augustine has no wish to extend the glory of history, honorable though it may have been in its kind and in its time and place. For him, there is no *Roma aeterna*. What so many of his contemporaries experienced as the end of Rome, given Alaric's sack of the city in 410, did not mean anything to him—and he undertook to write *The City of God* both to allay anxieties concerning the end of the "world" and to quash false expectations that had arisen through substituting for the longevity of the Roman Empire that of the church on earth.

If Kantorowicz is correct in arguing that, as the temporal characterization of the mystical body, *aevum* succeeded in merging time and eternity, thereby opening up the possibility of institutional history, in *The City of God* we can also discern an intertwining of time and eternity, albeit it in reverse order. Whereas the *corpus mysticum*, as the body politic of the pope and subsequently the king, sought to achieve extension as durability by imposing its lasting presence on time and history, Augustine's *civitas permixta*—in which the city of God as well as the city of the devil, the *civitas caelestis* as well as the *civitas terrena*, are represented—is defined in terms of the brevity and unsustainability of temporality and historicity. As we have seen, Augustine does not shy away from talking about history—the history of the Roman Empire, for instance. Glorious though that may, in its own way, have been, however, its beginning and end must be measured against the priority of the one and only *civitas* fully deserving that name, the *gloriosissima civitas dei*. This priority of the city of God is made abundantly clear in the majestic opening sentence of the book: "The most glorious city of God, both in the present course of time when it is on pilgrimage amidst the ungodly while living by faith and in the stability of its eternal seat which it is waiting for in patience: that is what I have undertaken to defend."[14]

In fact, however, "priority" is not the right designation for the city of God, since its presence is founded on an all-pervasive love and its rival is based on a distorted imitation of that love. This creates many problems concerning how it can be identified.[15] The *corpus mysticum*, to begin with its point of origin, the externalization of the Eucharist in the shape of the host's turning into the real, material, tangible, and measurable presence of Christ in and through transubstantiation, may, if we can believe Kantorowicz, have developed into the increasingly discernible contours of institutions.[16] The longer one looks at the city of God from a noninstitutional, historical point of view, however, the more elusive and remote it becomes. It looks, indeed, as though the ghosts of the unresolved aporias of time, discussed in book 11 of the *Confessions*, have come back to haunt Augustine's attempts at "making history." Even if, on the face of it, in *The City of God* Augustine recoils from trying to account for the enigmatic presence of time as present, he cannot avoid that dilemma and somehow draws a line between time and eternity along the lines of change and movement, on the one hand, and immobility, on the other:

> If we are right in finding the distinction between eternity and time in the fact that without motion and change there is no time, while in eternity there is no change, who can fail to see that there would have been no time, if there had been no creation to bring in movement and change, and that time depends on this motion and change, and is measured by the longer or shorter intervals by which things that cannot happen simultaneously succeed one another? Since God, in whose eternity there is no change at all, is the creator and director of time, I cannot see how it can be said that he created the world after a lapse of ages, unless it is asserted that there was some creation before this world existed, whose movements would make possible the course of time.[17]

Yet the moment we try to interpret this passage in terms of the different *civitates*, its problematic status comes to the fore. Temporality may be in place all right, as the core of the created world. But that self-same temporality is created and sustained by a duration that, ultimately, derives its qualities not from movement and change but from the presence in its midst of the city of God, however hidden, entangled in the embrace of the other city, the *civitas terrena*. This entanglement is responsible for the *civitas permixta* being a mere *saeculum*, sheer temporality and historicity. No one can tell how to measure this temporality, however, or how to distinguish one city from another. Moreover, any possible relationship between the two is bound to be of an unequal nature. The city of God is intrinsically as timeless as God's eternal love, a timelessness that is reflected inside history itself. On the one hand, Cain is said to have founded a city. "Abel, on the other hand, as a pilgrim, has not founded a city. For the City of the saints is up above, although it produces citizens here below, and in their persons the City is on pilgrimage until the time of its kingdom comes. At that time it will assemble all those citizens as they rise again in their bodies; and then they will be given the promised kingdom, where with their Prince, 'the King of ages,' they will reign, world without end."[18] At the same time, Cain's earthly city is not as clear-cut as the cruel and evil behavior of its founder would seem to suggest, since at its best even that city, in its state of servitude and quest for freedom, can be called a shadow of the eternal one: "a certain part of the earthly city is made an image of the celestial city, not by signifying itself but by signifying the other city, and, therefore, in servitude."[19] No wonder efforts have been made to fill up the space thus seemingly created between a third city, in the guise of the *saeculum*. This shadowland of factual life is no substitute for a city, however. Nor is this shadow, in Platonic fashion, to be seen as the reflection of an ideal state of affairs up there behind the screen. It is time that prevents the city of God from materializing as a lesser copy of a fuller original: "For the development of these two societies which form my subject lasts throughout this whole stretch of time, or era, in which the dying yield place to the newly-born who succeed them."[20] History is presented not as ambiguous but as fathomless. No institutional extension, duration, or clarity exists where there is no guarantee of any clarity or durability of personal or corporate identity. Augustine makes this abundantly clear in a passage in which time is revealed to be utterly temporal (i.e., as not allowing for any extension), yet at the same moment utterly entangled in the grip of eternity:

> She [the city of God] must bear in mind that among these very enemies are hidden her future citizens; and when confronted with them she must not think it a fruitless task to bear with their hostility until she finds them confessing the faith. In the same way, while the City of God is on pilgrimage in this world, she has in her midst some who are united with her in participation, but will not join with her in the eternal destiny of the saints. Some of these are hidden; some are well known, for they do not hesitate to murmur against God, whose sacramental sign they bear, even in the company of his acknowledged enemies. At one time they join his enemies in filling the theatres, at another they join us in filling the churches.[21]

So much, then, for finding a way to raise the *civitas permixta* above a "river-run" flow of time by articulating something in time's depths. But what about my other promise, to demonstrate that there is in time not only more flux but also more stability than the *civitas permixta* seems to allow? Surely, inside the *saeculum* we have no reason to expect the durability of a mystical body. Conversely, the fact that "the world is being made *with* time" is hardly promising with regard to any extension of its existence beyond time. We must then face the question of how to reconcile the presence of the city of God inside the heart of the created world—that is, within time—with its atemporal status. How can we measure what is beyond measure yet conditions, underlies, and is present within the very temporality and historicity in which we live and move? Just as, in the *Confessions*, continuous attention and focus ultimately direct and contain the *distentio animi*, the spreading out of the soul in the the world (the *regio dissimilitudinis*), or, to put it in terms of history, in the pilgrimage of the heavenly city on earth, so, in *The City of God*, the stretch of time between the beginning and the end, between Creation and the Last Judgment, is given durability in the Jerusalem that is above and yet imposes a stronger presence upon time and history than their own weak selves could produce. When God created the world and established the days, Augustine says, he purposely omitted to mention the creation of night as one of his activities:

> Now the knowledge of the creature is a kind of twilight, compared with the knowledge of the Creator; and then comes the daylight and the morning, when that knowledge is linked with the praise and love of the Creator; and it never declined into night, so long as the Creator is not deprived of his creature's love. And in fact Scripture never imposes the word "night," in the enumeration of those days one after another. Scripture never says, "Night came"; but, "Evening came and morning came; one day." Similarly on the second day and all the rest. The creature's knowledge, left to itself, is, we might say, in faded colours, compared with the knowledge that comes when it is known in the Wisdom of God, in that art, as it were, by which it was created. For that reason it can more appropriately be described as evening than as night. And yet that evening turns again to morning, as I have said, when it is turned to the praise and love of the Creator.[22]

There is more to this passage than just allegorical niceties. Leaving out *nox* does the trick and "solves" our problem. If anyone has spent his energy in measuring and describing the night of human sin, it surely is Augustine. Consequently, eliminating *nox* from specifically being created should not, of course, be taken as an attempt to overlook the problems of evil and sin. Nor are we supposed to put up with life as one uninterrupted twilight. This skipping of the night prevents the city of God from materializing as a Platonic idea come true or, for that matter, from being present throughout as the inner structure of being. Duration has become a matter of a voice exorcising the invading, alien night. Evening turns to morning only so long as—and on the condition that—the song of God's praise and love be sung. Of course, the *attentio* required to sustain time and history as the permanence underlying the intermingled occurrence of the two cities—no night—is immense, the more so since no clear lines of identity, whether personal or institutional, can be discerned. Nor are those cities governed and held together from a center. And yet, from the viewpoint of durability and perseverance—from grace, that is—the city of God is what it is, anytime and anywhere, no more, no less.

The Scandal of Religion

Luther and Public Speech in the Reformation

Antónia Szabari

Although Luther is generally viewed as the creator of a homogeneous, modern German vernacular, after even a cursory sampling of passages in his immense oeuvre, one is struck by how artificial, hybrid, and strange his language is. Luther mixes Latin and German, biblical references and vernacular idioms, and blessings and curses. This mixing of registers was not entirely unprecedented in the sixteenth century—for example, the French author Rabelais did the same—but its effect on public speech was. Trained in the liberal arts and in the canonical literature of the Church, and being a particularly astute reader and translator of the Bible, Luther was familiar with widely different languages and rhetorical conventions, which he both skillfully exploited and drove to their limit. But his oddest idiom, the one I undertake to analyze in this essay, may be the hybrid of pious and (from the Church's point of view) blasphemous language. It is aptly illustrated by the following statement, from a pamphlet entitled *Against the Murderer of Dresden*:

> For I am unable to pray without at the same time cursing [*fluchen*]. If I am prompted to say "Hallowed be Thy name," I must add "Cursed, damned, and outraged [*verflucht, verdampt, geschendet müsse werden*] be the name of papists and of all those who slander [*lestern*] your name." If I am prompted to say, "Thy Kingdom come," I must perforce add, "Cursed, damned, and destroyed must be [*verflucht, verdampt, verstöret müsse werden*] the papacy together with all earthly kingdoms that are against your kingdom." If I am prompted to say, "Let there be Thy will," I must also add, "Cursed, damned, outraged, and destroyed be [*Verflucht verdampt, geschendet und zu nichte müssen werden*] all the ideas and attacks of the papists and of all those who strive against your will and decision."

Indeed, I pray thus orally every day and in my heart [*mit dem herzen*], without inter-mission, and all those who believe in Christianity pray thus with me. And I am well convinced that God will hear our prayers.[1]

Luther published these words in 1531, against an anonymous "papist" pamphleteer who had sold his "mean-spirited little book [*Schmachbuchlin*]" in the previous year at the fair of Leipzig—one of the publishing centers of Catholic propaganda. The author of the pamphlet to which Luther responds could have been Georg, the staunch Catholic duke of Saxony, or any of the numerous monks and lay publicists who worked under his patronage. Luther feels that the anonymous book calls for a counterattack against all papists, admitting that, although he will aim at the "sack," he may hit the "donkey." With this proviso, Luther is referring to the religious practice of correcting the other's error in the name of charity. Luther's curses, aiming at the errors ("the sack") but possibly injur-ing the persons ("the donkey"), show little concern for brotherly love. Furthermore, Lu-ther is distinguishing between the formal level of belief, which one carries like a sack, and the psycho-physical human being, the donkey, suggesting that the actual consequences of his objections to Catholic dogma may involve his adversaries' affective reactions. With this statement, Luther signals that he is self-consciously stretching the limits of the religiously sanctioned rhetoric of blame and correction circumscribed by Christian moral-ity to create a more effective and injurious language. Just how far does Luther stretch conventional rhetorical and religious practices? What are the consequences of his rudeness?

Luther's rhetorical practice at once evokes existing conventions and calls these con-ventions, along with established authorities and the entire rationale of Christian society, into question. He relies on a tradition of verbal violence rooted not only in satire and the rhetoric of blame, *pugna verborum*, but also in inherently religious forms of speech such as ritual cursing and Bible-based provocative and violent language. Many of Luther's insults are drawn directly from or mimic the Bible, whose language, he insists, is inher-ently contentious, a "war cry."[2] The practice of cursing to which Luther has recourse is not alien to the enormous textual canon under the power and jurisdiction of the Church, which availed itself of ritualized curses and anathemas against heretics and those responsi-ble for "scandals."[3]

The provocative nature of Luther's rhetoric lies in the claim that it is not provocative at all, a claim that is designed to disarm all critics by implicitly accusing them of the error they seek to correct. As we will see, this essentially satirical reversal of positions is intri-cately tied to Luther's theology of the performative and to his reading of the Bible-based notion of "offense" or "scandal." Luther does not simply indulge in negative forms of speech. He seeks to justify his use of rhetorical conventions such as the *pugna verborum* and the religious conventions such as cursing. As a result, he succeeds in disengaging the definition of violent and nonviolent, pious and impious language from the external, fixed norms (both rhetorical and moral) that determine the medieval and early modern ethics of public speech. The most lasting consequence of his rhetorical practice consists in the transformation of public speech while maintaining its reference to the sacred. According to the analysis presented in this paper, at the historical basis of the modern arena of public speech are not only eighteenth-century coffee houses (as the Habermasian notion of the public sphere might suggest) but also the violent pamphlet wars of the Reformation. If true, this insight should contribute to our understanding of the modern public sphere and of public speech.

Luther's Double Tongue

With its triple aim—*docere, movere, delectare*—in the early modern period classical rhetoric provided a conceptual framework for thinking about speech as an interpersonal act in which a speaker produces an effect on an interlocutor. Seen as formal (oration, poem, tract, etc.) or informal (dialogue, colloquy, letter, etc.), rhetoric conceives of speech as originating in a rational individual producing an intellectual effect and sometimes also an affect in another individual or in a collective. The aim of rhetoric is to lodge the effect produced by speech in a rational interlocutor capable of calculating the interlocutor's thoughts and affects; in the strict sense, classical and Renaissance rhetoric is interested in the act of speaking insofar as its effects can be predicted and circumscribed. Defining speech as *ratio*, it cautions against an excessive use of affective language. Within the framework of classical and Renaissance rhetoric, Luther's rhetorical practice of intensifying the injurious effect of language can only be described as transgression and excess. This is not to dispute the fact that Luther's practice lends itself to analysis in the terms of classical rhetoric, even less to argue that Luther ignored the rules of rhetoric, but rather to argue that his texts tend to operate at the limits of the norms that classical rhetoric prescribes.[4] Luther liked consciously to stretch the boundaries that in traditional rhetoric separate *elegantia* and *urbanitas* from licentious, obscene, or hurtful speech.[5] With considerable self-irony, he referred to his own rhetorical excesses by calling himself a "chatterer [*Ich bin ein Wäscher*]."[6]

In early modern Europe, a good reputation conveyed social power, and the goal of humanist education and rhetorical training was to attain it. Culturally, slander was sanctioned as a form of challenge only within a culture of glory and political fame.[7] Dishonoring one's enemies or rivals was one of the "uses of works of art" (e.g., in the defamatory images of traitors and rebels in the Italian Renaissance).[8] As the cultural elite, however, Renaissance humanists promoted an ethics of moderation and control, one that relied on the intellectual and moral ideal of the educated subject of humanism. The prominent Dutch humanist Erasmus, observing the success and the popularity of the printing press, laments in the 1508 edition of his *Adages* that this new invention not only makes possible the fast dissemination of classical works but also provides numerous opportunities for authors to criticize and insult each other. He cautions printers to "hasten slowly" in printing slanderous books.[9] Erasmus promoted an ethical way of using language—one that implied at once a plenitude of styles, traditions, and convictions, and a form of sophisticated linguistic self-control.

In his 1525 tract *The Tongue*, Erasmus describes in detail the forms of linguistic use that he considers excessive. As the title indicates, he sees language, embodied in the tongue, that agile "lump of flesh," as able to act on its own and speech as a speech act that has specific moral consequences. Speaking and, by extension, writing can have beneficial or harmful effects, the latter arising from the essential slipperiness of speech, since, much to Erasmus's regret, speech can never fully avoid being in a state of excess. When language thus lapses into excess and into unreason, the outcome is never a good one, for Erasmus believes that nothing can stop it from continuing to slip from *stultitia* to *malitia*, from foolish chatter to deliberately evil usage, such as lying, flattery, manipulation of opinion, perjury, sedition, slander, whispering, blasphemy, heretical teachings, and calumny. Because of the numerous ways in which language transgresses the boundaries of reason, Erasmus's unrelenting struggle with linguistic excess is also a never-ending one:

> but the tongue of man no man can tame. It is a restless evil, full of deadly poison. With the tongue we praise our God and Father, and with the same we abuse men who have been made in the image and likeness of God. From the same mouth come forth blessing and cursing. My brethren, these things ought not to be so. Does a fountain send through the same passage sweet and bitter water? Can the fig tree, my brethren, bear grapes, or the vine figs? So neither can salt water yield sweet. And yet we think ourselves splendidly scrupulous with our Pharisaical pretences, while we carry with us the fire of hell in our tongues, when we say one thing seated and another standing, and when we constantly turn our tongue into more forms than any polypus can take on.[10]

Although these words are obliquely aimed at the duplicitous practices of Erasmus's Catholic critics, in his debate with Luther concerning the will Erasmus has no other argument to use against Luther than the same one of linguistic excess.

Erasmus's disagreement with Luther is a good example of minimal doctrinal differences slipping into an irreconcilable disagreement. Doctrine was not the principal bone of contention between the two prominent scholars, each of whom had originally sought the other's alliance. When Erasmus initiates the debate with the publication of *De libero arbitrio* (1524), even though he defends the Church's position on the issue of the will, he presents his theological position in the weakest possible form. Luther holds that individual freedom amounts to nothing; in Erasmus's view, it amounts to "almost nothing." Erasmus's responses to Luther (he produced two more sizable books, *Hyperaspistes I* and *II*) became increasingly impatient, however. Humanist studies and, in particular, the Christian humanism upon which Erasmus staked his studious life and his public reputation could only exist in a precarious balance between criticizing conventional religion and knowing when to stop. In Erasmus's view, divulging one's convictions "before unlearned masses . . . would cause great scandal [*magno cum offendiculo diceretur*]" because the uneducated cannot be expected to master moderation and linguistic control.[11] Unlike Luther, Erasmus does not find religiously based violent language justifiable. In his view, Luther's manifest inability and unwillingness to maintain his speech within the limits of *urbanitas* destroys his credit: "Very many things prevented me from believing it [i.e., the authenticity of Luther's message], but among the principal reasons were the bitterness of your pen, your unbridled urge to hurl insults, the utterly scurrilous *bons mots*, the saucy moues and mocks which you employ against all who dare to open their mouths against your dogmas."[12] Erasmus advocates an ethical ideal of public speech that consists in moderation and the avoidance of injurious language (although he found controlled satire acceptable),[13] and Luther's rhetorical practice stretches the limits of classical and humanist rhetoric to the point where its ideal of a moderate disagreement becomes impossible. Erasmus stages the debate with Luther in *Hyperaspistes I* as a defeat suffered not by him personally but by Christian humanism: "Your courage, Luther, has brought us to an era when we are prohibited not only from speaking badly about Christ but even from speaking well of him."[14]

Erasmus's resolute adherence to the rhetorical ideal of sophisticated self-control did not permit him to describe Luther's bent toward excess, his "double tongue," effectively, nor, for that matter, effectively to counter it. Both Luther's practice and present-day reflections on linguistic injury, however, confirm that, while norms can be established, laws and rules laid down to curb the injurious effect of language, verbal injury implies a flexible, situational, and interpersonal verbal act whose impact cannot be contained by norms or laws.[15]

Luther with Austin?

Austin's idea of the performative has a constative kernel, as Shoshana Felman argues in *The Scandal of the Speaking Body*. This constative kernel has to do with a metaphysical or theological presupposition that is best illustrated by the condition of the felicitous promise, that is, the speaker's corresponding intention and the continuity of this intention into the future act after the promise: "every promise is above all the *promise of consciousness*, insofar as it postulates a noninterruption, continuity between intention and act."[16] The theory of the performative reveals a second presupposition as well, that of the transparent representation of this intention: "the 'I' who is understood by Austin to be the presumption of illocutionary utterances is presumed to be a pure consciousness, a will, an intention, cognitive content, adequately and transparently represented by language in time."[17]

This intentional unity, continuity, and clarity is the very "illusion" that performative speech acts create.[18]

In the Judeo-Christian tradition, speech acts belonged first and foremost to the domain of theology. They were modeled upon the age-old idea of the magic power of the creative divine *verbum* that called into being the existing universe, time and space, in seven days. This one-time act, which is then disseminated into the created things, the given world about which one can make constative statements, true or false, is not what interests Luther, however. Instead, he re-reads the Bible as a speech act performed by a transcendental consciousness. But because the intention of this consciousness is never fully disclosed (God remains forever *deus absconditus*), it takes a corresponding consciousness, the assurance of the human subject of the continuity and the transparency of the promise, to recognize the divine promise. This recognition is what Luther calls faith, and faith manifests itself in the subject's dealings with the revealed God (*deus relevatus*), as well as in his social dealings with other subjects. Luther's theology of the performative has nothing to do with the magic power of the divine word; rather, it describes speech acts as dynamic processes: not as magic words that produce static substances but as essentially social and intersubjective events.

God revealed himself in Scripture, and the subject's primary obligation is to recognize Scripture as a transparent, consistent message, as essentially one and the same promise made by God (Christ, the Spirit). Luther describes the effect of the divine speech act as analogous to an orator's performance: the "holy spirit" is a speaker. It teaches and exhorts but also knows how to blame—and "faith" has an affective component. It is a passion to which alone the "spirit" is able to move the "heart" of the reader or listener.[19] Yet faith is not to be understood, in rhetorical terms, as persuasion; the "assurance" of the believer contains a surplus of conviction that separates "faith" (a theological term) from merely being persuaded (a rhetorical term).[20] The former requires the interlocutor's active participation, while the latter is an effect to which she submits. Scripture, Luther insists, is essentially reducible to an oral announcement, a locutionary act, a gospel: "we can . . . take it for certain that there is only one gospel, just as the new testament is only one book. . . . *Evangel* is a Greek word meaning glad tidings, good news, welcome information, a shout, something that makes one sing and talk and rejoice." The good tidings constitute a promise, for "there is only one faith and only one God: the God who makes promises."[21] Luther understood the unique spoken word as iterable and took this iterability to guarantee the continuity of intention: "This gospel may be proclaimed in few words or in many."[22] Thus the logocentric idea of the gospel hinges on its repetition through writing. The privileged example of the iterability of writing in the period was the reproducibility and variability of printed type. The four gospels do nothing other than repeat the *same* one gospel, as do all the texts that Luther considers to constitute authentic Scripture. "Now God, in order to strengthen such faith, often promised this evangel, this Testament of his, through the prophets of the Old Testament."[23] Moreover, Luther claims that their message is equally clear and identical. This absolute iterability of the promise is embodied in the printed word, always reproducible, repeatable, both orally and in writing. Thus the printed word is arguably an essential weapon of Lutheran propaganda, as well as a decisive element in shaping Luther's theology and rhetoric.[24]

Of particular significance is Luther's theology of the sacraments, whose number he reduced from seven to three, especially his interpretation of the Last Supper, the pivot of his sacramental theology. Luther's attack on the Catholic Mass hinges upon reading the Last Supper as Christ's speech act, in which he made his testament: "Hoc est corpus meum; hic calix novum testamentum est in sanguine meo."[25] Luther's insistence on communion in both kinds in the Lord's Supper and his vehement opposition to the doctrine of transubstantiation are presented as necessary consequences of his reading Scripture as an iterable speech act rather than as a true or false statement. According to Luther, scholastic theologians who wondered how Christ could state of the bread that "this is my body" and avoid contradicting Aristotelian logical and grammatical criteria of truthfulness (which require a strict semantic correspondence between subject and predicate in affirmative statements) simply miss the performative force of Christ's words. Luther's theory of sacraments makes the Lord's Supper into the ritualized and conventional repetition of the testament of Christ. It is an *opus operans*, the dynamic repetition of the active work of the divine word; thus all priestly ceremonies, vestments, music, images, and, in general, all "works" (*opus operatum*) can be eliminated. In Luther's sacramental theology, the three sacraments he recognizes—the Lord's Supper, baptism, and penitence—are "signs" that serve as reminders of this speech act of promise.

Luther's theology of the iterable divine speech act is exemplified in the claim he makes, in the "Babylonian Captivity of the Church," that baptism performed as a joke and a mockery is still valid. It is not the intention of the person who pronounces the words and carries out the ceremony that counts, but the transcendental intention, which includes the interlocutor's recognition called "faith." "Faith" thus reformulated is essentially an act of recognizing a divine intention.[26] For this reason, neither ecclesiastical tradition nor sacerdotal hierarchy can offer guarantees against blasphemy or idolatry. The concrete and immediate socio-historical significance of this radical reinterpretation was to empower the believer and to undermine the power of the clergy, but its lasting effect was to destabilize the normative definitions of piety and blasphemy, serious and comic, and religious and profane. Because the transcendental consciousness called "God" makes the recognition of it called "faith" into an obligation, not external formal characteristics of speech and action but the individual's conviction determine whether they are pious or blasphemous.

Scandal

The papal bull that eventually led to Luther's excommunication condemned him for heresy and scandal—standard charges against those who deviated from the Church's dogma.

But the Church's problem with Luther was not simply dogmatic. In the Hebrew Bible, "scandal" signifies "trap," "tangle," and "obstacle" in both literal and figurative senses; the word reappears in the New Testament closely associated with the "stumbling block" and signifies a (mostly spiritual) harm done to oneself or another. It receives its most elaborate formal expression in the *Summa Theologica* of Thomas of Aquinas, as "something less rightly said or done [*dictum vel factum minus rectum*] that occasions spiritual downfall."[27] Aquinas worked in the wake of Augustine and the early canonists, who transformed the ambiguous biblical image of scandal into a moral concept, signifying a grave transgression against *caritas*, which, as Ludwig Buisson argues in his study *Potestas und Caritas*, formed the legal basis for the strengthening of papal power from the twelfth to the fifteenth centuries.[28]

Relying on a long tradition established by interpreters and legal scholars, Aquinas elaborates the notion of scandal in order to establish what became the classic distinctions in the idea. Aquinas's "scandal" ("something less rightly said or done") defines action and speech deviating from rectitude (a moral ideal of the right way of acting); both action and speech are seen as interpersonal, social, and public. He also sought to define action's complex relation to intention and to others in society. The first important distinction he introduces is between "active" and "passive" scandals. Active scandal ("scandal given") can be intentional ("demonic") if one wants to do evil, or it can be unintentional if one's actions or words lead to scandal without meaning to. Passive scandal ("scandal taken") can arise out of spiritual weakness, which involves no scandal given, when the other's actions are impeccable ("scandal of the weak"). Passive scandal can also arise out of the malice of the taker ("scandal of the Pharisees"). The gravity of the transgression differs according to these four basic distinctions, but a scandal is always a transgression, always "less right."

Scandal is a public matter; in this it differs from sin, for the mere appearance of sin is enough for scandal. Thus, it always and by necessity involves recognition by a person other than the acting or speaking subject; mere desire to act in a certain way that remains inaccessible to others cannot constitute a scandal, nor can actions that remain entirely concealed. Aquinas relies on the Augustinian understanding of the importance of *bona fama* for conduct: Christian love commands *famae bonae cura* and the avoidance of scandal.[29] This public aspect of the theological notion of scandal is the link between this notion and the vernacular and secular use of the word. In Romance languages, from the fourteenth or fifteenth century on, the form *esclandre* (the etymological root of modern English *slander*) and its variants (OF *escandele, escandle, eschandele, escanle, escandre, esclaundre*, etc.; MF *esclandre*)[30] designated verbal injury and hostile or polemical language (insult, slander, dispute, quarrel, anger, bad example, public quarrel, divulging of defamatory information, dishonoring somebody, spreading of malicious rumor, etc.). Medieval popular morality requires the public eye and the interpretation of others in society. In this, it imitates and reproduces the all-pervasive authority of the Church, the guarantor of social order, unity, and justice, diffused into the realm of everyday life. Since Paul's letters, scandal has been used as a term to impose moral order on society and to prevent it from lapsing into the chaos of individual differences.[31] In the Christian world of the Middle Ages, to transgress against *caritas* meant to transgress against and seek to destroy the *ratio* of society, which as a whole was subject to Christian morality, represented and safeguarded by the Church. Renaissance humanists did not fully accept the Church's absolute right to determine the rational order of Christian society. Notably, Erasmus delegates the responsibility of acting and speaking in society in accordance with the principle of Christian love to the educated individual, a position not always welcomed by the Church. Erasmus believes, as we have seen in his debate with Luther, that this idealized Christian humanist subject should be allowed the freedom to disagree or be skeptical about some tenets of Church doctrine, so long as he does not go too far in putting into questioning the authority of the Church.

By reinterpreting the biblical word *scandal*, Luther transforms this legal, theological, and ethical notion into a subversive polemical tool to use against the Catholic Church.[32] In his programmatic tract *The Freedom of a Christian* (1520), he accuses the Catholics of impiety—offending the "faith" of the "weak" with false doctrines—and proclaims that one does not need to worry about offending such people. For Luther the theologian, the greatest scandal, the only one that really matters, is false doctrine. While a Christian should behave charitably to other Christians "[the impious] he must resist, do the very opposite, and offend them boldly lest by their impious views they drag many with them into error. In the presence of such men it is good to eat meat, break the fast, and for the sake of the liberty of faith do other things which they regard as the greatest of sins."[33] In this citation, Luther is paraphrasing a passage from Paul's letter to the Corinthians, in which Paul exhorts the Corinthians *not* to scandalize their brothers. Luther's paraphrase of the passage from the Corinthians is probably influenced by Luther's favorite Pauline epistle, the one to the Galatians, to whom Paul preaches Christian freedom. Luther shifts the meaning of the term *scandal* to signify words rather than deeds, first by declaring that the "false doctrine" of the Catholic Church is the greatest scandal, then by providing the Christian with the right to challenge those who scandalize "the weak." His lesson for the sixteenth-century Christian is that it is allowable to offend the impious. This justified offence, in Luther's eyes, is best done in words. It means to proclaim one's conviction, one's faith, to combat the adversary with the word of Scripture—itself a stumbling block.

The Outrageous Book

By the early 1520s, with the publication of the New Testament in German, Luther had transformed Scripture (his own translated and printed version of it) into a weapon against the Church. This was made possible by his reading of it as a divine speech act, one that is both felicitous and binding—one that demands to be viewed as felicitous by the reader or hearer. Moreover, Luther challenged the Church to refute him on the basis of this Scripture; for him, the battle had to be fought with words—and those were, most often, printed words. Whereas "the papists have washed the mouth of the Gospel," Luther claims to go back to the "original" gospel—realized in his translation—the original one, the "stumbling block."[34] In so doing, he reached back to the moral teachings and language of late-medieval preachers. The fourteenth-century Dominican preacher Johannes Tauler emphasizes the dangerous consequences of the improper reception of Scripture by comparing the malevolent reader or hearer to a "venomous spider" who is able to draw only deadly poison, instead of honey, from a beautiful rose. Luther also zooms in on the negative effects of reading Scripture. The paradox Luther elaborates is also expressed in Sebastian Franck's *Paradoxa* (1534): "the Gospel creates subversion in the world and is an obstacle to truth."[35] Luther insists that the "good news" is for those who are "poisonous spiders" a source of venom.[36] Luther here equates the rhetorical figure of the venomous spider with the term *scandal*. New Testament uses of this complex figure allow Luther to do this: the "word" is a scandal for those who lack perseverance; Christ is a scandal for his disciples and the Pharisees; and the gospel is a stumbling block for the Jews, according to Paul. These images allow Luther to underscore the potentially subversive effects of the book. Luther not only reinterprets the theological notion of scandal, breaking the normative legal and moral hegemony for which it served as a tool, but also exploits the passages in the Bible that define scandal as a positive and powerful speech act.

Scripture is not only a promise but also a threat or warning. In this double quality, it polarizes its readers.[37] The Bible is a potentially "scandalous" text; what it "does" depends on the reader's disposition, her felicitous or infelicitous reading act. By extension, Luther's books possess the same essential ambivalence. The most significant effect of this rhetorical practice is not political division (or sedition, as the charge went) but the politicization of public speech. In his writing practice, Luther makes blasphemous statements that can be interpreted in opposite ways: one is either offended or converted by them. In other words, they have the effect of being perceived either as deeply religious or as deeply antireligious. Their *modus loquendi* is inextricably tied to the *modus audiendi* (and hence also the *modus agendi*) of the audience. The politicization of public discourse feeds on the creation of what Bakhtin, reflecting on the inseparable interplay between formal and ideological (hence also political and confrontational) elements in literary texts, called a *dialogic* situation, in which words do not have a meaning independently of the situation in which they are spoken by a speaker and understood—and appropriated—by an auditor. They have no neutral meaning and cannot be taken in a sense that is independent of the interlocutor's ideological position.[38] Although the term *ideology* did not appear until the eighteenth century, Donald Kelley has shown that the shift from dogma to conviction ("assurance") in Luther's theology led to the development of a Protestant ideology and, later, to the development of different kinds of religious ideologies *avant la lettre*.[39] The aim of Luther's inherently violent and destabilizing rhetorical practice was to claim that what was conventionally accepted as pious language is in fact blasphemy and that what appeared to be blasphemy is in fact true piety. This rhetorical strategy is manifest in a pamphlet in which he fashions the tool of popular satire for the purposes of his own theology of offense.

"Be not offended"

Among the "angry little booklets" that Luther published for popular consumption was one entitled the *Monk-Calf*; it is a mock exegesis, and as such singular in Luther's œuvre, an occasional piece that corresponds to the literary form of satire. The pamphlet's patent antipapist polemical agenda is underscored by the fact that Luther's text appeared together with a satirical piece by the humanist Melanchthon concerning the Pope-Ass, a fictional monster allegedly found on the banks of the Tiber in Rome after the flooding of 1496. Unlike Melanchthon's Pope-Ass, Luther's Monk-Calf has a kernel of historical truth: indeed, a disfigured calf was born near Freyberg, Saxony, on December 8, 1522. In response to satirical poems that termed this "monster" "Luther,"[40] Luther picked up his pen and responded with the *Monk-Calf*. As both Luther's text describes and the accompanying woodcut illustrates, the Monk-Calf pokes fun at the depravity of monks, nuns, and, in particular, the preachers of the mendicant orders. He is blind, is dressed in the cassock of a monk, wears the tonsure, and preaches, standing on his rear legs with an outstretched tongue. His upper jaw is human, but his lower one is bovine. His enormous ears, Luther explains, signify the tyranny of the sacrament of confession:

> As a first and comprehensive point of this sign: Be not offended [*laß dir das keyn schimpff seyn*] that God has clothed a calf with a clerical garb, a holy cassock: through this he signified many things with one figure, namely, that it must become manifest that all the monks and nuns are nothing but false, deceitful phantoms and secular hypocrites [*ein falscher lugenhafftiger schein und eußerlich gleyssen*] of a spiritual, godly life.[41]

What is noteworthy about this passage is not so much the message or the manner of Luther's critique, which appears at first sight to be a crude satire of Catholic religious practices and institutions, but rather Luther's stretching of the popular view that monsters (*monstra*) are divine portents that indicate (*monstrare*) the future.[42] In sacramental theology, Luther condemns ordination and confession as man-made ceremonials, refusing the Church the power to initiate a rite. This the divine word alone, as the act of promise, has the authority to do: "For the church was born by the word of promise through faith, and by this same word is nourished and preserved. That is to say, it is the promises of God that make the Church, and not the Church that makes the promise of God. For the word of God is incomparably superior to the church."[43] The Monk-Calf represents the "golden calf," both idol and idolatry—or, with Austin, the "false" speech act—of the Church, by contrast to the solely felicitous promise as the revealed truth of Scripture.

In the sixteenth century, monsters abounded in satirical and popular literature because they represented the distortion of reality that satire operates. Yet "while normal satire distorts reality in order to unmask the discord in a given situation, Luther's treatise, by adding the eschatological dimension, goes full circle: what is presented as a blasphemous deviation and perversion turns out to be the actual state of affairs! Satire changes from an attack into recounting the actual conditions. Satirical imagery is, in Luther's perspective, transformed into depiction of realities."[44] This is what really distinguishes Luther's pamphlet from ordinary, realist satire. In a satire, one is never asked to believe, but a cognitive effort is necessary to keep in mind the difference between "reality" and the fictional distortion of it carried out by the satire. Of course, the distortion serves to bear out the reality, what otherwise might remain hidden. It also produces, mediates the representation of, a reality. Nonetheless, fiction and reality are never allowed to collapse into one another. But this is what Luther is asking his readers to do: to believe in the reality of it. The crux of the matter lies in his claim not that this distortion is simply a convenient fiction that helps to open the reader's eyes to what actual, concrete reality is and should be, but that it is not fiction at all—being instead the truth, a true image of a reality not (yet) visible.

Luther's belief in the apocalypse has been somewhat of an embarrassment for a theologian who purportedly purged religion of the contamination of superstition and thus greatly contributed to the "disenchantment" of the modern world. Heiko Oberman has argued against those who would dismiss Luther's eschatology as a leftover of late-medieval superstitious and popular beliefs, showing that, rather, it constitutes an essential element in Luther's theology, indeed, that we "will not get closer to Luther's mission if we do not enter into his graphic, dramatic eschatology."[45]

Oberman argues, moreover, that whenever Luther speaks of "Reformation" he never means an improvement brought about on the social level but envisions it as a divine act that takes place at the end of time.[46] God alone can bring about the general renewal of the world, but such a renewal also marks the end of the world as we know it, that is, the world with its established order, values, and morality. And such an end is announced by preliminary signs such as the Monk-Calf.

The Monk-Calf, a preacher of false doctrine, is a sign of the divine act of Reformation and at the same time a perfect example of Luther's scandal. In the footsteps of late-medieval preachers, Luther translated that term into German as *ergernis*, the sixteenth-century equivalent of the modern German word *Ärgernis*. The meaning of this German word is different from the meaning of the Hebrew-Greek *skandalon*. *Ärgernis* is derived from the root *arg-*, which means "evil" or simply "bad," and *ärger*, the comparative, signifies "worse." The *Ärgernis*, the "worsening" of the world, heralds the ultimate divine act of Reformation, the apocalypse. Luther liked to repeat the popular saying "The longer the world goes on, the worse it becomes [*Die Welt wird je länger, je ärger*]": this proverb became the expression of his open endorsement of the increasing number of religious offenses, *scandala*—even including (what he considered to be) blasphemy, heterodoxy, and inauthentic forms of worship.[47] Luther thus exploits and intensifies the eschatological significance of the figure of the "stumbling block": *Ärgernis* is the worsening of the world. The Monk-Calf is a scandal in this sense; it is a divine sign, a warning.

While the Christian is not supposed to pry into the secrets of divine election, in his social dealings with others he can see the visible Church, the preliminary revelation of the final, invisible Church of the elect, emerge. This is why Luther is able to find consolation in the fact that the elect, the ones who will not stumble—however small their number may be—are protected, while the rest of the world deviates from orthodoxy as a consequence of his teachings. Moreover, all he can do to promote a Reformation is to provoke more *scandala*, the falling away of many from faith, in other words, to provoke through injurious language to which others take offense: "Cursed, damned, and destroyed must be the papacy together with all earthly kingdoms that are against your kingdom."

Luther does not intend to amend people with his "interpretation"; rather, he anticipates a deterioration of the entire "papal kingdom" as the consequence of the appearance of the Monk-Calf and as the effect of his pamphlet: "For this reason they [the faithless] should not believe me in this matter but rather take offense more and more and be stubborn, after which they will not know the truth or improve their faithless lives."[48] Let us consider the provocative core of Luther's claim. While the "testament" in which God reveals himself, speaks, transforms the reader-listener into a believer who understands it, *bona fide*, to be a felicitous speech act, scandalous rhetorical practice, theologically speaking, produces the "faithless"—a category that is also produced by a language whose "effect" the "faithless" is and through which it becomes recognizable as such. The end of the world is already happening—thanks to Luther's insults. The outrageous language of this pamphlet is modeled upon the language of the Bible. There is only one way in which the Monk-Calf can (at least textually) be redeemed: by not being offended by it, in other words, by fully subscribing to the satire as if it were as true as the Word of Scripture. It all comes down to the reader's interpretation, to his willingness to read the message. With this strategy, Luther increases the significance of insulting considerably, while he also wards off responsibility for it. If you are insulted by Luther, if you take offense, if you do not see the real state of affairs in this satirical image, you have already stumbled over the stumbling block that is an ineluctable manifestation of the will of a *deus absconditus* whose full revelation is postponed until the Last Judgment.

The use of the notion of scandal as a polemical concept did not stop here. Luther's adversaries, both Catholics and dissidents within the Reformed movement, turned his weapon against him. The moral use of this concept in the Reformation continued to rely on the normative idea of a "respectable majority" (corresponding to each of the various congregations and churches that began to proliferate in Europe and throughout the world during the Reformation), whom it permits to accuse and ostracize those whom it deems to be "other." *Scandal* as a polemical term undid the moral-religious unity of the public space, all the more so as various groups tried to enforce their norms of morality and piety.

A careful look at Luther's theology of offense reveals, however, a point of even greater division than the fragmentation of the homogeneous public space into heterogeneous and, possibly, hostile groups representing different beliefs and norms. The French author Montaigne sums up Luther's public effect: "I note that Luther has left behind in Germany as many—indeed more—discords and disagreements [*autant de divisions et d'altercations*] because of doubts about his opinions than he himself ever raised about Holy Scripture. Our controversies are verbal ones."[49] Montaigne's nominalist disclaimer that religious controversies are merely verbal disputes reveals his anxiety about the power of words to divide. While writing these lines, he was no doubt also thinking of France, caught both in an on-going civil war, the "wars of religion," and in a fierce pamphlet war. Luther's objections to Catholic dogma and to the moral and political order represented by the Church, Montaigne claims, have had grave effects on society. But disagreements about dogma or about the right interpretation of Scripture do not stop at the formal level of beliefs. Montaigne's important insight is that disagreements about dogma are also disagreements among people, and this social effect of dogmatic disputes is the principal problem. Although aiming at "the sack," Luther hit those who carried their beliefs on their backs; he upset people, who in turn upset each other. In his *How to Do Things with Words*, Austin terms this capacity of language to produce effects outside the locutionary act "perlocutionary": "Saying something will often, or even normally, produce certain consequential effects upon the feelings, thoughts, or actions of the audience, or of the speaker, or of other persons."[50] The greatest "scandal of religion" in the sixteenth century is precisely this perlocutionary aspect of dogmatic disagreements, that is, their capacity to offend people and, spreading, to create a "hydra's head" of argumentation.[51] This is why the consequences of Luther's theology of offense have to be measured by the proliferation of slanderous books whose principal aim was to offend the adversary.

In the early years of the Reformation, German Catholics were reluctant to give up their long-won position of *auctoritas* by arguing with a monk from Wittenberg. For this reason, the number of Catholic pamphlets published in German against Luther is relatively small in comparison with the number of pamphlets produced by Luther's "media campaign."[52] French Catholics were much less reluctant to engage in a pamphlet war with their French-speaking Protestant adversaries. Just to mention one example, the pamphleteers Artus Desiré and Fremin Capitis did not shy away from parodying Protestant French translations of the Book of Psalms, de facto espousing Luther's and the Reformers' view that it is not the external, formal characteristics of a speech act but the consciousness of the speaker that determines whether it is blasphemous or not. Thus the words of Scripture translated and spoken by Calvinists were blasphemous words that could and should be parodied.

If the Reformation—rather than the Enlightenment, as has often been assumed—can be said to create the modern structure of the public sphere, that is because it calls into question all conception of the public sphere as transparent: curses can be prayers and prayers curses. Enlightenment or secularist theories of the emergence of the public realm have missed the Reformation's genuine modernism, which consists in bringing out the potentially contentious, "excitable," character of religious and, perhaps, any speech. Luther is a case in point, a *novum* inexplicable in the terms of classical rhetoric and Humanism, inexplicable also within the secularist modernist paradigm.

On the Names of God

Ernesto Laclau

Eckhart asserts:

> God is nameless for no one can either speak of him or know him.
> . . . Accordingly, if I say that "God is good," this is not true. I am
> good, but God is not good! In fact, I would rather say that I am
> better than God, for what is good can become better and what can
> become better can become the best! Now God is not good, and so
> he cannot become better, he cannot become the best. These three
> are far from God: "good," "better," "best," for he is wholly tran-
> scendent. . . . Also you should not wish to understand anything
> about God, for God is beyond all understanding. . . . If you under-
> stand anything about him, then he is not in it, and by understand-
> ing something of him you fall into ignorance, and by falling into
> ignorance, you become like an animal since the animal part in crea-
> tures is that which is unknowing.[1]

If God is nameless, that is due to His absolute simplicity, which
excludes from itself all differentiation or representational image:

> You should love God non-mentally, that is to say, the soul should
> become non-mental and stripped of her mental nature. For as long
> as your soul is mental, she will possess images. As long as she has
> images, she will possess intermediaries, and as long as she has inter-
> mediaries, she will have no unity or simplicity. As long as she lacks
> simplicity, she does not truly love God, for true love depends upon
> simplicity.[2]

The only true attribute of God is Oneness, because it is the only
attribute that is not determinate. If I say that God is good, "goodness"

is a determination that implies the negation of what differs from it, whereas God is the negation of the negation. As such, Oneness, being a nonattribute that involves no difference and, therefore, no negation, is the only thing that we can predicate of Him.

> Oneness is purer than goodness and truth. Although goodness and truth add nothing, they do nevertheless add something in the mind: when they are thought, something is added. But oneness adds nothing, where God exists in himself, before he flows out into the Son and the Holy Spirit. . . . If I say that God is good, then I am adding something to him. Oneness, on the other hand, is a negation of negation and a denial of denial. What does "one" mean? One is that to which nothing has been added.[3]

> If we call God "Lord," or "father," we are dishonoring Him, because those names are incompatible with Oneness—a Lord requires a servant and a father, a son. So "we should learn that there is no name we can give God so that it might seem that we have praised and honored him enough, since God is 'above names' and is ineffable."[4]

It seems apparently necessary to conclude, with Dionysius Areopagite, that "the cause of all that is intelligible is not anything intelligible." This paves the way for the mystical way, the *via negativa*. God is

> not soul, not intellect,
> not imagination, opinion, reason and not understanding,
> not logos, not intellection,
> not spoken, not thought,
> not number, not order,
> not greatness, not smallness,
> not equality, not inequality,
> not likeness, not unlikeness,
> not having stood, not moved, not at rest.[5]

And so on. What we are presented with here, through all these negations, is a certain manipulation of language by which something that is ineffable gets expressed. This is a generalized tendency within mysticism: a distortion of language that deprives it of all representative function is the way to point to something that is beyond all representation. In some primitive texts, such as those related, for instance, to Merkabah mysticism, this effect is obtained by giving each organ of the body of the Creator, in their descriptions, such an enormous length that all visual representation becomes impossible. As Gershom Scholem points out: "the enormous figures have no intelligible meaning or sense-content, and it is impossible really to visualize the 'body of the shekinah' which they purport to describe; they are better calculated, on the contrary, to reduce every attempt at such a vision to absurdity."[6] In a highly intellectualized discourse such as that of Eckhart, the devices are, obviously, much more sophisticated—they rely on the redemptive nature of language, according to which "words come from the Word." But in any case it is a distortion of the normal use of language that is at stake. What is involved in such a distortion?

Let us concentrate for a moment on the series of negations through which Dionysius attempts to approach the (non)essence of the divinity. In the first place, all the contents that are negated are part of an enumeration that has no internal hierarchy or structure. They are in a purely paratactic relation with each other. In the second place, the enumeration is an open one: many more contents—actually, all representational content—could have been part of the same enumeration. Now this enumerative operation is crucial to produce the effect of meaning that Dionysius is looking for. If he had just said, for instance, that God is not "imagination," the possibility would always have existed that He is something else, endowed with a positive content. It is only the location of "imagination" in an enumerative chain with "opinion," "logos," "number," "intellection," and so on, as well as the open character of the enumeration, that guarantees that God can be identified with the "ineffable." But in that case, the enumeration is not just an enumeration, in which each of its terms would express the fullness of its own isolated meaning (as when we say, for instance, that the U.S.A. was visited last year by many British, French, and Italian people). In the case of Dionysius' text, each of the terms in the enumeration is part of a chain which, *only when it is taken as a totality*, expresses the nonessence of that Who is the Cause of All Things. That is, that we are dealing with a peculiar type of enumeration, one whose terms do not simply coexist one beside the other but instead can replace each other, because they all, within the enumerative arrangement, express the same. This is the type of relation that I call *equivalence*.

It could perhaps be objected that this possibility of an equivalential substitution is simply the result of the negative character of each of the terms of Dionysius' enumeration. But I do not think that this is the case. If the only thing that we had in the succession of negative terms was the negation of which they are bearers, the possibility of expressing the ineffable would be lost. If all we are saying is that God is not *A*, not *B*, and not *C*, this by itself does not exclude the possibility that He is *D*, *E*, or *F*. That is, if we focus exclusively on the *not* of the negation, there is no way of meaningfully constructing the open-ended dimension of the enumeration (on which the possibility of expressing the "ineffable" depends). We are apparently dealing with two contradictory requirements: we want to maintain the ineffable character of the experience of the divinity, and we want at the same time to show through language such an ineffable presence. As we said, no pure concentration on the *not* will help us to meet these two requirements. The enumeration of Dionysius has another dimension, however, for what he is saying is not that God is "not imagination"—paragraph—"not logos"—paragraph, and so on. What he is actually saying is, first, that God is something that goes *beyond* the specific meaning of terms such as *imagination*, *logos*, *intellection*, and so on, and, secondly, that this transcendence, this going *beyond* the specific meanings of these terms, is shown through the equivalence that the terms establish between themselves. It is clear that an equivalential enumeration—as different from a purely additive one—destroys the particularized meanings of its terms as much as a succession of negations does. I can perfectly replace "not imagination," "not logos," and "not intellection" with the equivalential succession "imagination," "logos," and "intellection." In both cases I would be saying exactly the same thing, for if I have to concentrate—in order to establish the equivalence—on what "imagination," "logos," and "intellection" have in common, I have to drop most of the particularized meanings of each of these terms, and if the chain of equivalences is extended enough, it can become the way of expressing something that exceeds the representational content of all its links— that is, the "ineffable." The advantage of eliminating the *not* from the enumeration is that in that way its equivalential character becomes more ostensible, and its infinitude—its open-ended nature—becomes fully visible. When I enumerate "not-A," "not-B," "not-C," and so on, I can incorporate D into that chain, in the fullness of its positive meaning, without any further requirement. But if I have the equivalence between the positive terms A, B, and C, I cannot incorporate D into that chain without the added requirement of reducing D to what it has in common with the three previous terms.

So from the previous analysis we can conclude that to say "God" is something different from any particular attribute that we can predicate of Him and to say that He expresses Himself through the *totality* of what exists is to say exactly the same thing.[7] Likeness (= equivalence) between things is the way in which God—actualizes Himself? expresses Himself? Listen to Eckhart:

> God gives to all things equally and so, as they flow forth from God, all things are equal and alike. Angels, men and women and all creatures are equal where they first emerge from God. Whoever takes things in their first emergence from God, takes all things as equal. . . . If we take a fly as it exists in God, then it is nobler in God than the highest angel is in itself. Now all things are equal and alike in God and are God. And this likeness is so delightful to God that his whole nature and being floods through himself in this likeness. . . . It is a pleasure for him to pour out his nature and his being into this likeness, since likeness is what he himself is.[8]

Insofar as the experience of the ineffability of God passes through the equivalence of contents that are less than He, He is both beyond those contents and, at the same time, fully dependent on them for His actualization. Indeed the greater his "beyond," the more extended the chain of equivalences on which His actualization depends. His very transcendence is contingent upon an increased immanence. Let us quote Eckhart again: "God is in all things. The more he is in things, the more he is outside them: the more in, the more out and the more out, the more in."[9] As David says in Browning's *Saul*:

> Do I task any faculty highest, to imagine success?
> I but open my eyes,—and perfection, no more and no less,

In the kind I imagined, full-fronts me, and God is seen God
In the star, in the stone, in the flesh, in the soul and the clod.[10]

Now if God is present "in the star, in the stone, in the flesh, in the soul and the clod," it is clear that mystical experience does not lead to an actual *separation* from things and daily pursuits but, on the contrary, to a special way of joining them, so that we see in any of them a manifestation of God's presence. According to Eckhart:

Those who are rightly disposed truly have God with them. And whoever truly possesses God in the right way, possesses him in all places: on the street, in any company, as well as in a church or a remote place or in their cell. No one can obstruct this person, for they intend and seek nothing but God and take their pleasure only in him, who is united with them in all their aims. And so, just as no multiplicity can divide God, in the same way nothing can scatter this person or divide them for they are one in the One in whom all multiplicity is one and is non-multiplicity. . . . This experience of daily involvement as one in which multiplicity is not denied but is lived as the variegated expression of a transcendent unity is the distinctive mark of the "unitive life" required by mystical consciousness.[11]

Eckhart gives two metaphoric examples of what it is to live multiplicity in unity. The first is the case of somebody who is thirsty: their thirst will accompany all the activities in which they are engaged, irrespective of their variety. The other refers to somebody who is in love: that person's feeling will taint the multifarious pursuits of his or her daily life.

A last important aspect to be considered is mystical *detachment*, whose inner structure is most revealing for our purposes. The detachment in question cannot be that of an anchorite, who lives a segregated existence, for the mystic is not refusing involvement in daily life. The mystic should be fully engaged and, at the same time, strictly detached from the world. How is this possible? As we know, actually existing worldly things—Browning's star, stone, flesh, soul, and clod, Julian's small thing like a hazelnut—can he considered from two perspectives: either in their isolated particularity, in which each of them lives a separate existence, or in their equivalent connection, in which each of them manifests the divine essence. Thus, the mystic has to love each instance of his worldly experience as something through which the divinity shows itself; however, because it is not the particular experience in its own naked particularity that shows God but instead its equivalential connection with everything else, only by the latter connection, the contingency of the fact that it is *this* experience rather than any other than the one that I am having at the moment, do I approach the divinity. Essential detachment and actual involvement are two sides of the same coin. It is like the formation of the revolutionary will of a subordinated class: each participation in a strike, in an election, in a demonstration counts less as the particular event concerned than as a contingent instance in a process that transcends all particular engagement, namely, the education of the class, the constitution of its revolutionary will. On the one hand, the latter transcends all particular engagements and, in that sense, requires that the class be detached from them; on the other hand, without serious engagements in particular events there is no constitution of the revolutionary will. Paradoxically, it is the detached nature of what is invested in a particular action, its purely contingent link to it, that guarantees that involvement in that action will be a serious one. Let us allow Eckhart to speak for a last time:

> We must train ourselves not to seek or strive for our own interests in anything but rather to find and to grasp God in all things. . . . All the gifts which He has granted us in heaven or on earth were made solely in order to be able to give us the one *gift*, which is himself. With all other gifts He simply wants to prepare us for that gift, which is Himself. . . . And so I tell you that we should learn to see God in all gifts and works, neither resting content with anything nor becoming attached to anything. For us there can be no attachment to a particular manner of behavior in this life, nor has this ever been right, however successful we may have been. Above all, we should always concentrate upon the gifts of God, and always do so afresh.[12]

Let us draw two important conclusions from our brief exploration of mysticism. The first concerns the specific problems involved in naming God. God being ineffable, we could use whatever name we might want to refer to Him, insofar as we attribute no determinate content to that name. Eckhart says that, precisely because of this, it is best just to say "God," without attributing anything to Him. So the name of God, if we are not going to soil His sublime reality (and our experience of it), has to be an empty signifier, a signifier to which no signified can be attached. And this poses a problem. Is "God" such an empty signifier, or is this name already an *interpretation* of the sublime, of the absolute fullness? If the latter is the so, to call the sublime "God" would be the utmost irreverence. In other words, while the mystical experience underlies an ineffable fullness that we call "God," that name—*God*—is part of a discursive network that cannot be reduced to this experience. And in actual fact the history of mysticism has provided a plethora of alternative names to refer to that sublimity: the Absolute, Reality, the Ground, and so on. There have even been some mystical schools—like some currents of Buddhism—that have been consequently atheistic. If the mystical experience is really going to be the experience of an absolute *transcendens*, it must remain indeterminate. Only silence would be adequate. To call it "God" is already to betray it, and the same would be the case for any other name that we choose. Naming "God" is a more difficult operation than we would have thought.

Let us now move to our second conclusion. As we have seen, there is an alternative way of naming God, which is through the self-destruction of the particularized contents of an equivalential chain. We can refer to God by the names of *star, stone, flesh, soul,* and *clod* because, insofar as they are part of a universal chain of equivalences, each of them can be substituted for any other other. *Ergo*, they are all indifferent terms for naming the totality of what exists—that is, the Absolute. Here we are confronted, however, with a different problem from that of naming God in a direct way—or, perhaps, with the same problem seen from another angle—because, if that operation could be achieved, we would have accomplished something more than obtaining a universal equivalence: we would have destroyed the equivalential relation and made it collapse into simple identity. Let us consider the matter carefully. In a relation of equivalence the particular meanings of its terms do not simply vanish; they are partially retained, and it is only in some aspects that the replacement of one term by the others operates. Some currents of Hindu mysticism have advocated a total collapse of differences into undifferentiated identity, but Western mysticism has always played around the Aristotelian-Thomist notion of analogy, grounded in an equivalence that is less than identity. A mystic like Eckhart was trying to think "unity in difference," and that is why the analogic relation of equivalence was crucial in his discourse. The universe of differences had to be brought into unity without the differential moment being lost. But it is here where we find a problem, for, if the equivalence becomes absolutely universal, the differential particularism of its links necessarily collapses. We would have an undifferentiated identity in which *any* term would refer to the totality, but in that case the totality—the Absolute—could be named in an immediate, direct way, and its transcendent dimension, which is essential to the mystical experience (and discourse) would have been lost. If, by contrast, the equivalence remains an equivalence and does not collapse into identity, it will be *less* than universal. In that case, as it remains an equivalence, it will be able to be the means of representing something transcending it, but, as the chain will be less than universal, *clod, flesh,* and *stone* will be not only the transparent medium of expression of the Absolute but also its jailers: the remainder of particularity will be back with a vengeance—as it cannot be eliminated, it will transform the mystical intervention from a free walk into the Absolute into the attribution of an absolute value to a particularity that is entirely incommensurable with it.

If we put our two conclusions together, the result is only one: God cannot be named; the operation of naming Him, either in a direct way or indirectly, through the equivalence of contents that are less than Him, involves us in a process by which the residue of particularity, which mystical intervention tries to eliminate, proves to be irreducible. In that case, however, mystical discourse points in the direction of a dialectics between the particular and the Absolute, which is more complex than it claims to be and which we must now explore.

. . .

Let us concentrate for a moment on this double impossibility around which mystical discourse is organized and see to what extent it belongs exclusively to the field of mystical experience or whether it should rather be conceived as the expression, in mystical garb, of something belonging to the general structure of all possible experience. Naming God is impossible, we said, because, being the absolute *transcendens*, He is beyond all positive determination. If we radicalize the logical implications of this impossibility, we see that even the assumption that God is an entity, even the assumption of Oneness—if Oneness is conceived as the unicity of an entity—is already an undue interpretation, because it is to attribute a content to that which is beyond any possible content. If we remain within the realm of discourse, of the *representable*, the "sublime"—the "numinous," as Rudolph Otto calls it—is that which is radically not representable. So unless we espouse the rationalistic assumption that there is nothing in experience that cannot be translated into a positive representational content, this impossibility—as the limit of all representation—will not be simply a logical impossibility but an experiential one. A long tradition has given a name to it: the experience of finitude. Finitude involves the experience of fullness, of the sublime, as that which is radically lacking—and is, in that sense, a necessary beyond. Let us remember the way in which Lacan describes the imaginary identification that takes place at the mirror stage: it presupposes a constitutive lack; it is the primary identification that functions as a matrix for all subsequent secondary ones—so the life of the individual will be a vain search for a fullness of which he or she will be systematically deprived. The object that would bring about such an ultimate fullness is the beyond that the mystic claims he or she is directly experiencing. As such, it is something that accompanies *all* possible experience. The historical importance of mystical discourse is that, by radicalizing that "beyond," it has shown the essential finitude that is constitutive of all experience; its historical limit has been, in most cases, its having surrendered to the temptation of giving a positive content to that "beyond"—the positive content being dictated not by mystical experience itself but by the religious persuasion of the mystic. This can be seen most clearly in the argument that God shows Himself in everything that exists. If the argument is taken in all its implications, we should conclude that actions that we would call immoral express God as much as all the others. This is a conclusion that has been accepted by some extreme mystical sects: insofar as I live in God, I am beyond all moral limitations. But in most cases the mystic accepts conventional religious morality. It is clear, however, that the latter is dictated not by the mystical experience but by the positive religion to which the mystic belongs.

Let us move to the other side of what we have called the double impossibility of structuring mystical discourse: representation of the "beyond" through a chain of equivalences. As we have said earlier, the condition of this form of representation of the Absolute is that the equivalence does not collapse into unity (for in that case we would be dealing with a *direct* representation and the dimension of "beyond" would be lost). To arrive at a *true* equivalence, the differential particularity of its terms must be weakened, but not entirely lost. What are the effects of that remaining particularity? The main one is to put limits on those links that can become part of the equivalential chain. Let us suppose, for instance, that we have in a relation of equivalence *chastity, daily prayer,* and *charity.* If the equivalence collapses into identity—that is, if all differential meaning is obliterated—there will be no obstacle to *free love* becoming part of the chain. But if the chain is a chain of *equivalences*, the particular meanings will not be entirely eliminated and, in that sense, *chastity* would resist the incorporation of *free love* into the chain. The differential meanings are a limitation but, at the same time, a condition of possibility for the equivalence. The equivalence is, however, as we have seen, a condition of representation of the "beyond." Because the equivalence requires partial retention of the differential meanings of its terms (which involves putting limits on its expansion), the only possible conclusion is that the very constitution of the "beyond" is not indifferent to the differential contents whose equivalence is the condition of its representation. We could present the argument in a syllogistic fashion:

> Limitation and retention of particularity is the condition of equivalence;
> Equivalence is the condition of any "beyond";
> So, limitation and retention of particularity is the condition of any "beyond."

The consequences of this sequence are momentous for the structuration of mystical experience (i.e., for the possibility of an absolutely empty signifier that would represent a beyond for all particularism and difference). The only possible conclusion is that there is no possibility of a beyond of differences that is not ancillary to an operation of reintroducing difference. That remainder of difference and particularism cannot be eliminated and, as a result, necessarily contaminates the very content of the "beyond." Here we have a process that can be described in either way: either as a "materialization" of God, giving Him a differential content that is His very condition of possibility, or as the deification of a particular set of determinations that are invested with the function of incarnating the Absolute. But both ways arrive at the same deadlock: a pure expression of the divine essence, which proved to be impossible through straight naming, is no more possible when we use, in an indirect way, a chain of equivalences. We see why a mystic like Eckhart has to rely on the contents of a positive religion: because mystical experience, left to itself, is incapable of providing the differential remainders that are, nonetheless, its condition of possibility.

In this way, mystical discourse reveals something belonging to the general structure of experience: not only the separation between the two extremes of radical finitude and absolute fullness but also the complex language games that it is possible to play on the basis of the contamination of each by the other. It is to the strategies made possible by this unavoidable contamination that I want to refer now. I will give two examples, one from the field of politics, the other from ethics.

As I have argued, *hegemony* is the key concept in thinking politics.[13] I understand by *hegemony* a relationship through which a particular content assumes, in a certain context, the function of incarnating an absent fullness. In a society suffering deep social disorganization, for instance, "order" can be seen as the positive reverse of a situation of generalized *anomie*. The initial situation to which "order" is opposed is the experience of deprivation, finitude, and facticity. Now, once this experience takes place at different points in the social fabric, all of them will be lived as equivalent to each other because, beyond their differences, all of them will point toward a common situation of dislocation and incompletion. So fullness as the positive reverse of this situation of constitutive lack is that which would bring about the completion of the community. Here, however, a second dimension comes to the fore. We know that a relation of equivalence weakens differential meaning: if we must concentrate on what all differences have in common (which is that to which the equivalence points), we must move in the direction of a "beyond" of all differences that will be tendentially empty. "Order" cannot have a particular content, given that it is the simple reverse of all situations lived as disordered. Like mystical fullness, political fullness needs to be named in terms deprived, as much as possible, of any positive content. Where the two start diverging is at the point at which mysticism will deploy all kinds of strategies to have the ultimately unavoidable positivity of content reduced to a minimum, whereas a hegemonic practice will make that ultimate impossibility its raison d'être: far from increasing the gap between fullness and differential content, it will make of a certain particular content the very name of the fullness. "Market economy," for instance, will be presented in some discourses as the *only* content that can bring about the fullness of the community and, as such, as the very name of that fullness. At that point, however, a third dimension comes into operation. We pointed out earlier that the condition of an equivalential relation is that differential meanings, although weakened, do not disappear, and that they put limits to the possibility of an indefinite expansion of the chain of equivalences. Now these limits are obviously more important in a political discourse than in a mystical one, given that the former tries to establish a stable articulation between fullness and difference. Once *market economy* has become, in a discourse, the name of the fullness of the community, some equivalences will become possible while some others will be more or less permanently excluded. This situation is certainly not fixed, for discursive configurations are submitted to deforming pressures— some equivalences, for instance, can change the meaning of *market*—but the decisive point is that, if the function of representing the fullness deforms the particular content which assumes that function, that particular content reacts by limiting the indeterminacy of the equivalential chain.

My second example concerns ethics. There has been a lot of discussion in recent years about the consequences, for moral engagement, of "postmodernity" and, in a more general sense, of the critique of philosophical essentialism. Does not the questioning of an absolute ground deprive moral commitments of any foundation? If everything is contingent, if there is no "categorical imperative" that would constitute a bedrock of morality, aren't we left with a situation in which "everything goes" and, consequently, with moral indifference and the impossibility of discriminating between ethical and unethical actions? Let us see what the theoretical preconditions of this conclusion are. I think that here we must distinguish between two aspects. The first concerns the possibility of a serious moral engagement with *any kind* of action (leaving aside for the moment its actual content). What the critique of essentialism implies is that there is no way of morally discriminating a priori between particular courses of action—not even in the sense of establishing a minimal content for a categorical imperative. This, however, does not logically imply that serious moral commitments could not be attached to engagements taken by less than courses of action dictated a priori. To conclude the opposite would be the same as saying that only the particularity of a course of action conceived as particularity could be the source of a serious moral engagement. But this is exactly what the whole of mystical experience denies. Let us remember what we said earlier about the dialectics between *detachment* and *engagement* in Eckhart. It is only insofar as I experience my contact with the divinity as an absolute, beyond all particularized content, that I can give to my particular courses of action their moral seriousness. And if we generalize in the way we pointed out earlier: only if I experience the absolute as an utterly empty place can I project into contingent courses of action a moral depth that they, left to themselves, lack. As we can see, the "postmodern" experience of the radical contingency of any particular content claiming to be morally valid is the very condition of the ethical overinvestment that makes possible a higher moral consciousness. As in the case of "hegemony," we have here a certain "deification" of the concrete, whose ground is, paradoxically, its very contingency. Serious moral engagement requires a radical separation between moral consciousness and its contents, so that no content can have any a priori claim to be the exclusive beneficiary of the engagement.

Let us now move to our second aspect. Even if we grant that this gap between the experience of the absolute as an empty place and an engagement with the particular contents that are going to incarnate it becomes permanent, does this not leave us entirely without guidance about what are the *right* incarnating contents? It certainly does. This lack of guidance is what we earlier called facticity, finitude. If there were an a priori logic linking the experience of the absolute to particular contents, the link between the incarnated absolute and its incarnating content would have become a necessary one, and the absolute would have lost its dimension of beyond. In that case we would be able to name God in a direct way, or at least to claim to have a discursive mastery of His essence, as Hegel did in his *Logic*. To claim the opposite does not mean that *any* content, at any moment, can be an equal candidate for the incarnation of the absolute. This is only true *sub species aeternitatis*. But historical life takes place in a terrain that is less than eternity. If the experience of what we have referred to in terms of the dual movement "materialization of God" and a "deification of the concrete" is to live up to its two sides, neither the absolute nor the particular can find a final peace with each other. This means that the construction of an ethical life will depend on keeping open the two sides of this paradox: an absolute that can only be actualized by being something less than itself, and a particularity whose only destiny is to be the incarnation of a "sublimity" that transcends its own body.

The Permanence of the Theologico-Political?

Claude Lefort

There was, in the nineteenth century, a widespread and lasting conviction that one cannot discern the transformations that occur in political society—that one cannot really take stock of what is appearing, disappearing, or reappearing—without examining the religious significance of the old and the new. In both France and Germany, philosophy, history, the novel, and poetry all testify to that. This conviction is not, of course, entirely new, and it can be traced far back in history. I am not thinking of the work of theologians and jurists, or of their disputations over the links between the authority of kings and emperors, and that of popes; no matter how they exercised it, their thought was still confined within the limits of a theologico-political experience of the world. It is, it seems to me, in the sixteenth century that we detect the first signs of a modern reflection upon politics and religion; it is then that a new sensitivity to the question of the foundations of the civil order is born as a result of the combined effects of the collapse of the authority of the Church and of the struggles that accompanied the Reformation, as a result both of the assertion of the absolute right of the prince and of challenges to that right. It is, however, still true to say that at the beginning of the nineteenth century a much wider debate is inaugurated as a result of the French Revolution. It is while that event is still a living memory that there arises a feeling that a break has occurred, but that it did not occur within time, that it establishes a relationship between human beings and time itself, that it makes history a mystery; that it cannot be circumscribed within the field of what are termed political, social, or economic institutions; that it establishes a relationship between human beings and the institution itself; that it makes society a mystery. The religious meaning of this break haunts the minds of the men of the period, no matter what verdicts they may reach—no matter whether they look for signs of a restoration of Catholicism, for signs of a renewal of Christianity within Catholicism or Protestantism, for signs of the fulfillment of Christianity in political and social life, outside the old framework of the Churches, or even for signs of its complete destruction and of the birth of a new faith. To mention only the case of France, we might say that at one extreme we have legitimists like De Maistre, that at the other we have socialists like Leroux, and that, between the two extremes, we have such individual thinkers as Ballanche, Chateaubriand, Michelet, and Quinet; they all speak the same language, and it is simultaneously political, philosophical, and religious.

It is true—and let us not forget it—that the same period sees the assertion of a new state of mind, of a tendency (traces of which can be found in the sixteenth century, and which became clearly outlined during the French Revolution) to conceive of the state as an independent entity, to make politics a reality *sui generis*, and to relegate religion to the domain of private belief. As early as 1817, Hegel was already denouncing this tendency in terms that foreshadow its future developments. Arguing in the *Encyclopedia* that "the state rests on the ethical sentiment, and that on the religious," he adds this valuable commentary:

> It has been the monstrous blunder of our times to try to look upon these inseparables as separable from one another, and even as mutually indifferent. The view taken of the relationship of religion and the state has been that, whereas the state had an independent existence of its own, springing from some source and power, religion was a later addition, something desirable perhaps for strengthening the political bulwarks, but purely subjective in individuals:—or it may be, religion is treated as something without effect on the moral life of the state, i.e., its reasonable law and constitution, which are based on a ground of their own.[1]

Before long, similar criticisms became widespread in France, but they were based upon different premises, were inspired by humanism or by a socialism tinged with a new religiosity, and were addressed to adversaries who came to the fore when the reign of Louis-Philippe ensured the triumph of a pragmatic or even cynical politics, which Victor Cousin painted in more favorable colors as eclecticism. This "bastard philosophy," to use Leroux's expression, certainly celebrates the indestructible virtues of religion, but it does so in order to subordinate them to the preservation of a political order that, to cite Hegel once more, is based on a ground of its own.

We therefore have to recognize that what is now the dominant conception of politics goes back a long way. Its origins seem to merge with those of the bourgeois spirit—with the spirit of a bourgeoisie that has become politically dominant. Without wishing to dwell on the vicissitudes of ideology that drove it from the intellectual scene, we ought, then, to say that it is not in the work of the thinkers we first mentioned that we find the first signs of our modernity, but in eclecticism. The "monstrous blunder" that Hegel denounces would therefore appear to designate the truth of modern times, the truth of our own times. The judgment of history, which he evokes so often, appears to have gone against him, to have denounced his blunder. In more general terms, we would then have to conclude that, if those thinkers who sought the religious truth of the political revolution they had witnessed (and I am referring to the democratic revolution) seem so alien to the sensibilities of our time, it is because they had no understanding of the new. But can we leave matters at that, and wax ironic about their wild imaginings? For these thinkers, the ancien régime was something that had existed in living memory. They still lived in the gap between a world that was disappearing and a world that was appearing, and their thought was still haunted by questions that knew no limits—by which I mean that it was not yet restricted by any presuppositions as to how to define objects of knowledge or as to how to define politics, religion, law, economics, or culture. Might we not ask ourselves whether these thinkers may, even if they were mistaken, have had a singular ability to grasp a symbolic dimension of the political, of something that was later to disappear, of something that bourgeois discourse was already burying beneath its supposed knowledge of the real order of society?

Before we attempt to answer that question, we must first define our terms.

It is certainly a fact that political institutions have long been separated from religious institutions; it is also a fact that religious beliefs have retreated into the realm of private opinion.[2] The phenomenon is observable even in countries where Catholicism remains the dominant religion. True, this statement has to be qualified if we also take into consideration those European countries that have come under totalitarian domination. But, while that phenomenon is thought-provoking, let us ignore it for the moment in order to concentrate on our general observation. Does it have any meaning in itself? Can we say that religion has simply disappeared in the face of politics (and survives only on the periphery of politics) without asking ourselves what its investment in the political realm once meant? And do we not have to assume that it was so profoundly invested therein as to have become unrecognizable to those who believe its effects to have been exhausted? Can we not admit that, despite all the changes that have occurred, the religious survives in the guise of new beliefs and new representations, and that it can therefore return to the surface, in either traditional or novel forms, when conflicts become so acute as to produce cracks in the edifice of the state?

According to the former view, the "modern" notion of politics is not in doubt and derives from our actual experience. According to the latter, it is an index of our ignorance or disavowal of a hidden part of social life, namely, the processes that make people consent to a given regime—or, to put it more forcefully, that determine *their manner of being in society*—and that guarantee that this regime or mode of society has a permanence in time, regardless of the various events that may affect it. Following that line of argument would not necessarily take us back to those interpretations (and they are, moreover, contradictory) that regarded the link between the religious and the political to be indissoluble, but we would at least have to recapture something of their inspiration.

If, however, we specify the terms of our question in this way, we cannot fail to notice that they are closely related to the meaning we give to the words *the religious* and, more important still, *the political*. We must, then, examine their meaning.

We can define *the religious* in broader or narrower terms, and the threshold beyond which the word loses all pertinence is a matter for debate; it would, however, seem that we can readily agree that certain beliefs, attitudes, and representations reveal a religious sensibility, even though the agents concerned do not relate them to any dogma; even though they do not imply any fidelity to a church; and even though they may, in certain cases, go hand in hand with militant atheism. The expression "religious sensibility" retains a fairly precise content if we relate it to historically and culturally determined phenomena: in other words, not to religion in general but to the Christian religion, whose various manifestations we can identify without any risk of error. The word *political*, on the other hand, brings us face to face with an ambiguity that must be resolved if we are to know what we are talking about. The fact that we can choose to say either *the political* [le politique] or *politics* [la politique] is, as we all know, an index of this ambiguity. What is certain is that the delimitation of the domain known as "the political" does not result from methodological criteria alone. The very notion of "limits" in fact derives from a desire for an "objective" definition—a desire that lies at the origin of the political theory, political science, and political sociology that have developed in the course of our century. No matter whether we attempt, for example, to circumscribe an order of social relations that are intelligible in themselves, such as power relations; to conceive of a body of social functions whose necessary articulation signals the coherence of a system; to distinguish a superstructural level, based upon relations of production in which class domination is at once expressed and disguised by institutions, practices, and representations that supposedly serve the general interest; or, finally, to identify from empirical observation which of the mass of social facts relate directly or indirectly to the exercise of power, the underlying assumption is always the same: we assume that the object can have substance only if it is particular. In other words, the epistemological operation through which we relate to the object—be it posited as "real" or as "ideal"—makes it appear by separating it from other defined or definable objects. The criterion of what is *political* is supplied by the criterion of what is *nonpolitical*, by the criterion of what is economic, social, juridical, aesthetic, or religious. This operation is not innocent; it hides behind a truism borrowed from the domain constituted as that of exact knowledge: science deals only with particulars. It need scarcely be pointed out that this disposition has never prevented anyone from looking for articulations between that which pertains to politics and that which pertains to different realities or different systems; on the contrary, it usually acts as an encouragement to do so. How, for example, do power relations combine with juridical relations? How is the political system integrated into a general system as a subsystem? How are the political institutions, practices, and representations that are essential to the preservation of a mode of production determined, and what is their specific efficacy in different socio-historical formations? How do they, in their turn, exploit a given state of culture, law, or religion? Theorists and observers are only too willing to formulate such problems. Indeed, those who take a relational, a Marxist, a functionalist, or a descriptive stance urge us to use our historical experience as a means to identify the various modes of the articulation of social relations, subsystems, and superstructural levels. But it is still true to say that any attempt to conceptualize the ways in which the combinations vary derives from the preliminary operation of breaking down social data in order to find something intelligible. And it is also true to say that that operation is inspired by a principle that erects the subject into being a pure subject of knowledge, gives it a scientific neutrality, and guarantees it its self-assurance by virtue of the coherence of its constructs or observations.

We arrive at a very different idea of *the political* if we remain true to philosophy's oldest and most constant inspiration, if we use the term to refer to the principles that generate society or, more accurately, different forms of society. It would be absurd to claim that we then apprehend the political in its wider acceptation. We are elaborating a different idea, and we are guided by a different requirement of knowledge. We do not need to evoke the centuries-old debate that makes up the history of political philosophy in order to specify the meaning of this idea or of this requirement, for it is not relevant to our purposes to ask how the philosopher's search was, in the past, guided by his investigations into the essence of man, into the transition from a state of nature or into reason's self-realization in history. The idea that what distinguishes one society from another is its *regime*—or, to be more accurate and to avoid an overworked term—its *shaping* [mise en forme] of human coexistence has, in one form or another, always been present, and it lies, so to speak, behind the theoretical constructs and behind advances in philosophical thought that are tested against the transformation of the world. In other words, it is simply because the very notion of society already contains within it a reference to its political definition that it proves impossible, in the eyes of the philosopher, to localize the political *in* society. The space called "society" cannot in itself be conceived as a system of relations, no matter how complex we imagine that system to be. On the contrary, it is its overall schema, the particular mode of its institution, that makes it possible to conceptualize (either in the past or in the present) the articulation of its dimensions, and the relations established within it between classes, groups, and individuals, between practices, beliefs, and representations. If we fail to grasp this primordial reference to the mode of the institution of the social, to generative principles, or to an overall schema governing both the temporal and the spatial configuration of society, we lapse into a positivist fiction; we inevitably adopt the notion of a presocial society and posit as elements aspects that can only be grasped on the basis of an experience that is already social. If, for example, we grant to relations of production or the class struggle the status of reality, we forget that *social division* can only be defined—unless, of course, we posit the absurd view that it is a division between alien societies—insofar as it represents an internal division, insofar as it represents a division within a single milieu, within one "flesh" (to use Merleau-Ponty's expression); insofar as its terms are determined by relations, but also insofar as those relations are themselves determined by their common inscription within the same space and testify to a common awareness of their inscription therein. Similarly, if we make a rigid distinction between what belongs to the realm of economics or politics (defined in modern science's sense of the term), or between what belongs to the juridical or the religious in an attempt to find within them signs of specific systems, we forget that we can arrive at that analytic distinction only because we already have a subjective idea of the primal dimensionality of the social, and that this implies an idea of its primal *form*, of its political *form*.

The difference between the idea of the political (in all its variants and all its moments) and political science (in all its variants and all its moments) is not that the latter is concerned with society as a totality and that the former rejects "totality" as an illusory object. Marxist science, for example (and I am not referring here to Marx himself; his thought is at once more ambiguous and more subtle than this), does indeed claim to be able to reconstruct a real or ideal totality; Parsonian science also claims to be able to rearticulate systems of functions within what it terms a "general system." The opposition manifests itself at a different level. The philosopher is not necessarily in search of an elusive object such as a totality; he looks at different regimes or forms of society in order to identify a principle of internalization that can account for a specific mode of differentiation and articulation between classes, groups, and social ranks, and, at the same time, for a specific mode of discrimination between markers—economic, juridical, aesthetic, religious markers—that order the experience of coexistence.

We can further specify the notion of shaping [*mise en forme*] that we have introduced by pointing out that it implies both the notion of giving meaning [*mise en sens*] to social relations (the expression *mise en sens* is taken from Piera Aulagnier) and that of staging them [*mise en scène*]. Alternatively, we can say that the advent of a society capable of organizing social relations can come about only if it can institute the conditions of their intelligibility, and only if it can use a multiplicity of signs to arrive at a quasi-representation of itself. But we must again stress that the shaping or institution of the political cannot be reduced to the limits of the social as such. As soon as we posit as *real* the distinction between what is social and what is not social, we enter the realm of fiction. We have just said that the principle of internalization that enables us to conceptualize the political presupposes a mode of discriminating between the various markers that organize the experience of coexistence, and that experience is inseparable from the experience of the world, from the experience of the visible and the invisible in every register. It need scarcely be stressed that discrimination between real and imaginary, true and false, just and unjust, natural and supernatural, and normal and abnormal is not restricted to the relations people establish in social life. The elaboration attested to by any political society—and not simply the society in which the subject who is trying to decipher it lives—therefore involves an investigation into the world, into Being as such. Understanding how the experience of an *objective* world, of a world that is what it is independently of particular collective experiences, arose—at least partially—in the course of history (and it is tempting to describe it in Husserlian terms as a transition from the socio-political *Umwelt* to the *Welt*) would, of course, be a formidable task, and a further task for political thought.

For the moment, however, we will restrict ourselves to an examination of the difference between political philosophy and political science. We can agree that the latter encounters problems that bear the hallmark of philosophical research, but for political science they are of course no more than *problems* to be circumvented, along with other problems, during the process of reconstructing or describing the workings of society. In fact, the theorist who analyzes politics in terms of power relations cannot but ask himself how and why they stabilize in any given configuration in such a way that the dominant power does not have to exercise its authority openly, irrespective of whether he grants them their own logic or sees them as a reflection or a transposition of class relations that are themselves determined by a mode of production. He cannot but ask how and why they succeed in eluding the understanding of actors, how and why they appear to be legitimate or in accordance with the nature of things. Apparently, then, his problem is how to account for the process of the internalization of domination. But he resolves that problem by looking beyond the frontiers of politics for the nature and origins of the process, by appealing to the mechanisms of representation he finds in the spheres of law, religion, or technical-scientific knowledge. Similarly, the theorist who defines the specificity of political action by subordinating it to functional imperatives (ensuring the unification or cohesion of the social whole, making it possible to formulate and achieve general objectives) is not unaware of the fact that his definition is purely formal. He therefore accepts that such functions can be performed only if social agents internalize the political imperative. And in order to account for that, he invokes the values and norms that determine behavioral models within a given system of culture. But he then assigns specific functions to those norms and values; he seeks to find the preconditions for their efficacy within the coherence of the system whence they derive. In short, whatever the schema of the reconstruction or description may be, his approach always consists in isolating relations and combining them in order to deduce *society* from these operations. The fact that certain of these relations are assumed to provide a key to the modes of the internalization of the social should deceive no one. The theorist is moving to an external element. When he speaks of law, religion, science, values, norms, and categories of knowledge, he is simply filling in the blanks in a pregiven schema of actions, practices, and relations (defined in either materialist or formalist terms). The second operation depends upon the first. Precisely how the object is repositioned to allow the transition from the level of the real or the functional to the so-called level of the symbolic is of little import. Precisely how the element of the imaginary or of language is introduced is of little import. The conclusion that, in the last analysis, power relations, relations of production, or functional relations are always "represented" or "spoken" by religious, juridical, or scientific signs is also of little import. This notion of the symbolic does not help us to escape an artificialist conception. It is deployed in a play of articulation whose terms have already been separated out, and it is grafted onto something that is assumed to contain within it its own determination.

The opposition between philosophy and science is one between two intellectual requirements. For science, knowledge finds its self-assurance by defining functional models; it operates in accordance with an ideal of objectivity that introduces a sovereign distance between the subject and the social. The externality of the knowing subject is of necessity combined with the idea that the social can stand outside itself. Conversely, any system of thought that takes up the question of the institution of the social is simultaneously confronted with the question of its own institution. It cannot restrict itself to comparing structures and systems once it realizes that the elaboration of coexistence creates meaning, produces markers for distinguishing between true and false, just and unjust, and imaginary and real; and that it establishes the horizons of human beings' relations with one another and with the world. It attempts to explain itself and, at the same time, to explain its object. In that respect, it seems to me that there is no radical difference between our present requirement and those of the philosophy of history or of ancient philosophy. We have lost the criteria of classical reason, refuse to distinguish between healthy and corrupt regimes, between legitimate and illegitimate authorities—a distinction based upon the idea of a human essence—and find it impossible to invoke the idea of the development of Mind—which would allow us to see the constitution of the modern state as both the completion of an itinerary and the meaning of the stages (progression, regression, and digression) that go to make it up. Nevertheless, we are still traversed by our investigation into the meaning of the human adventure that unfolds in different forms of political society, and that investigation is still a response to our experience of the political in the here and now. We look for signs of truth and signs of legitimacy, for traces of the concealment of truth and right, and we do so because of the tension inherent in any thought that is trying to define what it has the *right* to think.

To return to the question with which we began: that of the historical disentanglement of the religious and the political. In the context of sociology or political science, their disentanglement is an obvious fact, which leaves intact the categories of knowledge of the social. The political and the religious are regarded as two separate orders of practice and relations; the problem is one of understanding how they are articulated, or how they cease to be articulated, by examining empirical history. The fact that for hundreds or, rather, thousands of years human beings made no such distinction, and that they gave a religious expression to the functions exercised by authority or to the power relations whence it arose, does not detract from the need to recognize the pertinence of a distinction whose value is self-evident in terms of objective analysis. Now this approach brings us up against a double difficulty. On the one hand, history, like society before it, loses all depth; the phenomenon of separation becomes an index of one general system among others; and science assumes a resolutely relativist stance. When this happens, science conceals the conditions of its own formation and, along with them, the basis for the claim that its operations have a universal validity, as it is the fact of separation that allows it to identify the specificity of politics. On the other hand, we have a combination of a dialectical or evolutionary theory and the idea that the elimination of religion from the political field marks the formation of a rational, or potentially rational, type of society in which institutions and practices appear, or begin to appear, for what they really are. But in that case, the fact of the separation of the religious and the political tells us nothing in itself; its meaning is established by reference to a law of historical development or to the laws of the dynamic of social structures.

The philosopher finds himself in a different position. When he thinks of the principles that generate society and names them "the political," he automatically includes religious phenomena within his field of reference. This does not mean that, in his view, the religious and the political can coincide. It does, however, mean that one cannot separate the elaboration of a political form—by virtue of which the nature and representation of power and social division (divisions between classes and groups) can stabilize, and by virtue of which the various dimensions of the human experience of the world can simultaneously become organized—from the elaboration of a religious form, by virtue of which the realm of the visible can acquire death, and by virtue of which the living can name themselves with reference to the dead, whilst the human word can be guaranteed by a primal pact, and whereas rights and duties can be formulated with reference to a primal law. In short, both the political and the religious bring philosophical thought face to face with the symbolic, not in the sense in which the social sciences understand that term, but in the sense that, through their internal articulations, both the political and the religious govern access to the world. This does not make it inconceivable that there is, in any society, a potential conflict between the two principles, or even that it is universally, if tacitly, recognized to exist. Nor does the fact that there is in the modern world an imperative to make a clear distinction between the realms they regulate create difficulties for political thought; this state of affairs in fact meets its requirements, as it has never been able to submit to the authority of religion without demeaning itself, and as it demands the right to seek its foundations within its own activities. In a sense, this revolutionary event is the accomplishment of philosophy's destiny; philosophy is bound up with that event in that it finds the conditions for its own emancipation at the very moment when human beings acquire a potential grasp of their own history, a means to escape the fatalism imposed on their lives by the subjugation of the social order to religious law, and a means to detect the possibility of a better regime in their practices and the novelties they create. But it would be quite illegitimate to leap to the conclusion that religion as such must disappear or, to be more accurate, that it must be confined to the realm of personal opinion. How, in fact, could we argue this, without losing all sense of the symbolic dimension of religion, of the dimension that constitutes the relations human beings establish with the world? The fact that differences of opinion are now recognized to be legitimate does, of course, have a symbolic meaning, but only, it would seem, within the limitations of a political system that guarantees every individual the right to enjoy the respect he must show others. What philosophical thought strives to preserve is the experience of a difference that goes beyond differences of opinion (and the recognition of the relativity of points of view that this implies); the experience of a difference that is not at the disposal of human beings, whose advent does not take place *within* human history, and that cannot be abolished therein; the experience of a difference that relates human beings to their humanity, and that means that their humanity cannot be self-contained, that it cannot set its own limits, and that it cannot absorb its origins and ends into those limits. Every religion states in its own way that human society can only open onto itself by being held in an opening it did not create. Philosophy says the same thing, but religion said it first, albeit in terms that philosophy cannot accept.

Philosophy's critique of religion is therefore ambivalent. Whereas, for example, it rejects the truth that the Christian churches find in Revelation and, in theory, escapes the authority of the Text and refuses to accept the image of a God who comes down to earth and is incarnated in the person of his Son, it does not assume that untruth is a lie or a lure. Nor, when it remains true to its inspiration, does it want to preserve untruth for the simple reason that it may contain beliefs that help to preserve the established political order. What philosophy discovers in religion is a mode of portraying or dramatizing the relations that human beings establish with something that goes beyond empirical time and the space within which they establish relations with one another. This work of the imagination stages [*met en scène*] a different time, a different space. Any attempt to reduce it to being simply a product of human activity is doomed. Of course, it bears the mark of human operations in that the script for the performance bears witness to a human presence and borrows from human sense experience. Human beings populate the invisible with the things they see, naively invent a time that exists before time, organize a space that exists behind their space; they base the plot on the most general conditions of their lives. Yet anything that bears the mark of their experience also bears the mark of an *ordeal*. Once we recognize that humanity opens onto itself by being held in an opening it does not create, we have to accept that the change in religion is not to be read simply as a sign that the divine is a human invention but as a sign of the deciphering of the divine or, beneath the appearance of the divine, of the excess of *being* over *appearance*. In that sense, modern religion or Christianity proves to be teaching the philosopher what he has to think. He rejects religion insofar as it is the enunciator of Revelation but, insofar as it is a mode of the enunciation of the divine, he at the same time accords it a power of revelation that philosophy cannot do without, if, that is, it ceases to divorce the question of human nature from the question of human history.

To simplify the argument to extremes: what philosophical thought cannot adopt as its own, on pain of betraying its ideal of intelligibility, is the assertion that the man Jesus is the Son of God; what it must accept is the meaning of the advent of a representation of the *God-Man*, because it sees it as a Change that recreates humanity's opening onto itself, in both the senses in which we have defined it. Modern philosophy cannot ignore its debt to modern religion; it can no longer distance itself from the work of the imagination or appropriate it as a pure object of knowledge; once it finds itself grappling with the question of its own advent, once it no longer conceals from itself that there is also such a thing as the philosophical *work of thought* and that the focus of its investigations can be displaced, even though it may indulge in the fantasy of being able to put a halt to its displacements. The philosopher's pretensions to Absolute Knowledge notwithstanding, the substitution of the concept for the image leaves intact the experience of alterity in language and of a division between creation and unveiling, between activity and passivity, and between the expression and impression of meaning.

These last remarks may, perhaps, bring us closer to the most secret reasons for the philosopher's continued attachment to the religious. Justified as his demand for the right to think may be, and even though it frees him from every established authority, he not only realizes that any society that forgets its religious basis is laboring under the illusion of pure self-immanence and thus obliterates the locus of philosophy, he also senses that philosophy is bound up with religion because they are both caught up in an adventure to which philosophy does not possess the main key. And so when he proclaims that Christianity's end has come, he still invokes the birth of a new faith, because he is unable to divorce his knowledge from a primordial knowledge that is at once latent and widely shared. Despite appearances, he therefore refuses to accept the historical fact of the separation of the religious and the political. As we have said, he argues that those who accept it as an established fact have a mistaken notion of the political. But in doing so he runs the risk of denying that appearances have sufficient consistency to represent a new practice, to inscribe themselves in some way in the reality of power and the state. But, given that he accords representation a symbolic status and that he still thinks it impossible to divorce the position of power from its representation, a problem should now arise as to how to evaluate the change implied by the representation of a form of power that has no religious basis. Unless this problem arises, a philosophical critique will have no import or will consist simply in the denunciation of erroneous opinions. But, as we have already seen, that was not its objective; its object was the possibility of so shaping society that the religious world would be merely misrecognized or disavowed.

. . .

The future that the thinkers of the nineteenth century were attempting to decipher is to some extent our past and our present. The meaning of our present itself is, of course, dependent upon an indeterminate future; but we enjoy the advantage of an experience that was denied them and that brings a new relief to their debates. In their day, the political form we know as modern democracy was only just coming into being. All its premises had been established, but it still kept its secret, even though its dynamic and its ambiguities were partly visible, as we can see, in particular, from certain of Tocqueville's extraordinary insights into the future. The project of totalitarianism, however, still lay beyond the horizons of their political thought, and there can be no doubt that it both helps shed light on the secret of democracy and urges us to investigate anew the religious and the political.

Modern democracy testifies to a highly specific shaping [*mise en forme*] of society, and we would try in vain to find models for it in the past, even though it is not without its heritage. The new determination—representation of the *place of power*—bears witness to its shaping. And it is certainly this distinctive feature that designates the political. I deliberately refrained from stressing this earlier because I was concerned with bringing out the difference between political science and political philosophy by showing that the former attempts to circumscribe an order of particular facts *within* the social and that the task of the latter is to conceptualize the principle of the institution of the social. But now that the danger of ambiguity has been removed, we no longer need to be afraid to advance the view that any political philosophy and any political science is governed by a reflection upon power. Precisely because of this, they do not deal with specifics but with a primal division that is constitutive of the space we call society. And the fact that this space is organized as *one* despite (or because of) its multiple divisions and that it is organized as *the same* in all its multiple dimensions implies reference to a place from which it can be seen, read, and named. Even before we examine it in its empirical determinations, this symbolic pole proves to be power; it manifests society's self-externality and ensures that society can achieve a quasi-representation of itself. We must, of course, be careful not to project this externality onto the real; if we did so it would no longer have any meaning for society. It would be more accurate to say that power makes a gesture toward something *outside*, and that it defines itself in terms of that outside. Whatever its form, it always refers to the same enigma: that of an internal-external articulation, of a division that institutes a common space, of a break that establishes relations, of a movement of the externalization of the social that goes hand in hand with its internalization. I have for a long time concentrated upon this peculiarity of modern democracy: of all the regimes of which we know, it is the only one to have represented power in such a way as to show that power is an *empty place* and to have thereby maintained a gap between the symbolic and the real. It does so by virtue of a discourse which reveals that power belongs to no one; that those who exercise power do not possess it; that they do not, indeed, embody it; that the exercise of power requires a periodic and repeated contest; that the authority of those vested with power is created and re-created as a result of the manifestation of the will of the people. It could, of course, rightly be pointed out that the principle of a power that men are forbidden to appropriate had already been asserted in classical democracy, but it need scarcely be pointed out that power still had a positive determination in that the representation of the city and the definition of citizenship rested upon a discrimination based upon natural criteria or—and this comes to the same thing—supernatural criteria.

The idea that power belongs to no one is not, therefore, to be confused with the idea that it designates an empty place. The former idea may be formulated by political actors, but not the latter. The first formulation, in fact, implies the actors' self-representation, as they deny one another the right to take power. The old Greek formula to the effect that power is *in the middle* (and historians tell us that it was elaborated within the framework of an aristocratic society before being bequeathed to democracy) still indicates the presence of a group that has an image of itself, of its space, and of its bounds. The reference to an empty place, by contrast, eludes speech insofar as it does not presuppose the existence of a community whose members discover themselves to be subjects by the very fact of their being members. The formula "power belongs to no one" can also be translated into the formula "power belongs to none of us" (and in historical terms, this appears to be the earlier of the two). The reference to an empty place, by contrast, implies reference to a society without any positive determination, which cannot be represented by the figure of a community. It is because the division of power does not, in a modern democracy, refer to an *outside* that can be assigned to the gods, the city, or holy ground; because it does not refer to an *inside* that can be assigned to the substance of the community. Or, to put it another way, it is because there is no materialization of the *Other* (which would allow power to function as a mediator, no matter how it were defined) that there is no materialization of the *One* (which would allow power to function as an incarnation). Nor can power be divorced from the work of division by which society is instituted; a society can therefore relate to itself only through the experience of an internal division that proves to be not a de facto division, but a division that generates its constitution.

It should also be added that, once it has lost its double reference to the *Other* and to the *One*, power can no longer condense the principle of Law and the principle of Knowledge within itself. It therefore appears to be limited. And it therefore opens up the possibility of relations and actions that, in various realms, in particular in those of production and exchange, can be ordered in terms of norms and in accordance with specific goals.

If we wished to pursue this argument, we would have to examine in detail the processes that regulate the establishment of democratic power, in other words, the controlled challenge to the authority vested in its exercise. It is enough to recall that this requires an institutionalization of conflict and a quasi-dissolution of social relations at the very moment of the manifestation of the will of the people. These two phenomena are both indicative of the above-mentioned articulation between the idea that power is a purely symbolic agency and the idea that society has no substantial unity. The institutionalization of conflict is not within the remit of power; it is rather that power depends upon the institutionalization of conflict. Its institutionalization is the result of a juridical elaboration, and, in this first sense, it allows us to identify a field specific to politics: the field of competition between protagonists whose modes of action and programs explicitly designate them as laying claim to the exercise of public authority. This immediately reveals the link between the legitimacy of power and the legitimacy of a conflict that seems to constitute politics, but it must also be noted that this phenomenon presupposes the coming together of a number of conditions relating to social life as a whole: freedom of association and of expression, and the freedom of ideas and of people to circulate. In this respect, the idea of a division between the sphere of the state and the sphere of civil society, which is so often invoked, seems to blur rather than to elucidate the features of the democratic phenomenon. It prevents us from identifying a general configuration of social relations in which diversity and opposition are made visible. It is, I believe, also noteworthy that the delineation of a specifically political activity has the effect of erecting a *stage* on which conflict is acted out for all to see (once citizenship is no longer reserved for a small number) and is represented as being necessary, irreducible, and legitimate. That each party claims to have a vocation to defend the *general* interest and to bring about *union* is of little importance; the antagonism between them sanctions another vocation: society's vocation for division. It is also of little importance that what is at stake in the political conflict does not coincide with what is at stake in the class struggle, or the struggle between interests; whatever the degree of distortion introduced by the shift from the political level to the social level, the important point is that all de facto divisions are transfigured and transposed onto a stage on which division appears to exist de jure. This phenomenon is, as we have noted, combined with the singular procedure of universal suffrage, which is based upon the principle of popular sovereignty but which, at the very moment when the people are supposed to express their will, transforms them into a pure diversity of individuals, each one of whom is abstracted from the network of social ties within which his existence is determined—into a plurality of atoms or, to be more precise, into statistics. In short, the ultimate reference to the identity of the people, to the instituting subject, proves to mask the enigmatic arbitration of number.

Let us stop and retrace our steps after this first stage in our analysis. The representation of politics that lies at the origins of social science is, it must be agreed, generated by the very constitution of democracy, for it is indeed true, as social science asserts, that power no longer makes any gesture toward an *outside*, that it is no longer articulated with any *other* force that can be represented, and that, in that sense, it is disentangled from the religious. It is indeed true that power no longer refers to any point of origin that coincides with the origins of Law and Knowledge and that, in that sense, the type of actions and relations that cluster around its pole can be distinguished from other types of actions and relations that might be termed juridical, economic, and cultural, and it is therefore true that something can be circumscribed as being *politics* [la politique]. The one thing that remains hidden from the gaze of the scientific observer is the symbolic form that, as a result of the mutation in power, makes this new distinction possible: the essence of *the political* [du politique]. The illusion that the political can be localized within society is therefore not without a certain consistency, and to dismiss it as a mistaken opinion would mean surrendering to one more illusion.

Modern democracy is, we have said, the only regime to indicate the gap between the symbolic and the real by using the notion of a power that no one—no prince and no minority—can seize. It has the virtue of relating society to the experience of its institution. When an empty place emerges, there can be no possible conjunction between power, law, and knowledge, and their foundations cannot possibly be enunciated. The being of the social vanishes or, more accurately, presents itself in the shape of an endless series of questions (witness the incessant, shifting debates between ideologies). The ultimate markers of certainty are destroyed, and at the same time there is born a new awareness of the unknown element in history, of the gestation of humanity in all the variety of its figures. It must, however, also be made clear that the gap is merely indicated, that it is operative, but that it is not visible, that it does not have the status of an object of knowledge. It is the attributes of power that are exposed to our gaze, the distinctive features of the contest in which power appears to be the prize. The things that capture our attention and that are designated as objects to be known are the mechanisms that control the formation of a public authority, the selection of leaders, and, more generally, the nature of the institutions vested with the exercise and control of that authority. And so the symbolic dimension of the social passes unnoticed, precisely because it is no longer masked beneath a representation of the difference between the visible world and the invisible world.

This, then, is the paradox: regimes in which the figure of power stands out against an *other* force do not completely obscure the political principle behind the social order. Where the religious basis of power is fully affirmed, it appears to be both the guarantor and the guardian of the certainty that supports the experience of the world; at the same time, it appears to be the keeper of the law that finds its expression in social relations and that maintains their unity. By contrast, democracy, in which the figure of the *other* is abolished, in which power is not divorced from the division that generates it—I will not say that power is stripped bare, as that would imply surrendering to yet another realist fiction—and in which power therefore eludes our grasp (escapes appropriation and representation), is a regime that cannot be apprehended in its political form. While the contours of society become blurred, and while the markers of certainty become unstable, there arises the illusion of a reality that can explain its own determination in terms of a combination of multiple de facto relations.

Now, does not an analysis of this type also lead us to ask whether political philosophy, which does, for its part, continue to search for the principles that generate modern society, might not be caught in the trap of appearances in that it takes the view that society's religious basis is indestructible? That conviction is no doubt based upon the idea that no human society, whatever it may be, can be organized in terms of pure self-immanence.

But is this the only reason for its attachment to the religious? Is not political philosophy guided by a quest for an ultimate knowledge that, although it is won in response to the requirements of reflection, is still formulated in terms of knowledge of the *One*? Is not this the inspiration it wishes to preserve, and does it not sense that the advent of democracy threatens to do away with it? I am not forgetting that, in its effective movement, it contradicts this inspiration, places thought in the realm of the interrogative, and deprives it of the religious element of certainty and that, in that sense, it is, as we have noted, bound up with a political constitution that no longer permits human activities to be placed beneath the sign of a primal law. But taking its effective movement into account does not mean that we must ignore its representation of its aims. And does not the fact that it is drawn toward the religious indicate that it is retreating in the face of a political form that, by subjecting human beings to the experience of division, fragmentation, and heterogeneity in every register, and to the experience of the indeterminacy of the social and of history, undermines the ground on which philosophical knowledge was built and obscures the task it sets itself? The assertion that a society can never lose its religious basis can, in other words, be understood in one of two ways. The philosopher may mean to say that it would be illusory for society to claim to be able to confine the principle of its institution within its own limits. But in that case he fails to see that, whereas modern democracy does foster that illusion, it does so by breaking down old certainties, by inaugurating an experience in which society is constantly in search of its own foundations. He fails to see that it is not the dimension but the figure of the *other* that it abolishes and that, while there is a risk involved in the loss of the religious, there is also something to be gained by calling the law into question, that freedom is a conquest. Alternatively, he may mean to say that religion elaborates a primordial representation of the One, and that this representation proves to be a precondition for human *unity*, but we then have to ask ourselves about the reasons for the attractions of unity. We have to ask how much its attractions owe to its opposite, namely, the repugnance inspired by division and conflict. We have to ask how the philosophical idea of the One colludes with the image of a united society. We have to ask why unity must be conceived beneath the sign of the spiritual, and why division must be projected onto the material plane of interest.

· · ·

In order to evaluate fully this reluctance to admit that there is a separation between the political and the religious, we must go beyond the level of analysis at which we have been working. It is in fact impossible to ignore the fact that the image of union is generated or re-generated at the very heart of modern democracy. The new position of power is accompanied by a new symbolic elaboration, and, as a result, the notions of state, people, nation, fatherland, and humanity acquire equally new meanings. If we take no interest in these notions or restrict our discussion to the function they may play in the process of legitimating power, we adopt the artificial point of view that we described as characteristic of science. They derive, of course, from what we have called the shaping [*mise en forme*] and staging [*mise en scène*] of society, and from the process of giving it meaning [*mise en sens*]. The only problem is to determine whether or not they are essentially religious.

It is also true that, even if we do take the view that these notions are essentially religious, we will not necessarily agree as to how they are to be interpreted. It is one thing to say—in a society based upon individual freedoms—that Christianity delivers human beings from the domination of needs and from the image of their temporal finiteness, that it inspires in them a feeling of community, fraternity, and obedience to an unconditional moral principle, and that, in the absence of Christian belief, there would be no place for an ethic of service to the state or for patriotism. It is quite another thing to say that the very principle of Christianity implies a depreciation of worldly values, that religious feeling has broken with Christianity, is being re-created, and is now invested in love of the nation or of humanity. According to the former argument, social morality and the state still rest upon religion, to cite Hegel once more; according to the latter, social morality is self-sufficient because it has become religious. But, important as that distinction may be, it does not alter the terms of the question we are asking, for both interpretations appear to accept that anything that expresses the idea of having social roots, of sharing a feeling of belonging, of identifying with a principle that shapes human coexistence, must derive from a religious feeling.

Is this beyond all doubt? Do we not have to ask whether the religious might not be grafted onto a more profound experience as a result of some *determinate* representation of origins, community, and identity?

Our brief comments on the notion of the ''people'' in democracy suggest that it is bound up with an ambiguity that cannot adequately be translated into religious terms. The people do indeed constitute a pole of identity that is sufficiently defined to indicate that it has the status of a subject. The people possesses sovereignty; they are assumed to express its will; power is exercised in their name; politicians constantly evoke them. But the identity of the people remains latent. Quite apart from the fact that the notion of the people is dependent upon a discourse that names the people, that is itself multiple, and that lends the people multiple dimensions, and that the status of a subject can only be defined in term of a juridical constitution, the people are, as we have noted, dissolved into a numerical element at the very moment of the manifestation of their will.

A similar ambiguity arises if we examine representations that have been accorded a religious significance. When we speak of the state as a transcendent power, we mean that it has its own raison d'être, that in its absence society would have neither coherence nor permanence, and that, in that sense, it demands unconditional obedience and the subordination of private interests to the imperative need for its preservation. But we then fail to see that democracy disassociates political power from the existence of the state. It is no doubt as a result of that disassociation that the state acquires its great might, that the characteristic impersonality of its operations allows it to subdue all social activities and relations to its interests and even to foster the illusion that it is a great individual, that everyone has to recognize its will as its own, to paraphrase Hegel. But it is equally certain that this tendency is held in check, because the political competition and social conflict mobilized by the democratic process of contesting the exercise of power led to an indefinite transformation of right and to a modification of the public space. Reason of state threatens to become an absolute, but it is powerless to assert itself, because it remains subject to the effects of the aspirations of individuals and groups in civil society and, therefore, to the effects of such demands as can be inscribed within the public space. When we evoke the nation, we look to it as the source of a religious faith. But do we not have to ask how it is defined, and to evaluate its debt to the discourse that enunciates it? Do we not have to ask how the nation and the feelings it inspires were, in Europe, transformed as a result of the discourse of the French Revolution and, in the nineteenth century, as a result of the new constructs of the historians who contributed so much to the formation of a new political consciousness? In the case of France, we have only to think of the role Thierry, Guizot, Mignet, or, somewhat later, Michelet played in portraying the nation's destiny, in introducing a new perspective, in reshaping values, in giving events a new depth, and in breaking history down into significant sequences. We have only to observe how effective this "composition," which was modified as a result of both the progress of knowledge and ideological imperatives, was in molding our collective memory, how it is imprinted on monuments, commemorations, place names, school textbooks, popular literature, and both major and minor political discourses. We would be wrong to conclude that a new religion is inscribed within this phenomenon simply because it implies the depiction of the origins and permanence of a community, for all signs and symbols that mobilize belief lend themselves to interpretation, to reinterpretation, and are bound up with modes of anticipating the future, with the idea of the goals that social actors imagine to be real and legitimate. The idea of the nation does not refer to a text that exists prior to the commentary; it is, of course, supported by an accretion of materials and representations, but it can never be separated from a discourse on the nation—a discourse that, while it enjoys a privileged relationship with the discourse of power, is still not amenable to appropriation. Paradoxically, it is because it is a historical entity that the nation eludes the religious imagination, which always tries to establish a narrative, to master a time that exists outside time. While the nation bestows a collective identity, it is at the same time implicated in that identity. It remains a floating representation, and the origins of the nation, the stages of its foundation, and the vectors of its destiny are therefore constantly being displaced and are always subject to the decisions of social actors—or those who speak for them—who want to establish themselves within a duration and a time that allows them to name themselves.

And why should this demand for a *name* be wholly ascribed to either the register of religion or that of ideology? Perhaps more than any other, the idea of the nation urges us to make a distinction between the symbolic, the ideological, and the religious.

. . .

The difficulty of analyzing modern democracy arises because it reveals a movement that tends to actualize the image of the people, the state, and the nation, and because that movement is necessarily thwarted by the reference to power as an empty place and by the experience of social division. The movement of which we are speaking must be described with greater precision: when society can no longer be represented as a body and is no longer embodied in the figure of the prince, it is time that people, state, and nation acquire a new force and become the major poles by which social identity and social communality can be signified. But to assert, in order to extol it, that a new religious belief takes shape is to forget that this identity and this community remain indefinable. Conversely, to find in this belief a sign of pure illusion, as liberal thought encourages us to do, is to deny the very notion of society, to erase both the question of sovereignty and that of the meaning of the institution, which are always bound up with the ultimate question of the legitimacy of that which exists. It means, for example, reducing power—or the state, which is wrongly confused with power—to an instrumental function, and the people to a fiction that simply masks the efficacy of a contract thanks to which a minority submits to a government formed by a majority; and, finally, it means regarding only individuals and coalitions of interests and opinions as real. If we adopt this view, we replace the fiction of unity-in-itself with that of diversity-in-itself. We thereby deny ourselves the means to understand that, far from signaling a regression into the imaginary, the aspirations that have been manifested in the course of the history of democratic societies under the slogans of establishing a just state or emancipating the people have had the effect of preventing society from becoming petrified within its order, and have re-established the instituting dimension of right in the place of the law that served to establish both the respective positions of rulers and ruled, and the conditions for the appropriation of wealth, power, and knowledge.

If we reject both these modes of interpretation (not forgetting that they were outlined as a result of the constitution of a new type of society), might we not finally be able to detect the paths by which a return to the religious might be effected?

A return? It will be objected that the term presupposes that the religious never disappeared. Indeed. But it is one thing to say that beliefs have survived in their traditional form and quite another to accept that a fire which has gone out can be relit. It is, moreover, worth asking, as Merleau-Ponty used to ask, whether anything in history has ever been superseded in an absolute sense. In the present case, the analysis we were outlining reveals the possibility of situations in which the symbolic efficacy of the democratic system is destroyed. If, in effect, the mode of the establishment of power and the nature of its exercise or, more generally, political competition prove incapable of giving form and meaning to social division, a de facto conflict will appear throughout society. The distinction between power as symbolic agency and power as real organ disappears. The reference to an empty place gives way to the unbearable image of a real vacuum. The authority of those who make public decisions or who are trying to do so vanishes, leaving only the spectacle of individuals or clans whose one concern is to satisfy their appetite for power. Society is put to the test of a collapse of legitimacy by the opposition between the interests of classes and various categories, by the opposition between opinions, values, and norms—and these are no less important—and by all the signs of the fragmentation of the social space, of heterogeneity. In these extreme situations, representations that can supply an index of social unity and identity become invested with a fantastic power, and the totalitarian adventure is under way.

For our purposes, it is not important to distinguish between the various modes of the formation of totalitarianism. We cannot, of course, ignore the fact that in one case the image of the people is actualized through the sanctification of the proletariat, and that in the other it is actualized through the sanctification of the nation, that the former process is shored up by a redefinition of humanity and that the latter is shored up by a redefinition of a race: communism and fascism are not to be confused. But, in terms of the question we are posing, the similarity between the two is striking. Both attempt, in one way or another, to give power a substantial reality, to bring the principles of Law and Knowledge within its orbit, to deny social division in all its forms, and to give society a *body* once more. And, it should be noted in passing, we find here an explanation as to why so many contemporary philosophers—and by no means only minor figures—have become compromised in the adventures of Nazism, fascism, or communism. The attachment to the religious that we noted earlier traps them in the illusion that unity and identity can be restored as such, and they see signs of its advent in the *union* of the social body. It is not because they submit to a charismatic authority that they lend their support to totalitarian regimes, particularly not if they rally to communism; they surrender to the attractions of a renewed certainty and, paradoxically, they use it as a pretext to assert their right to contemplate freely the basis of any experience of the world.

We should, of course, be careful not to reduce the totalitarian phenomenon to its religious aspects, as certain imprudent commentators have done. It is, rather, by exploring the genesis of ideology, by identifying the metamorphoses of a discourse that, by placing itself under the aegis of knowledge of the real, claims to escape the indeterminacy of the social, to master the principle of its institution, to rise above division so as to enunciate its terms and conditions and to inscribe it within rationality, either by preserving it in its present state or by subjecting it to the movement of its own abolition; it is by detecting the new relationship that is established between the viewpoint of science and the viewpoint of the social order that we can best arrive at an understanding of totalitarianism. This regime represents the culmination of an artificialist project that begins to take shape in the nine-teenth century: the project of creating a self-organizing society that allows the discourse of technical rationality to be imprinted on the very form of social relations and that, ultimately, reveals "social raw material" or "human raw material" to be fully amenable to organization. It would, however, be futile to make a sharp distinction between the ideological and the religious, for while the latter is disavowed insofar as it indicates an *other* place, we can also see that it is reactivated in the quest for a *mystical* union and in the representation of a body, part of which—the proletariat, the political party, the lead-ing organ, the egocrat (to use Solzhenitsyn's phrase)—represents both the head of the people and the people in its entirety. The reproduction of this model in one sector of society after another then converts individuals into members of multiple micro-bodies.

Within the framework of ideological discourse, it is even conceivable that the repre-sentation of the organization (or, more accurately, of the machine) can combine with that of the body. Not only does extreme artificialism tend to be interchangeable with extreme organicism because of the demand for the full affirmation of the social entity, this dis-course can only hold up if the social entity becomes a body and only if—no pun in-tended—it can embody the subjects who speak it: it tends to abolish the distance between enunciation and utterance, and to be imprinted on every subject, regardless of the signi-fication of words.

The increasingly perceptible effects of the failure of totalitarian ideology are no less instructive. The reappearance of a divide—deeper here than in any other regime—between the discourse of power and people's experience of their situation indicates the impossibility of precipitating the symbolic into the real, of reducing power to a purely social definition, of materializing power in the persons of those vested with it, of repre-senting society as a body without supplying it with an external guarantor of its organiza-tion and limits, and of abolishing social division. The nature of this discourse is in fact such that the subject either loses all notion of its own position or perceives it as being totally alien, as a mere product of a group that manipulates words in order to conceal facts. Once belief in communism is shaken, it gives way to the image of a party or a power that rules through force; to the image of an external force that subjugates the society it claims to embody; to the image of a law that is its property, of a law that is designed to conceal the rule of the arbitrary; to the image of a truth of history that is designed to conceal lies. And when signs are inverted, when the plenitude of communism reveals a void, when the people break up and morals break down, or when, to use Hegel's language once more, social morality and the state collapse, we see the return of democratic aspira-tions and, along with them, the old faith, which means primarily the Christian faith. In response to the fantastic attempt to compress space and time into the limits of the social body, there reappears a reference to an absent body which symbolizes a time-span that can be neither appropriated, mastered, nor reduced. Certainty is reborn, together with a singular ability to attack the image of the "new man" and of the "radiant future" by deriding it.

Might it not, however, be a further mistake to believe that the new links that are being forged between the democratic opposition and the religious opposition bear witness to the democratic essence of Christianity or to the Christian essence of democracy? If we accept that, do we not lose sight of the meaning of the adventure that began when they became disentangled in the nineteenth century? To put it more simply, do we not have to admit that they come together in a restoration of the dimension of the *other*, which totalitarianism tries to suppress with its representation of the People-as-One?

. . .

We have until now been asking how we can conceive the links between the religious and the political, and the possibility of their being broken. But is this the appropriate language to use? Is there any sense in trying to apprehend the religious as such by extracting it from the political and then specifying its efficacy in one or another form of society? Or, to be more specific, and since the scope of our investigation has from the beginning been restricted, are we entitled to refer to an essence of Christianity and to relate certain features of modern political societies (that is, societies instituted since the beginning of the Christian era) to that essence? The question may be disconcerting insofar as Christianity is based upon a narrative, or a body of narratives, to which we are free to refer, whatever degree of veracity we may accord it, in order to identify it as a specific religion that appeared at a given epoch in the history of humanity. Even at this stage, however, we cannot ignore the fact that the birth of this religion has a political meaning. That fact was, of course, stressed and discussed by theologians for centuries, long before Dante based his apologia for a universal monarchy on the argument that the Son of God resolved to come to earth and to take the form of a man at a time when humanity was united under the authority of the Roman emperor, who was, metaphorically, the emperor of all humanity—and that, more specifically still, He resolved to do so at a time when the first census of all the emperor's subjects was being carried out. It is, however, more pertinent to note that one cannot derive the principles of a political order from the sacred texts. Attempts to do so were made over and over again, but the point is that they involved digressions through multiple and often contradictory interpretations. The new religion reformulates the notion of a duality between this world and the next, and between man's mortal destiny and his immortal destiny; it depicts a mediator who is a God-made-man. It is believed to bring together not only one people but the whole of humanity; the body of Christ symbolizes the unity between men and God, and the union of all men in the authority. Christ lives on in a Church of which he is simultaneously the head. The very fact that the event of his birth took place at a specific time and in a specific place indicates that he was born to be the new Adam. A link is established between the idea of the fall and the idea of redemption, and thus makes tangible the historical dimension of the divine. All these themes lend themselves to political elaborations, but their meaning is in itself uncertain. It is when a definite relationship is established between a certain type of political institution and a certain type of religious institution that the religious basis of the political order becomes legible, as does the political basis of the Church, for the Church ceases to merge with Christian humanity and is circumscribed within a space, organized under the aegis of a power, and imprinted on a territory.

Let us now, then, qualify a formula that appeared to take us to the heart of the problem. We asked ourselves whether religious belief might not have been transferred onto philosophical thought at the very moment when the latter claimed to be able to discern the persistence of the religious in the political; whether, in short, it might not have misrecognized itself by misrecognizing the meaning of the new society that began to take shape in the last century. It might be more accurate to ask: Does not this thought bear the imprint of a theologico-political schema? Is it not because it is secretly governed by a curious identification with the *royalty of the spirit* that it is drawn to the One?

. . .

The work of Michelet appears to me to provide the perfect justification for asking this question. He is not, of course, a "philosopher" in the sense in which scholars understand that term, but the reader has already been warned that we are not using it in its restrictive sense. The fact is that he does not belong to the species "scientific historian," which had yet to come into being; his history is interpretive and is bound up with an investigation into the meaning of humanity's development and, more specifically, into the political and religious revolution that he thought was going on before his very eyes, despite the forces that were trying to hinder it or to reverse its course. I find his thought exemplary because it testifies to a debate that we rarely see taking place within the mind of one man. His initial stance is to espouse and combine two conceptions that see the Revolution as being heir to the work already accomplished by Christianity and by the monarchy, respectively. Breaking with this inspiration, he then makes a radical critique of the ancien régime as a theologico-political formation, whose destruction was inaugurated by the Revolution. But his critique is such that it re-exploits seemingly discredited theologico-political categories to make an apologia for modernity. Yet this very operation, and we may well wonder to what extent it is conscious or unconscious, brings him up against the idea of a right or a freedom that can found itself, the idea of a humanity that displays signs of its self-transcendence, of a heroism of the spirit (the expression is an early borrowing from Vico), of an infinite questioning of any given configuration of knowledge.

The movement that takes us from the *Introduction to a Universal History* or the *Origins of French Law [droit]* to the *Bible of Humanity* or the 1869 Preface to the *History of France* via *The French Revolution* describes a trajectory in which we find a constant tension between the idea that religion is the ultimate horizon of human life and the idea that right [*droit*] is the ultimate source of human self-creation or, to be more accurate, that right is an internal principle that allows human beings to transcend themselves. These two ideas determine, respectively, the notion of having roots in a place and a time—the notion of tradition and of an identity between self and being (people, nation, humanity)—and the notion of the rootlessness, the wandering, and the turmoil of being, the notion of a wild assertion of the self as being free from all authority, as being supported only by the work that is being accomplished.

It is obviously my intention not to summarize Michelet's itinerary but, by making a digression, to shed light on the question that concerns us here. Let us go back, then, to the starting point provided by the *Introduction to a Universal History*. What is its relevance? It is not that it reveals the author's originality. To put it briefly, it is a condensation of the interpretations of Guizot and Ballanche. The monarchy is seen as a leveling and centralizing agent, which has the virtue of creating conditions of equality and of making society increasingly homogeneous. Michelet sees in Christianity the advent of a religion of equality and fraternity, of a religion based upon a love of humanity. The idea that the old monarchy became useless once the construction of society had been completed is borrowed from Guizot; the idea that the spirit of Christianity has been invested in social institutions is borrowed from Ballanche. It is important to note that Michelet rapidly arrives at a double reading of the history of France, that he reads it in both religious and political terms. In his view, the distinctive feature of France is that the "feeling of social generality" was born in that nation. Despite inequality of condition and of morals, and despite the regional differences that survived until the Revolution, a people comes into being thanks to the double effect of a principle of material unification and a principle of spiritual unification. We will not dwell upon the formulas that signal France's pre-eminent role in "bringing heaven to earth"; a few examples will suffice: "the moral world found its Word in Christ, the son of Judaea and of Greece, and France will explain the Word to the social world"; France's role is to "break the news of this new revelation"; France speaks "the Word of Europe" and holds "the pontificate of the new civilization." We will, however, pick out at least this judgment, which he will later invert: "The name of the priest and the king, of the representatives of what is most general, that is, most divine in the thought of a nation lent, as it were, the obscure right of the people a *mystical envelope* in which it grew and became stronger" (emphasis added).

In *The French Revolution*, Michelet transforms this "mystical envelope" into an illusion: he completely divorces right and justice from the name of the king and the priest, who are now seen as concealing them in order to stifle them. And yet he still finds the basis of ancien régime society in the "priestly monarchy." Indeed, if we are to believe his own account, his conversion to the struggle against Christianity and his decision to write his *Revolution* originated in something similar to a religious revelation. The authenticity of the scene he reconstructs in 1869 is irrelevant; it is an admirable illustration of how symbols change place in the construction he himself built and of how that construction survives despite inversions of meaning.

His *History of France* had, he tells us in the Preface, brought him to the threshold of the "monarchical ages" when an "accident" upset his plans.

> One day when I was passing through Reims, I saw the magnificent cathedral, the splendid Coronation Church, in great detail. When one walks around the internal gallery eighty feet above the ground, one sees the ravishing wealth of its flowery beauty as a permanent alleluia. In this empty immensity, one always seems to be able to hear the great official clamor that was once called the voice of the people . . . I reached the last little tower. There, I found a spectacle that astonished me greatly. The round tower was garlanded with sacrificial victims. One has a rope around his neck; another has lost an ear. The mutilated are sadder than the dead. How right they are! What a terrifying contrast! The church of festivals, the bride, has adopted that lugubrious ornament for her wedding necklace! The pillory of the people has been placed above the altar. But might not those tears have fallen down through the vaults and onto the heads of the kings? The tearful unction of the Revolution, of the wrath of God. "I will not understand the monarchical ages," I said to myself, "unless I first establish within me the soul and the faith of the people, and, after *Louis XI*, I wrote my *Revolution*. (1845–53)

This astonishing description is more eloquent than many historically or theoretically based arguments, and it does more than they ever could to help us understand the position Michelet adopts to mount his attack on the theologico-political. Where is his position? Inside the cathedral of the coronation, the very place where Christian France was shaped and then reshaped. It is there that he takes up his position; indeed, he explores it thoroughly. He ascends its heights, just as the souls of the kings were believed to ascend to take their place at the side of God, to the acclamation of the people, and, in this new liturgy, his thought takes its place at the side of the people. Michelet moves through the church like an actor. He makes it undergo a true metamorphosis, but he is still there. He watches the king being crowned, but he secretly transforms the coronation into a deposition so as to reveal a second coronation that, so to speak, reduplicates it. He uses all the old symbols: the coronation, the acclamation that welcomes the elect into the communion of saints, the marriage between the Church and Christ, between the kingdom and the king, the sacrificial victim, the cross that stands above the altar, the unction that raises the king head and shoulders above his assembled subjects. But for Michelet the coronation is that of the people. It is the true voice of the people that he hears in the nave; he imagines the celebration of a different marriage; the garland of sacrificial victims replaces the martyred Christ; the pillory stands above the altar; tears replace the sacred liquor; the Lord's anointed becomes the anointed of the Revolution, which becomes God's epic poem. And, it must be added, he becomes sensitivized to a time that, while it does not exist outside time, does not exist within time either: the time of a people, of the people who await their incarnation, who are in a sense always invisible, but who reveal themselves for one moment in history—and who demand faith.

It must not be believed that the scene in Reims Cathedral is simply a phantasmagoria; it is a condensation of many of the themes that determine the intellectual work which went into *The French Revolution*. It is not necessary to identify all the references, even though they are explicitly religious. The image of the Church appears in both the 1847 and 1869 prefaces. Michelet's reply to those who mourn the fact that the Revolution could not use the spirit of the Reformation to combat Catholicism is that it adopted no Church for the very good reason that "it was itself a Church" (a criticism addressed specifically to Quinet, although he is not mentioned by name). Michelet's reply to those who criticize his book and claim to be the heirs of the Girondins or the Jacobins is that he is reluctant to argue with them because he "did not want to destroy the unity of the great Church." But the mystical conception of the Revolution is at least as important as the words themselves, if not more so. The Revolution was, of course, an event that occurred in a specific place, but, as he writes at one point and as he constantly suggests, "it knew nothing of time or space." The event was modeled on Christ's appearance on earth. It bears witness to the fullness of time, to use St. Paul's expression, but it also abolishes time. It inaugurates an era, but it escapes all temporal determination and represents a spiritual unity that allows humanity to accede to its own presence. In that sense, it proves to be indestructible, to exist outside the field of continuing political battles, and to condemn all attempts to restore the old order as being in vain. With the Revolution, humanity rises above itself, and henceforth it is only from these new heights that it can relate to itself and survey the vicissitudes of its history. When he analyzes the Fête de la Fédération, Michelet adopts the language of the theologian, and speaks of it as though it were France's marriage with France, as though it were modeled on the marriage between Christ and the Church or that between the king and the kingdom. And when he returns to the theme of humanity's search for its own body, he evokes the moment when the world said to itself: "Oh, if only I were one. . . . If only I could at last unite my scattered members, and assemble my nations." And when, in the 1869 Preface, he returns to 1790, he adds: "No other *agape*, no other communion was comparable to this." In the same passage, he turns the war of 1792 into a "holy war." We saw then "the absolute, infinite nature of sacrifice." This is enough for him to refute once more Quinet's thesis that the Revolution could not find new symbols: "Faith is all; form counts for little. What does it matter how the altar is draped? It is still the altar of Right, of Truth, and of Eternal Reason. Not a stone from it has been lost, and it waits peacefully."

It is the establishment of certainty and the new relationship that has been forged between certainty and revelation, which bear witness to the reinscription of Michelet's thought within the matrix of the Christian religion. But we must never lose sight of the fact that the monarchical reference is combined with a Christological reference. Michelet does not simply adopt the notion of a duality between the temporal and the nontemporal, transpose it onto a new register, and link it to an event that allows the nontemporal to be read within the temporal; he reappropriates the image of the king and the idea of the sovereignty of the One in order to celebrate the people, spirit or reason, and justice or right. Like the Revolution, the people are divided in their existence. Insofar as the people exist within time and space, they can appear fallible, divided, or even despicable, as when they take on the features of "mob rule" or "popular caprice," as when they adopt the gross gesticulations of the parvenus of the Paris Commune, and as when they grotesquely allow themselves to be ruled by "buffoons": they can become "the most dangerous of judges" when they are "in ferment" (the references are to the chapter on the trial of Louis XVI). In their atemporal existence, they win their true identity and reveal themselves to be infallible and at one with themselves, to be in legitimate possession of an absolute right. And when they take on this status, they occupy the position of the king. Michelet is not indulging in rhetoric when he says that, as a historian, he has taken the "royal road" and comments that: "to me, that word means popular" (book 3); in raising the question of the legitimacy of the condemnation of Louis XVI, he is asserting that "the people are all" and designating "the true King: the people." One cannot fail to see in certain of these formulas a resurgence of the theologico-political myth of the double nature of the king.

The repeated eulogies to right as the sovereign of the world (a formula borrowed from Rousseau) are equally significant, as is the moment when, in the course of his pitiless description of the wrong-doings of the priestly monarchy, Michelet elevates Buffon, Montesquieu, Voltaire, and Rousseau to the status of the founding fathers of the new humanity (he even calls them "the great doctors of the new Church") and when, reappropriating an expression whose illusory effects he never ceases to denounce, he elevates "royalty of spirit" above the world. We see here the workings of the transference to which we referred earlier. "Until then, unity had been based upon the idea of a religious or political incarnation. A human God, a God made flesh, was required to unite Church and State. Humanity was still weak, and placed its union under the sign, the visible sign, of a man, an individual. From now on, unity will be purer, and will be freed from this material condition; it will lie in the union of hearts, in the community of the spirit, in the profound marriage of feelings that joins each to all." A more detailed analysis of Michelet's language would further reveal a symbolic architecture which is very similar to that elaborated at the end of the Middle Ages, an architecture which placed the king in a position to be a sovereign mediator between justice and people, and justice in a position to be a sovereign mediator between reason and equity.

As we have already said, the fact that we find in Michelet's thought the imprint of the theologico-political he is so determined to destroy does not, however, discredit his interpretation of the mutation that occurred in the transition from ancien régime to

Revolution. He is one of the few thinkers of his day to recognize the symbolic function of power in shaping social relations. Anyone who doubts that this is so has only to read or reread the introduction to *The French Revolution*, a veritable essay in political philosophy, whose major insight seems to me to have lost none of its acuity, despite the fragility of the historical reconstruction. Compared with that made by Tocqueville, Michelet's analysis of the ancien régime may, of course, seem summary and sociologically poor. But we do not have to choose between them, and the difference between them is not that between an ideological history and a conceptual history. In fact, Michelet sees and tries to conceptualize something that escapes Tocqueville's thought. The latter notes every sign of the gradual centralization of the state and of the increasing equality of condition, and interprets them as proof that society is indeed being transformed, despite the seeming permanence of its order. It could not be said that he is insensitive to the symbolic dimension of the social. In one sense, it does not escape him, for, rather than the de facto growth of equality and centralization, it is, I believe, the establishment of a principle of similarity governing both conduct and morals and the establishment of the *point of view of the state* that attracts his attention. But it is precisely because he erects this into a model—an ideal model whose coordinates in time and space are never defined—that he loses interest in the figure of power and tends to reduce the history of the ancien régime to the breakup of aristocratic society to such an extent that the new society appears to be no more than the final product of that process, and the Revolution becomes unintelligible except insofar as it designates the moment of a flight into the imaginary. Michelet, by contrast, decodes the symbolic by transposing it onto another register; within this register, the mainspring behind domination and behind the organization of institutions is, as he puts it, the most *obscure* and the most *intimate* element in the position and representation of power (and let me repeat that one cannot exist without the other). He expresses his views most clearly when, having drawn up a balance sheet of the state of France on the eve of 1789, having noted that "I see the Revolution everywhere, even at Versailles," having judged inevitable and visible to all "the defeat of the nobility and the clergy," and having described the boldness and blindness of Calonne, he concludes: "The only obscure question was that of royalty. This is not, as it has so often been said, a question of pure form, but a fundamental question, a question more intimate and more perennial than any other question in France, a question not only of politics, but of love and of religion. No other people so loved their kings." This interest in the obscure, the profound, and the primal, which inspires all Michelet's works from *The Origins of French Law* to *The Sorcerer*, helps him to discover something that Tocqueville fails to see: the mystery of the monarchical incarnation. Beyond the conscious representation of a divine-right king whose power restores something of the presence of Christ and thereby makes justice appear in his person, there lies an unconscious representation of a society embodied in a king, of a society whose political institutions are not simply ordered in accordance with a "carnal principle" but whose members are so captivated by the image of a body that they project onto it their own union, that their affects are precipitated in an amorous identification with that body. If we read him carefully, we find that Michelet in fact combines two arguments that, while they are connected, do not overlap.

The first relates the political law of the ancien régime to religious law—indeed, it would not be going too far to say that the one is derived from the other. Christianity proves to be both the system that shaped the monarchy and the body of institutions that supports it. This is in fact obvious from the very plan of the Introduction: the first part is entitled "Of Religion in the Middle Ages" and the second, "Of the Former Monarchy." Michelet therefore immediately formulates the question: "Is the Revolution Christian or anti-Christian? Logically and historically, this question comes before all others." And the answer is not long in coming: "On the stage, I still see only two great facts, two principles, two actors, and two persons: Christianity and the Revolution." He even goes so far as to assert: "All the civic institutions that the Revolution invented either emanated from Christianity, or were modeled on its forms and authorized by it." From this point of view, the schema is simple: Christianity is "the religion of grace, of free, arbitrary salvation, and of the good pleasure of God." The human monarchy is constructed in the image of the divine monarchy: both govern on behalf of an elect. Arbitrary power, masked as justice, has taken up its abode in society: it is found "with depressing regularity in political institutions." It is a "carnal principle" that supports social organization, the division between the orders, and the hierarchy of conditions; this is a principle that "puts justice and injustice in the blood, that makes them circulate along with the flux of life from one generation to the next." The theologico-political system is, he suggests, such that it glorifies love, the personal relationship that exists between man and God, between man and king; the spiritual notion of justice is materialized; love is put "in the place of law." To paraphrase freely, using the same terms that we used earlier: when the law is fully asserted and when divine might and human might are condensed within a single person, Law is imprinted upon power; Law as such is abolished; the motive behind obedience is no longer fear, but a loving submission to the monarch. At the same time, the obverse of the love demanded by Christianity is revealed to be its hatred of all who perturb order: "The incredible furies of the Church during the Middle Ages," the Inquisition, the books that were burned, the people who were burned, the history of the Vaudois and the Albigenses. Compared with that terror, the revolutionary Terror makes one smile. The love inspired by the king also has its obverse: torture, the Bastille, *lettres de cachet*, and the *Livre rouge*.

But Michelet's second argument, which first emerges in the articulation between the first and second parts of the Introduction, takes a different direction. The might of the king does not simply descend from the heights of Christian arbitrariness; it is also constructed by his subjects. It is they who built "this sanctuary, this refuge: the altar of the kingdom." It is they who invented "a series of legends and myths embroidered and amplified by all the efforts of genius: the holy king who was more of a priest than the priests himself in the thirteenth century, the knight-king in the sixteenth century, the good king with Henri IV, the God-king with Louis XIV." In one sense, they are obeying the same inspiration as the great thinkers of the period, observes Michelet: Dante was similarly inspired to seek the salvation of humanity in unity and to imagine a monarch who, because he embodied the One, would possess unlimited authority and would be set free from mortal passions. But "we must dig deeper than Dante, we must dig into the earth, and uncover and contemplate *the profoundly popular basis on which the colossus was built*" (emphasis added). Men did not simply believe that they could "save justice in a political religion," and they did not simply create "a God of Justice out of a man"; they made kings the object of their love. Theirs was a singular love: "an obstinate, blind love, which saw all its God's imperfections as virtues. Far from being shocked at seeing the human element in him, they were grateful for it. They believed that it would bring him closer to them, that it would make him less proud and less harsh. They were glad that Henri IV loved Gabrielle." The remarkable thing about the description of this love, about the evocation of Louis XV, the "well-beloved," a God-made-flesh, and about the pages devoted to Louis XVI as he returns from Varenne to his execution is that they suggest that we have to re-examine the representation of the king's two bodies. This, as formulated in the Middle Ages, was based upon the notion of the two bodies of Christ and, in sixteenth-century England, generated the juridical fiction that the king was two persons in one, one being the natural king, a mortal man who was subject to time and to common laws, who was vulnerable to ignorance, error, and illness, and the other being the supernatural king, who was immortal, infallible, and omnipotent within the time and space of the kingdom. This representation gave rise to numerous commentaries by English historians, and Ernst Kantorowicz analyzes them with unrivaled erudition and subtlety.[3] Michelet does not, of course, bring this out, but he does deal with the issue indirectly, and in such a way as to reveal the limited extent to which this representation can be formulated in juridical or theologico-political terms, even though it was primarily such a formulation that caught the attention of contemporaries. As we read Michelet, it becomes apparent that, over and beyond this representation, it is the natural body that, because it is combined with the supernatural body, exercises the charm that delights the people. It is insofar as it is a sexed body, a body capable of procreation and of physical love, and a fallible body that it effects an unconscious mediation between the human and the divine; the body of Christ, although mortal, visible, and fallible as well as divine, cannot ensure that mediation because, while it indicates the presence of God in man, it cannot fully indicate the converse: the presence of man and of the flesh in God. By breaking with the argument that derives the human monarchy from the divine monarchy, Michelet uncovers an erotico-political register. In his view, that register is, no doubt, established simply because religion has put love in the place of Law. But he does outline a logic of love in the political, and it is surprising that he does not see that it is older than Christianity. The modern king, who is portrayed as God's representative on earth, as a substitute for Christ, does not derive all his power from that image. It is through the operation of sacrifice alone, in the element of suffering alone, that man becomes like God, identifies with Christ, and shuffles off his mortal coil. At this point, love values the king above life itself. And it is through the double operation of sacrifice and pleasure [*jouissance*] that the king's subjects experience rapture. Love both nourishes their life and justifies their death. It is the image of the natural body, the image of a God made flesh, the image of his marriage, his paternity, his liaisons, his festivals, his amusements, and his feasts, but also the image of his weaknesses or even his cruelties, in short, all the images of his humanity, that people their imaginary, that assure them that the king and the people are conjoined. A carnal union is established between the great individual and his mass of servants, from the lowliest to the most important, and it is indissociable from the mystical union between king and kingdom. According to theology and the jurists, the immortal king possesses the gift of clairvoyance as well as that of ubiquity, but, at the same time and even as he escapes the gaze of his subjects, he has the gift of attracting the gaze of all, of concentrating upon himself the absolute visibility of man-as-being: since he is a unique focal point, he abolishes differences between points of view and ensures that all merge in the One.

Michelet's extreme sensitivity to the enigma of the monarchical incarnation and of the role it gives to the natural body within the supernatural body is particularly evident in his analysis of the condemnation of Louis XVI. We will examine only those elements that are relevant to our purposes. The question of whether or not the trial should have taken place is not an issue for Michelet. It is obvious that it should have taken place. It had a double utility. On the one hand, it restored royalty to its rightful place—"within the people"—by making the people a judge; on the other, "it brought out into the light that ridiculous mystery which a barbarian humanity had for so long turned into a religion: the mystery of the monarchical incarnation, the bizarre fiction that the wisdom of the people is concentrated in an imbecile." Given that royalty was embodied in a man, the problem was to establish how the evil could be excised so as to destroy the incarnation and so as to prevent any man from ever becoming a king. The historian gives his answer immediately, and then supports it with numerous arguments. "Royalty had to be dragged into the broad light of day and exposed on all sides; and it had to be opened up to reveal what was inside the worm-eaten idol, to reveal the insects and worms inside the beautiful golden head. Royalty and the king had to be condemned usefully, judged, and placed under the blade. Did the blade have to fall? That is another question. When he merged with the dead institution, the king was no more than a head made of wood, empty, hollow, no more than a thing. If, when that head was struck, even a single drop of blood flowed, that was proof of life; people began to believe once more that it was a living head; royalty had come back to life" (book 9).

This penetrating analysis can be reformulated as follows: men regard royalty as a condensation of immortal life, and that life takes the form of a living man: the king. It has to be demonstrated that the symbol of life is the product of an illusion; belief has to be rooted out; and the idol has to be shown to be an idol. In short, the inner shadows of this pseudo-visible entity have to be destroyed; he must be laid low and torn to pieces. That action alone will ensure that the living individual loses his life. The empty head of Louis XVI appears in the empty crown. If, on the other hand, Louis XVI is struck, and if his blood is shed in the belief that this will annihilate his body, it will be found that we have here a living man, and, given that this living man represents eternal life, royalty will be resurrected. In general terms, Michelet is trying to explain that, because royalty is embodied in a man, the royal phantasmagoria is revived when the man is turned into a spectacle. Hence his bitter commentary on the detention of Louis XVI in the Temple. It was believed, he suggests, that the deposition of the individual would have the effect of desanctifying him. On the contrary: "The most serious and the cruelest blow that could have been struck against the Revolution was the ineptitude of those who constantly kept Louis XVI before the eyes of the population, and who allowed him to relate to the population both as a man and as a prisoner." Why? Because the more he was revealed in his human singularity, and the more visible the living individual became, the more he remained a king. His sufferings inspired love even before he was executed, but beyond that love there lay, so to speak, *the attraction of the unique object of every gaze.* Michelet succeeds admirably in showing that Louis XVI appears to be unique precisely because he is so commonplace, because he is seen in the bosom of his family, a mere man amongst mere people, caught up in the insignificance of everyday life. All the signs that designate him to be a man restore his kingship.

I cannot refrain from pointing out the remarkable manner in which the writer portrays Louis XVI. He shows him to his readers, but he does so in order to prevent him from delighting the eye. He describes him as "ruddy-faced and replete," as eating too much over-rich food, as walking along with "the myopic gaze, the abstracted expression, the heavy gait, and the typical swaying walk of the Bourbons," and as giving the impression that he is "a fat farmer from the Beauce." By doing so, he does not make him any less commonplace, but his neutral observations do tend, as it were, to dissolve his individuality into a genre painting.

The crucial moment in the interpretation, however, concerns the execution. Michelet is not insensitive to the arguments of the Montagne, as it believes that it did have the merit of recognizing the imperative need to destroy the incarnation. The Montagne believed, "not without reason," he adds, that "a man is as much a body as a spirit, and that one could never be certain of the death of the monarchy until one had touched, felt, and handled it in the shape of the dead body of Louis XVI and his severed head." He suggests, in a sense, that if the people were to be elevated to the rank of royalty, they needed, perhaps, more than the image of the Law; they needed, perhaps, an image of punishment. But he also suggests that, while the imagination is not extinguished by the light of justice, nothing stimulates it more than the sight of a corpse. The blood of the dead man does not destroy the incarnation; it revives it. Royalty and religion are reborn at the very moment when the revolutionaries lapse into the illusion that sustained them: namely the illusion that they were imprinted upon a real body. Such, then, are "the terrible effects of the legend of the Temple," of the legends that were unleashed by the execution:

> The kings of the scripture are called Christs; Christ is called a king. There was not a single incident in the king's captivity that was not seized upon and translated into an episode in the Passion. The Passion of Louis XVI became a sort of traditional poem that peasants and women passed on by word of mouth: the poem of Barbarian France.

How can the thinker who is so devoted to rooting out beliefs that give rise to, sustain, or restore the mystery of the monarchical incarnation consent to their being transferred onto the sacred image of the People, the Nation, Humanity, and the Spirit? The problem would become more complex if we were to follow a further strand in Michelet's interpretation of the Revolution, but to do so would be beyond the scope of the present essay. These all too brief remarks must suffice: although he posits an antithesis between the ancien régime and the Revolution, Michelet is still blind to the internal contradictions of the Revolution. He sees Robespierre's acquisition of power as a resurrection of the monarchy (a process that began with the death of Danton, he notes in the 1868 Preface); he attacks the Jacobin doctrine of public safety by comparing it to the absolutist idea of reason of state and the Christian doctrine of salvation. He denounces both the Montagnards and the Girondins as arrogant intellectual elites ("There is a terrible aristocracy among these democrats"); he even goes so far as to say of Robespierre that "On the day that the director was revealed to be the future king of the priests [after the trial of the Mother of God], a reawakened France set him at the side of Louis XVI" (book 3). He wishes, we said, to ensure that the Revolution will not be confused with any one of its episodes, and to prevent it from being appropriated by any one clan; but, while he temporalizes it in one sense, in another he restores to it a temporality that cannot be mastered and describes its progress in such a way that the creation and destruction of men and ideas become indissociable; although he asserts the unity of the spirit of the Revolution, he sees it as being deployed in different places and as stirring up so many currents that he makes a distinction between a truly peasant revolution and an embryonic socialist revolution.

Perhaps the contrast between two of his formulas reveals just how ambiguous his conception of the Revolution is. Both, as it happens, have become famous: "History is resurrection" and "History is time."

. . .

The reader of the rapid sketch we have outlined cannot have failed to sense the weakness in Michelet's argument. When he derives the human monarchy from the divine monarchy and political institutions from religious institutions, he is relying upon an outrageous simplification of Christianity. This does not invalidate his thesis that both types of institution are inscribed within single schema, but it is by no means proven that the latter are modeled on the former. As we have indicated, any such proposition presupposes that one can conceive of an essence of Christianity without taking into account the political fact. Michelet, in fact, half glimpses the arbitrary element in this hypothesis when he states that the Gospel contains no specific teachings: "Its vague morality," he concedes to his adversaries, "contains almost none of the doctrines that made Christianity such a positive, absorbing, and compelling religion and that gave it such a hold on men" (Introduction). He therefore makes it clear that he is taking as his object religion as it is fully instituted by Catholicism. As, however, he discovers that the theme of grace is the principle behind its doctrine, one might have expected him to take the phenomenon of Protestantism into consideration and to look at the mode of its insertion into modern political societies, rather than simply remarking in passing that it merely "formulates in harsher terms" the doctrine of the Catholic world. He remains silent about this point. When he outlines his major opposition between Christianity and revolution, he deliberately ignores events in America. It escapes his notice that it was the Puritans who founded free institutions in New England, and that they constantly referred to the Bible in their political proclamations, whereas his contemporary Quinet finds in the combination of Protestantism and freedom a lesson that has considerable implications for any understanding of modern democracy. Yet this lacuna in Michelet's argument, or rather, this occultation of a Puritan revolution, is relevant to our argument, not so much because it is a sign of his failure to understand or recognize the true nature of Christianity as because we can see in it an index of his determination to circumscribe the efficacy of the religious. Michelet's purpose is, of course, to show how Christianity shaped the European monarchies and, more specifically, the French monarchy. It should, however, also be noted that, while Quinet is careful to distinguish between Christianity and Catholicism, and even to stress the liberating virtues of Protestantism, he has no more insight than Michelet into the specific efficacy of the religious. Also, for his part, he is looking for a formula for a new faith that can be invested in the People, in the Nation, in Humanity and, at the same time, in Right, or Justice, and Reason. It is also pertinent to ask whether the ideal of political freedom that is affirmed by the break with the values of the monarchical regimes might not, thanks to Puritan discourse, be able to coexist alongside a definite increase in conformism at the level of opinions and morals, and whether, in that sense, it might not coexist with a new disavowal of the effects of the social division that sets democracy free. It is, in fact, as though, although they are working on different premises, the thinkers who are most alert to the advent of modernity and to the irreversibility of the course of history (and, in the case of France, I am not thinking only of Michelet and Quinet, but also of liberals like Guizot and Tocqueville and of socialists like Leroux) all looked to the religious for the means to reconstitute a pole of unity that could ward off the threat of the breakup of the social that arose out of the defeat of the ancien régime.

. . .

This, then, is the question to which we return after our digression through Michelet's problematic and which we must now reformulate. Rather than attempt to redefine relations between the political and the religious in order to assess the degree to which one is subordinated to the other and to examine the question of the permanence or nonpermanence of a sensitivity to religious thought in modern society, might it not be more appropriate to posit the view that a theologico-political *formation* is, logically and historically, a primary datum? We might then be able to see in the oppositions it implies the principle of an evolution or, if we prefer to put it this way, the principle of a symbolic operation that takes place in the face of events and to detect how certain schemata of organization and representation survive thanks to the displacement and transference onto new entities of the image of the body and of its double nature, of the idea of the One, and of a mediation between visible and invisible, between the eternal and the temporal. We would then be in a better position to ask whether democracy is the theater of a new mode of transference, or whether the only thing that survives in it is the phantom of the theologico-political.

If this is so, what we will discover is a network of determinations, of which the "priestly monarchy" supplies only one element, albeit a constituent element, and in which the development of city-states, urban corporations, and trade guilds, and the exploitation of the heritage of classical humanism, all become caught up in their turn. We will also discover a dynamic schema imprinted upon the complex play of chiasmata that Kantorowicz analyzes with such subtlety. These are not, I repeat, chiasmata between the theological and the political, as his formulations sometimes suggest, but, if I may be forgiven the barbarism, between the already politicized theological and the already theologized political.

It need scarcely be stressed that this schema is legible only if we bear in mind the horizons of the real history in which take place changes in the economic, technological, demographic, and military realms, changes in the balance of power between the dominant actors, and changes in the categories of knowledge—and in that realm, the renaissance of Roman law and of ancient philosophy marks a decisive moment. If, moreover, we accept Kantorowicz's argument, that schema cannot be projected in its entirety onto empirical history, even though its articulations can be grasped within a temporal dimension. The four formations identified by the author—Christo-centric, juridico-centric, politico-centric, and humano-centric kingdoms—testify to a displacement of the representation of the king's two bodies, but what is displaced on each occasion is not eradicated and proves to contain the kernel of a future symbolic configuration. Thus, the fact that royalty is originally supported by the image of Christ does not mean that it must abandon that image when the Christological reference loses its efficacy as a result, in part, of the strategy of the pope and his exclusive claim to be the Vicar of Christ. Long after the disintegration of the tenth-century Othonian myth, the *Traité du sacre* written for Charles V explicitly makes him a substitute for Christ, and indeed, as Michelet rightly notes, Louis XVI could still benefit from that identification. Similarly, the fact that in the age of Frederick II and Bracton the representation of the king is firmly supported by that of Justice and Right should not make us forget that a veritable religion of Right was reformulated in the sixteenth century and that it contains within it elements of a future system in which the body politic or the kingdom will appear to be the sacred body of the king. Nor should we forget that when, in his *De Monarchia*, Dante paints a portrait of an emperor who, insofar as he possesses a universal authority, can represent the One and can therefore represent the coming together of humanity as a body, despite the multiplicity of its members and the sequence of generations, his theologico-political vision of humanism cannot be explained away in terms of contemporary conditions (still less can it be reduced to a nostalgic longing for empire). Dante's vision was prefigured by the lengthy labors of the Italian jurists, and it will be reactivated in the period of Charles IV, Elizabeth, Francis I and Henry III. When imperial ambition is combined with a universal language, the ideas of the *De Monarchia* and the double figure of Augustus and Astra, of might and justice, will be exploited anew and will be used to promote the edification of a new monarchy and the conquest of the world. The essentials remain unchanged: the theologico-political is revealed in the deployment of a system of representations whose terms may be transformed, but whose oppositional principle remains constant.

When royalty is made by the institution of unction and coronation, it is possible for the king to argue the case for a sovereignty that removes him from the rest of humanity, that allows him to be a Vicar or minister of Christ, to seem to have been made in his image, and to have both a natural, mortal body and a supernatural, immortal body. At the same time, it is possible for the pope, who controls the rite of coronation, to seize the emblems of the monarchy and to imprint his power on the temporal realm (and this possibility was later realized through the Gregorian reforms and in the dispute over investitures). When, in an attempt to undo the imbrication of secular and priestly functions that came about as a result of the sanctification of royalty, the Church acquires the strength to circumscribe its domain and to become a functional body modeled on the emergent states, it tries to differentiate itself radically from all other political entities and to preserve its spiritual mission by claiming to be a mystical body (*corpus Ecclesiae mysticum*)—the very body of Christ, who also represents its head. At the same time, a religious vocation is reimprinted on the kingdom, which defines itself as a mystical body (*corpus Republicae mysticum*)—the body of the king, who also represents its head. When the reexploitation of Roman law and of Aristotelianism provides theology and political theory with a new conceptual framework, the ancient concepts of *imperium, populus, communitas*, *patria*, *perpetuitas*, and *aevum* (a notion intermediate between that of time and that of eternity) are reworked to represent, in their respective registers, a new relationship between the *particular*, which is still inscribed within the limits of a body, of an entity that is organized spatially and temporally, and the *universal*, which is still related to the operation of transcendence. The ideas of reason, justice, and right, which inspire both a return to the principles of classical thought and a movement toward a secularized ethic, are themselves caught up in a theologico-political elaboration. The prince (and we have already alluded to this event) comes to occupy the position of the mediator between Justice and his subjects; the old Roman definition of the emperor as being at once above the laws and subject to Law is modified to put him in that position; he appears to be both his own superior and his own inferior; grace makes him divine, but his nature makes him human. He both institutes and reveals justice, and is both its vicar and its image within the state—and, symmetrically, Justice, like Christ, becomes an object of worship, and insinuates itself into a position in which it can mediate between sovereign reason and equity, between a substitute for divine law and a substitute for human law.

Particular attention should be paid to the series of divisions that accompanies and sustains the representation of bodies, a representation that was originally inspired by the model of Christ. Not only can they be substituted for one another, they support one another. The principle of the schema is, let me repeat, established when a new kind of royalty is instituted by the rite of coronation. As Marc Bloch demonstrates, we are now in the presence of a complex phenomenon that calls into question both the status of temporal power and the status of spiritual power . . .[4] When the king is blessed and crowned as the Lord's anointed, his power is spiritualized, but, although he is the earthly replica of Christ, he differs from his model in that, while grace makes him divine, his nature makes him human. It is not simply that he cannot truly take the place of the sacred one (and no doubt no one has ever been able to do so), it is also that his person makes visible both the union of natural and supernatural, and the division between them. Despite the attempts made by the Othonian emperors, the path to a complete identification with a God-made-man remains blocked. At the same time, the king comes up against another earthly force: the priest, from whose hands he receives his rank, and who is in a position to claim to be his superior. The division of the body of the king therefore goes hand in hand with the division between royal (or imperial) and papal authority. What happens at the latter pole is equally significant, for the claim that the pope is superior to any temporal power is bound up with his ambition to imprint his own spiritual power on a territory. In that respect, it should be recalled that the circumstances surrounding the pact signed between Pépin le Bref and Etienne II—the first pact between a pope and a king—are not anecdotal; they have a symbolic significance. Pépin converts his father's bid for power into an act of usurpation: he asks the Church to establish the basis of his legitimacy. Etienne, for his part, tries to enlist the king's help in seizing the Exarchate of Ravenna by exploiting a forged document—the so-called Donation of Constantine, which surrenders Rome's possessions into his hands. A doable fraud is thus covered up by a new combination of religious law and human law. The new formation is indeed theologico-political through and through, by which I mean that it is determined by a double struggle for power. It is, however, even more important to note that we can from the outset discern two simultaneous movements toward a universal authority that is both scriptural and temporal. But neither can be carried through to completion: unrestricted political domination is impossible, and so is the creation of a theocratic monarchy.

The fragmentation of authority that is characteristic of feudal organization, by contrast, has the result of outlining the position of a king who, within the framework of a limited territory, appears to have no superiors—that is, no temporal superiors—and who is defined as being an emperor within his own kingdom (*imperator in suo regno*). And it is at the very moment when this claim is being so clearly asserted—in, that is, the mid-thirteenth century in both France and England—that the monarchical configuration begins to be deployed in its Western singularity.

The work of inscribing power and laws within a territory, the delineation of a political society with definite frontiers, and the winning, within that space, of the allegiance of all to the authority of the king are accompanied by the process of the sanctification and spiritualization of the kingdom. The process of secularization and laicization, which tends to deprive the Church of its temporal power within the framework of the state and which tends to include the national clergy within the community of the kingdom, is paralleled by the process of the incorporation of those religious representations that are capable of investing a "natural" space and social institutions with a mystical signification. Throughout the fabric of society, a division is effected between the realm of the functional and the realm of the mystical, though, given that it is revealed in terms of that representation, it would be more accurate to speak of it being effected throughout the fabric of the *body politic*. The division of the body politic occurs together with the division of the king's body; at the same time, the body politic is part of his body; his immortal and supernatural body remains that of a person whom race makes divine and in whom God dwells but, at the same time, it migrates into the body of the kingdom; while a single body is defined both as the body of a person and as the body of a community, its head remains the symbol of a transcendence that can never be effaced. Thus, in the famous essays he devotes to the reign of Philippe le Bel, Joseph Strayer shows how the conquest of the unity of political society under the slogan "defense of the kingdom" succeeds in mobilizing religious affects—the defense of the kingdom is a continuation of the defense of the kingdom of Christ; a feeling for the earthly fatherland replaces a feeling for the heavenly fatherland; the warriors who sacrifice their lives become brothers to the crusaders who fell in order to deliver Jerusalem and who were promised to the glory of God.[5] The historian reveals how the figure of the warrior king becomes that of the Most Christian King, just as the territory is transformed into a *holy land*, and the mass of subjects into a chosen people (see his essay "The Most Christian Country, the Chosen People, and the Holy Land"). It is pointless to dwell upon precisely how the Roman notions of *patria*, *communitas*, and *populus* are reactivated and reshaped within a religious symbolic; I would simply like to draw attention to what is by now a well-known phenomenon: the installation of representations of the People, the Nation, the Fatherland, of Holy War and of the salvation *or* safety [*salut*] of the state, within the theological configuration of the medieval monarchy. With reference to Kantorowicz's analyzes, it would be no less instructive to examine the process inaugurated in the twelfth century whereby a public domain becomes detached from the person of the king and is defined as a domain of inalienable property, and whereby a further division is introduced between reference to an objective order and reference to a sacred order: the *res publica* becomes a *res sacra* modeled on the possessions of the Church, which are themselves the property of Christ. The crown and the treasury are placed beneath a pole of impersonality that will later become the pole of the state and, thanks to the same inversion of signs, are defined as persons, as mystical bodies. (Bracton even ventures to define the king as the Vicar of the Treasury, in accordance with the model of the Vicar of Christ.)

Finally, it would also be appropriate to re-examine the relationship that was established between the notion of a power that is confined to a limited territory and a restricted community (a notion unknown in the period of the empire), and the notion of a power that has a vocation for universal domination. And it would be appropriate to re-examine the symmetrical relationship that was established between the notion of a kingdom, a nation, and a people that are accorded a definite identity, and the notion of a land and a community in which humanity is imprinted and embodied in a privileged manner. The formula that makes the king an emperor in his own kingdom contains a contradiction: it makes a gesture toward both an unlimited authority and a limited authority; it indicates that modern monarchs' tacit acceptance that their might is restricted by the might of others has not done away with the fantasy of imperial might—a fantasy that has been revived again and again throughout the ages. And this contradiction drifts into the framework of the kingdom; it is as though empirical frontiers are conceivable only if the kingdom finds itself to be entrusted with universal values. In order to appreciate its full import, we would perhaps have to elucidate it further by re-examining the role played by the idea—which receives its initial impetus from Dante—that humanity will become *one* and will live in peace under the sole authority of the *One*, an idea that combines the power of the spirit or sovereign reason with political power. This idea was strongly challenged by those who saw humanism as providing the basis for a critique of the temporal monarchy—a critique that began to be formulated by the end of the fourteenth century in Florence and that spread throughout Europe in the sixteenth—but it may also be worth asking whether it might not have retained its theologico-political efficacy in the realm of philosophy, and whether it might not resurface whenever philosophy attempts to reformulate the principle of what, following Michelet, we have termed the royalty of spirit.

. . .

What conclusions are we to draw from this brief incursion into the theologico-political labyrinth? That we must recognize that, according to its schema, any move toward immanence is also a move toward transcendence; that any attempt to explain the contours of social relations implies an internalization of unity; that any attempt to define objective, impersonal entities implies a personification of those entities. The workings of the mechanisms of incarnation ensure the imbrication of religion and politics, even in areas where we thought we were dealing simply with purely religious or purely profane practices or representations.

If, however, we look back at the democratic society that began to take shape in the nineteenth century and that the philosophers and historians of the period were exploring, do we not have to agree that the mechanisms of incarnation were breaking down? The disincorporation of power is accompanied by the disincorporation of thought and by the disincorporation of the social. The paradox is that any adventure that begins with the formulation of a new idea of the state, the people, the nation, or humanity has its roots in the past. In that sense, Tocqueville has more reason than he might suspect to denounce the illusion that the French Revolution was a radical beginning and to want to reconstruct the prehistory of democracy. Although we have been able to do no more than allude to the fact, there was at the time of the Renaissance a humanism tinged with a political religiosity, and Michelet could still find traces of it, almost without realizing it. Far from leading us to conclude that the fabric of history is continuous, does not a reconstruction of the genealogy of democratic representations reveal the extent of the break within it? And so, rather than seeing democracy as a new episode in the transfer of the religious into the political, should we not conclude that the old transfers from one register to the other were intended to ensure the preservation of a *form* that has since been abolished, that the theological and the political became divorced, that a new experience of the institution of the social began to take shape, that the religious is reactivated at the weak points of the social, that its efficacy is no longer symbolic but imaginary, and that, ultimately, it is an expression of the unavoidable—and no doubt ontological—difficulty democracy has in reading its own story, as well as of the difficulty political or philosophical thought has in assuming, without making it a travesty, the tragedy of the modern condition?

—*Translated by David Macey*

Violence in the State of Exception

Reflections on Theologico-Political Motifs in Benjamin and Schmitt

Marc de Wilde

Two months after the events of September 11, President George W. Bush issued a Military Order authorizing the "indefinite detention" of certain noncitizens in the "war on terror."[1] The Military Order effectively resulted in the suspension of fundamental rights of "enemy aliens," such as the right to be brought before an impartial tribunal within forty-eight hours and to seek the assistance of an attorney, and eventually legitimized a biopolitical violence against those detained at U.S. interrogation centers in Guantánamo Bay, Baghram, and Abu Ghraib. In his recent book *State of Exception* (2005), Giorgio Agamben argues that Bush's Military Order has introduced a "state of exception" in which enemy aliens are no longer subject to positive law and have completely lost their juridical identities. The "bare lives" of these enemy aliens are directly exposed—without any legal mediation—to a sovereign violence: "neither as prisoners nor as accused, but only as 'detainees,' they are the object of a pure de facto rule, of a detention that is indefinite not only in the temporal sense but in its very nature as well, since it is entirely removed from the law and from judicial oversight."[2]

Agamben's argument suggests that understanding the violence inherent in contemporary "states of exception" involves not merely a critical analysis of U.S. detention policies but also a genealogical investigation into the formation of new figures of sovereignty emerging in an age of post-secular reason. Contrary to the classical forms of sovereignty, constituted by a public, even theatricalized or ritualized manifestation of state violence, its new post-secular forms seem to be dependent upon a more elusive, spectral violence, related, for example, to classified rules and "ghost detainees." The center of gravitation in Agamben's genealogical analysis is the work of Walter Benjamin and Carl Schmitt, written during the Weimar Republic (1919–33), a time in which state sovereignty constantly threatened to dissolve into countless acts of nonstate violence. Two of their early texts, especially, Benjamin's "Critique of Violence" (1921) and Schmitt's *Political Theology* (1922), mark a new sensibility in the transformation of sovereignty's manifestations, which, though secularized, bear witness to a reappearance of theologico-political figures of thought.[3]

In the present essay, I want first to determine the status of theologico-political motifs in the work of Benjamin and Schmitt, simultaneously seeking to lay bare an affinity underlying their seemingly opposed intellectual positions (Critical Theory versus Conservative Revolution). Second, against the background of this theologico-political affinity, I try to reconstruct their respective concepts of sovereignty, relating them to notions of law, violence, and responsibility. Finally, I examine whether Benjamin's and Schmitt's theologico-political understanding of the concept of sovereignty can indeed, as Agamben maintains, provide clarification of the violence inherent in contemporary states of exception, that is, in the border zones between positive law and bare life, within the United States as well as outside its territory, in the camp at Guantánamo Bay and its doubles. I will argue—with Benjamin and in a certain sense against Schmitt and Agamben—that it is not so much the absence of positive law that characterizes these states of exception as the possibility of a depersonalizing juridical violence, which tends to escalate in the presence of a certain kind of political theology.

A Hidden Dialogue: The Political Theologies of Benjamin and Schmitt

Benjamin belonged to the early Frankfurt School, a philosophical movement that attempted to save the critical impetus of Enlightenment thought. In the eyes of the Frankfurt School, the First World War had discredited the Enlightenment's dominant cultural and philosophical expression in Germany, that is, idealism. Drawing upon Hegel's justification of conflict as a valuable source of cultural rejuvenation, idealism had succeeded in supplying even a patently senseless war with a reasonable appearance. The crisis of idealism thus caused the members of the Frankfurt School to search for a radical alternative, which they eventually found in an unorthodox Marxist approach.[4] Benjamin considered his main philosophical task to be reconciling Marxism's critical materialism with the tradition of Jewish religious thought. This resulted in his political theology, which consists in a historical materialism in the service of hidden theological convictions.

Schmitt, in every sense Benjamin's opposite, belonged to the Conservative Revolution, an intellectual movement situated at the extreme right of the political spectrum. A characteristic feature of this movement was its revolutionary attitude in seeking to reshape society according to the ideals of community (*Gemeinschaft*) and culture (*Kultur*). It strove to mobilize modern means (e.g., modern propaganda techniques) and even a modernist aesthetics (e.g., Ernst Jünger's prose) in the service of a nationalist project. By continuously undermining the fragile democracy of the Weimar Republic, the conservative revolutionaries in fact paved the way for National Socialism. Schmitt had a considerable career during the Third Reich and became an influential state lawyer.[5] An (unorthodox) interpretation of Catholicism, which permeates his juridical and political concepts, is at the origin of his political theology.

In the mid 1920s and early 1930s, just before Hitler's takeover, Benjamin and Schmitt mutually influenced each other and even corresponded briefly.[6] In the open climate of the Weimar Republic, it was not unusual for intellectuals to cross political dividing lines. Intellectuals of opposite political convictions would discuss freely with one another, as is exemplified by the contacts and affinities between such thinkers as Martin Heidegger and Herbert Marcuse, or Ernst Bloch and Ernst Jünger.[7] In some instances, political theology seems to have functioned as an (implicitly) shared theoretical approach, which made possible the crossing of political dividing lines. This phenomenon is especially significant in light of the massive breakdown of political frontlines in January 1933 (National Socialism itself having been an amalgam of various political elements, originating in both conservative and revolutionary thought[8]). The hidden dialogue between Benjamin and Schmitt, to which not only their correspondence but also important references in their work testify, can be adequately understood only in the light of their shared theologico-political convictions.

In the work of Benjamin and Schmitt, the concept of political theology covers more than the political and less than the strictly theological. "Political theology" does not refer to what is usually called "politics," but to "the political [*das Politische*]." Benjamin and Schmitt argue that the political no longer takes place in the classical political institutions, such as parliament or political parties, but has become omnipresent: in modern societies the political is present and active in media, the economy, technology, and so on.[9] What is usually meant by "theology," that is, comments on revelation and theories of the religious, is scarcely to be found in their work. Hence, the concept of political theology implies neither a political form of theology nor a "theology as politics." Political theology actually seems to indicate the reappearance of theological figures of thought in a secularized political sphere, in which their original meanings and functions have become obsolete. The theological (re)surfaces not only in fundamental political beliefs, ideologies, and myths, but also, silently, in theories of sovereignty, decision, and the "force of law."[10]

Two dominant interpretations of theologico-political motifs in the work of Benjamin and Schmitt can be found in the secondary literature. Representatives of the first interpretation (Norbert Bolz, Michael Rumpf, Lutz Koepnick, et al.) suggest that Schmitt, being a Catholic theorist, is able to justify a top-down conception of political power, since Catholicism accepts a moment of materialization, namely, the Incarnation, that allows divine violence to be represented within the juridico-political sphere.[11] According to this interpretation, Benjamin, contrary to Schmitt, embraces a radical critique of power, since Judaism doesn't acknowledge this moment of materialization and thus denounces any attempt to appropriate divine violence within the sphere of politics and law. Thus, while Schmitt defends a sovereign decision, in which he recognizes the theological *creatio ex nihilo*, Benjamin attempts to expose this decision as an unjustifiable act of violence. Representatives of this interpretation argue that Schmitt decides in favor of law and order, in which he recognizes the hidden workings of salvation, whereas Benjamin sides with the revolution, in which he sees the embodiment of a law-destroying violence that alone does justice to the impossibility of anticipating redemption.[12]

Representatives of the second interpretation (Suzanne Heil, Wolfgang Fietkau, Michael Makropoulos, et al.) suggest that Benjamin's political theology is comparable to Schmitt's because he eventually risks abandoning his strict anti-theocratic approach for a more positive "theologization of revolutionary politics."[13] According to this interpretation, Benjamin's "theological-anarchistic program of abolishing the law" is in danger of becoming the mirror image of Schmitt's polemic against the law in favor of the exception, onto which the promise of redemption is projected.[14] In the revolutionaries' law-destroying violence, Benjamin recognizes the "sparks of a spontaneous ontological evidence," which can only be explained as brief instances of a "theological revelation."[15] Thus, representatives of this second interpretation suggest that Benjamin, like Schmitt, acknowledges the possibility of a direct manifestation of divine violence in the juridico-political sphere.

The first interpretation fails to do justice to a certain conceptual ambivalence in Schmitt's political theology. On the one hand, Schmitt rejects the notion that after secularization a juridico-political order can provide the justification for, or prove the necessity of, its establishment in theological terms. Instead, the sovereign decision, which founds and guarantees the juridico-political order, always extends beyond itself into a normative openness. "The decision," Schmitt writes, "is, considered normatively, born out of nothing."[16] On the other hand, Schmitt recognizes the inclination of the political community to represent itself in terms of a redemptive truth, which in fact denies this normative openness. When, in the wake of secularization, awareness of a lack of legitimacy becomes unbearable, the need arises for an embodiment of the community, which can again provide certainty. This need results in the tendency to reason away the normative openness from which the sovereign decision, as well as the political, stems. The sovereign decision can no longer be undetermined and open—can perhaps no longer be a real "decision" at all—but appears as the actualization of a mystical unity.[17]

Against this background, the first interpretation is not false but clearly one-sided: it explains only the second aspect of Schmitt's political theology, that is, his understanding of the juridico-political order as the embodiment of a mystical unity. It ignores the first aspect, that is, his conceptualization of the political as a normative openness, which no worldly power can appropriate. The need for sovereign decisions and the inevitable return of the political actually reveal the impossibility of forcing a mystical body into juridico-political substance. Positive laws, Schmitt suggests, need sovereign decisions because they fail to prescribe the rules unequivocally. This is no temporary failure, but a permanent inadequacy—an inadequacy that affects the core of these laws' legitimacy. A similar imperfection characterizes the concept of the political: the sovereign can only create a political community by identifying enemies, reconciling his citizens by excluding others. Since there is no foundational norm, the political is defined by the "real possibility" of a conflict that cannot be permanently mediated.[18] Schmitt's understanding of the juridico-political order as the embodiment of a mystical unity can therefore be adequately interpreted only if its counterpoint, that is, an urgent awareness of the imperfection marking its laws and decisions, is also taken into consideration.

The second interpretation fails in a similar way by identifying Benjamin's political concepts *as* theology, thus ignoring his conviction that theology has to keep out of sight, be hidden in a radical materialism. In Benjamin's view, theology is not completely absent from the juridico-political sphere, but neither can it be described in explicitly theological terms. His materialist understanding of politics and law relates, as he famously puts it, "to theology like blotting paper to ink."[19] On the one hand, understanding the juridico-political order as a historical phenomenon in the light of redemption would be, according to theology itself, inadmissible.[20] On the other hand, without theology history would, in the final analysis, be incomprehensible; it would become a senseless conjunction of events. Benjamin therefore understands the juridico-political order with the help of theology, though he avoids the use of explicitly theological concepts. Although representatives of the second interpretation emphasize the theological implications of Benjamin's juridico-political vocabulary—for example, by claiming the positive identity of theological illumination and revolutionary politics—Benjamin actually underlines the impossibility of an explicitly theological interpretation of the political, emphasizing that "nothing historical . . . can of itself relate to the Messianic."[21]

Schmitt's Theory of Sovereignty

The state of exception, Schmitt argues in *Political Theology*, can be proclaimed when the existence of the legal order as such is threatened, for example, in the case of an impending civil war or a large-scale terrorist attack. This proclamation results in the temporary suspension of the law, so that the threat can be countered without any legal restrictions. In the state of exception, Schmitt claims, the normal legal order "recedes," making way for an "authority that is unlimited in principle [*eine prinzipiell unbegrenzte Befugnis*]." The one who proclaims the state of exception can thus be identified as the sovereign ruler.[22] In the state of exception, the sovereign has carte blanche to take all measures he deems necessary to suppress the threat posed to the legal order and to restore a normal situation in which the law can again be applied. He is even authorized to suspend constitutional rights and freedoms, if necessary, to safeguard the constitution as such. Thus, the state of exception should neither be confused with a legally regulated "state of emergency" nor with "martial law." The state of exception is, on the contrary, beyond the scope of positive law. There are no legal limits whatsoever to the sovereign's emergency powers.

Schmitt is fully aware of the risks involved in this suspension of the law. The emergency powers designed to defend the legal order can instead erode it. The sovereign could, for example, seize the emergency merely as a pretext to create a situation in which fundamental norms can be ignored with impunity. Schmitt suggests that the legal order cannot be defended from the sovereign body that was created in its defense.[23] As long as those invested with emergency powers choose to take responsibility for the legal order, transgressing the law only in order to preserve its underlying aims and convictions, the state of exception might in the end be suppressed and the rule of law might prevail. The legal order will inevitably crumble, however, in the face of a sovereign who doesn't support its most fundamental principles. In that case, the transgression of the law threatens to result in the destruction of the norms, and the "state of exception" is in danger of becoming the rule. Thus, Schmitt warns, within the state of exception the legal order is always exposed to the risk of being abolished by an irresponsible sovereign.[24]

Within the state of exception, Schmitt argues, a sovereign violence comes to light that simultaneously constitutes and threatens the existing legal order. This violence is essentially normalizing; it consists in "a normal forming of life relations [*eine normale Gestaltung der Lebensverhältnisse*]." Because positive laws cannot apply to chaos, the force of law presupposes a normalization of life itself. "The exception," Schmitt claims, "appears in its absolute form when a situation in which legal prescription can be valid must first be brought about."[25] In the state of exception the sovereign's normalizing violence creates and shapes a "homogeneous medium [*ein homogenes Medium*]," in which the law mirrors itself, forcing its image and form upon actual life relations. Only thus, by creating a homogeneous medium, can juridical norms acquire the force of law. In Schmitt's understanding, this "normalization is not merely an 'external presupposition' [of the norm], which can be ignored by the jurist"; instead, normalization belongs to the "immanent force [*immanente Geltung*]" of juridical norms.[26] In the state of exception, Schmitt suggests, the sovereign ruler violently coerces his subjects to adopt fundamental norms, so that the normal legal order can have force and effect.

Contrary to the claims of some commentators, Schmitt's concept of "life relations" should not be read as referring to a somewhat naïve "philosophy of life [*Lebensphilosophie*]."[27] Schmitt's is a politically mediated concept: when he writes, for example, that "in the exception the force of 'real life' breaks through the crust of a mechanism that has become torpid by repetition," he is not referring to some kind of unmediated authentic life but to life as it is produced by the decision.[28] The decision, moreover, does not produce life as such but a violent *separation of life relations*. As the German philosopher Jakob Taubes points out in his reading of Schmitt, the *Ent-Scheidung*, the decision, is simultaneously a *Scheidung*, a separation—this *Scheidung* being, in the final analysis, a separation of friend and foe. The concept of real life is thus parasitic upon the political.

Whoever ignores the political—or polemical—origin of the decision is, according to Taubes, "immoral, for he does not understand the human condition, which is finite and, *because of this finiteness*, has to separate, that is, to decide."[29]

According to Schmitt, legal rules need sovereign decisions because they fail to prescribe their application to specific cases unequivocally: "Every concrete juristic decision contains a moment of indifference from the perspective of content, because the juristic deduction is not traceable in the last detail to its premises."[30] For at least three reasons, the decision becomes independent of the rule's normative content. First, a legal rule cannot anticipate the specific characteristics of the concrete case, that is, its possible exceptional character, so that all cases that are not merely ideal textbook cases but originate in "real life" itself (*wirkliches Leben*) need a decision to bring them under the scope of the rule. Second, assuming that the rule is indeed applicable, it does not prescribe *how* it should be applied: for example, what aspects of the case should be taken into consideration in the light of the rule's *ratio*. Third, the rule does not contain any provisions concerning which institutions would be authorized to decide the case, since, as Schmitt remarks, "a distinctive determination of which individual person or which concrete body can assume such an authority cannot be derived from the mere legal quality of the maxim."[31] Therefore, according to Schmitt, even in the normal juridical situation a real decision is inevitable.

By refusing to accept the reality of the decision, that is, its reality as a violent separation, the sovereign ruler can seek to escape responsibility. Schmitt mentions the concept of responsibility only twice, in the concluding passages of the text. There he claims—together with the Catholic theorist of the state Donoso Cortés—that attempts to repress the notion of a radical exception are to be understood merely as a "method of circumventing responsibility [*eine Methode die Verantwortung zu umgehen*]."[32] Schmitt seems to be aiming primarily at liberals, who, as he remarks ironically, would even consider answering the question "Christ or Barabas?" with a request for postponement or the establishment of a commission of inquiry.[33] Postponing such an extremely urgent decision—one that doesn't allow for any delay, and thus presents itself only in an "instance of danger"—will inevitably result in a furtively festering violence, and only a decision taken with inner conviction will provide a chance, albeit an exceptionally small one, to bring that violence to an end. Hence, Schmitt reproaches the liberals not only for denying the presence of state violence but also for gambling away the chances of redemption.

The question seems to be, then, how the state of exception and the sovereign decision should responsibly be seen in the light of political theology. Schmitt conceives of secularization as a complex historical process, in which theology is banned from the political sphere without completely disappearing. After secularization, theological expressions, which have decisively marked the form of juridico-political discourse, can reappear at any moment, though their original meanings and functions have become obsolete. Schmitt, for example, points to similarities between the secular concept of the state of exception and the theological concept of the miracle.[34] His claim actually consists in two separate arguments: he argues, on the one hand, that "all the central concepts of the modern doctrine of state" are in fact secularized theological concepts, and, on the other, that a "structural analogy" exists between theological and legal concepts.[35] Schmitt thus emphasizes both a genealogical and a systematic affinity between the state of exception and the miracle, without, however, claiming that these concepts are positively identical.[36]

According to Schmitt, theological expressions, images, and metaphors continue to haunt a secularized juridico-political discourse. Thus theology is not completely absent from the legal sphere, but neither can it be described in directly theological terms. Schmitt's argument that the sovereign "decision is, considered normatively, born out of nothing" should be read against this background.[37] On the one hand, Schmitt implicitly aims at an analogy between the legal concept of the decision and the theological concept of the *creatio ex nihilo*, the divine creation "out of nothing." On the other hand, he consciously avoids the use of explicitly theological terms. In Schmitt's eyes, a positive identification of both concepts—the legal decision and the theological *creatio*—would only amount to the formation of quasi-theological myths. Far from being identical to the *creatio ex nihilo*—that is, a pure original creation—the sovereign decision remains violent and impure. By understanding the decision in light of the *creatio*—not claiming an identity, but focusing on an analogy—Schmitt attempts to dramatize responsibility, stressing the possibility of radical violence in the case of failure.

Benjamin's Critique of Violence

In "Critique of Violence," Benjamin, like Schmitt, examines the relationship between law and violence in the light of theology. By exposing the legal order's dependence on violent "lawmaking" decisions, Benjamin likewise attempts to articulate a certain kind of responsibility, which he understands theologically. Benjamin begins by suggesting that the existing critiques of violence are entangled in a conceptual confusion concerning both the violence to be criticized and the violence inherent in critique itself. A critique that understands violence to be merely a means to effect the norms of either positive or natural law will not be able to get a hold on state violence, for that critique will focus on the illegitimacy or illegality of a juridical practice instead of grasping violence "as a principle." That critique, moreover, tends to mobilize violence as itself a means, that is, as a "means of pressure," and thus risks becoming implicated in the very violence it seeks to criticize. Benjamin suggests that the critique of violence can only be effective if it succeeds in overcoming this conceptual confusion: neither the violence to be criticized nor the violence inherent in critique itself is merely a means. It is not a means, but a "manifestation."[38]

In the first part of the text, Benjamin examines what this notion of violence as a manifestation entails for the understanding of sovereign state violence. In the juridico-political order, he recognizes traces of an immediate violence that does not refer to a goal or a cause outside itself and that, in consequence, cannot be understood by reference to its normative meaning or function. Benjamin identifies this violence as a "lawmaking violence [*rechtsetzende Gewalt*]," to be distinguished from a "law-preserving violence [*rechtserhaltende Gewalt*]." Lawmaking violence seems to reside in the "force of law [*Gesetzeskraft*]," guaranteeing the laws' applicability. The juridico-political order betrays its dependence on lawmaking violence in at least four cases: those of military law, the death penalty, the police, and the parliament. These "legal institutions" are meant, according to the text's structure, to illuminate the various aspects of lawmaking violence: military law serves to prove the originality, the death penalty the excessiveness, the police the omnipresence, and the parliament the furtiveness of lawmaking violence.

With his reflections on *military law*, Benjamin seeks to demonstrate that sovereign state violence is not merely a "predatory violence" outside of and opposed to the legal order but a force capable of *founding and modifying* relations of law. The sovereign's unlimited authority to wage wars seems, at first sight, opposed to the existing relations of law, and even a threat to the continuity of the legal order as such. The peace ceremony that formally ends all military operations, however, implies that a new de facto situation will be recognized as new law. Through what Benjamin describes as the "necessary sanctioning of every victory," military violence, which at first seemed opposed to the legal order, is in retrospect recognized as being legitimate and in accordance with the law. In this moment of sanctioning, a lawmaking violence comes to light that is original, a priori, and independent of any formerly existing relations of law. Thus military violence, as a result of being legalized after the event, can cause a permanent modification of the legal order.[39]

According to Benjamin, the critics of the *death penalty* are well aware that they are not just aiming at one legal institution among others but at the origins of the law as such. What motivates their critique is not the punitive measure itself but the *absence of any measure*; they reject capital punishment as being "out of proportion." At the core of the legal order seems to reside a kind of lawlessness, a violence that escapes every attempt at legal regulation. Confronted with this elusive violence, the laws prove to be fragile and powerless, incapable of checking the excess upon which their applicability seems to depend. According to Benjamin, the death penalty thus reveals "something rotten in the law [*etwas Morsches im Recht*]": originating in a lawless violence, the legal order is always already exposed to the possibility of its decline, its internal corruption.[40]

The institution of the *police*, Benjamin argues, embodies a "spectral mixture" of lawmaking and law-preserving violence, for the police's law-preserving function always also entails the possibility of extending or restricting the application of the rules in exceptional cases. Thus, the police are capable of reformulating the rules that they pretend merely to apply. Because of this fusion of lawmaking and law-preserving violence, Benjamin suggests, both forms of violence lose their mutual limitations. Lawmaking violence can thus penetrate all the regions of the legal order, also those of mere administration and preservation. The laws are constantly threatened by their possible suspension in the "exceptional case." Benjamin therefore calls police authority "ignominious": "its power is formless, like its nowhere-tangible, all-pervasive, ghostly presence in the life of civilized states."[41] In modern democracies, the police even bears witness to the "greatest conceivable degeneration of violence."[42]

Parliaments, Benjamin claims, cultivate a politics of compromise that has supposedly banned all forms of violence. Denying the reality of lawmaking violence, parliaments are in fact only taking refuge in a more *concealed* violence, for compromises always presuppose a moment of compulsion. Benjamin quotes Erich Unger: "it would be better otherwise, is the underlying feeling in every compromise." Thus parliaments can only issue legal decrees of which "the origin and outcome are attended by violence."[43] According to Benjamin, the parliaments' illusion that they embody a perfectly peaceful discussion turns out to have a high price. The fact that a politics of compromise has to accept any position as negotiable inevitably undermines the parliaments' legitimacy. Parliaments fall into decline as soon as they lose awareness of the presence of violence. In modern democracies, Benjamin argues, parliaments offer a "woeful spectacle" because they have lost consciousness of the lawmaking violence originally represented in them. They have fallen prey to indecision.[44]

After having discussed the notion that state violence is a manifestation of lawmaking violence, Benjamin shifts his focus to the violence represented in critique itself. To escape the aporia of positivism and natural law, he introduces the concept of "pure means [*reine Mittel*]." Pure means do not serve any purpose outside themselves and are, strictly speaking, no means at all but *media*: they open up a sphere of pure mediation, in which any intention to intervene in moral relations is absent.[45] As Benjamin suggests, only a politics of pure means can effectively criticize state violence, thus bringing the dialectic of lawmaking and law-preserving violence to an end. This politics of pure means can "under certain conditions" take the form of a revolutionary strike. Following the French anarcho-syndicalist Georges Sorel's *Reflections on Violence* (1908), Benjamin distinguishes between, on the one hand, a "political general strike," which uses the threat of violence as a means of forcing the state to accept compromises, and, on the other, a "proletarian general strike," which categorically rejects the use of violence and aims at the complete abolition of the state.[46] Whereas the first form of work interruption is the *means* of a lawmaking violence, the second is the *medium* of a law-destroying violence.

In the political strike's lawmaking violence, Benjamin recognizes the manifestation of a mythical violence, which, by threatening retribution, only creates new boundaries and thus causes a continuation of guilt. By contrast, the proletarian strike's law-destroying violence bears witness to a divine violence, which at the end of time will destroy the law as such, thus expiating all possible guilt. Whereas the first form of violence is a "bloody violence over mere life for its own sake," the second is a "pure violence," which does not spill any blood and aims at saving "the soul of the living."[47] Benjamin claims that mythical violence demands the sacrifice of its victims, with the goal of preserving "mere life [*blosses Leben*]," whereas divine violence can only "accept" that sacrifice for the sake of justice. What is divine in life, Benjamin argues, is not mere life itself but its possible righteousness, that is, the moral task invested in life, the fulfillment of which is postponed to an unforeseeable future. Thus, only the sacrifice of mere life in an attempt to save the "soul of the living," that is, justice, can bear witness to the presence of divine violence.

Analogous to Schmitt's theologico-political convictions, Benjamin's concept of divine violence seems related to a certain notion of responsibility, originating in an awareness of the radical exception. In his famous interpretation of the text, Jacques Derrida argues that Benjamin's concept of "divine violence" should be read as a call for justice beyond positive law.[48] Because the creation and application of positive law is always attended by violence—an exclusion of that which escapes the generalizing language of rules and norms—justice must consist in a deconstruction of the law. In Derrida's reading, divine violence resides in the silent call to *remember* the specific otherness of all cases originating in life itself—an otherness that remains unrepresentable within the order of general laws. He suggests that, according to Benjamin, divine violence will only "accept" sacrifices that aim to save otherness from oblivion. Although these sacrifices cannot count on a certain result, since they are withdrawn from an economy of calculating intention, they can at least give voice to an otherness that the violence of myth threatens to silence.[49]

In this reading, whereas divine violence will refuse to accept sacrifices of life, insofar as they have been enforced *under* the law, it will accept those sacrifices originating in a responsibility *before* the law. Thus, like Schmitt's political theology, Benjamin's seems to imply the task of inventing a politics that bears witness to divine violence, though without being able to understand itself as a direct representation of that violence. The relation between a profane politics of pure means and a divine violence—if it makes sense to speak of a "relation" at all—can only be an *indirect* one, mediated by solitary struggles before the law. The possibility of the worst, the risk of life's being sacrificed to an illusion, that is, the specter of a justice that turns out to be mere myth, will only be realized if that indirect relationship is misunderstood to be a direct one. As soon as the revolutionary begins to think of his law-destroying violence as an instrument of salvation, redeeming history through the direct intervention of the divine violence it supposedly represents, he is bound to cause the worst, that is, a senseless sacrifice of "mere life" to myth.

Contemporary States of Exception

Schmitt's concept of the state of exception is still relevant in our times, for various reasons. We will have to restrict ourselves to the most urgent one. According to Schmitt, within the state of exception, when the worst violence has become possible, the sovereign ruler is simultaneously subjected to an unrestricted responsibility. Contemporary sovereigns, by contrast, most often represent their decisions within the state of exception as *apolitical*, that is, as not separating but harmonizing "life relations." Although they sometimes employ a polemical language—for example, that of a "war on terror"—the metaphors they use, especially the theological ones, suggest that their decisions are beyond the political.[50] According to Schmitt, the sovereign ruler should, on the contrary, take responsibility for the *Scheidung,* that is, for the violent separation his decisions actually bring about. He should understand that, within the state of exception, when an unlimited authority emerges, his responsibility is likewise without limits.

For at least one reason, however, Schmitt's concept is inadequate to illuminate contemporary states of exception. As we have shown, Schmitt considers the state of exception primarily from the perspective of sovereignty. His concept thus implies a complete absence of legal restrictions to state violence. In the specific case under consideration, however—Guantánamo Bay and, more generally, the indefinite detention of "enemy aliens"—the law is not absent at all. On the contrary, the enemy aliens have lost their rights *by and in agreement with the law,* and what is more, their seemingly lawless status is in fact imposed on them by juridical rules and decisions. On January 12, 2004, for example, the U.S. Supreme Court ruled that the policy of the federal government to withhold the names and detention places of enemy aliens was in agreement with American positive law, and on June 28 it accepted, though under certain conditions, the policy of military tribunals that decide in these cases without the possibility of appeal.[51] Moreover, as we know, even the detention circumstances at Guantánamo Bay, though outside the scope of the normal legal order, are narrowly regulated by juridical rules and decisions, of which Bush's Military Order is the most important.[52]

Contrary to Schmitt's thesis, not the complete withdrawal of the legal order but the possibility of a depersonalizing juridical violence characterizes the state of exception. What strikes us in the case of Guantánamo Bay is not some kind of unrestricted physical violence but rather a certain juristic, or at least narrowly regulated, disciplinary violence. The sovereign authorities, as a rule, restrain from brutalizing the detainees' "bare lives" ostentatiously, subjecting them instead to an almost invisible violence, controlling their bodies and concealing their faces. The state of exception can indeed be characterized by the desubjectivication of the detainees, that is, by their loss of rights and legal protections. The process of desubjectivication is realized, however, through the law and remains incomplete, that is, *the detainees are subjected to law without being subjects of law.* The detainees' loss of rights does not open up a lawless sphere within the legal order, but the desubjectivization is itself—its result included—governed by a strict regime of rules and decisions.

This depersonalizing juridical violence has found its most extreme manifestation in the Abu Ghraib prison in Iraq. What is decisive is not that fundamental rights were withheld from the detainees; rather, what is decisive is that they have lost the "right to have rights" as such. This circumstance is even more troubling than the physical mutilations and sexual abuses. The detainees of Abu Ghraib were deported from society with bags over their heads. Terrorists? Maybe. No judge will confirm that they are what they are taken for. Those detainees have completely lost their juridical personalities, effectively meaning the possibility to be acknowledged as a subject of the law before a competent tribunal.[53] They are not outside the legal order, but handed over to what Benjamin characterized as a "formless" and "faceless" police violence beyond all accountability. The anonymous and strikingly mobile interrogation units, moving from Guantánamo Bay to Abu Ghraib to Baghram, seem to have the "nowhere-tangible, all-pervasive, ghostly presence" Benjamin ascribed to that police violence.[54] Its mixture of law-preserving and lawmaking violence comes to light in the interrogators' authority to suspend the laws' applicability in exceptional cases. In the continuing war on terror that exception seems to have become the rule.

The published photos depicting sexual humiliations of those detained at Abu Ghraib cannot be understood as the expression of a regression into earlier forms of sovereignty that depended on a public, even theatrical staging of cruelty. The informal way the perpetrators are posing for their portraits to be taken—almost as if these pictures were meant to be sent home to their families—betrays the privatized idiom of these images (which the sexual character of the abuses seems to confirm). This privatization may indicate that modern forms of sovereignty have become increasingly dependent on the invisibility of state violence. Furthermore, the pictures testify to an obsession with excess, highlighting the absence of limits to state violence. In the case of enemy aliens, even the death penalty, in which Benjamin recognized an excessiveness of state violence escaping all attempts of legal regulation, seems to have been removed from the public sphere.[55] The military tribunals have the authority to pronounce the verdict of capital punishment, if required by an exceptional state interest, behind closed doors. In this sense, the war on terror has indeed resulted in a durable modification—not a mere extension but a qualitative change—in the American legal order.[56]

A distinctive feature of violence in the state of exception is the radicalization of its impersonal character. Schmitt represents the state of exception simultaneously as a "state of necessity [*Notfall, Ernstfall*]," in which a de facto situation—for example, the threat of an imminent terrorist attack—makes it necessary to suspend the normal legal order. Thus, sovereign decisions in the state of exception are supposed to be grounded in sheer necessity of fact. Because of this necessity and, moreover, because of its formal and impersonal character, the violence can acquire a reasonable appearance in the eyes of the perpetrators. Stressing its theological background, Schmitt is in fact attempting to make the "necessity" even more pressing. When he emphasizes the analogy between, on the one hand, the state of exception and, on the other, the theological Last Judgment, he risks legitimizing a violence that, because of its assumed impersonal origins, will itself depersonalize. Perhaps we should, on the contrary, question the necessity itself, thus seeking—with and against Schmitt—to politicize the state of exception and to articulate the responsibility it entails.

Critique, Coercion, and
Sacred Life in Benjamin's "Critique of Violence"

Judith Butler

I would like to take up the question of violence, more specifically, the question of what a critique of violence might be. What meaning does the term *critique* take on when it becomes a critique of violence? A critique of violence is an inquiry into the conditions for violence, but it is also an interrogation of how violence is circumscribed in advance by the questions we pose of it. What is violence, then, such that we can pose this question of it, and do we not need to know how to handle this question before we ask, as we must, what are the legitimate and illegitimate forms of violence? I understand Walter Benjamin's essay "Critique of Violence," written in 1921, to provide a critique of *legal* violence, the kind of violence that the state wields through instating and maintaining the binding status that law exercises on its subjects.[1] When Benjamin offers a critique, he is offering at least two different kinds of accounts: in the first instance, he is asking: How does legal violence become possible? What is law such that it requires violence or, at least, a coercive effect in order to becoming binding on subjects? But also, what is violence such that it can assume this legal form? In asking the latter question, Benjamin opens up a second trajectory for his thought: Is there another form of violence that is noncoercive, indeed, a violence that can be invoked and waged against the coercive force of law? He goes further and asks: Is there a kind of violence that is not only waged against coercion, but is itself noncoercive and, in that sense if not some others, fundamentally nonviolent? He refers to such a noncoercive violence as "bloodless," and this would seem to imply that it is not waged against human bodies and human lives. As we will see, it is not finally clear whether he can make good on this promise. If he could make good on it, he would espouse a violence that is destructive of coercion, shedding no blood in the process. This would constitute the paradoxical possibility of a nonviolent violence, and in what follows I hope to consider that possibility in Benjamin's essay.

Benjamin's essay is notoriously difficult. We are given many distinctions to handle, and it seems as if we handle them only for a few moments, then let them go. There are two sets of distinctions that one must work with if one is to try to understand what he is doing. The first is the distinction between *law-instating* (*rechtsetzend*) and *law-preserving* (*rechtserhaltend*) violence. Law-preserving violence is exercised by the courts and, indeed, by the police and represents repeated and institutionalized efforts to make sure law continues to be binding on the population it governs; it represents the daily ways in which law is made again and again to be binding on subjects. Law-instating violence is different. Law is posited as something that is done when a polity comes into being, and law is made, but it can also be a prerogative exercised by the military in innovating coercive actions to handle an unruly population. Interestingly, the military can be an example of law-instating and law-preserving power, depending upon context; we will return to this when we ask whether there is yet another violence, a third possibility for violence that exceeds and opposes both law-instating and law-preserving violence. If we focus, though, on law-instating violence, Benjamin seems clear that the act of positing law, of making law, is the work of fate. The acts by which law is instituted are not themselves justified by another law or through recourse to a rational justification that precedes the codification of law, nor is law formed in some organic way, through the slow development of cultural mores and norms into positive law. On the contrary, the making of law creates the conditions for justificatory procedures and deliberations to take place. It does this, as it were, by fiat, and this is part of what is meant by the violence of this founding act. In effect, the violence of law-instating violence is summarized in the claim that "This will be law" or, more emphatically, "This is now the law."[2] This last conception of legal violence—the law-instating kind—is understood to be an operation of fate, a term that has a specific meaning for him. Fate belongs to the Hellenic realm of myth, and law-preserving violence is in many ways the byproduct of this law-instating violence, because the law that is preserved is precisely the law that has already been instated. The fact that law can only be preserved by reiterating its binding character suggests that the law is "preserved" only by being asserted again and again as binding. In the end, it would seem, the model of law-instating violence, understood as fate, a declaration by fiat, is the mechanism by which law-preserving violence operates, as well. The fact that the military is the example of an institution that both makes and preserves law suggests that it provides a model for understanding the internal link between these two forms of violence. For a law to be preserved is for its binding status to be reasserted. That reassertion binds the law again, and so repeats the founding act in a regulated way. We can see here, as well, that if the law were not to make itself anew, not to be preserved, it could very well be that the site where a given set of laws would cease to work, cease to be preserved, cease to be made binding once again, would be the military, since it seems to be the institution that is exemplary by at once preserving and enforcing law, and thus the site where law might be arrested, cease to work, even become subject to destruction.

If we are to understand the violence at work in both law-instating and law-preserving violence, we must consider another violence, one that is to be understood neither through the notion of fate nor, indeed, as Hellenic or "mythic violence." Mythic violence establishes law without any justification for doing so, and only once that law is established can we begin to talk about justification at all. Crucially, law is founded without justification, without reference to justification, even though it makes reference to justification possible as a consequence of that founding. First the subject is bound by law, and then a legal framework emerges to justify the binding character of law. In consequence, subjects are produced who are accountable to the law and before the law, who become defined by their relation to legal accountability. Over and against this realm of law, in both its founding and preserving instances, Benjamin posits a "divine violence," one that takes aim at the very framework that establishes legal accountability. Divine violence is unleashed against the *coercive force* of that legal framework, against the accountability that binds a subject to a specific legal system and stops that very subject from developing a critical, if not a revolutionary point of view on that legal system. When a legal system must be undone, or when its coerciveness leads to a revolt by those who suffer under its coercion, it is important that those bonds of accountability be broken. Indeed, *doing the right thing according to established law is precisely what must be suspended in order to dissolve a body of established law that is unjust.*

This was surely the argument of Georges Sorel in his *Reflections on Violence*, which profoundly influenced Benjamin's discussion of the general strike, the one that leads to the dissolution of an entire state apparatus. According to Sorel, the general strike does not seek to implement this or that particular reform within a given social order, but seeks to undo the entire legal basis of a given state. Benjamin brings the Sorelian position together with a messianic thinking that gives his view a theological and political meaning at once. Divine violence not only releases one from forms of coerced accountability, a forced or violent form of obligation, but this release is at once an expiation of guilt and an opposition to coercive violence. One might respond to all of this with a certain fear that only anarchism or mob rule might follow, but there are a few propositions to keep in mind. Benjamin nowhere argues that all legal systems should be opposed, and it is unclear on the basis of this text whether he opposes certain rules of law and not others. Moreover, if he traffics here with anarchism, we should at least pause over what anarchism might mean in this context and keep in mind that Benjamin takes seriously the commandment "Thou shalt not kill"—to whose meaning I will shortly return. Paradoxically, Benjamin envisions the release from legal accountability and guilt as a way of apprehending the suffering and the transience in life, of life, as something that cannot always be explained through the framework of moral or legal accountability. This apprehension of suffering and transience can lead, in his view, to a kind of happiness. Only through recourse to Benjamin's notion of the messianic can one see how the apprehension of a suffering that belongs to the domain of life that remains unexplained through recourse to moral accountability leads to, or constitutes, a kind of happiness. In my conclusion, I'll try to make clear what I take this conception to be when I consider his "Theologico-Political Fragment."

Benjamin was working with several sources when he wrote "Critique of Violence"; they included Sorel's *Reflections on Violence*, Hermann Cohen's *Ethic of the Pure Will*, and Gershom Sholem's kabbalistic inquiries. In a sense, he was working along two trajectories at once: a theological one and a political one, elaborating, on the one hand, the conditions for a general strike that would result in the paralysis and dissolution of an entire legal system, and, on the other, the notion of a divine god whose commandment *offers a kind of injunction that is irreducible to coercive law*. The two strands of Benjamin's essay are not always easy to read together. There are those who would say that the theology is in the service of the theory of the strike, whereas others would say that the general strike is but an example of—or an analogy to—divine destructiveness.

What seems important here, though, is that divine violence is communicated by a commandment that is neither despotic nor coercive. Indeed, like Franz Rosenzweig before him, Benjamin figures the commandment as a kind of law that is neither binding nor enforceable in a way that requires legal violence.[3] When we speak about legal violence, we are referring to the kind of violence that maintains the legitimacy and enforceability of law, the system of punishment that lays in wait if laws are broken, the police and military force that back up a system of law, and the forms of legal and moral accountability that make sure individuals remain forcibly obligated to act according to the law, indeed, to gain their civic definition by virtue of their relation to the law.

Interestingly enough, it is through a reconsideration of the biblical commandment, specifically, the commandment "Thou shalt not kill," that Benjamin articulates his critique of state violence, a violence that is in many ways exemplified by the military in its double capacity to enforce and to make law. Although we are accustomed to thinking of the divine commandment as operating in an imperative way, mandating action on our part and ready with a set of punitive reactions if we fail to obey, Benjamin makes use of a different Jewish tradition of understanding the commandment, which strictly separates the imperative that the law articulates from the matter of its enforceability. The commandment delivers an imperative precisely without the capacity to enforce in any way the imperative it communicates. The commandment is not the vocalization of a furious and vengeful God, and in this view Jewish law more generally is decidedly *not* punitive; moreover, the commandment associated with the Jewish God is here *opposed* to guilt, even seeks an expiation of guilt, which, according to Benjamin, is a specific inheritance from the mythic or Hellenic traditions. Indeed, Benjamin's essay offers in fragmented and potential form the possibility of countering a misconception of Jewish law that associates it with revenge, punitiveness, and the induction of guilt. Over and against the idea of a coercive and guilt-inducing law, Benjamin invokes the commandment as mandating only that an individual struggle with the ethical edict communicated by the imperative. This is an imperative that does *not* dictate, but *leaves open* the modes of its applicability, the possibilities of its interpretation, including the conditions under which it may be refused.

We have in Benjamin a critique of state violence inspired in part by Jewish theological resources, one that would oppose the kind of violence that strikes at what he calls "the soul of the living [*die Seele des Lebendigen*]." It is important to tread carefully here, since it would be a mistake to say this essay constitutes a "Jewish critique," even though a strand of Jewish theology runs through it, and certainly it makes no sense to call this a "Jewish critique" because Benjamin was a Jew. If the critique can justifiably be called "Jewish," that is only as a result of some of the critical resources Benjamin brings to bear. And it is important to remember that Sorel, who was not Jewish and who brings no clearly Jewish resources to bear in his critique (unless we consider Bergson in this light), has surely influenced this essay as much as Scholem or Cohen. Although Benjamin clearly equivocates about the possibility and meaning of nonviolence, I will suggest that the commandment, as thought by Benjamin, is not only the basis for a critique of legal violence but also the condition for a theory of responsibility that has at its core an ongoing struggle with nonviolence.

Here I will insert an aside, to make clear what I think are some of the political implications of this reading, since I see two that I would want to embrace. If part of the vulgar representation of Judaism is that it subscribes to a concept of God or to a conception of law based on revenge, punishment, and the inculcation of guilt, we see an illuminating remnant of a different Judaism in the Kabbalistic strains that inform Benjamin's thought. Thus, if part of the reduction of Judaism that we confront in popular representations of its meaning consists in identifying Judaism with a wrathful and punitive God, and Christianity with a principle of love or *caritas*, we would have to reconsider these distinctions. We also see, I think, the traces of a counter-rabbinic movement in the early twentieth century that informed the work of Rosenzweig and ultimately Martin Buber, one that was associated with the notion of spiritual renewal and that worried about both assimilationism, on the one hand, and rabbinic scholasticism, on the other. This movement was also critical of efforts to establish a legal and political territoriality for Judaism, and some of these arguments have important resonance for rethinking Zionism today. Rosenzweig, for instance, both opposed legal coercion and invoked the commandment as way of figuring a noncoercive law. He remarks that, whatever the specific stipulations of a commandment, each and every commandment communicates the demand to "love God." Indeed, in *The Star of Redemption* Rosenzweig writes that God's commandments can be reduced to the statement "Love me!" In the 1910s and 1920s, both Rosenzweig and later Buber opposed the idea of a "state" for the Jewish people and thought that the critical and even spiritual power of Judaism would be ruined or, in Buber's words, "perverted" by the establishment of a state with legal coercion and sovereignty as its basis.

Rosenzweig died too early to revise his stand, but Buber came to embrace a version of Zionism that would include a federated state jointly and equally administered by "two peoples." Benjamin, so far as I know, took no such view of the founding of a state in the name of Zionism, and he deflects the question time and again when pressed by his friend Scholem in their correspondence.[4] What seems to matter here, for those who seek to make use of his text as a cultural resource for thinking about this time, is at least twofold: it opposes what sometimes amounts to an antisemitic reduction of Jewishness to so much blood-letting at the same time as it establishes a critical relation to state violence, one that might well be part of an effort to mobilize critical Jewish perspectives against the current policies, if not the constitutional basis of citizenship, of the state of Israel. As you may know, it is sometimes said that to criticize the state of Israel is to criticize Judaism itself, but that view forgets that Judaism offers an important set of perspectives that were critical of Zionism before its triumph in 1948 and that now continue in some forms on the left, both within Israel/Palestine and throughout the diaspora.

Of course, Benjamin's essay has its present-day detractors, many of whom would doubtless argue that it fails to anticipate the assault of fascism on the rule of law and parliamentary institutions. Between the writing of Benjamin's essay in 1921 and its contemporary readers, several historical catastrophes have ensued, including the extermination of more than ten million people in Nazi extermination camps. One could argue that fascism ought to have been opposed precisely by a rule of law that was considered binding on its subjects. But it follows equally that if the law that binds its subjects is itself part of a fascist legal apparatus, then it would appear that such an apparatus is precisely the kind of law whose binding force should be opposed and resisted until the apparatus fails. Benjamin's critique of law, however, remains nonspecific, so that a general opposition to the binding, even coercive character of law seems less savory once we consider the rise of fascism, as well as the flouting of both constitutional and international law that characterizes U.S. foreign policy in its practices of war, torture, and illegal detention. But it was surely in light of the rise of European fascism that some critics have taken distance from Benjamin's essay.

Benjamin's essay received a trenchant reading by Jacques Derrida in his "Force of Law" and became a controversial foil for Hannah Arendt in her "On Violence." At the time that Derrida wrote his essay on Benjamin, he worried openly about what he called "the messianic-marxism" that runs through "Critique of Violence" and sought to distance himself from the theme of destruction and to value an ideal of justice that is finally approximated by no specific or positive law. Of course, later Derrida would revisit messianism, messianicity, and Marxism in *Specters of Marx* and in various essays on religion. In the essay on Benjamin, Derrida made clear that he thought Benjamin went too far in criticizing parliamentary democracy, and that Benjamin's critique of legal violence could lead to an antiparliamentary political sentiment that was associated too closely with fascism. At one point, Derrida claims that Benjamin rides "an antiparliamentary wave" that was the very wave that carried fascism.[5] Derrida also worries that Benjamin wrote to Carl Schmitt in the same year that he published "Critique of Violence," but we don't learn what, if anything, in that letter gives cause for concern. Apparently the letter is about two lines long, indicating that Benjamin is thankful for Schmitt for sending on his book. That formal expression of thanks hardly forms a basis for inferring that Benjamin condones Schmitt's book in part or in whole.

Arendt, in "On Violence," also worries that views such as Benjamin's do not understand the importance of law in binding a community together and maintains that he failed to understand that the founding of a state can and should be an uncoerced beginning, and in that sense nonviolent in its origins.[6] She seeks to base democratic law on a conception of power that makes it distinct from violence and coercion. In this sense, Arendt seeks to solve the problem by stabilizing certain definitions, engaging in what might be termed a stipulative strategy. In her political lexicon, violence is defined as coercion, and power is defined as nonviolent, specifically, as the exercise of collective freedom. Indeed, she holds that if law were based in violence, it would therefore be illegitimate, and she disputes the contention that law can be said to be instated or preserved by violence.

Indeed, whereas Arendt understands revolutions to instate law and to express the concerted consent of the people, Benjamin maintains that something called "fate" originates law. And whereas Derrida, in his reading of the essay, locates the messianic in the performative operation by which law itself comes into being (and so with law-establishing power, with fate, and with the sphere of the mythic), it is clear that for Benjamin the messianic is associated with the destruction of the legal framework, a distinct alternative to mythic power. In what remains, I would like to examine this distinction between fate and divine violence, and to consider the implications of Benjamin's messianic for the problem of critique.

. . .

Let us remember that Benjamin is making at least two sets of overlapping distinctions, one between law-founding and law-preserving violence, and then another between mythic and divine violence. It is within the context of mythic violence that we receive an account of law-founding and law-preserving violence, so let us look there first to understand what is at stake. Violence brings a system of law into being, and this law-founding violence is precisely one that operates without justification. Fate produces law, but it does so first through manifesting the anger of the gods. This anger takes form as law, but one that does not serve any particular end. It constitutes a pure means; its end, as it were, is the manifesting itself.

To show this, Benjamin invokes the myth of Niobe. Her great mistake was to claim that she, a mortal, was more fecund and greater than Leto, the goddess of fertility. She offended Leto immensely and also sought, through her speech act, to destroy the distinction between gods and humans. When Artemis and Apollo arrive on the scene to punish Niobe for her outrageous claim by taking away her children, these gods can be understood, in Benjamin's sense, to be establishing a law. But this lawmaking activity is not to be understood first and foremost as punishment or retribution for a crime committed against an existing law. Niobe's arrogance does not, in Benjamin's words, offend against the law; if it did, we would have to assume that the law was already in place prior to the offense. Rather, through her hubristic speech act she challenges or tempts fate. Artemis and Apollo thus act in the name of fate, or become the means by which fate is instituted. Fate wins this battle and, as a result, the triumph of fate is the establishment of law itself.

In other words, the story of Niobe illustrates law-instating violence because the gods respond to an injury by establishing a law. The injury is not experienced first as an infraction against the law; rather, it becomes the precipitating condition for the establishment of law. Law is thus a specific consequence of an anger that responds to an injury, but neither that injury nor that anger are circumscribed in advance by law.

The anger works performatively to mark and transform Niobe, establishing her as the guilty subject, who takes on the form of petrified rock. Law thus petrifies the subject, arresting life in the moment of guilt. And though Niobe herself lives, she is paralyzed within that living: she becomes permanently guilty, and guilt turns into rock the subject who bears it. She becomes permanently petrified, and the retribution that the gods take upon her is apparently infinite, as is her atonement. In a way, she represents the economy of infinite retribution and atonement that Benjamin elsewhere claims belongs to the sphere of myth.[7] She is partially rigidified, hardened in and by guilt, yet full of sorrow, weeping endlessly from that petrified well-spring. The punishment produces the subject bound by law—accountable, punishable, and punished. She would be fully deadened by guilt if it were not for that sorrow, those tears, and so it is with some significance that it is those tears to which Benjamin returns when he considers what is released through the expiation of guilt. Her guilt is at first externally imposed. It is important to remember that it is only through a magical causality that she becomes responsible for her children's deaths. They are, after all, not murdered by her hand, and yet she assumes responsibility for this murder as a consequence of the blow dealt by the gods. It would appear, then, that the transformation of Niobe into a legal subject involves recasting a violence dealt by fate as a violence that follows from her own action, and for which she, as a subject, assumes direct responsibility. To be a subject within these terms is to take responsibility for a violence that precedes the subject and whose operation is occluded by the subject who comes to derive the violence she suffers from her own acts. The formation of the subject who occludes the operation of violence by establishing herself as the sole cause of what she suffers is thus a further operation of that violence.

Interestingly enough, fate characterizes the establishment of law, but it does not account for how law, or legal coercion in particular, can be undone and destroyed. Rather, fate establishes the coercive conditions of law by manifesting the subject of guilt; its effect is to bind the person to the law, establishing the subject as the singular cause of what she suffers and steeping the subject in a guilt-ridden form of accountability. Fate also accounts for the perennial sorrow that emerges from such a subject, but fate cannot be the name that describes the effort to abolish those conditions of coercion. To understand the latter, one must move from fate to God, or from myth, the sphere to which fate belongs, to the divine, the sphere to which a certain nonviolent destruction belongs. We have yet to understand in what precisely this nonviolent destruction consists, but it seems to be the kind of destruction that Benjamin imagines would be directed against the legal framework itself and, in this sense, would be distinct from the violence required and waged by the legal framework.

Quite abruptly toward the end of his essay, Benjamin resolves that the *destruction* of all legal violence becomes obligatory (249). But we do not understand whether this is a violence that is exercised by particular legal systems, or a violence that corresponds to law more generally. His discussion remains at a level of generality that leads the reader to assume that it is law in general that poses a problem for him. When he writes that the destruction of all legal violence is obligatory, it would appear that he writes at a moment and in a certain context that remains undelineated within the essay.

Earlier, he has distinguished between the political general strike, which is lawmaking, and the general strike, which destroys state power and with it the coercive force that guarantees the binding character of all law—legal violence itself. He writes that the second kind of strike is destructive, but *nonviolent* (246). Here he is already proposing a nonviolent form of destructiveness. He turns in the final pages to a discussion of God to exemplify and understand this nonviolent form of destructiveness. Indeed, it may be said that God has something to do with the general strike, since both are considered to be destructive and nonviolent at once. God will also have to do with what Benjamin calls an anarchism and not with lawmaking. Thus if we think that God is the one who gives us the law or, through Moses, relays a dictation of what the law should be, we must consider again that the commandment is not the same as positive law, which maintains its power through coercion: as a form of law, the commandment is precisely noncoercive and unenforceable.

If what is divine in divine violence neither gives nor preserves the law, we will be left in a quandary about how best to understand the commandment and, in particular, its political equivalent. For Rosenzweig, the *commandment is emphatically* not an instance of legal violence or coercion. We think of the God of Moses as giving the commandment, and yet the commandment is not an instance of law giving for Benjamin. Rather, the commandment establishes a point of view on law that leads to the destruction of law as coercively binding. To understand the commandment as an instance of divine violence may seem strange, especially since the commandment cited by Benjamin is "Thou shalt not kill." But what if the positive legal system to which one is bound legally demands that one kill? Would the commandment, in striking at the legitimacy of that legal system, become a kind of violence that opposes violence? For Benjamin, this divine violence has the power to destroy mythical violence. God is the name for what opposes myth.[8]

It is important to remember not only that divine power destroys mythical power, but that divine power *expiates*. This suggests that divine power acts upon guilt in an effort to undo its effects. Divine violence acts upon lawmaking and the entire realm of myth, seeking to expiate the marks of misdeeds in the name of a forgiveness that assumes no human expression. Divine power thus does its act, its destructive act, but can only do its act if mythic power has constituted the guilty subject, its punishable offense, and a legal framework for punishment. Interestingly enough, the Jewish God, for Benjamin, does not induce guilt and so is not associated with the terrors of beratement. Indeed, divine power is described as lethal without spilling blood. It strikes at the legal shackles by which the body is petrified and forced into endless sorrow, but it does not strike, in Benjamin's view, at the soul of the living. Indeed, divine violence acts in the name of soul of the living. And it must also then be the soul of the living that is jeopardized by the law that paralyzes its subject through guilt. This guilt threatens to become a kind of soul-murder. By distinguishing the soul of the living from "life" itself, Benjamin asks us to consider what value life has once the soul has been destroyed.

When we ask what motivates this turn against legal violence, this obligation to destroy legal violence, Benjamin refers to "the guilt of a more natural life" (250). He clarifies in "Goethe's Elective Affinities" that a "natural kind" of guilt is not ethical and is not the result of any wrong-doing: "with the disappearance of supernatural life in man, his natural life turns into guilt, even without his committing an act contrary to ethics. For now it is in league with mere life, which manifests itself in man as guilt" (308). He does not elaborate on this notion of a natural life in "Critique of Violence," though elsewhere in the essay he refers to "mere life [*blosse Leben*]." He writes, "mythic violence is bloody power [*Blutgewalt*] over all life for its own sake [*um ihrer selbst*]; divine violence is pure power over all life for the sake of the living [*reine Gewalt uber alles Leben um des Lebendigen*]" (250). Positive law thus seeks to constrain "life for its own sake." Divine power does not safeguard life itself, however, but life only for the sake of "the living." Who constitutes "the living" in this notion? It cannot be everyone who merely lives, since the soul of the living is different, and what is done "for the sake of the living" may well involve taking away mere life. This seems clear when Benjamin refers, for instance, to the plight of Korah—a biblical scene in which an entire community is annihilated by the wrath of God for not having kept faith with his word—as an example of divine violence.

It is with some consternation, then, that we must ask whether the commandment "Thou shalt not kill" seeks to safeguard natural life or the soul of the living, and how it discriminates between the two. Life itself is not a necessary or sufficient ground to oppose positive law, but the "soul" of the living may be. Such an opposition may be undertaken *for the sake of* the living, that is, for those who are alive by virtue of that active or living soul. We know from the early part of the essay that "the misunderstanding in natural law by which a distinction is drawn between violence used for just ends and violence used for unjust ends must be emphatically rejected." The kind of violence that he calls "divine" is not justified through a set of ends but constitutes a "pure means." The commandment "Thou shalt not kill" cannot be a law on the order of the laws that are destroyed. It must itself be a kind of violence that opposes violence, in the same way that the mere life controlled by positive law differs from the soul of the living, which remains the focus of divine injunction. In a rather peculiar twist, Benjamin appears to be reading the commandment not to kill as a commandment not to murder the soul of the living, and therefore as a commandment to do violence against the positive law that is responsible for such murder. An example of the positive law's seizure of mere life is capital punishment. In opposing legal violence, Benjamin would now seem to oppose capital punishment as the legally mandated violence that most fully articulates and exemplifies the violence of positive law. Over and against a law that could and would sentence a subject to death, the commandment figures a kind of law that works precisely to safeguard some sense of life against such punishments—but which sense? Clearly this is not a simply biological life, but the deathlike state induced by guilt, the rocklike condition of Niobe with her endless tears. Yet it is in the name of life that expiation would be visited upon Niobe, which raises the question of whether the expiation of guilt is somehow a motivation or an end for the revolt against legal violence. Are the bonds of accountability to a legal system that reserves the prerogative of capital punishment for itself broken by a revolt against legal coercion itself? Does something about the claim of "the living" motivate the general strike, which expiates the guilt that maintains the hold of legal coercion upon the subject? *The desire to release life from a guilt secured through legal contract with the state—this would be a desire that gives rise to a violence against violence, one that seeks to release life from a death contract with the law, a death of the living soul by the hardening force of guilt.* This is the divine violence that moves, like a storm, over humanity to obliterate all traces of guilt, a divine expiative force and thus not retribution.

Divine violence does not strike at the body or the organic life of the individual, but at the subject who is formed by law. It purifies the guilty, not of guilt, but of its immersion in law and thus it dissolves the bonds of accountability that follow from the rule of law itself. Benjamin makes this link explicit when he refers to divine power as "pure power over all life for the sake of the living." Divine power constitutes an expiating moment that strikes without bloodshed. The separation of legal status from the living being (which would be an expiation or release of that living being from the shackles of positive law) is precisely the effect of the blow, the strike, and its bloodless effect.

But is this violence truly bloodless, if it can involve the annihilation of people, as in the Korah story, or if it relies on a questionable distinction between a natural life and the soul of the living? Is there a tacit Platonism at work in the notion of the "soul of the living"? I would like to argue that there is no ideal meaning attached to this notion of the "soul," since it belongs precisely to those who are living, and I hope to make clear how this works in my concluding discussion.

Benjamin begins to articulate this distinction when he concedes that violence can be inflicted "relatively against goods, right, life, and suchlike," but it never absolutely annihilates the soul of the living (*die Seele des Lebendigen*; 297–98). Although divine violence is violence, it is never annihilating in an absolute sense, only relatively. How do we understand this use of the term "relatively [*relativ*]"? And how, precisely, does it follow that Benjamin proceeds to claim that it cannot be said that his thesis confers on humans the power to exercise lethal power against one another? "The question 'May I kill?' meets its irreducible [*Unverruckbare*: unmoveable, fixed—literally, not able to make crazy or to make veer from the path] answer in the commandment 'Thou shalt not kill'" (250). That the commandment is irreducible and unmovable does not mean that it cannot be interpreted and even contravened. Those who heed the commandment "wrestle [*sich auseinanderzusetzen*] with [it] in solitude and, in exceptional [*ungeheuren*] cases, . . . take on themselves the responsibility of ignoring it" (250).

Over and against the mythic scene in which the angry deed establishes a punitive law, the commandment exercises a force that is not the same as a marking by guilt. The divine word, if it is a performative, is a perlocutionary speech act, which depends fundamentally on being taken up to take hold. It works only by being appropriated, and that is surely not guaranteed. Benjamin describes the commandment's nondespotic powers: "the injunction becomes inapplicable, incommensurable, once the deed is accomplished," which suggests that any fear that the commandment provokes does not immediately bind the subject to the law through obedience. In the example of mythic law, punishment instills guilt and fear, and Niobe exemplifies the punishment that lays in wait for anyone who might compare him or herself to the gods.

Benjamin's commandment entails no such punishments and lacks the power to enforce the actions it requires. The commandment, for Benjamin, has no police force. It is immoveable, it is uttered, and it becomes the occasion for a struggle with the commandment itself. It neither inspires fear nor exercises a power to enforce a judgment after the fact. Hence, he writes, "no judgment of the deed can be derived from the commandment" (250). Indeed, the commandment cannot dictate action, compel obedience, or level judgment against the one who complies or fails to comply with its imperative. Rather than constituting a criterion of judgment for a set of actions, the commandment functions as a *guideline* [*Richtschnur des Handelns*]. And what is mandated by the commandment is a struggle with the commandment, whose final form cannot be determined in advance. In Benjamin's surprising interpretation, one wrestles with the commandment in solitude.

As a form of ethical address, the commandment is that with which each individual must wrestle without the model of any other. One ethical response to the commandment is to refuse (*abzusehen*) it, but even then one must take responsibility for refusing it. Responsibility is something that one takes in relation to the commandment, but it is not dictated by the commandment. Indeed, it is clearly distinguished from duty and, indeed, obedience. If there is a wrestling, then there is some semblance of freedom. One is not free to ignore the commandment. One must, as it were, wrestle with oneself in relation to it. But the wrestling with oneself may well yield a result, a decision, an act that refuses or revises the commandment, and, in this sense, the decision is the effect of an interpretation at once constrained and free.

One might expect Benjamin to safeguard the value of life over violence and to coin a notion of nonviolent violence to name this safeguarding action, this strike against the shackles of the law, this expiation of guilt and resuscitation of life.[4] But he makes clear that those who prize existence over happiness and justice subscribe to a position that is both "false" and "ignominious [*niedrig*]." He objects to the understanding of "existence" as "mere life" and suggests that there is "a mighty truth" in the proposition that existence is to be prized over happiness and justice if we consider existence and life to designate the "irreducible, total condition that is 'man' . . . man cannot, at any price be said to coincide with the mere life in him" (251). As is clear in Benjamin's agreement with the Jewish view that killing in self-defense is not prohibited by the commandment, the commandment against killing is based not on the sacredness (*heiligkeit*) of life itself (a notion that correlates with guilt) but on something else. He does not refuse the notion of the sacred in trying to establish the grounds and aims of the commandment against killing, but he wants clearly to distinguish what is sacred in life from mere or natural life.

The temptation to read Benjamin as subscribing to an otherwordly doctrine of the soul or the sacred emerges temporarily when he refers to "that life in man that is identically present in earthly life, death, and afterlife" (251). Even then, he only refers to the sacred through a conjecture and a parenthetical appeal: "however sacred man is [*so heilig der Mensch ist*], . . . there is no sacredness in his condition," which includes bodily life and its injurability. What is sacred is some restricted sense of life that is identical in this life and the afterlife—but what sense are we to make of this? Benjamin introduces the problem of the sacred and of justice only in the context of a conjecture, suggesting that it belongs to an indefinite future, if to any time at all. How are we to adjudicate Benjamin's claims? Is this appeal to another life, to a sense of life that is beyond the body, the maneuver of the "spiritual terrorist [*der geistige Terrorist*]" who supplies the "ends" that justify violence? That would seem to be at odds with Benjamin's earlier claim that divine violence does not act according to specified ends, but rather as a pure means. By the latter phrase, he seems to suggest that divine violence consummates a process but does not "cause" it, that we cannot extricate the "ends" it achieves from the "means" by which it is achieved, and that instrumental calculations of that sort are overcome.

Let us first understand the restricted sense of life that emerges within Benjamin's conjecture. If there is something sacred or divine in this restricted sense of life, then it would seem to be precisely that which opposes guilt and the law-enforcing violence of positive law. It would consist in that which resists or counters this form of legal violence,

213

and we have seen that this kind of hostile counter-violence is itself the expression of what remains unbound, unguilty, or expiated. In this essay, however, we see that divine violence is allied with the general strike and what is revolutionary, and this in turn is allied with what contests and devastates the legal framework of the state. I would suggest that this sacred or divine sense of life is also allied with the anarchistic, with that which is beyond or outside of principle. We saw this anarchistic moment already when the solitary person is conjured as wrestling, without model or reason, with the commandment. It is an anarchistic wrestling, one that happens without recourse to principle, one that takes place between the commandment and the one who must act in relation to it. No reason links the two. There is in this solitary coming to terms with the commandment a nongeneralizable moment that destroys the basis of law, one that is called forth by another law in the name of life and in the hope of a future for the living outside the shackles of coercion, guilt, and accountability that keep the legal status quo unchallenged. The destruction or annihilation of state power belongs neither to lawmaking nor to law-preserving violence. Although an epoch is founded through this abolition or revolutionary destruction of legal violence, no law is made from this place, and the destruction is not part of a new elaboration of positive law. Destruction has some odd permanence to it, and this makes sense if we consider that the anarchistic moment in any effort to come to terms with the commandment is one that destroys the basis of positive law. It also makes sense when we consider the theological sense of the messianic with which Benjamin himself is coming to terms in this essay, which not only informs the restricted sense of life we have been investigating but counters the Platonic reading of his understanding of the soul.

I would suggest that the anarchism or destruction that Benjamin refers to here is to be understood neither as another kind of political state nor as an alternative to positive law. Rather, it constantly recurs as the condition of positive law and as its necessary limit. It does not portend an epoch yet to come, but underlies legal violence of all kinds, constituting the potential for destruction that underwrites every act by which the subject is bound by law. For Benjamin, violence outside of positive law is figured as at once revolutionary and divine—it is, in his terms, pure, immediate, unalloyed. It borrows from the language in which Benjamin describes the general strike, the strike that brings an entire legal system to its knees. There is something speculative here when Benjamin claims that expiatory violence is not visible to men and that it is linked to eternal forms: the life in man that is identically present in earthly life, death, and afterlife. Reading "Critique of Violence" together with the "Theologico-Political Fragment,"[9] written at about the same time, we can discern claims worth careful consideration: first, that nothing historical can relate itself to the messianic; second, that this expiatory violence can be manifest in a true war or divine judgment of the multitude against a criminal (252).

At this point, there still seems to be cause for worry. Is Benjamin offering justification for a true war outside of all legality, or for the multitude to rise up and attack a criminal designated as such only by themselves? His final reference to a sacred execution would seem, as well, to conjure similar images of lawless masses rising up to do all sorts of physical violence in the name of some sacred power. Is this Benjamin riding "an antiparliamentary wave," one that brings him perilously close to fascism? Or does so-called sacred execution attack only the totalizing claims of positive law? He has already claimed that divine or sacred violence is not to be justified by a set of ends, though he seems to claim that a specific relation between the actor and the divine is stake in divine violence.[10]

So how do we interpret what he claims here? Benjamin does not call for violence, but rather suggests that destruction is already at work as the presupposition of positive law and, indeed, of life itself. The sacred does not designate what is eternal, unless we understand destruction itself as a kind of eternity. Moreover, the notion of the sacred invoked by Benjamin implies that destruction can have no end and that it is redeemed neither by lawmaking nor by a teleological history. In this sense, destruction is at once the anarchistic moment in which the appropriation of the commandment takes place *and* the strike against the positive legal system that shackles its subjects in lifeless guilt. It is also *messianic* in a rather precise sense.

In conclusion, then, let us consider the precise meaning of *destruction* in the messianic conception with which Benjamin is working. Consider first the claim from the "Fragment" that "in happiness all that is earthly seeks its downfall [*im Glück erstrebt alles Irdische seinen Untergang*]" (312–13). This downfall does not happen once, but continues to happen, is part of life itself, and may well constitute precisely what is sacred in life, that which is meant by "the soul of the living." For the Benjamin of the "Theologico-Political Fragment," the inner man, linked to ethical solicitude, is the site of messianic intensity. This makes sense if we keep in mind the solitary wrestling with the commandment that constitutes Benjamin's view of responsibility, one that remains radically distinct from, and opposed to, coerced obedience. The messianic intensity of the inner man is conditioned or brought about by suffering, understood as misfortune or fate. To suffer from fate is precisely not to be the cause of one's own suffering, is to suffer outside the context of guilt, as a consequence of accident or powers beyond one's control. When fate succeeds, however, in creating positive law, a significant transmutation of this meaning of fate ensues. The law wrought by fate succeeds in making the subject believe that he or she is responsible for her own suffering in life: in other words her suffering is the causal consequence of her actions. Fate inflicts a suffering that is then, through law, attributed to the subject as his or her own responsibility.

Of course, this is not to say that there is, or should be, no responsibility. On the contrary. But Benjamin's point is to show at least three interrelated points: (1) that responsibility has to be understood as a solitary, if anarchistic, form of wrestling with an ethical demand; (2) that coerced or forced obedience murders the soul and undermines the capacity of a person to come to terms with the ethical demand placed upon her; and (3) that the framework of legal accountability can neither address nor rectify the full conditions of human suffering. The suffering to which Benjamin refers is one that is coextensive with life, one that cannot be finally resolved within life, and one for which no adequate causal or teleological account can be given. There is no good reason for this suffering, and no good reason will appear in time. The messianic occurs precisely at this juncture, where downfall appears as eternal.

In the "Fragment," the perpetual downfall of human happiness establishes transience as eternal. This does not mean that there is only or always downfall, but only that the rhythm of transience is recurring and without end. What is called immortality corresponds, in his view, to "a worldly restitution that leads to the eternity of downfall, and the rhythm of this eternally transient worldly existence, transient in its totality, in its spatial but also its temporal totality, the rhythm of Messianic nature, is happiness" (313). Benjamin understands happiness to be derived from this understanding, this apprehension of the rhythm of transience. Indeed, the rhythmic dimension of suffering becomes the basis of the paradoxical form of happiness with which it is twinned. If the rhythm of the messianic is happiness, and the rhythm consists in an apprehension that all is bound to pass away, undergo its downfall, then this rhythm, the rhythm of transience itself, is eternal, and this rhythm is precisely what connects the inner life of the person, the person who suffers, with what is eternal. This seems to account for the restricted sense of life invoked by the commandment. It is not the opposite of "mere life," since transience surely characterizes mere life, but it is mere life grasped as the rhythm of transience. This provides a perspective counter to the view that life itself is sinful, that guilt must bind us to the law, and that law must therefore exercise a necessary violence on life.

There is, then, a kind of correlation between inner life and a suffering that is eternal, that is, unrestricted to the life of this or that person. The inner life, understood now as suffering, is also the nongeneralizable condition of wrestling with the commandment not to kill; even if the commandment is contravened, it must be suffered. This solitary wrestling and suffering is also the meaning of anarchism that motivates moves fatal to coercive law. Coercive law seeks to transform all suffering into fault, all misfortune into guilt. By extending accountability beyond its appropriate domain, however, positive law vanquishes life and its necessary transience, both its suffering and its happiness. It turns its subjects into wailing stones. If the positive law establishes a subject accountable for what she suffers, then the positive law produces a subject steeped in guilt, one who is compelled to take responsibility for misfortunes that are not of her own doing, or one who thinks that, by virtue of her will alone, she could put an end to suffering altogether. Whereas it is surely the case that humans cause harm to one another, not all of what any of us suffer can be traced to the actions of another. The expiation of the guilty subject through divine violence takes place when the self-centered notion of the subject as harmful cause is tempered and opposed by the realization of a suffering that no amount of prosecution can ever abate. This expiation unshackles the subject from the fugitive narcissism of guilt and promises to return the subject to life—not mere life, and not some eternal beyond, but life in this sense of its sacred transience. For transience to be eternal means that there will never be an end to transience and that perishing inflects the rhythm of all life. Benjamin thus does not defend life against death, but finds in death the rhythm, if not the happiness, of life, a happiness that requires an expiative release for the subject of guilt which would be the undoing of that subject itself, a decomposition of that rocklike existence.

In Benjamin's early writings on art, he refers to something called "critical violence," even "sublime violence," in the realm of the work of art.[11] What is living in the work of art moves *against* seduction and beauty. Only as a petrified remnant of life can art bespeak a certain truth. The obliteration of beauty requires the obliteration of semblance, which constitutes the beautiful, and the obliteration of guilt requires the obliteration of marks—so in the end both signs and marks must be arrested for the work of art to evince its truth. This truth is to take the form of language, of the word in the absolute sense (a view that proves problematic for understanding the visual field as distinct from the linguistic one). This word, in Benjamin's sense, gives organizational unity to what appears, although it does not itself appear; it constitutes an ideality embedded in the sphere of appearance as organizing structure.

In "Critique of Violence," the word is the commandment, the commandment not to kill, but this commandment can be received only if it is understood as a kind of ideality that organizes the sphere of appearance.[12] What is sacred in transience is not found outside that transience, but neither is it reducible to mere life. If the condition of "mere life" must be overcome by sacred transience, then it follows that mere life does not justify the commandment that proscribes killing. On the contrary, the commandment is addressed to that which is sacred and transient in human life, what Benjamin calls the rhythm of the messianic, which constitutes the basis of a noncoercive apprehension of human action. And though Benjamin claims that it cannot be the singularity of the body that stands in the way of killing, he does seem to suggest that the notion of an extra-moral transience allows for an apprehension of human suffering that exposes the limits of a notion of morality based on guilt, the metalepsis of moral causality that produces paralysis, self-beratement, and endless sorrow. And yet Benjamin seems to preserve something of endless sorrow from this account. After all, Niobe not only regrets what she has done but mourns what she has lost. Transience exceeds moral causality. As a result, Niobe's tears may provide a figure that allows us to understand the transition from mythic to divine violence.

Niobe boasted that she was more fecund than Leto, and so Leto sent Apollo to kill her seven sons. Niobe continued to boast, and Leto sent Artemis to kill her seven daughters, though some say that one daughter, Chloris, survived. Niobe's husband takes his life, and Artemis then turns Niobe into rock, but a rock from which tears stream eternally. One could say that Niobe caused her punishment, and that she is guilty of arrogant boasting. But the fact remains that it was Leto who thought up that punishment and ordered the murders of Niobe's children. It was, as well, Leto's children, Apollo and Artemis, who implemented her legal authority, thus constituting its legitimacy retroactively. Only with that punishment does law emerge, producing the guilty and punishable subject who effectively conceals and effects law-instating power. If divine violence is not involved in the making of law but mobilizes the messianic in its powers of expiation, then divine power would release the punished subject from guilt.

What would Niobe's expiation look like? Can we imagine? Would justice in this case require a conjecture, the opening up of the possibility of conjecture? We can imagine only that the rock would dissolve into water, and that her guilt would give way to endless tears. It would no longer be a question of what she did to deserve such a punishment, but of what system of punishment imposes such a violence upon her. We can imagine her rising up again to question the brutality of the law, and we can imagine her shedding the guilt of her arrogance in an angry refusal of the violent authority wielded against her and an endless grief for the loss of those lives. If that sorrow is endless, perhaps it is also perennial, even eternal, at which point it is her loss and also part of the "downfall" that links her loss to the rhythms of destruction that constitute what in life is sacred and what of life makes for happiness.

There remain many reasons to be suspicious of Benjamin's arguments in this early essay, since he does not tell us whether it is obligatory to oppose all legal violence, whether he would support certain forms of obligation that coercively restrain those in power from doing violence, and whether subjects should be obligated to the state in any way. Clearly he is not offering a plan for the future, but only another perspective on time. The essay ends on a note of destruction, but not transformation, and no future is elaborated. This does not mean, however, that there can be no future. Earlier he has noted that, for Sorel, the proletarian general strike engages a kind of violence that is, "as a pure means, . . . nonviolent." In explaining this, he writes, "for it takes place not in readiness to resume work following external concessions and this or that modification to working conditions, but in the determination to resume only a wholly transformed work, no longer enforced by the state, an upheaval [*ein Umsturz*] that this kind of strike not so much causes as consummates [*nicht so wohl veranlasst als vielmehr vollzieht*]" (246).

This consummating upheaval links the general strike with divine violence. The latter also breaks with modes of coercive enforcement and opens onto a sense of time that refuses teleological structure and prediction. Specifically, the messianic thwarts the teleological unfolding of time. (The messiah is that which will never appear in time.) The messianic brings about expiation, displacing guilt, retribution, and coercion with a broader conception of suffering in relation to an eternal or recurrent transience. In this sense, Benjamin's critique of legal violence compels us to suspend what we understand about life, loss, suffering, and happiness, to ask about the relationship between suffering, "downfall," and happiness, to see what access transience affords to what has sacred value, in order to oppose a deadening of life and a perpetuation of loss by means of state violence. Sacred transience could very well function as a principle that shows us what it is about mere life that is worth protecting against state violence. It might also suggest why the commandment "Thou shalt not kill" functions not as a theological basis for revolutionary action but as a nonteleological ground for the apprehension of life's value. When the suffering one undergoes becomes understood as a recurrent, even eternal rhythm of downfall, then it follows that one's own suffering might be dispersed into a recurrent rhythm of suffering, that one is afflicted no more and no less than any other, and that the first-person point of view might be decentered—dissipating both guilt and revenge. If this recurrent downfall gives life its rhythms of happiness, this would be a happiness that would in no sense be purely personal.

We can perhaps also discern in Benjamin's discussion the conditions of critique, since one must have already departed from the perspective of positive law to ask about and to oppose the violence by which it gains its legitimation and self-preserving power. The law legitimates the violence done in the name of the law, and violence becomes the way in which law instates and legitimates itself. This circle is broken when the subject throws off the shackles of law or finds them suddenly removed or undone, or when the multitude takes the place of the subject and refuses to implement the demands of law, wrestling with another commandment whose force is decidedly undespotic. The individual who struggles with the commandment is likened to the population that elects a general strike, since both refuse a certain coercion and, in the refusal, exercise a deliberative freedom that alone serves as the basis of human action. Benjamin notes that under the conditions of a rigorous general strike, especially when the military refuses to do its job, "the action diminishe[s] instances of actual violence" (247). Although we call a strike an "action" against the state, it is, as Werner Hamacher notes, an omission,[13] a failure to show, to comply, to endorse, and so to perpetuate the law of the state. If this refusal to act is itself violent, then it is directed against the imperative to act itself, a way of relieving the law of its power and force by refusing to instate it again and again, refusing the repetitions of implementation by which the law preserves and instates itself as law across time. The law can and will "go under," the law will have its "downfall," and that will link this action with the destruction of what has existed historically in the name of a new and different time—an "upheaval," as Benjamin remarks. To offer a critique is to interrupt and contravene law-preserving power, to withdraw one's compliance from the law, to occupy a provisional criminality that fails to preserve the law and thus undertakes its destruction. That Benjamin's essay ends so abruptly might be understood as a kind of sudden ending, the very operation of critique on the model of a destruction and upheaval that contravenes teleological time.

Imagine, if you can, that Apollo and Artemis tell their mother to get a grip and refuse to obey her command, or that the military, refusing to break up a strike, effectively goes on strike itself, lays down its weapons, opens the borders, refuses to man or close the checkpoints, all its members relieved of the guilt that keeps obedience and state violence in place, prompted rather to withhold their action by the memory and anticipation of too much sorrow and grief, and this—in the name of the living.

From Rosenzweig to Levinas
Philosophy of War

Stéphane Mosès

1

It seems that through the work of Franz Rosenzweig, and subsequently that of Emmanuel Levinas, the twentieth century has seen the birth of a radically new conception of ethics. It appeared against the horizon of the two great historical catastrophes that left their mark upon that century, the First World War, in the case of Rosenzweig, and in that of Levinas, the Second World War and the massive extermination of the Jews by Nazi Germany. Rosenzweig's generation experienced the First World War as the collapse of an age-old order bearing testimony to the stability of a European civilization that, wars and revolutions notwithstanding, had managed to guarantee a minimum of political equilibrium between nations and an appearance of civic tranquility in society, in which mankind seemed to occupy its natural place in the general harmony of the world. Rosenzweig's thought was born of that collapse. For him, the battlefields of 1914–18 marked not only the end of an old political order but also the ruin of any civilization founded, since the Greeks, on a belief in the capacity of the *Logos* to illuminate the ultimate rationality of the real. In his view, the entire Western philosophical tradition could be summed up in the affirmation that the world is intelligible, that it is ultimately transparent to reason, and that man himself only achieves his dignity to the degree that he is a part of that rational order. For Rosenzweig, it was precisely those two propositions that the First World War denied forever. Faced with the spectacle of the mad carnage to which the nations of Europe gave themselves over—the very nations that had embodied the philosophical ideal of a world ordered by the Logos—it was no longer possible to affirm that the real is rational or that in the light of reason original chaos is necessarily transformed into an intelligible cosmos. Moreover, the individual, who was supposed to blossom forth as an autonomous subject in a world regulated by reason, becomes, in a lethal logic instituted by warfare, a simple object of history, a negligible quantity, a faceless number, swept away despite himself into the whirlwind of battle, along with millions of others.

The Star of Redemption, conceived between 1916 and 1918 on the Balkan front and written between July 1918 and February 1919, opens with the evocation of an experience at the outer limits of the extreme: the anguished cry of the individual before the threat of imminent death. That cry expresses at once the instinctive revolt of man against the violence done to him (in this particular case, the violence of history), the affirmation of a basic, obvious truth: his irreducible identity as subject and the sudden collapse of all the philosophical constructions intended to make him forget the horror of death. It is at the moment when the individual, defined as a simple part of a whole, is threatened with annihilation that the subject awakens to the full consciousness of his uniqueness. This paradoxical reversal, in which the sudden illumination of the consciousness of man's mortal condition reveals to him the irrefutable reality of his personal existence, represents both the original experience from which Rosenzweig's thought emerged and the rhetorical figure that permanently subtends the unfolding of his system. That is what specifically initiates the very possibility of ethics, or more precisely, that is the point from which, beyond the violence that seems to make the very idea of ethics obsolete, the meta-ethical dimension of the subject emerges.

Forty years after the publication of The Star of Redemption, the preface to Totality and Infinity, which may be said to serve as the overture to the general themes of that work, begins with a meditation on war. War is seen as primal reality, casting doubt on classic philosophy's claim to found a universal morals. The homage Levinas pays to The Star of Redemption, "too often present in this book to be cited,"[1] confirms the impression produced by a comparative reading of the two texts. The preface to Totality and Infinity was conceived as a reworking, in a new historical and philosophical context, of the introduction to The Star of Redemption—prolonging it, echoing it, after the manner of a variation on the original theme.

What is philosophically common to these two openings is the critique of the idea of totality. The critique that is the starting point of The Star of Redemption has been reinterpreted and reformulated by Levinas as a radical overcoming of the system of being by the idea of the infinite. But the most remarkable thing about this parallel between the thought of Levinas and Rosenzweig is that in both cases the experience of war constitutes the horizon of a fundamental questioning of the whole Western philosophical tradition. Between these two experiences of historical violence, the 1914–18 war for Rosenzweig and the war of 1939–45 for Levinas, there are numerous analogies, but also something absolutely different. The Second World War, which from a historical point of view appears as the prolongation of the First and to a large extent as a direct consequence of it, is nevertheless radically different. Although the idea of "total war," that is, a war directed not only against opposing armies but equally against civil populations, was already in evidence in 1914–18, its systematic generalization dates from 1939–45. The main point is that the conflict of nationalisms, still characteristic of the First World War, gave way to confrontations between ideologies, or more precisely—in the case of national socialism—to the methodical application of an ideology aimed at the extermination of whole populations, first and foremost the Jewish people.

From this perspective, the Second World War not only involves, like the earlier war, the death of millions of individuals but also involves the systematic annihilation of human groups as such, and to a certain extent the putting into question of the very idea of humanity. That difference explains the difference of emphasis in the introduction to *The Star of Redemption* and the preface to *Totality and Infinity*, and in a more general way the difference between the philosophies of Rosenzweig and Levinas. While Rosenzweig still affirms the irreducible reality of the personal subject, that is, of the self (*das Selbst*) in the face of the tyranny of war, Levinas no longer believes in the possibility of any such individual resistance to the wave of historical violence, or even in its legitimacy. For Levinas, the subject's protest against the death that threatens it continues to bear witness to the vital egotism that stirs within all that seek to "persevere in being" and is the source of the war of each against all. As opposed to classic war, in which the revolt of the individual is sustained by the hope that he or she may be able to escape death, eliminative persecution makes every individual a potential victim, destined sooner or later for inevitable death. In this absolute forsakenness, there is for the self no beyond war; nor can there spring (as there could for Rosenzweig) the possibility of a meta-ethics from its anguished cry. That is why in Levinas the basis of ethics is not to be found in care for self but only in care for the other person. It is true that the idea of care for self is not absent from *Totality and Infinity*; it can be divined behind such notions as enjoyment, atheism, or separation, which refer back, as in Rosenzweig, to the "ipseity of the I,"[2] a first ipseity that will break apart with the absolutely new discovery of the transcendence of the other. But more originary than that primordial possession of self by self, its immemorial investment by the idea of the infinite carries it—from all eternity, so to speak—outside itself and assigns it to its responsibility for the other. On the "historial" horizon of total annihilation, the vision of ethics as it is still found in Rosenzweig—that is, as a second movement, as the rupture of a primordial egotism—appears anachronistic in relation to the revelation of a care for the other that is far more fundamental than care for self. Care for the other, to which, it seems, the last cries of many victims bore witness.

2

Rosenzweig's inaugural "speculative gesture" in the introduction to *The Star of Redemption* consists in the link he establishes between the world war and the crisis of Western ontology. This is not a simple analogy. The world war and the crisis of the philosophy of Being do not resemble one another; one is not the image of the other. Rosenzweig does not conceive of the history of philosophy as a war between different systems, nor of the war between nations as a confrontation between opposing metaphysical ideals. For him, the history of political events and the history of philosophy obey two distinct logics, and one cannot serve as an illustration for the other. But neither is this a causal link. Rosenzweig does not think that radical questioning of the metaphysics of Being waited for the world war to begin, nor does he think the war was due, even indirectly, to philosophical reasons. But beyond the empirical difference between the philosophical and the political, between theory and praxis, knowledge and action, the Western metaphysical tradition has always affirmed, according to Rosenzweig, the original identity of the rational and the real. That, for him, is the great secret hidden beneath the whole philosophical adventure "from Ionia to Jena," and that is what we must recall in a kind of anamnesis. There is, behind the history of Western metaphysics, an implicit axiom: the identity of being and totality. It is precisely that initial axiom that the preface of the *Star* sets out to question. Does the idea of being necessarily coincide with that of the one? Does experience not show us, on the contrary, that being reveals itself precisely in multiplicity and dispersion? And inversely, does the idea of totality necessarily involve that of being? Should we not, rather, see in this a purely conceptual synthesis of experiences that are on each occasion singular—the gathering of a multiplicity of concrete events into a common category? Moreover, is the being-one idea truly constitutive of human experience? Is it not, rather, a utopian category that would designate the limit or ultimate horizon of all our experience?

These questions eventually converge in an original interrogation concerning the place of man—qua person in each case unique—at the heart of the idea of totality. That idea aims to grasp phenomena in their generality, understanding them by integrating them into a network of rational explanations: in short, by enclosing them within one intelligible system. Thus, the specificity of each individual, the singularity of his destiny, the uniqueness of the events that make up his life, will be perceived as mirages of subjective consciousness, behind which rational knowledge will decipher the play of various constraints—biological, psychological, and social—that determine him despite himself. The uniqueness of the self is then dissolved in the totality of being, and the subject itself, stripped of its illusory singularity, will henceforth appear as but a simple element of the system enveloping it. That vision of being as absolute knowledge, the intelligible grouping of all particular phenomena, underlies, according to Rosenzweig, the entire history of Western philosophy, culminating in German idealism and finally triumphing in Hegel. In Hegel's system, the history of philosophy as ontology is at once concluded and realized in the identity of being, reason, and totality. The fact that in such a system the diversity of individual views is always unmasked as the illusions of a subjective conscience leads necessarily to a conception of morality as the submission of subjective aspirations to a more general system of laws. It is true that, in that subordination of particular interests to a higher order, free will is transcended and realized as rational freedom; but in this permanent movement toward greater generality, freedom does not cease denying itself in favor of the Law, so that ultimately the moral subject also finds realization in its identification with reason.

It is this eclipse of self in the totality of the Logos that Rosenzweig divines behind the general mobilization of individuals and their transformation into so many anonymous elements lost in the great machinery of war. In that, he is merely following the spirit of Hegel's philosophy, in which the dialectic of history is nothing but the dialectic of reason itself. But Rosenzweig's reading of that identity is the opposite of the one Hegel suggests. While for Hegel the historical process, through which the unfolding of the absolute is manifested, reveals the deep rationality that informs the universal spirit, Rosenzweig sets out from the empirical observation of the chaos into which Europe has been plunged and denounces the conception of reason to which that nameless catastrophe bears witness. Thus, it is on the basis of the spectacle of historical reality that Rosenzweig completely subverts the spirit of Hegel's philosophy, which represents for him, as we have seen, the last metamorphosis of the history of Western ontology.

In order to bring about this reversal, all he has to do is concentrate on the developments Hegel devotes to war in the last part of the *Philosophy of Right*. True, it is not a case of direct reference: Hegel's theory of war, alluded to in Rosenzweig's *Hegel and the State* in the context of the Hegelian vision of the state, is not explicitly quoted in the *Star*. But it is constantly present—negatively, so to speak—behind the analyses of the role of war in the "messianic politics" of modern nationalisms, especially behind the meditation on war and death with which the book begins. The revolt of the individual against the violence war inflicts on him, this central theme of the introduction to the *Star*, must be read as a response to the Hegelian metaphysics of war, as expressed in a passage from *The Phenomenology of Spirit*:

> In order not to let them become rooted and set in this isolation, thereby breaking up the whole and letting the [communal] spirit evaporate, government has from time to time to shake them to their core by war. By this means the government upsets their established order, and violates their right to independence, while the individuals who, absorbed in their own way of life, break loose from the whole and strive after the inviolable independence and security of the person, are made to feel in the task laid on them their lord and master, death. Spirit, by thus throwing into the melting-pot the stable existence of these systems, checks their tendency to fall away from the ethical order, and to be submerged in a [merely] natural existence; and it preserves and raises conscious self into freedom and its own power.[3]

For Hegel, the ethical vocation of the individual can be carried out only within ever more general communities to which he belongs: the family, the civil society, and the state.

When he is cut off from this context, which alone ties him to the universal, he falls back into a purely natural existence, that is, into his particularity, which is egotistical and therefore fundamentally amoral. From this point of view, war is the paroxysmal event in which the individual is called back, despite himself, to his ethical destination: "This relation and the recognition of it is therefore the individual's substantive duty, the duty to maintain this substantive individuality, i.e. the independence and sovereignty of the state, at the risk and the sacrifice of property and life."[4]

Now it is precisely the annulment of the self at the heart of the totality that, for Rosenzweig, ruins the very foundations of true ethics. In his view, ethics can only spring from a radical freedom, an original possession of self by self. The Hegelian deduction of ethics, in which the individual rises to ever-increasing generality, realizing himself finally in the renunciation of selfhood, defines him from the outset as a simple part of a whole, as an element, insignificant in himself, of a system that alone confers meaning and dignity on him. Against the horizon of war, this speculative construction falls apart. The imminence of a death that strikes at random, far from lifting the individual above himself, casts him down upon the most elementary affirmation of his physical existence. In relation to that foundational experience, in which "the compassionate lie of philosophy" is demystified once and for all,[5] ethics only becomes possible again after the vindication by the individual of his most personal existence, that is, his refusal to allow himself to be caught up in the system of the totality. Whereas in Hegel it is in war that the ethical destination of man is accomplished, for Rosenzweig it can only be revealed beyond war.

3

In the conceptual structure of *The Star of Redemption*, the emergence of ethics from the experience of the anguish of death, that is, the rupture of the totality, is only one step, though admittedly a primordial one, in a more essential process, which leads the ego (*das Selbst*) toward the discovery of the central experience of its history, revelation. Revelation will, in turn, lead it to the conclusion of its adventure, its new conception of life. The dual link of revelation with death, on the one hand, and life, on the other, explains the secret logic that commands the spiritual itinerary of the ego.

In the history of Rosenzweig's thought, the notion of an original subjectivity, positing itself outside the system of being, is prior to *The Star of Redemption* but not to the experience of war. It was in October 1917, on the Macedonian front, that this groundbreaking intuition came to him. A few weeks later, he developed its implications in a letter to a friend, in which he would later recognize the "original cell [*Urzelle*]" of *The Star of Redemption*. In it, the affirmation of the radical extraterritoriality of man with respect to the domain of Being corresponds to the interpretation of the Hegelian system as the consummation of philosophy, the definitive closure of the history of Western metaphysics.

> After it [reason] has thus taken up everything within itself and has proclaimed its exclusive existence, man suddenly discovers that he, though he has long been digested by philosophy, is still there. . . . "I, who am indeed dust and ashes." I, a completely common private subject, I with my first and last name, I dust and ashes, I am still there. And I philosophize, i.e., I have the insolence to think philosophy, that sovereign mistress of all.[6]

A few lines further on, Rosenzweig summarizes that intuition in the following formulation: "Man has a twofold relation to the Absolute, one where it has him, but still a second where he has *it*."[7] In the wake of Kierkegaard and Nietzsche, Rosenzweig subverts the Hegelian thesis of the end of philosophy from top to bottom. If everything has become philosophy, each individual should be able to begin philosophizing on his own. Against the background of the historical catastrophe of European civilization, it is this repossession of the subject by itself that the introduction to *The Star of Redemption* comes to proclaim.

It is the primordial autonomy of man as subject in his own right that Rosenzweig qualifies as "meta-ethical." This meta-ethical dimension refers back to the root of his ipseity, the original self-sufficiency of his identity. From this point of view, the primary foundation of the ego is in a sense beyond good and evil, an elementary affirmation of self preceding all morals, which Rosenzweig associates with the idea of an "intelligible character" in Kant,[8] that is, with an "anamnesis of the concept of freedom," setting out from which it will be possible to "discover the *nuevo mondo* of Revelation."[9] This meta-ethical root of the ego, characterized by an original form of perseverance in being, is illustrated in the history of Western culture by the hero of Greek tragedy. He represents for Rosenzweig man in his elementary separation, in his pure self-affirmation. Closed up in his tragic solitude, he does not succeed in truly communicating, either with other men or with the gods. In this sense, he incarnates the nexus of inviolable narcissism on which the identity of each of us rests. This faithfulness to oneself, this stubbornness of the ego in affirming itself in spite of everything, is very far from morality conceived of as a submission to the Law. Yet it appears in Rosenzweig to be the necessary condition for the inner revolution that will let man accede to true humanity.

This revolution, which parallels the one accomplished in the history of Western civilization by the passage from paganism to Judaism and then to Christianity, is accomplished when the meta-ethical ego breaks out of its elementary narcissism and opens itself to the double reality of the neighbor and God. The exit from self, which is preeminently a break from ipseity, a renunciation by the ego of self-sufficiency to the benefit of the other, is nonetheless simultaneously a measure of faithfulness to oneself, in which the originary separation of the ego is maintained. This is why the transformation of the tragic hero (that paradigmatic figure of the meta-ethical ego) into the man of revelation is presented as both radical conversion and expression of a profound continuity. In Rosenzweig's thought, accession to the world of revelation implies no renunciation of the pagan substructure of life. The latter is neither forgotten nor disowned, but remains present and legible beneath its obliteration. There remains, in the figure of the man of revelation, something heroic and quasi-Nietzschean: it is in the name of a radical freedom that he decides to give up his autonomy and submit to the call of the other. More generally, for Rosenzweig the order of revelation is dependent on the temporal order. "Life, all life, must first become wholly temporal, wholly alive, before it can become eternal life."[10]

In the conversion of meta-ethical man into the man of revelation, the elementary self is transformed into "I," a substantivized adverb into a speaker. Indeed, this is not a return to traditional morals but rather the discovery of a different conception of ethics, based on the structures of dialogical discourse. In the experience of revelation, as Rosenzweig lays it out in the central chapter of the second part of the *Star*, what was self becomes I, the subject of a discourse addressed to a Thou; but this I does not become itself except to the degree that, even before that first word, in an anteriority more anterior than all anteriority, it had been addressed as a Thou by another I.[11] There is, at the origin of this linguistic model of revelation, a fundamental asymmetry: the experience of the I is always preceded by that of the Thou, or to put it another way, the I does not become what it is except in response to the call of the Thou. That perennial anteriority of the other—"immemorial anteriority," Levinas will say—is inscribed in the very stuff of experience, since the moment self-consciousness is awakened, the others, those surrounding the ego, are already there (always there since forever). That is why the I is defined in Rosenzweig as an essential *heteronomy*. More precisely, the moment of revelation, the moment in which the meta-ethical ego is transformed into I, is exactly the moment it discovers its dependency upon a reality investing it from without. That reality, interpreted as the reality of God in the foundational experience that is revelation, immediately takes on the form of the other, the neighbor, as soon as the I, in the second moment of its constitution, turns toward the world. The truth is that the subordination of the I to God and its subordination to the other are two aspects of the same structure of experience. (Let us note in this connection that, in the analysis of the constitution of the divine identity in the Bible that Rosenzweig develops in the same passage, God himself only defines himself as I after man has been constituted as I opposite him.)

This fundamental asymmetry in the I-Thou relation, in which the Thou always precedes the I, translates, from the ethical point of view, into the subordination of the subject to the commandment. The commandment, independently of its specific content, signifies a shattering of human autonomy, the submission to an absolutely other who invests subjectivity from without. From this point of view, the commandment shatters the autonomy of the subject and deprives it of its freedom—or so it appears. But more profoundly, the I cannot face a radical exteriority unless it bears within itself the memory or trace of an original independence, precisely that of the meta-ethical ego. The relation of the I to the commandment is absolutely different from the relation of the autonomous subject to the moral Law in Kant's philosophy. In the first part of the *Star*, Rosenzweig criticizes Kant's ethics (and, more generally, the theory of ethics of German idealism) by showing that the freedom of the subject, believed to be accomplished by submission to the moral law, in reality disappears in the system of being, which alone confers upon it its supreme dignity. Through the dialectic of autonomy and the Law, it is in reality the impersonal principle of reason that, in a continuous process of emanation, takes possession of personal subjects and entirely absorbs them. Paradoxically, then, it is the relation of the heteronymous subject to the commandment, that is, to a word come from elsewhere, a word that constrains us to accomplish even the undesirable, that maintains it in its identity and its separation. That identity, prerequisite to all injunction and continuing to subsist after the injunction, is the identity of the meta-ethical ego, the elementary root of the I, sign of a primordial ipseity that still remains alive at the very moment when it is being radically put into question. Such is the primordial intuition on which *The Star of Redemption* is constructed: the authentic relation can only be established between beings necessarily separated beforehand. Here, in place of the movement of the procession of meaning by which, in idealism, the absolute pours forth into the particular, Rosenzweig sets in opposition the movement of conversion by which the same opens itself to the call of the absolutely other.

4

To a certain extent, the preface to *Totality and Infinity* takes up the meditation on war at the point where *The Star of Redemption* had left it. The whole conceptual edifice of the *Star* is constructed on the dissidence of the ego in relation to the system of the totality, or, if you will, on the possibility of the transcendence of the person in relation to the immanence of being. In other words, Rosenzweig's point of departure is the postulate according to which there can be a space of peace outside a totality entirely governed by war. That space of peace is that of the I, which the experience of revelation wrests from the grip of the system of being, and, looked at on the collective scale, that in which the Jewish people lives its religious existence beyond the tragedies of history. The question Levinas asks at the beginning of *Totality and Infinity* is then: Is the dissidence of the person in relation to the totality really possible? Is it not, as Hegel thought, an illusion of subjective consciousness? Specifically, must we not recognize the obvious and admit, again with Hegel, that war is the necessary law of relations between individuals, and consequently between nations and states? And if that is true, is morality not the ultimate naiveté? Indeed, war—the "exceptional state" par excellence—suspends morality for the sake of the immediate defense of each one's vital interests. That, writes Levinas, is why "War is not only one of the ordeals—the greatest—of which morality lives; it renders morality derisory."[12] War is, without doubt, the permanent state of humanity, and thus: "The art of foreseeing war and of winning it by every means—politics—is henceforth enjoined as the very exercise of reason. Politics is opposed to morality, as philosophy to naïveté."[13] Like Rosenzweig, Levinas here has as his reference point Hegel's political philosophy, but he follows its logic to the end. The unfolding of reason in history leaves nothing outside itself, and the ego's pretension to affirm itself as an exception *paralleling* the general system of Spirit is nothing but a chimera of subjective consciousness. In placing himself within the Hegelian logic, then, Levinas unmasks Rosenzweig's procedure as an illusion engendered by the ego's narcissism. The point is not, he writes, to set up an opposition between the experience of the totality and "the protestation of one person in the name of his personal egotism or even of his salvation. Such a proclamation of morality based on the pure subjectivism of the I is refuted by war, the totality it reveals, and the objective necessities."[14] In other words, at the time Levinas was writing *Totality and Infinity*, that is, fifteen years after the end of the Second World War, the obvious fact that no one could avoid getting caught up in war, and that individual protest would immediately be negated in the name of a collective logic that usually takes on the appearance of rationality, had long made the individual revolt championed by Rosenzweig obsolete.

Like Rosenzweig, Levinas turns to Hegel to interpret war as a metaphysical event that reveals the fundamentally agonistic essence of the real, and therefore of reason itself. But while for Rosenzweig the link between the experience of war and the idea of totality, even though it underlies the entire edifice of the *Star*, remains implicit, Levinas sees in war (war between consciousnesses, war between states) the very essence of Hegelian philosophy—in other words, the truth of ontology itself: "Being reveals itself as war to philosophical thought, . . . war affects it as the very patency, or the truth, of the real. . . . Harsh reality . . . harsh object-lesson, war is produced as the pure experience of pure being."[15] It is in this perspective that Levinas outlines, in the preface to *Totality and Infinity*, a phenomenology of war, in which the concrete experiences by which it is characterized are reduced to their essence. So it is with the experience of *general mobilization*, described as "a mobilization of absolutes, by an objective order from which there is no escape."[16] Similarly, the suspension of individual freedom in a society at war corresponds to a vision of being as absolute determinism, of freedom as knowledge of necessity, and of man as "a part of nature": "The visage of being that shows itself in war is fixed in the concept of totality, which dominates Western philosophy. Individuals are reduced to being bearers of forces that command them unbeknownst to themselves."[17] Indeed, in Levinas the notion of totality designates a vision of man perceived essentially as an object of knowledge, like a phenomenon given to our observation, which is to be made intelligible by reducing its apparent uniqueness to the result of a combination of various causal series. Indeed, man can be perceived from two radically opposed points of view: one quantitative, in which he appears to be an undifferentiated element in a measurable manifold, as a barely perceivable unit in a mass that obeys its own laws; the other qualitative, in which he emerges, *without context*, as a unique and irreplaceable person. The second point of view is the only one that permits the founding of an ethics, in that it focuses attention on the uniqueness and singularity of each man as a being endowed with freedom and responsibility.

The question, for Levinas as for Rosenzweig, is then the following: How can we exit the totality? Is there a place beyond being, a place thought can identify and speech describe, a place of pure transcendence, in which man can signify outside all context? For Rosenzweig, as we have seen, this place of extra-territoriality is the ego, the subject anchored in the affirmation of its irreducible singularity. It is precisely this attempt to recommence philosophy setting out from the pure experience of the ego that Levinas rejects. His inaugural "speculative gesture" does not, however, consist in refuting Rosenzweig's procedure, but rather in radicalizing it, which he does by thinking the idea of totality through to the end. Totality, in the very logic of Hegel's logic, cannot leave outside itself the existence of a supposedly autonomous ego. Despite all its vehemence, the existential protest of the ego, the desperate affirmation of its desire to live, bears witness, ultimately, to a naïve egotism, an unawareness of the necessary laws governing the real. As opposed to Rosenzweig, Levinas seems to agree with Hegel in thinking that the universality of reason transcends the point of view of the individual ego. *Totality and Infinity*, Levinas writes, "does present itself as a defense of subjectivity, but it will apprehend subjectivity not at the level of its purely egoist protestation against totality, nor in its anguish before death."[18] Hence the completely radical reversal of perspective Levinas carries out in relation to Rosenzweig. There is, exterior to the system of totality, no place for any substance whatsoever, *except for exteriority itself*. There is, in fact, something that infinitely exceeds the idea of an all-encompassing totality in which all differences, all particularities (whatever their place in the hierarchy of the system), are ultimately absorbed into the identity of the same: namely, the notion of a pure exteriority itself. It is this exteriority that Levinas, inspired by a famous passage by Descartes in the *Meditations*, calls the idea of the infinite. In the context of the *Meditations*, what Descartes has in mind is that if I, a finite creature, am capable of thinking the idea of the infinite, that is because it was placed within me by a truly infinite being. What Levinas retains of this reasoning is the idea according to which thought is capable of thinking "beyond what is capable of being contained in the finitude of the *cogito*."[19]

But for Levinas, the idea of the infinite is not graspable as such; it is not a theme given to thought. Precisely because by its very definition it surpasses all thought, it gives itself only indirectly, in a roundabout way or a displacement, in which it shows itself, as if by metonymy, through a lived experience: that of the revelation of the exteriority of others. The other man, in his radical exteriority, is imposed upon me as the unintegrable itself, as the one who cannot be reduced to one element among others in the totality of which I am a part. The place outside the system of being, and setting out from which the notion of totality itself loses its meaning, is not the ego: it is the other. The situation in which the totality breaks up is that in which "the gleam of exteriority or of transcendence in the face of the Other" is revealed.[20]

But even in *Totality and Infinity*, in which ethics is still described in terms of encounter and the face-to-face, that is, against the background of a metaphysics of presence, the uniqueness of the person as the locus of transcendence in relation to the system of being is no longer, as in Rosenzweig, that of the ego, but that of the other. For Levinas, the radical questioning of Western ontology implies the repudiation of the concept of the ego in which Rosenzweig still believed: the ego that, according to Pascal's expression, quoted at the beginning of *Otherwise than Being*, demands its "place in the sun." Levinas's implicit denunciation of the meta-ethical ego in Rosenzweig, qualified as a "impotent subjectivism" in which "the protest of a person in the name of his personal egotism or even his salvation" is expressed,[21] marks the distance separating the crisis of Western civilization—whose downfall was presaged by the First World War and consummated during the Second—from *the collapse of the idea of humanity* as Europe had conceived it.

—*Translated by Michael B. Smith*

Levinas, Spinoza, and the Theologico-Political Meaning of Scripture

Hent de Vries

At intervals of about ten years, Levinas devoted articles to Spinoza.[1] At first glance, these readings stand out for their critical, indeed, polemical tone. In his 1955 "The Case of Spinoza," Levinas accepts Jacob Gordin's summary verdict: "Spinoza was guilty of betrayal [*il existe une trahison de Spinoza*]" (108 / 155–56). Indeed, in this text we find an even more startling hypothesis, that, by "proposing that Spinoza's trial be reopened," Israel's founding father, David Ben-Gurion, was, Levinas surmises, "seeking to question—more effectively than the missionaries installed in Israel—the great certainty of our history; which ultimately, for Mr. Ben-Gurion himself, preserved a nation to love and the opportunity to build a State" (110 / 157).

Levinas gives as the main reason for his condemnation that Spinoza sought to overcome Judaism with Christianity, then Christianity with a philosophical wisdom considered to represent the proper—that is, the intellectual—love of God. Spinoza thus ascribes no more than a transitory role to Judaism in the general economy of being, even while retaining a quasi-permanent role for "religion [*religio*]," more precisely, piety, in the form of obedience and charity.

But in the same articles the harsh judgment about Spinoza's "betrayal" is mitigated and qualified in importantly nuanced ways, to the extent that Levinas praises Spinoza's writings, especially the *Theologico-Political Treatise* and the *Ethics* (despite their major blind spot in a probable ignorance of rabbinic literature, especially the Talmud), for their remarkable, albeit largely latent, "anti-Spinozism." It is this "anti-Spinozism" that Levinas, relying on Sylvain Zac's *Spinoza and the Interpretation of Scripture*,[2] seeks to bring out. In Spinoza, the argument goes, Spinozism and anti-Spinozism keep each other, if not in balance, then at least in a necessary relation of partial correction. This, I would like to suggest, by implication, inversion, and simple extension gives Levinas's anti-Spinoz-ism—the metaphysical position with which he is most often identified—a remarkable element of Spinozism, as well. Here I would like to bring out this intellectual horizon and ethical aim, which is characterized by what Levinas comes to call "interiorization." Specifically, I will ask whether or to what extent this horizon and ethical interiorization presuppose an interrogation of the theologico-political or, what amounts to the same here, of the theologico-political meaning of Scripture.

I am fully aware that the textual basis for such a comparison or confrontation is extremely limited. Extensive and explicit discussion of Spinoza's scriptural and directly metaphysical writings—let alone of his smaller treatises or letters—is almost entirely ab-sent from Levinas's major works. Exceptions are his remark, in his 1961 magnum opus, *Totality and Infinity*, that the thought of the other is "at the antipodes with Spinozism" and his adoption and extension, in his second major work, *Otherwise than Being or Beyond Essence*, published in 1973, of one of Spinoza's most important concepts, the *conatus essendi*. Taken to its extreme, the *conatus* is used there to express a deplorable and inevita-ble ontological truth, namely, the bad positivity and negatively valorized plenitude of being and its self-centered interest as such. Spinoza, Levinas writes, is the "philosopher of being, of being explaining itself by its unfolding," or again, for Spinoza:

> The divinity of being or nature consists in the pure positivity of *esse*, in the very strength of its being, which expresses itself in the deductive engendering of *natura naturata*. This is an unsurpassable force or rationality, for there is nothing beyond that positivity and that *conatus*, no value in the sense of a surpassing of being by the good; it is a totality without *beyond*, affirmed perhaps more deeply than in Nietzsche himself—a totality that is but another name for the non-clandestineness of being, or for its intelligibility, in which inner and outer coincide.[3]

Indeed, Levinas's whole later thought seems increasingly organized around a critique of Western ontology, egology, and all philosophies of the "Neuter," which he sees as premised upon and culminating in this peculiar Spinozistic affirmation of the striving or desire (the *conatus* or *appetitus*) of all things, whether living or inanimate, to persist in their being. One of the central axioms underlying the edifice of the *Ethics* formulates this assumption succinctly: "The striving by which each being strives to persevere in its being is nothing but the actual essence of the thing" (part III, proposition 7). No further dem-onstration or deduction of this claim is ever given, either in Spinoza or in Levinas, though its metaphysical, epistemological, ethical, and aesthetic implications are spelled out at great length, as the *conatus* comes to express the totality, identity, indeed, sameness that are supposedly involved in the very idea of being and its conceptual schemes, in its lin-guistic structures and language games, in its forms of life and pursuit of economic interests, in the maximization of pleasure, and in cultural and aesthetic expression no less than in the discursive formation of institutional power (of science, medicine, the state, etc.).

Surely there could be no difference greater than the one between the encompassing Spinozistic definition of desire as perseverance for all individual beings (indeed, of *esse* as *interesse*, as Levinas repeatedly says) and the specifically Levinasian idea of infinitizing desire as the enigma of *disinterestedness* revealing itself in human passivity (rather than in what Spinoza calls "active affects")? Is the comparison not simply implausible, because Levinas leaves no doubt that—since the primary basis of understanding between Judaism, Christianity, and Islam can be found in "the Reason that the Greek philosophers revealed to the world"—there remains every reason to believe that "we still have more chance of finding an unsullied [*sans mélange*] rationalism in Plato and Aristotle than in Spinoza" (109 / 157)? Is our attempt to read Levinas and Spinoza together not from the outset doomed to fail? Yes and no.

Even when the early articles from which I take my lead are read through the lens of the mature works, Levinas's assessment of Spinoza's betrayal and his condensation of Western philosophy's single essential tendency demonstrates a subtle appreciation of a central ambiguity in this author's intellectual and theologico-political undertaking as a whole. This interpretation of Spinoza reveals, for Levinas, a structural ambivalence in philosophy in general, just as, Levinas writes, "in the context of today's French anti-humanism, as in that of Brunschvicq's humanist idealism of the recent past, [Spinoza] expresses philosophy's truth."[4] The ambivalence of this truth, Levinas suggests, becomes nowhere clearer than in philosophy's problematic—more precisely, unappeasable—relation to Scripture, on the one hand, and to the ordering of the political, on the other. For Spinoza as for Levinas, these two domains are inseparable. The interpretation of Scripture yields a theologico-political meaning. The political and politics find their meaning—their hermeneutic model, as it were—in Scripture.

More than a difference in nuance between Levinas's overall critique of Spinoza's ontology (i.e., his understanding of God and Nature as the geometrically structured system of an infinite chain of causes, i.e., of infinite modalizations of infinite attributes) and his appreciation of this author's biblical criticism in the *Theologico-Political Treatise* is at stake in the confrontation that interests me here. In fact, Levinas's critique and appreciation of Spinoza do not exclude but rather imply each other, for reasons that I will spell out.

But what leeway could Levinas's appreciation of Spinoza's theologico-political understanding of Scripture offer for a careful reconsideration of his apparent all-out condemnation of this thinker's larger metaphysical project, as encapsulated in the *conatus essendi*? What would it mean to read Spinoza—and, by implication or retroactively, perhaps, also Levinas—against the grain *at this specific point*? To answer this question, we must take a step back and reconstruct the precise elements and general thrust of Levinas's analysis. Speaking of the *Theologico-Political Treatise*, Levinas writes:

Within the history of ideas, [Spinoza] subordinated the truth of Judaism to the revelation of the New Testament. The latter is of course surpassed by the intellectual love of God, but Western being involves this Christian experience, even if it is only a stage.

Henceforth we cannot ignore the harmful [*néfaste*] role Spinoza played in the decomposition of the Jewish intelligentsia, even if for its representatives, as for Spinoza himself, Christianity is only a penultimate truth, and the adoration of God in spirit and in truth must still surmount Christianity. . . . It was by prefiguring Jesus with Judaism that Spinozism managed to introduce [or accomplish, *accomplir*] a movement into [or in] irreligious Judaism which, when it was religious, it opposed for seventeen centuries. How many Jewish intellectuals detached from all religious belief [*croyance*] do not regard the figure of Jesus as fulfilling the teaching of the prophets, even if this figure or these teachings are succeeded in their minds by the French Revolution or Marxism? For a Léon Brunschvicg, whose memory we venerate, or a Jankélévitch, whom we admire, a quotation from the New Testament is much more familiar than one from the Old Testament, and it is often the former that illuminates the latter. . . .

Thanks to the rationalism patronized by Spinoza, Christianity is surreptitiously triumphing, bringing conversion without the scandal of apostasy! (108 / 155–56)

In other words, "Western being," in its philosophical concept, represented here by these political ideas and thinkers, does not involve Jewish experience (albeit as a stage) in the same way as it does Christianity, given the emphasis placed on acknowledging the Gospels as "an inevitable stage on the road to truth" (108 / 155). To avoid this "mixture [*mélange*]" (cf. 109 / 157) of philosophical reason and Christian "atmosphere" (109 / 156), one would, we have seen, need to return to Plato and Aristotle rather than Spinoza. Rather than presenting a "cryptogram" (111 / 158) in which philosophy enters into mortal combat with religion *in obliquo* or *a tergo* (i.e., secretly and indirectly), as Leo Strauss suggests in his influential interpretation of the *Theologico-Political Treatise*, Spinoza, in Levinas's reading, amalgamates reason and revelation—especially in its Christian articulation—*far too much*. This is the treacherous and, it would seem, *un*-Spinozistic or even anti-Judaic moment in Spinoza, which is not to be confused with the positive, anti-Spinozistic element on which Levinas chooses to dwell at greater length. Interestingly, and in close proximity to and distance from Heidegger's diagnosis of the onto-theological constitution of Western metaphysics, the moment that amalgamates reason and revelation (as a wooden iron, of sorts) foregoes philosophy's truth (the *conatus essendi*), whose relentless self-satisfaction Levinas exposes to its ultimate limitation (which is not so much religious as ethical, an "otherwise than being and essence"). Both this un-Spinozistic moment and the anti-Spinozistic element operate side by side, but do not sit very well with the Spinozism of the overall rationalist project, which, Levinas agrees with Zac, should not be confused with the inauguration of the historical critique of Scripture for which the

Theologico-Political Treatise has become known. The invention of the "higher criticism" was not Spinoza's primary intention. As Levinas notes: "The idea of applying a historical method to the Bible is . . . born from a concern to protect true philosophy [*la vraie philosophie*] in the City, just as America was discovered by navigators who were expecting to reach the East Indies" (112 / 160). But this derivative method restores Scripture to its proper rights and becomes the key to reading—if not necessarily explaining ("in terms of cause")—the political text and texture from biblical times up to the emergence of early modern nation states.

Spinoza's un-Spinozistic solution of amalgamating reason and revelation, along with its legacy, differs from Franz Rosenzweig's (to which Levinas refers approvingly) in that it leaves intact no separate, parallel, and compatible path to salvation for Judaism. Unlike Rosenzweig, in Levinas's reading, Spinoza conceives of "eternity" only in the most abstract terms—terms that are theoretical and atemporal rather than ritual, calendrical, or cyclical. But then, like Rosenzweig, "whose homage to Christianity consists in showing it a different destiny than the one Judaism accomplishes all the way to the end" (109 / 156), Spinoza develops a position far removed from Hegel's sublation of *all* religion as merely a transitional dialectical moment in the self-unfolding of reason. Spinoza's *modernity*, Levinas surmises, lies in what amounts to a profoundly anti-Hegelian stance, even though his historical and contemporary—read systematic-philosophical—importance reveals a profound ambivalence as well:

> In our day, the history of ideas is the godless theology that stirs the soul of unbelievers. . . . Spinoza exerted an influence on this history of ideas that was decisive and anti-Jewish.
>
> It does not have to do with biblical criticism, which he inaugurated. Biblical criticism can ruin only a faith that has already been shaken [*ébranlée*]. Does not the truth of eternal ideas shine forth all the more when they are denied the external support of a dramatic and theatrical revelation? When they are studied for themselves, do they not bear witness to the divine value of their inspiration and the purely spiritual miracle of their union? This miracle is all the more miraculous the more we are dealing with numerous and disparate fragments, a marvel that is all the more marvelous to the extent that rabbinic study develops a form of teaching that tallies with it. (107 / 154)

The all the more miraculous miracle of Spinoza's genius—not necessarily of Spinozism, but of its correlative, parallel, perhaps constitutive, "anti-Spinozism," which is not to be confused with its un-Spinozistic "treason"—is that two possibilities (more precisely, two necessities), two paths of life, of (Jewish) religion (and, as we shall see, indirectly, of philosophy), are acknowledged in his writing, however obliquely. Levinas leaves no doubt that these two paths, which are also two methods, are not given equal privilege by Spinoza or by most of the traditions on whose shoulders he stands or that stand on his shoulders in turn.

What, then, is treacherously "anti-Jewish" in Spinoza? Is it the occasional Greek-Christian amalgamation of reason and New Testament doctrine, notably the views of Jesus and Paul—"none of the Apostles did more philosophizing than Paul" (*Theologico-Political Treatise*, chap. 11)—and hence the mixing of ontology and onto-theology, the political and the theologico-political (an amalgamation that would, on close scrutiny, contradict Spinoza's own hermeneutic principle of *sola scriptura*)? If so, what remains of Levinas's appreciation of the *Theologico-Political Treatise*'s perceived modernism and its central scriptural and, more indirectly, philosophical claim (namely, the necessity of limiting the claim that philosophy can bring to bear upon Scripture and, through it, upon the political)? Or is Spinoza's un-Spinozistic moment the forgetfulness—or rather "ignorance"—of the rabbinic written and oral tradition, of the Talmud, a forgetfulness that Levinas suggests, basing himself on the historical research of van Dias and van der Tak, may already have taken root in the Jewish community of Amsterdam well before Spinoza's excommunication? If this is so, is there in Spinoza's writings any single philosophical, ethical, theological, or political statement or idea (that is to say, any definition, axiom, proposition, demonstration, etc.) that Levinas should consider untrue or, rather, "inadequate" (to use the terminology so often deployed by both authors, albeit it with such different connotations and, perhaps, ulterior aims)?

As we have seen, Levinas (and Zac) do not consider the historical critique of Scripture, for all its historicist-naturalist reductionism—that is, its presuming to offer a genetic philology without philosophy—to have been "Spinoza's fundamental project" (111 / 159). The fundamental project is, instead, to protect the freedom of thought in the commonwealth and thereby to ensure the commonwealth's integrity and stability, in turn. This aim, paradoxically, yields a secondary result, namely, insight into how the text and texture of the state must be read. Genetic philology doesn't equal archeology, let alone causal explanation, but entails an altogether different hermeneutics of its own:

> The neutrality of the Scriptures with regard to philosophy presupposes the possibility of interpreting *Scripture through Scripture*. To prove the truth of a text, one must make it accord with reality [*réel*]; to understand its significance [*signification*], it suffices to have it accord with itself. By right, certainly, everything human [*tout l'humain*] is explained by Nature—that is, through causes. But before explicating ideas, one can understand them as significations: "Spinoza's great discovery consists in showing that, in order to understand the exact meaning [*sens*] of the ideas contained in the sacred texts, we can use a method that is as rigorous as the method of learned men, without seeking to explicate things in terms of causes."[5]

In so doing, Spinoza, having denying Judaism—that is to say, rabbinicism and Talmud—the place it is due, nonetheless grants its irreducibility to categories of the Western spirit, whether Greek or modern, and hence guarantees it an independence of sorts. True, Levinas continues, the "colligation of literary facts" on which Spinoza's biblical hermeneutics is based (in full accord with Bacon's method for the "intellection of natural facts") may seem to lack "an anticipatory project of the whole" (113 / 161), without which such textual data and strata, at first glance, would seem to make no sense. On closer scrutiny, this ascetic withholding of the larger metaphysical project may, paradoxically, open up a philosophical path in its own right: the interpretation of signs, that is to say, of good theologico-political sense. In the *Theologico-Political Treatise,* as Levinas reads it: "Spinoza thinks that a discourse can be understood without the vision of the truths enlightening it. But isolating the fundamental significations of an experience while practicing an 'epochē' in relation to its truth involved indicating one of the paths upon which philosophy may embark, even after the end of speculative dogmatisms" (113 / 161).

What is least plausible in Spinoza's engagement with the biblical text—his withholding of the philosophical totality implied in his very undertaking—is precisely what renders it most promising and significant, for not only "religious philosophy, but . . . all philosophy." It is with this procedure that he makes place, "in the life of the Spirit," for what Levinas calls "'prophetic' light." Prophecy speaks in its own voice—and does so, as Spinoza says, "without irony," as the "Word of God"—"next [*à côté*]" to that of reason, which, for its part, must cast its "natural light" on seemingly contingent things and events. Religion is thus a category "*sui generis*" just as much as it forms part of a larger scheme (113 / 161). This is the dual-aspect character of all there is and all there is to say:

> Of course, Spinoza does believe that the Word of God ultimately comes from the nature of God and if one understood this nature, wisdom and the future would derive from it in a rigorously determinist way. But in the complexity of things, this future cannot be known philosophically. . . . Since the impenetrable complexity of things is not contingent, the Word is not dedicated to the silence of the day in which "everything will be clear." (113 / 161)

The lack of conceptual rigor for which the expression the "Word of God"—to be distinguished, though it is not numerically or ontologically distinct, from the metaphysical idea (existence and essence) of God or Nature—stands can, by Spinoza's own account, not be provisional, that is to say, temporal. Hence the noise of biblical language will not cede to the silence of the philosophical concept. Already in Spinoza, who in this differed from many of his contemporaries, there is, Levinas says, "a way of reading the Bible that comes down to listening to the Word of God. This manner remains irreplaceable in spite of the privileges to be gained by philosophy (that is to say, Spinozism)" (117 / 168).

Furthermore, Spinoza's alleged betrayal hardly squares with Levinas's no less emphatic claim that the *Ethics*—in what Stuart Hampshire calls its metaphysical "dual-aspect" view of reality [6]—assumes, in the name of rationalism, a "freedom of spirit," which is co-extensive rather than amalgamated with the very ethical interiority Levinas seeks to bring out. Indeed, it is as if Athens and Jerusalem were neither opposed nor confused, but oscillate and alternate in an elective affinity that allows them to make common cause in purging superstition and idolatry:

> It is to reason that Spinoza's work offers supreme and certainly approving homage. It is ultimately the interiority of rational relations, and their equivalence to the highest forms of life, that are illuminated by the *Ethics*. Judaism cannot separate itself off from this, just as it cannot turn its back on mathematics; it cannot remain disinterested in democracy and social problems, any more than it can choose to ignore the injuries man and things inflict on man in favor of intelligible relations, such as dialogue, gentleness and peace. Beyond its credo and its ritualism, Judaism in its entirety, by means of its faith and its practices, has perhaps sought only to bring an end to mythologies and the violence they exert on reason and perpetuate in customs.
>
> Rationalism does not menace the Jewish faith. (107 / 153)

Where, then, lies the opposition between Levinas's and Spinoza's projects, if their principal disagreement is not primarily theoretical, philosophical, theological, or metaphysical—and, we should add, if their agreement in a few remarkable points is, indeed, *near total*? How could Spinoza's metaphysical monism and Levinas's ontological pluralism (which, like the Spinozistic affirmation of the univocity of being, is not based upon any dualism or upon an analogical representation of the relationship between infinite and finite being) reveal any convergence, parallelism, or compatibility, let alone find a shared ground? Put differently, how could a broadly conceived causal determinism and a narrowly defined indeterminism—in short, a philosophy of immanence and a thinking of transcendence, the affirmation of positive, active affects or emotions versus the suffering of an ever more patient passivity—make common cause at any point at all?

As Jean-François Rey insightfully writes: "Far from opposing ethics and morality, as Deleuze proposes, Levinas wants to see in the spinozist enterprise of desacralization and de-theologization an 'ethical interiorization.'"[7] As Levinas himself formulates it: "Through [*à travers*] the multiple authors whom the historical method discovers in sacred texts, the Word of God invites men to obey the teachings of justice and charity. Through [*à travers*] historical criticism of the Bible, Spinoza teaches us its ethical interiorization" (117 / 168–69).

But is this to suggest that there is, after all, an elective affinity between the extreme rationalism and rational mysticism of the second and especially third kinds of knowledge (*ratio* and *scientia intuitiva*) of which the *Ethics* and the *Treatise on the Emendation of the Intellect* speak so compellingly, on the one hand, and the equally relentless rationalism of Levinas's own conception of ethical metaphysics, with its increasing emphasis on infinitizing desire and saintliness, on the other? Does the reference to "ethical interiorization" simply mean that Levinas's insistence on philosophy's scriptural (more precisely, rabbinic and Talmudic) counterpart and its exegesis or hermeneutics—even within the terms laid out by Spinoza's treatise—is characterized by a universality, interiority, and hence rationality of its own? This is what Levinas, with Zac, seems to suggest: "Without opening onto [*déboucher sur*] Spinozism, without being 'of the order of reason in the philosophical sense of the word,'[8] these truths [i.e., the "eternal truths of faith"] involve an interiority of their own." In short, it has a nonphilosophical intelligibility, "a religious liberalism, but without philosophy" (114 / 163). Is this interiority and intelligibility—indeed, liberalism—already implied and acknowledged in Spinoza's use, in the *Theologico-Political Treatise*, of the formulations the "Word of God" and, in the *Ethics*, "piety," both of which call for "obedience" and "charity" and entail no more than a "minimal creed"? Finally, do these two possible perspectives—the dual aspects of the philosophical or theoretical, on the one hand, and the scriptural, practical, and, as we shall see, theologico-political, on the other (to which both Spinoza and Levinas seem deeply committed), constitute a real alternative?

Indeed, what *is* the difference between the epistemic truth that adequate, philosophical knowledge conveys and the nonepistemic, moral "*sui generis* certitude" (113 / 161) that Spinoza reserves for faith? The latter, Levinas comments, is a "subjective certainty, a risk, but 'the customs [*l'usage*] of life and society oblige us to give our consent to a large number of things that we cannot demonstrate.' The moral word thus has a special rank [*statut*], placed beside speculation and above the realm that falls to imagination" (115 / 164).

There is no simple answer to these questions. At one point Levinas writes that "the motives for obedience are not of a *rational order*. They are motives of an affective order, such as fear, hope, fidelity, respect, veneration, and love" (114 / 163). In this reading, Scripture's many—and often seemingly incomparable—motifs motivate in a way different from adequate ideas and deductive reasoning (and, ultimately, the third kind of knowledge, or intellectual love of God). More precisely, they move, mobilize, set in movement (as ideas and intuitive science would not). And yet, Levinas claims following Zac, they do not resort to the laws of "vague experience," but have a separate status as a fourth kind of knowledge, of sorts, irreducible to imagination, ratiocination, and intuition:

> What counts is the difference between those who regard the Scriptures, even if they are judged to be inspired or naïve, as a text like any other, and those who regard them, in spite of the traces they retain of their evolution, as an essential form of the spirit, irreducible to perception, philosophy, literature, art, science, or history, yet compatible with political and scientific freedom. Although incapable of being transmitted *more geometrico*, the Word of God, which is religion and not merely wisdom, can be presented as agreeing with philosophy. . . . In that lies not its inconsistency but its originality and its universality, its independence in the face of the order that

philosophy declares to be final and where it claims to reign without division [or sharing, *partage*]. This gives it its power to survive at the end of philosophy. . . . Spinoza—while substituting, in the *Ethics*, a philosophy for the religion of the Bible— was careful to retain in this philosophy the incontestable plenitude of the Scriptures. Spinozism was one of the first philosophies in which absolute thought also tried to be an absolute religion. (117 / 167–68)

Formally, but—as Deleuze says in his commentaries on Spinoza—*not numerically distinct*, philosophy and religion are thus considered to be two complementary, parallel sides of one and the same phenomenon, which is the quest for the *vera vita*, the true way of life, in other words, a spirituality that has nothing ethereal but is deeply steeped in affect and thereby, perhaps, betrays its "difficult freedom." Yet what the parallelism suggests, Levinas goes on to say, is that, in the final analysis, it is already implicit in Spinoza's own account that:

Philosophy does not engender itself. To philosophize is to move toward the point where one sees the light as it illuminates the first meanings, which nonetheless already have a past. What Spinoza called the Word of God projects this clarity and carries language itself. The biblical commandments concerning justice are no longer a sublime stammering to which a wisdom transmitted *more geometrico* would restore absolute expression and context. They lend an original meaning to being. (118 / 169)

Irreducible, the scriptural commandments are no less constitutive of being—including the being that we are—than the causal nexus among bodies or among ideas that Spinoza postulates as much as he deduces in axioms and definitions of his supposedly fully deterministic system. Starting out from the doctrine of the univocity of being, of which Duns Scotus (as Deleuze reminds us) was the most original defender—and whose presuppositions Levinas by and large accepts in his negative evaluation of the telos of Western being in its totality and "essance"—Spinoza's system does not fully realize its wider implications. Yet in its acknowledgment of Scripture and the "minimal creed"—the "Word of God"—it signals exteriority, or, what comes down the same, "ethical interiority," *from within*.

This is not to forget that Levinas believed Spinoza to be ignorant of Talmudic modes of reasoning, which do not model truth according to the fixed laws of Nature but, on the contrary, presuppose a continuing discussion, a production of sense and hence of revelation (in analogy with the *creatio continua* of which Christians—up to Descartes and the occasionalists—continued to speak). In his response to Richard McKeon, Levinas insists that "even though he knew medieval Jewish philosophy and certain Kabbalistic writings perfectly, Spinoza had had no direct contact with the pre-medieval work of the Talmud."[9] And yet, Levinas continues, it is quite possible that:

This contact, moreover, could already have been broken in the community itself in which he was born, where the ideas, customs and preoccupations of Marranism were still very vivid memories, and interest in the Kabbalah and eschatological waiting were prevailing over the attraction that the advanced dialectic of the Talmud and rabbinical discussion had to exercise. . . .

. . . . This is significant beyond its biographical importance. In the critique that the *Theologico-Political Treatise* makes of it, rabbinical exegesis of Scripture is, as it were, separated from its Talmudic soul, and consequently appears as a blind and dogmatic apologetic of the "Pharisees" who are attached to the letter (but who are quick to give it an arbitrary meaning) and as a forced reconciliation of obviously disparate texts.[10]

Spinoza might therefore not have been acquainted with the "open-ended dialectic" of "oral Law," of an "'ontology' of meaning" that the "life of the Talmud" exemplifies more than anything else.[11] Or again: "For Spinoza, all knowledge that sums up a temporal experience, everything that assumes a poetic style, bears the mark of the imaginary. The Bible, conditioned by time, is outside adequate ideas."[12] In other words, Spinoza failed to see a certain hermeneutic whose "polysemy of meaning" is premised on exegesis, not on a text's genesis, and whose effective history moves well beyond the subjective intentionality of the author's—or first readers'—ideas, presupposing a creative role in the "production of meaning [*sens*]."[13] This is the "gift of prophecy," whose structure has, according to Levinas, become the model for all *modern* interpretation of Scripture, literature, and, indeed, philosophy: "the religious moment of any reading of books and of all poetic pleasure." To affirm such polysemy even has philosophical repercussions, since it "permits us to understand in what sense, while there may be numerous possible interpretations of Spinozism itself, they do not exclude its truth but testify to it."[14]

Furthermore, Spinoza does not allow for the possibility that Derrida, speaking of Kant's philosophy of religion, calls a principle of "verification":[15] the possibility that the imagination (or superstition, myth, and, by implication, even idolatry and blasphemy) might become true. Or, as Levinas says: "It is in Spinoza that images—associated with knowledge of the first kind—receive from the second and third kind only an explanation, not a deepening. . . . The Spinozan way of 'explaining' images instead of seeking within them a knowledge (however embryonic) of the true, is in Descartes, in whose writings the sensible is not the source of the true, but the sign of the useful."[16] But Levinas takes a more nuanced view than Jean Lacroix's interpretation (who in this echoes Zac), according to which Spinoza, in the *Theologico-Political Treatise*, indicates merely a "nonphilosophical" route to salvation. In this view, the "understanding of Scripture through Scripture" implies that "it is forbidden to seek philosophical concepts in Scripture"—a "thesis," Levinas comments, to which Spinoza's "enterprise" in this work cannot be "reduced," even though it is "a very important one."[17] True enough, Levinas goes on to suggest, in his review of Lacroix's work, "Scripture may be salutary, like truth—but it is not the latter's implicit prefiguration. It is not an infused wisdom, an interiority, or a reason without knowing it."[18] In Levinas's view, the relationship between Scripture (and the political) and philosophy is more complicated and this already in terms of Spinoza's own philosophy, in both the *Ethics* and the *Theologico-Political Treatise*.

There is thus a certain duality in Spinoza's understanding of the theologico-political meaning of Scripture, which allows for the enduring value of the positivity of revealed religion, at least at its minimal core. For Spinoza, this is Christian piety and charity; for Levinas, the spiritual life of the Talmud as taught by the masters and, more broadly, the "religion of adults."

Since the possibility of 'verification' is ignored, the "ethical interiorization" of the biblical "Word of God" that Levinas discerns in Spinoza's *Theologico-Political Treatise* and in the many interspersed *scholia* of the *Ethics* has already taken place at the a priori, that is to say, transcendental or metaphysical-ontological level. "Interiorization" is not distilled or abstracted from a learning process in which the true gradually—and, as it were, teleologically—sheds its cultural-cultic vehicles, which were necessary yet inessential or inadequate, though not for that reason arbitrary or false. Scriptural religion is not, as Schopenhauer mused, "truth in the garment of a lie."[19] Although this impression is certainly given by the early beginnings of genetic or higher criticism of the biblical text, the stripping off of all *adiaphora* hardly captures the formal structure and acknowledgment of the "ethical interiorization" that Levinas, reading Spinoza, singles out. The distinction is subtle:

> Between the interiority of the Divine inscribed in the hearts of men and the interiority of fitting thought [i.e., of the ideas of the second and third kind of knowledge], on the one hand, and the exteriority of opinion [i.e., imagination, the first kind of knowledge], on the other, Spinoza would not have recognized, in history, a work of interiorization that reveals the inner meaning [*sens*] of something that had previously passed for opinion. But to his credit, Spinoza did reserve for the Word of God a *proper status* outside opinion and "fitting" ideas. (117 / 167)

More than the metaphysical inconsistency of which we spoke earlier—and given the fact that he does not assume any "verification" in the sense of the becoming true and adequate of the false or inadequate—Levinas is drawn to "this side of Spinoza that is perhaps the least Spinozist," for, as he says, the "fact that non-Spinozism can make an appearance in Spinoza remains itself indicative. We are far from so-called Spinozists to whom the believer-non-believer alternative is as simple as pharmacist-non-pharmacist" (117 / 167). So is the fact that it does this in a *theologico-political*, that is to say, scriptural context, where ethics and ethical interiority take the form of an exegesis and hermeneutics whose production of polysemic meaning has relevance well beyond the Bible, beyond rabbinic writing and the Kabbalah, and beyond the Talmud and its oral tradition. That relevance extends into literature, poetics, philosophy and even everyday speech (undoing its rhetoric and restoring its drama).

Spinoza, we saw, "had no direct contact" with the proper argumentative style of the Talmud, its "'ontology' of meaning." Yet a critical question imposes itself here. Is it possible that the model of exegesis, hermeneutics, and inspiration that Levinas attributes to the Talmud presupposes the very ontology of "expression" that, according to Deleuze, organizes (and unsettles) the Spinozistic system, as well as a long lineage of thought that runs from Neoplatonism via Duns Scotus, Hume, and Leibniz all the way up to Nietzsche, Heidegger, and the philosophy of *Difference and Repetition* itself? After all, the polysemy of Talmudic exegesis is not so very different, Levinas says, from the methods Rudolf Bultmann and Paul Ricoeur adopt in their engagements with the New Testament, just as it is co-extensive with literature, that is to say, with the "coming and going from text to reader and from reader to text" that forms "the distinctive feature [*le propos*] of all written work, of all literature, even when it does not pretend to be Holy Scriptures."[20] Levinas writes that the "unique structure" and "genre" of the Talmud is that "It maintains problems in a state of discussion. Theses oppose each other, yet they remain, to use its own expression, 'the words of the living God.' It authorizes [*accrédite*] the idea of a *single* spirit, despite the contradictions of dialogues which have no conclusion. An open-ended dialectic which does not separate itself from the living study whose theme it becomes. This study reflects and amplifies the disturbing dynamism of the text."[21] If there is a "polysemy of meaning," it thus takes the form of an *infinite modalization* of the Word, whose effect—or, as Levinas says, "result"—is from the outset indistinguishable from the "origin," which is nothing outside them. As Levinas will suggest throughout *Totality and Infinity*, there is no existing infinite, in and for itself, which preexists only to subsequently reveal—or, in the Spinozistic idiom, express and modalize—itself in its creation (or to its creatures). In the response to McKeon, Levinas writes:

> The various epochs and the various personalities of the exegetes are the very modality in which this polysemy exists. Something would remain unrevealed in the Revelation if a single soul in its singularity were to be missing from the exegesis. That these renewals may be taken as alterations of the text is not ignored by the Talmudic scholars.[22]

It is interesting to note that, in this context, Levinas recounts a Talmudic suggestion, according to which the teaching of the School of Rabbi Aquiba would be incomprehensible to Moses while nonetheless constituting his very own teaching. A critical question arises here. Might not the same hold true for Levinas's teaching with respect to Spinoza, or, if we are allowed the temporal inversion, for Spinoza with respect to Levinas? Would not their respective teachings, while incomprehensible in terms of each other, *express each other more faithfully than each of them could do on its own?* But also, paradoxically, could not the Talmud unwittingly anticipate *both*, just as both, even in their most philosophical, supposedly nonscriptural writings, echo, mimic, recreate—albeit, precisely, by ignoring this—the Talmud, in turn? In other words, might not the very model of exegesis, hermeneutics, and inspiration that Levinas attributes to the Talmud presuppose the ontology of "expression" that, according to Deleuze, organizes (and unsettles) the Spinozistic system?

And how distinct is Talmud (in Levinas's reading) from any other written work, from any other "production of sense"? Levinas writes: "If Spinoza, the genius [*genial*] Spinoza, had intimately known the life of the Talmud, he would not have been able to reduce this ontology [i.e., the polysemic production of meaning] to a bad faith on the part of the Pharisees, nor explain it away by the fact that 'many more ideas can be constructed from words and figures than from the principles and notions on which the whole fabric of reasoned knowledge is reared' (*nam ex verbis et imaginibus long plures ideae componi possunt quam ex solis principiis et notionibus, quibus tota nostra naturalis cognitio superstruitur*; chap. 1)."[23] A different logic—of revelation qua expression and modalization through cultural-cultic forms of life—is at work here. Yet it resembles the very Spinozistic expression of the infinite substance (of God or Nature) in the infinite (and infinitely modalized) attributes. In both scriptural and philosophical models, the absolute origin or cause is nothing outside (i.e., before or beyond) its "result," that is to say, its effects, which, in turn, are not independent of their interpretation—their idea, their imagination, their perception, their affect, their understanding, their comprehension, their intuition.

In Levinas's view, the "imaginative faculty" is not what "constitutes the social world." It is not "the source of human diversity," of "the differences between how we live," as political theorist Steven B. Smith suggests.[24] The "social imaginary" is above all construed religiously, more precisely, theologico-politically. Beyond the tripartite epistemological and ontological distinction between the three forms of knowledge, Spinoza, in Levinas's interpretation, thus indirectly allows for a fourth domain that links to all three kinds of knowledge without itself constituting knowledge, whether adequate or inadequate:

> The Word of God therefore opens up a dimension that is proper to the Spirit and like no other. We must not confuse it either with Philosophy or with Science or with Politics.
>
> Spinoza the rationalist would have seen this admirably. Philosophical systems, scientific and political doctrines can, depending on the age, rally souls around this Word. The Word remains independent even while being able to attach itself to these doctrines for a while. (298n.6 / 168n.1)

Levinas, using a curious terminology, speaks further of an "*innexion* of the Word to the activities—which resound from the outset—of the intellect [*innexion de la Parole aux activités, d'emblée retentissantes, de l'intellect*]" (298n.6 / 168n.1, my emphasis), from which it absolves itself as well.

If this is so, on what grounds does Levinas accept Spinoza's view of the ontico-ontological specificity of the social, more precisely, of relationships that exceed the domain of the familial and of friendship, of love and enmity, and hence imply our dealing with what Levinas would call the realm of "the third," that is to say, of "justice"? And why is their meaning above all theologico-political, that is to say, expressive or revelatory of "obedience" and "charity" rather than of any supposed theoretical knowledge or metaphysical truth? Further, if expression is the way of the infinite (i.e., of revelation, prophecy, and eschatology) from beginning to end, how could exegesis, homily, and liturgy—in short, the whole domain of cult and, in Spinoza's view, superstition—retain a relative autonomy, marked by "separation," indeed, by "interiority," a restricted "economy," of sorts?

This is only possible if *expression carries the principle of its own interruption—its stasis no less than its stability—within itself*. Its purely gestural (some would say performative) Saying—which is a doing, indeed, a "doing before hearing"—requires the fixity of a Said that "betrays" it in the dual sense this term connotes: the Said conveys and distorts or hides and obscures the Saying, and must do so necessarily. Left to its own devices, it signals—indeed, expresses—nothing; more precisely, in its very purity it is no better than (or distinguishable from) the worst. Strange mimicry of the best and the worst, of the *illéité* and the *il y a*, both of which call for the mitigation no less than for the polarity of their opposition.

Levinas can thus rightly claim that there is a certain novelty in Spinoza's treatment, in the *Theologico-Political Treatise*, of the relationship between reason, on the one hand, and history and the political, on the other. This novelty enables Spinoza to escape the summary judgment that Levinas felt obliged to pass on Hegel and, more generally, on the philosophies of the same and the Neuter, from Parmenides to the later Heidegger. Spinoza's *Theologico-Political Treatise* testifies to a greater ambiguity: "European philosophy, in Spinoza's age, has not yet come to regard political life as a moment in its own unfolding process, but Reason for Spinoza does enter [or carry with it, *comporte*] certain political conditions" (111–12 / 159).

Spinoza and, in his footsteps, Levinas do not merely presuppose these political conditions of reason, they affirm and even *justify* them by granting them their own constitutive, albeit limited, right. In consequence, the balanced assessment of Spinoza's ontological and theologico-political views that Levinas provides offers an important key to his *own* understanding, in the major philosophical writings, of the relationship between his ethico-religious metaphysics and its Saying, on the one hand, and the public space of the *res publica*—that is, of the realm of the third, of the Said—on the other.

Levinas's position thus seems very close to the one that Y. Yovel ascribes to Spinoza in the first volume of *The Marrano of Reason*, where he claims that "Spinoza holds that even arbitrary laws are preferable to the fierce dangers of lawlessness and anarchy (of which Europeans had a recent experience in the thirty-year war). The civil state is a realistic middle term between two hypothetical extremes: the state of universal strife where no government is available, and the state of universal rationality where no government is necessary."[25] For Spinoza, an intrinsic tendency toward sociality—and hence toward ecclesial communities and cultic practices, but also commerce and the commonwealth, in short, the whole domain of the political—is inscribed into the very concept of reason. Such a tendency announces itself with the first duality—"on s'amuse mieux à deux," as Levinas used to say—and extends to the third. Yet in Spinoza this social dimension of "ethical interiority" takes a peculiar form, as is clear from his statement that "The reasonable man is one who seeks out other like-minded people to enjoy together the life of the intellect, or freedom."[26]

Such Spinozistic sociality hardly reveals the asymmetry or passivity of which Levinas writes. Nor are like-mindedness or the life of the intellect, let alone the idea of Spinozistic-deterministic freedom, categories for which Levinas has much use. And yet the parallels between the two philosophers are difficult to ignore. Reason requires sociality, the political, the theologico-political, whose constitutive function and relative autonomy—and hence relative exteriority, heteronomy—it cannot (fully?) draw within its orbit or reduce to a mere dialectical moment in its own unfolding.

Spinoza's "betrayal" was his calculated departure from the community, rather than his espousal of a monistic metaphysics, which, in Levinas's reading, leaves room and, perhaps, for the first time in modernity, establishes a nongeometrical "space" for "interiority," not least because "interiority," in the Levinasian idiom, figures an "exteriority" within and beyond being and the *conatus essendi*. Add to this the explicit meditation upon philosophy's intrinsic limit and its no less internal link to the realm of the theologico-political, whose relative autonomy religion—in all of its cultic manifestations and, indeed, phenomenality—presents ecclesially and liturgically, that is to say, figuratively, dramatically, theatrically, and performatively, and it becomes difficult to see in Spinoza the greatest antagonist of the Levinasian project. On the contrary, although Spinoza doesn't draw on all the available resources that Scripture implies, he nonetheless conveys an eminently modern—and, indeed, Jewish—point of view, which Levinas summarizes as follows:

> Modern man no longer belongs, via his religious life, to an order in which propositions on the existence of God, on the soul, on miracles or a future revealed by the prophets would remain, in spite of the abstract nature of their pronouncements, on the level of truths of perception. At least, present-day Judaism in the West does not understand them in this way. Hence, for a modern religious conscience, the idea that Scripture contains the Word of God, but is not that actual Word, frustrates [or undoes, *dejoue*] only an infantile representation of the Revelation without discrediting a text to which a Jew nowadays can bring many more resources, when investigating

this word, than Spinoza could have dreamed. The theological formulations of his tradition transport [*charrient*] the accumulated riches [*l'acquis*] of a long inner experience. (115–16 / 165)

Nonetheless, we may conclude that Spinoza does make a significant contribution that outweighs his "betrayal." As Levinas acknowledges, " 'Judaism is a revealed Law and not a theology': this opinion from Mendelssohn came, then, from Spinoza" (117 / 169). This task, Levinas continues, has lost nothing of its urgency:

Can Jewish consciousness in our days deny this teaching of interiorization, when it is capable of giving such teaching a new meaning and new perspectives? Does it want to side with a Kierkegaard in regarding the ethical stage as surpassable? . . . The ethical significance of Scripture, whose irreducibility was perceived by Spinoza's genius and which he knew to single out in an age in which axioms, still superb, had nothing to fear from axiomatics, has survived the dogmatism of adequate ideas. (117–18 / 169)

Neither the precritical dogmatism of opinion nor the dogmatism of common notions—and perhaps not even the intuitive science that grasps the essence of particular things—can cover the proper domain of ethics, of the spiritual life of Scripture, whose hermeneutic richness the Talmud expresses and whose no less important theologico-*political* sense Spinoza formalized and phenomenologically concretized for modernity.

If there is any invective against Spinoza—beyond the claim that Spinozism harbors, within its most vivid imaginations, within its most rigorous demonstrations, and within its most intellectual intuitions, the seeds of a certain anti-Spinozism (which now no longer necessarily means Judaism)—it is much less pronounced than the distance marked in these pages from another Judeo-Christian philosopher, Henri Bergson, of whose *The Two Sources of Morality and Religion* Levinas notes in passing that, in privileging historical Christianity (albeit in its most dynamic and mystical forms), it is far less hesitant than Spinoza. Following Zac's analysis, Levinas recalls that Spinoza interprets Judaism as a "State religion" and Christianity as a "religion of the individual," while leaving no doubt that "Christian universalism has remained a pure pretension" (297n.3 / 162n.). Not so in Bergson. Hence, Levinas surmises: "On this point, did Bergson have other teachers than Spinoza in order to forget the entire preceding point?"[27]

PART II

Beyond Tolerance:
Pluralism and Agonistic Reason

On the Relations Between the
Secular Liberal State and Religion

Jürgen Habermas

1

The suggested theme for our discussion today is reminiscent of a question that Ernst Wolfgang Böckenförde, in the mid-1960s, succinctly put as follows: Is the liberal secular state nourished by normative preconditions that it cannot itself guarantee?[1] The question expresses doubt that the democratic constitutional state can renew the normative preconditions of its existence out of its own resources. It also voices the conjecture that the state is dependent upon autochthonous conceptual or religious traditions—in any case, collectively binding ethical traditions. Were the doubt substantiated and the conjecture proven true, the state would find itself in trouble, for it is obliged to maintain ideological neutrality in the face of the "fact of pluralism" (Rawls). This conclusion doesn't, however, invalidate the conjecture.

I would like to begin by specifying the problem in two respects. Cognitively, the doubt refers to the question of whether, once law has been fully positivized, political rule is at all open to a secular, that is, a nonreligious or postmetaphysical justification. Even if such legitimation is granted, with respect to motivation it remains doubtful whether such an ideologically pluralist community could be stabilized normatively—that is, beyond a mere modus vivendi—by presuming an at best formal background consensus, one limited to procedures and principles. And even if this doubt could be removed, it remains a fact that liberal systems are dependent upon the solidarity of their citizens—a solidarity whose sources could dry up completely as a result of a "derailed" secularization of society. While this diagnosis cannot be dismissed, it must not be understood to mean that the learned among the defenders of religion can generate an argumentative "surplus," as it were, on the

251

basis of it. Instead, I will suggest that cultural and societal secularization should be understood as a twofold learning process, one that requires both Enlightenment traditions and religious doctrines to reflect upon their respective limits. With regard to post-secular societies, the question finally arises: Which cognitive views and normative expectations must the liberal state demand of its religious and nonreligious citizens as they interact with one another?

Political liberalism (which I defend here in the special form of Kantian Republicanism[2]) understands itself to be a nonreligious and postmetaphysical justification of the normative foundations of the democratic constitutional state. This theory is part of the tradition of rational law [*Vernunftrecht*], which does without the cosmological or divine-historical [*heilsgeschichtlich*] assumptions found in classical and religious teachings of natural law. The history of Christian theology in the Middle Ages—particularly late Spanish scholasticism—belongs, of course, in the genealogy of human rights. But the fundamental principles that legitimize the ideologically neutral authority of the state are, in the end, derived from the profane sources of seventeenth- and eighteenth-century philosophy. Only much later did theology and the church come to terms with the intellectual challenges of the revolutionary constitutional state. If I understand correctly, however, from the perspective of Catholicism, given its relaxed attitude toward the *lumen naturale*, nothing in principle stands in the way of an autonomous foundation of morality and law—a foundation independent of the truths of revelation.

The post-Kantian foundation of liberal constitutional principles has, in the twentieth century, been forced to come to terms less with the painful aftermath of objective natural law (such as material value ethics [*materiale Wertethik*[3]]) than with historicist and empiricist forms of critique. In my opinion, weak assumptions concerning the normative content of the communicative condition of socio-cultural forms of life are sufficient for defending a nondefeatist notion of reason against contextualism and a nondecisionistic concept of law's validity against the positivism of law. The central task lies in explaining the following:

1. Why the democratic process counts as a legitimate legislative procedure: insofar as the democratic process complies with the conditions of an inclusive and discursive opinion- and will-formation, it justifies the presumption that the results are rationally acceptable; and

2. Why democracy and human rights co-originally interpenetrate each other in the process of drafting a constitution: the legal institutionalization of the procedure of democratic legislation requires that *both* liberal *and* political basic rights [*Grundrechte*] be guaranteed simultaneously.[4]

This grounding strategy refers to the constitution that the consociated citizens give to themselves and not to the domestication of an existing state authority, as the latter should be created only through the democratic drafting of the constitution. A "constituted" (rather than a merely constitutionally tamed) state authority is juridified [*verrech-*

tlicht] to its very core, so that the law completely penetrates political authority. The statuary positivism [*Staatswillenspositivismus*] of the German theory of public law (from Paul Laband and Georg Jellinek to Carl Schmitt), which was rooted in the *Kaiserreich* [Imperial Germany], provided a loophole for a nonlegal ethical substance "of the state" or "of the political." By contrast, in a constitutional state no sovereign exists who could draw upon a prelegal substance.[5] Once it is gone, the preconstitutional sovereignty of the prince leaves no gap that would subsequently need to be filled—in the form of an ethos of a more or less homogeneous people—by an equally substantial popular sovereignty.

In light of this problematic heritage, Böckenförde's question has been understood to imply that a fully positivized constitutional order would be in need of religion or some other "sustaining force" in order to secure cognitively the foundations of its validity. According to this interpretation, positive law's claim to validity needs to be backed up by the prepolitical-ethical convictions of religious or national communities because such a legal order cannot be self-referentially legitimized on the basis of democratically generated legal procedures alone. If, by contrast, one conceptualizes the democratic process, not positivistically, like Hans Kelsen or Niklas Luhmann, but rather as a method by which legitimacy may be generated out of legality, there arises no validity deficit that would then need to be filled by "ethical life." As opposed to the right-Hegelian understanding of the constitutional state, the proceduralist, Kant-inspired view insists upon an autonomous foundation of constitutional principles that, at least in its intention, is rationally acceptable to all citizens.

2

In what follows, I will assume that the constitution of the liberal state is self-sufficient with regard to its need for legitimation, that is, that it can draw upon the resources of a set of arguments that are independent of religious and metaphysical traditions. Even given this premise, however, doubt regarding motivation persists, for the normative, existential presuppositions of the democratic constitutional state are more demanding with respect to the role of citizens [*Staatsbürger*], who regard themselves as authors of the law, than with respect to the role of citizens of society [*Gesellschaftsbürger*], who are merely the addressees of the law. Addressees of the law are expected only, when exercising their subjective freedoms (and claims), not to overstep any legal boundaries. Such obedience in the face of laws binding on freedom differs significantly from the motivations and attitudes expected from citizens [*Staatsbürger*] in their capacity as democratic fellow lawgivers.

Citizens should actively exercise their communicative and participatory rights, not only with regard to their own best interests but also with respect to the public good. This requires a greater motivational outlay, one that cannot be legally commanded. To require participation in elections would, in a democratic constitutional state [*Rechtsstaat*], be as out of place as to prescribe solidarity. The readiness, if need be, to vouch for one's fellow citizens, although they are and remain unknown to oneself, as well as the willingness to sacrifice one's own concerns for the general interest may only be suggested to the citizens [*Bürger*] of a liberal community. This is why political virtues, even when "levied" in small doses, are essential for the continued existence of a democracy. Political virtues are a matter of socialization and of acclimating oneself to the practices and modes of thinking within a liberal political culture. The status of citizen is, in a certain sense, embedded in civil society, which derives sustenance from spontaneous and, if you like, "prepolitical" sources.

From this it does not yet follow that the liberal state is incapable of reproducing its motivational preconditions out of its own secular resources. Of course, the motives for citizens' participation in political opinion- and will-formation draw upon ethical conceptions of life as well as cultural forms of life. But democratic practices develop their own political dynamic. Only a *Rechtsstaat* without democracy—and in Germany we have long enough been accustomed to just such a state—would suggest a negative answer to Böckenförde's question: "To what extent can peoples united in a state live solely on the guarantee of individual freedom, without a 'common bond' which precedes that very freedom?"[6] The democratically constituted *Rechtsstaat* not only safeguards negative freedoms for citizens of society [*Gesellschaftsbürger*] concerned with their own welfare; by relaxing controls on communicative freedoms, the state also mobilizes its citizens to participate in the public debate on issues that pertain to all of them. The missed "common bond" is a democratic process in which the correct understanding of the constitution is ultimately under discussion.

In current discussions concerning, for instance, the reform of the welfare state—as well as immigration policies, the war in Iraq, and the abolition of compulsory military service—what is at issue is not just individual policies, but always also the contentious interpretation of constitutional principles. And implicitly, what is at issue is the question of how—in light of the diversity of our cultural ways of life, of the pluralism of our worldviews and religious convictions—we want to understand ourselves as citizens of the Federal Republic [*Bundesrepublik*] as well as Europeans. Certainly, looking back historically, a common religious background, a common language, and, most of all, a newly awakened national consciousness were conducive to the emergence of a highly abstract civic solidarity. But republican sentiments have, in the meantime, largely broken away from these prepolitical anchorings—that we are not prepared to die "for Nice" is simply no longer an objection to a European constitution. Think of the political-ethical discourses about the Holocaust and widespread criminality: they have made the citizens of the Federal Republic aware that the constitution is an achievement. The example of a self-critical "politics of memory [*Gedächtnispolitik*]"—by now no longer an exception, since examples can be found in other countries—illustrates how the ties of constitutional patriotism form and renew themselves in the political medium itself.

Contrary to a widespread misunderstanding, "constitutional patriotism" means that citizens make the principles of the constitution their own, not simply with regard to abstract content, but from within the historical context of each individual national history in its concrete meaning. If the moral contents contained within basic rights are to gain a foothold as part of our convictions, the cognitive process is not enough. Moral discernment and worldwide consensus in the form of moral indignation at severe violations of human rights are sufficient only for the integration of a constitutionalized cosmopolitan society (if there should one day be one). Solidarity among the members of a political society, however abstract and legally mediated it may be, emerges only when the principles of justice find their way into the more densely woven network of cultural values.

3

Accordingly, the secular nature of the democratic constitutional state shows no weakness inherent to the political system as such, that is, no internal weakness that would cognitively or motivationally endanger its self-stabilization. External reasons are not, however, thereby excluded. A derailing modernization of society as a whole could very well erode the democratic bond and drain the democratic state of the kind of solidarity upon which it depends, without being able to command it legally. In this instance, the very constellation that Böckenförde had in mind would come to pass: the transformation of citizens of affluent, peaceful, and liberal societies into isolated monads who act only in their own self-interest, wielding their rights as subjects against one another like weapons. Evidence for such an erosion of civic solidarity can be seen in the larger context of a politically uncontrolled world economy and world society. Markets—which, unlike state administrations, cannot, of course, be democratized—are increasingly assuming allocative functions over the areas of life that had, until now, been held together normatively by either political or prepolitical forms of communication. It is not only private spheres that are increasingly being given over to the mechanisms of action that is oriented toward success and unfolds according to its own respective preferences: the segment subject to the constraints of public legitimation is also shrinking. Civil privatization is strengthened because democratic opinion- and will-formation, discouragingly, fails to function properly. At the moment, it operates reasonably well only in national arenas and no longer influences decision-making processes that have been displaced to supra-national levels. Dwindling hope that the international community has the power to shape politics also contributes to the de-politicization of citizens. In view of the conflicts and outrageous social injustices of a highly fragmented world society, disappointment grows with the failure of each new attempt along the path, initially adopted after 1945, toward the constitutionalization of international law.

Postmodern theories comprehend these crises in a manner that is critical of reason: not as a result of a selective exhaustion of the potential of reason that, after all, was always inherent in Western modernity but rather as logically following from the program of a self-destructive spiritual and societal rationalization. It's true that a radical skepticism concerning reason is alien to the very nature of the Catholic tradition. But Catholicism has, as recently as the 1960s, struggled with the secular thought of humanism, Enlightenment, and political liberalism. Thus, the theorem that only a religious orientation toward a transcendental reference point could help a remorseful modernity out of its impasse again finds resonance today. A colleague in Tehran once asked me whether, from a culturally comparative and religio-sociological perspective, it wasn't in fact European secularization that was the special path [*Sonderweg*] in need of correction. The question reminds one of the situation during the Weimar Republic, recalling Carl Schmitt, Heidegger, or Leo Strauss.

I think it is better not to exaggerate, in the manner of a critique of reason, the question of whether an ambivalent modernity will be able to stabilize itself merely by drawing upon the secular forces of communicative reason. I would prefer to approach it undramatically, as an open, empirical question. By this, I do not intend to introduce the phenomenon of the continued existence of religion in a continually secularizing environment as a mere social fact. Philosophy also needs to take this phenomenon seriously, as a cognitive challenge from within, as it were. But before I take up this thread in the discussion, I would like to mention an obvious turn, in another direction, that the dialogue could take. As a result of the tendency to radicalize the critique of reason, philosophy has allowed itself to be moved to a self-reflection upon its own religio-metaphysical origins and to occasionally become entangled in conversations with a theology that, for its part, has sought to connect with philosophical attempts at a post-Hegelian self-reflection of reason.[7]

· · ·

A digression. The starting point for the philosophical discourse on reason and revelation is a continually recurring topos: reason, reflecting upon its most basic foundation, discovers that its origin lies in an Other; and it must recognize the fateful power of this Other if it is not to lose its rational orientation in an impasse of hybrid self-empowerment. What serves as a model here is the exercise of a reversal, of a conversion of reason through reason—accomplished or at the very least initiated by reason's own efforts. This is the case whether reflection begins with the consciousness of the discerning and active subject, as in Schleiermacher, with the historicity of the always individualized existential self-assurance, as in Kierkegaard, or with the provocative disintegration of ethical relations, as in Hegel, Feuerbach, and Marx. With no initial theological intention, a reason that is becoming aware of its own limits steps beyond itself toward an Other—whether in mystical union with an encompassing cosmic consciousness, in the despairing hope of the historical event of a redeeming message, or in the form of a forward-pressing solidarity with the downtrodden and humiliated, a solidarity that desires to hasten the arrival of messianic salvation. These anonymous gods of post-Hegelian metaphysics—encompassing consciousness, the inconceivable [*unvordenklich*] event, an unalienated society—are easy prey for theology. They offer themselves up to be decoded as pseudonyms for the trinity of the personal God engaged in *communicatio sui*.

Still, these attempts to renew philosophical theology after Hegel are more agreeable than the kind of Nietzscheanism that simply borrows the Christian connotations of hearing and understanding [*Vernehmen*], devotion and expectation of grace, arrival and event, in order to call a thinking that has been propositionally emptied out back into the undetermined archaic that precedes Christ and Socrates. By contrast, a philosophy that is aware of its fallibility and fragile position within the differentiated framework of modern society insists upon the generic, but by no means pejoratively intended, distinction between a secular mode of speaking, which requires itself to be generally accessible, and a religious mode of speaking, which depends upon the truths of revelation. Unlike in Kant and Hegel, this grammatical distinction does not bring with it the philosophical requirement of determining for itself what part of the contents of religious traditions—above and beyond the societally institutionalized knowledge of the world—is true or false. The respect that goes hand in hand with this cognitive decision to refrain from judgment is founded on respect for persons and for ways of life that clearly derive their integrity and authenticity from religious convictions. But respect is not everything: philosophy has reasons to be willing to learn from religious traditions.

4

Unlike the ethical restraint that characterizes postmetaphysical thought—which eludes every generally binding concept of the good and exemplary life—holy writings and religious traditions articulate, subtly spell out, and hermeneutically keep alive over thousands of years intuitions about fall and redemption, about a saving exit from a life experienced as being without salvation. That is why something that has elsewhere been lost and that cannot be restored using the professional knowledge of experts alone remains intact in the life of religious communities, so long as they avoid dogmatism and the moral constraint of a prescribing of conscience. By this something I mean sufficiently differentiated possibilities of expression and sensibilities for misspent life, for societal pathologies, for the failure of individual life plans and the deformation to be seen in distorted life contexts. Philosophy's willingness to learn from religion can be grounded in the asymmetry of epistemic claims, not, to be sure, for functional reasons, but—bearing in mind its successful "Hegelian" learning processes—for reasons of content.

The mutual penetration of Christianity and Greek metaphysics did not, of course, bring about only the spiritual form [*geistig Gestalt*] of theological dogmatics and a Hellenization—not in every aspect beneficial—of Christianity. It also promoted philosophy's appropriation of genuinely Christian content. This work of appropriation found its expression in heavily laden, normative conceptual networks such as: responsibility; autonomy and justification; history and memory; beginning anew, innovation, and return; emancipation and fulfillment; externalization, internalization, and embodiment; individuality and community. It is true that the work of appropriation transformed the originally religious meaning, but without deflating or weakening it in a way that would empty it out. The translation of the notion of man's likeness to God into the notion of human dignity, in which all men partake equally and which is to be respected unconditionally, is such a saving translation. The translation renders the content of biblical concepts accessible to the general public of people of other faiths, as well as to nonbelievers, beyond the boundaries of a particular religious community. Benjamin, for instance, sometimes succeeded in such translations.

Based on this experience of the secularizing release of religiously encapsulated potentials of meaning, we can now give a defused interpretation of Böckenförde's theorem. I have mentioned the diagnosis that the balance that has emerged in modernity between the three major media of societal integration is now threatened because markets and administrative power drive societal solidarity—that is, a coordination of action in accordance with values, norms, and a usage of language oriented toward communication—out of ever more areas of life. It is therefore also in the constitutional state's own interest to treat with care all cultural sources upon which the consciousness of norms and the solidarity of citizens draw. This consciousness, which has become conservative, is reflected in the talk of a "post-secular society."[8]

This term refers not only to the fact that religion continues to assert itself in an increasingly secular environment and that society, for the time being, reckons with the continued existence of religious communities. The expression *post-secular* does not merely acknowledge publicly the functional contribution that religious communities make to the reproduction of desired motives and attitudes. Rather, the public consciousness of post-secular society reflects a normative insight that has consequences for how believing and unbelieving citizens interact with one another politically. In post-secular society, the realization that "the modernization of public consciousness" takes hold of and reflexively alters religious as well as secular mentalities in staggered phases is gaining acceptance. If together they understand the secularization of society to be a complementary learning process, both sides can, for cognitive reasons, then take seriously each other's contributions to controversial themes in the public sphere.

5

Religious consciousness has been forced to engage in processes of adaptation. Every religion is originally a "conception of the world" or a "comprehensive doctrine" in the sense that it claims the authority to structure a form of life in its entirety. Under the circumstances of the secularization of knowledge, of the neutralization of state authority, and of the generalized freedom of religion, religion has had to give up this claim to interpretive monopoly and to a comprehensive organization of life. As functional differentiation brings about societal subsystems, the life of the religious community also separates itself from its social context. The role of a member of a community differentiates itself from that of a citizen of society. And because the liberal state is dependent upon a political integration of its citizens that goes beyond a mere modus vivendi, this differentiation of memberships has to amount to more than a cognitively undemanding aligning of religious ethos with the imposed laws of secular society. Rather, the universalistic system of law and the egalitarian morals of society must be connected to the ethos of the community from within, in such a way that one follows consistently from the other. To represent this "embedding," John Rawls chose the metaphor of a module: the module of secular justice should, despite the fact that it was constructed with the help of ideologically [weltanschaulich] neutral reasons, fit in with each of the orthodox foundational systems.[9]

This normative expectation with which the liberal state confronts religious communities accords with the latter's own interests insofar as it gives them the possibility of exerting, via the political public, their own influence on society as a whole. It is true that the resulting costs of tolerance, as the more or less liberal abortion regulations show, are not distributed symmetrically between believers and nonbelievers. But neither does secular consciousness enjoy negative religious freedom without cost. It is expected to acquire, through practice, a self-reflexive handling of the limits of Enlightenment. The conception of tolerance in liberally constituted, pluralistic societies demands that believers recognize that they must sensibly reckon with the continued existence of dissent in their dealings with nonbelievers, as well as with those of other faiths. And the same recognition is demanded, within the framework of a liberal political culture, of nonbelievers in their dealings with believers.

For the religiously unattuned citizen, this constitutes the by no means trivial request that he or she self-critically determine the relationship between faith and knowledge from the perspective of a general knowledge of the world. The expectation of a continuing disagreement between faith and knowledge only deserves the predicate "reasonable" if, from the perspective of secular knowledge, religious convictions are also accorded an epistemic status that is not irrational per se. By no means, therefore, do naturalistic conceptions of the world, conceptions that owe their existence to the speculative processing of scientific information and that are relevant for the ethical self-understanding of citizens,[10] enjoy in the political public a prima facie priority over competing ideological or religious conceptions.

The ideological neutrality of state authority, which guarantees the same ethical freedoms for every citizen, is incompatible with the political generalization of a secularistic worldview. Secularized citizens, insofar as they act in their role as citizens of a state, may neither deny out of hand the potential for truth in religious conceptions of the world nor dispute the right of believing fellow citizens to make contributions to public discussions that are phrased in religious language. Liberal political culture may even expect its secularized citizens to participate in efforts to translate relevant contributions from a religious language into a publicly accessible one.[11]

—Translated by Anh Nguyen

Prepolitical Moral Foundations
of a Free Republic

Pope Benedict XVI

In the acceleration of the tempo of historical developments in which we live, two factors, it seems to me, stand out above all others as characteristics of a development that, earlier, began only slowly. The first is the formation of a world society in which individual political, economic, and cultural powers depend, more and more, on each other, and come into contact and permeate each other in their different spheres of life. The other is the development of man's possibilities, of his power to make and to destroy, possibilities that, exceeding everything to which we have previously been accustomed, raise the question of the legal and moral control of power. Thus, this question is quite pressing: How can cultures, as they encounter each other, find the fundamental ethical principles that can guide their cooperation along the right way and build a common, legally responsible body to tame and organize power.

That the project of a "world ethos [*Weltethos*]," proposed by Hans Küng, has been so well received shows that the question is in the air. This is true even if one accepts Robert Spaemann's sharp-sighted criticism of this project.[1] A third factor enters in, in addition to the two already mentioned above: as cultures meet and penetrate each other, ethical certainties that had previously been normative are more or less shattered. The basic questions of what the Good actually is in any given context and why one must do the Good, even if it is harmful to oneself, remain largely without an answer. Now, it seems clear to me that science as such cannot produce an ethic, and that scientific debates cannot, therefore, generate a renewed ethical consciousness. Yet it cannot be disputed that a fundamental change in the conception both of the world and of man, a change that is the result of growing scientific knowledge, contributes significantly to shattering old moral certainties. In this respect, science now clearly has a responsibility for the human being as human being, and philosophy, in particular, has a responsibility to follow critically the development of the individual sciences and to probe critically any rash conclusions and false certainties about what man is, where he comes from, and why he exists. Put differently, it is philosophy's responsibility to separate the nonscientific element from scientific results with which it is so often intermingled, and in this way to remain attentive to the whole, to the further dimensions of the reality of human existence, only some aspects of which can reveal themselves in science.

Power and Law

Concretely, it is the task of politics to bring power within the norm of law and in this way to order its sensible application. Not the law of the strong, but the strength of the law must prevail. Power in ordering and serving law is the opposite of violence, by which we understand lawless and illegal power. That is why it is important for every society to overcome suspicion of law and its ordinances. Only in this way can arbitrariness be averted and freedom lived as communally shared freedom. Lawless freedom is anarchy, and hence the destruction of freedom. Suspicion of the law, revolts against the law, will always break out when the law itself no longer appears to be the expression of a justice in the service of all, but rather the product of arbitrariness, the presumption of right on the part of those who have the power to do so.

For this reason, the task of bringing power within the norm of law points to further questions: How does law come into being, and how must law be constituted so that it is a vehicle for justice and not a privilege of those who have the power to establish the law? This is, on the one hand, a question of the coming into being of the law, but, on the other hand, it is also the question of the law's own inner norms. That the law must not be an instrument of power for the few, but rather needs to be the expression of the common interest of all, seems, at least at first, to be solved by means of the democratic formation of a common will. Because the process of democratic will-formation allows everyone to take part in the making of the law, the resulting law is the law of all and as such can and must be respected. Indeed, the guarantee of a collaborative participation in the construction of the law and in the just administration of power is the main reason for arguing for democracy as the most appropriate form of a political order.

Nevertheless, it seems to me that there remains yet another question. Since unanimity among people is rarely achieved, democratic will-formation must rely on one of two essential tools, either delegation or majority decision, in which, according to the importance of a question, different ratios for a majority might be required. But majorities too can be blind or unjust. History makes this quite clear. When a majority, however large it may be, represses a minority—for example, a religious or a racial one—by means of oppressive laws, can one still speak of justice, of law? It is in this way that the principle of majority rule still leaves the question of the ethical bases of the law unanswered, still leaves open the question whether there is anything that can never become law, that is, anything that always remains unlawful in essence or, conversely, anything that by its very nature is unalterably a right and precedes every majority decision and must be respected by it.[2]

Modernity has formulated a reserve of such normative elements in the different declarations of human rights, thereby withdrawing them from the discretion of majorities. Now, one may well, in the present state of affairs, be content with the inner evidence of these values. But even such a deliberate restriction of the question has a philosophical nature. There are, then, values that follow, in and of themselves, from the essence of human existence and that are, for that reason, inviolable for everyone who is human. We will need to return to the question of the scope of such a conception, particularly as the evidence for it is by no means recognized in all cultures today. Islam has defined its own catalog of human rights, one that differs from the Western one. And while it is true that China is today determined by a cultural form that originated in the West, namely, Marxism, China—so far as I know—is nonetheless asking whether the issue of human rights is not just a typically Western invention that needs questioning.

New Forms of Power and New Questions about How to Manage Them

If what is at stake is the relationship between power and law, including the sources of the law, the phenomenon of power itself must be examined more closely. I don't want to attempt to define the nature of power as such, but rather to sketch the challenges that confront us as a result of the new forms of power that have developed in the past half-century. In the period initially following the Second World War, shock at the new destructive power that man had gained with the invention of the atomic bomb was dominant. Man saw himself suddenly capable of destroying himself and his world. The question arose: What political mechanisms are needed to avert this destruction? How can such mechanisms be found and made effective? How can ethical forces that shape such political forms and lend them effectiveness be mobilized? In reality, competition between the opposing blocs of power and the fear that the destruction of the other would lead to one's own destruction protected us for a long time from the terrors of atomic war. The mutual limitation of power and fear for one's own survival proved to be saving forces.

What causes anxiety now is no longer so much fear of the great war, but rather fear of an omnipresent terror that can effectively strike anywhere and be everywhere. Humanity, we have come to realize, doesn't actually need the great war to make the world unlivable. The anonymous powers of terror, which can be present everywhere, are powerful enough to affect us even in our everyday lives. But the haunting possibility remains that criminal elements could gain access to means of wholesale destruction and so deliver the world to chaos, outside the political order. For that reason, the question of law and ethos has shifted: What sources does terror draw upon? How can we succeed in averting this new illness of humanity from within? An alarming thing here is that terror legitimizes itself—at least partly—morally. The pronouncements from Osama bin Laden present terror as the answer of powerless and oppressed peoples to the arrogance of the powerful, as just punishment for the latter's presumption and for their blasphemous arrogance and cruelty. For people in certain social and political situations, such motivations are apparently convincing. Terroristic behavior is presented partly as a defense of religious traditions against the godlessness of Western society.

At this point, a question arises to which we must return: If terrorism is also fed by religious fanaticism—and it is—is religion then a healing and saving power, or is it not, rather, an archaic and dangerous one, which constructs false universalisms and thus leads to intolerance and terror? And if this is so, mustn't religion be placed under the guardianship of reason and carefully contained? The question then surely arises: Who can do that? How does one do that? But the general question also remains: Is or is not the gradual abolition, the overcoming, of religion to be looked upon as a necessary human advancement, so that humanity can enter on the path to freedom and universal tolerance?

Meanwhile, another form of power has come to the fore. But what at first seems to be purely beneficent and wholly worthy of praise could in fact turn into a new kind of threat for mankind. Humans are now capable of making humans, of producing them, so to speak, in a test tube. Humans have become a product, and with that, their relationship to themselves changes radically. They are no longer a gift of nature or of God the Creator. They are their own product. Humans have descended into the wellspring of power, into the source of their own existence. The temptation now to construct the proper human being, the temptation to experiment with humans, the temptation to view humans as trash and to cast them aside, are not fantasies of antiprogressive moralists. If a short while ago the question of whether religion is actually a positive moral force presented itself, now doubt about the reliability of reason arises. Finally, the atomic bomb must also be considered a product of reason; finally, the breeding and selection of humans was conceived by reason. Should it, then, not now be the other way around, with reason placed under supervision? But under the supervision of whom or what? Or should religion and reason perhaps limit each other mutually, with each showing the other its respective limitations, while also pointing the other in the right direction? Here a question again arises: In a world society, with its mechanisms of power, its unchecked forces, and its different views of what law and morality are, how and where can there be found effective ethical evidence with sufficient motivational and assertive force to help answer and successfully meet the above-mentioned challenges?

Prerequisites of the Law: Law—Nature—Reason

It at first seems obvious that we should look at historical situations that are comparable to ours, insofar as there are comparable ones. At any rate, it is worthwhile to consider briefly that ancient Greece had its enlightenment, that the law founded on the gods lost its evidence, and that it became necessary to seek a deeper grounding for the law. And so the thought arose that there must, in contrast to positive law, which can be unjust, be a law that is derived from nature, from the being of man itself. This law, which would constitute the corrective to positive law, must be found.

Nearer to us is the example of the double rupture that occurred in European consciousness at the beginning of modernity and that compelled us to lay the foundation for a new reflection on the content and source of the law. First, one broke out of the borders of the European, Christian world with the discovery of America. One then encountered peoples who did not belong to the Christian system of faith and law, which, prior to this, was the source of law for everyone and gave law its form. There was no common legal ground with these peoples. But were they then lawless, as some contended at the time and as was reflected in their practice, or is there a law that transcends all legal systems, joining and guiding men as men in their mutual relationships? In this context, Francisco de Vitoria developed the already-latent idea of the "law of peoples," of the *ius gentium*—where *gentes* also has the sense of heathen, of non-Christian. What is meant here is a law that precedes the Christian form of law and that is to organize the just cooperation of all peoples.

The second rupture in the Christian world took place within Christianity itself as a result of the schism that divided the community of Christians into communities that stood—at times hostilely—in opposition to one another. Once again, it was necessary to develop a common law that precedes dogma, or at least to develop a legal minimum whose principles would no longer be derived from faith, but rather from nature, from man's reason. Hugo Grotius, Samuel von Pufendorf, and others developed the idea of natural law as a law of reason that institutes reason as the organ of communal lawmaking beyond the limits of any particular faith.

Natural law—especially in the Catholic Church—remains the topos with which the Church, in conversations with secular society as well as with other communities of faith, appeals to a shared reason and searches for the foundations of a communication about the ethical principles of the law in a secular, pluralistic society. But this instrument has unfortunately become dull, and I don't, therefore, want to use it to support my position in this conversation. The idea of natural law presupposes a concept of nature in which nature and reason interlock, in which nature itself is reasonable. With the triumph of evolutionary theory, this view of nature has been demolished. Although there may be instances of reasonable behavior in nature, nature, according to evolutionary theory, is, as such, not rational: this is the diagnosis that has come to us and that today seems widely incontrovertible.[3] Of the different dimensions of the concept of nature upon which the former notion of natural law was based, only the one articulated by Ulpian (early third century A.D.), in the following well-known sentence, remains: "ius naturae est, quod natura omnia animalia docet."[4] But this does not suffice for our questions, which are not about what pertains to all *animalia*, but rather about the specific human tasks that human reason has created and that cannot be accomplished without reason.

Human rights have remained the last element of natural law, which essentially—in modernity, at any rate—sought to be a law of reason. Human rights are incomprehensible without the premise that man as man, simply by virtue of being a member of the human species, is the subject of rights, and that inherent in his being itself are values and norms that are to be found but not invented. Perhaps the doctrine of human rights today should be supplemented by a doctrine of human duties and of the limits of man. Now, this addition could help renew the question of whether there might be a reason of nature, and thus a law of reason for man and his existence in the world. Today, such a conversation would need to be laid out and designed interculturally. For Christians, this would have to deal with Creation and the Creator. In the Indian world, it would correspond to the concept of "dharma," the inner lawfulness of being; in the Chinese tradition, it would correspond to the idea of the Tao of Heaven.

Interculturality and Its Consequences

Before I attempt to come to any conclusions, I would like to elaborate a little on the ideas just laid out. Interculturality seems to me today to be an essential dimension of the discussion of the basic questions about what it is to be human, a discussion that can be conducted neither solely within the Christian tradition nor solely within the Western tradition of reason. It's true that both traditions see themselves as universal—which, de jure, they may well be. De facto, however, they must recognize that they are accepted only by certain parts of humanity and are also understandable only to certain parts of humanity. The number of competing cultures is, of course, much smaller than it may at first appear.

Above all, it is important to note that unity no longer exists within individual cultural spheres. Rather, all cultural spheres are marked by far-reaching tensions within their own cultural traditions. This is entirely evident in the West. And while the secular culture of a strict rationality, of which Habermas has given us an impressive picture, is predominant and understands itself to be a cohesive force, the Christian understanding of reality also continues to be an effective one. Both poles exist in varying proximity to or tension with one another, in mutual willingness to learn or in more or less decisive rejection. The Islamic cultural sphere is marked by similar tensions; it is a long way from the fanatical absolutism of a bin Laden to attitudes that are open to a tolerant rationality. The third large cultural sphere, Indian culture or, more accurately, the cultural spheres of Hinduism and Buddhism, is in its turn also marked by similar tensions, even if these, at any rate from our perspective, appear to be less dramatic. These cultures also see themselves exposed to the claims of Western rationality and to the inquiries of Christian faith, both of which are present within them. They assimilate both of these in different ways, while attempting to maintain their own identities. African and Latin American tribal cultures, the latter of which have been reawakened by certain Christian theologies, complete the picture. They seem, to a large extent, to call Western rationality into question, but also to call into question the universal claim of Christian revelation.

What follows from all of this? First, it appears to me, the de facto nonuniversality of both major cultures of the West—the culture of Christian faith as well as that of secular rationality—much as they might both, each in its own way, be involved in the shaping of all cultures throughout the world. It is for this reason that the question of Habermas's colleague in Tehran—namely, whether, from the point of view of comparative culture and sociology of religion, it might not be European secularization that is the exception in need of correction—seems to be of considerable weight to me. I would not really, at any rate not necessarily, reduce this question to the atmosphere associated with Schmitt, Heidegger, and Lévi-Strauss—that is, so to speak, to a European context that has tired of rationality. It is, in any case, a fact that our secular rationality, plausible as it might seem to our Western reason, is not plausible to every *ratio*. It is a fact that secular rationality, as rationality, in its attempt to make itself evident, comes up against limits. Its evidence is, in actuality, closely connected with certain cultural contexts, and it must recognize that, as such, it is not comprehensible to the whole of humanity and that it cannot therefore be operative throughout it. In other words, there is no rational or ethical or religious universal formula about which everyone could agree and which could then support everyone. In any case, such a formula is presently beyond our reach. It is for this reason that the so-called world ethos remains an abstraction.

Conclusion

What, then, is to be done? With regard to practical consequences, I find myself largely in agreement with what Habermas has articulated concerning a post-secular society, the willingness to learn, and mutual self-limitation. I would like to conclude by summing up my own view in two theses.

1. We have seen that there are pathologies in religion that are highly dangerous and that make it necessary to regard the divine light of reason as a tool, so to speak, a means by which religion must be purified and put in order again and again—which, by the way, was also the intention of the Church Fathers.[5] But our reflections have also shown that there are—and mankind today is, in general, not as aware of this—also pathologies of reason, a hybris of reason that is not any less dangerous but that, considering its potential efficiency, is even more threatening: the atomic bomb; man as product. And because of this, reason must, in its turn, also be reminded of its limits and learn to be ready to listen to the great religious traditions of humanity. If reason puts aside this correlativity, this willingness to learn, and fully emancipates itself, it will become destructive.

Kurt Hübner has recently formulated a similar demand and said that such a theory is not, in the first instance, about a "return to faith" but rather about "freeing oneself from the epochal misconception that it [i.e., faith] has nothing more to say to contemporary man because it contradicts his humanistic idea of reason, enlightenment, and freedom."[6] I would, accordingly, speak of a necessary correlativity of reason and faith, of reason and religion, which are appointed to mutually cleanse and heal one another, which mutually need one another and mutually must recognize this need.

2. This basic principle must be, in practice, concretized in our present intercultural context. Without a doubt, the two primary partners in this correlativity are Christian faith and Western secular rationality. One can and must be able to say this, without any kind of false eurocentrism. Both determine the state of the world to a degree that no other cultural force does. But that still does not mean that one may push other cultures aside as a kind of *quantité négligeable*. This would indeed be a Western hybris, one that we would pay for dearly and to a certain extent already do. It is important for the two large components of Western culture to allow themselves to listen, to involve themselves in a true correlativity with these cultures as well. It is important to involve the latter in an attempt at a polyphonic correlation, in which they would open themselves up to the essential complementarity of reason and faith. As a result, a universal process of cleansing can grow, one in which the essential values and norms that are somehow intuited by all people can finally attain new power to illuminate, in order that what holds the world together can again have an effective influence on humanity.

—*Translated by Anh Nguyen*

Bush's God Talk

Bruce Lincoln

Most discussions of George W. Bush's religious faith draw heavily on his campaign autobiography, *A Charge to Keep: My Journey to the White House* (1999), which puts religion at the beginning, middle, and end of the story.[1] Deliberately vague in its chronology, the book describes a man who drifted until middle age, when Billy Graham "planted a mustard seed" in his soul and helped turn his life around.[2] Modifying the conventions of conversion narratives, the book acknowledges Bush's youthful indiscretions but downplays the nature and severity of his sins. It does not single out one decisive, born-again moment, but describes a gradual transformation that included such steps as Bible study, repudiation of drink, and a recommitment to God, church, and family.

All this took place in 1985 and 1986, as Bush's oil business in Texas was floundering, his marriage was in trouble, and his father was preparing his White House run. The following year, Bush became senior adviser on the campaign team. One of the core responsibilities assigned to him, probably as a result of his newfound faith, was to serve as liaison with the religious right. He was coached and assisted in this by Doug Wead, an Assemblies of God minister, good friend of Jim and Tammy Faye Bakker, and longtime Republican operative.

Wead introduced him to the right people and taught him to win their support by showing he shared their values and spoke their language. "Signal early and signal often," he counseled, urging that the candidate's speeches be larded with biblical allusions. The elder Bush demurred, but his son took the lesson in earnest.[3]

A Charge to Keep opens portentously: "Most lives have defining moments. Moments that forever change you. Moments that set you on a different course." The first such moment for Bush is "renewing my faith." Marriage and fatherhood are listed next, and the last is a sermon he heard in January 1999 as he began his second term as governor of

Texas.[4] Taking as his text Exodus 3–4, the familiar story of how God appeared to Moses in the burning bush and called him to free Israel, Pastor Mark Craig emphasized the way Moses initially hesitated to respond to God's call, feeling himself unworthy. Connecting this critical moment in sacred history to concerns of the present, Pastor Craig observed that America was hungry for leadership, moral courage, and faith. Good men, when called, could not hesitate. This prompted Barbara Bush to inform her son: "He's talking to you."

Bush's response was attractively modest: "The pastor was, of course, talking to us all, challenging each of us to make the most of our lives."[5] His words sit side by side with his mother's in this doubly coded tale. Those so inclined will see a humble man of faith, moved to do the right thing by good advice and a thoughtful sermon. Others will recognize a divine call, issued through an inspired preacher and accepted, after initial hesitation, by the Lord's chosen: the new Moses. The text is designed to admit both readings. It suggests the stronger interpretation to those who find it congenial, but allows for a more modest reading for anyone who considers such views either presumptuous or preposterous.

Yes, Bush believes God called him to office. But he is careful to *say* this obliquely and to connect it with a broader theology of vocation, in which all are called to take their place and do their best. People's stations may vary, but we all receive God's grace and serve his will. The title of Bush's book foregrounds these concerns. It comes from a well-known hymn, which was played at the church service with which he began his first term as governor in 1995. Written by Charles Wesley, its words and music are much beloved by evangelicals throughout Texas and the South.

> A charge to keep I have,
> A God to glorify,
> A never dying soul to save,
> And fit it for the sky.
> To serve the present age,
> My calling to fulfill;
> O may it all my powers engage
> To do my Master's will!

In his book, Bush tells America what he told Texas with the hymn: he regards public office as God's calling and a sacred trust. He shares the hymn's inspiration with his staff, whom he expects to give their highest and best. To dramatize the point, he invites them to come see the picture hanging over his desk, where a determined rider on horseback charges up a steep hill, a picture also titled *A Charge to Keep*. "This is us," he tells them, "we serve One greater than ourselves."

At the end of the chapter devoted to this theme, Bush cites a Bible verse, 1 Corinthians 4:2: "Now it is required that those who have been given a trust must prove faithful."[6]

The verse is appropriate for the theme, but the way he introduces it feels a bit awkward and heavy-handed. Although Bush often alludes to Scripture, he does not frequently cite chapter and verse this way. But this is a signal for his core constituency, making strategic use of their specialized reading practices. Full citation invites those with such habits to consult the passage. Anyone who does will find that the verse is embedded in this paragraph:

> This is how one should regard us, as servants of Christ and stewards of the mysteries of God. Now it is required that those who have been given a trust must prove faithful. With me it is a very small thing that I should be judged by you or by any human court. I do not even judge myself. I am not aware of anything against myself, but I am not thereby acquitted. It is the Lord who judges me. Therefore do not pronounce judgment before the time, before the Lord comes, who will bring to light the things now hidden in darkness and will disclose the purposes of the heart. Then every man will receive his commendation from God.

One has to wonder: Is this how Bush regards himself? Is this how he would like to be regarded? More likely, this is another instance of double coding. If such things please you, he wants you to know he thinks of himself as a faithful servant of Christ, and feels himself accountable to no law save God's, no court save the Last Judgment. But if such things make you uneasy, he would prefer that the question never arise. Following the strategy of "Signal early and signal often," Bush employs biblical citation to communicate with his base, the linguistic equivalent of winks and nudges.

The practice lets him convey things the faithful love to hear, while letting them feel that they enjoy a privileged relation to him by virtue of sharing biblical reference points. At the same time, it lets him veil these things from people who would be put off by biblical language or might challenge its propriety. Should anyone point out what he is doing, it is easy to deny any but a general meaning, while dismissing the criticism as verging on paranoia.

A Charge to Keep ends with a chapter explaining how the virtue of compassion informs Bush's policies and makes him a visionary leader. Here and elsewhere, however, he invests the term *compassion* with a particular meaning. To appreciate this, one has to consider his mythic account of the fall in American culture:

> During the more than half century of my life, we have seen an unprecedented decay in our American culture, a decay that has eroded the foundations of our collective values and moral standards of conduct. Our sense of personal responsibility has declined dramatically, just as the role and responsibility of the federal government have increased. . . . We can now say, without question, that the belief that government

could solve people's problems instead of people solving people's problems was wrong and misguided.[7]

The reason government cannot deal with social issues, he asserts, is its lack of compassion. He understands compassion to be a quality of spirit that characterizes (religious) individuals and groups, but is categorically different from the soulless, bureaucratic nature of the state. When government attempts to care for the needy, it does so for practical and political, not moral and spiritual, reasons. And in doing so, it obscures and inhibits the compassion of godly individuals, thereby compounding the problem.

However rhetorically attractive it may be, "compassionate" conservatism differs only slightly from rougher forms of the same creed. It remains laissez-faire in its approach to social welfare and justice, and it justifies this stance by claiming the state has no ability (rather than no right or no reason) to intervene in such matters. Since compassion is a spiritual quality, according to this perspective, social welfare and justice are best left to religious institutions, whence the specialized form of privatization (and patronage) that is the president's "faith-based initiative."

> For our culture to change, it must change one heart, one soul, and one conscience at a time. Government can spend money, but it cannot put hope in our hearts or a sense of purpose in our lives. This is done by churches and synagogues and mosques and charities that warm the cold of life. They are a quiet river of goodness and kindness that cuts through stone. . . . Government should welcome the active involvement of people who are following a religious imperative to love their neighbors. . . . Supporting these men and women—the soldiers in the armies of compassion—is the next bold step of welfare reform.[8]

Bush made compassion a centerpiece of his 2000 campaign, actively courting religious people as well as "suburban soccer" moms, who found other conservatives too callous.[9] To counter the risk that his emphasis on compassion might make him seem effeminate, however, he often paired it with courage, describing these two as the quintessential American virtues. Like the other attributes that mark the U.S. as exceptional among nations, these are not just secular qualities. Rather, they are gifts of grace and the instruments of grace through which Americans do God's work in the world. Though the state, in Bush's view, is somehow incapable of compassion, nothing inhibits its capacity for courage, especially in the form of military action.

For about eight months after his inaugural, Bush held courage and compassion in rough balance. If anything, the latter seemed to prevail, albeit in his specialized sense. Tax cuts, a smaller role for government, and a shift of social service to the faith-based "armies of compassion" were his chief agenda items.

The events of September 11, 2001, changed things. Initially rendered almost speech-less, Bush searched for a way to comprehend and describe what had happened. "A difficult moment for America" was his first attempt, quickly followed by "a national tragedy" and "an apparent terrorist attack"[10] Once the plane crashes had been confirmed, he promised to "hunt down and punish those responsible for these cowardly acts," and he asked the country for prayer.[11] In his third speech of the day, he renewed this request and quoted the 23rd Psalm: "Even though I walk through the valley of the shadow of death, I shall fear no evil, for You are with me."[12]

The verse was well chosen, and it resonated with other aspects of this address, in which Bush first introduced a discourse on "evil." He used the term four times (more than any other, save "terror/terrorist/terrorism"), and it let him characterize the situation with a stark moral simplicity. Elsewhere he spoke of America as defender of all that is good and just, "the brightest beacon for freedom and opportunity," thereby implying a struggle of light and darkness ("And no one will keep that light from shining.") His dualistic vision was best captured, however, in another passage: "Today, our nation saw evil, the very worst of human nature. And we responded with the best of America—with the daring of our rescue workers, with the caring for strangers and neighbors who came to give blood and help in any way they could."[13]

Courage here was of a defensive sort—the daring of rescue workers—while compas-sion took varied forms (caring for strangers, etc.). Both showed America at its godly best, confronting demonic evil. In subsequent days, Bush recalibrated the balance between the two virtues so that courage overshadowed compassion but never eclipsed it completely. At the same time, the kind of courage he invoked was increasingly aggressive. He pledged to pursue and destroy not just Al Qaeda, but terrorism; not just terror, but evil. Mean-while, he informed the world there could be no neutrality in the coming struggle. "Every nation, in every region, now has a decision to make," he announced on September 23. "Either you are with us, or you are with the terrorists."[14]

To his credit, Bush never (with a single unfortunate exception) cast the conflict as a crusade.[15] When influential evangelists (Franklin Graham, Pat Robertson), academics (Samuel Huntington, Bernard Lewis), and generals (William G. Boykin) have construed Islam as the enemy, Bush has not rebuked them, thereby permitting some to believe he shares their views. In his own statements, however, he has staked out a more temperate and prudent position, speaking of Islam as a religion of peace. Our enemies are not those of a different faith, but "barbaric criminals who profane a great religion by committing murder in its name," a phrase he used when commencing war in Afghanistan (October 7, 2001).[16]

Countless changes can be rung on Manichaean chimes once the binary opposition of Us and Them is aligned with plots pitting Good against Evil. Among the many variants Bush employed during and after the Afghan war were: narratives of American courage versus cowardly terrorist attacks; American goodness and compassion versus blind hatred and resentment; true American piety versus self-deluded fanaticism; and modem civilization versus medieval resistance to progress. The last of these binaries implies a temporal sequence: the good future will succeed an evil past, just as surely as spring follows winter. Toward the end of the Afghan war, Bush began to develop this into a theological position, as when he told the United Nations: "History has an Author who fills time and eternity with his purpose. We know that evil is real, but good will prevail against it."[17]

When the time came to make his case for another war, Bush returned to this idea. In his third State of the Union address, after rehearsing charges about weapons and terrorist ties and portraying Saddam Hussein as evil incarnate, the president lifted his argument to the grandest of terms:

> We go forward with confidence, because this call of history has come to the right country . . . Americans are a free people, who know that freedom is the right of every person and the future of every nation. The liberty we prize is not America's gift to the world, it is God's gift to humanity. We Americans have faith in ourselves—but not in ourselves alone. We do not claim to know all the ways of Providence, yet we can trust in them, placing our confidence in the loving God behind all of life, and all of history.[18]

Ten months later, when the situation in Iraq had turned ominous and sour, he reaffirmed these views in an address to the National Endowment for Democracy (November 6, 2003). He began by observing that between the 1970s and the present, the number of democratic governments in the world had grown from 40 to 120. "Historians in the future will offer their own explanations for why this happened," he said and went on to anticipate their speculations. Such human factors as American leadership or the rise of a middle class paled, however, in comparison with the hand of the unmoved mover. "Liberty is both the plan of heaven for humanity and the best hope for progress here on Earth," he announced. These are no secular matters:

> The advance of freedom is the calling of our time. It is the calling of our country. . . . We believe that liberty is the design of nature. We believe that liberty is the direction of history. We believe that human fulfillment and excellence come in the responsible exercise of liberty. And we believe that freedom, the freedom we prize, is not for us alone. It is the right and the capacity of all mankind. And as we meet the terror and violence of the world, we can be certain the author of freedom is not indifferent to the fate of freedom.[19]

Much the same language was recycled in the speech with which Bush accepted his party's nomination.[20] The sole major addition was the passage with which he concluded the address and moved to his benediction: "Like generations before us, we have a calling from beyond the stars to stand for freedom. This is the everlasting dream of America, and tonight, in this place, that dream is renewed. Now we go forward—grateful for our freedom, faithful to our cause, and confident in the future of the greatest nation on earth. God bless you, and may God continue to bless America."[21] All of these texts convey a sophisticated theology of history that rests on five propositions: (1) God desires freedom for all humanity; (2) this desire manifests itself in history; (3) America is called by history (and thus, implicitly by God) to take action on behalf of this cause; (4) insofar as America responds with courage and determination, God's purpose is served and freedom's advance is inevitable; (5) with the triumph of freedom, God's will is accomplished and history comes to an end.

This is the fullest and most sophisticated theological position Bush has articulated in the course of his presidency. As we have seen, it follows several earlier systems, each of which had its own force, rationale, and moment. These include: an evangelical theology of "born again" conversion; a theology of American exceptionalism as grounded in the virtue of compassion; a Calvinist theology of vocation; and a Manichaean dualism of good and evil.

In developing these concepts, however, he has shown little concern for consistency and coherence. His theological systems simply pile up, much like his rationales for war in Iraq—of which twenty-seven appeared over the course of one year.[22]

What is more, there are serious tensions and contradictions among the various systems. The one with which Bush ends, for example, differs sharply from the one with which he started. In his theology of history, salvation is an impersonal and inevitable process of gradual world-perfection, in which the Creator's goals are achieved through the collective actions of a chosen nation. By contrast, his evangelical faith makes salvation individual and by no means inevitable; it comes in a blazing moment of faith and decision, when a lost soul accepts Jesus as personal savior. If the theology of the early Bush is Pauline, his more recent stance is Hegelian, but without the dialectic and with America, not Prussia, in history's starring role. It is hard to imagine how one man can hold both doctrines.

I am persuaded that Bush's evangelical convictions, which he embraced decades ago in a period of life crisis, matter to him deeply. The other parts of this theology are more recent overlays. They took shape after he learned his trade as a successful politician, and they were worked out in collaboration with a talented staff. It is hard to say how committed he is to any one of these later formulations. Indeed, it is hard to know in what sense they are his, or what it means to speak of "belief" in such a context. Does he own and inhabit these beliefs, or simply profess and perform them? When he has tried to explain his theology of history without a prepared text, the results have not been pretty:

See, what's happening is that freedom is beginning to rise up in a part of the world that is desperate for freedom, a part of the world where people are resentful because they are not free human beings. And we believe that freedom is the Almighty's gift to every person in this world. It is the basic belief of the American system. And so—I say this to the families of the soldiers I meet. I tell them their sons and daughters or husbands and wives are on an incredibly important mission for history. See, when Iraq is free, it will begin to change the vision of those in Iran who want to be free. When Iraq is free, it will say to the Palestinians, who have been subjected to leadership that has not led in their interest, that it's possible to live at peace with our close friend, Israel.[23]

When this text is placed beside Bush's more formal addresses, the contrast is revealing. In the speeches written by his staff, the same phrases (or more elegant versions thereof) articulate sophisticated ideas that are born of serious reflection.[24] In his version, they are reduced to a jumble of feel-good slogans, with which the president rallies a loyal constituency to support controversial, even dubious policies (in the current example, the Iraq war and his Middle East policies).

When speaking in his own voice, the president transforms his writers' subtle instruments of persuasion into clumsy parodies of themselves. Even Manichaean dualism—a doctrine not known for its subtlety—can be vulgarized in this fashion: "I see things this way: The people who did this act on America, and who may be planning further acts, are evil people. They don't represent an ideology, they don't represent a legitimate political group of people. They're flat evil. That's all they can think about, is evil. And as a nation of good folks, we're going to hunt them down."[25] Bush made these remarks two weeks after 9/11, as the Patriot Act was being drafted, and he made them to employees of the FBI. In this heated context, his blunt language construed Al Qaeda not just as quintessentially evil, but as having no political beliefs and no legitimacy. It also appears that its followers have no legal rights, since his words convert criminal suspects into beasts fit for hunting.

One is forced to conclude that Bush's theology and his deployment of it are less systematic than pragmatic. Although he fosters the impression that his policies are grounded in deep religious conviction, the reality is often the reverse. Vague notions and attractive terms such as *compassion*, *history*, and *freedom* are given rhetorical, sometimes even intellectual, coherence by his staff. Bush may resonate to some of the ideas and some of the language they prepare for him, but for the most part he uses these to justify policies that have already been decided on quite other grounds. Preemptive wars, abridgments of civil liberty, cuts in social service, subsidies to churches, and other like initiatives are not just wrapped in the flag; together with the flag, they are swathed in the holy.

Many of those responsible for shaping these policies are tough-minded neoconservatives who share with political philosopher Leo Strauss a cynical view of religion as unfit for elites, but useful in swaying the masses. To Bush falls the task of securing broad support for this team's agenda from his fervently evangelical base. It is not an easy business, and it requires all the linguistic skill, theological ingenuity, and tactical acumen his staff can muster. The apparent sincerity with which Bush displays his convictions while delivering their lines is a significant piece of his own very real, if very limited genius. It has also been, up to this date (October 2004), a primary condition of his success.

Pluralism and Faith

William E. Connolly

Relativism and Faith

Straussianism is the only professorial movement in the United States
that has attained the standing of a public philosophy. Since at least the
late 1970s, its proponents have not only played a significant role in the
academy but have served as advisers to the president when a Republican
holds office and as talking heads on news channels such as Fox News,
CNN, and MSNBC when Republicans are in or out of office. The tendency is to counsel respect, in the name of civic virtue, for the presidency when a Republican holds office and to subject the incumbent to
sharp critique when a Democrat holds office. Reagan and the two
Bushes have been recipients of the first honor; Carter and Clinton recipients of the second line of attack. Let's explore the contribution that Leo
Strauss himself has made to contemporary Straussian public philosophy, as well as limits he may set to such a movement.

In Liberalism: Ancient and Modern, published in the 1960s, Strauss
argues in favor of a classical liberal education and against the shape
modern liberalism has taken. Liberal education, in the classic sense,
prepares an elite of gentlemen to lift mass democracy to a higher level
of achievement:

> Liberal education is the counterpoison to mass culture, to the cor-
> roding effects of mass culture, to its inherent tendency to produce
> nothing but "specialists without spirit and voluptuaries without
> heart." Liberal education is the ladder by which we try to ascend
> from mass democracy to democracy as originally meant. Liberal
> education is the necessary endeavor to found an aristocracy within
> democratic mass society. Liberal education reminds those members
> of a mass democracy who have ears to hear, of human greatness.[1]

Waiving reservations about his use of the term *mass*, I agree that liberal education makes an indispensable contribution to the nobility of democracy. The issue is: What type of nobility to foster? What kind of civic virtue to nourish? A chapter entitled "The Liberalism of Classical Political Philosophy" provides insight into Strauss's view. Here Strauss reviews a book by Eric Havelock on liberalism in classical Greek political philosophy. Havelock writes before the philosophy of John Rawls had achieved hegemony among liberal academics in America. Strauss, while rebuking Havelock for "unsurpassed shallowness and crudity" in his reading of Greek classics, also gives us an idea of how the "modern liberalism" of which Havelock is a prototype looks to him.[2] My purpose is not to defend Havelock's reading of ancient Greek thinkers but to probe Strauss's account of modern liberalism through his critique of Havelock.

Havelock, he says, thinks that every value is "'negotiable' because he is extremely tolerant."[3] Strauss himself wonders whether tolerance can be spread so widely, "whether Tolerance can remain tolerant when confronted with unqualified Intolerance."[4] The modern liberal also asserts, crucially, "that man's being is accidental to the universe,"[5] though he is mistaken if he imagines that most classical Greek thinkers agreed with him. The modern liberal also thinks "that man's nature and therewith morality are essentially changing."[6] Strauss, reasonably enough, objects to Havelock's critique of Plato for not having set forth liberalism before criticizing it. "Plato failed to set forth the liberal view," Strauss says, "because the liberal view did not exist."[7] Plato criticized sophistry, not liberalism. But why did he use myth as well as argument to do so?

> We on our part suggest this explanation. Plato knew that most men read more with their "imagination" than with open-minded care and are therefore much more benefited by salutary myths than by the naked truth. Precisely the liberals who hold that morality is historical or of merely human origin must go on to say . . . that this invaluable acquisition . . . is "too precious to be gambled with": the greatest enemies of civilization in civilized countries are those who squander the heritage . . . ; civilization is much less endangered by narrow but loyal preservers than by the shallow and glib futurists, who, being themselves rootless, try to destroy all roots and thus do everything in their power in order to bring back the initial chaos and promiscuity. The first duty of civilized man is then to respect his past.[8]

Again: "There is undoubtedly some kinship between the modern liberal and the ancient sophist. Both are unaware of the existence of a problem of civilization, although to different degrees. For Protagoras supplies his assertions with important qualifications which do not come out in Havelock's paraphrases. . . . The utmost one can say about his whole discussion is that it sheds some light on present day liberalism."[9]

In this context, he offers his most grave objection to Havelock and, by implication, to modern liberalism:

Through that philosophy the humane desire for tolerance is pushed to the extreme where tolerance becomes perverted into abandonment of all standards and hence of all discipline, including philological discipline. But absolute tolerance is altogether impossible; the allegedly absolute tolerance turns into ferocious hatred of those who have stated most clearly and most forcefully that there are unchangeable standards founded in the nature of man and the nature of things.[10]

I find Strauss's use of such phrases as "enemies of civilization," "squander," "perverted," "shallow and glib futurists," "rootless," "utmost," "abandonment of all standards," and "ferocious hatred" to express a degree of virulence outstripping the intellectual vices of his object of attack. I do, however, agree that every political regime must set limits and seek to secure them through education and discipline. A pluralistic society, for example, inculcates the virtue of relational modesty between proponents of different faiths and creeds, and it seeks to limit the power of those who would overthrow diversity in the name of religious unitarianism.

Most importantly, pluralism is not the same as cultural relativism, "absolute tolerance," or "the abandonment of all standards," though many of its critics, Straussian and otherwise, tend to treat these perspectives as if they were the same. Cultural relativism is the view that you should support the culture that is dominant in a particular place. The terms *culture* and *place* are key, for relativism is most at home with itself when it is situated in a concentric image of territorial culture. Here culture is said to radiate from the family to larger circles such as neighborhood, locality, and nation. The largest circles of belonging in turn radiate back to the smaller ones, with each circle entering into relations of resonance with the others. Given such an understanding of culture, a relativist is one who supports whatever practices and norms prevail in each concentrically ordered "place." Indeed, it is the concentric image of culture that allows you, first, to isolate each territorial regime as an enclosed "culture" and then to support the content of each territorial culture so defined. I don't, in fact, know many cultural relativists, for many called "relativists" by others do not in fact embrace a concentric image of culture. Rather, absolutists are apt to support such an image of culture and then to project their own image back on those they define as relativists.

A pluralist, by comparison, is one who prizes cultural diversity along several dimensions and is ready to join others in militant action, when necessary, to support pluralism against counter drives to unitarianism. A pluralist is unlikely to define culture through its concentric dimension alone, the definition of culture that allows both relativism and universalism in their simple forms to be. Pluralism, of the sort to be supported here at least, denies the sufficiency of a concentric image of culture to territorial politics. Pluralists are also alert to ec-centric connections that cut across the circles of family, neighborhood, and nation, as when ecologists in different parts of the world align to put pressure on several states at once, or gays and their supporters from different families, neighborhoods, communities, and religious faiths press for laws and norms that extend marriage and family, or an alliance of oil magnates from different countries puts pressure on oil-producing states, or a cross-state coalition of citizens presses the United States, Israel, and Palestine together to forge a real state in the occupied territory of Palestine. Pluralists are attentive both to established connections that exceed the concentric image of culture and to ec-centric flows that surge against the grain of the concentric dimension of being, as when new rights for women are taken through political insurgency, or a new right to doctor-assisted death for terminally ill patients is pressed into being from below the previous threshold of recognized rights, or a cross-country citizen movement is organized to alter state environmental practices.

Pluralists, given the complexity of culture, are often pressed to decide which of these parties to support, which to oppose, and which to meet with studied indifference. A pluralist thus seldom bestows "unqualified tolerance" on any specific place or circle of being, because the image of culture adopted does not divide territorial places up into intercoded circles. Pluralists are not relativists, in the first instance, because our very commitment to pluralism makes it incumbent upon us to embrace some things in this particular place, to be indifferent to others, to be wary of others, and to fight militantly against the continuation of yet others.

Pluralists set limits to tolerance to ensure that an exclusionary, unitarian movement does not take over an entire regime, that is, to ensure that a territorial regime does not become too concentric and too closed. Moreover, we also define a set of *general virtues and limits* needed to nourish a pluralist ethos within a territorial regime. Granted, we are cautious in setting *final* limits in advance to the scope of diversity, for we are attuned to the dicey history of how absolute limits posed at one time in Europe or America were revealed later to have fostered grave suffering and to be unnecessary to effective governance. Take, for starters, ideas, heretofore widespread in the West, that the citizens of a regime must be Christian, that only men can be citizens, that only heterosexuals can participate openly in public life, that racial mixing is misogyny, that only landed gentlemen are qualified to govern a state, that marriage must be restricted to the relation between men and women, and that avowed atheists are too unreliable to be serve as elected public officials. It is thus necessary to set limits, *but pluralists are critical of the self-confidence with which many unitarians endow already-existing limits with eternal necessity.*

It is necessary to set limits, partly because it is impossible to house every possible mode of diversity in the same regime at the same time. And it is necessary to organize militantly when pluralism is under grave duress from unitarian movements. You encourage a wide range of religious faiths, sensual habits, household organizations, ethnic traditions, gender practices, and so on, and you encourage the civic virtues of pluralism to inform relations between these constituencies. But a democratic pluralist won't willingly, for instance, allow: murder to go unpunished, parents to refuse to give their children the opportunity for education, the public school system to deteriorate, wealthy citizens to evade taxes, orphaned children to be placed under the care of incompetent adults, adult citizens to be unemployed for too long, the gap between the real cost of living in a system and the income-earning ability of most citizens to grow too large, the income hierarchy to become too extreme, or narrow unitarians of whatever stripe to take charge of the regime. Pluralists thus agree with Strauss that "absolute tolerance is altogether impossible," even as we may set the limits in question at different points and places.

Moreover, a diverse culture is one in which pluralistic *virtues* of public accountability, self-discipline, receptive listening, gritted-teeth tolerance of some things you hate, and a commitment to justice are widespread. Pluralism, particularly of the multidimensional, embedded variety supported here, requires a set of civic virtues to support itself.

But what is the "ground" or "basis" of pluralist virtues? Must it, at least, not come from a single, universal source? And how authoritative or self-certain is that ground? When Strauss alludes to the liberal's "ferocious hatred of those who have stated most clearly and most forcefully that there are unchangeable standards founded in the nature of man and the nature of things," it seems reasonable to assume that he endorses unchangeable standards anchored in a single source. Perhaps he does. But he also says, in a statement quoted earlier, that "Plato knew that most men read more with their 'imagination' than with open-minded care and are therefore much more benefited by salutary myths than by the naked truth." And several times Strauss says that he sometimes inserts his own beliefs into the words of others rather than stating them directly. So it is at least possible that, while Strauss thinks the untutored must be made to believe that there is an eternal, undeniable basis of fixed virtue, he himself doubts that the source needed can be demonstrated. If so, one way to protect this politically necessary but philosophically unanchored idea would be to attack vociferously those who publicly call the weight of the anchor into question. The virulence of Strauss's attack on Havelock, then, might express a desire to identify the single, universal basis of virtue *or* a desire to veil his own skepticism about the ability to provide the ground that civilization needs. It is hard to tell.

Let's pursue this question a step further, turning to an essay in which Strauss engages a great thinker of the past, an essay, therefore, less freighted with the political passions of Strauss's day. In the "Preface to Spinoza's Critique of Religion," Strauss explores the relation between reason and religious tradition in Spinoza's philosophy. Spinoza is pivotal because he helped launch the modern idea that reason is sufficient to itself, that it need not invoke an element of faith to support itself. After a rich account of responses by Jewish intellectuals in Weimar Germany to Spinoza's thought, Strauss turns to the fundamental issue dividing Jewish orthodoxy from Spinoza's heterodox philosophy. With respect to faith in "an omnipotent God whose will is unfathomable, whose ways are not our ways, who has decided to dwell in the thick darkness," Strauss says, "The orthodox premise cannot be refuted by experience nor by recourse to the principle of contradiction. An indirect proof of this is the fact that Spinoza and his like owed such success as they had in their fight against orthodoxy to laughter and mockery. . . . One is tempted to say that mockery does not succeed in the refutation of the orthodox tenets, but is itself the refutation."[11]

Indeed, we can now see that Strauss himself inverts Spinoza's strategy, replacing Spinoza's mockery of a personal God with invective concerning Havelock's faith in the contingency of the universe. Mockery weakens orthodox faith, Strauss says, when it taps into dissonance between the expressed belief of the faithful and other tacit judgments they make in daily life. If you already doubt at some level that every word in the Pentateuch was asserted by the divinely inspired Moses, Spinoza's presentation of textual evidence that Moses died before the books were finished might threaten your faith. But if your faith in divine inspiration runs deep, or if you think it is a faith that the masses must accept even if you do not, evidence of the untimely death of Moses merely adds a minor complication to be met in a variety of creative ways. So Spinozian mockery can take a toll on some believers, but Spinozian reason and argument, Strauss asserts, is incapable of providing a definitive refutation of orthodox faith.

> The genuine refutation of orthodoxy would require the proof that the world and human life are perfectly intelligible without the assumption of a mysterious God. . . . Spinoza's *Ethics* attempts to be that system but it does not succeed; the clear and distinct account of everything which it presents remains fundamentally hypothetical. As a consequence its cognitive status is not different from that of the orthodox account. Certain it is that Spinoza cannot legitimately deny the possibility of revelation. But to grant that revelation is possible means to grant that the philosophic account and the philosophic way of life are not necessarily, not evidently, the true account and the right way of life; philosophy, the quest for evident and necessary knowledge, rests itself on an unevident decision, on an act of will, just as faith. Hence the antagonism between Spinoza and Judaism, between belief and unbelief, is ultimately not theoretical, but moral.[12]

This is a superb formulation. I endorse much in it. Being a neo-Spinozist of sorts myself, I concur, for instance, that Spinoza did not demonstrate his philosophy of substance as univocal, or prove parallelism of mind and body. His is a highly contestable philosophy, one in which faith and argument are interwoven. Moreover, no secularist or rationalist after Spinoza has demonstrated the sufficiency of reason to itself, either, though it is understandable that a variety of scientists and atheists are impressed by the evidence and arguments to be brought on behalf of such a creed. Orthodox faith in a created world has not been eliminated by argument and laboratory results, though recourse to this piece of evidence or that argument might press some of the faithful to sharpen their thinking through alteration. Many modern Christians and Jews, for instance, have modified elements in their received faiths to render them compatible with evolutionary theory—

treating, for instance, biblical statements that appear to contravene that story as allegorical.

Faith is sustained by a mixture of cultural devices, including induction at a young age, common rituals, shared stories, epiphanic experiences, scientific research, and public arguments, all mixing into each other. Occasionally, an argument, unexpected event, expression of mockery, or startling piece of evidence hits a person of this or that faith in just the right way at a susceptible moment, prompting eventual conversion from one faith to another. Surely Spinoza's traumatic excommunication as a youth by Jewish Elders in Amsterdam played a role in the later evolution of his thought, for instance. Argument alone seldom, if ever, suffices to lodge or dislodge faith. It is even hard to say what "argument alone" would look like in such a context.

I also embrace a variant of the Straussian contention that the "antagonism between Spinoza and Judaism, between belief and unbelief, is ultimately not theoretical, but moral." To bring out the points of contact and difference, let me expand the formulation a little. The difference (which does not always have to take the form of an "antagonism") is not exactly between "belief and unbelief," with the implication that one side is filled with belief and the other has a vacancy where belief might have been. It is better articulated as the difference between a positive belief in *transcendence over the world* and a positive belief in the *immanence of the world.* Those inspired, say, by Moses, Paul, Augustine, or Mohammed hold that the world is created, that (in some cases) eternal life is possible, that the human obligation to morality is founded on a divine command in the last instance, and that divine revelation is fundamental to cultivation of religious truth. Those inspired by the likes of Buddha (in some readings), Epicurus, Lucretius, Spinoza, Hume, Nietzsche, and Havelock, by contrast, confess faith that the world is eternal rather than created, that it is a world of becoming without an intrinsic purpose, and that goodness and nobility are anchored, in the first instance, in a nonjuridical source such as human love of the complexity of world or the abundance of life over induction into a specific identity. The debate between these two faiths has not to date been resolved, despite what some parties on both sides say. The adversaries are inspired in part by contrasting moral judgments, with one set asserting that the world would fall apart unless most people profess belief in transcendence and the other contending that overcoming resentment of contingency is what is needed and that violent struggles between different visions of transcendence have brought a load of otherwise unnecessary agony into the world. Strauss himself may believe in a created world, or that the masses require such a belief even if he does not, or that Platonic reason is sufficient unto itself.[13] I will not try to decide that question.

My view is that the most noble response to this persisting conflict is to seek to transmute it into debates salted with agonistic respect between the partisans, with each faith-constituency acknowledging that its deepest and most entrenched faith is legitimately contestable by others. It may be, as "pessimists" eagerly retort, that many believers will refuse such an invitation. But if the late-modern time is one in which most territorial regimes find themselves populated by partisans of different faiths/creeds/philosophies, if much violence within and between states is traceable to dogmatism on this score, and if the cultural *need* for such a public ethos is therefore high, then public intellectuals should lead the way in setting the example, rather than decrying the refusal of others to follow one that they do not instantiate sufficiently in their own practices. The assumption enabling such a pursuit is that *between* a fundamental image of the world as either created or uncreated and a specific ethico-political stance resides a *sensibility* that infuses how the creed is lived, how it is expressed, and how it is portrayed to others. The sensibility flows into the creed, rotating its ethico-political compass in this way or that. An existential faith, then, consists in a creed or philosophy plus the sensibility that infuses it.

The most urgent need today is to mix presumptively generous sensibilities into a variety of theistic and nontheistic creeds, sensibilities attuned to the contemporary need to transfigure relations of antagonism between faiths into relations of agonistic respect. The idea is not to rise either to one ecumenical faith or to a practice of reason located entirely above faith, but to forge a positive ethos of engagement between alternative faiths/philosophies. Of course, the difficulties are great and the probabilities may even point in other directions, but the contemporary need is great. Those who invoke the cover of pessimism to forgo pursuit of the possibility do not contribute enough to the end they purport to support.

Such a pluralism of creeds, again, does not devolve into relativism. Pluralists think it is extremely important, for instance, *how* people of diverse faiths hold and express their faiths in public space. And we seek to limit the power of those who would invest their faith with unquestioned territorial hegemony. We think that, in a world marked by the co-existence of multiple faiths on most politically organized territories, the horizontal relations between faiths require as much attention as the vertical dimensions of each. *Expansive pluralism, then, supports the dissemination of general virtues across diverse faiths.*

To the extent that Strauss seeks to realize a regime in which one creed rules over others, he folds an exclusionary sensibility into his faith. The exclusionary imperative is an effect less of the creed he embraces than of the type of sensibility infused into it. To the extent that he seeks to realize a world in which multiple faiths interact productively on the same terrain, that, too, is influenced by the kind of sensibility infused into faith. The same goes for me. My faith in immanence, in the last instance, might be joined to a presumptively generous sensibility or to an exclusionary, imperious sensibility.

But why do I, a believer in immanence and supporter of deep pluralism between creeds, join Strauss in drawing attention to the ubiquity of faith? Why do so, in particular, during a time when so many brim over with faith and many of the faithful in several traditions vindicate violence to nationalize the states they inhabit? Here I follow William James, to whom the same question was posed. James says, "I quite agree that what mankind at large most lacks is criticism and caution, not faith."[14] Among many, it is the relational sensibility attached to faith that needs work, not the admission that faith plays an important role in life. But, James asserts, he writes in the first instance to other philosophers, most of whom profess either to rise above faith or, more often, to bracket it when they participate in the domains of science, literary theory, philosophy, social theory, and public life.

James, like Strauss and me, is dubious about these latter claims. While many express their faith with less relational modesty than need be, the intellectual class tends to repress the role that faith plays in the intellectual enterprise itself. It is when you press the ubiquity of faith upon the intellectual class that you see that faith need not always be everything or nothing. There is a lot of room between denying faith a constitutive role in life and making it into everything. When you see how faith commitments vary in intensity, content, and imperiousness, you set the stage to explore what it takes to engender modesty in the relations between faiths co-existing on the same territory. And when you include yourself and your faith in the equation, rather than pretending to float above the fray, you place yourself in a better position to commend the ethos to others.

Americanism and Terrorism

Let's fast-forward from the age of Strauss to today. William Kristol, a leading Republican publicist, Paul Wolfowitz, the Deputy Secretary of Defense under George W. Bush who orchestrated the Iraqi invasion, and William Bennett, a leading publicist of neoconservatism, all profess debts to Leo Strauss. I will focus on Bennett, who until recently served as the most visible media spokesperson for Reagan-Bush-Bush Republicanism. Between Leo Strauss of the 1950s and 1960s and William Bennett of the onset of the twenty-first century, a host of events has transpired. There have been new movements in decolonization, civil rights, feminism, gay/lesbian rights, sexual liberation, and ecology. On the register of dramatic events, there has been an intensification of the Palestinian-Israeli conflict, the rise of a global corporate plutocracy, the collapse of the Soviet Union, the emergence of a neoconservative majority on the American Supreme Court, the intensification of a large evangelical Christian political movement, the near takeover of the electronic news media in the U.S. by the moderate and bellicose right, the rapid rise of neoconservative think tanks, 9/11, the war against Al Qaeda in Afghanistan, the Guantánamo Gulag, the invasion and occupation of Iraq by an American-led coalition of the willing, and Abu Ghraib.

William Bennett is no Leo Strauss. Is he, though, one of the gentlemen Strauss says philosophers need to help infuse virtue into the currency of public life? There is, in one respect, a clear line of descent from Strauss's philosophical politics, propagated through readings of classic philosophers, to William Bennett's political admonitions, delivered in popular books, public speeches, and TV interviews. Bennett also sees relativism, self-indulgence, and rootlessness all around him, particularly among those who support multidimensional pluralism. He finds organized religion, particularly Christianity, to provide an essential source of value to America and Western civilization. And he focuses on weaknesses in American education, attacking in strong terms the "secularism" and "anti-Americanism" of the "professoriate."

Bennett, like Strauss, looks back to a time when values were solid and the middle class had self-confidence. His descriptions of decadence resonate with those Strauss gave of the 1950s and 1960s in America. Unlike Strauss, however, he does not measure modernity against the ancient Greek world. Rather, he measures the present against the 1950s in America, the period in which Strauss himself saw classical virtues succumbing to the rootlessness and relativism of modern liberalism. When you read Bennett alongside Strauss, seeing the same terms applied to different eras, you discern how efficacious the relentless use of that rhetoric can be by those hell-bent on occupying the authoritative center around which other minorities are expected to revolve.

Bennett, unlike Strauss, is not wary of the electronic news media. He lives on and for it. This gentleman, who loves to gamble, would bet a large sum against my wager on the positive relation between pursuing an expansive ethos of multidimensional pluralism and the survival of democratic civilization. I think that today it has become even more important to mobilize a cross-state citizen movement to press Israel and the United States to support either a new state of Palestine or a greater Israel with equal citizenship for all residents. Such a direction is not only just to the occupied residents of Palestine, it is also important to the future of democracy in the United States and Europe. In *Why We Fight*, written shortly after the trauma of 9/11, Bennett proceeds in a different direction. He explains why it is necessary to wage aggressive cultural and military war against the evils of Islam. The American reaction to the trauma of 9/11 has filled him with hope, for he discerns a new unity of purpose in America.

The war on terror, he says, is above all a religious war. In that war, America must be wary of the liberal distinction between moderate and extreme Muslims, in either the Middle East or the United States. The first attack against America in 1993 "should have brought home the folly of the then fashionable distinction between 'moderate' and 'extreme' Muslim militants and the absolute need to 'err on the side of caution' in protecting the safety of our citizens."[15]

Bennett, like Strauss, has been critical of secularism in the West because it does not give enough importance to religious faith in supporting essential republican virtues. He would be pleased to know that at least 58 percent of Americans say that you cannot be moral unless you believe in God, while the figure is only around 13 percent in France.[16] He would also be pleased to learn that 81 percent of Americans believe in hell, though it might trouble him that less than 1 percent think they themselves are going to hell. Given Bennett's previous focus on the indispensability of religion to public life, it is fascinating to see how he now thinks the Islamic world needs to undergo "the equivalent of the eighteenth-century Enlightenment,"[17] though he is hardly confident it will do so.

Here I am closer to Strauss along one dimension and critical of both along another. I think, first, that exclusionary variants of Judaism, Christianity, Islam, and atheism could all profit from going through the Enlightenment and, second, that the secularism emerging from the Enlightenment is today too unalert to the role that enactment and ritual play in its own mode of being and too self-confident in projecting a separation between reason and faith. We need to pass *through* the Enlightenment, in its dominant modes, coming out at a place that respects its opposition to theocracy while simultaneously moving beyond the overweening confidence in reason the two dominant wings within it pursued.[18] If and as you call upon Muslims in Europe and America to be receptive to co-existence with other faiths on the same territory and across territorial divisions, it is indispensable to work upon your own faith—theistic or nontheistic—to come to terms affirmatively with its deep contestability in the hearts and minds of others.

Bennett also believes that both "we" and "they" need to rethink things, but he means that we need to affirm our superiority more confidently, while they need to admit our superiority more humbly. When we identify the sources of attacks on us:

> Too often we have tacitly accepted a share of that blame, tacitly behaved as if we needed to ask forgiveness for the weakness and backwardness, the corruption and evil, that others have brought on themselves and for which they are solely responsible. If the Islamic world is ever to experience the uplift it has demanded, all this will have to change—on both sides. They will have to cease rejecting Western civilization and instead begin to study it; we will have to cease indulging ourselves in guilt and instead, as the writer Shelby Steele has finely put it, "allow the greatness of Western civilization to speak for itself."[19]

For Bennett, Arabs should study the greatness of Western civilization, not, however, as it today unveils itself in film, TV dramas, novels, pop music, the professoriate, many Protestant Christian churches, and liberal politicians. Its greatness stands against such relativistic and rootless forces. "Western civilization" functions, in his hands, as a weapon to wield against traditions outside the West *and* the majority of things that now constitute the West. He seeks to wage cultural war within "the West" and cultural-military campaigns against Islam outside it.

Bennett does praise Islam in the late Middle Ages. But I can find no moment where a crack opens to encourage him to listen with new ears to faiths different from those already on his official register of those to be honored. Cultural pluralism, for him, is not something you draw upon to open yourself a bit. It is a weapon to wield against places and faiths that do not conform to the fixed range of diversity you now accept.

The neoconservative policies of invasion and occupation, combined with efforts to tighten borders and security arrangements at home, both humiliate and outrage many in the Middle East and turn pluralist democracies against themselves, fostering more closed surveillance states. New patterns of surveillance can easily be installed. But every time you make progress on one front without addressing Muslim grievances abroad and at home, new holes, cracks, border porosities, and potential targets automatically emerge elsewhere. If the border between the U.S. and Mexico is secured, that between it and Canada becomes more porous; if air travel is tightened, the food-supply system, trains, the computer network, and urban targets of dirty bombs become available. Airport surveillance, Internet filters, passport-tracking devices, legal detention without criminal charges, security internment camps, secret trials, "free speech zones," DNA profiles, border walls and fences, erosion of the line between internal security and external military action, and translation of large sections of the electronic news media into embedded conduits of mass mobilization—these security activities resonate together, engendering a national-security machine that pushes numerous issues outside the range of legitimate dissent and mobilizes the populace to provide abstract readiness to support new security and surveillance practices against under-specified enemies.

Bennett is a publicist who has lost touch with subtle elements in the thought of the master who inspires him, even as he applies the master's rhetoric of relativism, rootlessness, self-indulgence, misguided tolerance, and superficiality against Democrats, liberals, and pluralists in his own state.

A Special Minority

Strauss is insightful about the predicament of Jews in Europe before the Second World War. He sees that prewar, secular responses to Judaism promoted legal equality without becoming deeply embedded in public culture. Judgments about who belongs and does not belong are not inscribed in law alone. They also reside in the daily practices of the majority, in how it responds in public places, the workplace, the stage, in commercial life, at dinner parties, in the courtroom, at the police station, and so on. Strauss quotes Theodor Herzl, who said, "We are a nation—the enemy makes us a nation whether we like it or not."[20] The enemy defined Jews as a nonterritorial nation within a territorial state, guaranteeing in so doing that Jews would be treated as a special minority unlike other minorities. Strauss does not think that early Zionism was capable of resolving "the Jewish problem" either.

It is not clear to me how Strauss would extrapolate from these insights today. But the condition of the Jew in Europe prior to the Second World War parallels in one respect the condition of Muslims in Europe and the United States today. There are differences. The Muslim minority here and now, unlike the Jewish minority there and then, has another region to turn to, where its faith is in charge. The similarity, however, is that many Europeans and Americans today define Muslims as a special minority, as the minority that constitutes a nation within a nation which does not honor the Enlightenment distinction between private faith and public reason.

Talal Asad, an anthropologist of Islamic heritage, studies the religious practices of both Christians and Muslims. He explores an obscure dimension of contemporary European secularism that unconsciously contributes to the politics of double minoritization of Muslims.

Consider his critique of Wilfred Cantrell Smith, who sought to distill the essence of "religion" from several world cultures and then drew upon that distillation to compare Islam, Christianity, and Judaism. Smith, Asad says, thinks of a religious tradition "as a cognitive framework, not as a practical mode of living, not as techniques for teaching body and mind to cultivate specific virtues and abilities that have been authorized, passed on, and reformulated down the generations."[21] Smith treats the palpable operation of ritual in some variants of Islam as a sign of its underdeveloped character. His secular, Protestant reading of religion in general obscures an important component of culture—*its embodiment in repetitive practices that help to constitute the dispositions, sensibilities, and ethos through which meaning is lived, intellectual beliefs are settled, and relations between constituencies are negotiated.* Smith's very distillation of "religion" and "faith" from the materialities of culture situates them within a secular image of a world divided between private rituals and publicly articulated beliefs. It treats belief as neatly separable from ritual practice. This unconscious generalization of one image of religion then sets the standard he uses to measure one "religion" against others.

The political upshot of Smith's interpretation becomes visible in Asad's book *Formations of the Secular.* Here Asad traces how the dominant European idea of religion expresses a larger cultural unconscious discernible in Smith's work. He contrasts this self-understanding to devotional practices of Christianity in the European Middle Ages. Then when the Christian "devotee heard God speak there was a sensuous connection between the inside and outside, a fusion between signifier and signified. The proper reading of scripture depended on disciplining the senses (especially hearing, speech, and sight)."[22] This inner connection between devotional practice and education of the senses gets obscured in secular, Protestant representations of religion: "where faith [within Europe] had once been a virtue, it now acquired an epistemological sense. Faith became a way of knowing supernatural objects, parallel to the knowledge of nature (the *real* world) that reason and observation provided."[23] Now, rituals and exercises are understood only to *symbolize* a belief or faith already there, not to participate in the very constitution of faith itself. You can hear echoes of Strauss's account of the ubiquity of faith in Asad's genealogy, even if the sensibility of the two theorists—their sensory orientations and sensual dispositions to diversity—differ.

Of course, if Asad is right, the body/brain/culture network in which we participate still continues to flow back and forth between human enactment, institutional discipline, embedded experience, and the constitution of belief. But many secularists, ministers, theologians, anthropologists, philosophers, and social scientists place such practices within a cognitive framework that either ignores the embedded character of embodied faith, diminishes its importance, or reduces it to modes of cultural manipulation to be transcended by cognitively pure belief. Cultural theorists often speak of the body. But many who do so continue to reduce ritual to a mechanism through which beliefs are *represented* rather than a medium through which embodied habits, dispositions, sensibilities, and capacities of performance are also *composed and consolidated*. Atheists, too, participate in this tendency when they act as if the only question is whether you "believe" in a transcendent God, accepting, in doing so, the assumption that cognitive belief or disbelief is both the only critical element and separable from the education of the senses: "The idea that there is a single clear 'logic of atheism' is itself the product of a modern binary—belief or unbelief in a supernatural being."[24]

Euro-American Protestants and secularists are thus apt to obscure those practices of dress, demeanor, perception, gesture, dreaming, and prayer that help to compose *their* orientations to being, even as they focus on them in a relatively unfamiliar constituency. They are apt, that is, to reduce their own faith to a set of abstract *beliefs*, while concluding that a Muslim minority lacks the secular division between private belief and public behavior that marks a tolerant society.

Many contemporary Euro-American secularists—both the majority who privately profess belief in a transcendent God and the minority who do not—fasten onto this issue, contending that the problem of "Islamic faith" inside and outside Europe is generated by the failure of its adherents to accept the division between freedom of private faith and participation in democratic governance of the state by citizens who bracket their faith when they enter the public fray. Both nationalists on the right and secular liberals contend that "the de-essentialization of Islam is paradigmatic for all thinking about the assimilation of non-European peoples to European civilization."[25] The critical point is that as and if you discern how faith and demeanor are connected you also become less confident about the secular picture of a wall between private faith and public reason.

Asad does not claim that Muslims in Europe make no contribution to the difficulties they face. Those who constitute their faith as the universal faith that should govern others on the same territory may experience themselves to be persecuted merely because the political regime in which they participate does not make their faith the governing one. In that respect they mirror the demands of those Jews, Christians, and atheists who have demanded territorial hegemony for their faiths. Asad suggests, however, that the negotiation of a new pluralism in Europe will *also* involve reassessment on the part of secular, enlightened Europeans of their own tendency to treat belief as neatly separable from disciplinary practices, cultural routines, and the education of sensory experience. Augustine knew these things, too. He knew, for instance, that confession voiced in the right way in the proper mood of devotion helps to embed the faith it articulates. Even Kant knew better.

Indeed, the most popular definition of contemporary "Europe" itself—as presented by those constituencies who define themselves as embodying its essence—is that to be European is to express religious belief in the private realm and to participate as abstract citizens in the public one. This tolerant-sounding definition quietly elevates modern Christian believers into the center of Europe and shuffles Muslim believers into a minority unlike other minorities.

I would add that, for secularists, religion is safely relegated to the private realm only because secularists also contend that there is an independent way of reaching authoritative public agreements without recourse to the diverse religious faiths of citizens. The problem is that different secular sects nominate different instruments to fill this role, and each instrument diverges significantly from the others on what that authoritative practice is or could be. Some place their faith in the dictates of public reason, others in deliberative consensus, others in transparent procedures, others in implicit contractual agreements, and others in a "myth" of equality citizens accept *as if* it were ontologically grounded. None of these images of public life folds the reflexivity needed into faith-practices themselves. They do not, in my view, because they pretend to identify *a forum above faith through which to regulate diverse faiths*. If the nobility of secularism resides in its quest to enable multiple faiths to co-exist on the same territory, its shallowness resides in the hubris of its distinction between private faith and public reason.

Embedded Faith and Relational Diversity

If Asad clarifies an element in the double minoritization of Muslims in Europe and America, he also speaks to many orthodox Catholics, Jews, evangelical Protestants, and obdurate atheists. Taken together, these minorities may make up a majority of minorities in several countries.[26] Many of them feel that the privatization of religion and the corollary reduction of faith to a pile of epistemic beliefs has minoritized them in a double way too, if not as radically. Thus the issue posed with reference to Muslims in Europe is important to Muslims, to other faith-practices, and to the larger question of how to forge a robust, pluralist ethos of engagement out of multiple minorities of religious being.

What, from the point of view of secularism, does it take to "de-essentialize" faith? In the case of John Rawls, for instance, it seems to involve three things: first, to subtract from each creed the demand that it provide the authoritative center around which state politics rotates; second, to disconnect belief (but not its symbolic expression) from devout enactments and ritual performances; third, to reach consensus on a discourse of public justice that rises above the diversity of private faiths while being compatible with most.[27] The doctrine of embedded pluralism I embrace concurs with Rawlsian secularism in asking advocates of each faith-practice, including Christianity, to give up the first demand, doing so because this is the minimal concession each must make to foster common governance on the same strip of territory without significant violence or oppression. It breaks, however, with classical secularism on the second expectation. That expectation, as I have already suggested, rests upon a superficial reading of the complex relation between devotional mood, performance, and belief. Once you modify the second condition, it becomes pertinent to reconstitute the third expectation, as well. To put the point briefly, you transfigure the drive to reach a consensus on justice above contending faiths into the effort to negotiate a positive ethos of engagement between multiple constituencies who bring chunks and pieces of their faiths with them into the public realm.

It is pertinent to see how the Rawlsian image of secularism also coalesces with the image of the state assumed in realist and neorealist international relations theory. According to these accounts, the Westphalian accord in early modern Europe recognized the sovereignty of each European state over its citizens by pushing religious differences into the private realm. Thus domestic liberal theory and international-relations theory in the West converge upon the assumption of privatized religion. But, again, if Asad is correct, Christendom has never been privatized in Euro-American states to the degree publicists of secularism and the Westphalian accord assume. To pursue a new pluralism appropriate to the contemporary world is to come to terms, then, with the expansion of religious diversity inside Western states, the critical role that practice plays in constituting each religious faith as well as in representing it, the effects the acceleration of speed and interdependence have had on citizen movements to foster multidimensional diversity within and across states, and the effects all of these process have had on the double minoritization of many Muslims within Euro-American states.

Here we focus on what it takes to pluralize political culture within Europe and the United States. Two ingredients are critical. First, there is the extension of the *dimensions* or *types* of legitimate diversity within the state. In a culture of multidimensional pluralism, you not only honor a diversity of faiths and ethnic practices, you also extend diversity into gender practices, marriage arrangements, linguistic use, sensual affiliations, and household organization. If and as multidimensional diversity becomes embedded in corporations, schools, the military, and the composition of elected officials, *a host of constituencies now acquire more leverage to press their faith communities from within to honor that variety.* The cumulative effect is a healthy politics of creedal ventilation within and between faiths.[28] Such creedal ventilation uncovers an elasticity of language and governance already simmering in each creed, particularly when each is considered across a long stretch of time. The new social movements within faith communities make this element of elasticity more transparent to the faithful.

More importantly yet, together such movements disperse the mythic assumptions through which defenders of the religiously centered nation portray the common life. Such movements disperse the appearance of a national center occupied by one constituency affirming the same faith, using the same language, displaying the same skin color, conforming to the same marriage practices, and/or participating in the same sensual affiliations. *The image of a national majority around which minorities of different types revolve is eventually transfigured into the image of interdependent minorities of different types, each of which needs to sustain connections with numerous others to generate practices of common governance.* This effect is accomplished both by drawing multiple minorities out of the closet and by amplifying public awareness of a multidimensional diversity that is already in motion below the static images of national self-representation. The most positive result of such a process is to transfigure the myth of a uniform majority that tolerates or represses a set of discrete minorities ranged around it into a visible culture of interdependent minorities of multiple types negotiating a generous ethos of governance between them. In the most promising scenario, every individual and every constituency now becomes a minority along one or more dimensions.[29]

No automatism governs this process; it can be derailed at any point. It is almost as susceptible to derailment as the pursuit of the unified nation is to the violent repression of selected minorities or devolution into a civil war between militant contenders seeking to occupy the authoritative center.

If and when muiltidimensional pluralization is well underway, it *amplifies* within each institutional faith an experience already there. Most institutional faiths are punctuated by a moment of mystery, abyss, rupture, openness, or difference within the faith that complicates or confounds the experience of faith. It is precisely at this point in their own practices that the faithful identify a stutter in their own creed, sometimes drawing upon this sense of creedal insufficiency to inspire presumptive generosity toward other creeds. For Christians, this might be the element of mystery or trembling that Augustine and Kierkegaard respectively emphasize; for Buddhists, it might be the point at which the apparently solid self encounters the absence of the ego in a world without a designing God; for Muslims, it might be the moment of mystical reception of the difference between finitude and infinity; for nontheists, it might be the element of abundance, creativity, and unpredictability that inhabits a world of becoming; and for Jews, it might be the ineffable dimension of divinity that makes it inappropriate to name the nameless one. In each case, the gap opens up an element of mystery, rupture, or difference that evades or resists definitive interpretation.

This internal element is fateful to the politics of pluralism, for at this juncture some of the faithful are moved to deny or repress such a moment in the interests of asserting political hegemony over other faiths. It is the moment when, in effect, many are tempted to call the devotees of other faiths faithless, nihilists, subjectivists, relativists, or rootless, on the way to vindicating their marginalization, or worse. There is a long history of this. Sometimes it acquires an ironic twist, as when Kantian Christians asserted that Jewish legalism makes its proponents unalert to the rupture in faith and therefore not qualified to be full citizens in Europe. Today, I call attention to a variant of this phenomenon that still falls below the radar of many defenders of the religions of the Book, for many of these assert with confidence that, while faith in *transcendence*—which might assume the shape of Christ, Allah, the nameless one, or a more faint whisper yet—draws you to the experience of the rupture or difference in faith, faith in *immanence*, in a world of becoming without a divine force above the world, projects confidence that the world is without rupture, or knowable in the last instance, or subject to consummate human control. Such a reading, however, misrepresents several philosophies of immanence by failing to come to terms with the image of time as "out of joint" in which they are set. Such misrepresentations can have fateful consequences, as the ugly history of Euro-American orientations to paganism and atheism testify.

Assuming, then, that most faiths encounter a disruptive moment within their own faith, the response of participants to this internal rupture is fateful for the possibility of pluralism. The response might open the door to pluralism or marshal its repression. There is, in my judgment, no definitive causal process or undeniable moral law that governs the outcome. It depends, as our earlier foray into Straussian theory may have indicated, upon the sensibilities the faithful cultivate, the decisions they make, and the ethos they seek to negotiate. That's why, at this point and others too, pluralism emerges as a possibility to pursue rather than as the certain effect of determinate conditions. To the extent it is attained, it remains a fragile achievement to be cherished rather than an outcome to be taken for granted.[30]

The most that can be said, then, is that, in an age of multiple minorities of numerous types co-existing on the same territory, considerable pressures emerge to amplify the dimension of difference or mystery within each faith. To the extent that pressure is affirmed without resentment rather than repressed or resented, negotiation of a positive ethos of engagement becomes more promising.

In a political culture of deep pluralism with a twist, each faith practices its specific rituals, and each faith-minority brings pieces and dimensions of its faith into the public realm when the issue in question makes it pertinent to do so. Deep pluralism thereby reinstates the link between practice and belief artificially severed by secularism; and it also overturns the impossible counsel to bracket your faith when you participate in politics. But, to support the possibility of multiple faiths negotiating with dignity on the same territory, each faith-minority now amplifies awareness of the element of rupture or mystery already simmering within it. It responds affirmatively to the preliminary sense of rupture in faith, as well as to other ingredients that counsel generosity to others. It does so by mixing into its faith-imbued practices a secondary set of practices that prepare it to participate with forbearance and presumptive generosity in a larger ethos of multidimensional pluralism. Each faith thereby *embeds* the religious virtue of hospitality and the civic virtue of presumptive generosity in its own relational practices.

But what are the attractions of such an agenda? Negotiation of such an ethos of pluralism, first, honors the embedded experience of faith; second, gives expression to a fugitive element of care, hospitality, or love for difference simmering in most faiths; third, speaks to a compelling need during a time when most territorial states house multiple faiths; and, fourth, offers the best opportunity for diverse faiths to co-exist without vio-lence while supporting the civic conditions of common governance. It does not issue in a simple universalism, in which one image of transcendence prevails everywhere or in cul-tural relativism, in which one faith prevails here and another there. It is neither universal-ism nor relativism in the simple mode of each.[31] It is pluralism. A pluralism that periodically must be defended militantly against this or that drive to religio-state unitarianism.

The public ethos of pluralism pursued here, again, solicits the active cultivation of pluralist virtues by each faith and the negotiation of a positive ethos of engagement be-tween faiths. Unlike the versions of liberalism and relativism Strauss and Bennett oppose, I am thereby a proponent of civic virtue. But the public virtues embraced are pluralist virtues. The civic virtues of pluralism, in turn, must become embedded in numerous institutional practices for a positive ethos of pluralism to be.

Such modulating practices are already operative, to some degree, in many, perhaps most, faith-practices. They are also more densely sedimented in nontheistic practices than many theological and secular intellectualists admit.[32] They find expression in the multi-media worlds of family ritual, neighborhood gossip, classroom routine, dormitory living, urban apartments, occupational disciplines, professional practices, individual exercises, films, and TV dramas. Such cultural practices mix image, word, rhythm, music, and other nonconceptual sounds to help compose the relational, thought-imbued moods that in-habit us.

The ennobling of pluralism, to the extent it occurs, moves back and forth between microscopic negotiation of mundane issues among multiple minorities, reflexive work upon the relational dimension of their own faith-practices by specific constituencies, and public engagement with larger issues of the day. It is the endless circuits back and forth that do the most productive work.

The motives to support multidimensional pluralism are themselves diverse, irreduc-ible to any single model of moral obligation or self-interest. Support is grounded partly in care for the late-modern condition that multiplies minorities on the same territory; partly in a desire to ensure that you do not become a minority persecuted by others; partly in an interest to protect the survival of democracy under the distinctive conditions of late-modern life; partly in recognition of the embedded character of your own faith as well as that of others; partly in specific injunctions to love, generosity, charity, or hospital-ity that help to compose your own faith-practices; partly in a desire to avoid participation in otherwise unnecessary modes of violence fomented by the clarion call of national unity; and partly in a mixture of these motives, which will vary in texture from case to case. The hope is that these motives will mix into one another, engendering a positive resonance machine.

Tolerance of negotiation, mutual adjustment, relational modesty, and agonistic re-spect are, up to a point, cardinal virtues of embedded pluralism. The limit is reached when pluralism itself is threatened by nationalist forces in the name of defeating "relativism," "nihilism," or "rootlessness." At a certain point of danger, a militant assemblage of pluralists, with each constituency drawing upon its own sources of sustenance, must coalesce to resist such an onslaught. Before that point is reached, it is important to point out muted ways by which the politics of anathematization proceeds, for when intercultural connections are intensive and extensive, the anathematizations of one day readily degenerate into policies of repression, cleansing, invasion, torture, or liquidation on the next.

Deep, multidimensional pluralism provides a viable corrective to cultural relativism, shallow secular diversity, and national models of exclusionary politics. To the extent that it responds to the contemporary acceleration of pace and diversification marking the contemporary age, the new pluralism carries forward through alteration noble elements in the Enlightenment, democracy, and the religions of the Book.

Subjects of Tolerance

Why We Are Civilized and They Are the Barbarians

Wendy Brown

Primitive men . . . are uninhibited: thought passes directly into action.

> —Sigmund Freud, *Totem and Taboo*

If intolerance and narcissism are connected, one immediate and practical conclusion might seem to be: we are only likely to love others more if we also learn to love ourselves a little less.

> —Michael Ignatieff, "Nationalism and Toleration"

Since a group is in no doubt as to what constitutes truth or error, and is conscious, moreover, of its own great strength, it is as intolerant as it is obedient to authority. It respects force and can only be slightly influenced by kindness, which it regards merely as a form of weakness. What it demands of its heroes is strength, or even violence. It wants to be ruled and oppressed and to fear its masters. Fundamentally, it is entirely conservative, and it has a deep aversion to all innovations and advances and an unbounded respect for tradition.

> —Sigmund Freud, citing Gustav Le Bon, *Group Psychology*

The murder of [a U.S. civilian working in Saudi Arabia] shows the evil nature of the enemy we face—these are barbaric people.

> —President George W. Bush, June 18, 2004

In recent years, culture has become a cardinal object of tolerance and intolerance. This is not only because liberal democratic societies have become increasingly multicultural as a consequence of late-modern population flows and the affirmation of cultural difference over assimilation. It is also because political conflict has become, in Mahmood Mamdani's phrase, "culturalized": "It is no longer the market (capitalism), nor the state (democracy), but culture (modernity) that is said to be the dividing line between those in favor of a peaceful, civic existence and those inclined to terror."[1] Mamdani credits Samuel Huntington and Bernard Lewis with conceptually catapulting culture to the status of a political dividing line between good and evil, progress and reaction, peaceability and violence. In a 1990 article "The Roots of Muslim Rage," Bernard Lewis put forward the "clash of civilizations" thesis to describe relations between what he termed the "Judeo-Christian" and "Islamic" civilizations; a few years later, Huntington generalized the thesis to argue that "the velvet curtain of culture" had replaced the Cold War "iron curtain of ideology."[2]

When political or civil conflict becomes culturalized, whether in international or domestic politics, tolerance emerges as a key term, for two reasons. The first is that some cultures are depicted as tolerant while others are not, that is, tolerance itself is culturalized insofar as it is understood to be available only to certain cultures. The second is that the culturalization of conflict makes cultural difference itself into a (if not *the*) salient site for the practice of tolerance or intolerance. The border between cultures is taken to be inherently volatile if those cultures are not subdued by liberalism.[3] Thus tolerance, rather than, say, equality, emancipation, or power sharing, becomes a basic term in the vocabulary describing and prescribing for conflicts rendered as cultural.

The culturalization of conflict and of difference discursively depoliticizes both, while organizing the players in a particular fashion, one that makes possible that odd but familiar move within liberalism: "culture" is what nonliberal peoples are imagined to be ruled and ordered by, but liberal peoples are considered to *have* culture or cultures. In other words, what Mamdani terms the "ideological culturalization" of politics does not reduce all conflict or difference to culture in a uniform way. Rather, "we *have* culture, while culture *has* 'them'"; or we *have* culture, while they *are* a culture. Or we are a democracy, while they are a culture. This asymmetry turns upon an imagined opposition between culture and individual moral autonomy, in which the former vanquishes the latter unless culture is subordinated to liberalism. The logic derived from this opposition between nonliberalized culture and moral autonomy then articulates a further set of oppositions between nonliberalized culture and freedom, and between nonliberalized culture and equality. This essay maps this logic in order to reveal how and why liberalism conceives of itself as unique in its capacity to be culturally neutral and culturally tolerant, and conceives of nonliberal "cultures" as disposed toward barbarism.

. . .

The overt premise of liberal tolerance, when applied to group practices (as opposed to idiosyncratic individual beliefs or behaviors), is that religious, cultural, or ethnic differences are sites of natural or native hostility. Tolerance is conceived as a tool for managing or attenuating this hostility to achieve peaceful co-existence. Yet within a liberal paradigm, this premise already begs a number of questions: What makes groups cohere in the first place, that is, what binds them within and makes them hostile without? What makes group identity based on culture, religion, or ethnicity, as opposed to other kinds of differences, an inherent site of intolerance? Within liberal society, what are culture, religion, or ethnicity imagined to contain within and repel without that makes their borders so significant? What do we imagine deposited in these sites such that they feature a relatively solidaristic inside and inherently hostile outside? Given a liberal account of human beings as relatively atomized, competitive, acquisitive, and insecure, what makes common beliefs or practices a site for overcoming this prickliness? What kinds of beliefs are thought to bind us, and is it something in the nature of the beliefs themselves or is the binding achieved through an order of *affect* attached to belief? Put differently, what is the relation between the binding force of the social contract and the binding force of culture or religion? Why isn't the social contract sufficient for reducing the significance of subnational group hostilities?[4]

In short, what, according to liberal theory, makes multiculturalism a political problem that tolerance is summoned to solve? And from what noncultural, nonethnic, or secular place is tolerance imagined to emanate for this work? These are not easy questions to ask, or even to formulate properly, from within a liberal, modernist, or rationalist paradigm. This is partly because the methodological individualism of liberal theory produces the figure of an individuated subject by abstracting and isolating deliberative rationality from embodied locations or constitutive practices. The formulation of rationality that has nonreason as its opposite presumes a Cartesian splitting of mind from embodied, historicized, cultured being. Across Lockean, Kantian, Millian, Rawlsian, and Habermasian perspectives, rationality transcends, or better, exceeds embodiment and cultural location to permit a separation between rational thought, on one side, and the constitutive embodiment of certain beliefs and practices, on the other. For deliberative rationality to be meaningful apart from "culture" or "subjectivity," the conceit must be in play that the individual *chooses* what he or she thinks. This same choosing articulates the possibility of an optional relationship with culture, religion, and even ethnic belonging; it sustains as well the conceit that the rationality of the subject is independent of these things, which are named as context rather than constitutive. But if the deliberative rationality that generates choice entails the capacity of the subject to abstract from its own context, then individuation itself posits a will (to reason as well as to other things) that enables such independence. The idea of individuation is thus enabled on the one side by rationality and on the other by a notion of will; together they produce the possibility of the autonomous liberal subject.

The quintessential theorist of this formulation, of course, is Kant, for whom intellectual and moral maturity consists in using "one's own understanding without the guidance of another."[5] Rational argument and criticism, indeed, the rationality of criticism, is not simply the sign but also the basis of the moral autonomy of persons, an autonomy that presupposes independence from others, independence from authority in general, *and* the independence of reason itself. From this perspective, a less individuated person, one who has what social theorists term an organicist identity, appears as neither fully rational nor fully in command of a will. That is, the liberal formulation of the individuated subject as constituted by rationality and will figures a nonindividuated opposite who is so *because of* the underdevelopment of both rationality and will. For the organicist creature, considered to lack rationality and will, culture and religion (culture *as* religion, and religion *as* culture–equations that work only for this creature) are saturating and authoritative, while for the liberal one, culture and religion become "background," can be "entered" and "exited," and are thus rendered extrinsic to rather than constitutive of the subject.

Through individuation, so this story goes, culture and religion as forms of rule are dethroned, replaced by the self-rule of men. But this very dethroning changes the meaning of culture and religion within liberal and organicist orders. In liberal societies, culture is positioned as the "background" of the subject, as something one may opt in or out of and also deliberate about. (This is what makes rational-choice theory intellectually coherent as a form of social theory for liberal societies, but only for liberal societies.) Put the other way around, if not only rule but also subject constitution by culture and religion are equated with organicist orders, this rule and this constitution are imagined to disappear with the emergence of the autonomous individual; indeed, their vanquishing is the very meaning of such autonomy. For liberal subjects, culture becomes food, dress, music, lifestyle, and contingent values. Culture *as* power and especially as rule is replaced by culture as merely a way of life; culture that preemptively oblates the individual transmogrifies into culture as a source of comfort or pleasure for the individual, akin to the liberal idealization of the domestic sphere as a "haven in a heartless world." Similarly, religion as domination, tyranny, or source of irrationality and violence is presumed to transform, where the individual reigns, into religion as a choice and as a source of comfort, nourishment, moral guidance, and moral credibility. This is the schema that allows President Bush's prayers about political matters, his routine consultations with radical Christian groups on foreign policy, and even his personal conviction that his military mission in the Middle East is divinely blessed to be sharply differentiated from the—dangerous— devotion to Allah of a Muslim fundamentalist. Bush's religiosity is figured as a source of strength and moral guidance for his deliberations and decisions, while the devotee of Allah is assumed to be without the individual will and conscience necessary to such rationation.[6]

Moral autonomy, the name liberalism gives to this individuated figure, is widely understood by theorists of tolerance to constitute *the* underlying value of the principle of liberal tolerance.[7] Susan Mendus writes, "the autonomy argument is sometimes referred to as the characteristically liberal argument for toleration."[8] For Will Kymlicka, "liberals are often defined as those who support toleration because it is necessary for the promotion of autonomy."[9] And for Bernard Williams, "if toleration as a practice is to be defended in terms of its being a value, then it will have to appeal to substantive opinions about the good, in particular the good of individual autonomy."[10] But if autonomy is the liberal good that tolerance aims to promote, tolerance is also understood as that which can only be generated by autonomous individuals—that is, in part, the significance of its status as a civic offering rather than a legal mandate. Tolerance thus requires in advance what it also promotes. Conversely, tolerance as the abiding of behaviors or convictions other than those to which one subscribes is conceived within liberalism as unavailable to the unindividuated or nonliberal subject. The making of a tolerant world, then, literally requires the liberalization of the world, a formulation endorsed by liberal democratic theorists, pundits, and political actors ranging from Will Kymlicka to Thomas Friedman. As Michael Ignatieff argues, "the culture of individualism is the only reliable solvent of the hold of group identities and the racisms that go with them." The "essential task in teaching 'toleration,'" he adds, " is to help people see themselves as individuals, and then to see others as such."[11]

While Kant functions as the foundation stone for contemporary liberal theorists subscribing to this formulation, the contribution of Freud to the ideology of the tolerant liberal self and its intolerant organicist other is an interesting one. Many liberal theorists concerned with tolerance implicitly or explicitly place Freudian assumptions at the heart of their work or have tucked him into their arguments as a kind of authorizing signature. What Freud offers, among other things, is an account of why liberal orders, in their affirmation of the individual, represent themselves as the only possible regime type for cultivating and practicing tolerance, while simultaneously promoting the pluralistic belief structure understood to necessitate tolerance. Though Freud ratifies the "mature" (or "advanced") status of the individuated Westerner in this regard, he does not make an ontological or permanent distinction between the individual and the group. In Freud's view, individuated subjects can regress into organicist formations at any moment, forfeiting the definitive elements of proper individuation when they do so. Strong group identity thus constitutes not an opposition to but a regression from the mature individuated psyche. Even though Freud pathologizes the group (as irrational and dangerous), he does not reify the rational individual as a permanent cultural achievement radically differentiated from organicist subjects.

In what follows, then, Freud's thinking will be both criticized and appropriated for a critique of liberal thinking about tolerance. On the one hand, Freud's progressive historical-anthropological narrative, in which tolerant liberal orders represent the highest stage of "maturity" for man and are equated with civilization, will be read critically, especially insofar as these themes are manifest in contemporary theorists of tolerance.[12] That is, Freud's equation of individuation with both ontogenetic and phylogenetic maturity, and of solidarity or organicism with primitivism or regression, will offer a basis for grasping the civilizational discourse that frames contemporary tolerance talk and converts it to the purposes of liberal imperialism. On the other hand, Freud's appreciation of the contingency of groups, their basis in affect rather than essential traits, is valuable in deconstructing the ontologization of "blood and belonging" at play in the modern liberal theory and practice of cultural tolerance.[13]

Freud

In *Civilization and Its Discontents* and *Totem and Taboo*,[14] Freud is conventionally read as explaining how men overcome what he posits as a natural asociality rooted in sexual rivalry and primary aggression. As accounts of how men come to live together without perpetual strife, these stories have been read as Freud's version of the emergence of humans from a state of nature into social contract and from primary satisfaction of the instincts to the instinctual repression productive (via sublimation) of civilization. But another current cuts across Freud's depiction of our struggle for sociality, one that concerns how subjects progress not just from primary hostility to relative peaceability but from organicist identities—groups—to civilized individuals. These two tales are neither identical nor fully reconcilable—fact, they represent two different tropes of "the primitive": the lone savage and the submissive tribal follower. The second figure is the problematic of *Group Psychology and the Analysis of the Ego*,[15] and it makes a shadowy appearance in *Civilization and Its Discontents*, as well. It is the narrative of this figure, with its "ontogeny recapitulates phylogeny" trajectory from childlike primitivism to mature liberal cosmopolitanism, that can be detected at the foundations of most liberal tolerance talk. Although this talk does not actually reference Freud, it remains convergent with Freud's accounts of what binds groups, what signals primitivism and civilization, what the tensions are between the individual and the group, and what is so dangerous—internally oppressive, externally threatening—about organicist societies. Together these accounts coin tolerance as something available only to liberal subjects and liberal orders and constitute the supremacy of both over the dangerous alternatives. They also establish organicist orders as a natural limit of liberal tolerance, as intolerable in consequence of their own intolerance.

Freud's challenge to himself in *Group Psychology and the Analysis of the Ego* is to explain *Massenpsychologie*—variously translated as mass, mob, or crowd psychology but inherently pejorative across these translations—as consonant with, rather than a departure from, the individual psychology he devoted his life to mapping. Unlike others working on the problem (whom he considers at length in the book's first chapter), Freud does not treat group behavior or feeling as issuing from a structure of desire different from that of individual affect. His concern here, in addition to ratifying the basic architecture of the psyche he spent years theorizing, is to affirm the individual as a primordial unit of analysis and action *and thereby* to pathologize the group as a dangerous condition of de-individuation and psychological regression. Freud's beginning point, then, works normatively to align maturity, individuation, conscience, repression, and civilization and to oppose these to childishness, primitivism, unchecked impulse, instinct, and barbarism. This is the alignment and opposition that makes its way into contemporary tolerance discourse.

Yet Freud's contrast between primitive groups and civilized individuals is not a straightforward story of emergence from an undifferentiated mass to self-reflective individuality. As is well known, it is the repression of *individual instinct*, and not the disaggregation of a group, that animates the drama of *Civilization and Its Discontents*, in which human happiness, satisfaction, and self-love are all sacrificed on the altar of civilization. It could even be said that for Freud there is only ever the individual, that is, the individual is both the ontological a priori and the telos of civilization; groups are not primary or natural, nor are they stable. To the contrary, Freud's insistence upon our "primary mutual hostility" and natural "sexual rivalry" makes associations of any sort an achievement, whether they are relatively permanent and organized structures arrived at through the complex covenant of the totemic system depicted in *Totem and Taboo* or more contingent and unstructured, as with those diagnosed in *Group Psychology*.[16] Man is not a "herd animal" but a "horde animal," Freud writes at the conclusion of his lengthy critical discussion of other theorists of group psychology.[17] A herd animal has an instinctual affinity for closeness, a primary gregariousness, while the horde animal is constituted by an external organizing principle that brokers a complex need for, rivalry with, endangerment by, and aggression toward others.

Still, Freud, like other nineteenth-century European thinkers, conceives "primitive" peoples as organized by principles of tribalism rather than individualism. Individuation is both the agent and sign of civilization for Freud, while groups signify a condition— whether temporary or enduring—of barbarism. Organicist orders, in other words, denote not simply pre-civilized social relations and subject formations but *de-civilized* ones, in which the demands of civilization have been loosened or shed. This is why, despite his quarrel with their analyses of the source of *Massenpsychologie*, Freud allows fellow psychologists Gustav Le Bon and William McDougall to characterize the problem he joins them in wishing to understand, namely, that the mental life of "unorganized" groups is comparable to that of primitive people *and* of children.[18] For Le Bon, "by the mere fact that he forms part of an organized group, a man descends several rungs in the ladder of civilization. Isolated, he may be a cultivated individual; in a crowd, he is a barbarian—that is, a creature acting by instinct. He possesses the spontaneity, the violence, the ferocity, and also the enthusiasm and heroism of primitive beings."[19] McDougall says the behavior of the group "is like that of an unruly child or an untutored passionate savage in a strange situation, rather than like that of its average member; and in the worst cases it is like that of a wild beast, rather than like that of human beings."[20]

So we have in Freud the paradox of an analytical a priori individualism (the lone savage) and a colonial historiography of the emergence of modern individualized man out of organicism (the primitive tribalist). Savage man is a nonhuman animal, lacking instinctual repression, while primitive man is a human infant, lacking individuation and rationality. This paradox, which is distributed across the several Freudian texts mentioned thus far, also appears in many contemporary liberal discussions of culture and tolerance. If there is a reconciliation of the paradox in Freud, it is hinged to the very a priori status of the individual: regressed man, unindividuated man, isn't regressed *to* the group but *by* the group to a more instinctual psychic state. And his de-individuation derives not from his relation to others but from his own instincts. He is without the independence of will and deliberation yielded by a developed super-ego. Man in a group does not simply merge—Freud quarrels overtly with "contagion theory"—but bears both a shared attachment to something external to the group and a shared lack, a lowered or absent super-ego. Man in a group ceases to be directed by his own deliberation and conscience. He ceases to be organized by free will and rationality, those two crucial features of the individuated liberal subject.

Through this lens, the brutal murders and public torching of four American civilians by a Fallujan mob in March 2004 converge with the torture scenes orchestrated by American troops in Abu Ghraib revealed a month later. Both could be read as a decline of individual deliberation, conscience, and restraint in the context of morally depraved group enthusiasms.[21] Yet this convergence still permits a divergent assessment of the two peoples from which the acts emerged—such that President Bush could declare the Fallujan incident or the Nicholas Berg decapitation to confirm the "true nature of the enemy," while insisting that the torture at Abu Ghraib did not express the "the real nature of American women and men fighting in Iraq." We shall return to this matter after we examine the basis for the liberal conviction that group ties cancel rational deliberation and moral conscience.

For this purpose, we need to enter the story Freud tells in *Group Psychology and the Analysis of the Ego*. Freud's commitment to a methodological and social individualism requires that his analysis of group psychology commence with the question of how a group is possible at all before considering why certain group formations induce or produce animal-like, passionate, and mentally defective behavior among its members. That is, primary rivalry and atomization have to be overcome, an overcoming that can only issue from the drive that binds humans, namely, eros. Love for another is all that can challenge the primary narcissism generative of social hostility and rivalry. Immediately, however, Freud cautions against imagining that the bonds of a group consist in a simple love of group members for one another—that would be to eschew both our primary self-regard and what Freud, borrowing from Schopenhauer, identifies as the "porcupine problem," which goes as follows. A number of porcupines, feeling cold, huddle together in order to benefit from each other's warmth. But in drawing close, they feel one another's quills and sense danger, leading them to draw apart again, but this returns them to suffering from the cold. The repetition of this movement, in which "they were driven backwards and forwards from one trouble to the other," produces for Freud a metaphor of human desire and explains an oscillation he associates with inherent ambivalence in love.[22] If eros impels us toward closeness with another, this very closeness makes us terribly vulnerable to injury and suffering. So we pull away, only to feel endangered by loneliness and fearful isolation.[23]

Explaining the phenomenon of the human group, then, necessitates explaining how this oscillation between two unacceptable dangers—closeness, which produces terrible vulnerability to another, and isolation, which produces a sense of unprotectedness—is overcome in favor of prolonged closeness. How do we become continuously huddling porcupines? The answer lies not in the dynamics of eros within the group but rather in the fact that the group is constituted by something external to which we are each libidinally bound—a leader or an ideal. A group is formed out of mutual identification in love or idealization (they turn out to be the same) of something outside the group. But what is the nature of this identification such that it actually binds those who share it? In *Group Psychology*, Freud specifies three types of identification in love:

> First, identification is the original form of emotional ties with an object; secondly, in a regressive way it becomes a substitute for a libidinal object-tie, as it were by means of introjection of the object into the ego; and thirdly, it may arise with any new perception of a common quality shared with some other person who is not the object of the sexual instinct. The more important this common quality is, the more successful may this partial identification become, and it may thus represent the beginning of a new tie.[24]

Freud hypothesizes that "the mutual tie between members of a group is in the nature of this [third] kind," meaning, we are bound to members of a group by virtue of a perceived shared quality, in this case love for the leader or external ideal.[25] But this hypothesis in turn calls for understanding the psychic phenomenon of "being in love" to appreciate why identification with others in this state would produce a strong bond.

So, what is it to be in love? In the beginning, goes Freud's oft-rehearsed tale, there is only sexual desire. What we call love precipitates out of the inhibition of this desire. Love—whether that of a child for its parents or an adult for a lover or friend—is aim-inhibited eros. Aim inhibition entails a displacement or rerouting of libidinal energy; in the case of love, this energy goes into idealization of the object. But idealization itself, Freud explains, is more than reverence for the object. Rather, it is a way of satisfying one's own need to be loved by projecting one's ideals of goodness onto another. Idealization thus involves a circuitry of projection from the ego-ideal of the lover onto the love object, which produces a feeling (being in love) that in turn gratifies the ego's own desire for love or self-idealization.[26]

In short, the idealization of a loved one, in which the object is inevitably "sexually overvalued" (only the lover sees the beloved's bottomless charms) and rendered relatively free from criticism, involves a great deal of our own narcissistic libido spilling onto the object. Here is Freud's account of how these two sources of the affect of love—the inhibition of eros and the gratification of the lover's own ego—combine:

> If the sensual implications are more or less effectively repressed or set aside, the illusion is produced that the object has come to be sensually loved on account of its spiritual merits, whereas on the contrary these merits may really only have been lent to it by its sensual charm.
>
> The tendency which falsifies judgment in this respect is that of *idealization*. . . . We see that the object is being treated in the same way as our own ego, so that when we are in love a considerable amount of narcissistic libido overflows on to the object. . . . in many forms of love choice . . . the object serves as a substitute for some unattained ego ideal of our own. We love it on account of the perfections which we have striven to reach for our own ego, and which we should now like to procure in this roundabout way as a means of satisfying our narcissism.[27]

Idealization is narcissistic projection necessitated by aim inhibition. But precisely because this experience of narcissism is so heady for the ego—headier, indeed, than any mere sexual satisfaction, which, Freud notes, "always involves a reduction in sexual overvaluation"—idealization can grow quite extreme. And as the idealization intensifies, so also does the narcissistic gratification it produces, with the effect of eventually overtaking the ego-ideal of the lover altogether: "the ego [of the lover] becomes more and more unassuming and modest, and the object more and more sublime and precious, until at last it gets possession of the entire self-love of the ego, whose self-sacrifice thus follows as a natural consequence."[28] Here lies the secret of the love of individual group members for a leader or ideal. Originally driven by eros, the (sexless) love for the leader or ideal develops into an ardent idealization of the loved object, starting as a gratification of the ego's own narcissism and ending with the idealized object taking the place of the ego-ideal itself and consuming the ego. This last move explains the familiar phenomenon in group psychology of strongly deteriorated individual judgment and conscience:

> Contemporaneously with this "devotion" of the ego to the object, which is no longer to be distinguished from a sublimated devotion to an abstract idea, the functions allotted to the ego ideal entirely cease to operate. The criticism exercised by that agency is silent; everything that the object does and asks for is right and blameless. Conscience has no application to anything that is done for the sake of the object; in the blindness of love remorselessness is carried to the pitch of crime. The whole situation can be completely summarized in a formula: *The object has been put in the place of the ego ideal.*[29]

So this is the nature of the love that individual group members bear toward the leader or idea. But what binds group members to one another? How do these individual lovers of a distant figure or ideal become attached to one another, especially given Freud's hypothesis of primary rivalry in love? Here Freud returns to identification: *a group is a number of individuals who have put one and the same object in the place of their ego ideal and in so doing, identify with one another in their ego*. The group coheres to the extent that individual ego ideals have been replaced or absorbed by a common object. In doing so, the group not only shares a love object and ego ideal but becomes something of a common ego, a "common me" to a degree that no mere social contract could produce.[30]

A group based on the collective experience of being in love with something external to it is what engenders mutual identification rather than mutual rivalry among the lovers. The distant (or abstract) character of the love object secures the impossibility of any group member actually, and hence exclusively, possessing the object. The nonsexual nature of the love both perpetuates the idealization and assures this impossibility.[31] Nonsexual love also allows for a persistent oscillation between love of a leader and love of an ideal—the group is bound by idealization that is at once detachable from a particular person and sustained through a particular person. The person remains abstract and idealized because sexual consummation, which would reduce the idealization, does not occur.

Through this rendering of love and identification as the basis of groups, Freud believes he has explained two crucial things: (1) how groups can exist at all when we are naturally rivalrous and antisocial, that is, when we are porcupines; (2) why groups represent a regressed state of the psyche, that is, why group behavior episodically becomes mob behavior, even among the highly educated or civilized. With regard to the first, our natural rivalry is resolved through collective identification, the mechanism of which is love for an external object or ideal. We do not actually love each other but are bound together through identification that is experienced as love, even as it is a way of living our love for the unattainable object. With regard to the second, for Freud, being in love inherently entails a certain regression, a withdrawal from the world and a loss of boundaries—a state of abandon as well as slavishness. Moreover, being in love entails a loss of the individual ego-ideal and of the conscience and inhibition it sustains. It is not the group as a group that is in this condition but rather the aggregate of individuals who are each in this state vis-à-vis something external to the group. Collective identification of group members with one another's love heightens this state and also forms the basis for the group tie.

Freud's theory of group formation is quite suggestive for thinking about nationalism, not to mention fascism. However, we have rehearsed this story not for its explanatory value but in order to explore its assumptions and explanations as they operate in liberal figurations of the inherent intolerance and dangerousness of organicist societies. In *Group Psychology*, Freud masterfully articulates an ideology of the civilized, individuated subject and pathologizes groups and group identities. Basing the group tie on the dynamics of love and identification produces group enthrallment as a regression from rationality, conscience, and impulse control. The group is dangerous for having these qualities and also signifies a literal undoing of the individuated subject, who must be, in Freud's words, "conquered" by the requirements of civilization.[32]

While Freud elsewhere links civilization, instinctual repression, and maturity at both the ontogenetic and phylogenetic levels, only in *Group Psychology* does he elaborate the politico-theoretical implications of these relatively conventional metonymies: organicist societies are inherently less civilized than liberal individualistic ones because nonindividuation signals a libidinally charged psychic economy, which constrains rational deliberation and impulse control. This renders individuation both an effect and a sign of instinctual repression, conscience, and the capacity for self-regulation. It renders groups inherently dangerous because of the de-repressed human condition they represent—the psychic state of urgency, unbridled passion, credulousness, impulsiveness, irritability, impulsiveness, extremism, and submissiveness to authority that Freud, drawing on Le Bon and McDougall, takes to be characteristic of the group.[33]

Freud also defines organicist societies as problematic because in them love operates in the public or social realms, instead of being (properly) confined to the private and familial ones. Such societies represent the dangerousness of public ardor and signify the importance of containing love in the domestic domain for civilization to produce the rationality and individuation that is its mark.[34] If love civilized is love domesticated, then ardent attachments of any sort—to a God, a belief system, a people, or a culture—must remain private and depoliticized if they are not to endanger civilization and the autonomous individual who signifies a civilized state. Culture is thus dangerous if it is public rather than private, a formulation that is significant in distinguishing liberal from nonliberal states, and even more so, "free" societies from "fundamentalist" ones. What is achieved by starting with the egoistic individual who then (consequentially and detrimentally) sacrifices his individuality as a member of the group is the valorization of the liberal individual as a rational, self-regulating subject, and hence as a modestly free subject. This becomes especially clear if we remember that Freud's pathologization of the group pertains not just to its crude and dangerous behavior but also to its enthrallment, its constitution through domination: "It wants to be ruled and oppressed and to fear its masters."[35] If what holds a group together is slavish devotion to something external to it, and if such devotion incites the naturally egoistic subject to give up a significant part of its individuality, then Freud has succeeded in defining group belonging as the inherent sacrifice of individual freedom (rooted in deliberation, self-direction, and conscience) on the altar of love for that which dominates it. Strong social bonds arise only and always as an effect of domination and as a sign of dangerous regression to a de-individuated and hence derepressed state.

Above all, Freud has made organicist societies signify a condition in which subjects are less conscience-bound and civilized than the mature individual and less individualized *because* they are less conscience-bound, that is, because their ego ideals are conferred on the external ideal or leader. If the fall into primitivism is a fall away from super-egoic self-regulation, "civilization" becomes coterminous with self-regulating individuals and the diminution of groups inherently dominated by a leader or ideal on the one hand, and unrepressed instincts on the other. Individuation (vis-à-vis one another and authority) represents the throwing off of ontogenetic and phylogenetic "childhood" and the acquisition of instinctual repression, deliberation, conscience, and freedom.[36] In this light, the gleeful mob violence against the American security workers in Fallujah appears iconographic of an absent liberalism—such violence appears as the rule rather than the exception for an order construed as desperately in need of the very liberal democratic transformation that it is resisting. Indeed, such violence becomes vindication of George W. Bush's newfound liberation theology, his mission to free the unfree world both in the name of what is good for others and in the name of what makes the world a safer place.[37] By this account, to be without liberalism is not simply to be oppressed but to be exceptionally dangerous.[38] Conversely, American and British torture and humiliation of Iraqis at Abu Ghraib was rendered as sheer aberration: "not the America I know" as Bush put it. Or, in the words of British Prime Minister Tony Blair, "what we came to put an end to, not to perpetrate," a formulation that deftly reverses the source of violence, attributing it to Iraqi political culture while ruling it out of character for the Western occupiers.[39]

This argument implies that the individual must be cultivated and protected and that group identities of all kinds must be contained insofar as they represent both the absence of individual autonomy and the social danger of a de-civilized formation. Organicist orders are not only radically other to liberalism but betoken the "enemy within" civilization and the enemy to civilization. Most dangerous of all would be transnational formations imagined as organicist from a liberal perspective, which link the two—Judaism in the nineteenth century, communism in the twentieth, and today, of course, Islam.[40]

Liberalism and Its Other: Who Has Culture and Whom Culture Has

The governmentality of tolerance as it circulates through civilizational discourse has, as part of its work, the containment of the (organicist, non-Western, nonliberal) other.[41] As pointed out earlier, within contemporary civilizational discourse, the liberal individual is uniquely identified with the capacity for tolerance, and tolerance itself is identified with civilization. Nonliberal societies and practices, especially those designated as fundamentalist, are not only depicted as relentless and inherently intolerant but as potentially intolerable for their putative rule by culture or religion and concomitant devaluation of the autonomous individual, in short, their thwarting of individual autonomy with religious or cultural commandments. Out of this equation, liberalism emerges as the only political rationality that can produce the individual, societal, and governmental practice of tolerance, and, at the same time, liberal societies become the broker of what is tolerable and intolerable. Liberalism's promotion of tolerance is equated with the valorization of individual autonomy; the intolerance associated with fundamentalism is equated with the valorization of culture and religion at the expense of the individual, an expense that makes such orders intolerable from a liberal vantage point.

These logics share the assumptions about individuals and groups that appear both in Kant's grammar of moral autonomy and in Freud's pathologization of groups. They entail two particular conceits about autonomy in liberal orders: the autonomy of the subject from culture (the idea that the subject is prior to culture and free to choose culture) and the autonomy of politics from culture (the idea that politics is above culture and free of culture).

. . .

"*Culture* is one of the two or three most complicated words in the English language," Raymond Williams begins the entry "Culture" in *Keywords*.[42] The term emerges as a noun, he tells us, only in the eighteenth century and is not commonly used as a noun until the middle of the nineteenth century.[43] Originally deployed mainly as a synonym for civilization, the noun described the secular process of human development.[44] In our time, however, Williams writes, culture has acquired four broad categories of usage: (1) a physicalist usage that reaches back to the old, synonymic relationship that the verb *culture* had with husbandry; (2) a usage that approximates "civilization" and refers to a general process of intellectual, spiritual, and aesthetic development; (3) an anthropological usage that indicates a particular way of life of a people, period, group, or humanity in general; and (4) a usage that refers to a body of artistic and intellectual heritage or activity.[45]

Williams mentions briefly that these meanings do not remain distinct today, but their admixture requires closer scrutiny for us to appreciate the problematic of culture within contemporary liberal democratic discourse. If culture signifies a material process, a common way of life, a process of development of the distinctly human faculties of intellect and spirit, and a valuation of selected products of these faculties, then this very complex of meanings represents a certain vexation within liberalism. On the one hand, liberal societies generally regard themselves as representing the world-historical apex of culture and cultural productions. On the other hand, liberalism conceives of itself as freeing individuals from the mandate of culture in any of its senses, that is, as producing the moral and intellectual autonomy of the individual to self-determine the extent of participation in culture(s) in every sense of the word. Whether construed as high art, as the acquisition of knowledge, or as an ethnically inflected "way of life," culture in liberal societies is largely deemed an objectifiable good that is optional and privately enjoyed, hence the common reference in multicultural schools today to "sharing one's culture" (by which is usually meant sharing food, holiday rituals, or performing arts) or "respecting another's culture" (by which is usually meant respecting another's dietary practices, holidays, or ways of dress). But this means liberalism cannot feature culture as a public good or even a public bond. The closest liberals generally come to the notion of a publicly shared culture is "national culture," which conveys a loose link between particular national histories, social mores, and habits of thought, or "market culture," which, ironically, redounds to the physicalist meaning of culture as a form of husbandry or cultivation that exceeds individual choice and that produces conditions of subsistence and existence. Some liberal theorists also speak of "Western culture," by which they are usually alluding to the habits of life and thought organized by liberalism, Christianity, and the market.

The conceptual positioning of culture as extrinsic to the liberal subject (and to the liberal state, about which more shortly) is exemplified by the normative conditions Seyla Benhabib sets out for the resolution of multicultural dilemmas, each of which presumes the capacity to grasp and negotiate culture from the outside: universal respect, egalitarian reciprocity, voluntary self-ascription, and freedom of exit and association.[46] Benhabib is attempting to establish limits to the claims of culture that would respect individual autonomy without violating the fabric of culture, certainly an admirable endeavor. But in order to assess and limit the claims of culture according to such criteria, it must be possible to grasp culture as knowable and as containable from some noncultural place. Similarly, Benhabib speaks about limiting minority cultural claims in terms of the "rights" they have over their members: these "communities do *not* have the right to deprive their children of humankind's accumulated knowledge and civilizational achievement. . . . they *do* have a right to transmit to their children the fundamentals of their own ways of life *alongside* other forms of knowledge shared with humankind."[47] Again, the very language of rights implies an ability to isolate various parties—the culture and the individual, respective forms of cultural knowledge—that rests upon an autonomous, precultural, Kantian subject to whom such judgment and assertion is available.[48]

From such ground, it is not surprising that a range of contemporary theorists of tolerance—Bernard Williams, Joseph Raz, Michael Ignatieff, Will Kymlicka, along with the Rawlsians and the Habermasians—tacitly or expressly argue that a tolerant worldview is only available to peoples or societies with a deep value and practice of individualization, an investment in individual rather than group identity. If collective identity, linguistically denoted as "culture" today, is affirmed as important to human beings by these thinkers, it is also problematic for liberalism's attachment to the secularism that guarantees both individual autonomy and deliberative rationality. Culture represents not simply a local claim upon the individual and, in this regard, an attenuation of individuality and autonomy, but it undermines the aspiration to a public rationality that overcomes cultural particularism in favor of putatively acultural concerns with justice as fairness. Thus, even as a deliberative democratic theorist such as Benhabib struggles to recognize cultural belonging and identity in excess of what is offered by the nation-state and dismisses as "institutionally unstable and analytically untenable" efforts to separate "background culture" from "public political culture," she also insists upon a set of norms, metanorms, and principles to produce "free and reasoned deliberation among individuals considered as moral and political equals" as the basis of democracy.[49]

Most importantly, if, for liberals, collective identities represent the dangerousness of the group, liberalism stands for that which has coined a solution to this dangerousness without abolishing collective identity altogether. Liberalism prides itself on having discovered how to reduce the hungers and aggressive tendencies of collective identity while permitting individuals private enjoyment of such identity. This solution involves a set of interrelated ideological moves in which religion and culture are privatized and the cultural and religious dimensions of liberalism itself are disavowed. Culture and religion are private and privately enjoyed, ideologically depoliticized, much as the family is, and, like the family, situated as "background" to *homo politicus* and *homo oeconomicus*. Culture, family, and religion are all formulated as "havens in a heartless world" rather than as sites of power, politics, subject production, and norms. In this way, far from being that which constitutes the subject, culture becomes something that, in Avishai Margalit's and Moshe Halbertal's phrase, one may "have a right to."[50]

These analytic moves to situate culture as extrinsic to the individual, as forming the background of the individual, as that which the individual "chooses" or has a right to, not merely confirm the autonomy of the individual but also figure culture as inherently oppressive when it saturates or governs law and politics. In liberalism, the individual is understood to have, or have access to, culture or religious belief; culture or religious belief does not have him or her. The difference turns upon which entity is imagined to govern: sovereign individuals in liberal regimes, culture and religion in fundamentalist ones. The same move identifies liberal legalism and the liberal state as fully autonomous of culture and religion. These two forms of autonomy, that of the individual and that of the state, are importantly connected: liberalism is conceived as juridically securing the autonomy of the individual from others *and* from state power through its articulation of the autonomy of the state from cultural and religious authority. Liberal politics and law represented themselves as secular not only with regard to religion but also with regard to culture, and above and apart from both. This makes liberal legalism at once cultureless and culturally neutral (even though legal decisions will sometimes allude to standards of "national culture" or "prevailing cultural norms"). Put the other way around, liberalism figures culture as separable from political power and political power as capable of being cultureless. These moves render liberal legal principles universal and culture inherently particular, a rendering that legitimates the subordination of culture to politics as the subordination of the particular to the universal. These moves also permit principles of liberal democracy to be *universalizable* without being culturally imperialist; as universals, these principles are capable of "respecting" particular cultures. Conversely, nonliberal orders represent the crimes of particularism, fundamentalism, and intolerance, as well as the dangerousness of unindividuated humanity.

This distinction and presumed separation between politics and culture within liberalism is crucial to sustaining the fiction of the autonomous individual and the fiction of its imagined opposite—the radically de-individuated, culturally or religiously bound creature of a fundamentalist order. Seen from the other direction and in a more deconstructive grammar, the liberal construction of its fundamentalist other as one ruled by culture and religion enables liberal legalism's discursive construction of culture as a form of power only when it is formally imbricated with governance, which is how this discourse represents most nonliberal regimes. The autonomy of the state from culture is therefore just as important as the autonomy of the individual from culture in distinguishing liberal orders from their other. Nonliberal polities are depicted as "ruled" by culture or religion; liberalism is depicted as ruled by law, with culture dispensed to another domain, a de-politicized and voluntary one. In this way, individual autonomy is counterposed to rule by culture, and subjects are seen to gain their autonomy not through culture but against it. Culture is individual autonomy's antinomy and hence what the liberal state presumes to subdue, de-power, and privatize, as well as detach itself from.[51]

The twin conceits of the autonomy of liberal legalism from culture and the autonomy of the self-willing and sovereign subject from culture enable liberal legalism's unique positioning as fostering tolerance and liberal polities' unique position as capable of brokering the tolerable. Tolerance is extended to almost all cultural and religious practices seen to be "chosen" by liberal individuals but may be withheld for those practices seen to be imposed by culture inscribed as law, as it may be withheld for whole regimes considered to be ruled by culture or religion. This logic effectively insulates all legal practices in liberal orders from the tag of "barbarism" while legitimating liberal aggression toward non-Western practices or regimes deemed intolerable. And this logic allows for the disavowal of the cultural imperialism that such aggression entails because the aggression is legitimated by the rule of law and the inviolability of rights and choice, each of which is designated in liberal discourse as universal and noncultural. Ubiquitous in all liberal theoretical discussions of tolerance and the intolerable, this logic was succinctly expressed by George W. Bush during the initiation of the U.S. war on Afghanistan in 2002:

> We have a great opportunity during this time of war to lead the world toward the values that will bring lasting peace. . . . We have no intention of imposing our culture. But America will always stand firm for the non-negotiable demands of human dignity: the rule of law, limits on the power of the state, respect for women; private property; free speech, equal justice; and religious tolerance.[52]

None of these "non-negotiable demands"—which do not hail from the United States but from a paradoxically transcendent or sacred place called "human dignity" where the individual is a priori—are portrayed as cultural, not as conditioned by the sovereignty of states or nations.[53] Instead, each is set out as a universal political principle both independent of culture and capable of being neutral with regard to culture, as well as innocent of the particulars of political regimes. Each, importantly, presumes the autonomy of the subject and the state from culture. And each so-called demand also figures a dark other against which it obtains its own identity. The "rule of law" is opposed to rule by the sword, religious leaders, or cultural custom; "limits on state power" are opposed to absolutism or state power imbricated with other powers such as culture or religion; "respect for women" is opposed to the degradation of women (by culture or religion) but also, interestingly, the equality of women; "private property" is opposed to collective ownership, national or state ownership, or public property; "free speech" is opposed to controlled, bought, muffled, or conditioned speech; "equal justice" is opposed to differentiated justice; and "religious tolerance" is opposed to religious fundamentalism. These dark others, metonymically associated with each other, together signal the presence of barbarism, liberalism's putative opposite. This implies that liberalism itself is inherently clear of all of these dark others, that each belongs exclusively to nonliberal regimes and cultures, and moreover, that where liberalism does not prevail, neither does civilization.

· · ·

This essay began with a consideration of the anxiety about organicist orders evident in liberal thought, and it has explored Freud's theory of group identity to plumb liberal assumptions about the civilizational supremacy of orders featuring high levels of individuation. Freud's story reveals the ways in which liberal thought equates organicism with primitivism, and especially with subjects who lack the capacity for self-regulation, conscience, instinctual repression, and rational deliberation. Such organicism, I have been suggesting, is equated with rule by "culture," "religion," and "ethnic identity"; liberal legalism is the sign that these things do not rule, the sign that a secular state and an autonomous individual have usurped their power and put them in their appropriate place.

Liberal tolerance, which simultaneously affirms the value of autonomy and consecrates state secularism, is understood to be a virtue available only to the self-regulating individual, a political principle available only to secular states, and a good appropriately extended only to individuated subjects and regimes that promote such individuation. Conversely, those captive to organicism and organicist practices are presumed neither to value tolerance, to be capable of tolerance, nor to be entitled to tolerance. The governmentality of tolerance deploys the formal legal autonomy of the subject and the formal secularism of the state as a threshold of the tolerable, marking as intolerable whatever is regarded as a threat to such autonomy and secularism.

Yet, even as tolerance is mobilized to manage the challenges to this logic posed by the eruptions of subnational identities in liberal polities occasioned by late modern transnational population flows, this invocation of tolerance also functions as a sign of the breakdown of this logic of liberal universalism. Tolerance arises as a way of negotiating "cultural," "ethnic," and "religious" differences that clash with the hegemonic "societal culture" within which they exist. The conflict that emerges when those differences erupt into public life poses more than a policy problem, for example, whether Muslim girls in France can wear *hijab* to public schools, or whether female circumcision or bigamy can be practiced in North America. Rather, the conflict itself exposes the nonuniversal character of liberal legalism and public life; it exposes its cultural dimensions.

This *exposé* is managed through the supplement of tolerance discourse in one of two ways. The difference is designated either as dangerous in its nonliberalism (hence as not tolerable) or as merely religious, ethnic, or cultural (hence as not a candidate for a political claim). If it is a nonliberal political difference, it is intolerable; and if it is tolerated, it must be privatized, converted into an individually chosen belief or practice with no political bearing. Tolerance thus functions as the supplement to a liberal secularism that cannot sustain itself at this moment. Still, the very fact of the eruption that challenges liberalism's putative aculturalism, and the mobilization of tolerance to respond to it, suggest other political possibilities, ones that might affirm and productively exploit rather than disavow liberalism's culturalism.

In a passing remark about the contemporary language of "cultural or ethnic minority," Talal Asad identifies another site of contemporary leakage in the aspirations of liberal legalism to purity. Within liberalism, Asad notes, *majority* and *minority* are political terms with political relevance. As such, these terms "presuppose a constitutional device for *resolving* differences," which is not, of course, how the language of tolerance approaches difference. "To speak of cultural majorities and minorities is therefore to posit ideological hybrids," Asad continues. "It is also to make the implicit claim that members of some cultures truly belong to a particular politically defined place, but those of others (minority cultures) do not."[54] Without acknowledging or thematizing this slippage between the cultural and the political within liberalism, tolerance is adduced to handle it, indeed, to re-depoliticize what erupts into the political as a cultural, religious, or ethnic claim. Again, tolerance appears as a supplement for liberalism at the point of a potential crisis in its universalist self-representation. And again, the alternative is not abandoning or rejecting liberalism but, rather, using the occasion to open liberal regimes to self-reflection on the false conceits of their cultural and religious secularism, and to the possibility of being transformed by their encounter with what liberalism has conventionally taken to be its constitutive outside and its hostile other. Such openings would involve deconstructing the opposition between moral autonomy and organicism, and between secularism and fundamentalism, both for the polyglot West and for the polyglot Islamic world.[55]

These deconstructive moves bear the possibility of conceiving and nourishing a liberalism more self-conscious of and receptive to its own always already present hybridity, its potentially rich failure to hive off organicism from individuality, culture from political principles, law or policy. This would be a liberalism potentially more modest, more restrained in its imperial and colonial impulses, but also one more capable of the multicultural justice to which it aspires. Above all, it would be a liberalism less invested in the absolute and dangerous opposition between us and them, thereby losing one of its crucial justifications for empire under the flag of liberal democracy.[56]

Religion, Liberal Democracy, and Citizenship

Chantal Mouffe

Contrary to what many liberals had predicted, instead of becoming obsolete thanks to the development of "postconventional identities" and the increasing role of rationality in human behavior, religious forms of identification currently play a growing role in many societies. Yet the question of what should be the place of the church in a liberal democracy is a burning issue in several of the new Eastern European democracies. It seems, therefore, that the old controversy about the relationship between religion and politics, far from being on the wane, is again on the agenda.

My aim in this paper is to examine some of the issues related to this debate from the point of view of the model of agonistic pluralism that I am currently elaborating. I hope to be able to show that this model provides a better framework than many versions of deliberative democracy for acknowledging the role played by religion in the formation of personal identity and the consequences that this entails for politics.

Liberal Democracy as Agonistic Pluralism

In order to situate my reflection and to avoid misunderstandings, a few general remarks concerning liberal democracy are needed at the outset. First, I consider it important to distinguish liberal democracy from democratic capitalism and to envisage it in terms of classic political philosophy as a *regime*, a political form of society that needs to be defined exclusively at the level of the political, leaving aside its possible articulation within an economic system. Understood in those terms, liberal democracy is much more than merely a form of government, since it concerns the symbolic ordering of social relations. It refers to a specific form of politically organized human coexistence, which results from the articulation between two different traditions: on one side, political liberalism (rule of law, separation of powers and individual rights), and on the other side, the democratic tradition of popular sovereignty.

Second, it should also be clear that when I am speaking of liberal democracy, I am referring to the ideal type of a *political* form of society and not to the "really existing liberal democratic societies" in their complexity. Envisaged from that angle, liberal democracy—in its various appellations: constitutional democracy, representative democracy, parliamentary democracy, pluralist democracy, modern democracy—cannot be viewed as the application of the democratic model to a wider context, as some would have it. In other words, the difference between ancient and modern democracy is not one of *size* but of *nature*. The crucial difference resides in the acceptance of *pluralism* that is constitutive of modern liberal democracy. By "pluralism" I mean the end of a substantive idea of the good life, what Claude Lefort calls "the dissolution of the markers of certainty." Pluralism indicates a profound transformation of the symbolic ordering of social relations. This is something that is totally missed when one refers, like John Rawls, to the *fact* of pluralism. There is, of course, a fact, which is the diversity of the conceptions of the good that we find in a liberal society. But the important difference is not an empirical one; it consists in the legitimation of division and conflict and concerns the *symbolic* level. What is at stake here is the emergence of individual liberty and the assertion of equal liberty for all.

When liberal pluralist democracy is envisaged in that way, and its specificity as a new regime acknowledged, we can, I believe, formulate questions that were impossible before, and we can also offer a solution to problems that had appeared insoluble. For instance, the question of the relation between democracy and liberalism has long been a very disputed issue. According to Carl Schmitt pluralist liberal democracy is a contradictory combination of irreconcilable principles: whereas democracy is a logic of identity and equivalence, its complete realization is rendered impossible by the logic of pluralism, which constitutes an obstacle to a total system of identification. Franz Neumann, for his part, points to the fact that, while both sovereignty and the rule of law were constitutive elements of the modern state, they were irreconcilable with each other, for highest might and highest right could not be realized at one and the same time in a common sphere. So far as the sovereignty of the state extends, there is no place for the rule of law. According to him, all attempts at reconciliation come up against insoluble contradictions.

It cannot be denied that, through the articulation of liberalism with democracy, two logics that are ultimately incompatible have been linked together. But I do not consider that we should therefore accept Schmitt's conclusion concerning the nonviable character of liberal democracy. We can, it seems to me, envisage this question in a different way. It is evident that the complete realization of the logic of democracy, which is a logic of identity and equivalence, is made impossible by the liberal logic of pluralism and difference, which impedes the establishment of a total system of identifications. But I consider precisely the existence of such a tension between the logic of identity and the logic of difference to define the specificity of pluralist democracy and make it a regime particularly suited to the undecidability that is the specific character of modern politics. To be sure, the liberal logic that aims to construct every identity as positivity and difference necessarily subverts the project of totalization inscribed in the democratic logic of equivalence. But far from complaining about it, this is something that we should see as very positive. Indeed, it is the existence of such a tension, which also manifests itself between the principles of equality and liberty, and between our identities as "citizens" and our identities as "individuals," that constitutes the best guarantee against the dangers of final closure or of total dissemination that would be the consequence of the exclusive dominance of one of the two logics. Far from aiming at its suppression—that would lead to the elimination of the political and the end of democracy—we must preserve and enhance it. Between the project of a complete equivalence and the opposite one of pure difference, the experience of modern democracy consists in acknowledging the existence of those contradictory logics as well as the necessity of their articulation—an articulation that constantly needs to be recreated and negotiated, with no final point of equilibrium where a final harmony could be reached. Only in that precarious space "in-between" can pluralist democracy exist. To believe that a final resolution of conflicts is eventually possible, even if this is seen as an asymptotic approach to the regulative ideal of a free, unconstrained communication, as in Habermas, does not provide the necessary horizon of the democratic project. Rather, this belief is something that puts it at risk. Indeed, it implicitly carries the desire for a reconciled society, where pluralism would have been superseded.

· · ·

Once liberal democracy is seen as a regime whose political principles are the assertion of liberty and equality for all, we must acknowledge that the consensus required for a pluralist democracy to function well and to reproduce itself cannot be envisaged as merely an agreement concerning procedures. Those who conceive the pluralism of modern democracy as needing only to restrict an agreement about *procedures* do not realize that there can never be pure procedural rules without reference to normative concerns.

Wittgenstein's conception of practices and languages games can help us to clarify this point. For Wittgenstein, to have agreement about opinions there must first be an agreement about the language used. He also alerted us to the fact that agreements concerning opinions are in fact agreements concerning forms of life. As he says: "So you are saying that human agreement decides what is true and what is false. It is what human beings *say* that is true and false; and they agree in the *language* they use. That is not agreement in opinions but in form of life."[1] With respect to the problem that interests us here, this points to the fact that a considerable number of "agreements in judgments" must already exist in a society before a given set of procedures can work. For Wittgenstein, to agree about the definition of a term is not enough, for we need agreement in the way we use it. He puts it in the following way: "if language is to be a means of communication there must be agreement not only in definitions but also (queer as this may sound) in judgments."

Procedures only exist as a complex ensemble of practices. Those practices constitute specific forms of individuality and identity that make possible allegiance to the procedures. It is because they are inscribed in shared forms of life and agreement in judgments that procedures can be accepted and followed. They cannot be seen as rules created on the basis of principles and then applied to specific cases. Rules, for Wittgenstein, are always abridgments of practices; they are inseparable from specific forms of life. The distinction between procedural and substantial cannot, therefore, be as clear as some would have it. In the case of justice, for instance, I do not think that one can oppose, as so many liberals do, procedural and substantial justice without recognizing that procedural justice already presupposes acceptance of certain values. Democracy, therefore, is not only a matter of establishing the right procedures independently of the practices that make possible democratic forms of individuality. Procedures always involve substantial ethical commitments. For that reason, they cannot work properly if they are not supported by a specific type of ethos. This means that, contrary to what Rawls believes, comprehensive doctrines cannot be excluded from the political realm. In my view, important consequences follow from that, and a new way of thinking about religion and the role that it could play in the creation of such ethos is made possible.

· · ·

The previous reflections indicate that there is a serious misunderstanding involved in the liberal tenet of the *neutrality* of the state. To be sure, in order to respect individual liberty and pluralism, a liberal democratic state must be agnostic in matters of religion and morality. But it cannot be agnostic concerning political values, since by definition it postulates certain ethico-political values that constitute its principles of legitimacy. Far from being based on a relativistic conception of the world, liberal democracy is the expression of specific values that inform the way in which it establishes a particular mode of ordering social relations. This new symbolic ordering constitutes its specificity as a distinct regime. As a new political form of society, liberal pluralist democracy is characterized by a certain number of crucial separations: between the public and the private, between church and state, between civil law and religious law. Those separations make possible the emergence of civil society as a distinct realm. Moreover, the liberal notion of a secular state implies not only the distinction between church and state, but also the conception of the church as a voluntary association. This underlines the important difference that exists between our belonging to the state and our belonging to a religious group. For some people, this means a necessary separation between religion and politics. But such a distinction is not at the same level as the other ones, and we will have to examine later in which way it should be understood.

. . .

Against the view defended, for instance, by the pluralist school of Harold Laski and G. D. Cole, it is important to acknowledge that membership in the political community, that is, citizenship, should not be envisaged as constituting one identity among others, located at the same level as other identities linked to inscriptions in voluntary associations. Citizenship is indeed one of the weak points in liberal doctrines. This is why they are vulnerable to the communitarian critique. In order to delineate a conception of citizenship that would reconcile the strong meaning it had in the civic republican tradition with the pluralism constitutive of modern democracy, I have argued that we need a conception of citizenship as a political identity that consists in identification with the ethico-political principles of liberal pluralist democracy and with a commitment to defend its institutions. Citizenship, when conceived as allegiance to the ethico-political values constitutive of pluralist democracy, reveals the impossibility for democratic politics to do without an idea of political community and a reference to the common good. Citizenship refers to the dimension of political community, and, pace liberals, it is not something that can be understood in individualistic terms. It always entails a collective element. I want to stress, however, that, in order to be compatible with pluralism, political community needs to be conceived as a discursive surface and not as an empirical referent. Politics is about the constitution of political community, not something that takes place inside a political community. Political community, as a surface for inscribing demands where a "we" is constituted, requires the correlative idea of the *common good*, but a common good conceived as a "vanishing point," a "horizon of meaning," something to which we must constantly refer but which cannot exist under modern conditions. In such a view, the common good functions as a "social imaginary," that is, as that on which its very impossibility of achieving full representation bestows the role of a horizon that is the condition of possibility of any representation within the space that it delimits. In other words, it is once a condition of possibility and a condition of impossibility.

The common good can also be envisaged as specifying what we can call, following Wittgenstein, a "grammar of conduct" informed by the ethico-political principles of modern democracy: liberty and equality for all. Citizenship understood as allegiance to the ethico-political values constitutive of modern democracy could, I believe, provide the type of consensus required in a pluralist democracy. Indeed, such a consensus concerning principles does not imply negation of conflict and division, and in consequence the creation of a homogeneous collective will. Conflicting interpretations of those principles will always exist. And this is why there will always be different conceptions of citizenship.

Politics, therefore, can be envisaged as the terrain where competing interpretations of shared principles struggle in order to define the "common sense" and establish their hegemony. For instance, a social democratic conception of citizenship will put forward a specific understanding of liberty, of equality, and of who belongs to the "all," which will enter into contestation with conservative and neoliberal interpretations of the same principles. In this way, the common good is "pluralized," and it becomes an object of contestation. This type of dissent about the common good, far from being negative for democracy, is, in my view, the very condition of a vibrant democratic life. This is, indeed, what the agonistic debate should be about.

· · ·

In order to render intelligible the agonistic perspective that I am putting forward, I must say something about the distinction that I have proposed between "the political" and "politics."[2] By "the political," I refer to the dimension of hostility and antagonism that is an ever-present possibility in all human society, antagonism that can take many different forms and emerge in diverse social relations. "Politics," by contrast, refers to the ensemble of practices, discourses, and institutions that seek to establish a certain order and to organize human coexistence under conditions that are always potentially conflictual because they are affected by the dimension of the political. This conception, which attempts to keep together the two meanings of *polemos* and *polis* present in the idea of politics, is, I believe, crucial for democratic politics.

Politics aims at the creation of unity in a context of conflict and diversity. It is concerned with the formation of a "we" as opposed to a "them." The novelty of democratic politics is not overcoming the we/them distinction but the different way in which it is established. Once this dimension of "the political" is acknowledged, we can envisage "politics" as the attempt to tame hostility and to defuse the potential antagonism that exists in human relations. According to such an approach, the fundamental question for democratic politics is not, pace the rationalists, how to arrive at a rational consensus reached without exclusion. This, in other words, would imply the construction of an "us" that would not have a corresponding "them." This is impossible because the very condition of constituting an "us" is the demarcation of a "them." The real issue at stake in democratic politics is how to establish the us/them distinction in a way that is compatible with pluralist democracy.

A pluralistic democratic order supposes that the opponent is not seen as an enemy to be destroyed but as an adversary whose existence is legitimate and must be tolerated. We will fight against his/her ideas, but we will not put into question his/her right to defend them. This category of the adversary does not eliminate antagonism, however. And it should be distinguished from the liberal notion of the competitor, with which it is sometimes identified. An adversary is a legitimate enemy, an enemy with whom we have in common a shared adhesion to the ethico-political principles of democracy. But our disagreement concerning their meaning and implementation is not one that can be resolved through rational agreement, hence the antagonistic element in the relation. To come to accept the position of the adversary is to undergo a radical change in political identity. To be sure, compromises are possible; they are part of the process of politics. But they should be seen as temporary respites in an ongoing confrontation.

Hence the importance of distinguishing between two types of political relations: one of antagonism between enemies, and one of agonism between adversaries. We could say that the aim of democratic politics is to transform an "antagonism" into an "agonism."[3] Contrary to the liberal model of "deliberative democracy," which excludes all divisive issues from the public sphere in order to allow for free and unconstrained deliberation on all matters of common concern, the model of "agonistic pluralism" that I am advocating asserts that the prime task of democratic politics is not to eliminate passions or to relegate them to the private sphere in order to establish a rational consensus in the public sphere. It is, rather, to attempt to mobilize those passions toward democratic designs. It is necessary to understand that, far from jeopardizing democracy, agonistic confrontation is in fact its very condition of possibility. To be sure, pluralist democracy demands consensus on a set of common ethico-political principles. But it also calls for the expression of dissent and the institutions through which conflicts can be manifested. This is why its survival depends upon the possibility of forming collective political identities around clearly differentiated positions and choice among real alternatives. When the agonistic dynamics of pluralism are hindered because of a lack of democratic identities to identify with, the ground is laid for various forms of politics articulated around essentialist identities and for the multiplication of confrontations over non-negotiable moral values.

Separation Between Church and State

Now that I have presented the main ideas of the "agonistic pluralism" that I am advocating,[4] I want to examine some of its implications for the relation between church and state.

As we have seen, the agonistic model denies that the liberal state is or should be neutral. The separation between church and state cannot, therefore, be justified with the argument that the state should be neutral toward all religions. According to such a view, the separation between church and state is a defining feature of liberal democracy, since that is what makes possible a regime of toleration, where the state tolerates a multiplicity of religious groups and forces these groups to tolerate one another. But the justification for this regime of toleration does not pretend to be made by appealing to supposedly neutral arguments. Toleration is justified on the ground that it is required by the values constitutive of the liberal democratic regime and the form of human coexistence that they inform. It is because the ethico-political principles of the liberal state are the assertion of liberty and equality for all that a regime of toleration is necessary and that the state should not be permitted to favor one religion over another. Those who do not share those values will of course claim that this is "liberal fundamentalism," and they will see the institutions of liberal constitutionalism as a form of violence imposed upon them. This is, I think, unavoidable, and it is not by declaring that their opponents are "unreasonable" that liberals will ever solve the problem. Antagonism is indeed ineradicable.

· · ·

The separation between church and state is, in my view, one of the central tenets of liberal democracy envisaged as a new "regime"—which does not mean that it is fully realized in existing liberal democracies. Nevertheless, we need to scrutinize what this implies. I want to argue that, contrary to some interpretations, it does not require that religion should be relegated to the private sphere and that religious symbols should be excluded from the public sphere. As Michael Walzer has argued, for instance, what is really at stake in the separation between church and state is the separation between religion and *state power*. This implies that the state must have the monopoly on legitimate violence and that religious associations should not be given any control over coercive power.

To speak of the separation between church and state, therefore, is one thing; another is to speak of the separation between religion and politics; and still another is to speak of the separation between the public and the private. The problem lies in the fact that those three types of separation are sometimes presented as in some way equivalent and requiring each other. In consequence, the separation between church and state is seen as implying the exclusion of all forms of religious expression from the public sphere.

It is, I submit, the tendency to identify politics with the state and the state with the public that has led to the mistaken idea that the separation between church and state means the absolute relegation of religion to the private. I do not think that such a view can be defended. As long as they act within constitutional limits, there is no reason why religious groups should not be able to intervene in the political arena to argue in favor of or against certain causes. Indeed, many democratic struggles have been informed by religious motives. And the fight for social justice has often been enhanced by the participation of religious groups.

· · ·

Since it does not postulate that comprehensive views should be excluded from the public sphere, the agonistic approach makes room for religious believers in the political realm in a way that is not open to other models. To believe that the field of politics should be envisaged in terms of "interests," as in the aggregative model of interest-group pluralism, or of "reason" and "morality," as in the deliberative model, is to miss the crucial role played by passions, values, beliefs, and all the various forms of collective identification in political action. This is not to deny that these can have consequences that are not always welcome. But by attempting to impede all those motivations for playing a role in the political domain, many democratic theorists end up eliminating the very forces that move people to political participation.

This is why the "agonistic" model of democracy seems to me much better suited to deal with the question of religion than the "deliberative" one. According to the advocates of the deliberative model, all divisive issues, like religion, should be relegated to the sphere of the private in order to allow for a rational consensus to be established in the public realm. In their view, religious considerations do not have a legitimate place in political deliberation, since they are the expression of particularistic passions. The "priority of the right over the good" requires that only moral, universalizable concerns be considered legitimate. As a result, in both the Rawlsian and the Habermasian versions of deliberative democracy—albeit in different ways—religious arguments are excluded from politics. By contrast, the model of agonistic pluralism that I am proposing acknowledges the importance of religious forms of identification as legitimate motives for political action and does not attempt to keep them outside the political realm. This does not mean, of course, that it would allow legal recognition of demands that would put into question the very basis of the constitutional order and that could abolish, for instance, the separation between church and state. The principles of liberal constitutionalism are to be respected. But as long as they accept to adhere to those rules, religious believers will not be forced to keep their concerns out of the democratic public arena.

Once distinctions of church/state, public/private, religion/politics cease to be considered equivalent, it is possible to imagine the multiplicity of forms in which religion could begin to play a legitimate role in liberal democratic societies. What liberal democracy requires is not the elimination of religion from the public sphere, as most versions of deliberative democracy argue. Indeed, the agonistic view of democracy that I have just delineated asserts that there is a place for religious forms of intervention within the context of agonistic debate. What a liberal democratic regime requires is that those interventions should be made within the constitutional limits set by its principles of legitimacy. Those constitutional limits will, however, vary according to the way different societies interpret the ethico-political principles that are constitutive of modern democracy and the type of hegemonic articulation established between its liberal and its democratic components. It is therefore a mistake to imagine that there is a single correct, universal way of envisaging liberal democracy. How the ethico-political principles of liberal democracy are institutionalized in specific conditions is part of the agonistic struggle. And this is an issue that should always remain open to contestation.

Toleration Without Tolerance

Enlightenment and the Image of Reason

Lars Tønder

> The experience of chaos, both on the speculative and the other level, prompts us to see rationalism in a historical perspective which it set itself on principle to avoid, to seek a philosophy which explains the upsurge of reason in a world not of its making and to prepare the substructure of living experience without which reason and liberty are emptied of their content and wither away.
>
> —Maurice Merleau-Ponty, *Phenomenology of Perception*

The Ontological Imaginary of Reason

Contemporary attempts to justify tolerance and toleration converge on the importance of reason. The argument for this, on behalf of what we might call the "model of reasonable toleration," is that reason is available to everyone who is willing to give to others what they want for themselves. Its laws apply universally, and even though its results are more reliable than those that come from other sources of knowledge, it is always open to revision. This makes it the right candidate for being the "neutral" yet "case-sensitive" arbitrator in societies with conflicting notions of the common good. As Rainer Forst, a prominent advocate of reasonable toleration, argues, "Persons are tolerant to the extent that, even though they disagree with others about the nature of the good and true life, they tolerate all other views within the bounds of reciprocity and generality. This is why toleration is a *virtue of justice* and a *demand of reason.*"[1]

This essay addresses the ontological presuppositions that circumscribe this kind of argument. It does so through the notion of what I call "the ontological imaginary of reason." This term of art designates a loose gathering of world images that seek to make sense of what rea-

327

son is. The way it does so may change over time, but its purpose is always to connect abstractions about human existence with the embodied expressions through which citizens "image" their social circumstances. The imaginary is in that sense akin to what Hegel calls *Gedanken in das Vorstellen*, that is, a mode of "picture thinking" that presents itself through performances and storytelling.[2] But unlike Hegel, who seeks to overcome picture thinking, this essay makes no such attempt. To the contrary, I suggest that we view the underlying performances and stories as the most profound way of expressing the nature of reason. I do so because the performances and stories, invoking the embodied circumstances under which reason arises, operate just as much in the register of affect as in the register of explicit consciousness. They connect, we might say, the procedural nature of reason to the bodily dispositions that sustain this nature.

The importance of this connection is evident once we realize how the model of reasonable toleration legitimizes itself through privileging a limited group of Enlightenment thinkers, among which the most prominent are Locke and Kant. At first, this privileging may seem uncontroversial because of the originality with which these thinkers approach the issues of tolerance and toleration. But the closer we look, the more evident it becomes that at stake is a particularly contentious version of the ontological imaginary of reason. This version begins by depicting reason as a disembodied faculty of cognition. It then draws a strict dividing line between those aspects of human existence that matter ontologically and those that are indifferent. Moreover, it tries to ensure that any analysis of tolerance and toleration adheres to three imperatives of thought: namely, neutrality, dispassionateness, and systematicity. Both aspects—the identification of the indifferent and the three imperatives—then lead to an image of reason in which reason organizes its activities independently of how those who embody these activities experience the world on an everyday basis.

I claim that this image is flawed because of its tendency to misrecognize the bodily dispositions from which reason arises. I also claim that this tendency prevents the model of reasonable toleration from approaching the issues of tolerance and toleration in a way that appreciates the unique nature of both. But I would like to emphasize that the defense of these claims is not the prospect of articulating the real essence of tolerance and toleration. It may be that there is such an essence, but it is unlikely that we, in the event it appeared, would be able to recognize its form and content. Rather, I defend my claims by showing how the effect that the image produces (as opposed to, say, its truthfulness or authenticity) is a disconnection of *tolerance* from *toleration*: that is, a disconnection of the disposition to endure pain and suffering (tolerance) from the institutional framework accommodating minority groups, through principles such as free exercise of religion and separation of church and state (toleration).[3] The stakes of this disconnection are high. Not only is the ability to endure pain and suffering an important part of our commitment to the principles of toleration, but also, since the disconnection implies relegating tolerance to the unexamined background, it entails a lopsidedness in how we approach the issues of tolerance and toleration. We may think of this lopsidedness as a "theory of toleration without tolerance," a theory that has difficulty responding to questions such as: What kind of pain and suffering should citizens tolerate? What makes it possible to endure pain and suffering? What kind of agency does this endurance entail? And what kind of sensibility nourishes this agency in the most effective way?

This essay seeks to prepare the ground for a project that could answer these questions without falling into the pitfalls created by the image of reason just outlined. I begin by discussing how any reading of the Enlightenment is just as much a reflection of the desires and interests of the present as it is a reflection of past events. This will help us to address the ontological presuppositions that circumscribe the contemporary model of reasonable toleration.

Enlightenment(s)

There are obvious reasons for connecting the Enlightenment era with issues of tolerance and toleration, the most significant of which is the way in which the Enlightenment itself followed from the internal fragmentation of the Christian faith. This fragmentation increased the level of religious pluralism—at least if we count the sheer number of Christian denominations that emerged after the Reformation (for example, Lutheranism, Presbyterianism, and Anabaptism)—and it led to the search for a way to justify the principles of religious freedom that would go beyond the theological motives informing previous discussions of these principles. This search, in turn, motivated Enlightenment thinkers across Europe, who, more than anyone else, were concerned with finding a way to liberate the foundations of knowledge from the influence of medieval theology. The result was, thus, what many today think of as a happy marriage between the politics of religious freedom and a philosophical interest in knowledge based on reason alone. As historians such as Ole Peter Grell and Roy Porter argue, "it was the thinkers of the Enlightenment who most clearly voiced arguments for toleration, in all their strengths and weaknesses, which continue to envelop us in our present multicultural and multireligious societies. Here, as in so many other ways, we are the children of the Enlightenment."[4]

The problem with this proposition is that, while we may be children of the Enlightenment, it is not self-evident that this says anything specific about what or who "we" are. In fact, a number of historians have over the past ten years argued that to speak of the Enlightenment in the singular is to betray what this era is all about.[5] The Enlightenment, they argue, is a complex phenomenon, which includes opposing paradigms of thought. It crosses its own lines of division—lines that follow distinctions between "radical" and "moderate," "early" and "high," "conservative" and "liberal," "civil" and "metaphysical"—and it remains nothing but an infinite network of ideas about what it means to be a reasonable person. Because of this, these historians propose, each from his own perspective, we are better served if we speak of Enlightenment(s), in the plural. Moreover, because there is no such thing as *the* Enlightenment, any attempt to construe one is just as much a reflection of the embodied circumstances—that is, the desires, prejudices, and habits—in which the historian's interpretation is set as it is a reflection of what actually took place in the past. This means that we must see the business of historical interpretation as an attempt either to define or to transform oneself in light of some limited section of what we call "history." As Ian Hunter argues, invoking the embodiment of his own argument, interpretations of the Enlightenment are "intellectual practices or 'spiritual exercises' whose special role is to permit attention to and transformation of the self."[6]

What follows seeks to heed these considerations by paying close attention to the way in which the valorization of Enlightenment thinkers such as Locke and Kant has changed over time. It also tries to show how this valorization entails a marginalization of other Enlightenment thinkers—Voltaire, in particular—promoting an image of reason that prevents the contemporary model of reasonable toleration from engaging the endurance of pain and suffering (what I earlier referred to as the disconnection of tolerance and toleration).

The Lockean Paradigm

Today, there are few who would disagree with James Tully's remark that the *Epistola de tolerantiam*, by Locke, is "a classic in the European struggle for [tolerance] and toleration," one that poses the issue of democratic pluralism "within a recognizably European problematic, the terms of which were set by the generation of Grotius and Lipsius."[7] This makes Locke a natural starting point for our discussion.

Let us first note that only in recent years has the *Epistola* attained the status of being a "classic" in the history of tolerance and toleration. In the 1960s, for example, historians such Henry Kamen and Joseph Lecler saw no reason to make Locke the centerpiece in their accounts. To the contrary, they argued that Locke's discourse is, above all, a demonstration of "Nonconformist thought, with all its narrow-mindedness" and added that the Lockean arguments are "neither as original nor as liberal as defenses [of tolerance and toleration] penned by other European writers."[8] These remarks, which no longer appear to be prominent in the literature, may not reflect the actual legacy of Locke, yet they do invite us to pursue another kind of questioning: How has the *Epistola* become so central to contemporary discussions of tolerance and toleration? What kind of desires and interests does this reevaluation reveal? And what are the ontological commitments that underpin it? Answers to these questions say more about contemporary political theory than they say about the *Epistola*.

We can now turn to Locke's argument for the rationality of toleration. The historical events that led to this argument are well documented. Locke wrote the major part of the

Epistola in November 1685, while living in exile in Utrecht, and it is for the most part a reiteration of another essay from 1667—entitled "An Essay Concerning Toleration"—which Locke refused to have published. One reason for this might be that the 1667 essay represents a change in Locke's thinking, which until then had been rather conservative, favoring the right of the civil powers in matters of religious worship. But mindful of what he had learned from the early Earl of Shaftesbury, who defended the Whig Revolution against King Charles II, Locke became convinced that the time was ripe for another kind of government, one that would guarantee the liberty of individuals who live in opposition to their government. This led to the theory of private property that lies at the heart of Locke's *Second Treatise of Government* (1690). It also led to what a majority of contemporary theorists see as the foundation upon which the *Epistola* relies.[9]

Without oversimplifying, we might say that Locke's theory of private property has two parts. The first part shows how religion belongs to the jurisdiction of the private sphere, based on the assumption that religious beliefs, like other modes of private property, are a product of the labor that individuals put into the land given by God to mankind in general. The second part shows that it is impossible to regulate the private sphere politically, since politicians, being subject to the jurisdiction of the public sphere, only have the means to *protect* property, leaving it to each individual to decide how he or she wants to *appropriate* this property. These insights demonstrate not only the irrationality of persecution but also the rationality of a policy that limits the jurisdiction of the state. Indeed, they lead Locke to conclude that we must distinguish the business of the church from that of the state. "If this be not done," Locke warns, "there can be no end put to the controversies that will be always arising between those that have, or at least pretend to have, on the one side, a concernment for the interest of men's souls, and, on the other side, a care of the commonwealth."[10]

Needless to say, the distinction between church and state earned Locke a place in the canon of modern secular liberalism. It anticipates the idea of limited government, and it shows why this kind of government should stay neutral in debates about religion. But what seems like a purely secular theory is more than a cornerstone in the history of modern liberalism. It is also a party to the controversy concerning the reasonable, and, hence, true nature of the Christian faith, which, Locke argues, shows both "the necessity and advantage" of, if not *tolerance*, then at least *toleration*.[11] More than a few commentators have been critical of the Christianization that this proposition entails. They argue that it compromises the neutrality of liberalism and that it makes Locke's argument "uninteresting from a philosophical point of view."[12] It may be true that Christian belief, no matter how charitably we define it, compromises the neutrality of liberalism. But the lesson is not that this makes Locke's discourse uninteresting. Rather, it shows how issues like tolerance and toleration depend upon arguments that do not distinguish sharply between politics and religion. The way we negotiate this dependency hinges on the connection between the image of reason that legitimizes these arguments and the bodily dispositions that sustain them.

Locke's own contribution to this negotiation follows from his intervention in the controversy about *adiaphora*—what we may translate as "things indifferent"—which dates to an early essay from 1660 (published in 1967 under the title *Two Tracts on Government*). There Locke argues: (1) that there are things indifferent to salvation and blessedness, (2) that things indifferent concern aspects of religious worship not mentioned explicitly in the Scripture, and (3) that civil government has a right to legislate things indifferent in order to maintain the peace and security of the commonwealth.[13] Of these claims, the last is the most controversial, something Locke realizes in his more mature writings, turning his interpretation of things indifferent into an argument in favor of a certain distance with regard to disputes over religion. He argues this in the *Epistola*:

> [If] I be marching on with my utmost vigour, in that way which, according to the sacred geography, leads straight to *Jerusalem*; why I am beaten and ill used by others, because, perhaps, I wear not buskins; because my hair is not of the right cut; because, perhaps, I have not been dipt in the right fashion; because I eat flesh upon the road, or some other food which agrees with my stomach; because I avoid certain by-ways, which seem unto me to lead into briars or precipices; because, amongst the several paths that are in the same road, I choose that to walk in which seems to be the straightest and cleanest; because I avoid to keep company with some travellers that are less grave, and others that are more sour than they ought to be; or in fine, because I follow a guide that either is, or is not, clothed in white, and crowned with a mitre? Certainly, if we consider right, we shall find that for the most part they are such frivolous things as these, that, without any prejudice to religion or the salvation of souls, if not accompanied with superstition or hypocrisy, might either be observed or omitted; I say, they are such like things as these, which breed implacable enmities among Christian brethren, who are all agreed in the substantial and truly fundamental part of religion.[14]

What role does the endurance of pain and suffering play in this performative account of human experience? At first, it would seem that pain and suffering are everywhere—after all, we are talking about a person who is being "beaten and ill used by others" because of his or her religion. But the way in which Locke connects pain and suffering to the image of reason suggests, nonetheless, a misrecognition of their nature. This is so because the connection itself relies on the doctrine of empiricism, which emphasizes the role that sensory experience plays in the pursuit of knowledge. Locke is the first to reckon how this leads to a condition of contingency that not only causes difference of opinion but also frustrates the attempt to reduce or increase the effects of pain and suffering. We might say that for Locke pain and suffering are dispositions of the body that, at least in principle, have the potential to elude strict control. But the conclusion Locke draws from this does not account for this elusiveness. To the contrary, with the doctrine of empiricism as his reference point, Locke maintains that the human mind, upon careful examination, is free to distinguish between what is essential and what is inessential to the happiness of everybody. It is this freedom—a freedom independent of the bodily dispositions that empower it—that makes it possible to reduce or increase pain and suffering at the behest of the person who encounters them. Locke explains about the relationship between free will, agency, and examination of the body: "Examination is *consulting a guide*. The determination of the *will* upon enquiry is *following the direction of that Guide*: And he that has a power to act, or not to act according as such determination directs, is a *free Agent*."[15]

This account of the relationship between self-examination, agency, and free will defines Locke's contribution to the contemporary model of reasonable toleration. The contribution is an image of reason as a disembodied faculty of cognition that, without being involved in day-to-day dealings, is capable of deciding the extent to which difference of opinion matters to the pursuit of happiness. This implies an instrumental stance with regard to the construction of knowledge, a stance that supports the development of what Charles Taylor calls "the punctual self."[16] Locke also more directly influences the way in which contemporary theorists approach the issues of tolerance and toleration. First, it follows from his analysis that the duty to tolerate wrong does not extend to things that touch upon substantial truths of morality or religion. This point is the implicit upshot of the notion of things indifferent, and it shows that to be tolerant depends upon knowing when not to be tolerant. Second, it follows that the raison d'être of toleration is the pursuit of happiness, understood as the opposite of pain and suffering. This puts the issue of *toleration* in opposition to *tolerance* because the latter includes the attitude or sensibility that makes it possible to endure pain and suffering. Thus, we may conclude that Locke takes us to a crossroad: either we disconnect the two issues—tolerance and toleration—or we rethink the ontological imaginary of reason empowering this disconnection.

Three Imperatives of Thought

The stakes at this crossroad are high. On the one hand, it seems "natural" to follow the route of Locke because it directs us to someone like Kant, who gives the doctrine of empiricism a transcendental foundation. On the other hand, it seems equally "natural" to replace the Locke-to-Kant route with one that appreciates the intellectual diversity characterizing the seventeenth- and eighteenth-century Enlightenment. Such an alternative route would take us to a variety of other thinkers, among whom Voltaire might be the first to come to mind, because he, more than anyone else, was seen as a champion of the Enlightenment in his own time. That Voltaire no longer has this status is clear from the way in which contemporary theorists of reasonable toleration interpret his work as an intellectual curiosity in the history of political thought. It is to this revalorization that we now turn; to understand the reason behind it is to gain insight into the tacit exclusions that determine the reasonableness of toleration.

Voltaire arrives at the basic insight—that "tolerance . . . is the endowment of humanity [*l'apanage de humanité*]"[17]—through his engagement with the Calas case. This is the case in which Jean Calas, a Protestant father living in Toulouse, was executed on March 10, 1762, for having killed his son Marc-Antoine, who, the prosecutor alleged, was in the process of converting to Catholicism. Convinced that Jean Calas was innocent and that Marc-Antoine had committed suicide for personal reasons, Voltaire set out to protect Mme Calas and her family from further harassment. His focus on how the deliberations of the thirteen judges responsible for the case were shaped by the broader context challenges the image of reason that Locke promotes.

Voltaire begins his defense—published in *Traité sur la tolérance*—with the suggestion that the *Toulousaines* have an innate disgust for other religious faiths.[18] He substantiates this by reminding his audience of the tradition in Toulouse that celebrated the deaths of more than three thousand Protestants killed in a massacre by their Catholic adversaries on May 17, 1562. He also points out how one of the religious fraternities in Toulouse influenced the opinion of the judges by honoring Marc-Antoine at a commemorative mass, at which he was presented as a martyr who died for his struggle against evil (that is, Calvinism). Both of these observations help Voltaire establish the claim that the people of Toulouse, and not the Calas family, were responsible for the suggestion that Marc-Antoine had been in the process of converting to Catholicism. They also help Voltaire to understand that, if the virtues of tolerance and toleration are to flourish, they can do so only if we place them in a climate of enlightened forbearance. This, stresses Voltaire, is not something that happens in a disinterested manner. To the contrary, it depends on the partisanship of those who are prepared to appreciate the embodied nature of reason. Voltaire argues this in an often-quoted passage: the "great means to reduce the number of fanatics . . . is to subject that disease of the mind to the regime of reason [*régime de la raison*], which slowly, but infallibly, enlightens men. Reason is mild and humane. It inspires forbearance and drowns discord; it strengthens virtue and makes obedience to the laws agreeable rather than compulsory."[19]

There is no doubt that this alternative image of reason had a great impact on the political climate of France during the eighteenth century, epitomized in Condorcet's comment that Voltaire was the *idole de la nation*. Voltaire maintained this status in early-twentieth-century commentaries by scholars such as Ernest Cassirer, who saw in the *Traité* an attitude of sober engagement, which made it possible for Voltaire to focus "in one point all the intellectual convictions and tendencies of the Enlightenment."[20] But Voltaire no longer occupies the epicenter of the Enlightenment. In fact, we might describe the more recent reception of Voltaire as a shift from seeing him as key to the discussion of tolerance and toleration to viewing him as a curiosity in the history of these issues. Preston

King, for example, finds that "only the most general comments are called for on Voltaire," because he was "more of an impressionist and journalist than a thinker," who swung "wildly from a desire to defend the right of religious views" to a "somewhat contradictory desire" to fight the Catholic Church.[21] Rainer Forst, whom we encountered earlier, is more generous in his commentary, although he too finds Voltaire's defense of religious pluralism to be inherently flawed, arguing that "although reason speaks *against* any dogmatic pretension of unconditionality . . . , it does *not*, as Voltaire thought, speak *for* a religion of reason." In fact, Forst argues, if reason is to provide a solid foundation for the issues of tolerance and toleration, it must approach its own regime as more than yet "another particular belief."[22]

My interest in these comments stems not so much from what they say about the legacy of Voltaire as from what they say about the kind of argument that counts as reasonable in the contemporary discussion of tolerance and toleration. They do so in an implicit manner, one in which the criteria by which we judge other images of reason are hidden in the judgment itself. Even so, if we listen carefully, we find three imperatives of thought at work in the commentaries by King and Forst. These imperatives seek to regulate the way contemporary theorists approach the issues of tolerance and toleration:

1. *The imperative of systematicity.* The first imperative states that our approach must be systematic and coherent. This may sound uncontroversial, because these are the terms that lend credibility to theory in general. To demand systematicity and coherence, however, is also to demand independence of context, a demand that detaches the theorist from the circumstances in which everyday politics is lived. It also detaches the theorist from the bodily dispositions in which his or her theoretical apparatus is set. Both detachments make it difficult to approach the issues of tolerance and toleration in light of concrete experiences where pain and suffering elude strict control. Since this elusiveness is an important part of tolerance proper, we might thus say that the first imperative encourages the separation of tolerance from toleration, relegating the former to the unexamined background.

2. *The imperative of dispassionateness.* The second imperative that we find in the comments by King and Forst states that our approach must be dispassionate. Again, this may not sound controversial, because the practice of being tolerant of others entails the ability to curb one's inclination to anathematize or persecute. But the imperative of dispassionateness also implies that we can be neither ardent nor enthusiastic about being a tolerant person. This takes away the inspiring dimensions of this kind of subjectivity. It also impairs the attempt to imagine, not to mention encourage, a political sensibility (as opposed to, say, a disinterested procedure or formal institution) in which tolerance is cardinal. Thus, it may be that a certain kind of wildness or affective intensity is desirable when it comes to the way in which we approach the issues of tolerance and toleration.

3. *The imperative of neutrality.* The third imperative embodied by Voltaire's critics is that our approach to the issues of tolerance and toleration must be neutral with regard to

partisan politics and ideological commitments. It is important to be clear about this kind of neutrality. It does not imply, for example, that our approach should be indifferent to various ways of interpreting tolerance and toleration, like a skeptic who refuses to make any kind of judgment about the world. Nor does it imply acknowledgment of the way in which any approach to this world is deeply contestable. Rather, it implies that our approach should be available across a variety of beliefs and other commitments. This requires a kind of intellectual superiority—one in which the standard of reason is the ultimate arbitrator regardless of its own biases—which implicates the imperative of neutrality in its own kind of dogmatism. It assumes the possibility of placing a set of moral and religious convictions beyond the realm of contestation.

My point about these three imperatives is not only that they situate Voltaire's appreciation of the embodiment of tolerance and toleration on the margins of contemporary political theory but also that they contribute to the depiction of reason as that which stands apart from our everyday involvement with the world. They do so by solidifying the idea, which comes from Locke, that to think politically is to systematize, in a neutral manner, what is essential and what is inessential to human happiness. Indeed, we might say that the political theorist is like a Newtonian physicist, who operates under the assumption that his or her movements are irrelevant to what he or she measures. There is thus no real sense of tragedy or untimeliness in this image of reason. Moreover, the three imperatives marginalize those political theorists who seek to follow a route different from the one that Locke outlines. This is not because the Lockean theory is fully finished. Among other things, Locke has neither established the autonomous nature of reason nor freed the motivation of toleration from hedonism. Even so, the imperatives help to define the Lockean theory as the starting point of political reasoning, limiting the diversity of the eighteenth-century Enlightenment to a question of securing the claims that Locke could not secure. This is what turns Locke's "theory of toleration without tolerance" into an anticipation of what Kant (and those who follow him) has to say about this theory. It is the task of Kant's transcendental philosophy to complete what is incomplete in Locke.

The Purity of Toleration

Kant's attempt to define what one commentator calls the "grounding of reason" makes him the historical endpoint in the path toward the model of reasonable toleration.[23] It is Kant who completes the image of reason that underpins this model, and it is Kant who provides it with the authority needed to fend off competing images. The latter, however, may also be why the Kantian project is an obstacle to a project that appreciates the unique nature of both tolerance and toleration. The following seeks to show why this may be so, beginning with the way in which Kant establishes toleration (but not tolerance) as a demand of reason.

The overall ambition of the Kantian project is to show that it is possible to be both the legislator and the judge of our own laws. This kind of self-government is possible, argues Kant, if intelligent individuals surrender themselves to the discipline of reason— what he calls *die Disziplin der reinen Vernunft*[24]—which holds that it is in the interest of reason never to take anything for granted, but instead to be engaged in what Foucault later would call the "critical attitude of modern civilization."[25] This is an attitude that, first, encourages those who reason to think for themselves and, second, obliges them to listen to the better argument, permitting them to embody the motto of the Enlighten- ment—*sapere aude*—have courage to use your own understanding.[26] What is more, al- though this discipline may expose the reasonable to the unreasonable, Kant is certain that reason will emerge vindicated from such an exposure. The argument for this is that reason thrives in an open society, where citizens are able to speak their minds in public and where reason can test its claims. So what appears to be contrary to reason—that someone should listen to unreason or speak unreasonably—is, in fact, part of reason itself. It is because of this that we may say that toleration (understood as a system of government accommodating minority groups) is a demand of reason. Kant argues this in *Critique of Pure Reason*:

> Reason must in its entire undertakings subject itself to criticism; should it limit free- dom of criticism by any prohibitions, it must harm itself, drawing upon itself a dam- aging suspicion. Nothing is so important through its usefulness, nothing is so sacred, that it may be exempted from this searching examination, which knows no respect for persons. Reason depends on this freedom for its very existence. For reason has no dictatorial authority; its verdict is simply the agreement of free citizens, of whom each must be permitted to express, without let or hindrances, his objections or even his veto.[27]

It is easy to find the democratic tendencies in this statement. Even so, we should be extra attentive to presuppositions that support these tendencies.[28] A few surprises await us here. For example, despite his praise of freedom of religion—and, thus, of toleration—Kant is not eager to affirm tolerance proper, but states instead that a prince must decline the presumptuous title of this concept (*den hochmütigen Namen der Toleranz*) if he wants to call himself enlightened.[29] Likewise, although he affirms the value of reason's listening to unreason—and, thus, of letting reason encounter pain and suffering—Kant is not eager to affirm the questioning of reason "all the way down" but states instead that there are certain limits to what we can bring into question in order to be reasonable. These limits— which surface in the discussion of the categorical imperative and the postulates of rea- son—prevent Kant from appreciating the unique nature not only of toleration but also of tolerance.

The first set of limits has to do with the way we justify the categorical imperative. Kant argues that we cannot grasp the imperative the way we grasp conventional objects in time and space, which are subject to what he calls the "speculative usage of reason,"[30] simply because the imperative itself does not appear in any concrete manner. Even so, although the imperative is nonphenomenal, it is still necessary for us to know whether it respects the discipline of reason. Only if it does can we accept the imperative as legitimate. Kant solves this problem by introducing a second mode of reason—"practical reason"— which is not subject to any critical deduction but instead is what makes critical deduction possible in the first place. This implies that all we must demonstrate is that there is practical reason and that this kind of reason is sufficient to determine the will without the influence of any empirical condition. However, because this assumes what we seek to prove—that is, the categorical imperative—Kant finds it unreasonable to question the imperative itself. Instead, he argues that we should accept it as a fact of what it means to be reasonable, something without which intelligent individuals could not be who they are. Kant argues this in a passage that establishes the apodictic character of the moral law: the "moral law is given, as an apodictically certain fact, as it were, or pure reason, a fact of which we are a priori conscious, even if it be granted that no example could be found in which it has been followed exactly."[31]

The second set of limits to the practice of critical reasoning has to do with what Kant calls "postulates of pure practical reason." These postulates, which may appear to be so "out-dated" that we should eliminate them from the Kantian corpus altogether, include: (1) the immortality of the soul, which is necessary for the perfection of the moral law; (2) human freedom, affirmatively regarded, which is necessary for the possibility of human agents' not being subject only to the laws of nature; and (3) the existence of a divine creator—that is, God—who is necessary for the existence of a world other than that of the senses, that is, the existence of the nonphenomenal, intelligent world.[32] As I said, it is tempting to eliminate these postulates, especially because not even Kant believes that it is possible to demonstrate their validity by way of reason alone. They are indeed postulates and not, say, arguments. Even so, Kant insists that we affirm the postulates. Why? Because they establish the condition under which a finite being will obey the moral law, accepting the way in which it determines the will that directs his or her actions. The postulates in that sense make intelligent individuals—those with an ability to be reasonable—feel reverence for the moral law. What is more, the postulates provide the same individuals with a sense of orientation within the domain of action, since the postulates determine their perceptions of what is morally right in any given case. This alone makes it necessary not only to state but also to affirm the validity of the three postulates.

We can now turn to the reason why these two sets of limitations—that is, the apodictic certainty of the moral law and the three postulates of pure practical reason—prevent Kant from appreciating the unique nature of not only toleration but also tolerance. The main point is that the moral law and the three postulates are committed to a certain kind of purity. What is "pure," Kant implies, is that which holds the conditions of possibility in its own hands.[33] Moreover, it arises spontaneously, without influence from some cause other than reason itself, and it maintains its autonomy insofar as it does not mingle with that which individuals experience through their senses, through their engagement with the world. Both the moral law and the three postulates of pure practical reason hinge on this kind of purity. But does this commitment to purity allow us to address the pain and suffering around which the issue of tolerance revolves? Much suggests the contrary, because pain and suffering are the kind of phenomena that challenge Kantian autonomy. They do so, first, by making the one who experiences them feel vulnerable and, second, by suspending the very idea of reason, putting into question the criteria that define it. Because of this, we might say that to address tolerance proper (and not only toleration) would require the opposite of what it means to be pure and, thus, autonomous in the Kantian sense. It would require that we set out from the presumption that individuals are not the cause of their own actions, from the assumption that they are not autonomous, reckoning the way in which they are under the influence of affects and moods that they do not control. Only with these alternative assumptions at hand will we be able to address the pain and suffering that circumscribe the issues of tolerance and toleration.

Rethinking Tolerance and Toleration

We have now uncovered the ontological presuppositions underpinning the model of reasonable toleration. These presuppositions depict reason as a disembodied faculty of cognition—a faculty capable of detaching itself from everyday experience—and they lead to an image of reason that demands a disconnection of tolerance and toleration. To be clear, this image does not exist *in concreto*, but instead emerges between the events of the seventeenth- and eighteenth-century Enlightenment and contemporary appropriations of these events. Indeed, it shapes the spiritual exercises from which our sense of what it means to be a tolerant subject emerges. The way it does so entails: (1) an ontology drawing a strict line between the essential and inessential aspects of the world; (2) a set of postulates stating the immortality of the soul, the autonomous character of our freedom, and the existence of God; and (3) a mode of political inquiry expressing itself in a tone of neutrality, dispassionateness, and systematicity.

Theorists of reasonable toleration are confident that the result of this image of reason—what I have referred to as a "theory of toleration without tolerance"—represents the best way of adjudicating the tolerable in a neutral yet case-sensitive manner. But the preceding discussion has brought this confidence into question. It has done so by suggesting that a theory of toleration without tolerance has few answers to questions such as: What causes pain and suffering? What defines the kind of pain and suffering that the citizenry should endure? What characterizes a political culture in which this endurance is cardinal? My point is that the effects of not answering these questions are far more important than the theorists who follow in the footsteps of Locke and Kant are willing to anticipate. My point is also that the effects reveal the need for a new project of tolerance and toleration, one that approaches these two issues as equally important. The following two points seek to define the contours of such a project.

The first item that a new project on tolerance and toleration must engage is the nature of bodily dispositions. If it is the case that tolerance concerns the endurance of pain and suffering, and if it is the case that this endurance is what determines the difference between the tolerable and the intolerable, then it is also the case that these dispositions are of great importance to the overall discussion of tolerance and toleration. We should not be put off by the fact that pain and suffering can be difficult to define. In fact, we should see this as an invitation to think of pain and suffering as layered phenomena that inscribe themselves on the bodies from which they arise. This attempt would proceed not so much by talking about the inexpressible void that is pain and suffering—about how pain and suffering have no voice of their own—as by exploring the way in which these phenomena color bodily dispositions at the intersection of physical stimuli and cognitive activity.[34] The upshot would be an appreciation of the multiple circuits of pain and suffering, each of which has its own level of intensity, temporal permanence, and overall direction. It would also be a better way of differentiating between these circuits, among which some would be appropriate for a new politics of tolerance and toleration.

The second item that a new project on tolerance and toleration must engage is the need to develop an alternative language of enlightenment. This language need not be one of unreason or wildness. Instead, it should be one that puts the reasonable into question, placing us at the brink of thought itself in order to explain "the upsurge of reason in a world not of its making" (to quote the epigraph of this essay).[35] I would wager that we do this most effectively if we pursue a double strategy—what we may characterize as "disruptive engenderment." On the one hand, this strategy appreciates old categories of thought but tries to refresh their meaning, creating a tension between the familiar and the unfamiliar. On the other hand, the strategy also draws on unconventional material in order to create new categories of thought. These categories may seem idiosyncratic, but this is only because they seek to chart uncharted terrain. The idiosyncrasy is in that sense part of the attempt to rethink tolerance and toleration. What is more, the categories that this new language creates cannot be judged according to existing conventions. To the contrary, we should judge them according to the way in which they alter the network of meanings and significations that we put them back into. It is only if we do so that *re*thinking becomes a possibility.

Saint John

The Miracle of Secular Reason

Matthew Scherer

JOHN RAWLS IS A SAINT. In the words of Amy Gutmann, who remarked, when delivering his eulogy, that she felt "privileged to have lived in his time," Rawls was "saintly as well as wise."[1] Within certain communities of political theorists, such sentiment appears to be widespread, as is evident from expressions of personal admiration in the wake of Rawls's death. The general fact of this sentiment presents a number of problems, not only for a highly private man who by all accounts went to great lengths to avoid celebrity, let alone sainthood, but also for secular liberals who share in these feelings of reverence, as well as for those engaged in contemporary political thought more generally. How is it that, after all these centuries, and in the face of all its protestations to the contrary, even an avowedly secular, liberal, democratic politics still needs a saint?

This is a serious question about the persistence of political theology within a discourse that disavows it. There is also a hint of scandal if it can be maintained that what is commonly taken to be the paradigmatic postfoundational secular liberal-democratic discourse is intimately bound up with and permeated by religious modes of thought and action. The wager in pursuing this point is that a continued acquiescence in secular discourse's attempts to sever itself cleanly from the domain of the religious, consigning certain dimensions of human experience to one or the other domain and defining each domain against the other, can only serve to obscure vital dynamics of both secular and religious conduct. Rawls, for example, argues that the variant of political liberalism he articulates is the natural fruit of European historical experience, that it therefore represents no cultural innovation, and that it therefore requires no moment of political founding. More specifically, he argues that it emerges from the detachment of politics from religion through a largely realized process of secularization and that adopting his political liberalism therefore requires no interference between, or conversion of, interests. Yet anyone who looks at the experience of Rawlsianism over the past fifty years will find that it belies these claims. One need only notice that Rawls's work is shrouded in the myth of having originated a new departure for political philosophy and having resurrected political philosophy from a "moribund state."[2] In short, a central feature of the reception of Rawls's work, accepted by critics and adherents alike, is that it marks an unanticipated and seemingly inexplicable point of discontinuity in the recent tradition of political thought. It is a modest claim to call this a miracle. Just as Rawls has been elected for sainthood, *A Theory of Justice* has been elected for canonization among the ranks of great books. This has contributed to a studiously dispassionate text's being received with genuine passion—gratitude and affirmation in some places, indignation and denunciation in others—on either side of what Sheldon Wolin has referred to as the "Liberal/Democratic Divide" pressed open by Rawls.[3] It is another modest claim to associate this divide with the division between rival faiths.

Doctrines of political liberalism, from their earliest articulations to their most recent variations, seek to exclude theology, both when it underwrites political authority and when it makes claims upon the deep currents of faith that flow beneath individual conscience. This exclusion may, in fact, be the most economical way of stating liberalism's intellectual stakes: continuing a gesture exemplified by Spinoza and Hobbes, liberalism prohibits talk of miracles and closes the pathways to the domain of individual belief that would support such talk. So, while its miraculous appearance is agreed to be a central characteristic of Rawlsianism, this finding should sound scandalous. Indeed, one could write a history of liberalism by tracing subtle and unavowed reincorporations of the theological, despite its formal exclusion. Here I will ask how, if there has in fact been a Rawlsian miracle, theological modes have been reinscribed in political liberalism.

If Rawls's political liberalism, rather than simply excluding religious motifs, articulates a new relation between theological and political experience, one route into this problematic runs through *conversion*, which is to say that grasping this relation may follow from asking how this particular doctrine takes root and what particular dimensions of human experience it appeals to and depends upon. Whether Rawlsian liberalism is seen as something that needs to be extended, refined, tempered, combatted, overcome, given therapy, or otherwise treated, any of these aims will be better aided by examining the discourse's mechanisms and mapping its sense than by clarifying or refuting the project on the level of formal argumentation or, worse, by avoiding it on the pretense that it consists in shallow, innocent, or impertinent nonsense, illusion, or error. In short, adequately addressing Rawlsian liberalism requires taking seriously the nature of the claims it makes on its audience.

Critical responses to Rawls can be divided into two general categories. On the one hand, there is an internal criticism that scrutinizes the order of liberties, the enumeration of basic goods, the propriety of assuming a greater or lesser risk aversion on the part of rational actors, and the like but evinces little attention to the larger political and philo-sophical significance of such arguments. Critics internal to the project of formulating a theory of justice tend to produce highly technical and strictly analytical inquiries concern-ing the coherence, clarity, and consistency of the project. On the other hand, there is an external criticism that seeks to detect the project's basic defects, oversights, evasions, or obfuscations but shows little appetite for engaging with those engaged in the internal mode of criticism. This division tracks two major pathways of avoidance of the text: one either quibbles with it or denies that it is worth quibbling with.

Thus, approaches to Rawls have generally ignored the relations established between reader and text, either, in the terms of political theorists, by assuming that the theory of justice elaborated in the text has no purchase on the political situation of the reader, in which case it is at best a distraction, or, in the terms of political philosophers, by assuming that the reader's own situation is superfluous to the purposes of articulating a philosophi-cal theory, because this situation can only introduce empirical confusion into what should be an endeavor of a priori knowledge. Both assumptions obstruct inquiry into how a conversation, or circuit, is formed between a reader and Rawls's text. While most com-mentators acknowledge that many theorists and philosophers have come to care about Rawls, nobody asks how they come to care, assuming that the answer is either self-evident or evidence of nothing worth noting: either Rawlsians are predisposed to find this work meaningful—perhaps because, in the course of their education, they absorbed the con-ventions of a community that endorses such work—or Rawls's work carries its own seal of meaningfulness, perhaps because, as for Kant, like the starry heavens above, the moral law inspires awe in its beholders.

One could say, however, that to be convinced of the importance of a theory of justice one must first be convinced that people act out of a sense of justice; and to be convinced that people act out of a sense of justice, one must first be convinced of the importance of a theory of justice. Accepting that, according to what seems a reasonable historical reconstruction, the mid-century Anglo-American world of political thought was marked by an absence of concern both for the sense of justice and for the principles of justice, then it would seem that there is, indeed, an air of the miraculous in the success of Rawls's work. Two distinct but internally related points then call for investigation: (1) the me-chanics by which Rawls's work comes to seem credible to those working within its param-eters (call this the element of conversion), and (2) the tenor and limitations of the variant of liberalism elaborated by Rawls in terms of the kind of thought, sorts of interest, and fields of sense opened by the project (call this a question of the character of what one is converted to).

If one takes seriously the suggestion that *A Theory of Justice* and *Political Liberalism* should be placed in the company of Plato's *Republic* and other great books of the tradi-tion, one should recognize that approaching Rawls's texts requires attention to their liter-ary qualities. What Rawls rhetorically does in those texts lies very close to the practice of democratic politics as he engages in persuasive dialogue, imparts conviction, and seeks to convert individuals and institutions. This is neither to justify the terms of the conversation Rawls conducts nor the reverse; rather, it is to ask: How is it that his voice has been such a powerful force both in stirring and in conducting this conversation? In other words, if we take Rawls to be a saint, how can elements of belief, passion, myth, yearning, and suffering be incorporated into the account of his doctrine's, or of any doctrine's, circulation? If there is neither sufficient reason for this conversation nor adequate compulsion to engage in it, how do we account for its occurrence? One could call this an investigation into the politics of the liberal everyday, or research into the circuits between a society's articulation of its experience and the institutions of a society's basic structure that condition this experience.

In what follows, I will: first, articulate the problem of miraculous events and place Rawls's theory of justice in connection with the social-contract tradition as articulated by Rousseau, to indicate how a moment of political paradox originally dissolved by the hands of God finds resolution in the miraculous works of a saint; second, holding to the criterion that saintly or miraculous works inspire wonder, explore the captivating power of Rawls's saintly persona; and, finally, adducing a second criterion of saintliness, suggest how the private dimensions of Rawls's persona illuminate the peculiar needs and experiences the rhetorical mechanics his texts express and appeal to.

Miracles Wrought by God's Hand and by the Touch of a Saint.

Owing in great measure to their central importance in the life of the Christian church, miracles, saints, and conversion have been the subject of intense disputation within the various traditions of theological, political, and philosophical discourses throughout the history of Western Christendom. It will not be possible to provide an historical account of the shifting relations between these terms here, given the overwhelming complexity of the topic, but it will be possible to indicate the barest traditional sense of them in order to show how they will function with respect to my argument.[4] Miracles appear as disruptions of the natural order that defy explanation in accord with the canons of human reason. An interest in miracles derives in no small measure from their relation to revelation, which is to say, from their power to testify to the presence of the divine. As one reference work puts it, miracles are "events inexplicable by the operation of natural forces and therefore regarded as manifestations of special divine activity."[5] But it is also in the nature of the miraculous to be subject to contestation. Philosophical engagements, from Spinoza's and Hume's on, have centered on the necessarily dubious quality of any *evidence* that can be offered for the occurrence of miracles. Political engagements, such as Hobbes's and Locke's, have centered on the problem of sovereign *authority* that is motivated by the necessity of deciding on such dubious evidence. And the Christian gospels themselves countenance the problem of distinguishing true from false miracles, motivated by nothing less than the problem of distinguishing true and false messiahs. The Greek text employs a range of terms for events that we now gather under the Latinate term *miracle*—such as *erga* ("works"), *semia* ("signs"), *dunameis* ("powers"), and *terata* ("wonders")—and this may be seen as a relic of the variability and uncertainty of the terrain they demarcate.[6] Miracles, in short, stand at the center of a complex relation between faith and reason: on the one hand, the recognition of a miracle depends upon faith, as the evidence offered for it must appear contrary to all reason; on the other hand, the occurrence of a miracle functions as evidence for one's faith in the truth of any revelation. It is at this intersection that miracles take on their most political valence: as Hobbes recognized, deciding upon the truth or falsity of a miraculous event is a function of authority, on the one hand, but, on the other—as can be seen in the cases of prophets, apostles, and saints—miracles themselves produce authority, serving as warrants for the legitimacy of the figures who perform them. The significance of our other two terms can be laid out more quickly: saints are those who, above all else, work miracles, the wonder of which, in turn, is capable of effecting conversion.

That Rawls has produced works is beyond dispute: he has written a great deal that has been read widely with deep appreciation for some time. To recapture the sense of a miracle, paradox, or scandal here, it should be noted that it is not entirely clear why these works should have been attended by wonder, why, that is, anybody has cared, continues to care, or should come to care about Rawls's work. Rawls's oeuvre comprises: a first major statement, *A Theory of Justice* (1971), around which revolves all his subsequent work; the revision of his *Theory* in *Political Liberalism* (1993); its extension to international relations in *The Law of Peoples* (1999); its working notes in his *Collected Papers* (1999); and the teaching that went on concurrently with its formulation in *Lectures on the History of Moral Philosophy* (2000) and in the forthcoming *Lectures on Social and Political Thought*; and its final restatement in *Justice as Fairness* (2001). These texts comprise some two to three thousand printed pages, and yet they are devoted exclusively to what had been, and in some quarters continues to be, the dubious topic of justice. It is certainly remarkable, then, that by one recent estimate *A Theory of Justice* alone has sold somewhat better than a quarter of a million copies in English and has been translated into two dozen languages since its initial publication.[7] To this one might add some three or more thousand academic publications generated in response to Rawls, countless more citations made of his work in the work of others, conferences convened, institutions established, funded, and secured under his name, as well as the students he has instructed personally or by proxy, his work long having served as a staple of undergraduate and graduation education.[8]

A measure of his work's more concrete political impact could be based upon its circulation among and influence upon policy makers, public institutions, and, perhaps above all, judges and other legal practitioners, though these are more difficult to trace.

Though the animus expressed in the piece, not to mention the forum in which it is published, renders it suspect, there is probably some truth in Alan Ryan's claim in the *Washington Times* that "through the invisible medium of Supreme Court clerks and the more visible medium of the Harvard, Yale, Stanford, Chicago, etc. law reviews, Mr. Rawls's ideas have crept into the law of the land."[9] Though it circulates only on the level of hearsay, a somewhat more credible, commonly found narrative attributes to Rawls not only responsibility for having shifted analytical philosophy away from its concern with "small-scale problems" to return to the care for public problems exemplified by John Dewey, but also for having shifted a philosophical discourse of governance regulated by the Utilitarian principles championed by John Stuart Mill toward a discourse that accords a central place to individual rights.[10]

But to say Rawls's influence has been widespread is not to attest to the sense of wonder it has created: the latter claim requires a different kind of justification. The most direct measure of an individual's status within a given discipline is the extent to which other members of that discipline feel an obligation to engage with his or her work and formulate an opinion about it: everyone working in the field of political theory or political philosophy, it seems, has an opinion about Rawls. What is noteworthy in these opinions is not their general approval of or admiration for what Rawls has done but the collective sense that his work has effected a shift in the pathways of disciplinary interest. Stuart Hampshire is about as guarded on this point as anyone, but, in the *New York Review of Books*, he writes of *A Theory of Justice*, "I think that this book is the most substantial and interesting contribution to moral philosophy since the war."[11] More forcefully, Sheldon Wolin, writing in *Political Theory*, maintains that "Insofar as it is possible to attribute to one man and one book the principle responsibility for both developments, [namely, the intellectual superiority of liberalism over its critics and the return of analytic philosophy to the subject of politics] John Rawls incontestably would be that man and his *A Theory of Justice* would be that book. His accomplishment is nothing less than to have set the terms of liberal discourse in the English-speaking countries."[12] Likewise, according to a piece written for *Dissent* by Amy Gutmann, "Political thinking in the academy has changed since the 1950s and early 1960s in at least three significant ways. . . . All three of these changes are attributable to the influence of *A Theory of Justice*."[13] And even Stanley Cavell is compelled to admit, in a moment of admiration no doubt tinged with regret, introducing a series of lectures addressed to the American Philosophical Association, that "John Rawls's *A Theory of Justice* . . . has, more than any other book of the past two decades, established the horizon of moral philosophy for the Anglo-American version or tradition of philosophy (at least)."[14] In a more personal register, H. L. A. Hart notes in the *University of Chicago Law Review*, "No book of political philosophy since I read the great classics of the subject has stirred my thoughts as deeply as John Rawls's *A Theory of Justice*."[15] Michael Sandel, having made a career out of inciting debates with Rawls's work, aptly notes in the *Harvard Law Review*, "rare is the work of political philosophy that provokes sustained debate. It is a measure of its greatness that John Rawls's *A Theory of Justice* inspired not one debate, but three."[16] And in more popular publications such as the *New York Times Book Review*, the *Times Literary Supplement*, *The Economist*, the *Listener*, the *Nation*, the *New Republic*, the *New Statesman*, the *Spectator*, the *Observer*, the *Washington Post*, and so forth—all of which, remarkably, published reviews—the "broad critical acclaim, even fame" of *A Theory of Justice* has been even more pronounced.[17] However they determine its influence and assess its substance, these sources agree that Rawls's project has decisively influenced the direction of political thought. They all mark Rawls's intervention as a turning point.

Yet the critical reception of Rawls has failed to sufficiently appreciate the significance of his project's success as an event in the life of political thought. Apart from my summary in the preceding paragraph, no theorist or philosopher, to my knowledge, has undertaken to address, in a serious and sustained fashion, the basic fact of this importance or to attend to the logic of its miraculous appearance. Instead, commentators note that Rawls has "set the terms" or "established the horizons" of philosophical discourse and then proceed to rebut, critique, or repudiate his position as they would rebut, critique, or repudiate any other. Rawlsian discourse has yet to encounter a form of criticism that, seeking neither to discern whether or not it truthfully represents something else, namely, our current political condition, nor whether it provides a serviceable tool with which to intervene in this condition, seeks rather to discern and describe what its particularity and its particular appeal consist in. The concern that has been lacking, then, is to articulate and diagnose Rawls's work in terms of its capacity to claim and hold one's interest, in other words, in terms of its miraculous capacity to fascinate, to incite wonder, and to effect conversion.

Placing his work in closer connection with the social-contract tradition from which it departs will help to demonstrate how the claim for the miraculous nature of Rawls's works and for his own saintly status can be made serious. A recent survey of the critical literature, undertaken by one of Rawls's former students, indicates that the question of what Rawls's project was remains open even for internal critics who find themselves working squarely within the parameters he established.[18] One might begin to examine Rawls's relation to his own chosen tradition by recalling that the key moments of this tradition are Hobbes, Locke, Rousseau and Kant.[19] It can reasonably be said that these authors are concerned with two points: (1) addressing the concrete historical conditions of the emergence and consolidation of nation-states and the extension of suffrage, as well as the congruent civic turmoil, revolution, war, and conquest; and (2) addressing the ideational condition of a failure of traditional religious worldviews and the emergence of scientific and philosophical thought oriented toward and governed by the threat of skepticism (namely, the threat that our words cannot enable us to reach the world, each other, or our own selves). This moment in political thought has been treated as coextensive with either: (1) a new departure given by the age of Enlightenment or, more darkly, as Nietzsche has given it to us, as the culmination, though still unwitting, of the long goodbye European culture pays to its dead God, or (2), as Carl Schmitt has given it to us, as the latest installment in a long line of sociological reinscriptions of the theological tradition.[20] Whatever precise determinations one settles upon, and no historian would be satisfied to settle upon any one, both the concrete and ideational tendencies can safely be said to have pressed political theory to articulate afresh its own foundations, thus giving birth to the theory of the social contract. However the relation is stated, the emergence of new forms of state power in need of justification, together with the need to secure the certainty of human knowledge and meaning as they slipped free of tradition, conditioned modernity and the articulation of contract theory.

But to say that Rawls's politics responds to the pressures of the modern condition and that this modern condition is marked by a theological order waning in the face of an ascendant secular power says too much and too little at once. The relation between theo-logical and secular orders of authority has been the object of continuous, delicate, and varied treatment starting with the contract tradition's earliest formulation in the work of Hobbes; indeed, as recent scholarship asserts, this delicate treatment has been central to these theories.[21] It has been clear from the outset that Rawls is most directly indebted to Kant: he and his critics have undertaken what, by now, must be considered an exhaustive exploration of this debt.[22] To trace the lineage back a step further, to Rousseau, will shed more light on the theological problematic, however, as well as the peculiar political rein-scription of this problematic performed by Rawls's work. What is to be shown, then, is how Rawls is continuous with Rousseau, how he inherits what is known in contemporary political theory as the Rousseauean "paradox of politics," and how his mode of negotiat-ing this paradox is no less original than Rousseau's, no less forceful, and no less to be contended with.[23] It is worth noting that the contract tradition has never been silent about this paradox and that one remarkable feature of Rawls's work is that, far from neglecting this political moment, he has *performed* a solution of the paradox that has elsewhere only been indicated at a formal or theoretical level. Call this either the politics or the theology of Rawlsian liberalism.

In *The Social Contract*, Rousseau faces the problem of founding a just and enduring polity given man's imperfect (whether innocent or corrupt) political, cultural, and moral state. This is Rousseau's way of introducing his project: "I want to inquire whether there can be a legitimate and reliable rule of administration in the civil order, taking men as they are and laws as they can be," where *taking men as they are* acknowledges that while "man is born free . . . everywhere he is in chains."[24] From the hands of God, man comes well formed; by virtue of life in this world, he is corrupt: only by establishing the proper order of political association can this perfection be reclaimed. In this sense, Rousseau comes as close as a truly modern thinker can to the classical Christian problematic of conversion or, at least, to the Augustinian form of this problematic as we are given to witness it in his *Confessions*. Rousseau departs from Augustine in imagining that the conversion to be achieved turns man toward the life of republican, or civic, virtue rather than toward God. He continues his introduction by asking, "How did this change [i.e., man's enslavement in his fallen state] occur?" and answers, "I do not know," as the modern condition to which he is responding is largely determined by the recognition that men are incapable of comprehending the laws of heaven. But concerning the question "What can make it legitimate?" what can serve as an *earthly* resolution of the problem, he maintains, "I believe I can answer this question," and the answer is that a good-enough redemption of the situation consists in approximating the proper form of the social contract and establishing the agency of the general will, by which the split in man's nature between private and public interest, between inclination and reason, can be resolved. In its more famous form, the solution is one in which man is forced to be free and made desirous of his own bondage to the law through his reconciliation with his society.[25]

But this account omits stating clearly the conditions of the paradox. Elsewhere, Rousseau puts the central problem as follows: "How will a blind multitude, which often does not know what it wants because it rarely knows what is good for it, carry out by itself an undertaking as vast and as difficult as a system of legislation?"[26] It is helpful to recall the force of the *Two Discourses*: for Rousseau, man is irresolvably split—even in the rightly constituted order he remains, necessarily, divided or "doubly engaged," as citizen and subject, private and public being—and in his current condition, moreover, both his will and his reason are corrupt. This is at once a theological and a sociological assessment: human nature and human society mirror one another in their corruption. But if Rousseau's doctrine is controlled by a distinct understanding of man's condition as a fallen being and his culture as marked by a corruption of nature, it is equally governed by a concern to hold out the hope of, indeed to formulate a plan for, the redemption of his soul and of his society. Having placed man in the world, Rousseau's God is not Hobbes's God, retreating on high, nor is he Spinoza's God, retreating into nature, but, rather, he personally touches upon the social contract at two significant points, both of which determine and authorize the precise form of Rousseau's democratic hope.

The figure of God is evident in all the books of the *Social Contract*, but it is in the second and fourth that His presence is most significant. There, in the chapters "On the Legislator" and "On Civil Religion," He can be seen supervening upon the contract in its founding moment and subtending its continuation in time. In "On the Legislator," Rousseau notes that "Gods would be needed to give laws to men."[27] This is not only because a patient, disinterested, and dispassionate knowledge of man's good exceeds his capacity for comprehension, not only a problem of limited knowledge or insufficient reason— rather the problem is that nothing in man's nature guarantees his acceptance of the law, even when it is given its proper formulation. This is where making a connection with Kant would be misleading. Were demonstration of the proper form of the social contract, and steady reflection upon this form, sufficient to establish it, Rousseau's having drafted *The Social Contract* would have been sufficient to solve the problem, or paradox, of politics. But, according to Rousseau, *there is nothing in man's original nature to stir in him reverence for the law*, and we have no right to hope, as Kant does at the conclusion to the *Critique of Practical Reason*, that "Two things fill the mind with ever new and increasing wonder and awe, the oftener and the more steadily we reflect on them: the starry heavens above me and the moral law within me."[28] Where right, for Kant, inspires reverence of its own accord, and right, for Hobbes, inspires reverence only when it comes bearing a sword or threatening war, and right, for Locke, requires only the tacit consent granted it by virtue of one's mere presence in society, Rousseau has nothing to guarantee the needed reverence for the law, save for the grace of God or, what amounts to the same, the proper education of man's social spirit. In the *Social Contract*, the agent of this education alternately takes the form of the profession of civil religion, which ensures one's continued compliance with the law, and the figure of the wise legislator, who gives the law and whose "great soul is the true miracle that should prove his mission."[29]

The problem of our condition, and this is what makes it a paradox calling for miraculous resolution, is double: man's reason is benighted, and his will is corrupt. Were one intact, it could suffice to correct the other, but because neither is in order, to establish and maintain a just order, God must touch twice, once through the legislator upon reason and again through the doctrines of civil religion upon the mass of man's habits, mores, and moral sentiments. Here is the classical formulation of the paradox given in "On the Legislator": "In order for an emerging people to appreciate the healthy maxims of politics, and follow the fundamental rules of statecraft, the effect would have to become the cause; the social spirit, which should be the result of the institution, would have to preside over the founding of the institution itself; and men would have to be prior to laws what they ought to become by means of laws."[30] Without the "social spirit," which men lack because they have been raised in an unjust society, the "rules," which could alone serve to order a society just enough to conjure this spirit, cannot be formulated. Likewise, without the "fundamental rules of statecraft," which are nowhere written and which would be necessary to constitute the kind of society that could produce men able to "appreciate" its maxims, the "social spirit," which alone could guide the formulation of such rules, cannot be conjured up.

Rousseau continues: "Since the legislator is therefore unable to use either force or reasoning, he must necessarily have recourse to another order of authority, which can win over without violence and persuade without convincing."[31] Here, because a political wisdom that uses its "own language, rather than that of the common people," fails to persuade in the absence of a social spirit that would animate conviction and because force, in the form of another's violent dominion, fails to win one over by failing to accord with the dictates of one's own reasoning, the legislator must have recourse to something other than reason or force.[32] In short, what is called for is nothing less than the revealed authority of the miraculous event.

Therefore, Rousseau concludes: "This [paradox] is what has always forced the fathers of nations to have recourse to the intervention of heaven and to attribute their own wisdom to the Gods; so that the people, subjected to the laws of the State as to those of nature, and recognizing the same power in the formation of man and of the City, might obey and bear with docility the yoke of public felicity."[33] Only through the appeal to heaven, then, can spirit and reason come to obey what is made to appear as a law of nature, just as it is only through a "purely civil profession of faith" that "the sentiments of sociability without which it is impossible to be a good citizen or a faithful subject" can be maintained.[34] Rousseau reasserts, then, the centrality of myth and miracle to the problem of political founding: specifically, he affirms the necessity of a discourse that exceeds reason and law, that appeals to powers beyond the scope of these faculties, beyond the proper functions of reason and law.

Where God's place has been so elegantly suppressed in Kant's critical system that contemporary Kantian liberals can proceed as though he were never there, he strides unavoidably to the foreground in Rousseau's work. The theological basis of the civil order, which is so clear in Rousseau's *Social Contract*, is renegotiated but preserved throughout Rawls's work. Whatever else changes between *A Theory of Justice* and *Political Liberalism*, the negotiation of Rousseau's paradox persists in the procedure of *reflective equilibrium*, where an adequate "sense of justice" must be present in advance for an individual to adopt the "principles of justice," as well as in the procedure of Kantian, or constitutional, *construction* as it is undertaken by a society in *Political Liberalism*. What has gone unnoticed is the persistence not only of the paradox, but of its theological negotiation, as well: rather than placing his "wisdom" in the mouth of gods, through an array of textual procedures, and through the agency of those who have been drawn to follow him and enshrine him as such, Rawls is made to accede to the position of a "saintly as well as wise" interlocutor capable of stirring the needed conviction without express recourse to gods.

In its new form, the problem goes something like this. On the one hand, Rawls's logical demonstrations aren't sufficient to compel a reader to change his or her principles, certainly not if he or she does not accept the norms operative in the demonstration. As Rawls himself might have put it, "principles of justice" cannot direct one's conduct if the corresponding "sense of justice" is not in place, or, perhaps more directly, there's no way of reasoning with the unreasonable. On the other hand, it certainly cannot be maintained that Rawls has—or, at least, when he launched his product, that he *had*—at his disposal an institutional apparatus sufficient to inculcate such a sense of justice through disciplinary practices alone. In other words, while it's not satisfying to say that he's made his point through propositional reasoning, it's not satisfying, either, to say that he's had his way through literal force. As Rousseau so carefully put the point, what is required is an appeal to "another order of authority." In what follows, I will call this, alternately, the saintly measure, the rhetorical form, and the micropolitical circulation of his doctrine and will insist that the better part of Rawls's saintly wisdom depends upon his unacknowledged appeals to registers of thought and feeling that circulate throughout his texts. It has been a source of frustration for his interpreters from early on that his arguments do not adhere to the norms of pure game theory, or to the confines of Kantian philosophy, or to any other single level of argumentation. In the literature, this eclecticism is generally seen as a lamentable eccentricity, a regrettable lapse of rigor, but much of the authority wielded by Rawls's arguments within each level of argumentation derives precisely from his creative concatenation of these levels of discourse.

The First Basis of Rawls's Sainthood

Paul Ricoeur has suggested something like a concern for the mode of fascination in which readers are held in thrall to Rawls's texts: "I propose to say that justice as fairness . . . attempts to solve the difficulty of Rousseau's famous paradoxical legislator . . . [so that] justice as fairness may be understood as the *earthly* solution to this paradox," and, more to the point, switching from the register of philosophical logic to that of the philosopher's lived experience, "the awesome magnitude of the attempt to devise such a solution may explain the fascination Rawls' book has exerted for nearly twenty years over friends and adversaries alike."[35] Accounting for the fascination that Ricoeur notes, I would suggest, requires accounting for the experience of confronting the text not as a collection of abstract arguments but as a rhetorically sophisticated and affectively nuanced performance. Though it is not uncommon to hear complaints about the prosaic qualities of Rawls's prose—that it is turgid, that it is dry, that there is no poetry to it—in fact, there is a great deal of style to the exposition. Among his reviewers, Stuart Hampshire has come closest to recognizing this, writing that *A Theory of Justice* "is a very persuasive book, being very well argued and carefully composed, with possible objections and counterarguments fairly weighed and considered: at the same time it conveys a moral vision and a ruling idea, and a strongly marked personal attitude to experience."[36] A good part of understanding the general "fascination" with Rawls noted by Ricoeur involves understanding the textual operations that contribute so forcefully to producing it.

The triangle of *ethos*, *pathos*, and *logos* that constitutes the classical arrangement of persuasive devices described in Aristotle's *Rhetoric* provides an apt framework within which to begin investigating Rawls's procedure:

Of the modes of persuasion furnished by the spoken word there are three kinds. The first kind depends on the personal character of the speaker; the second on putting the audience into a certain frame of mind; the third on the proof, or apparent proof, provided by the words of the speech itself. Persuasion is achieved by the speaker's personal character [*ethos*] when the speech is so spoken as to make us think him credible. We believe good men more fully and more readily than others . . . his character may almost be called the most effective means of persuasion he possesses. Secondly, persuasion may come through the hearers, when the speech stirs their emotions [*pathos*]. . . . It is towards producing these effects, as we maintain, that present-day writers on rhetoric direct the whole of their efforts. . . . Thirdly, persuasion is effected through the speech itself when we have proved a truth or an apparent truth by means of the persuasive arguments suitable to the case in question [*logos*].[37]

Commentaries on Rawls's work have consistently avoided the first two modes of persuasion identified by Aristotle, *ethos* and *pathos*, taking his work to be purely argumentative and focusing exclusively on the third mode, *logos*. This is hardly surprising: what constitutes the remarkable power of the character Rawls projects and the emotional appeal he makes is also what renders these dimensions virtually invisible. That character and those emotions are perfectly congruent with the arguments made: in other words, the proponent of a politics based in reasonable conduct inflects his arguments with the force of his own exemplary reasonableness so as to induce in his audience the desired form of reasonable response. In the form of the prose, one finds projected what William James calls the philosopher's "essential personal flavor" or "philosophical temperament," or what Stanley Cavell designates the achievement of a distinctive "personal voice." A large part of Rawls's saintly measure inheres in the force of his personal character and the power of his emotional appeals to inspire conviction in a reader who would otherwise be unprepared for it, thus producing a conversion of interest that cannot be explained with reference to argumentative force alone. In what follows, we will consider in turn examples of the appeal of character and the appeal of emotion.

To begin with, the essential outlines of Rawls's philosophical character can be specified rather easily. The foremost quality of his writing is to establish Rawls as a judicious speaker with eminent good will and abundant common sense: (1) he constantly calls to attention, explains, and duly weighs what he considers to be the most salient of opposing viewpoints; (2) he is punctilious almost to the point of fault in crediting others for their corrections of his errors and contributions to his understandings; and (3) he is painstaking in giving the reader his own arguments and ideas in thoroughly analyzed form, couching them in brief sentences and short subsections that can be immediately grasped and easily digested. This mixture of judiciousness, good will, and common sense is tempered by a pronounced humility. Rawls even goes so far as to disavow any claim for originality in his work, preferring that we see him only to be setting in order and clarifying certain prominent elements of our tradition. "Indeed," he writes in a striking moment of self-effacement, "I must disclaim any originality for the views I put forward. The leading ideas are classical and well known. My intention has been to organize them into a general framework by using certain simplifying devices so that their full force can be appreciated."[38] In the place of bold assertion, apt metaphor, piercing depth of vision, or fine discernment, we find in Rawls's prose the passive voice, demonstrative sentences, myriad simple formulations, and the careful arrangement of subsections. Abjuring the fine, rare, challenging, creative, and counterintuitive in language (and concept), such prose has the cumulative effect of accentuating the propriety of its author's conclusions, which, the author insists, carry "their full force" in themselves, and whose force depends only upon the author's "simplifying devices" to clear the obscurity that might impede it. Rawls claims for his prose, then, what Aristotle identified as the power of the best "arguments suitable to the case," and he disavows both the role his character plays in shading these arguments and the role the emotional responses produced in the reader play in conditioning his or her reactions to the argument. It is the very lack of apparent audacity in his argumentation, however, that allows these disavowed modes of persuasion to find their way into a reading of his text, producing its subtle and distinctive powers of fascination.

The manner in which Rawls disqualifies moral perfectionism from playing a role in his own theory provides an excellent example of how his character functions to produce conviction. In Rawls's taxonomy, perfectionism is a subclass of the larger group of teleological doctrines, which include utilitarianisms and communitarianisms (of Aristotelian or other stripe), against which Rawls distinguishes deontological theories, including his own. Rawls argues against perfectionism at the point where he distinguishes theories of the right from theories of the good and declares the primacy of the former. This argument has touched off decades of intramural controversy among Anglo-American political theorists: it is of paramount importance, then, for Rawls to establish that the capacity for a "sense of justice," or one's "liability" to suffer guilt in the face of principles, conceived as an inherently human capacity, is a more appropriate basis for moral worth than any of the excellences that a doctrine of perfectionism asks one to achieve. The position Rawls takes is not striking in itself: it is merely a modest reformulation of the argument, familiar from Kantian moral philosophy, that one's rational nature constitutes one as a moral agent and qualifies one for moral consideration. What is interesting, however, is how he takes it.

Although there are well-tried arguments for taking the capacity to reason to be the sole basis for moral consideration, when Rawls works his way down to brass tacks, the character conjured by his prose carries more weight than his arguments strictly conceived. At a decisive moment in "The Sense of Justice," Rawls demurs on the level of propositional argument, writing that he "cannot discuss here the propriety of this [competing, perfectionist] assumption," and offering in place of such a discussion his assessment that "it suffices to say" what he needs to say.[39] Rawls tends to refer potential points of contention to arguments developed elsewhere, allowing the larger edifice's coherence to bear the burden of proof for its individual points. At this moment in "The Sense of Justice," however, rather than being referred to a larger project, an argument for selecting the capacity for reason over the contending bases for moral consideration is deferred indefinitely. How is this gesture made plausible?

Rawls does present summary accounts of what utilitarian and perfectionist theories hold to be competing bases for moral consideration. These bases represent potential alternatives to the capacity for having "a [rational] sense of justice" that Rawls will ultimately hold to be "necessary and sufficient for the duty of justice to be owed to a person."[40] For utilitarianism, the capacities in question are those "for pleasure and pain, for joy and sorrow." Rawls dismisses this variant of moral naturalism with the estimable argument that it is insufficient to account for the moral indignation we do, in fact, feel at the sight of injustices perpetrated upon others. It has never been hard to argue against utilitarianism. On the more difficult question of perfectionism, Rawls proceeds as follows:

> Such an aristocratic doctrine can only be maintained, I think, if one assumes a specific obligation on the parties in the original position: namely the obligation to develop human persons of a certain style and aesthetic grace, or the obligation to the pursuit of knowledge and the cultivation of the arts, or both. *I cannot discuss here the propriety of this assumption*, or whether if it were accepted it would justify the inequalities commonly associated with aristocracy. *It suffices to say* that in the analytic construction no such obligation is assumed. The sole constraints imposed are those expressed in the formal elements of the concept of morality, and the only circumstances assumed are those exhibiting the conflicts of claims which give rise to questions of justice. *The natural consequence of this construction* is that the capacity for the sense of justice is the fundamental aspect of moral personality in the theory of justice.[41]

That is as far as justification reaches. The point is not to catch Rawls in a dogmatic preference for a moral universe fueled by one's susceptibility to guilt, resentment, and indignation about transgressions of right over an associational universe driven by feelings such as shame and pride concerning failure or achievement of the good. In fact, Rawls is more supple on this point than is commonly recognized: he maintains that "a complete moral doctrine includes both" motivation from shame and motivation from guilt.[42] But this claim is decisively argued neither here nor elsewhere in his texts; rather, it is continuously deferred. Having excluded the possibility of a purely Kantian appeal to the "fact of Reason" as the foundation for morality, Rawls employs a rhetorical strategy that invites us to accept this position on his authority without reason, but clearly without force.

The argument against perfection is, moreover, layered with nuanced shades of feeling, and these shades of feeling ultimately bear the weight of the argument proper. Rawls's commonsensical manner establishes an implicitly antipathetic disposition toward an "aristocratic ethic which takes as necessary certain attributes and capacities such as strength, beauty, and superior intelligence" precisely by abjuring the qualities of "imagination and wit, beauty and grace," that serve as standard criteria of perfectionist virtue.[43] There is a direct relationship between the propositional content of Rawls's argument, namely, that the human capacity for reason is the basis for moral considerations, and the force of his rhetorical ethos, more precisely, the implication that Rawls's procedure is more direct, natural, and trustworthy than his contenders'. The exclusion of "imagination and wit, beauty and grace," from the discussion at a rhetorical level functions as a micro-political device of persuasion, and a reader senses the inadequacy of perfectionism before coming to know what it is. At work here is an appeal by Rawls's reasonable character to the respect owed to reason itself.

Another example will draw out some of the ways in which Rawls mobilizes his readers' emotional responses to bolster his arguments. In the preface to *Political Liberalism,* Rawls writes, "I try to preserve, perhaps unsuccessfully, a certain conversational style," and this "conversational" style invites the reader to embrace the very receptiveness to reasoning, in the sense of hearing, weighing, and selecting the best available argument, congruent with Rawls's moral and political program.[44] Consider the opening lines of *Political Liberalism,* and the tone they set for the text. Rawls says, "Perhaps I should, then, begin with a definition of political liberalism and explain why I call it 'political.' But no definition would be useful at the outset. *Instead I begin with a first fundamental question* about political justice in a democratic society."[45] Rawls introduces his *Theory of Justice* with a similar gesture. There he begins: "I sketch some of the main ideas. . . . The exposition is informal and intended to prepare the way for the more detailed arguments that follow."[46] Were Rawls not so closely identified with the tradition of analytical philosophy, his embarkation upon these projects of rigorous philosophical argumentation by beginning a "conversation" with his audience and posing a question or a sketch rather than offering a definition would not be remarkable. But he is correctly identified with that tradition, and thus it is pertinent to see what he derives from departing from its norms. That Rawls begins with a question or a sketch signals his intent, present throughout *Political Liberalism* and *A Theory of Justice,* to elicit the reader's active involvement in the work at hand.

While the conversation that takes place in what Rawls has called the "original position" has been justly criticized as no real conversation at all, the conversation opened by *Political Liberalism* is of another order. There, to pose a question to the reader is to imply that it is to be answered—it is to level a challenge and, perhaps, to open an engagement. Rawls is not in the least naïve on this count: he knows that the conversational form implied by the back and forth rhythm of question and answer tends to elicit a certain range of normative considerations. The demands of attentiveness, responsiveness, politeness, and so forth come to mind. It may well be that the more powerfully the norms of conversation are installed in the text, the less apt the reader will be inclined to dissent radically from the conclusions of the theory. It's not inconceivable, either, that he or she should become less likely to turn away from the discussion altogether. Or, to borrow the language of Rawls's own moral psychology, a reader may feel worthy only if he or she does not shirk the obligation to give and take reasons that all parties to the conversation could accept when these obligations have been so diligently, carefully, judiciously, sensibly, and painstakingly observed by Rawls himself—and this thought may be accompanied by a feeling of shame at perhaps not being worthy. Alternatively, the thought may arise that one ought not to make "unreasonable" rebukes to a decent and "reasonable" interlocutor such as Rawls—a thought accompanied, perhaps, by a feeling of guilt by any reader tempted in this direction. While the conversational style of *Political Liberalism*, in particular, should be kept distinct from what one imagines the parties to the original position to be doing in their conversation, and Rawls's remarks on moral psychology should be kept distinct from either of these conversations, Rawls violates these distinctions rhetorically as much as he defends them argumentatively, and these are strategic violations, not errors. Keen-sighted analytical philosophers such as Bernard Williams have long noticed this slippage between levels of argumentation, but, because they have failed to concern themselves with the rhetorical functions of Rawls's texts, they have responded to such maneuvers only by crying foul or faulting them as mistakes and lapses in rigor, rather than acknowledging them as part of an efficacious technique.[47]

Recall the three levels of deliberation announced in *Political Liberalism*: carried on (1) by the representative figures imagined in the original position, (2) by the ideal citizens of the theoretically constructed, well-ordered society, and (3) by us, that is, John Rawls, you, and me, citizens of the world as we know it, who on the occasion of confronting a text such as *Political Liberalism* are meant to be engaged in a discussion about the proper conception of political justice.[48] Where these distinctions cross is precisely where Rawls's argument gains its force, when it does. Everything, for Rawls, depends upon one's willingness to be reasonable, and to be reasonable in a particular sense of the word, meaning primarily to make judgments in accordance with the criterion of reciprocity, that is, to propose and accept only principles that strike oneself and one's interlocutors as fair. I would claim that the rhetorical genius of Rawls's conversational prose is to incline *our* discussion, which takes place at the third level, to proceed in "reasonable" terms, where "reasonable" is understood in the sense given within the first two levels of deliberation, and to do so without our yet having explicitly accepted these terms. To accept these terms explicitly, we must already be reasonably inclined, and being reasonably inclined consists precisely in expressly accepting these terms as the ones that best describe this inclination. This, of course, recalls the condition of Rousseau's paradox of politics, and the measure of Rawls's saintliness is the extent to which he has, by mobilizing disavowed and largely unrecognized rhetorical modes, managed to negotiate this paradox. Put in other terms, the miracle of Rawlsianism lies in its subtle renegotiation of the registers of reason and faith.

Although, Rawls says, philosophy and logic cannot coerce us, he admits that they might leave us "feeling coerced." This is a fantastic distinction to make. Here is Rawls's precise formulation: "Political philosophy cannot coerce our considered convictions any more than the principles of logic can. If we feel coerced, it may be because, when we reflect on the matter at hand, values, principles, and standards are so formulated and arranged that they are freely recognized as ones we do, or should, accept. . . . Our feeling coerced is perhaps our being surprised at the consequences of those principles and standards, at the implications of our free recognition."[49] Or perhaps it is the result of a powerful circuit of resonant thought and feeling being established between various values, principles, standards, images, emotions, identifications, aspirations, and arguments Rawls has brought into circulation. All the while Rawls is arguing for a moral and political order based upon the normative force of reason, a force derived from the individual feelings of guilt and shame one feels on account of one's actions in the face of this reason, he relies on putting something like this force into play to make his argument, or to make one listen long enough for him to make his argument, while his readers are held captive on pain of inchoate feelings that may only later come to be called guilt or shame. Indeed, he seems to assume that the disposition to have those feelings is already in place, working on and through the reader before the principles that would give them their name, their moral form, and their political authorization. In short, the reader is drawn to accept the very terms under discussion by the circulation of thought between multiple layers of the discussion itself, by way of a discourse that touches argument, feelings, and norms of conversational propriety at once, creating an internal circulation among them.

At his most provocative, Rawls is engaged in a sophisticated and rhetorically nuanced effort to foster the conditions of agreement needed to carry the convictions his arguments are supposed to support. For Rawls's argument, everything depends upon his reader being *inclined* just so. And for a rhetorical analysis of this argument, everything depends on coming to understand how a reader is encouraged to become so inclined. Though it can be forcefully argued that Rawls's project fails as a diagnosis of our political condition and that it amounts to an unappealing account of what our politics should be, neither of these descriptions captures what Rawls is doing most effectively. And neither claim engages the modalities through which faith in his project is established and maintained. On the contrary, such critiques of Rawls, in arguing that he displaces politics or otherwise denies its importance, glide over the immense and, to judge from the broad, sympathetic reception of his work, effective effort he makes to convert his readers: such critiques take his strong performance to be a weak description, mistaking the character of a saint for that of a fool.

The Second Basis of Rawls's Sainthood

I would like to conclude by suggesting a second, related basis for the claim that Rawls was a saint. Along with the production of miraculous works, another central criterion of sainthood is that the story of a saint's life teaches something that cannot be taught in any other way. As one reference work puts the matter, "the designation of a man or a woman as a 'saint' is the judgment by the Christian community of the day, both in its local and universal form, as to the desired qualities of the exemplary Christian Life."[50] Hagiography functions to preserve the saint's example, which is seen as worthy of preservation because his or her life will have *instantiated* values whose viability and desirability cannot be suggested by reason or historical precedent alone. Saints, then, serve as sources of inspiration: they are exemplary figures who make possible what, but for their example, would be inconceivable. They embody human possibilities that call for identification and imitation. And, as is suggested by the shifts in character from the saints who attended the church's origins in a marginal community to those chosen after its ascent to an institutionalized state religion, the shifting values and political circumstances of a community are reflected in the lives of those it chooses to designate as saints.[51] While I have sought to trace the significance of liberalism's having a saint, I will here identify why it might have this saint in particular. Having argued that much of Rawls's appeal lies in the authoritative style of his personal voice and its capacity to imbue discussion of political arrangements with the qualities of judiciousness, good will, and common sense, I will claim that the example of Rawls's life makes clear a source of the impulse to moral philosophy, philosophical justification in general, and the current imagination of what liberal political life entails, embodied in his *Theory of Justice* and *Political Liberalism*. To what needs might these qualities appeal? In what might the appeal of Rawlsian reasonableness, and the practices of liberal politics its spirit is intended to govern, consist?

Following James's contention that a philosopher's "temperament" or "essential personal flavor" determines the course and outcome of his or her work as well as the extent of its effect upon its audience allows us to see, in another way, the pertinence of biography, or hagiography, to political thought. On this point, James writes: "The books of all the great philosophers are like so many men. Our sense of an essential personal flavor in each one of them, typical but indescribable, is the finest fruit of our own accomplished philosophic education. What the system pretends to be is a picture of the great universe of God. What it is,—and oh so flagrantly!—is the revelation of how intensely odd the personal flavor of some fellow creature is."[52] James is far from lamenting this personalization of philosophical argument; he maintains, on the contrary, that "the one thing that has *counted* so far in philosophy is that a man should *see* things, see them straight in his own peculiar way, and be dissatisfied with any opposite way of seeing them."[53] Philosophical voices worth listening to, James tells us, will be distinctly inflected, and grasping the nature of these inflections is the highest measure of philosophical education. Rawls's rhetoric is not just a collection of various devices but a collection of devices used to present his own distinctive character and to inspire the reader to adopt that character by participating in conversation with it. What is the nature of this inflection of character and, thus, of its appeal?

Insofar as Rawls was famous, personally famous, it was for his intensely private life and for his largely successful attempt to avoid celebrity.[54] Throughout his career, he gave very few interviews, and these never on personal topics. Toward the end of his life, however, Rawls did consent to undertake some form of autobiography. He authorized Thomas Pogge, a former student and friend, to publish a biographical sketch based on a series of conversations. Two vignettes from this biographical sketch suggest that the story of Rawls's life presents with dazzling clarity dimensions of the appeal that fashioning and defending a theory of justice holds out:

> John (Jack) Bordley Rawls was born on February 21, 1921, in Baltimore as the second of five sons of William Lee and Anna Abell Rawls. The most important events in Jack's childhood were the losses of two younger brothers, who died of diseases contracted from Jack. The first of these incidents occurred in 1928, when Jack fell gravely ill. Although [his younger brother] Robert Lee (Bobby) had been sternly told not to enter Jack's room, he did so anyway a few times to keep Jack company. Soon both children were lying in bed with high fever. The correct diagnosis and antitoxin came too late to save Bobby. His death was a severe shock to Jack and may have (as their mother thought) triggered his stammer, which has been a serious, though gradually receding, handicap for him ever since that time. Jack recovered from the diptheria, but the very next winter caught a severe pneumonia, which soon infected his brother Thomas Hamilton (Tommy). The tragedy of the previous year repeated itself. While Jack was recovering slowly, his little brother died in February of 1929.

> Rawls proceeded to teach in the Harvard Philosophy Department from 1962 until his retirement in 1991. Rawls was an unusual person among the self-confident divinities of the Harvard Philosophy Department. With his caring interactions with students and visitors, his modesty, his insecurity and conciliatory attitude in discussions, one could have taken him for a visiting professor from the countryside next to his famous and overwhelmingly brilliant colleagues Quine, Goodman, Putnam, Nozick, Dreben, and Cavell. Rawls has always found it difficult to function in larger groups, especially with strangers, and even more so when he himself is the center of attention. On such occasions he may seem shy or ill at ease and is sometimes still bothered by his stammer.[55]

This is delicate ground, ground that some will want to avoid, much as, after his death, Ludwig Wittgenstein's friends and followers sought to avoid questions about his apparent homosexuality for fear that discussion of what was then seen as an acutely embarrassing subject could only diminish the importance, and impede the proper reception, of his work. But if we take seriously the idea that the force of Rawls's project is constituted largely by its capacity to bring the desire for justice into circulation by rhetorical means, and the idea that political argument more generally is continuously informed by similar circuits of thought and feeling, the very real grounds of personal fault, regret, guilt, shame, envy, and resentment are ones it would be best not to avoid. The most remarkable feature of Rawls's semi-autobiographical sketch, which takes up a mere fourteen printed pages, is the power with which it conjures this range of feelings. The scenes sketched above are compounded by further thematic threads: Rawls's recounting of his childhood exposure to the racist and classist dispositions of his parents and those of his own privileged, or "lucky," social milieu; his recollection of following behind an older brother who excelled in sports and distinguished himself in war, both of which distinctions Rawls markedly failed to attain; and Rawls's humiliation by an influential undergraduate instructor in philosophy, Norman Malcolm, who in an "unpleasant" early encounter subjected "a philosophical essay which he [Rawls] himself thought rather good" to "very severe criticism," refusing to accept it and demanding its rewriting—oddly enough, Rawls remembers this event as having led to "a gradual deepening of . . . [his] interest in philosophy."[56] I would like to suggest that these accounts can sharpen our focus on how forms of intense social suffering—from guilt, shame, envy, resentment, humiliation, and so forth—accompany both our need to appeal to a notion of justice and our attachments to such a concept. I mean to imply that, far from impoverishing a discussion of Rawlsian liberalism by hinting that it can be reduced to the personal experience of its author, attention to the affective registers it engages and the everyday circumstances of the still "lucky," if less so of late, political experience of contemporary Western liberal democracies can enrich that discussion.

Consider for a moment the bearing of this on Bonnie Honig's and Stanley Cavell's responses to the modes of exclusion central to the practice of Rawlsian liberalism. Honig explores the manner in which "Rawls's ideal of institutional justice" continuously engenders "remainders"—criminal subjects, in short—who fall outside the bounds of this ideal and consequently call for punishment and reform.[57] In a complementary moment, Cavell engages the implications of Rawlsianism for the practice of democracy, suggesting that a threat of callousness or, worse, moral blindness inheres in *A Theory of Justice*'s promise of allowing privileged citizens to accede to positions "above reproach," which is to say, above hearing the claims of injury entered by their less privileged fellows.[58] While both find admirable elements in Rawls's project, they seek to supplement it, Honig with a more agonistic vision of politics, Cavell with the concerns of what he calls Emersonian perfectionism. Once the desirability of such supplementation has been theoretically established, however, the further problem of resistance to its demands remains. I would suggest that the scenes from Rawls's life help make plausible the extent to which his, and our own, affirmations of something like a theory of justice, our commitments more generally to giving justifications for what we do, and our attachments to a form of liberalism that depends on legal protections from social injury, despite the limitations of all these, are bound to individual experiences of the cycles of reproach, guilt, and shame recurrent in political life. While they find acute expression in his own memoirs, such experiences are not at all peculiar to Rawls. I would suggest in conclusion, then, that part of confronting the basis of social suffering in Rawlsian liberalism entails recognizing more generally that liberal appeals to rights—in particular, the right to draw boundaries that allow one to refrain from certain conversations—serve the function of assuaging persistent modes of suffering. What this suggests, in turn, is that modes of suffering that often find their calls for relief answered in religious modes of experience may also be central to the appeal of secular liberalism. This, in turn, may begin to cast light on the nature of our persistent attachment both to the promises of religion and to the promises of secular liberalism. While Honig's and Cavell's critiques can help us recognize the need to supplement the central juridical forms of liberal politics, the scenes from Rawls's life, insofar as they find resonance with scenes from one's own life, can help us recognize the sources of resistance to enacting these supplements.

I began this essay by noticing that John Rawls has been called a saint and have attempted to give this claim a serious basis by demonstrating that where, in Rousseau's classical articulation, a persistent political-theological paradox of founding through recourse to gods has been dispensed with, the same paradox has been eased in Rawls's work by way of nuanced rhetorical appeals to the sensibilities it assumes to be installed in its readers and attempts both to mobilize and to inflect in new directions. The measure of Rawls's saintliness, I assert, lay in his skill at deploying these rhetorical means to the miraculous end of inspiring convictions that would otherwise remain unavailable. Insofar as political life contains a moral dimension—that is, insofar as a concept of justice is somehow applicable to political life—the dimension of morality, justice, or social spirit that this further dimension represents stands in need of something like a miracle for its inception. Failing this, the arguments for morality lack sense, just as, in the absence of a sense of justice, the principles of justice lack lived significance. I would suggest, however, that admirable appeals to justice may find their root in the ineliminable experiences of personal suffering that they tend to obscure. And that the faith Rawls seeks to inspire in his conception of liberalism is much more closely analogous, in the needs it serves, to modalities of religious faith, which Rawls has been taken to have escaped. In the end, then, it would appear that even an avowedly secular, liberal, democratic politics stands in deep need of its saints, and that this very need can serve as a vital source of moral and political instruction.

PART III

Democratic Republicanism, Secularism, and Beyond

Reinhabiting Civil Disobedience

Bhrigupati Singh

To clarify it again, what, then, is the difference between religion and philosophy? A core distinction would be that the latter can subsist without a conception of the divine. In other words, philosophy does not necessitate a conception of another, higher world, with which to slander or to beautify, or to authorize its work in this world. It need not traffic in super-earthly hopes. Of what consequence then, is this emergent conception of a "post-secular" world where it is religion that is (so much stronger? or only more distinctly?) an intervening force in the practical affairs of this world, enmeshed in public-creating technologies of such recent origin? Take another aspect of this question: What space do these same technologies grant to philosophy? Contemporary communication media such as newspapers or television are hardly a forum for philosophical disputation. Indeed, an argument about the concept of being as a current affairs TV program would be comical. The market would hardly desire it. So then, philosophical problems are not current affairs. And religious problems are? Or is it that these issues, reported as such, actually have nothing to do with religion at all? As for philosophy, I can neither doubt nor prove that there have been few points in human history when philosophical speculation, variably defined to include both mystics and scholastics, has been considered as unnecessary or out of place an occupation as it is today in neo-liberal societies. Is this a secular or a theological development?

As regards the contemporary world, we are urged to speak on supposedly more important matters, such as globalization or terrorism. For anyone wanting to approach these discussions with a philosophical step, there is cause for much diffidence, both about the quality of the ensuing conversation and about the question of what a specifically philosophical contribution to it might look like (as distinct from say, the need for historical analysis to diffuse some of the hyper-presentness surrounding terms such as *globalization* and *terrorism*). Surrounded by such blurry, opinionated terms, the first question would be: How can one set oneself a topic? Keep in mind that thinkers as different as Thoreau, Marx, Kierkegaard, Nietzsche, and Gandhi all warn against reading the newspaper every day. The first step might be to listen: Is philosophy even being referred to, anywhere at all?

In fact, it is, both within the academy and outside. In recent years a request for philosophical perspective has begun to be heard from people from a wide spectrum of political leanings and denominations, and conceptual inquiry seems vaguely relevant again, even in the public domain. Charitably worded, many people are of the opinion: "After the events of September 11 and the return of religion, it has become increasingly crucial to reconsider (to revise/reject/reinforce) the heritage of the Enlightenment." For all its well-intentioned self-reflexivity (or not), the violence of this correlation immediately erases all differences internal to cultures and selves, wholly obscuring the constitutive heterogeneity of the Enlightenment itself, falsely bridging the Atlantic gap between America and Europe, a move that fantastically places Immanuel Kant and George W. Bush in the same camp, even as it sustains, in however harsh or mild a form, the pernicious thesis of the "clash of civilizations." Such a thesis, with its concomitantly false call to philosophy, is equally upheld by many of those who claim to speak with some intellectual authority on the "non-West," conceived as such only through poor, negative, and resentful conceptions of identity and difference. A note for progressives and for conservatives: what seems like a battle against a single Goliath can also yield a harvest of false Davids. In a discussion framed as such ("Enlightenment versus the non-West," or "religion in the post-9/11 era," or the "return" of religion—where had it gone?), it might be bolder to remain silent. This is not to deny the importance of such discussions, but rather to re-examine our angle of participation in them. In other words, the terms on which we accept this urgency, since to think again, in crisis, is indeed to reexamine the ways in which we are both joined and separate, to others and to ourselves.

This last sentence takes us toward the domain of ethics, which we might count as another step, since this is one of the few terms from academic philosophy that still seems to resonate in the public domain. Not that there is any kind of monopoly even here. In the "real world" (as they often call it nowadays; a christening that should itself be cause for sociological inquiry, or for philosophical wonderment), the cumulative pressure of all manner of claimants exerts itself—economists, scientists, environmentalists, journalists, marketing professionals—all have something to say on the topic of ethics. If these domains are somewhat specialized, there is also the more holistic theological claim on morality, or the religious dictation of a way of life (and the wide range of variations possible, internal to a set of norms, for instance, in sectarian, or social, or individual differences, or in adaptation to technological changes). Philosophy, inasmuch as it is separate from these domains, still has a crucial stake in such a conversation—that is, it earns its right to speak. With this confidence the argument that follows will revisit or begin to freshly map out a certain terrain of ethics, sensing resonances internal to philosophy and its relations with the world. But philosophy is hardly a single entity (and if it is, it contains a variety of competing forces), so a sentence in anticipation of our own sectarian battles is in order: the ethical terrain inhabited and expressed by this essay will be regarded with some suspicion, from an institutional, we might even call it a "mature" perspective, say that of Kant specifically as he reappears in Rawls, or Hegel as he reappears, very differently, in Charles Taylor or in Slavoj Žižek (who, in a recent essay, formulates his distrust of some of the conceptual terrain we shall soon cover as a "critique of the ongoing soft revolution"[1]), or by more recent "identity"-based formations such as the postcolonials (and their critique of "the West" or of "Europe"). This argument hopes to elaborate rather than to abate those suspicions, since their continued friction might create some potential energy (that is to say, our battles might strengthen, rather than weaken us).

As a point of departure, we can return to the question of globalization. Of the many significations gathered in this term, let us catch one that is presently dominant, say, from an oppositional perspective. In recent years, now more so than ever, it is impossible to speak about this topic without bringing up the subject of "America," which is accused, and not unjustly so, both internally and internationally, of being dominated and ruled by stupid white men (to quote the title of Michael Moore's popular book). If this is indeed the case, then perhaps it won't serve us well to constantly point out just how belligerent, stupid, and white America has always been, since without an alternative this is a doctrine of cynicism and despair. In other words, what would it be like to demand intelligence, to show that there is evidence of it in this milieu, that thinking has been possible here? If we are to preserve some link, not necessarily given or self-evidently pacifist, between thinking and philosophy, we might pose the question as follows: In what ways has America expressed itself philosophically? This has been one of the abiding questions for the American philosopher Stanley Cavell over the last few decades in his numerous writings on Emerson, Thoreau, and Hollywood cinema.[2]

If thinking in America is still premature, in the "new" world still constrained by its adolescence, a dominant strand of early- to mid-twentieth-century Western European philosophical thought seems to face the opposite problem, that of completion or absurdity, the exhaustion or nausea of old age, evident, for instance, in different ways, in figures such as Heidegger and Sartre. But much has happened since then, and it is with Gilles Deleuze most powerfully that one might again find a youthful demeanor, a new lease on life in this territory of philosophy, retaining and inheriting its formative concerns. The crucial Heideggerian problem of "dwelling" and its oblivion, "the real dwelling plight lies in this, that mortals . . . must ever learn to dwell," from *Building, Dwelling, Thinking,*[3] a reinscription of the problem of *What Is Called Thinking?*, which began with Descartes, is turned in Deleuze from a "plight" into an affirmative, nomad thought. This is to say that what were taken to be grim, irredeemable crises across numerous strands of writing—the impasses of representation, the nonunity of the subject, the presence of the unthought in thought and of nonsense in sense, the constitutive ambiguities of morality, movement, and inconstancy—are turned away from despair, as Deleuze uses these very paradoxes to form the conditions of possibility for a new image of thought, outlined, for instance, in *Difference and Repetition* as a move away from the "dogmatic image of thought."[4]

Moving between these lines of thought, Cavell and Deleuze, which is also to say between a certain expression of America and of Europe, we might find ourselves at a loss to account for the startling resonances that arise between them. It is remarkable that these resonances exist, even though neither philosopher ever makes a single reference to the other's work and that seem, for all practical purposes, unaware of each other's existence. In what follows, we will explicitly map certain relations on the terrain of ethics. Implicit in this kinship are certain key conceptual moves, made separately by both Cavell and Deleuze, which provide the scaffolding for this argument, although in the space of this essay we will be able to do no more than gesture toward them. Some of these conceptual relations are:

1. A mode of philosophical writing that is neither that of critique nor that of dialectics.[5] Alongside this is a conception of philosophy as a specific kind of activity, or way of life, far in excess of individual writers or the specific positions from which they speak. That is to say, philosophy is limited neither to a subject (being rather "a-subjective" or "pre-individual," virtually, prior to its actualization, in Deleuze's terms), nor to a set of polemical positions (the "achievement of the un-polemical" is the way Cavell describes a possibility, and a threat, inherent in the kind of writing that he holds up as exemplary).[6]

2. A movement away from the framework of representation toward the problem of expression (such that in our argument we will not ask if Cavell is adequately "representative" of America or Deleuze of Europe, but rather what kinds and degrees of changeable forces each *expresses* in relation to a dynamic milieu).[7]

3. A conceptualization of difference as internal to being.[8]

4. The conception of an internal, mobile relation between sense and non-sense.[9]

5. The centrality of immanence to their respective philosophical projects.[10]

A crucial point to keep in mind is that this is not a comparison (since we are not looking for equivalences, to show that *x* is the "same" as *y*) but rather the co-habitation of a certain conceptual plane, facilitated by these signals and affinities.[11]

But still, one might ask, why these names, and genealogies, and lists? Why not just say what I have to and be done with it? It is one of the preconditions of thought, both disabling and enabling (more so for philosophy than for others?), that before anyone can begin to say anything, a lot has already been said. In this regard, for both Cavell and Deleuze, the continuation or task of philosophy is taken up, first as a mode of inheritance, undertaking the construction of what we might call a counter-tradition in each case, primarily Spinoza, Bergson, and Nietzsche for Deleuze, and Austin, Wittgenstein, and in recent years, most importantly Emerson for Cavell (his *Cities of Words* attempts to render a history of the philosophical impulse to moral thought from Plato to Rawls in relation to what he names Emersonian moral perfectionism).[12] Moving between these series, we will assert that, as attempted inheritors of Nietzsche and of Emerson respectively, Deleuze and Cavell move tantalizingly close along this particular trajectory of their work.[13] This mutual hospitality or resonance surely has something to do with a previous alliance, on which Cavell has written a number of times, namely, Nietzsche's admiration for the writings of Emerson, an engagement sustained over two decades of the most productive phase of his career. Here is Nietzsche in 1881: "Emerson. I have never felt so much at home in a book, so much in my own house as,—I ought not to praise it, it is too close to me."[14] Cavell works through texts, particularly Nietzsche's "Schopenhauer as Educator," as well as portions of *Ecce Homo, The Gay Science,* and *Human, All Too Human,* in which Nietzsche can be seen to be transfiguring and absorbing Emersonian sentences into his own.[15] Aside from conceptual overlap, this sympathy rests on the resonating tonality of a passionate antimoralism and on a profound similarity of attitude, that of a turning away in dismay from one's given culture, particularly its institutionalized forms, a distrust of the present or the actual state within which one finds oneself, which is not a withdrawal but rather a turning toward the eventual, in the task of attempting to sense the new, to create a philosophy of the future. Cavell reads Emerson's recurrent references to "my constitution" not only as it has most often been interpreted, as a celebration of his own individuality or nonconformity, but also as a reference to the constitution of the United States, which he is attempting to amend in finding or founding philosophy for America.

To be done with morality is not to be done with ethics. If these vibrations outward from Nietzsche and Emerson are noteworthy, inasmuch as we are trying to align what might at first seem contradictory banners, Emersonian transcendentalism and Deleuzian immanence, then let us add a third series to disperse things even further and see if the resonance can still be maintained. Consider my surprise, sometime back, in a U.S. bookstore, to open distractedly the pages of *Hind Swaraj* (translated as *Home Rule for India* or *Freedom for India*), the text in which Gandhi first set out his political-philosophical ideas, and to find that the preface sums up its entire intellectual debt in only four proper names, thanking: "Tolstoy, Ruskin, Thoreau, Emerson and others, besides the masters of Indian philosophy."[16] A sentence or two of background to situate Gandhi's text, in what is also a footnote on the theme of globalization, and how unclear the conceptual significance of this term is apt to become when we stop to consider varied trajectories or histories of travel, migration, and displacement, likewise critiques of Western civilization, trade policy, and the violence thereof. *Hind Swaraj,* or *Home Rule for India,* was published not in India but in South Africa, where Gandhi spent the first twenty years of his adult life, part of a wave of trader migration from Western India in the 1880s that followed a previous wave of indentured labor two decades earlier. The text is written in dialogue form between an Editor and a Reader. (Gandhi translated Plato's *Apology* into Gujarati a few years earlier, a fact probably significant for his use of the dialogue form.) *Hind Swaraj* was addressed mainly to expatriate Indians, particularly those living in London who were advocating the use of violence in the struggle against the British.

This might be a familiar sound, to hear an Indian bring up the name of Gandhi, participating in something like a critique, say, of "the West," in whatever form, by invoking what is assumed to be familiar or near, itself supposed to be a function of identity by birth. My move here is quite the opposite, based more on what Nietzsche calls the throw of the dice. As an undergraduate in Delhi University, in admiration of older but still quite young leftist student unionists, I learned to say, with some conviction: "Gandhi was the pet dog of imperialism," a phrase handed down to us from decades-old Indian Communist Party pamphlets. Gandhi successfully earned the distrust of both the left and the right in India, and he was finally assassinated by a member of the Hindu right, an offshoot of the political parties that were in power in the central government of India until April 2004. In my own case, suffice it to say that had it not been for Deleuze writing on Nietzsche, for Cavell reading Nietzsche reading Emerson, and for Emerson appearing in the preface of Gandhi's text, I would have put *Hind Swaraj* down in a matter of minutes. And since the "I" in this text refers less to an individuality and more to a conglomeration of milieus, forces, and affects, we might take philosophy to be a realm where private acts take on public significance.

Let us insert this book a little further into the resonating series outlined above. Gandhi's critique of "the West" is reasonably well known, as that of a society based primarily on relations of force (could we call this, as Deleuze does, a Newtonian or thermodynamic image of thought?) and on a vision of human nature based on selfishness or rational self-calculation ("rational choice"). However, finding oneself at a loss, enchained, the move away from despair and resentment, or more accurately, from Nietzsche's term *ressentiment*, is enabled by the premise of *Hind Swaraj*: this is a critique that begins from oneself, above all, in an attempt to invent a form of political association that does not yet exist. "The people are missing," as Deleuze would say. How does one analyze oneself when it is not simply a matter of an "I," but rather of numerous potential selves? What we find here is an analysis too "untimely" to be called sociological, being instead a diagnostic account of the presently available technologies and modes of being in the world: *Hind Swaraj* has chapters on "Lawyers" (Gandhi himself, as is well known to Indian schoolchildren, was trained as a lawyer in England), "Doctors," "Education," "Machinery," and "Railways." Why would such exegesis be necessary in an anticolonial manifesto? The method, in this case, offers a striking parallel to Nietzsche's conception of the philosopher-physician, a "doctor" of civilizations (which reappears in Deleuze as the problem of "the critical and the clinical"), attempting to perform what Gandhi names "surgery of the soul," which takes the form of diagnosis (symptomatology) and therapy. While the conditions of external subjection, say that of colonialism, are not inconsequential, the key concern is something more like an "internal" situation, that is, a relation to the self that evaluates present ways of life in order to form what Cavell calls an unattained but attainable self. This is a process of constant experimentation, coping with recurrent difficulties, the central topic, for instance, of Gandhi's autobiography, *My Experiments with Truth*, rather than the finalism of a prespecified end or a goal (this book is not, for example, called "How I Finally Found the Truth"). Though historically Gandhi appears as the leader of a nationalist movement, when India was declared an independent nation-state in August 1947, he was nowhere near the official celebrations in Delhi, and he didn't send the leaders of the new state so much as a congratulatory note. Instead, he was in Noakhali, near Calcutta, employing his signature technique of fasting in an effort to stem the tremendous inter-religious violence that had broken out in various parts of the subcontinent as a result of the partition of India and Pakistan. "No virtue is final, all are initial," as Emerson puts it in "The Conduct of Life."[17]

To put it another way, this is an impulse to the perfectibility of the self that is at the same time a call for the transformation of the world as a whole, not a lament for a world gone by but a summons to one still to be borne, witnessed. "The transformation of the world as a whole," a world "still to be borne," phrases of such ambition that more often than not they are apt to lose their force entirely. In any case, does anyone still have such hopes? It depends on where we look. For the last few years, people from very diverse backgrounds, from a hundred and fifty countries, have been meeting in large numbers in what has come to be called the World Social Forum (WSF), an outgrowth of what was earlier called the antiglobalization movement, held together for the moment in a fragile coalition, united by very little except the slogan "Another world is possible."

Let us take the philosophical relations we have been building closer to a more familiar set of questions, through which philosophy opens out to the problem of associations, politics, or ethics. Our point of departure here is the relation between the individual and the community on the question of obedience or consent (the "social contract"), and the distinct but related problem "Why ought I obey the State?" and the Kantian formulation "Morality takes the form of Law." On a weak reading of either series, Nietzsche and Emerson would be said to celebrate the individual as a continuation of Romanticism, while Gandhi would be said to set forth a communitarian ethics. But listen to Gandhi respond to the question of "socialism and communism" in India: "Their one aim is material progress. . . . I want freedom for full expression of my personality. I must be free to build a staircase to Sirius if I want to."[18] In his response, Gandhi invokes "the viewpoint of Sirius," a version of the "view from above," a crucial problematic of the eighteenth and nineteenth centuries, found, for instance, in Goethe's understanding of poetry as an exercise consisting in spiritually elevating oneself high above the earth, or, as with Ernest Renan, writing in 1880: "Viewed from the solar system, our revolutions have scarcely the extent of the movement of atoms. Considered from Sirius, they are even smaller still."[19] At the outset we asked about the difference between religion and philosophy. Now we are in a position to gesture toward their kinship. The problem of transcendence, or an "ascent of the self," is perhaps the first question of, or impulse to philosophy and to philosophical cultivation (and the grounds of its overlap is also the very point of its separation from or competition with religion), particularly in the ancient Greek conceptualization of spiritual exercises and of philosophy as the ascent of the soul into the celestial heights, a conception common to the Epicureans, the Stoics, and the Cynics, continued by Plato in the discussion of the "transmigration of souls" in the *Republic*, and of "the soul's flight into the infinity of the heavens" in the *Theaetetus*.[20] While the eighteenth- and nineteenth-century dream of producing a new Lucretius all but disappears by the twentieth century, the terrain of this problematic falteringly reappears, for instance, in the late Foucault (with his discussion of the Stoics and the "cultivation of the self") and is present throughout Deleuze, as perhaps the central question of his entire oeuvre, that of the "outside" or the "virtual" ("thought comes from the outside").[21]

How transcendence turns to immanence in Deleuze, Cavell, and Gandhi respectively must wait for a longer discussion elsewhere. Closer to the matter at hand, in his invocation of this philosophical genealogy of what Cavell would call an unattained but attainable self, Gandhi is activating a conception of freedom ("I must be free to build a staircase to Sirius") that displaces the demand for or threat of uniformity that might accompany a call for equality (say that of socialism), or national or cultural unity (say that of nationalism). The question of consent and its potential transgression stands in relation both to the state, to being ruled, and to morality, or obedience to society, more generally. "The virtue most in demand in society is conformity. Self-reliance is its aversion." This is Cavell's favorite Emerson quote, the stimulus for his essay "Aversive Thinking in Nietzsche and Heidegger,"[22] a line of thinking that continues into Deleuze's *Difference and Repetition*, where the beginning of the refusal of the dogmatic image of thought is "a question of someone—if only one—with the necessary modesty not managing to know what everybody knows, and modestly denying what everybody is supposed to recognize."[23] Gandhi claimed of Thoreau's "Civil Disobedience" that it had offered him "scientific proof" for his own method of struggle, Satyagraha.

Let us try to make this formulation a little more precise. Disobedience is not "resistance." The question of consent is constitutively ambiguous, since it is unclear in which instances one's consent to a presently existing state, a state of affairs, has already been given and in what manner it might be withdrawn, or if we are even actually aware of the manner of our participation or perpetuation. After the age of national consciousness, colonialism now seems an unfathomable outrage, but for more than two hundred years it was lived habitually, taken to be a tolerable state of affairs. How is the seemingly normal, the accepted, to be brought into crisis? If the stability of the social demands that morality take the form of law, in what context is it necessary to insist that this law be broken, and in what manner might this be done? Since this is not knowable in advance, disobedience being both a threat and a possibility, philosophy of this genre and its related form of politics courts both tragedy and farce. How, then, might one proceed? Fundamentally, disobedience is based on a simultaneously positive and evaluative relation to desire, from Emerson through Nietzsche all the way to the "desiring-machines" of Deleuze and Guattari's Capitalism and Schizophrenia books. The Emersonian constraint, or necessity, is not expressed as an "ought" or an obligation but rather as a form of attraction, an attraction to my further self, which is also to another world, the eventual, struggling to emerge from the actual. The underlying fear of this strand of aversive thinking is not disorder or lawlessness but rather the complete impoverishment of desire and of capabilities, the impossibility of the emergence of newness (of becoming), self-directed (bewitched in some cases, sacrificed in others) to the powers of conformity and the requirements of obedience. But to affirm desire and speak ill of restrictions in a neo-liberal regime is a tricky matter, since the entire socio-economic apparatus seems organized to constantly multiply needs and cravings, worldly attractions joined to a sense of affirmation. ("Express yourself," says the mobile phone; "Excel yourself," says the business suit, and ever so often it is experienced as such. "Satisfaction guaranteed.") Keep in mind that we mentioned a positive and an *evaluative* relation to desire.

So by what criteria are human desires to be evaluated, those of this world or of another? Consider that the practical work of almost every religion, at least in its ascetic forms, has been to set replicable limits, to design a regime of the body to train and guide human desire in quest of a realm above worldly ends. But can these limitations, or regimes, or criteria, be fixed, once and for all, as a source of judgment? This would be the aim of a moral law, which we are saying we turn against. So let us leave this question of evaluation in limbo for the moment and continue with the consideration of positive desire, or affinities. The question of attractions rather than obligation creates a line of flight back toward (Deleuze's materialist, antimoralist) Spinoza: his *Ethics*, a potentially productive link that remains to be made, since Gandhian politics is above all about new arrangements of bodies (consider the self-imposed restrictions, the voluntary frugality that was briefly experienced as *freedom* by a generation of Gandhians), the relations between bodies (his own) and the body politic. At the same time, the centrality of the body and the question of modes of existence puts substantial pressure on the relation between the "private," say, the domain of religion, and the "public," say, that of politics. "Anyone who thinks that religion and politics can be kept apart, understands neither religion nor politics": this is probably one of Gandhi's most famous statements. Yet this must be countenanced by his lack of endorsement for the officially existing forms of organized religion, and their concomitant distrust of him—Christian missionaries who told him to convert, since he had drawn so heavily on the teachings of Jesus, or those belonging to the Hindu right, who accused Gandhi of being a "Muslim-lover," for which reason he was finally assassinated.

A statist suspicion: discussions regarding the "self" or "modes of being" are usually met with some distrust when confronted with talk of, say, global inequality or the duties of the welfare state. Cavell, Deleuze, and Gandhi, each from very different intellectual quarters, are accused of being uninterested in the modern state and its regulatory institutions. Taking this charge to have an element of truth, let us ask: What, then, is the primary focus of their concerns? Rather than necessarily negating or opposing the state and its institutions (although in some cases this might be crucial to do), the force of their praxis and the crux of their concerns lie in the domain of sensibilities, or the directions in which the body and desire are trained, to enable one to live in a particular way. This also tells us that theirs is not a libertarian philosophy, since the suspicion of the state extends only insofar as the law can neither fix morality nor enforce ethics. The modern state cannot replace an ancient God. Sensibilities take the form of the "micro" or "molecular elements" of politics for Deleuze (related to but distinct from the molar accretions of the state and its institutions);[24] in Cavell's and Gandhi's lexicons, the conceptual plane of this word is absorbed into its adjacent term, the soul. We might take this to be Deleuze-Cavell-Gandhi's collective inheritance from Romanticism, which refuses to leave the soul either to be denatured and ignored by the certainties of predictive science or to be obediently shepherded by the earthly legislators of an omnipotent God. [25] It is commonly said of Romanticism that it naturalized or secularized theological concerns. The drawback of such a formulation is that it trivializes the scope and the achievements of the Romantic quest, renders it banal, without an element of wonderment, as if it were self-evident why one should need a secular "theology" in the first place, how such a need might persist in the wake of the Copernican revolution, or what struggles its actual expression might entail. Turning toward, or returning to, this region of thought, we encounter the distinct but related problems of souls and of saints. Here we also gradually reenter the question of the evaluation or training of desire. *Souls* and *saints*: perhaps no one in my generation remembers how to use these words. These terms need not be taken only in their Christian sense, since Romanticism also has strong pagan leanings, usually involving some variant of nature worship or passionate contemplation. The Romantic aspiration for the soul lay not in its final salvation but rather in its earthly up-building or cultivation, which is why the Romantic genre of the confession, in Rousseau, for instance, is empirical: an analysis of "successive states of the soul," accountable first and foremost to itself and its desire for self-knowledge, movement and stasis, reception and transformation.[26]

Does this sound very personal, very subjective? That would be precisely the wrong interpretation. The soul, for Romanticism, lies not in the individual but in specific forms of life: the interrelations of nature, culture, and individuation or actualization. That is to say, the soul is primarily impersonal. It is hard to rescue terms such as *nature* and *culture*, *body* and *soul*, from common sense or, rather, to lead them back to a conceptual force field where they might have some sense and value. Turn again to the following common-sense proposition: the soul is private, or interior, belonging to the individual, while the body is the exterior, or public, or common, human form. Working into this problem from different routes, Cavell and Deleuze both invert this relation: the soul is preindividual, or asubjective, while it is the body and its capacities that individuate and actualize. Now we are in a somewhat better position to receive Gandhi's recurring invocation of "soul-force," his work on bodies, on himself, to produce a more general political effect. Does culture have a soul?[27] The answer may not, in most cases will not, be in the affirmative. If culture had a birth, it might also decline. This is the crux of Cavell's essay "Declining Decline: Wittgenstein as a Philosopher of Culture" and the more general conception, through Spengler and others, including much of Romanticism, of culture as a garden requiring nourishment, tending, and cultivation (a matter of nutrition, Nietzsche might say). The garden has often been falsely conceived on the model of a tree, while the concern should really be with grass, *Leaves of Grass*, the rhizome, immanence, such that a change in sensibilities is something like a tectonic shift, creating thereby not only a genealogy, but also a geology of morals.[28]

A postcolonial suspicion: by reinserting Gandhi into this line of thinking, indebted to Emerson, alongside Nietzsche and Thoreau, have we secretly reinscribed the primacy of "the West"? To say this would be to ignore a previous set of resonances internal to the lines of thought we have been describing. Thoreau structured *Walden* in eighteen sections to mimic the *Bhagavad-Gita*. Emerson, in what Cavell describes as his "Eastern longings," refers constantly to Vedanta philosophy, much in circulation in New England at the time. Nietzsche's texts have extended discussions of the law book of Manu, of *ArthaShastra*, and recurrently seek to absorb Sanskrit terms (Nietzsche describes the speed of his writing as *Gangasrotagati*, strong as the flow of a river, and that of his rivals as *Mandukagati*, like the hopping of a frog), alongside reverential invocations of "the ancient sages" (or "the masters of Indian philosophy," as Gandhi refers to them in *Hind Swaraj*), quite apart from the fact that the key Nietzschean concepts of the Eternal Return and the dice throw are direct transfigurations of the *Rig Veda*.

It is hard to discuss such matters sensibly, for the time being, while one is as yet uncertain what manner of classification the term *Hindu* provides. (We have been reclassifying such identities throughout this argument. On closer scrutiny, we might find Gandhi, for instance, to be more Christian than Thoreau, but we shall leave that aside for now, since it is not directly relevant to this essay.) Meanwhile, within a certain kind of international scholarship, which could have pursued such inquiries further, a term of abuse has emerged to attack, or to inhibit, what could, until even one generation earlier, innocently be described as Emerson's "Eastern longings." This would now be called "Orientalism," a term and a world-historical sensibility, once vibrant, that has degenerated into a mode of resentment in cruder hands, now stultifying and inhibiting rather than encouraging research. In the interactions we have been describing, rather than a strict West/non-West demarcation, what we have are attractions, or rather rhizomes (as described by Deleuze and Guattari in *A Thousand Plateaus*), "that pertain to a map that must be constructed . . . that is always detachable, connectable, reversible . . . and has multiple entryways and exits and its own lines of flight."[29] Based on the principle of heterogeneity, we can make connections that have everything to do with resonance, stimulus, and response, although they may or may not have anything to do with conscious intention. Extended relations might be drawn further: Schopenhauer is deeply indebted to Buddhism, Nietzsche learns from Schopenhauer, Tolstoy is indebted to Schopenhauer, Gandhi learns from Tolstoy. Or: Tolstoy sets forth his own theory of moral perfectionism, Lenin calls him "a reactionary in the most literal sense of the term," the Indian organized left in the 1920s and at various other points accuses Gandhi of being "a reactionary." And so on to the nth degree.

But in what way are these lines of resonance, internal to our rhizome, productive for their constitutive terms—for Gandhi, for example, who in any case is such a monster of fame that his deeds scarcely need repetition, much less our meager philosophical scaffolding? In many ways, that is precisely the point. If it is Cavell's claim that Emersonian thought is repressed or denied in America, it is hard to convey the extent to which Gandhi has been deadened in India, even when he is praised or commemorated, attached to little else but the moral pieties of a nativist, nationalist, guilt-provoking imagination, which has begun, for more than two generations now, to seem oddly anachronistic, exhausted, and, most damningly, impractical, which is to say, without any future. "It's too Romantic," one might say, to use another currently prevalent term of abuse, since the reception of Romanticism itself lies in ruins. This is in part because Gandhi's political terminology seems difficult to stomach, so far from the bureaucratic, technocratic rationalism that has been at home in India, as elsewhere. "Force of the soul," "all-pervading cosmic spirit," "experiments with truth," such terms may not seem so utterly foreign after a particular route through Deleuze, through Cavell.

The latent global scope of this rhizome does not, however, make the potential inheritability of Gandhi, or of Emerson, any less difficult. And inheritance is a crucial stake here, since we are turning, returning to yesterday in order to prepare for the day after tomorrow. The first difficulty: it begins to sound deadly when someone, anyone, who has not earned the right to speak, in that manner, in that milieu, at a particular moment, begins to produce ethical noises, or what Cavell calls the sound of moral perfectionism. (How does one earn the right to speak as such? Such a question is usually both asked and answered subconsciously, or preconsciously; it is a feeling, or an affect, or an ongoing set of relations, more than a statement. As a result, it is a difficult matter to "change one's mind" about such things, since most of the action has already taken place long before the matter reaches the mind. Which is why such changes are tectonic, for good and for ill: an unforeseen co-habitation, a mutation, the geology of morals.) Statements regarding perfectibility can sound poisonous, or ridiculous. In matters of discredit our attention is usually directed upward, say, toward George W. Bush in his debasement of the language of democratic aspiration ("Freedom is on the march," "Infinite Justice"—such words are, in any case, not the stock-in-trade of Emersonian moral perfectionists or Deleuzians, who are both passionately antimoralist in tone).

Much harder to notice is a more pervasive threat, internal to any line of thinking, not that of error or of misunderstanding but of what Deleuze names, following Nietzsche, the problem of "stupidity," moments in which we ourselves come to embody or to will vacuousness, which could be within our scope to notice, or not. Take an example: "Above all to thine own self be true." This maxim could be sensibly asserted through Emerson, Nietzsche, or Gandhi (keeping in mind that in none of these cases is the "self" necessarily equal to an "I"), but Shakespeare puts it in the mouth of Polonius, as Laertes makes fun of him behind his back, pointing us to the ease with which the bestowal of such an injunction can be perverted. Or how utterly pious and vacuous it can seem to a succeeding generation, which has no predetermining criteria with which to differentiate between education, indoctrination, paternalism, or piety. In other words, a loss of knowledge, or of faith, or of a corresponding form of life: who or what to be disobedient to?

Thus any continuation of Gandhi, for instance, requires us to consider him not only as a rhizome, but also as a singularity, in his status as a saint, Mahatma. Who would be the equivalents of saints in secular life? Whom should one admire, be attracted to, as to a higher self? This was another pressing concern for Romanticism and its inheritors. Here we find the sense of the nineteenth-century theme of "the Hero" in Carlyle, whom Gandhi also admired, transfigured into the problem of "representative men" in Emerson, the "man of action" in Bergson, the "exemplar" or "specimen of the species" in Nietzsche. Gandhi, it would seem, is an outstanding personification of these hopes of the philosophers of the nineteenth and early twentieth centuries. In such a reading (an influential one, since Romanticism in contemporary sensibilities is best remembered for its cult of the genius, or the author) it would seem that no one but Gandhi himself could speak that language, perform those actions. This would leave no hope for Gandhianism to re-emerge as a future politics, since all that is then left for us ordinary mortals to do is wait, in that most theological of gestures, for another such Messiah to appear.

This is the point at which Cavell and Deleuze reopen the lines of experimentation, in what Cavell calls the "democratization of moral perfectionism."[30] Difference precedes repetition. What would constitute a repetition of Gandhi? How many variations are possible within the theme "Gandhi," without losing its sense? My experiments with truth, Gandhi might say, were mine alone, for everyone and no one to follow. What then? Here is a phrase to restart with: a way of life. In a recent paper, Ajay Skaria points out that Gandhi was criticized by members of the nationalist movement for spending too much time tending to the daily upkeep of the ashrams.[31] The empirical connection back to our philosophical route here is Gandhi's engagement with two texts by Henry Salt, *A Plea for Vegetarianism*, which he read in his early years as a student of law in London, and Salt's *Life of Henry David Thoreau*, which he read during his first incarceration in South Africa in 1908, an engagement that can be traced in Gandhi's correspondence with Henry Salt and his discussion of Thoreau's *Walden* and experiments in living.[32] For Cavell and for Deleuze, philosophy bears a crucial relation to ways of life. How might one live? What should one eat? How is the soul to be nourished? Who should one look up to? Is anyone still interested in such questions? A sampling of pop bestsellers in a train-station book-store would confirm that such discussions continue (*Chicken Soup for the Soul*; *The Atkins Diet*; *The Art of Living*; *My Life*, by Bill Clinton; and other "exemplary men" autobiographies). Are these books of philosophy or of religion? Or are they simply indefinably debased pop (dare we even call it "culture"?) mishmash, answering to no genuine need other than that of capitalist profit?

Whether or not this question can be definitively answered in terms of need, one can at least ask: Is there intelligence in evidence here? If so, what manner of nutrition is it, if these books are, in fact, food for thought? We might say that these books are the textual equivalents of the junk food (that uniquely American invention), lying on the adjacent shelf of the same train-station shop, alongside a shelf of pharmaceuticals, that other great contemporary opiate. What, then, would be healthier, or more nourishing for the soul, than *Chicken Soup*? The rarefied diet of philosophers? But that is hardly digestible, or even producible or replicable on a mass scale. What then? Genuine religion? But would that, then, be food for *thought* (or opium for the masses, as we once called it)? What is food for thought? What is called thinking?

Most thought-provoking in this thought-provoking age of ours is the fact that we are still not thinking. After "reversing Platonism" we are left, not with the problem of false competitors for the form of the good, requiring, say, the expulsion of the poets or the Sophists—that is, of a particular type of speech—but rather with the threat of lifeless expression, words in exile, habits deadened by conformity, stupidity.[33] So what do we need, a reawakening? A new moral law? Enlightenment? At this point Deleuze looks to lunatics, drug addicts, primitive nomadic hordes; Cavell, to a vaguely defined figure of the child. Hardly material for a Sunday-school sermon. At the end of the day, Nietzsche tells us, Kant was a cunning Christian, a moralist. Enlightenment is humanity's passage to its adult status: "Enlightenment is man's release from his self-incurred immaturity," this is the first line of Kant's "What Is Enlightenment?"[34] *Unmundigkeit*, the word used by Kant to describe the state of bondage from which the human seeks freedom, or transcendence, translates both as "tutelage" and as "minority." It is in relation to the force of this word that we must place Deleuze and Guattari's central concept of "minority-becoming,"[35] or Cavell's stress on the problem of re-education, rebirth, or coming into language, the figure of the child that haunts his reading of Wittgenstein's *Philosophical Investigations*, or Emersonian passivity: "All I know is Reception." The Gandhian paradox: freedom through submission. Civil disobedience, then, is also about learning or creating a different obedience, in uncertain variation between a potential transgression and a necessary limitation. Rather than arguing for or against the Enlightenment, this is more a problem of embodiment, of actualizing an attitude, of staking one's territory in a line of flight (the claim of reason), for an ethos, and the variations it might attain, or need to attain, over time, over barely noticeable tectonic or technological shifts and upheavals.

This is the problem with maturity: it ossifies so easily, so democratically, as common sense; it finds roots rather than rhizomes.

But let us not be too quick in posing the realm of experimentation as a convenient or easily attainable alternative. Here again stupidity resurfaces, not only as that committed by others, but one's own, internal to thought. Take another example. Distinct from Polonius is the stupidity of Pangloss in Voltaire's *Candide*, relentlessly satirized for his deluded optimism in the ultimately harmonious nature of the universe. Emerson, Thoreau, indeed, all the theorists of this line have often been accused of not understanding the true nature of evil, for their seemingly inexplicable faith or optimism, a charge leveled by Indian political theorists such as Bhikhu Parekh and others against Gandhi.[36] Then there is also the question of what an "antimodern" attack on modernity might look like, in terms of a way of life, or technologies, a charge leveled as much against Rousseau or Romanticism as against Gandhi. At the end of *Candide*, the novel's chief characters decide that European, or indeed all earthly institutions relating to politics, religion, and war are so irredeemably disastrous that they will spend the rest of their days in the Orient, working their garden on a little farm near Constantinople. That this bears some resemblance to Gandhi's experiments with collectives or with Thoreau's *Walden* should alert us to the specific danger of an incomprehensible asceticism or rarefied withdrawal that this line of thinking manifests. It is in relation to these threats, nativist nationalism, pious moralism, naïveté, or ascetic snobbery, in light of which most inheritors of Gandhi (of Thoreau?) have appeared already lost, that Nietzsche, Cavell, and Deleuze, with their sympathetic but relatively distinct lines of positivity, appear as forces of resuscitation.

Resuscitation toward the eventual. Let us return to the company of those today who desire that, from within this world, another might emerge. Having invoked the World Social Forum in this discussion, which has also been about globalization, we cannot leave it once mentioned as only a utopian possibility. In WSF-Mumbai in India, in January 2004, over one hundred thousand people from various activist groups, NGOs, national self-determination movements, and political organizations, from one hundred and fifty countries, gathered to discuss strategies in their respective domains against a common enemy, neo-imperialism. The excitement and carnival atmosphere of such an event (the first international institutional arrangement of its kind not wholly determined, or organized, by states, or by commerce, on its first journey out of Brazil, where it began) coexisted with great anxiety, expressed in many of the discussions, about the lack of positive proposals and an incipient disappointment with the feeble and generalized consensus, based mainly on negations. These forums are now held annually across four continents as a response to globalization in the most recent sense of the term: processes put in place by Bretton Woods institutions such as the World Bank and the International Monetary Fund (IMF), mainly through their structural adjustment programs, that facilitate the formation of a network of internationally mobile finance capitalism. It would seem that a struggle against neo-imperialism would do well to take suggestions from Gandhi, one of the most revered anticolonial leaders in world history. But matters are rarely so straight-forward. Consider the first line of Thoreau's "Civil Disobedience," often quoted by Gandhi: "I heartily accept the motto,—'That government is best which governs least.'"[37] Does the opposition to contemporary neo-liberalism hinge on a generalized demand for a return to national protectionism? It would seem so listening to several key participants of the WSF, such as the Brazilian and the Indian organized left, or Jose Bove and the Via Campesina group from France. Would Gandhi and Thoreau, then, seem neo-liberal in comparison? (And what significance does the phrase "self-reliance" have, in Emerson's inflection of it?) Keep in mind that, with the mutual implication of sense and nonsense, the same phrases can also be empty, or poisonous. (A finance minister, for instance, announces a cut in agricultural subsidies, declaring that it will "foster self-reliance.") The problem would hinge on what it means to be governed "least." At the bare minimum, one could say that the efforts of the WSF are directed toward ensuring some form of accountability, or care, or the possibility of upward mobility, for those who find themselves on the receiving end of large-scale, profit-oriented economic processes.

But a trickier problem arises here regarding NGOs and international activists, the other relatively distinct set of major players internal to the WSF, alongside the organized left. Consider that, alongside its predatory qualities, neo-liberalism also produces an international welfare mechanism. The World Bank itself funds large-scale initiatives in social forestry, health, education, and disaster management, through both national governments and NGOs. Are these to be entirely mistrusted? (In Gandhian or Emersonian terms, as we have been describing them, the question would return to a consideration of a "way of life," although that would be a digression at this point). Whatever the case may be, it would seem harder to organize a protest against a global "poverty alleviation" or "corporate social responsibility" program. A more obdurate radical might say that these are mere discharge mechanisms, the palliative measures of capitalism, gently releasing tensions, rather than letting them build up (although the question would arise, build up toward what?). If one gives up the idea of a final, decisive battle to redeem this earth, once and for all (re-read the lyrics of "The Internationale"), then, we could ask, in what way are recurrent tensions built up, and how are they discharged? A state of equilibrium in one milieu might be the result of a great strain on another. This becomes particularly germane when we consider that many of our daily requirements, say, petroleum or wheat, are fulfilled by intense pressure on finite resources, often necessitating transfers over great distances. How does one disrupt the ordinariness of a society that has lost the tools, or gained too many, by which to estimate its own needs and the effects it is having on others and on itself, and on the earth as a whole? Secularism is supposed to be the realm of doubt, but no faith is stronger, or less prone to actual skepticism among its adherents today, than neo-liberal democracy.

What is a faith? A translatable and mobile set of bodily practices, habits, modes of dress and social organization, the direction of thought, forms of leisure, the training of desire, a conception of the good life, affective and cultural tendencies, all of which possess relative variations over space and time, say, in social or sectarian differences, or in relation to the raw materials they inherit, or the technological innovations they absorb (which all faiths do). The masterstroke of this faith is to make even heresy potentially profitable. Dialogue? How does one converse with a polity that is saturated with technologies of communication? It would be achievement enough to catch their attention for a few seconds. An argument still quite unclear in this regard is the relation between violence and nonviolence. In which cases and to place what demand in front of whom is the use of violence justifiable, and to what degree? The charter of the WSF turns against violence per se. Participating groups must have pledged to use only "non-violent methods of social change."[38] Paradoxically, this denies participation to many of the groups, such as the Zapatistas from Mexico, Ya Basta!, and the Black Bloc from Europe, that began the entire process in the late 1990s, when it was still referred to as the antiglobalization movement. It is perhaps too early or too late to say anything definitive about such matters, but given that Gandhian practice practically invented the possibility of nonviolent direct-action politics, there surely remains here an inheritance not to be lost, or rather, one to be recurrently rebuilt. Such that one can say, of the "ongoing soft revolution," that, at the very least, it remains ongoing.

And what about the concerns regarding philosophy with which we began this essay? It may well come to pass that these supposedly unfavorable conditions, the lack of a readily available public, turn out to be for the best. Bereft of all pre-existing authority, philosophy can once again begin to be persecuted, or ignored long enough to wait, to gather its own forces, and to go in search of the few companions to whom it is meant to speak. And in this privacy plant the seeds that will bear fruit the day after tomorrow.

Rogue Democracy and the Hidden God

Samuel Weber

"America will have been my subject"—it is almost in passing, and yet with considerable emphasis, that Jacques Derrida makes this announcement early on in a lecture that was to become the major portion of *Rogues* (*Voyous*).[1] And yet the passing remark could hardly have been more significant. America—in particular, the United States—always held a special importance for Derrida's work.[2] It was in American universities that Derridean "deconstruction" first began to establish its international reputation, and it was also in the United States that the backlash against deconstruction first emerged and then crystallized in connection with the revelations concerning Paul de Man's youthful writings in a Belgian collaborationist newspaper. Whatever other effects that affair had, it called attention to the political dimension of Derrida's work, an aspect that had been largely overlooked in its early reception in this country. Whereas the social upheavals of the sixties and seventies provided the context in which deconstruction emerged in France, its reception and resonance in the United States tended, initially at least, to be confined to the university. To be sure, the American university of the late sixties and seventies had become a highly politicized place, but its politicization was of a very different kind from that which prevailed in Europe. There, the intellectual context in which structuralism and poststructuralism, including the work of Derrida, emerged was dominated by state institutions, including the universities, whereas in the United States the very word *state*, in the singular, has always been regarded not just with suspicion but indeed as something of a foreign interloper, an unwelcome guest in the precincts of American English. Thus, although Derrida resolutely rejected attempts to *position* him and his work in terms of established French and European political categories—in particular those of Marxist "materialism," as in the series of interviews published in 1972 under the title *Positions*[3]—the political context of intellectual activity, such as the kind he was engaged in, was impossible to ignore. But it was associated more with institutions than with individuals. This is already reflected in the title *Positions,* which, like that of *Rogues* many years later, is not by accident formulated in the plural, for a certain plurality—and we will have occasion to return to this—is mobilized throughout his writings to unsettle the unity often attributed to political concepts in general and to that of "democracy" in particular.

Shortly after these interviews were published, Derrida, with others, embarked upon a series of political initiatives involving issues that at first, at least, tended to be local in character: politics with a small *p*. The first major project of this kind was the founding in 1975 of an organization of teachers and scholars, GREPH, aimed at elaborating critical alternatives to a governmental plan to eliminate the teaching of philosophy in the last year of high school (the *Réforme Haby,* named after the then Minister of Education). GREPH, which stands for the Research Group on the Teaching of Philosophy, proposed that philosophy should not merely continue to be taught in the last year of the *lycée* but be extended to earlier school grades, as well as integrated into professional training in the fields of law, medicine, and so on. The idea was to question the logic of specialization that informed the *Réforme Haby,* not just by retaining the status quo but by transforming it. Another such localized intervention involving the development of border crossings was the 1985 founding of the International College of Philosophy (CIPh), which was designed not only to serve as a forum for interdisciplinary study among academics but also to create the possibility for high-school teachers of philosophy, and others, to pursue research aims not possible in secondary schools. The conviction that informed the founding both of GREPH and of CIPh was that the efficacy of political intervention often requires informed experience of the institutional practices involved, including knowledge of their history and structure.

Initially, then, and for quite some years, the political dimension of Derrida's work was more evident in such micro-political institutional interventions. Although such contexts were local, they were tied to larger issues by virtue of being situated within the highly centralized and hierarchized French state apparatus, which includes virtually all of the country's educational and research institutions.

It is this link between the local and the national, between the micro- and the macro-political—a link that is in great measure a result of the specific institutional situation of French higher learning and research—that allows and indeed impels those participating in educational and research institutions, whether as teachers, researchers, students, or staff, to connect their immediate concerns to much larger political issues, involving the French state, the nation, and its relation to other nations in an increasingly "globalized" world. One example of this tendency was the April 2006 protests and demonstrations of high-school and college students—soon joined by many of their teachers, as well as substantial numbers of workers and their unions—against the revision of the labor law (in French known as the "CPE": contract of first employment) proposed by Prime Minister

Dominique de Villepin. The CPE would have allowed employers to fire young workers employed for the first time without having to justify their action before an independent tribunal. Confronted by massive protests, the government abandoned the CPE—at least for the time being.

To return to Derrida: as his international reputation grew, it was inevitable that he would move from his largely local institutional interventions of the seventies to increasingly global, macro-political concerns in the eighties, whether they involved the apartheid policies of South Africa or the rights of Palestinians to an independent state. In his writings, a growing engagement with macro-political questions became legible through a problematization of the question of nation, nationality, and national languages, and then through the enlargement of institutional perspectives to more general questions of law and its relation to justice, but also including questions of copyright, the right of asylum, and many other issues. Such macro-political concerns, which undertook to reinterpret practical political questions in terms of the often unthematized and unconscious assumptions that made them possible, produced major works such as *On Spirit: Heidegger and the Question* (1987), which examines the political implications of Heidegger's endorsement of the notion of Spirit in the early thirties in view of his previous critique of it; or the essays collected in 1988 as *On the Right to Philosophy*. This turn toward what I have been calling "macro-political" questions culminated in what can be considered a final "political" trilogy: *Specters of Marx* (1993), "Faith and Knowledge" (1996), and *Rogues* (2003). But if this trilogy can be called "political," that is only insofar as it enjoins its readers to rethink the very limits of what has been designated as "politics," and in so doing to envisage its transformation. It is significant that all three of these texts grew out of talks that Derrida gave in conferences or colloquia: his writing remained, in this sense, tied to the *singular* occasions that called it forth, to which it responded but which it also sought to re-address—that is, to reinscribe in a larger and generally unexpected historical and cultural context.

To come now to the specific case of *Rogues*, the situation to which this text both *responds*, addresses, but above all seeks to *re*address, was a very particular conference: the fourth dedicated to his work at the French conference center at Cérisy-la-Salle, in Normandy. It was also to be the last. This possibility endowed the question of time with a special urgency. But this urgency was not just tied to the singular person of Derrida. Here, perhaps more than elsewhere, the date cast a long shadow. For the general question of "democracy to come"—a phrase that had occurred and recurred in his writing over many years, without ever having received anything like an extended elaboration—could not be discussed in the summer of 2002 without some consideration of the attacks of September 11, 2001, and, above all, of their aftermath. To address this situation responsibly and responsively, could for Derrida only mean to raise questions concerning the discursive traditions that dominated thinking about democracy and their link to a situation in which the "war on terror" had become the public leitmotif of the country that had long been regarded, and that continued to present itself, as the world's leading democracy, the United States. To attempt to readdress the question of democracy in this particular situation had thus to proceed through a rereading of certain of the discourses and traditions out of which the notion of democracy emerged and to which it remained indebted.

With respect to one of the terms that Derrida chose to serve as the title of his talk, and then of the book of which it composed the major part—*rogue*, and in particular, *rogue state*—he recalls that its use in political discourse was by no means limited to the current American administration. Rather, he reminds his readers, the use of the phrase reaches a high point "between 1997 and 2000 . . . first of all in the speeches of Clinton himself and those of his top advisors (particularly Madeleine Albright)" (95–96 / 138). Previously, he notes, "Ronald Reagan had preferred the term *outlaw*, and George Bush tended to speak of *renegade* regimes." As to the word *rogue* itself, its use goes back to the sixteenth century, when it designated "a dishonest, unprincipled person . . . a rascal." "From there," Derrida notes, its "meaning is extended, in Shakespeare as well as in Darwin, to all nonhuman living beings, that is, to plants and animals whose behavior appears deviant or perverse. Any wild animal can be called rogue but especially those, such as *rogue elephants,* that behave like ravaging outlaws, violating the customs and conventions, the customary practices, of *their own* community" (93 / 135). The word *rogue* thus acquires the significance of "a mark of infamy," involving a "banishing or exclusion that then leads to a bringing before the law." Here Derrida underscores one important distinction of the English word with respect to its French and German counterparts, *voyous* and *Schurken*: whereas the latter two words always signify human beings, the English word comes to be applied to plants and animals, endowing the term with a particularly dangerous connotation manifest in the following remark from an article published in the *Chronicle of Higher Education:* "In the animal kingdom, a rogue is defined as a creature that is born different. It is incapable of mingling with the herd, it keeps to itself, and it can attack at any time, without warning" (94 / 135).

The fact that in English the word *rogue* is not limited to any one class of beings seems to endow it with a particular, and dangerous, capacity: impossible to place or classify, it is also difficult to predict and defend against: "It can attack at any time, without warning." Although Derrida does not mention it here, just such considerations inform the 2002 National Security Strategy (NSS) document of the Bush government, which reacted to the attacks of September 11, 2001, by declaring long-established procedures of international law to be obsolete and by endorsing "preemptive" military action as an integral and legitimate part of official American policy:

For centuries, international law recognized that nations need not suffer an attack before they can lawfully take action to defend themselves against forces that present an imminent danger of attack. Legal scholars and international jurists often conditioned the legitimacy of preemption on the existence of an imminent threat—most often a visible mobilization of armies, navies, and air forces preparing to attack.

We must adapt the concept of imminent threat to the capabilities and objectives of today's adversaries. *Rogue states and terrorists* do not seek to attack us using conventional means. They know such attacks would fail. Instead, they rely on acts of terror and, potentially, the use of weapons of mass destruction—weapons that can be easily concealed, delivered covertly, and used without warning. . . .

The United States has long maintained the option of preemptive actions to counter a sufficient threat to our national security. The greater the threat, the greater is the risk of inaction—and the more compelling the case for taking anticipatory action to defend ourselves, even if uncertainty remains as to the time and place of the enemy's attack. To forestall or prevent such hostile acts by our adversaries, the United States will, if necessary, act preemptively.[4]

This statement, written by then National Security Advisor Condoleezza Rice, links "rogue states" to "terrorists": the phrase thus is used to designate not only a state that "relies on acts of terror" itself, but also "terrorists," who presumably are not integral parts of the state. Rogue states thus are held to subcontract out what traditionally has been regarded as their exclusive prerogative: the massive and systemic use of violence. The notion of "rogue" thus marks the turning point at which the legitimate use of violence by the nation-state is delegated to nonstate agents who, precisely because they do not wear the uniforms or uniformity of the state, are increasingly difficult to identify, localize, and anticipate. They are less visible than official agents of the state, and they are also less accountable. It is as though the rogue state is a state in the process of being taken over by the parasitically private interests and agents it itself has produced.[5] This takeover constitutes the threat against which the world's one remaining "superpower" seeks to react by promulgating its doctrine of preventive and preemptive military action, even and especially in situations where no "imminent" threat can be established. The very notion of "imminence" and the temporality upon which it depends is thereby called into question, if indeed not entirely emptied of meaning, as was the case in regard in the American decision to attack Saddam Hussein's Iraq in March 2003, and as appears to obtain once again at the time of this writing in certain arguments being brought forward ostensibly to prepare for and justify military action against Iran.[6]

Used as an adjective, then, to modify or qualify the notion of "nation-state," the term *rogue* raises the question of the relationship between the monopoly of violence historically accorded the state and a state-delegated use of violence to nonstate agents whose very heterogeneity positions them to be effective producers of "terror."[7] Analyses of the notion of "rogue state," such as those by Noam Chomsky, Robert Litwak, and William Blum, whose works Derrida gratefully acknowledges (96 ff. / 138 ff.), all make the point that the use of this phrase by the United States to designate—and often attack—other countries is made to justify violations of the very international law to which the term seems to appeal. In other words, the use of the term to designate and condemn an enemy actually describes the user. Derrida by no means disagrees with this account, but he does find something decisive missing in it: the link between rogue states and the concept of legitimate political sovereignty itself:

> It is not a criticism of these courageous works to wish for a more fully developed political argument [*pensée*], especially with regard to the history, structure, and "logic" of the concept of sovereignty. This "logic" would make it clear that, a priori, the states that are able or are in a state to make war on rogue states are themselves, *in their most legitimate sovereignty*, rogue states abusing their power. As soon as there is sovereignty, there is abuse of power and a rogue state. Abuse is the law of use; it is the law itself, the "logic" of a sovereignty that can reign only by not sharing. More precisely, since it never succeeds in doing this except in a critical, precarious, and unstable fashion, sovereignty can only *tend*, for a limited time, to reign without sharing. It can only tend toward imperial hegemony. (102 / 145–46)

This, of course, assumes a very general account of sovereignty. But even without going into the question in detail, much of what has happened in the few years since Derrida pronounced these words argues for their plausibility. Sovereignty seeks to transcend time, as well as language, insofar as both require it to partition and share, to divide and compromise its unity and integrity—in short, to *compose* with alterity, rather than simply *impose* itself upon it.

It is therefore fitting that Derrida mobilizes precisely the media that such sovereignty seeks to absorb and to neutralize: language and time, in his account of the specific historical conditions leading up to the emergence of the word *rogue* in American political discourse.

The background for this situation, Derrida asserts, lies in the fact that today the international institution founded after the Second World War to adjudicate conflicts between nations, the United Nations, no longer provides the United States with a reliable majority, neither in its General Assembly nor in its Security Council, both of which are required to legitimate the use of force between member nations. Without this majority, the United States is no longer entirely sovereign in its ability to use force to regulate international conflicts. However, the United Nations Charter does allow for one significant exception—and exceptions to such founding charters are almost always significant—to the authority invested in the Security Council, and through it the United Nations, to adjudicate conflicts and prohibit the use of force: the right of individual states to self-defense, a right preserved in Article 51 of the UN Charter. This article, which constitutes "the only exception to the recommendation made to all states not to resort to force" in the settling of international conflicts, would, in the perspective developed by

Carl Schmitt, constitute the very essence of sovereignty. The sovereign would be "he who is able to decide on the state of exception"—or, translated into the situation of the United Nations, sovereign would be the nation-state able to decide what constitutes a threat to its survival, and thus a situation of self-defense. For Schmitt, however, the "state" is already present in that which exceeds it as an exception, for the exception is merely the state in its negative form: it is above all a "*state* of exception [*Ausnahmezustand*]," or more precisely, as the German word translated by "state" literally says, it involves a bringing "to stand"—a *Zu-stand*.[8] The force of the decision that constitutes sovereignty is to bring the exception as a temporal movement of alterity and difference to a standstill, thus making it the negative mirror image of the state, which constitutes itself as negation of the negation. Thus, writing about the League of Nations in 1925 (in *Roman Catholicism and Political Form*), Schmitt argues that, although the League might seem to constitute a "super-state" or "super-sovereign" capable of adjudicating disputes between nations, it would inevitably betray "the idea of an impersonal justice" by developing "its own powerful personality."[9]

The argument that Derrida develops in *Rogues,* however, although indebted to Schmitt, diverges from his notion on decisive points. For Derrida, the enabling "other" of sovereignty is not the "*state* of exception," which later, in Schmitt's *Concept of the Political,* will be identified with, or rather *as* the "enemy," generally understood either as another state or as a group seeking to take over the state. By thus determining the "other" of sovereignty as a "state of exception," Schmitt defines the exception as essentially a negative mode of the state or, which amounts to the same, as a state of negation. It is this determination of alterity as state of exception that Derrida problematizes in his reconsideration of certain discourses on and practices of democracy.[10]

Before we turn to this argument itself, it is worth noting that what Schmitt, writing in 1925, refers to as a "super-state" or "super-sovereign" has since undergone a significant terminological shift: today it is called a "superpower." This shift seems to acknowledge that the claims of states or sovereigns to transcend their particularity and relativity can only be based on sheer power—military in the first instance, economic in the second, cultural in the third—rather than on any sort of political legitimacy. But if it is power rather than legitimacy that determines sovereignty today—and perhaps always has, although not as obviously—then where does this leave the distinction between legitimate and "rogue" states?

The title that Derrida gives to his study of "democracy to come" already entails a partial response to this question. It designates "rogue states" in the plural, a plurality that will ultimately call into question the survival of the concept itself. If there are *many* rogue states, including those that most loudly pronounce and denounce other states as being "rogue," and if this plurality depends not simply on the perfidiousness or self-interestedness of any one state—on its "personality," as Schmitt might have said—but on the traditional understanding—and practice—of sovereignty as essentially indivisible, one and the same, then the plurality of rogue states also announces the disappearance or irrelevance at least of the term as a political concept, if not of the behavior it stigmatizes.

From this situation, Derrida draws the aporetical conclusion: "There are thus only rogue states. Potentially or actually," but also that precisely *because* there are always "more" rogue states, there will soon be *no more* rogue states, since the difference between legitimate and rogue states will have collapsed into a sovereignty that by its nature refuses to be shared, to recognize anything outside of itself—and thus is in essence "roguish." All of this is condensed in the French phrase that provides the title of the penultimate chapter: "Plus d'États voyous," which, depending on how it is pronounced, can mean either "*more* rogue states" (the final *s* is pronounced) or "rogue states *no more*" (the final *s* is mute), but which, therefore, when written, can, and in this case does, mean both at once. Roguishness, as Derrida interprets it, is rooted in nothing other than the structure of sovereignty itself—of sovereignty *as* a structure *of* the *self*. Sovereignty, without which law is unthinkable, must place itself outside the law, for reasons that the following passage from *Rogues* associates with its relation to language, or rather, to silence:

> Unavowable silence, denegation: that is the always unapparent essence of sovereignty. . . . A pure sovereignty is indivisible or it is not at all, as all the theoreticians of sovereignty have rightly recognized and that is what links it to the decisionist exceptionality spoken of by Schmitt. This indivisibility excludes it in principle from being shared, from time and from language. . . . As soon as I speak to the other, I submit to the law of giving reason(s), I share a virtually universalizable medium, I divide my authority, even in the most performative language, which always requires another language in order to lay claim to some convention. The paradox—always the same—is that sovereignty is incompatible with universality even as it is appealed to by every concept of international, and thus universal or universalizable—and thus democratic—law. (101 / 144)[11]

This "silence" that belongs to the "essence of sovereignty" does not, Derrida clarifies, mean that sovereignty cannot speak—it speaks all the time—but rather that its discourse lacks meaning (*sens*). The use of the term *rogue state* is an exemplary instance of this lack of sense and of its historical dynamics. It seeks, by negation and by demarcation, to invest the nonrogue, sovereign "superpower" with meaning and legitimacy. But in its own tendency to ignore established international and domestic legal traditions—whether in its endorsement of preemptive warfare as a principle of foreign policy or in its suspension of habeas corpus with respect to the "terrorist suspects" imprisoned at Guantánamo as a principle of domestic policy (of "homeland security")—the democratic superpower increasingly resembles that which it seeks to oppose as its mortal enemy, the "terrorists" or "rogue states." This has to do, Derrida insists, not simply with the specific set of policies pursued by a particular American administration but with the claim of sovereignty itself to be indivisible and self-identical:

> To confer sense or meaning on sovereignty, to justify it, to find a reason for it, is already to compromise its decisive exceptionality, to subject it to rules, to a code of law, to some general law, to concepts. It is thus to divide it, to subject it to partitioning, to participation, to being shared. And [this] is to turn sovereignty against itself, to compromise its immunity. This happens as soon as one speaks of it. . . . But since this happens all the time, pure sovereignty does not exist; it is always in the process of positing itself by refuting itself, by denying or disavowing itself; it is always in the process of auto-immunizing itself, of betraying itself by betraying the democracy that nonetheless can never do without it. (101 / 144)

Sovereignty, which seeks to be above language and time, finds itself caught up in both as media of alteration and transformation that it seeks to appropriate as media of self-positing and self-preservation.

If, then, the ambiguous quality of roguishness proceeds from what can be called the aporia of sovereignty, in which the claim to a certain universality—or, at least, to a certain superiority—undercuts the constitutive and aporetical claim that the sovereign is indivisibly self-same, then "democracy," by associating the notion of "sovereignty" with something called the "people"—the *demos*—sets the stage on which what Derrida calls "auto-immunization" begins to play itself out.

Without being able to delve here into the intricacies of the idea of "auto-immunity" as it emerges in the later writings of Derrida—Michael Naas has written a remarkable text on the subject, in which he describes "auto-immunity" as "the last iteration" of "deconstruction" itself[12]—I will note only that it continues a line of thought that goes back to his early writings on Husserl, in particular *Speech and Phenomenon*, where Derrida deconstructed the Husserlian notion of "auto-affection," thus introducing a concern with the notion of the "self"—*autos*—and the related but distinct concepts of "sameness" and "ego" that was to remain throughout his writings and indeed to assume increasing importance over the years.[13] The shift, however, from the philosophical notion of "auto-affection"—the mind speaking to itself without the intermediary of anything exterior or other, whether temporal, corporeal, or linguistic—to that of "auto-immunity," borrowed from the life sciences, recenters Derrida's discourse around the process by which the "self," in seeking to "protect" itself against external dangers, tends to weaken its own defenses and thus to debilitate or even destroy that which it is seeking to safeguard. One example of the auto-immune tendency of democracy that Derrida discusses in *Rogues* is the suspension of the Algerian elections of 1992 by the ruling party, the FLN, after it had won only 15 seats in the first round against 188 that went to its opponent, the Islamic Salvation Front (FIS). Reacting to this election result, the FLN outlawed the FIS, imprisoned, tortured, and often murdered its leaders, adherents, and sympathizers, and thus ushered in a bloody civil war. Given the highly undemocratic character of the FLN, even if it was "elected" prior to 1992, this example strikes me as unfortunate and not entirely appropriate. A better one, or at least one closer to home, would be measures such as "The Patriot Act," the suspension of habeas corpus, domestic surveillance without due process, and other policies of the current American government, which are justified as necessary to safeguard the "homeland."[14] But since such measures, which restrict individual liberties, do not affect the electoral mechanism, which today is widely presented as and considered to be the single most important institution identified with "democracy," they attract less attention—and indignation. Similarly, the structure of the electoral process itself, its increasing dependency upon private financing, is also an issue that receives little attention from the public—not surprisingly, given that the media which largely shape that attention are themselves part and parcel of the problem.

However this may be, the specificity of the example given by Derrida can obscure the more general tendency that he is concerned to emphasize, which resides in the particular propensity of democracy toward autoimmunity: "Democracy has always been suicidal, and if there is a to-come for it, it is only on condition of construing otherwise life, and the force of life" (33 / 57).[15] This tendency does not, therefore, depend simply on a particular government or its policies, however suicidal they may seem. At the core of this propensity is the difficulty of determining the nature of sovereignty in democracy. Rule of the people, liberty and equality—these notions have historically imposed themselves in regard to democracy and yet also have proved difficult to reconcile with one another in a coherent synthesis. Sovereignty, for instance, is traditionally understood as indivisible, whereas democratic sovereignty, expressed in some sort of elective process, entails rotation and alternation—but always understood as a "return of and to the self" (10 / 30). Similarly, freedom tends to be construed as an element of self-determination, once again implying the power of a sovereign subject to say, "I can." Thus, the notion of the "self" as an autonomous instance tends to inform most conceptions of democracy. And yet at the same time, an examination of certain discourses on democracy reveals something very different: not a determinate self or subject at the core of democracy but an irreducible alterity.

In analyzing a number of passages from Plato and Aristotle, Tocqueville and Rousseau, Derrida retraces certain aspects of this unstable and even aporetical configuration. On the one hand, at the very beginning of Western philosophy, there is the Platonic distrust of a regime that not only confounds liberty with license, *eleutheria with exousia*, but also discovers "indetermination and undecidability in the very concept of democracy" (25 / 47). Reviewing the discussion of democracy in the *Republic*, Derrida points to Plato's emphasis on its seductive power to fascinate, which in turn is associated with its phenomenal multiplicity: "Democracy *seems* . . . the most beautiful (*kallistē*), the most seductive of constitutions (*politeiōn*; Republic, 557c). Its beauty resembles that of a multi- and brightly colored (*poikilon*) garment. . . . The same attribute defines at once the vivid colors and the diversity, a changing, variable, whimsical character, complicated, sometimes obscure, ambiguous. Like the fanning wheel [*la roué*] of a peacock, which women find so irresistible" (26 / 43). Derrida insists on the importance of the feminine quality that Plato attributes to democracy, a quality that he both associates with desire and also mistrusts; such femininity diverges from the masculine, patriarchal, and fraternal perspective that will dominate theories of democracy and politics throughout most of the history of Western thought.[16]

This masculine, patriarchal, and fraternal perspective is linked, according to Derrida, to the conception of sovereignty as intrinsically indivisible, including the sovereignty of the people. A famous passage from Tocqueville's *Democracy in America* points to the theological origins of such a perspective. In summing up his impression of the distinctiveness of American democracy as he experienced it in the 1830s, Tocqueville concludes that: "The people reign over the American political world as God rules over the universe. It is the cause and the end of all things; everything rises out of it and is absorbed back into it" (14 / 34). Tocqueville's comparison of "the people" ruling over the "American political world" with God ruling the universe suggests that this popular-democratic notion of sovereignty, even in its most secular appearance, retains a strong theological and monotheistic character. Derrida contrasts this monotheistic perspective—God as One and the Same—with a Greek precursor, Aristotle's conception of the Prime Mover (*to proton kinoun*), which, although itself neither moving nor moved, sets everything else into motion. It is, he notes, "a motion of return to self, a circular motion." And yet, Derrida adds, the circular motion of self-return initiated by the Prime Mover is associated by Aristotle with "a desire. God, the pure actuality of the Prime Mover, is at once erogenous and thinkable." He is desirable as "thought thinking thought [*hē noēsis noēseōs noēsis*]" (*Metaphysics*, 12.1072a-b, 1074b; 15 / 35).[17] The movement initiated by the unmoved Prime Mover *desires* to come full circle as the return of thought to itself—thought thinking thought. Thinking is thus defined as a movement by which the self, through a process of self-reflection, takes "pleasure in the self," which is to say, in the ability to *stay the same* over time and space and thus to be—that is, *to remain—one and the same.*

To the extent, then, that "democracy" always implies some degree of self-determination and of popular sovereignty, it is informed by what Derrida designates as "ipseity" or "ipsocracy,"[18] as rule of the *self-same.* Over what does this self rule? Over everything *other,* to be sure, not merely in the form of beings or entities, but even more in that of *time* and *space* as media of proliferation, dissemination, and alteration, and over *language* as medium of sharing and partitioning. The self rules by asserting its unity and unicity as *one-self,* as a self that stays the same over time, through space, and throughout languages—in the image of a God construed as One and the Same.

This is not the only way in which the uniqueness of the one can be conceived, however. If, as Derrida observes, democracy always involves a "question of number," the

response to that question has never been univocal. It can, as in Tocqueville's interpretation of the American experience of "the people," be understood as implying an instance
that is one and the same, which is to say, as "ipseity" (15 / 35). But it can be understood
differently, namely, as "the truth of the other," as "heterogeneity," as "anonymity," as
indeterminate or indefinite. In French, these two options converge in the little word *un*,
which can designate both the number *one* and also what in English is called the *indefinite
article*: *a* or *an*, *anyone*, and thus *no one—no one in particular*, no one definite, defined,
or definitively definable. Thus Derrida places great emphasis on the fact that Aristotle
describes the Prime Mover as both finite and indefinite at once: as "*a* life" rather than
simply as "life" in general—and yet at the same time, as a life "that exceeds that of
humans" insofar as it is lived "in a constant manner." "A" life in this sense is thus neither
the life of an individual human being nor life in general. Its constancy can be read to
imply a certain overcoming of time and space as media of alteration. The life of the Prime
Mover would then constitute the life of the self, life *as* self-same. But Aristotle also seems
to retain the notion of an irreducible *singularity* at the very origin of life. At the origin of
life would be not just "life" as such, life in general, life that can be lived constantly, but
"a life," life in the singular, life that is finite: once and for all. The question of how these
two notions of "life" relate to one another constitutes one of the questions that informs—or should one say "tortures"?—Derrida's discussion of democracy, and it also
suggests why he is eager to retain the possibility that it must be construed as "a concept
exceeding the juridical-political sphere" (35 / 59). If Derrida never mentions the notion
of the "biopolitical," it is perhaps because this emphasis on "*a* life"—on life in the *singular*—is incompatible with the generalizing perspective of biopolitics.

Aristotle is, however, not the only writer mobilized by Derrida to offer an alternative
to Tocqueville's description of the godlike character of the popular sovereign in American
democracy. It is striking, and perhaps not without a certain irony, that Derrida also turns
to the writer who many years before, in *On Grammatology*, he had invoked to name the
"age" that "deconstruction" was called upon to transcend: Rousseau. In this late text of
Derrida, Rousseau returns, but in a very different guise. In the chapter of the *Social Contract* dealing with democracy, Rousseau emphasizes, in a Platonic vein, how singularly
unsuited to human life democracy seems, above all because of its protean quality: "No
government tends more forcefully and continuously to change its form," he observes.
And yet Rousseau does not conclude from this that democracy is simply to be disqualified
or dismissed as a form of government. Rather, he emphasizes the extraordinary demands
it places on those who would practice it: "It is under this constitution that the citizen
ought to arm himself with force and constancy, and to say each day of his life from the
bottom of his heart what a virtuous Palatine said in the Diet of Poland: *Malo periculosam
libertatem quam quietum servitium* [I prefer liberty fraught with danger to tranquil servi-
tude]" (75 / 110). This danger—which, as Derrida adds, often concerns "nothing less than
life itself," leads Rousseau to conclude that "if there were a people of gods, it would

govern itself democratically. So perfect a government is not suited to humans" (75 / 110). Rousseau's "people of *gods*" contrasts sharply with Tocqueville's people-as-*God*, namely, as the One God, the God that is One and the Same. Rousseau, by contrast, sees not the One God but "gods" in the plural as defining the kind of "people" required by "democracy," which is difficult to come by, being "not suited to men." Or, one is tempted to add, not suited to those "men" who see themselves as created in the image of God, of the One God as a Self that strives to stay the Same.

Rousseau's emphasis on the plurality of gods supposed and demanded by democracy leads Derrida to reflect on how this alters the very notion of the divine, and with it, of the sovereignty it informs:

> This *plus d'un*—*more than one*—that then affects the word *gods*, the dissemination by which it is literally taken into account (the gods, yes, but how many, and will they be as equal as they are free?), this *more than one* [plus d'un] announces democracy, or at least some democracy, beyond government and democratic sovereignty. This "more than one" affects God with divisibility precisely there where sovereignty, that is, force, *cracy*, does not suffer division, where the force of the One God, single and sovereign . . . will have been called single, one and indivisible by all those who have analyzed sovereignty, from Plato and Aristotle to Bodin, Hobbes, and Rousseau. (75 / 110)

Thus, with the same formulation that disqualifies democracy as a political regime or government ill-suited for humans, Rousseau, by associating it with a plural divinity, breaks with the tradition of political discourse that from Plato and Aristotle to Schmitt insists on the indispensable unity and indivisibility of the sovereign. Democracy, as a regime of "gods" rather than of men, is called into question as a regime at all.

If, then, the essence of sovereignty has traditionally been construed on the basis of a force that is *indivisible*, and if democracy has generally been construed as "a government of number, of the greatest number" (76 / 111), the question posed by the formulation of Rousseau concerns that which makes number great: Is it the indivisible individuality of the One as the basic unit of all numerical calculation? Or is it a singular and irreducible divisibility that makes each and every number always more—and less—than itself, more and less than one—and thus not so much a number as an indefinite article?

Could this also be why the word *rogues* is set in the plural in Derrida's title? And could it be that this plurality also affects its link to the state, as in the phrase *rogue state*? What of rogues *within* the state, subverting its stability and dislocating its unity? Could the emergence of the word *rogue* as a political term be a symptom of such irrepressible disunity?

I, at any rate, have a very different memory of my first encounter with this word in political discourse. For me, it is forever associated with what in retrospect appears increasingly to be one of the watershed events of recent—a highly relative term, to be sure—American political history: the assassination of President John F. Kennedy on November 22, 1963. Of all the many reactions and discourses that emerged in response to that fateful event, not the least memorable was the theory of a conspiracy possibly involving elements of the state apparatus, above all its security agencies. It is in this connection that I first encountered the term *rogue* in a political context. At that time, however, it was used not to stigmatize illegitimate foreign states but rather as a term for one aspect of what Colonel L. Fletcher Prouty called, in a book of the same name, *The Secret Team*. Prouty, who from 1956 to 1963 served as liaison officer between the Department of Defense and the CIA, became convinced that the murder of President Kennedy was the result of a coalition of forces operating both within various defense, intelligence, and other governmental agencies, and outside. The intra-governmental grouping he designated as a "secret team" not merely because it operated in secret but because its secret operation was designed to circumvent scrutiny and control through the representative and accountable organs of the democratic state.[19]

Whatever one may think of this notion of a "secret team" as responsible for the assassination of President Kennedy (and perhaps other assassinations as well), Prouty's approach and his information, which reflected the experience of someone who had long worked within and reflected upon the organizations he was analyzing, suggests that the divisibility of sovereignty and of so-called sovereign states upon which Derrida insists proceeds from their innermost elements and institutions, which are no more unified and legitimate than are the states as a whole.

The fact is that long before the term *rogue* was used to delegitimize foreign states, it was used to designate elements working *within* the domestic state apparatus but *outside* the official chain of command and control. In this perspective, it also seems appropriate that the phrase *rogue elements* emerged in connection with the assassination of a chief of state, for if, as Tocqueville put it, the people in American democracy are felt or expected to "rule over the political world as God rules over the universe," the public, visible elimination of the one political figure and office that *manifests* the unity of that people as a whole, but also its accountability and possibility of self-transformation, stands as a challenge to the capacity of that people to *rule itself*, or at least to rule itself *democratically*.

As Plato already emphasized, the distinctive quality of democracy seems inseparable from a certain form of manifestation, above all, a certain visibility. From this standpoint it may be highly significant that the assassination of President Kennedy in Dallas was performed as a public and visible act. Reported by the media "live," audible on radio and visible on television—and subsequently viewed innumerable times on various recordings, including the famous "Zapruder film," the killing of this president established once and for all, albeit in a complex and ambiguous manner, the political power both of what is called "media coverage" and of obscure, unidentifiable—or at least unidentified—forces acting outside of the established structures of accountability. The relation of the latter to the former gave new meaning to the ambiguous term "media coverage." The televisual and print media *covered* the event but revealed neither its causes nor its significance. Indeed, by focusing its "live coverage" on individual figures, such as Oswald and Ruby, it may have participated in a cover-up of the event in its complexity. At any rate, ever since, the realm of the visible, in politics as elsewhere, has been increasingly framed by that of the invisible, the accountable by the unrecounted. Thus, the communication of visible and invisible has in recent political history been very different from that which allowed Plato to compare democracy with a "multi- and brightly colored (*poikilon*) garment" (Republic, 557c). Visible and invisible have, rather, been presented as symmetrical mirror images, as simple oppositions, as light and dark, rather than "like the fanning wheel of the peacock, which women find so irresistible" (26 / 43).

In place of the many-colored, spangled quality of democratic multiplicity described by Plato (and deeply mistrusted by him), the perceptual field of American democracy, as propagated by the televisual media, has assumed a rigorously binary and oppositional character, with figure framed by ground, foreground framed by background, and the whole framed by the discourse and appearance of "anchors," whose function seems above all precisely that: to anchor—fix in place—all movement of uncertainty that might exceed or complicate the simplicity of the individual, isolated frame. The familiar figure of the "anchor" is the audiovisual correlative, condition, and confirmation of the self, exhibiting the possibility of its staying the same over time—for a while, at least.

This relation of democracy, and in particular American democracy, to a certain experience of image and sound as meaningfully unified, transparent, and self-contained can be illuminated by recurring to a different but perhaps not unrelated discussion of another kind of image, one that involves not democracy but the economic organization of society, which in many circles today is proclaimed as being structurally inseparable from it. This discussion is found in a short and unfinished text written in 1921 by Walter Benjamin and bearing the title "Capitalism as Religion." Consisting of only a few pages, it can be divided into two sections. The first is devoted to the elaboration of four theses on the relation of capitalism to religion. The second comprises a series of notes, written in telegraph style and lacking all elaboration: they seem to be notes for further study. In order to make any sense of the very brief allusion to images that interests me in our context, it will be helpful first briefly to summarize Benjamin's four theses. His first and primary thesis is that capitalism is not just the product of a religion, as argued by Max Weber,[20] but is itself a religion, in particular, what Benjamin calls a "cult." What he means by "cult" is never entirely elaborated in this short fragment (or elsewhere, so far as I can see[21]), but certain of its characteristics are made clear: first, cult is distinguished from "dogma" and also, implicitly, from "faith." It is less theoretical, mental, or internal than practical. Second, capitalism is religious insofar as it responds to the cares and concerns to which religions traditionally have sought to respond. As a cult-religion, capitalism responds to these cares and concerns through a form of practice—of doing. Third, in contrast to traditional religions, the capitalist cult abolishes the distinction between "weekday" and "holiday." Instead, the capitalist cult is *constant*: it is celebrated all the time; it is "permanent," thus turning time into a homogeneous medium of duration at the same time that it consumes all the energies of those who practice it. And finally, in sharp contrast to the religions of the Book, "capitalism is presumably the first case of a cult that is not expiatory but rather culpabilizing [*verschuldend*]."[22] The German word that Benjamin uses and that is translated here as "culpabilizing"—*verschuldend*—has, as he himself notes, a "demonic ambiguity," since it signifies both *guilt* and *debt*.[23] This does not mean that the expiatory perspective is absent from this religion—far from it—but rather that its practice involves not the "reformation of being but its "demolition [*Zertrüm-merung*]." What is thus celebrated without interruption or respite in the capitalist cult is a universalization of indebtedness that knows no bounds. Indeed, "God himself [*Gott selbst*] is included in this debt and guilt." God himself—God as the name of a certain Self—"is not dead" but "has been implicated [*einbezogen*] in human destiny." The result, however, of such "implication" is that that God can be worshiped by the capitalist cult only by being kept secret (*verheimlicht*): "The cult is celebrated before an unripe and immature deity [*einer ungereiften Gottheit*]; every representation, every thought of it violates the secret of its maturity [*Reife*]."

The indebted deity ripens, but unlike a bond or a tree never reaches full maturity, not, at least, in the capitalist cult-religion. Lacking maturity, it cannot provide the *return* that alone would justify the faith, the credit and credibility, extended to him. Instead, that debt (and guilt) only accumulate. And so this unripe deity of debt and guilt must be hidden in order to provide a suitable object of worship for the capitalist cult. It is hidden, however, not simply by being withheld from view but by being represented by something else. By what else? It is here that a short note, written by Benjamin probably more to himself than to anyone else, a note for future research, points toward what might possibly constitute a missing link in our previous discussion of Derrida's roguish reading of democracy to come, not to mention some of the more recent vicissitudes of democracy in America.

Here, then, is the note that Benjamin telegraphs to himself:

Capitalism developed itself in the West parasitically out of Christianity . . . so that in the end [the] history [of Christianity] is in essence that of its parasite, capitalism.

Comparison between the pictures of saints of different religions on the one hand, and the banknotes of different states on the other. The spirit, that speaks out of the ornamentality of the banknotes.

Methodologically what should be investigated first are the (various) connections money establishes with myth during the course of history until it could extract so many mythical elements from Christianity that it could constitute its own myth.[24]

The cult of an indebted and guilty deity that must be worshiped unremittingly and yet, by virtue of its immaturity, must also be kept secret requires a surrogate in which indebtedness and the promise of redemption are credibly merged. This surrogate must be recognizable in its singularity and yet at the same time endowed with a durability, a constancy, a permanence that no singular being can hope to attain so long as it is merely alive. It is this capacity to endure in and through a certain circulation that provides the basis of the comparison—the *Vergleich* that does not establish simple equality (*Gleichheit*) but only a *likeness*—between "pictures of saints of different religions" and the "ornamentality of banknotes of different states." The pictures of saints depict the mortality of singular living beings whose sanctity, however, turns mortality into a promise of redemption. The ornamental designs of modern banknotes, by contrast, reinscribe the pictures of individuals, living or dead, in a context that is not merely representational but allegorical, in the sense that Benjamin, a few years later, in his study *Origin of the German Mourning Play*, was to demarcate sharply from the symbolic by virtue of allegory's nonimmanent, discontinuous, and *never entirely visible* mode of signification.[25] In this sense, *allegory reckons* with the Lutheran doctrine of *sola fides* and its critique of the redemptive power of "good works"—and *counters* it as well. It takes it into account by "ornamentalizing" all manifest likeness, including the likeness of the image of man to his creator (and redeemer). It counters it by treating its images as *legible*. Their problematic legibility, however, is apparently rendered calculable in the relation of ornamentality to monetary value, always made explicit—and hence legible—by numbers. In this way, the ornamentality of banknotes links the "faith" of *sola fides* to a system of calculable *credit* that is *measured numerically* but *manifested* through *effigies*. As with the pictures of saints, however, what those effigies signify is that in the cult-religion of capitalism, the hope of redemption will henceforth be inseparable from the medium of circulation, which renders every "one" equal to every other "one" in order to render calculable the "bottom-line" of the balance sheet. The "myth" of "money" that informs the capitalist cult thus becomes the historical heir to the redemptive promise of Christianity. To spend is to save—and to be saved! "Datsun saves!"[26]

Let me conclude—or rather, break off—with a question. With respect to Plato's emphasis on democracy as more (and less) than just a form of government or the name of a constitution, Derrida notes that "in addition to the monarchic, plutocratic, and tyrannical democracies of antiquity," a number of other types of political regimes claiming to be democracies have arisen in the modern period. Among these he lists "parliamentary democracy (whether presidential or not)," "constitutional monarchy" working in tandem with parliamentary democracy, "popular democracy," "liberal democracy, Christian democracy, social democracy, military or authoritarian democracy, *etc.*" (27 / 49). What, however, of this "etc."? Does it, for instance, include, stand for, or conceal "economic democracy," and if so, in what way? Does it include it as a mere extension of all the other variations of democracy that seek to name themselves properly, in the present, with proper names? Defined properly, "economic democracy" would designate a political system in which the people, as a collective self, is at home (*oikos*) with itself, keeping its wealth to itself and keeping its own house in order according to its self-given laws.

Economic democracy in this sense would designate home rule, rule of the people *at home with itself*. In view of such home rule, all the efforts of that people would be directed at the preservation, maintenance, and defense of its homeland security, building ever higher walls of defense to protect its home against intrusion from the outside—but also against subversion from the inside, from those rogue elements that are always already pursuing their own self-interest and that continue to do so. And yet, since today, more than ever before, walls are not enough, such homeland security would necessitate forays outside: not just into the world, but throughout the world, to identify and neutralize potential threats to the home and to the homeland. All of this could be part of what might be called "economic democracy." We would also have a picture not so very different from the image presented today by many if not most states that call themselves "democratic," and first and foremost, by democracy in America.

It can happen, however, that this pursuit of homeland security produces exactly what it seems to fear: the extension of indebtedness and guilt, which can reach a point where the very notion of the "homeland," as a geopolitical basis for democracy, has to be called into question. The linking of a territorial entity to a specific ethnic or national grouping tends to dissolve in the face of such indebtedness, which confirms the dependency of the group "itself" upon other groups, other "selves." The celebration of the "immature" and "secret" deity—money—both promotes and undercuts the adherence to other groupings (ethnic, religious, local, fan clubs, etc.) that seek to define themselves through visible representations and binary opposition.

The question then can become, in the face of a tendency that can also be designated as "auto-immune," just what the relation of "life" and "death" will be, and whether it will continue to be defined within an "economy" of the self—an "autocracy."

The question is not simply when such a point is reached, but perhaps even more significantly, if it will allow for a reconsideration of the processes that have led up to it, and of the alternatives that have been marginalized along the way. If democracy can be induced to reconsider itself, to reconsider its relation to the sovereignty of the self, to a self that defines its liberty in terms of its power to say "I can"—which is to say, its power to *stay the same* over time and space, and perhaps this is the not so secret message of "globalization" today—it may be able to recall that, although the images and effigies on which it relies *circulate* like banknotes, they do not necessarily come full circle and provide a return. From the tortured—and torturing—experience of a democracy seeking to control past and future in the name of "Number One," a democracy to come could begin to envisage itself otherwise than as an incessant capitalist cult of consumption and reproduction celebrated in an unremitting series of holiday sales, promising to "save" but only within the scope of their limited duration. Or in the incessant binarism of professional sports, with its regular and recurrent calendar celebrating and inculcating the logic of winner take all, which is also the principle of the distinctively American model of the democratic electoral process, which refuses the proportionality common in the rest of the world. And in their place, a democracy reconsidered—reconsidering its "self"—could leave room and time for a banal and unspectacular *week,* in which one day makes way for the next without seeking to impose itself as the first, last and only one—and yet which remains once and for all.

To be sure, as Derrida remarks at the end of *Rogues*: "All that is not for tomorrow [*c'est pas demain la veille*]" (114 / 161); more literally, "tomorrow is not the eve." And yet, like images in rear-view mirrors, that eve may be nearer than it appears and getting closer all the time.

Intimate Publicities

Retreating the Theologico-Political in the Chávez Regime?

Rafael Sánchez

Para Edmundo Bracho y Diómedes Cordero

> The current space of sovereignty . . . , which is also the space of the finish-
> ing of identity in general, is solely a distended space full of holes, where
> nothing can come to presence.
>
> —Jean-Luc Nancy, *Being Singular Plural*

On January 10, 2001, television screens across Venezuela filled with an
extraordinary image: surrounded by a forest of microphones and journalists, the nation's Defense Prime Minister, General Ismael Eliécer
Hurtado Soucre, suddenly produced and held up in his right hand a
pair of lightly colored women's panties, which he waved at the cameras
while delivering a volley of fiery accusations against enemies of the regime. In the wake of the avid succession of flash pans that greeted the
general's press-conference revelations, and after brief hesitation, most
members of the audience burst into irrepressible laughter. Soon that
laughter would be echoed all over the globe. Carried by local television
and newspapers, the electronically reproduced image of the general and
his panties instantly traveled everywhere, so that, at least for some brief,
discontinuous moments, the most distant points of the planet burst into
globalized laughter at the unintended prank of this South American
general. Or so, at any rate, I like to imagine General Hurtado's worldwide reception. Whatever happened elsewhere, in Venezuela the laughter still resonates, and it is anyone's guess how long its waves will keep
rippling into the future.

I argue in this essay that the general's colored panties blew a gaping
hole in the theologico-political balloon of the Venezuelan Chávez re-

El ministro aseguró que han llegado 140 pantaletas de todos los colores

FIGURE 2   "The minister has assured the public that the army has received 140 panties in as many different colors." (*El Universal*, January 11, 2001.)

gime, which keeps growing bigger day by day. Even if by one or another spectacular means the regime constantly puffs itself up, since that moment its theologico-political substance has not ceased leaking through this hole. Indeed, if things continue as they are, one Schmittian scenario would be a total collapse of the political amid proliferating conflicts. As Schmitt and others after him have argued, given the world's radical indeterminacy, the political can only come about as the result of constantly reiterated, inherently violent decision. Akin to the miracle in a certain theological tradition, such a decision, the sovereign exception, makes both lawful regularity and the political community possible. Thoroughly transcendent to the political, this decision brings it into being as a more or less delineated, cohesive totality, while designating the enemies or enemy vis-à-vis which the political totality defines itself.[1] Given such an understanding of how, in all its seriousness and gravity, the political totality comes about, I now wish to consider the opposite, largely comical possibility, that is not how totalization happens or how it triumphantly succeeds but rather how, precipitated by laughter, it hilariously fails.

Considering the awesome, transcendent force that goes into the making of the political community—the sheer constructivist bent of the decision that so deliberately puts it together as an articulated, ordered totality—it is not surprising that laughter can have a wondrous effect. After all, according to Bataille, "laughter exposes the relation between reason and unreason," in an eruptive moment of excess that momentarily reveals the unknown that dwells within the known, ruining from within any reasonable construct, in this case the state.[2] As Bataille puts it, "that which is laughable may simply be the unknowable," and "the unknown makes us laugh."[3] Simon Critchley offers a related way of understanding how laughter and, more generally, the comic expose the boundaries of any objectivity to an ineradicable alterity. For him, humor issues from a "disjunction . . . between expectations and actuality," which, defeating "our expectations" about reality or causality, produces "a novel actuality." "The comic world," Critchley writes, "is the world with its causal chains broken, its social practices turned inside out, and commonsense rationality left in tatters." The Venezuelan instance may be confidently added to Critchley's list of examples of such subversive disjunction between expectations and actuality, from "talking dogs" to "farting professors and incontinent ballerinas."[4] Indeed, given our everyday expectations about generals, what could be more jarringly discrepant than for one of them, the nation's Defense Prime Minister, no less, to be caught on national television beside himself with anger, with a pair of women's panties clutched in his right hand?

It is enough to focus briefly on the televised, electronically reproduced image of the general and his panties to see why, within seconds, the effects of the panties episode, the laughter it provoked, spread like a virus throughout the regime. Invoking an epidemic is not all that outlandish, considering that for Bataille laughter falls under the "principle of contagion" that is constitutive of "society" or the "community" (provided, I might add, the latter is understood as "infinite resistance to presence, foundation and essence").[5] If the theological imbues the state with its capacity to shape or totalize "society," laughter, in Pierre Clastres's formulation, may be a case of "society against the state."[6] Though in the wake of the incident the regime has steadily kept losing its aura of authority, probably it still does not quite know what hit it. Probably, too, most if not all local actors, for whom the panties episode is by now a receding memory, would not accord it as much consequence as I do. Yet a cursory glance at the local media, overwhelmingly in the hands of the opposition, would confirm that a momentous shift in the overall tone of public discourse did take place in the wake of the incident. Before General Hurtado's fateful press-conference revelations, public communications by even the most uncompromising critics of the regime were suffused with the modicum of deference that a democratically elected government extracts from its audience. After the incident, however, such deference all but disappeared. Increasingly, the regime has been publicly portrayed in the media as either a joke, an illegitimate autocracy, or both. Ludicrous operetta, quintessential banana republic, rapidly deflating balloon—these are some of the tropes that increasingly recur in public portrayals of the regime, and they do not hesitate to point out the violent intolerance peeking through the crumbling façade of its legitimizing rhetoric. The initial responses to the 2001 incident indicate just how momentous it was for the local political imagination and suggest why this shift could have happened.[7]

Take, for example, one journalist's label for the entire episode: climaxing in the generals' press conference appearance: "the mysterious case of the multicolor panties."[8] By labeling it a whodunit, the journalist hints at the episode's huge potential to deflate by alluding to a form of emplotment that could not but signal the depths of triviality to which the regime had suddenly sunk. Even more telling is the expression *el pantaletazo*, with which the media all alluded to the repercussions that the general's decision to wave his panties in front of the cameras had both in the army and, more generally, throughout the regime. Added to any noun, the Spanish ending *azo* enlarges it to the point of bursting. Formed from the Spanish noun *pantaletas*, "panties," the expression *el pantaletazo* signals literally an explosion of multicolored panties, which threatened to blow the regime's transcendental claims and illusions to smithereens.

Humor, perhaps more than anything else, best captured the enduring significance of the panties episode. Shortly after the media revelation, a group of local comedians announced the opening in a local theater of their new production *El Pantaletazo*, advertised as a follow-up to their previous theatrical production. Both in the capital city Caracas and elsewhere in Venezuela, for over two years the group had been presenting to full houses and great public acclaim a satirical comedy called *La Constituyente*, whose characters and events kept changing as they followed, day by day, the main events in and developments of the Chávez regime. The comedy featured local personalities from both politics and the media, including, of course, Chávez, impersonated to great satirical effect by a local actor, who, occasionally, mockingly shows up in the media parading as the president. Since the sequel figured the same cast of characters, when it opened President Chávez could rest assured that for the foreseeable future every one of his public gestures, interventions, and appearances would reverberate in the antics of his theatrical double.

As I was toying with the idea for this essay, it occurred to me that both the title of the original comedy, *La Constituyente*, and that of its sequel, *El Pantaletazo*, admirably characterize the two main moments that, I argue, the regime has undergone since it was elected in December 1998. An initial period, lasting for approximately two years, was distinguished by a radical constitutionalism (hence the title *La Constituyente*), bent on founding anew all aspects of the nation through recourse to the originary constituting powers of the people. This was followed by a *pantaletazo*, or explosion of multicolored panties that possibly signaled the beginning of the regime's unraveling. Whether inadvertently or not, by their decision to switch titles from *La Constituyente* to *El Pantaletazo*, the local comedians registered a transition from radical constitutionalism to its undoing. In any event, just when references to the panties episode began to peter out in the media, the decision of the local comedians to name their new production *El Pantaletazo* brought the whole affair back into the limelight. Given how long *La Constituyente* stayed in local theaters, it is not surprising that its successor, *El Pantaletazo*, kept the panties affair highly visible until relatively recently.

The whole affair began with a letter sent to the Venezuelan journal *El Nacional* by one Pablo Aure, who is a lawyer, a sometime university professor, and a failed politician from one of the Venezuelan states, where he occasionally writes for the local newspapers. Titled "Generals in Panties," the letter berates the army for its lack of courage vis-à-vis President Chávez and alludes to how "generals have been lately receiving as presents delicate and intimate feminine garments."[9] On the whole, the letter belongs to an unsavory genre that consists in messages sent to prominent figures, especially in the military, accompanied by feminine garments meant to shame the addressees into action by suggesting their unmanly, cowardly behavior vis-à-vis those in power. Although I have not been able to check their accuracy, I have come across references in the Venezuelan press to an episode during the Allende years in Chile in which panties were sent to officers in the military in order to provoke them into staging a coup against the democratically elected president, one in which no less than the Prussian army humiliates an enemy with a similar gift, and references to various other incidents in Venezuela from several years ago.[10] The sexism implicit in this form of humiliation is unquestionable. Examining the local gender economy is not my purpose here, however, although gender will remain a crucial dimension in much of what follows. In order to prevent any easy generalizations about local gender relations, I will say that throughout the weeks after General Hurtado's press conference, there was no dearth of feminist voices deploring the incident in the local media. Nothing, including its insults, misogyny, and vulgarity, sets the letter that Aure sent to the Venezuelan army apart from the sexism characteristic of the genre overall.

In light of later developments, especially the electronically reproduced panties of the televised press conference, one of the letter's passages stands out, however, suggesting not only what might be unique about the latest Venezuelan instance of the genre but also why, in this instance, things went so awry. Immediately after mentioning the intimate gifts sent to the generals, the letter says: "The image of courage that once we had of Venezuelan generals has nowadays altogether vanished and we simply imagine them in the presidential palace, Miraflores, or in the president's residence, La Casona, parading their multicolored panties."[11] There is something excessive, is there not, about the image of these middle-aged generals parading their multicolored panties in the public space and in full view of their president? Surely panties are meant not for such serial exposure but to be demurely worn close to the body and out of public view. Also, curiously anticipating in its very seriality the panties' serialized TV transmission, in Aure's mediatized imaginings not only are the generals' panties serially laid in row after row of scantily clad generals but all come in different colors. Blue, orange, violet, pink . . . I can only imagine the delicate commercial transactions in which the mysterious senders of the panties engaged in order to avoid overlaps, making sure that the color of every panty differed, however subtly or minutely, from the rest. Not a mean task, considering that, as it turned out, no fewer than 140 different panties were sent to the generals, so that simply to grasp the color spectrum induces vertigo.

One final oddity in the passage concerns the usage of the Spanish word *desfilando*, which I translate "parading." In Spanish *desfilar* means both "to march," what the military does, and "to parade" or display something in the presence of some significant other or others. Thus, for example, in a fashion or a military parade either models or army personnel march in front of an audience while parading their couturier designs or their uniforms and weapons before an audience. Interestingly, in Aure's passage the generals do not parade *in* panties but are, rather, parading *their* panties before the President. The construction is so odd in Spanish that I believe it betrays intention on the part of the writer. By imagining the generals parading not *in* panties but *their* panties, the writer reduces the generals' bodies to the status of mannequins, arranged in rows to display what is truly important: namely, the multicolored panties serially displayed on the generals' bodies as waiting to be bought by customers in a clothing store. In sum, a radical desubjectification is added to a no less radical commodification of the body, to which the intended feminization of the letter's addressees is surely not indifferent.

I cannot think of anything farther removed from the auratic depth that I imagine intrinsic to the earlier panties episodes as public instances of private debasement, and thus necessarily sparing graphic details that would break that privacy open, than the intense graphicality, even the exhibitionism of Aure's commodified imaginings. I can easily envisage, some twenty or thirty years ago, a high military personage from any country being overcome by shame as he opens, in the chiaroscuro of his public office, a box containing the anonymous gift of a translucent, delicately vulnerable panty.[12] By contrast to the recent Venezuelan affair, the social efficacy of the whole episode would reside in the public presumption of secrecy, not on serialized exposure, and on the swirling of rumors about an unavailable and invisible chamber of power where an ominous reversal and defilement is thought to take place. In these earlier episodes, at least part of the efficacy of the panties depends on their ability to provoke in private a catastrophic reversal, collapsing all distinctions and separation between gazing male subjects and gazed-at feminine objects, or between public and private spaces, while violently returning the generals' bodies to a stage that presumably they had left behind. As in some fantasy scenarios where the onset of male adolescent sexuality is ambivalently played out against the embracing phantasm of the mother's body, through this gift of feminine panties the generals are once again brought in dangerous proximity to the mother. Yet this time the repetition does not harbor detachment but rather is a dreaded return that leaves the generals paddling in sticky maternal stuff.[13] I bring up all this Freudian imagery, whatever its merits may be, simply to make salient how well it fits the closed economy of the patriarchal subject of modernity, which, as Lacoue-Labarthe and Nancy insist, occludes the nonsubjective "wider stage" of inscription that antedates the subject, as well as to underscore how far removed both this imagery and probably also this subject are from the recent Venezuelan incident.[14]

A few days after the publication of Aure's letter, military intelligence broke into his residence and took him into custody, on the accusation of "offending, insulting, and despising the armed forces."[15] After thirty-six hours in detention, at the request of both the nation's attorney general and the Defensoría del Pueblo, who insisted that the military had no jurisdiction over a civilian,[16] and in the wake of spirited protests from several public instances, including NGOs and other civil rights organizations, Aure was freed. Amid such widespread criticism of the armed forces, Minister Hurtado decided to call his fateful press conference. It was in this mediatized context, after justifying Aure's detention on the grounds of his suspected involvement in the affair (Why did he mention panties and not, for example, "brassieres or men's underwear," given that, before his letter, all official references were only to "intimate garments"?), that the General produced his colored panties, out of a box presumably containing the remaining 139.[17]

In the wake of this mediatized exposure, all hell broke loose, both in the press and in the media, and innumerable jokes started to circulate in the streets. For a while, a pandemonium of discordant voices crowded the public space, some high pitched and strident, others grave and ponderous, most comically deflating. One journalist hinted at the reasons for the universal hilarity when he spoke of the incident as "the first time ever in the history of Venezuelan TV that panties and epaulets came together on the screen."[18]

The juxtaposition was seen as so outrageously incongruous that in its wake any gravitas and majesty that the Prime Minister General had ever claimed for himself thoroughly dissipated. Like a balloon, such claims deflated in sight of everyone, amid general laughter. One weekly magazine from Caracas chose General Hurtado as that week's looser "for a press conference that will pass into the history of Venezuelan humor." For its probable victims, this laughter threatened to engulf everything the General had ever touched or

FIGURE 3 Caricature by UGO from *El Nacional*, January 13, 2001, featuring a general in women's underwear.

FIGURE 4 "The panties affair has allowed us to observe the great 'importance' that a general loses when not wearing his uniform. (Caricature by Weil, *TalCual*, January 12, 2001.)

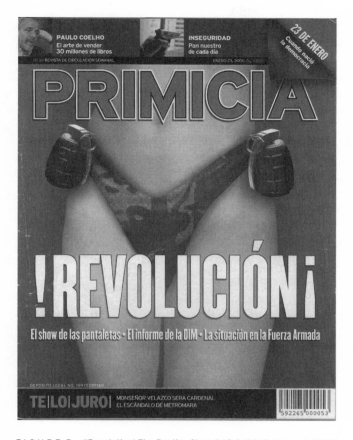

FIGURE 5   "Revolution! The Panties Show." (*Primicia*, February 1, 2001.)

been in contact with. To begin with, the entire armed forces, which he publicly represented, now stood exposed in the media as good only for handling a rather fragile opponent. Even more threatening, however, was the fact that, because of the regime's militarism, President Chávez himself, along with the entire regime, risked dissolving in this corrosive laughter. Indeed, the media event was seen as so damaging for everyone and everything concerned that one political commentator wondered why the prime minister had been so reckless as to appear before the cameras in such a dubious company without first having listened to the advice of an expert in image management.[19]

As with the surrealist montage of an umbrella and a sewing machine on a dissecting table, the mediatized coupling of epaulets and panties aroused such surprise and hilarity in part because their public juxtaposition troubled the boundaries between domains that not only are customarily kept separate but whose very identities depend on such strict demarcation, as the gendered identity and auratic authority of the public domain of the state are largely contingent upon its being demarcated from the domain of privacy and feminine sexuality alluringly evoked in women's lingerie ads, or the corporate identity of the armed forces as the state's means for the monopolistic control of violence is still, in many places, made contingent upon the exclusion of women. For one dangerous moment, the televised spectacle of a single, lightly colored panty held in the Defense Prime Minister's right hand put all such identities publicly under erasure. By triggering all kinds of funny, wild associations playing on the motifs of the generals' uncertain gendered identities and unabashed transvestism, the media event briefly made the army's claims to masculine purity and virility appear rather foolish.

It would be easy to pile up example after example from the Venezuelan press, many of a feminist bent, that in one way or another betray awareness of the high stakes involved in the whole panties episode. In general, the multicolored panties' ability to trouble established identities and boundaries was largely contingent on their serialized exposure in the electronic media, already foreshadowed in Aure's mediatized imaginings. In other words, their efficacy was contingent on their value as exposition, not, as in the earlier panties episodes, on any public assumption of secrecy. Drawn into the open from the private niches where modernist sensibilities had confined them, the panties, in their serialized reproduction in both the media and the mediatized imaginings of some of the regime's opponents, were unleashed in public space. There they took on a life of their own as mobile signs drifting across the public surfaces of the nation. Hitherto repressed in the domains of privacy, the panties' commodity lineage was sharply brought out by such mediatized exposure. Spread across the nation's public surfaces, their sedimented significance as quintessential tokens of privacy subverted institutionally established boundaries, among them those of the state, which trembled at the public sight of the general's multi-colored panties.

Two examples drawn from the Venezuelan press eloquently illustrate how, on the one hand, the panties' new life focused public awareness on their status as commodities, and, on the other, this very publicity entailed a breaking open, with unpredictable consequences, of the private sphere where heretofore panties had alluringly glowed. In one, a dreamily mournful piece written for the literary supplement of one of the two main local newspapers, after stating that "intimate garments hound us in the darkness," its writer mulls over the reasons why, lately, Caracas's advertisers have "resorted to the intimacy of closed spaces," especially to the walls of the metro, as preferred public sites for the outdoor advertising of women's lingerie. Unproblematically assuming a male gaze as the advertisements' target, he explains that "lust is reserved for obscurity." Interpellated "amidst the nocturnal buzz of the trains" by "the anonymous voice from that gigantic body" unexpectedly stretched out on the neon-lit billboard, the masculine passer-by is catapulted out of the "urban scene" and into the "very center of her bed." Such a rewarding fantasy is, however, frustrated by the recent media event, concerning which he says:

we have been abruptly coaxed out of the darkness like fish lifted on an invisible line. They take away from us the secret passages and the reveries to which all self-respecting passers-by succumb. . . . There are those who wish to bring the garments to the surface, denying the night in which they are surrounded and enveloped. . . . A solitary garment has emerged from the catacombs to be hung from a pen or a pencil, where, to our shame, it oscillates before the world's astonished gaze.[20]

Under such a crude glare, the panties' repressed life as commodities also comes into focus. In another, outrageously funny piece from about the same time, two other journalists, in a joint article, propose that, rather than take it so much to heart, the army should rejoice at the aggregate monetary value represented by the no fewer than 140 multicolored panties sent by mail to the generals over the past few weeks. They then go on to enumerate different possible models—Panty, Dental Floss, Boxer, Sash, Turtle Neck, Touché—insisting that, paradoxically, the smaller the item, the more expensive it is. Given their impression that what General Hurtado flashed at the cameras was a "tiny tanga," they find it safe to assume that the army has recently come into a nice sum of money. Switching tone, the journalists hint that perhaps the true reason the Defense Ministry is so upset is "the panties' nationality." Most of the panties that circulate in the Venezuelan market, whether smuggled or legally imported, come from neighboring Colombia, where lingerie figures among the 10 leading export items, with annual sales of 10.6 million dollars. In view of this situation "the gift may have constituted an unforgivable intrusion from neighbors in the internal affairs of the Bolivarian Republic of Venezuela." The moral that the authors extract from the whole affair is "that behind every panty always hides a serious matter."[21]

The serious matter hidden behind the alluring presence of the panties as tokens of intimacy is nothing less than their status as both commodities and mediatized images within an expanding, anonymous realm of ceaseless circulation and mobility resilient to any attempts at closure, whether by the state or by any other totalizing instance. No matter how briefly, what the *pantaletazo* explosively brought into public awareness, hence its subversive potential, is that more and more, as Nancy puts it, the givenness of being "is given to us as meaning . . . that is, in turn, its own circulation—and we are this circulation."[22] For a brief interval, the explosion of multicolored panties opened up a gap through which being intruded into public awareness as an "explosion of presence" that "is the spacing of meaning, spacing as meaning and circulation."[23] From "presence to presence," this circulation is carried in all directions—for example, here, across the boundaries of the nation-state, which the migrant, multicultural panties infiltrate by means legal and illegal—by touches among things, dead or alive, animate or inanimate: "stones, plants, nails, gods, . . . humans,"[24] and now, also, multicolored panties. The in-betweenness that arises every time two or more entities or things touch one another does not amount to any connective tissue that could lend itself to the beautiful sublation of

Subió cotización de pantaletas

El regalo recibido por las Fuerzas Armadas podría llegar a Bs. 7 millones.
Entre las marcas preferidas están las colombianas, pero entran de contrabando

Andrés Urbáez
Delia Meneses

El general Eliécer Hurtado Soucre no debería tomarse tan a pecho el obsequio de 140 pantaletas, de variados colores, que le han hecho supuestos subversivos desestabilizadores a las Fuerza Armada Nacional. Antes bien, debería considerar que sumando el valor del regalo contenido en los múltiples sobres que, de manera parcial, mostró en su rueda de prensa, este podría alcanzar los siete millones de bolívares.

Si los generales recibieron una pantaleta Touché, es posible que les haya tocado un regalo de 50 mil bolívares. El valor también depende del modelo.

Paradójicamente, mientras más pequeña la prenda, más cara. Así, si los generales recibieron un mayor número de las llamadas "hilo", es posible que el obsequio haya sido más costoso que si, en cambio, les tocó las "cuello tortuga". Bien mirado el ejemplar mostrado en cámaras por el ministro se aprecia una diminuta tanga.

PRENDA DE VALOR

Parte del enfado ministerial puede deberse a la nacionalidad de las pantaleticas. Desde hace no poco tiempo, la mayoría de las pantaletas que utilizan las venezolanas son importadas a Venezuela desde Colombia, por lo que el obsequio podría constituir una intrusión imperdonable de los vecinos en los asuntos internos de la República Bolivariana de Venezuela.

Por otra parte, un porcentaje importante de estas importaciones se hace de manera ilegal, por la vía del contrabando, a causa de la negligencia de los encargados de vigilar los límites fronterizos, lo que constituye una comprensible causa de molestia en predios castrenses.

De hecho, en el intercambio comercial binacional, la ropa interior constituye uno de los rubros más transados. En el Boletín de Comercio Exterior publicado por la Dirección de Impuestos y Aduanas Nacionales colombiano, correspondiente al lapso enero-septiembre del 2000, el rubro "sostenes y sus partes, incluso de punto" aparece entre los 10 principales productos de exportación hacia Venezuela, representando un monto de 10,6 millones de dólares, un incremento de 53%, con respecto a 1999. Venezuela es, después de Estados Unidos, el principal destino para las exportaciones colombianas.

Lo único que demuestra todo este caso es que detrás de toda pantaleta se esconde, siempre, un asunto de fondo.

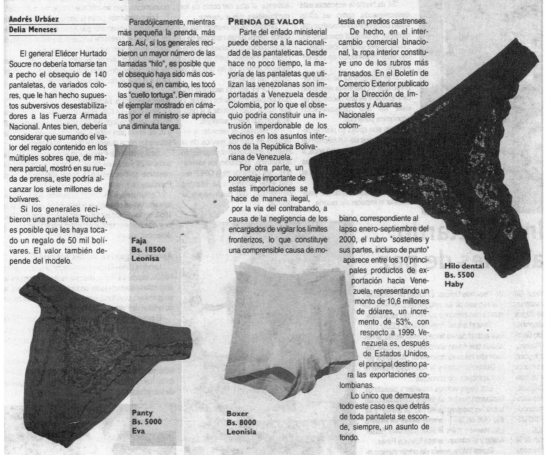

Faja
Bs. 18500
Leonisa

Hilo dental
Bs. 5500
Haby

Panty
Bs. 5000
Eva

Boxer
Bs. 8000
Leonisia

FIGURE 6   Humorous article in *TalCual*, January 22, 2001, entitled "The Prices of Panties Went Up," concerning the different models of panties supposedly received by the army.

everything into one or another higher-order instance or totality. Rather, it is precisely because its "law . . . is separation"[25] that this touch of circulation opens up, in all possible directions, unprecedented space-times: for instance, the unprecedented space-time opened up by the touch, in front of the cameras, between the (touché?) colored panty and the right hand of the general.

The Chávez regime came to power in December 1998 as the result of general elections, which Lieutenant Colonel Hugo Chávez Frías surprisingly won by a devastating margin. One of the leaders of a clandestine cell within the army, Chávez had, in 1992, led a failed left-wing coup against the then democratically elected government. Permeated by a fundamentalist nationalist ideology, from the start Chávez's secret organization, the MBR200, sought to regenerate the nation's decay by returning it to the teachings of its founding fathers, especially those of Simón Bolívar, father of the fatherland. Such an impulse to regeneration is already discernible in the fraternal oath that, in a mythical moment of foundation, presumably gave birth to the organization. Sworn before a sacred tree that is one of the telluric emblems of the nation, such an oath amounts to a striking instance of the "politics of friendship" that Derrida has recently deconstructed. In it the nation's very soil, along with its putatively autochthonous people and founding ancestors, are all summoned to co-presence through a performative that asserts a mystical "bond between the political and autochthonous consanguinity." In sum, the organization's founding oath is "the place of fraternization as the symbolic bond alleging the repetition of a genetic tie."[26]

Since the establishment of the regime, this political theology has run an extraordinary course. Characterized by a radical constitutionalism, the regime aims at nothing less than founding anew the entire people/nation, along with its main domains, institutions, and authorities. Armed with a newly approved Constitution, this project makes constant appeals to the originating powers of the sovereign people. It is not, however, these powers but the unifying will of the nation's dead founding hero, Bolívar, that the regime's political theology identifies as the source of the totalizing energies on which the official project draws. As I argue elsewhere, it is largely on account of his symbolic status in the nation's political imaginary as Rousseauean Great Legislator and People's Delegate that the regime's political theology puts Bolivar in charge of healing the nation's fractures by once again uniting the nation in an inclusive totality, needless to say, through the ventriloquizing agency of President Chávez.[27] Although a series of innovations may be discerned, some registering the intensely globalized times, along with this ventriloquism, the regime's political theology is anything but new. In many ways, it is a citation of a theologico-political formation that, repeatedly recycled throughout the nation's history, goes back to the founding of the country some two hundred years ago in the two decades of unimaginable violence that followed Venezuela's declaration of independence in 1811.

It is surely not irrelevant that the kind of political theology that concerns me here posits the nation as a matter of absolute, radical beginnings, claiming a radical break with the colonial past. To make a long story short, it all has to do with the Spanish king's awesome disappearance some two hundred years ago and the catastrophic consequences that followed. Among these were the collapse of the entire colonial order, with its articulated orders and estates, now bereft of the kingly "thing" that had glued it together, and the freeing of mimetic subjects from corporate niches as the colony crumbled.[28] The colonial order could be described as a well-oiled machine for reducing mimesis to codified identity. To put it in Lacoue-Labarthe's terms, with the collapse of this order into "terrifying instability . . . mimesis" returned "to regain its powers."[29] In an exorbitant mimetic expropriation of the panoply of hegemonic roles and identities, the new subalterns sought to fill the postcolonial spaces now made vacant and flattened—flattened because, although in reconfigured ways some of the hierarchies and partitions of old were still precariously in place, in principle, at least, the new democratic syntax that emerged in the king's wake symbolically rendered postcolonial space as a flat, horizontal domain of abstract exchangeability among autonomous, interchangeable individuals.

It was these flattened spaces that, amidst an unstoppable circulation of masks in which all government capsized, the subalterns now filled with a homicidal metonymic slippage "from one term to the next,"[30] bent not just on killing the whites but on stealing their identities. Hence all the anxieties about imitation that are voiced in the writings of the founding fathers and in the archives from the moment of independence. A kind of "modernity from below," confronted with this maelstrom of torn bodies and stolen identities, the founding fathers unsurprisingly saw their task as being to create the nation from scratch, since, like their Jacobin predecessors, it ws indeed from scratch or from the crowd's violent mimesis that they had to proceed. Hence all the emphasis on the nation's absolute, radical beginnings in Venezuela's and Latin America's other foundational charters, which these tribunes envisaged as tools to mould or create the nation ex nihilo as the exclusive aftereffect of the law enshrined in the Constitution.[31] In its abstract universality, only the law could provide a fitting mirror where, as bearers of equality, the postcolonial crowds could see themselves reflected as the homogeneous people of a nation. It was a matter, in other words, of arresting through reflection the crowd's lateral mimetic flight by holding up to them the mirror of the law as allegedly expressing their latent "general will."[32]

To be effective, however, the law needs to be enunciated. Therefore the founding fathers monumentalized themselves as representatives of the law, or, what amounted to the same, of the people's "general will" on the stage of the polity, so as at least temporarily to stop the postcolonial masses in their tracks by asking them to focus on and identify with these tribunes' words and gestures on stage as on that which, deep within their hearts yet already enshrined in the text of the Constitution, everyone presumably shared, namely, the "general will." Given the Rousseauean quality of the nation's beginnings, its distinctively Jacobin origins, such a putatively shared "will," amounting to the nation's law, is close to the definition of what the "nation" was. Theatrical through and through, such tribunal performances required that the domain of political representation be sealed off from "society" so as to be constituted as a (bourgeois) theater where, as on a stage, the claims of the Jacobin tribunes to represent the new nation could be sustained. Where but in such an enclosed space can re-presentation or the representative relation, instituting a radical demarcation between a theatrical "inside" and an excluded "outside," thrive? As Lyotard and others argue, only in such a well-demarcated theatrical space is it at all possible for any entity enduringly to re-present one or more absent ones.[33] Nothing was more urgent for the founding fathers than to erect such a sealed representational domain so as to constitute themselves as the representatives of the nation left outside its walls.[34]

Over time, such efforts crystallized in *monumental governmentality*, which I describe elsewhere.[35] Brought about by a wide range of discursive and nondiscursive practices, from historiography and the theater to civic rituals and various forms of domestic and public bodily training, for over two hundred years, since the time of independence, such monumental governmentality has been sculpting the voices, gestures, expressions, and overall bodily demeanor of the nation's tribunes, so that, appropriately monumentalized, these "tribunes" can "speak" the law to their assembled audiences from the raised stage of the polity, thereby making them, after the fact, into the nation's sovereign that was supposed to be there all along. Such *après-coup* performatives, though incessantly repeated, eventually fail. Because of tensions between the universal and the particular *and* the aporetic nature of the "general will," republican audiences eventually vacate the scenes of interpellation contrived for their benefit, once again becoming republican crowds. No matter how much they try to constitute themselves as impossible sites for reconciling the universal and the particular, thus submitting to the hyperbolic frenzy of "dancing Jacobins" that, I argue, is endemic to the continent's populism, Venezuela's and Latin America's other "tribunes" eventually lose their audiences. Vacating the republican theater through any crack available, such audiences eventually leave these tribunes gesticulating in an empty theater.

As that happens, once again the "terrorizing instability" of the origin returns as crowds resume the lateral mimetic flight from which the tribune's monumentalized yet dancing performances had temporarily wrested them.[36] If, as Lacoue-Labarthe and Nancy have argued, ours is an age of the "retreat" of the theologico-political as the withdrawal of any communal figure of identification,[37] then, as the preceding scenario suggests, since independence Latin America has lived such a withdrawal as a chronic, catastrophic occurrence. All of which is to say that, rather than "biopolitics" succeeding "politics" or, to stay with Foucault, a "society of discipline" one predicated on "sovereignty,"[38] with all the horror and promise involved, in Venezuela, at least, no such means of pacifying the republican crowds became widely available. Instead, in Venezuela (and Latin America generally) the politics of exemplarity of an early republicanism crystallized in a form of monumental governmentality, and as a result the whole continent froze in an inaugural moment of modernity: that when a Jacobin tribune or one of his present-day populist successors addresses his or her popular audiences, swelling with republican sentiment, just across the stage.

Yet, nearly since independence, there has been, at least in Venezuela, one way available to temporarily arrest, or at least slow down, the inevitable dispersal of the general will imminent in the scenario to which I have just alluded. I am referring to the "Bolívar" way, whereby, monumentalized as a Great Legislator and as such symbolically made into a foreigner with no stakes in the local order of things, Bolívar "returns" once again to totalize "society" or a nation about to blow up into a myriad disparate fragments.[39] Unlike the "horizontal" tribunal prosthesis, which is subject to endless metonymic decay, Bolívar is what, following Geoffrey Bennington,[40] I call a "vertical prosthesis" of the general will, that is, a thoroughly transcendent, theological means of supplementing this will's originary lack of self-presence by totalizing it, thus temporarily arresting the general will's fall into the singularity of its cases, of the sovereign into the individual's maddeningly conflicting (mimetic) desires.[41] Given that it came to power in the wake of an acute economic crisis and an even more acute crisis in political representation, where all available representative instances, especially the political parties, were thoroughly delegitimized, it is not surprising that from the beginning the Chávez regime appealed to Bolívar with a vengeance. Considering the combined centrifugal forces of a huge international debt, the unemployment and poverty that had followed an IMF-imposed program of structural adjustment, a colossal crisis in the nation's banking system, and the alarming rate at which capital kept flying out of Venezuela, such a widespread appeal is hardly surprising. After all, it is during such times that Bolívar "returns" in order, precisely, symbolically to suture the nation.

From the beginning, Chávez employed an extraordinarily aggressive rhetoric as a weapon to dismantle the last remnants of the ancien régime, and his and his regime's constant use of "Bolívar" as a rallying cry and point of identification immediately paid handsome dividends. After coming to power in December 1998, Chávez rapidly called for a referendum to elect delegates for a Constituent Assembly charged with drafting a new Constitution. Claiming originary powers and staffed by an overwhelming majority of Chávez supporters, this assembly from the beginning went beyond its electoral mandate, declaring itself to be "the sole legitimate authority of the land," dissolving the opposition-controlled Congress, and assuming the right "to fire judges, majors, and governors."[42] From Congress to the judiciary, after a series of elections won in quick succession, in little over a year the regime was firmly in control of all the main institutions of the Venezuelan state. By the end of 2000, just two years after assuming power, it seemed as if, with the exception of the national media, which were controlled by powerful private interests, nothing stood in the way of the regime's revolutionary project of state recentralization. Whatever elements of an organized opposition may have survived did not seem to amount to much. These were the *escuálidos*, or "emaciated," whom Chávez incessantly mocked in his weekly radio program *Aló Presidente*. In sum, with a few annoying blips, at the time everything suggested that the regime's project of tightly collecting the entire nation around the ancestral figure of Bolívar via the ventriloquizing agency of Chávez, thereby refashioning it in the dead hero's image, had succeeded. As if drawing on a "mystical foundation,"[43] the realization of the old theological dream of a "common existence" entirely defined by the state form, by "the decisions and reach of sovereignty," seemed at hand.[44]

And then, as if out of thin air, in April 2002 the opposition staged a huge rally in the streets of Caracas. Since then, things have drastically changed, in a political landscape marked by a string of momentous events: a frustrated coup d'état by radicalized right-wing sectors after nineteen people had been shot dead and more than a hundred wounded in the streets of Caracas during an opposition rally, an incident still shrouded in mystery; a series of huge rallies and counter-rallies, staged either successively or simultaneously by the opposition and the followers of the regime; a vast business and workers' strike that brought the national oil industry to a halt and that may have wrecked the local economy for years to come; and, most recently, sanctioned by the Constitution, a huge effort by the opposition to collect signatures calling for a referendum to decide upon Chávez's stay in power, a possibility that the beleaguered regime tried unsuccessfully to prevent by declaring null more than a million of the over three million signatures collected. What has happened? What can possibly explain that in a little over a year the escuálidos, or "emaciated," of yesterday have become the relatively plump characters of today? Moreover, how are we to account for the suddenness of the transformation?

To begin with, this recovery did not mean that two well-defined, consolidated enemies or antagonists now confront each other on the political stage, so that eventually one will displace or cannibalize the other. Things are more porous and complicated than that. For one thing, the supposed victories of the opposition are at best pyrrhic. Every one of its actions either immediately met with a commensurate reaction from the forces of the regime or, especially in the case of the opposition's most ambitious initiatives, eventually dissipated into a chorus of discordant voices, images, and happenings in the face of a regime that, like the living dead, keeps coming back. Such a string of faux pas by the opposition could not but be subject to considerable laughter. The sort of laughter that concerns me here is not at all choosy about its targets. It does not, for example, single out some special entity or entities as objects of mockery and derision while neatly sparing the rest. True, the Chávez regime was primarily affected by the panties incident, its hollow principles momentarily deflated by thunderous, omnivorous laughter. Such contagious laughter has, however, a tendency to lead a life of its own, rippling out from the throats of those who laugh first to resonate in the proliferating and ever-widening gaps in the polity. It acts like a corrosive solvent and tends to become endemic. Eventually, everything and everyone concerned is overcome by it, including those who laughed first but, amid the growing laughter, regardless of what they try or do, eventually are left looking silly or somewhat ridiculous on the political stage.

Such laughter does not affect this or that political party, personality, or entity: rather, it afflicts the political as such. From left to right, and right down the middle, such comprehensive laughter envelops the entire political topography, delivering it over to a scary, unfathomable otherness. Regardless of any informing ideologies, or of the actors' desires, worries, or programmatic intentions, it eventually overtakes every site where the political is at all enunciated, leaving them all encompassed by a troubling, advancing obscurity, the night of not knowing where every (postpolitical?) initiative is being tried out. It may even be said that this laughter is the anonymous sound that the theologico-political makes in its irrepressible retreat. In Venezuela it is so prevalent than one local caricaturist goes so far as to suggest that, if prices keep going down, "comicalness" may eventually overtake oil as the nation's most profitable export item.[45] Moreover, in Venezuela such laughter affects the opposition perhaps even more than it does the government. Bereft of any credible leadership, organization, or program and affected even more than the regime by the institutional debacle of recent years, the opposition, in its urgency to get rid of Chávez, often abruptly descends from the heights of tragedy into the lowly bosom of comedy. If the circumstances were not the uncertain mess that they presently are, it might even be said that he who laughs last laughs best, with the government uttering the final, deafening laughter before the sorry spectacle of the opposition's many trials and tribulations.

FIGURE 7 "If oil prices continue to go down, we will have to increase exports in humor." (Caricature by Rayma, *El Universal*, November 6, 2001.)

As one cartoon intimates, however, under the prevailing circumstances it is impossible once and for all to award the prize for the greatest laughingstock. Laughter is a great equalizer, democratically afflicting all the contending parties. Saying to whom the last laugh will go is not just hard to decide, it is radically undecidable. As a result, even if often the regime laughs even harder than the opposition does, this does not mean that it achieves any more success in quashing or subduing its opponents. As in some virulent replay of the nation's implosive origins, the more that the regime exerts overwhelming force at some point or another in the political landscape, trying to bring everything within its grasp, the more, in their lateral flight, such things elude its sovereign grasp. Much like the electronically reproduced panties of the general, things fly in all directions, briefly touching each other to form fleeting figures where, amidst tumbling monuments, the face of the sovereign state does not catch its reflection. In a political landscape increasingly crisscrossed by NGOs, manifold media images, Internet messages, cellular phone commu-

FIGURE 8 "At the moment, I don't know whether I work for the leaders of the government or for those of the opposition." (Caricature by Rayma, *El Universal*, May 8, 2004.)

nications, and human rights organizations, where some of the traditional functions of the nation-state are increasingly taken over by a congeries of transnational instances, such as granting agencies, financial organizations, multinational corporations, or multi-state political corporations, the local state finds it increasingly difficult to do its job. Paradoxical as it may seem, a tell-tale sign of such difficulty is the regime's inflationary use of the "Bolívar" sign, which, as concerned local historians insist, can only bring about its devaluation.

It is not, then, surprising that, to borrow a revealing expression from a local analyst, in this era of "diminished sovereignties" Venezuela's political antagonists have found themselves mired in an endless, exhausting war of attrition, since, as he insightfully suggests, every time these actors make a move they must look behind their backs and seek approval from the relevant international instance or instances.[46] The very notion of a sovereign decision falls victim to such a play of mirrors, increasingly incapable, as all decisions are, of attaining the kind of self-identity and consistency that, by totalizing the political field while designating one or more enemies significant, renders them sovereign. There are enough indications that, lately, in Venezuela something may be seriously amiss with the sort of political theology that, explicitly or implicitly, makes national sovereignty the obverse of a delineation of the nation's enemies. Take, for example, the nervousness with which the Chávez regime keeps vertiginously reiterating its founding constitutional gesture, serially to found anew all imaginable aspects of the nation—from the parliament, to worker and neighborhood organizations, to the university and a string of other similar institutions. Some local commentators have even spoken of the "constitutional franchise" that the regime has extended to the most varied personalities and groups in their efforts incessantly to found everything anew. Or the jitteriness with which President Chávez, in his self-appointed role as media mogul, keeps adding new political enemies to a list that already including oligarchs, the Church, landlords, and the media, without that list in any way congealing into the single enemy of the people that thinkers like Ernesto Laclau have identified as populism's unsurpassable other, the necessary foil against which this sort of regime establishes and defines itself. In this regard, even if the Chávez regime is often viewed as populist, so far it has failed to achieve that which, according to Laclau, is distinctive of populism—as, I might add, of a singularly virulent version of the Schmittian logic of the political—namely, the ability to totalize the social field or, what amounts to the same, the field of the popular by designating an imaginary enemy.[47]

Little wonder if, in such weak, or *debole*, circumstances, as Vattimo might have it, *fuerza*, or "force," is one of the most insistent demands of the agents. Much like the members of the Venezuelan María Lionza possession cult—who for hours chant to achieve "force" while, paradoxically, seeing it dissipate along an endless, metonymic chain of spirits, from "Vikings" and "Barbarians" to Mexican movie stars, by whom they are routinely possessed—so Venezuelan political subjects see their force dissipate just as they ask for more.[48] Considering what has been said of the Hegelian State as "the thought of the social totality" and, as such, "the final truth of the entire regime of subjectivity," it may very well be that the very notion of the subject is now at stake.[49]

I will conclude with an image that brings home the kind of unhomely explosion of privacy into public space that Roland Barthes called the "publicity of the private" and that in Venezuela today is playing such havoc with the nation and the regime's political theology.[50] Just when references to the multicolored panties were petering out in the media, an article in one of the major national newspapers cast a strange light on the entire episode. In it a local humorist describes repeatedly arriving home to traces of a rebellion that all of his domestic objects, especially his clothing, have staged during his absence. He finds hints of underwear, socks, or shirts having fallen in love and taken off together, clothing lying everywhere as if exhausted from the wild party of the night before, or buttons nibbled like crackers on top of little dishes in the living room. And everywhere his most beloved public gala dressing, tuxedos and the like, is entirely covered over with feminine underwear, especially panties, in a scene resembling an "orgy of cloth, synthetic textiles, 100% cotton and silk." After swearing that his "clothing is alive," the author ends his piece with a vision of this clothing folding him into a luggage and, much "like a departing sock," sending him packing.[51]

By contrast to the sense of subjective destitution in our earlier dreamily mournful example, in which the panties no longer hound the masculine subject in the dark, here such a subject is well on the way to becoming an object. What was salient in that earlier scene was the subject's intense shame as the solitary panty migrated from the alluring domains of privacy into the glare of public exposure. In thus shaming the masculine subject, such a migration by the object disclosed how much the domains of publicity and the political thrive on suppressed viscerality, a point that Michael Warner has effectively made.[52] Regardless of all of their claims to universalism and neutrality, the self-identity and perpetuation of such domains of unmarked masculinity require that they be rigorously sealed off from the realms of privacy and sexuality. This means that the boundaries between the public and the private must be carefully policed, so that no unauthorized passage occurs. Hence the subversiveness of the panty's solitary emergence from the catacombs of privacy, a passage sharply revealing how, in Venezuela at least, sexuality remains the unavowed truth of the subject.[53] It also brings out how much the perpetuation of the kind of political theology addressed here requires that masculine subjects take their pleasures privately, so that they may be freed to declare publicly the sober truths of the state.

Not that these neat demarcations have ever quite worked in Venezuela, where the sexualization of the political and the politicization of privacy have long been the norm. Yet, largely due to globalization and the media, the increasingly promiscuous quid pro quos and exchanges between the public and the private threaten to wreck any residual integrity that such domains might formerly have possessed, a possibility that in Venezuela arrives amid growing violence. In an equivocal space—where public statues "walk,"[54] mysteriously migrating from their assigned sites to reappear in the city's most unexpected places; the president sings on national TV or hands over recipes for combatting the common cold or improving one's diet; open-air public art, escalators, and rails surreptitiously yet constantly shrink, their materials chipped away by a nocturnal army of anonymous "workers" and perhaps later redeployed as components in, for example, a variety of domestic appliances; or retired army officers march against the government with their military uniforms neatly and somewhat quaintly arranged on hangers so as to circumvent a prohibition on wearing them[55]—in such a space all denominations falter. About to become something else, common names (and what they stand for) totter at some unfathomable edge, undermined by uncertainty. To call such a space "public" is to indulge in a misnomer, considering how, increasingly, virtually everything within this space is irrepressibly (and glaringly) contaminated by its canonical opposite. Something similar can be said of the "private." As every inside yields to an unmasterable outside, more and more this domain's most intimate souvenirs, mementos, and fetishes are unceremoniously delivered to a faceless, borderless exterior. What becomes of these in such a mobile, hybrid terrain—neither straightforwardly "public" nor unabashedly "private"—cannot safely be predicted. Indeed, what subjects, politics, entities, or identities might still be possible is a question that, amid growing violence, must remain up for grabs.

In this undecidably utopian or dystopian scenario lurks a possibility other than random violence: that of a freeing of all objects from the subjective regimes, the subject-object dialectics to which objects have hitherto been subjected. If in one of my earlier examples the solitary panty summons the subject sexually in the dark only to deflate him,[56] the scenario in which all domestic objects, including panties, rebel may have less to do with sex per se than with what the Italian philosopher Mario Perniola recently called the "sex appeal of the inorganic" or Nancy calls "the touch,"[57] a condition in which, as objects among objects, former subjects, sent packing from their homes, enter an oceanic realm where the theologico-political "retreats," while a touch circulates among stones, stars, generals, or multicolored panties, multiplying the gaps through which laughter erupts.

Postscript, August 2005

Since the first version of this paper, written now some three years ago, much water has gone under the proverbial bridge in Venezuela. While at the time things appeared undecided, with the main political opponents locked in a war of attrition with an unforeseeable outcome, the situation today is quite different. Against the expectations of many, on August 15, 2004, the Chávez camp won, by a large margin, a referendum called by the opposition to revoke its mandate. The regime now seems firmly in control of virtually all the nation's main political institutions and levers of power. Taking advantage of the disarray that the largely unexpected defeat inflicted upon its adversaries and making effective use of its precarious majority in parliament, following the referendum the regime swiftly went on the offensive. Rapidly it passed a series of laws and undertook initiatives that both expanded and consolidated its grip over such crucial institutions as the armed forces, the oil industry, the central bank, and the judiciary, while criminalizing many forms of protest that heretofore opposition forces had used to great effect in their efforts to bring down the government. To give one crucial example, though previously the privately owned media had been one of the main weapons wielded by the regime's opponents in their crusade against Chávez, in the months after the referendum a law was passed by the government-controlled parliament that, insidiously, encourages self-censorship by the media. Given the apparent consolidation of the regime, its seeming solidity and power, it should come as no surprise that I regarded publishing this paper, originally written under quite different circumstances, with some trepidation.[58] Indeed, how is one to accommodate the notion of a politico-theological retreat and the image (and the reality) of a regime triumphantly basking "in the shadow of the liberator,"[59] that is, in the rich afterglow of a Bolívarian political theology? The difficulties are compounded when one considers that such an apotheosis unfolds against the backdrop of a floundering and thoroughly disarticulated opposition.

A total of six months of fieldwork in Venezuela, conducted in two stages, in 2005 and in the fall of 2004, has convinced me that realities on the ground are less of a piece than reporting in the global media might suggest, hence, that the image of an all-powerful regime secure in its totalizing reach is overblown. I cannot here go into all the reasons that sustain my conclusions—or, for that matter, account for the regime's ability so thoroughly to quash its opponents under circumstances that, like the ones addressed in this paper, should have rendered such an outcome unlikely. Doing this would mean writing a new and different paper, something that I leave for another occasion. Suffice it to say two things. One, that the notion of a retreating, or even imploding political theology in principle does not preclude the possibility of relatively unstable configurations of force contingently coming into being, in which one or more political actors temporarily gain the upper hand against some crushed opponent(s). In retrospect, such a result was something of a foregone conclusion in Venezuela, where, with a few notable exceptions, an opposition narcissistically locked in the mantralike recitation of a few sound bytes—"civil society," "democracy," and the like—showed itself singularly unable to address the aspirations, predicaments, and grievances of the vast majority of the population. And this in a country that, during the last few decades, has experienced dramatically increased rates of poverty, amid the near-total collapse of its representative institutions. Little wonder if, confronted with a regime that, whatever its shortcomings, came into power and defines itself precisely in reference to such dire circumstances, the opposition floundered.[60] Best exemplified in the campaign slogan *Chávez vete ya!* ("Chávez, go now!"), insistently heard in opposition rallies during the closing days of the campaign for the referendum, the shortcomings of a media-driven politics have perhaps never been so glaring.

Which does not mean, contrary to what some local commentators think, that the overall significance of the recent Venezuelan events comes down to the notion of a deficit of politics that can simply be remedied by injecting more of the same into the activities and programs of the opposition. Without clarifying how, in the present circumstances, doing so would be possible, these analysts draw from the opposition's defeat in the referendum the lesson that more politics is needed if in the future this sector is to have a fighting chance against Chávez. In other words, according to them, any opposition comeback is contingent upon the ability of this sector to shake off its dependency upon the media and to get on with the reconstitution of the political parties and other representative instances that have been washed out by the catastrophic socio-political upheavals of recent years. While there is some truth in this—certainly, the opposition will somehow have to improve upon that (political) score if it wishes to leave its mark on the future course of local events—the question still remains as to how doing so would be possible in Venezuela today. That is, how, beyond wishful thinking, would it be possible effectively to reconstitute political instances that the drift of events has perhaps rendered hopelessly ineffectual?

With this, I arrive at my second point concerning what has transpired in Venezuela since the referendum, one that is considerably more disturbing than just saying that politics was lacking so as to better pave the way for the return of the (theologico-)political. It is, after all, not politics but its retreat—that is, the retreat of the theologico-political—that, in such events, is ultimately at stake. While the excess of the regime's politics, if that is what it was, bought it some time, allowing it momentarily to prevail over its politically deficient opponents, abundant signs suggest how fragile such an outcome really is, how much, in other words, the present configuration of forces is an equilibrium that is highly volatile, largely because, no matter how numerically overbearing it may be,[61] the victory of the regime in the referendum has not stopped the hemorrhage of politico-theological substance with which, after a relatively brief honeymoon in the beginning, it has ceaselessly been afflicted.

The distinction Louis Marin makes between "force" and "power" may be useful here. If, for Marin, "force" results in the struggle to the death among contending parties right now, "power" is the ability of some signs to hold such force in reserve, thereby introducing a necessary delay, which somewhat defuses the devastations of the present.[62] While at present the Chávez regime enjoys considerable amounts of "force," as measured by its success in the polls or its ability to control virtually all of the nation's main economic and political institutions over and against the will and desires of its opponents, the same cannot be said of its capacity to accumulate "power." Bedeviled by a rosary of calamitous ills that instantly reverberate in the media,[63] from rampant corruption to faltering government-sponsored programs for the poor, a failing oil industry, and proliferating conflicts among its rank and file, the regime seems constitutionally unable to capitalize on its successes so as enduringly to totalize the social and political field in reference to some

424

significant enemy or enemies. This bespeaks a retreating political theology that, accelerated by globalization and the media, no amount of inflammatory rhetoric on the part of Chávez or other spokespersons of the regime can suffice to slow down. As in the case of the Defense Prime Minister and his panties, such forceful rhetoric and sovereign acts seem caught in a horizontal drift in which any auratic height they seek to secure for themselves fatefully dissipates.

To put all this in terms that slightly stretch Marin's, yet I believe are compatible with his, in spite of its avowedly politico-theological inclinations, the regime seems fatefully unable to gather enough political-theological signs around itself so as to translate, not just the destructively divisive play of forces in the present, but also its gaps, oblivions, and lacunae into an enduring socio-political constellation. As a result, no sooner does it quench a fire than another flares up with equal or greater intensity, a situation still rife with laughter, even if nowadays somewhat frozen or contained by the regime's official spectacle of might. Thus the regime goes on, from one fire to the next, in a disconcerting drift that, if not somehow halted (but how, given the difficulties of adopting any unabashedly authoritarian solutions under the current global and local preconditions?), cannot but endanger, if not its survival, then its overall, long-term revolutionary design. No wonder that lately the term *implosion* has repeatedly surfaced in the writings of a series of local political analysts in reference to the regime's current predicament. In a recent newspaper article, one of these insightfully summarized the situation by pointing out that, curiously enough, given how much it has overcome any overt challenges to its rule, "the recurrent trait of this government has been its incapacity to consolidate the dominion over institutions that were already regarded as definitively controlled."[64] Another way of saying this is that, as in a dream, at least according to some indications, the more the government assumes complete control of any particular institution or domain, the more things slip out of its hands, any illusion of control rapidly dissolving into thin air.

I will end this postscript with an event that recently filled all the main Venezuelan media and that I believe illustrates much of what I have been saying. This is the assassination in the streets of Caracas, on November 18, 2004, of Danilo Anderson, the state prosecutor in charge of bringing to trial all those accused of participating in the failed coup attempt against Chávez of April 2002. He was killed by a car-bomb, and, if one is to judge from the government's immediate response, it is hard to come up with any other incident that so instantly raised local political temperatures. A series of rallies was swiftly organized, which, besides blaming the oligarchy, attempted to canonize Anderson as the first martyr of the revolution. The government went so far as to rapidly commission a series of busts of the young prosecutor, which were to be placed in all official institutions to honor his memory. Such an effervescent state of affairs did not last long. Before the official pathos had any chance to settle into anything like a collective state of grief and rightful indignation, news started to percolate in the media that suggested an altogether different scenario than the one the regime wished to impress on the public: namely, that, rather than being a virtuous martyr, Anderson might have been simply a crook, the hub of a clandestine network of blackmailers secretly extorting great sums of money from the accused in exchange for having their names removed from the list of those allegedly involved in the plot to bring Chávez down. In light of these accusations, the reasons for Anderson's killing would have been chrematistic rather than political, his assassination ordered by some big banker or some other fat cat unwilling to pick up the tab the accusers were putting on his or her head.

Whatever truth there may be in these revelations—and some argument concerning their merit is still going on in Venezuela—the fact is that, ever since they started to emerge, the official commemoration has stopped dead in its tracks, with a stony silence filling the void that the receding official rhetoric has left behind—so dead, in fact, that, at least according to some media reporting, all the busts that at a considerable cost the government had commissioned in order to commemorate Anderson were rapidly and surreptitiously melted down.[65] Even if they had just been paid for but not yet actually made, or simply put aside until some hypothetical vindication of Anderson takes place,[66] the fact is that at least for now the dead prosecutor has dropped far down the list of topics that the government wants to see addressed in public. I will leave the reader with this image of melting official busts, which, even if not factually true, in light of all that I have said about Venezuela's monumental governmentality and the role of statuary therein is, at the very least, poetically so.[67] The state's inability even to lastingly canonize its martyrs is a paradoxical monument or reminder of the continuous retreat of the political theological in Venezuela today.

The Figure of the Abducted Woman

The Citizen as Sexed

Veena Das

Writing in 1994, Gyanendra Pandey, the well-known historian of the subaltern, took the neglect of the Partition in the social sciences and in Indian public culture to be a symptom of a deep malaise.[1] Historical writing in India, he argued, was singularly uninterested in the popular construction of Partition, the trauma it produced, and the sharp division between Hindus, Muslims, and Sikhs it left behind. He attributed this blindness to the fact that the historian's craft has never been particularly comfortable with such matters as "the horror of Partition, the anguish and sorrow, pain and brutality of the 'riots' of 1946–47."[2] The analytical move in Indian historiography, Pandey further argued, was to assimilate the Partition as an event in the intersecting histories of the British Empire and Indian nation, which left little place for recounting the experience of the event for ordinary people.

In recent years, many writers, including Pandey himself, have produced impressive testimonial literature on the Partition in an attempt to bring ordinary people's experiences into the story of this event.[3] Corresponding to this development is the scholarly effort to show how anxiety about Hindu-Muslim relations, especially about the sexuality and purity of women, circulated in the public domain in the late nineteenth and early twentieth centuries in the popular forms of cartoons, comic strips, posters and vernacular tracts. Part of the burden of this essay is to try to understand how public anxieties about sexuality and purity might have created the grounds on which the figure of the violated woman became an important mobilizing point for reinstating the nation as a "pure" and masculine space.[4] At stake, then, is not simply the question of "silence" but also that of the genres that enabled speech and gave it the forms it took. It is instructive that there has been no attempt to memorialize the Partition in the form of national monuments or museums. No attempt was made, for that matter, to use the

427

legal instruments of trials or public hearings to allow stories of mass rape and murder to be made public or to offer a promise of justice to the persons violated.[5] There was no dramatic enactment of "putting history on trial," which Shoshana Felman sees as a particular feature of twentieth-century collective traumas.[6] Instead, the trope of horror was deployed to open up space for speech in the formal setting of the Constituent Assembly debates and in popular culture. It gave the recounting of the event a tonality of rumor.

Consider, first, the numbers and magnitudes as these are cited in official reports. As Pandey argues, numbers are not offered here in the sober register of a judicial tribunal or a bureaucratic report based upon careful collection of data—rather, they function as gestures toward the enormity of the violence. I might add that this mode of reporting was not peculiar to the Partition. It was part of a wider bureaucratic genre, which used numbers and magnitudes to attribute all kinds of "passions," such as panic, incredulity, or barbarity, to the populace when faced with a crisis, such as an epidemic or a riot—thus constructing the state as a rational guarantor of order. We shall see how the figure of the abducted woman allowed the state to construct "order" as essentially an attribute of the masculine nation, so that the counterpart of the social contract becomes the sexual contract, in which women as sexual and reproductive beings are placed within the domestic sphere, under the control of the "right" kinds of men.

The Abducted Woman in the Imaginary of the Masculine Nation

How did the gendering of suffering allow a discourse of the nation to emerge at the time of the Partition? What precise work does the figure of the abducted woman and her recovery do in instituting the relation between the social contract and the sexual contract at the advent of the nation? I will take the figure of the abducted woman as it circulated in political debates soon after the Partition and ask how this was anchored to earlier figures available through myth, story, and forms of print culture in the early-twentieth-century discourse on this figure. How was the figure of the abducted woman transfigured to institute a social contract that created the nation as a masculine nation?

One of the earliest accounts of the violence of the Partition renders the story as follows:

> The great upheaval that shook India from one end to the other during a period of about fifteen months commencing with August 16, 1946, was an event of unprecedented magnitude and horror. History has not known a fratricidal war of such dimensions in which human hatred and bestial passions were degraded to the levels witnessed during the dark epoch when religious frenzy, taking the shape of a hideous monster, stalked through the cities, towns, and countryside, taking a toll of half a million innocent lives. Decrepit old men, defenseless women, helpless young chil-

dren, infants in arms, by the thousand were brutally done to death by Muslim, Hindu, and Sikh fanatics. Destruction and looting of property, kidnapping and ravishing of women, unspeakable atrocities, and indescribable inhumanities, were perpetrated in the name of religion and patriotism.[7]

The Government of India set up a Fact Finding Organization to investigate the communal violence. Although the files containing these reports were never made public, G. D. Khosla, who was a justice of the Punjab High Court and was in charge of producing this report, interviewed liaison officers of the Military Evacuation Organization, which had been in charge of the large-scale evacuation of minorities from one dominion to another. Based on this information, Khosla put the figures of loss of life in the warring communities altogether at between 200,000 and 250,000, and the number of women who were raped and abducted on both sides at close to 100,000. Support for this is provided by information given in the context of legislative debates in the Constituent Assembly, where it was stated on December 15, 1949, that 33,000 Hindu or Sikh women had been abducted by Muslims and that the Pakistan government had claimed that 50,000 Muslim women had been abducted by Hindu or Sikh men.

Joint efforts made by the Governments of India and Pakistan to recover abducted women and restore them to their relatives led to the recovery of a large number of women from both territories. It was stated, on behalf of the government in the Constituent Assembly on December 15, 1949, that 12,000 women had been recovered in India and 6,000 in Pakistan. The figures given by Khosla on the basis of the Fact Finding Organization were that 12,000 Hindu or Sikh women had been recovered from the Punjab and the Frontier regions in Pakistan, and 8,000 Muslim women from the provinces of the Indian Punjab.

As I said earlier, Pandey makes the subtle point that numbers function here not as forms of reporting, in which we can read bureaucratic logic, but rather as elements of rumor, in which the very magnitudes serve to signal both excess and specificity. He argues that in the official reports, as well as in reports by leading political figures, the circulation of such stories served to transform hearsay into "truth."[8] What Pandey misses, it seems to me, is that the magnitudes established that violence was taking place in a state of exception, which, in turn, opened the way to authorize the state to undertake extraordinary measures by appeals to the state of exception. I argue that the circulation of the figure of the abducted woman, with its associated imagery of social disorder as sexual disorder, created the conditions of possibility in which the state could be instituted as essentially a social contract between *men* charged with keeping male violence against women in abeyance. Thus, the story about abduction and recovery acts as a foundational event that authorizes a particular relation between social contract and sexual contract— the former being a contract between men to institute the political and the latter, the agreement to place women within the home under the authority of the husband/father figure. The "foundational" event inaugurating the nation then is anchored in the imaginary of the abduction of women, which signaled a state of disorder, since it dismantled the orderly exchange of women. The state of war, akin to the Hobbesian state of nature, comes to be defined as one in which Hindus and Muslims are engaged in mutual warfare over the control of sexually and reproductively active women. The origin of the state is then located in the rightful reinstating of proper kinship by recovering women from the other side. If one prefers to put it in the terminology of Lévi-Strauss, one could say that the state reinstates the correct matrimonial dialogue among men.[9] The foundational event of the inauguration of the state brings something new into existence, but the event does not come from nowhere—it is anchored in imagery that already haunts Hindu-Muslim relations.

The Discourse of the State

A conscious policy with regard to abducted women and children born of sexual and reproductive violence was initiated in the Indian National Congress on November 23 and 24, 1946, when delegates expressed grave concern about the fate of women who were violated during the communal riots.[10] Dr. Rajendra Prasad, who was later to become the first president of independent India, moved a resolution that received wide support from prominent leaders of the Congress Party, including Jawaharlal Nehru. This is how it was worded:

> The Congress views with pain, horror, and anxiety the tragedies of Calcutta, in East Bengal, in Bihar, and in some parts of Meerut district. The acts of brutality committed on men, women, and children fill every decent person with shame and humiliation. These new developments in communal strife are different from any previous disturbances and have involved murders on a mass scale as also mass conversions enforced at the point of a dagger, abduction and violation of women, and forcible marriage.

The operative part of the resolution then states the obligation of the Congress Party toward such women:

> The immediate problem is to produce a sense of security and rehabilitate homes and villages which have been broken up and destroyed. Women who have been abducted and forcibly married must be restored to their homes. Mass conversions which have taken place forcibly have no significance or validity, and the people affected by them should be given every opportunity to return to their homes and the life of their choice.

This resolution was adopted in November 1946. The situation, however, worsened after March 1947. Thus three weeks after India and Pakistan achieved their independence as separate states, representatives of both dominions met on September 3, 1947, and agreed that steps should be taken to recover and restore abducted persons. Both sides pronounced themselves against recognition of forced marriages.

The All India Congress Committee met in the middle of November and reiterated that "During these disorders large numbers of women have been abducted on either side and there have been forcible conversions on a large scale. No civilized people can recognize such conversions, and there is nothing more heinous than abduction of women. Every effort, therefore, must be made to restore women to their original homes, with the co-operation of the Governments concerned."

An inter-dominion conference followed the Congress session, at which the two dominions agreed to the steps to be taken to recover abducted women and children. The implementation of these decisions led to the recovery of large number of women from both sides—between December 1947 and July 1948, 9,362 women were reported to have been recovered in India and 5,510 in Pakistan. At this time, both governments worked to create a legal instrument for the work of recovery. As a result, appropriate ordinances were issued in India on January 31, 1948, and in Pakistan in May 1948. The ordinance in India was renewed in June 1949. In December 1949, the Constituent Assembly passed the Abducted Persons (Recovery and Restoration) Act, 1949, which remained in force until October 31, 1951.

These events point to the manner in which the state took cognizance of the sexual and reproductive violence directed against women. To some extent this obligation was generated by the expectations of the populations affected. The devastated refugees, who had lost their homes, their families, and their possessions in the bloody riots and were housed in refugee camps in Delhi, thought it appropriate to address the leaders of Independent India as recipients of their laments. In this manner, they were not only creating a framework for the state legitimately to take up the task of recovering abducted women but also discovering that claiming entitlement over women of one's own community could be seen as a legitimate affair of the state.

Khosla reports that refugees in distress made loud and frantic appeals to all departments of the government. Pandit Nehru received letters in the months of August, September, and October seeking his personal intervention to save a relative or to recover a piece of property or a precious possession left behind in Pakistan. People wrote accusing him of enjoying a victory that had been won at the expense of the Hindus of West Punjab. Khosla quotes a letter addressed to Pandit Nehru by a retired schoolmaster, who states that "What has compelled me to write this to you is the fact that in casting about my eyes I fail to find anyone in the world except you who can help me in my calamity." How was the nation to respond to such investment of both despair and hope in its leaders?

The Question of National Honor

For the new nation-state of India, the question of the recovery of abducted women and children then became a matter of national honor. There was a repeated demand, publicly enunciated, that the state take upon itself responsibility for such recovery. The new government in India tried to reassure the people of its intentions in this regard via several press notes. Rajashree Ghosh, for instance, cites a press note, published in *The Statesman* on November 4, 1947, that "forced conversions and forced marriages will not be recognized and that women and girls who have been abducted must be restored to their families."[12] Various administrative mechanisms for the recovery of women were operative in the early stages of the recovery operations, including the Office of the Deputy High Commissioner, the Military Evacuation Organization, the chief liaison officer and the Organization for Recovering Abducted Women. They were made up of social workers and other officials. All these efforts culminated in an Inter-Dominion Agreement signed on September 3, 1947, and finally in the Abducted Persons (Recovery and Restoration) Act of 1949. Through these legal instruments, each country provided facilities to the other for conducting search and rescue operations. Both agreed that the exchange of women should be equal in number. Wide powers were given to the police to conduct the work of recovery, and arrangements were made for housing the recovered women in transitory camps. Disputed cases were to be referred to a joint tribunal for final settlement.

In terms of procedure, the Indian government set up Search and Service Bureaus in cities in the Punjab where missing women had been reported. This information was then passed on to the relevant authorities, and a search for these women and children was mounted. The Indian government enlisted the help of women volunteers, especially those with a Gandhian background, to help in the recovery process. Prominent among these women were Mridula Sarabhai, Rameshwari Nehru, and Kamlabehn Patel. In her memoirs of this period, Kamlabehn Patel reports that "In those days it wasn't prudent to trust any male, not even policemen, as far as the safety of women was concerned."[13] Several transit camps were set up, such as the Gangaram Hospital Camp in Lahore and Gandhi Vanita Ashram in Amritsar. Kamlabehn herself was in charge of the transit camp in Lahore. Recovered women and children were then transferred to India or Pakistan, under police escort. A woman or child who was claimed by a close relative in India could be handed over to the relative only at Jullundher, in the presence of a magistrate.

Taken at face value, it would appear that the norms of honor in the order of the family and the order of the state were mutually supportive. The families with whom I worked relate generalized stories praising heroic sacrifices made by women, but to speak in the first person about the facts of abduction and rape was not easy.[14] Normalcy was seen as the restoration of women "to their families." Men appear here as heads of households rather than as individuals sprung from the earth, as in the famous mushroom analogy with which Hobbes conceptualizes the makers of the social contract. It is my contention that once the problem of abducted women moved from the order of the family to the order of the state (as in the demand for legislation), it sanctified a sexual contract as the counterpart of the social contract by creating a new legal category of "abducted person" (one applicable, however, only to women and children) within the regulatory power of the state. An alliance was forged between social work as a profession and the state as *parens patriae.* This rigidified the official kinship norms of purity and honor by transforming them into the law of the state.

The discussion in the Constituent Assembly concerning the Abducted Persons (Recovery and Restoration) Act 1949 focused on three issues. The first was the definition of a civilized government, and especially the responsibility of the state to women against whom violence had been unleashed. The second was the definition of an abducted person, including the rights of women abducted by men. The third was the rights of children born of "wrong" sexual unions and the obligations of the state toward them. The connecting thread between these three issues is the notion of national honor and the preservation of the purity of the population, through which the sexual contract is made grounds for a social contract that institutes the nation as a masculine nation.

In introducing the bill, Shri N. Gopalaswami Ayyangar, a distinguished lawyer then minister of transport, stated that, concerning experiences associated with the Partition, "most of us will have to hang our heads down in shame." He went on to say that "among the many brutalities and outrages which vitiated the atmosphere . . . none touched so low a depth of moral depravity as these mass abductions of women on both sides . . . those of us who think of civilized government and want to conduct the government on civilized lines should feel ashamed."[15]

As is clear from this statement, the state distanced itself from the "depths of moral depravity" that the population had shown and took upon itself the task of establishing a civilized government. Part of the definition of this civilized government was not only to recover women defined by the new nation as "our" women but also to restore to the opposite side "their" women. The interest in women was premised, however, upon their definition not as citizens but as sexual and reproductive beings. In the recovery of women held by the "other" side, what was at stake was the honor of the nation, because women as sexual and reproductive beings were being forcibly held. This was explicit in the demands, made by several members, that not only should the recovery of women on both sides be more or less equal but also women in their reproductive years should be "recovered." Shri Gopalaswami Ayyangar referred to this criticism, saying that several critics alleged that "while in India we have recovered women of all ages and so forth, in Pakistan they had recovered for us only old women or little children." He went on to counter this criticism by citing figures to show that the distribution by age of recovered women from both dominions was, in fact, roughly equal. Of the total women recovered, he said, girls below the age of twelve from Pakistan and India were 45 percent and 35 percent respectively. In the age group between twelve and thirty-five years, the recovery was 49 percent in Pakistan and 59 percent in India, while the percentage drops to about 10 percent for women older than thirty-five years. This clearly shows that national honor was tied to regaining control over the sexual and reproductive functions of women. The social contract that would legitimate both nations was seen as one instituted by men, in which they would be capable of recovering their own places as heads of households by firmly placing the sexuality and reproductive powers of women within the family.

In fact, however, the figure of the abducted woman signals the impossibility of the social contract, because the sexual contract that would place men as heads of households (not as a matter of kinship but as matter *for the state)* was in jeopardy. Pandit Thakurdas Bhargava explicitly drew on this figure when he stated:

> You will remember, Sir, how when one Ellis was kidnapped by some Pathans the whole of Britain shook with anger and indignation and until she was returned Englishmen did not come to their senses. And we all know our own history, of what happened at the time of Shri Ram when Sita was abducted. Here, where thousands of girls are concerned, we cannot forget this. We can forget all the properties, we can forget every other thing, but this cannot be forgotten.[16]

Then there was the question of whether Muslim women needed to be returned to their families. It is interesting to note the particular tonality that creeps into Pandit Thakur Das Bhargava's statement: "I don't suggest for a moment that the abducted Muslim girls should be kept here because I believe that not only would it be good for them to be sent away but it is equally good for us to be rid of them. I don't want immorality to prosper in my country."

It is important to mark here that to be a citizen as a head of a household demands that men's own sexuality be disciplined, oriented to the women who have been placed "correctly" within the family, and that children who would claim citizenship be born of the right kind of union of men and women. I have elsewhere analyzed courtroom talk in the cases of rape in Indian courts of law to argue that "male desire" is construed as a natural need in the judicial discourse on rape, so that whenever the cultural and social constraints are removed, men are seen as falling into a state of nature in which they cannot control their appetite for sex. In an earlier paper, I argue that:

> it is male desire which is considered as "natural," hence "normal," and the female body as the natural site on which this desire is to be enacted. Women are not seen as desiring subjects in the rape law—as wives they do not have the right to withhold consent from their husbands, although the state invests its resources in protecting them from the desires of other men. Paradoxically, women defined in opposition to the wife or the chaste daughter, i.e. women of easy virtue, as the courts put it, also turn out to have no right to withhold consent. . . . A reading of female desire as

interpreted by the courts demonstrates that while men are seen to be acting out their "natural" urges when engaging in "illicit" sex, women who show any kind of desire outside the confines of marriage are immediately considered "loose." By escaping the confines of male-centered discourses of sexuality and alliance, these women are then castigated by becoming the objects of any kind of male desire. Rape is not a crime but is reduced to an act that she herself deserves or seeks.[17]

Clearly, deeply rooted assumptions about the husband/father figure continued in the juridical unconscious even when the figure of the abducted or raped woman appeared in the singular in postindependence India.

Let us consider next the question: Who is an abducted person? According to the bill, "An 'abducted person' means a male child under the age of sixteen years or a female of whatever age, who is, or immediately before the 1st day of March 1947 was, a Muslim and who, on or after that day, has become separated from his or her family, and is found to be living with or under the control of a non-Muslim individual or family, and in the latter case includes a child born to any such female after the said date."[18]

We shall take up later the question of children defined as "abducted" under the provisions of the bill. As for the women, it was clear that the bill failed to make any provision for ascertaining whether a woman wished to return to her original family or not. This question was raised by several members. The sharpest criticism came from Thakur Das Bhargava, who stated that: "You want to take away the rights of a major woman who has remained here after the partition. . . . My submission is that the law of nations is clear, the law of humanity is clear, the Indian penal Code is clear, the Constitution we have passed is clear, that you cannot force a woman who is above 18 to go back to Pakistan. This Bill offends against such a rule."

In addition to the manner in which the rights of a woman to decide her future course of action were taken away by the state in order to protect the honor and purity of the nation, there was also the question that the bill gave wide powers to the police to remove a woman forcibly if she came under the definition of an abducted woman under the clauses of the bill. This, as Shri Bhargava pointed out, took away the rights of habeas corpus from a person who was treated as an abducted person even if she were mistakenly so labeled.

When several members of the house pointed to increasing evidence that many women were refusing to go back to their original families and were practically coerced by social workers to return, Shrimati G. Durgabai, speaking on behalf of both the social workers and the women's movement, defended the social workers on the grounds that they knew best what the women's true preferences were. Shrimati Durgabai's statement is worth quoting in detail:

Questions are also asked: Since these women are married and settled here and have adjusted themselves to the new environment and to their new relatives here, is it desirable that we should force them to go back? It is also argued: These women who have been able to adjust themselves to their new surroundings are refusing to go back, and when they are settled, is it desirable that we should force them to go back? . . . These are the questions we have to answer. May I ask: Are they really happy? Is the reconciliation true? Can there be a permanent reconciliation in such cases? Is it not out of helplessness, there being no alternative that the woman consents or is forced to enter into that sort of alliance with a person who is no more than the person who is a murderer of her very husband, her very father, or her very brother? Can she be really happy with that man? Even if there is reconciliation, is it permanent? Is this woman welcomed in the family of the abductor?

Paradoxically the authority of the woman social worker was used to silence the voice of the woman as subject, and to put upon her an obligation to *remember* that the abductor to whom she was now married was the murderer of her husband or her father. The disciplining of sentiment according to the demands of the state collapsed duty to the family and duty to the state. The women themselves seemed to have been caught in an impossible situation, where the obligation to maintain a narrative continuity with the past contradicted the ability to live in the present. At one place, Shrimati G. Durgabai herself testified to the apprehensions of women at the prospects of returning to their original homes:

> Sir, we the social workers who are closely associated with the work are confronted with many questions when we approach a woman. The women say "You have come to save us; you say you have come to take us back to our relatives. You tell us that our relatives are eagerly waiting to receive us. You do not know our society. It is hell. They will kill us. Therefore, do not send us back."

Yet at the same moment that these apprehensions were expressed, the authority of the social worker was established by the statement that "The social workers associated with this work know the psychology of these abducted recovered women fully well. They can testify to it that such a woman only welcomes an opportunity to get back to her own house." The refusal of many women to go back and the resistance that the social workers were encountering in the field was explained away by an attribution of false consciousness or a kind of misrecognition to the women. The appropriate sentiment in all such cases was coercively established as a desire for the original home that allowed men on both sides of the border to be instituting the social contract as *heads of households* in which women were "in their proper place."

Children and Reproductive Futures

We come now to the category of children defined as abducted. As stated earlier, the bill defined any child born to a woman after March 1, 1947, as an abducted person if its mother came under the definition of an abducted person. These, in short, were children born through "wrong" sexual unions. The discussion in the Constituent Assembly focused on the following issues. First, how were rights over a child to be distributed between the male and the female in terms of their relative contributions to the process of procreation? Second, what legal recognition was to be given to children whose parents were not considered to be legally married, since the bill held all forcible marriages to be null and void? Third, was there a contradiction between the legality established by the state and the customary norms of a community regarding the whole question of determining the legitimacy of a child? Finally, if only one parent was entitled in these cases to transmit filiation as a basis for establishing citizenship, was the relationship with the mother or with the father to be considered relevant for creating the necessary credentials for citizenship?

While there was no explicit enunciation of a theory of procreation and the relative contributions of the male and the female to the procreative process, analogies drawn from nature were sometimes used. Pandit Thakur Das Bhargava stated at one point, for instance, that he did not understand how a general rule could be formulated by which the child was to be handed over to the mother rather than the father:

> It takes only nine to ten months gestation during which the child has to remain in the mother's womb. . . . It should not be made a rule that in every case the child is to be given over as a matter of rule. It is something like the rule that when you plant a tree it grows on the ground; therefore the tree goes with the land and the fruit of the tree goes with the tree. A child is the fruit of the labour of two persons. There is no reason why the father should be deprived in each case. Why should we make this rule?

Analogies from nature, especially from the activities of agriculture or horticulture to conceptualize procreation, are part of the repertoire of ideas contained in Hindu texts and in the popular ideas regarding procreation.[19] Importantly, a theory about the "labour" of reproduction enters into the state's repertoire of ideas, even as it is articulated in opposition to the provisions of the bill. Although Srimati Durgabai did not pose the question in these terms, she questioned the rights of the male on the grounds that he was an abductor. Men who had forcibly abducted women, sold them, and used them for commercial purposes, she argued, could not claim rights over the children born to these women. In contrast to the earlier argument, Durgabai's interpretation would be that not the joint labor of a man and a woman but the plunder by men of women's bodies had created such a child. Hence, "What right has the abductor to keep the child? The child has to go with the mother."

Another member, Shri Brajeshwar Prasad, also evoked the notion that in nature there was no question of illegitimacy or legitimacy of a child, and that it was only the conventions of society which made children legitimate or illegitimate. In his words:

> Sir, I do not know how a child born of a man and a woman can ever become illegitimate. This is a notion I have not been able to grasp, but still knowing full well the attitude of the present Government, knowing full well the attitude of the Hindu society, we have to take the facts as they are and the illegitimate children if they are to live in India, they will remain as dogs, as beasts.

In the above discussion, it was clear that the question of the legitimacy or illegitimacy of the children was related to the fact that it was the provisions of the bill that had made all such unions, which may have started with abduction and ended with marriage, illegal and thus the children born to such unions illegitimate children. As one member (Shri Brajeshwar Prasad) put it, even if a natural attachment had developed between the abductor and the abducted woman, the law did not recognize such marriages. Therefore, a woman could continue to stay with her abductor "only as a prostitute and a concubine," while her children could remain in the country only as illegitimate children, who would be a "standing blot on Hindu society."[20]

A contradiction between state-defined legality and community-based legality was pointed out by Chaudhari Ranbir Singh, at least as he saw the matter, for he thought it would be a mockery to the country if children born to Muslim women were sent away on the grounds that they would be mistreated as illegitimate children here. "There is a general custom in our Punjab," he stated, "particularly in the community to which I and Sardar Bhupinder Singh Man belong, that, regardless of the religion or community of the woman one marries, the offspring is not regarded as illegitimate, and we give him an equal share." Clearly a wide variety of customary norms regarding children born to women through wrong sexual unions had existed. These were now standardized into a single law through which illegitimacy was defined. How are we to understand this moment as foundational in terms of the relation between the social contract and the sexual contract in defining the nation-state? I suggested earlier that the figure of the abducted woman had circulated in the late nineteenth and early twentieth centuries as a site of anxiety for defining the place of men as heads of households.[21] It is important to note that the question of a father's rights over his children after his conversion to another religion was not a new question—it had legal precedents. Whether a man who had converted to Christianity could continue to claim conjugal rights over his wife had been debated, for instance, before the colonial courts, as had the issue of whether a man's "natural" rights over his child overrode the dissolution of marriage after conversion. I have argued elsewhere that, while the courts were reluctant to apply English common law to these cases, arguing that the legal imagination must contend with people of one faith living under a political sovereign who owes allegiance to another faith, the general consensus was that the father's right could not be denied.[22] It now became possible to set aside the legal precedents on these questions and to take custody away from the father in the case of children born to women who had been forcibly possessed, precisely because the foundational event was located within an imagination of a state of emergency, when normal rules were set aside. In the next section, I will discuss these issues briefly, then conclude with the question: Why is the state interested in women as sexual and reproductive beings?

Anchoring the Figure of the Abducted Woman

Recent work on the nexus between ideas of sexuality, obscenity, and purity shows that images of lustful Muslim males and innocent Hindu women proliferated in the propaganda literature generated by reform Hindu movements such as the Arya Samaj and political organizations such as the Hindu Mahasabha and the Rashtriya Sevak Sangh.[23] Charu Gupta has recently marshaled impressive material from the vernacular tracts published in Uttar Pradesh in the late nineteenth and early twentieth centuries to show that mobilization of the Hindu community, especially by new forms of religio-political organizations such as the Arya Samaj and the Hindu Mahasabha, drew upon the image of the lustful Muslim as a threat to Hindu domesticity. Consider the following passage, which Gupta cites, from a speech delivered by Madan Mohan Malviya in 1923 on the subject of kidnapping:

> Hardly a day passes without our noticing a case or two of kidnapping of Hindu women and children by not only Muslim badmashes and goondas, but also by men of standing and means, who are supposed to be very highly connected. The worst feature of this evil is that Hindus do not stir themselves over the daylight robbery of national stock. . . . We are convinced that a regular propaganda is being carried on by the interested party for kidnapping Hindu women and children at different centers throughout the country. It is an open secret that Juma Masjids at Delhi and Lahore are being used as headquarters of these propagandists. . . . We must do away with this mischievous Muslim propaganda of kidnapping women and children.[24]

Reference to the lustful Muslim and the appeal to the innocence of Hindu women, who could easily be deceived by Muslim men, were plentiful. In some cases, the harshness of Hindu custom against widows was invoked to explain why Hindu women fell into the traps of seduction laid by wily Muslims. Gupta is surely correct in concluding that evocation of these fears provided an emotive basis for arguments in favor of Hindu "homogeneity and patriarchy."[25] I think we can go further, for the story of abduction has implications for the very staging of sovereignty, so that, when this story appears magnified at the time of the Partition, it becomes the foundational story of how the state is instituted and also its relation to patriarchy. It invites us to think the story of the imaginary institution of the state in Western theory from this perspective rather than the other way around.

In proposing this line of argument, obviously I do not see family simply as an institution located in the domain of the private but suggest that sovereignty continues to draw life from the family. The involvement of the state in the process of recovering women shows that, if men were to become ineffective in the control they exercise as heads of families, thus producing children from "wrong" sexual unions, then the state itself would be deprived of life. The figure of the abducted woman acquires salience because it posits the origin of the state not in the mythic state of nature but in "correct" relations between communities. Indeed, the *mis-en-scène* of nature itself is that of heads of households at war with other heads of households over control of the sexual and reproductive powers of women, rather than unattached "natural" men at war with each other. There is an uncanny address here to Lévi-Strauss's notion of the original state as one in which men are posited as relational beings and the exchange of women is the medium through which this relational state is achieved.[26] The disturbance of proper exchange then comes to be construed as a disturbance in the life of the state, robbing it of the sources from which it can draw life. Does this story, located at the juncture of the inauguration of the nation-state in India, tell us something about the nature of sovereignty itself?

In an acute analysis of the relation between fatherly authority and the possibility of a woman citizen, Mary Laura Severance argues that in Hobbes we find a predication of fatherly authority based on consent rather than something that is natural or originary, as was claimed by Sir Robert Filmer.[27] But, she notes, the consent of the family to be ruled by the father in effect neutralizes his power to kill. By grounding the power of the father in the consent of the family, Hobbes is able to draw a distinction between fatherly and sovereign authority as two distinct but artificial spheres. This is done, however, within the framework of the seventeenth-century doctrine that women are unfit for civil business and must be represented (or "concluded") by their husbands. The sexual contract and the social contract are, then, two separate realms. As Severance notes, however, the idea of the state of nature as being that in which every man is in a state of war with every other man should be modified to read that every *father*, as the head of the family, is at war with every other *father*. In her words, "the members of each individual family 'consent' not to the sovereign's but to the father's absolute rule; they are not parties to the 'contract' that brings the commonwealth into existence."[28] I would claim that this war of "fathers" is what we witness in the acts of abduction and rape. The state's commitment to the recovery of women is the acknowledgment of the authority of the father as the necessary foundation for the authority of the state. I find it useful to invoke Rousseau's analysis of the figure of the woman in the discussion of sovereignty in *Emile* to show that the notion of the sexed individual as the basis of the political is deeply linked to the idea of the life of the sovereign.[29]

As I have argued elsewhere, in Rousseau the figure of the woman is introduced not as the symmetrical opposite of the man but rather as the obligatory passage through which the man moves along the road to marriage, paternity, and citizenship.[30] While the scene of seduction is necessary for the pupil in *Emile* to be inserted into the social, he proves his capability to be a citizen by learning how to renounce the very lure of the woman that was his passage into sociality. The parable of Sophie, whom Emile must learn to love and through whom he must learn to overcome his fear of death, points to the close relation, for a man, between learning how to inhabit society through engagement with sex and how to become a good citizen by overcoming the fear of separation and death. It is worth pausing to reflect on this.

From Emile's journey into citizenship, we learn the multiple chains of signification into which the figure of Sophie is inserted. She is the chimera inserted into the text—a figure of seduction, the future mother of a family, and one through whom Emile learns that to be a good citizen is to overcome his fear of death by giving a law to the desires of his heart. Hence, she is seductress in the present, maternal in the future, and teacher of duty and code of conduct. Without her, he can overcome physical ills, but with her and then despite her, he will become a virtuous citizen. "When you become the head of a family, you are going to become a member of the state, and do you know what it is to be a member of the state? Do you know what government, laws, and fatherland are? *Do you know what the price is of your being permitted to live and for whom you ought to die*?"[31]

There are two thoughts here. The first is that, in order to be a citizen of the state, you must be the head of a household; the second is that you must know for whom you ought to die. For the woman, the duty of a citizen is confounded with her duty to her husband. A woman's comportment must be such that not only her husband but also his neighbors and friends must believe in her fidelity. When she gives her husband children who are not his own, we are told, she is false both to him and to them and her crime is *"not infidelity but treason."*[32] Thus, woman as seductress holds danger for the man, because she may use her powers of seduction to make the man too attached to life and thus unable to decipher who and what are worth dying for. In her role as mother, she may deprive him of being a proper head of a household by giving him counterfeit children. That this is treason and not infidelity shows how the mother, who was completely excluded as a figure of thought in Hobbes, comes to be incorporated into the duties of citizenship. For Rousseau, the individual, on whose consent political community is built, is, no doubt, a sexed individual, but the woman has the special role not only of introducing the man to forms of sociality but also of teaching him how to renounce his attachment to her in order to give life to the political community.[33]

Within this scheme, women's allegiance to the state is proved by their role as mothers in bearing legitimate children (recall the remark that the crime of bringing illegitimate children into the world is not infidelity but treason); and men learn to be good citizens by being prepared to die in order to give life to the sovereign. Once the individual is recognized as social because he is sexed, he is also recognized as mortal. In Rousseau, we see that man is said to receive life from the sovereign. Political community as population is dependent upon reproduction: thus, the citizen's desire to reproduce and to give the political community legitimate "natural" children attests to his investment of affect in the political community. A corollary is that a woman's infidelity is not only an offense against the family but also against the sovereignty of the state.

We can see now that the *mise-en-scène* of abduction and recovery places the state as the medium for reestablishing the authority of the husband/father. Only under conditions of ordered family life and legitimate reproduction can the sovereign draw life from the family. Gupta's work allows us to see that the earlier imagination of the Hindu woman as seduced or duped by the Muslim man is complemented by the idea that her attraction to Muslim practices is an offense against the patriarchal authority of the Hindu man, imagined within the scene of colonialism. Thus, for instance, Gupta gives examples from many vernacular tracts in which the practice of Hindu women praying to Muslim *pirs* (saints), a common religious practice of Hindus and Muslims alike, is construed as a betrayal of the Hindu man—a mocking of his potency. To my ears, these sound remarkably like the act of treason that Rousseau attributes to women who bring "wrong" children into the world. The following quote from a vernacular tract offers a particularly telling example:

> God believes in the worship of only one husband for women, but they pay service to Ghazi Mian for many years. . . . Where before Hindu women worshiped their husband for a lot of love and produced a child, today they leave their husband and go to the dead Ghazi Mian and at his defunct grave, ask for a child. It is not women but men who are to be blamed for this hateful act. Even when they are alive, instead of asking their wife to become a true *pativrata*,[34] they allow her to go to the dead grave of a Turk to ask for a child and become an infidel.[35]

I began this essay by juxtaposing the problem of the silence concerning the Partition with an excess of speech in the mode of rumor encountered not only in the popular imagination but also at the heart of official documentation of the event. my analysis takes the legal and administrative discourse concerning the abducted woman to be an important site for understanding how the social contract is grounded in a particular kind of sexual contract. In the trope of horror through which this space of (excess) enunciation and action opened up under the sign of the state, not only were the voices of women drowned out, but their suffering was recognized as relevant only for the inauguration of sovereignty. The repression of voice and what it is to recover it—not through speech generated in collecting oral history or in the process of psychotherapy but as part of an everyday life in which women give expression to their violation. I have tried to pursue this question in my larger work, where I suggest that in a world torn by violence it seems to be the task of women to attend to everyday life by looking after children, lighting the cooking hearth, containing hurts, and thus putting the world together stitch by stitch. It is to those gifts that I look for a picture of healing the world. How else are we to overcome the taint of the official discourses that could see the suffering of women who were abducted and violated, but only for establishing the correct order of the family and the State?

How to Recognize a Muslim When You See One

Western Secularism and the Politics of Conversion

Markha G. Valenta

> Whatever else the project of the Enlightenment may have created, it aspired to create persons who would, after the fact, have wished to become modern.
>
> —Arjun Appadurai

> And yet most individuals enter modernity rather as converts enter a new religion—as a consequence of forces beyond their control.
>
> —Talal Asad

> I think we lack a name around which a radical politics can take shape.
>
> —Simon Critchley

> Was du ererbt von deinen Vätern hast
> Erwirb es, um es zu besitzen.
>
> —Goethe

Prelude

One of the most dramatic aspects of the encounter between the West and Islam today is the urgency with which both are being driven to reexamine their most fundamental assumptions and worldviews—and to reinvent them. Striving, forced, fearing to live together, we are creating a new world, now, this very minute.

Yes, there is caricature, aversion, and fear; and yes, these sow the seeds for what has been imagined by some to be an epic "clash." So we speak of the West and of Islam, we write down these words, black on white, ink to paper. Yet this makes them no more real or true. Less so, if truth be told. The West and Islam encompass histories too varied, too porous, too centrif-

ugal to be coherent powers. They lack that which war requires: a central intelligence, an authorized authority that we follow as One—as a Holy Body—into the vortex of History. That isn't to say that we might not yet create them, or that they might not clash. But for the moment it is precisely the mythic nature of the battle that makes it so appealing to the fantasies of our politicians and lesser commentators, while it is only a minor drama relative to the so much more grand drama of invention that is taking place. An invention of collaboration, through difference. What is at stake is the possibility of imagining a role for the power and practice of religion, of belief, of fundamental conviction within democracy, rather than beyond or against it. Not just our own religion, our own conviction, but also another's. And not just democracy at home, but democracy across the world. It means making minorities of us all, risking my conviction as it touches yours. Which is to make the world ours. This requires all our ingenuity and dedication, for the answers we already have fail us now. Private belief, blessed nation, and sacred state. Beyond these, in our passions, as in democracy, beats life. And it is up to us to say what kind of life it will be.

The Problem

The problem is not the veil itself. For more than a thousand years, Muslims, Christians, and Jews engaged each other (and before them Persians, Greeks, and Romans) without its becoming an issue. Only an odd hundred years ago, in the second decade of Europe's colonization of the Islamic worlds, did this simple piece of cloth on a woman's head become a primary site of attack and counterattack. Since then, the veil has been an astoundingly pregnant source of social, political, religious, and judicial conflict. The question is: Why?

The first point to note is that the veil's prominence in the encounter between Islam and the West depends on a fundamental collaboration among all those involved: whatever their standpoint, however opposed and far removed from each other, all have agreed that this is to be a primary site at which to take their stand. Precisely the intensity and expansiveness of the conflict means that the veil—the veiled woman—is a point at which the many Muslim and Western worlds stand especially close to each other, touch each other. The veil is a medium of translation, communicating power and resistance, desire and otherness to each other, from West to East and East to West, from faction to faction, across a gap of difference. So there is much at stake.

The second point to note is that the discussion of the veil within the West's public space, which is the space that concerns me in this essay—our media, governments, judiciaries, scholarship, and arts—takes place in terms that are themselves largely secularist and modern.[1] So the operative epistemological and ontological concepts are those of the individual, self-expression, culture, choice, identity, independence, and so forth. Though the veil is closely imbricated with religious experience and belief, the concepts and concerns of religion—the question of the relations among the human, the sacred, and the divine; the question of our spiritual life; even that of finding a haven, a sanctuary, a spring of hope and beauty to challenge the mundane world of consumerism, sexual saturation, inequality, injustice, and violence—are repressed. Man's relation to man squeezes out the question of man's relation to her ultimate horizon, to the final terms of her being. And the question of human agency is reduced to a nitty-gritty materialism, a petty, dreary tug-of-war between man and man barely able to imagine anything else, least of all the fullness—whether we call it God, or desire, or our infinite responsibility to the other—whose call to us has been there before we ourselves were. Overflowing with norms, the debate achingly struggles for an ethics, a means of relating self to other, far beyond its grasp. As do I.

The problem, then, is not so much the debate's modernism or secularism per se as the fact that it is an impoverished modernism, a hollow secularism. Once, perhaps, these were ideological constellations, processes, ways of life whose vision—however faulty—was universal in the sense of striving to bind together self and world; but now, in the contemporary debate about Islam in the West, they most often are terms of division. They make the other wish not so much, in the words of Arjun Appadurai, to have become modern as to convince her of modernity and secularism's limits, their provincialism, their inability to grasp and enfold this other life, my life. Most fundamentally, the power of these two—as of any faith system—once lay (and perhaps still lies) in their ability to imagine and project human unity and redemption through sacrifice and commitment, including unto death if necessary[2]—as, for example, the myth of "the white man's burden," for all its vicious and violent arrogance, did for modern colonialism. If profit and brute power were the obvious base motives for colonialism, sacrifice—the risking of life and limb in the name of "King" and "God" and "civilization"—is what gave colonialism its golden aura: what allowed the West to sanctify its violence, as well as its greed. In this sense, you might say that the failing point of colonialism was the moment at which indigenous resistance made colonialism a true burden, unprofitable, brought home the sacrifice and killed the romance. So, too, the modernism and secularism of the contemporary West—whether that of "fortress Europe" or "benevolently" expansionist America—is one in retreat from the universal, from the true universalism that dares to imagine sacrificing the self for the other, for the world. The only modernism and secularism capable of rallying the world, including the world within the West, to its banner today would be one capable of imagining itself taking on the veil—if only for a moment, a day, a lifetime. Belief, to be powerful, must be a risk of faith as much as its buttressing.

The third point to note is that the debate about the veil is the debate about Islam in the West; that the debate about Islam is the debate about the future of the Western nation-state; and that at the heart of the debate about the nation-state is the question of the nature of the West and its democracy.[3] Each of these—the veil, Islam, the nation-state, the West, and democracy—certainly constitutes a discrete terrain of its own, with its own set of distinct themes, discourses, and histories. But at the same time they are continually made to flow through each other; almost invariably any discussion of one generates references to all the others. So the veil is not only the meeting point between East and West, is not only a border phenomenon, but has made its way to the very heart of contemporary Western history and identity. Today the West cannot answer the question of its nature and its future without going through Islam. In this sense, the West has already been as "Islamicized" as the Islamic world has been Westernized.

The fourth point to note is the centrality of territoriality to this discussion. In fact, this is the heart of the matter. The most fundamental socio-political trend of modernity, as the historian Charles Maier argues, has been the control of space as the primary principle not only for organizing and regulating power but also for our very imagination of the world.[4] The role and conception of space over past centuries has, of course, been far from universally consistent. Yet since the sixteenth century societies across the world have increasingly linked both their identity and their security to bounded space—by force as much as by choice. More specifically, since the mid-nineteenth century, new technologies have mandated and enabled a rescaling of territoriality, all too often through civil war, in the course of which decentralized (proto-)national regimes transformed themselves into increasingly centralized, coherent nation-states. From Meiji Japan to Canada, from Argentina to the states of Italy, and from Thailand to the German Confederation, this development has been both too global and too simultaneous to be understood (though it often still is) as a matter of diffusion, as the gradual spread of the European nation-state model to the rest of the world. Instead, what we see is that the combined effect of new technologies, human migrations, and the spread of revolutionary ideologies led to a comprehensive disruption of rural hierarchies: in China and Japan, in the Americas, and in Europe itself "the land was escaping the control of its traditional rulers."[5] Responses of the elites varied, of course, but the most successful were those where, as in Meiji Japan, old and new elites joined together to deploy the newest resources at hand—steam power, the railroad, the telegraph, the market—to expand the geographical scale of their political control. If the Peace of Westphalia initiated the "invention of the frontier" in Europe and the seventeenth and eighteenth centuries were the great "epochs of enclosure," then by the late nineteenth century spatial partition had become the hegemonic form of global politics and social imagination, turning frontiers into "the razor's edge on which are suspended the modern issues of war and peace, of life or death to nations," as the triumphant colonialist Lord Curzon declared.[6] "The modern world," Maier writes, "was gripped by the episteme of separation":

When the boundaries were transgressed or could not be stabilized, social orders degenerated. Liberals and revolutionaries as well as expansionists shared the conviction that tribal peoples lacking territorial structures must succumb to modern states. . . . Something there was that must have loved a wall. . . . For not only geographical frontiers: social and class upheaval at home as well as renewed international competition compelled an obsession with social enclosures of all sorts: the boundaries that separated nation from nation, urban from rural, and the zones within cities, the conceptual frontiers that divided church from state, public from private, household from work, alleged male from reputed female roles [and the civilized from the barbarian]—social and political order was conceivable only through spatial partition.[7]

Equally crucial to this project of late-nineteenth-century territoriality—to the gradual or eruptive, intentional or forced shift from confederal organization to centralized nation-states depending on bounded space for their power, security, and identity—is the mechanism of saturation, the "filling" of the national space with the authority, the institutions, the ideology, and the economics of the nation. The territory is to be continually mapped, interconnected, exploited, mobilized, shaped, and reshaped at an ever-increasing level. All points are to be made accessible to the movement of military and police power, raw resources, goods, and people through vast railroad projects; the intensified gathering and dispersal of information is to be administered by new strings of government agencies and post offices, linked by an ever-expanding grid of telegraphic and electrical cables (note that in France government bureaucracy sextupled in the nineteenth century); and the transfer of ideology is to be seen to through schools, national media, holidays, and so forth: "no point inside the frontiers could be left devoid of the state's control."[8] Which is not to say that there is not resistance, that resistance does not have its own place within the realm in the name of progress, democracy, liberalism, or even conservatism. Only that resistance must accept the principle of centrality, its totality, the concentration of wealth, agency, knowledge, formation, and culture at the center.[9] Resistance might question the current centrality's constitution and intentions or, taking on the form of radical rebellion, it might strive for centrality itself in a zero-sum bid for power. But the principle and authority of centrality remain untouched. Aspiring to remain total, centrality thus "lays claim, implicitly or explicitly, to a superior political rationality (a state or "urban" rationality)," as the French historian Henri Lefebvre has argued.[10]

This, then, is the doubled logic of modern territoriality: the simultaneous necessity to saturate and to separate, to centralize and to expand, to fortify against the alien and make coherent the own—nation, home, self—through the control of space at all levels, material, ideological, and ontological. Danger and abjection lie in the realm not so much of the known other (which, after all, has a crucial function as the self's mirror image across the border) but most especially in the territorially impure and the unaligned, the open and the vulnerable, the unbounded, the incoherent, the uncentered. These threaten not only the sovereign and secure subject—national or individual—but the very possibility of territoriality. But because the logic of territorialism is a contradictory one—at once uniting and dividing, homogenizing and differentiating—territorialism both produces and contains its own disruption. In this sense, as with capitalism, the preeminent mode of territorialism has been that of (regulated) crisis. There has, of course, been a crucial conjunction between territorialism and capitalism since the mid-nineteenth century, insofar as each complexly obstructs as well as enables the other. I can't delve into this here, though we might say in brief that the intent of territorialization is that of fixing location and identity (ever anew), while that of capitalism is dislocation, a universal uprooting and co-option of the local, the eccentric, the self-conscious, and the self-constraining in the interests of capital itself. But the point that I do want to make is that the persistence of these modes of organizing modern life, each of them disruptive of established social relations even as it imposes others, has depended on their adaptability, their ability to recuperate precisely what challenges them. If, as Simon Critchley rightly argues, "rather than evolving toward a revolution that would take us beyond it, one might say that *capitalism capitalizes itself* . . . it simply produces more capitalism," then so too territorialism territorializes itself, it simply produces more territorialism.[11] That is, the crises generated through these respective socio-political and socio-economic systems—by the resistant, the avant-garde, the radical—are time and again defused and redirected in the interests of the system itself.[12] In territorialism as much as capitalism, structural contradiction is as likely to fuel as to disrupt such powerful systems, more likely to nurture inventive art than to instigate the final rupture.

In the case of Western European colonialism, by the late nineteenth and early twentieth centuries this logic was being extended to the colonial domains themselves. Like the European nation's internal peripheries (urban as well as rural), these external peripheries were decreasingly seen as simply the sites of raw resources, supply posts, and markets, but instead as jurisdictions to be "transformed into cloned territories offshore that must themselves be clearly bounded,"[13] the stronger the work of territoriality in the nation-state, the stronger the conviction that the colony too was to be integrated and reformed into the image and the extension of the national self, the center. This, for example, was the argument so fervently made by the influential Dutch orientalist Snouck Hurgronje in his *Nederland en de Islâm* (*The Netherlands and Islam*; 1911/1915). Hurgronje's most responsive audience, however, remained not the government but the missionaries, who shared his territorial intentions of reforming the Dutch East Indies to the point that the differences between the Eastern and Western halves of the empire would disappear. Even in the case of such "successful" empires as Britain, the problem in practice was how to balance the intention to integrate the other with the equally necessary one of separation and hierarchy, which made colonialism possible in the first place. And the answer was to continue to assume—and assure—that the colonial lay far from the center, peripheral not only in place but in time and culture.[14] Some day they would be like us, it was said, but not now. The duty of the colonized, as of all marginals, was to take their place in the waiting room of history; ours to bear the heavy burden of transforming and reshaping them.[15]

Territoriality, then, is as much about the politics of time as those of space—and this is where religion comes into play. But first, a note about the veil, for this is the time and the terrain within which the politicized veil emerges. As with all beginnings, such emergence is multiple and constructed after the fact—today, at this moment. Beginnings, after all, are all about the present. They are all about ourselves, but also all about that beyond ourselves—the vital beyond, the third force, in and through which we understand our encounter with the world as we struggle to sustain and to pressure today through yesterday. And I have gone in search of just such an axis of pressure, to give what lies before me, the course and discourse of the veil as it is today, a quarter-turn, away from war. Let me break the hold of the words we have here with a story from there.

The place is late-nineteenth-century Egypt, at the moment Qassim Amin publishes *Tahrir al-Mar'a* (*The Liberation of Woman*) in 1899, some seventeen years after the beginning of the British occupation.[16] From there, the debate over the veil, its power to define a whole complex of forces and tensions in a nutshell—through the simple choice for or against—spreads in a great wave. So much of Britain and so much of Egypt come to be in its grasp. All have something to say about the veil, are taken by it as by fantasy or dread. From there it moves easily and swiftly outward, carried by horse and camel, by letter and fiction, and, most especially, by word of mouth, across the borders of the world. The infrastructure, the means of transportation from one nation, state, and language to another, are provided by the concrete lines of colonial and regional power. Even as Britain is preeminent among the European imperial nations, so Egypt is preeminent in the Middle East, drawing its neighbors' attention and energies to itself, exporting its ideas and concerns. Alongside the Ottoman Empire (by which it had been ruled for nearly three hundred years, until Napoleon's incursion in 1798), Egypt is the first Islamic country both to experience the full effect of European commercial expansion and to engage practically and conceptually with Western modernism, including the concept of women's rights. This actual and imagined "representativeness" of the encounter between Britain and Egypt, not only as colonizer and colonized but as, respectively, preeminent Western and Middle Eastern nations, sets the stage for the globalization, the extension, of the debate on the veil to the rest of the world beyond this British-Egyptian "locale." That is, even as British imperialism fueled and relied on universalizing (Western) cultural discourses, so Egyptian discourses on the veil—and on women, modernity, and Europe more generally—likewise have easily been projected and received as a universalizing (Middle Eastern / Islamic) cultural discourse.[17]

The irony, of course, is that once upon a time ancient Egyptian society was the most, and most uniquely, egalitarian in the entire Mediterranean region—patriarchal but neither systematically oppressive nor misogynist.[18] Only with the arrival of the northern Mediterranean powers—the Greek conquest of 333 B.C. (by soldiers bearing under their arms learned Aristotle's treatise on women's natural inferiority to men), followed by the

Romans and the spread of Christianity—did the practice of veiling and, more broadly, of women's enclosure, devaluation, and repression spread. In this sense, veiling was the material measure of ancient Egypt's Hellenization and Romanization, its "Europeanization," if you will, even as that process simultaneously integrated Egypt just as surely into the surrounding Levantine culture. Until that point, Egypt had been the exception to the rule of women's occlusion, the trussing of female voice and body between walls of cloth and mortar common to the worlds around it north and south, east and west. And so, through Europe and in line with most of the Levant, the reification, the setting into stone and law of the binary between veiled mistress and unveiled slave, of secluded virgin and public whore, all founded on the fancy of woman as prime(d) receptacle for men's libidinal projections and economic intentions came to Egypt, too.

INTERLUDE: ANOTHER VEIL

That isn't the whole story, of course. We must consider as well the *sitr*–the curtain behind which the Fatimid caliphs were concealed at the opening of an audience session. This *sitr* was removed by a special servant at the opening of a session in order to unveil the enthroned ruler, and it was put back in place at the close of the session. It is at such a moment the mark of authority, of law, of power, corresponding to the *velum* of the Roman and Byzantine emperors. So our Latinate name for women's fabricate seclusion–the "veil"– contains within it, itself screens, a plethora of royal, divinely justified masculine predecessors.

And then there is Allah, whose Most Beautiful Names at once designate and veil the Named: Allah *al-Batin* and Allah *as-Satîr*, Allah the Hidden and Allah the Veiler / the Protector, and Allah *al-Ghafûr*, the One who veils our faults and forgives our sins so they are not seen by anyone else, even the angels.

This is the Allah to whom is called out in time of need: *Yâ Sattâr!* "O Veiler, O Coverer, O Protector, O Shelterer!"

In this sense, the modern debate about the veil—as it begins, at least, in Egypt under British occupation—dramatizes Europe's encounter not just with the Islamic world but with its very own foundations. What this Egyptian veil literally embodied was in fact Islam's ties to the very Greco-Roman culture that Europe drew upon to sustain its own Enlightenment and, subsequently, its nineteenth-century self-construction as a superior "Europe" distinct not only from the "Orient" on the other side of the Mediterranean but from the Islamic Moor, Ottoman, and Balkan *within* geographical Europe. Which is to say: the veil cannot easily stand, as so many have assumed or asserted, for the difference, the boundary, between Europe and some repressive Oriental/Byzantine/Islamic other. What the veil in fact marks is one of the many moments of difference's dissolution, of the historical interweaving of Occidental and Oriental to create the very thing that today at moments most seems to divide the two.

This is a crucial point to the extent that many in the West argue that Islam itself must undergo a process of "enlightenment" and advancement—a process of modernization, even secularization—whose success depends on making it, in Western eyes, more akin to the West they know. For many this step entails dropping the veil, read simultaneously as a symbol for a "medieval" past that Europe itself has left behind and as resistance to universal norms of secular democracy and equality.

INTERLUDE: WHAT'S IN A HOME?

Federal [Dutch] Equal Treatment Commission–Judgment 2003-157. On April 4, 2003, the director of a nursing home in The Hague gave a radio interview in which she described her institution's dress code prohibiting nursing-home staff from wearing headscarves, caps, or any other head-coverings. The director explained that the code was required because of the nursing home's "lifestyle-based" approach to geriatric care. This consisted in having demented and thus easily frightened residents live in an environment familiar to them. Islamic headscarves, she believed, didn't fit in with the culture in which these residents had been raised. Correspondingly, some Indonesian nurses who refused to remove their veils were transferred to another nursing home. Following the radio interview, the Office of Discrimination Issues (The Hague) brought a suit against the nursing home for religious discrimination. The Equal Treatment Commission hearing the case agreed, remarking that headgear of all sorts, including headscarves, had been part of the daily street scene when these residents had been growing up during the 1920s, '30s, and '40s. The nursing home therefore was found to have made a "not objectively justified" (indirect) religious distinction, in violation of the equal treatment law.

Some Questions

Why is it that the nursing-home director moved to foreground Islamic scarves as a site of particularly disruptive potency, in curious contrast to her (assumed) tolerance for such drastically "foreign" entities as blue jeans and sneakers, plastic, fresh nonlocal produce, racial and ethnic minorities, central heating, male nurses, women with short hair, and so forth?

Does it perhaps "cover up" the fact that nursing-home residents by definition are bound to be subject to a temporal, spatial, and physical regimen utterly foreign to them, to their memories and desires, and so inclined to disrupt most senses of being "at home" on a regular basis, no matter how well intentioned the nursing-home policy?

Some Conclusions

Certainly, in this way the whole onus of all that is "alien," "fearful," and "intrusive" in the nursing home comes to reside in the veil and the Muslim.

It is precisely this movement, however, that the commission in exemplary fashion rejects by refusing specifically to recognize the highly selective, strategic partition between present and past, Dutch and Muslim, headscarf and veil, on which this move so vitally depends.

Consistent with the principled "pragmatism" of Dutch judicial decisions though it is, the commission's judgment at the same time stands in sharp contrast to the general tenor of public discourse on the veil in the Netherlands. As I write, for example, the board of my university is considering enacting its own dress code barring full facial veils and requiring students to make eye contact and shake hands with their professors, all in the name of protecting "Dutch cultural norms" and "Western values."

This is, to be sure, a triple elision. On the one hand, it is an erasure of the ancient Mediterranean world's "coherence" as a constellation of intersecting, mutually influencing cultures as these contributed critically to the evolution of both the West and Islam. In this sense, it makes as much sense to claim ancient Greek and Roman thought and achievements for "Islam" as for "Europe"—considering that *both* these identities developed long after their object. In the second place, a blindness to the fact that the veil we have today is not that of yesterday. The coverings on women's heads that the British encountered in Egypt were, in fact, one variation on the whole range of head-coverings common for women (and men) throughout Europe as much as throughout the Middle East. It was the colonial encounter that made of specific women's head-coverings something more, a covering not like all others but instead a category all its own, a "Muslim veil," symbolizing the line between West and East, enlightened and oppressed, the familiar and the fearful. Finally, this is an obfuscation of the comprehensive misogynist collusion, of the ease with which all these societies—including an originally egalitarian Egyptian one—were able to find each other in women's containment and comprehensive oppression. Certainly, women's possibilities, roles, and "nature" varied from one place to the next; certainly women had their own forms of resistance, indirect power, and creativity. Yet the veil's survival over the course of thousands of years traces the shared traffic in and through women, their collectively separate condition relative to men's in the midst of a realm of differences between ancient Judaic, Greco-Roman, Christian, Zoroastrian, and

453

Islamic worlds. In this sense, much of the contemporary discourse concerning the veil is a matter of patriarchy's encounter with itself.

Moreover, arguments about the veil have by and large been discussions *about* women rather than *with* women. This is a point that, for all its obviousness—to the point of cliché, to the point of tears—has yet to be actively addressed. At the most general level, it is of course an outgrowth of the tradition within patriarchal cultures, both in the West and in the Middle East, of mediating relations between men through exchanges of and contestations over women. Thus there exists a long heritage within the West, going back to medieval times, of articulating Islamic inferiority in terms of Islam's purported degradation of women. At the same time, the fervent foregrounding of gender relations as a primary, explicit site of political, social, and judicial conflict is itself relatively new. This, again, has everything to do with the elaboration in the nineteenth century of the territorial distinction between private and public spheres, leading, on the one hand, to the conviction that women's proper location was in the private sphere and, on the other hand, some decades later, to the feminist repudiation of the doctrine of separate spheres. Crucially, this repudiation was achieved *through* rather than in opposition to extant territorial divides between men and women. As Linda Kerber and Jane DeHart-Mathews argue, it was through their increasing participation in social, religious, and reform organizations that women were:

> transforming women's sphere from the private, family-oriented world of domesticity into the formerly male world of politics and public policy. . . . The "womanhood" identified with "mothering" was becoming less a biological fact—giving birth to children—and more a political role with new ideological dimensions. The traditional word *motherhood* was being reshaped so as to justify women's assuming new, ever-more-public responsibilities. Women now clearly meant to transform the domestic housekeeping responsibilities of their grandmothers into an attack on the worst abuses of an urban, industrial society. The household now included the marketplace and city hall.[19]

It is within this context—of Western women's energetic extension, remapping, and transformation of their territory within the local nation, even as Western nations attempted the same at the global level through colonialism—that Muslim women's veil first became a visceral political and cultural issue.[20] Precisely the parallels in these processes, their shared foundation in a logic of territorialism, enabled Western colonial administrators and residents in the Middle East to shamelessly blend feminist discourse into colonial apologetics. The veil, they said (back then, as today), held women back, under men's thumb. The veil, they said (back then, as today), was proof of Islamic backwardness and inferiority. Oppression of women and backwardness are intrinsic to Islam, they said (back then, as today). So, they said, only by casting off such "practices 'intrinsic' to Islam (and therefore Islam itself) . . . could Muslim societies begin to move forward on the path of civilization."[21] Only then would Muslims develop the same high mental, moral, and social standards as the West, enabling them to participate fully in modern life. Notably, the colonialist critique of Islam was only one instance of the more universal colonial assumption that the liberation of non-Western women oppressed by indigenous religions and cultural traditions was a crucial and morally validating component of the modern colonial enterprise throughout the world.

As a result, contemporary Western feminist critiques of Islamic gender relations—having helped to sustain colonialism so effectively in the past—all too easily have a colonialist ring to them today. The categorical assertion of Ciska Dresselhuys, head editor of the Netherlands' primary feminist magazine, *Opzij*, that she would never hire a (Muslim) woman wearing a headscarf comes to mind. Western feminism needs a new vision of Islam, one able, for example, to address the ways in which Muslim women in the Middle East and Asia, as well as in Europe, have been using the veil to remap, reform, and extend women's territory from the private to the public—deploying it to create a new space for the veiled female self in the public, male realm.[22] At the same time, Western feminism has itself something to learn from veiled women's critique—however variously articulated and (in)consistent—and from their resistance to the omnipresent sexualization and commodification of women in the West today, what Peter van Rooden calls the "pornographization" of the public space.[23] Such a reform of mainstream Western feminism is not a choice but a necessity: the continued widespread use of traditional feminist arguments to sustain assumptions of Western superiority demands this. As does the all too common habit among the West's general populace of focusing on others' oppression of women to deflect critique of women's position within the West. But is it possible?

INTERLUDE: VIOLENCE AGAINST WOMEN

Vignette 1. The Dutch government recently conducted a study of domestic violence, seeking to establish its extent and nature. The government, specifically Minister Donner, was shocked to find that it is still highly prevalent. So prevalent, in fact, that the government decided not to conduct a public educational campaign on the issue because the state was unable (unwilling) to free up the resources required adequately to meet the needs of all those who might come to the government for help. So the violence continues.

Vignette 2. A Dutch high-school principal recently attempted to initiate a public discussion of the pressures and violence brought to bear on (Muslim) immigrant girls and women by male family members—fathers, uncles, brothers, cousins—seeking to force these girls and women to conform to codes of conduct prohibiting free interaction with boys and men, divorce, and unregulated movements in public spaces. The discussion fizzled.

Inference 1. There is considerably greater public interest in and affective commitment to deriding Islam's oppression of women than there is to preventing actual violence against women. So the violence continues . . . as does the derision of Islam.

Inference 2. While a veil on the heads of a handful of girls is perceived throughout much of continental Western Europe as having the potential to undermine the West's hard-fought democratic values, the continued battering of women—much like the lucrative traffic in Eastern European women, girls, and boys forced into prostitution—apparently poses little danger to European societies. No one argues that it should be allowed to continue; they just assume (I must assume) that it will stop some day, die a silent death, as we become ever more democratic. At least it's not un-Western.

Significantly, those Western colonizers of a century ago most opposed to the veil in Muslim societies (in the name of Muslim women) were often the ones most fiercely resistant to feminism at home. The point, after all, was to transform non-Western women into the ultimate civilized woman as she had *already* been established within Western bourgeois society (even as at home, bourgeois society had taken as its task the reform and elevation of the working classes). The British consul general in Egypt at the turn of the nineteenth century, Lord Cromer, offers a fine example: an uncompromising proponent of unveiling Muslim women in the colonies, he was also a founding member and sometime president of the Men's League for Opposing Women's Suffrage.[24] What we might call "colonialist feminism" was activated, then, not only in the interests of the imperial project but of a patriarchal territorialism that sought to strengthen established gender relations and identities at the center, most particularly women's exclusion from the political realm and the restriction of motherhood to the world of biology. After all, as Edward Said notes, by this point "imperialism was considered essential to the well-being of British fertility generally and of motherhood particularly."[25] The doubled logic of territorialism is again at work: striving to enclose and saturate Muslim space with its authority, in the name of liberation, while fortifying the dividing walls between the sexes in the name of nature. The veil is the frontier zone, the borderland, the zone of ephemerality between a concrete here and there, male and female, the body politic and the politicized body.

At the same time, it is important to see here the mechanism, the logic, by which at one and the same time colonized peoples were pressured to transform fundamentally—to accept having Western understandings of the process of Modern History, which is to say, Westernization, forced upon them—even as Western women were required to remain true to their established gender position. While the colonized are then radically historicized, the contemporary West, as the culmination of History, is itself removed from History. In this way, the threat posed then, as now, by the colonized (the feminists, the immigrants, the peripheral) was the reintroduction of History into the West in the face of all those who proclaimed the end of history—whether the Fukuyamas of today, or the British imperialists of yore.[26]

. . .

We believe without belief, beyond belief.

—Wallace Stevens

After you've spent a whole morning seeing through the illusions of politics, of love, of family and God, of art and meditation, have had to declare them unfit, when yet in the course of another morning you've left nothing whole of all that mankind believes in—not because you *want* to destroy, but because it already was broken, torn, ravaged in the first place, because the scales must finally fall from peoples' eyes—then, sometime around lunchtime, you feel a need for spirituality.

—Arnon Grunberg, *The Asylum Seeker*

The debate on the veil is part of the larger—and as yet unresolved—problem of minorities in representative democracies; the difficulty, perhaps even the impossibility, that minor positions and experiences have in being heard—recognized—by the majority. At the same time, of all the minorities within the West's nation-states, the case of Islam stands out at this moment by virtue of the urgency with which it is experienced as an issue in need of immediate and drastic attention; the intensity with which it links local, national, and international currents; the degree to which the representation of Islam, and correspondingly of the West as Islam's other, are contorted and distorted; and the range and extent of the political, social, and human consequences of such distortions.[27]

So, in the Netherlands, a land with a long tradition of religious and cultural tolerance, the events of September 11 released a flood of anti-Islamic commentary, practices, and legislation (most recently, the effective if indirect suppression of Islamic schools in a country committed to state support of religious education), which shows no signs of abating soon. If all Western nations have their own history of anti-Islamic orientalism, the shift in the Netherlands from a national commitment to antidiscrimination before September 11 to a national commitment to the forceful integration, marginalization, and repression of divergent Muslim elements after the September attacks has been, quite possibly, the most dramatic of all European responses—notwithstanding the French commitment to Muslims' "laicization" and the British and German willingness to discriminate against Muslims relative to Christians and Jews. And so a tide of anti-Islamic "common sense" now infects the public realm, vociferously and blindly—as in the columns of the late Theo van Gogh, or in essays by the writer Leon de Winter, or in the LPF's echoes of Pim Fortuyn's jeremiad against the "Islamicization" of Dutch society—asserting Islam's "backward" nature, its aggressive resistance to conversion into the modern, Western fold, and its disruption of moral citizenship.[28]

This development has captured virtually the entire spectrum of Dutch public thought, from the Liberals and Christian Democrats to the Labor Party and Socialists, and from the ever crudely provocative antiestablishment Theo van Gogh—who imagined that Islam's presence reintroduces the possibility of religious war in Holland, "a kind of

Belfast, with bomb attacks and burned-out churches and mosques . . . a fight to the death. An unequal fight that we're going to lose"—to the explicitly progressive, gay, mixed-race writer Stephan Sanders, who can likewise only see in the veil a gaping wound that marks the destruction of a woman's individuality and expressiveness, her subjection to a male or divine hand, a "moral masochism . . . [a] danger, in the form of someone who thinks that she must hide herself from sight."[29] Spying a girl whose headscarf has slid back, Sanders imagines that she wrestles with the question of whether or not to put the veil back in place. And in watching her, Sanders himself takes on the role of "witness," documenting her grand "personal struggle like that of all struggles for freedom in history"—a struggle for the freedom, Sanders in fact implies, to become like him, an individual unfettered by tradition, religion, or social ties.

To a significant extent, these developments are, of course, the continuation of a traditional Eurocentrism that to this day quite unself-consciously values and foregrounds classically "Western" views and concerns, including anti-Islamic stereotypes that have changed little since they were first developed during the Crusades. Crucially, the dominant terms of this discourse are those of modernism and secularism, concepts equated and exchanged regularly and unself-consciously with those of democracy and tolerance. Correspondingly, all parties in the public discussion now being held throughout Western Europe are in fact required to enact modernist (which is also to say: territorial, nationalist, rationalist, individualist) secularity even when secularity itself, and modernism, are the ideologies they most seek to challenge and resist. If secularity and modernity are to be questioned, their discursive and political priority force critics to question them on their own terms. To consider the veil—or the nation—outside this framework is to risk placing oneself outside the public discussion itself.

This, in fact, is what has happened. On the one hand, the significant analyses of the veil not framed in exclusively modernist, Western-centric terms—such as, among others, the work of the historian Leila Ahmed (*Women and Gender in Islam*), the anthropologists Fadwa El Guindi (*The Veil*) and Lila Abu-Lughod (*Writing Women's Worlds*), the sociologists Fatima Mernissi (*Beyond the Veil*) and Monique Gadant ("Femmes alibi"), the radical anticolonial writer Frantz Fanon ("L'Algérie se dévoile"), the literary critic Winifred Woodhull (*Transfigurations of the Maghreb*), the psychoanalyst Luce Irigaray (*Speculum of the Other Woman*, among others), the filmmaker Yamina Benguigui (*Femmes en Islam*), and the philosopher-theologian-activist Tariq Ramadan (*Western Muslims and the Future of Islam*)—continue to be generally marginalized and ignored by Western politicians, policymakers, journalists, pundits, and public intellectuals. And not only by them but by feminists, as well, deeply indebted as the majority are to Western humanism, including its most recent antifoundationalist variation. I've touched on this above, but it is still important to observe how spare, how watery and thin, has been the Western feminist engagement with Islamic critical thought, including with Islamic feminism.

To this extent, our public discussions of the veil, that marker of Islamic difference, are vitally impoverished. Democratic principles certainly are abided by in the sense that the state's suppression of those views it deems a threat to itself and the nation—"anti-Western," "fundamentalist," and "refusing to integrate"—remains within the framework of constitutional law. Yet divergent views of all stripes, whether explicitly religious or pacifist or anticonsumerist, only reach the public sphere with difficulty, and then all too often are distorted.[30] The problem is that precisely the privileging of selected segments of Western society—those enacting and representing mainstream, Western self-conceptions—over others in the public space is itself fundamentally undemocratic. In essence, what takes place is the propagation of undemocratic practices in the name of democracy.

The crucial point here is that Western nations' public debate around the veil, representative as it is for the debate about Islam, has failed according to the standards not only of progressive multiculturalism but of democracy itself *once democracy is conceived as a comprehensive rather than a nationalist project*—that is, once we commit ourselves to democracy in the name of democracy and not of this or that authority, this or that nation. The key point is that while it may be the nation's intention to realize democracy, it cannot be democracy's intention to preserve the nation. True democracy, as Simon Critchley argues, at once strives for and never achieves "the fantasy of the society as one, as a unity or fullness."[31] It is the perpetual incompleteness of the intention, as well as the intention itself, that must be recognized and kept alive. The moment democracy is imagined as truly achieved, or as the particular achievement/property/essence of only one people or civilization, is the moment of its death. That is to say: democracy is as much an ethics as a politics. In this sense, the actual participation of democratic subjects is at least as vital as the legislative creation of the possibility to participate. In this specific regard, the growing alienation of individual citizens from collective democratic practices in Western nations since the Second World War is all the more flagrant in light of the knee-jerk frequency with which contemporary Western democracy is presented as a corrective to Islam's ostensibly inherent repressive and calcifying deficiencies.[32]

INTERLUDE: AN INTERVIEW WITH THE MINISTER

Below are some excerpts from a recent conversation between the journalist Folkert Jensma and Rita Verdonk, the Dutch Minister of Aliens Affairs and Integration. She is a member of the Liberal Party and a former prison director. It was printed a day after the AIVD, the Dutch domestic intelligence and security agency, published a report documenting that the harsh attacks on Islam in the media and government are alienating minority youth, possibly to the point of driving them into the hands of fundamentalists (*NRC Handelsblad*, March 13-14, 2004, 17).

RV: If your child goes to school in the Netherlands, then it can't be that he hears something completely different at home. That has to be changed.

FJ: So that means government intervention. I exaggerate now in the interests of the conversation: while appealing to the principles of liberalism, there has never been so much state intervention propagated as at this moment, with regard to this subject.

RV: Look, as minister, I stick to the Basic Agreement [of the coalition government]. A liberal vision allows the government to set limits. It's not just about individual freedom.

FJ: [(Jewish) Amsterdam mayor Job] Cohen says that integration through the mosques is a good possibility. Then it's held against him that he's being naïve.

RV: If all kinds of things are being said in those mosques that go against our constitutional rights, then we have to do something about it. But say that the mosque has an open-house day in order to show that a religion is being preached there, just like any other religion in the Netherlands, then I think that's excellent.

FJ: That's how I think too, gladly. But then you and I are typically Dutch consensus-thinkers, not used to battle, to polarizing orthodox Muslims—it's exactly us they want to challenge.

RV: If it's really the case—we're now right on top of all the radical mosques—that things happen there that don't fit into our system of norms and values, then you have to intervene. There are all kinds of possibilities for that. Mosques are sometimes organized as a foundation. You can dissolve those if you see a reason for doing that.

FJ: It's struck me that integration is now a matter of judiciary policy, as if it's a crime, a question of the public order. There are also countries that consider integration and [maintaining one's] own identity a positive value that benefits the country. This is of course old-fashioned multicultural thought, but I still put it to you.

RV: I don't find it defensive. We don't want to write off disadvantaged *allochtonen* ["foreign-born," i.e., minorities of non-Western descent], but to take them by the hand. We want to teach them about our norms and values. It's very good that integration is the task of the Ministry of Justice. Aliens policy plus integration forms a whole.

The debate's dominant terms are those of modernism, secularism, and the European nation (this nation, that nation, or "Europe" as a whole), concepts equated and exchanged regularly and unself-consciously with those of democracy and tolerance. So naturalized is this equation that its politics—the ways in which it enables very particular relations and authorizations of power processes—all too often remain invisible. In other words, we have forgotten both their contingency and their historicity. Indeed, the marginalization of other voices in debates concerning Islam and the veil results not only from the persistent vigor of Eurocentrism but—at the very same time and in the same place— from the fact that the object of the West's discussion is not only the veil or Islam but, simultaneously, the West's own current crisis of identity and historical destiny. The immense energy and affect invested by Western Europeans in discussions of the veil can be traced to the fact that it is the site at which not one but two highly charged discourses encounter, intermingle, and disrupt each other: one concerning the relation between Islam and the West, the other, the relation of the West to its own past and future.[33]

Talal Asad's essay "Muslims as a 'Religious Minority' in Europe" is important, among other reasons, for foregrounding the extent to which the problem of Islam in Europe is the problem of Europe's own self-representation.[34] Such representation has never been easy, for the multiple peoples, cultures, politics, and religions that inhabit the territory of "Europe" mean that any definition of Europe's boundaries is bound to be political. Telling the story of Europe has meant implicitly or explicitly excluding the putatively non-European within Europe: the Jewish, the Scandinavian, the Roma, the Eastern (Orthodox/Russian), the Muslim, the African. What then survives this onslaught is the narrative of a civilization and a history understood in terms of a fundamental, essential Europeanness developing across homogeneous space and through linear time. So the notion of "Europe" is used—by the historian Michael Wintle, for example—to designate the peoples and cultures that have been subjected to the successive formative events of the Roman Empire, Christianity, Enlightenment, and industrialization.[35] Each event in turn is understood as having shaped the subjects within its bounds into respectively Roman, Christian, Enlightened, and modern European subjects (such that the modern both transcends yet contains within it the Roman, the Christian, and the Enlightened). At the same time, the multivarious foreign ideas and techniques that entered Europe from outside its bounds are likewise reworked into "Roman," "Christian," "Enlightened," and "modern" ones, to be cultivated and passed down as Europeans' own inheritance.[36]

Though not based in notions of race, this still is, in Edward Said's terms, a deeply filiative vision, founded on historical lines of descent that determine contemporary distributions of authority, authenticity, and hierarchy—and the distribution of property, in the sense that Europeanness becomes a distinct characteristic, nature, or essence subject to laws of inheritance and ownership. To embody Europe, to represent and be represented by Europe, is to enact its history—where History itself, as Dipesh Chakrabarty has quite brilliantly argued, is understood as the matter of becoming modern and secular as Europe did. That is, History—as it most often continues to be practiced by our scholars and embodied by our national narratives the world over—entails becoming (of failing to become) "Europe," where "Europe" consists not so much in the specific cultural, political, and religious content of modern Europe but rather in the constellation of assumptions, ideologies, and worldviews—modern Europe's notions of time, of the relation of the secular to the sacred, and of the nature of human agency—structurally embedded in the scholarly methods we have inherited from modern Europe and to this day use to understand our world from Bombay to New York to Istanbul.[37] The important point here is that, at its most fundamental, this problem is not a matter of lacking adequate knowledge of Europe's actual Islamic history and heritage, which is well documented if not well known. Rather, it is that that history cannot be told within the logic of a History that allows for only one trajectory through space and time, one reality per territory.

So within Europe's dominant self-narration, divergence from the Roman-Christian-Enlightenment-modern trajectory places one, at one and the same moment, outside Europe, outside history, and beyond belief—irrespective of one's historical, cultural, political, or residential ties to material, geographical Europe. All that is understood to be opposed to the "Roman," the "Christian," the "Enlightened," the "modern," and the "secular"—as these successively contain and succeed each other—can neither be imagined as European nor lay claim to Europe. Those considered incapable or found unwilling—whether in body or in spirit—to believe in and to reflect Europe back to itself as "Europe" are excluded. So to this day the second- and third-generation descendents of non-Western immigrants to the Netherlands are called "allochthonous," which is to say, "foreign-born." And it is the continuing power of this mechanism that ensures that Islam—and its veiled markers—continue to feared as alien.

In this sense, the reigning European history is fundamentally intolerant, fundamentally unwilling to take the risk of an active tolerance, one that asks as much as it gives. As Thomas Scanlon clearly explains: "Toleration is, for all of us, a risky matter, a practice with high stakes. . . . What tolerance expresses is a recognition of common membership that is deeper than these conflicts, a recognition of others as being just as entitled as we are to contribute to the definition of our society. Without this, we are just rival groups contending for the same territory."[38] It is the difference between easy tolerance and rigorous tolerance—as these, in turn are linked to easy and rigorous democracy. If easy tolerance is a willingness to accept the existence of an insignificant, because impotent, minority, rigorous tolerance means recognizing that divergent minority as vitally constitutive of the nation and its future. It is to give these people, whoever they may be, a say not just over themselves, but over us.

Time and again, however, a politics of (cultural-ideological) descent trumps that of dissent. Most obviously, perhaps, what is at issue here is the fact that the operative principle in these discussions again and again is the assumption that the West's *current* sociopolitical stability, moderate state violence, and material success validate maintaining a privileged set of (what are presented as) *traditionally* Western standpoints. This is not simply a theory of power, but also one of history; which is to say: power makes its own past as much as its own truth. In the process, the division between East and West, the veiled and unveiled, is *doubly* mapped onto the grid of Western history: it marks the divide not only between past and present but also between two *sorts* of past—implicitly framed as two sorts of morality—that which we repudiate (the oppressive, the violent, the exploiting, the hypocritical, the antidemocratic, and in all these senses "un-Western") and that which we today have realized (the liberating, the democratizing, the tolerant, the moral). The crucial thing to remark is that, taken to its logical conclusion, this is a deeply ahistorical—and in that sense impotent—vision. It is a vision, in essence, incapable of addressing our new conditions: post-territorial, post-secular, postmodern.

In making this argument, let me begin with the proposal that the organizing logic of modernity was Europe—Europe as the center of the West, Europe as the powerful constellation of Western European nation-states materially at work in the world, and "Europe" as an epistemological and ontological ideology intent on universalizing its vision of history and being. At the heart of postmodernism, then, we might say, lies Europe's collapse. So postmodernism marks the failure of Eurocentrism, of Europe as a global principle, and a new start at re-creating the world—a world, incidentally, in which religion returns from the margin.

INTERLUDE: THE BEGINNINGS OF POSTMODERNISM

It is a little-known fact that the first book on postmodernism was written from an explicitly Christian standpoint by one of the more successful American religious educators and cultural critics of the interbellum period. Disturbed by the emptying of religious content from religious practices and theologies, Bernard Iddings Bell in 1926 published *Postmodernism and Other Essays*, outlining his vision for a new understanding of Christian religion and its role in contemporary society. In 1939, he following this up with *Religion for Living: A Book for Postmodernists*. The crux of the matter for Bell was to get beyond the recently formulated opposition between fundamentalism and modernism. In practice this meant an acceptance of both the historicity of the Bible and the truth of miracles, including Jesus' divinity.

While Bell was popular on the college lecture circuit and published in such highbrow national magazines as *The Atlantic Monthly*, his argument appears to have had little impact. Not only does the opposition between fundamentalism and modernity remain a highly popular one to this day, but Bell's vision of postmodernity appears to have been unable to make headway outside the privatized ghetto to which religion had been assigned, or even to have been picked up within the religious community itself. It was as such too little, too late, too new . . . though recent events suggest that, notwithstanding the significant flaws in his argument, Bell might better be seen as impressively prescient, as one of the first to herald and enact the "return of the religious," of a postmodern religiosity beyond territorialism.

Of course, it makes sense that Western Europe should be among the most resistant to this new phase of history. Even as it attempts practically to realize a new Europe, a new and closer union of the battered old states, the primary stance is defensive rather than creative. In facing the present—in politics, education, social welfare, citizenship, and intellectual life—too much of Western Europe is still in flight from its past, from totalitarianism, violence, and gross inhumanity, rather than seeking to realize the future. Having again achieved a level of stability and wealth, it strives to protect what it has, fears what is different, trills at the slightest perceived threat to its current democracy and economic security—rather than risk seeking for itself and the world truly new forms of life and being. Just consider the current Dutch government's pending draconian expulsion of 26,000 long-time resident illegal immigrants; or German Christian Democrats' fundamental refusal to imagine Turkey as a member of Europe; or, more generally, the lack of vision that marks European leadership across the board and has stymied all attempts to respond creatively and with daring to Europe's own problems, as well as those of the world: from the framing of a visionary European constitution, to Bosnia and Iraq, to Israel and Palestine, to the American behemoth's unilateralism. European political leaders have boldly asserted that the challenge facing Europe is to become the most powerful economy in the world within the next decade. But the true challenge, in fact, is to imagine Europe's role and identity in the world after the end of Eurocentrism—and the failure is remarkable. Instead, what we are offered is simply a new, shrunken provincialism, as fearful of the postmodern rupture of territorialism as of Islam and multiculturalism. It salvages what is to be salvaged of Europe's modern heritage, but cowers from going beyond it—beyond the regional and the economic, the rational and the secular, the fortified bounds of its imaginary territory.

In this sense, it is the continuing resonance of Europe's bestial implosion half a century ago that today spurs Europe's continued resistance to engaging fully the most fundamental challenges it faces. These challenges are kept at a perpetual pitch of urgency by precisely the forces on which Europe today is depending for stability and succor— those of capitalist economics and territorialist politics. In running from the past, Europe in effect keeps that past continually before it. Its current security and stability can only be imagined as a precarious eye in the storm, an oasis between the actual past and a potential future of the instability, irrationality, and danger that dervishly orbit the circled wagons of the present, of Fortress Europe today. Under such conditions, under such an imaginary, the trick is to make that present, and that Europe, extend as far and as long as possible; to snatch security from the jaws of an unstable future and a threatening world. The tragedy of such a vision is that it erases the future to the point that the new—the postmodern, the Islamic—can only be conceived as a return of the past, and the imagination needed to engage it as the present-future is effectively suppressed.

The problem is a fundamental discrepancy between the West's self-image and actuality—the problem of how to assert fundamental assumptions, standpoints, and intentions while accounting for their continued disruption, contradiction, and even failure in practice. So the former French Prime Minister Michel Rocard argues that, while Europe has historically played a much greater role than the rest of the world in generating war and carnage, it now can give the world "the assurance . . . that wars will no longer originate in Europe." Not only does the Union respect human rights, but this is the first great economic power to have "been born without force."[39] The Second World War as an inalienable primary impulse to the Union utterly disappears here—as, more generally, does the crucial fact of colonialism and its contribution to Europe's material, social, intellectual, and aesthetic development. Rocard's account is in effect a narrative not only of self-birth but of stillbirth—for the "Europe" he imagines is one not transforming through time but only expanding in space, "first to ex-Yugoslavia, then to Turkey, then one day to the Middle East and the Islamic world." It is capable of "assuring peace and development" to all humanity and yet, at the same time, incapable of politics, for it is "only a space of proximity."

This fundamental discursive rupture between "peace" and "development," on the one hand, and "politics," on the other, critically masks the politics of peace and liberal-market economics themselves—the extent to and ways in which the forms these take are historically determined and contingent, even as they themselves are held in place forcefully by Europe's nation-states. The notion of "development"—as it entails the fantasy of effective bureaucratic government by secular states opening the way to universal welfare—is one of the most deeply political notions of our day, at once powerfully productive *and* destructive. Most crucially, Rocard's portrait is both blind to and unable to account for the forms of violence that today confront Europe *from within*. This same logic of splitting, between present and past and between good past and bad past, is at work in Dutch (former) Prime Minister Wim Kok's assertion not so very long ago that "The Netherlands have been completed [*Nederland is af*]"—a statement meant to refer to the completion of Holland's postwar project of reconstruction, but quickly taken to mean much more. The present has been freed from the past's limitations, even as that past's intentions in the present have been realized. And behold, he saw that it was good.

So it is the conjunction between, on the one hand, an essentialist narrative of Europe's history and, on the other hand, an ahistorical account of Europe's present that explains why Islam, and the veil as its symbol, today are widely represented as simultaneously *alien* intrusions on Western ground, *premodern* holdovers, and *antimodern* threats to what we have achieved today. The essence of the Western present is constructed as the continuation and embodiment of a very particular quasi-sacred modern, Enlightened "origin" (at once centuries old and purely contemporary), from which all contradiction and multivalence have been bleached out. Correspondingly, the Western present likewise can only with difficulty be imagined as a site of contradiction, divergence, and as-yet-unknown becoming. The diffusion of what is into what has been and what will be makes history impossible, and with it a West whose (post)modernity is ours to continue making rather than simply to inherit and steadfastly defend.

. . .

Yet even as we speak, there is a crucial rupture. Precisely the inability of the modernist narrative of Europe to account for either the return of the religious or the presence of the Islamic in its midst means that its veneer of "naturalness" is stripped away. In being confronted with contemporary events and forced to defend itself, Europe finds its own historicity and contingency to be revealed—and thus also the possibility of an alternative. Central to this development has been the dislocation of the once so powerful link between modernity and the world's disenchantment—to the point that today intellectuals and politicians can no longer assume religion's irrelevance and inevitable demise under (post-)modernity. Crucially, however, the language and conceptual tools necessary for considering this condition as a domestic, Western development, like those necessary for articulating a new democracy, are highly impoverished after years of repression by the secularization thesis. It is under such pitiable conditions that our public discussions turn to substitutes—including the veil, and Islam more generally—as a way both of articulating their distress and of masking our failures. It is easier in Western Europe to speak of the return of the religious as the threat of an *alien* religiosity, opposed both to secularization *and* the West. In this sense, the West returns to and engages its own inherited religiosity through that of the (Islamic) other—much as it once returned to its Greek roots through Muslim scholarship. And just as that Muslim scholarship had left its own improvements in the thought of the Greeks before it was translated back to the West, so too our engagement with Islam in the West today is bound to mark and re-form Western religiosity itself.

This crisis of the secularist assumption, then, is central to European discourses of the veil, particularly in societies such as France and the Netherlands, committed strongly to both a secularist understanding of modernity and a universalist account of human progress inclined to place their respective nations at history's forefront.[40] Within such a framework, minorities' refusal to be absorbed fully into the reigning national culture and narrative, particularly their persistent, resistant religiosity—even while abiding by the laws of the political state—are necessarily understood as not only a challenge to the superiority of the particular nation but a more general resistance to and disruption of modernity. To tolerate such deviation—in the rigorous sense of tolerance as the recognition of others' equal right to define the nature and future of our society—would mean critically reconsidering the nature of both the nation and modernity itself.[41] It is at this point that the issue of conversion arises—both modernity's hunger to convert the other, and its own resistance to conversion.

It is modernity's logic of conversion, tied as it is to the Western project of colonialist territoriality, that continues to define the limits of the contemporary Western engagement with the Islamic veils in its midst. In fact, you might say that conversion is the politics of secularism. At the religious level, conversion, of course, played a crucial role through the collaboration of European missionary activities with their nation-states' colonial projects: a close—if at times testy—partnership between state, religious institutions, and/or lay religious societies in the interests of converting savage "them" into loyal, if lesser, members of "our" empire. At the same time, Western missionary activity itself—the active imagining of converting the world to Christianity—only emerged subsequent to and as a result of Christianity's own "conversion to modernity."[42] That is, modern conversion can be distinguished from religious expansion in medieval times both by the fact that for the first time its intentions were literally universal—seeking to extend a religion's reach without reference to extant geo-political borders—even as it operated quasi-independently of political and material conquest.[43] In the sixteenth and seventeenth centuries came the first wave of modern missionary activity, as the Roman Catholic Church's Counter-Reformation sought to reconsolidate its fragmented power within Europe to become a universal authority once again, while translating this vision into an independent global mission, complete with new religious orders that extended themselves to Japan, China, and India. The collapse of the papacy's European venture by the end of the eighteenth century, ruptured by the growing effectiveness of territorialist power structures, however, meant the dissolution of its missionary endeavors as well.

At the same time, the dramatic transformations of Western society through industrialization, revolution, and economic expansion likewise disrupted Protestant ecclesiastical authority to such an extent—in the United States and Britain to begin with—that space opened up for the development of new evangelical churches, along with new forms of voluntary, interdenominational religious association. The crucial thing to note is that it was precisely the shared, new conception of religion as located in the sphere of the private that enabled these groups to imagine themselves as "missionary bodies, existing in a free social sphere, apart from the structures of public and national authority."[44] This foundational understanding of themselves in terms of private religiosity, while reinforcing institutional churches' actual separation from the secular world of politics, at the same time spurred increased socio-political involvement by individuals in the name of religious conviction and consciousness. Not only did the new religious groups become the first examples of modern, professional, and sophisticated mass organizations, but their work to convert their fellow citizens, along with colonized subjects, entailed an explicitly political concern for reforming their nation in the name of a moral citizenship, expressed in such movements as Christian Republicanism and Abolition. In other words, it was precisely the location of religion in the sphere of the private that freed up new critical energies and political spaces in the realm of the public—even as conversion became the privileged discourse under modernity for conceptualizing both personal religious practice and worldly, political intent, national(ist) commitment, and transnational collectivity.[45]

Interesting in this regard is the attempt by the internationally influential orientalist Snouck Hurgronje to elaborate a new—"ethical" rather than crudely "exploitative"—Dutch approach to expanding control of the Dutch Indies (Indonesia) in the early twentieth century. More than all others, Hurgronje asserts, the missionaries in the field sympathize with his recognition of "the duty that our people must fulfill toward Island society," consisting in the need to develop a unified position regarding "our national pedagogical task toward the Mohammedan subjects of the Dutch state" and the need to address the "great questions of 'East and West' that our people have had put before them."[46] In Hurgronje's writing, "national mission work" and "Christian mission work" labor side by side, and he praises highly the missionaries' commitment to the great task of achieving "a unity that, if it came into being, would remove all obstacles to a unification of the civilization and national consciousness in the Eastern and Western part of the kingdom of the Netherlands."[47] Yet at the same time he reprimands the missionaries for their religious fervor, fearing that it will stoke indigenous peoples' resistance to Dutch control. Instead, he argues, all Dutch in the East Indies, including missionaries, must work first for national, political, and epistemological conversion of the indigenous (or what he calls their "spiritual annexation"), after which there will be all the time necessary to struggle with the arduous and extended task of converting Islamic inhabitants to Christianity.

Crucially, Hurgronje explicitly rejects Protestantism as an essential unifying factor for Dutch national culture—in a society that includes not only "Christians of the most diverse confessions, but also Jews and Free Thinkers," all of whom "feel themselves at home to such an extent that they resist with all their might, even to the sacrifice of goods and blood, all attempts to make them take on another nationality or another state-alliance."[48] While quite accurate in practical terms, Hurgronje misses two crucial facts here. First, it is precisely the religious content of the missionaries' intentions that sustains their transnational vision—their commitment to converting the indigenous peoples of the East Indies to nationalized Dutch-Protestant modernity—while the government officials who so frustrate him remain trapped in what amounts to a provincialist and preterritorialist secular pragmatism, incapable of looking farther than the possibility of short-term economic profit. At the same time, it is his nation-state's fragmentation into separate religio-socio-political "pillars"—which is to say, its incomplete territorialization due to the absence of a coherent, all-powerful "center"—that makes any saturation and conversion of the colonial territories likewise impossible. The very diversity of the Netherlands, which prevents Protestantism from being a unifying factor, also ensures the impossibility of "spiritually annexing" the periphery. And yet, early-twentieth-century Holland's conversion to modernity was not so much disrupted by fragmentation but rather *created* the fragments of the nation-state, as such. That irony today haunts the nation's renewed encounter with Islam. More generally, this is the eternal irony of territorial modernity, of modernity as the capitalist nation-state: the necessary persistence of instability, the perpetual incompletion, the staggered segmentation of a nation-state simultaneously imagined as always already whole and complete.

· · ·

While secularization's disruption has generated a wide variety of responses within the West today, there also are clear patterns that allow us to locate these relative to each other. To begin with, the first division is between those who, on the one hand, continue to see the religious and the secular modern as opposed categories of thought and life and those who, on the other hand, approach them as fundamentally interrelated and interdependent. The important point here is that this gathers together in the first group—their mutual antipathy notwithstanding—those to whom such a return of the religious is a relief, seeing in religion a site of socially redemptive, moral, and political possibility, and those to whom religion marks the triumph of irrationality, inequality, repression, and violence. While the former call for a repudiation of the secularist thesis, the latter (including the proponents of *laïcité* in France, such absolutist Dutch atheists as the strident Islam-fighter Ayaan Hirsi Ali and Herman Philipse, and the American philosopher Richard Rorty) argue that the return of the religious in fact calls for an even more radical reinforcement and enforcement of a secularism that essentially boils down to a secularist nationalism. Yet, however elegantly articulated, there exists a fundamental flaw in such standpoints, in that they ultimately require the critic to present the religious or secular other being opposed in terms of caricature rather than complex reality. Such a position necessarily represses the long and intriguing actual history of shifting coexistence, dialogue, and collaboration between the secular and the religious.

More interesting and useful than this first group is the second group of critics, who recognize the fundamental historical and conceptual imbrication of the secular and the religious. These too can be divided into two groups: on the one hand, those, such as the philosopher Charles Taylor, who see in secularism a neutral and independent political ethic, whose value lies in enabling diverse traditions and worldviews to live together peaceably—that is, secularism not as a bulwark against religion but as an enabler of religious diversity in the face of the return of the religious—and those, on the other hand, such as the postcolonial thinkers Talal Asad, Dipesh Chakrabarty, Peter van der Veer, and Gauri Viswanathan, who argue that secularism's fundamental implication in the project of European colonialism requires us not so much to reject secularism outright as critically to engage the nature of its political, cultural, and historical intentions.

While Taylor, in his essay "Modes of Secularism," explicitly seeks to trace both secularism's origins in religious history and its subsequent historical development, his argument is marred by two significant weaknesses.[49] The first of these, as Talal Asad has pointed out, is that Taylor's vision of secular democracy as a form of voluntary self-discipline obscures the extent to which secularism becomes the political ideology through which the state justifies its monopoly on violence—a violence it uses not simply to impose order but to assert what are to count as the core political principles according to which political disputes are resolved. So while Taylor suggests that the state works through negotiation and persuasion and Asad recognizes "the generous impulse behind this answer," the latter is forced to point out that "the nation-state is not a generous agent and its law does not deal in persuasion." The moment that "parties to a dispute are unwilling to compromise on what for them is a matter of principle (a principle that articulates action and being, not a principle that is justifiable by statements of belief," the state is free to resort to intimidation, command, and the threat of legal (which is to say, indirectly or directly violent) action.[50] The French government's recent decision—in the name of *laïci-té*—to ban all *ostentatible* ("conspicuous") public religious expression, directed particularly at Islamic veils, comes immediately to mind. Believing its commitment to the principle of secularism threatened by the principle of freedom of religion, the state moved decisively to curtail such freedom.

The second weakness in Taylor's argument derives from the fact that he implicitly structures his account of the beginnings of modern secularism according to a teleological vision of Western progress that not only posits an advance from violence to peace but links it to the shrinking of Christian demands in the public sphere. This not only fails to account for the persistence of Western violence and for the crucial role Christian societies and theologians played in creating and enabling that very public sphere—a widespread error, as insidious to Habermas's account, for example, as to Taylor's[51]—but also for the extent to which it was the development of secularism itself that transformed conversion from a marginal consideration into one of Western modernity's central tropes and mechanisms.

The confusion in Taylor's representation of Western democracy foregrounds the extent to which our problem is that, as nations and societies, we still lack the adequate concepts and tools to think *collectively* about our democracies' current flaws, about the ways in which and the extent to which they remain unrealized. Certainly, there exists an extensive body of scholarly and popular works energetically criticizing our societies' failures. The problem in this case, however, is not only that the existence of such critique is itself used to validate the idealized vision of democracy—"see, we're an open society composed of independent, critical individuals free to state our minds"—but that these critiques are all too often made in the name of a likewise idealized democracy. Disagreement, then, primarily comes from divergent views concerning *how* to achieve the ideal, while that ideal itself remains underarticulated and undertheorized, as if we all—not so much political theorists as the public at large—knew what we mean by "democracy." The question becomes one about means *rather than* ends, when what we need is the rigorous challenge of reconfiguring *both* means *and* ends.

The dramatic global changes of the past fifty years—the vast human migrations; the immediacy of travel, communications, and weapons technology; the new diasporic, transnational and international communities to which this has given rise; the (thus far unsuccessful) pressures on the West to extend its democratic commitments to international economic and socio-political relations; the vast mass and influence of American cultural productions and their imbrication with American global economic-political intentions in the name of "benign imperialism"—all these emphasize the need fundamentally to reconsider our conceptions of democracy. Can, in such a setting, democracy still be "representative," or do we need a new mechanism and logic for articulating and authorizing power? Is the concept of "citizen" still the right one for naming an individual's relation to the most significant socio-political institutions structuring her life? And how can we best resolve the tension between nation-states' decreasing control over their own economic, social, and cultural territories, even as such states are still the only institutions we have to guarantee the protection and enforcement of human rights?

It is at this point—the question of the West's identity and historical intention—that discussions of the veil become most "local," most shaped by national, regional, even municipal differences in historical vision, political tradition, and socio-cultural life. So, for example, while all the debates on the veil throughout Europe express a deep-seated anxiety and sense of strident urgency, the discourse varies significantly across the continent. It centers, for example, on the issue of *laïcité* in France, whereas the question of the state's religious toleration is the organizing principle in the Netherlands. The question of Judeo-Christian social and cultural superiority predominates in Germany, while that of Catholicism's cultural and institutional centrality preoccupies discussion in Italy. Just as importantly, within nations themselves there exist significant internal differences. In the Netherlands, for example, at the municipal level public responses to Islam encompass everything from the controversial multi-religious, dialogic, and inclusive policies of Amsterdam's mayor Job Cohen to the equally controversial anti-Islamic intentions of Rotterdam's influential Leefbaar Rotterdam (Livable Rotterdam) faction. Even more locally, at the level of the city district, individual neighborhood schools and other institutions are developing intentionally inclusive and exclusive policies regarding headscarves and veils, religious education, and holiday celebrations. While certain traditionally Christian schools in the Netherlands are once again foregrounding their respectively (orthodox/reformed) Protestant or Catholic identities and principles in the hopes of discouraging poor Muslim/migrant students, other historically "Dutch" and even Christian schools are developing and integrating Muslim religious educational materials in order to strengthen their ties to the predominantly migrant neighborhoods surrounding them. Such integration of an Islamic trajectory, however, can in turn frustrate new Muslim schools competing for the same students with their own mix of Islamic/migrant and Dutch pedagogical structures, which now are less likely to obtain a license for establishing educational facilities for those neighborhoods. The majority of migrant parents indicate a preference for having their children attend "integrated" schools, yet the demand for Muslim schools has expanded phenomenally in recent years.

In this way, the abstractions of much larger continental and national debates are concretely re-enacted in funding and policy decisions made neighborhood by neighborhood, street by street, family by family. These operate within the framework of an intricate local politics of money, religion, and culture, articulated in terms of institutional, neighborhood, city, and personal life-worlds that bedevil any simple opposition between "Islamic" and "Western" standpoints. At the very same time, each conflict and development cannot help but be deeply formed by the ongoing and unresolved question of European nations' individual and collective future in the face of their growing multi-culturalism and multi-religiosity. So even as local developments follow their own complex logic of syncretism and multiple contestation, they become fodder for these larger national, continental, and global debates concerning the relation between the West and the Rest. These debates, in turn, not only erase much of the local politics involved but then themselves become the terms within which, at crucial moments, the local debates are conducted. The crucial point here is that the local and the global are not discourses and developments that can be isolated from each other, as if they took place in different locations at different moments, cleanly separated—the local city council and CNN news; the sidewalk, migrant café, and the world's great halls of power; the line at the cashier and (inter)national policy statements. No, they flow through each other and become each other, one after another after another, as we shift from word to word, moment to moment, place to place. We take them from each other's mouths, give them shape, and pass them on.

. . .

The discourse concerning the veil within the West, then, is hardly about the veil itself. Or, rather, the veil is continuously postponed and interrupted—as it has been within my own essay in its attempt to clear the ground for a constructive, critical consideration of its object.

And there is still so much more to tell. What about the veil's centrality to modern Western epistemology itself, how it is that in placing man where God had been, we took as our task the unveiling of reality. Is this not the central trope of modern thought, of science, of politics, of our work as scholars and intellectuals? Going one step farther, when we realize the complexity of the world and the limits of our human mind, is it not again the veil to which we refer—as do, not surprisingly at all, Hélène Cixous and Jacques Derrida in their collaborative bundling of "loosely" autobiographical/confessional texts under the title *Veils,* reflecting on the obscured and obscuring nature of vision, identity, and knowledge?[52]

And what about the beginnings of modern philosophy, of Kant, who called up the veiled goddess Isis to visualize "the moral law within us," to which we listen and whose command we understand, though "we are in doubt whether it comes from man, from the perfected power of his own reason, or whether it comes from an other, whose essence is unknown to us and speaks to man through this, his own reason."[53] It is the question of the metaphysical itself that is veiled, its existence at once unresolved and other. Here, too, the veil is a medium of translation, not only between self and other, between me and the law, between reflective and active being, between man and spirit, but also, as Hent de Vries points out, between the extremes of philosophy and obscurantism—pedagogy and mystagogy, in Kant's own words—as these touch one other.[54]

Going back further still, what are we to make of the homeward-bound Odysseus putting on the sea goddess Ino's veil in order to keep from drowning, a magical transvestism (the only one in the Homeric world) that aligns the hero with the feminine, both to save his life and to ritually mark his transition to a new, domestic existence far from the exotic world of vice and danger he has traversed?[55]

Finally—leaving Europe but remaining in the West—there is the veil's distinctive symbolic life in America and the possibilities it provides for reading the European discourse against the grain, a reading replete with the potential for creating both a more complex understanding of the veil's life in the West and revealing potential resistances hidden from the generally derisive Western view. We might begin with Hawthorne's "veiled lady" in *The Blithedale Romance*, situated amid the growing tension between the commercialized public realm and the private domestic realm. And then there is Madame Blavatsky's *Isis Unveiled*, the founding work of theosophy, which not only sought to bring together the living and the dead, but also—through the figure of Annie Besant—Western and Eastern religiosity, in the process transforming both. Most powerful of all, however, is the way in which the great radical African American activist, scholar, and writer W. E. B. Du Bois deploys the trope of the veil in his *The Souls of Black Folk* (1903). While in the first instance the veil marks the oppressive divide between white and black, it also becomes the site of resistant difference—a difference at once racial, gendered, ontological, and spiritual—which has as its object of critique not only reigning racist ideology but also the rationalism of Western Enlightenment discourse.

As Cynthia Schrager has explained, Du Bois's intention in representing the "spiritual strivings" of African Americans is explicitly to counter Booker T. Washington's foregrounding of the economic sphere as the primary site of integration—what the critical editors of the March 1905 issue of *The Voice of the Negro* called Washington's "soulless materialism."[56] Crucially, this articulation of the divergences between Du Bois and Washington in terms of materialism versus spiritual(ism) both followed the structure of the larger debates of the day between (empiricist) science and (mystical) religion and referenced the popular practice of spiritualism, whose intention it was to materialize those who had gone beyond the veil of death. In this way:

> Du Bois's use of the trope [of the veil] joins "race" to "spirit," figuratively installing blacks "on the other side" as a kind of spiritual counterculture to white materialism. . . . Du Bois's utopian image recalls the heterosexual complementarity at the heart of sentimental culture's gendered division of the public and private realms. Occupying a position analogous to that of the "feminine" in sentimental culture, "blackness" functions in *Souls*—to borrow Kenneth Warren's apt formulation—as a "posture of dissent" against the materialism of American culture. At times romanticized, even essentialized, *Souls* offers a powerful and problematic critique of the nexus of the terms determinism, materialism, realism, and positivism . . . Du Bois's use of premodern images and resources in *Souls* represents an important location for his critique of the enlightenment rationalist project, a project that is problematically complicitous with the institution of slavery.[57]

There as here, then as today, the veil marks the intersection of white and black, male and female, public and private, the material and the ephemeral, the economic and the human, the rational and the spiritual, dispassionate science and passionate moral commitment. In this way, the veil becomes not only the trope for marking conflicted social divisions but also the nature of our own work as scholars mediating between the academic and the political. That is, the importance of Du Bois's work lies in the conjunction between his critique of the American racial regime, of American materialism, *and* of the fundamental methods and assumptions of empiricist rationalism. Throughout, the question is that of how to make visible the invisible, "how to make intelligible that which has been relegated to the outside of normative cultural boundaries."[58] By taking this as his challenge, Du Bois transforms the veil from an agent of black invisibility into an active site of renewal, creation, and critique: the mark of silenced difference becomes the site of innovative, visionary dissent.

Applied to the West's dominant accounts of Islam's alienness, these resistant configurations of the veil by critical minorities, particularly Du Bois, offer the possibility not only of disrupting the currently hegemonic discourse but of interrupting and rewriting "Europe," "modernity," and History themselves (along with "America")—to the point where they become not simply territories of homogeneous space and empty time to be fought over under a political regime of conversion but sites of rigorous and visionary tolerance. Lest I be assumed to naively idealize what today in the Netherlands is considered by too many to be an old-fashioned and discredited commitment to diversity, I want to conclude with a sketch of a very real historical alternative offered by Australian aboriginal territorial practices:

> Unlike countries that mutually exclude one another, this aboriginal conception of country allows one country to span the territory occupied by peoples who speak mutually unintelligible languages or different dialects, and who have different social structures and kinship systems. It also allows for countries, tracks, to cross one another, to occupy the same objective space. Typically one country crosses another at a specific location that is important to both. Each group's story of their dreaming tells of the encounter with the other group at the place of intersection. When a group performs rites at a totem location shared by other groups, they all meet together, share their knowledge through dance drama performances, and form relationships based on the terms of these crossings.[59]

The point is not that we need to create this in the West. It is already here; just veiled. All we need to do now is find the words, and through them the worlds to match them.

Yâ SATTâR!

Laïcité, or the Politics of Republican Secularism

Yolande Jansen

The fact that citizens inhabit several public spheres that overlap and extend laterally and do *not* coincide with national boundaries produces difficulties for the modern secular state.

—Talal Asad

Laïcité creates the religious by turning it into a separate category, which should be isolated and circumscribed. It reinforces religious identities instead of letting them dissolve into more diversified practices and identities.

—Olivier Roy

In the end it is not the girl who is excluded, but the scarf.

—Henri Pena-Ruiz

Laïcité—the French version of secularism, which insists on the strict separation of church and state or, more generally, of politics and religion—has become well known internationally in the context of the March 2004 law prohibiting pupils at public schools from wearing "signes religieux ostensibles [conspicuous religious signs]."[1] Historically, however, it is important to view *laïcité* in the context of the struggle between Catholicism and Republicanism during the first decades of the Third Republic (1870–1905). This contextualization will allow us to critique the use of *laïcité*, but also of secularism more generally, as a frame within which to conceptualize contemporary questions concerning ethno-religious diversity and, in particular, the presence of Islam. I will argue that, if we want to try to answer contemporary questions concerning the deep diversities and inequalities that have arisen in the context of postcolonial migration, we need to deconstruct the opposition between *laïcité* and *communautarisme*, the generic term used in French discourses to denote most versions of multiculturalism and identity politics, often associated with a challenge to equal republican citizenship. Moreover, we also need to deconstruct the underlying opposition between freedom and *appartenance* ("belonging") inherited from the French Enlightenment. To develop an alternative frame, we will need to pay systematic attention to the distribution of power and to minority-majority relations and critically to rethink the relation between religion and culture in the sociological concept of secularization that underlies the political-philosophical concept of *laïcité*.

Laïcité as a Cultural Concept

In principle, *laïcité* is a juridical-political concept institutionalizing the separation of the republican state from religion.[2] French political philosopher Cécile Laborde has said that it does not fundamentally differ from other liberal principles when it comes to dealing with religious diversity.[3] Since 1905, French law has separated church and state more rigorously than do countries such as Britain, Germany, or Denmark, but this is only a matter of degree. Moreover, contemporary French political practice, like that in other Western countries, creates ample space for religious pluralism, as well as encouraging the exercise of religious freedom. To give just one small example, contrary to what the law of 1905 prescribes and what received opinion thinks is still in practice, the French state does finance private religious schools and religious associations. It has also been recognized that the French state, despite its ideology of the strict independence of religion and state, has a long tradition of the *gestion* ("management") of religion.[4] This implies not only its accommodation within the public sphere but also, more strongly, its centralization and at least partial control by the state.[5]

Though the concept of *laïcité* needs to be set against the backdrop of the secularization of the French state in a centuries-long struggle with the Catholic Church, the term was first used in the 1870s, as were its counterparts the verb *laïciser* ("to secularize"), and the nouns *laïcisation* (the action and result of *laïcité*), and *laïcisme* (the doctrine of *laïcité*). Only the adjective *laïque*, derived from the Greek *laos* ("people"), is much older (1487; it means "that which does not form part of the clergy"). The meaning of *laïc* is very close to that of *séculier*, which denotes that "which belongs to the *siècle*" (the first meaning of *saeculum* in Latin; in English, "century"), that is, to the temporal order, the *monde* (the second meaning of *saeculum* in Latin; in English, "world"), as opposed to the religious, atemporal order. *Le Petit Robert* lists the derivations of *laïque* and *séculier* as synonyms, yet the grammatical equivalent of *laïcité, secularité,* is not recognized as a word.

It is no coincidence that the combatant hypostatic nouns of the more neutral adjective gained prominence during the struggle of the Third Republic finally to rid itself of the Catholic heritage and of the pope's and the aristocracy's shared aspirations to overturn the results of the Revolution. After the defeat of France in the Franco-Prussian War in 1870, the Second Empire was replaced by the Third Republic. At the outset, the Third Republic confronted a country divided in an ongoing struggle between *les deux France*. The first France was the prerevolutionary "eldest daughter" of the Catholic Church. After the Revolution, traditionalists and counterrevolutionaries claimed it to be (and constructed it as) the real, authentic France, the romantic Catholic "tradition" that would have been passed on to new generations had it not been so rudely destroyed by the Revolution.[6] The other France was the post-Revolutionary *État-nation*, the political nation founded during the Revolution. As the negative of the first France, which received its rulers from God (the king) and, most frustratingly, partly from Rome, the new, modern France constructed itself as an autonomous, self-constituting political nation.[7]

During the struggle between *les deux France*, Republicans needed to develop an ideology that could replace Catholic morality and that would spread the ideal of secular citizenship across the country. Due in particular to the introduction of *suffrage universel*, public schooling became crucial to prevent the people from voting for an authoritarian (Catholic) regime. As the famous Republican Ferdinand Buisson, one of the great proponents of public education, aptly stated in 1899: "Two conditions must be fulfilled to set a republic on its feet. One is easy: you must provide it with a republican constitution. The other is difficult: you must provide it with a people of republicans."[8]

Thus, from the beginning it was clear that Republicanism required more than just a juridically defined secularity; it needed a pedagogy to institutionalize a culture of Republicanism.[9] The perception of this need gave a dimension to *laïcité* that persists in its contemporary understandings, where the concern is not so much with freedom of conscience and the disestablishment of religion as with a "communitarian concern for civic unity," which tries to "substitute democratic civic loyalty for religious and traditional allegiances."[10] Three political cartoons from the time of the separation of 1905 will help us to grasp the symbolic aspects of the struggle around public education in French culture.

Figure 9, Charles Fournigault's "The Declaration of the Rights of Man and of the Citizen," is a didactic image. It has frequently been used as an educational poster to advocate *laïcité*. We see "once upon a time" opposed to "today." In parallel, Catholic icons such as the castle, serfdom, and community are opposed to the republican institutions of school and the vote. The transition from the premodern "once" to modernity's "today" takes place through the teaching of the Declaration of the Rights of Man and of the Citizen. Note the strong symbolic opposition between religious belonging and the freedom of citizenship. Public school is presented as a crucial institution for the transition from a "natural" provincial situation of communal social hierarchy to a "civilized" urban democracy figured through the orderly, partitioned windows, which act as mediators of a modern, mathematized view of the natural world "outside" and, if we push the interpretation a little, function as symbols for the equality of all individual citizens.

FIGURE 9   Charles Fournigault, 1905: "La Déclaration des droits de l'homme de du citoyen [The Declaration of the Rights of Man and of the Citizen]." (From Pierra Nora, ed., *Les Lieux de mémoire* [Paris: Gallimard, 1992], 98.)

Figures 10 and 11 are ironic answers to the didactic efforts of cartoons such as Fournigault's. They suggest that the transition from premodern to modern times also meant, to some, the replacement of one monistic state system, heading toward strong centralization, with another. These cartoons, drawn by the famous political cartoonists Jules-Félix Grandjouan and Gustave Henri Jossot, were both published in the critical anarcho-syndicalist magazine *L'Assiette au beurre*.

"Choose, you're free" suggests that the struggle between church and state was a struggle about the center of (pedagogical) power. The cartoon deconstructs the opposition between Catholic belonging and traditionalism, on the one hand, and the freedom associated with modern citizenship, on the other. It is either *catholicité* or *catholaïcité*, as *laïcité*

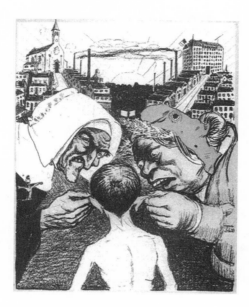

FIGURE 10   Jules-Félix Grandjouan (1904): "Choisis, tu es libre [Choose, you're free]." (*L'Assiette au beurre*, 1904; http://www.payer.de/religionskritik/karikaturen6.htm; accessed on June 6, 2005.)

FIGURE 11   Gustave Henri Jossot (1907): "Respect." (*L'Assiette au beurre*, 1904; http://www.assietteaubeurre.org/respect/respect_f1.htm; accessed on June 6, 2005.)

was famously dubbed by Edgar Morin, and there is little freedom for the pupils on either side of the spectrum. It is not accidental that the two teachers depicted are women. The first great *laïc* educational law, of August 1879, obliged every department of France to have a teachers' training college for women. Jules Ferry, the minister of education, argued that Catholicism upheld its influence through women, positing that "women must belong to Science (and not) to the Church."[11] The smoking factories in the background of the cartoon suggest that underneath the superficial difference between public and private schools is the same inescapable "capitalist hell."[12]

The cartoons contain some key concepts from the present-day discourse of multiculturalism. The concepts of respect and commune are particularly striking.[13] It is as though the slogans of those forms of pluralism that seek to overcome the neglect of difference and inequality in formal conceptions of liberal citizenship, well known from the philosophies of Will Kymlicka, Iris Marion Young, or Charles Taylor, were anticipated in France in such a way that, as a cultural memory, they appear to imply a return to a premodern traditionalism linked with predemocratic structures of society. Thus, these forms of pluralism seem themselves to imply inequality.

"The Declaration" and "Choose, you're free" share a specific conception of history. They conceive of societal change as taking place in either radically backward or forward movement. The direction of modern society is not a gradual mediation between group belonging and formal citizenship, but sudden change through revolutionary steps; only such change can move inherently immobile systems. We can only fall back into premodern, that is, communal social structures or be dragged in the direction of an inescapable "capitalist hell"—or perhaps in the direction of a second Revolution, which would promise an entirely new form of community. Because of this revolution-based conception of history, it is difficult for memory, tradition, community, and religion to be interwoven or entangled with modernity, freedom, and democratic politics.

In contemporary questions surrounding the presence of Islam, we are now dealing with the religion of a minority that has no history of political domination, as Catholicism did. Rather, both in the colonies and in contemporary France, Islam is associated with a history of a lack of power, a history that, moreover, involves ethnic othering. This affects the applicability of the frame of *laïcité*. We cannot responsibly transpose the imaginary structure of the struggle between church and state into an abstract opposition between politics and religion, then translate it into a concern about the role of "political religion" in contemporary society. This, however, is precisely what happens in the discourse of *laïcité*, as Olivier Roy has argued.[14] I think a deeper critique should also be made. In what follows, I try to demonstrate that it is not enough to distance ourselves from the *laïcité de combat* ("combatant *laïcité*") inherited from the Third Republic (as, for example, the Stasi committee does), or even to distance ourselves from the frame of *laïcité* in general (as Olivier Roy does). Instead, we should also criticize the unhelpful conceptual schemes inherited from *laïcité's* cultural history, showing the traces of the modernist abstract opposition between *appartenance* ("belonging"), on the one hand, and freedom, on the other. I will substantiate this in both the moderate discourse on *laïcité* of the Stasi committee and Olivier Roy's critique of it.

The Stasi Report

In July 2003, the president of the Republic, in the midst of ongoing conflicts about girls who came to school wearing headscarves, appointed a commission of prominent French philosophers, jurists, sociologists, historians, and pedagogues, led by the Christian-Democratic politician Bernard Stasi, to examine the situation. (In particular, in the early summer of 2003 a lot of media attention had been devoted to the case of two daughters of an atheist Jewish father in Aubervilliers, Paris, who had presented themselves at school wearing scarves, had refused to take them off, and had been sent away from school. Their father, a lawyer at the antidiscrimination organization MRAP, did not like their decision but defended their right to wear the scarves.) At the end of its deliberations, the committee issued the "Stasi Report," which provides a lengthy analysis and redefinition of *laïcité* and imparts to the French government the crucial recommendation that it issue a law prohibiting the wearing of "conspicuous religious signs" in schools.[15]

The headscarf conflicts provided the major focus of the report, but other struggles were at least as important. The report mentions, among other things, Islamic women's refusal to be treated by male doctors, Islamic pupils' refusal to participate in physical education, the refusal of Islamic pupils or their parents to acknowledge the authority of female teachers, Islamic pupils' refusal to attend classes on the Holocaust, the general rise of anti-Semitism, the increase in group thinking at schools in general, and the pressures brought to bear on young people, girls in particular, to define themselves as members of a "different" community. Although the Stasi Report does not mention September 11, a fear of terror and the generally acknowledged possibility that, with its large Muslim population, France too could once more fall victim to a terrorist assault probably also inspired the French government to rethink the merits of *laïcité*. After all, as recently as 1995, members of the Algerian GIA had exploded three bombs in the Paris Metro, killing eight and wounding two hundred.

The Stasi committee sought to answer these challenges by rethinking the compatibility of *laïcité* and pluralism, as well as their limits. The explicit aim of the committee's redefinition of *laïcité* was to provide a common ground on which to live in diversity, not a denunciation of diversity itself in the name of a Jacobin heritage. When read superficially, the Stasi report is one of the most pluralistic documents ever produced in French official circles. The committee explicitly distances itself from *laïcité de combat* (2.3). Quite symbolically, the concluding words of the report are "le pluralisme, la diversité [pluralism, diversity]" (Conclusion). These two concepts occur throughout the report. With regard to education, the committee proposes that more attention should be paid to immigrants' histories, to colonial history, and to "the religious fact."

By proposing the prohibition of "conspicuous religious signs," however, the committee not only created an exception to this multicultural attitude but also revealed how deeply problematic ethno-religious pluralism remains in French society, at least among republican intellectuals. The committee explained its decision as follows. It does not oppose pluralism, but it does resist a *communautarisme* intent on drawing legal or political boundaries between ethnic or religious groups within France, as well as the practicing of a "prosélytisme agressif [aggressive proselytism]" (1.2.3). Today, therefore, in addition to indicating the neutrality of the state and the separation between church and state, *laïcité* also implies "la défense de la liberté de conscience individuelle contre tout prosélytisme [the defense of individual freedom of conscience against all proselytism]" (1.2.2). Here, rather than a bipolar relation between state and individual, a triangular relation between individual, community, and state is at stake. We are dealing not only with the protection of the freedom of individual consciousness from intrusion by the state, but also with the protection of freedom of conscience—by the state—from a "devoir d'appartenance [duty to belong]" (4.1.2.2). This duty to belong is imposed upon individuals by communities that want to keep their members from merging into the melting pot of general individual citizenship. Headscarves have become the symbol of this struggle.

The result of the duty to belong is that Islamic girls living in the (ghettoized) *banlieus*, where *communautarisme* is strongest, are under severe pressure to wear the headscarf. The committee reported that it had been particularly sensitive to the "cri de détresse [cry of distress]" of girls forced to wear headscarves, which the many teachers interviewed by the committee contended formed the "silent majority" (4.2.2.1). If these girls do not wear the scarf, they pay the price of being harassed, socially excluded, even sexually assaulted—of being considered *putes, infidèles,* or *impudiques* ("whores, adulterers, or shameless women"). Some girls had to be interviewed behind closed doors because it would have been dangerous for them to speak of their experiences in public.[16] The most acute formulation of this concern is a phrase in the Stasi report stating that the headscarf now provides the girls, paradoxically, with the very protection that the Republic should offer (3.3.2.1.).

This new constellation of the relation between individual, state, and community has convinced some of those known as "new secularists," who for years opposed *laïcité de combat* and promoted a moderate multiculturalism, to endorse the new law on *laïcité*, including the prohibition of the scarf in public schools. To the surprise of many, for example, Alain Touraine, who had always opposed the prohibition of the scarf and who had defended interpretations of it as a *bricolage* of the new and the old, came out in support of the new law. Explaining his change of mind, he said that *he* had not changed but France had and that, to his great dismay, it had become a *communautarian* country. Whereas at first the scarves could be interpreted as symbols of hybridity and cultural negotiation, as signs of an integration that preserved the agency of the migrants themselves, now Touraine had concluded that the girls and organizations defending the scarf were proposing, in the same bargain, an undesirable *communautarisme*.[17] According to this reasoning, the scarf has become the sign of a segregationist *communautarisme*, or of "political Islam," which is frequently used as a synonym. It is no longer seen as an aspect of a possibly private Islamic belief, and options less dependent on the public-private divide are not taken into account.

One might ask a few questions here about diagnosis and treatment. If we are concerned with violence perpetrated against women in the name of specific religious claims, should our answer take the form of a general prohibition of "conspicuous religious signs" at school? Why not concentrate on providing Islamic women with as many possibilities for participation in the larger society as possible, instead of putting this participation at risk when they wear a headscarf?[18] Why not concentrate on issues of ghettoization, economic exclusion, and the incapacity of the educational system to deliver inclusion for everyone? Why is the idea of political religion, or, more generally, of *communautarisme*, perceived as so problematic that even its harmless symbols, like scarves and kippas, must be prohibited?[19]

Here, I think we must refer back to the cultural meaning of *laïcité*, which not only problematizes a duty to belong, but all kinds of belonging to "communities" smaller than the nation, which are perceived as competing with citizenship and therefore as problematic, as traditionalist, and something that should be overcome. The committee sometimes forgot that its primary concern was the *devoir d'appartenance* of the oppressed girls and squarely returned to a concern with the appearance of religion in public places. This is apparent, for example, when the report states that the headscarf affairs have symbolized the "delicate questions" posed by the wish to realize "la conciliation entre liberté de conscience et exigences de la neutralité du service public [the reconciliation of the freedom of conscience with the demands of the neutrality of the public sphere]." The committee's slippage into the old problematic might explain why, if the *problem* is girls being forced to wear the signs of belonging to a separate community, the *solution* is thought to lie in the prohibition of headscarves in schools.

The heritage of old *laïcité*'s problematically abstract distinction between freedom and belonging becomes more apparent when we analyze in detail the Stasi committee's general normative standpoint on the desirable relation between *laïcité* and *communautarisme*. We have already noted that the committee distances itself from the classical Republican political philosophical tradition, which defended the unity of the social body and perceived difference as "threatening."[20] Yet the report is reluctant actively to endorse diversity. It deploys passive constructions or indefinite pronouns like "certains [some people]":

Aujourd'hui la diversité est parfois présentée sous un jour positif; le respect des droits culturels est revendiqué par certains qui les considèrent comme un aspect essentiel de leur identité. Conserver culture, croyance, mémoire—réelle ou imaginée—apparaît comme une forme de protection tout en participant à un monde mouvant d'échanges.

Today, diversity is sometimes presented in a positive vein; respect for cultural rights is claimed by some who consider them an essential aspect of their identity. To preserve culture, belief, and memory—real or imaginary—appears to be a form of protection while participating in a changing, moving world. (1.2.4.)

This explanation actively endorses neither cultural rights nor the conservation of culture, memory, or belief. By not distinguishing between the two, the committee implies that little distinction can be made between the various possible multicultural claims. Talking about "conservation" implies that multicultural claims are usually put forward with conservative goals in mind. Such an approach does not take the relational aspects of these claims into account: for example, how they may be part of a negotiational process designed to improve the power position of a minority. Nor does it consider the transformative aspects of these claims, which may aim not at conservation but at a transformation that is not assimilation at a rapid pace.[21]

In the next quote, we can see the strong terms in which the link between communitarian sentiment and the exacerbation of cultural identity is perceived: "Nier la force du sentiment communautaire serait vain. Mais l'exacerbation de l'identité culturelle [ne saurait] s'ériger en fanatisme de la différence, porteuse d'oppression et d'exclusion. [To deny the force of communitarian sentiment would be vain. But the exacerbation of cultural identity (should not) establish itself as a fanaticism of difference, bearer of oppression and exclusion]" (1.2.4). Diversity is accepted only because it is inevitable. It is perceived as something to be tolerated rather than embraced. Communitarian sentiment is accepted, but the perceived danger is immediately noted: the exacerbation of cultural identity should not turn into fanaticism. Again, diversity is seen as almost immediately turning into violence, through the assertion that it should not lead to fanaticism, oppression, and exclusion, as if this were to be expected.

The next sentence of the report is designed to specify what underlies the tendency of diversity toward fanaticism: it states that "chacun doit pouvoir, dans une société laïque, prendre distance par rapport à la tradition [in a secular society, everyone should be able to distance him- or herself from his or her tradition]." This does not at all imply a "reniement de soi, mais un mouvement individuel de liberté permettant de se définir par rapport à ses références culturelles ou spirituelles sans y être assujetti [denial of self, but an individual movement of freedom, permitting the individual to define him- or herself with regard to his or her cultural or spiritual references without being subjected to them]" (1.2.4). This phrase repeats the old dichotomous distinction between tradition and belonging, connoted here by subjection, on the one hand, and individual freedom, on the other. As a specification of what is necessary to avoid fanaticism, such a generalized claim concerning how an individual should relate to tradition should be rejected, for it is questionable that there is an either/or choice between distancing oneself from one's tradition and being subjected to it. The phrase repeats the freedom of conscience, but now makes it something assigned by the state. This spills over into a concept of "liberal" individual autonomy that is incompatible with recent moderate liberal views of the "reasonable pluralism of the good life."[22] Moreover, fanaticism is not intrinsically linked to profound religious beliefs. Those who seek to formulate normative views of society should reflect on the social and political conditions of freedom rather than attempt to indicate how an individual should conceive of an "individual movement of freedom."

Perhaps a more important question is whether this normative stance on how individuals should relate to their tradition is appropriate for Muslims in France. The Stasi committee interprets demands for the right to wear headscarves in public schools in terms not of a premodern traditionalism but of political religion as a reaction to modernity, as an act of will. With Islamism, we are not talking about the *capacity* to distance oneself from one's tradition, but about the *will* to do so. The committee claims, for example, that the scarf was affirmed in the Muslim world as a new tradition in the 1970s with the emergence of radical political-religious movements, and that the scarf appeared in French schools only at the end of the 1980s.[23] The committee does not reflect on this transition in the interpretation of the scarf, from being a sign of premodern traditionalism to signifying a postmodern refusal to distance oneself from one's constructed tradition. In its normative explanation of what *laïcité* requires, the Stasi committee refers to tradition rather than to this political-religious movement of postmodern identity politics, merges traditional religion with specific forms of political religion, and falls back into a generalized distrust of religion.

Moreover, the interpretation of the scarf in terms of postmodern identity politics suggests that those who do not endorse the laïcist frame either cannot distance themselves from their tradition or have constructed a political religion from scratch. This again does no justice to the intricacies of actual religiosity, nor, for that matter, to the intricacies of secularity. For both religious and nonreligious persons, elements of autonomy and heteronomy, of being defined by (a fragmented but partially transcendent) tradition and by oneself, are always entangled and interdependent. The ideological turn of the debate lies in the way we conceive "modern" French people as being able to distance themselves from their traditions "rationally," while, when others do the same and partly construct and transform their traditions, they are considered as exacerbating their cultural identities, if not worse.

We encounter the heritage of a dichotomy between belonging and freedom in explanations of the function of the public school in terms of *laïcité*. The neo-republican philosopher Cathérine Kintzler, for example, recently formulated the republican idea of the public school as a place pupils attend not as consumers or in order to enjoy our rights but in order to "s'autoconstituer comme sujet [constitute oneself as a subject]."[24] According to Kintzler, this means that pupils get the opportunity—but are also obliged—to distance themselves from all prerational, social, and religious forms of belonging. Pupils should be encouraged to evaluate critically all kinds of worldviews without having to decide to become a member of any particular one. In other words, public school is the space where *laïcité* realizes itself as an actual place:

> Toute l'argumentation revient à dire que les élèves présents à l'école ne sont pas des libertés constituées (comme c'est le cas des citoyens dans l'espace civil), mais des libertés en voie de constitution et que l'école est une institution productrice de la liberté.

> The whole argument boils down to the idea that the students present in the school are not constituted liberties (as is the case with citizens in the public space), but liberties that are in the process of being constituted, and that the school is an institution that produces freedom.[25]

The Stasi committee gave a similar definition of what *laïcité* should entail in the context of public school, but it adds the making of the *citoyen* in the process:

> À l'école de la République sont accueillis non de simples usagers, mais des élèves destinés à devenir des citoyens éclairés. . . . [L'école] doit favoriser une mise à distance par rapport au monde réel pour en permettre l'apprentissage.

> At the school of the Republic we do not welcome simple users but pupils destined to become enlightened citizens. . . . [The school] must encourage a distancing from the real world, to permit its being learnt. (4.2.2.1)

One criticism of Kintzler's and the Stasi committee's laïcist arguments concerning the role of public education might be that they present the transition from *appartenance* to *autoconstitution* as something quite unproblematic that we can decide on when we pass the threshold of the school. A critical reply from "within" to this advocacy of the school as the place to constitute oneself as a subject, or a *citoyen éclairé*, could be found in Émile Durkheim's rethinking of Kantian morality, which so inspired Republicans at the end of the nineteenth century.[26] Figure 12, Grandjouan's "Always the idols," illustrates the enormous force of (neo-)Kantian thought in the development of the official secular philosophies of pedagogy at the turn of the nineteenth century. In this cartoon, Victor Hugo, the hero of nineteenth-century anticlerical pedagogy, is carried aloft, accompanied by the idols from both Republican and Catholic sides: Joan of Arc, Kantian morality, duty, the moral law, and immortal principles. Durkheim was the first Republican professor of peda-

FIGURE 12   Jules-Félix Grandjouan: "Toujours les idoles." (From Pierre Nora, ed., *Les Lieux de mémoire* [Paris: Gallimard, 1992], 118.)

gogy at the Sorbonne; he was also the first to be sensitive to the mediation between republican morality and the religious heritage, and to detranscendentalize the idols in the process of acknowledging this mediation. He thought that Republican morality could not be entirely derived from an imagined, ideal, universal, but ultimately nonexistent reason. Therefore, he translated Kant's idea that reason produces the moral law into the idea that the law is the product of a collective labor. By doing so, he subtly transformed Kant's antinomy of morality into a sociological view of humanity.

In Kant's view, morality implies, on the one hand, that the law should be produced by reason. In that sense, the law is given to the subject rather than constituted by it: it implies heteronomy. On the other hand, morality implies that the subject gives him- or herself the law: it implies autonomy. In his explanation of Kant's antinomy, Durkheim translates it into a slightly different one. At the autonomy pole, Durkheim stays close to Kant: we cannot think that "the will can be fully moral when it is not autonomous, when it passively receives a law of which it is not itself the legislator." But in his explanation of the heteronomy pole, Durkheim distances himself from Kant. According to Durkheim, heteronomy means that "the moral rule is the product of a collectivity, we receive it much more than that we make it."[27] What precedes the subject for Durkheim is not pure reason but collectivity, and with this argument, he makes the Kantian concept of morality, oxymoronically, "sociologically transcendental."

For Durkheim, it is important that Kantianism, like Protestantism, supposes the translation of the heritage of religious, transcendent morality into moral principles:

> With Protestantism, the autonomy of morality becomes even more apparent, because the strictly cultic element diminishes. The moral functions of the divine become the only reason for its existence; this is the only argument invoked to prove it. . . . We must look, at the very heart of religious conceptions, for moral realities that here are as if lost and dissimulated; we must free them to find how they are consistent, to determine their proper nature, and to express them in a rational language. We must, in a word, discover the rational substitutes for these religious notions, which, for so long, have served as carriers of the most essential moral ideas. . . . We must discover these moral forces, which man, up to the present, has not learned to represent to himself except in the form of religious allegories.[28]

Durkheim considers the heritage of the religious past to be an indispensable reservoir of moral forces. Autonomy does not mean that we reject the religious heritage or that we rise above it in order to evaluate it critically from an Archimedan point of view. What we need, rather, is a translation of the concretely developed, historical moral forces that religions have carried with them.

A preliminary examination of *laïcité* through its history reminds us that its moral-philosophical basis is much more complex than is suggested by contemporary claims concerning the ways in which public schools embody its ideals. I would propose that the prohibition of religious signs in public schools is at least partly the result of a wish to reaffirm the laïcist foundations of public schooling in the struggle with a religion, Islam, that is perceived to be as threatening as clerical Catholicism once was. In that sense, the prohibition is not only an answer to the violence perpetrated against girls in their struggle against their "duty to belong," but more fundamental. By this affirmation of the laïcist foundations of public schools, it is not this violence but religion in general that is once again brought into competition with a modernist conception of subjectivity.

In fact, even before the philosophical problematic Durkheim formulated, Kant himself already problematizes this conception of subjectivity. Ironically, the great philosopher of autonomy refers to veiling in order to make clear how "transcendental" the sources of our moral sense are: "The veiled goddess before whom we of both parties bend our knees is the moral law in us, in its inviolable majesty. We do indeed perceive her voice and also understand very well her command. But when we are listening, we are in doubt whether it comes from man, from the perfected power of his own reason, or whether it comes from an other, whose essence is unknown to us and speaks to man through this, his own reason. At bottom we would perhaps do better to rise above and thus spare ourselves research into this matter; since such research is only speculative, and since what obliges us (objectively) to act remains always the same, one may place one or the other principle down as a foundation."[29] A questioning of this modernist self-understanding is imperative at a time when more and more people, not only Muslims, come to understand themselves (partly) in religious terms. If we do not question the frame of *laïcité* and its counterpart, *communautarisme*, we risk reducing our analyses of the problematic place of Islam in contemporary France to accusations that political religion, or identity politics in general, are the underlying cause of violence. Instead, we should analyze the constellation of this violence, its social context and the place of religion within it, without any predeterminations from the modernist philosophical heritage.

Olivier Roy on *Laïcité* and Globalized Islam

The dichotomous conception of belonging and freedom that we have discerned in the discourse of *laïcité* also appears in Roy's sociological analysis of contemporary Islam, developed most recently in *Globalized Islam* and *Laïcité in the Face of Islam*.[30] Roy is critical of approaches to Islam within the framework of *laïcité,* as well as those that use the framework of multiculturalism. According to him, both *laïcité* and multiculturalism assume the existence of Islamic "communities" or contribute to their formation. He considers *laïcité* the ideology of a republic "obsessed with the religious" and "fascinated by monarchy."[31] *Laïcité* frames the claims of an Islam that wishes to become visible in the public sphere in terms of a contest for political power, thus translating *social* religious identities into political ones. In doing so, *laïcité* enhances the formation of religious identities linked with political contestations, instead of facilitating their merging with more diverse identifications and practices. Multiculturalism, by contrast, links Islam to migrants' cultures of origin and tends to grant power to conservative elites supposedly representing entire ethno-religious groups. For Roy, however, these elites at most represent the purely religious neo-communities of those who explicitly declare themselves their "members." Underlying Roy's critique of contemporary normative philosophies of integration is a sociological analysis of contemporary Islam, particularly of the "public" Islam challenging the diverse European secularisms.

Roy argues that this public Islam is not a traditional Islam inherited from migrants' cultures of origin. Rather, it forms part of a wider "return of the religious" in a globalizing world, one also apparent in, for example, Christianity and Hinduism. In the case of Islam, the emergence of such a "neo-fundamentalism" is politicized because of the history of the Middle East, but this does not prevent Islam from taking part in a dynamics of globalization and secularization just like other religions. This is particularly so in the West, where Islam has become a minoritarian religion and has thus been brought to recognize a secular realm "outside" religion. Moreover, in globalized neo-fundamentalist Islam, all ties to specific cultures (and states) are deliberately cut in the search for a "pure," universal religious community, the *ummah*.[32] Second- and third-generation migrants, in particular, feel attracted to this form of Islam, because they can use it as an apology for the "deculturation" and "uprootedness" that have resulted from migration.[33] Global Islam is thus linked to the individualization processes demanded of individuals living in the West. New global media such as the Internet fit this new, deterritorialized religion perfectly. Being a Muslim, like being a believer in other religions, has become a matter of choice, and those who choose to make it a crucial element of their identities should be considered *born-again* Muslims rather than Muslims in any cultural (ethnic) sense.

Roy considers the results of viewing contemporary Islam through either the framework of *laïcité* of that of multiculturalism equally disastrous. *Laïcité* squeezes this neo-religion into the old frame of a religion aspiring to state power, when the level of the state is precisely *not* relevant to this Islam. The emphasis on *laïcité* creates fears of an Islamic *communautarisme* by majorities, analogous to those in the nineteenth century of the *classes dangereuses*—when in actuality these "communities" hardly exist. Only very weak forms occur. These develop at the level of neighborhoods or in even weaker, more imaginary, forms at the global level—but not, however, at the level of the nation-state. Moreover, laïcists tend to create a divide between "good" (liberal and secular) and "bad" (fundamentalist) Muslims, thus excluding from dialogue those that should be included (and *gérés* ["dealt with"]).[34] Multiculturalism, by contrast, addresses conservative elites as representative of predefined ethno-religious groups. These elites can acquire political power over nonbelievers and over those who consider themselves secular Muslims by claiming the right to protect these ethno-religiously defined communities from pressures to assimilate. Policies based on a better understanding of neo-fundamentalist Islam would avoid creating or imagining more extensive communities than there actually are. They would exclude no religious groups from dialogue and would not interfere with other people's dogmas, but, at the same time, they would never consider the spokesmen of religious groups to be the representatives of entire ethno-religious communities.

Although I think Roy's criticism of the frameworks of *laïcité* and of a top-down, conservative multiculturalism is welcome, I find problematic the interrelated use of the concepts of culture, multiculturalism, and secularization in his understanding of globalized Islam, which he deems necessary in order to be able to present his critique. To talk of the "deculturation" of second-generation immigrants and endorse the theoretical possibility of a strict separation of religion from (ethnic) culture is to assume an essentialist notion of culture that links it to an ethnic particularity and immediate belonging, which members of the second generation lose or can even actively reject. But what about the relation of neo-Islam to a more general concept of culture, which encompasses practices, beliefs, and ways of doing, seeing, and thinking, as well as ways of negotiating with the members of majorities and "making" culture in the process? Moreover, by not distancing himself clearly from the neo-fundamentalist concept of Islam's "deculturization" into a pure religion, indeed, even deploying it in his own conceptual scheme, Roy assumes a problematic understanding of secularization. He (and the neo-fundamentalists) seem to follow the modernist understanding of secularization as the radical individualization of religion, leading to religion's complete break with tradition and belonging. In short, with the strong opposition between (ethnic) culture and (individualized) religion, we seem to reencounter in Roy's sociological notion of secularization the dichotomy between belonging and freedom criticized in the discourse of *laïcité*.

The suggestion of a possible "deculturization of religion" is based on what we could call a "strong theory of secularization," inherited from Durkheimian sociology. Historically, this notion of secularization is linked to the interpretation of Protestantism as an individualized "religion of the heart" that severs itself from the *culte*, from tradition, and from institutions. We came across this notion of secularization when discussing Durkheim's pedagogy, where he suggested the full autonomy of morality from the *culte* in Protestantism.[35] Roy's endorsement of a similarly strong version of secularization overlooks the many criticisms of the modernist concept of secularization as privatization and individualization, even within the context of Protestantism. Veit Bader, for example, distinguishes three versions of the secularization thesis: it can refer to the privatization of religion, to its individualization (the two are often conflated), or to the separation of religion from politics. Bader refutes them all. First, believers may recognize that their beliefs and practices are contingent and, in Roy's words, "minoritarian," but this does not mean that they will (or must) privatize their religion. Second, religious belief may individualize to a certain extent, but never to the point of becoming purely subjective, "asocial," or "deculturized"—this point is directly relevant to a critique of Roy. Third, organized religions may develop as public religions while at the same time being "modern" in the sense of open to democracy.[36] Yet another way to launch a systematic critique of religion as a "pure" or invisible religion of the heart, or as a pure "belief" without rule or ritual, would be via Wittgenstein's philosophy of meaning.[37] Wittgenstein rejects the possibility of (Cartesian) subjectivities by refuting the possibility of a "private language" and by arguing that meaning-making is an inevitably social, cultural practice, a matter of *Gepflogenheit* ("custom").[38] This is also so in religious matters.

In conclusion, the return of the religious does not only designate a changed state of affairs in society. In contemporary philosophies of religion, it also corrects earlier theories of secularization, which Roy seems to endorse without question. Understanding global Islam as a fully secularized, individualized religion presses it into a frame that is as old as the frame of *laïcité* Roy criticizes. This frame, moreover, is based on the same modernist divides between belonging and freedom, autonomy and heteronomy, private and public inherited from the nineteenth century.

This is problematic not only theoretically but also politically: it draws boundaries between an Islam inextricably linked to immovable "cultures of origin," on the one hand, and to a supposedly deculturalized, deterritorialized "neo-Islam" as the *Islam des jeunes* on the other. Furthermore, it links images of a (dangerous) "deculturization" and "up-rootedness" to young Muslims. Like the Stasi committee, Roy is not specific enough in tracing the causes of violent behavior: by concentrating on Islam as a religion, he fails to address in any systematic manner the difficult knots linking contemporary Islam with questions concerning ethnicity, poverty, othering, and global politics.

I would like to suggest that a sophisticated notion of culture should play a mediating role in understanding these questions, linking the emergence of globalized Islam to the particular cultures with which it interacts. I do not mean culture in the sense of a reified copy of the (past) culture of origins, but culture as a nodal point linking (in this case) religious experience and practice to memories, power positions, and the experiences of others in the present. To substantiate this, before returning to the headscarf issue, I would like briefly to discuss the definition of culture Bonnie Honig proposes in her reaction to Susan Okin's famous thesis that multiculturalism is bad for women:

> "Culture" is a way of life, a rich and time-worn grammar of human activity, a set of diverse and often conflicting narratives whereby communal (mis)understandings, roles, and responsibilities are negotiated. As such, "culture" is a living, breathing system for the distribution and enactment of agency, power, and privilege among its members and beyond. Rarely are those privileges distributed along a single axis of difference such that, for example, all men are more powerful than all women. Race, class, locality, lineage all accord measures of privilege or stigma to their bearers. However, even those who are least empowered in a certain setting have some measure of agency in that setting and their agency is bound up with (though not determined by) the cultures, institutions, and practices that gave rise to it.[39]

This definition has the advantage of being packed with contrasting elements. To my mind, it grasps what culture can mean once we put aside both its essentialist definition in terms of "original belonging" and the antiessentialist or constructivist attempt to empty out the concept of culture to the point of denying its relevance. Honig's definition grasps the complexity and pervasiveness of culture. This definition inextricably links belonging and freedom, or, analogously, structure (system) and agency. What might have been added is a note on the relational and negotiational elements of culture as it is made by different groups occupying different power positions. Culture thus defined is relevant to contemporary discussions about Islam in relation to secularism in at least two ways.

We need to conceive of a systematic link between Islam and culture if we wish to analyze the position of Muslims in France not only in terms of their self-definition but also taking into account the ways in which they are positioned and made into ethnic others by cultural majorities. There is a subtext of ethnic othering and xenophobia linked to Islam that is difficult to address if we stay within the discourses that focus exclusively on Islam as religion. Let us not forget that the first headscarf affairs coincided with Marianne wearing a *hijab* or *tchador* in political cartoons.[40] Ethnic othering is not the exclusive domain of the Front National, but also penetrates the framework of *laïcité*. Most strikingly, this was demonstrated by the fact that, the day before the Stasi committee presented its report, *Le Monde* published a petition signed by many famous French feminists claiming to defend the rights of women: "The Islamic veil pushes all of us, Muslims and non-Muslims alike, towards an intolerable discrimination against women. All complacency in this regard would be perceived *by every woman of this country* as a personal attack on her dignity and freedom."[41] We need to link Islam and culture (in the sense of ethnic culture but *not* in the sense of inherited ethnicity) theoretically so that we can analyze and criticize the mechanism of exclusion that betrays itself here: "if you do not think like us, you do not belong to us." Roy's concentration on the nonmatch between the framework of *laïcité* and neo-fundamentalist Islam as a fully secularized religion makes this as difficult as the framework of *laïcité* itself.

A notion of culture is also relevant for understanding the position of Islam in France in relation to intercultural memory, which should be a memory that links religion to power positions. This is an evident and necessary step in the case of Islam in France, with its colonial background. In the summer of 2003, I spent a long day with Samia, a young Algerian woman studying in Paris who wears a headscarf. That day, she taught Arabic at a *centre culturel* in St. Denis—where she hospitably took me. In reply to my questions about her scarf, she at first said that the scarf was something between her and Allah. We could interpret this, à la Roy, as a sign of neo-fundamentalist individualism, but we would at least have to admit that the personal relation of the believer to God is also a crucial element in classical Islam. This was not the only motive she gave for wearing the scarf, however. Her second answer, that "our mothers wore headscarves when they cleaned the houses of the French and it was never a problem," contains a postcolonial and class-based argument. For Samia, the headscarf had only become a problem in the eyes of the French when Muslims started to be public *citoyens*. Perhaps her argument evoked the fact that, in Algeria until 1947, Muslims were considered *sujets* and could only become *citoyens* after abandoning their religion, while Christians and Jews were considered *citoyens*. Taking seriously these shared memories—of a long period of shared experiences of exclusion—does not imply the use of a reified concept of culture. A definition like Honig's will do. Such a concept of culture is more dynamic than Roy suggests; it can help us to embed cultural and religious claims in history and to connect them with agency without declaring them purely constructed or ideological beforehand.[42]

Trying to Understand French Secularism

Talal Asad

In modern society there is typically a multiplicity of religious beliefs and identities, and—so we are told—they can be held together only by a formal separation between religious belonging and political status, and by the allocation of religious belief to the private sphere. To be fully part of a democratic community, citizens holding different religious beliefs (or none) must share values that enable them to have a common political life. These values reflect the unity of the state that represents them. Without shared values there can be no integration, without integration no political stability, without some measure of stability no justice, no freedom, and no tolerance. Secularism provides the framework for realizing all these things.

But what do people mean when they say that the integration of a national population requires them to "share fundamental values"? Partly they mean that all citizens should "respect the law," and that therefore they should accept the final authority of the national state (but foreign nationals resident for varying periods in the state as well as tourists and visitors from many lands are also expected to "respect the law" without sharing fundamental values). Sometimes they also mean that if members of society share verbal and behavioral codes they can communicate better with one another (although good communication is as likely to facilitate dispute and disagreement as it is to secure consensus). Mostly what people have in mind, I think, is something that they all value equally and that *therefore* holds them emotionally together. An interesting question is why everyone's having essentially the same values should be thought to be so crucial for urban societies in which most interactions are between strangers, more often than not ephemeral in character, and in which most people are probably thankful they do not have to bond emotionally with one another in every urban encounter. In each society there are circles of trust and mistrust, archipelagos of solidarity set in seas of danger or distaste, that do not coincide with state boundaries.

It will quickly be pointed out that this sharing of values and sentiments is not about quotidian life but about collective decision making at a nation-state level by which diversity is managed and a sense of national belonging is fostered, and that the latter can only happen if civil status is separated from religious affiliation. But although it is normal for liberal democracies to insist that all citizens have the same civil and political rights—for example, that they are entitled to due process, to political and legal representation, and so on, irrespective of belief, race, or gender—it does not follow that religious, racial, or gender criteria are necessarily excluded from consideration in assessing or improving the status of legal persons who are citizens.[1] In other words, neither the qualities that make all citizens politically equal in a liberal democracy nor those that differentiate them in it require "the general sharing of core values"—a homogeneity that defines *the nation* as a community of sentiment rather than the state as a structure of law.

In relation to the European Union, one often reads that "A shared religious heritage based on Christian values . . . may be seen as one formative cultural influence at the heart of and giving substance to 'European' civilization."[2] Although the constitution of the European Union excludes any reference to Christianity, the sentiment that Christianity is central to its heritage remains quite common in Europe. Many French people, while strongly opposed to any mention of religion in the EU Constitution,[3] have no difficulty in speaking of their "Judeo-Christian legacy"[4]—a pregnant phrase now that "Islam" has become the Stranger Within. A history of shared cultural values is taken to be a sound basis for political union. What it means to say that Europe shares a religious heritage, however, given its recent history of bitter conflicts and wars, is not clear. Nor is it obvious what "Christian values" (or "Judeo-Christian values") are, given that historically Christians (and Jews) have valued a wide range of often inconsistent things on the basis of different interpretations of traditional texts. Nevertheless, the idea that a successful modern nation-state rests on a dominant culture that encodes shared values is now commonplace.

The assumption that there are core values, a national culture that secures political unity, enables many people in Europe to ask: How do the values of Muslim immigrants affect the unity of the nation? Many non-Muslims express anxiety because of their belief that "Islam" does not negotiate with "non-Islam." One response to that has been to insist that both in the past and today many Muslims *have* negotiated with non-Muslims, and *have* adapted to life in polities ruled by non-Muslims—especially in colonial countries. But beyond such attempts at liberal reassurance it can be argued that even in liberal societies politics is not merely about toleration and adjustment. Because of the emphasis on autonomy in modern secular society, democratic politics is also about resisting power that demands adjustment to privileged norms, about exerting pressure to alter laws that underwrite social conditions regarded as unjust or unreasonable. The liberal claim that societies must be "open" implies that majorities do not have an absolute right to remain undisturbed. Even in a democracy the majority may have to learn to reorient itself. "Assimilation" is never a one-way process, but the attitude of the majority to its signs is always critical: Is the process to be read as enrichment (never tidy, often unpredictable in its consequences) or as contamination ("adulteration," "debasement," "mongrelism")? There is in fact no "final solution" to political problems—other than death.

The preoccupation with unity has been a central feature of authoritarian discourse, and the requirement of loyalty to symbols of the nation is central to that political tradition. I do not mean to suggest that it is always an indicator of authoritarianism. My thought is that the call for "unity" and "integration" may be seen as part of the problem of *centralized state control*. Those who are to be unified or integrated are required to submit to a particular normative order. The solution to that problem has taken various forms. The genocidal horror inflicted on European Jews by the Nazi state, including Jews who had assimilated, was one such "final solution." Effacing public signs of religious difference in order better to integrate with the abstract state they inhabited did not save them. For this racist state, assimilation was itself highly dangerous because it carried the implication of degeneration.

Racist states seem to have emerged in Europe at the threshold of modernity. The Spanish historian Rodrigo de Zayas describes how, during the latter part of the sixteenth century, Spanish ruling elites came to the conclusion that Moriscos (Spanish Muslims who had been forcibly converted to Catholicism) had to be eliminated in order to attain a unified nation. They discussed ways of attaining that end, including genocide, assimilation, and deportation. Being assimilated to the state religion did not save the Moriscos. In 1609 a law was finally passed in favor of deportation, resulting, Zayas writes, in the first racist state in European history.[5] True, there was an earlier "racist" law forbidding anyone who didn't have "clean blood" from taking up a paid position in Spain—the person concerned having to prove that no Jew or Muslim had been a member of his family for at least four generations.[6] Zayas argues, however, that this was a confused way of trying to identify "religious purity" in *specific* cases. By contrast, the 1609 law focused neither on religion nor on the individual case but on an entire minority population identified formally as "a different nation" according to cultural signs (dress, language, habits, etc.). This reading amounted, in effect, to a "secular" response to the problem of integration, even though it had emerged from the realm of Catholic Kings. In many respects, Zayas claims, the "Morisco question" in the sixteenth century anticipates the "Jewish question" in the first half of the twentieth: a concern with the "political health" of a governed population.

In what follows I want to look in some detail at another secular reading recently rearticulated in France in relation to its Muslim citizens, which is certainly not as drastic as either of the two I have mentioned. France is, after all, a democratic country, in which various liberties are safeguarded, legally and in everyday intercourse. I reflect on the recent restatement of *laïcité* from an anthropological perspective, by which I mean simply trying to see a particular public event—or series of interlinked events—as the articulation of a number of organizing categories typical of a particular (in this case political) culture. The event on which I focus is the so-called Islamic veil affair and its central articulation is the Stasi commission report. But first a caveat: much has been written on this subject, some arguing for and some against the right of young Muslim women to wear the headscarf in school; my essay is not part of that debate. Nor is it in any sense an attempt to offer solutions to what is often called "the crisis of *laïcité*." Its more modest aim is simply to try to understand some concepts and practices of French secularism.

For most of 2003 and much of 2004, following a speech by then Interior Minister Nicolas Sarkozy in April 2003,[7] French public opinion was exercised by the affair of "the Islamic veil." Should Muslim girls be allowed to wear a covering over their hair when they are in public schools? The dominant view was definitely that they should not. A considerable amount of polemic has been published on this topic, in France as well as elsewhere.[8] This was not the first time that the matter had been publicly discussed, but on this occasion the outcome was a law prohibiting the display of religious differences in public schools. The headscarf worn by Muslim schoolgirls has become a symbol of many aspects of social and religious life among Muslim immigrants and their offspring to which secularists object. Researchers have inquired into the reasons for their lack of integration into French society,[9] and especially for the drift of many of their youth toward "fundamentalist Islam" (*l'islamisme*), a drift that some trace to pervasive racism and to economic disadvantage, but that others see as a result of manipulation by conservative Middle Eastern countries and by inflammatory Islamist Web sites. Intellectuals have debated whether and if so how it is possible for religious Muslims to be integrated into secular French society. The passions that have led to the new law are remarkable, and not only on the part of French Muslims. The majority of French intellectuals and politicians—on the left as well as the right—seem to feel that the secular character of the Republic is under threat because of aspects of Islam that they see as being symbolized by the headscarf.

Grace Davie, a well-known British sociologist of religion, has written extensively on contemporary European religion. Referring to France, she writes, "It is . . . the country of Western Europe which embodies the strictest form of separation between church and state. The French state is rigorously secular—or '*laïque*,' to use the French term. It is conceived as a neutral space privileging no religion in particular and effecting this policy by excluding the discussion of religion from all state institutions, including the school system."[10] Statements like this assume that French secularism is built on relatively simple and austere principles. As I shall argue, this is far from being the case.

People commonly find the origin of *laïcité* in the constitution of the Third Republic at the end of the nineteenth century. But secularism has many origins, and I find it useful to begin the story in early modern times. At the end of the sixteenth-century wars of religion, the states of Western Christendom adopted the *cuius regio eius religio* principle (the religion of the ruler is the religion of his subjects). This agreement is part of the genealogy of secularization in that it attempted to resolve *particular religious* problems by adopting *a general political* principle at a time when "the core of religion" was coming to be seen as an internal matter. Contrary to what is popularly believed, it was not the modern world that introduced a separation between the religious and the political. A separation was recognized in medieval Christendom, although of course it meant something very different from what it means today. For one thing, it articulated complementary organizing principles. Although in theory distinct, "temporal power" (the monarchy) and "spiritual power" (the church) together embraced the entire realm through a multiplicity of mutually dependent—and sometimes conflicting—*personal* relations. The medieval idea of the king's two bodies (the body natural and the body politic, the one physical and the other metaphysical) was eventually transfigured.[11] The state became de-Christianized and *depersonalized*: political status (a new abstraction) could be separated from religious belonging, although that doesn't mean it was totally unconnected with religion. The dominance of "the political" meant that "religion" could be excluded from its domain or absorbed by it. That in turn presupposed a political concern with identifying religion either in its nominal or adjectival forms. The reading of uncontrolled religion as dangerous passion, dissident identity, or foreign power became part of the nation-state's performance of sovereignty. Defining religion's "proper place" while respecting "freedom of conscience" became both possible and necessary.

Put another way: once the state became an abstract, transcendent power, independent of both rulers and ruled (as Hobbes famously theorized it), it was possible to argue about the scope of its national responsibilities toward social life as a whole—the space in which subjects with different (religious) beliefs and commitments live together. It became natural for *the state*—now seen as an overarching function distinct from the many particular purposes of social life, and distinct also from the national bureaucrats, parliamentary representatives, judges, and other officials who carried out that function—to decide not only who was deserving of (religious) tolerance in that life but what (religious) tolerance was. And it became possible to think about mobilizing the sentiments of *both* rulers and ruled in support of the integrity of beliefs that could be obeyed. Signs (emblems) were needed for the abstract state to represent itself, of course, and beyond that, it needed the ability to deal with signs that defined what it represented. Signs are important to all political authority, but especially so to the modern state because of the several domains that it carves out and the diverse activities it regulates.

In 1589 the Edict of Nantes gave French Protestants the right to practice their religion in a Catholic realm, at the very time when Spain was on the verge of expelling its Muslim converts to Christianity. Although the Edict was revoked in 1685, the French Revolution a century later denounced all "religious intolerance" and attacked the ecclesiastical hierarchy in the name of Liberty, Equality, and Fraternity. The political oratory and pamphleteering of the Revolution crystallized a public space that was national in its focus and ambition. By then, of course, the essence of religion had come increasingly to be defined as consisting essentially of personal belief, so that the Church as a public body appeared primarily to be a rival for political authority. The result was nearly a century of bitter conflict between the state and its internal competitor for sovereignty, a conflict finally resolved under the Third Republic, which was dedicated to a civilizing mission in the name of the Revolutionary ideals of humanity and progress.[12] When in 1882 the Third Republic made secular schooling compulsory for six- to thirteen-year-old children, national education became a means of inculcating positivist humanism in its future citizens and weaning future generations away from the historical Church. It was coincidentally then, under the Third Republic, that a significant extension of France's colonial conquests took place, justified by its *mission civilisatrice*, the crusading complement to its positivist nation-building at home. (Although Algeria had been conquered earlier in the century, in 1830, Tunisia was annexed in 1881 and Morocco in 1907, both under the Third Republic—as were other places in the Pacific, Southeast Asia, and West Africa.) Anticlerical schooling at home, unequal agreements with the Church, and imperial expansion abroad were the pillars on which *laïcité* was established under the Third Republic, a significant moment in the formation of modern French nationalism. Algeria was an exception to the onslaught of positivist schooling. Here Church and state worked hand in hand, with the former being encouraged by the latter to organize the religious conversion and appropriate schooling of Muslim Algerians.[13]

Interestingly, with the coming of the Third Republic, established after the ignominious defeat of France by Prussia in 1870, some people sought to present the secular Republic as "a Muslim power" and even tried to invent an "Islam of France." Established together with Catholicism, Protestantism, and Judaism as religions entitled to state funding for schools, Islam differed from those three in being recognized only in one part of France: Algeria. Patriotic orientalists like Louis Massignon, who survived the Great War, became applied Islamologists in the service of France, enthusiasts for the project of emancipating Muslims within the framework of the French empire.[14] It was the Republic that would decide who was worthy of being emancipated, and *how*, by bringing to bear its own passion for *laïcité* as the exercise of benevolent power.

I want to suggest that the French secular state today abides in a sense by the *cuius regio eius religio* principle, even though it disclaims any religious allegiance and governs a largely irreligious society.[15] In my view, it is not the commitment to or interdiction of a particular religion that is most significant in this principle but the installation of a single absolute power—the sovereign state—drawn from a single abstract source and facing a single political task: the worldly care of its population regardless of its beliefs. As Durkheim points out in his writings on integration, the state is now a transcendent as well as a representative agent. And as Hobbes had shown, it could now embody the abstract principle of sovereignty independent of the entire political population, whether governors or governed, and independent of any supernatural power.

One way of looking at the problem that interests me is this: since "religion" directs the attention of subjects to *otherworldly* concerns, state power needs to define its proper place for the *worldly* well-being of the population in its care. (This doesn't include the guarantee of life; the state may kill its own or let them die while denying that right to anyone else. But it does include the encouragement of a flourishing consumer culture.) An image of worldly well-being that can be *seen* in social life and so *believed in* is needed, but so is an answer to the question: What are the signs of religion's presence? *Laïcité* therefore seems to me comparable to other secularisms, such as that of the United States, a society hospitable to religious belief and activism in which the federal government also finds the need to define religion. In the American case, however, there is more reliance on courts than on legislation.[16]

Reading Signs

Because religion is of such capital importance to the lay Republic, the latter reserves for itself the final authority to determine whether the meaning of given symbols (by which I mean conventional signs) is "religious." One might object that this applies only to the meaning of signs in public places, but since the legal distinction between public and private spaces is itself a construction of the state, the scope and content of "public space" is primarily a function of the Republic's power.

The arguments presented in the media about the Islamic headscarf affair were therefore embedded in this power. They seemed to me not so much about tolerance toward Muslims in a religiously diverse society, not even about the strict separation between religion and the state: they were first and foremost about the structure of political liberties—about the relations of subordination and immunity, the recognition of oneself as a particular kind of self—on which this state is built, and about the structure of emotions that underlies those liberties. The dominant position in the debate assumed that in the event of a conflict between constitutional principles the state's right to defend its personality would trump all other rights. The state's inviolable personality was expressed in and through particular images, including those signifying the abstract individuals whom it represented and to which they in turn owed unconditional obedience. The headscarf worn by Muslim women was held to be a religious sign conflicting with the secular personality of the French Republic.

The eventual outcome of such debates about the Islamic headscarf in the media and elsewhere was the president's appointment of a commission of inquiry charged with reporting on the question of secularity in schools. The commission was headed by ex-minister Bernard Stasi, and it heard testimony from a wide array of persons. In December 2003, a report was finally submitted to the president, recommending a law that would prohibit the display of any "conspicuous religious signs [*des signes ostensibles*]" in public schools—including veils, kippas, and large crosses worn around the neck. On the other hand, medallions, little crosses, stars of David, hands of Fatima, or miniature Qur'ans, which the report designates "discreet signs [*les signes discrets*]," are authorized.[17] In making all these stipulations, the commission clearly felt the need to appear evenhanded. The proposed law was formally passed by the National Assembly in February 2004 by an almost unanimous vote. There were some demonstrations by young Muslims—as there had been earlier when the Stasi commission had formally made its recommendation—but the numbers who protested openly were small. Most French Muslims seemed prepared to follow the new law, some reluctantly.[18]

I begin with something the Stasi report does not address: according to the Muslims who are against the ban for reasons of faith, the wearing of the headscarf by women in public is a religious *duty* but carrying "discreet signs" is not. Of course there are many Muslims, men and women, who maintain that the wearing of a veil is *not* a duty in Islam, and it is undoubtedly true that even those who wear it may do so for a variety of motives. But I do not offer a normative judgment about Islamic doctrine here. My point is not that wearing the veil *is* in fact a legal requirement. I simply note that *if* the wearer assumes the veil as an obligation of her faith, *if her conscience impels her to wear it as an act of piety*, the veil becomes for that reason an integral part of herself. For her it is not a *sign* intended to communicate something but *part of an orientation, of a way of being*. For the Stasi commission, by contrast, all the wearables mentioned *are* signs, and are regarded, furthermore, as *displaceable* signs. But there is more to the report than the veil as material sign.

The Stasi commission takes certain signs to have a "religious" meaning by virtue of their synecdochic relation to systems of collective representation—in which, for example, the kippa stands for "Judaism," the cross for "Christianity," the veil for "Islam." What a given sign signifies is therefore a central question. I stress that, although the Stasi report nowhere defines "religion," it assumes the existence of such a definition because the qualifying form of the term ("religious signs") rests on a substantive form ("religion").

Two points may be noted in this connection. First, precisely because there is disagreement among contemporary pious Muslims as to whether the headscarf is a divinely required accoutrement for women, its "religious" significance must be indeterminate for non-Muslims. Only by rejecting one available interpretation ("the headscarf has nothing whatever to do with real religion") in favor of another ("the veil is an Islamic symbol") can the Stasi commission insist on its being obviously a "religious" sign. This choice of the sign's meaning enables the commission to claim that the principle of *laïcité* is breached by the "Islamic veil," and that since *laïcité* is not negotiable the veil must be removed. (To some extent this variability of interpretation was played out subsequently in relation to the meaning of the Sikh turban.[19])

The second point is that the "religious" signs forbidden in school premises are distinguished by their gender dimension—the veil is worn by women, the kippa by men, and the cross by both sexes. The object of the whole exercise is, of course, to ban the Islamic veil partly because it is "religious" but also because it signifies "the low legal status of women in Muslim society" (a secular signification). The girls who are the object of the school ban are French, however, living in France; they are therefore subject to French law and not to the *shari'a*. Since French law no longer discriminates between citizens on grounds of gender or religious affiliation, *since it no longer allows, as it did until 1975, that a man may chastise his wife for insubordination*, the sign designates not a real status but an imaginary one, and therefore an imaginary transgression.

Ideally, the process of signification is both rational and clear, and precisely these qualities make it capable of being rationally criticized. It is assumed that a given sign signifies something that is clearly "religious." What is set aside in this assumption, however, is the entire realm of ongoing discourses and practices that provide authoritative meanings. The precision and fixity accorded to the relationship of signification is always an arbitrary act and often a spurious one, insofar as embodied language is concerned. In other words, what is signified by the headscarf is not some historical *reality* (the evolving Islamic tradition) but *another sign* (the eternally fixed "Islamic religion"), which, despite its overflowing character, is used to give the "Islamic veil" as a stable meaning.

Assuming, for the sake of argument, that certain signs are essentially religious, where and how may they be used to make a statement? According to the Stasi report, secularism does not insist on religion's being confined within the privacy of conscience, on its being denied public expression. On the contrary, it says that the free expression of religious signs (things, words, sounds that partake of a "religious" essence) is an integral part of the liberty of the individual. As such, it is not only legitimate but essential to the conduct of public debate in a secular democracy—so long as the representatives of different religious opinions do not attempt to dominate.[20] But what "domination" means when one is dealing with a religiously defined minority, whose traditional religion is actively practiced by a small proportion of that minority, is not very clear.

It is interesting that the determination of meanings by the commission was not confined to what was *visible*. It included the deciphering of psychological processes such as desire and will. Thus the wearer's *act of displaying the sign* was said to incorporate the actor's *will* to display it—and therefore became part of what the headscarf meant. As one of the commission members later explained, its use of the term "displaying [*manifestant*]" was meant to underline the fact that certain acts embodied "the will to [make] appear [*volonté d'apparaitre*]."[21] The *Muslim identity* of the headscarf wearer was crucial to the headscarf's meaning because the will to display it had to be read from that identity. (Another aspect of its meaning came from equating the will to make the veil appear with "Islamic fundamentalism" or "Islamism," terms used interchangeably to denote a range of different endorsements of public Islam.) Paradoxically, Republican law thus realizes its *universal* character through a *particular* (i.e., female Muslim) identity, that is, a particular psychological internality. However, the mere existence of an internal dimension that is accessible from outside is felicitous for secularism. It opens up the universal prospect of cultivating Republican selves in public schools. At any rate, "the will" itself is not seen but the visible veil points to it as one of its effects.

"Desire" is treated in an even more interesting way. The commission's concern with the desires of pupils is expressed in a distinction between those who didn't really want to wear the headscarf and those who did. It is not very clear exactly how these "genuine desires" were deciphered, although reference is made to pressure by traditional parents and communities, and one assumes that some statements to that effect must have been made to the commission.[22]

It is worth remarking that solicitude for the "real" desires of the pupils applied only to girls *who wore the headscarf*. No thought appears to have been given to determining the "real" desires of girls *who did not wear the headscarf*. Was it possible that some of them secretly wanted to wear a headscarf but were ashamed to do so because of what their French peers and people in the street might think and say? Or could it be that they were hesitant for other reasons? However, in their case surface appearance alone was sufficient for the commission: no headscarf worn *means* no desire to wear it. In this way "desire" is not discovered but semiotically constructed.

This asymmetry in the possible meanings of the headscarf as a sign again makes sense if the commission's concern is seen to be not simply a matter of scrupulousness in interpreting evidence in the abstract but of guiding a certain kind of behavior—hence the commission's employment of the simple binary "coerced or freely chosen" in defining desire. The point is that in ordinary life the wish to do one thing rather than another is rooted in dominant conventions, in loyalties and habits one has acquired over time, as well as in the anxieties and pleasures experienced in interaction with lovers and friends, with relatives, teachers, and other authority figures. But when "desire" is the objective of *discipline*, there are only two options: it must either be encouraged (hence "naturalized") or discouraged (hence declared "specious"). And the commission was certainly engaged in a disciplining project.

So the commission saw itself as being presented with a difficult decision between two forms of individual liberty—that of girls whose desire was to wear the headscarf (a minority) and that of girls who would rather not. It decided to accord freedom to the latter on majoritarian grounds.[23] This democratic decision is not inconsistent with *laïcité*, although it does conflict with the idea that religious freedom is an *inalienable right* of each citizen— which is what the Rights of Man (and, today, human rights) articulate.[24] But more important, I think, is the detachment of desire from its object (the veil), so that it becomes neutral, something to be counted, aggregated, and compared numerically. Desires are essentially neither "religious" nor "irreligious," they are simply socio-psychological facts.

Now I have been suggesting not only that government officials decide what sartorial signs mean but that they do so by privileged access to the wearer's motive and will—to her subjectivity—and that this is facilitated by resort to a certain kind of semiotics. To the extent that this is so, the commission was a device to *constitute* meanings by drawing on internal (psychological) or external (social) signs, and it allowed certain desires and sentiments to be encouraged at the expense of others. A government commission of inquiry sought to bring "private" concerns, commitments, and sentiments into "public" scrutiny in order to assess their validity for a secular Republic. The public sphere, guarantee of liberal democracy, does not afford citizens a critical distance from state power here. It is the very terrain on which that power is deployed to ensure the proper formation of its subjects.

From its beginning the idea of the secular Republic seems to have been torn in two conflicting directions—insistence on the withdrawal of the state from *all* matters of religion (which must include abstention from even trying to define "religious signs") and the responsibility of the state for forming *secular citizens* (by which I do not mean persons who are necessarily "irreligious"). The Stasi report seizes this basic contradiction as an occasion for creative interpretation. The trouble with the earlier legal judgments relating to the veil, it says, is that "the judge did not think he had the power to pronounce on the interpretation of the meaning of religious signs. Here was an inherent limit to the intervention of the judge. It seemed to him impossible to enter into the interpretation given to one or another sign by a religion. Consequently, he was not able to understand that the wearing of the veil by some young women can mean discrimination between man and woman. And that of course is contradictory to a basic principle of the Republic."[25] The Stasi report regrets that judges in these cases had refused to enter the domain of religious signs. It wants the law to fix meanings, and so it recommends legislation that will do just that. But first it has to *constitute* religious signs whose meanings can be deciphered according to objective rules. For what the commission calls "a sign" is nothing in itself. "Religious signs" are part of the game that the secular Republic plays. More precisely, it is in playing that game that the abstract being called the "modern state" is realized.

One might suggest that for the Stasi commission the headscarf worn by Muslim schoolgirls is more than a sign. It is an icon in the sense that it does not simply designate but evoke. What is evoked is not a "headscarf [*un foulard*]" but "the Islamic veil [*le voile islamique*]." More than an image, the veil is an imaginary—a shrouded difference waiting to be unveiled, to be brought into the light of reason, and made indifferent.

Dealing with Exceptions

The Stasi report insists that secularism presupposes the independence of political power as well as of different religious and spiritual choices; the latter have no influence over the state, it says, and the state has none over them.[26] What emerges from the report, however, is that the relationship is not symmetrical. It is claimed that the Republic treats all religions equally. But this does not preclude its taking certain decisions that affect religion, although religion may never intervene in matters of state. This asymmetry is, I suggest, a measure of sovereign power.

Schmitt pointed out that sovereignty is the ability to define the exception. *Laïcité* is made up of exceptions, and it is the function of sovereignty to identify and justify them—to forestall thereby the Republic's "disintegration." But in view of the famous doctrine that France is "la République une et indivisible," it is not entirely clear how the fear of "disintegration" relates to the singular, invisible state as opposed to those many persons (officials and citizens) who *represent* it.

Defenders of *laïcité* (and they include most assimilated Muslims[27]) argue that the debate over the headscarf is to be understood as a reluctance on the part of the French state to recognize group identity within a Republic that is represented as a collection of secular citizens with equal rights, inhabiting a level public sphere. Of course there are differences in France, they say, and these must be recognized as aspects of people's identities so long as they do not threaten the unity of society. In articulating national unity, state neutrality, and legitimate diversity, secularism creates, over and beyond the traditional attachments of each person, that larger community of affections (*la communauté d'affections*), "that collection of images, values, dreams, and wills that sustain the Republic."[28] For this reason religious liberty must be subject to the demands of public order, as well as to the efficient performance of economic tasks.[29] "The Republic" itself stands apart from all its members, and although it depends on images, values, dreams, and wills that bind them together *as a community of sentiments*, it imposes the principle of abstract equality on all citizens irrespective of individual emotions, in a rational process of signification that is at once semiotic and political.

The first question here is whether there is any place in *laïcité* for rights attached to religious groups. And the answer is that indeed there is, although such groups are usually thought of as exceptions. Perhaps the most striking are Christian and Jewish schools, private establishments "under contract [*sous contrat*]" to the government, which are heavily subsidized by the secular state. In these state-supported religious schools, where it is possible, among other things, to display crosses and kippas, and where religious texts are systematically taught, pupils nevertheless grow up to become good French citizens. How important is this educational sector? According to the latest government figures, slightly over 20 percent of all high-school pupils are enrolled in religious schools.[30] (Incidentally, even in public schools, where "conspicuous religious signs" are now forbidden, separate dining arrangements are made for Muslim and Jewish pupils who wish to follow their religious dietary laws.)

Here are some other examples of "religious groups."

Alsace-Moselle is the one region in which the state pays the salaries of priests, pastors, and rabbis, and owns all church property. (In the rest of the country, only churches built before 1905 are owned and maintained by the state.) There are historical reasons for this exception,[31] and the Stasi report suggests these exceptional arrangements be retained on the ground that the population of that area is especially attached to them—that is, because they are part of its regional identity. Retaining these arrangements does not, the report insists, conflict with the principle of secularism.[32]

Another exception is this: although the Republic is secular, the Church of Rome has a very special position within it. The modus vivendi put in place from 1922 to 1924 between France and the Holy See allows the Republic to recognize "diocesan associations" within the framework of the 1905 law.[33] These autonomous associations are territorially defined, and they have complicated financial rights and obligations in relation to the state. Today they are the bodies representing the Catholic Church in official dealings with the Republic. In addition, there are religious councils—such as the so-called Muslim council (Conseil Français du Culte Musulman) and the highly respectable council that represents the Jewish community (Conseil Répresentatif des Institutions Juives de France). On the analogy of the Catholic Church, these organizations constitute *interlocutors* of the secular state as it aims to define "the proper place of religion."[34]

There are more exceptions that re-enforce the attachment of individuals to religious communities: chaplains in the army, in colleges, schools, prisons, and hospitals, are all provided and paid for by the state. Jewish and Muslim funerary rites are permitted in cemeteries, although the cemeteries are all owned and maintained by the state. According to the 1987 law, gifts made to religious associations benefit from tax concessions—like other associations that provide a general public service. The Stasi report acknowledges these exceptions to the principle of the state's absolute neutrality but sees them as "reasonable modifications" that allow each person to exercise his/her religious liberty.[35]

France is not—and never has been—a society consisting only of individual citizens with universal rights and duties. Signs are not neutrally distributed in the Republic. French citizens *do* have particular rights by virtue of belonging to religious groups—and they have the ability to defend them. Thus early in 1984, when the Mauroy government attempted to introduce limited state intervention in religious schools, massive demonstrations in Paris and Versailles (about a million in the former) led to the government's fall. Although demonstrations are not in the normal sense part of a reasoned *debate*, they do of course express and defend political positions in a passionate yet legally permitted way.

Thus the subsidized religious schools throughout the country, the diocesan associations, the special arrangements in Alsace-Moselle, the religious associations that lawfully receive donations and hold property, as well as the religious gatherings that have the right to perform burial rituals in public spaces or march in funeral processions through public thoroughfares, all have a politico-legal presence in the secular structure of the French Republic. To these organizations belong many citizens, clerical and lay, whose sensibilities are partly shaped by that belonging. Do such groupings amount to "communitarianism"? The term is less important than the fact that France consists of a variety of groupings that inhabit the public space between private life and the state. And since they dispose of unequal power in the formulation of public policy, the state's claim of political neutrality toward all "religious" groups is rendered problematic.

The Stasi commission is aware of exceptions to the general rule of *laïcité*. It explains them by distinguishing between the founding principle of secularism (that the lay Republic respects all beliefs) and the numerous legal obligations that issue from this principle but also sometimes appear to contradict it. The legal regime, it points out in its report, is not at all a monolithic whole: it is at once dispersed in numerous legal sources and diversified in the different forms it takes throughout mainland France and in its overseas territories.[36] The scattered sources and diverse forms of French secularism mean that the Republic has constantly to deal with exceptions. I want to suggest that *that* very exercise of power to identify and deal with the exception is what subsumes the differences within a unity and confirms Republican sovereignty in the Schmittian sense. The banning of the veil as a sign can therefore be seen as an exercise in sovereign power, an attempt by a centralized state to dominate public space as the space of particular signs.

A salient feature of Republican political theology is its postulate of an internal enemy. For much of the nineteenth century, this enemy was the Church. In fact, in the latter part of the nineteenth century French Catholicism was not a politically unified force. Thus the historian Émile Poulat has identified four tendencies among French Catholics in that period—integrism and liberal, bourgeois, and popular Catholicism—each of which took different positions on political, economic, and devotional matters.[37] Integrists, for example, hoped for a restored Catholic monarchy and a reempowered Church that would guide the nation, but bourgeois Catholics, committed to a faith of personal salvation and therefore content with a "private" place for religion, supported a Republic that stood for the freedoms won in the Revolution of 1793. But the unity sought by secularism needed a recognizable enemy, and a homogenized Catholic Christianity filled that role. Out of its struggle with Catholicism, *laïcité* produced its own ideology, which has now become vital in the struggle with another enemy—a homogenized "fundamentalist Islam."[38]

I want to stress that my interest is not in arguing that France is inadequately secular or that it is intolerant. I should certainly not be taken to be arguing for the veil as a right to cultural difference or for the girls' right to practice their faith. My concern is to try and identify some of the questions addressed or excluded by *laïcité*, to begin an analysis of its economy of public signs, to try to locate some of the subjects in its public spaces. I have been implying that no actually existing secularism should be denied its claim to secularity just because it doesn't correspond to some utopian model. Varieties of remembered religious history, of perceived political threat and opportunity, define the sensibilities underpinning secular citizenship and national belonging in a modern state. The sensibilities are not always secure, they are rarely free of contradictions, and they are sometimes fragile. *But they make for qualitatively different forms of secularism.* What is at stake here, I think, is not the toleration of difference but sovereignty, which defines and justifies exceptions, and the quality of the spaces that secularism defines as public. The "crisis of *laïcité*" seems to me uniquely embedded in a political struggle over two idealized models of France's future, a division that cuts across left and right parties: a highly centralized and controlling state versus a decentralized and minimalist one, in both of which the need to exercise sovereignty seems to be taken for granted. This struggle has somehow come to be linked to the state's principled definition of religion and its "public" limits in the interest of creating "a community of sentiment."

At any rate, in my view it is wrong to see secularism primarily as the modern formula for toleration (enduring a difference that strikes one as intolerable). There are obviously rigid secular societies and relaxed religious ones. Besides, the idea of tolerating difference—itself a complicated idea, ranging as it does from indifference to endurance—predates the modern political doctrine of toleration. Secularism has to do with particular structures of freedom and sensibilities within the differentiated modern nation-state. It has to do with conceptualizing and dealing with sufferings that appear to negate or discourage those freedoms and sensibilities—and therefore it has to do with agency directed at eliminating sufferings that conflict with them. In that sense secular agency is confronted with having to change *a particular distribution of pain*, and while in that capacity it tries to curb the inhuman excesses of what it identifies as "religion," it allows other cruelties that can be justified by a secular calculus of social utility and a secular dream of happiness. It replaces patterns of premodern pain and punishment with those that are peculiarly its own.

Here are some familiar examples (I leave aside Stalinist and Nazi atrocities): the deliberate destruction of civilian populations in the Allied bombing of German and Japanese cities during World War II, the ruthless American prison system, the treatment of non-European asylum-seekers by EU countries. All of these actions by liberal democracies are based on calculations of worldly pain and gain, not on religious doctrines and passions. Anything that can be used to counter attempted subversions of the state—any cruelty or deception—acquires justification as a political technique. In "a state of exception," liberal democracies defend "the rule of law" not only by issuing administrative orders to eliminate public disorder but also by the extrajudicial means of secret violence (the inflicting of pain and death), so long as that contradiction doesn't cause a public scandal.[39] Deliberately inflicted suffering in modern war and government blends into the widespread social misery produced by neo-liberal economic policies. Thus apart from the enhanced scale of suffering due to modern techniques, the quality of human suffering is often shaped by changed relations and ideas. People are taught that they are free and equal and find to their anguish that they are not: encouraged to believe that they can fulfill all their "normal" desires—even be desired by others—they find they cannot and are not. The modern sufferer's sense that pain is always worldly, or that it no longer has any moral significance, perhaps makes it less easy to bear. Certainly, modern poverty is experienced as more unjust—and so as more intolerable.

Incidentally, I do not suggest that the distribution of pain engendered by modern power is worse than the distribution in premodern societies but only that it is different. Nor do I make the foolish claim that there has been no progress in matters of suffering. The cure of various illnesses and improvements in public health and welfare are undeniable social facts that have led to the amelioration of distress and affliction. My point is only that more is at stake in secularism than compassion for other human beings in plural democratic societies. And nothing is less plausible than the claim that secularism is an essential means of avoiding destructive conflict and establishing peace in the modern world. Secular societies—France among them—have always been capable of seeking solidarity at home while engaging in national wars and imperial conquests. They are also likely to pay greater attention to problems of political order and social solidarity than to the distress that might be caused to members of one or another religious group by government policies aiming at national unity.

Today, France is being incorporated into the fiscal structure of the European Union. This situation, as well as the transnational movements of peoples and resources, of words and images, affect it in unpredictable ways. The state *appears* to be less strong than it was. Problems of political order and social security begin to seem ever more urgent.

Passionate Subjects

"Liberty, Equality, Fraternity" is a well-known image of the lay Republic. It is claimed that the secular state will not tolerate any intolerance within its jurisdiction. Its law inscribes "freedom of conscience" and "liberty of expression," "equality of political rights" and "equal access to the benefits of the welfare state." Liberty and equality thus refer to the legal status of citizens but fraternity is essentially a matter of affect, one's bond with the nation. It is thus an indication of the fact that *laïcité* is not simply a matter of legal inscriptions and political arrangements (the law state).

So how fraternal are the relations the nation oversees among its religiously diverse members? Is the nation simply the unit that is bound together in sentiments of solidarity? Vincent Geisser documents the growing tide of hostility toward Muslims and Arabs living in France today and recounts the many public statements and actions that have sought to connect this population with concerns about national security.[40] According to Geisser and others, dislike of Muslims and Islam has roots in a bitter colonial history—especially its troubled relations with Algeria—which is kept alive by a million colonial settlers who "returned" to France after its independence. "French" as an identity is commonly opposed, as it was in Algeria, to the inferior categories of "Arab" or "Muslim" (or "maghrebin"). This public attitude is now reinforced by a new concern about international terrorism. Yet in the nineteenth century a long line of French writers and travelers (including Nerval, Lamartine, and Flaubert) depicted Arabs and Muslims sympathetically—

reflecting, as they did so, their nostalgia for a world being ravaged by modernity. The passions involved then and now should not, therefore, be seen as a product of straightforward enmity. The sensibilities they express are now, as in the colonial past, sometimes fragile and contradictory. The point I wish to stress, however, is that these sensibilities go beyond "the historic conflict with the lands of Islam"; they are integral to the secular project attached to the Republic, which is to promote a certain kind of national subject who is held to be essentially incompatible with an "Islamic subject"—not merely in the legal but also in the psychological sense.

In a book that appeared a year before Geisser's,[41] Daniel Lindenberg (professor of political science in the University of Paris VIII) maintains that this wave of Islamophobia is part of a wider reactionary movement that has acquired new force and includes hostility to mass culture, feminism, and antiracism. On the one hand, popular writers like Michel Houellebecq and Oriana Fallacci (an Italian but widely read in France) attack Muslims in language that is very reminiscent of Céline's anti-Semitic obsessions in *Bagatelles pour un massacre*. On the other, eminent Catholic intellectuals such as Alain Besançon and Pierre Manent are able to get a sympathetic audience for their anti-Muslim sentiment.[42]

One aspect of this sentiment is evident in the way public talk about Muslims in France has become entangled with public concern over hostility toward Jews. For the Stasi report the rise of anti-Semitism is a major theme, to which it devotes an entire section. "The threats to secularism," it notes, "go hand in hand with a renewal of violence toward persons belonging to, or thought to belong to, the Jewish community."[43] Rémy Schwartz, *rapporteur* to the commission, was more explicit, in a statement to a journalist from *The New Yorker*. The old judgment about the veil in schools may have been adequate in 1989, he observed, but now the situation was very different. Wearing the veil had become part of an Islamic threat: "What we have now is part of a global politics of anti-Semitism, and it had to be limited."[44] According to this authoritative statement, the Stasi commission's major concern was to confront the symbol of this new global danger because it threatened the founding values of *laïcité*—Liberty, Equality, Fraternity—*from outside*.

Animosity toward Muslims is now more pervasive than toward any other religious or ethnic group.[45] Put another way: anyone who wants to be taken seriously in public life cannot afford to be known as an anti-Semite—even the National Front now attempts to avoid appearing anti-Semitic in public—but the same cannot be said of people hostile to Islam.[46] (Incidentally, even the common claim that political criticism of the state of Israel is often "a mask for anti-Semitism" acknowledges in effect that this prejudice needs to be disguised when expressed publicly.[47]) By contrast, there are many prominent intellectuals in France who publicly express opinions Muslims say they find offensive, intellectuals who remain highly respected.[48] Acts and statements offensive to Jews, on the other hand, issue largely from sections of the population that are already far from respectable: extreme right-wing elements (neo-Nazis) or Muslim youth in the "sensitive" *banlieus*. (It need hardly be said that the neo-Nazis are no friends to Muslims either.)

Sometimes the anti-Jewish acts of young Muslims are explained as a consequence of their identification with Palestinians living under Israeli military occupation or of the social exclusion and economic disadvantage suffered by Muslims in contemporary France. Invariably such explanations are denounced by some in the media as tantamount to "excusing criminal violence," and blame is placed instead on a world-wide Islamic movement.[49] Nothing, it seems, could be clearer than this as an example of the social danger of religious passion. And yet a very small proportion of French Muslims are practicing followers of their faith.[50]

The complicated emotional relationship of many French Jews with the Israeli state is too sensitive a subject for most non-Jewish commentators to deal with publicly. A thoughtful piece entitled "The Jews of France, Zionists without Zionism,"[51] written by Esther Benbassa (professor of the history of modern Judaism at the École Pratique des Hautes Études), underlines the tension between the passionate attachment of French Jews to the state of Israel and the ideological claim by the latter that all Jews belong in Israel, "in their own state." Israel's liberal democracy is, of course, distinctive in many ways. As the state of the Jewish nation, it is *not* the state of all its citizens (there is a Palestinian minority in Israel), and at the same time it *is* the state of a large population of noncitizens who are also nonresidents (Jews in other countries). Does the French state also include and exclude citizens from the French nation? Not in quite the same way, for although French Muslims tend to have strong sympathies with the predicament of Palestinians under Israeli occupation (and Iraqis since the U.S. invasion), no foreign state beckons them *as Muslims* to come and join "their own state."

Nevertheless, my point is that both Jews and Muslims in France have complicated imaginaries of distance and closeness, complicated emotions of belonging and rejection. What is missing in Benbassa's account, therefore, is a discussion of the implications this tension has for the relations of French Jews with French Muslims, for both of whom identity is at once local and transnational, and for whom memories embrace many different times and tempos. And notably missing too is a consideration of the ambivalent feelings of French Jews of Algerian origin for "Algeria"[52]—at once nostalgic and fearful.[53]

There is, in other words, a conceptual problem that lies beyond the friction between Jews and Muslims in France. It concerns the idea—on which *laïcité* is premised—that secular citizens are committed to a *single nation* (a single collective memory, as Renan put it in his influential disquisition on "the nation") and therefore to a *bounded* culture. Benbassa's article shows that precisely because secularism is a *state* doctrine, devised for the purpose of dealing with *state* unity, it does not fit well with a world of multiple belongings and porous boundaries, nor can it acknowledge the fact that people identify emotionally with victims in the past and with victims in other countries as "their own." Her article helps one to understand that, for subjects occupying different sites, different things are politically imaginable and therefore possible within networks of uneven constraint and sentiment. There is much more to national emotions than selective memory and forgetting (Renan), as I shall argue in a moment.

However salient anti-Semitism is today, as a social phenomenon it seems to me to be given greater emotional recognition by French politicians, public intellectuals, and activists than parallel expressions of prejudice against Muslims.[54] This asymmetry is due in part to a general sense that anti-Semitism has been the cause of greater cruelty in modern Europe than anything perpetrated by anti-Arab racism or by anti-Islamic phobias. It is not easy to measure experiences of cruelty against one another, but there is no doubt that the systematic attempt by the Nazis to eliminate all of Jewry within the modern nation-state is without parallel. Yet the cruelties perpetrated by the French in Algeria were not minor. They stretch from destroyed villages, orchards, wells, and fields during the conquest in the nineteenth century through numerous massacres of Muslims to the torture chambers of the Battle of Algiers in the twentieth century.[55] But all this is remembered (and therefore reexperienced) as having taken place "outside France," and the victims are thought of as "non-Europeans" (as their successors in France still are), and therefore to be taken less seriously.

In an interesting book on the symbolic role of the Holocaust in France, Joan Wolf has shown how the meaning of that event for Jews has been appropriated by diverse groups for their own discursive purposes. "After the 1990 desecration of a Jewish cemetery at Carpentras," she writes, "the nation denounced the 'fascist' Le Pen in a narrative that was tantamount to a repudiation of Vichy and an identification with its Jewish victims, and the Holocaust came to stand for the suffering and innocence of the French people at the hands of the evil and guilty Vichy regime."[56] Wolf points to the gap between the Jewish experience of trauma and the non-Jewish political rhetoric of victimhood under the Vichy regime. Certainly the Nazi racial persecution of Jews followed by their mass murder remains the dominant element in Jewish collective memory—and therefore in their sense of victimhood. Wolf has virtually nothing to say, however, about the involved and evolving relations between Christians, Muslims, and Jews in Algeria both before and after the struggle for independence. These relations tend to be differently nuanced in the collective memory of each group of immigrants in secular France. French Muslims have their own collective sense of victimhood (apart from contemporary Islamophobia in France, there are memories of colonial Algeria, images of Israeli suppression of Palestinians, etc.). But here I want to draw attention to the symbolic dependence of a morally restored France on the public recognition of Jewish suffering. This linkage, I suggest, carries its own emotional charge, one that makes it easy to substitute "Islamic fundamentalism" (read "Islam"—and so "Muslims") for Vichy's *ideological* anti-Semitism, and thereby intensifies public distrust of French Muslims as dangerous outsiders within the gate. The values espoused by Vichy are now claimed to be an interruption of "real France." although Vichy was no less a part of modern France than the *maquis* was.[57]

The shame-faced awareness on the part of many French that they themselves participated in the historic cruelty against the Jews under Vichy encourages not only their calling publicly for exceptional vigilance against anti-Semitism but also their denouncing with exceptional fervor any incident that might be called anti-Semitic. Thus criticism of the state of Israel is often said to be a sign of suppressed anti-Semitism. When politicians condemn "anti-Semitism" in their opponents, their personal motives may be unclear but the effect of intimidation in public debate is evident.[58] But for most people the expression of concern about anti-Semitism seems to indicate a hope that a nation's virtue once lost can be reclaimed, that moral damage it has done to itself can be repaired. At any rate, my main point is this: the attempt by many intellectuals and much of the media to shift the entire question of anti-Semitism to "confronting the danger of Islamism" has the comforting effect for many of diverting attention away from the historical prejudice against Jews in France and away, therefore, from the more general question of the role of anti-Semitism (*as well as of Islamophobia* and of varieties of racism) in the construction of French national identity. And the demands of national identity in France today are deeply rooted in the idea of a secular Republic with its own glorious history.

This web of emotions indicates how fraught the very idea of neutrality is in the politics of secularism. Guilt, contempt, fear, resentment, virtuous outrage, sly calculation, pride, anxiety, compassion, intersect ambiguously in the secular Republic's collective memory and inform attitudes toward its religiously or ethnically identified citizens. *Laïcité* is not blind to religiously defined groups in public. It is suspicious of some (Muslims) because of what it imagines they may do, or is ashamed in relation to others (Jews) because of what they have suffered at the hands of Frenchmen. The desire to keep some groups under surveillance while making amends to others—and thus of coming "honorably" to terms with one's own past, of reaffirming *France* as a nation restored—are emotions that sustain the integrity of the lay Republic. And they serve to obscure the rationality of communication and the clarity of signs that is explicitly assumed by the Stasi commission.

"Fraternity" is surely too simple a sentiment—even as a secular ideal—for the densities of national politics. Put another way, all modern states, even those committed to promoting "tolerance," are built on complicated emotional inheritances that determine relations among their citizens. In France one such inheritance is the image of and hostility toward Islam; another is the image of and (until recently) antipathy toward Judaism. For long, and for many, Jews were the "internal other." In a complicated historical readjustment, this status has now been accorded to Muslims instead.

This is not to say that there is no criminal activity among young Muslims who live in the "sensitive" *banlieus,* and that patriarchal attitudes don't characterize most Muslim "immigrants." But then neither crime nor patriarchy is foreign to French society. Interpreters of *laïcité* who object to French Muslims on these grounds do not consider what makes criminality and patriarchal relations *defining* features of an ethnic or religious "culture." Thus although the Napoleonic Code allowed a man to chastise his wife physically—a right abrogated only in 1975—it has not, to my knowledge, been argued that "French culture" was essentially barbaric.[59] Male violence against women is not unique to Muslim societies, and not all women who wear the headscarf in those societies are subject to male violence.[60]

It is also true that the Iranian Revolution of 1979 and the increasing prominence of Islamic militancy in many parts of the Muslim world have frightened many secularists in France. But it is unclear just how all these things have come to be construed as a threat to the "foundational values" of the secular Republic. I refer not just to the obvious fact that Islam as a minority religion today is not comparable to the Catholic Church engaged in the nineteenth-century struggle for the soul of France. It is the notion of "foundational values" that is obscure here, given that *laïcité* predates the legal recognition of the principle of gender equality by about a century.

One might therefore wonder whether the headscarf affair wasn't generated by a displacement of the society's anxieties about its own uncertain political predicament or its economic and intellectual decline. In a witty and incisive review of the Stasi report, the French anthropologist Emmanuel Terray has recently claimed that this is how the headscarf affair should be understood—as an example of "political hysteria," in which symbolic repression and displacement obscure material realities.[61] Terray points out that in discussing the "threat to the functioning of social services," the Stasi report makes no mention of inadequate funding but focuses instead on the minor difficulties created when some Muslims make "religious" demands in schools, hospitals, or prisons (see especially pp. 90–96 of the report). Of course, this is precisely what *laïcité* is. Its overriding concern is with transcendent values (the neutrality of the state, the separation of "religion" from politics, the "sacredness" of the republican compact) and not with immanent materialities (the distribution of resources, the flexibility of organizations, etc.). Isn't this why the strong defenders of *laïcité* seem unwilling to explore the complicated connections between these two?

Terray's article is a tour de force, and although his primary concern is with explaining the *origin* of the headscarf affair (unlike mine, which is to try to use it as a window into *laïcité*), I think that affair should not be seen simply as an irrational attempt to respond to a real political-economic crisis. I suggest that for many the antipathy (even hostility) evoked in this event is, quite simply, part of what it means to be a secular Frenchman or Frenchwoman, to have an identity formed by layers of educated emotions. The affair *is* about signs and about the passions evoked by them. The signs *do* have political and economic implications, but they do not stand as empty masks. The advocates of secularism claim that signs are important when they signify the worldly equality of all human beings and invite compassion for human suffering. There is a special sense in which this claim is right, although the game of signification is much more complicated than spokespersons for the Republic declare it is.

Defenders of the veil claim that it is integral to their religious beliefs. Whether this is true or not interests me less than the following question: How does the secular state address the pain of people who are obliged to give up part of their religious heritage to show that they are acceptable? The simple answer is: by expecting them to take beliefs lightly. Most liberals are not passionate in expressing their beliefs. It is worth recalling that in early modern Europe neo-stoic thinkers who supported the emergence of the strong, secular state—the state that became the foundation of modern nationalism—did so because they saw passion as a destructive force that threatened the state. Since for them passion was identified with religious belief, this meant in effect a detachment from the latter—a skepticism in matters of faith. This virtue seems to have been absorbed into the style of liberalism, so that religious passion has tended to be represented—especially in a modern political context—as irrational and divisive. After the Revolution, passionate investments even in personal relationships were often frowned upon. Louis de Bonald's well-known condemnation of divorce is an expression of just that attitude.[62] (The Revolution had legalized divorce in 1791, but it was again made illegal in 1816.) The moral basis of the family would be undermined, de Bonald argued, if love were to be accepted as the criterion of its formation and dissolution. Although de Bonald was not a liberal, his distrust of passion finds echoes in the bourgeois cultivation of self-presentation in public through the nineteenth century into the twentieth. As in the political domain, so in the private—the sense among many is that passion is a disturbing force, the cause of much instability, intolerance, and unhappiness.

Passionate support of *secular* beliefs was not—is not—regarded in the same way. *That* passion is felt to be more like the public expression of "objective principle" rather than "subjective belief"—a criterion supplied by the Positive philosophy. Where, as in the French Revolution, secular passion led to Terror, this was precisely because it was a *revolution*, a divided people in the process of being made into a united Republic. In general, distress is a symptom of irrational and disrupted social conditions. "Good" passion is the work of secular enlightenment, not of religious bigotry. Yet ironically, although the emotional concern about anti-Semitism (or Islamophobia) is always an example of "good" (because secular) passion, being emotionally steeped in the *object* of anti-Semitism or Islamophobia (the traditions of Judaism or Islam themselves) may not be.[63]

When Science and Progress are pursued in an orderly fashion, when the fatherland expands to include all of Humanity, when Universalism has conquered the world, then social tolerance, stability, and harmony will finally prevail. That, at any rate, has been the promise of *laïcité* since the Third Republic. The reality, however, is one of continuous instability and ruptures, and of the emergence of new threats. This requires a political theology.

Notes on the Political Theology of *Laïcisme*

"The state's vocation," declares the Stasi report, "is to consolidate the common values on which the social bond in our country is based. Among these values is the equality of men and women. Being a recent conquest, it occupies a place of great importance in our law. It is part of today's Republican contract. The state will not remain passive in the face of any attack on this principle."[64] The object of the report's equalizing discourse is, after all, the young Muslim woman or schoolgirl. How is that equality conceived in this lay Republic, which is also (following the claim of its guardians) the inheritor of a "Judeo-Christian" legacy?

In August 2004, the Vatican published a document entitled "On the Collaboration of Men and Women in the Church and in the World," which criticized social tendencies that it saw as trying to obliterate differences between men and women. The document was critically received in France as an attack on feminism and homosexuality (although the Republic's representatives remained noticeably silent in the face of this attack on a basic Republican value). Among the critics was the eminent sociologist of religion Danièle Hervieu-Léger, who described the publication with some contempt as a sign of the inability of the Catholic Church to keep up with the times. She stressed, however, that historically Christianity had contributed greatly to the recognition of women's dignity in cultures, such as the Roman, where women were inferior but went on to say that it now appeared to want to shut the door to progress again. She reminded her interviewer of Saint Paul's statement to the Galatians: "in Christ there is no longer either master or slave, neither Jew nor Greek, neither man nor woman."[65] The full verse (in the English Revised Version) reads: "There can be neither Jew nor Greek, there can be neither bond nor free, there can be no male and female: *for ye all are one in Christ Jesus.*" What this verse affirms is not, strictly speaking, the equality of these couples but their *unity in Christ.* The slave is not redeemed in the world according to this famous utterance, the Greek does not become a Jew. Christ died on the cross so that in him believers might have life everlasting *despite their differences.* What one is offered is not a legal entitlement but a refusal to read signs. By citing Saint Paul, Hervieu-Léger wishes to invoke the Republic, which, in its representative capacity, unifies all its citizens: male and female are one in France. Are we to understand that the ideological roots of modern secularism lie in Christian universalism?

The acquisition of the vote by French women in 1944 made explicit a unity that had hitherto been implicit. The right to vote now gives the individual woman power, albeit temporary power. A woman's vote is equal to the vote of a man. But the *result* of that act is not social equality—it simply converts her individual identity as a woman with a unique biography and social position into a political unity. The vote itself is of no significance—it is the result of voting that is important. Through it both man and woman, whether they actually cast a vote or not, are bound to a representative body—in the semiotic as well as the political senses. It is that body that offers the promise of freedom in the world. That body is co-terminous with the law, and the law doesn't only accord the same rights and freedoms to all citizens (redeem them) but demands obedience from them under threat of punishment. In Paul's utterance, by contrast, it is precisely *not* the law that promises redemption, *not* politics, but God's infinite love for all—regardless of difference. This freedom is not political; it does not rest on the circulation of political signs. It is the freedom and bondage that comes from *being in love*.

For Rousseau, the great theorist of freedom as will (and advocate of a civil religion), the domain of politics was a public space of male activity; the entry of women into politics would, he thought, be against nature. Most feminists have long been highly critical of Rousseau for this reason, but Mona Ozouf—following Pierre Rosanvallon—has recently offered an interesting interpretation.[66] The Rousseauean opposition between men (culture) and women (nature) radicalized the Jacobin conception of the citizen as someone whose abstract quality was connected to his autonomy. Precisely because women were seen as socially dependent on someone else, they were not eligible for full citizenship. That, says Ozouf, explains the late acquisition of the vote by women in France. In America and Britain, by contrast, women were given the vote much earlier, but as women and not as individuals. She then goes on to make a more intriguing if controversial observation to account for the singularity of French feminism: "If Frenchwomen experience their specific attributes in a less anguished and less recriminating way than do American women, is it not because, in France, differences are subordinate—and not contrary—to equality? When everyone has an intimate conviction that the abstract equality of individuals must inevitably triumph over differences, these differences can be experienced without being violently rejected *or* fetishized."[67] The national genius of France, Ozouf believes, rests on the general conviction that "an essence [is] shared by all French people,"[68] and it is this essence that facilitates the French sense of gender equality.

But if women are at once equivalent and individually different, two questions arise. First, how do atomized individuals form a unity in the national community? The answer for some seems to be: by virtue of the essence they share (perhaps Durkheim's idea of "mechanical solidarity"). An abstract equality is already built into the notion of *French* citizenship, defining the necessary unity through equivalence. Second, what *differences* are accepted and why? Can the "Islamic veil," as worn by French schoolgirls, be a site for rearticulating *conjunction and disjunction*? My impression is that this possibility is rejected because the veil is seen as essentially having *a veiling function* (it is a symbol that can be removed). It hides the truth of signs from the light of reason, which would allow difference to be read as it should be read: as—in Ozouf's formulation—difference subordinate to equality. What that truth points to is not the veil itself nor even its absence *but the command that it be removed*.

An argument is sometimes made by supporters of gender equality that the veil is intolerable because it symbolizes the attribution to women of an absolute or innate responsibility for the violence that may be done to them by men on the basis of gender difference, and that this responsibility is what generates the *subsequent* demand for its veiling by them. This argument is interesting for several reasons. First, it indicates an analytic misunderstanding, because the veil does not hide gender difference, it advertises it. Second, the argument betrays an unfamiliarity with Islamic law, because the latter does *not* attribute an absolute or innate responsibility to women for all violence done to them by men—which is *not* to say that men and women are always treated as equal subjects before that law, or that the law never sanctions violence against women. But the veil as a sign is at once less and more than the law. Third, the argument regards the headscarf independent of context or use, so that it becomes part of a theological rhetoric applicable equally to Afghan women under the Taliban and to French women living in France under French law. It obscures the distinction between causes and excuses, and therefore muddies the meaning of the veil as an "origin" or "justification" of violence. Finally, the argument makes it difficult to see how Muslim youths in the *banlieus* who assault young Muslim women for going about unveiled in public are dealt with by imposing a sartorial ban in public schools in the name of Republican values.

I should stress again that my concern here is not with defending the right to veil. My modest aim is to examine the argument that because veiling is a symbol of gender inequality and a cause of sexual violence against women it should be legally prohibited in public schools. I am persuaded that various powerful affects underpin this demand and that their presence facilitates the use of theological language in this debate.[69]

Whatever the case may be, it is worth noting the distance of the Republican notion of gender equality (sexual difference is always subordinate to legal sameness) from the Pauline model of indistinction. There it is not that abstract equality *must* inevitably triumph over difference, it is that difference does not matter because in Christ Jesus men and women are one. It is not that they have the same power, that each has a vote of equal value. (Paul even admonishes husbands and wives to take their proper places *in this world*: "Wives, be in subjection to your husbands, as is fitting in the Lord. Husbands, love your wives and be not bitter against them"; Colossians, 3:18–19.) My point is not that Paul makes his "reactionary" meaning explicit here—if indeed it was Paul who wrote Colossians. It is quite simply that his affirmation about being one in Christ is not a sociological statement, for even the statement from Colossians does not contradict that oneness in Christ, a oneness that refers to those redeemed by Christ's sacrifice, those who have let him enter them. "For the mind of the flesh is death; but the mind of the spirit is life and peace," says Paul, "Because the mind of the flesh is enmity against God. . . . And if Christ is in you, the body is dead because of sin; but the spirit is life because of righteousness" (Romans 8:6–10). It is therefore in the universality of the spirit, in the fact that men and women, as subjects *in* the Lord, can live in righteousness, that the inequalities of particular bodies (dead because of sin) can be equalized—that is, brought equally to life and the same life.

This theology of unity has a coherence that the political theory of equality for which it is sometimes used does not. In her historical study of French feminism, Joan Scott supplies a dimension that is largely missing in Ozouf by problematizing what the latter takes for granted. The debate over gender equality has been indeterminate, Scott argues, because the terms in which it is carried out—"man," "woman," "individual," and so on—are subject to continuous transformation. "Post-suffrage feminism," she writes, "was constructed in the space of a paradox: there was the declared sameness of women and men under the sign of citizenship (or the abstract individual), and there was the exclusionary masculinity of the individual subject. On the one side was the presumed equality that followed from the legal metaphysics of universal rights: on the other was the inequality that followed from the presumed natural facts of sexual difference. It is in terms of this inconsistency . . . that we can understand . . . the conflicts that have characterized the most recent history of feminism."[70] Scott is aware that there is a paradox in asserting both abstract individualism *and* individual differences as valid. If the former "must inevitably triumph over" the latter, it is only by fiat, by an arbitrary decision, because the interpretability of signs makes it possible to represent differences as inequalities and vice versa.

Her interesting approach points to another conclusion: universal equality and particular difference are not diametrically opposed "principles." They are generalizations, the one relating to collectivities, the other to the individual. And as there is no such thing as an absolutely valid generalization (descriptive or prescriptive), one must decide whether certain generalizations (e.g., universal equality or particular difference) are relevant to the case at hand, and if so, why and in what way. Such "casuistical" reasoning is not necessarily an arbitrary concession to self-interest, a failure to uphold justice. It is the sustained investigation into and assessment of circumstances and forces in which the problem being considered is actually embedded. Instead of beginning with the axiom that difference is always subordinate to sameness, one asks: What are the arguments for saying that *this* difference—between woman and man, Jew and Muslim, employer and employee, and so on—is relevant *here*? How viable—politically, legally, morally—are the arguments for claiming that they are essentially the same or crucially different? One does not ask why the exercise of sovereign power justifies the exception to a universal rule but how ways of reasoning in this particular case can yield the conclusion they do. One is still, of course, left with the question: What sensibilities enable one to recognize what is relevant and reasonable in *this* case? (Why does one feel that it is reasonable, even in France, to take account of gender difference in providing public toilets but not in providing public schools?)

It is often pointed out by defenders that *laïcité* does not require citizens of the Republic to be identical. On the contrary, it encourages them to develop their individuality. The flowering of individuality that *laïcité* encourages, however, is founded on positivism and humanism.[71] It is only a *particular* kind of individuality that is sought. Secular humanism, the philosophy that interprets the Republic, holds that what individuals share above everything is life in this world, human life. The worldly life of the individual is the object of protection and welfare for every progressive republic; life is also "the ultimate sacrifice" the individual can make for its sake. It is the "sacredness" of the Republic, its legibility as "the sacred," that gives it the authority to dissolve the paradoxes of gender equality. This assumption of "sacred" authority contrasts with Scott's insistence that the tension between individual difference and general equality must be accepted as a paradox.

The modern, abstract republic is invisible in itself. It therefore needs to represent itself through signs. But can an image represent the invisible? Or, in theological terms: How can the unrepresentable God be represented for humans? One way, famously, is through the icon, an image that mediates and organizes the relationship between the invisible God and his human worshippers. The icon is *dynamic*, linking the presence of the divine to the cultivation of the human spirit. By analogy, it is in the very *act* of sign deployment that the republic realizes itself in its citizens.

Régis Debray, politician, philosopher, and member of the Stasi commission, argues that the myth of the social contract is a sacred principle, functionally equivalent to divine revelation. In proposing that the Republic's respect for what is sacred to others requires that others respect the sacred principle on which the Republic is founded (a social compact defining citizenship), he seems to imply that the toleration of difference is a more appropriate attitude *between* "civilizations" than within them.[72] At any rate, simple invocations of the sacred in secular arguments of this kind dissolve the old Christian pair "spiritual" and "temporal" into the Republican "sacred." By attaching the sign of sanctity to the modern concept of the abstract, de-Christianized state, it seeks to make political power exercised in the name of *the nation* untouchable, even as it is unspeakable.

Some members of the Stasi commission are also members of a nation-wide organization called "le Comité Laïcité République" (CLR), whose purpose is to defend and further the principles of French secularism. Founded in 1991, it includes members with Jewish, Christian, and Muslim backgrounds, many of whom are well-known personalities. CLR is clearly inspired by the positive philosophy of Auguste Comte and of his followers (especially Émile Littré). It can rightly claim to be at the ideological center of "the French Republic."

The Web site that advertises the aims of this organization reflects the spirit and sometimes the wording of the Stasi commission report:

> The school is the sacred place of the Republic, where one learns to become a citizen, where all children are taught to become free women and men, equal in rights and interdependent, regardless of their color, their origin, and their religious, philosophical, or cultural belonging. It is there that liberty, equality, and fraternity acquire their full, concrete meaning. That is why the school must remain a protected sanctuary, and with regard to it secularism should never allow commercial, communitarian, or dogmatic interests to intrude.[73]

The school is sacred because proper formation is integral to the founding myth of the secular Republic.

Ironically, it is not religious schools that are said to be sacred but secular schools, those directly administered by the state, in which no "religious signs" may appear. Pupils may move between the sacred space and time of public schools and the profane space and time of the street (and of home, mosque, and Internet in the *banlieus*). Because the public school is sacred, it should not be exposed to contamination by worldly interests. One might expect that it was therefore also the protected space of imagination and fantasy in contrast to the "real" world of constraint. But for defenders of *laïcité* that does not appear to be so.

The public school is a pedagogic structure that "the Republic" presents as a space of emancipation. That space sustains contradictory demands, however: on the one hand, that the individual define herself, and on the other, that she be bound by an unconditional obedience to the nation-state and hence submit to schoolteachers and other state officials. This contradiction is nicely brought out in the following statement by a member of the Stasi commission, who insists that secular schools do not deny differences:

> They simply take care that these differences are asserted in a way compatible with the universalism of rights and the personal freedom to define or even redefine oneself without being tied down by group loyalty. . . . An attitude of inquiry and of open-mindedness to knowledge is incompatible with the peremptory assertion of an identity more fantasized than freely chosen [*une identité plus fantasmée que librement choisie*], especially at an impressionable age. . . . Many of the pupils are minors, and it is unrealistic to maintain that they know clearly who they are and what they do.[74]

According to positivism, fantasy is the very essence of "religion" because it asserts the possibility of existing in "another world." If fantasy has any role in the formation of adults in the ultimate—scientific, industrial—phase of human progress, says positivism, it is to provide inconsequential amusement, play that must never be taken seriously. (The Romantic tradition has a more positive view of fantasy, allowing that it is necessary to both morality and sanity. As does Freud.) Only the disciplined subject, positivism insists, can choose freely, by breaking away from the traces she has inherited. This is possible only when she has been properly taught what is real and rational, which is why boys and girls must be subject to the same secular regime. What seems to emerge from *this* discourse is not that secularism ensures equality and freedom but that particular versions of "equality" and "freedom" ensure *laïcité*.

Laïcité is the mode in which the Republic teaches the subjects in its care about what counts as real, and what they themselves really are, in order better to govern them by letting them govern themselves. There is something more important at stake than the individual's desire to decide for herself: what is to count as knowledge of reality on the basis of which the autonomous self can make a "truly free choice" (moral, political, or economic). In the real world of capitalism in which the market imposes conditions of work and profitability and in which advertising manipulates zones of ignorance and desire among individual consumers, the idea of "free choice" means a happy immersion in a consumer culture. How far can the offspring of North African immigrants, unemployed and stigmatized, secure in *that* world an identity "freely chosen" in school? French positivism seems to conceive of "free choice" on the basis of two quite distinct forms of the liberal individual: the subjective version, which chooses in response to an "authentic, distinctive core," and the forensic version, according to which the citizen can choose as a matter of "universal right."

But *laïcité* has great ambitions. Like American Christianity, it aims to redeem the world.[75] A lyrical passage entitled "Secularism: A Hope for the Twenty-first Century" concludes the declaration of principles by the CLR:

> Secularism faces not the past but the future of mankind. Carrier of reason's future, it is open to the progress of thought. It wishes to be the liberator of intelligence. Secular humanism, living force of History, addresses itself to all women and all men, to all peoples. Rejecting all ethnocentrism and bearing emancipation for all, it attests more than ever—in a world becoming increasingly smaller—to the permanence and universal mission of the values of Liberty, Equality, and Fraternity. Today, secular humanism alone can nourish and guide the march of all peoples toward knowledge, toward a better existence and justice, toward peace and freedom.[76]

The philosophy of secular humanism invoked here presupposes the existence of subjects who can find (or make?) an inner core that can be claimed to be authentic, an authentic self that needs to be both freed and regulated by an abstract, transcendent (state) power and by the impersonal power of the market, because each individual acquires his or her *proper* freedoms only through those powers. The maintenance of "universality" is a function of the state, which at the same time represents and speaks to a *particular* essence. But the limits to the state's transcendence, as well as the excess generated by its passions, both continually undermine the clarity of its theology of signs.

Conclusion

Defenders and critics of the Islamic veil law represent it in different ways, but secularists, whether pro or con, employ the same political language, in which they assert something about the proper place of religion.[77] I think that in doing so most of them miss just how certain discourses can become part of the powerful practices that cultivate particular sensibilities essential to a particular kind of contradictory individual—one who is morally sovereign and yet obedient to the laws of the secular Republic, flexible and tolerant yet fiercely principled. The liberal idea is that it is only when this individual sovereignty is invaded by something other than the representative democratic state, which represents his individual will collectively, and by something other than the market, which is the state's dominant civil partner (as well as its indispensable electoral technique), that free choice gives way to coerced behavior. But the fact that the notions of moral and political sovereignty are not coherent as descriptions of contemporary individual and collective life is less important than the facts that they are part of the apparatus of techniques for forming secular subject-citizens and that the public school has such an extraordinary ideological place in the Republic's self-presentation. Central to that apparatus is the proper deployment of signs, a topic with which I began this essay. So I end with a few further remarks about it.

The internationally famous Egyptian activist Nawal al-Saadawi describes a protest march of young women against the new law in February 2004:

> The slogan raised by the girls and young women who demonstrated against the announcement made by the government of France was "the veil is a doctrine not a symbol." Another argument used as a part of the brain-washing process is to consider the veil an integral part of the identity of Islamic women and a reflection of their struggle against Western imperialism, against its values, and against the cultural invasion of the Arab and Islamic countries. Yet in these demonstrations the young women and girls who marched in them wearing the veil were often clothed in tight fitting jeans, their faces covered with layers of make-up, their lips painted bright red, the lashes around their eyes thickened black or blue with heavy mascara. They walked along the streets swaying in high-heeled shoes, drinking out of bottles of Coca Cola or Sprite. Their demonstration was a proof of the link between Western capitalist consumerism and Islamic fundamentalism, how in both money and trade ride supreme, and bend to the rule of corporate globalization. It was an illustration of how a "false consciousness" is shot through with contradiction.[78]

What upsets Saadawi, of course, is the apparent mystification of the young women demonstrating against the French ban, which led them to express their self-negation, as it were. The interesting assumption that she and many others make is that a concern with adornment is incompatible with religious expressions, which, to be really "religious," ought to be concerned only with the transcendental and the unworldly, and that what is asserted to be mandatory Islamic behavior cannot be authentic if it is at the same time combined with "capitalist signs." (As always, particular definitions underlie the discourse about "religion," but it is curious that the *normative* character of this definition should so often go unnoticed by the "nonreligious.")

I have cited Saadawi for another reason, however. Contrary to the slogan of the young demonstrators—"the veil is a doctrine not a symbol"—Saadawi insists, like the Stasi commission, that it is precisely as a symbol that it is important. The interesting thing about symbols (i.e., conventional signs) is that they invite one to do a reading of them independently of people's stated intentions and commitments. Indeed, the reading becomes a way of retrospectively constituting "real desires." It facilitates the attempt to synthesize the psychological and juridical concepts of the liberal subject. Are these immature girls aware of what they are *really* saying when they assert their wish to wear the headscarf? Is their "contradictory" appearance an index of their confused desire to be modern? Can *that* desire be deciphered as a modern passion repressed by—and therefore in conflict with— the "fanatical" religiosity expressed by the Islamic veil? Doesn't emancipation require the freeing of what is repressed and the dismantling of fanaticism? These are the kinds of question that suggest themselves and that seem to demand authoritative answers.

Vincent Geisser records some of the authoritative answers that appeared in the French media. At first, he notes, the young women with headscarves were represented as victims of their relatives. But then, in response to the latest sociological studies on the wearing of the veil, which showed a complicated picture of the young women's motives for wearing it, the media chose an even more alarmist interpretation. "Henceforth it is the idea of 'voluntary servitude' that prevails in media analyses: that young French women should themselves choose to wear the headscarf is precisely what makes them even more dangerous. This act is no longer to be seen as the consequence of family pressure but as the sign of a personal—and therefore *fanatical*—commitment."[79] This, as Geisser points out, makes the veil appear even more threatening to the state school and to Republican values in general. Once one is in the business of uncovering dangerous hidden meanings, as in the Spanish Inquisitor's search for hidden beliefs, one will find what one is looking for. Where the power to read symbols includes the construction of (religious/secular) intentions attributable to practitioners, even the distinction, made in the 1905 law of separation between church and state, between "freedom of conscience" (a moral immunity) and "freedom of religious practice" (a legal right) becomes difficult to maintain with clarity.

Secularism is invoked to prevent two very different kinds of transgression: the perversion of politics by religious forces, on the one hand, and the state's restriction of religious freedom, on the other. The idea that religion is a system of symbols becomes especially attractive in the former case, I think, because in order to protect politics from religion (and especially certain kinds of religiously motivated behavior), in order to determine its acceptable forms within the polity, the state must identify "religion." To the extent that this work of identification becomes a matter for the law, the Republic acquires the theological function of defining religious signs and the power of imposing that definition on its subjects, of "assimilating" them. This may not be usually thought of as *coercive* power, but it is undoubtedly an intrusive one. The Stasi report does not pretend otherwise. The secular state, it insists, "cannot be content with withdrawing from all religious and spiritual matters." [80]

Pierre Tevanian, a critic of the new law, has written that secularism as defined by the laws of 1881, 1882, and 1886 applies to the premises, the school curricula, and the teachers, but not to the pupils. The latter are simply required to obey school rules, to attend all lessons properly, and to behave respectfully toward others.[81] These founding texts appear to be echoed in the Council of State judgment of November 27, 1989 (issued on the occasion of an earlier crisis concerning the veil), which the Stasi report cites ("education should be provided with regard, on the one hand, to neutral curricula and teachers and, on the other hand, to the liberty of conscience of the pupils"[82]) and which it then glosses in its own fashion. Instead of withdrawing completely from anything that describes itself as "religion" (while insisting that no behavior be allowed that disrupts the proper functioning of education) the Stasi report chooses to interfere with "religion" by seeking to define its acceptable place.

Today it seems that "religion" continues to infect "politics" in France—partly as parody (the "sacred" foundation of the secular Republic) and partly as civilization ("Judeo-Christian" values in the education of secular citizens). Whatever else *laïcité* may be, it is certainly not the total separation between religion and politics said to be required for living together harmoniously in a diverse modern society. It is, by contrast, a continuous attempt by state apparatuses to encourage subjects to make and recognize themselves through appropriate signs as properly secularized citizens who "know that they belong to France." (Only to France? Ultimately to France? Mainly to France?) Like other modes of secularism, *laïcité* is a modern form of political rule that seeks to define a particular kind of secular subject (whether "religious" or not) who can take part in the game of symbols—the right kind of conventional signs—to demonstrate his or her loyalty to the state.

Where does all this leave the notion of "a community of shared values," which is said to be minimally secured in a modern democratic society by secularism? My simple thought is that differences in class, gender, region, and ethnic origin do not constitute a community of shared values in France. Besides, modern France has always had a sizable body of immigrants, all bringing in "foreign" ideas, habits, and experiences. The only significant difference is that since the Second World War they have been largely from North Africa. The famous slogan "la République une et indivisible" reflects a *nationalist* aspiration, not a social reality. Like people everywhere, the French are imbued with complex emotions about their fellow citizens,[83] including a simple feeling that "France" belongs to *them* but not to Others. In any case, the question of feelings of belonging to the country is distinct from that of the rights and duties of citizenship; the former relates to dreams of nationalism, the latter to practices of civic responsibility.

Public arguments about equitable redistribution of national resources exist in France as they do in every liberal democracy. Like other political matters they are negotiated—secretly as well as openly, to the satisfaction of all parties or of only a few. The state's integrity is, of course, fundamental to this. Its administrative institutions may be able to carry through decisions politically arrived at, or they may find themselves confronted with obstacles. But logically this process does not seem to me to require a principled reference by the state to "the proper place of religion" in a secular society—any more than it needs to have a principled reference to "the proper place" of *anything*. Viewed in historical perspective, the political culture of the modern nation-state is never homogeneous or unchanging, never unchallengeable or unchallenged. The ways in which the concept of "religion" operates in that culture as *motive* and as *effect*, how it mutates, what it affords and obstructs, what memories it shelters or excludes, are not eternally fixed. That is what makes varieties of secularism—including French *laïcité*—always unique.

If one accepts this conclusion, one may resist the temptation to think that one must either "defend secularism" or "attack civic religion." One might instead learn to argue about the best ways of supporting particular liberties while limiting others, of minimizing social and individual harm. In brief, one might content oneself with assessing *particular* demands and threats without having to confront the *general* "danger of religion."

Pim Fortuyn, Theo van Gogh, and the Politics of Tolerance in the Netherlands

Peter van der Veer

In August 2004, a short film that dealt with the theme of violence against women in Islamic societies was broadcast on Dutch television. The key scene showed four topless women in transparent clothing; their bodies had been covered with calligraphically inscribed verses from the Koran that legitimate the subjection of women. Working from a script written by Member of Parliament Ayaan Hirsi Ali, the filmmaker Theo van Gogh had created the ten-minute movie *Submission*, a direct translation of the word *Islam*. Van Gogh had a long-established reputation for being a provocateur, which included insulting the Jewish community and references to Muslims as "the secret column of goat-fuckers." He was fat, purposefully unkempt, antiauthoritarian, satirical, and immoderate in his language—in short, a personification of the Dutch cultural ethos since the 1970s. He had frequently been sued for libel and slander, but managed to defend himself successfully under the rubric of freedom of speech.

After the movie was released, both van Gogh and Hirsi Ali received death threats. Van Gogh was murdered in the early morning of November 2, 2004, in Amsterdam by Muhammad Bouyari, a young man of dual Dutch and Moroccan nationality who had grown up in the Netherlands. The murder of van Gogh triggered a nationwide panic. The Minister of Finance referred to a clash of civilizations, declared that there was a war going on between Islam and the West, and boasted that if extremist Muslims wanted war, they could get it. This seemed to give license to those who wanted to set arson in the country's mosques, as immediately happened. There was fear of widespread reprisals against Muslims and their property, but the situation was brought under control by the more responsible elements among Dutch state authorities. The murder of van Gogh, though generally taken to be a sign of growing

Islamic terrorism, also seemed to mark the end of an era of cultural transformation in the Netherlands.

These events did not fit the Netherlands' global image and tourist branding as a wealthy, tolerant, and perhaps excessively liberal society. Discussions in Holland after van Gogh's murder focused on the intolerance of Islam, the threat of Muslim extremism, and, perhaps most significantly, Muslims' lack of humor. As many Dutch commentators remarked, Muslims simply could not take a joke; they took life and especially their religion too seriously. Much emphasis was placed on freedom of speech and artistic expression. The terms of the debate resembled those generated by Salman Rushdie's *Satanic Verses*, in which Muslim illiteracy in satire was identified as a sign of deep cultural backwardness. Nevertheless, *Submission* was not an especially funny film, and scriptwriter Hirsi Ali saw it as a quite serious political challenge to Islam's sexual violence against women. Before the film was broadcast, the leading Dutch liberal newspaper had already described it as a "new provocation by Hirsi Ali." Rather than the supposed lack of humor among Muslims, what needs to be explained is the aggression of the Dutch against a Muslim minority that forms some 7 percent of the Dutch population and is by and large a socially and culturally marginal group. Most discussions in the Netherlands, however, have not been about Dutch society and culture but about the nature of Islam and global terrorism. Van Gogh was indeed killed by a Muslim fanatic, who made his religious motivations and desire for martyrdom explicit in a letter pinned to the breast of the murdered filmmaker. Islam is a global signifier of trouble and terrorism, and the Dutch follow the general tendency of explaining incidents like the murder of van Gogh within the framework of the rise of militant Islam. It is important to understand, however, how these global images of Islam are appropriated and used in different arenas to interpret very different situations.

The main issue in the murder of van Gogh is not Islam but Dutch culture. But whenever Dutch culture comes under scrutiny, the focus has been on its tolerance and liberal values. Jonathan Israel, for instance, who has written extensively on early modern Dutch society and especially the Radical Enlightenment of Baruch de Spinoza, has argued in the Pierre Bayle Lecture of 2004 that tolerance was an Enlightenment value developed by thinkers like Spinoza and Bayle in the Netherlands. His analysis of the events surrounding the murder of van Gogh was that the Dutch had forgotten their own history of tolerance because the Dutch educational system had suffered from financial cuts. While I agree that one has to look to the majority population to understand what is going on today, Israel is wrong in his understanding of the history of Dutch tolerance. What I want to argue here is that current events in the Netherlands must indeed be understood in relation to Dutch culture rather than Islam, but that such an analysis requires a different genealogy from the one laid out by Israel.

The murder of van Gogh was preceded by another murder, one committed not by a Muslim but by a radical animal-rights activist. On May 6, 2002, a day after the national celebration of the liberation of Holland in 1945 and only six days before the general elections, the Dutch were shocked to learn that the politician Pim Fortuyn had been killed in Hilversum, the center of Dutch media activities. That same evening riots broke out in The Hague near the parliament buildings, and the prime minister (who usually commuted by bicycle) had to be escorted to his home by police. The next day the widely read populist newspaper *The Telegraph* published a photo of the slain politician with his shoes sticking out from under a white sheet. Emotions ran unusually high in the Netherlands, and several leftist politicians received police protection after death threats, which came mostly in the form of bullets in letters sent by the mail. These quickly became a token of such political importance that some politicians took to mailing such letters and bullets to themselves.[1] Fortuyn's mansion in Rotterdam, with the kitsch name Palazzo di Pietro, was flooded with flowers brought by growing numbers of people, not unlike the public outpouring of grief at Princess Diana's violent death. Thousands participated in a huge procession in Rotterdam led by the mayor. The government, in consultation with Fortuyn's family and the party leaders of the List Pim Fortuyn (LPF), decided to go on with the elections, which on May 15 produced an unprecedented loss for the ruling Labor Party and a huge victory for the LPF. His friends brought Fortuyn's ashes to his holiday villa in Italy, and the Dutch were regaled with endless gossip about the men and women financially backing Fortuyn's party. These were mostly rich real-estate developers with a somewhat shady reputation and a total lack of political savvy. It is perhaps relevant that they had greatly benefited from the real-estate boom of the 1990s (when house prices rose 300 percent), and in this sense were close to the populist emotions that are intimately related to real-estate prices. One of them, the developer Harry Mens, a personal friend of Fortuyn, claimed to have a direct line to the leader in heaven. Since the LPF had to take part in the government coalition, candidates for ministerial positions had to be found overnight in an almost nonexistent, chaotic party that had centered completely on the personal charisma of Fortuyn. This drama continued for half a year and ended with new parliamentary elections that wiped out the LPF. While other societies have such fun all the time, never in history, one may assume, had the Dutch been so entertained by their politicians.

Indeed, one of the key elements behind Fortuyn's incredibly fast rise in Dutch politics was his mission of eliminating the tedium of Dutch politics. Within the space of one year, his flamboyant media performances had gained him a huge following. He was a tall, elegant man, a dandy whose choice of suits and ties was as important as his statements. Fortuyn earned a handsome income as a public speaker and organizer of discussions at large business meetings and had developed into a formidable public debater. Being gay undoubtedly helped his public persona. The Dutch are not trained to be great public speakers, and there is no tradition of debate in the political culture. Campy, extroverted gay entertainers have become hugely popular in the Netherlands, whose population tends to be reticent rather than eloquent.[2] "They say what everyone thinks," is how such entertainers are usually described, and Fortuyn precisely fitted that image. He could say things in a strident manner and combined a feminine vulnerability with a sharp and entertaining irony. Being gay was also important to the content of his politics, since he always saw himself as an outsider who was capable of expressing the feelings of those who felt excluded from power. In this sense, Fortuyn fitted the classic definition of the populist. To an unprecedented degree, he brought his personal life into politics, and the public responded with emotional sympathy.

Fortuyn had had a checkered career. He studied sociology and became a student activist and fanatical Marxist during the 1960s. His first job was as a lecturer in Marxist sociology at the University of Groningen, and his syllabi were filled with the writings of Lenin. Later, Fortuyn transformed himself into a spokesman for the silent majority and entrepreneurial Holland. He wrote a column for a right-wing weekly and became a media personality. In sum, he followed a very common trajectory from the radical left to neo-conservative. Despite his new emphasis on entrepreneurship, he was not an entrepreneur but a member of the managerial and media class. In the 1990s, Fortuyn railed against politicians of the established parties, who he claimed had abandoned their voters, did not care about the people, and were indecisive, uninspiring technocrats. This was evident in the way they dealt with Muslim immigration into the country: the common people were not protected against the influx of criminal foreigners, who threatened the hard-won freedoms of the Dutch. Fortuyn was vocal especially in defense of individual sexual freedom, and his public gay identity enabled him perfectly to take up the defense of Dutch progressive sexual politics against Islamic traditions. Asylum seekers, foreign immigrants, and especially Islam as a backward religion represented threats to the Dutch way of life, and it was time to be proud of our advanced nation and defend it. This was the message that secured Fortuyn top place (over Erasmus and Rembrandt) in a recent poll to determine the greatest Dutchman in history. This kind of populism had been virtually unknown in Dutch politics, which had been dominated by coalitions of Christian-Democrat, Socialist, and Liberal parties for the past century. Politicians outside of these parties with a direct appeal to the public never stood a chance. How can we explain the unprecedented success of this kind of populism in the Netherlands? In answering this question, I focus on the production of a certain cultural politics in the Netherlands after the decline of religion. This cultural politics feeds on desires and anxieties that make the Dutch incapable of dealing with globalization and immigration. But first, I must sketch the political arena in which Fortuyn and, later, Hirsi Ali became so successful.

Dutch Politics at the End of the 1990s

In 1992, the Dutch had been governed for eight years by a so-called purple coalition, which included the Labor Party and the Liberal Party but excluded the Christian-Democrats, who had been part of coalition governments for a century. This reflected the decline of the significance of religious identity in society, as evident from statistics of church attendance and its effect on voting patterns. The 1990s were a period of economic growth and of strong consensus among employers, trade unions, and politicians about the direction of policy making. Political opposition came from marginal radical leftists and from the largely impotent Christian Democrats, who were expected only further to decline in power. The two traditional opponents, the Labor Party and the Liberal Party (which in Holland is more or less a conservative, right-wing party), were both in the secular government coalition and could thus not politicize differences of opinion. Since consensus was the basis of both politics and civil society, parliamentary debates became boring. At the end of the 1990s, the socialist prime minister, Wim Kok, stated with great complacency that the Dutch welfare state was now complete and only minor technical details were left for political discussion. How little did he guess that everything would be overturned by events in 2002! It at least shows that technocratic politics tends to ignore the emotional side of mass politics.

Something seems to have upset Dutch collective well-being at the end of the 1990s. First there was the issue of migration and asylum. Asylum seekers flooded into Western Europe and also into Holland. The asylum seekers were put in "conditions of exception," sometimes for five or six years, in which they could not work but lived in nicely furnished camps before any decision was taken to send them back or grant them asylum. When asylum was denied, feeble attempts were made to escort the rejected immigrants over the border, but the media quickly showed how unsuccessful this approach was. Most of the rejected asylum seekers became illegal immigrants, and a whole range of measures was taken to regulate illegality. This situation, especially in the big cities like Rotterdam, Utrecht, and Amsterdam, has become a source of anger among the so-called autochthonous population.

In addition, the Netherlands faced a problem with Turkish and Moroccan so-called guest workers, who had immigrated in the 1960s. Most of these workers had remained in Holland but lost their jobs with the decline of manufacture and lived on welfare. Most had brought their families, and their children tended to marry native Turks and Moroccans, thus creating ethnic enclaves that were as much connected to their countries of origin as to the Netherlands. Immigrants developed a reputation for being criminals, as a growing underclass of Moroccan youths, in particular, became involved in petty crimes like purse snatching and auto theft. Since many asylum seekers and guest workers were Muslim, Islam was increasingly understood as the unifying symbol of these unwelcome foreigners. In Holland far-right parties, leaning toward fascism, had taken up this issue with slogans like "Our own people first," but the mainstream parties more or less declined to politicize immigration. It is this vacuum that was so eloquently exploited by Fortuyn.

In this sense, his political role was similar to that of Jörg Haider in Austria, Filip de Winter in Belgium, and Jean-Marie Le Pen in France, but Fortuyn himself most closely identified with Silvio Berlusconi, given his savvy with media politics and his ideological and emotional distance from the traditional far right. Fortuyn understood that there was an incipient backlash against migration and globalization. He capitalized on it, but did not create it. The recent rejection of the European constitution is another manifestation of this backlash. The European Union is often seen to stand for the slow disintegration of Dutch national integrity, and it became decidedly unpopular after the introduction of the euro.[3]

At the end of the 1990s, one could also sense an alienation of the Dutch from their established image in the international area. The Srebenica tragedy of 1995, in which over seven thousand Muslim men were killed under the eyes of a Dutch U.N. battalion (Dutchbat) that had come to protect them, festered for some time in Dutch politics. One thing that became clear in the aftermath of the massacre was that the Dutch peacekeepers had developed a strong dislike for the Muslim population of the area, whom they considered to be poor, dirty, and cunning. While it is unclear whether one has to like the people whom one protects, the dislike expressed by some of the soldiers became an element in the public perception of the Dutchbat's performance. The Dutchbat came to stand for the total failure of Dutch goodwill in international politics, for a lack of political realism, and for the corrosive effects of the welfare state on masculine valor. Footage of Dutchbat soldiers celebrating their evacuation, which had been shown on Dutch television, was seen as especially distasteful when the genocide of Srebenica Muslims later became known. In 1996 the government asked the NIOD (a Dutch research institution for war documentation that was founded to deal with Dutch history during World War II) to do a thorough historical investigation of what really happened. This research received ample funding and was probably the largest research project ever undertaken by historians and social scientists in the Netherlands. The NIOD's final report was presented in 2002 and led to the resignation of the Dutch cabinet a few months before the general elections took place.

The political situation in which Fortuyn emerged as a formidable contender was one in which the ruling parties had lost credibility in dealing with both the most important domestic issue, immigration, and the most important international issue, Holland's superior moral standing among the nations. Moreover, the ruling parties had run out of steam in managing the economic downturn and political instability that affected the world economy. Even voters who were not especially attracted to Fortuyn's message felt that a fundamental change was needed, and Fortuyn seemed to have the charisma to bring this about. The attacks on the United States on September 11, 2001, seemed further to confirm Fortuyn's message that the world had changed and that fearsome Muslim terrorists were ready to attack Western civilization. To respond to these new challenges, one needed new leaders, and Fortuyn seemed to fit the bill.

The Collapse of the Pillars and the Rise of Liberty

The 1960s were a turning point in Dutch history, as in Europe and the United States more generally. In Holland, that turning point was deeply connected to a shift in the social location of religion. A popular narrative among the Dutch is that during this decade they finally liberated themselves from the constraints of religion. Declines in church membership and church attendance were very steep during the 1960s, and in a relatively short period Holland was transformed from a highly religious to a highly secular society. Until the 1960s, political scientists defined Holland as a pillarized, consociational society divided into tightly integrated communities (i.e., pillars) formed on the basis of religion or ideology. The most important of these pillars emerged as a result of political mobilization in the nineteenth century and centered on Protestantism, Catholicism, socialism, and liberalism. This goes back as far as the days of the Dutch Republic (1568–1795), which was a particularistic and highly fragmented socio-political infrastructure. At the end of the previous century, attempts to modernize and integrate Dutch political, social, and administrative institutions took the form of a pillarized, and subsequently corporative and consensual, system. When I was growing up during the 1950s and 1960s, I was raised as a Protestant, and we had our own church, political party, sports teams, schools, shops, and welfare organization, as if we formed an ethnic community. Everything in society was organized according to these pillars. The Dutch pride themselves on their long tradition of tolerance, but this was part of a broader system of noninterference with other pillars. Marriage patterns in the Netherlands also followed such divisions. This is well expressed in the Dutch proverb "When you have two beliefs on one pillow, the devil will sleep in between." Much of this well-organized system collapsed at the end of the 1960s under the pressures of the sexual revolution, the student revolt, and the rise to power of the postwar baby boomers. The elements that remained, such as a political orientation toward consensus and corporatism, came under constant pressure from a volatile electorate. Political parties continued to be based on the old ideological divisions, but voters were now motivated by issues primed and framed by the media.

The silent revolution of the 1960s is celebrated in the Netherlands as a liberation, especially from obstacles to enjoyment. Although Catholics were a majority in the country before the 1960s, the Calvinist ethos of frugality and moral strictness had spread to the entire population, including Catholics, socialists, and communists. It is always striking, for instance, to see how closely Dutch communists resemble Dutch Calvinists. This ethos portrayed enjoyment as something potentially sinful. As in other Western European nations, Christian life was more or less bourgeois life, and the lower classes were targeted in a whole range of missionary activities to improve their habits, and especially to keep them from drinking and abandoning their families. The power of religious organizations in a pillarized society was in this respect quite formidable, since low morals might mean loss of one's job with a Christian employer or loss of welfare. In the 1950s, the Catholic

Church was still politically strong enough that bishops could threaten to refuse Catholics the sacrament if they voted for the Socialist Party.[4] The Dutch Catholic Church province was at the time a key supplier of missionaries, and Protestants were also deeply involved in missionary activities, especially in the Dutch colonies. This declined following the de-colonization of the 1950s but was followed by the rise of pillarized organizations of development aid, with a secularized missionary spirit. This commitment to international charity is still present today, and the distribution of aid plays a central role in Dutch foreign policy.

The 1950s saw the rise of the Dutch welfare state, with a range of provisions for social security and for the elderly. The Dutch were now taken care of from cradle to grave, but no longer through religious or other ideological organizations. People became increasingly independent of the social arrangements of their communities thanks to generalized state provisions. This coincided with the huge impact of the youth rebellion of the 1960s, in which students rebelled against their professors, the state, and religious authority and valorized drug use. The anarchist Provo movement and the riots surrounding the marriage of Princess Beatrix in 1965 were the clearest signals that Dutch society was changing. The most important change in my view, however, was a growing emphasis on enjoyment. Enjoyment became the hallmark of consumer societies everywhere in the West, but for the Dutch the transition from deeply ingrained frugality to boundless consumption seems to have been particularly stark. Holland is among the ten wealthiest countries in the world, and the Dutch take more foreign vacations than anyone else in the world. Holland itself has become a major tourist destination for young people (backpackers and the like), fueled by its international reputation for liberal policies toward drugs and sexual behavior. Pornography is ubiquitous, even on commercial television. Soccer games have developed into large, riotous rituals, in which the police must control periodic outbursts of hooliganism. Divorce rates shot up after the 1960s, and the law accepts gay marriage. This feast, which began in the 1970s, was threatened in the late 1990s by only two things: Muslim immigration and globalization.

For the Dutch, Muslims stand for theft of enjoyment. Their strict sexual morals remind the Dutch too much of what they have themselves so recently left behind. There is indeed very little difference between strict Christian ideas about sexuality and enjoyment and strict Muslim ideas about these matters. Dutch orthodox Christians (both Catholic and Protestant) and orthodox Muslims refer to very similar textual traditions to authorize their views. In a society where consumption and especially the public performance of sexual identity have become so important, the strict clothing habits of observant Muslims are an eyesore. Dutch universities have now issued dress codes in which the *niqaab* (veil) and the *burkha* are prohibited for students. In an interesting move, in 2004 the (Protestant) Free University of Amsterdam not only banned these forms of Islamic dress but also excessively sexy clothing that reveals belly-buttons or underwear. The wearing of headscarves by Muslim girls, in particular, is regarded as a total rejection of the Dutch way of life. The government has recently proposed exams for prospective citizens that use pictures of topless women and gay marriages to determine whether the applicants are comfortable with the "Dutch way of life." While much of public debate is focused on the integration of Muslims into Dutch society, few Dutch would declare openly that they consider Muslim views of sexuality to be a rejection of integration. Sexuality is subsumed under the rubric of female liberation, and feminists have led the attacks on Muslims in the Netherlands. One leading feminist in the Netherlands recently declared that she would not allow a woman with a headscarf to become a member of the editorial board of a feminist magazine. In response, it was pointed out that immigrant women with head-scarves surely cleaned the offices of that magazine. This fine observation of the relation between class, gender, and race was only marginally taken up in the Dutch debate. The relation between Islam and homosexuality has also received public attention: quotes from the Koran about the punishment of unnatural sex, as well as statements by Moroccan imams about homosexuality, are taken as a sign of the backwardness of Islam and the need for Muslims to catch up with the times. This is seen as related to similar condemnations of homosexuality found in the Bible and articulated by conservative Christian preachers. In short, the Dutch feel that they have just recently freed themselves from Christian conservatism, only to be confronted by Islamic injunctions. Precisely this fueled Pim Fortuyn, but with a twist. He declared that he liked fucking young Moroccan boys but did not want to be restrained by backward imams. This pointedly recalled homosexual desires and Orientalist fantasies about Morocco that had been part of the Dutch imagination for a century. Something here goes beyond the public discussion of the position of women and homosexuals, and this is the contradictory politics of desire.

Liberated Muslim immigrants, especially the Somalian Ayaan Hirsi Ali, play a special role in the debate about liberty and Islam. According to her own account, Hirsi Ali fled Somalia when her father wanted to arrange a marriage for her. She received asylum in the Netherlands and studied political science, after which she worked for a think tank of the Labor Party and became involved in fighting the abuse of women in the Muslim community. Her work focused on the issue of clitoridectomy, which is prevalent among Somalians but not among the vast majority of Muslim women in the Netherlands, who are of Turkish and Moroccan descent. Hirsi Ali's struggle for the liberation of Muslim women was felt to be authentic by Dutch feminists in all parties and politically correct, since she belonged to the attacked community. In the Liberal Party, she was nominated to a parliamentary seat with the objective of making anti-Islamic, pro-women issues a major plank in election campaigns. In this sense, her emancipatory campaign was directed primarily toward gaining votes from the majority community rather than transforming the Muslim community. The subaltern can speak, but in order to be heard she has to express the feelings of the dominant community. Refugees from Islamic countries, such as Somalia and Iran, have gained special prominence in the attack on Islam, since they can manifest authenticity. They tend to be more strident in their tone either because of personal experiences or because of an insecurity about their expertise beyond these experiences. Certainly in a political climate that favors "the personal," an attractive black woman with good media presence who accuses the prophet Muhammad of having been a pedophile can be a political, though controversial, asset. The Liberal Party, which she represents in parliament, is generally conservative and rather staid, and Hirsi Ali's position is not unchallenged within it, but, as with Fortuyn, it is precisely the controversy and media attention she generates that has kept her political career going.

Recently, tensions within the Liberal Party over the issue of immigration have come to the surface. In May 2006, Minister of Immigration Rita Verdonk, a prominent leader of the Liberals, collided with Hirsi Ali when she found out that Hirsi Ali had lied about her name and other details when applying for asylum in the Netherlands. Hirsi Ali had to step down from her membership in parliament. In the row that followed, it was unclear whether she could retain her citizenship, since on similar grounds others had been sent back to where they came from. In the end that did not happen, but Hirsi Ali accepted an offer of work from the Enterprise Institute, a neo-conservative think tank in Washington. She was vehemently defended by Richard Perle, one of the architects of Bush's foreign policy in the Middle East, Salman Rushdie, and Mario Vargas Llhosa, an interesting group of anti-Islamists.

Conclusion

In a recent national survey, a majority of Dutch respondents declared themselves satisfied with their own lives but very unhappy with society at large and pessimistic about the future.[5] They worried about a decline in norms and values in social life and about the decline of social welfare. Sixty percent of the autochthonous Dutch felt uneasy about the presence of ethnic minorities, and 75 percent perceived Muslim fundamentalism as a threat. The general picture is one of considerable fear for the future, fear of a globalization that will disturb the arrangements of Dutch society. Migrants are made to stand for the major transformations in Dutch society and are felt to be part of a threatening phase of globalization. Many Dutch are ambivalent about the freedoms brought to them since the 1960s; they want these freedoms to be preserved in the private sphere but complemented with more restrictive regimes in the public sphere. Religious traditions disturb such distinctions. Islam is a public religion, and it manifests itself both within and outside of the private sphere. It reminds the Dutch too much of what they have recently left behind.

My argument has been that one must look at broader Dutch cultural transformations in order to understand recent events in the Netherlands. These transformations, while typically Dutch, do not necessarily distinguish the Netherlands from the rest of Europe. Similar processes can be recognized in other European societies, where the arrival of primarily Muslim immigrants has triggered strong emotional and political responses. In this respect, the Netherlands bears particular comparison with Scandinavian countries. The anthropologist Unni Wikan has recently published a passionate critique of Norwegian policies toward immigrants in a book with the telling title *Generous Betrayal: Politics of Culture in the New Europe.*[6] Her main argument is that excessive respect for the "culture" of immigrants has subverted human rights, especially for women and children. A subsidiary argument is that the welfare society has segregated immigrants into an underclass. Much of this discussion is immediately recognizable in the Dutch case. It is now generally accepted in Dutch public opinion that the 1980s and 1990s suffered from an excessive "political correctness" that has made an open discussion of immigrant criminality or practices such as clitoridectomy among Somalian women impossible. The public attacks on immigrant culture, and especially Islam, by Theo van Gogh are thus accounted for as a backlash against the political correctness of the past.

While Wikan provides an interesting analysis of how the culture of immigrants is reified in Norway and of the effects of such reification on the production of ethnic enclaves, she gives us hardly any critical analysis of Norwegian culture, which is essentialized as one of humanitarian values of equality and human rights. In such an analysis, minorities tend to have cultures that can be deconstructed, while majorities have cultures that are taken for granted. The historical development of Norwegian egalitarianism and secularism and their precise natures are not taken into account at all.

In a recent work, the social philosopher Nancy Fraser has highlighted the complications of an ethos of equality confronted with multiculturalism.[7] In a discussion of notions of redistribution and recognition in contemporary philosophy, she argues that these two notions should be seen in connection if one wants to enhance justice in the age of identity politics. This would be an appropriate response to Wikan's argument, but, like Wikan, Fraser does not question the basic assumptions of liberalism. The key term in Fraser's discussion is *parity*, according to which justice requires social arrangements that permit all (adult) members of society to interact with one another as peers. While she wants to create a space for the recognition of difference, this can be done only within a secularist perspective, as is made clear by her discussion of the debate over headscarves in France. According to Fraser, those who protest the prohibition of the headscarf in state schools must show, first, that the ban denies educational parity to Muslim girls and, second, that permitting the scarf would not exacerbate female subordination. The ban on headscarves would be unjust if Christian crosses and Jewish yarmulkes were allowed in school. For Fraser, then, the issue is whether the school treats everyone equally and is, in this case, sufficiently laic, secular. But if we recognize Islam as a tradition different from the liberal tradition, and Muslims as a community informed by that tradition in their engagement with modern conditions, it is clear that Fraser's notion of parity is irrelevant to many Muslims. For them (as for some Jewish and Christian groups), the issue may be that because hair has sexual potency, covering it is a sign of female modesty and, as such, a disciplining of the body that is central to being a devout Muslim woman. As in every living tradition, there is much Islamic debate surrounding the issue; but if we want to recognize difference, we must acknowledge the debate on its own terms and not replace it with one about parity.

Fraser's view on the second issue, whether wearing the headscarf exacerbates female subordination, fails to engage conceptions of male-female relations that are hierarchical in nature, but rather condemns these conceptions as univocally patriarchal and thus as acceptable only in a strategy that leads to gradual emancipation from them. That is fine as an expression of value pluralism, but the real clash comes with the power of the state to enforce equality against the wishes of the Muslim minority. In fact, the banning of the headscarf is a direct result of majoritarian democratic politics in the framework of the nation-state; it has everything to do with governmentality and little with emancipation, and will probably result in strategic essentialism on the part of Muslim girls who want to assert their difference. Even if a defense of headscarves is accepted by the state, it must be phrased in Fraser's secular language of autonomy and freedom and not in the religious language of moral reasoning that the minority uses. Fraser's fine attempt to bridge the gap between redistribution and recognition in social philosophy does not question its underlying secularism and will thus fail to effectively recognize difference.

My account of the events in Holland goes beyond the contradictions generated by policies of equality or parity. These events have been triggered by open disrespect and even aggression by the majority population against Muslims. The common perception in the Netherlands is that Muslims must be secularized and integrated into society; otherwise they will be a threat to the unity of the nation. The perceived need for this secularity and unity is embedded in a society's history and is clearly different in different societies. In the Dutch case, it is not an elaborated theory of *laicité* that is the foundation of the state, as in France; it is, rather, the shared and recently developed values of liberty of choice in consumption that are the ideological basis of Dutch unity. The fact that the clash with Muslims in European societies commonly centers on the headscarf does not imply that that issue means the same thing everywhere. In Holland, I think it reflects not so much a perceived challenge to the secularism of the state as a perceived rejection of sexual liberty and consumer values.

Can a Minority Retain Its Identity in Law?

The 2005 Multatuli Lecture

Job Cohen

Ladies and Gentlemen,

It is an honor and a pleasure for me to address you here today in the Grote Kerk of Breda in the context of the 2005 Multatuli Lecture. The theme about which I have been asked to say something is: Can a minority retain its identity in law?

Introduction

Since this is the Multatuli Lecture, let me start out from his work, with a quote from "Idea Number 7" about the relationship of majorities to minorities:

> Ruling by a majority of votes is the law of the strongest applied amicably. It means: if we fought, we would win . . . so let's skip the fighting. This system leads not so much to truth as to quiescence. Yet only for the moment, and as a palliative, since the members of the minority usually think they are right and are individually stronger, not so much because of their awareness of being right as because of their more closed ranks and their greater incentive to make an effort. When a minority grows into a majority, it loses the specific value it initially gained by enlarging its numbers. It adopts all the errors of its defeated opponents, who, in their turn, make a virtue of defeat. The upshot is sad.

Asking about minorities presupposes that there is a majority. Today's story therefore concerns not only "minorities" but also the "majority."

Moreover, talking about minorities is always a question of time and context. What a majority denies a minority may in turn be denied to that majority if it later finds itself in the minority position.

Let us keep Multatuli's idea in mind as we examine today's question in greater detail. I propose to approach the subject as follows. First, I will discuss what we in the Netherlands understand by the term *minorities* and what we have understood by it in the past, as there is a significant difference in this respect between today and yesterday. I will then go on to discuss, from the perspective of fundamental rights, the main question, that is, whether a minority can retain its identity in law. The final question I will deal with is what social problems are concealed by today's question. I will conclude by outlining how we can best tackle the problem to which the question points.

What Is a Minority?

The Netherlands: Traditionally a Country of Minorities

The Netherlands is the country of minorities par excellence. It is a country in which no group is so dominant that it can lay down the law to other groups. The country therefore has a long tradition in which not unity but the individual parts have played the central role. It is in these parts that it has all happened. The struggle has been not so much between the parts as within the parts, and this struggle has sometimes been bitter.

In his book *Republic of Rivalries*, historian Piet de Rooij formulates this as follows. The most characteristic feature of Dutch society can be described as "unity in diversity."[1] In his view, the Netherlands has been a country not of bitter disputes between parts but of continuing rivalries. The parts have not always been the same. Originally they were, above all, a person's own city or region, but the nineteenth century saw a division of society along denominational or ideological lines. Until recently, Dutch society was nothing more than a combination—or rather, a cohabitation—of different groups (Protestants, Catholics, Socialists, and Liberals, to mention just the largest groups), all of which were minorities. No matter how the dividing lines ran, it was generally accepted that pragmatic compromises had to be reached in which it was important that all groups should feel that they had benefited equally. At the top the leaders of the different denominational or ideological "pillars [*zuilen*]" came together to discuss how matters should proceed. But others in these pillars had little if any contact with members of other pillars. And people readily accepted this. In the course of the twentieth century, the unity of the Netherlands evolved mainly through the recognition of the right of others to be different. Tolerance of being different became the norm and was directly and above all linked to maintaining scope for the interests and rights of one's own group. This right to be different and yet to be treated equally benefited not only the denominational or ideological pillars, but others, too: it was pivotal in the emancipation of workers, women, and homosexuals and to their aspirations to participate fully in Dutch society.

Major Changes

In the 1960s, history took a turn that has an important bearing on a number of matters that play a role today:

1. The system of denominational or ideological pillars began to crumble. Now, in 2005, it can be regarded as a thing of the past. The end of this system of pillars also brought an end to a particular model of leadership. The leaders of the denominational or ideological pillars enjoyed the confidence of the members to settle disputes. No good alternative to this system has yet been found. In an individualized society in which everyone wants to "do his or her own thing," leadership is a complicated issue.

2. Almost at the same time, the Netherlands was confronted, for the first time in its modern history, with a substantial wave of immigration. First from Italy, Spain, Portugal, and Yugoslavia; later from Morocco and Turkey; and, since the late 1970s, from all over the world. Today, the populations of Amsterdam and of Rotterdam comprise over 170 nationalities.

Since the 1970s, Dutch society has endeavored to apply the principle of equality strictly to all aspects of life. Whereas inequality was formerly a fact of life that was taken for granted, major differences in our society—between men and women, between social classes, between experts and lay people, between the different political parties, and so forth—have become blurred. Or perhaps I should say these differences have become less explicit. And hence, to quote Piet de Rooij again, much experience of dealing with major differences has been lost.

All of this has happened within a national and international context of ongoing individualization, democratization, globalization, privatization, smaller government, and, last but not least, secularization.[2] In my Cleveringa speech of 2002, I described the consequences of these five major developments for our society. At the time, I said that these are developments that interact with one another, reinforce each other's consequences, and have gradually led to a position in which people face one another as individuals and as strangers. The report of the Social and Cultural Planning Office entitled "The Social State of the Netherlands 2005" mentions another new development in the Netherlands, namely, the frequent occurrence of social and emotional loneliness as a result of individualization, divorce or the loss of a partner in some other way. More and more people feel that they stand alone in a society that is in a state of flux, that offers people little certainty, and that comes across as very menacing.

These effects are exacerbated by tensions in the international arena—tensions of which we are becoming increasingly aware and which have a major influence on us. I am not the first to note that the terrorist attacks by the fundamentalist Muslim organization

Al Qaeda on New York and Washington on September 11, 2001, were a turning point. Since then we have experienced two wars, in Afghanistan and Iraq, in which Dutch troops have participated. Since 9/11, terrorist attacks have been carried out by Muslim fundamentalists at various places in the world—Bali, Casablanca, Istanbul, Madrid, and London, to mention but a few—causing dozens of fatalities and casualties. And, yes, in Amsterdam we too were confronted by this violence when the filmmaker and publisher Theo van Gogh was murdered by Muhammad Bouyari, a Dutch citizen of Moroccan descent, in November 2004.

The international climate is undeniably contributing to the present climate of menace and alienation. Individuals who face one another as strangers do not know what norms and values they share with one another (or do not share—because this too creates clarity, as was apparent in the era when the Netherlands was divided along denominational and ideological lines) and therefore do not know what they can expect of other people. We merely suspect that the other person will act on the basis of his or her own norms and values, which are often unknown to us. As strangers facing one another, we suspect that if everyone merely acts on his or her own authority or on the basis of his or her own norms and values (and this also immediately explains the concern, or even the fear, as criminologist Hans Boutellier has said[3]), things will become a real mess.

This is why one can hear calls for clarity from all segments of Dutch society: clarity about the applicable rules, both about the content of the rules and about how they are to be applied; clarity about the rules that one must observe and can expect others to observe in the public domain; clarity about the role of government. It goes without saying that observance of the laws and rules of our country is a precondition for the functioning of our society, and hence for the integration of all population groups in the same society; indeed, this is so self-evident that I will not discuss it today. In everything that follows I will assume that this requirement is fulfilled. What is much less clear is the form that these rules should take. This also explains the question we are dealing with this afternoon: "Can a minority retain its identity in law?" with the emphasis on "in law." As we shall see, though, this term "in law" is probably not the nub of the matter.

Minorities and Majority in the Netherlands in the Year 2005

If we try to define the Netherlands, in 2005, we might say that it is a society of individuals who face one another as strangers in a country that has traditionally comprised minorities that cohabit but are unable, because of their size, to dominate one another. In such a country, everyone has an interest in ensuring that the rights of "minorities" are properly defined and properly regulated. The Netherlands is, after all, a country in which minorities have traditionally been treated with a degree of respect less commonly found in other countries. This came about only because everyone belonged to a minority or was aware that they could one day become a member of a minority. But it is debatable whether this is still the prevailing view.

After all, if I ask what we mean in the Netherlands by "minorities," I hear many people thinking, "Well, of course, we mean Surinamers, Antilleans, Turks, Moroccans, and all those others who have come to the Netherlands in the past forty years." In other words, non-Western immigrants, or *allochtonen*, as they are known in the Netherlands, a term that we wish to jettison but seemingly cannot. And I also hear "Muslims." In other words, it is about the presence of *new* groups, of ethnic minorities, and of a new religious minority (the Muslims) in our midst. Most people are no longer aware that there is a chance that they themselves belong to a minority.

According to James Kennedy, professor of modern history at the Free University in Amsterdam, the Dutch tradition of respecting minorities has come under fire in recent years. In his view:

> for the first time a majority culture has come into being that can be described as liberal, secular, and white. As these people no longer feel that they belong to a minority culture, they are less inclined to recognize the value of respect for minorities. As it is no longer part of their own experience, they find it harder to understand why minorities should be accorded a certain respect. This is an important and ongoing development.[4]

Sjoerd de Jong, a columnist with *NRC Handelsblad* (a Dutch daily), saw the contours of Dutch society entirely redrawn following an interview with Ayaan Hirsi Ali. He expressed it as follows:

> From Hirsi Ali's radical engagement emerges the picture of a different, more abstract country from the plodding polder nation with which we are familiar. Now the Netherlands seems, above all, to be the expression of a high ideal: "the West," "modernity," or "the Enlightenment." From this perspective the culture of consultation and compromise, of give and take, that is so often referred to as "typically Dutch" can signify only one thing: betrayal of the Enlightenment. A complex intellectual tradition thus becomes a complete and pure ideal that must not be tampered with.[5]

According to Kennedy, the development of a liberal, secular, and white majority culture is bound to have consequences.

1. For the first time in the history of the Netherlands, it is conceivable that something in the nature of a "Dutch identity" can be constructed, behind which a majority of Dutch would be willing and able to shelter. This would have been inconceivable when Dutch society was divided along denominational and ideological lines.

2. There is a tendency to view this Dutch identity as a "mono-identity" opposed to ethnic and religious identities, which are incompatible with Dutch identity.

3. Freedom of religion is no longer regarded as a key concept of a free society. This represents a break with three centuries of Dutch tradition because, as Kennedy observes, "the entire modern order is based on freedom of religion, on the freedom of minorities to exercise their consciences without compulsion from the State." Many liberal thinkers now believe—out of fear of Islam—that this is no longer necessary. Freedom of religion is even viewed as an obstacle to a free society.

4. Freedom of education has become a matter of debate, too, once again out of fear of Islam. Prior to 9/11 this was never an issue; now people argue that we must change tack.

Another consequence of the new majority thinking is that people tend to regard themselves as enlightened and emancipated, and they take a stand vis-à-vis minorities that are seen as being neither. This has two consequences: (1) the minority is put under pressure to adapt; and (2) the burden of being tolerant shifts from one addressed to oneself to a reproach to the other. Instead of asking "Am I sufficiently tolerant?" we berate the other person: "You are not sufficiently tolerant." In addition, this shift takes place without due reflection on the quality of one's own tolerance. On this point, Kennedy observed, after the murder of Theo van Gogh: "I am in no doubt that double standards were applied in relation to what Theo van Gogh said about Muslims. This was widely accepted, whereas the discriminatory remarks of Muslims were accepted to a much lesser extent."[6] This is a "worrying development," says Kennedy, and I very much agree with him.

Can a Minority Retain Its Identity in Law?

Collective Rights?

Now that I have outlined the social context within which the debate on minorities and between majority and minority is taking place in the Netherlands in 2005, we must pause and consider the concept of "retaining one's identity." Let us assume that this is intended to mean the complex of factors that characterize a particular group, such as culture, religion, language, daily customs, structure of family life, and sexuality. "Retaining one's identity" is therefore closely connected with the exercise of universal human rights and fundamental rights, both as a group and as an individual.

The question "Can a minority retain its identity in law?" is therefore above all the question of whether in the Netherlands immigrants or Muslims can remain themselves in law *as a group*. If the question is couched in such terms, I can give a short, categorical answer: no. This has been the case since the beginning of this year, when the Dutch government ratified the European Framework Convention for the Protection of National Minorities. The Framework Convention was approved by the Dutch Parliament by Act of 2 December 2004.[7]

The convention protects the rights of national minorities, namely, minority groups that belong, literally, to a different nation, even though they have citizenship of the state in which they live. The convention requires all member states to create laws that will protect minorities in their countries. Under the convention the protection of minorities implies that they may not be persecuted on account of their ethnic, linguistic, or religious identity and that they may maintain their culture. The convention expressly imposes obligations on the participating parties, namely, the European states. First, they are required to respect human rights, both generally and as regards members of national minorities (although this, of course, was already regulated in the European Convention on Human Rights). And, second, the Framework Convention introduces rights that may in fact be regarded as collective rights. Member states are required, for example, to "take measures in the fields of education and research to foster knowledge of the culture, history, language, and religion of their national minorities" and "in areas inhabited by persons belonging to national minorities traditionally or in substantial numbers, if there is sufficient demand, the Parties shall endeavor to ensure, as far as possible and within the framework of their education systems, that persons belonging to those minorities have adequate opportunities to be taught the minority language or to receive instruction in this language." Furthermore, member states must "endeavor to ensure, as far as possible, the conditions that would make it possible to use the minority language in relations between those persons and the administrative authorities."

In the Netherlands, Frisians are the only national minority recognized by the Dutch government within the meaning of the Framework Convention.[8] It follows that immigrants or Muslims in the Netherlands have no collective group rights, no rights to retain their group identity, and no recognition as a national minority, except for the human rights laid down in the Constitution and in various European and international conventions on human rights. This is my provisional conclusion.

Individual Rights?

So if there are no group rights, are there individual rights? After all, the smallest minority is always the individual. Almost everyone in the Netherlands spontaneously answers this question with a "yes"—and rightly so. Our entire legal system, including the Constitution, is geared to this. The question that arises in particular is: Can an immigrant, particularly a Muslim, remain a Muslim *in law* in the Netherlands?—with the emphasis on "in law." In the light of Article 1 of the Dutch Constitution, the answer to this can only be "yes." The text of Article 1 of our Constitution reads: "All persons in the Netherlands shall be treated equally in equal circumstances. Discrimination on the grounds of religion, belief, political opinion, race, or gender or on any other grounds whatsoever shall not be permitted." It follows from this article that all individuals in the Netherlands, including immigrants and Muslims, are entitled to equal treatment in our constitutional democracy and to the fundamental rights set forth in our Constitution. Important fundamental rights are: freedom of speech and expression (Article 7),[9] freedom of religion and belief (Article 6),[10] freedom of association and assembly (Article 9),[11] freedom of education (Article 23),[12] and freedom from invasion of privacy (Article 10).[13]

As the law provides, fundamental rights may be exercised not only individually but also collectively, in association with others, albeit always subject to each person's responsibility to the law. Whether a person has remained within the limits of the law in exercising fundamental rights is a matter to be decided by the courts. The courts determine whether or not limits have been exceeded—this is *not* a matter that is decided in the lower house of parliament. Nor is it a matter decided by the media.

An Important Role for the Courts

It follows that the question whether Imam El Moumni was guilty of discrimination in 2002 in making hurtful comments about homosexuals and could be prosecuted for this was a matter for the courts. It was held both at first instance and on appeal that the spiritual leader of the Rotterdam Nasr mosque should be acquitted. According to the judges, El Moumni had not intentionally discriminated against homosexuals or incited discrimination and hate. The judges took the view that the statements by the Imam were covered by the constitutional freedom of religion. The way in which he had done this was within the limits of what is acceptable, in the view of The Hague Court of Appeal.[14] In this case, freedom of religion took precedence over the hurt feelings of homosexuals.

An example of a case in which freedom of speech and expression prevailed over the hurt feelings of Muslims is the judgment of The Hague District Court of March 15, 2005. Ayaan Hirsi Ali, a member of parliament for the Liberal Party (VVD), was sued by four Muslims at the start of the year in connection with her intention to make a sequel to the film *Submission Part I*, directed by Theo van Gogh. The four Muslims had applied to The Hague District Court for an interim injunction restraining the defendant from "making hurtful or derogatory statements in public about the Muslim population group, the Muslim faith, Muslim culture, and the prophet Mohammed and from expressing views offensive to Muslim believers." They also wished to have an order restraining Hirsi Ali from releasing the second part of *Submission* or a film with a similar content.

The key question was whether Hirsi Ali had overstepped the mark in her criticism of Islam and had been needlessly offensive. The case turned on the use of the words *pedophile* and *perverse*. The court held as follows:

> It seems as though by using these words the defendant has sought to explore the bounds of what can still be deemed acceptable. The choice of the term *pedophile* is unfortunate as it at least presupposes a pattern of behavior, whereas this account concerns a one-off event. Moreover, the word in its present connotation is used about

a situation that occurred centuries ago. The defendant used these terms once or at the most on a few occasions. It follows that in the context of the exaggeration she is permitted she remained within the bounds of what is acceptable. It is debatable, however, whether frequent use of these or similar words would still fall within the bounds of proportionality and subsidiarity. Although the defendant has submitted that the use of these terms precisely illustrates that the Koran is not a practical guide for daily life, it is considered that she could illustrate this view in a different (more effective) way and in better-chosen words.[15]

The Hague judge held that the plaintiffs had failed to show that Hirsi Ali had *intended* to offend or insult them or to make blasphemous statements about Muslim belief. Nor did he see any reason to ban her from releasing another film similar to *Submission Part I*. In other words, the constitutional freedom of speech and expression prevailed in this case over the interests of the four Muslim plaintiffs.

The judgment of The Hague court is a fine example of how our constitutional democracy functions, because:

1. The four Muslims made use of the courts and thus demonstrated that they were abiding by and wished to respect the rules of our constitutional democracy;
2. The judgment showed that Hirsi Ali had the right to exercise her freedom of expression as she saw fit and that in doing so she had not exceeded the bounds of what is acceptable;
3. At the same time, the judgment of the court indicated that there are bounds that must be observed in exercising freedom of speech and expression, which in turn affords legal protection to the Muslims who felt that their religious feelings had been offended.

I have dealt at length with these two examples in order to show that, in my view, there is not much wrong "in law" in the Netherlands when it comes to the question of whether a minority can retain its identity *in law*. We have a system of protecting fundamental rights: everyone who lives in the Netherlands (and this includes immigrants and Muslims) can make use in the same way of the system of fundamental rights, and if there is disagreement about whether the bounds of the law have been observed in exercising a fundamental right, the Dutch courts are on hand to give judgment—and actually do so. The fact that the system works and that the Constitution does not therefore need adjustment is also evident from the policy paper "Fundamental Rights in a Plural Society," which was published by the Ministry of the Interior and Kingdom Relations in 2004.[16] The entire system is geared to ensuring that a minority can retain its identity, even if the minority consists of immigrants or Muslims acting either individually or together. Our legal system is structured—or rather, has grown historically—in this way because its object is to guarantee the plural society that has always been a basic characteristic of the Netherlands, because as a country we have derived our identity and unity from respecting the rights of others to be different. We can be proud that our system still functions in this way.

In my view, the conclusion is clear. The question "Can a minority retain its identity in law?" must be answered as follows:

1. Immigrants or Muslims in the Netherlands have no collective group rights, no right to retain their identity as a group, and no recognition as a national minority save for the human rights contained in the Constitution and in various European and international conventions on human rights.
2. Immigrants and Muslims are protected as individuals, however, even when they act together or collectively, in order to retain their identity on the basis of the constitutional freedoms that apply to everyone in the Netherlands.

In other words, what a minority can do "in law" in the Netherlands is clear. So, this is not really the issue.

Social Problems

The main problems between minorities and the majority occur not in relation to the Dutch authorities or Dutch law but in *society*, in the relations between citizens and other private parties. In the Netherlands there is great tolerance of different lifestyles, but at the same time there is great pressure to be like everyone else and to press others into a mold. It seems that, in some circles, some lifestyles are not or are only barely tolerated. Clashes between fundamental rights and between lifestyles must be solved not in court but in practice.

Here are some examples:

1. A homosexual teacher at a predominantly ethnic school is openly disobeyed in class and shown disrespect on account of his sexual orientation. The very same children, however, demand respect from their teacher for their ethnic background and culture.
2. An imam whose belief precludes him from shaking hands with a woman and is nonetheless obliged to do so feels that his beliefs are not respected. An emancipated woman who insists on shaking hands with the imam in turn feels that she has not been shown respect and has been treated differently if he refuses (quite apart from the fact that, according to her, shaking hands is a norm that the imam should learn to observe).
3 The desire of a Muslim minority to build a mosque can be completely at odds with the wishes of a secular majority, who do not wish to be confronted with other people's expressions of belief and certainly not those of Muslims.

4. Muslim women and girls with headscarves have difficulties in the Netherlands in school, in employment, and even in public places, where they are regularly exposed to verbal harassment.

5. Jews with yarmulkes dare not go to some places because of verbal harassment by young Moroccans.

6. Intolerant attitudes exist between ethnic minority groups or within an ethnic minority community (e.g., Berbers and Arabs in the Moroccan community, Hindustanis and Creoles in the Surinamese community).

7. In some secular circles, it is not the done thing to say that you are against euthanasia, donor codicils, or gay marriage.

These are relatively harmless examples compared with the violence committed by young Moroccans against Jews during the Palestine demonstration in Amsterdam in April 2002, or compared with the murder of Theo van Gogh by Muhammad Bouyari; freedom of expression was brutally smothered by someone who considered that his religious feelings had been insulted and offended. Or take the fact that some members of the lower house of parliament and other politicians have to go through life surrounded by heavy security, as their lives are not safe on account of their opinions.

There has undeniably been an atmosphere of fear, alienation, and menace in the Netherlands since the terrorist attacks of 9/11 and the murder of Pim Fortuyn in 2002 and of Theo van Gogh almost a year ago. But the five major changes that have occurred in the past forty years and have led to a society in which people face one another as strangers—as I outlined at the start of my lecture—have also contributed to this atmosphere. These feelings of fear and alienation are being compounded by the fact that people must confront the nuisance or criminality of groups of young people from ethnic backgrounds in their own neighborhoods or districts. The same applies to the threat of a terrorist attack in the Netherlands, which has become a reality since the murder of Theo van Gogh. So, in a nutshell, this is the explosive cocktail served up with the debate on minorities in the Netherlands in 2005.

To this must be added the fact that many people in the Netherlands feel threatened by the presence of Muslims in general. It is not merely the threat of terrorist attacks that is feared; the fear is deeper and is connected with various factors:

1. The fear that the clock will be turned back and that freedoms won in the 1960s and 1970s, particularly in the sexual field (namely cohabiting, more relaxed divorce laws, homosexuality, abortion, the Pill, "free" sex), in the field of women's rights, and in respect of self-determination (euthanasia) will be lost.

2. Demographic factors: the Dutch population is aging; people are having fewer and fewer children; and there are more and more single people. At the same time, the number of non-Western immigrants is growing. In 2005, 10.3 percent of the Dutch

population consisted of non-Western immigrants.[17] They are concentrated in the big cities: in Amsterdam the figure is 36 percent. The report of the Social and Cultural Planning Office (SCP) entitled "Keeping Out of Each Other's Way: The Influence of Ethnic Concentration on Integration and Perceptions" shows that a majority of Dutch society (60 percent) believes that there are too many people from ethnic minorities in the Netherlands and that two out of three indigenous Dutch people have little if any contact with them. The fact that the ethnic minorities and the indigenous Dutch have little to do with one another is closely connected with the fact that they live apart. This alone greatly increases the chances of meeting members of one's own group and reduces the chances of meeting others outside that group. If many people from ethnic backgrounds live in a neighborhood, they are much less likely to have contact with the indigenous Dutch. This is particularly true in the four largest cities. Nonetheless, we can see that the ethnic minorities and the indigenous Dutch view each other fairly positively once they do come into contact. The more dealings they have with one another, the more positive is the view. According to the SCP report, however, a rapid influx of people from ethnic backgrounds into a neighborhood leads to a more unfavorable assessment.[18]

3. A fear of the Islamicization of Dutch society. The primary fear is that the Muslim minority will eventually become the majority and impose its will on the former majority. Naturally, this fear is fueled by the picture that we have of Muslim states as places that lack a democracy but not, in many cases, repression. What also does not help in the slightest is that such manifestly bad guys as Osama bin Laden and Saddam Hussein are perceived to be prominent Muslims.

The crucial point is that fundamental rights and above all lifestyles, norms, and values clash, and that conflicts must be solved not in court but on the streets in practice. Although government can guarantee the fundamental rights of any person—as will indeed be honored in court in the event of a conflict between fundamental rights—in daily practice this is time-consuming and other means of resolving dilemmas must be sought. But we are often at a loss as to how this must be done. It is precisely because everyone has the right to be "him- or herself" that there is a clash with the right of the other person to be "him- or herself." Everyone wants to do his or her own thing and to be disturbed by others as little as possible in the process. The desire for rules is above all about curbing the behavior of *other* people—we ourselves should of course be allowed maximum freedom!

And so we find ourselves in the Netherlands in an era in which many people wish to pursue their own individual courses and no longer wish to spend much time respecting the right of others to be different, certainly not if the other person is from an ethnic minority or, even worse, a Muslim. And people tend to have even less patience when confronted not by individual Muslims or immigrants but by Muslims or immigrants who act collectively in the public arena and invoke their fundamental rights.

In such circumstances it is sometimes easier simply to insist that you are the "majority" and to demand that "people either adapt to our ways or leave the country." This adaptation is, in fact, not as easy as it sounds. It is no longer just about our laws and rules—which ethnic minorities and Muslims should (rightly) observe—or about the norms and values that people should know and, preferably, share (even if this has never been the case in the Netherlands). Now it is also about whether or not people subscribe to a new Dutch identity—the "mono-identity" observed by Kennedy—as opposed to ethnic and religious identities that are incompatible with it. This excludes rather than includes large groups of individuals in the Netherlands, and people do not stop to consider whether this has a positive effect on Dutch society as a whole. The mirror image of this trend can be seen in some members of the ethnic minority and Muslim communities: they are withdrawing more and more into their own groups and undergoing a process of radicalization.

In such circumstances, the question no longer concerns what a minority can do in law: instead, it concerns what a majority can demand of a minority in the sense of adaptation and integration. It is important to realize that questions about adaptation and integration will produce different answers both in the case of the so-called majority and in the case of the different minorities in the Netherlands. It is also important to realize that there is no consensus between majority and minority, no consensus among ethnic minority groups or within ethnic minority and Muslim groups, or even within the so-called Dutch majority, and no consensus about Dutch identity or the direction in which Dutch society should move. Hence the enormous confusion and the shrill tones in which the debate is conducted.

Future Scenarios

We must bear in mind that, ultimately, it is the majority (or rather the behavior of the majority) that determines how far minorities are integrated into a society and not the reverse, as is sometimes thought.[19] Ultimately, the majority must create room for this—or not, as the case may be. In either case, we are responsible for the consequences. It is always about "us" and not about "them," and in many cases "them" means "us."

We must ask ourselves the following questions:

1. What form should a new Dutch identity take? Is it to be tailored along enlightened lines? Is this identity to be inclusive or exclusive of all individuals and groups resident in the Netherlands?

2. Will minorities, if they are unwilling or unable to join the "majority," retain a place *within* society as a minority, but with equal rights and duties and respect for the fact

that they are different? One possibility would be to revamp the old model of a society divided along denominational and ideological lines (the "pillars") for the common purpose of developing a new model for Dutch citizenship.

3. Or are we moving toward a model of society in which minorities fall *outside* society (whether or not they are confined to certain neighborhoods) and do not count in society, with all the consequences that this entails? The aftermath of Hurricane Katrina in New Orleans should serve as a warning to all of us in this respect.

My preference would be for an inclusive society, one in which minorities have equal rights and duties and are treated with respect for their differences. Other options involve a majority imposing its will on minorities. I need only remind you of Multatuli's "Idea Number 7" to predict that this could only lead to even greater entrenchment and polarization and, in the long run, to even greater radicalization. And I am not talking just about minorities. To combat fear, we need clarity and guarantees, clear rules that must be enforced. This is understandable, but fear is also a bad counselor. Our behavior must not lead to a situation in which we push a group toward the very place we do not wish them to be. If people do not feel at home in the Netherlands, they will always feel that their loyalties lie elsewhere. Integration, belonging, and taking part cost time, more time than we usually therefore care to give. We will have to do everything possible to prevent further polarization, while realizing that this takes time. To this end we will have to mobilize many forces in society, both among the majority and among the minorities. It would be better for us to start thinking in terms of "we" rather than making an unproductive distinction between "Dutch people" and "immigrants," between "Dutch people" and "Muslims," or between the "majority" and the "minority."

Preventing Polarization and Mobilizing Positive Forces—Ervin Staub

This is an approach that we have adopted in Amsterdam. Following the murder of Theo van Gogh, the municipal executive drew up an action plan titled "We Amsterdamers." The aim of the plan is to:

1. Combat terrorism, as an addition to the activities of the police and judicial authorities;
2. Combat radicalization;
3. Prevent polarization and mobilize positive forces.

The plan thus combines a hard and a soft approach. It is intended to bring the different groups in Amsterdam closer together and to increase society's ability to avoid polarization and escalation.

The first two lines of action (combating terror and preventing radicalization) are less relevant in the context of today's subject. I can, however, assure you that the necessary measures have been taken in this respect, too. It is the third line of action—namely, preventing polarization and mobilizing positive forces—that is relevant to this afternoon's subject. One of the persons whose advice we have sought is Professor Ervin Staub of the University of Massachusetts, who is an expert in dealing with conflicts between population groups. Professor Staub has been involved in the reconciliation process following the genocide in Rwanda; he therefore has experience of situations much more serious than that in which our society now finds itself.

Professor Staub has written a report for Amsterdam entitled "Understanding the roots of violence and avenues to its prevention and to the developing of positive relations between the local ethnic group and Muslim minorities in Amsterdam, in the Netherlands—and the rest of Europe." Most of what now follows is derived from his ideas.

1. A first step toward preventing polarization is to organize a real debate. At present, much is said in Dutch homes, on the television, in newspapers, and on the Internet *about* each other and *to* each other, but there is little dialogue *with* each other. In addition, many voices are not heard, and I am not only referring to those of the ethnic minorities. The vote against a European constitution is a sign that many people in the Netherlands feel excluded.

2. This is not very surprising, as we hardly ever meet one another. To be honest, things were not much better formerly, when the Netherlands was divided along denominational and ideological lines. People met other members of their own particular group, but had little contact outside the group. Perhaps meeting one another is not in keeping with the Dutch mentality. We are probably perfectly content if we can go our own way in our own particular surroundings. But the consequence is a lack of contact between groups, a lack of social cohesion, and an absence of integration of minorities. "Integration into what?" is then a justified question. Whatever the case, meetings are a precondition for establishing a real dialogue, and for this purpose meeting places are necessary: at school, at work, in the public domain, and on television. This is the second step.

3. The third step is to ensure that in the dialogue we treat each other with respect. The other person must not be demonized or humiliated. We all have a responsibility when it comes to what we say. We may not like hearing it, but cursing and swearing causes pain. Freedom of expression is highly prized in the Netherlands. This means that a lot may be said, but what is at issue is whether what *may* be said *should* be said. The debate prompted last year by the murder of Theo van Gogh is very valuable in this respect and must be continued. Dutch author and columnist Remco Campert was the first to make this point. Writing in the newspaper *De Volkskrant*, he inquired:

"Surely freedom of expression is rather different from the right to hurt people right to the quick?"[20]

4. The fourth step is to learn about each other's cultures, religions, norms, and values, as well as about each other's fears and pain. The media could—and in my view should—play an important role in this. They could produce programs that enable people to appreciate and identify with the dilemmas facing Dutch society at present, programs that portray Muslims and unbelievers, indigenous Dutch people and immigrants as fellow Dutch citizens who have their own ordinary cares and problems. And they certainly need not be intellectual programs. The Dutch series *Zeg eens A* in the 1980s was crucial to the acceptance of homosexuals (the series portrayed a lesbian relationship) and of mixed couples (a white daughter with a black boyfriend). And in the U.S.A., programs such as *The Cosby Show* and *Oprah Winfrey* have done more for the rights of black Americans than any law. So why shouldn't we do the same here? Reality TV is "in," and we like nothing better than a bit of voyeurism.

5. The fifth step is to ensure that the basic criteria of the debate are clear to the parties involved.

   a. Requirements for integration? Yes, requirements can and should be made in relation to how large groups of newcomers are integrated.

   b. Rules? Yes, without clear rules there can be no society. In addition, the rules need to be soundly enforced.

   c. Limitation of the fundamental rights of minorities? No. Fundamental rights apply to everyone. This principle may not be compromised. It would be contrary to everything that we hold dearest: constitutional democracy and rule of law.

   d. A national immigration policy? Yes, this is necessary in order to ensure better coordination of the efforts to integrate minorities. The aim should be to ensure that it is clear both to the present population and to future immigrants why the Netherlands needs immigrants both now and in the future, in the light of demographic trends such as aging, the falling birth rate, and the international orientation of our economy. We can then actually welcome the people whom we need and who wish to be here with us.

   e. Combating the radicalization of Muslim youth? Yes. In Amsterdam we are now working on a model in which enforcement and prevention are mutually reinforcing.

6. The sixth step is to make the switch in due course from dialogue to the "Netherlands Joint Project"—that is, the development of a shared and nonexclusive vision of society and Dutch identity. This brings me to the concept of citizenship as a possibly binding concept. On other occasions I have spoken of this and will now therefore simply refer to what I have said before.[21]

Finally, when we talk about combating polarization and mobilizing positive forces, we must bear in mind that this is a lengthy process and that it must continue even in the case of extreme threats such as terrorist attacks. There is simply no other option.

. . .

Ladies and Gentlemen,

This brings me to the conclusion of my remarks. We have been talking about the relationship between minorities and the majority in the Netherlands in the year 2005. We have paused to consider the traditional characteristics of the Netherlands: "unity in diversity" and "respect for the right of others to be different." These traditional characteristics are perhaps subject to change in our era owing to the development of a mono-identity, as James Kennedy has said, an identity that may be endorsed by a majority of the population for the first time in Dutch history, to the possible exclusion of others who do not wish to adopt this identity, and what consequences this entails. My answer to today's question "Can a minority retain its identity in law?" has been as follows:

1. Immigrants or Muslims in the Netherlands have no collective group rights, no rights to maintain a group identity, and no recognition as a national minority, except for the human rights contained in the Constitution and in various European and international conventions on human rights.
2. There should, however, be protection for ethnic minorities and Muslims as individuals, even when they act jointly or collectively, to remain themselves, that is, to continue in their own beliefs and customs, on the basis of the constitutional freedoms that apply to everyone in the Netherlands.

We have examined our legal system, with its emphasis on guaranteeing the traditionally plural nature of Dutch society, and have found that the system functions properly. This is something of which we may be proud. We have also found that when it comes to the position of minorities in our society, it is not so much the law as the relationship between citizens that causes friction. Individuals and groups of individuals who "wish to retain their identity" generate friction with others who also "wish to retain their identity." They then clash with one another and do not know how to resolve their conflicts. This leads to unease and an atmosphere of fear, alienation, and menace. The social background to this, including both national and international factors, has been considered. We have seen that we must do everything we possibly can to prevent further polarization, and that we must mobilize many forces in Dutch society to this end. I have attempted to indicate how this should be done by referring to the opinion of Ervin Staub, who recommends a process of discussion, meeting, respect, and dialogue. This is a process for which we must allow sufficient time and with which we must persevere even in difficult times.

I have told you all this in the full realization that *minority* and *majority* are political terms that sometimes have little bearing on how people live their lives, and in the realization that life is much more beautiful and complex, and that a person—and certainly a modern person—may have several identities, several loyalties, and several worlds, no matter from what country he or she comes. What that life looks like, however, is not a matter for government, but for dreams and literature.

—*Translated by Liesbeth van Looijengoed*

Prophetic Justice in a Home Haunted by Strangers

Transgressive Solidarity and Trauma in the Work of an Israeli Rabbis' Group

Bettina Prato

Trauma, Identity, and the Israeli-Palestinian Conflict

What does it mean to practice a peace activism simultaneously rooted in Judaism and in human rights, in a context in which trauma-influenced readings of Jewish identity are invoked to justify violating the rights of other people(s)?[1] How can the language of universal rights be reconciled with a belief in Jewish uniqueness that includes a history of exceptional suffering and a divinely granted claim to a Promised Land inhabited by others? And, most importantly, what are the theoretical and practical consequences of affirming not just the possibility but the need for such reconciliation in the name of Jewish identity itself, when the latter is routinely interpellated via trauma discourses and institutions?

Rather than address these questions in the abstract, this essay sets them in the context of today's Israel/Palestine, where identity is not just a matter of borders, citizenship, or religious heritage but also the terrain on which traumatic investments born of past and present history are negotiated. This is particularly true in the past two decades, as public references to moments of exceptional suffering in Jewish-Israeli and Palestinian histories—notably but not exclusively the Shoah and the *Nakbah*[2]—seem to have acquired growing significance in discourses on the two ethno-national identities. In particular, and in parallel with a growing popularization of the vocabulary and institutions of psychic trauma in both societies, such moments are increasingly included in national identity narratives as paradigms of "unspeakability," in line with psychoanalytic views of trauma as suffering that overwhelms people's ability to turn events into objects of speech.[3]

Despite the very different realities of Jewish Israelis and Palestinians, for both peoples the public and private articulation of ethno-national (or ethno-religious) identity takes place today in spaces pervaded by narratives of victimization, partly but not exclusively fed by ongoing conflict.[4] In consequence, experiences of suffering seem to acquire a certain inescapability in contemporary narratives of Jewish-Israeli and Palestinian identities, ranging from personal memoirs to the rhetoric of political parties and religious groups. Even when that is not so, the recurrent affirmation of past victimization in authoritative spaces of socialization and identity formation makes it difficult for individuals to at once claim loyalty to one's ethno-national identity and stand outside the "national consensus" to be critical of narratives of "innocence" and "victimhood." In addition, the recent popularization of a variety of trauma discourses (from psychotherapeutic discourses to secular and religious discourses of ethno-national trauma) and their integration into narratives and practices of Jewish-Israeli identity has resulted in certain temporal disturbances. In particular, the discursive centrality of a genealogical bond between today's Israelis and the victims of "unspeakable" and in a sense "unwitnessable" past episodes of Jewish victimization (notably the Shoah) sustains a temporal logic in which past and present insecurities lend each other exceptional urgency. In this context, a possible repetition of the past sometimes seems to outweigh narratives of historical progress, such as those linked to the early phases of Zionist and Israeli history, as if Jewish and Israeli past and present were condemned to merge in the endless repetition of certain moments of "unwitnessable" violence.

Taken to its extreme, the temporal logic of collective trauma may lead to the identification of any possible "content" of Jewish-Israeli identity with (past) victimization, as the traumatic elusiveness of events such as the Shoah enables them to be rhetorically transmuted from historical facts into a sort of genealogical "essence" of identity. In today's Israel, the essentialist merger of ethno-national identity and trauma is for the most part only a possibility, though one that seems at times implicitly affirmed by certain institutions feeding into contemporary discourses of ethno-national Jewish-Israeli trauma. These include psycho-social institutions offering assistance to terror victims, civil-society organizations helping terror survivors and their families, a variety of institutions targeting Holocaust survivors, and certain political and religious groups justifying their political projects with reference to the traumatic "fate" of Jews. More than a mere possibility, however, is the affirmation of a sort of Jewish-Israeli "calling," a set of ethical, political, and affective obligations advocated as a corollary of ethno-national membership and partly deriving from the very "unspeakability" of an exceptionally violent and painful past. In contemporary trauma literature, the normative force of such an affirmation is rendered by equating trauma with the threatened disappearance of the individual and collective witness,[5] that is, of a subject of speech who can articulate a testimony of victimization, thereby countering the power of trauma to defeat the most properly *human* faculty (speech). In some authoritative discourses on Jewish-Israeli identity, the proper relationship of ethno-national subjects to an "unspeakable" past is articulated as a call to lend uncritical support to ethical-political projects advocated in testimonial terms, that is, as ways to "speak" the past while securing the continued existence of a testimonial community thanks to a Jewish state that will prevent a repetition of the "unspeakable."

Both in Israel and among Palestinians, it has been right-wing political groups who have most explicitly appropriated the vocabulary of testimony, to shore up political projects centered on a neat overlap of physical state borders and ethno-religious identity. The quasi-normalization of trauma-influenced discourses of identity, however, makes it difficult for political forces that seek to take a distance from traumatic genealogies (e.g., most of the left) to relate to national insecurities in "secular" terms, that is, as historical realities subject to the grammar of linear time, causality, and mundane justice. At a minimum, even these groups must somehow engage the testimonial legacy of the past in ways that are respectful of taboos such as that against even hinting at some form of mutual comparability between the Shoah and the *Nakbah*. More generally, the question of how to engage this legacy *through moral witnessing* is present even in initiatives aiming to restore ethical and political agency to Israelis and Palestinians as ethno-national communities by delivering Israeli-Palestinian politics from the all-consuming preoccupation with avoiding repetition of past traumas.

One of the key obstacles confronting these projects is that the combination of recurrent evocations of traumatic histories with insecurities born of ongoing conflict tends to interpellate the bearers of each ethno-national identity as subjects whose existence (both physical and as bearers of identity) depends upon the pursuit of a pure, sovereign space emptied of all potentially "traumatizing" others. In other words, this combination seems to intensify and in a sense to "individualize" what Derrida calls an "ipsocentric" tendency of sovereignty (as well as of democracy) in general, in the sense of a logic of affirmation of the self-centered, tendentially exclusionary power of the self or of a community of "semblables" or peers.[6] At least on the surface, this seems to invite a generalization of individual trauma theory on a broad socio-political scale: in Freud's work, the etiology of psychic trauma is marked by the psyche's attempt retroactively to master a moment of utter powerlessness (i.e., the traumatic event). Specifically, trauma results from a momentary defeat of psychic mechanisms tasked with defending the inner metabolism of human life, which in turn depends on the successful mediation of organic individuality coexisting with its "other" (i.e., the world, in the form of stimuli constantly testing the quasi-inertial pace of organic life).[7] Hence trauma results from an interruption in a sort of "filtering" process through which individuals maintain a sense of mutual compatibility between the pace of organic existence and that of "the other/world." Since it reveals the precariousness of that compatibility, trauma generates for Freud a need retroactively to annul its own occurrence, which may lead to neurotic symptoms, such as the compulsive repetition by a trauma victim of elements of a traumatic event. In addition, contemporary studies of a "post-traumatic stress syndrome" (PTSD) stress the role played by symptoms such as "avoidance," that is, behavior that aims to create around the individual a space emptied of all elements that might evoke the trauma or its causes/agents (i.e., all "others"), as well as the common occurrence of phenomena of role reversal, where trauma scripts are reenacted by victims, who take on the role of their past victimizers.[8]

Though properly applicable only to individuals, such notions are sometimes generalized to entire ethno-national groups, particularly in situations of conflict.[9] In Israeli-Palestinian politics, for example, some authors might emphasize the apparent ability of two ethno-national histories marked by moments of collective trauma to "entrap" people into strategies of avoidance and role reversal. A historical analysis of the role played by references to such moments in Israeli and Palestinian politics, however, shows that there is nothing automatic in the apparent analogy between individual post-traumatic strategies and politics sustained via narratives of collective victimization, unspeakability, and testimonial crisis. Rather, the possibility of drawing such an analogy appears to be linked largely to the progressive institutionalization of a number of trauma discourses (including medical, psycho-social, ethno-national, and religious discourses) both in Israel and in Palestinian society since the 1970s.[10] In this discursive context, religious discourse is also sometimes an instrument to reinforce exclusionary attachments, whether these derive from traumatic events themselves or from political and cultural choices concerning the proper construction of the legacy of the past. Thanks to the overlap of religious and ethno-national identity in Israel, religious discourse may infuse this legacy with a sort of divine logic, so that political choices that resemble post-traumatic avoidance and role reversal can be advocated as testimonial obligations to the nation and to God, sustaining a quasi-redemptive attachment to the pursuit of national security and marking national boundaries with a series of quasi-religious taboos.

But is this the only way religious discourse can play a significant role vis-à-vis the politics of sovereign identity in contemporary Israel? In this essay, I want to explore a different, even opposite possibility. Through a study of the work and ideology of Rabbis for Human Rights (RHR), a group of Israeli rabbis engaged in acts of solidarity with Palestinians, I want to pose the question of whether the religious appropriation of human rights discourse may generate opportunities for transgressing the exclusionary loyalties that trauma-laden identity narratives seem to encourage in today's Israel. Given the tension ethno-national and religious trauma narratives of Israeli identity bring about between discourses and practices that affirm the universality of human rights and those that affirm Jewish-Israeli particularity, such an appropriation may seem bound to be characterized by paradoxes and contradictions. Nevertheless, contradictions and nonreconciliation between the supposed universality of a human rights ethics and the trauma-laden particularity of Jewish-Israeli identity need not result in a paralysis of ethical and political action On the contrary, my study of RHR shows that this very lack of reconciliation can be the occasion for testimonial practices of religious and political identity that are ethically and politically life-enabling both for Israelis and, to a lesser degree, for Palestinians, thanks to the creation of concrete, perhaps untheorizable spaces where the other/enemy can be faced beyond the exclusiveness of Jewish trauma-related obligations.

I will suggest that the tension between religious identity and human rights discourse, intensified by the traumatic subtext of many Jewish-Israeli identity narratives, pushes RHR to exceed its own theoretical foundations by letting human rights practice push the limits of its understanding of prophetic Judaism. In particular, what is exceeded is a notion of justice and of the prophetic that relies on a clear distinction between self and other/stranger, a distinction central both to the discourse of religious identity and to the logic of trauma and post-trauma. I will argue that this excess is not accidental and that the tension between human rights and religious discourse heightened by trauma narratives may provide a concrete terrain for the exercise of ethical-political responsibility in the quasi-Levinasian sense of an ability to respond directly to the presence and needs of others/strangers rather than delegating that response to the institutions of formal politics. At the same time, my focus on the practical, contingent nature of such responsibility is meant to suggest that merely theoretical reconciliations of human rights and religious identity discourses are unlikely to be able to counter the tendency of trauma-bearing identity narratives to sustain the pursuit of exclusionary politics (or a radical version of Levinasian "ontology"). In the case of RHR, for instance, the combination of a prophetic reading of Judaism and of human rights discourse creates theoretical opportunities for acts of solidarity that in practice defy exclusionary politics; yet such opportunities must then be translated into concrete, individual choices, which entail taking risks and negotiating the costs of transgressing identity.

In the end, RHR's example appears significant neither as an ideal model nor as a collection of individuals with exceptional abilities to resist the temptation to self-closure around individual or collective "Jewish wounds." Rather, it is significant because it offers religious Israelis a possibility for working around discourses of ontology/identity designed as a shield against traumatic anxieties, as well as repositories of narcissistic affirmation, without asking Jewish Israelis to abandon those anxieties or to bear them without the practical, affective support of a Jewish state. Despite the obvious limitations of such an approach, a focus on human rights practice allows RHR to remain attached to discourses of Jewish woundedness and testimonial obligations, but to do so in a way that is both critical and self-compassionate. Unlike some secular Israeli peace groups, RHR thus refrains from advocating a non-Jewish Israeli state, nor does it uphold a notion of justice rooted in a radical openness to the "other" as not (only) a stranger. Instead, the group seeks in human rights practice a viable niche for its pursuit of justice on behalf of Palestinians and marginalized Israelis.

Thanks to a pragmatic negotiation of conflicting commitments to identity and to universality, RHR's pursuit of "limited" responsibility does not, then, replace Zionist narratives with narratives of a Derridean "unconditional hospitality" or a "hospitality of visitation."[11] Rather, this notion and practice of responsibility works in counterpoint to these narratives. One might add that it actually exists only thanks to these narratives and the state of Israel as a Jewish state. On the one hand, RHR initiatives are examples of limited, practical resistance to the "ontological closures" of political Zionism. On the other hand, RHR's theoretical and practical engagement with Jewish trauma narratives may also be a starting point for a new, peace-oriented approach to the implications of such narratives for Israeli-Palestinian relations. While far from representing an ideal of justice, RHR's work shows how Judaism and human rights can at least provisionally turn the privileges of state sovereignty into a sort of Levinasian "dwelling" for some Jewish Israelis, that is, a home that is visited by (and vulnerable to) "strangers" but that nonetheless offers concrete possibilities for taking on ethical responsibility and negotiating one's interpellation by discourses of collective trauma. The result is a multiplicity of small acts that engage people as bearers of relative power "to do," pushing the limits of ethno-national, trauma-laden identity from *within*, rather than from *beyond* the discourse and institutions of ethno-national ontology, toward a politics neither of recognition nor of love,[12] but rather of cautious togetherness, occasional friendship, and respectful distance.

Human Rights, Politics, and Religion: The "Compatibility" Debate

The ethical and political ambiguities of a universalistic human rights discourse in a world organized not only around civic and ascriptive singularities but also around power inequalities have not gone unnoticed in political and ethical philosophy. While the universal promise of this discourse makes it emblematic of the emancipating potential of the Enlightenment for many theorists of democracy (notably those who follow in Kant's steps, like Habermas), or at least of a positive limit to violence beyond the *ratio* of sovereign legitimacy in the liberal tradition, Marxist critiques have emphasized the active disregard of socio-economic inequalities by a politics based on "the Rights of Man."[13] Moreover, postfoundationalist authors writing in the footsteps of Nietzsche or Foucault, postcolonial theorists, and theorists of the politics of gender, race, or sexual identities have all critiqued some of the presuppositions of liberal human rights discourse, notably the naturalization" of a certain notion of individuality, humanness, and subjectivity associated with the "bearer of human rights."

Levinas approached the question of the "Rights of Man" understood as "human rights" from a particularly original critical standpoint. His critique suggests that human rights discourse cannot provide a "just" *ratio* for politics, thereby moderating the unlimited demands of ethical responsibility,[14] so long as these rights are not understood as the "rights of the *other*." In his words:

> The formal characteristics of the Rights of Man, such as they are conceived of since the Renaissance, consists in their being attached to every human person independently from any prior granting by any authority or tradition. . . . But the right of man, signifying the right to a free will, is exercised in the concreteness of the empirical

order of man—of man among men, in being-there—as the right to being-there or to live, and hence as the right to satisfy the needs that sustain life.[15]

Given the multiplicity of potentially conflicting holders of rights, Levinas believes that the Kantian idea of a common rationality of wills, whereby we are led by practical reason to the universal, cannot guarantee that human rights discourse will moderate the infinite demands of ethics through justice. Rather, what enables the convergence of rights in a polity that upholds "the Rights of Man" is the primacy of a will rooted in "An attachment to the other in his alterity to the point of granting him a priority over oneself. . . . That the Rights of Man are originally the rights of the other man, and that they express, beyond the burgeoning of identities in their own identity and their instinct for free perseverance, the for-the-other of the social, of the for-the-stranger—such appears to me to be the meaning of their novelty."[16]

The tension between universality and particularity in certain debates about human rights is sometimes linked to the idea of this ever-possible gap between the realm of ethics, which may not be (entirely) regulated by various forms of *ratio*, and that of politics, where the possibility of relying on certain sources of (legal, political, economic, and even moral) *ratio* remains generally dominant, despite trauma discourses and also despite what Derrida regards as a tension with regard to the "uncountable" in certain political forms, notably democracy. Given the frequent overlap between human rights and humanitarian discourses in contemporary international politics, the tension between universality and particularity is often the object of critique, especially where the language of human rights is assimilated to psycho-social discourses (e.g., in some postconflict interventions). Beyond these settings, the rhetoric of human rights is sometimes called into question because of the violent policies it can be used to justify, since its apparent "neutrality" makes it particularly appealing as political currency. Finally, "universalistic" human rights discourse has been challenged about the compatibility of its claims with non-Western or nonliberal cultures. This challenge has emerged, for instance, in the work of authors who question the idea that codified human rights are a "second-level theory," that is, one that has universal validity because it does not engage interests, values, or beliefs but rather "places itself outside and above the arena of doctrinal disagreement and seeks only to regulate people's relations with one another," based on universal consensus concerning "what people are owed merely by virtue of being human."[17]

As already noted, the view that human rights discourse constitutes a "second-level theory" has been challenged by different authors (e.g., Nietzschean, Foucauldian, Marxist, feminist, and psychoanalytic theorists, among others). In addition, some have attempted to ground this discourse in different substantive moral and religious theories instead of merely exposing its filiation with certain Western liberal premises. In so doing, these authors have generally defied liberal warnings that cultural traditions strongly committed to certain notions of the "good" tend to be inhospitable to human rights. Religious traditions in particular have often been regarded by liberals as problematic from a human rights perspective, because doctrinal coherence may require giving precedence to divinely sanctioned values over respect for individual rights such as freedom of thought, creed, and conscience.[18] Although the issue has often been framed in terms of "compatibility" between human rights and religious discourses, what is generally at stake in these debates is a very concrete political problem, namely, the possibility of anchoring what Western liberalism understands as human rights in a universal and normatively binding "overlapping consensus," as Rawls would put it, that is, a consensus bridging ethical-philosophical positions built on normative "foundations" supposedly beyond scrutiny. In the case of substantive moral or religious traditions overlapping with ascriptive identities marked by trauma, moreover, both the "compatibility" problem and the political problem of identifying a terrain for such consensus may be particularly complex. In these cases, not only different substantive values but also exceptional existential dangers *and* testimonial obligations may be invoked by certain groups or polities to justify selective definitions of who is the proper bearer of human rights.

The problem of "compatibility" surrounding human rights discourse thus generally appears as not primarily a theoretical or doctrinal problem but rather a political and ethical one, and this is perhaps especially true of situations where collective identification with certain substantive traditions and membership in "wounded" biopolitical communities overlap, at least discursively. For one thing, different authors, including Levinas, have noted the virtual impossibility of a universal realization of human rights in the absence of appropriate (notably liberal or democratic) political institutions, which nonetheless tend to betray these rights by virtue of their perhaps inevitable incarnation in particular (ascriptive, civic, and/or economic) identities. In addition, if we look at the context of debates on the compatibility of human rights with foundationalist traditions in Israel/Palestine, we find that even supposedly universal terms like *human* and *right* are marked by the power effects of nation-specific histories, practices, and affects, as well as by discourses of trauma. Consequently, the key question concerning the role that human rights discourse may play in Israel/Palestine today is not one of its abstract compatibility with supposedly "foundationalist" discourses like Judaism or Islam. Rather, the question concerns the contextual significance of affirming such compatibility or, more importantly, of practically making room for it against exclusive, conditional, or humanitarian readings of this discourse. It is in this sense that the discursive strategies of RHR are a source of insights into the possibility that human rights and trauma discourses may be engaged together to mitigate both the disempowering effects of testimonial humanitarianism and those of trauma-laden violence.

Human Rights Discourse in the Work of RHR

Founded in 1988 "in response to serious abuses of human rights by the Israeli military authorities in the suppression of the Intifada," as well as to the "indifference of much of the religious leadership and religiously identified citizenry to the suffering of innocent people seen as the enemy,"[19] RHR chose from the beginning to present itself under a "human rights" label. This was partly due to the narrow scope of its original intentions, which were to bring human rights violations against Palestinians to the attention of the Israeli public, in close partnership with B'tselem, one of the leading (secular) human rights institutions in the country. The human rights label also signaled a desire not to take a "political" stance, because it was felt that this would reduce the power of RHR's ethical message and its ability to reach people at different ends of the political spectrum. Over the years, however, the scope of RHR's work has gradually expanded to include activities that are not only testimonial or documentary, nor solely focused on Palestinians, but rather cover a broad spectrum of issues including social and economic justice in Israeli society, health care and housing rights, trafficking in women, and more.[20] According to a flier describing a recently initiated study program, the "Rabbis for Human Rights Yeshiva," issues of relevance to the group now include the crisis of the welfare state in Israel, gender (in)equality, domestic violence, the environment, and the rights of foreign workers. The Yeshiva program also draws upon a broad spectrum of sources, including conventional human rights literature, humanistic philosophy, the *Halakha* (Jewish law), and miscellaneous sources on the religious imperatives of justice and *tikkun ha olam*, that is, "repair" or "care" of the world.[21]

Despite the human rights label, it is clear from an analysis of RHR publications, statements, and activities that the group is concerned with something that goes beyond internationally codified principles concerning such rights, particularly if these are interpreted in individualistic, liberal terms. Indeed, as was apparent from various interviews I conducted with member rabbis, their understanding of the relationship between the work of RHR and the specific content of human rights discourse is far from rigid.[22] For one thing, human rights appear to them to be a relatively nonthreatening, supposedly "nonpolitical" (in the sense of nonpartisan) kind of public discourse, which can be embraced across religious divisions and even span the religious-secular divide without the need to engage political (i.e., party) affiliations. Moreover, the discourse of human rights both is relatively "soft" and draws upon the power of the hegemonic liberal discourse in an Anglo-American West, to which Israel feels very close.[23] Essentially, however, human rights are first and foremost a way to translate the biblical call to justice ("Justice, justice, you shall pursue"; Deuteronomy 16:20) into a set of principles with practical relevance to the present Israeli-Palestinian situation, suggesting concrete ways to focus one's moral malaise in a context in which posing political questions of "who is right" and "who is wrong" can otherwise have paralyzing effects.

The translation of biblical calls to justice into human rights discourse is not a self-evident move in Judaism. Indeed, one of the most authoritative voices in Israeli public discourse, the late Yeshayahu Leibowitz, stated that no notion of rights can be derived from Jewish religious foundations. This is a common claim among Jewish critics of ethical doctrines based on rights, and even those who believe in an essential identity of human rights ethics and Judaism acknowledge that the latter is primarily a religion of *mitzvoth*, or obligations, although they argue that rights are the logical correlate of obligations. In Leibowitz's view, however, "Right is a legal term that designates a concept which is inapplicable apart from an institutional framework defined in terms of a legal system established by men. Its application to natural reality is invalid."[24] Moreover, he rejects any attempt to reconcile Judaism with ethical discourses in general, suggesting that "religion and ethics are antagonistic" because they stem from utterly different concerns (the one with obeying the Torah, the other with proper will and intention, molded either by knowledge of truth or by adherence to duty).[25] In relation to human rights ethics, in particular, Leibowitz claims that there is no basis in Judaism for placing specific value in the human being, who is nothing but an *image* of the divine.[26]

Against such a view, and in line with a humanistic Jewish tradition that counts among its members Moses Maimonides (1138–1204) and Saadiah Gaon (882–942), RHR takes the biblical theme of creation *b'tselem (Elohim)*, "in the image" (of God), as a foundation for the infinite value of the human person. In so doing, it aligns itself with Jewish humanists such Haim Cohn or Lenn Goodman, who argue that human rights are a natural consequence of man's being in God's image, and "elements of a larger scheme of natural justice, which situates humanity in creation vis-à-vis God's law, as articulated in Scripture and as implicit in the human frame and condition."[27] To some extent, RHR literature recognizes that the notion of *b'tselem* can ground different understandings of human personhood, ranging from phenomenological humanism to a reading of human rights that allows them to be applied in a manner that privileges the rights of Jews, especially when Jewish lives are at stake.[28] The theoretical position of the group seems to lie somewhere between an undifferentiated humanism and a humanism rooted in the peculiar calling of the Jewish people, with tones that more or less accentuate the universal or the Jewish-specific features of *b'tselem* depending on the circumstances.

To the extent that a common group position exists it seems to be close to that of David Novak, for whom *b'tselem* does not indicate some intrinsic quality of the human being as such, since, as he points out, "the problem with seeing the image of God as an inherent characteristic of human nature is that such a characteristic can be constituted phenomenologically without reference to God." Rather, that notion marks a continuous intimacy between man and God, which transpires as "that which God and humans share in what they do together." In other words, "Essential human action, which is the practice of the commandments, is unlike all other things that are made by the Creator. Rather, it is done along with the Creator. In rabbinic teaching, even God himself is imagined to observe the commandments of the Torah in order to share with his people the basic reality of their active life. Thus the basis of a positive relationship between God and humans is the human capacity, designated as the image of God, to be able to respond to God's commandments with a sense of authentic obligation."[29]

Novak's nonphenomenological approach to the value of the human person as something that is rooted in a dynamic, relational understanding of "being in the image" resonates with the limited "theoretical" literature of RHR,[30] though the action-oriented implications of such an approach are most evident in its practice and practice-focused online postings and news commentaries. In a recent text that summarizes some key aspects of RHR thinking concerning human rights,[31] for instance, the concept of human personhood as reflection of the divine is presented as the basis for a "religious humanism" that makes the value of each individual equal to that of a whole world, paving the way for equal ethical obligations toward Jews and non-Jews. Concerning the right to life, in particular, the author Noam Zohar writes: "The unique attribute of a human is in one's being part of the divine presence, an attribute which characterizes each and every offspring of the first person, each minted from the same stamp—'loved is man who is created in God's image.' Indeed, whoever destroys a single life not only causes a quantitative decrease in the presence of God, but actually destroys a unique manifestation of this presence, for which 'the world was created,' and qualitatively and irreparably diminishes the image, 'as if one had destroyed a whole world.'"[32]

This is not to say that the notion of *b'tselem* necessarily affirms the absolute or equal value of every human being, however, as this would amount to a religiously sanctioned phenomenological humanism. On the contrary, for Zohar the search for religious grounding for a human rights discourse requires maintaining a gap between what, following Levinas, we could refer to as the "ontological contraction" represented by a (human) being bearing a specific identity and the divine infinity of which such being is a trace.[33] In Zohar's words, "almost every language of values that describes human nature must emphasize that certain human attributes are not manifested equally among each and every person. Humanism is not just a declaration of human value, but also a challenge for everyone to realize their great hidden potential as human beings."[34] This is not to suggest, however, that people who are not Jewish or have committed crimes against Jews and violated divine law forfeit some of their dignity as beings made *b'tselem*, which would in turn reduce their (human) rights to life, property, or freedom. The act of taking human lives, for instance, is said to cause divine sorrow in all cases, even when divine law itself enjoins capital punishment for certain categories of criminals. Moreover, offering a sort of generalized version of Arendtian forgiveness as a form of human interaction rooted in the "excess" of *who a person is* vis-à-vis *what she does*,[35] Zohar suggests that there is always a capacity for bearing witness to infinity in each human being, which demands to be preserved unless a person's being alive directly endangers other lives.

In David Novak's view, this capacity exists differently at the universal level and at that of the "chosen people," since humanity as a whole partook in a first covenant between God and Noah, while Israel alone was chosen (at least for the time being) to be God's partner in the Abrahamic covenant. From Novak's standpoint, this means that there is continuity between universal human rights, which were granted to humanity through the first covenant as a precondition for meaningful life after the deluge, and Jewish law and values, which stand as a perfect, but also more demanding model for acts that enable humans to perform their intimacy with God. In other words, though there are different degrees of meaningfulness of human life, which entail a qualitative gap between the life of Jews and that of others, the life of non-Jews also has a value that is beyond the biological, because it is also rooted in a fundamental orientation of the human being toward the divine. Moreover, human rights represent divinely sanctioned safeguards to such meaningful life and cannot therefore be violated or suspended by recourse to the exclusionary character of the second covenant.

On some level, then, it seems clear from these texts that religious foundations can be found in Judaism (as in other religions) to advocate respect for meaningful human life or life that serves to reflect the divine image, whether or not that meaning is reached through the performance of God's commandments as entrusted to Israel. The right to life, however, is not the only human right that can be found within or appropriated from Jewish tradition: in fact, some of the authors who argue for a full compatibility of human rights and Jewish values find textual or traditional foundations for a wide range of civil, social, and economic rights, including workers' rights to fair compensation, association, and freedom to break employment contracts.[36] Most authors writing about a Jewish human rights tradition stress the centrality of freedom of speech and of opinion in Judaism, which Cohn, for instance, regards as best represented by the prophets and sages.[37] Zohar himself highlights a tradition of "free speech" and of institutions meant to ensure that people may follow different interpretations of the law according to conscience in the ancient Jewish polity. According to him, the reason for this is that the content of divine revelation and of divine law is not always totally clear or sufficiently comprehensive in scope, making it necessary to maintain institutions that can support different interpretations not only for practical purposes but also in the interests of the continued vitality of Judaism.

Supported by a series of authoritative Jewish sources, Zohar claims, first, that no coercion should be used to force Jewish people to obey a particular reading of the Torah, let alone to support the ethical or political implications of such a reading (contrary to contemporary pressures not to challenge the "Israeli consensus"). Second, he offers a rather liberal notion of the ability of individual conscience to contribute to determining one's proper relationship with people and with God, given inevitable uncertainty about how God's word should be interpreted at different times and in different situations. The need to ensure that people can realize their full human potential by living according to the Torah *and* their conscience demands institutions that guarantee civil and political liberties, and that also protect individuals from political authorities claiming to identify their own word with God's. Indeed, Jewish tradition recognizes that statehood as such tends to erode liberties and just institutions, and that values such as human rights and freedoms cannot be fully entrusted to the state but rather require the periodic intervention of the divine through the voice of prophets. This is not a contingent human necessity but rather an instrument that God has used in Jewish history to keep His people from becoming too settled in the ways of a sovereign community. Although the historical role of Jewish prophets has not been an easy one, as they have generally been "disturbing" figures for the powers of the day, RHR identifies its work on behalf of human rights with this role, particularly since this work requires precisely the liberty of religious interpretation and of political criticism that past prophets exercised. In the next section, I will address the significance of the prophetic theme for the group, both as a complement to human rights discourse and as a potentially *political* language of resistance to the state, particularly in its role of supreme incarnation of the Jewish people as a testimonial community in the wake of collective trauma.

Rabbis for Human Rights as the Prophetic Conscience of Today's Israel

RHR's reading of the Jewish tradition and of its place in it centers on a prophetic call for justice that periodically surfaces in the history of Judaism as a necessary corrective to its "ontological" tendencies (in a way echoing the "work" constantly performed by Levinasian "infinity" in the midst of "being"[38]), notably at times when a Jewish polity exists. According to Rabbi David Forman, American-born founder and former Chairman of the organization, RHR was established "to give a voice to a Jewish tradition, which speaks of a prophetic vision of social justice, equality and humanity."[39] As noted by current RHR chairman Rabbi Zvi Weinberg, this call stands today in contrast to an official Israeli Judaism that seems more preoccupied with questions of ritual than with moral commandments. Beyond the circle of RHR, however, others have articulated this contrast in sharper tones, referring to the Israeli religious establishment as an example of "Constantinian Judaism." This term has been used by American scholar Marc Ellis to indicate "complicity" between right-wing secular nationalism and mainstream Jewish institutions, whose present key objective seems to him to be to mark out the space of what/who is untaintedly Jewish rather than to uphold the ethical content of Judaism.[40] As for the precise form taken by such complicity, Ellis and others hint at a "state of emergency" Judaism that lends itself to be used to justify rights violations for the sake of a pure Jewish space, where state and citizens may bear witness in isolation to their exceptional fate of trauma and redemption.

Violations of Palestinian rights are disregarded or even justified by some religious authorities in Israel for the sake of realizing God's promise of *Eretz Israel* (the Land of Israel). This happens especially with settlement policies, whether within or beyond the confines of political consensus and the law (as in the extremist fringes of the settlers' movement). In mainstream religious discourse, however, the argument for ignoring or even justifying human rights violations is usually articulated at least in part in defensive terms, based on claims that "they started it first" and that acts of terror violate the human rights of Israelis. Such arguments are linked to themes of security and survival in addition to (and sometimes more than) that of *Eretz Israel*. The popularity of the "defensive" argument may be in part a result of Israelis' constant exposure to narratives of Jewish history marked by reference to collective trauma. It seems reasonable to assume, however, that the persistent insecurity of life in what was once supposed to be the "safe-haven" of world Jewry significantly contributes to making present-day violence amenable to interpretations that obscure Israeli responsibilities in the conflict.

In religious terms, the argument that Jewish Israelis have no alternatives to self-defense at all costs, even when that requires violating human rights, finds support in the notion that Jewish survival is not just a matter of self-interest but also a divine prescription, since the existence of the Jewish people is a precondition for the realization of God's law, and their presence in Israel is an expression of the Abrahamic covenant. The power of such argument may explain why, though concern with Jewish and Israeli survival (and the continued dependence of the former on the latter) spans the religious-secular divide, public-opinion surveys indicate that it is religious Israelis who most often express the belief that *Jewish* survival is at stake in the conflict, and all necessary measures are therefore legitimate to preserve state security.

This opinion is recognized by members of RHR. In fact, the organization was born from a need on the part of founding rabbis to dissociate themselves from the political and moral consequences of what they refer to as an "intolerant and uncompromising" understanding of Judaism and Israeliness. It is a bitter confirmation of the validity of their claim to represent the "prophetic conscience" of Israeli Judaism that religious Jewish Israelis generally regard its members as "radicals" and even anti-Zionists. Few of the Orthodox majority even know the group, but RHR workers often encounter religious settlers "in the field," as they assist Palestinians tending their farms in areas occupied by settlers. Government institutions, notably judicial courts and the military, tend to be similarly unsympathetic toward the group, despite regular efforts by RHR fieldworkers to coordinate with the Israeli army. This unsympathetic view is fueled by frequent confrontations between the army and members or sympathizers of the group, which have led to several arrests of RHR's executive director, Pennsylvania-born Arik Ascherman, and to his recently concluded trial for "obstructing the work of government officials" by acts of solidarity with Palestinians.[41]

Although the group counts among its members representatives from all three main strands of Judaism in Israel,[42] including a small number of Orthodox rabbis, its understanding of the concrete implications of a Jewish embracing of human rights seems to place it beyond the Israeli consensus and at times openly against the institutions and laws of the state. RHR ethics and practices take a position against the merging of religious discourse with a political culture of "security at all costs," demanding endless sacrifice of Israeli and Palestinian lives. This places members (often against their will) on a collision course with other religious Israelis and with the state, insofar as these uphold visions of Judaism and of Israeliness that draw exclusionary and militant implications from a combination of trauma and religious narratives with which RHR refuses to become complicit. Apart from its involvement with other groups in the Israeli "peace left," RHR thus cannot be seen as representative of a large front in Israeli society, let alone of a majority among religious Israelis.[43] On the contrary, the group is a self-consciously marginal but vocal phenomenon, in line with the prophetic tradition they consider themselves to inherit.

What, exactly, is at stake in this self-positioning in prophetic terms? First, evoking the prophetic bestows a form of traditional legitimization on the group's dissent vis-à-vis the religious majority and the state, at a time of great pressure to "close ranks" behind state policies due to insecurity, which trauma-influenced narratives present as capable of escalating into the "unspeakable," which has come to mean the destruction of Israel as a Jewish state or as a safeguard for the Jewish people as a testimonial community. By contrast, RHR calls Jews to find a sense of courage and integrity in the prophetic tradition, combined with a particular sensitivity to the ethical and political needs of today's Jewish Israelis as the bearers of a complex legacy made of past quasi-annihilation, present insecurity, and sovereign power. In particular, Rabbi Ascherman suggests that the challenge for rabbis who seek to "restore morality to Israeli politics" is to acknowledge the traumatic entanglements that complicate the self-positioning of Jewish Israelis vis-à-vis their ethnonational identity and the state, yet to try to resist the temptation to offer consolation to their communities or an illusion of divine intelligibility beyond suffering caused by conflict. Recognition of past and present traumas makes it necessary for "prophetic rabbis" to speak compassionately to their people, rather than in the stern style of ancient prophets. A greater challenge, however, is for rabbis to find a way to *live* (in an active sense, as opposed to "surviving") as Jews and Israelis in a time of darkness, when it appears as if God has ceased to speak, to take an interest in the history of His people, and to suggest how it may be possible to reconcile Jewish survival and the Covenant.

What, then, is the relationship between RHR's recourse to the prophetic and this acknowledgment of the present "darkness," in which Jews must operate as if the key to changing their reality were in their hands, even though their only hope resides in God's being at work in this very obscurity? Is the biblical call to "justice, justice" not beyond the capacities of normal human beings, who find themselves facing an environment that generates anxieties echoing those fed by authoritative identity narratives? The answers to these questions lie, perhaps, in the second level of significance in the reference to the prophetic in the work of RHR. Beyond legitimizing dissent, this reference also hints at an ideal of perfect justice that the Jewish polity is called upon to realize yet cannot until the coming of the Messiah. In other words, prophetic calls are God's way to pose to His people, time and again, an impossible challenge of perfect justice combined with sovereign power, while reminding them (through repetition) that He is aware of their vulnerability and of their other weaknesses that stand in the way of such a combination. This vulnerability and these weaknesses, then, are not accidental but rather necessary to keep people's eyes oriented toward the time of the Messiah, rather than focused only on the present and on the limited promises of statehood and earthly power. Prophetic time, the time when the Jewish community needs prophets to call it back to God, is thus similar to the time of the Augustinian earthly city, in the sense that it is full of darkness and compromises, with no clear path toward salvation. The work of contemporary inheritors of the Jewish prophetic tradition, however, may bring some light into this darkness by creating spaces for human responsibility that may moderate people's vulnerability and confusion. Framed in prophetic terms, human rights discourse may provide a practical key to turn the messianic ideal into a moral imperative that Jewish Israelis can address in social and political life, even in the present "darkness."

The content of the prophetic interpretation of the Torah evident in RHR statements and weekly biblical commentaries written in light of current events encompasses but also exceeds human rights discourse. As Forman suggests, the prophetic call taken up by RHR can best be encapsulated in words from Deuteronomy, "Justice, justice you will pursue," which he takes to mean that pursuing just ends is not enough, and that just means (i.e., means that are not merely "justified" by the "justice" of their ends) are also needed. Interpreting the prophetic call in terms of human rights may, of course, facilitate a reading of Deuteronomy that foregrounds the question of "just means," leaving aside the question of just ends as if it were self-evident. From the perspective of RHR, however, this question is not unproblematic, but rather incapable of being addressed outside the realm of politics and ideological interpretations of identity, which the group generally engages only in the rather abstract terms of a Zionism respectful of the rights of Palestinians.

By identifying the biblical call to justice with a commitment to human rights, RHR seems to evade the question of whether the Zionist project itself, in its concrete historical realization, should enjoy the same status as "just end" as do Judaism or Jewish survival. Indeed, by framing the question of a compatibility between a Jewish Israel and human rights in terms of the compatibility of human rights and Judaism, RHR literature seems to "normalize" Israeli history and Zionism as natural outgrowths of Judaism (hence essentially compatible with justice identified with human rights), thus precluding the possibility of questioning the historical justifications for a Jewish state. In this sense, RHR members can be regarded (and generally see themselves) as Zionists, though critical of the consequences of Zionist history in violations of the rights of Palestinians.

A univocal RHR stance on the historical "justice" of the Zionist project as an "end" is not easy to find, both because the group represents a plurality of views and because it operates from within a context marked by trauma narratives, which sets limits to the extent to which Israel's historical trajectory can be critically discussed without incurring the accusation of questioning its right to exist. RHR publications and interviews with members generally suggest that the dominant theme underlying the group's call to prophetic justice is the survival of the Jewish people not only in general but specifically as a national community in *Eretz Israel*. The question of Israel's right to exist within the boundaries of 1949, however, is not always approached in the same terms, since references to national rights and international law by various rabbis mix with themes of Jewish history, values, and survival, yielding sometimes an impression of equal appreciation of secular-political and religious justifications for state survival, and at other times a sense of identification of the survival of individuals with that of the Jewish people and of the state, as transpires in the discourse of right-wing religious groups. Unlike the latter, however, RHR considers sovereign control by Jews over the whole land of biblical Israel not a "just" end but rather a conditional entitlement, whose "justice" depends on whether it is an instrument for the realization of properly *Jewish* life in a land that Jews both have been promised and have fought for. Given the presence of Palestinians in the West Bank and Gaza, control over these areas cannot, according to this view, be a means to ensure the realization of such Jewish life today, nor to secure Jewish survival or the survival of the state of Israel. Contrary to the views of religious settlers, Jewish land claims in biblical Judea and Samaria may, therefore, have to be relinquished, despite their apparent "justice" in light of the covenant, because the realization of these claims cannot be undertaken with just (hence properly *Jewish*) means. In this regard, Rabbi Ascherman often quotes the biblical story of Abraham's decision to part ways with his nephew Lot by splitting with him the Land that was entirely promised to him, so as to avoid strife. This story suggests to Ascherman that Abraham's moral inheritance (hence a properly *Jewish* understanding of justice in relation to the state of Israel) includes the capacity to forfeit some Jewish land claims out of desire to live in peace with others.

It is not clear that most Palestinians would accept such a notion of justice, which seems to call only for ending the occupation or its human rights violations, leaving the historical trajectory of the Zionist enterprise until 1967 essentially beyond discussion. Nor does this notion account for the fact that Palestinians remain silent "others" and "strangers" in whose name justice must be done, rather than being recognized as people who can articulate their own vision of justice, which may be quite different from Abraham's or RHR's. Despite these limitations, the conjunction of human rights pragmatism with a prophetic sense of Jewish chosenness in RHR hints at a vision of the significance of a Jewish Israel that may at least provisionally work around the difficulty of questioning the Jewish character of the state as a "just end." Such a vision is not new: for instance, in his writings about Zionism, Levinas argues that the most authentic justification for the creation of Israel was the need to bear a torch of witness to infinity that would shine as an example to all peoples.[44] Similarly, though not necessarily in religious terms, other Jewish intellectuals of the early twentieth century, such as Hannah Arendt, Judas Magnes, and Martin Buber, believed that a Jewish homeland in Palestine might generate forms of political belonging of unprecedented openness. Even for Yeshayahu Leibowitz, who claimed that there was no such thing as a national Jewish right to set up a state in today's

Israel, the existence of such a state was crucial to provide "a framework within which the struggle over Jewish identity took place," as this "would awaken something in the consciousness of Jews throughout the world who have an interest in their Jewishness."[45]

Such notions of Israel as an example to the world are neither foreign nor secondary to the work of RHR. The way the group seems to interpret such notions, however, is profoundly marked by trauma, in recognizing vulnerability as a decisive factor in the environment in which the "torch" must be held up and seeing that Israel's exemplariness respects a traumatic grammar that defines what can be discussed (or become "speakable" at all). Against this backdrop, the language of human rights serves as a relatively "non-traumatic" response to the predicament of noninnocent Jewish-Israeli victimization by making room for limited but direct assumption of responsibility by individuals for what *can be* changed, that is, Israeli policies and perhaps laws and institutions, while standing back from what *cannot* (apparently) be changed, that is, Israel's existence as a Jewish state. The latter, in turn, is supposedly redeemed as a "just end" not through recourse to religious discourse but through a call for practical engagement with a present that may "justify" the past.

Is this sufficient from the standpoint of those who dispute the "justice" of the trajectory of Jewish ethno-national and religious "ontology" toward statehood? Are human rights a way to retroactively depoliticize certain historical processes and to normalize their crystallizations in the present by reducing everything to the issue of how to "humanize" a polity that, more than any other, is often called upon to justify its origins? A way into such questions may be found by following another thread of RHR discourse, namely, that of Jewish exile and the exodus from Egypt as the pivot of the traumatic genealogy of Jewish-Israeli identity that the group upholds, hinting at a constantly interrupted understanding of belonging to and citizenship in the state of Israel and at practices of dwelling in the land haunted by the shared strangeness of all its inhabitants.

A Dwelling among Strangers

> And for the sin which we have sinned against You through insolence—
> Saying that only Jews have rights to the Land.
> —RHR Vidui prayer for Yom Kippur, the Day of Atonement

As I mentioned at the outset, the Shoah and other moments of great suffering and danger for a Jewish testimonial community occupy an important place in contemporary authoritative narratives of Jewish Israeliness. In particular, the Shoah and the traumatic connotations of the quasi-annihilation of the community have been repeatedly elaborated in a variety of discourses and narratives, lending them the uncanny sense of a constant proximity to catastrophe. In the religious realm, in particular, part of this elaboration has taken the form of rethinking the meaning of a Jewish covenant with God in the context of a set of theologico-political perspectives that is sometimes referred to as "Holocaust theology." This literature has implications for a religious legitimization of the testimonial role of the Israeli state, entitling it to exceptional political loyalties because it bears witness to (and serves to prevent a repetition of) an exceptional history of victimization. The writings of authors such as Irving Greenberg, Elie Wiesel, and Emil Fackenheim, grant this legitimization to Israel by affirming a connection, not only historical but also theological and ethical, between the Shoah as paradigm of the suffering and quasi-annihilation of Jews as a testimonial community, on the one hand, and the creation of the state of Israel, on the other. After the Shoah, supporting the Zionist project is to these authors the "614th commandment" for Jews, as Fackenheim put it,[46] one that has as much religious value as the other 613 because it is the only way to ensure the survival of the chosen people in a history from which God can be absent.

As authors such as Marc Ellis have noted, the influence of Holocaust theology on Israeli Judaism, as well as on the discourse of the religious and even secular right in Israel, has grown significantly since the 1970s. Beyond the basic notion that support for Israel should be advocated as part and parcel of the Jewish imperative to bear witness to the Shoah, neither such theology nor the religious and political discourses that echo it offer univocal positions concerning how the Jewish state should best bear witness to the Shoah, what kind of support it may rightly claim from world Jewry, and whether or not such support may be conditional upon how it plays its testimonial role. In the history of institutions tasked with "creating the Israeli citizen," the significance of the Shoah has also been interpreted in different ways, and its presence in public discourse, identity narratives, and socialization practices has not always been central. On the contrary, only since the 1970s has the Shoah become a prominent component of mainstream narratives of Jewish Israeliness, and this process has continued through the 1980s and 1990s, partly in response to significant emigration, which has led Zionist institutions to seek ways to reassert the link between Israel as a Jewish state and the ever-present possibility of a repetition of the Shoah. Today, a recrudescence of anti-Semitism in Europe and precarious security conditions in Israel contribute to keeping the Shoah at the center of public discourse, despite open debate concerning its historical significance and its implications for Israeli politics and for the Israeli-Palestinian conflict.

According to Rabbi Ehud Bandel, a founding member of RHR and chair of the conservative movement in Israel, the centrality of Holocaust trauma to contemporary Israeli identity cannot be stressed too much, but it does not amount to clear support for a specific political project. The peculiar legacy of the Shoah rests in its unspeakable enormity, which can only generate a call to "bear witness" and to ensure that "never again" will such horror be allowed. The specific ethical, political, and religious responses that can be given to such interpellation vary, however, both in relation to Israeli politics and for Jewish communities in other countries. In general, Bandel's view is that a proper response to the testimonial call of the Shoah can resist the temptation to fall into the vicious circle of trauma discourses that tends to blur the line between past and present and therefore to reduce the act of bearing witness to a mimetic identification of the living with the dead. In the case of Israeli Jews, in particular, the temptation to be resisted is that of a mimetic appropriation by living Israelis of the predicament of the Jewish victims of the Shoah. This is a risk to be avoided first of all because such identification encourages the living to take on the mantle of "innocence" that belongs to the dead of the Shoah. Second, collective witnessing modeled upon the logic of individual trauma risks being trapped in the same pattern of repetition of traumatic neurosis, leading a testimonial community to sacrifice meaningful present life on the altar of the past. In the case of a community that identifies with a state, such as Jews in Israel, this risk is particularly great because it entails the possibility that state institutions may also become trapped in a vicious circle that does not lead them to seek ways to sustain life, as states must do vis-à-vis their citizens. On the contrary, such institutions are ideally placed to nurture and perpetuate violence toward "others" as a self-nurturing reaction to what Judith Butler recently called a "narcissistic preoccupation of melancholia" born of the forced realization of the vulnerability of a certain community (in this case Jews).[47]

How can an Israeli rabbi preach and practice a balance between bearing witness and a taste for life, and at the same time remind his people that they do not have a perpetual claim to innocence, or to suffering, even when their present reality lends itself to being rhetorically appropriated as a threatened repetition of past trauma? Like Rabbi Ascherman, Bandel suggests a combination of compassionate recognition of present Jewish-Israeli suffering and acknowledgment of the historical reality of other traumatic moments to which Jewish Israelis are linked by religious and political belonging but from which they are also relatively independent by virtue of living in a different time and place. While Ascherman stresses the importance of focusing on what Jewish Israelis can do through practical human rights work as a form of *tikkun ha olam*, Bandel suggests also the need to cultivate alternative readings of Jewish history and identity to counter the negative effects of trauma-centered approaches to the Jewish past. The point is not to minimize the significance of past Jewish victimization, its traumatic character, or its testimonial legacy, but rather to search for positive counterpoints in Jewish history that can be integrated into a Zionist project that may enable Jewish Israelis to take responsibility for their future.

While there is no official preference for one particular narrative of Jewish history in RHR literature, certain historical and biblical references recurrently provide interpretive keys in discussions of Israeli affairs by group rabbis. One particularly interesting reference is to the memory of a "traumatic departure," to borrow a term from Cathy Caruth's analysis of trauma in Freud's meta-historical story of Moses.[48] This is the memory of Jewish slavery and liberation from Egypt, which was the prelude to the assumption of political power in a "promised land," as well as to a covenant based on God's giving of

His law to the Jews. In Jewish tradition, the story of the exodus is essentially one of divine deliverance, but it is also a paradigm for Jewish identity as a reality to be affirmed collectively through testimony and respect for divine law. At the center of this testimonial affirmation, however, is not only a story of salvation but also one of slavery and strangeness. In the words of David Forman, "Jewish national identity was forged on the anvil of the Egyptian experience of slavery. It was against the background of collective suffering that we were born as a people, charged with becoming a "holy nation." Our wanderings in the desert were to teach us that the maintenance of our freedom would be dependent upon the definitive rejection of the social model of power and its abuse, as symbolized by ancient Egypt. Did we return to our ancestral homeland only to become like the ancient Egyptians? If so, then we will never be ourselves, as was historically prescribed for us at the moment of our national birth."[49] Forman's words suggest that "being ourselves" for Jewish Israelis means taking up the legacy of an experience of trauma and departure (toward salvation and toward the law). As for the implications of this legacy, the Bible itself seems to condense them in the call: "You shall not wrong a stranger or oppress him, for you were strangers in the land of Egypt." In other words, the memory of suffering and injustice born of living as powerless strangers should prevent any temptations Jews may feel to identify with their former oppressors and reenact the tragedy of victimizing a people as a sort of retroactive triumph over the past. Instead, Jews must always think and feel what it was like to be strangers in Egypt, maintaining commemorative practices such as the eating of matzo bread at Passover and, most importantly, upholding an ethics of power exercised from a position of "strangeness" to it.

The practical implications of such a position can be drawn in different ways vis-à-vis the validity of the Zionist project as an embodiment of Jewish identity claiming to represent the legacy of Exodus, since the Zionist enterprise includes the building of a state in which non-Jews would always be strangers, at least to some degree. As a whole, RHR does not seem to have a definite position on this point. By insisting on the experience of Egypt in their writings and in the curriculum of their yeshiva program, however, the rabbis seem to suggest that being authentically Jewish in today's Israel is not about matching a set of requirements for Jewish "purity" upheld by the Chief Rabbinate, but rather about being able to identify with the experience of being "strangers among strangers." This understanding of Jewish identity shows a Benjaminian sensitivity to history in its call to bear testimony to a past that is one simultaneously of ruins and of redemptive possibilities. Those possibilities, moreover, do not appear to be exhausted by the historical event of a divine intervention that interrupted a certain condition (i.e., slavery) once and for all, but rather remain as a sort of hidden treasury in the Jewish past, which can continue "haunting" the present, like trauma but differently from the compulsive, potentially self-destructive relationship between living and dead warned against by Bandel. The historical fact of liberation from Egypt, which led to ancient Israeli statehood, need not, then, be seen as the end of the Jewish experience of strangeness, either in historical terms or in terms of its ethical significance. On the contrary, this event (like the creation of contemporary Israel) seems to be perceived by RHR rabbis who discuss the contemporary relevance of Exodus as the disclosure of a possibility to redeem both past and present "strangeness" of the Jews from the Promised Land through the gift of Sinai, namely, Mosaic law.

What can this mean, concretely, for contemporary Israeli politics? A possible response is contained in the words of Rabbi Samson Raphael Hirsch, whose teachings are used in the RHR yeshiva curriculum. According to Rabbi Hirsch, the story of exile in Egypt means that "it is not race, not descent, not birth or country or property, altogether nothing external or due to change, but simply and purely the inner spiritual and moral worth of a human being, which gives him all the rights of a man and of a citizen." Moreover, "your whole misfortune in Egypt was that you were *gerim*, 'foreigners,' 'aliens,' there, as such, according to the views of other nations, you had no right to be there, had no claim to rights of settlement, home, or property. . . . Therefore beware, so runs the warning, of making rights in your own State conditional on anything other than that simple humanity which every human being as such bears within him."[50]

If RHR were to apply Hirsch's words literally to today's Israeli state, it might conclude that the state of the Jews ("your own State") should be one in which strangers are not really such, in the sense that none of their rights (including the right to expand and occupy space freely, which Hirsch stresses elsewhere) should be based on Jewishness or lack thereof. To Hirsch, all rights of citizenship appear indeed to be a matter of mere "human rights," suggesting that even in a "state of the Jews" citizenship may be detached from ascriptive identity, as potentially foreshadowed by the democratic strand in the genealogy of Israeli statehood. Although Hirsch seemed to write with a rather unproblematic notion of the state of Israel as one that would be self-evidently "of the Jews," in the sense of having a large Jewish majority (he was, after all, writing several decades before the creation of modern Israel), a notion of citizenship that would de facto eliminate strangeness might pose different problems were demographics to call into question the Jewish character of the state, which presupposes a distinction between Jewish citizens and "strangers," whether or not this affects state recognition of human rights. In such a situation, which is indeed Israel's reality today, the exclusionary effects of defining Israel merely as the "state of the Jews" could not be disregarded, and Hirsch's interpretation of the biblical call may no longer be as viable as it may once have seemed.

The difficulty of reconciling citizenship based on identity with the desire to overcome divisions between self and stranger in the name of the legacy of Exodus is also visible in the writings of RHR rabbis, whose views about the implications of that legacy for today's Israel appear "more moderate" than Hirsch's. In a recent RHR newsletter, for instance, Yehiel Grenimann writes about non-Jewish minorities in Israel and their rights in a language that is characteristic of the group, that is, in terms of vulnerability and powerlessness, requiring the intervention of Jews to act and speak on behalf of these people. In his words: "The duty to protect and defend the rights of the socially disadvantaged is repeatedly emphasized in both biblical and Talmudic texts. The message is clear. We are responsible for 'the widow, the stranger in our midst and the orphan.' We are responsible for the well-being of those who work for us. In these matters the distinction between Jews and non-Jews is not significant."[51] Thus, to Grenimann the stranger has claims upon "us" because of her very defenselessness, which is intrinsic to her "strangeness" and is therefore (potentially) forever able to call upon us to take responsibility on her behalf. Hence the presence of the stranger as a powerless person (despite her ability to "work for us") requires an assumption of responsibility on the part of the Jewish majority in Israel, but it also enables this majority to affirm its power to speak and act on behalf of others. In consequence, the existence of the stranger *as such* need not be regarded as problematic, nor does the Jewish experience of strangeness necessarily demand establishing a situation of equal citizenship that would enable today's "strangers" to assume responsibility toward their Jewish fellow citizens (since the Jews' own strangeness is past, but also yet to be redeemed).

While this limited appreciation of the significance of Jewish strangeness in Egypt is rather common in public RHR pronouncements, in line with the group's general commitment to the Jewish character of the Israeli state, this need not necessarily result in a sort of benevolent paternalism, whereby non-Jews in Israel are forever confined to the position of vulnerable subjects awaiting the caring speech of others. According to Rabbi Benjamin Hollander, for instance, the presence of strangers within Israel is not just an inevitable social evil that Jewish Israelis must deal with by taking responsibility for these people's well-being. On the contrary, this presence is a key reason for the very creation of a Jewish state, which was needed "so that Jews could obey the mitzvah not to oppress the stranger,"[52] a commandment mentioned in the Bible no fewer than thirty-six times. In other words, without such strangers the state would somehow forfeit some of its Jewish character in the sense of being a space for the realization of biblical commandments. Moreover, the concrete meaning of "nonoppression" in a contemporary democracy cannot be interpreted in paternalistic terms, but rather means granting non-Jews all the rights attached to modern citizenship, on an equal footing with their Jewish fellow citizens. According to Hollander, the biblical term *oppression* must be understood in light of what contemporary Western societies consider necessary for the dignity of the human being, both as an individual and as a member of an ethno-national group, rather than relying on idiosyncratic interpretations of the mitzvoth by Israeli politicians.

The question of how contemporary Israelis should "remember" being strangers in Egypt thus appears as an essentially political one rather than one of human rights alone, as it begs further questions about the concrete contemporary meaning of "nonoppression" and the distinction between rights of citizenship and human rights. The question of the relationship between rights of citizenship and human rights is also familiar in Western political discourse, for instance, in the context of debates about multiculturalism and about various liberal, republican, or "deliberative" understandings of human rights as more or less originally implicated in certain possibilities of political participation or "public autonomy." In the case of Israel/Palestine, however, these issues take on a different character due to the ill-defined boundaries of what constitutes a sovereign public space. Indeed, this question takes on particular urgency in debates concerning the "promised land," its borders, and the nature of Jewish claims to all or part of it. If wielding sovereign power in a particular territory is to enact the memory of being strangers elsewhere and not to oppress other strangers, as Hollander suggests, how is one to understand the relationship between the Jewish people and the Land? And what, exactly, is the land of Israel? What are its boundaries? Where can one legitimately draw a line to say "here you are strangers, here you are at home"? Again, this set of questions clearly exceeds both religious and human rights discourse taken separately. The conjunction of human rights discourse with a particular reading of the prophetic call summed up in the commandment to remember one's own strangeness, however, paves the way for engaging questions of politics and national rights in relation to the Land.

One of the most explicit RHR statements concerning the political implications of the convergence of human rights and prophetic discourse for the issue of land rights is offered by Rabbi Forman, who writes that "Being wedded to a Divine promise of Eretz Yisrael Hashleima (the Greater Land of Israel), whose roots are found in a biblical narrative that took place thousands of years ago, is no longer theological viable."[53] In similar tones, Rabbi Hollander notes that recognizing the human rights of Palestinians today means recognizing their national aspirations and the right to live in a land that has been theirs for centuries, by creating their own state alongside Israel. In his view, there are practical as well as theological reasons for foregoing the interpretation of Eretz Israel proposed by the settlers' movement and by the religious right, starting from the fact that it is not possible today to occupy the entire territory of Mandate Palestine for strategic, legal, humanitarian, and political reasons. Moreover, in religious terms the value of human life must, for Hollander (and RHR in general), be put above that of the land, and saving lives requires confining Israel to internationally recognized borders. While this is also the position of other Israeli religious peace groups, such as Netivot Shalom, the human rights focus of RHR enables it to ground this stance not only in the human cost of a "Greater Israel" in terms of Israeli lives, as these groups do, but also in the costs inflicted on Israel's "others." As Rabbi Ascherman put it: "We have no right to force ourselves on others and then justify these kinds of human rights abuses in order to protect our presence."[54]

If this is the case, however, how does RHR as a group understand and justify the *right* of Jews to live as citizens *in a Jewish state*, the creation of which turned hundreds of thousands of people into "strangers" in their own land and elsewhere, in refugee camps that predate by twenty years the occupation of the West Bank and Gaza? In principle, the notion of dwelling in power (i.e., achieving statehood) *as a means* to obey the commandment to bear witness to one's legacy of strangeness may suggest a fully egalitarian approach to citizenship in Israel, as well as to questions of justice vis-à-vis the consequences of the Zionist project. In practice, however, the relative political neutrality of RHR's human rights discourse and the dependence of the very notion of "strangeness" in the texts discussed above on the existence of a state "of the Jews," combined with the limits posed by discourses of collective trauma on what kind of articulations of Jewish political-religious identity may be "heard" in today's Israel, tend to prevent such a "radical" RHR reading of citizenship and justice. The question then is how the group can negotiate the resulting tension between its declared commitment to prophetic justice rooted in divine law and in the memory of strangeness and its attachment to a project that recalls a Levinasian crystallization of being or "thematization" (which corresponds here to Jewish national identity and statehood). For Levinas, thematization (like ontology) is both a manifestation and a betrayal of infinity, but a betrayal without which no responsibility, substitution—in sum, no ethics—would be possible.[55] In what follows, I will attempt to show how RHR seems to live out a practical negotiation of a similar "betrayal" through a systematic practice of excess of concrete solidarity work vis-à-vis its narrative references (including human rights discourse). In this way, the group realizes what may be seen as a series of fragile approximations of prophetic justice on the contingent terrain of multiple acts of engagement with others, which are so many instances of "betrayal" of infinity and divine justice, as well as transgressions of the closures through which such betrayal (i.e., exclusionary statehood) operates.

Subversive Solidarities: Working by Candlelight in Prophetic Times

As I noted at the outset, my interpretation of the work of RHR largely revolves around a tension between its literature and its activities, a tension that is in part a product of a discursive environment in which it is difficult to give narrative expression to acts of solidarity between Israelis and Palestinians save in the relatively "nonpolitical" languages of human rights and of religious ethics. In the previous section, I suggested that the failure or unwillingness of RHR and other peace groups to elaborate narratives of Jewish Israeliness that could serve as alternatives to religious Zionism limits their ability to claim the role of Israel's "testimonial conscience," at least as concerns the events of 1948. Perhaps paradoxically, however, the very decision to refrain from giving an overtly "political" signification to certain activities in which the group engages seems to allow it to be concretely responsive to specific violations of Palestinian rights. Thanks to its nonpartisan stance, the group can mobilize the energies of its members and of a potentially broad section of Israeli society sensitive to "Palestinian suffering" without having to confront the implications of each initiative for the legitimacy of Israeli and Palestinian national narratives. RHR finds ethical and symbolic coherence, as well as life-enabling power, in the choice to invest not only in testimony but also in productive or restorative (economic) work *in partnership with Palestinians.* In this kind of work the group finds practical ways to transcend normative categorizations inherited from ethno-national trauma discourses without feeling the need to find alternative narratives of identity as a precondition for practices having economic and symbolic power.

A key aspect of this choice to focus on testimonial, productive, and restorative solidarity work is a "traumatic" reading of the Covenant and of God's presence in history, neither of which seems to yield a blueprint for premessianic Jewish politics. In other words, this choice acknowledges the absence of a Fatherlike Symbolic principle (e.g., a God who speaks clearly about how to reconcile ethics, sovereignty, and survival). This may allow a representational and life-enabling order alternative to that centered on statehood, ascriptive citizenship, and borders. RHR members repeatedly affirm their awareness of the Arendtian warning that justice (both that which comes from the recognizing distinct national narratives and that which allows a family to have a roof over its head) depends in part on the ontological consolidation of potentially exclusionary subjectivities into rights of sovereignty, borders, and citizenship. Instead of advocating a Levinasian ethics of responsibility shorn of context, RHR's work thus builds on the unequal power effects of a specific political and economic context that includes Israeli statehood, the fragmentation of Israeli and particularly of Palestinian economies under the Occupation, and unequal citizenship rights. RHR uses these inequalities to achieve concrete results through solidarity work, but also seeks opportunities for contrapuntal interruptions of the exclusionary aspects of Jewish-Israeli nationhood. Again, this occurs not at the level of narratives that provide symbolic signification for certain events or forms of violence but rather through a multiplicity of testimonial, restorative, or preventative initiatives to which the group invites Israelis, through a network of volunteers and via e-mail appeals.

As I mentioned at the outset, RHR is essentially a group of activists, although only a minority of its roughly ninety members (2004 figure) are directly involved in daily activities such as farming, tree planting, house (re)building, demonstrations, lobbying with government agencies, and so forth. Much of this work is done by volunteers, some of them students in its yeshiva program, as well as any other person who has time and energy to contribute. For some initiatives, individuals who can take on the burden of heavy labor or bear the risk of violence are especially encouraged to participate, while in other cases entire families are invited, for instance, when Palestinian farmers celebrate the harvest or the successful (though often temporary) reconstruction of their homes. RHR may engage with Palestinian farmers (and often with members of the International Solidarity Movement) in plowing, pruning, harvesting, helping to sell Palestinian agricultural produce (particularly olives and oil), and planting trees uprooted by soldiers or by settlers. Moreover, the group collects information on families who have received demolition orders for homes built without permit on their own land in East Jerusalem or in neighboring areas. When a legal case to defend these families cannot be made successfully, RHR volunteers often participate in initiatives to resist demolitions by standing in the way of bulldozers. Nonviolent resistance is also used in demonstrations in which the group participates at the invitation of village committees in West Bank areas affected by the construction of the Israeli Separation Barrier.

While explicitly motivated by desire to uphold the human rights of Palestinians, the presence of RHR rabbis and volunteers is often perceived by observers (both Israeli and Palestinian) as having political meaning in transgressing the Israeli consensus. This is true on a variety of levels, starting with that of spatial transgression, though RHR members usually refrain from breaking laws regulating Israeli presence in areas populated primarily by Palestinians (those labeled under Oslo regulations as areas A). By crossing "borders" into areas B or C to stand by Palestinians who try to secure a livelihood by tending to their farmland, RHR members challenge the state politically in the sense that they ask its institutions (notably the army, police, and courts) to show their power to protect these people's rights according to commitments the state has openly made. As Rabbi Ascherman has often stated, what RHR wants is often just to see that police and soldiers "do their job" in preventing settlers from encroaching upon Palestinian farmland or attacking farmers. In practice, the presence of RHR alongside Palestinian harvesters sometimes encourages security forces to restrain settlers, aids communication when farmers are not fluent speakers of Hebrew, and ensures that someone is present at the site of possible rights violations who can report to Israeli authorities and, if necessary, appeal to the Israeli judicial apparatus (something that Palestinians are unlikely to be able to do). Needless to say, however, soldiers (not to mention settlers) often also experience this presence as a provocation, and at times settlers react by doubling their efforts to damage Palestinian fields when RHR members return to their homes. Furthermore, though there is no official RHR position on settlements as such, the presence of group members during confrontations between settlers and Palestinian farmers pushes them to take contingent stances that, though framed in terms of human rights or of Israeli law, take on clearly political significance in the context of debates around settlements in Israel. As for house demolitions, the political import of the group's stance came out, for instance, in Ascherman's speech at the final hearing of his trial in the spring of 2005, when he stated that there is a gap between law and justice in Israel that obliges its citizens to practice civil disobedience until legal institutions can once more acquire legitimacy from a religious point of view.[56]

How, exactly, do these various acts of solidarity exceed the discursive references of RHR, whether in terms of human rights discourse or in terms of an ethics of Jewish strangerness combined with sovereign power in the Promised Land? The answer may vary depending on the kind of activity at issue, as well as on its context. To the extent that any degree of generalization is possible, one might say that a first level of "excess" can be found in the way in which subject positions and power relations are shaped by the very fact of Palestinians and Israelis working together in a given situation. Although the presence of RHR rabbis supposedly brings an element of security to joint demonstrations, planting, or harvesting thanks to their religious standing and to their being Israelis, in reality participation in these activities entails a relative blurring of nationally marked subject positions with respect to power and vulnerability. Israeli rabbis and volunteers accept vulnerability to violence, at least for the duration of the activities, but they also do all they can to avoid that violence, most importantly, by refusing to give up their superior power to "represent" that violence by "speaking the same language" as soldiers and settlers (i.e., not only Hebrew but also the language of Zionism and of the laws of the state).

At a demonstration against the Barrier in the village of Biddu, for instance, Rabbi Ascherman approached Israeli border police to stop them from beating a young Palestinian boy, only to be arrested himself and then tied to the front of a police jeep as a human shield "protecting" the front window from stones thrown by demonstrators. On other occasions, RHR members and supporters have been harassed, beaten, and arrested while demonstrating with Palestinians or working in the fields. Generally both they and their partners understand that the privileges attached to an Israeli ID card (or even to a skullcap) may be temporarily forfeited in these situations. In sum, the space where joint actions take place is one in which identity lines are often partly and temporarily suspended, but the effectiveness of these actions also depends on the preservation of the privileges of Israeli identity, without which the presence of group members would not render Palestinians safer or their situation more available to potentially empowering instruments for representation (e.g., Israeli courts).

Despite the temporary suspension of these privileges, the specific prerogatives of an Israeli national or rabbi in a situation of joint work with Palestinians are thus part of what makes RHR's acts of solidarity possible and effective. This is contrary to Levinas's view of ethical responsibility (though not his notion of political justice), which requires that people confront the other's suffering and his practical (including economic) misery while shorn of all qualities of their own, including the capacity for doing, or what he calls "I can." Besides relying precisely on this capacity, RHR's work constitutes a very *political* sort of responsibility in the sense that it engages Israelis with an "other" whose "suffering" is not unrelated to their own history or to their power, both in the sense that these have contributed to it and in the sense that they are necessary in order to enable its witnessing and its alleviation under the Occupation.

On a second level of "excess" beyond its symbolic referents, much RHR practice goes beyond the principle of "nonoppression" of the stranger (which is affirmed by the symbolic order of prophetic Judaism) by actively cultivating Palestinian presence in the landscape of biblical Israel. By rebuilding homes, replanting orchards, and assisting with harvesting, RHR members seem to signal a desire to nurture the "economic" fabric of Palestinian life as a nontransient factor in this land, whether in the West Bank (including East Jerusalem) or in Israel proper. In this respect, there is an important difference between the call not to oppress "strangers," which the group upholds in theory, and the act of building *with them* (as opposed to *for them*) the capacity to provide for themselves, in the process strengthening their roots in the Promised Land.[57] This difference is not only theoretical but also political, since "life-enabling" or "economic" power—the power both to provide concrete livelihoods and to cultivate "forms of life" supported by distinctive symbolic orders—is not just claimed by Israelis to be used on behalf of others but is ascribed to and recognized in others both as individuals and as communities, suggesting that their "strangerness" to the Land does not make their roots in it any less vital or rich in economic and symbolic value than those of Jewish Israelis. Importantly, it is almost always Palestinian farmers, homeowners, or village committees who invite RHR members and other activists to come to work with them. It is also Palestinians who invite RHR members to celebrations in *their* homes and villages, that is, in places to which they are tied not only by bonds of property or of economic need but also by bonds of symbolic signification in ethno-national, familial, or religious terms. On these occasions, Palestinians and Israelis are capable of life-enabling solidarity only by virtue of their different access to certain "qualities" that make up the Levinasian "I can," that is, a capacity for economic and symbolically significant work that is partly, though not exclusively, rooted in ethno-national membership.

For RHR members, neither human rights nor Zionist identity are set aside in the work of solidarity, and yet each of these discourses is either exceeded or transgressed while working literally "in the field." Ultimately, there is no mimesis, no identification of RHR members with their Palestinian "others," either as abstract human beings or as a national community. On the contrary, my participation in some RHR initiatives and my reading of the group's literature suggest that Israeli members retain a sense of primary responsibility toward their national community, state, and religious tradition, as well as to their own past and present traumas. Their Palestinian partners are often aware of this, though they are not always willing to accept it, despite the expediency of contingent cooperation. In fact, this sense of primary responsibility toward one's people and one's own symbolic referents (e.g., Jewish values and understandings of terms like *justice*) is often reinforced by the ascriptive identity into which RHR people are interpellated by their Palestinian partners. While accompanying an RHR member on a visit to a Bedouin resettlement camp whose families he has helped for many years and with whom he maintains very warm relations, I once witnessed a group of children (who had run to meet the rabbi with friendly enthusiasm during all his previous visits) ask him, "You are Jewish, so tell me: why did your people kill Rantisi?"[58] When the rabbi expressed his sadness for this event and tried to challenge the children's assumption that as a Jew he must respond for all actions committed by the state of Israel, a child retorted: "Then [i.e., if you are indeed sad] why did you Zionists come to take our land?" By asking that, the child seemed to draw a line that could not be crossed by human rights discourse or by the strong personal bond between his family and the rabbi, demanding not only friendship or practical solidarity but rather a clear assumption of responsibility *by an Israeli* for what he saw as an inextricable combination of the historical trajectory of Zionism and of specific acts of violence authorized by the Israeli state today.

A similar, though less open manifestation of Palestinian perceptions of the ambiguity of the stance of RHR with respect to the politics of Zionism was visible in the attitude of a Palestinian family I visited with some RHR volunteers on the outskirts of Jerusalem in early 2004. The family, which had received a house demolition order after having built an additional floor to a house it had owned since 1962 (i.e., since before the Israeli occupation of East Jerusalem), had contacted RHR to provide data that could be used to build a legal case. The meeting initially concentrated on collecting details that could be used for the case, and the family presented its situation in a language designed in part to awaken a "humanitarian conscience" in its audience and in part to demonstrate its familiarity with the grammar of citizenship and of formal rights. After the family discovered that I spoke Arabic and was not Jewish (unlike the other group members), however, I became the recipient of a very different kind of discourse, one that showed great political self-awareness and a sense of shame at having to play the role of "trauma victims" in need of the testimonial aid of Jewish Israelis. In addition, there was a sense of resignation (possibly temporary and not uncritical) to the fact that making their case and securing the basic essentials for a decent life by keeping a roof over their heads required subjecting their situation to two systems of signification (i.e., Israeli legality and human rights) that did not correspond to what they saw as its *authentic* meaning (i.e., that Israelis have no right to decide Palestinian rights to build on Palestinian land).

If we assume, like Levinas, that justice is a precondition for life-enabling work that does not merely depend on the goodwill of individuals but is also sustained by institutions, identities, and even borders as sources of *ratio* and of the power to discern the "countable" from the "uncountable" (to paraphrase Derrida) does it follow that RHR's practices are a sort of "trauma-bearing" surrogate of the justice preached by past prophets, not to mention a poor substitute for secular justice grounded in equal citizenship? Shouldn't Jewish prophetic politics aim for the kind of justice that can be enforced by institutions that do not conceal power behind trauma narratives and that do not impede people's pursuit of signifying economies of life by cultivating existential anxieties and even by demanding symbolically disruptive violence?

Although this brief discussion of RHR cannot provide final answers to such questions, it does suggest caution concerning the possibility of finding better alternatives to this sort of limited justice contrapuntal to trauma-laden narratives of Jewish Israeliness *under the present circumstances* of the Occupation. In particular, it is difficult to imagine an alternative that could less contingently address the combined pressure of traumatic genealogies, the covenantal faith of religious Israelis, and the power dynamics of a situation in which the capacity to transgress requires some of the privileges of sovereignty. In the practice of RHR, the conjunction of human rights discourse and of religious Zionism seems to make possible acts of solidarity that, by translating the biblical call to justice into concrete life-enabling practices for the "other," provisionally confront injustices that are sometimes defended on the grounds of trauma-laden Israeli nationhood. Further exploration of the possibility of understanding and practicing Israeli sovereign power as the enabler of testimony to (one's) "strangerness" may perhaps require recognizing that there is intrinsic value, rather than mere "tragic necessity," both in transgressive solidarity and in certain economies of life based on practical solidarity work *with* and *as* "strangers." For the time being, RHR's work suggests that productive or restorative work *with* others can at least be an occasion to gain ethical and political agency when the order of nation-hood is marked by a crisis of symbolic guarantors.

PART IV

Opening Societies and the Rights of the Human

Mysticism and the Foundation of the Open Society

Bergsonian Politics

Paola Marrati

In his 1920 Oxford lecture "The Possible and the Real" (published in 1934 in *La Pensée et le mouvant*, rather unhappily translated as *The Creative Mind*[1]), Bergson returns to a question of method: the importance of the position of problems in philosophy. Solutions, or answers to problems, are implied in the way in which problems are stated; they are their empirical results. It is critical, then, to avoid the danger of the confusion resulting from "badly put or badly analyzed problems." Philosophy, or at least its significance, stands or falls with the problems it is capable of setting up.

Among the examples of badly analyzed problems that Bergson provides, the one of the category of the possible is certainly one of the most striking. In the history of philosophy, as well as in everyday language, it is usually assumed that the category of the possible contains less than the category of reality. In other words, we have the habit of thinking that a possibility is necessarily and obviously something less than its corresponding reality, even though in fact, Bergson argues, the possible "contains more than the real."[2] How is this mistake made? Where does its supposed evidence come from? And, more importantly, what is the "badly put problem" from which this mistake results? Let me cite the following passage:

> During the great war certain newspapers sometimes turned aside from the terrible worries of the day to think of what would have happened later once peace was restored. They were particularly preoccupied with the future of literature. Someone came one day to ask me my ideas on the subject. A little embarrassed, I declared I had none. "Do you not at least perceive," I was asked, "certain possible directions? I shall always remember my interlocutor's

591

surprise when I answered, "If I knew what was to be the great dramatic work of the future, I should be writing it." I saw distinctly that he conceived of the future work has being already stored up in some cupboard reserved for possibilities. . . . "But, I said, the work of which you speak is not yet possible."—"But it must be, since it is to take place."—"No, it is not. I grant you, at most, that it will have been possible." . . . Thus in judging that the possible does not presuppose the real, one admits that the realization adds something to the simple possibility: the possible would have been there from all time, a phantom awaiting its hour; it would therefore have become reality by the addition of something, by some transfusion of blood or life. One does not see that the contrary is the case, that the possible implies the corresponding reality with, moreover, something added, since the possible is the combined effect of reality once it has appeared and of a condition which throws it back in time.[3]

Our understanding of future events is shaped by the pervasive belief that the possibility of things precedes their existence, like the ensemble of possible worlds Leibniz's God contemplates, like the a priori structures that lay out in advance the form of all experience, or like a logical space in which all events are supposed to place themselves in preestablished compartments. Hence it becomes understandable that the concept of the possible is supposed to contain less than that of the real: one being the image of the other, existence would give a body to its own phantom, add to it the only thing it still is missing—a little bit of reality. The final consequence, as Gilles Deleuze points out in *Difference and Repetition*, is that existence becomes inexplicable: because it adds nothing to the concept of a possibility that precedes it, existence remains outside the domain of the conceptual, without reason and, paradoxically, without importance.[4]

According to Bergson, the opposite, rather, is the case. The possible is just the real with the addition of an act of the mind that throws its image back onto the past: "the possible is the mirage of the present in the past." We are mistaken to assume that the possible is less than the real. There is more in the category of the possible than in that of the real because the former also contains the very act of the mind that projects a possible unto the past. The possible is constituted *retrospectively*, indeed *retroactively*.

What is at stake, however, is much more than a question of method in the academic sense of the term, or a question of conceptual analysis. Behind the illusion of the possible, a mistake can be discerned that compromises the very task of philosophy as Bergson conceives of it or, to be more precise, the task of a *conversion* that philosophy must achieve. The task is no longer to think the eternal—in another world or in this one, since there also is a modern way of attaching thought to that which is removed from time—but to think the *moving* (*le mouvant*), the new in the process of making itself. It is from this perspective that Bergson's critique of the traditional concept of possibility acquires its full importance and unfolds its consequences. The philosophical failure to provide a conceptual determination of existence we have just discussed may seem a paradoxical outcome when expressed in the way Bergson states it, but it is nonetheless perfectly consistent with traditional philosophy's desire to capture eternity in time, the unchangeable laws of change itself, to conceive movement only as the realization of an untimely possibility.[5] In the account Bergson provides of the history of ancient and modern philosophy, all their important differences notwithstanding, the Platonic idea that knowledge is of the eternal remains unchallenged and continues to guide, explicitly or implicitly, philosophical inquiries.[6] What comes into existence, what is born in time, has its law, reason, or cause elsewhere; it is nothing but the incarnation of a possibility that precedes it.

The conversion Bergson is calling for is thus a conversion of philosophy to time. As the term *conversion* suggests, for philosophy it is not so much a matter of changing the objects of inquiry (it could hardly be argued that 'time' has not been a philosophical topic prior to Bergson) as of changing its way of looking at them, of transforming its own desire. Philosophy should become capable of turning away from the longing for eternity if it has to think the power of time, which, according to Bergson's famous claim, "is invention or it is nothing at all."[7] That such a conversion is not an easy task, or that such a claim is not an easy one to grasp, is proven by the long series of remarkable philosophers and readers—from Heidegger to Adorno, from Merleau-Ponty to Foucault, to name just a few—who dismiss Bergson's conception of time on the grounds of its supposed subjectivism and the dichotomy between time and space, thus sidestepping the question of the new, and with it the entire Bergsonian philosophical project.[8]

The assumption that the possibility of things precedes their existence comes down to denying the reality of the new, to speaking of time without thinking it, to erasing the only feature that defines time, its power of creation. But how, then, should the power of time be thought? In *Creative Evolution*, Bergson seeks to show that his project is not merely an abstract metaphysical hypothesis. The Darwinian discovery of the evolution of life, with the production of new and unpredictable forms of life, as well as of new ideas and new concepts that can grasp them, imposes on both science and philosophy a rethinking of time. Time can no longer be thought of as an exterior frame, in which events follow upon one another, but rather in itself has to be conceived as constituting a genuine force of agency—to the extent that Bergson identifies the very essence of time with a creative power along the lines of what could be called a properly ontological pragmatism: if time *does* nothing, it *is* nothing.[9]

The critique of the category of the possible is the necessary consequence of thinking time as *duration*. Bergson explores the psychological and subjective dimension of duration in his first book, *Essai sur les données immédiates de la conscience* (1889; also rather unhappily translated as *Time and Free Will*); he gives a metaphysical and ontological account of it in *Matter and Memory* (1896), his second book. But it is not until *Creative Evolution* (1907) that he establishes the missing link between a subjective experience of time and a philosophical hypothesis by means of the "fact" of the evolution of life. If some examples of the retrospective illusion of the possible come from art and politics (Romanticism and democracy), the concept of duration has been elaborated elsewhere: between psychology and biology.

Thus, the strange phrase that concludes the second part of the *Introduction to Metaphysics*, published two years after the Oxford lecture, in 1922, becomes understandable: "One is never compelled to write a book."[10] Bergson has just discussed, in a concise and systematic manner, the achievements of his method, and the contribution he has been able to make to the solution of a number of problems. He has also recalled what elsewhere he names "the need for precision in philosophy,"[11] which amounts to the necessity of producing singular concepts that fit each singular object instead of considering knowledge to be a given set of categories or conceptual schemes ready to be applied to any new fact, object, or event we happen to encounter.[12] Bergson could have ended his *Introduction* in this way without feeling obliged to declare that nobody is obliged to write a book, which is, after all, nothing more than a logical consequence of what he has just affirmed and which only becomes strange, if not enigmatic, when it is enunciated as such. To be sure, the book he did not feel compelled to write is not just any book. Bergson knew very well what was expected of him because of his philosophical authority, his institutional responsibilities, and the political functions in which he served.[13] It was a book of moral and political philosophy that was expected of him and about which one wondered why Bergson still had not written it.

As is well known, Bergson ended up writing this book: *The Two Sources of Morality and Religion*, which came out in 1932. As is also well known, expectations were not fulfilled, and *The Two Sources* did not find the immense resonance that his other books had done. Still today, and despite the renewed interest in Bergson's philosophy, this book remains somewhat on the margins. Nevertheless, it is an important text, not only in its relation to Bergson's œuvre as such, but also, and above all, with regard to the specific questions it raises.

How is one to think the origin of morality, the history and future of human societies, or the function of religion once one situates oneself—as Bergson does—outside any historicist perspective, as well as outside any abstract rationalism? Bergson's problem in considering human history is that he can take neither a Hegelian nor a Kantian position. Human history—the becoming of societies, of morality, of forms of political organization—is a part of the movement of the evolution of life and shares with it a radical lack of teleology. One of the crucial arguments of *Creative Evolution* is the absence of any pre-established direction that could underlie and orient the paths taken by forms of life in the course of evolution. According to Bergson, the opposition between deterministic and finalistic approaches to evolution is only a superficial one: they both share the same mistaken assumption that "all is given." For determinism, on the one hand, "all is given" in the past in the form of a linear causal chain that makes of evolution the unfolding of a previously given program. For finalism, on the other hand, the movement of evolution aims at the achievement of a finality and is thus oriented toward the future, but a future whose shape is known in advance. It is of little importance whether the development of evolution is understood in terms of an impulse from the past or an attraction to the future; in both cases, the succession of species and of forms of life is nothing but a surface phenomenon, and time is deprived of its power of creation.

Any attempt to think the becoming of human societies in the light of a philosophy of history shares, for Bergson, the same teleological delusion of finalism. Human becoming cannot be an exception to evolution: no law of history traces the movement of human societies in advance; humans live in duration, as does everything else. From this point of view, the notion of progress is nothing but one of the forms of the retrospective illusion of the possible.

But a Kantian position that would locate the origin of morality in reason is equally untenable for Bergson, not only because the regulative ideas of reason introduce a form of teleology but also because, for Bergson, reason itself is a product of the evolution of life. Reason belongs to evolution's becoming, a becoming that produces new ideas and new concepts at the same time as it produces new forms of life.[14] It is precisely from the perspective of the becoming of forms of life that Bergson will attempt to think the sources of morality, religion, and the political, and of their reciprocal articulation.

The Two Sources opens with the question of moral obligation. It is a fact that we all obey—most of the time, in any case. But why? Children obey their parents and their teachers, but whom exactly do they obey? Bergson remarks that this obedience is not so much granted a singular person as it is granted the place this person occupies: children obey parents insofar as they are parents, teachers insofar as they are teachers, because parents and teachers occupy a well-determined place in society. Their authority derives first and foremost from a social position. Behind moral obligation, society can be discerned. As one would have expected, the comparison between society and an organism appears right away (even if, as we shall see, Bergson will change the meaning and value of this traditional comparison). In organisms, the different parts are subordinate to one another according to biological necessity. Human societies, too, are in need of such "biological links," but since they are made up of individuals who are, at least in part, free, cohesion comes from elsewhere. In human societies, the link is established by the force of *habit*. We take up habits, sometimes of giving orders, more often of obeying, that make us stay in the place that society assigns us. In other words, habit is the equivalent in human societies to what instinct is in animal societies. It is not by an antlike instinct that we play the social roles that are ours, but by habit.

We must not be mistaken, however: Bergson by no means affirms that social and political forms of organization are biologically determined or determinable. Every habit is radically contingent. The only thing that is not contingent is the *habit of taking up habits*. This is, furthermore, the difference Bergson establishes between human and non-human living beings; it is human beings' largest margin of liberty, it is the non-necessity of any given social structure. Nonetheless, no human society could constitute itself or even survive without the cohesion guaranteed by a network of habits. Moral obligation (in any case, its first source) has no other origin or function; it is the pressure that society exerts on us to give form to the network of habits of which our everyday life is made up. Bergson further insists on the fact that obligation does not come from the outside, because every individual belongs to society as much as to him- or herself. A subject outside of society is nothing but an illusion, and obligation, prior to linking humans to each other, "links each one of us to ourselves." This is not to say that our subjectivity is purely social or that there are no other threads to give consistency to our psychic life, but rather that most of the time, as Bergson would have it, "it is at the surface, at the point where it inserts itself into the close-woven tissue of other exteriorized personalities, that our ego generally finds its points of attachment; its solidity lies in its solidarity."[15]

Made up of a set of everyday habits that attaches us as much to ourselves as to others, moral obligation, according to Bergson, is never punctual or singular. Each obligation implies others and would have no meaning by itself. That is why Bergson speaks of the "totality of obligation." Society sketches the program of our lives and we follow this sketch without particular effort, almost without noticing it. Thus, the origin of morality is not to be found in an austere and rigid conception of duty demanding the "over-human" effort of conforming to a categorical imperative. There is no need to be a hero of pure reason to fulfill our many duties. Bergson certainly realizes that in moments of "crisis," when the temptation to no longer follow the good path is strong, "to do one's duty" can cost us much, and moral obligation thus loses its anodyne aspect. In these moments, reason can help us lean toward duty; yet, from the fact that reason can make us return to duty, it does not at all follow that the origin of moral obligation is rational. The totality of obligation, with its system of habits, does not rely on pure reason: on the contrary, it is the human equivalent of or supplement to the social instinct that makes animal societies function.

Not without a little malice, Bergson remarks that no human being obeys by virtue of pure logical coherence; the "one must because one must" of a categorical imperative is never encountered in human conduct. And the thought experiment of a pure categorical imperative suggested by Bergson does not look very Kantian:

If we want a pure case of a categorical imperative, we must construct one a priori or at least make an arbitrary abstraction of experience. So let us imagine an ant who is stirred by a gleam of reflection and thereupon judges that she has been wrong to work unremittingly for others. Her inclination to laziness would indeed endure but a few moments, just as long as the ray of intelligence. In the last of these moments, when instinct regaining the mastery would drag her back by sheer force to her task, intelligence at the point of relapsing into instinct would say, as its parting words: "You must because you must."[16]

Social life is immanent to instinct as well as to intelligence, and the "habit of taking up habits" that lies at the origin of morality and religion produces results comparable to those produced by instinct. There is thus a "natural," "biological," or "evolutionary" ground under the layer of acquired habits, of culture, if you like. It is a ground that is always present and at work in human societies, which does not change, or changes very little, and which one would be wrong *philosophically* and *politically* not to take into account. According to Bergson, the "primitive" are not the only others: we, the "civilized," are just as "primitive" in this respect.[17]

The biological ground Bergson is speaking of, however, should not be confused with any form of "social Darwinism," "evolutionary sociology," or the like. True, for Bergson, humans are, in the first place, "living animals," and if there is in his philosophy a metaphysical desire to go beyond the human condition, such a desire is not one of stripping humanity of its bodily life in favor of a purely spiritual, ghostly existence. There is nothing about animality, about biological forms of embodiment, to be despised, for the very reason that life as such is identified by Bergson with a tendency to change, with an essential mobility, an aspiration to novelty that runs through all living forms. The privilege of humans, what singles out humanity, is a greater capacity for freedom and change. This privilege, however, does not separate humanity from the realm of the living; it does not open up an ontological gap in a Kantian or Heideggerian manner. Rationality itself is, in Bergson's view, deeply rooted in life to the extent that life as such is endowed with a highly cognitive competence: the capability of solving problems. More precisely, life is *defined* by this capability. In *Creative Evolution* the fundamental biological category is that of the *problem*, not that of *need*. Nutrition, before being a need to be satisfied, is a problem to be solved. According to Bergson, the problem of nutrition is addressed, and solved, in "different but equally elegant" ways by vegetal and animal forms of life. Living beings are thus cases of solutions to problems. The superiority of humanity, if one wishes to use this vocabulary, lies in the wider range of different solutions it can make available to itself, in the greater, though not absolute, freedom of coming up with new and different solutions to new—and old—problems. Instruments and machines prolong and extend such a capacity. According to Bergson, not only does technology play a crucial role in human history, a role that exceeds the one played by political events, but its transformative power in turn affects and modifies biological forms of life. Bergson clearly understands that no absolute line can be drawn between organic and inorganic tools, between organs and machines. Once life is conceived in terms of a creative capacity to solve problems, organic and inorganic tools certainly differ—namely, in the way in which they are produced—but they do not belong to different ontological domains; rather, they supplement each other in multiple and unpredictable ways.[18]

If we now return to the question of human societies, from which the "natural ground" never disappears, we can see that they resemble each other in one decisive respect: they are *closed* societies. The fact that modern nation-states are much, much larger than the ancient Greek cities or certain "primitive tribes" does not change anything about the principle. A society is closed because its essence is to include a certain number of individuals and to exclude all others. The boundaries that define a society as closed have nothing simply factual about them, just as the consequences they imply are far from neutral. The morality and religion that Bergson has just described in their function of providing social cohesion belong to closed societies: they would have no role to play in an *open society*. This open society does not yet exist and would have to embrace all of humanity.

But why can the whole of obligation and the institutional, or institutionalized, religions not broaden the systems of moral and civic habits to include the whole of humanity? Why is a break required and a different kind of morality and religion called for? Bergson knows well that in each nation there is much talk about "duties toward humanity" (today, this would be "human rights," but the difference is not one of kind) and that these duties are made out to be the natural prolongation, so to speak, of duties toward the family, the institution, or the state, as if there were only a quantitative difference but no gap, no tension. Yet, according to Bergson, this discourse is nothing but a façade, whether it be pronounced in good or in bad faith. It is enough to look at what happens when a war breaks out: borderless human fraternity gives way to an outburst of violence; everything is allowed against the enemy—murder, pillage, rape, torture, cruelty. To respond that these are exceptional and rare events is but a delusion; there is nothing exceptional about wars except our desire not to see them coming, to exclude them from "the normal path things take," of which they would only be an unfortunate accident.

In reality, the outburst of violence illustrates the nature of closed societies (to which parliamentary democracies belong) and shows the other face of morality and religion. Behind the peaceful regularity of habits, so necessary to social cohesion, an attitude can be discerned: the attitude of discipline in confronting the enemy. No closed society, democratic or not, can escape its instinct of cohesion, which is an instinct of war. The exclusion that founds closed societies is thus not neutral or vaguely benevolent: it is essentially hostile.[19]

That is why, to Bergson's mind, the belief that we could pass from love of the family and of the nation to love of humanity in general by a continuous broadening of our sympathy, by the progress of a sentiment that would grow while remaining the same, is a mistake with grave consequences. We will never arrive at humanity in stages, via the family and the nation: "Neither in the one case nor the other do we come to humanity by degrees, through the stages of the family and the nation. We must, in a single bound, be carried far beyond it, and, without having made it our goal, reach it by outstripping it."[20]

The leap does not, properly speaking, give us the "love of humanity in general." An object so vague would, rather, be apt to "cool the most ardent souls." In any case, the leap does not give us anything at all, and certainly no determined or determinable object.

What it does is to lead us elsewhere, toward another morality, another religion. The totality of obligation in its moral or religious versions has its source in the pressure exercised by society inside and outside of ourselves; its natural function is to ensure the group's bond, to—in a way—imitate organic and instinctual links to ensure that collective life is possible, even if it demands the sacrifice of personal interests. Human societies rest neither on utilitarianism nor on a contract, but on a biologico-evolutionary "social instinct," of which the closure of the group is an essential aspect. According to Bergson, between this type of morality and religion, which springs from closed societies, on the one hand, and an open morality and open religion, on the other, there is neither continuity nor rupture, because they are not of the same nature; their respective sources are different. To say it in a formula dear to Bergson, what separates them is a "difference of kind and not one of degree." One is the effect of a pressure, the other is but an opening. But an opening onto what? Onto everything or nothing, and there is no difference whatsoever:

> The other attitude is that of the open soul. What, in that case, is allowed in? Suppose we say it embraces all humanity: we should not be going too far, we should hardly be going far enough, since its love may extend to animals, to plants, to all nature. And yet not one of these things which would thus fill it would suffice to define the attitude taken by the soul, for it could, strictly speaking, do without all of them. Its form is not dependent on its content. We have just filled it; we could as easily empty it again.[21]

The opening is nothing but a tendency or an attitude, and it is precisely in this sense that the opening is essentially mystical, at least in the definition Bergson gives of mysticism (which, incidentally, remains rather faithful to certain strands of mysticism). Yet it seems important to insist on the fact that the opening has no object, not because its object would be too large or too vague and consequently difficult to describe but because the opening *as* opening does not have an object. Every object assigned to it from the outset, even if it were the entire universe, would close it. This does not imply, however, that open morality and open religion do not apply to all sorts of different objects according to situation and context. Quite the contrary, mystics are, to Bergson's mind, men and women of action: they do not retire from the world, they act in it, and the force of mysticism is a force of agency. It is in another sense that the mystic opening does not and cannot have a determinate or determinable object. If the passage from the closed to the open is not one of degrees, of a progressive broadening, that is because closed societies always have a determinate object: a people, a nation, a community, and so on. They have a figure, an identity, however precarious and provisional it might be. The open society is neither the sum of these different faces nor the sum of a certain number of characteristics that they all share. In *Creative Evolution*, Bergson defines the essence of life and of forms of life as a tendency toward change. Humanity is not an exception: no one can know in advance what would define humanity, what would indicate the unbridgeable boundaries of the human. Also, if the open society is to include all of humanity, the mystic opening, as we have seen, passes through humanity, so to speak, without tying itself down. To put it in different, non-Bergsonian terms: the universal has no figure, the universal is empty. But this emptiness is not structural. The universal is a movement, a movement without preestablished direction and without continuity. It is a fragmented movement that stops itself and freezes, suddenly to reappear, elsewhere and differently. Much later, in 1991, Deleuze will remember Bergson when he writes in *What Is Philosophy?* that the first principle of philosophy is that universals do not explain anything because they need to be explained themselves.[22]

But what is the source of mysticism, of a morality, a religion, and a politics of opening? What opposes itself to the pressure of social obligation (all along entering into compromise with obligation, because for Bergson pure mysticism does not exist as a state that one could enter once and for all and remain there)? For the reasons we have seen, the second source cannot be habit or pure reason: it is the power of affects and feelings. The example of music, which Bergson chooses, is significant. Certainly, it is a commonplace to attribute to music a particular power to excite emotions, but what is important to Bergson is that this power is all the stronger for being detached from any object. Music is able to create new feelings and introduce them into us or, more precisely, Bergson writes, to introduce us into them. The force of a feeling has to do with this power to open us up to the new: the mystical source of morality and religion lies in this force; instead of being derived from social pressure, it is aspiration.[23]

The absence of any determinate object on which I have so insisted certainly has a counterpart in Bergson's thought. That which can communicate open morality, propagate it, cannot be a corpus of doctrines or an institution. The power of a feeling cannot be triggered except by an example; hence the necessary role of a hero of morality, famous or anonymous (the exemplary figure among these being the Christ of the Gospels). We must not believe, however, that the figure of the exemplary hero fills the void of the open: if imitation is necessary, it is also, strictly speaking, the imitation of nothing. There is no set of rules, norms, or conduct to follow: what must be imitated is an attitude, a tendency of the mind, and a capacity to act.

Bergson is not calling for a morality and a politics of irrational emotions or sublime sensibility. His claim is, rather, that no morality and no politics—whether "open" or "closed"—can ever take place within the limits of reason alone.

Insofar as the author of *Creative Evolution* is concerned, with his faith in living beings' power of creation, we now find ourselves in a strange situation. We are confronted, on the one hand, with "natural" societies, sustained by an evolutionary instinct that leads to the closed group, always ready to close itself even further in order to attack the enemy. On the other hand, we also see a demand for an opening, a second source of morality, which is, from this point of view, "against nature," and whose only chance, politically, is, precisely, to "fool nature." (Bergson credits human beings for having developed very quickly this capability to fool nature, by turning sexuality, for example, away from its goal, the reproduction of the species.) Nonetheless, there is no break between *Creative Evolution* and *The Two Sources*. The second source expresses an aspect of life, too, and its capacity to "fool nature" is nothing but a way of linking up once more with the power of life. And Bergson does not hesitate to invoke a philosopher otherwise not very dear to him: Spinoza. Between the two sources, there is the same difference, and the same relation, as between *Natura Naturans* and *Natura Naturata*: "Hence in passing from social solidarity to the brotherhood of men, we break with one particular nature, but not with all nature. It might be said, by slightly distorting the terms of Spinoza, that it is to get back to Natura Naturans that we break away from Natura Naturata."[24]

To Bergson's mind, we will never be able to pass from closed societies to the open society by means of a progressive broadening. Dreamt of from time to time by some, as he writes, the open society sometimes succeeds in tearing apart closures and in actualizing something of itself before closing itself again in the network of habits, in the whole of social obligation. What is at stake in these moments is thus a qualitative, not a quantitative, leap. One could call these moments "progress" if one would like to believe that these steps are all taken in the same direction. But that would once again be the retrospective illusion of the possible because in reality there is no direction established in advance. If that were the case, moral and political renovations would be foreseeable and there would be no need to create, no need to produce or invent them.

Without being willing to subscribe to a philosophy of history or to a universalism of pure reason, Bergson puts the emphasis on the new, the unforeseeable, which is never contained in the past, not even as possible. He trusts the powers of time and of life, which are nothing but a production of the new—all along knowing that these forces are fragile and that nobody can guarantee us a better future.

Bergson's political theology—if he has one, which is not certain—is an act of belief in the moving and in change; an appeal to act in order to open up societies and institutions, which by their very essence seek to freeze. But if there is no explicit teleology, is there any finality to this mysticism of movement? Maybe there is, but it is a finality without either form or content, a desire to break through the boundaries, to go beyond that which presents itself as possible. It is in this sense that I would like to read the famous and enigmatic claim with which *The Two Sources* ends: "Theirs the responsibility, then, for deciding if they want merely to live, or intend to make just the extra effort required for fulfilling, even on their refractory planet, the essential function of the universe, which is a machine for the making of gods."[25]

—*Translated by Nils F. Schott*

The Agency of Assemblages and the North American Blackout

Jane Bennett

The Agency of Assemblages

One thing that globalization names is the sense that the "theater of operations" has expanded greatly. Earth is no longer a category for ecology or geology only, but has become a political unit, the whole in which the parts (e.g., finance capital, CO_2 emissions, refugees, viruses, pirated DVDs, ozone, human rights, weapons of mass destruction) now circulate. There have been various attempts to theorize this complex, gigantic whole and to characterize the kind of relationality obtaining between its parts. Network is one such attempt, as is Michael Hardt and Antonio Negri's empire.[1] My term of choice to describe this whole and its style of structuration is, following Gilles Deleuze, the assemblage.[2]

The electrical power grid is a good example of an assemblage. It is a material cluster of charged parts that have indeed affiliated, remaining in sufficient proximity and coordination to function as a (flowing) system. The coherence of this system endures alongside energies and factions that fly out from it and disturb it from within. And, most important for my purposes here, the elements of this assemblage, while they include humans and their constructions, also include some very active and powerful nonhumans: electrons, trees, wind, electromagnetic fields.

I will be using the idea of an assemblage and offering an account of the blackout that struck North America in August 2003 in order, first, to highlight the conceptual and empirical inadequacy of human-centered notions of agency and, second, to investigate some of the practical implications, for social scientific inquiry and for politics, of a notion of agency that crosses the human-nonhuman divide.

The *International Herald Tribune,* on the day after the blackout, reported that "The vast but shadowy web of transmission lines, power generating plants and substations known as the grid is the biggest gizmo ever built . . . on Thursday [August 14, 2003], the grid's heart fluttered. . . . complicated beyond full understanding, even by experts—[the grid] lives and occasionally dies by its own mysterious rules."[3] What can it mean to say that the grid's "heart fluttered" or that the grid lives "by its own rules"? What is this power it wields? Can it be described as a kind of agency, despite the fact that the term is usually restricted to intentional human acts? What happens to the idea of an agent once nonhuman materialities are figured less as social constructions and more as actors, and once humans are themselves assessed as members of human-nonhuman assemblages? How does the agency of assemblages compare to more familiar notions, such as the willed intentionality of persons, the disciplinary power of society, or the automatism of natural processes? How does recognition of the nonhuman and nonindividuated dimensions of agency alter established notions of moral responsibility and political accountability?

My strategy is to focus attention on the distributive and composite nature of agency. Are there not human, biological, vegetal, pharmaceutical, and viral agents? Is not the ability to make a difference, to produce effects, or even to initiate action, distributed across an ontologically diverse range of actors—or *actants*, to use Bruno Latour's less anthropocentric term?[4] Some actants have sufficient coherence to appear as entities; others, because of their great volatility, fast pace of evolution, or minuteness of scale, are best conceived as forces. Moreover, while individual entities and singular forces each exercise agentic capacities, isn't there also an agency proper to the groupings they form? This is the agency of assemblages: the distinctive efficacy of a working whole made up, variously, of somatic, technological, cultural, and atmospheric elements. Because each member-actant maintains an energetic pulse slightly "off" from that exuded by the assemblage, such assemblages are never fixed blocks but open-ended wholes.[5]

Before elaborating such a distributive and composite notion of agency, let me say a bit about the materialist ontology with which it is allied. This faith, or better, this wonder, can be described as a kind of vitalism, an enchanted materialism. Within this materialism, the world is figured as neither mechanistic nor teleological but rather as alive with movement and with a certain power of expression.[6] By "power of expression," I mean the ability of bodies to become otherwise than they are, to press out of their current configuration and enter into new compositions of self, as well as into new alliances and rivalries with others.[7] Within the terms of this imaginary, there are various sources or sites of agency, including the intentionality of a human animal, the temperament of a brain's chemistry, the momentum of a social movement, the mood of an architectural form, the propensity of a family, the style of a corporation, the drive of a sound-field, and the decisions of molecules at far-from-equilibrium states.

So, my profession of faith (with a nod to the Nicene Creed): I believe in one Nature, vibrant and overflowing, material and energetic, maker of all that is, seen and unseen. I believe that this pluriverse "is continually *doing things,* things that bear upon us . . . as forces upon material beings."[8] I believe that this "generative mobility"[9] "resists full translation and exceeds our comprehensive grasp."[10] I believe that to experience materiality as vital and animated is to enrich the quality of human life. Or, as Spinoza suggests, the more kinds of bodies with which a human body can productively affiliate, the greater the prospects for an intelligent way of life: "as the body is more capable of being affected in many ways and of affecting external bodies . . . so the mind is more capable of thinking."[11]

More needs to be said to flesh out this materialism. But let me return to the focus of this essay: a distributive, composite notion of agency; an agency that includes the nonhumans with which we join forces or vie for control. Back, then, to the blackout of August 2003.

The Blackout

The electrical grid is a volatile mix of coal, sweat, electromagnetic fields, computer programs, electron streams, profit motives, heat, lifestyles, nuclear fuel, plastic, fantasies of mastery, static, legislation, water, economic theory, wire, and wood—to name just some of the actants. There is always some friction among the parts, but for several days in August 2003 in the United States and Canada the dissonance was so great that cooperation became impossible. The North American blackout was the end point of a cascade—of voltage collapses, self-protective withdrawals from the grid, and human decisions and omissions. The grid includes various shutdown valves and circuit-breakers that disconnect parts from the assemblage whenever they are threatened by excessive heat. Generating plants, for example, shut down just before they are about to go into "full excitation,"[12] and they do the same when the "system voltage has become too low to provide power to the generator's own auxiliary equipment, such as fans, coal pulverizers, and pumps."[13] What seems to have happened on August 14 was that several initially unrelated generator withdrawals in Ohio and Michigan caused the electron flow pattern to change over the transmission lines, which led, after a series of events including one brush fire that burnt out a transmission line and several wire-tree encounters, to a successive overloading of other lines and a vortex of "disconnects." One generating plant after another separated from the grid, placing more and more stress on the remaining participants. Within a one-minute period, "twenty generators (loaded to 2174 MW) tripped off line along Lake Erie."[14]

Investigators still do not understand why the cascade stopped—on its own—after affecting fifty million people over approximately twenty-four thousand square kilometers and shutting down over one hundred power plants, including twenty-two nuclear reactors.[15] The U.S.–Canada Task Force Report was more confident about how the cascade began, insisting that there were a variety of agential loci.[16] These include: electricity, with its internal differentiation into "active" and "reactive" power (more on this later); the power plants, which are understaffed by humans but overprotective in their mechanisms; the wires of transmission lines, which tolerate only so much heat before they refuse to transmit the electron flow; the brush fire in Ohio underneath a transmission line; Enron FirstEnergy and other energy-trading corporations, who, by legal and illegal means, had been milking the grid without maintaining its infrastructure; consumers, whose demand for electricity is encouraged to grow without concern for consequences; and the Federal Energy Regulatory Commission, whose Energy Policy Act of 1992 deregulated the grid, separated the generation of electricity from its transmission and distribution, and advanced the privatization of electricity. Let me say a bit more about the first and the last of these actants in this assemblage.

First, the nonhuman actant: electricity. Electricity is a stream of electrons moving in a current, which is measured in amperes, and the force of that current, the pressure pushing it through the wires, is measured in volts. In a system like the North American grid, electrical current and voltage are constantly oscillating like a pair of waves.[17] When the two waves are in phase with each other (rising and falling at exactly the same time) there exists "active power," or the type of power used most heavily by lamps, blow dryers, and other appliances. But some devices (such as the electric motors in refrigerators and air conditioners) rely also on "reactive power," where the waves are not in sync. Reactive power, though it lends no help in physically rotating a motor, is nevertheless vital to the active power that accompanies it, for reactive power maintains the voltage, or "electricity pressure," needed to sustain the electromagnetic field required by the system as a whole. If too many devices demand reactive power, then a deficit is created. One of the causes of the blackout was a deficit of this reactive power. In order to understand how this deficit occurred, we need to turn to a human actant, the Federal Energy Regulatory Commission.

In 1992, the Commission gained U.S. Congressional approval for legislation that separated the production of electricity from its distribution: companies could now buy electricity from a power plant in one part of the country and sell it to utilities in geographically distant locations. This greatly increased the long-distance trading of electric power—and greatly increased the load on transmission wires. But here's the rub: "as transmission lines become more heavily loaded, they consume more of the reactive power needed to maintain proper transmission voltage."[18] Reactive power doesn't travel well, dissipating over distance, so it is best if it is generated close to where it will be used.[19] Technologically speaking, power plants are quite capable of producing extra amounts of reactive power, but they don't have a financial incentive to do so, for reactive-power production reduces the amount of salable power produced. What is more, under the new regulations, transmission companies cannot compel generating plants to produce the necessary amounts of reactive power.[20]

Reactive power, vital to the whole, was a profitless commodity and thus became in short supply. Here emerged what Garrett Hardin has called a tragedy of the commons. Though rational for each individual user of reactive power to increase demand, the aggregate effect of such acts is disastrous: in a world of finite resources, "freedom in a commons bring ruin to all."[21] The reactive power deficit was an effect unanticipated by the lobbyists who pushed the new regulations in order to create a huge, continent-wide market in energy trading. But the market economy was not the only site of surprise. Electricity too contributed swerves and quirks—idiosyncrasies, deviations, and declinations internal to the functioning of the grid system. Electricity is a *flow* of electrons, and because its essence is this mobility, it always is going somewhere. But where this will be is not entirely predictable. "In the case of a power shipment from the Pacific Northwest to Utah, 33 percent of the shipment flows through Southern California and 30 percent flows through Arizona—far from any conceivable contract path."[22] What is more, in August 2003, after "the transmission lines along the southern shore of Lake Erie disconnected, the power that had been flowing along that path" dramatically and surprisingly changed its behavior: it *"immediately reversed direction and began flowing in a giant loop counterclockwise* from Pennsylvania to New York to Ontario and into Michigan."[23] Seeking to minimize its role in the blackout, a spokesman for FirstEnergy, the Ohio-based company whose Eastlake power plant was an early actant in the cascade and an early target of blame, said that any analysis needed to "take into account large unplanned south-to-north power movements that were part of a phenomenon known as loop flows, which occur when power takes a route from producer to buyer different from the intended path."[24]

This condensed account of the blackout identifies an assortment of agentic sites, from quirky electron flows to cocky economists' assumptions about market self-regulation. It sketches a world where agency is distributed along an ontological continuum of beings, entities, and forces, and it offers an example of what it means to say that a grid lives a life of its own.

How does this preliminary understanding of a distribution of agentic capacities compare with more conventional notions of agency? In the next section, I survey several philosophical approaches to the notion of agency, including the phenomenology of Maurice Merleau-Ponty, who, though he recognizes a kind of body intentionality, refuses the idea of nonhuman materiality as agentic. I look also at the notion operative in the "agency-structure debate" within anthropology, sociology, and political science, where agency attaches exclusively to persons and where social structures "act" only insofar as they *thwart* human agency. Taken as a whole, these discussions suggest that the concept of agency is very closely bound to a desire to celebrate the distinctive power of human intentionality and, more generally, to elevate the human mode of being above all others. They also reveal a close link between this human exceptionalism and the notion of moral responsibility. To affirm that agentic capacity is distributed along a continuum of ontological types and that it also issues from composite groupings of them is to unsettle a host of inherited concepts, including cause, time, culture, nature, event, life, kinship—and also responsibility. The fear is that to distribute agency more widely would be to jeopardize attempts to hold individuals responsible for their actions or to hold officials accountable to the public. I respond to these challenges in the final section of the paper.

Human Exceptionalism

Kant, whose impact upon our thinking about agency remains profound, conceived of agency as the capacity for morality, where moral agency consists in rational obedience to the moral law, whose form is inscribed in the minds of all men. The agentic act is rational in the sense that submission to the form of law is untainted by sensuous motive or influence. Kant's image of this moral autonomy, like his vision of the mind as an elegant composition of faculties capable of an ethereal, disembodied kind of action, is quite arresting. My guess, however, is that few nonphilosophers recognize themselves to be practitioners of such fantastic agency, which is as indifferent to sense perception as it is to the social consequences of an action.[25]

Recent philosophical accounts of agency focus more on intentionality and decision than on obedience and submission. The regulative ideal operative here is agency as the accurate translation of ideas into effects. This approach too chafes against everyday experience—where it seems that one can never quite get things done, where intentions are always bumping into (and only occasionally trumping) the trajectories of other beings, forces, or institutions. But its advocates acknowledge this: the extensive literature on intentionality is full of subtle and refined accounts of the conditions of possibility and complexities of intentionality—conditions that are of course absent in the ideal case.[26] And so challenges to this approach must do more than charge that the ideal is unrealizable in practice. The issue for me, rather, is whether figurations of agency centered around the rational, intentional human subject—even considered as an aspirational ideal—understate the ontological diversity of actants.

A phenomenological conception of agency, in the tradition of Martin Heidegger or Merleau-Ponty, cautions against placing more weight on intellectual reason than it can bear. Instead, a theory of agency must begin by acknowledging the essentially embodied character of human action and the intersubjective field of all human acts. This is because, as Diana Coole puts it, "the operation of agentic capacities . . . will always exceed the agency exercised by rational subjects," even as these subjects "acquire differential agentic capacities depending upon their intersubjective context."[27] Instead of agents, Coole speaks of a variety of agentic capacities distributed across a spectrum: discrete, reflective selves occupy the middle range, with the human body and its "motor intentionality"[28] at one end, and a nonpersonal, phenomenal force field at the other. Coole rightly emphasizes that not all agentic capacities are possible at every location on the spectrum, precisely because different actants are differently embodied. The self-conscious intentionality (occasionally) exercised by humans finds a counterpart—not an equivalent—in the feedback loops operative in nonhuman (e.g., chemical) systems.

Coole's attempt to dislodge agency from an exclusive mooring in the individual, rational subject is an important touchstone for my attempt to extend agency even beyond embodied intersubjectivity, to materiality per se and thus to human-nonhuman assemblages. But Coole restricts her spectrum to a range of *human* actants because her interest in agency is tied to a political project (a kind of radical democracy), and politics is for her an exclusively human affair. Here I disagree. Though human reflexivity is indispensable for transforming political life, on many occasions and in a variety of ways the efficacy of political change is not a function of humans alone. It is better understood, I think, as the conjoined effect of a variety of kinds of bodies. The prevention of future blackouts, for example, will depend upon a whole host of cooperative efforts: Congress will have to summon the courage to fight industry demands at odds with the common good, but reactive power will also have to agree to do its part, on condition that it's not asked to travel too far.

In short, though Coole's phenomenological account tries not to hierarchize agentic sites, and though it names bodies as bearers of agentic capacities, it continues to give conceptual hegemony to human actants. A distributive theory of agency does not deny that human persons are capable of reflective judgments and thus are crucial actants in many political transformations. But it attempts a more radical displacement of the human subject from the center of thinking about agency. It goes so far as to say that effective agency is *always* an assemblage: even what has been considered the purest locus of agency—reflective, intentional human consciousness—is from the first moment of its emergence constituted by the interplay of human and nonhuman materialities.[29] Everyday events—blackouts, traffic jams, power surges, upset stomachs, mood swings—repeatedly indicate the presence of a wide variety of actants, some that are personal and some that don't take the form of persons. But even persons are always engaged in an intricate dance with nonhumans, with the urgings, tendencies, and pressures of other bodies, including air masses, minerals, microorganisms, and, for some people, the forces of fate, divine will, or karma.

Perhaps the "agency-structure debate" of the last several decades in the social sciences was initially provoked by a similar hunch about the agentic capacity of collectivities. But the very terms of the debate precluded more explicit articulation of this insight. The active power of assemblages is concealed under the rubric of (social) structures, (cultural) contexts, (religious) settings, (economic) climates, or (environmental) conditions—terms that denote passive backgrounds or, at most, states of affairs whose sole power is the negative one of constraint or resistance.[30] Structures, surroundings, contexts, and environments name background settings rather than spirited actants. Expressly creative or productive forms of activity remain the preserve of humans, and should an active form of power—an agentic capacity—seem to issue from a governmental institution, a virus, an architectural structure, or an arrangement of public space, this vitality is nervously referred back to its origin in persons—to avoid the mortal sins of anthropomorphism, vitalism, or fetishism.[31]

Let me state the obvious in order to make it a problem: wherever it looks, social science tends to see only the social activity of *humans*. The agency it examines, describes, or explains is normally confined to that exercised by humans, exercised directly in the case of individuals and indirectly in the case of collective practices, institutions, or rituals. The agentic power of human-nonhuman assemblages (e.g., of artifacts, weather, conscious desires) appears as merely an effervescence of the originary agency of persons.

The actor network theory of Bruno Latour, Michel Callon, and John Law is a powerful voice contesting this anthropocentric tendency.[32] Seeking to theorize agency without presupposing the priority of human intentions, projections, or even behaviors, it refuses the conceit of a humanity that pictures itself as the wellspring of any agency deserving of the name. A branch of science studies, it affords natural-technological materialities a more active role than that possessed by surroundings, structures, or contexts. In *Aramis* (1996), for example, Bruno Latour shows how the machinic equipment (cars) and the material forces (electricity, magnets) of an experimental Parisian mass transit system enacted agential powers in an assemblage with human bodies, words, and regulations.[33] Latour's later work continues to chastise social science for reducing vital materiality to the passivity of an object: "Why don't things count? Why are social scientists afraid? Because they can't imagine roles for things other than the typical boring roles that they have in their social science journals. Firstly, things carry necessity. . . . Secondly, they are plastic and are just there to bear the human ingenuity. . . . Thirdly, [they form] . . . a simple white screen to support the differentiation of society."[34] It might be added that social scientific models of agency tend also to ignore the efficacy of materialities that, though they operate inside the human body, are neither unique to human bodies nor susceptible to the intentions of the individual, and thus are not quite "human." Examples of this include the chemical-electrical relays that enable brain activity or the various hormonal agents connected to them.

Parsing Agency

Curled up inside the idea of human agency are several related notions, including efficacy, directionality, and causality. These form what Theodor W. Adorno would have called a *constellation*: a sticky web whose "elements entwine into a more and more total context of functions."[35] Efficacy names the productivity of agency, its power to create. It points to the fact that something new has been made to appear or occur. In much of moral philosophy, in order to qualify as efficacious, an effect needs to bear a sufficiently close relationship to a preexisting plan (i.e., not be accidental or random); it needs to have come into existence through a parsimonious process, (i.e., in the fewest possible steps); and it must be of sufficient magnitude (i.e., have changed the situation is a way that matters to its participant-residents).

A distributive notion of agency does not so much reject this model of efficacy as shift its focus. Instead of honing in on a single effect, it pays attention to a linked series of them, for an unstable cascade spills out from every "single" act. To take the cascade as the unit of analysis is to locate intentions within an assemblage that always also includes their wayward offspring. An intention becomes like a pebble thrown into a pond, or an electrical current sent through a wire, or a neural network: it vibrates. Actants are "entities with uncertain boundaries, entities that hesitate, quake, and induce perplexity";[36] each one harbors a simultaneous variety of virtual modes of expression, and which subset will be actualized at any given moment is not predictable with confidence.

To focus on the cascade of becomings is not to deny intentionality or its force, but to see intentionality as less definitive of outcomes. It is to loosen the connection between efficacy and the moral subject, and bring efficacy closer to the idea of the power to make a difference, to generate changes that call for responses. This is a power possessed by an ontologically diverse range of actants. Neither does this understanding of efficacy claim that anything can happen at any time, that there is no limit to the variety of effects likely to emerge from an initial impetus. The cascade of effects, precisely because it is a *material* process, tends to follow a habitual trajectory; action in a material world tends to form grooves and follow patterns.

Thus we arrive at the second item in the constellation of agency, directionality, or the sense that agency entails a movement away from some initial condition or configuration and toward something else. In moral philosophy, this directionality is typically figured on the model of purposiveness, or as a goal-directedness linked to a mind with a capacity for choice and intention. Hegel depicted this orientedness as *Geist,* an increasingly self-conscious purposiveness in nature and history; and in at least one strand of Catholic theology, directionality is figured as an unfolding of divine intentionality. Jacques Derrida offers an alternative to such consciousness-centered conceptions of directionality in his notion of "messianicity," by which he means the *promissory* quality of a claim, image, or object. This promise of something to come is, for Derrida, the very condition of possibility of phenomenality: things appear to us only because they tantalize and hold us in suspense, alluding to a fullness that's elsewhere and a future restlessly on its way. For Derrida, this promissory note is not and can never be fully redeemed: the "straining forward toward the event" never finds relief. It entails instead a waiting "for someone or something that, in order to happen . . . must exceed and surprise every determinate anticipation."[37] Derrida argues that it is not only phenomena that obey this logic: language, and thus thought too, operate only in the promissory mode.[38]

In framing the directionality of perception and language as an unfulfillable promise, Derrida offers one way to think about an open-ended kind of directionality, a directionality delinked from the strict logic of purpose or intentionality. I myself remain agnostic about whether messianicity names the very structure of experience. Instead of the aporia of a promise continually deferred, my materialism suggests that at the heart of things is a matter-energy tending toward some settlements and not others, an impetus issuing from material assemblages whose elements include an ontological variety of actants.

The idea of impetus brings us to the third, and perhaps trickiest, item in the constellation of agency: causality. Again, the easiest way to imagine causality is as "efficient causality," where an active force is isolated as the author of a clearly identifiable effect. To understand agency as distributive is not to deny this kind of causality. George W. Bush and his advisors, for example, can be said to be the efficient cause of the post–9/11 invasion of Iraq. But if one extends the time frame or widens the angle of vision on the action, such billiard-ball causality falters and appears as only one of the operative modes of causality. Alongside singular and integral agents, one finds a more diffuse or distributed series of actants, with partial, overlapping, and conflicting degrees of power. Henri Bergson, for example, notes that, in addition to efficient causality, there is also the causality of "releasing" and "unwinding":

> The billiard-ball that strikes another determines its movement by *impelling*. The spark that explodes the powder acts by *releasing*. The gradual relaxing of the spring that makes the phonograph turn *unwinds* the melody inscribed on the cylinder. . . . What distinguishes these three cases from each other is the greater or less solidarity between the cause and the effect. . . . Only in the first case, really, does cause *explain* effect; in the others the effect is more or less given in advance, and the antecedent invoked is—in different degrees, of course—its occasion rather than its cause.[39]

Emergent causality is another way of conceiving a nonlinear, indirect causality, where instead of an effect obedient to a determinant, one finds circuits where effect and cause alternate position and redound back upon each other. If efficient causality seeks to rank the actants involved, treating some as external causes and others as dependent effects, emergent causality places the focus on the process as itself an actant, as itself in possession of degrees of agentic capacity.[40] This sense of a melting of cause and effect is also expressed in the ordinary usage of the term *agent*, which can refer both to a human subject who is the sole and original author of an effect—as in "moral agent"—and to someone or something that is the mere vehicle or passive conduit for the will of another—as in "literary agent" or "insurance agent."

If ordinary language intuits the existence of a nonlinear, nonhierarchical, non–subject-centered mode of agency, Hannah Arendt makes the point explicitly by distinguishing between cause and origin in her discussion of totalitarianism. "Causes" entail singular, stable, and masterful initiators of effects, while "sources" invoke a complex, mobile, and heteronomous enjoiner of forces:

The elements of totalitarianism form its origins if by origins we do not understand "causes." Causality, i.e., the factor of determination of a process of events in which always one event causes and can be explained by another, is probably an altogether alien and falsifying category in the realm of the historical and political sciences. Elements by themselves probably never cause anything. They become origins of events if and when they crystallize into fixed and definite forms. Then, and only then, can we trace their history backwards. The event illuminates its own past, but it can never be deduced from it.[41]

For Arendt, it is impossible to discern in advance the cause of totalitarianism. Instead, the political phenomenon is such that its sources can only be retroactively revealed. These sources are necessarily multiple, made up of elements unaffiliated before the crystallization process began. In fact, what makes the event happen is precisely the contingent coming-together—the crystallization—of a set of elements. Here Arendt's view is consonant with a distributive notion of agency. But if we look at what spurs such crystallizations for her, we see her revert to a more traditional, subject-centered perspective. Whereas the theorist of distributive agency would answer that anything could touch off the crystallization process—a sound, a last straw, a shoe, a blackout, a human intention—Arendt concludes that while the "significance" of an event can exceed "the intentions which eventually cause the crystallization," intentions are nevertheless the key to the event. Once again, human intentionality is positioned as the most important of all agential factors, the bearer of an exceptional kind of power.[42]

Shi

The history of agency as a philosophical concept is, in general, a history of attempts to mark the uniqueness of humans. Extraordinary attention has been given to a relatively small subset of human actions, that is, those whose effects appear to have been faithful to our intentions. It might be asked, then: if the raison d'être for the concept of agency is this desire to celebrate the distinctive power of humanity, why insist upon applying the concept to something like electricity, and to the assemblage of humans and nonhumans called the grid? Why not speak more modestly of the capacity of materialities to form a "culture," or to "self-organize," or to "participate" in effects?[43]

While such vocabularies are worthy of theoretical exploration, I am not ready to yield the term *agency* to humans alone, to one side of an "agency-structure debate." This is because, first, it seems to me that the rubric of material agency is a more effective counter to human exceptionalism—to, that is, the human tendency to understate the degree to which people, animals, artifacts, technologies, and elemental forces share powers and operate in dissonant conjunction with each other. And, second, no one really knows what human agency is, or what humans are doing when they are said to act. In the face of every analysis, human agency remains something of a mystery. If we don't know just how it is that human agency operates, how can we be so sure that the processes through which nonhumans make their mark are qualitatively different? A more plausible hypothesis is that the eventing of both shares a series of family resemblances, even operates isomorphically.

Humans and nonhumans live and act in open wholes that pulse with energies, only some of which are actualized at any given time and place. The point that I would like again to underline is that, in addition to the agential propensity of each member of an assemblage, there is also the agency proper to the grouping itself. Deleuze and Guattari describe this force field as a milieu, the agentic force of human-nonhuman assemblages: "Thus the living thing . . . has an exterior milieu of materials, an interior milieu of composing elements and composed substance, an intermediary milieu of membranes and limits, and an annexed milieu of energy sources and actions-perceptions."[44]

Something like this agency, which attaches to assemblages, is called *shi* in the Chinese tradition. *Shi* helps to "illuminate something that is usually difficult to capture in discourse: namely, the kind of potential that originates not in human initiative but instead results from the very disposition of things."[45] *Shi* is the style, energy, propensity, trajectory, or élan inherent to a specific arrangement of things. Originally a word used in military strategy—a good general must be able to read and then ride the *shi* of a configuration of moods, winds, historical trends, and armaments—*shi* names the dynamic force emanating from a spatiotemporal configuration rather than from any particular element within it.

But again, the *shi* of an assemblage is vibratory; it is the mood or style of an open whole where both the membership changes over time and the members themselves undergo internal alteration. Each member "possesses autonomous emergent properties which are thus capable of independent variation and therefore of being out of phase with one another in time."[46] When a member-actant, in the midst of a process of self-alteration, becomes out of sync with its (previous) self—when, if you like, it is in a "reactive power" state[47]—it can form new sets of relations within the assemblage, leaning toward a different set of allies. The members of an open whole never melt into a collective body, but instead maintain an energy potentially at odds with the *shi*. Deleuze invented the notion of "adsorbsion" to describe this part-whole relationship: adsorbsion is a gathering of elements in a way that both forms a coalition and yet preserves something of the agential impetus of each element.[48] It is because of the creative activity *within* actants that the agency of assemblages is not best described in terms of social "structures," a locution which designates a stolid whole whose efficacy resides only in its conditioning recalcitrance or capacity to obstruct.

Like the agency of individual actants, the *shi* of a milieu can be obvious or subtle. It can operate at the very threshold of human perception and detection or more violently.

A coffee house or a schoolhouse is a mobile configuration of people, insects, odors, ink, electrical flows, air currents, caffeine, tables, chairs, fluids, and sounds. Their *shi* might at one time consist in the mild and ephemeral effluence of good vibes, and at another in a more dramatic force capable of engendering a philosophical or political movement—as it did in the cafes of Sartre and Beauvoir's Paris and in the Islamist schools in Pakistan.

Responsibility and Distributive Agency

The electrical grid, by blacking out, lit up quite a lot: the shabby condition of the public-utilities infrastructure, the law-abidingness of New York City residents during the blackout, the disproportionate and accelerating consumption of energy by North Americans, and the element of unpredictability marking assemblages composed of intersecting and resonating elements. Thus spoke the grid. One might even say that it exhibited a communicative interest. It will be objected that such communication is possible only through the intermediary of humans. But is this really an objection, given that even linguistic communication necessarily entails intermediaries? My speech, for example, depends upon the graphite in my pencil, the millions of persons, dead and alive, in my Indo-European language group, not to mention the electricity in my brain and laptop computer. (The human brain, properly wired, can light up a 15-watt bulb.) Humans and nonhumans alike depend upon a "fabulously complex" set of speech prostheses.[49]

To be clear: the agency of assemblages of which I speak is not the strong kind of agency traditionally attributed exclusively to humans. To make such a claim would be simply to anthropomorphize. The contention, rather, is that if one looks closely enough, the productive power behind effects is always a collectivity. Not only is human agency always already distributed in tools, microbes, minerals, and sounds, it only emerges as agentic *by way of* a distribution into the "foreign" materialities its bearers are eager to exclude. My essay, which speaks of a radical kinship of people and things, is indebted to a rich and diverse tradition of ecological thinking, including a variety of pantheisms, vitalisms, and materialisms. Its ontological monism is a riff on the ecological theme that "all things are interconnected." There was never a time when human agency was anything other than an interfolding network of humanity and nonhumanity. What is perhaps different today is that the higher degree of infrastructural and technological complexity has rendered this harder to deny.

Does the acknowledgment of nonhuman actants relieve individual humans of the burden of being held responsible for their actions? The directors of the FirstEnergy corporation were all too eager to make this point in the Task Force Report: no one really is to blame! Though it's unlikely that the energy traders share my ontological imaginary—a kind of distributive monism where organic and inorganic possess shares of agency—I too find it hard to assign the strongest or most punitive version of moral responsibility. Autonomy and strong responsibility seem to me to be empirically false, and thus their invocation seems tinged with injustice. In emphasizing the ensemble nature of action and the interconnections between persons and things, a theory of vital materialism presents individuals as simply incapable of bearing *full* responsibility for their effects.

A distributive notion of agency does interfere with the project of blaming, but it does not thereby abandon the project of identifying (what Arendt called) the sources of harmful effects. To the contrary, such a notion broadens the range of places to look for sources. Look to long-term strings of events: to selfish intentions and energy policy that provides lucrative opportunities for energy trading while generating a tragedy of the commons; but look also to the stubborn directionality of a high-consumption social infrastructure, the unstable power of electron flows, wildfires, exurban housing pressures, and the assemblages they form; and to the psychic barriers to acknowledging the link between American energy use, American imperialism, and anti-Americanism. In each of these cases, humans and their intentions participate but are not the sole or necessarily the most profound actant in the assemblage in play.

Though it would give me great pleasure to assert that deregulation and corporate greed are the real culprits in the blackout, the most I can honestly affirm is that corporations are one of the sites where human efforts at reform can be applied, that corporate regulation is one place where intentions might initiate a cascade of effects. Perhaps the responsibility of individual humans may reside most significantly in one's response to the assemblages in which one finds oneself participating—do I attempt to extricate myself from assemblages whose trajectory is likely to do harm? Do I enter into the proximity of assemblages whose conglomerate effectivity tends toward the enactment of nobler ends?

In a world where agency is distributed, a hesitant attitude toward assigning blame becomes a virtue. But sometimes moral outrage, akin to what Plato called *thumos*, is indispensable to a democratic and just politics. The doctrine of preemptive war, the violation of human rights and the Geneva accords at Guantánamo Bay, the torture of prisoners in Iraq, the restriction of protesters at President Bush's public appearances to a "free speech zone" out of the view of television cameras, the U.S. military's policy of not keeping a count of Iraqi civilian deaths—all these are outrageous. Outrage will not and should not disappear completely, but a politics devoted too exclusively to moral condemnation and not enough to a cultivated discernment of the web of agentic capacities can do no good. A moralized politics of good and evil, of singular agents who must be made to pay for their sins—be they Osama bin Laden or George W. Bush—becomes immoral to the degree that it legitimates vengeance and elevates violence to the tool of first resort. A distributive understanding of agency, then, reinvokes the need to detach ethics from moralism, and to produce guides to action appropriate to a world of vital, cross-cutting forces.

These claims need more flesh, and even then remain contestable. Other actants, enmeshed in other assemblages, will surely offer different diagnoses of the political and its problems. It is ultimately a matter of political judgment what is more needed today: Should we acknowledge the distributive quality of agency in order to address the power of human-nonhuman assemblages and to resist a politics of blame? Or should we persist with a strategic understatement of material agency in the hopes of enhancing the accountability of specific humans?

Automatic Theologies

Surrealism and the Politics of Equality

Kate Khatib

To write about surrealism and theology seems an almost heretical act, on both sides of the equation. Like other Romantic and post-Romantic artistic movements of the late nineteenth and early twentieth centuries, surrealism owes a debt to mysticism and the occult that is already widely acknowledged, as is the occurrence of religious symbolism throughout its corpus. Were these works of art equal to the sum total of the surrealist interventions in the theological realm, there would be little more to discuss. A less cursory inspection reveals, however, that the presentation of surrealism as a fleeting moment in the artistic history of the twentieth century fails to capture the full breadth of the critical project that is at stake. Indeed, one would do better to define surrealism as a unique epistemological tradition, one that touches not only the artistic and literary world of 1920s Paris but also the revolutionary political world of 1960s Chicago, insurgent movements in Latin America, and the networked communities of the *altermondialisation* movement. If we are able to make such a claim, we can do so only on the basis of the shared project at the center of all surrealist praxis: nothing less than the total reenchantment of the world.

In fact, surrealism's central aims and activities have never been entirely devoid of spiritual tendencies; while calling for a total rebellion against the authoritarian structures of church and state, and ultimately against the concept of *any* singularity—god *or* sovereign—incarnated as a higher power, surrealist discoveries such as automatism, chance, and the Marvelous share striking aspects with the messianic notion of a return to an all but forgotten unity of the profane and the divine, the actual and the possible, and the real and the imaginary. Thus, the exploration of the relationship between the surrealist tradition and the theological one must deal with a situation far more complex than the equation of a particular moment in the history of artistic practice with a particular set of messianic categories. If lines of resonance appear between elements of the surrealist project and certain theological constructs—revelation, the miracle, and the sacred are all present in various forms in surrealist thought—one must tread lightly in this dangerous territory of making theological claims on behalf of a group of thinkers whose collective intent was the total destruction of all repressive systems, including church and state, and who, in 1925, composed an open letter declaring war on the pope; indeed, in more than seventy years of theoretical development, surrealism's adherents have never failed to continue the project of scathing theological critique because, following Marx, "the criticism of religion is the prerequisite of all criticism."[1] Exclusionism, authoritarianism, the hierarchically dominant position of the Church—the surrealists have cited all of these as justification for their belief that the greatest enemy of human imagination is organized religion, which centers on a purely phantasmagoric and fundamentally mythical and *unreachable* central body. "God is a hallucinatory projection of humankind's own misery, fear, and loathing," Don LaCoss wrote in 2001, "refracted back onto ourselves, and incorporated into our individual psyches as well as the larger society."[2]

Yet the surrealists' position as critics of organized religion should not prevent their inclusion within the field of "post-secular" studies. The surrealists may have set their cause in opposition to the traditional theological arsenal, but they also mined the rhetoric of religious criticism for useful tools, taking bits and pieces and investing them with new significance outside the archaic language of heaven and hell, forging direct links between such lofty concepts as "revelation" or "the sacred" and the concrete understanding of objects in the everyday world. The surrealists reoriented these concepts and their ultimate aims toward something that might best be described as *practical truth*. In fact, surrealism's interventions in the theological-political field throughout the first half of the twentieth century foreshadow the rethinking of religion that Hent de Vries seems to have in mind when he writes, in the introduction to *Philosophy and the Turn to Religion*:

> as a sociopolitical force and as a theoretical problem . . . the "return of religion" remains inexplicable as long as one continues naïvely to oppose religion, not only to critique, autonomy, and self-determination, to the profane and the finite, to the technological and the mechanical, to the modern and the postmodern, but also to their concrete manifestations in the secular nation-state and republicanism, the nature of international law, and the future of transnational forms of identity (individual and collective).[3]

Seeking, in the movement's earliest incarnations, to break out of the Enlightenment context of life lived by virtue of reason alone and to shed the theological baggage that weighed down all post-Enlightenment European critical and artistic practice, surrealism's adherents envisioned a world in which binary oppositions were brought to the breaking point, a world in which language was flexible enough to allow any and all concepts—theological and otherwise—to be violently ripped from their places within a traditional historical trajectory. Old notions were invested with an entirely new significance as they were recast amongst the myriad surrealist theories of knowledge and experience; chance replaced reason as the guiding logic of interpretation; and the old binaries of "sacred" and "profane" became stand-ins for largely the same categories of experience.

Surrealism's contribution to the growing discourse on political theologies and the "return of religion" is something of a post-secular *via negativa*: in seeking to represent "whole races deprived of life and liberty for the 'crime' of not believing man unfit for heaven on earth," Surrealism's critical theory unwittingly provides exactly the negation of religious tropes that is necessary if we are to begin the process of reaffirming post-secular theology.[4]

. . .

Surrealism has only recently resurfaced as an object of theoretical interest in both the academic world and the public sphere. Major exhibitions in the last ten years—at the Tate Modern Gallery in London, the Guggenheim and Metropolitan museums in New York, and the Pompidou Center in Paris, among others—coupled with the hotly debated sale of André Breton's famous personal collection in 2003,[5] have brought surrealism and its adherents back into the public eye. While the movement's investment in questions of visual and aesthetic practice cannot be ignored, the surging popularity of surrealist "art" (a somewhat dubious term, depending on whom you ask) precipitated by these recent exhibitions has little to do with the explicitly critical and epistemological methodology upon which these paintings, drawings, and objects are based. While lauding the surrealists' innovations, these exhibitions have done little more than prematurely historicize a method of political and social praxis that is still in and *of* great use today.

"Generalizations about surrealism based entirely on painters are bound to be misleading," wrote Penelope Rosemont, co-founder of the Chicago Surrealist Group, in her introduction to the 1997 collection *Surrealist Women*, "because surrealism never has been primarily a movement of painters."[6] Viewed primarily as an aesthetic movement, surrealism's innovations as a school of political thought are often overlooked or dismissed as artistic enterprise. Conspicuously absent from the walls of museums and galleries are the political declarations, the tracts, the manifestos—the voluminous programmatic and methodological writings—that charted surrealism's course at every step. It is, of course, undeniable that surrealism's adherents have invested a great deal of energy and critical praxis in questions of aesthetics, as well as in questions of the visual, the literary, spectatorship, and the revolutionary potential of a variety of artistic media; in fact, much of the movement's critical power—and its legitimacy as a form of mysticism in its own right—is derived from its close relationship with the realm of art. Yet surrealism's actual involvement with aesthetics, like its involvement with theology, has been premised, more often than not, upon the spectacular demise of art itself. In the wake of Dada, surrealism's engagement with art was really a question of anti-art, although the surrealists, unlike the dadaists, carried this dialectical demise through to its complete end, making a full cycle past the destruction of art to arrive at a point where something new—a radically new approach to artistic production—could arise like a phoenix from the ashes. In a monograph on the minimalist painter Ad Reinhardt—not a surrealist himself, but not entirely unsympathetic to surrealist sensibilities—Susan Sontag outlines the mystical movement between art and anti-art:

> As the activity of the mystic must end in a *via negativa*, a theology of God's absence, a craving for the cloud of unknowingness beyond knowledge and for the silence beyond speech, so art must tend toward anti-art, the elimination of the "subject" . . . , the substitution of chance for intention, and the pursuit of silence. . . . Therefore, art becomes estimated as something to be overthrown. A new element enters the artwork and becomes constitutive of it: the appeal (tacit or overt) for its own abolition, and, ultimately of art itself.[7]

This description holds true for surrealism as well as for minimalism: as a critical practice, surrealism carefully balances on this fine line between art and anti-art, or perhaps more legitimately, between the development of anti-art as a productive strategy and the call for the ultimate overthrow of art, whose limitations were far greater than those of the human imagination.

Were one hard-pressed, then, to establish the fundamental structure of the confluence of artists, authors, thinkers, and ideologues known collectively as the Surrealist Movement, it would not be along the lines of a theory of aesthetics. Rather, surrealism might best be described as a theory of experience, a critical—indeed, political—epistemology, whose greatest goal was to develop a radically new way of experiencing the world and of understanding the very structure of thought. From its self-acknowledged beginnings during the dark days of the First World War to its rebirth in the heated climate of late 1960s activism in the United States—Chicago Surrealism is a direct offshoot of one of the anarchist chapters of Students for a Democratic Society (SDS)—and onward to its involvement with the global *altermondialisation* movement, surrealism was, and remains today, one of the most novel attempts to clear a pathway through the underbrush of a disenchanted world, giving rise to the possibility of a more spontaneous, joyous experience of everyday reality. What André Breton, Philippe Soupault, Paul Eluard, Louis Aragon, Benjamin Peret, and their fellow adventurers uncovered in their surrealist experiments was something more than an artistic, or even rhetorical, approach to the expression of the subconscious. Surrealism is unavowedly *not* an attempt at a do-it-yourself theory of psychoanalysis, nor does it reach outside reality to grasp at some straws of the supernatural. Basing their project in reality itself, surrealism's founders put forth their collective epistemology as purely immanent, never seeking to transcend the boundaries of the human mind, only to find a new, more authentic way of experiencing the world.[8]

In 1929, Benjamin wrote that "anyone who has perceived that the writings of [the surrealist] circle are not literature but something else—demonstrations, watchwords, documents, bluffs, forgeries if you will, but at any rate, not literature—will also know, for the same reason, that the writings are concerned literally with experiences, not with theories and still less with phantasms."[9] Benjamin was, in fact, one of the first theorists—perhaps the *only* theorist—to recognize the philosophical, indeed, *revolutionary* importance of surrealist praxis, discovering in the movement's early texts a welcome antidote to the epistemological disenchantment that plagued the Neo-Kantian paradigm against which he struggled throughout his career. Surrealism played an integral role in Benjamin's later philosophy, providing an unexpected but ideal bridge between his early messianic and later materialist writings: it filled the gap Benjamin perceived between mystic and Marxist theories, a gap that had to be bridged if theory was to overcome the "temporally-limited" Kantian epistemology, which remained unable to move past its own time, forever mired in the "religious and historical blindness of the Enlightenment."[10] In opposition to the Enlightenment paradigm, Benjamin had in mind a more revolutionary system, a way of reading history against the grain of traditional temporal boundaries. Surrealism, by placing the utmost importance upon the collection of individual experiences that defined its critical *oeuvre*, was, for Benjamin, the most radical expression of human freedom that had graced European thought "since Bakunin."[11]

Particularly interesting for Benjamin was the surrealists' willingness not only to accept but actually to privilege individual experiences that were not based solely in empirical fact.[12] "The loosening of the self by intoxication"—and not only drug-induced intoxication, but religious and artistic ecstasies, as well as madness and manic fits—"is, at the same time, precisely the fruitful, living experience that allowed [the surrealists] to step outside of the charmed space of intoxication."[13] The belief that any individual's experience of the world carries within it a grain of truth was surrealism's great weapon in the battle for the reenchantment of the world, for a "new world society in which the imagination would constitute the only power," as Franklin Rosemont, co-founder of the Chicago Surrealist Group, wrote in 1973.[14] The politics of equality that defined the movement, especially in its later, more radical incarnations, dictated that the surrealist experience of the world—considered the authentic, even *redemptive* experience of the world—must be freely accessible and flexible enough to encompass the most far-reaching manifestations of human freedom. "Poetry must be made by all. Not by one," reads the dictum of Isidore Ducasse, Comte de Lautréamont and surrealist fellow traveler, a serious statement for a group of ideologues who were, by their own admission, committed to living the "poetic life."[15] If Surrealism was to welcome all the disenchanted into its secret bond, then by its very definition it had to integrate everything with which it came into contact, which meant taking intoxication and madness, dreams and delusions, and the most ignoble of actions in stride, incorporating them into the collective character of the surrealist world while maintaining each one as pure individuality. To say that the surrealist world was a world composed of fragments is not altogether untrue, but it is important to realize that these fragments form a collectivity, a unified multiplicity in which equal importance was placed upon each instance of surreality, instances that could be widely shared, transmitted across all boundaries—physical, mental, and otherwise.

The strong Communist tendencies in the surrealist politics of equality are obvious, and Walter Benjamin was quick to pick up on these glimmers of a political project at work. At the same time, what most fascinated Benjamin in the surrealist politics of equality was something more subtle, something that reached back to the problematic opposition between the divine and the profane that he had written about in his earlier texts.[16] In taking the traditional figure of the vice and turning it into a methodological principle, surrealism created a space in which human baseness could stand on an equal footing with traditional conceptions of goodness. Thinking about Dostoevsky's Stavrogin—"a Surrealist *avant la lettre*"—Benjamin wrote:

> No one else understood, as he did, how naive philistines are when they say that goodness . . . is God-inspired, but that evil stems entirely from our spontaneity, and in it we are independent and self-sufficient beings. No one else saw inspiration, as he did, in even the most ignoble actions, and precisely in them. . . . Dostoevsky's God created not only heaven and earth and man and beast, but also baseness, vengeance, cruelty. . . . That is why all these vices have a pristine vitality . . . they are perhaps not "splendid," but eternally new, "as on the first day."[17]

Not only vice and evil—themes historically associated with the fallen state of man—played a role in the surrealist epistemology, but so did human imperfection. Breton's early interest in the writings of Freud, in theories of madness, and in psychoanalysis led him to locate moments of enchantment in a variety of conditions that were usually considered to be abnormal and were certainly not included in the traditional paradigm of redemption. Surrealism turned the traditional hierarchy of redemption on its head, eschewing the blunt distinction between good and evil in favor of a more inclusive paradigm that saw the possibility of true freedom in all instances of human imperfection.

Yet this narrative of madness and intoxication may be misleading, for it often results in the perception of Surrealism as nothing more than a kind of dream logic, a psychic movement entirely divorced from everyday reality, a perception that is far from accurate. What was at stake in the surrealist explorations of the psyche was a kind of redemption that ultimately embraced the profane world instead of attempting to transcend it, a redemptive system in which the potential for reenchantment was located squarely within the reality of a base, imperfect, and sometimes even vile everyday world; this is, perhaps, the truest understanding of Benjamin's *profane illumination*. The surrealists, by their own admission, were explicitly engaged in the project of freeing the world from a system in which an enchanted (or redeemed) experience of the world is postulated but ultimately withheld, set apart from reality like a sacred object to be worshipped but never touched. The surrealist world is a world of *things*, of everyday objects, each one of which might contain within itself the potential to push experience to its limits, to explode the spheres of art, religion, politics, and even time itself. Breton was the first, Benjamin argues, to discover the "revolutionary energies" contained within "enslaved and enslaving objects," which, however closely related to the present, still belonged to times past. He had in mind things that appeared "outmoded," "destitute," like the first iron constructions, the Paris arcades, factory buildings, and old photographs, the objects of technology and science, as well as objects from the natural world.[18] In many ways, what surrealism really developed was a way of interacting with the world, with everyday objects, that allowed the magical forces contained within them to come to the fore. It was a way of treating the past *politically* rather than *historically*, not suggesting the irrelevance of history but instead demonstrating the immense force that the past exerts on any present, no matter how future-oriented it may be. Breton, Soupault, Aragon, and the others embraced the outmoded, destitute objects of an increasingly industrialized and nationalist France and thus adopted the intermingling of past and present, of dream and reality, as a methodological principle. While remaining politically grounded in the present, the Paris surrealists railed against Sartre's positing of the engaged intellectual and invoked their own central concept: *automatism*, a radical form of spontaneous experience that was intended to bring the world of intoxication into balance with the world of objects. Rather than move away from either real or imagined objects, surrealist praxis aimed to bring the two together, by way of something like a purely immanent, internal model: "a real *insulation*, thanks to which the mind, on finding itself ideally withdrawn from everything, can begin to occupy itself with its own life, in which the attained [reality] and the desired [imaginary] no longer exclude one another."[19]

The surrealists saw these encounters with the lives of objects both as an engagement with the world of created things—technological objects, buildings and structures, in short, objects constructed by man—and, at the same time, as an engagement with the natural world. According to Penelope Rosemont, "Meret Oppenheim identified the key methodological principle [of surrealism] when she pointed out in 1955 that works produced via psychic automatism 'will always remain alive and will always be revolutionary . . . because they are in organic liaison with Nature.'"[20] The surrealist appreciation of nature stems not from a view of the natural world as fixed and immutable, as defined by a set of transcendentally predetermined conditions, but rather springs forth as an irreverent, organic materialism. Instead of opposing an image of a fixed natural world to an image of the constantly shifting world of human progress—a world indicated by the scores of outmoded, forgotten objects left by the wayside—surrealism sought to bring the two together, suggesting that a redemptive potential could be unleashed if one could manage to interact with the world of human progress as one interacted with nature. What surrealism privileged in nature was its unpredictability, its close relationship with the world of chance—a concept that arose time and again in the movement's theoretical armature. The figure of the chance encounter defines the automatic experience of the world that is at the center of all surrealist production, and what is at stake in the chance encounter is a moment in which something is experienced as radically new, "eternally new," as Benjamin describes it in relation to Dostoevsky's theology of vice and as Breton demonstrates when, in *Nadja*, he describes how he was suddenly able to experience the city of Paris as though it were his first encounter, while never losing sight of the historical implications— the past lives, if one prefers—of the places and objects he encountered. Rosemont cites this liaison between surrealism and nature, between surrealism and the objects with which it engages, as the central issue at stake in the surrealist politics of equality:

> This is the very basis of surrealism as a revolutionary community: the unity of theory and practice at the highest point of tension of individual and collective creation. . . . Such a conception of life and the world, defined by audacity and readiness for change, is the opposite of all the dominant ideologies of our time. . . . All here is urgency and expectation, and the conviction that a poetics of revolt is the only way that might— just might—lead us all to something at least a little closer to earthly paradise.[21]

Understanding exactly what takes place in the chance encounter, and exactly what it means to say that these moments contain a redemptive potential that might lead one closer to realizing an "earthly paradise," is a rather perplexing problem. The notion is not entirely divorced from the logic of the divine manifestation or the articulation of the numinous element of the sacred in the language of the profane. In *The Sacred and the Profane*, Mircea Eliade introduces the compelling notion of the "hierophany," a figure that is perhaps best understood here as the way in which the sacred may be experienced in the profane world. "Man becomes aware of the sacred because it manifests itself, shows itself, as something wholly different from the profane."[22] For Eliade, this earthly appearance is tinged with the uncanny sensation of having encountered something that seems not entirely of the everyday world, a "manifestation of something of a wholly different order, a reality that does not belong to our world, in objects that are an integral part of our natural 'profane' world."[23] The notion of the hierophany is bound up with the paradoxical notion of a convergence between the mystical and the physical body that troubles classical Christian theology and runs through the work of more loosely theological thinkers like Benjamin. Surrealism, with its emphasis on the commingling of reality and imagination, and its insistence on the potential of every object to make manifest a chance encounter with something magical, seems not too distantly related to Eliade's notion, a point underscored by Paul Ricoeur when he suggests that objects imbued with a special significance in the hierophany are "transformed into something supernatural—or, to avoid using a theological term, we may say that [they are] transformed into something superreal [*suréel*], in the sense of being superefficacious while still remaining a part of common reality."[24] The theological concept of the hierophany and the surrealist chance encounter are indeed similar, even to the point of suggesting that automatism's products are so many hierophanies, manifestations of, if not the numinous element of the sacred, then at least its secular counterpart. Yet there remains a central point of divergence between these concepts in that each implies a different notion of "presence." The Eliadian hierophany suggests that the sacred may manifest itself in any object, at any time, without warning. But surrealism's central theory seems to be a step ahead: the numinous element—not God, but at least the potential for earthly redemption—*already* exists in every object; what is at stake is finding a way to experience what is already present.

· · ·

"Everything I love, everything I think and feel," André Breton wrote in 1941, "predisposes me to a particular philosophy of immanence according to which surreality would be embodied in reality itself and would be neither superior nor exterior to it."[25] Though Breton would only articulate the relationship of the real and the surreal as one of internality late in the Parisian movement's development, the concept of surrealism as a mode of communication and as a tool for the understanding of reality is present throughout the Paris years. It becomes even stronger in the later incarnations of surrealist epistemology in the 1960s and 1970s outside of France. Breton continues, "And reciprocally, too, because the container would also be the contents. What I envisage is almost a communicating vessel between the container and the contained."[26] The image of the communicating vessel is an important one, in part because it later frames and entitles one of Breton's most self-revealing texts, written in 1955, but more interestingly because it indicates a sensitivity to "the natural sweep of a merging universe, where an element from one field crosses over into the next like the elements in surrealist games" or like the flow of water and potential energy between vertical tubes in the elementary-school science experiment that shares its name with Breton's text.[27]

The image of the communicating vessel also indicates one of the most serious divergences between surrealism and the religious forms with which it shares the most attributes. Messianism—even when unorthodox and heretical—may be loosely defined as seeking to rebuild a lost unity between antinomous concepts; surrealism's aim is, conversely, not so much *unity* as *equality*. Just as in the communicating vessel, unity, or the potential for communication across the boundaries between binary oppositions, is presupposed in the surrealist world, but equality between divergent concepts and, importantly, equality in the access one may have to the beyond from within the here and now, is yet to be won. For the messianic thinkers closest to the surrealist project, Benjamin among them, human time is fallen time. Man inhabits the profane realm and is charged with the task of rediscovering the sacred in the everyday and, in some way, restoring or recreating the *analogia entis* between the divine and earthly realms. For the surrealists, by contrast, the sacred is not lost, but inaccessible. Entirely bound up with the restrictive structures of authority and used as an ontological velvet rope to keep certain objects and ideas out of the reach of everyday individuals, the sacred becomes, for the surrealists, little more than a tool of repression. Because it is indicative of a hierarchy that makes true human freedom unattainable, the sacred is transformed into exactly that which must be overcome in pursuit of true spirit, which is perhaps best known in surrealist parlance as the Marvelous.

The experience of the Marvelous is best described as the experience of a world suddenly brought into balance by a chance encounter. And the surrealists were, as Benjamin was quick to point out, not always up to the challenge of recognizing the moment in which the Marvelous flashed before them.[28] Benjamin illuminated an interesting and even crucial point: surrealism itself, if we define it not as a confluence of thinkers but solely as the experience of the Marvelous in the everyday world, becomes an object in the game of chance, an unlikely revelation, entirely profane in nature, which Breton enigmatically defines as a quasi-divine "state of grace."[29] Surrealism, then, is something that *happens*, that takes one by surprise, although, to be sure, one must already be open to the idea and *believe* in its possibility. The concept of the automatic—automation, automated, automaton—becomes far more complex and, if one dare say so, dialectical than it seems at first glance. *Auto*, derived from the Greek reflexive pronoun that roughly translates as "self," carries in our modern tongue the dual connotation of self and other, in the sense of both an internal and an external influence; more problematically, the entire word *automatic* has, in English at least, the double weight of indicating both something spontaneous, which happens without forethought, and an occurrence so mundane, so carefully studied and planned, that it is, for lack of a better phrase, entirely internalized by a droning system of rhythmic, repetitive actions.

This complexity is not usually grasped in the manifold literature on the subject; even within the literature produced by the Surrealist Movement itself, automatism and its associated concepts are used in such myriad ways, and in so many divergent contexts, both theoretical and pragmatical, that a comprehensive historical treatment of its artistic, political, and literary usage is becoming more and more difficult, even as it becomes more and more urgent. Such a history lies outside the scope of this text, but in focusing in on specifically surrealist adventures in automatism, one may at least begin to illuminate this intriguing concept. Conveniently, surrealism preserves the double connotation of the automatic, making it an ideal manifestation on which to focus.

That automatism is invoked as the central concept in what one might call surrealism's critical practice should come as no surprise. Breton himself links the "discovery" of automatism with the birth of surrealism in the first "Manifesto of Surrealism" in 1924. Five years earlier, he had already collaborated with Soupault on *The Magnetic Fields*, the first set of texts that would explicitly be classified as "*Surrealist* (and in no sense Dada) since it is the fruit of the first systematic use of automatic writing," as he told André Parinaud in 1952.[30] *The Magnetic Fields* was, in a sense, the systematized expression of surrealist automatism par excellence, a collaborative collection of texts composed entirely of "spontaneously irrupting autonomous phrases," suggestive of a state of waking dream, a hallucination, or even a revelation—words and phrases that were culled together without forethought or examination, whose collective meaning became clear only in retrospect.[31] Before the surrealists came to understand the true weight of what they had discovered, Breton had already begun to set forth what was to be a basic method for achieving automatism in his now famous "Secrets of the Magical Surrealist Art":

> After you have settled yourself in a place as favorable as possible to the concentration of your mind upon itself, have writing materials brought to you. Put yourself in as passive, or receptive a state of mind as you can. Forget about your genius, your talents, and the talents of everyone else. Keep reminding yourself that literature is one of the saddest roads that leads to everything. Write quickly, without any preconceived subject, fast enough so that you will not remember what you're writing and be tempted to reread what you have written. The first sentence will come spontaneously, so compelling is the truth that with every passing second there is a sentence unknown to our consciousness which is crying out to be heard.[32]

Automatic writing, which Breton describes in this passage and which is an explicit example of how to catalyze objective chance in a productive manner, requires a fair amount of discipline. It is neither an exercise in absurdity nor a free-form literary genre. If one engages in the practice of automatic writing, then one is charged with the difficulty of vigilantly resisting the temptation to interrupt the flow of words by reading, examining, or altering what has been set down upon the page. This is not to say that the products of automatic writing resist interpretation; however, interpretation, illumination, or learning from what is produced and from what has taken place comes only afterward, almost as an afterthought. The automatic method requires the participant to make a leap of faith in opening up completely to the unfettered flow of thoughts, having absolute faith in the process about to be undertaken. What is of importance is, as always, the actual *experience* one has during the process of automatism, *not* what one produces, for the products of truly automatic writing arise randomly rather than in the form of reflections upon a preselected topic. Just as the early surrealists could never anticipate which objects might suddenly emerge as catalysts for a chance encounter with the Marvelous while they ambled along the streets and through the arcades of 1920s Paris, the topics that arise during the process of automatic writing can never be specifically anticipated.

This last point is of crucial importance. Automatic writing, in the surrealist sense of the term, was not, is not, and was never intended to be a literary (or artistic) mode of expression. Breton and Soupault may have derived some inspiration from Rimbaud's *Alchimie du Verbe* and Lautréamont's *Les Chants du Maldoror*, but the project they undertook in the spring of 1919 was unparalleled. Automatism is nothing less than an entirely new way of looking at the world. While its products might serve as so many expressions and as works of art in their own right, it is the lived experience of the process that is of critical importance. This focus differentiates surrealist automatic practice from more literary processes such as stream of consciousness writing: the stream of consciousness method, loosely derived from the psychological writings of William James on the flow of the inner consciousness and adapted to literary practice by Édouard Dujardin, James Joyce, Virginia Woolf, and William Faulkner, among others, depends upon a radical leap outside of conventional narrative sequence and logical argumentation, and is intended to fully reflect the multiple forces—both internal and external—that might influence a character at any given time.[33] On the surface, automatism and stream of consciousness bear some resemblances; upon a deeper investigation, however, one notices that stream of consciousness proceeds from exactly the type of external reflection that automatism precludes. At base, the stream of consciousness method depends upon a mental movement that is best described as "thinking through something," and its ultimate aim is the unfettered expression of thoughts; surrealist automatism, by contrast, aims at a total revolution of the mind.

As with most unorthodox theories of praxis, surrealist automatism cannot be approached from a single direction or point of view. In one sense, automatism is wholly individualistic (even solipsistic) in character and intrinsically related to certain categories of experience that fit within a largely mystical rhetoric: the surrealist experience of the world is magical and revelatory, an unbridled state of joy, free from intention, and flowing through it is something formerly unknown that is manifestly, unquestionably true. At the same time, in its other, more practical sense, automatism has an explicitly political and universal goal: the surrealist experience of the world provides a creative framework that allows one to gain some measure of control over the language that shapes our knowledge of, and thus our experience of and interaction with, the everyday world and the objects within it. Surrealism in this second sense—which is intimately bound up with its other, more metaphysical aims—has the power to "liberate language from its utilitarian and prosaic regimentation" and in so doing "to assist in creating the revolutionary situation, which, as Marx put it, 'makes all turning back impossible.' "[34] Two moments are at work in Surrealism's critical practice, one joyous and the other revolutionary, yet both share a common goal and a common character. The Marvelous, that great surrealist watchword, is, in fact, what is always at stake in automatism. More than a by-product of a psychic experiment, more than a beautiful object, the Marvelous is an active mode of experiencing the world. In its own way, every surrealist experience is what we might call *self-revelatory*, its goal being not so much a greater understanding of the self (this would be, for example, the goal of something like stream of consciousness), but rather a "profane illumination," by which we are to understand an inspiration that comes from within, that is drawn from deep within the memories generated by lived experiences, called forth when human intentionality gives way to the logic of chance. Unlike automatism's historical predecessors—prophets, psychics, and psychoanalysts—this automatically emerging revelatory moment draws nothing from outside everyday reality as it is experienced by the human psyche; there is no "beyond," no higher power from whom a divine, prophetic word is communicated, filtered down through a human medium.[35] Rather, surrealism furnishes its own concept of the sacred in the form of the Marvelous and locates it in the workings of the mind itself, looking toward everyday language as the privileged site from which to access "a moment in which . . . antinomies no longer have any meaning, in which knowledge completely takes hold of things, in which language is not speech, but reality itself, yet without ceasing to be the proper reality of language."[36]

That automatic writing has, over time, become the primary expression of surrealist automatism is no coincidence, then. Language had been the site of the surrealists' first discovery of the "magical aspect of things" that would so entrance Benjamin, as it would entrance all of surrealism's fellow travelers. "Surrealists became well aware," Maurice Blanchot writes in his 1949 reflections on the movement, "of the strange nature of words: they saw that words have their own spontaneity . . . [they] understand, moreover, that language is not an inert thing: it has a life of its own, and a latent power that escapes us."[37] Automatism is a way of harnessing a latent, productive power of language that continually eludes the grasp of the mind in the disenchanted world. It is, perhaps, no great surprise that Benjamin would become so inspired by the surrealist project: he saw this sort of experimentation with language as a way of closing the gap between words and concepts, between the disassociated graphical marks upon a page and the real and concrete objects to which they referred. "Language seemed itself only where sound and image, image and sound, interpenetrated with automatic precision and such felicity that no chink was left for the penny-in-the-slot called 'meaning,'" he writes in "Surrealism."[38] In Benjamin's interpretation of surrealist praxis, language as a way of achieving an absolute (surreal) experience—a way of getting at the essence of things—rather than a tool to aid in the communication of meanings or theories.

Of course, Benjamin's interpretation of surrealist praxis is just that: an interpretation. Though it remains one of the most salient, most intuitive investigations of surrealism to date, it falls short of the mark in its understanding of the central goal of automatic practice. True, surrealist automatism did aim to abolish the line that separates the real from the imaginary; Breton's philosophy of immanence, defined by the image of the communicating vessels, could hardly have had anything less as its object. But the surrealists would not have been likely to agree that their approach to language was in any way intended to abolish meaning—the total destruction of all meaning is more dadaist in character than it is surrealist. It is crucial to realize that the decades-long language game that ensued after the "discovery" of automatism has a practical, everyday application. Breton, Soupault, Aragon, Peret, and later the Rosemonts, following in the footsteps of Lautréamont, realized that poetry—and here we mean something more than the setting down of rhyme upon a page—had to have *practical truth* as its goal: Lautréamont charged those who followed him with the task of expanding poetry in such a way that it could enunciate the relationships between primary epistemological principles and the secondary truths of everyday life.[39] If the poetic endeavors that the surrealists undertook had to have practical truth as their goal, and if, as Penelope Rosemont and others have suggested, surrealism can be seen as a revolutionary form of community, then meaning must be of the utmost importance in the surrealist world, rather than something to be overcome or cast away. Instead, what becomes apparent in surrealism's engagements with the linguistic field is a desire to recast language as flexible enough to allow words to cease to be inextricably tied to just *one, historically determined* meaning. After all, surrealism is as much about leaving a door always open for novelty as it is about anything else: if one proceeds always according to the logic of chance, as the surrealists tried to do, even if they were not always successful, then anything could happen—would happen, in fact—at any point, and without warning.

Nowhere is this relationship between language, poetry, and surrealism better outlined than in Breton's "An Introduction to the Discourse on the Paucity of Reality." Written in 1924 and published in pamphlet form in 1927, this little-known text is one of Breton's most prescient investigations into the political position of language in everyday reality. First explaining, then lamenting the "immutable reality" to which language is doomed to refer, he writes that words "deserve to have another decisive function. . . . I believe it is not too late to recoil from this deception, inherent in the words we have thus far used so badly."[40] Breton's intention was to harness the poetic power of automatism—this text was composed just months before the publication of the first "Manifesto," where he would outline the productive process of automatism for the first time—by "throwing disorder into this order of words, to attack murderously this obvious aspect of things. . . . Language can and should be torn from this servitude."[41] The desire to rescue language from its dependency upon an immutable reality did not, however, play out as a movement away from meaning; rather, as things turned out, rescuing language meant allowing more and more meanings to develop for the simplest combinations of words. In effect, it meant leaving behind interpretation in favor of acceptance:

> A rather dishonest person one day, in a note contained in an anthology, made a list of some of the images presented to us in the work of one of our greatest living poets. It read:
>> "The next day of the caterpillar dressed for the ball" . . . meaning "butterfly."
>> "Breast of crystal" . . . meaning "carafe."

Etc.

No, indeed, sir. *It means nothing of the kind.* Put your butterfly back in its carafe. You may be sure that Saint-Pol-Roux said exactly what he meant.[42]

. . .

"The surrealist intervention on the poetic plane," Franklin Rosemont wrote in 1973:

> consists of short-circuiting the whole gamut of rationalizations (aesthetic, moral, etc.) to express the real functioning of thought, thereby liberating images of concrete irrationality in poetry that escapes the clutches of realistic appearances, breaks through the meshes of everyday action, and, breathing the flames of inspiration and revolt in all directions at once, calls for and prepares the dictatorship of the imagination.[43]

In claiming, not just to bring together figures of the actual and the possible on a rhetorical level, but actually to bring the imaginary to bear on everyday reality in a way that is both spontaneous and redemptive, surrealism makes a move that is not without glimmers of a covertly theological project intimately tied up with its overtly political project of establishing at least some small part of heaven on earth. The "state of grace" that Breton saw as the goal of all surrealistic endeavor is, in fact, a point at which the equality between dialectical oppositions reigns supreme: "Here at last . . . the world of nature and things makes direct contact with the human being who is again in the fullest sense spontaneous and natural. Here at last is the true communion and the true knowledge, chance mastered and recognized, the mystery now a friend, and helpful."[44]

The surrealist politics of equality, then, is dependent upon a notion of communicability that transcends all human boundaries while allowing the distinctions between concepts to continue to exist (albeit in a more lackadaisical fashion). It was exactly this fluidity between concepts, between the opposing forces of the real/imaginary, profane/sacred, disenchanted/reenchanted dialectics that made the surrealist project so attractive to thinkers, like Benjamin, with some stake in the development of a radical political epistemology. In many respects, the artistic success of the by-products of surrealist automatism is unfortunate, because it has obscured the political project that is fundamentally at stake in surrealist methodology, leading to the movement's canonization within the halls of great writers, poets, and painters and to the belief that automatism is nothing more than a method for the creation of sublime objects. Surrealism's aim was, however, and still is something more egalitarian. In 1933, Breton writes:

> Surrealism's achievement is to have proclaimed that all . . . humans are completely equal in relation to the subliminal message [for lack of a better term, the secular numinous element] and to have maintained constantly that this message is a com-

mon heritage of which we each have only to claim our share, and which must at all costs soon cease to be seen as the preserve of the few. Every man and every woman deserves the personal conviction that they, themselves can, by right, have recourse at will to this language which is not in any way supernatural, and is the vehicle, for each and every one of us, *of revelation*.[45]

Perhaps it is the case, as Anne Olsen suggested in 2001, that there is nothing "sacred" in surrealism, that the Marvelous—ostensibly surrealism's secular version of the sacred— "expresses all that is beautiful, passionate, and liberating according to each individual's imagination . . . [while] what is deemed 'sacred' is sanctified and imposed upon us."[46] One cannot, should not, and would never want to link surrealism to the canon of religious interpretations of profane experience. Yet at the same time it becomes increasingly clear that there is something theological at work in the automatic moment, however irreligious, however base and profane, it may be. Perhaps it is going too far to call the surrealist revelation, the point at which everyday life becomes "a life worth living," an automatic theology, in the sense of a new, suddenly emergent redemptive moment, but it is at least, picking up again on Eliade's powerful notion, an automatic hierophany, the sudden and profane manifestation of something more, something "superreal," in the objects of the everyday world. Benjamin once again provides interpretive guidance, this time with his notion of a dialectical time, inspired by his own interpretation of Judaic messianic theory: every present moment is imbued with a redemptive potential, every second is, famously, the "strait gate through which the Messiah might enter."[47] Surrealism, however, harbors no such dreams of gods or messiahs: a total revolution is what is at stake, and at every moment each individual holds the power to call forth this universal revolt in an encounter with chance.

Theoscopy

Transparency, Omnipotence, and Modernity

Stefanos Geroulanos

To be forever seen without seeing back is to succumb to a mercy and grace carved in religious force, to walk in fear and faith of a tremendous power one cannot face. It is to live a paranoid existence of nakedness before a God who is all-seeing, hence omniscient and omnipotent, and who accordingly metes out a social experience and a knowledge of one-self and one's history that is based on this awareness of being seen. I will name this condition *theoscopy*. Widespread from patristic texts to contemporary media artifacts and works of social theory, theoscopy involves the establishment of a site of perfect vision in the political, a site endowed with transcendental, theological power, which then turns into the sovereign structuring principle of the theologico-political.[1] Reconstructing the world around an axis in which visual, theological, and political problematics intermesh, theoscopy orients knowledge and history to an ethics and a social ideal of transparency before this gaze. Because it radicalizes constant imbalance between seeing and being seen into an absolute difference in which every man becomes entirely visible to what watches him, theoscopy enforces a political theology of the gaze that survives proclamations of a death of God in modernity.

The religious tradition itself offers a long series of considerations and interpretations of theoscopy. Citing Paul's letter to the Hebrews, for example, Augustine writes: "Indeed, Lord, to your eyes, the abyss of human consciousness is naked. What could be hidden within me, even if I were unwilling to confess it to you? I would be hiding from myself, not myself from you."[2] Augustine compares this penetrative divine gaze (which, a propos, sees through sin) to his own torment over the indiscernability of the shape and materiality of God—God who sees him, but who is visible, recognizable, and present to him *only insofar as* He remains perpetually unseen and insufficiently imagined by him.[3] More

633

recently, in an attempt to explain why the invisible and unavailable Creator-God served, in the Middle Ages, as a guarantor of truth and necessity against the potentially debilitating force of contingency in human affairs, Niklas Luhmann imputes to Him (whom he describes as no more than a "Judeo-Christian invention") the status of quintessential second-order observer, one who can create and observe without being affected by His creation:

> God is the quintessential observer who created everything, who continually re-creates . . . everything in the form of the *creatio continua*, who sees everything and knows everything. . . . The attribution of personality and power serve to establish Him as the observer of the entire world. . . . In this process God provides us the chance to observe Him, even though only as "Deus absconditus," as an unobservable God.[4]

Referencing Nicholas of Cusa, Luhmann treats divine observation as an explanation of medieval man's limited capacity to observe and create. Because of God's unobservable observation, His ability to create and to know the world is of an entirely other order than man's. What appears to man as contingent is in fact a necessity imposed by God, the observer for whom there are no limitations and no necessity.

If Luhmann's concept of observation corroborates a creative God, what happens once the *Deus absconditus* becomes evidence of God's inexistence rather than of His creativity? How does the structure of spectatorship change, and how does it continue to affect the theologico-political once society and social theory have done away with the centrality and authority of God? First, a series of texts crucial to the history of secularization maintained the premise of the self's construction through its relation to an imputed yet ever-present spectator.[5] In maintaining the ideality of this spectator and the failure of the seen subject to fill the void left behind by God's death, these texts treat the site of seeing as sovereign over the subject, as at once human and superhuman. Similarly, the transparency of the subject, once intimately connected in Catholicism with the purity of the soul before God (and thus with confession), survives as a social and ethical ideal of citizenship and community, reinforcing the dependency of the self on its visibility.[6]

Recent nonreligious theories of society and subjectivity have once again brought up this connection between optics and theology.[7] In the present essay I will trace the force of *theoscopy* in two such theories—the accounts of vision and modern power in Michel Foucault and Guy Debord.[8] As I will show, these two thinkers treat the modern economies of spectatorship and force in mutually constitutive terms on the basis of an analogy with older, theologically based forms of sociopolitical organization.[9] I will focus on their responses to two problems: (1) the emergence of modernity out of a religious and theologically conceived past; and (2) the significance of visually coded interpersonal relationships as bearers of that past. In these responses we will see how and why a theologically inflected concept of vision returns to organize modern everyday life, how theoscopy is reconstructed in a society devoid of God.

Foucault and Debord? Overtures

The philosophical universes, political reference points, and intellectual genealogies of Foucault and Debord scarcely overlap.[10] Debord never mentioned Foucault, in whom he undoubtedly saw a conformist academic. Foucault rejected Debord as philosophically obsolete:

> Our society is one not of spectacle, but of surveillance; under the surface of images, one invests bodies in depth; behind the great abstraction of exchange, there continues the meticulous, concrete training of useful forces; . . . it is not that the beautiful totality of the individual is amputated, repressed, altered by our social order, it is rather that the individual is carefully fabricated in it, according to a whole technique of forces and bodies. . . . We are neither in the amphitheatre, nor on the stage, but in the panoptic machine, invested by its effects of power, which we bring to ourselves since we are part of its mechanism.[11]

Nonetheless, there are considerable points of theoretical congruence, which also help explain the analogous intellectual roles each of them had within their respective philosophical traditions.[12]

First, both Foucault and Debord worked in and against philosophico-political contexts that they perceived as overdetermined and antiquated. Within and against these backgrounds, both authors attempted to explain modernity through analyses that emphasize the dynamics and status of power over its totalizing impetus.[13] Objecting to Sartrean, Marxist, and psychoanalytic accounts of power, Foucault perceived his work as originating in phenomenology, history of science, and structuralism. For him, power, at once constructive and narcotic, is not *per se* totalizing (or "evil"), yet in its reorganization of society it is always able to become so and always seeks to engage society as a whole.[14] Debord's adventures in Western Marxism began with the recognition of Soviet failure (for which he relied on Socialisme ou barbarie, Georg Lukács, and Henri Lefebvre[15]), retaining certain teachings in aesthetics and politics and rejecting the contemporary left as insufficient or stupid.[16] Debord wrote almost obsessively of totality and unity, though he rejected its Western Marxist treatments: he understood spectacular society to be hopelessly divided, broken down, and reunited only in the falsehood of the spectacle itself, a totality as boundless as it is all-encompassing, destructive, and mystifying.[17]

Second, both Foucault and Debord granted the gaze, and the visual realm in general, an imperious position in this approach to power and totality. For both, as Martin Jay has shown, just as the visual realm forms a blueprint for analyses of power, so it is rife with problematic formulations and often sickening consequences.[18] Foucault made the connection as early as his 1963 *Birth of the Clinic,* recognizing the clinical gaze's management of near-absolute power and medical knowledge through "a logical armature, which exorcised from the outset the naïveté of an unprepared empiricism."[19] Debord's understanding of a "social relationship mediated by images" as attacking "directly lived reality" dates to his writings from the late 1950s,[20] and returns strongly in his 1967 *Society of the Spectacle,* which presents the spectacle as the fundamental socioeconomic form and medium of modernity.[21] Commentators have noted that the spectacle, whether as a term of social analysis or as a rhetorical element, is so central, even voracious, in Debord's writing that it faces two dangers: (1) the failure to distinguish between various "spectacles" (cinema, advertising, etc.) and "the spectacle" as socioeconomic totality,[22] and (2) the potential collapse of "the spectacle" into no more than a catchword.[23] This presentation situates the gaze at once as a powerless faculty (for it can in no way overcome the near omnipotence of the spectacle) and as the site of all sensation in modern life, the site that demonstrates the limits of a modernity of the spectacle.

A third and often underappreciated shared element is Foucault's and Debord's respect for and reliance on a theological origin of modern power—a sort of allegory, mimetic history, and structural analogy between modern power and the divine. As I will try to show, theirs are not modernities of secularization but accounts that reconstruct theological structures in contemporary society, giving them not only metaphorical but paradigmatic significance.

Foucault, Scopic Asymmetry, and Theoscopy

From its emergence as a central category in Foucault's thought during the early 1970s, power contained a certain theological dimension, which it often occluded as an awkward shadow. It is indicative (and quite remarkable), for example, that Foucault's essays and interviews on panopticism resist religious allegorization and explicit theological interpretation of the panoptic machine and its effects.[24] At least until his 1979 essay "Governmentality,"[25] and despite his long and serious treatment of religious themes,[26] not one of Foucault's works demonstrates his "uncanny ability to discern history and contingency where others see nature and necessity" with regard to the theological dimensions of such "nature and necessity."[27]

While an unwillingness explicitly to present theology as prowling in the realms of power might be explained by Foucault's focus on the Enlightenment, it is important to appreciate his project of a negative anthropology as also one of negative theology.[28] Religion provided him with (often mostly Christian[29]) categories and concepts, which fundamentally affected his fascination with the historical construction of possibilities and forms of transcendence. "The sacred," for example, functions in his thought as both a modality of power and a quasi-theological category: without signifying (or denying) divine presence, it points to a historicized philosophical capacity or strategy that produces and formulates transcendence in a society or culture.

Foucault's link of negative anthropology to religious concerns is discernable from early on: before explicitly advancing a theory of power, Foucault connected man and God, qua absolutes, in their deaths amidst the order of things: "Nietzsche rediscovered the point at which man and God belong to one another, at which the death of the second is synonymous with the disappearance of the first, and at which the promise of the superman signifies first and foremost the imminence of the death of man."[30] A space for questioning opens up with Foucault's evaluation of tensions in the "order of man," just as another does with his problematization of *transparency, finitude,* and *self-knowledge* in this context.

More evocative still is the category of *power*, which, though not strictly transcendental, cannot be reduced to immanence or pinned to its endless empirical permutations. In his introduction to panopticism, echoing not only Jeremy Bentham but also Etienne de la Boétie, Foucault asks: "Is it not somewhat excessive to derive such power from the petty machinations of surveillance? How could *they* achieve effects of such scope?"[31] He then defines power: "We must cease once and for all to describe the effects of power in negative terms: it 'excludes,' it 'represses,' it 'censors,' it 'abstracts,' it 'masks,' it 'conceals.' In fact, power produces."[32] Power can be religious in three ways:

1. Certain kinds of power are strictly religious (e.g., Christian pastoral power and its development into a sociopolitical force);[33]
2. Within a certain group or society, power can be inflected religiously (e.g., in the addition of a parish church to a panoptic factory);[34]
3. Power, in modernity, may have a fundamentally religious basis.

I will refrain from demonstrating the first two and concentrate on the last, whose demonstration is more complicated and whose implications reach further. I will read Foucault's treatment of modern power through four types of theological connection, namely, *historical derivation, structural isomorphism, self-referential knowledge,* and *paradigmaticity.*

Derivation

Characteristic of both Max Weber's *Protestant Ethic and the Logic of Capitalism* and Carl Schmitt's *Political Theology* (though Schmitt did not stop there[35]), *derivation* implies that the organization and regulation of the political domain in modernity follows from a historically anterior theological set of concepts and practices. Foucault openly relies on such a model: "The modern Western state has integrated into a new political shape an old power technique that originated in Christian institutions."[36] On the one hand, power, in its very transcendental basis, does not exactly have a history, much less a history that begins in the Christian Middle Ages. On the other hand, the modern *apparatus* of political, penitentiary, and disciplinary power, as described in *Discipline and Punish*, begins with what, in homage to Ernst Kantorowicz, Foucault calls "the least body of the condemned man."[37] It is out of Kantorowicz's era of a political theology of royalty and its Christological theme of bi-corporeality that the modern construction of the "soul" arises. This, for Foucault, led to a modern historical reality of the soul, which, "unlike the soul represented by Christian theology, is not born in sin and subject to punishment, but is born rather out of methods of punishment, supervision, and constraint."[38] Out of a Christian and Christomimetic model of subjectivity arises a machine of power that enforces a subjectivity at once different from and consequent to this original model. Hence the move from the ritual spectacle of "the least body of the condemned" through the surveillant society of the carceral. Similarly, modern political rationality explicitly relies on the same religious past; for Foucault, the connection between pastoral power and reason of state is one of analogy and latency: "Political rationality has grown and imposed itself all throughout the history of Western societies. It first took its stand on the idea of pastoral power, then on that of reason of state."[39]

Structural Isomorphism

Schmitt writes of a structural analogy between the theological and the political realms. In Foucault, one could write instead of a structural isomorphism of modalities of power.[40] As is well known, Foucault postulates an "infinite," nonessentialist, and certainly nonempirical concept of power, which cannot be reduced to (or really distinguished from) the technological, architectural, mechanical, legal, and social dimensions that are, in a sense, its ways of shaping the subject.[41] Foucault's abstraction of power relations into "the objectivizing of the subject in . . . 'dividing practices'" immediately invokes an intersubjective space of regulation.[42] The subject exists in such a space, framed by the various operations that subject it, operations that, whatever their specific mechanics, are irreducibly visual and linguistic. Thus religiously inflected and divisive practices such as the pastoral are no different from modalities of power that are not fundamentally religious. While religious *frameworks* "disappear in part" following the Enlightenment,[43] Foucault demonstrates that certain *problematics* persist—for example, in a government's relation to the pastoral, which becomes a question of "people management" in a mode of shepherdhood. Though religious, this thematic is not limited to Christianity but provides a theoretical framework for ethical, political, and even aesthetic aspects of the rule over people and the direction of their lives, a rule that for him extends from Plato and early Christianity to the welfare state.[44]

This spiritual and theological isomorphism also underlies Foucault's rather strange sympathy for the Iranian Revolution—whose clerical claims he saw as somewhat incidental and not basic to the character of the revolt.[45] Here, the religious components of power, among which one may count its "infinite," transcendental dimensions, its historically determined religious practices, and its occasional expression in religious forces (as in Iran), become significant insofar as they help explain the pervasiveness of the theoretical isomorphism and suggest that it is impossible for power to exist strictly outside of, and in a different structural formation from, religious conceptualization and practice.

Self-Reflexive Knowledge

Other theologically inflected categories survive in Foucault's thought due to his approach to man as a construct of subjectivist self-knowledge, his insistence on the centrality of knowledge and self-knowledge in the definition of man. But man's knowledge of himself and the world, as Foucault repeatedly explains, constructs and helps to formulate both *man's conception of himself* in the world and his history/development in it—in his modern separation from an order of things, a separation that inversely created an "order of man."[46] This ensued in a "silencing" of a unified "order of discourse,"[47] because man turned to construct and know himself by contrast to the nonhuman rest of the world. The religious aspect emerges with self-referential knowledge (Foucault's "folding of representation back unto itself"[48] and his distancing of man from this "fold"), that is, in man's understanding of this separation. Above all, this happens because "Western discourse" cannot avoid its own relation to the past; it is tied to a self-construction, concurrent with the "death of God," through which it mimetically reorganizes its religiously constituted past.[49] This concurrence and mimetic self-construction helps foreground two concepts pertaining to knowledge in "the order of things" in a manner that is tied to both self-knowledge and religious influence. These concepts are *finitude* and *transparency*.

The analytic of finitude becomes a question with the rise of man as both "object of knowledge and subject who knows";[50] it addresses existential as well as epistemological finitude—the limits of "my life" and "my knowledge."[51] But the call to self-knowledge at this stage inverts the very basis of finitude: "Heralded in positivity, man's finitude is outlined in the paradoxical form of the *endless*; rather than the rigor of a limitation, it indicates the monotony of a journey which, though it probably has no end, is nevertheless perhaps not without *hope*."[52] If we accept the significance of derivation and structural isomorphism, then the secularization of a Judeo-Christian thematic of a life in aspiration and a salvation that lies beyond what is possible in the present can only be incomplete. Man's self-conception takes upon it permanence, hope, and the "paradoxical" inversion of finitude into a fantasy of a collective overcoming of death: it admits to no less than the impossibility of its quest for a pure anthropomorphism, the insertion of a religious address of finitude into the humanist defeat of religion.

Transparency also reappeared as a problem once the single order of discourse breaks down: "There was no longer any transparency between the order of things and the representations that one could have of them; things were folded somehow into their own thickness and onto a demand exterior to representation. It is for this reason that languages with their history, life with its organization and its autonomy, and work with its own capacity for production appeared."[53] Sidestepping the religious and secular philosophical problem of transparency (in Jansenism, Rousseau, Lukács, etc.), Foucault defines modernity as involving the breakdown of a transparent order of things and representations, man and the world of signs. In the breakdown of this order, transparency became a problem: its lack and its recognition as a lack denote man's inability to regulate properly his relation to things. As such a problem, transparency became a nostalgia for a world in which God, not yet dead, guaranteed the interaction between men and things, a fantasy that man should break through the new separation indicative of the limits of the order of man. As we shall see, transparency returns in Foucault's study of power as a social and ethical ideal of panopticism.

As knowledge became a fundamental aspect of Foucault's later conceptualization of power and the regulation of subjectivity, territory, and interactions, the two (religiously conversant) elements of finitude and transparency, which underpinned knowledge, maintained the theological premise of aspects and structures of power. Foucault articulates this reinvestment in the form of a question and an invocation, a camouflaged assertion: "What Great Observer will produce the methodology of examination for the human sciences?"[54] The demand for transparency and the impossibility of an admission of finitude pure and simple serve to elide both God and man: only a Baconian "Great Observer" will produce the methodology for a pure examination for the human sciences. Thus not only is the seemingly secular present shown to be isomorphic to and historically derivative of the political and social forms of the religious past, but man understands himself in a way that foregrounds, perpetuates, and religiously intones central theological themes that relate him to such a "Great Observer"—one that cannot be God (who is dead) and that cannot be a mere subject of observation and control, a mere man.

But whence the need for a "Great Observer"? The answer is brought out in Foucault's conception of the Panopticon as a paradigm for modernity. Bentham's device typifies power's production of reality as "the diagram of a mechanism of power reduced to its ideal form";[55] it is "a marvelous machine which . . . produces homogeneous effects of power." Through it:

one can speak of the formation of a disciplinary [*surveillante*] society in this movement that stretches from the enclosed disciplines, a sort of social "quarantine," to an indefinitely generalizable mechanism of "panopticism." Not because the disciplinary [*surveillant*] modality of power has replaced all the others; but because it has infiltrated the others, sometimes undermining them, but serving as an intermediary between them, linking them together, extending them and above all making it possible to bring the effects of power to the most minute and distant elements. It assures an infinitesimal distribution of power relations.[56]

Even if in their everyday life people do not *literally* and continually live under a watchful eye, they share these effects. At least four reasons account for the ubiquity of the power apparatus and turn it into the central paradigm of Foucault's disciplinary conception of power:

1. Scopic asymmetry;[57]
2. The subsumption, by the prisoner, of the ethic of visibility and transparency that "assures the automatic functioning of power";[58]
3. Social moralization" of the prisoner or subject;[59] and
4. A more general process of homogenization and disindividuation.[60]

These four categories are significant for several reasons, not least because they explain the connections between power/knowledge, power/gaze, and power/ethics, some of which lead in turn to the close connection between power, theology, and the gaze under the panoptic umbrella. In many ways they codify Foucault's attentiveness to the persistence of religion as ground (derivation, structural isomorphism, etc.) in the modern period— and locate this interest solidly within the question of panopticism. The Panopticon contains allusions to religious architecture and institutions,[61] analogies to a theologically conceived society in general, and crucial aspects that bring up the problematic of theoscopy.

The most important aspect of the Panopticon is *scopic asymmetry*. Scopic asymmetry encodes the power differend in the relation between two parties, one seeing and one seen. Here, it postulates that the prisoner is incapable of knowing when, how, by whom, and in what manner he can be observed. While the prisoner is entirely transparent to his observer, he cannot see back. As a result, he is made to believe that a gaze is always watching, watching him; as Foucault describes, he is also pushed to internalize that gaze. In other words, a gaze that can see every prisoner at once without being seen and that can be imputed to a presence (or even an absence) in the tower transforms the power imbalance built into spectatorship into an absolute foundation for disciplining the seen. Moreover, vision does not require an active or even an actual spectator, a body with eyes. Thus the imputed gaze becomes a technology that supplants the human observer or spy.[62] Power can be constantly and unfailingly enforced without any need for the actual or continuous presence of a guard in the tower; it acquires a ethical control over the prisoner's behavior.[63]

Lacking evidence of the presence of a supervisor, the subject turns a *visual* unavailability into an *epistemological* one. He assumes a spectatorial presence that is at once empirical and transcendental: empirical, because of the very real threat of punishment;

transcendental, because of its omnipotence and near-divine force.[64] And what acquires divine status (in a very real sense) is not the person in the tower but the very possibility of a person looking from the tower—in other words, the very center of the structure.[65] The architecturalized omnipotent gaze formalizes the all-seeing God, at once present and absent, and reinscribes him as a Great Observer: whether it is the whole of society or nobody that is watching, the Great Observer reappears, served by the precarious yet unconfirmed absence of any real gaze. The epistemological unavailability, the absence, of a divine observer confirms his existence.

A moral dimension to this argument points to the imposition of society's ethic and morality on the prisoner/subject. Foucault points to Bentham's postulate that the population of the entire town where the prison is built could take turns in the tower, thereby enforcing a morality common to the society that stands outside the Panopticon and profits from it.[66] The production of a religiously inspired morality, fueled by the omnipotence in the tower, follows from there: it is a local God, one that "agrees" with the jailer's world, that imposes the constraints of this local morality. Incarceration has precisely these effects: it ties a subject to a community in a manner that is conceptually as well as epistemologically inaccessible to this subject but involves the self-idealization of this community. The presence and power of the society in and around the prison, and the resulting reflexive and self-reflexive effect, serves precisely to produce morality. The moral implications of the Panopticon, of a society watching and imposing, also involve a connection to questions of the divine—for if God is to exist only insofar as he is epistemologically conceived and determined, then a local, indeed imputed God is reinscribed as the Great Observer.[67] In an ostensibly secularized realm, the indiscernible divine reappears in more than a merely aporetic form: as the ground of contemporary discourse, as the force behind the construction and homogenization of individuals, as the Great Observer, as the operator of human self-knowledge, as the constitutive nucleus of modern power.[68]

Debord, Religion, Time, and the Effusive Passivity of the Gaze

Guy Debord's engagement with religion was less extensive than Foucault's; there is, to date, no extended discussion of the religious thematics in Debord.[69] The occasional references to religious movements in the journals *Potlatch* and *Internationale Situationniste* are too occasional to form a consistent argument.[70] In fact, the best-known religious incident involving Debord's circle concerned a man who disguised himself as a Dominican priest during Easter Mass at Notre-Dame in 1950, to announce God's death before hundreds of shocked worshippers.[71]

Nonetheless, a religious dimension to the spectacle not only exists but is significant to an understanding of even the general aspects of Debord's thought.[72] Debord writes of the realm of the sacred and the problems of religion throughout *Society of the Spectacle*—

implicitly evoking an anthropological line from Lévy-Bruehl through Mauss up to Bataille.[73] Not only is the spectacle to be understood as "a specious form of the sacred,"[74] but Debord goes so far as to ignore the regressive and repressive tendencies in medieval millenarian cults and to argue for an analogy between modern revolutionary hopes and "the religious passion of millenarianism":

> Millenarianism, the expression of a revolutionary class struggle speaking the language of religion for the last time, was already a modern revolutionary tendency, lacking only the consciousness of *being historical and nothing more*. The millenarians were doomed to defeat because they could not recognize revolution as their own handiwork. The fact that they made their action conditional upon an external sign of God's will was a translation onto the level of thought of the tendency of insurgent peasants to follow outside leaders.[75]

Debord goes on to argue that the recoding of religious themes, institutions, and theologemes forms a fundamental part of modern society, even where "the most advanced forms of commodity consumption have seemingly broadened the panoply of roles and objects available to choose from."[76] Family and religion, "still the chief mechanism for the passing on of class power," not only survive, but their "vestiges . . . and thus too the vestiges of the moral repression that these institutions ensure, can now be seamlessly combined with the rhetorical advocacy of pleasure *in this life*. The life in question is after all produced solely as a form of pseudo-gratification which still embodies repression."[77] In other words, religion is significant both because it serves class (and spectacular) domination and because it forms an irreducible historical subtext to contemporary banalization and repression.[78] Such repression merely moves pseudogratification from the paradise it imagines to life in the present.[79]

Debord's most significant reference to religion comes at the opening of the book in a citation of Ludwig Feuerbach's preface to the second edition of *The Essence of Christianity*: "And undoubtedly our present era . . . favors an image over the thing it denotes, the copy over the original, representation over reality, appearance over existence. . . . That which is sacred for [the present era] is the illusion, while truth is profane. Worse, the sacred swells as truth decreases and illusion increases, so that the highest degree of illusion comes to be the highest degree of sacredness."[80] It is understandable that Debord uses for his exergue a quotation about truth and illusion—what surprises is the formulation of sacredness and profanity. Are we to understand that the spectacle, besides being the social, political, and economic ground of the contemporary world, a totality at once falsely united and infinitely divided,[81] is grounded in theological formulations at the same time that it forms the world's most profane moment? Why does Debord use this rhetoric of sacredness, apocalypse, and illusion in a theory propounding the spectacularization of commodity capitalism and the reduction to representation of "all that was once directly lived"?[82] Anselm Jappe writes that, for Debord:

> The spectacle is the heir of religion . . . the old religion projected man's own power into the heavens where it took on the appearance of a god opposed to man, a foreign entity. The spectacle performs the same operation on earth. The greater the power that man attributed to gods of his own creation, the more powerless he himself felt; humanity behaves similarly with respect to powers that it has created and allowed to escape and that now "reveal themselves to us in full force."[83]

While I am not convinced by Jappe's heavens/earth dichotomy, he is correct in presenting the spectacle/religion connection as one of analogy and historical derivation.[84] Indeed, it should be clear from the few quotes used above that, without speaking the language of religion, Debord's thought invokes theology both in terms of the derivation (the historical/genealogical descent) of the spectacle out of a medieval religious world and in terms of an isomorphism between past theocracies and the spectacular present.

But there is more to Debord's understanding of the connections between theology and spectacular domination. On the one hand, Debord's notion of the spectacle carries in it a theory of representation and idolatry that fundamentally defines his idea of modern life as a bastardized experience of the religious. On the other, his theory of time and history answers why one must take the spectacle not merely as the expression of a disenchanted, secularized, reified society with a religious past but also as the perfection and visualized realization of the potentials of such a past. Debord's version of theoscopy coimplicates these two approaches in constructing an anaesthetized subject dominated by a regime wherein the visual corrupts any sort of pure engagement or interaction and forces relations simulating faith to mask this effect.[85]

Spectacle

Debord insists that the power of the spectacle today retains and redeploys the religious aspect that it had possessed in earlier ages.[86] What it does *not* do is permit all that this aspect can claim to deliver—unlike the unified "mythical order" that masters arranged in prespectacular times.[87] While the sacred, *in its totality*, used to deliver a certain sort of existence and to promise other possibilities, the spectacle, in its ambiguous modernity, "depicts what society can deliver, but within this depiction what is permitted is rigidly distinguished from what is possible."[88] What one faces in the spectacle is nothing less than a false god, a poor parallel to promises of another age that today no longer hinge on their religious foundation or ideology.[89] Raised in the form of the commodity, such false gods offer only a present of illusion and consequently serve the very power that "creates [society's] concrete unfreedom."[90]

It is thus not entirely out of place to interpret many of Debord's critiques of the spectacle (and of spectacles—cinema, advertising, etc.) under the rubric of a critique of representation, more specifically, of a sort of *Bilderverbot*. Representation in and through the spectacle involves a critique of its false, illusive mask covering over a relation between individuals and things that would otherwise remain independent and largely unmediated—transparent—or at least mediated by value and not by its abstraction.[91] Other thinkers, notably Adorno—whose *Minima Moralia* Debord evokes, along with Marx's *Capital*, at the very beginning of his *Society of the Spectacle*[92]—have been discussed extensively in light of the thematic of the prohibition on images and its implications for representation.[93] Debord has not. Yet how else can one read Debord's elision between spectacle and spectacles,[94] his rejection of the imagist character of spectacles and of the spectacle in general qua nonlife,[95] if not as a rejection of idolatry mapped onto a terrain defined by the abstraction and false representation of capital, alienation, and merchandise?[96] Moreover, given Debord's rampant use of the opposition between the apparent and the real, is this conception of the spectacle anything but an aggressive conception of the immanence of modernity as universalized capitalist idolatry?

For one to whom the real world becomes real images, mere images are transformed into real beings . . . since the spectacle's job is to cause a world that is no longer directly perceptible to be seen via different specialized mediations, it is inevitable that it should elevate the human sense of sight to the special place once occupied by touch; the most abstract of the senses, and the most easily deceived, sight is naturally the most readily adaptable to present-day society's generalized abstraction. The spectacle is by definition immune from human activity, inaccessible to any projected review or correction.[97]

Through these operations, gods of the past have evolved into the form and structural force of images, have become nothing but images; these images in turn serve pseudo-gratification and social separation, adulating the socio-economically oppressive and providing a "world beyond" throughout the spectacle that turns human power against itself—the very "world beyond" that once served as the residing place of the gods, "those cloud-enshrouded entities" that "have now been brought down to earth."[98] More important than this "down to earth" is the idea that, once it has been brought down to earth, once it has become a part of the spectacle, the divine has lost itself and become recoded in the spectacle's power to dominate man and distance itself from him.[99] In the reinscription of idolatry, of the spectacle as a "specious form of the sacred,"[100] the critique of representation (as erasure of the real/apparent distinction and as destruction of a supposedly transparent relation of man to things) specifically reconstructs the subject (viewer, consumer) as an anaesthetized victim of images and economic power.[101]

In Debord, the consumer is thus a component of the spectacle insofar as he sees and almost automatically agrees with what he is shown—in other words, insofar as he fails to distinguish between the layers of capitalist exchange and domination that formulate and found the spectacle as the modern mode of being par excellence. The consumer is by no means a privileged viewer, indeed, any claim to capacious spectatorship is but a laughable effort to take upon oneself an impossible ideality, especially insofar as complete self-distantiation from the spectacle is not possible. Is it possible to say, then, that there is a spectacle without a proper, privileged spectator (except for Debord himself)?[102] Does the spectacle, in its very tautology, serve as the sole organizer of forces "in" it? Is it possible that the symbolism of "the sun that never sets on the empire of modern passivity . . . that covers the entire globe, *basking* in the perpetual warmth of its own glory" involves only the spectacle itself as the system that recognizes and can traverse the relations between men and things it sets up?[103]

I will return to this problem; it is important to suggest provisionally, nevertheless, that in its lack of epistemological tools to determine the status of seeing, the spectacular subject that fails to see and see through the spectacle reinforces the capitalist idolatry for which the epistemologically unavailable God of the spectacle is the spectacle itself, in its sublime position at once doomed and undefeatable.

Time and History

In sections 5 and 6 of *Society of the Spectacle*, Debord not only explains his notions of influence and historical derivation but, more significantly, answers why one must take the spectacle to be a world whose operational bases remain irreducibly religious.

In an elaborate and highly personal theorization of time and the meaning of history, which, due to its idiosyncrasy, has gone unnoticed, Debord conceives of time as fundamentally independent of man. The first sort of time that human societies experienced was *cyclical* (day/night, the seasons, etc.)—an era in which humans were incapable of controlling nature's repetitions in any way. The humanization of time (which, for Debord, is also the "temporalization of man"[104]) was effected only through the intervention of society. Rejecting and overcoming cyclical time, the ruling classes of masters separated themselves from other men and initiated the imposition of history. This overcoming cultivated kinship bonds and invented myth as a historical basis for the protection of mastery, but these changes combined to make rulership dependent on the construction of time and history it thought it had overcome. History (for Debord the masters' imposition of a temporalized archive) served in this sense to institute *irreversible* time, as well as, on certain occasions, to found separation at varying levels and to enforce conceptions of the present as radically distinguished from both past and future.

At this point in the development of man, semi-historical and monotheistic religions began to operate as "a compromise between myth and history, between the cyclical time which still dominated the sphere of production and the irreversible time which was the theater of conflicts and realignments between peoples."[105] *Semi-historical* religion presented itself in opposition to history by postulating an eternity based on cyclical time but superior to it, separated from it, which could be located in the future. Debord extends this to argue that religion, a radical opposition to historical time through the invention of *finality*,[106] served as a revolutionary turn to eternity qua promise of nonmastery, of return to a prehistorical, quasi-mythical past. As such, religion was revolutionary rather than cooperative, with classes representing mastery. The promise of an alternative sort of time was repeated in the early modern peasant revolts: "a millenarian utopianism aspiring to *build heaven on earth* brought back to the forefront an idea that had been at the origin of semi-historical religion, when the early Christian communities, like the Judaic messianism from which they sprang, responded to the troubles and misfortunes of their time by announcing the imminent realization of God's Kingdom, and so added an element of disquiet and subversion to ancient society."[107] But in each case the promise of a postapocalyptic fulfillment, first in the restoration of a prehistorical world, then *in the historical one*, turned to aid the oppressive regulation of society through irreversible historical time, engendering a society that could find temporary relief only in a *festival*. In their hopes and even their failures, Debord continues, "modern revolutionary hopes are not an irrational sequel to the religious passion of millenarianism."[108] The subsequent "victory of the bourgeoisie" brought about the instauration of two more types of temporality, *pseudo-cyclical* time and *reified* or *spectacular* time.[109] Pseudo-cyclical time is the investment of "false variants" (like the work day or vacations) with "the natural vestiges of cyclical time."[110] This final nail in the coffin of prehistorical time, Debord says, is time as we understand it today, a time of "homogeneous and exchangeable units" without "any qualitative dimension."[111]

With the reifying effect of commodities on culture, society living under pseudo-cyclical time has instituted the era of the spectacle, a time in which masters (and the world that has escaped them to produce a false order of its own) are able to organize *the entirety of human life,* even in the spheres of privacy and consumption. It is an era when the promise of a postapocalyptic time has become reality, even though it has become the reality of an empire of boredom, an era in which time is synonymous with the spectacle's antihistorical, unchanging, everlasting present.[112] In the spectacle, what has gone terribly wrong is that the humanization of time has collapsed into dehumanized reification, breaking the direct connection, even the equivalence, between man and time that supposedly existed in the past. With the rise of the commodity came the suppression of all that is human in humanized time and the transformation of time into the prime means of central, false promises.[113] If we are to drive Debord's consideration of millenarianism to its extreme, the spectacle is at once the time-epoch that cannot be saved and the preparatory era of an apocalyptic time: rather than a secular, atheist modernity dominated by images, the present is the culmination of the whole history of religious and temporal metaphysics, whose overcoming can only occur with the inversion of power and religious inflection of time in the exuberant festival.

It is indicative of Debord's intentions that section 5 of *Society of the Spectacle*, "Time and History," does not use a single word that can be understood visually. The exact opposite occurs in section 6, "Spectacular Time," where illusion, appearance, and spectacularity make a triumphant reentry. The significance of such a reentry is paramount. Not only is the appearance of the commodity equivalent to the entry of the visual realm into the realm of time, but *the spectacle is the only period in history whose structure is understood at once religiously and visually*. In other words, religion and the triumph of the visual coincide in *and only in* the spectacle to complete the commodity-based and disciplinarian aspects of society in a world moving toward closure and totality.

Theoscopy

It is in this coincidence that the spectacle appropriates for itself the privileged position of consequential spectatorship that it otherwise occludes from all those living under its reign. Debord's thought relies heavily on the construction of an implied spectator, a figurative, idealized counter to the infinite number of incompetent spectators who determine the present of the subject without locating themselves in a superior position vis-à-vis the spectacle. Every participant in the spectacle serves as its component, as an imperfect seer, an insufficient yet ever-present eye and object of another's eye—trapped in a temporality that extends almost infinitely, to envelop and undermine the possibility of an overcoming of the spectacle. Debord's subjects are *continuously* spectacularized, just as much as they themselves watch—what matters in the spectacle is that people unmistakably subject themselves to the economic, disciplinary, and visual conditions of separation by submitting their gaze and desire to it. Against Foucault's Panopticon of centralized vision, with the God hiding within its tower, Debord locates a weak and anaesthetized spectatorship at every possible position within the spectacle, quite literally everywhere, *and thus nowhere—in that none of these spectators can actually see the structure of the spectacle*. In this sense, the sheer proliferation of spectators and subjects of spectatorship, the all-pervasiveness of the empire of the spectacle and the multitude of individual spectacles help to suggest a larger epistemology of nonspectatorship—as in the Panopticon, whose central spectator is epistemologically unavailable yet nonetheless *ever-present*, implied *everywhere*.[114] Indeed, Debord seems willing to accept some sort of reversed Panopticon in his idea that spectators and subjects are all bound to a "center" through one-way relationships:[115] while they watch, they maintain the spectacle in its tautology, as an impossible divine spectator.

The positions of irreversible time and religion serve precisely to enclose man in this visual reign. Against spectacular time, which forces a relationship between man and God by reconstructing (while denying) the latter in a paralyzing barrage of exchange, image, and technology, Debord sets an apocalyptic humanist imagination based on communal participation, one whose temporal form and advent are not only incomprehensible to modern man but also dependent on man's hope of overcoming time itself.[116] This would be the "festival," which should be read within a tradition of apocalypse, prepared in the theory of time and coded as the triumphant arrival of transparency and the end of distorting representation. Just as the spectacle defines its temporality as the triumph of pseudocyclical time, the festival defines itself as the inversion of that time in a perpetual construction of situations—in fact, as a complete rejection of the role of time (cyclical, pseudocyclical, or otherwise) as a human order and as an attack on both "the visual" and "the religious" as they define the era of the spectacle. The dual character of time is then at once: (1) what locks man into the impossibility of overcoming this kind of existence, and (2) that whose overturning promises the end of the spectacle and its inexistent yet all-seeing God.

Identified with the time and observation of the spectacle itself, the inexistent God is here the impossible yet necessary eye that imposes time, the eye that the subject (even more, the situationist) fantasizes about controlling but from which it always suffers, to which it is always subject. The subject's position in the spectacle, suspended between the spectacular time of an eternal present and the fantasy of a nontemporal, nontheological, and postapocalyptic purity of the festival, is, once again, organized as a perfect believer, watched by a God that has extended from and escaped the subject's own powers and exists everywhere around him, controlling and ordering all of his moves, work, and leisure, even his own vision. Interpersonal relations come to bear the religious past—and to reconstruct it through the visual that masks socioeconomic power. What Debord demonstrates, in other words, is the modern world *as* empire of theoscopy, ruled by a highly advanced, diffuse, theocratic visuality in which everyone and everything is subject to the orders and order of the gaze in all its imperfect manifestations.

Eyes of an Absent God

The basic connection between the philosophical arguments of Foucault and Debord is their shared investment in theological and visual terms, the construction of a modern scene of existence as controlled by a spectator at once impossible and divine who organizes everything without ever acting or participating, by virtue of man's inability to control his own construction. It is significant, in this regard, that in each of them the historical derivation of modernity not only does not rely on a secularization process but implicates the religious and the historical aspects of this argument in the visual ones in this organization of modernity.

Accordingly, the role played by "the order of man" in Foucault is largely mirrored in Debord's conception of the temporal and metaphysical rise of the spectacle in the modern period. In the former, modernity is marked not only by the lack of a distinct

process of secularization but also by the survival and persistence of idealist and theologically laden motifs, according to which man comes to know and understand himself. In
Foucault, the historical shift between the classical age and modernity is thus set up, on
the one hand, in terms of an isomorphism, and, on the other, by a gradual emphasis on
the use and application of (fundamentally scopic) technologies and machines that, though
belonging to a religious and in some ways "premodern" worldview, come to the fore in
dechristianization. Social transparency, the analytic of finitude, and (above all) panoptical
modernity are the most important of these, regrounding *theoscopy* as a major marker of
the status and position of man in modernity. Debord, by contrast, dispenses with the
secularization thesis because he wants to present modern life and modern images not as
liberated from forms of the sacred but as reliant on their bastardization. His prehistory
of the spectacle can be read as a compounding of different kinds of time—and it is time
that determines historical epochs and the permeation of the religious tradition into everyday life. Rather than overcoming the gods of the past and the religious organization of
society, the rise of the spectacle is a new immanent idolatry, to which man is tied above
all through his submission to spectacular time and the weakness of his status as spectator.

Both Foucault and Debord thus present a modernity in which a decentralized and
pseudo-secularized form of control enforces powerful religious themes so as to maintain
a radical (one could even say totalitarian) subjection of modern man. Both code it in
terms of transparency, representation, and the rise of this modernity out of a theologically
conceived past. It is worth noting, however, that the locus of "God" in the theoscopic
organization or system is somewhat different in each of the two thinkers. For Foucault,
the univectoral gaze locates the spectator in a position that the panopticon's "inhabitants"
can only see and recognize as strictly transcendent. In Debord's writings, by contrast, it is
the very insufficiency of human spectatorship that suggests the formal possibility (and
formal significance) of a superhuman agency amidst men, one that results from their
construction of modernity and would see what they cannot. If such a metaposition is,
strictly speaking, available (to Debord himself), this is not to say that it is properly held,
for holding it would mean holding the capacity to impose time, to control perception, and
so on. For the spectacle to continue to function, embodied spectators must be incapable of
seeing through it, while such a possibility or position remains at least imaginable. In short,
both authors take the management of vision away from a embodied observer partaking
and coping in the world, and identify it—abstractly, formally, conceptually—with a perfect spectator who can only be emulated or fantasized in the world as it is.

Power and spectacle in Foucault and Debord accordingly result from their religious
and visual formulation; I have argued that these dimensions are best understood together.
This necessary epistemological unavailability of the God's-eye-view makes it possible to
speak of a cultural, theopolitical technology that is foundational in the two writers' contemporary pertinence. The peculiarity of theoscopy after Foucault and Debord is its need
to operate *without* God: it sets up a position of divine spectatorship but at the same time

leaves it empty, for neither of these authors is in any way prepared to argue that *God* will actually occupy this space. Nor is either of them prepared to accept that an idealized man or scientist can be hold such a status or position. Neither God nor Man: it is not just that God sees everything or just that the position of perfect spectator is reconstructed in terms that recall Him. Rather, the reconstruction also leaves open the possibility that the ever-present spectator's position cannot be filled in terms provided by the religious tradition. The role of technology and architecture is precisely this: to provide such a position but to make its operation distinct from any theological content that would tie it down to the affirmation of God. One could perhaps go so far as to say that precisely what institutes God, what grants him more than a metonymical status as the unfailing observer in Foucault and Debord's text, is precisely *His "death,"* his impossibility and conceptual unavailability, for it is only in such a circumstance that the formalization, dehistoricization, and discharging of all religious content in the divine can be emphasized, that a dechristianized Christian God can be reconstructed in order to fill in the divine where there is only nothing, to affirm a divine presence in its conceptual and empirical impossibility, to impose a "pure," unembodied, unfounded vision, God's gaze or His capacity to see, when there is no one there to see.

Come On, Humans, One More Effort if You Want to Be Post-Christians!

Thierry de Duve

And now abideth faith, hope, love, these three; but the greatest of these is love.

—St. Paul, I Corinthians 13:13

In the spring of 2003, the news came from the diocese of Helsingoer—Hamlet's country, quite appropriately—that Thorkild Grosboell, a theologian and minister in the Lutheran Church of Denmark, was an atheist. The pastor later retracted, but the fact remains: he had publicly stated that he believed neither in God the creator of the world, nor in the resurrection of Christ, nor in the eternal life of the soul. Mr. Grosboell is my post-Christian hero. I sincerely hope that history will remember his name as that of a pioneer in a new kind of enlightenment. To see the existence of God denied by rabid anticlerics, Marxist militants, disenchanted positivists, and materialists of all stripes is hardly a surprise. To see a minister trained in theology—and one, to boot, who has not at all renounced his spiritual mission, and whom his flock seems to appreciate and love—calmly and rationally declare his agnosticism is far more thought provoking. My bet is that some day Thorkild Grosboell will be canonized, when it will be clearly understood that the function of established religions—Christianity last but not least—was to prepare for humanity's definitive exit from the religious.

My admiration for Grosboell entails a somewhat paradoxical conception of religion, which I borrow from a liberating book—one of the few books, it seems to me, that offer new intellectual tools for disentangling the present-day confusion surrounding the so-called return of the religious. This book is Marcel Gauchet's *The Disenchantment of the World*—a book that proceeds from "the firm persuasion that there is very possibly somewhere beyond the religious age."[1] Gauchet clashes with a thesis current among historians of religions, namely, that the religious idea has become more developed, complex, and systematic as more and more refined religious practices and doctrines have come into being—all stemming from a primitive religious feeling that might have been the first existential response to the inescapable horizon of death and the earliest attempt to explain—in order to make tolerable—the extreme destitution of people cast into the thick of nature, whose hostility is *the* great mystery. This view of things, Gauchet suggests, is one-sided and overlooks the element of voluntary choice in the gesture of the earliest humans as they laid the foundations of religion. This gesture, in which Gauchet sees the essence of religion, is a kind of pact with nature whereby people consent to a cosmic order shot through with supernatural forces beyond their control in exchange for a stable place in this cosmos, guaranteed by respect for ancestral law and the perpetuation of the social order willed by the ancestors. It is evident that for a very long time we have been living in compliance not with this pact but rather with a contrasting one, in which nature is offered to us and is subject to the domination we exercise over it through science and technology, in exchange for the expulsion of the supernatural from the world and our fall into the irreversibility of history. According to Gauchet, the human species thus made two successive and contrary choices regarding what underpins and structures its being-together, the first of which alone yields religion. Gauchet doesn't explain why they succeeded one another in this order, but that is not hard to understand if we adopt a Darwinian point of view: for our barely hominized forebears, the animism of nature and the immobility of society must definitely have had a selective advantage. Once this choice was made, the possibility of the opposite choice could emerge only very slowly. This is why, Gauchet claims, "the most systematic and most complex religion occurs at the start," and, far from representing a development of the primitive religious gesture and advances in the conception of the divine, the stages through which the world's great religions have been formed "actually represent as many stages in the process of challenging the religious."[2] The three principal stages are: the emergence of the state, the advent of monotheism, and the internal development of Christianity, which Gauchet unhesitatingly proclaims to be the "religion of the exit from religion."

I shall not dwell any further on Gauchet's thesis, but I would like to emphasize the extent to which it refreshes and renews the issue of the religious and relieves it of the weight of historical fatality. By making the relationship to social foundations the center of gravity for the religious, Gauchet turns inside out the common view that makes the relationship to the religious the center of gravity for social foundations and, by the same token, makes it so hard to disentangle the political from the religious. There is no question of denying that religion constitutes a powerful social link, nor is there any question of refuting that, in the monotheistic religions, the horizontal link welding the community together depends upon the vertical link with a transcendent principle that, in return, organizes the community, either by retreating from it, as in Judaism, or by incarnating it, as in Christianity. It is simply a matter of seeing that, if the religion of incarnation seems to have taken the entanglement of the political and the religious to its limit, this religion also permits and prepares for its disentanglement. If Gauchet is right, humanity's exit from the religious, far from presupposing denial of and revolt against Christianity, implies going a long way with it, accompanying its thinking processes, coping with the results, and working through the consequences. "Come on, humans, one more effort if you want to be post-Christians!"—such might be the optimistic message of Gauchet's book, whose acknowledgment might be found in Pastor Grosboell's surprising new brand of enlightenment. I made Gauchet's message echo Sade's "Français, encore un effort si vous voulez être républicains" on purpose because, in this essay, I want to try my hand at a modest exercise in translation involving precisely that groundbreaking moment in modern, enlightened secularism, the French Revolution.

Its motto—*Liberty, Equality, Fraternity*—seems to me to translate the three Christian maxims expressed in the "theological virtues," *Faith, Hope,* and *Love,* into the political register. The two threesomes are congruent, and I don't think it will be hard to show that. But why do so? At first glance, to demystify the modern claim to secularism and state its failure to provide a (hasty and partial) explanation for the stubborn persistence or the vengeful return of the religious in the public sphere. Actually, I expect more than this from the exercise. I expect it to show, above all, that the motto of the French Revolution takes charge of the three Christian maxims and that it is only by doing so that it opposes superstitious, unenlightened religiosity and represents a major step forward on the way out of religion. Next, I expect it to show that the Revolution still insufficiently takes charge of the three Christian maxims. At the risk of seeming to condone religiosity, I shall argue that the maxims of faith, hope, and love must be endorsed, pondered, and understood for what they are before we can make out how their translation by liberty, equality, and fraternity really points to a possible exit from religion—at the same time, incidentally, as they offer an incipient response to the dead end of political thinking bequeathed by the Enlightenment.

To start with, it is striking that the three theological virtues should have been conceived and practiced in this order: first faith, then hope, and, last of all, charity or, better, love. It is striking, too, that liberty, equality, and fraternity should be listed in that order. This is enough to suggest a term-by-term match. That love and fraternity should be one and the same thing is readily understandable, provided we are not fooled by the gendering of the word "fraternity" (which, needless to say, we must address in due course). That faith and liberty should be inextricably linked is a little harder to understand, but only a little. Liberty only assumes its meaning if we understand thereby the freedom of the other. Laying claim to freedom for oneself without granting it to others obviously runs counter to liberty. It follows that an act of faith lies at the root of liberty—faith that the other will make good use of his or her freedom. The most enigmatic pairing is the link between equality and hope. Equality in the face of death is the only one that is certain. Yet hope entails the obverse certitude, or fortitude; it is a certain readiness for the redeeming event that will keep death at bay. Hope postulates equality in the face of life and is therefore the only maxim that acts as a barrier against death.

This was a very brief introduction to the issue at hand. We must now try to get a tighter grip on it, which I shall attempt to do by spiraling around the issue in a series of turns of the screw, the emphasis being on signs pointing to the exit from religion already contained in the Christian maxims, sometimes even more so than in their lay translation. Faith stands in opposition to belief. Animist religions are belief systems that are upheld not by any autonomous, subjective adhesion but simply by an absolute compliance with the authority of tradition. There is no distinction between the physical and metaphysical worlds: nature is the seat of magical forces that the individual can neither challenge nor doubt. There is no place for faith in any such system, nor is there in ordinary superstitions. Furthermore, faith has only a very limited place in all phenomena of religious fundamentalism, including contemporary variants. Belief is an abdication of thought, whereas faith is a explicit acknowledgment of the limits of thought. Belief is a state; faith is an act. One might think that it is essentially a religious act. If we go along with Gauchet, it appears, on the contrary, to be the supreme antireligious act, proclaiming the break with belief and the solitary destitution of the individual before the unknowable. Every act of faith declares the disconnection of the subject from the common rule and atavistic authority. Agreed, when faith in God is at issue, its declaration is an act of allegiance, but of individual and therefore free allegiance, which stands for the social bond only insofar as it presupposes the same adhesion, independently, on the part of others. The act of faith is an ethical act, which remained shielded behind the mask of the religious so long as there was not sufficient progress in the awareness of the disenchantment of the world—to quote Max Weber's expression that gave Gauchet's book its title.[3] With the advent of the Enlightenment, history thought it was ready for the religious maxim of faith to be translated into the political maxim of liberty. As it happens, the translation stopped midway, because the act of faith had not been sufficiently separated from its cangue of belief. As a result, the practical bases of ethics had been muddled together with theoretical antiobscurantism. Positivism would be the belated outcome of the fact that the Enlightenment (with the exception of Kant) did not take the postreligious virtualities of Christianity far enough.

Without faith, there is no hope. Without liberty, likewise, there is no equality. Christianity was the first religion to proclaim the equality before God of all his creatures and, among them, the equality of all human beings before the chance of salvation. This presupposed that human beings are beings of liberty and that the equality of all is based on shared faith. Hence the militant proselytism of the first universal religion. But because the faith of Christians radically distinguishes itself from belief, its main object is no longer the existence of God but rather the resurrection of his Son. Clearly, the twofold human and divine nature of Christ upholds the postulated existence of the Father, but based on a new link, virtually unknown to the Old Testament. This is the link of filiation that sustains the Father's fatherhood and that the believer reasserts by imitating Jesus. Already accomplished by Judaism, the gesture that posits the origin of the world beyond the world no longer involves renouncing an understanding of the here below—as in primitive animism. With Christianity, moreover, it is released from submission to the transcendence of the Law. This gesture has to do with the merely symbolic assertion of the separation between the creator and his creatures, under the novel form of paternity. God the creator is less the progenitor of the world than the symbolic father of men, who form a community of sons through the mediation of Christ's sacrifice. Men are equal in Jesus Christ because they are equal before the hope of salvation, that is, before the hope of resurrection. Faith in Christ's resurrection converts equality before death—the only certain equality—into equality before life. It is not hope in the eternal life of the soul after death that is the correlative of faith, rather, it is hope in the resurrection of the body on the day of the Last Judgment. When modern secularism arrived, history thought it was time to relegate the fable of the resurrection to those private closets where people keep their personal convictions and superstitions, and failed to realize that the place left vacant by the fable would sooner or later be forcefully filled in by death-dealing myths—the most fearsome of all being the myth that dared to proclaim inequality before death.

By being sons of one and the same Father, all men are brothers. When the French Revolution translated the Christian maxim of love as "fraternity," it merely took cognizance of a virtuality contained from the very start in the doctrine of Christ. As a corollary of equality in the hope for salvation, fraternal love extends to all. The only love that saves is universal love: this is the point that articulates the political and the religious, and it applies identically to St. Paul and to Marat. Because this point is one of articulation, and not one of confusion, it is, at the same time, the point at which the political and the religious can be disentangled. Not that they have been—at least not sufficiently—but we shall return to this in the second turn of the screw. What matters for the time being is to see that, just as faith is the condition of hope and hope is the condition of love, so liberty is the condition of equality and equality is the condition of fraternity. It is also important to see that, in both instances, it is the third term that retroactively feeds the first. Fraternity yields liberty; love gives faith. Or, if we cross the terms: love of another is what establishes the other in his or her liberty, which is thus never a liberation that is conquered but a gift that is received. And fraternity is what fuels the act of faith whereby I accept the liberty of my brothers. It goes without saying that faith can never be acquired once and for all, for it has to fight belief at all times; that acquiescence in the liberty of the other forever threatens to spill over into submission; that equality may remain formal and act as an alibi for injustice; that it is all too easy to muddle expectation with hope of retribution; that at any given moment fraternity runs the risk of closing in the cohesion of the most immediate group and taking up arms against the outsider; and that love is suspect so long as it can swathe itself in self-sacrifice or self-hatred. On many occasions, historical

Christianity has yielded to these temptations, to which theoretical Christianity neverthe-less contrasts this salutary antidote, which is its sole law: "Love thy neighbor as thyself." Such a maxim is political, what else? It is political because it is universal: my neighbor might be living far away, and my fellow humans are all of a kind. Why was the Revolution less radical than theoretical Christianity in its ideal of fraternity? The obvious and easy answer is because politics is the art of power, and it would be quite naïve and sentimental to base politics on the commandment to love. But this is not the nub: there will always be unequally distributed power. The real question—which we should try to consider out-side any legal framework—is the issue of the legitimacy of power. If the Revolution had carried out its fraternal maxim in a Christian way, it would have placed the legitimacy of political power in the reference of the brothers—in other words of the sons—to the shared symbolic father. It neither could nor would do so. Even if it hesitated, in the end it placed not the legitimacy but the illegitimacy of power in the paternal principle. Regicide was not unavoidable, but it took place, with, as its immediate consequence, the fantasy of a society of fatherless brothers. It is obvious that the Revolution was bent on beheading not a man but a symbol. When a symbol is beheaded, however, the head grows back again, and sooner or later a tyrant arises to pick up the stake of revolutions betrayed. Robespierre shows that this happened sooner rather than later.

Something awkward emerges with this first turn of the screw. Not only was the French Revolution largely unaware of the fact that by inventing the three maxims liberty, equality, and fraternity it was translating the three Christian theological virtues, faith, hope, and love, into the political register, it was also very unfaithful in its translation, and on a point that is not at all theoretical, since it involves the outbreak of violence, more precisely, parricide. There is nothing very Christian about this, and the question now is knowing—or deciding—whether the head of the king by divine right rolling in sawdust represents an advance in the direction of the exit from religion, or not. The least that can be said is that the execution of Louis XVI was a capital sin against the maxim of love. Neither morality nor sentiment is involved here; it is simply a matter of testing the hy-pothesis that the French Revolution did not take responsibility for the three Christian maxims radically enough and that therefore (I'll stick with Gauchet's paradox) it failed to take the postreligious virtualities of Christianity as far as it might have done. Because love retroactively gives and grounds faith, it is from faith and from its translation into liberty that we must embark on the second turn of the screw.

Whereas belief stems from closely held conviction and can cling to it, faith is declared. An act of faith stands for a declaration of faith, and this is one of the reasons why lay civil society deceives itself when it expects to see religious convictions confined to the private domain. Over and above the gesture that releases me from common belief and abandons me to my liberty, what is at issue in the act of faith? As we have seen: the freedom of the other. I make an act of faith whenever I surrender, in complete confidence, to the wager that you will make good use of your freedom. "You," not "he" or "she." The act of faith is addressed, which is why it cannot be separated from a declaration. It presupposes another, in the second person, facing me. Were my own freedom to be won at the expense of the freedom of others, it would not have any ethical dimension. In the third person, the freedom of the other has only a diminished ethical dimension. What does *their* freedom cost me (the freedom of slaves, the oppressed, the wretched of the earth) so long as I have not been confronted by them, in a face-to-face situation where their silent rebuke forces me to address them? *Your* freedom alone is altogether ethical: the freedom of the other in the second person. As soon as the dimension of the other as addressee is opened up, this other is recognized at once in his or her uniqueness and in his or her humanity, in other words, in the universality of his or her belonging to the human species. From this twofold recognition, apparently, stems the de jure equality of all others, as asserted by the Universal Declaration of Human Rights. In the rush to conclude as much, there was in fact something like a missed historical opportunity, the consequences of which—all too obvious today—can be seen in the confusion of issues of human rights with humanitarianism. Since the French Revolution, the disentanglement of the political and the religious has been a task for the judicial domain, and the judicial domain establishes a subject of law conceived in the first person, an "I" and not a "you." In its translation of the Christian maxim of faith into liberty, the French Revolution elided the address to the other. I might venture to say that this elision lies at the root of the tragic misunderstanding of political hope that has turned the two centuries separating us from the French Revolution into the repetitious history of revolutions betrayed.

The address to the other is an initiative, a beginning, an irreversible opening of time. Such, too, is one of the meanings of the word *revolution*. Its other meaning is "circularity," the hand of time rotating on itself, the initial openness closing in on the expected result. In this sense, any revolution is, from the outset, a revolution betrayed, and every hope is a promise I put into the other's mouth, from which I now inevitably deduce that it has not been fulfilled, at least not yet. Here initiative stems from expectation: addressing the other is demanding his or her response, and even (as is usual in the hopes of ordinary life), anticipating the desired response. Instead, we would need to devise an address that is absolutely not a request, so that revolutions not be betrayed and hope be freed from the cangue of ordinary expectations. There is something inhuman here, which verges on saintliness—but who would deny that this is what Christianity has aspired to? True, Christian hope veers toward the future—Christ's second coming and the resurrection of the body—yet it is a future that does not derive its meaning from the anticipation of the event to come but, on the contrary, from the conviction that the decisive event has already taken place. Compared with the various forms of political messianism that took off in the wake of the French Revolution, Christian messianism turns out to be strangely more "realistic" and disenchanted: the Messiah came, and the world's injustices are just the same as before. Henceforth, the act of faith in Christ's resurrection has to be renewed on a daily basis, and herein lies the root of hope, which thus turns out to be nothing other than the endurance of faith and absolutely not something akin to the daydream of revolution. Being equal in hope is not the same as being equal de jure and hoping one day to be equal de facto. The revolutionary maxim of equality has caused this confusion. It has put the law rather than the event at the ground-breaking moment: the right to liberty rather than the initial address that ushers in freedom; the right to equality in a future earthly life rather than victory over death, a one-time event but a decisive one; the right to fraternity, as if love were something due to men, rather than the ordeal of love that is proven in the triumph of Eros over Thanatos.

It is one of the ironies of history that as soon as the possible disentanglement of the political and the religious was envisioned, the two were reentangled once again. It is no coincidence that the French Revolution was marked by a parricide, and the invention of Christianity by the Father's consent to the Son's sacrifice. Christianity has been distinctly more anti-Oedipal than the Revolution, for which the social bond is still that of *Totem and Taboo.* The Revolution assigned the fraternity of the sons to the authority not of the father but of the mother—goddess of reason in the religious order, female figure of the Republic in the political order. By dint of this dual reference, the Revolution ran the risk of seeing all thinking about love forever torn between the utopia of its absolute rationality and its reterritorialization in blood ties, as if the only alternatives were either the old Platonic identification of love with the love of wisdom (philosophy) or the assimilation of love to the tribalism, pure and simple, of the only filiation that can be attested— filiation with the mother. There is a myth of fusional love in both: the hermaphrodite of the *Symposium*; the communion of the pure in the impure blood that waters our furrows (as the *Marseillaise* puts it). Fortunately, because the French Revolution was universalist, it did not give in to the temptations of ethnic tribalism. But it paid a very high price for its universalism, specifically, a considerable repression of the feminine. It is not just that the maxim of fraternity crushes sorority—even though there is a whole brand of feminism that, since Olympe de Gouges,[4] has legitimately attempted to grant sorority its rights. It is above all the fact that the feminine and maternal representation of the Republic— ranging from Daumier's extraordinary picture to the effigies of Marianne in France's town halls, once modeled on the features of Brigitte Bardot—inevitably presents it as a phallic mother (as psychoanalysis would put it), because she has been put in the symbolic place of a father, substituting for the father or the king beheaded by the Revolution, as if it were possible to behead a symbol.

At the end of this second turn of the screw, something emerges to back up the conclusions drawn at the end of the first, yet add something to them, as well. On the one hand, what the translation of the maxims faith, hope, and love by liberty, equality, and fraternity fails to think through revolves around the definition of paternity. Without lapsing into either morality or sentiment, it can be said that parricide involves a definition of paternity insofar as the Revolution was keen to behead a symbol, not just a man. On the other hand, the repression of the feminine—resulting from the fact that the denied paternal function surges up on the mother's side—indicates that the other thing the Revolution failed to think through revolves around sexual difference. The reduction of universal love to fraternity is the most obvious symptom of this; hence the hypothesis that, in order to advance toward the exit from the religious, it is perhaps necessary, at the present time, to "gender" the postreligious virtualities of Christianity left unattended to by the Revolution. Needless to say, I can only scratch the surface of this loaded issue. On the one hand, more than the other monotheistic religions, theoretical Christianity explicitly makes room for sexual difference at its very foundation; on the other hand, it does not fare any better in the historical responsibility for the repression of the feminine. Here, Christianity must be indicted as much as, if not more than, the Revolution. We shall not become post-Christian simply by taking the virtualities of Christianity to the limit. A break must be made. But where? The essential question seems to me to be deciding whether we must break with the doctrine of the incarnation, which is the great invention of Christianity, or whether we must break from within this doctrine. Will there be a way of rewriting it so that women have a different place in it, and that the repression of the feminine is no longer its consequence?

Whether to break with the doctrine of incarnation or not is a terribly delicate question because, in due course, it entails taking up positions with regard to the respective places of Judaism and Christianity in the matter of the exit from the religious. Given how monstrously the Shoah denied Judaism a place at all, caution is called for. Gauchet can be reproached for entertaining a teleological view of history that grants Christianity an irreversible surpassing of Judaism on the way out of religion. I myself admit to following in his footsteps when I base my optimism on his interpretation of Christianity as the "religion of the exit from religion." But I see no reason to exclude other exits from religion from being possible and desirable today, including one that takes as its point of departure Judaism and its ethics. There is room here for reflective efforts whose premises are divergent, but for which it would be premature to decide now that they will not one day converge. Indications of such an alternative route are found in the reflections of Hans Jonas about the concept of God after Auschwitz, or in the whole philosophical work of Emmanuel Levinas.[5]

As I embark on a third turn of the screw, which once again takes up the question of the address to the other as articulating faith and freedom, this mention of Levinas is not fortuitous. Levinas would say that otherness is the dimension of infinity revealed in the other's face. But it is one thing to *envisage* the other from within a religion of transcendence, such as Judaism, and it is quite another thing to do so from within a religion of incarnation, such as Christianity. For Levinas, the other is definitely not the other in the third person, the other about whom one speaks, but rather the other who is presented to me face to face. He is nevertheless not in the second person, as in the Christian act of faith. The Levinasian other is not primarily the other to whom I address my words but, first and foremost, the other who addresses me. The "me" starts by being a "you." This is why subjection to the other defines the subject as ethical: "the I always has one responsi-bility *more* than all the others."[6] Responsibility is asymmetrical and irreversible, nonreci-procal and nonegalitarian. It is the most fearsome aspect of ethics, according to Levinas. Whereas for a Christian the face of the other is the incarnation of his fellow man, for the Jewish philosopher it is the epiphany of infinity and the presentification of the Law.[7] Whereas for a Christian the act of faith is an addressed declaration that abandons the other to his freedom, for a Jew it is the reception of the address that declares to him that he belongs to the chosen people. May my Jewish readers please forgive me, but, insofar as I am following in Gauchet's footsteps, I can only see in the invention of Christianity an advance on the path to the exit from religion, articulated, needless to say, with the religion from which it issues. It is noteworthy that this invention should be signed with an act of faith that is altogether similar to the Jewish one—an act of faith that accommo-dates an election: it is Mary's acquiescence in Gabriel's "Blessed art thou among women." But it is no less noteworthy that this signature instantly entails a brand-new casting of roles based on sexual difference. God the Son was born from the womb of a woman fertilized by the divine Word—herein lies the foundation of the religion of incarnation. But at what price, given that from that day on, women have been condemned to being the medium and the vehicle of incarnation, receiving their own incarnation only as feed-back from this Word made flesh through their agency? They are virgins *and* mothers, bereft of their own flesh, or else they are fallen women. It is on the place of woman in the economy of incarnation that the status of images—and hence of art—has depended in Christianity, at least since the "economic" resolution of the ninth-century quarrel about iconoclasm.[8] I shall not dwell on this matter here except to say that I am calling for an incarnate image not born from the breath of a God and the womb of a Virgin, and that I know some artists—women artists, mostly—who are working to deliver it.

At the starting point of incarnation, we thus find an address to a woman and a "Jewish" act of faith—or a feminine one, since we can ascribe it to receptivity and acqui-escence. It is immediately followed by a second act of faith, which is little stressed in the Scriptures but is really the first in which it can be seen that faith is the retroactive gift of love. This is St. Joseph's acquiescence in Mary's pregnancy and the assumption of his role as "foster father." I have now and then quipped, as if it all resulted from a syllogism: Joseph knows he didn't sleep with Mary. Yet Mary is pregnant. So God exists. The effect is comical, with Joseph being propelled into the role of a cuckold with his head in the sand. The joke actually reveals more than conceals the profound beauty of Joseph's act of faith and its no less profound truth with respect to the paternal function. In the Gospels, of course, Joseph is alerted by an angel who appears to him in a dream and tells him that Mary is pregnant as a result of God's work. This is a concession to belief in a vein that often recurs in the Gospels, and is somewhat obvious to the eye of the modern reader. Like all dreams, according to Freud, Joseph's fulfilled a wish—the wish to find an un-alarming answer to the uncertainty of paternity. But this concession to belief can be bypassed, releasing the most subversive virtualities of Christianity in relation to the religious. Christianity is probably closer than any other mythology to recognizing what I think is the essential source of both the oppression of women by men and the repression of the feminine by the social order. This is the uncertainty of paternity, the anxiety and denial of men when it comes to admitting it, and the crazy inventiveness with which they have devised systems of kinship and apparatuses of power designed at once to conceal this truth from themselves and to deny women their freedom. Joseph does more than merely put his finger on what Lacan has called the paternal metaphor. He removes from paternity in general the fantasy of any father's certainty of his biological fatherhood. Accordingly, belief in God the creator—the progenitor—of the world takes a step backward. Such belief is essential to the dogma of incarnation only insofar as the twofold nature of Christ links up with the God of Abraham. But once incarnated in his Son, God the creator can withdraw from the world He has created much more radically than can the God of Abraham. He is pure Word, the simple name of the uncertainty in which humans are immersed when it comes to the origin of the world. By becoming Father, God admits to his purely symbolic existence. It is the same God, of course—the new alliance could only emerge from the virtualities of the old one—this God who created the world in seven days and produced out of the transgression of a woman the awareness of sin in men's hearts. Whence the equation that identifies Mary with the new Eve redeeming the old one. Isn't it time we changed our point of view? For twenty centuries, Christianity has been obsessed by Mary's virginity-maternity, in order not to have to deal with the consequences of Joseph's much more liberating virginity-paternity. It is not for nothing that the Marian cult has been reawakened, and the theology of the Virgin revamped every time the patriarchal order has had to cope with an upsurge of women's power on the historical stage, as occurred in the thirteenth and nineteenth centuries. From Joseph's viewpoint, God the Father is the name of his recognition of the uncertainty of paternity. And his act of faith in Mary's faithfulness—faith in faith, given by love—thereby becomes the nonreligious launchpad of the doctrine of incarnation.

The rest of the doctrine follows. Incarnation-birth yields incarnation-death. Once cast among mortals, the Son had no option but to be mortal himself. The Gospels have him dying an ignominious death, and I would not want to minimize either the dramaturgical effect and its effectiveness in Christian propaganda, or the revolutionary (Pasolinian) political novelty that makes the Son of God the weakest among the weak. But I would emphasize that if Christ's Passion led him to his death, it was for two unconnected reasons: because death is the logical consequence of incarnation, and because the humiliation of Christ, which is more essential than his physical suffering, is the sign of the Father's loss of power. The God of Abraham intervened in order to interrupt the sacrifice of Isaac, thus demonstrating both his omnipotence and his goodness. The God of the Christians does not intervene. His powerlessness is more than the patriarchate can bear, and it is quite understandable that, over the two thousand years of its existence, within a society in which the least that can be said is that the patriarchate has done pretty well for itself, Christianity has done its utmost either to deny the Father's powerlessness or to convert it into supreme glory. But the worm has been in the fruit of the patriarchate from the outset. Once the father is reduced to nothing more than a metaphor, power is no longer his inevitable attribute. If, for Lacan (who I cannot help thinking has achieved the Christian translation of Freud's Judaism), the name of the father is synonymous with the law, it is a law that fathers must obey, not a law that they decree. The father is merely the agent of the law of the signifier when he hands down his name, when he transmits the phallus.

I sometimes catch myself dreaming of a post-Lacanian utopia that makes the phallus not just the signifier of castration but rather the signifier of the uncertainty of paternity. It amounts to the same thing, but why does Lacan acknowledge it only with the greatest reservation? Didn't Lacan, who was something of a patriarch himself, stop halfway along the path in his Christian translation of Freud? I think he did, to the extent of imagining that the point where it is a matter of being post-Christian merges with the point where it is a matter of being post-Lacanian. (I don't think I am alone in thinking so; if I have understood correctly, Alain Badiou is on the same track.) If one wonders why the signifier of sexual difference (which applies to both genders) is on the masculine side and why, in addition, on the side of paternity rather than the side of masculinity in general, the answer is, obviously, because maternity doesn't need a signifier. The mother doesn't need her mother's status to be approved by a sign, acknowledged by a symbol. She knows in her flesh that she is mother. Man needs his paternity to be recorded in a symbolic act because he doesn't enjoy any physical signal of paternity. This is why *phallus* and *name of the father* are synonymous and *phallus* and *penis* are not. And why the phallus is a signifier and not a sign. It is not the father for which it substitutes, like a name for the thing it names, but the uncertainty of paternity. The phallus is a sign without any signified, or rather, referent. If a utopia at any price were needed for us to entertain hope, my post-Christian utopia would be simply this: when it has been understood that paternity consists in acquiescing in a basic uncertainty through an act of faith, and faith in the faith of the other—which is to say, that the man who gives his name to a child relies blindly on the trust he puts in the faithfulness of his woman—the power of the fathers evaporates. Obviously, this has been understood from the outset, but one doesn't wish to admit it because it calls for too much love. Foolish are those who think that a DNA test can be a substitute.

Let us be realistic and get back to the translation exercise under way: hope and equality. Now that the issue of sexual difference is on the table, equality between men and women is involved as much as equality between "undifferentiated" human beings. As I said earlier, hope is the endurance of faith, and Christian hope is buttressed by a quite specific faith—faith in the resurrection of the Son of God. Faith in his incarnation would seem to be merely its condition. In order to rise from the dead Christ had to die, and in order to die he had to have been born. Resurrection is the event, not incarnation. In a slim volume devoted to St. Paul—slim in size but big in terms of complex challenges—Alain Badiou minimizes faith in incarnation and maximizes faith in resurrection. *"Paul's thought dissolves incarnation in resurrection,"* he says.[9] Badiou does not believe in the fable of the resurrection any more than I do, so he does not dwell on the fabulous character of this particular event. Any event can take its place provided it grounds the uniqueness of the subject declaring it: "To declare an event is to become the son of that event."[10] For Badiou, the political meaning of the resurrection of Christ proceeds by way of human-kind's becoming the son—humankind transfixed by an event, like Paul on the road to Damascus. Revolutions, including the French one, may be such events. This becoming-the-son proceeds in turn by way of the deposition of the Father. Because, for Badiou, the event and its declaration alone "filialize," he is prompted to deny that Christian human-kind has been "filialized" by the mediation of Christ's sacrifice. He thus acts as if Christ's death did not count in his resurrection, and as if the ignominy of his death did not call the Father into question. For Badiou when he reads St. Paul, the deposition of the Father results from the spiriting away of mediation. This is a forceful reading, but it is not the only one possible, even if "With Paul, we notice a complete absence of the theme of mediation."[11]

Badiou clearly breaks with the doctrine of incarnation. His theme is not the exit from the religious—he reckons he is already free of that. Because my theme, which is more cautious, is to display the postreligious virtualities of the doctrine of incarnation, I am trying to make the break from within this doctrine. Like Badiou, however, I deem it necessary to disregard the concept of mediation—it is here, fairly and squarely, that the break will be made—but what interests me is whether incarnation itself can be conceived in nonmediatory terms. The emphasis put on Joseph's act of faith is a first step in this direction. As a nonreligious launchpad for the doctrine of incarnation, it shifts the question of the advent of the Son of God in the carnal, mortal world from maternity to paternity. We move from the mediation accomplished by the maternal womb, when it is touched by the received Word and responds by engendering, to the public declaration of the name of the Son / name of the Father, whereby the symbolic order records an addressed act of faith. But Christ's death issues from his birth, and I have the same reservations as Badiou when faced with the obligation to proceed by way of the mediation of Christ's Passion, sacrifice, and humiliation to justify the resurrection. My reasons are the same as his: the event does not have to be mediatory. It is clear that by refusing to minimize incarnation, I am forcing myself to conceive of not only Christ's birth but also his death in terms other than those of mediation. The fact is that sacrifice is a rather cumbersome and pathetic mediation in the dynamics of redemption. What purpose does it serve?

The real scandal is that God consented to the sacrifice of his Son. This was a profoundly ambiguous gesture. Granted that Christ's ignominious death on the cross is a structural consequence of the New Testament repetition of Isaac's sacrifice, this merely highlights all the more the difference between a God withdrawing into the purely symbolic function of paternity and a God, creator of the Law, and thus omnipotent, who from time to time manifests his power by intervening in earthly matters. It also highlights the fact that in the Old Testament Abraham is the father and God is the Law. The Old Testament had to take extraordinary measures to remind men that fathers are subject to the paternal law, the law of the signifier. The progress made by the New Testament is measured: God finds himself, so to speak, in the position of Abraham, and this is quite a blow for the patriarchate. You don't have to read the Scriptures (it's enough to go to the movies) to find out that when the patriarchate feels threatened, it never hesitates to sacrifice and humiliate its sons. It is reproduced in just this way when the Oedipus complex no longer plays its normative role (as in, e.g., Thomas Vinterberg's film *Festen*). Then the Oedipal conflict, settled by the humiliation of the son, is the perverse driving force behind the reproduction of a patriarchate that is all the more inured because humiliation and not the normative resolution of the Oedipal conflict is the channel through which the phallic torch is passed down; the phallus, henceforth, can be conceived only as a power to humiliate in turn.

But reproducing the patriarchate is not what the humiliation of Christ abandoned by his Father at Golgotha is meant to do. I would advance as a sign, though not a proof, of this the total absence of Oedipal conflict. "Thy will be done," the Son says to the Father, and the clouds darken—another concession to belief and to the miraculous, but one that ill disguises the new and scandalous powerlessness of the Father. Without this powerlessness, one could not understand why the resurrection is the event. It would just be a *coup de théâtre*, with the Father pulling the strings. But the Father is helpless and the Son arises on his own. It is only then that humankind is "filialized" in the equally shared hope of its own resurrection. This prompts Badiou to say that the death of Christ is merely the *site* of his resurrection. Yet it seems difficult to me to separate, as Badiou does, the resurrection from the Passion and to claim—a somewhat mechanical consequence of this refusal of mediation—that it is possible for us to take the place of the Son. It is his very own utopia. For my part, I think that Badiou is insufficiently disenchanted because he is too militant, that instead of disentangling the political and the religious, he ties them up in knots again, and that he runs the risk of once more eliding the issue of the feminine. For Gauchet, on the contrary, it is impossible for us to take the place of the Son because it is already taken.[12] In consequence, humankind is "filialized" for no more than the time it needs to be emancipated. Paradoxically, this will be humankind freed from its subordination to the power of the father because it refers its fraternity—and its sorority—to the empty place of the symbolic father rather than the filled place of the incarnated son. Because Badiou abstracts the event from its "site," he holds that "God renounces his transcendent separation" precisely where I would tend to see him renouncing his patriarchal omnipotence, that He "unseparates himself through filiation" precisely where I would tend to see him keeping stalwartly in his separate, symbolic father's place, and that

He "shares in a constitutive dimension of the divided human subject"—which is right, but in my view for quite different reasons.[13] Because God the Father relinquishes his power of intervention in the realm of the incarnate beings that we are, everything comes to pass as if He were acquiescing in turn to Joseph's acquiescence; Joseph too refrained from intervening in the process of incarnation. Or it is as if God were acknowledging receipt of the foster father's act of faith in the faith of his woman. It was addressed, but to whom? Or it is as if He were replying to the launch of incarnation by approving all its consequences, including the death of his Son and the radical redefinition of his own paternity. I read God's consent to the sacrifice of his Son in a light, almost disrespectful way, free of pathos, because I see in God's abstention from the course of earthly things the very opposite of a mediation. The abandonment of the Son by the Father is neither the negative moment in a dialectical process nor simply the "site" of the resurrection. It refers back to Christ's birth, and every birth is the particular resurrection of the life that is transmitted through it—there is absolutely no need to believe in the Christian fable to be in awe of this. In due course, women and the feminine should take, in this reading, a place quite different from that in historical Christianity.

All I can do in this essay is point to a few possible directions. One brings us back to the question of the other as recipient, as addressee. The universal address of the Christian "glad tidings" overlooks sexual difference, just as it overlooks ethnic and class differences. St. Paul writes: "There is neither Jew nor Greek, neither bond nor free, neither male nor female" (Galatians, 3:28). How should we read this leveling of differences in universality? It is fashionable to promote difference for difference's sake, and those who give in to fashion will be feminists, multiculturalists, and antiuniversalists, all in the same breath. Politically speaking, this is neither very clever nor very relevant. Organically without truth, says Badiou.[14] For all this, should the field be left open for the "ungendered" interpretation of Paul's universalist message, as broadcast by the French Revolution when it translated it as "fraternity"? We would be giving credit to the repression of the feminine when it uses the so-called neutrality of the masculine as a pretext. Or, as Badiou does, should we defend Paul by stressing the novelty of the "reversibility of the inegalitarian rule" introduced by him, in relation to the customs of the period?[15] I'm not sure that this is sufficient, because Badiou clings to the "necessity of traversing and attesting to the difference between the sexes *in order that* it become undifferentiated in universality."[16] In fact, the difference between the sexes is not just any old difference. It is not contingent but constitutive, and it is unclear whether it can or should be undifferentiated in universality, especially when one envisions both the problem of the universal and the problem of incarnation in terms of structure of address. It seems to me peculiar and quite valuable that in most languages—in any event, in those spoken by Christianity—the pronoun of address (the second person, *you*) makes no distinction between the genders, whereas the pronoun of the referent (the third person, *he, she*) does. If *you* did so, there would be a distribution of addressees as men and women. Let us not conclude that the pronoun of address is ungendered. It is two-gendered because it does not let us know the sex of the person, male or female, being addressed. Perhaps this uncertainty about the gender of the addressee is essential to the structure of address.

What, now, is the address structure of universal love? Love, Badiou reminds us, *is* the universal address, which faith alone does not constitute.[17] I wholeheartedly underwrite this definition (even if, as we shall see, I shall edge it in the direction of St. Joseph rather than St. Paul), and I stress the copula. If the act of faith is addressed, love *is* its address and its address to all. This dry and thoroughly unsentimental definition of love does justice to the loathing that may be inspired by Christianity, precisely because it presents itself as a religion of love. Who, even among practicing Christians, has never been irked by the intolerable certainty of those who know that they are doing good, by the dignified contrition of sanctimonious persons and the ostentatious self-sacrifice of charitable folk, by the inanity of "everyone is good, everyone is kind" broadcast by a schmaltzy Christianity, by the masochistic pride of those who offer the left cheek when someone has struck the right one, by the superiority of those who offer unilateral forgiveness—in a word, by the whole Christian paraphernalia of fawning modes of behavior, which reek of cassock and holy water? They are the outcome of the false belief in a reserve of infinite love spilling out, through pure goodness, over sinful humankind. In this respect, it matters little that the convinced Christian situates it in God and not in himself; the mere fact that he takes himself to be the dispenser is enough to make his claim a suspect one. This rightful loathing can be contrasted, by way of antidote, with the wholesomeness of the precept "Love thy neighbor as thyself." It reminds us, in the words of the proverb, that "charity begins at home." This is the basis. But if love is the address to all of the act of faith, wherein lies the proof of this universal address? In being in each and every instance singular, as if the declaration of faith placed in the freedom of an individual other was earmarked for a universal or indeterminate other. Love is not watered down in the universal (perhaps the difference between love and its mediocre translation by "charity" lies herein); it is felt for beings of flesh and blood taken one by one.

Joseph's acquiescence in Mary's pregnancy is an act of faith sustained by love. He loves Mary, not humankind in general. And it is because he loves her that he trusts her. Faith in Mary comes first, faith in God second. This is what the syllogism evoked earlier expressed as a joke. In the second stage, which coincides with Joseph's assumption of his purely symbolic paternity, his love for Mary is the address of his faith in God, and God, because he is One, is "for all."[18] Joseph's singular love for Mary thus becomes the universal address of his faith in God. But I am jumping the gun. Everything started with the dispatch of the archangel Gabriel, with God's address to Mary. It issues from a God who is not yet the God of Christians and who has chosen Mary among all women. Mary acquiesces in this choosing with a humility that is not just that of her feminine condition but also that of her people. As I have already suggested, the Jewish act of faith consists in the reception of and acquiescence in the mystery of one's being chosen. For both sexes, receptiveness and the assumption of the place of the addressee rather than that of the addressor in the structure of address are the substance of the Jewish act of faith, a substance that in this respect can be called feminine. (I wonder if it is not this cultural trait of Judaism that explains intolerance of the other to have been so frequently focused at once on hatred of the Jews and of the feminine). Badiou does not talk only about the God of Christians, he also talks about what the *mono* in *monotheism* means, and thus, above all, about the Jewish God, when he says that "The One is that which inscribes no difference in the subjects to which it addresses itself." Not even sexual difference? The pronoun of the address is two-gendered, and it becomes differentiated only on reception. Mary receives Gabriel's "I greet *thee*" as a woman. When Joseph acquiesces in Mary's acquiescence (and it doesn't matter whether it is to an angel appearing to him in a dream or to Mary directly), he also finds himself in a state of receptiveness vis-à-vis a message addressed to him, which the act of faith consists in welcoming. We can say that he welcomes it with his "feminine" side; we can also say that, in this act of faith in Mary, Joseph behaves "like a Jew." And it is the second stage of Joseph's act of faith, his act of faith in God whose address is his love for Mary, that transforms the Jewish God into the Christian God, the God-Law into the God-Love. It took the sequence of these two successive acts of faith on Joseph's part to make love become the universal address of faith. It is not my intent to minimize Mary's part, quite the contrary; I merely want to alleviate and shift her responsibility in the advent of the doctrine of incarnation. Even if they did not sleep together, she and Joseph needed to get together as a couple to make it happen. They in fact first brought God the Father into being, then God the Son only as the result of a ricochet, if you'll excuse the term. I use it with a dash of humor: like any earthly father, God the Father awakens to his paternity nine months before the birth of his Son. The unprecedented novelty is that He awakens at the very same time to a new definition of paternity: God gets "Josephized" by becoming Father. (He is very rarely called "Father" in the Old Testament.)

Thirty-three years later, this God who is still the God of the Jews, but who is now simply an agent of the law of the signifier and not the author of the Law, lets his Son die on the cross. I said earlier that everything came to pass as if He acquiesced in turn in Joseph's acquiescence or as if He acknowledged receipt of the foster father's act of faith in the faith of his woman. He who throughout the Old Testament was the Sole Enunciator, deaf—with a few memorable exceptions—to the prayers and entreaties of his people (this deafness is an essential factor of his transcendence), finds himself in the addressee's position—in a "Jewish" and "feminine" position. "*My God, my God, why hast thou forsaken me?*" God does not reply; He acknowledges receipt, which is not the same thing. Insofar as an acknowledgment of receipt is nonetheless a message sent back to the sender, God does as He has always done when men's prayers forced him to forego his deafness: He talks through signs; Christ dies and the clouds darken. What is Christ's death the sign of? Not only of the fact that the Father has lost his omnipotence, but also of his acquiescence therein. He is not deposed: He has lost his power but not his authority. He has just committed an act of faith, definitely not the first such act in his existence—Adam was also left to his freedom—but a far more decisive act of faith in the exit from the religious. The attribution to Adam of original sin was still a way of admitting that men, who are sinners by nature, will not pull through on their own, and that if they want salvation, they will have to wait for the Messiah who will deliver them. Basically, they did not deserve their freedom. But now the issue of merit has vanished, and it is this above all that is meant by the dispatch of the Messiah, and his death. He came, nothing has changed, so it's up to you from here on out. The God who abandons his Son to his ignominious death is under no illusions. In other words, he has no belief. He had to take things this far for the death of his Son to be the sign of his act of faith. God himself had to exit from the religious for his act of faith to be credible. The death of the Son attests to this. Through this death, God shows human beings that he leaves the use that they will make of their freedom up to them. He henceforth relies on them to disentangle the political from the religious, while He withdraws.

God exits from the religious when Christ dies, and men, at the same moment, enter the society of the spectacle. Let us remember Isaac's sacrifice, of which that of Christ at Golgotha was, mutatis mutandis, the New Testament repetition. I said earlier that the Old Testament had to take extraordinary measures to show men that fathers are subject to the law of the signifier, and do not decree it. Indeed, to force a father to sacrifice his son with the sole purpose of reminding him that fathers do not make the law is a bit excessive. Abraham obeys, and God, in his goodness, dispatches an angel who restrains his arm. The intervention is quite spectacular, and more than one Baroque painter made use of it. But Baroque painters are Christians and have received from the doctrine of incarnation the right to make images, even, since the Council of Trent, the injunction to put the full might of images at the service of the Church's propaganda. What their painting erases is the fact that there were no onlookers at Isaac's sacrifice, for God insisted that it be carried out in a remote and barren place. The contrast comes across: there are people at Golgotha, plenty of people. The mise-en-scène is highly successful: a long preamble with fourteen stations, each one with its moment of emotion; the simultaneous arrival of actors and spectators at the top of a natural hillock (much better than a raised podium); sound and fury, an incredible hubbub, the din of hammers, Roman soldiers all over the place; a man who is still young and quite handsome, wearing no more than a loin cloth; two thieves crucified to lend symmetry to the scene; a crown of thorns, a sponge soaked in vinegar, a spear wound, what a spectacle! And that cross! As Oliviero Toscani (the former Benetton photographer and art director), who knows about such things, says, a logo that holds up for twenty centuries has what it takes to make Madison Avenue jealous. Especially when the society of the spectacle has at its disposal today's technological means, when it has absorbed the lay civil society that issued from the French Revolution, when it has completely invaded the political stage, when it takes on the anthropological and sociological function of religion—being the bond that binds—the society of the spectacle is what most effectively shrouds the fact that we made good our exit from the religious two thousand years ago.

The society of the spectacle is the form taken by religion when society has exited from the religious. It starts with Golgotha, and with what luster! It gains new strength in ninth-century Byzantium, passing closer than ever to the mystery of incarnation, but straightaway mapping it onto economy, that is, onto mediation, a mediation that women and the feminine will pay for. It becomes the official politics of the Catholic Church with the Council of Trent and the energetic iconographic program of the Baroque period. And it lands in today's media industry, handed over to the semi-gods of entertainment and information alike. The society of the spectacle is in fine fettle. By saying that it is what most effectively shrouds the fact that we exited from the religious two thousand years ago, I do not mean to say that it is no more than a smokescreen that can be dispersed. I mean that religiosity is fighting back and standing up for itself, that it does not intend to die, that even at the end of the very long tale told by Gauchet, during which humans have very slowly learned to do without mediation with the invisible, the desire for such mediation is being fiercely defended—and all the more fiercely, it must be said, because the exit from the religious has by and large been accomplished. The blinding, dazzling excess of visibility of the spectacle is there to conceal that there are things that remain invisible and that between the visible and the invisible there is no mediation. There were no more witnesses at Christ's resurrection than Baroque painters at Isaac's sacrifice—something that remains to be pondered.

—*Translated by Simon Pleasance and Fronza Woods*

The Right Not to Use Rights

Human Rights and the Structure of Judgments

Werner Hamacher

The claim that human rights are *rights* and that they are the rights of *human beings* means two things. First, it means that they apply neither to the empirical totality of a bio- or zoological species nor to any individuals as the privileged (because exemplary) instances of such a species but rather to the human "as such" or "in truth." Human rights do not define man in his historically contingent appearance, but rather provide an explication of human essence as it presents itself in and of itself after all external attributes have been subtracted. Only human rights present man in his *right* light—in the unobstructed, undistorted, and direct light of his essence, his reason, and his concept. This, at any rate, is what the concept of human rights implied in the age in which they were first declared. The voice of the Declaration of Human Rights is therefore the voice of man himself: the voice of his right to have a voice and at the same time the voice that recognizes, preserves, and enforces this right, and therefore his essence. If the Declaration of the Rights of Man and of the Citizen of 1789 speaks of the "ignorance, neglect, or contempt of the rights of man," it does so in order to insist, following the tradition of natural law, that "man" and his "rights" are not a juridical fiction or an invention of this Declaration made at a particular historical moment that happens to bear the date 1789. They are, rather, the primary and foundational data that define man and have been given to him as "natural, unalienable, and sacred." Now they only need to be made accessible to reason, to be recovered from the obscurity of oblivion, and to be restored to universal respect. The declaration of human rights, by codifying and making public these rights, becomes at the same time an elucidation of human essence as it has always existed. It proclaims nothing new, but only makes explicit and public what implicitly has determined human nature for as long as the being called man has

671

existed. The goal of this reminder, this explication and publication of the rights of man, this opening up of something that, as such, is already revealed and accessible to all, is to eradicate the "sole cause of public calamities and of the corruption of governments." Political corruption, therefore, stems from a lack of cognition (whether through ignorance or forgetfulness) and from a lack in the practical application of such cognition (through contempt): it is a deficiency of the self-presence of man in his rights and of the presence of the Supreme Being in man. The Declaration becomes necessary only in order to mend this deficiency, "so that this pronouncement, being constantly before all the members of the social body, shall remind them continually of their rights and duties." The inalienable character of these human rights—and thus of human essence—finds a warranty "in the presence and under the auspices of the Supreme Being," because this is the only way in which the essential characteristics of the humanity of man can be secured. The inalienable and public substance of man, the substance of his rights, is therefore presented under the protection of the revelatory and inalienable qualities of the manifest.

The substance of man is the theological, the onto-theo-logico-political substance of the language of the Declaration itself. It is the kerygma of the kerygmatic, the manifestation of being manifest, the revelation of revelation. Man is not a blank spot in this declaration, but rather the one who, through it, assures himself of his own essence, the one who traces this essence back to its highest source, and the one who elevates his presence to a public, universal, and unforgettable fact, which is, precisely, his human nature. Human essence, correctly recognized and recognized as right, does not merely assert itself through this Declaration as through a foreign medium. The essence of the human and its humanity *is* itself and *consists in* this Declaration, since it makes itself manifest and actual in it. In the Declaration, the human announces itself *clare et distincte* as juridical essence, as the process and product of an autoenactment and autoverification carried out in universal consensus. In the very act of this self-declaration it declares—explicates, publishes, and enacts—each of the four fundamental rights enumerated in the first Declaration of 1789: liberty (in which the freedom of choice between action and nonaction is implemented), property (in which this freedom is asserted as *proprium* even before any possession of goods), security (in which human juridical essence is guaranteed as a perpetual right), and resistance to oppression (by which the oppression of man's freedom to proclaim himself is prevented).

The implication that human rights are the form in which human essence articulates itself and that this form is the juridical one of rights and their perpetual declaration is rendered more precise by the second implication of the rights of man: human rights, as enduring as they may be, arise from a moment of decision and form a conclusion. "The representatives of the French people," it is written in the Declaration of 1789, "have determined to set forth . . . the rights of man." And the Universal Declaration of Human Rights of December 10, 1948, which follows the rhetoric of the French Declaration in all decisive points, proclaims in its preamble that the General Assembly of the United Nations has declared the human rights because "the recognition of the inherent dignity . . . of all members of the human family" is the foundation of "freedom, justice, and peace in the world." The necessity of recognizing and declaring liberty and justice to be the foundation of human essence is drawn as a conclusion from this very foundation. A declaration, therefore, is the medium of an act of joining together: of a "General Assembly of the United Nations" or of the "Representatives of the French People." It corresponds to a conclusion, a decision, or a determination and serves to join together the essential ground of what in it is called "human" and the universal "recognition" and juridico-political enforcement of this ground. Although the UN (in contrast to the French nation-state) lacks an executive power and has to confine itself to recommendations for the enactment of its declared principles, the relationship between these principles and their declaration nevertheless remains the same as it is in the nation-state. This relationship has the form of a conclusion, no matter whether it presents itself as an executive or merely an instructive or educational power.

The conclusion is not only the political form in which the representatives of a people, or even of all peoples, *join together*, nor is it merely the technical form in which deliberations and negotiations can be *concluded* and brought to a consensus. In both the French and the UN declarations of human rights, a conclusion is, more importantly, the logical and ontological form in which the essential determination of man *is joined together* with its explicit recognition and public enactment. The essence of man establishes itself in the rights of man, and these rights explicate themselves in their public proclamation, which in turn presents itself as the first mode of their recognition and of their executive or educational actualization. In each case, right is conceived as a declaration—and therefore in the strict sense as a *category*—of human essence, and can therefore never appear independently of its categorical exhibition and of its conclusive connection with this human essence. In this sense, the UN declaration is no less instructive than the Declaration of 1789. If the latter once again makes present what has always been evident, even though it has been forgotten, denied, and treated with contempt, the UN General Assembly declares that the "recognition" of human dignity—of freedom, in other words—is the "foundation of freedom, justice, and peace in the world." If this sentence, the first in the declaration, is to be more than a trivial tautology, it can only be understood as claiming that the cognitive grasping of human essence is the condition for its political realization, and that the declaration is the connection—the *conclusio*—between the recognition and the actualization of human liberty and justice. But the possibility of such a cognitive-political conclusion, and therefore also the possibility of a declaration, presents itself only once the act of recognition grasps human essence *as such*, and only once the act of actualization transforms a preexisting foundation into a verifiable fact. The declarative "recognition" of the dignity of the human individual must therefore itself be an act of dignity. It has to enact its own grounding and must present an ontological tautology—an ontotautology—rather than a merely trivial one. Man unveils, explicates, and joins himself with himself in the declaration of his rights as a being that is, precisely, unveiling, declarative, and conclusive. These characters make up the juridical essence of man.

The structure of human rights proclamations shows that in them man shows himself to be self-showing and self-unveiling. All of these proclamations are essentially phenomenological and present themselves as procedures of fundamental phenomenology *in actu*: as speech acts and actualizations of concepts that do what they say and politically realize what they claim—even though at first only in the mode of an explication, publication, and instruction. They assert themselves as the performance of a grounding and install themselves—and stall—through this very assertion. The essence of man as it is explicated in the declaration, his dignity in freedom, is arrested into a right through the very process by which this explication proclaims this dignity and this essence as an object and an intentional correlate of its assertion. Freedom can be a "right" only because it is the theme of a declaration, and only for this reason does it have the status of a *category*: to be the public and publicizing manifestation of the essence of man. And this means not merely the status of any regional category whatsoever, but rather that of a practical foundational category: to be the ground of all ethical and political relationships between human beings. Right is a categorical declaration and a categorical thematization of man—and for this reason already a judgment and a *conclusion* about his humanity, an *exclusion* of all human possibilities that are not susceptible to juridical thematization and cannot be perceived by categorical thinking, and, in principle, the *occlusion* of all further deliberations that might be carried out or even just demanded by "human beings."

The declarations of human rights declare the trial about the essence of man to be, in principle, over.

The fact that human beings *as* human beings have a *right* to *be* human beings; that they must be made the theme of juridical statutes, orders, assessments and decrees, the object of legislative, judicial, and executive measures; that they are supposed to be fundamentally juridical beings—this scandal, this infinite and infinitely ambiguous scandal, which governs the movements of the process (and the movement *as* process) not only of effective politics and its respective propaganda but also of the ancient and constantly renewed alliance of jurisprudence, theology, and ontology, this restriction of the essence of man—of his freedom—to a legal entitlement, the amputation of man to an object of rights—is the foundational operation carried out by the declaration of human rights. In it, the rights of man are unveiled, proclaimed, and presented to the public; in it, they are brought, conjoined with their presentation, to recognition and their at least virtual realization; but this act of laying open is in no case a legislative act without being at the same time a juridical and potentially executive one, an act that is instructive, educative, or imperative.

The declaration of human rights is a judgment about man. It establishes the paradigm for every predicative judgment that men can make about men, and defines the human being as the one who is essentially judging, equally essentially judged and inescapably condemned to judge himself. The era of human rights is the era of judgment. It is the epoch not so much of philosophy as of philonomy.

The right of man is not only a category—and as such a public exhibition, a statement indicative of his essence (*kat agorein*)—it is an apophatic *logos* that arises from a decision, a conclusion, and a judgment and structurally determines that the essence of man consists in his right to submit himself and his world, his humaneness and all of humanity, to a judgment. The declaration of human rights carries out this judgment about the right to judgment and the jurisdictional essence of man. It posits the scene of a court of law—a court of law that is as much juridical as it is theological and philosophical—that claims to be the final arbiter of the structure of right and judgment in man. Whoever appeals to human rights submits, presumably always with the best of intentions, to the verdict of this court of law and turns himself, as judge and judged, into a figure of this scene and into both an agent and an object of this verdict. He not only pronounces judgment—and one that above all applies to himself—but declares in addition that there is nothing decisive to say about man except in the form of this judgment, this predication, and this verdict.

· · ·

The scene is old. Its age is already evident from one of its first descriptions to have been passed down, which also asserts—no less than the French Declaration and the UN declaration two thousand years later—that this scene springs from a reform that was intended to adjust traditional judicial procedures and to fit them better to the structures both of cognition and of man. This scene of a restitution of judgment to its purity, and therefore also of a restitution of the juridical nature of philosophy, is told in the form of a myth at the end of Plato's *Gorgias* (523a–26d). During the reign of Kronos, Socrates recounts, the living held judgment over the living (*zontes esan zonton*) on the day that someone was supposed to die. Their judgments lead to the complaint that souls were undeservedly appearing both on the Isles of the Blessed and in Tartarus. Zeus, the ruler of the new era, agreed with the complaint of Poseidon and Pluto, and gave as a reason for the wrongful verdicts passed by the living on the living that the people being examined were judged fully dressed, veiled by "handsome bodies, good stock, and wealth," which deceive both the witnesses and the judges, for the judges themselves are, since they are still alive, "fully dressed" and perceive those who appear before them only through the screen of their sensual eyes, their ears, and their whole bodies. The sight of the souls is obstructed by the sight of the judges' eyes, the hearing of the souls is hindered by physical ears—their perception and consequently also judgment are led astray by bodies. Zeus' reform institutes a court without veils. Judge and judged alike are supposed to be "stripped naked of all these things [*gymnos kriteon apanton touton*]." "They should be judged when they are dead. The judge, too, should be naked, and dead, and with his bare soul he should contemplate only the bare soul of each person [*aute te psyche auten ten psychen theorunta*] suddenly [*exaiphnes*] upon that person's death, when he's isolated from all his kinsmen and has left behind on earth all that adornment, so that the judgment may be a just one [*dikaia e krisis e*]" (523e). The *krisis*—the decision, the judgment, the sentence—thus finds its model in death, insofar as death is "the separation [*dialysis*] of two things from one another, the soul and the body" (524b). Death is the first, the archicrisis, which severs the merely accidental and contingent from the true nature of a being— and among these external, merely sensory and therefore misleading qualities Plato counts "handsome bodies, good stock, and wealth," just as the Declaration of Human Rights two thousand years later lists "race, color, sex, language, religion, political or other opinion, national or social origin, property, birth or other status" (Article 2 of the UN declaration of December 10, 1948). The soul is undressed of all these phenomenal particularities by death, and naked it presents its own relation to the sensory disfigurations that it still bears as traces to the gaze of *theoria*, which is in turn naked and nonphenomenological: "All that's in the soul is evident [*enthela*]" (524d). The judgment—*krisis*—that is passed on the souls by the souls refers not their sensory appearance but rather to their *physis* and their *ichne*, the traces of their ambitions and sufferings (*pathemata*). But if this judgment does not rest on phenomena, then it does not rest in phenomenal consciousness, either, for after the reform instituted by Zeus, mortals are no longer able to know their death ahead of the time of judgment. Death is not the theme of judgment, but rather the pure structure of judging, an aphenomenal and anepistemic separation, the ablation of the soul's essence itself, which does not enter into the horizon of a noetic act, but rather determines the horizon by which the judgment takes its course as a *pathos*, a *passio* and a passivity preceding any distinction between bodily passivity and psychic activity. The Platonic myth of the court of the dead therefore reaches its decisive point in the fleeting moment indicated by the word *exaiphnes*—"suddenly." Once the reign of Kronos, in which chronological time passes as a succession of phenomena and acts of consciousness and in which one can know the moment of one's death, is over, the judgment can no longer be anchored in the time of the thematizing consciousness. Even the time of objective consciousness needs to be put aside as a veil and obstacle to cognition in order to admit the time of *psyche* in its nakedness, its suddenness and bare proximity, not as a passing of discrete now-points but rather as the sheer moment beyond continuity and discontinuity, as the happening of discretion itself. Only in this ana-chronical temporality without before and after, without pre-sence or re-pre-sentation, without ideas and objects, can the *psyche* itself judge and at once be judged. It cannot, in other words, be judged fairly as an object to and from which certain characteristics could be added or subtracted, nor as a theme of predication.

The judgment passed by the court of the dead on the dead is therefore a very peculiar judgment. It does not judge phenomena, objects of knowledge, or intentional objects, and the judgment isn't passed by any subjects, whether empirical or transcendental. Since these are not a priori judgments, but rather ones that read the ambitions and sufferings of every soul from their traces, and since they judge each case only for itself, without subsuming its singularity under a general concept, a norm, an expectation, or a habit, all general models that the verdicts of the court of the dead could use as an orientation fall away. They are judgments of extreme singularity, even of ultra-singularity, since no "who" is being judged, but merely the question whether it is a "good one" or a "bad one"—in both cases, something supra-general and ultra-essential is being decided. When a judge of the dead, himself one of the dead, presides over someone's case, "he doesn't know a thing about him, neither who he is nor who his people are, except that he's somebody bad" or good (526b). The judgment of ultra-singularity is at the same time one of ultra-universality: the *singulare tantum* to which it applies is its own rule that surpasses every rule. The judgment does not refer to this *tantum* as a phenomenal or intentional object, but rather implements it as something supra-singular and supra-general; it does not estimate it according to its qualities but merely assigns and imparts it to the a-topian locus of these qualities. The relationship between the judge and the judged follows from the indication that the former receives from the latter; it is both a singular and a more than singular, both a universal and a more than universal *answer* to a corresponding *challenge*. But this answer cannot have the character of a performative act, which presupposes the minimal consensus of a community on the conventions of speaking, for such a consensus belongs to the phenomenal stock that alone is able to constitute a "who" and from which both the judge and the judged are severed in death. The only communities that Plato admits to his last court are the one between the Asian judge Rhadamanthus and the Asiatic people whom he judges, and the one between the European judge Aiakos and the European people of whom he, in turn, is the judge. But Minos presides over both of these, and he belongs to no community, ethnic or otherwise, suspending every community between the judge and the judged. The judgment of supra-singularity and supra-universality is therefore a judgment of *alterity*: of the separation between the one and everything else. This judgment is the creation of every singular being, the bringing about of its alterity and therefore the event of *alteration*. And since it is a final and therefore also a first and irreducible judgment, it is an initial separation [*Ur-teilung*], an archi-distribution very much like the one attributed to Minos in the eponymous pseudo-Platonic dialogue dedicated to the *nomos*. This original parting doesn't say something about something; it is no predicative identification of a theme or a thesis. It rests, rather, in the unthematic and athetic saying as a happening of *krisis*. The judgment passed by the dead on the dead is the event of mere saying—of a *logos*, as Socrates stresses—which must precede everything that is said, a judging that precedes the content of any judgment and therefore gives to every object and every being, every knowledge and every act of conscience, the very ground of its possibility. But as the event of mere saying, it cannot itself be something that is said or an object of knowledge; it instead—with structural irony—withdraws this ground. It is the separation that precedes every decision, an infinite and therefore always sudden, an unpredictable and therefore pretheoretical *krisis*.

The Platonic myth of the last judgment by a court of the dead attempts to give an answer to the question of the structure of a just verdict; the question, in other words, of what truly constitutes a judging discourse and also the question as to the nature of beings that relate to one another by way of such a discourse. The answer to this double question—the question concerning man and the question concerning language—must be a single one if it is to characterize a speaking that does justice to man by doing justice to language. The reformatory process that leads to the answer of the court of the dead is that of a reduction; not a phenomenological but rather a trans-phenomenological reduction, which subtracts the inessential attributes of the living in order to arrive at the bare, naked soul and the traces that are engraved in it. The judgment of the dead is issued in the ever singular event of *krisis*, and in it determines the individual and its language as the event of mere separation. The reduction, a laying bare, is a reduction to the act of reducing. The laying bare does not reveal a substantive something that lies hidden behind a veil—as later declarations of human rights suppose—but rather lays bare the event of laying bare, of the separation, the *krisis* and *dialysis*. It is a laying bare of laying bare, a *dénudation de la dénudation*, as Levinas calls it in *Otherwise than Being*, a work in which he devotes two important footnotes to the Gorgias myth.[1] This hyperbolic *krisis* of *krisis* is presented by Plato as a critique of the juridical practices by which the living pass judgment on the living, and presumably also as a criticism of the Areopagus and the lower courts of ancient Athens. Stripped of all references to its own time, it can also be read as a critical answer to all forms that right and judgment have taken since then, up to and including the declarations of human rights during the French Revolution and after the Second World War.

Socrates holds judgment over the structure of judgment and corrects what in it—even today—does not accord with justice either in language or in human affairs. Setting aside for the moment the complications of the Platonic body-soul distinction, which are solved in the *Gorgias* myth through the *ichne*, the trace, one can isolate three prominent, interrelated aspects in which the human rights of modernity are revised by the court of the dead. All three aspects agree in that they reduce the predicative judgment, the judgment in its sense of a predication, to a diction without a predicate, a mere *dicere* without eidetic correlate to and from which characteristics might be added or subtracted. The decision that something is good is not a predicate but a mere correlate to speaking and to the possibility of speaking at large.

a. The Gorgias myth at no point talks about rights. In the declarations of human rights, rights have the status of categorical exhibitions of human essence; they characterize the invariable substance of all human beings across all cultures and times and they are freed in both the Declaration and the Proclamation from the veil of oblivion and contempt. The explication and publication of these rights disrobes human substance of its inhuman distortion and incorporates it into the phenomenal stock of knowledge, of insight, and of practical recognition. For this reason, it is anything but a coincidence that both declarations of human rights count the right to property among the inalienable fundamental rights: knowledge is a possession, a possible or real form of property, founded in consciousness as the inalienable locus of convergence of the conscious and of life, and privileged as property in its extreme ideality. The Declaration of 1789 lists it in second place, directly after the right to freedom: "These rights are liberty, property, security, and resistance to oppression" (article 2). The UN declaration of 1948 proclaims in article 17 more cautiously, yet no less categorically, that "Everyone has the right to own property alone as well as in association with others." This right to property forms a systematic continuity with the right to security and freedom, for security means a *perseveratio in se ipsum*, while freedom is persistently determined as a limit against others, of which property figures as the material representation: "Liberty consists in the freedom to do everything which injures no one else; hence the exercise of the natural rights of each man has no limits except those which assure to the other members of the society the enjoyment of the same rights. These limits can only be determined by law"—thus article 4 of the French Declaration of 1789. Along the same lines, Kant writes in his essay of September 1793 "On the Common Saying: 'That May be Correct in Theory, but It Is of No Use in Practice'" that "all right consists merely in the limitation of the freedom of every other to the condition that it can coexist with my freedom in accordance with a universal law" (A239). Freedom, defined as a "choice limiting one another (which is called the civil condition)" and which characterizes "the rightful condition (*status iuridicus*) as such" (A240), is freedom only within its limitations with regard to the freedom of others. In his critique of the American and French human rights declarations in "On the Jewish Question," Marx accuses this egologically determined freedom of being the freedom of isolated social atoms and of blocking unlimited social freedom. Besides human rights declarations, Marx's analysis is also directed at John Locke's anthropological theory of property in the *Second Treatise of Government* of 1689, which had laid the groundwork for those declarations during the previous century. In the *Treatise*, Locke declares the purpose of all social compacts to be the "preservation of property" (§124) and further defines this "property" as "their lives, liberties, and estates" (§123). Since Locke identifies not just material goods and individual liberties but also life itself as "property," the grounding for all right to property must itself be an inalienable property, namely, the property of one's own person: "every Man has a *Property* in his own *Person*. This no Body has any right to but himself" (§27). The right to one's own person secures this person only as a property. Correspondingly, the right to freedom secures freedom only as a property, which stands in competition with other properties and turns the *status iuridicus* into a permanent condition of civil war, injuring all freedoms. The basic rights that are supposed to be the essential rights of man are national and international rights of civil war. Because they determine man in his *humanitas* as man-against-other-men and furthermore as man-against-man-himself, they are structurally (insofar as they are rights, rights of states and supra-national rights) not human rights but rather the rights of objects: nonhuman institutions not only of reciprocal limitation but also of reciprocal elimination. Right is right-against-right, and therefore, *ex definitione*, unjust. It is a category not of humanity but rather of self-reification and self-destruction. Every judgment that is also a predication is a judgment-against-judgment, a self-judgment, a de-predication and erasure of itself and its language. It does not open any prospects but closes itself against them and against its own future possibilities. Predication is, in every sense, a *conclusion* and an end. If it is to be a *beginning*, the *principle* of human rights must stop being a conclusion; it must take its distance from predicative judgments, become mere diction without predication and thereby introduce the possibility of justice both in human affairs and in those of language.

b. As for the second important aspect in which the justice dispensed by the Platonic court of the dead differs from human rights, rights are entitlements that one member of a society can claim vis-à-vis the other members of that society. In each case, a constituted society legitimates the individual claims and issues the "general" law that presides as sovereign over the rights of all members. But this sovereignty of the "general" law is only the sovereignty of a compromise reached through the mathematical criterion of majority and through a rationale by which this majority can hope to maximize its power and impact. That which is sovereign is always a foreseeable, calculable totality, combined with the equally calculable power of the conditions of preservation and expansion contained therein. (Only for this reason can a definition like that of Carl Schmitt be valid: "sovereign is he who decides on the state of exception"—for the decision on the state of exception takes place *with sole regard* to the rule of the maximization of power of a given or foreseeable totality, and therefore also the maximization of a majority and its privileges). Even in democracies a group of individuals therefore decides on the legislative totalities *against* or *before* other individuals. And this group decides—judges—according to the measure of *its own* will and the expansion of power of this will: not according to the measure of the incalculable singularity of individuals, taking into consideration their past and their futures, which cannot in all cases be defined by the will and the calculation of power. The sovereign community and its law submit that which is incompatible and resists all comparison to a measure that is only seemingly equal for everyone—the measure of numbers, of quantified will, ability, and power. But this makes the will—even if it may aspire to be a will to the good—a will to power and to the overpowering of others, and therefore a principle not of society or socialization but rather of selection, exclusion, and conflict. The human right that is founded upon it, regardless of whether it is the right to property, to security, or to formal-juridical equality, is always also the right of executioners and of calculators. Human rights are calculations with humans. The freedom that they grant to individuals, being the freedom established by the "universal" law of subjectivity, is only the freedom to expand and universalize the reign of individual wills: it is a freedom not of alterity but of assimilation; not of transformation but of conformity; not of dignity but of calculable value. The community established by this freedom is the community of rivalry and conflict, in which to be regarded as "human" means to figure as an item in a juridical calculation. Freedom isn't free so long at it finds its limit or its origin in the ego, even if it be the ego of another. Only the liberation of freedom from the principle of the majority of number, ability, and power could lead to its liberation *to another* other, and *another* "I"; only the invention of innumerably many liberated freedoms could bring about a human community. Only this community would indeed be "human" in its irreducible and thus nonformalizable plurality, in a sociality that cannot be monopolized or calculated by any state of right. It would be the "human" that has the *right not to need rights, not to use rights or be used and used up by them.*

c. The Platonic court of the dead at no point refers to rights, at no point to property, community, appearance, and the securities that may be guaranteed by them. These are, in fact, exactly the things that have to be discarded as a hindering and misleading veil before the judgment of the dead: gender, tradition, convention, community, ability, and appearance—and therefore the entire phenomenal apparatus that natural law and the American and French declarations define as *human rights*, including the freedom that is characterized as an exclusive *proprium* of the "I" as its person. That which remains as the praxis of this singular court of the dead is sheer judgment without predication, without a pregiven right, without corresponding duties that could be fulfilled or neglected; a judgment that corresponds neither to anything that has been said nor to a theme or an object of cognition or declaration, and therefore also not to a declared law. Instead, it lies this side of all manifestations and institutions, solely in the happening of *krisis*, and pertains only to another such happening. What, then, remains when only the act of judging as archi-distribution remains? Levinas asks this question in the two footnotes in *Otherwise than Being* in which he discusses the Gorgias myth. In one of them he insists that the judgment "remains judgment [*demeure jugement*]." In the preceding one, he emphasizes the question itself: "But one is right to ask what such a judgment consists in, a judgment that is not a priori and is not a judgment put on a given, is not a *judgment of experience.*" His answer to this not entirely rhetorical question confines itself to the reminder that the judgment of the dead is not, at first, a *jugement de justice* but, even before that, a responsibility for the single Other. It would thus be, even as an answer out of responsibility, a judgment: a judgment that comes *before* the judgment of the court, but nevertheless a judgment. One can put another answer beside the one given by Levinas as a response to his question about the judgment of Plato's court: the *krisis* of the anaphenomenal—of *psyche* and *ichne*—since it is bare saying, which refers neither to an object nor to a thematizable ground but only to itself in its alterity, can be nothing else than infinite, and, since it is an infinite judging without conclusion, it is withdrawn from all formalization and juridification. Being an event before any positing of laws, the *krisis* is an event without content, an event merely of the event, a *krisis* of *krisis*, in which the decision of judgment is nothing but a decision for the decision itself. Judging *remains*: but conclusive judgment is denied in the judging—and this naked event of judging resists every judgment about whether it itself constitutes a judgment or not. The fact that it can never be thought of and named with any certainty as itself, but only as something that it might not be, exposes the structural irony of this event.

As an infinite judgment it remains irreducible to a propositional content and is the *epochē* of judgment in the very act of judging: an abstention from judgment that arises neither from an intention nor from the particularity of the intentional object to which it could refer. Being an event, the act of judging precedes every intention and every object that could constitute itself in it. To the extent that the *krisis* evades all critical reflection directed toward it and *remains* as much a *krisis* as something that is athematical and an anathema, it also remains free of judgment: something that cannot be unveiled by any assertion, a secret without content. The unveiling cannot itself be unveiled. While declarations of human rights unveil (explicate and publicize) the hidden (misrecognized, disrespected) substantial character of man in order to place it under the protection and control of the political public at large, and while such declarations therefore pronounce a universal judgment on the unveiled essence of man as a judging being, the infinite *krisis* of the Platonic court of law removes every "what," every essence and every essentializing right as a veil. It judges only once, suddenly, *exaiphnes*, whether something is good—beyond being (*epekeina tes ousias*)—or bad (without being). It judges without the certainty or even the possibility of knowing whether a judgment has been passed. For this *krisis*, man is not a being that has to be unveiled and actualized, but rather a singular occurrence provoking a singular response, without a schema measuring its epistemic merits. The fact that Plato speaks of the court of the dead as a *mythos*—and a decidedly "demythologizing" one at that—may imply that one cannot talk about this *krisis* in predicative sentences. It is not the theme of a reflection, nor is it the reflection of a theme. Legal texts judge about right and wrong. "Literature," by contrast, and this includes the fabulations of the *mythos*, preserves the right of justice by pronouncing neither a judgment nor even a judgment on judgment.

But since it is an infinite *judgment*, even the *krisis* of the court of the dead still constitutes a judgment. It remains a judgment if for no other reason than that it refers to the remains, the traces, the *ichne*, of the phenomenal contexts in which somebody acts and desires. If this judgment is to be concerned with justice, then it must also deal with the justice of that from which the Platonic court cannot entirely abstain: the justice of social and genealogical contexts, conceived as their sense and use; the justice of tradition and its possibilities, and therefore of their appropriate transmission; the justice of appearances, defined as their just use; and the justice of goods, which implies their unlimited distribution and employment. Plato makes the judgment pass from soul to soul; the traces that lie between the souls as mediators must therefore be seen not merely as obstructions, but also as enablers of judgment. These traces are, like the *krisis*, instances of the immediacy of mere mediations. The remains of the phenomenal, which are also gates to the phenomenal, first necessitate judgments and thereby determine their structure. As athematical as the *krisis* may remain in its performance, it still remains a response—and therefore also the beginning of a reflection, a thematization and substantialization—of that to which it refers. And for this reason it is the ground of predicative statements and judgments, the inception of rights and of the juridification and institutionalization of the "human." Infinite judging is finite, and therefore—just like the *exaiphnes*—conceivable only outside of the opposition between the infinite and the finite.

The judgment thus always contains two traits that touch one another, accompany or cross each other: on the one hand, a bare event without ground or rest, without object or satisfaction, sheer transcendence; on the other, the fixation of a theme, the positing of a substance, the determination of an object, even if it be an ideal that serves as a frame of orientation. These two traits, which structure every language and which can be discerned in the Platonic myth, move to the foreground in the difference between the judgment of the dead and the judgment of human rights declarations. The judgment of juridical propositions presents the human being as belonging to a species governed by universal law; the judgment of *krisis* between good and bad testifies, *suddenly* (*exaiphnes*), for an individual, suspending all concepts and ideas that could be formed of him. The judgment of human rights identifies a substance; the judgment of infinite *krisis* dissolves all substantial determinations as phenomena in favor of their transessential movement. As conceived by human rights, man is the subject of his self-declaration, one who encounters all others only as a limit. Man as the court of the dead encounters him is, by contrast, the result of a *krisis*, from which both the one and the other emerge as from the event of their alteration. *Krisis* is the infinite critique of a predicating judgment; this predicating judgment is the resistance that *krisis* turns against itself. If the Platonic *krisis* introduces an adjustment of human rights as they have determined the practice of the ancient Aeropagus, and of all the other courts and institutions of declaration that have followed after, even unto the present, then it continues to demand (and demands ad infinitum) adjustments that would go beyond mere modifications, rectifications, and corrections of human rights. It demands adjustments that might release "the" human from the juridical obsession that its being be determined through rights as an object and subject of judgments, and it demands adjustments that correspond to the structural irony of any such adjustment. It does not demand them for any time in the near or far future, but rather *now, exaiphnes.*

. . .

Among the necessary adjustments to human rights—among those, in other words, that stem from the *structure of judgments as such and from the form of right that is grounded in them* rather than from a spontaneous emotion or from the juristic proof of the insufficiencies of human rights (already carried out in 1950 by Hans Kelsen in his *The Law of the United Nations)*—among these adjustments the most urgent are the ones that may be derived from the following demands:

1. That everyone "alone as well as in association with others" has the right to property, but loses this right whenever it is used for the social, political, or juridical definition of that which he himself, his community, or any other are or should be. Property, as well as the right to property and the right to have this right, are the means to do away with these means.

2. That everyone has the right to appear in any form whatsoever in and before his chosen public, so long as he does not deduce or demand to deduce from this the further right to regard this appearance as a representation of that which he is or should be. Each manner of appearing has its own right. This right is lost whenever it is used for the manipulation or overpowering of other manners of appearing—even before itself.

3. That everyone has the right to belong to one community or several communities, and to act upon them in such a way that all other rights are being furthered in every way. The furthering of these rights may not be limited by any of these communities or any cooperation between them. Wherever such limitation is enforced or threatens to be enforced, a right to part without sanction from the community or communities steps into place.

4. That sovereignty lies not in a people, nor in a nation or state and its representatives. Sovereignty is neither a category of right nor of its foundation or preservation.

5. That no community and no politically constituted society has the right to isolate any of its members, whether it be in order to protect itself or in order to exert punishment. Societies are associations of adoption. Every form of isolation, of segregation and arrest is a form of social murder. The killing of a human being can never be legal.

6. That everyone has the right to inform himself and others about these rights and to participate in the formulation of their consequences and the regulations concerning their enforcement. Everyone has the right to question these rights, to respond to them and to their insufficiencies, and to act to transform them, alone or in association with others, in view of their improvement.

7. That there is no *natural* or *positive* limit to the right to change all rights, including human rights in their traditional definition. The "everyone" to whom these rights are granted must include not only citizens, but also minors, permanent or visiting residents, as well as former and potential members of communities of rights. All rights therefore are transitional rights, which must prove their historical character by being open to future rights that are more just and by being open to a justice beyond right.

The myth of the transphenomenal *krisis* is devoid of all reference to rights. These are presented in a systematic combination in the human rights declarations; such declarations, however, neither unfold the full range of their implications nor even mention the one decisive implication that is common to all of them. It belongs to the very concept of rights, of natural rights as of positive rights, of human rights as of the individual rights that are deduced from them, that they include the "right" *not* to exercise them. Whoever is so disposed may decline to use the right to property and to security, the right to resistance to oppression, and even the right to freedom. But such a person neither renounces those rights nor forfeits them, but only declines to use them, to appeal to them, and to make them a ground for action. This undeclared implication of all rights propounds—in an equally undeclared manner—that the use of all rights and even of the sphere of rights itself may in principle be declined. It says that one can only be free if one is at liberty to refuse the *use* of the *right* to freedom; that one can only use a thing, even the "thing" of one's own proper person, if one can also refuse to do so; and that one can only resist coercion when one is free to resist the very *right* to resistance. The privilege not to use rights is not made explicit in any constitution or any declaration of rights, but is implied by all of them as a freedom *before* the law and *before* the right to freedom. This freedom is the ground for any right to clemency—the right, in other words, to suspend the execution of a verdict—that is reserved to the sovereign. It is an equivalent to the withholding of judgment *in* the judgment as it is practiced in the Platonic *krisis*. But anyone who puts clemency above right need not appeal to a "right" for this purpose. It is equally possible to appeal to uncertainties or omissions of right, and possible even to appeal to basic demands of rights that, due to imponderabilities, can never be translated into codified right. One such demand concerns the appropriate evaluation of singular occurrences or deeds, an *equity*—already demanded by Aristotle—that cannot be secured by a universal rule or even be brought about by a rule governing the application of rules to individual cases. The right to prevent a merely mechanical application of right and to therefore limit the limitations of rights and even right in general as a limit: this right to a suspension of right may not only intervene as the right to clemency in the transition from jurisdiction to execution. As the imperative to adjust the judicial evaluation to a particular case and to consider the interest and weight of conflicting rights, it must also guide any judgment passed by a judge or a court. In such cases, one no longer speaks of "rights" or "laws," but of procedural possibilities and liberties of application: in the English-speaking world, of *judicial discretion*; in the French law system, of *pouvoir d'appréciation du juge*.

If right defines the only universally recognized form of social relations, then social relations consist in a barrier between humans, and antisocial inclinations, linguistic inhibitions, and deadening of the senses is the sense of all social life. Compassion, however, may lift the barrier that right draws between the one who judges and the one who is judged, which may lead—both as a chance and as a danger for justice—to a Saturnalian inversion of the positions in the judicial theater. Tibor Déry, a Hungarian author who experienced the ruinous powers of the law system, draws a vivid picture of such a reversal in his parodic novel *Mr. G. A. in X.*, published in Budapest in 1964. There, an older woman explains the composition of the court:

> "Since the task of pronouncing law requires such great responsibility it is given to unhappy people, . . . because they can identify with the accused at every moment. By the end of the hearing they have changed to such an extent that it is impossible to discern any difference between the judge and the accused."
>
> "That is exactly right," said a man next to her, "I have seen more than one case in which the accused was unable to console the prosecutor, who was sobbing loudly, or the chief justice, who was writhing under the pains inflicted upon him by his professional duty. The latter tends to faint and lose his consciousness under the stress of any encouragement." . . .
>
> "But is it possible," said the young man, blushing with excitement, "that courts in other countries aren't composed of prisoners?"
>
> "It happens," said G.A.
>
> "I can't believe my ears," cried the young man and covered his mouth with his hand in shock.[2]

The possibility of declining to exercise one's rights, the possibility of suspending or overturning the execution of a judgment, and the possibility of employing rights in such a manner that they do justice to human beings and to language—all these possibilities are not local limitations placed upon the validity of the judicial corpus and the procedures of its application, but rather irreducible structural elements of right as a whole, by which it is opened to a realm that is in principle extrajuridical. The sphere of law, much as it is constituted to last, presupposes its own suspendability. This applies also to human rights, in which the essence of man is defined for all times and for every individual instance. Human rights declarations do not mention the possibility of declining the use of rights, along with the determination of the "human" suggested by them. They do not declare—and thus do not define as essential—that it is possible not to use the sphere of rights with its legislative, judicial, and executive powers and thereby to further the cause of justice. Instead, such a possibility remains merely implied. The joining together of rights and their nonuse, the joining together of an essential possibility and the possibility *not* to activate this possibility, the conclusion of rights and their suspension—this synthesis is not declared, nor can it be declared or explained in a juridical manner. The difference between the two introduces into each instance of right and to right itself the infinite *krisis* between the "human" as the substance of right and "humans," whoever and however they may be, as a *transcendens* of all essential determinations in the realm of law. This difference, a nonsynthesis, cannot be formulated in the predicative-synthetic language of judgment and can only be foreclosed by the judicial powers guided by it at the cost of justice and the probity of language.

. . .

A short fable by Walter Benjamin concerning the philosophy of law responds to this difference. It is probably the first note that he wrote after reading Kafka's works and was intended to serve as preparation for a longer essay on them. It was included in a letter written in November 1927 and sent to Gershom Scholem, the friend with whom Benjamin had exchanged his ideas about the structure of justice and the form of the complaint several years earlier. The text is entitled "Idea of a Mystery" ("Idee eines Mysteriums"), and, although it does not refer to human rights as such, it does refer to man and to the trial—and the historical process *as* trial—in which he is involved.

> History to be presented as a trial [*Prozeß*] in which man, as an advocate of mute nature, brings a complaint against all Creation and the persistent absence of the promised Messiah. The court, however, decides to hear witnesses for the future. The poet appears, who feels what is to come; the artist, who sees it; the musician, who hears it; and the philosopher, who knows it. Hence, their testimonies don't correspond with each other, even though they all testify to the coming of the Messiah. The court does not dare to admit that it cannot arrive at a conclusion. For this reason, new complaints keep being introduced, as do new witnesses. There is torture and martyrdom. The jury benches are filled with the living, who listen to man the plaintiff and to the witnesses with equal distrust. The jury members pass their duties on to their sons. At last, the anxiety grows in them that they might be driven from their benches. At the end, the entire jury has fled; only the plaintiff and the witnesses remain.[3]

The Hegelian conviction that world history is at once a world trial is dramatized—and reversed—in Benjamin's "mystery" in a quite un-Hegelian, but not entirely undialectical, manner. The court scene that he describes is the counterpart of the Platonic court of the dead, even though here it is "man" who is in charge of the prosecution and who apparently does not belong to "the living," who make up the jury. While Plato's myth posits a court that arrives at a judgment instantaneously, without a complaint and without witnesses, and that rests on nothing but the fact that it judges—and judges human beings—*exaiphnes*, Benjamin's "mystery" describes a prolonged trial, which in order to do right is supposed to arrive at a judgment but in reality is concerned with the fundamental categories of right itself, with judgment, and with its untenable relation to justice. The "mystery" is about a meta-juridical trial. The complaint that is filed addresses not only a deficit of Creation, the muteness of nature, but also the failure of the Messiah to appear, along with his promised reign of justice. The trial about the missing Messiah is a trial about justice—a trial, therefore, about the very form of the trial—and the question that the jury has to deliberate is presumably: whether messianic justice is *truly* absent or not; whether justice, even if it be a future justice, exists; and whether it would be just if it did exist, or just if it did not. Plato's myth of *krisis* strips souls of all their phenomenal veils. Benjamin's mystery, by contrast, invokes witnesses who testify to the coming of the Messiah and of justice by means of phenomena: the poet who feels them, the artist who sees them, the musician who hears them, and the philosopher who knows them. But the court listens to the witnesses with the same mistrust that it reserves for the grievance, since their testimonies don't match and arrive at anything but a synthesis or a synesthesia. The fact that the court comes to no decision and fears to be driven away because of its inconclusiveness; the fact that it finally flees out of *anxiety*, without having reached a judgment and pronounced right: this breakdown of the court constitutes—without a single word of judgment—the verdict passed on the court, the verdict passed on any possible conclusion, on any possible judgment, and on the entire sphere of right represented by it. That which *remains* in the Platonic court of the dead is the bare act of judging, suddenly and unendingly. Benjamin's world court, by contrast, knows no judgment but only the attempt to reach one. What *remains* are the prosecutor with his complaint and the witnesses with their contradictory testimonies. The last sentence of Benjamin's text states that "only the plaintiff and the witnesses remain [*bleiben*]" after "the entire jury has fled." The Messiah—and justice with him—have "failed to appear [*Ausbleiben*]" during the course of the entire world historical process. At the end of history *remains* the dispute about the one who persistently *remained absent*. The judgment should have brought about a decision about whether to admit the grievance or not, but also a decision about whether the accused, the one who remains absent, really remains absent and in what sense he might do so. The question that remains open is not about the sense of being but rather about the sense of the remaining [*Bleiben*] and remaining absent [*Ausbleiben*] of justice. This question is resolved neither through a judgment nor through a judicial decision; nevertheless, Benjamin's fable leaves the possibility open that a decision might still occur—yet occur precisely through the dissolution of the court.

It is evident that the Messiah does not enter into history. It is equally evident that messianic justice is not the object of a judgment. The mystery, however, lies in the fact that the collapse of the historical trial about justice could itself be just. It could, indeed, correspond to justice that it is not a theme of right, and it could be a testimony for justice that right has to fail when a decision about justice needs to be reached. But what does it mean that no judgment is possible about the Messiah—about justice and about the human, along with his complaint and his testimony?

It might mean that justice cannot be an object of judgment and of decision, of conclusion and the formation of consent, since it is itself a process (*Prozeß*) that *as a process* can only remain just if it isn't from the beginning concluded by a telos, a goal, or an intentional object. Justice would thus be not a purpose but an event; it would be history as the event of the juridical—and toward the end the no longer juridical—fight for justice, a fight that must be abandoned before the judgment is reached so as not to abandon justice itself. Justice would thus be not a cognitive category that refers to substantial determinations but an ethical—a messianic—event that invalidates all pretensions of substantiality.

Yet the experience that a judgment about the Messiah is impossible could mean that he may never come. The grievance about his remaining absent testifies to the fact that he isn't there; the testimony of the artists indicates, however, that he will come. Cognitive and juridical judgments refer to present objects, whether they be empirical or ideal. Where they refer to future objects, they do so only insofar as they will be present in the future. The Messiah, justice, and man, however, would remain absent *in* their very coming; they would arrive only in their failure to arrive, not in any present. Irresolvably aporetic events, they would remain unpredictable. What remains only by remaining absent is inaccessible to judgment, since it itself is the future that might make possible a judgment it nevertheless withholds. What may come doesn't allow itself to be judged, since the very possibility of its coming may at any moment turn out to be impossible. Every possibility of a future event is accompanied by the possibility of its impossibility; every prognosis about the future can be canceled by its remaining absent. The deactivation of judgment is a function of the future: for so long as there is historical time there will also be the possibility of a future and therefore the possibility of a Messiah. But so long as there is the possibility of his coming, there will also be the possibility of his not coming. Therefore, no conclusive judgment exists either about him or about the world in which he could possibly intervene. The Messiah—the justice to come—suspends with the judgment about him the entire sphere of right that is grounded in judgment.

That no judgment is pronounced about the Messiah—and this is the third explication—means neither that he will come nor that he won't come. It means neither that history is a messianic event nor that it is not. The inconclusiveness and flight of the court deactivate the form of judgment. The enduring dispute between the plaintiff and the witnesses devalorizes the illocutionary force of language—of the complaint and of the testimony—which might allow a decision about whether messianic judgment will arrive or remain absent, about whether history is messianic or not. If plaintiff and witnesses are the only ones to "remain" at the end of the world court, then the possibility that the complaint might be just also remains. But this complaint concerns at once the missing Messiah and the missing language of nature. Complaining—or lamenting—about the persistent absence of messianic language is therefore, although it pertains to messianic matters, not itself by any degree of certainty "messianic." It is *ammessianic*—both amessianic (without a messianic referent) and admessianic (relating to the possibility of a messianic event)—language that serves as an advocate for a language that remains absent, a language of a grief and an outrage that insists that a language for all and for everything should be possible and shall come, without, however, being certain of it and without being able to anticipate it as such. It is the language of a revolt not only of the unpredictable but also of the impracticable, imperformative, afformative; a revolt not only of the absence of judgment, but also of muteness—and therefore the insurrection of what Benjamin calls a "mystery." Mystery here has not only the sense of the Christian messianic mystery plays but also that of a structural secret. In the remaining of remaining absent, the perseverance of its lacking and the insistence on its own failure, language ceases to be a judgment or an act, a predication or a performance, an adjudication or execution, and leaves open the question of whether it can still be called language. It no longer has an addressee (for the jury flees), nor an object (for the very possibility of such an object is withdrawn from judgment), nor even a subject (which could constitute itself only in a language that would be more than a mere complaint or a testimony). Language, which at its extreme is complaint and testimony, is the language only of its own lack. *Language is its own stoppage*— and therefore the stoppage of all judicial powers that might appeal to it, of all judicial titles that might be claimed through it, and of all "human rights" that have been or might still be declared through it.

Some consequences concerning the structure of what are called "human rights" need to be drawn from the considerations that are condensed in Benjamin's short text. A judgment is not a form of justice, and right not a category of its integral realization. For as long as there are only human rights, there will not be human justice. The political, anthropological, and theological authorities who claim to be the advocates of human rights would serve the justice, freedom, and dignity of man best by expanding the zones of their indecision and by bringing about circumstances in which none of their rights need ever be appealed to—circumstances in which the right not to need and not to use rights could be exercised without any limits. Since this freedom to abstain from the use of rights cannot be brought about by force, and since the suspension of the sphere of right can only succeed if this sphere of right is internally developed to be as just as possible, everything must be done in order either to remove the degrading, incapacitating, and impoverishing elements from human rights or to render them harmless by transforming them. This applies in particular to the right to property, the right to sovereignty of the state, and the right of states to punish, exclude, and segregate their members and guests. Since justice cannot be expected, right must be furthered—foremost the right of those who don't have rights or cannot exercise them: the right of advocacy for everything that is silent, silenced, or mute, for the unborn and for the dead, for the natural as much as the technical in humans, for everything that is no more and not yet, for what has no voice, for the future and for the future of their pasts. The right of advocacy for everything that does not speak the language of right, of juridical argument and of judgment, including the right of both philosophy and literature, of myth and of mystery, of the court of the dead and of the fleeing world court in which the ruling forms of right and of judgment are suspended, along with the form of the human that they define.

—Translated by Tobias Boes

Contributors

Talal Asad was born in Saudi Arabia and educated in Britain. He now teaches anthropology at the Graduate Center of the City University of New York. His most recent book is entitled *Formations of the Secular: Christianity, Islam, Modernity* (2003).

Pope Benedict XVI is the 265th and reigning Pope, the head of the Roman Catholic Church, and the sovereign of Vatican City State. Formerly Joseph Cardinal Ratzinger, he served as a professor at various German universities and at the time of his election was Dean of the College of Cardinals. The most recent of his books to have appeared in English are *Values in a Time of Upheaval*, *Pilgrim Fellowship of Faith: The Church as Communion*, *The End of Time? The Provocation of Talking about God* (all 2005), and *Truth and Tolerance: Christian Belief and World Religions* (2004).

Jane Bennett is Professor of Political Science at The Johns Hopkins University and a founding member of the journal *theory & event*. She is the author of *The Enchantment of Modern Life: Attachments, Crossings, and Ethics* (2001), *Thoreau's Nature: Ethics, Politics, and the Wild* (1994; 2d ed. 2002), and *Unthinking Faith and Enlightenment: Nature and the State in a Post-Hegelian Era* (1987). She is currently working on a book that explores the ecological implications of different conceptions of materiality in contemporary political thought.

Wendy Brown is Professor of Political Science at the University of California, Berkeley. Her books include *Regulating Aversion: A Critique of Tolerance in the Age of Identity and Empire* (2006), *Edgework: Essays on Knowledge and Politics* (2005), *Politics out of History* (2001), and *States of Injury: Power and Freedom in Late Modernity* (1995).

Judith Butler is the Maxine Elliot Professor of Rhetoric and Comparative Literature at the University of California, Berkeley. Her most recent books are *Giving an Account of Oneself* (2005) and *Precarious Life: The Power of Mourning and Violence* (2004).

Job Cohen is Mayor of Amsterdam, a post he has held since January 15, 2001. Before that time, he was State Secretary of the Dutch Ministry of Justice, dealing chiefly with immigration, under Prime Minister Wim Kok. Prior to his entry into politics as a member of the Labor Party (PvdA), he was Professor of Methods and Techniques in the Faculty of Law of Maastricht University, and then the university's Rector Magnificus. In 2005, *Time* magazine awarded him the title "European Hero."

William E. Connolly is Krieger-Eisenhower Professor at The Johns Hopkins University, where he teaches political theory. His earlier book *The Terms of Political Discourse* (1993) won the Lippincott award for "a book of outstanding merit that is still significant after a time span of at least fifteen years." His recent publications include *Pluralism* (2005), *Neuropolitics: Thinking, Culture, Speed* (2002), and *Why I Am Not A Secularist* (2000).

Veena Das is Krieger-Eisenhower Professor at The Johns Hopkins University, where she teaches in the Department of Anthropology. She is a Foreign Fellow of the American Academy of Arts and Sciences and the Third World Academy of Sciences. She has published widely on questions of social suffering and violence. The last two books she has authored are *Life and Words: Violence and the Descent into the Ordinary* (2006) and *Critical Events: An Anthropological Perspective on Contemporary India* (1995).

Marcel Detienne is Gildersleeve Professor of Classics at The Johns Hopkins University. Some of his recent books are: *A Comparative Anthropology of Ancient Greece* (2006), *Les Grecs et nous* (2005), *Comment être autochtone: Du pur athenien au français racine* (2003), *Writing of Orpheus: Greek Myth in Cultural Context* (2002), and *Comparer l'incomparable* (2000).

Thierry de Duve is Professor of Aesthetics and Art History at the University of Lille 3. His work has long revolved around Marcel Duchamp's readymades and their implications for aesthetics; it is now finding a new center of interest in the work of Manet. He is the author of several books, including *Kant after Duchamp* (1996). He curated the exhibition "Voici—100 ans d'art contemporain" at the Brussels Palais des Beaux-Arts in 2000, as well as the Belgian pavilion at the 2003 Venice Biennale, shared by Sylvie Eyberg and Valérie Mannaerts.

Stefanos Geroulanos is a doctoral candidate in intellectual history at The Johns Hopkins Humanities Center and is currently completing his dissertation, "Man under Erasure:

Antihumanism and Philosophical Anthropology in French Thought (1925–1950)." He is also co-translating Georges Canguilhem's *Knowledge of Life*.

Jürgen Habermas is Professor of Philosophy Emeritus at the Johann Wolfgang Goethe-University in Frankfurt am Main and former director of its Institute for Social Research. He is also Permanent Visiting Professor at Northwestern University. The most recent of his many books in English translation are *Truth and Justification* (2005) and *Religion and Rationality: Essays on Reason, God, and Modernity* (2002).

Werner Hamacher is Professor of Comparative Literature at the Johann Wolfgang Goethe-University in Frankfurt am Main and Distinguished Global Professor at New York University. He is the author of *Pleroma: Reading in Hegel* (1999) and *Premises: Essays on Philosophy and Literature from Kant to Celan* (1997).

Yolande Jansen teaches history of philosophy and metaphysics in the Department of Philosophy at the University of Amsterdam. She is currently involved in a postdoctoral research project entitled "Laïcité's (French Secularism's) Interactions among France, Algeria, and Turkey" within the larger research project The Future of the Religious Past, sponsored by the Netherlands Organization for Scientific Research (NWO), and she is the author of *Stuck in a Revolving Door: Secularism, Assimilation, and Democratic Pluralism* (2006).

Kate Khatib is a doctoral candidate at The Johns Hopkins University Humanities Center. She is currently developing a dissertation project on surrealism, in both its historical and present incarnations.

Ernesto Laclau holds a chair in political theory at the University of Essex. Among the books he has authored are *On Populist Reason* (2005), *Emancipation(s)* (1996), and *New Reflections on the Revolution of Our Time* (1990). He is the co-author, with Chantal Mouffe, of *Hegemony and Socialist Strategy: Towards a Radical Democratic Politics* (1985).

Claude Lefort was a founding member of Socialisme ou barbarie, and later of Information et Liasons Ouvrières. He taught at the University of São Paulo, the Sorbonne, and the École des Hautes Études en Sciences Sociales. Among his books to appear in English are *Writing: The Political Test* (2000) and *The Political Forms of Modern Society: Bureaucracy, Democracy, Totalitarianism* (1986).

Bruce Lincoln is Professor of the History of Religions at the University of Chicago. Among his recent books are *Holy Terrors: Thinking about Religion after September 11* (2003) and *Theorizing Myth: Narrative, Ideology, and Scholarship* (2000).

Paola Marrati is Professor of Humanities and Philosophy at The Johns Hopkins University, where she directs the steering committee of the Program for the Study of Women, Gender, and Sexuality. She is also Directrice de Programme de Récherche at the Collège International de Philosophie. She is the author of *Genesis and Trace: Derrida Reading Husserl and Heidegger* (2005) and *Deleuze: Philosophie et cinema* (2003, forthcoming in an expanded English edition). She is currently completing a book project entitled *The Event and the Ordinary: On the Philosophy of Stanley Cavell and Gilles Deleuze.*

Stéphane Mosès was Professor of German and Comparative Literature at the Hebrew University from 1971 until 1997. He is Corresponding Member of the German Academy for Language and Literature and holds a Doctor honoris causa from the University of Tübingen. Among his books are: *Au-delà de la guerre: Trois Études sur Levinas* (2004), *Walter Benjamin and the Spirit of Modernity* (2003), *L'Ange de l'histoire: Rosenzweig, Benjamin, Scholem* (1992), and *System and Revelation: The Philosophy of Franz Rosenzweig* (1992).

Chantal Mouffe is Professor of Political Theory at the University of Westminster. Among her books are *On the Political* (2005), *The Democratic Paradox* (2000), *The Return of the Political* (1993), and, co-authored with Ernesto Laclau, *Hegemony and Socialist Strategy: Towards a Radical Democratic Politics* (1985).

Jean-Luc Nancy is Distinguished Professor of Philosophy at the University Marc Bloch, Strasbourg. The most recent of his many books to be published in English are *The Ground of the Image* (2005) and *A Finite Thinking* (2003).

M. B. Pranger is Professor of the History of Christianity at the University of Amsterdam. In his publications, which are mainly on medieval monasticism, he focuses on the relationship between religion and literature. His most recent book is *The Artificiality of Christianity: Essays on the Poetics of Monasticism* (2003), and he is currently completing a book on Augustine and Henry James, provisionally entitled *Augustinian Soundings.*

Bettina Prato recently completed her Ph.D. in political theory at the University of California, Berkeley, with a dissertation on the politics of responsibility, melancholy, and trauma in contemporary Israel/Palestine. In addition, she is an international consultant specializing in postconflict development interventions and gender-equality work in the Middle East.

Rafael Sánchez is a Research Fellow in the NWO-sponsored Pionier Program "Religion, Media, and the Public Sphere" at the University of Amsterdam. His publications have focused on media, mass politics, populism, and spirit mediumship. He is currently completing a book entitled *Dancing Jacobins: A Genealogy of Latin American Populism (Venezuela)* and a project entitled "The Fate of Sovereignty in the Landscape of the City."

Matthew Scherer is currently a Mellon Postdoctoral Fellow in the Department of Rhetoric at the University of California, Berkeley. He teaches courses in political theory and is preparing his dissertation, "The Politics of Persuasion: Habit, Creativity, Conversion," for publication.

Bhrigupati Singh is currently a Ph.D. student in the Department of Anthropology at The Johns Hopkins University. His current research project concerns starvation deaths and poverty in rural Rajasthan.

Lawrence E. Sullivan is Professor of World Religions in the Departments of Theology and Anthropology at the University of Notre Dame, after serving for many years as the Director of Harvard University's Center for the Study of World Religions. His *Icanchu's Drum: An Orientation to Meaning in South American Religions* won the 1989 Association of American Publishers award for best book in philosophy and religion and a 1990 best book award from the American Council of Learned Societies. He is associate editor of the sixteen-volume *Encyclopedia of Religion* and a Fellow of the American Academy of Arts and Sciences. He has served as President of the American Academy of Religion and deputy Secretary-General of the International Association for the History of Religions.

Antónia Szabari is Assistant Professor of French and Comparative Literature at the University of Southern California. She is currently completing a book entitled *Less Rightly Said: Scandalous Words in the French Reformation*.

Lars Tønder is Assistant Professor in the Department of Political Science at DePauw University. He is the co-editor of *Radical Democracy: Politics Between Abundance and Lack* (2005), and his current research focuses on questions of tolerance and toleration.

Markha G. Valenta is an interdisciplinary postdoctoral researcher at the Free University of Amsterdam. Her current project concerns the socio-cultural, imaginary, and institutional politics of Islam and Muslims in the West relative to larger processes of localization, globalization, and nation-state formation, in particular, through a close comparative reading of recent debates and events in the United States and the Netherlands.

Peter van der Veer is University Professor at Utrecht University. He is also a Senior Fellow and a Distinguished Visiting Professor at the India-China Institute of the New School in New York. He has published widely on religion and society, including *Imperial Encounters: Religion and Modernity in India and Britain* (2001), *Religious Nationalism:*

Hindus and Muslims in India (1994), and *Gods on Earth* (1988). He is currently engaged in a comparative project on spirituality in India and China.

Hent de Vries is Professor of Humanities and Philosophy at The Johns Hopkins University and Professor of Philosophy at the University of Amsterdam. He is the author of *Minimal Theologies: Critiques of Secular Reason in Adorno and Levinas* (2005), *Religion and Violence: Philosophical Perspectives from Kant to Derrida* (2002), and *Philosophy and the Turn to Religion* (1999). Among the volumes he has co-edited are, with Samuel Weber, *Religion and Media* (2001) and *Violence, Identity, and Self-Determination* (1998).

Samuel Weber is Avalon Professor of Comparative Literature at Northwestern University and Director of Northwestern's Paris Program in Critical Theory. He is the author of numerous books, most recently *Targets of Opportunity: On the Militarization of Thinking* (2005) and *Theatricality as Medium* (2004). He is the co-editor, with Hent de Vries, of *Religion and Media* (2001) and *Violence, Identity, and Self-Determination* (1998).

Marc de Wilde is Assistant Professor of Legal History at the University of Amsterdam. He is currently completing a dissertation on political theology in the work of Walter Benjamin and Carl Schmitt.

Notes

Hent de Vries and Lawrence E. Sullivan, Preface

1. Joseph Stiglitz, *Globalization and Its Discontents* (New York: W. W. Norton, 2002), 224–25.

2. Harlan Cleveland and Mark Luyckx, "Civilizations and Governance," background paper for the World Academy of Art and Science and EU Forward Studies Unit Joint Seminar, European Commission, April 1998, 9.

3. See Robert J. Barro and Rachel M. McCleary, "Religion and Economic Growth," National Bureau of Economic Research Working Paper 9682 (http://www.nber.org/papers/w9682).

4. In retrospect, the project also prepared the ground for an even more ambitious interdisciplinary research program, entitled The Future of the Religious Past: Elements and Forms for the Twenty-first Century and funded with a generous grant of more than five million euros by the NWO Research Council for the Humanities (GW), the NWO Research Council for the Social Sciences (MaGW), and the Netherlands Foundation for the Advancement of Tropical Research (WOTRO). The new program has intensified the rhythm of international exchanges started by the earlier collaboration. Assisted by its international advisory board, chaired by Professor Veena Das of The Johns Hopkins University, the program committee of The Future of the Religious Past, chaired by Hent de Vries, has now selected some thirteen projects of teams of researchers. Their most representative and challenging results, in conjunction with essays by internationally celebrated scholars, will be published in a series of five volumes under contract with Fordham University Press. The first of these is scheduled for publication in the fall of 2007.

Hent de Vries, Introduction: Before, Around, and Beyond the Theologico-Political

1. For the necessary cautions when speaking of "religion," see Tomoko Masuzawa, *In Search of Dreamtime: The Quest for the Origin of Religion* (Chicago: University of Chicago Press, 1993), and idem, *The Invention of World Religions: Or, How European Universalism Was Preserved in the Language of Pluralism* (Chicago: University of Chicago Press, 2005). See also Etienne Balibar, "Note sur l'origine et les usages du terme 'monothéisme,' in *Dieu*, special issue of *Critique*, no. 704–5 (2006): 19–45.

2. "*Vivre 'ensemble'*—Living 'Together'" is the title of the talk Jacques Derrida delivered at the conference entitled Irreconcilable Differences? Jacques Derrida and the Question of Religion, held at the University of California, Santa Barbara, on October 23–25, 2003. This was to be his last visit to the United States. He sought a new figure beyond any appeal to a quasi-biological notion of life and filiation, indeed, beyond even the human or humanity, or of the living restrictively defined.

3. Hans Joas, *Braucht der Mensch Religion? Über Erfahrungen der Selbsttranszendenz* (Freiburg im Breisgau: Herder, 2004), 124.

4. Cited in ibid.

5. Ibid., 124–25.

6. Ibid., 125.

7. The notion is aptly demystified in "Islam, America, and Europe," in *The Economist*, June 24, 2006.

8. Ibid.

9. Ibid.

10. Ibid.

11. Philippe Lacoue-Labarthe and Jean-Luc Nancy, eds., *Le Retrait du politique: Travaux du centre de recherches philosophiques sur le politique* (Paris: Galilée, 1983); *Retreating the Political*, ed. Simon Sparks (London: Routledge, 1997).

12. See Hent de Vries, *Religion and Violence: Philosophical Reflections from Kant to Derrida* (Baltimore: The Johns Hopkins University Press, 2002).

13. Scott Shane, "Terrorism Has a Global Impact but Is Often Rooted in Local Disputes," in *The International Herald Tribune*, July 17, 2006.

14. Robert Wright, "Progressive Realism: In Search of a Foreign Policy," in *The International Herald Tribune*, July 19, 2006. Wright attributes this view to Hans Morgenthau.

15. See my concluding chapter in Hent de Vries, *Philosophy and the Turn to Religion* (Baltimore: The Johns Hopkins University Press, 1999).

16. For deterritorialization, see Oliver Roy, *Globalized Islam: The Search for the New Ummah* (New York: Columbia University Press, 2004), 38. This book is a revised edition of *L'Islam mondialisé* (Paris: Seuil, 2002). Roy is hardly defending a present-day version of "Orientalism," which he defines as "the prevailing discourse among Islamic intellectuals" and its "mirror vision that still dominates a part of Western Islamic studies," namely, "the perception of Islam and of Muslim societies as one global, timeless cultural system" (Roy, *The Failure of Political Islam*, trans. Carol Volk [Cambridge: Harvard University Press, 1994], vii). On the meaning of *Orientalism*, see my lemma "Orientalism," in *Encyclopedia of Religion*, 2d ed., ed. Lindsay Jones (New York: Macmillan, 2005).

17. Roy, *Globalized Islam*, 39.

18. Ibid.

19. See the Global Attitudes Project of the Pew Research Center, reported in *Le Monde*, July 18, 2005, and in "Muslims and Europe: Surprisingly Positive. Pew Finds Changes in Attitudes," in *The International Herald Tribune*, July 7, 2006. See http://pewglobal.org/.

20. *The Economist*, July 16, 2005. A year after the attack, a video was broadcast by the Qatar-based news channel al-Jazeera in which one of the purported suicide bombers, Shezad Tanweer, announces that "what you have witnessed now is only the beginning," along with separate footage showing Ayman al-Zawahiri, Al Qaeda's number two in command, who thus sought to take credit for the attacks (see *The International Herald Tribune*, July 7, 2006).

21. Recruitment of volunteers in the targeted country by means of video appeals such as the one referenced in n. 20 may inaugurate a next phase in the logic of terrorism's de- and re-territorialization. See Jessica Stern, "Marketing Jihad: Al Qaeda Changes Its Pitch," in *The International Herald Tribune*, July 17, 2006. Stern refers to Adam Gadahn, a young American who invokes the widely mediatized abuses of prisoners and the increasing number of civil victims in Iraq to impute responsibility to American citizens, addressing himself to prospective local recruits.

22. Olivier Roy, "The Ideology of Terror," *The International Herald Tribune*, July 23–24, 2005.

23. Roy, *Globalized Islam*, 33.

24. Roy, *The Failure of Political Islam*, ix.

25. The Danish prime minister Anders Fogh Rasmussen was taken to task in the appendix to a recent report by scholars of the Center for Middle Eastern Studies at the University of South Denmark for not receiving a delegation that in October 2005 had requested an audition to protest "discriminatory tendencies" and "the abuse of Islam in the name of democracy, freedom of expression, and human rights." This blockage of dialogue, the researchers conclude, constituted "the real offense" in the whole affair, that is to say, "not the fact that the Prophet was insulted, but the fact that the insult was not recognized as such" (see *Le Monde*, June 6, 2006). A comment by scholars, made in a personal communication in Copenhagen in June 2006, was as simple as it was insightful: what the whole affair taught us, they said, was "there is no longer a local public sphere."

26. Olivier Roy, "The Ideology of Terror." See also Roy's "La Communauté virtuelle: L'Internet et la déterritorialisation de l'islam," in *Réseaux* (Paris: CENT/Hermes Science Publications, 2000).

27. See Roy, *Globalized Islam*, 42 ff. There is an element of autocritique in this comment, if we see it against the background of Roy's pre-9/11 statement that "aside from the Iranian revolution, Islamism has not significantly altered the political landscape of the Middle East. Political Islam does not pass the test of power. In the early 1990s the regimes of 1980 are still in place, and the Gulf War has established American hegemony. A strange Islamic threat indeed, which waged war only against other Muslims (Iran/Iraq) or against the Soviets (Afghanistan) and caused less terrorist damage than the Baader-Meinhof gang, the Red Brigade, the Irish Republican Army, and the Basque separatist ETA, whose small-group actions have been features of the European political landscape longer than hizbullahs and other jihad movements" (*The Failure of Political Islam*, ix). For a discussion of the cultural representation of the RAF, see Thomas Elsaesser, "Antigone Agonistes: Urban Guerilla or Guerilla Urbanism? The RAF, Germany in Autumn and Death Game," in *Giving Ground: The Politics of Propinquity*, ed. Joan Copjec and Michael Sorkin (London: Verso, 1999).

28. Roy, *Globalized Islam*, 43.

29. Ibid. Mutatis mutandis, this might hold true for changes in the balance of power within the Middle East itself, where an almost cynical calculation seems to hold sway over ideologico-religious considerations. See Olivier Roy, "L'Iran fait monter les enchères: La Stratégie de tension que Téhéran organise hors de ses frontières inquiète ses voisins arabes," *Le Monde*, July 21, 2006.

30. Roy, *The Failure of Political Islam*, ix.

31. Ibid., x.

32. Ibid., xi.

33. Ibid.

34. *The Economist*, June 24, 2006.

35. Marcel Gauchet, *Le Désenchantement du monde: Une Histoire politique de la religion* (Paris: Gallimard, 1985); *The Disenchantment of the World: A Political History of Religion*, trans. Oscar Burge, with a Foreword by Charles Taylor (Princeton: Princeton University Press, 1997).

36. Ibid., 44. See also Faisal Devji, *Landscapes of the Jihad: Militancy, Morality, Modernity* (Ithaca: Cornell University Press, 2005).

37. Roy, *Globalized Islam*, 49.

38. Ibid., 50.

39. Oliver Roy, "Get French or Die Trying," *The New York Times*, November 9, 2005.

40. David Brooks, "Gangsta, in French," *The New York Times*, November 10, 2005.

41. See *The New York Times*, January 30, 2006, and the "BondyBlog," to be found at www .hebdo.ch/indexBlogs.cfm and the corresponding volume edited by *L'Hebdo*, together with Serge Michel, *Bondy Blog: Des journalistes suisses dans le 9–3* (Paris: Seuil, 2006). The word *blog* comes from "weblog," then the pun "we blog." On the "New Social Critique" and "La République des

idées," inspired by the work of Pierre Rosanvallon, see the dossier in *Le Monde*, May 20, 2006, and the volume *La Nouvelle Critique sociale* (Paris: Seuil and *Le Monde*, 2006). See also David Lepoutre, *Coeur de banlieue: Codes, rites et langages* (Paris: Odile Jacob, 2001), and Loïc Wacquant, *Parias Urbains: Ghetto, banlieus, état* (Paris: La Découverte: 2006), and idem, "Burn Baby Burn, French Style? Roots of the Riots in the French City," an interview to be found on http://sociology.berkeley.-edu/faculty/wacquant/.

42. As I stated earlier, polls find little support for radical Islam: see "Muslims and Europe: Surprisingly Positive. Pew Finds Changes in Attitudes," in *The International Herald Tribune*, July 7, 2006.

43. Roy, "Get French or Die Trying."

44. See Jean-Marc Manach, "Échos de la guerre sur la blogosphère," in *Le Monde*, July 29, 2006. For Ramzi's blog, see http://ramziblahblah.blogspot.com, and Tom Zelter, Jr., "Anne Frank 2006: Web-savvy Youths Record Suffering in Mideast," in *The International Herald Tribune*, July 25, 2006. For the blog and video of Galya Daube, a fifteen-year-old inhabitant of Haifa, see www.snipurl.com/Galya).

45. See Thomas Crampton, "France's Mysterious Embrace of Blogs," in *The International Herald Tribune*, July 28, 2006. The article reflects on the intensity of blogging in France, where, interestingly, a far greater percentage (indeed, a majority) of Internet users visit blogs, "the personal and public journals of the Internet age." See also the survey of new media in *The Economist*, April 22, 2006, which details in what ways the "era of mass media is giving way to one of personal and participatory media," notably blogs, including photo and video blogs (or "vlogs").

46. See, for a report on the "One Laptop per Child" (OLPC) project, Éric Leser, "À 100 dollars, l'ordinateur des pauvres," in *Le Monde 2*, June 17, 2006, and Nicholas Negroponte, "One Laptop per Child," in *The World in 2006*, *The Economist*, 2006.

47. See *The Economist*, July 29, 2006, which leaves no doubt about the answer to this question: "Mobile phones are cheaper, simpler and more reliable than PC's, and market forces—in particular, the combination of pre-paid billing plans and microcredit schemes—are already putting them into the hands of even the world's poorest people. Initiatives to spread PC's in the developing world, in contrast, rely on top-down funding from governments or aid agencies, rather than bottom-up adoption by consumers. . . . There is no question that the PC has democratized computing and unleashed innovation: but it is the mobile phone that now seems most likely to carry the dream of the 'personal computer' to its conclusion." For the history of the personal computer, including its links to countercultural dreams of utopian social engineering in the sixties, see Thierry Bardini, *Bootstrapping: Douglas Engelbart, Coevolution, and the Origins of Personal Computing* (Stanford: Stanford University Press, 2000); the topic has recently also been taken up by Fred Turner, in *From Counterculture to Cyberculture: Stewart Brand, The Whole Earth Network, and the Rise of Digital Utopianism* (Chicago: University of Chicago Press, 2006).

48. Marjorie Garber and Rebecca L. Walkowitz, eds., *One Nation under God: Religion and American Culture* (New York: Routledge, 1999).

49. See Timothy Garton Ash, "New World Disorder," in *The Guardian Weekly*, July 28–August 3, 2006.

50. Mark Leonard, "The Geopolitics of 2026," in *The World in 2006*, *The Economist*, 2006. Leonard also sees a limited future role for what he—in a somewhat unhelpful expression—calls a "Faith Zone," that is to say, a consortium of Muslim countries, tied into the global economic market but distinguished from the supposedly secular (and expanding) "Eurosphere."

51. *Trouw*, May 15, 2006. For the report, see Jos de Haan and Christian van 't Hof, eds., *Jaarboek ICT en samenleving: De digitale generatie*, published under the auspices of the Sociaal en

Cultureel Planbureau and the Rathenau Institute (Amsterdam: Boom, 2006). On the general trends in the integration of young migrants, see Dirk Vlasblom, "Het beste van twee werelden: Internationale studie wijst uit dat de meeste jonge immigranten voor integratie kiezen," in *NRC Handelsblad*, January 8, 2006, which reviews a recent study by John W. Berry, Jean S. Phinney, David L. Sam, and Paul Vedder, entitled *Immigrant Youth in Transition: Acculturation, Identity, and Adaptation Across National Contexts* (Mahwah, N.J.: Lawrence Erlbaum Associates, 2006). In addition, see the contested report by the Dutch Scientific Council for Government Policy (WRR) entitled *Dynamiek is islamitisch activisme: Aanknopingspunten voor democratisering en mensenrechten* (The Hague: WRR, Amsterdam University Press, 2006), and the report by the Netherlands General Intelligence and Security Service (AIVD) of the Ministry of the Interior, *De geweldadige Jihad in Nederland: Actuele trends in de islamitisch-terroristische dreiging* (The Hague: Algemene Inlichtingen- en Veiligheidsdienst, 2006).

52. See the front-page article by Howard W. French, "Mob Rule on China's Internet: The Keyboard as Weapon," in *The International Herald Tribune*, June 1, 2006.

53. Patrick Haenni, *L'Islam de marché: L'Autre Révolution conservatrice* (Paris: Seuil, 2005), 10.

54. Ibid., 8–12. See also Samantha M. Shapiro, "Ministering to the Upwardly Mobile Muslim," *The New York Times Magazine*, April 30, 2006, on the media empire of Amr Khaled, a former accountant, whose Web site received 26 million hits in 2005 and is the third most visited Arabic Web site after al-Jazeera.

55. See Sonia Kolesnikov-Jessop, "Islamic Banking Seeks New Customers as Wealth Expands," in *International Herald Tribune*, May 24, 2006.

56. Haenni, *L'Islam de marché*, 17.

57. Ibid., 18.

58. Ibid., 18, 19.

59. Roy, *Globalized Islam*, 55, 56. Of course, one might point to a host of semi-official declarations that have now been assembled, translated, and interpreted. See: Bruce Lawrence, ed., *Messages to the World: The Statements of Osama bin Laden* (London: Verso, 2005); and Gilles Kepel and Jean-Pierre Milelli, eds., *Al-Qaida dans le texte: Écrits d'Oussama ben Laden, Abdallah Azzam, Ayman al-Zawahiri et Abou Moussab al-Zarqawi* (Paris: Presses Universitaires de France, 2005). See also Jason Burke, *Al Qaeda: The True Story of Radical Islam* (Harmondsworth, Middlesex: Penguin Books, 2003). These documents demonstrate a considerable heterodoxy and adaptability in discourse and strategy. In a recent public video statement, broadcast by al-Jazeera on July 27, 2006, Ayman al-Zawahiri, responding to the crisis in Lebanon, appealed to the "disinherited of the world" and the "victims of oppressors" for solidarity with Muslim jihadists. This was the first time Al Qaeda had directly appealed to non-Muslims to join its struggle (see *Le Monde*, July 29, 2006). This rhetoric may reveal that the perceived success of Hezbollah, a Shiite organization sponsored by Iran, may have tripped off mimetic rivalry in the Al Qaeda leadership, who, being Sunnis, consider Shiites to be heretics. Al Qaeda has always found it easier to assert solidarity with Hamas, a Sunni and Muslim Brotherhood organization. Conversely, Hezbollah has always disapproved of Al Qaeda's tactics.

To be aware of such distinctions is important, as Roger Cohen insists in "Sacrificing a Democracy While Supporting an Ally," in *The International Herald Tribune*, July 29–30, 2006: "'Everyone understands that a victory for Hezbollah is a victory for world terror,' said Haim Ramon, the Israeli justice minister. Not so: A victory for Hezbollah is a victory for Hezbollah. . . . Trying to turn the problems of the world into a single undifferentiated issues—the war on Islamic terror—does nobody any good."

An important source for the Muslim Brotherhood is Oliver Carré, *Mystique et politique: Le Coran des islamistes (lecture du Coran par Sayyid Qutb, Frère musulman radical (1906–1966)* (Paris:

Cerf, 2004); *Mysticism and Politics: A Critical Reading of Fi Zilal al-Qu'ran by Sayyid Qutb (1906–1966)*, ed. Reinhard Schulze (Leiden: E. J. Brill, 2003). For a view taken from everyday life, see Anne Nivat, *Islamistes: Comment ils nous voient* (Paris: Fayard, 2006).

60. Roy, "The Ideology of Terror."

61. Jessica Stern, "Terrorism: Jihad Is a Global Fad," in *The International Herald Tribune*, August 2, 2006.

62. Ibid.

63. Ibid.

64. Ibid.

65. See Gabriel Weimann, "Deadly Conversations: Terrorists on the Web," in *The International Herald Tribune*, July 21, 2006.

66. See *Le Monde*, August 6, 2005. That the very concept of electronic monitoring—as in the cooperation between the American National Security Agency (NSA) and phone companies such as AT&T, Verizon, and BellSouth—is problematic, not just for legal and moral but for logistical or mathematical reasons, is convincingly argued by Jonathan David Farley in "Getting the Terrorists on the Phone: The NSA's Math Problem," in *The International Herald Tribune*, May 17, 2006. See also the informative article "National Security Agency: Les Oreilles de l'Amérique," in *Le Monde*, June 1, 2006. Farley argues that "graph theorists" and "social network analysis specialists" have the greatest difficulty determining the exact factual patterns of communication, with its "central players" and hierarchies, based on a "chart with dots or 'nodes' representing individuals and lines between nodes if one person has called another." An unimportant person in the chain of command may take the most calls; a crucial person in the chain of events may show up only once.

The problem is hardly solved by the fact that, in addition to government agencies such as the NSA and CIA, private security companies, such as the *Search for International Terrorist Entities* (SITE), are either contracted for or volunteer information that they track on jihadist Web sites. See Benjamin Wallace-Wells, "Private Jihad: How Rita Katz Got into the Spying Business," *The New Yorker*, May 29, 2006. For the role of private Internet companies such as Yahoo and its Chinese partner Alibaba.com, Microsoft, Cisco Systems, and Google with regard to sites deemed "obscene" or "politically subversive" by Chinese authorities, see *The International Herald Tribune*, July 20, 2006, and also the special report "China and the Internet: The Party, the People and the Power of Cyber-Talk," in *The Economist*, April 29, 2006, which cites Bill Clinton's insightful comment that China's attempts to curtail Internet access and guide its use are "sort of like trying to nail Jell-O to the wall." China has the second largest group of Internet users after the U.S. and hence constitutes an enormous, growing market, even though it has its own—censored—search engines (such as baidu.com, which exploits approximately 56 percent of the available market).

The organization Reporters sans frontiers (Reporters Without Borders) has taken Google to task for indirectly being responsible for the arrest of Internet journalists. Indeed, of the fifty-eight online journalists who, according to some sources, are currently jailed, fifty are in China. The collaboration of Western Internet providers with the Chinese authorities is nothing exceptional. Telecom Italia owns a large portion of the Cuban Internet, and the French company Wanadoo offers broadband services in Tunisia (see Elda Dorren, "Online vrijheid in gevaar," in *NRC Handelsblad*, June 12, 2006). According to Reporters sans frontières (www.rfs.org), in 2005 there were some fifteen countries that censored the Web. The organization has urged Western countries to develop legislation for multinational Internet companies that offer services in countries with human rights violations.

67. One might argue that something similar is happening in the Israeli-Palestinian conflict in Lebanon. See Steven Erlanger, "How 'Winning' Might Be Defined by Israel and Hezbollah," in *The International Herald Tribune*, August 3, 2006. Erlanger sketches a "battle of perceptions" based

upon a dialectic of maximal force with minimal impact and the reverse, which perpetuates itself interminably: "Prime Minister Ehud Olmert wants to ensure that when a cease-fire is finally arranged, Israel is seen as having won a decisive victory over Hezbollah. . . . For Hezbollah, however, victory means simply avoiding defeat." The article, citing a former Israeli negotiator, calls this the "90–10 paradox": "Israel can eliminate 90 percent of Hezbollah's fighting capacity, but Hezbollah can still declare victory and claim to have fought the mighty Israeli Army to a draw." See also Martin van Creveld, "In This War, Too, Victory Is Unlikely," in *The International Herald Tribune*, August 3, 2006, and Robert A. Pape, "The Imagined Enemy, and the Real One," in *The International Herald Tribune*, August 4, 2006.

"Moderate and secular" Muslim countries have expressed concern about the effects of media images from the conflict in Lebanon on their populations. At an emergency meeting of the fifty-seven–nation Organization of the Islamic Conference in Kuala Lumpur, the president of Indonesia, Susilo Bambang Yudhoyono, echoing Samuel Huntington's much-decried thesis, was quoted as saying: "This war must stop or it will radicalize the Muslim world, even those of us who are moderate today. From there, it will be just one step away to that ultimate nightmare: a clash of civilizations" (Thomas Fuller, "Terrorism Could Grow, Leaders Say: Muslim Nations Warn of Lebanon Fallout," *The International Herald Tribune*, August 4, 2006).

68. "Rompre l'escalade," *Le Monde*, August 5, 2006.

69. Pierre-François Moreau, one of the editors of the critical edition of the *Tractatus Theologico-Politicus*, reminds us of this view in his *Spinoza: État et religion* (Paris: ENS Editions, 2005), 41 ff. See also Chantal Jacquet, *L'Unité du corps et de l'esprit: Affects, actions et passions chez Spinoza* (Paris: Presses Universitaires de France, 2004), chapter 3.

70. Moreau, *Spinoza*, 46–47.

71. Ibid., 47.

72. Ibid., 48.

73. Jacques Derrida, "Above All No Journalists!," in *Religion and Media*, ed. Hent de Vries and Samuel Weber (Stanford: Stanford University Press, 2001), 67.

74. Gilles Deleuze, *Spinoza: Philosophie pratique* (Paris: Minuit, 1981), 60, 61, 46; *Spinoza: Practical Philosophy*, trans. Robert Hurley (San Francisco: City Lights, 1988), 42, 43, and 31. Deleuze makes explicit reference to the motif of "auto-immune diseases" (ibid., 34n.5 and 42–49n.5 and 60).

75. Ibid., 34/49.

76. Indeed, the motif of mimetic transferal (not to say transference) works between individual bodies, between one individual and the body politic, between two or more social or political bodies, as well as inside of each of these composite individual or collective bodies. One might even assume, on the basis of Spinoza's model of imitation, that we might come (or, in fact, always already have come) to imitate ourselves and only thus become miracles, events, even special effects to ourselves.

77. For a sobering view, see the reflections of a former correspondent for the Dutch media in Cairo, Beirut, and East Jerusalem: Joris Luyendijk, *Het zijn net mensen: Beelden uit het Midden-Oosten* (Amsterdam: Uitgeverij Podium, 2006).

78. The medieval Iranian "Assassin" sect, founded by Hasan-i-Sabbah, opposed the regime of the Seljuq Turks in Iran. It comprised "a group of devoted and highly trained warriors who targeted high-profile government leaders and commanders and were ready to die in the attempt" (Carole Hillenbrand, "Unholy Aspirations," in *The Times Literary Supplement*, August 4, 2006). Hillenbrand cautions against identifying the Assassins too closely with Al Qaeda or with suicide attacks, claiming that "Al Qaeda's jihad is far removed from the theory in the classical Muslim books of Islamic law; it is all about sensationalism and shock."

79. See "Zarkaoui: Mort d'un tueur," in *Le Monde*, June 10, 2006.

80. Jan Assmann, *Herrschaft und Heil: Politische Theologie in Altägypten, Israel und Europa* (Munich: Carl Hanser, 2000), 15.

81. Ibid., 17. See Godo Lieberg, "Die 'theologia tripertita' in Forschung und Bezeugung," in his *Forschung und Bezeugung: Aufstieg und Niedergang der römischen Welt*, vol. 1.4, (Berlin: Walter de Gruyter, 1973), 63–115.

82. Ernst H. Kantorowicz, *The King's Two Bodies: A Study in Mediaeval Political Theology* (Princeton: Princeton University Press, 1957).

83. Jean-François Courtine, *Nature et empire de la loi: Études suaréziennes* (Paris: Vrin, 1999); cf., for a more general overview, Jean-Claude Eslin, *Dieu et le pouvoir: Théologie et politique en Occident* (Paris: Seuil, 1999).

84. Pierre-François Moreau, Introduction to *Traité théologico-politique*, vol. 3 of Spinoza, *Oeuvres* (Paris: Presses Universitaires de France, 1999), 3–17. See also Jacqueline Lagrée, *Spinoza et le débat religieux* (Paris: Presses Universitaires de France, 2004), 11.

85. Lagrée, *Spinoza et le débat religieux*, 11.

86. Cf. Luc Foisneau, *Hobbes et la toute-puissance de Dieu* (Paris: Presses Universitaires de France, 2000).

87. Cf. Gauchet, *The Disenchantment of the World*. Gauchet studies this process in detail with respect to the genesis, meaning, and fate of the French Declaration of Human Rights in 1789; see Marcel Gauchet, *La Révolution des droits de l'homme* (Paris: Gallimard, 1989).

88. Pierre Manent, *Cours familier de philosophie politique* (Paris: Gallimard, 2005), chap. 2.

89. Assmann, *Herrschaft und Heil*, 15.

90. Ibid.

91. Ibid., 28.

92. Ibid., 20–21.

93. Ibid., 16.

94. Ibid.

95. See Marcel Gauchet, "La Dette du sens et les racines de l'État: Politique de la religion primitive" and " Politique et société: La Leçon des sauvages," in idem, *La Condition politique* (Paris: Gallimard, 2005), 45–89, 91–180.

96. Jean-Luc Nancy, "La Déconstruction du christianisme," in *Les Études philosophiques*, no. 4 (1998): 503–19; "The Deconstruction of Christianity," trans. Simon Sparks, in *Religion and Media*, ed. Hent de Vries and Samuel Weber, 112–30. See also Jean-Luc Nancy, *La Déclosion: Déconstruction du christianisme, 1* (Paris: Galilée 2005), forthcoming in translation from Fordham University Press. For a useful introduction to Nancy's thought, see B. C. Hutchens, *Jean-Luc Nancy and the Future of Philosophy* (Chesham: Acumen, 2005).

97. See my "Winke: Divine Topoi in Nancy, Hölderlin, Heidegger," in *The Solid Letter: New Readings of Friedrich Hölderlin*, ed. Aris Fioretos (Stanford: Stanford University Press, 1999), 94–120.

98. These are all motifs upon which Derrida touches in his *Le toucher—Jean-Luc Nancy* (Paris: Galilée, 2000); *On Touching—Jean-Luc Nancy*, trans. Christine Irizarry (Stanford: Stanford University Press, 2005). Nancy's oblique response can be found in *Noli me tangere* (Paris: Bayard, 2003); forthcoming in translation from Fordham University Press.

99. See, for a further discussion of this motif in Nancy's thought, my *Religion and Violence*, chap. 2.

100. See Hutchens, *Jean-Luc Nancy*, chap. 5 ("Post-Secular Theology").

101. See Alexandre Dupilet, "Les Deux Corps de M. Chirac: Vivant physiquement mais mourant politiquement, tel est apparu notre président à la télévision," in *Le Monde*, April 5, 2006, on

Jacques Chirac's address to the nation, on March 31, to respond to the political crisis caused by the widely protested and later withdrawn plan of the CPE (Contrat premier d'ébauche) to fight France's massive youth unemployment, as part of the government's response to the November 2005 riots in the suburbs.

102. The rebounds of Jimmy Carter and Bill Clinton come to mind.

103. See Anselm Haverkamp, "*Richard II*, Bracton, and the End of Political Theology," *Law and Literature* 16, no. 3 (Fall 2004): 313–26.

104. Patrick Riley, *The General Will Before Rousseau: The Transformation of the Divine into the Civic* (Princeton: Princeton University Press, 1986); Dale K. Van Kley, *The Religious Origins of the French Revolution: From Calvin to the Civil Constitution, 1560–1791* (New Haven: Yale University Press, 1996); Michael Theunissen, *Hegels Lehre vom absoluten Geist als theologisch-politischer Traktat* (Berlin: Walter de Gruyter, 1970).

105. Hans Kelsen, "Gott und Staat," in *Logos* 11 (1922–23): 261–84; Heinrich Meier, *Das theologisch-politische Problem: Zum Thema von Leo Strauss* (Stuttgart: J. B. Metzler, 2003); Roberto Esposito, *Communitas: Origine et Destin de la communauté* (Paris: Presses Universitaires de France, 2000), and idem, *Catégories de l'impolitique* (Paris: Seuil, 2005). See also Myriam Revault d'Allonnes, *Le Dépérissement de la politique* (Paris: Aubier, 1999), and idem, *Le Pouvoir des commencements: Essai sur l'autorité* (Paris: Seuil, 2006).

106. Ernesto Laclau and Chantal Mouffe, *Hegemony and Socialist Strategy: Toward a Radical Democratic Politics* (London: Verso, 1985).

107. Ernesto Laclau, *Emancipation(s)* (London: Verso, 1996).

108. Ernesto Laclau, *New Reflections on the Revolution of Our Time* (London: Verso, 1990); idem, with Judith Butler and Slavoj Žižek, *Contingency, Hegemony, Universality: Contemporary Dialogues on the Left* (London: Verso, 2000).

109. Ernesto Laclau, *The Populist Reason* (London: Verso, 2005). For an overall discussion of Laclau's work, including his responses to his critics, see Simon Critchley and Oliver Marchart, eds., *Laclau: A Critical Reader* (New York: Routledge, 2004). This book contains a bibliography of his published work, as well as critical rejoinders to his position by William Connolly and Judith Butler.

110. From the description of the series Phronesis, edited by Ernesto Laclau and Chantal Mouffe. See Butler, Laclau, and Žižek, *Contingency, Hegemony, Universality*.

111. The distinction to which Lefort accords particular value as the "index" of conceptual "ambiguity" is well known from the collective project of Nancy and Lacoue-Labarthe entitled *The Retreat of the Political*. The opening chapter of Lefort's collection *Essais sur le politique*, entitled "La Question de la démocratie," was his contribution to this project. It appears in English as "The Question of Democracy," in Claude Lefort, *Democracy and Political Theory*, trans. David Macey (Cambridge: Polity Press, 1988), 9–20.

112. See *The International Herald Tribune*, June 30, 2006. See also David S. Cloud and Sheryl Gay Stolberg, "White House Offers Plan on Terror Suspects: Bush Draft Steers Clear of Courts-Martial," *The International Herald Tribune*, July 27, 2006. The United Nations Human Rights Committee, in its review of American compliance with the 1966 International Covenant on Civil and Political Rights, requested that the U.S. "immediately shut down any secret detention facilities and grant prompt access by the Red Cross to any person detained in connection with an armed conflict." The official response of the U.S. administration was that "the covenant applied only in the national territory of countries that had signed it and that it did not apply to the U.S. military or its installations abroad, which are governed by other domestic and international laws" (*The International Herald Tribune*, July 29–30, 2006). By the same token, the administration, represented by Attorney General Alberto Gonzales in an appearance before a congressional hearing (and first public

statement of policy after the Supreme Court's ruling), urged lawmakers to change the definition of war crimes prohibited by the Geneva Conventions. Asked by senator John McCain whether "evidence obtained through coercion" or "illegal and inhumane treatment" could be admissible as court evidence, Gonzalez, according to news reports, "paused for almost a minute before responding," and then said: "The concern that I would have about such a prohibition is, what does it mean? How do you define it? I think that if we could all reach agreement about the definition of cruel and inhumane and degrading treatment, then perhaps I could give you an answer" (cited in Kate Zernike, "U.S. Official Pushes for Clarity on Handling Terror Suspects," in *The International Herald Tribune*, August 4, 2006).

113. Judith Butler, *Precarious Life: The Powers of Mourning and Violence* (London: Verso, 2004); idem, *Giving an Account of Oneself* (New York: Fordham University Press, 2005).

114. Carl Schmitt, *Political Theology: Four Chapters on the Concept of Sovereignty*, trans. and introd. George Schwab (Cambridge: MIT Press, 1985); Jakob Taubes, *Die politische Theologie des Paulus*, ed. Aleida and Jan Assmann et al. (Munich: Wilhelm Fink, 1993); *The Political Theology of Paul*, trans. Dana Hollander (Stanford: Stanford University Press, 2005). For a discussion of the latter, see my *Religion and Violence*, chap. 3, and Joshua Robert Gold, "Jacob Taubes: 'Apocalypse from Below,'" in *Telos* 134 (Spring 2006): 140–56.

115. Assmann, *Herrschaft und Heil*, 16.

116. Jean-François Courtine, "Problèmes théologico-politiques," in idem, *Nature et empire de la loi*, 163–75. See also Myriam Revault-d'Allonnes, "Sommes nous vraiment 'déthéologisés'? Carl Schmitt, Hans Blumenberg et la sécularisation des temps modernes," in *Les Études philosophiques*, no. 1 (2004): 25–37.

117. Carl Schmitt, *Politisches Theologie II: Die Legende von der Erledigung jeder politischen Theologie* (Berlin: Duncker & Humblot, 1970).

118. Erik Peterson, *Der Monotheismus als politisches Problem: Ein Beitrag zur Geschichte der politischen Theologie im Imperium Romanum* (Leipzig: Jakob Hegner, 1935); idem, *Theologische Traktate* (Munich: Kösel, 1951); Hans Blumenberg, *Die Legitimität der Neuzeit: Erneute Ausgabe* (Frankfurt am Main: Suhrkamp, 1988). See, for an overview of these debates, Jean-Claude Monod, *La Querelle de la sécularisation: Théologie politique et philosophies de l'histoire de Hegel à Blumenberg* (Paris: Vrin, 2002).

119. For a different, psychoanalytic perspective, see Kenneth Reinhard, Eric L. Santner, and Slavoj Žižek in their collaborative volume *The Neighbor: Three Inquiries in Political Theology* (Chicago: University of Chicago Press, 2005).

120. More precisely, Enrique Dussel understands his work as a "Filosofía de la Liberacíon." See, for information on his extensive work and collaborative efforts, the Web site http://www.afyl .org. Catholic liberation theologies were inspired by Pope Paul VI's encyclical *Populorum Progressio* (1967) and the Vatican II document *Gaudium et Spes* (1962–65).

121. See the first issue of the new French journal *Controverses*, no. 1 (March 2006), which devoted a dossier to "La théologie politique des alter-mondialistes."

122. See, for an extensive discussion, Peter Scott and William T. Cavanaugh, eds., *The Blackwell Companion to Political Theology* (Malden: Blackwell, 2004).

123. For the complete English text of *Deus caritas est*, see http://www.vatican.va/holy_father/benedict_xvi/encyclicals/documents/hf_ben-xvi_enc_20051225_deus-caritas-est_en.html.

124. See Keith Bradsher, "Hong Kong Bishop Condemns China on Tiananmen Anniversary," in *The International Herald Tribune*, June 5, 2006.

125. Jürgen Habermas and Joseph Cardinal Ratzinger, *Dialektik der Säkularisierung: Über Vernunft und Religion*, ed. Florian Schuller (Freiburg im Breisgau: Herder, 2005).

126. See, for a general exposition of Joseph Cardinal Ratzinger's intellectual biography and general theological ideas, Aidan Nicols, O.P., *The Thought of Benedict XVI: An Introduction to the Theology of Joseph Ratzinger* (New York: Burns & Oates, 1988, 2005).

127. Francis Schüssler-Fiorenza, on the intellectual profile of the new pope, in the *Harvard Divinity Bulletin* 33, no. 2 (Autumn 2005), http://www.hds.harvard.edu/news/bulletin_mag/articles/33-2_fiorenza.html.

128. For a sustained discussion of Habermas's overall position in relation to the question of religion, see my *Minimal Theologies: Critiques of Secular Reason in Adorno and Levinas* (Baltimore: The Johns Hopkins University Press, 2005), 1–164. See also Joas, *Braucht der Mensch Religion?*, 122–28.

129. See Nichols, *The Thought of Benedict XVI*, 284 ff.

130. Joseph Cardinal Ratzinger, "Le Pluralisme: Problème posé à l'Église et à la théologie," in *Studia Moralia* 24 (1986): 307; cited in Nichols, *The Thought of Benedict XVI*, 287.

131. Ibid., 290–91.

132. Cited in Stanley R. Sloan, "All the President's Truths," *International Herald Tribune*, May 19, 2006.

133. Ibid.

134. Bruce Lincoln, *Holy Terrors: Thinking about Religion after September 11* (Chicago: University of Chicago Press, 2003).

135. The emergence of early modern absolutism, as epitomized by Hobbes's *Leviathan*, could likewise be said to capitalize on the "crises in the mediation" between heaven and earth "opened up by Protestantism" (Marcel Gauchet, *La Condition historique: Entretiens avec François Azouf et Sylvain Piron* [Paris: Gallimard, 2005], 295–96).

136. See also Philip Blond and Adrian Pabst, "The Twisted Religion of Blair and Bush," in *The International Herald Tribune*, March 11–12, 2006. See also Jean-François Colosimo, *Dieu est Américain: De la théodémocratie aux États-Unis* (Paris: Fayard, 2006), and, from a different perspective, Alan Wolfe, *The Transformation of American Religion: How We Actually Live Our Faith* (Chicago: University of Chicago Press, 2003).

137. For the debate concerning the legacy of Strauss and recent American politics, see Francis Fukuyama, "After Neoconservatism," in *The New York Times Magazine*, February 19, 2006, and, more extensively, his *America at the Crossroads: Democracy, Power, and the Neoconservative Legacy* (New Haven: Yale University Press, 2006), as well as Anne Norton, *Leo Strauss and the Politics of American Empire* (New Haven: Yale University Press, 2004), and the documentary film *The Power of Nightmares: The Rise of Political Fear*, written and directed by Adam Curtis, originally broadcast as a three-part mini-series on the BBC.

138. Heinrich Meier, *Leo Strauss and the Theologico-Political Problem* (Cambridge: Cambridge University Press, 2006). I am drawing here on my review of *Das theologisch-politische Problem: Zum Thema von Leo Strauss* (Stuttgart: Metzler, 2003). See Hent de Vries, "In der Gewalt des theologisch-politischen Dilemmas," *Deutsche Zeitschrift für Philosophie* 52 (2004): 823–29.

139. Leo Strauss, *What Is Political Philosophy? and Other Studies* (New York: Free Press, 1959), 13, cited in Meier, *Leo Strauss and the Theologico-Political Problem*, xvn.14.

140. Chantal Mouffe, *The Return of the Political* (London: Verso, 2005) and *The Democratic Paradox* (London: Verso, 2000).

141. Jacques Derrida, *Specters of Marx: The State of the Debt, the Work of Mourning, and the New International*, trans. Peggy Kamuf, introd. Bernd Magnus and Stephen Cullenberg (New York: Routledge, 1994); idem, "Faith and Knowledge: The Two Sources of 'Religion' at the Limits of Reason Alone," trans. Samuel Weber, in *Religion*, ed. Jacques Derrida and Gianni Vattimo (Stan-

ford: Stanford University Press, 1996), 1–78; and idem, *Rogues: Two Essays on Reason*, trans. Pascale-Anne Brault and Michael Naas (Stanford: Stanford University Press, 2005).

142. Jacques Derrida, "Autoimmunity: Real and Symbolic Suicides," in *Philosophy in a Time of Terror: Dialogues with Jürgen Habermas and Jacques Derrida*, ed. Giovanna Borradori (Chicago: University of Chicago Press, 2003), 120.

143. Ibid., 121.

144. Derrida, *Rogues*, 28.

145. For a sobering overview, see Philippe Sands, *Lawless World: Making and Breaking Global Rules* (Harmondsworth, Middlesex: Penguin Books, 2005).

146. I am thinking not of U.S. Defense Secretary Donald Rumsfeld's laconic "Stuff happens" but of his sophisms relating to the fabricated "evidence" of WMDs (weapons of mass destruction) in Iraq after the invasion: "Simply because you do not have evidence that something exists does not mean that you have evidence that it doesn't exist." And again, "Absence of evidence is not the evidence of absence. . . . There are thing we know that we know. There are known unknowns; that is to say there are things that we now know we don't know. But there are also unknown unknowns. There are things we do not know we don't know" (cited in Roger Cohen, "Rumsfeld Is Correct: The Truth Will Get Out," in *The International Herald Tribune*, June 7, 2006). Whether consciously or unconsciously, Rumsfeld seems to have been quoting Carl Sagan, who identifies this as the fallacy of "the appeal to ignorance—the claim that whatever has not been proved false must be true, and vice versa (e.g., *There is no compelling evidence that UFOs are not visiting the earth, therefore UFOs exist—and there is intelligent life elsewhere in the Universe. . .*). This impatience with ambiguity can be criticized in the phrase: absence of evidence is not evidence of absence" (Sagan, *The Demon-Haunted World: Science as a Candle in the Dark* [New York: Ballantine Books, 1996], 213).

147. Derrida, *Rogues*, 102.

148. Ibid., 101, trans. modified.

149. Samuel Weber, *Targets of Opportunity: On the Militarization of Thinking* (New York: Fordham University Press, 2005) and *Theatricality as Medium* (New York: Fordham University Press, 2004).

150. Rafael Sánchez, "Channel-Surfing: Media, Mediumship, and State Authority in the María Lionza Possession Cult (Venezuela)," in *Religion and Media*, ed. de Vries and Weber, 388–434.

151. *Laïcité et République: Rapport de la Commission de réflexion sur l'application du principe de laïcité dans la République remis au Président de la République le 11 décembre 2003, Commission présidée par Bernard Stasi* (Paris: La Documentation Française, 2004).

152. *The New York Times*, December 19, 2003. For representative documentation of the whole affair, see: Jean-Michel Helvig, ed., *La Laïcité dévoilée: Quinze années de débat en quarante "Rébonds"* (Paris: Libération, Éditions de l'aube, 2004); Pierre Tévanian, *Le Voile médiatique: Un Faux Débat: "L'Affaire du foulard islamique"* (Paris: Raisons d'agir, 2005); Alain Renaut and Alain Touraine, *Un Débat sur la laïcité* (Paris: Stock, 2005); and Olivier Roy, *La Laïcité face à l'Islam* (Paris: Stock, 2005).

153. Michèle Lamont and Éloi Laurent, "France Shows Its True Colors," in *The International Herald Tribune*, June 6, 2006.

154. For further development of this topic, see Yolande Jansen, *Stuck in a Revolving Door: Secularism, Assimilation, and Democratic Pluralism* (Amsterdam: Eigen Beheer, 2006).

155. Talal Asad, *Genealogies of Religion: Discipline and Reasons of Power in Christianity and Islam* (Baltimore: The Johns Hopkins University Press, 1993) and *Formations of the Secular: Christianity, Islam, Modernity* (Stanford: Stanford University Press, 2003).

156. David Scott, "The Power of Thinking: An Interview with Talal Asad," in *Powers of the Secular Modern: Talal Asad and His Interlocutors*, ed. David Scott and Charles Hirschkind (Stanford: Stanford University Press, 2006), 271.

157. Ibid., 272.

158. Ibid., 285.

159. Ibid.

160. Ibid., 298.

161. Asad, *Formations of the Secular*, 23.

162. Scott, "The Power of Thinking," 284.

163. That not all explosive issues revolve around the veil is illustrated by the recent international scandal triggered by the publication in Denmark of cartoons depicting the prophet Mohammed. Similar incidents have been reported with respect to Hinduism. See Salil Tripathi's article "The Right to be Offended," on the Indian painter Maqbool Fida Husain, in *The International Herald Tribune*, May 30, 2006. Husain repeatedly faced the risk of being prosecuted for painting Bharat Mata, Mother India, and several other Hindu female deities in the nude. As the writer of the article explains: "Because of the amount of attention Muslims have commanded when they have been offended by images they consider blasphemous—a concept alien to Hinduism—Hindus want equal treatment. They want the right to be offended."

164. Van Gogh's death was linked to his direction of the short film *Submission I*, in 2004, authored by Somali-born Ayaan Hirsi Ali, a defender of the "right to offend." A former member of parliament and an outspoken critic of Islam, Hirsi Ali nearly lost her Dutch passport over irregularities in her initial application. The ensuing uproar led to the fall of the Dutch government. A second film, entitled *Submission II*, whose script Hirsi Ali co-authored with van Gogh shortly before his murder, has been announced for the fall of 2006. Informed sources report that the Dutch government in The Hague has put a crisis team in place well in advance, anticipating new outrage and reprisals. Hirsi Ali has even announced a *Submission III*, which would feature God—Allah himself. No preparation for that release has been announced, however . . . See also Ian Buruma, *Murder in Amsterdam: The Death of Theo van Gogh and the Limits of Tolerance* (New York: Penguin, 2006).

165. Like Hirsi Ali, Job Cohen was singled out for a death threat in the letter stabbed onto van Gogh chest.

166. *Time Europe* 166, no. 15 (October 10, 2005).

167. On the issue of "Vreemden [Strangers]," Cohen pronounced the Cleveringa lecture at the University of Leiden, in November 2002. For the full text in Dutch, see http://www.amsterdam.nl/gemeente/documenten/toespraken/cohen/inhoud/cleveringa-lezing.

168. A recent government-commissioned report, published in June 2006 by the National Council Against Racial Discrimination, in collaboration with the Anne Frank Foundation and the University of Leiden, found that some 475,000 people (which is almost half of the Netherlands residents of non-Western origin, especially Moroccans, Turks, and descendents from families in the former colonies of the Netherlands Antilles and Surinam) indicated that they suffered from discrimination during job applications, at school, and in verbal and psychic abuse in public transportation, bars, etc. (*The International Herald Tribune*, June 15, 2006).

169. In the meantime, a host of publications and initiatives indicate a growing awareness of the urgency of these questions in relation to religion. See the special issue of *Christendemocratische Verkenningen*, the quarterly journal of the scientific bureau of the Christian Democratic Party, Christendemocratisch Appel (CDA), edited by Erik Borgman, Gabriël van den Brink, and Thijs Jansen, *Zonder geloof geen democratie* (Amsterdam: Boom, 2006), and Marcel ten Hooven and Theo

de Wit, eds., *Ongewenste goden: De publieke rol van religie in Nederland* (Amsterdam: Sun, 2006). The Wiardi Beckman Stichting, the scientific bureau of the Social-Democratic Labor Party, Partij van de Arbeid (PvdA), organized a symposium on religion and politics in June 2006, and the Netherlands Scientific Council of Government Policy, Wetenschappelijke Raad voor het Regeringsbeleid (WRR), in The Hague, has founded a project group entitled Religion and the Public Domain, to explore the possibilities of an official report with policy recommendations to the Dutch government.

170. The notion of universal human rights has been contested by multiculturalists for its Western bias and by some Jewish thinkers, even those on the left, such as Yeshayahu Leibowitz, for incompatibility with Jewish law and its commandments, i.e., *Halacha* and *mitzvoth*.

171. Jacques Derrida, *Adieu to Emmanuel Levinas*, trans. Pascale-Anne Brault and Michael Naas (Stanford: Stanford University Press, 1999).

172. See the informative introduction by Henri Gouhier to the centenary edition, Henri Bergson, *Oeuvres* (Paris: Presses Universitaires de France, 1959), xv.

173. Ibid., xi–xiv.

174. Ibid., xvi, cf. ix.

175. Ibid., xvi ; see Henri Bergson, in *Bulletin de la Société Française de Philosophie*, session of May 2, 1901, 63, reprinted in Henri Bergson, *Écrits et paroles; textes reassemblés par R.-M. Mossé-Bastide* (Paris: Presses Universitaires de France, 1957–59), 1:158–59.

176. Gouhier, Introduction, in Bergson, *Oeuvres*, xvi.

177. Ibid., xvi–xvii ; see Bergson, *Bulletin de la Société Française de Philosophie*, session of May 2, 1901, 63, in *Écrits et paroles*, 1:158–59.

178. Gouhier, "Introduction," in Bergson, *Oeuvres*, xxix.

179. Jane Bennett, *Thoreau's Nature*, 2d ed. (Lanham, Md.: Rowman & Littlefield, 2002), and idem, *The Enchantment of Modern Life: Attachments, Crossings, and Ethics* (Princeton: Princeton University Press, 2001).

180. For an examination of such a deconstructive turn, in particular in Derrida's writings on religion, see my *Philosophy and the Turn to Religion*.

181. The term is introduced by the Chairman and CEO of IBM, Samuel Palmisano, in "Multinationals Have Been Superseded," in the *Financial Times*, June 12, 2006.

Marcel Detienne, The Gods of Politics in Early Greek Cities

NOTE: This essay was original delivered as the 2002 Henry Myers Lecture at the Royal Anthropological Institute of Great Britain and Ireland, in London. It was published in *Arion* 12, no. 2 (Fall 2004): 49–66, and appears here courtesy of the author. © Marcel Detienne, 2004.

1. See the following works: Marcel Detienne, *Comparer l'incomparable* (Paris: Seuil, 2000); "Murderous Identity: Anthropology, History and the Art of Constructing Comparables," *Common Knowledge* 8, no. 1 (2002): 178–87; "Back to the Village: A Tropism of Hellenists?" *History of Religions* 141 (2001): 99–113; "L'Art de construire des comparables: Entre historiens et anthropologues," *Critique internationale*, no. 14 (2002): 68–78.

2. Robert Hertz Lecture (Paris, June 2002): Marcel Detienne, "Des comparables dans le champ du politique: Entre nous, ethnologues et historiens," *Gradhiva*, 2005, 1, 5–17.

3. *Qui veut prendre la parole?* under the direction of Marcel Detienne (Paris: Seuil, 2003).

4. Marcel Detienne, "Experimenting in the Field of Polytheisms," *Arion* 7, no. 1 (Spring/Summer 1999): 127–49; *Apollon, le couteau à la main* (Paris: Gallimard, 1999).

5. For a short introduction to these issues, see: "Dealings with the Gods," in Giulia Sissa and Marcel Detienne, *The Daily Life of the Greek Gods*, trans. Janet Lloyd (Stanford: Stanford University Press, 2000), 166–207. (A more precise phrasing might be "Gods at the Heart of Politics.")

6. I must confess that I am writing a book entitled *The Gods of Politics in Early Greek Cities*. I apologize for a few allusive mentions that may have slipped in.

M. B. Pranger, Politics and Finitude: The Temporal Status of Augustine's *Civitas Permixta*

1. A classic survey of this development—still—is: H.-X. Arquillière, *Augustinisme politique: Essai sur la formation des théories politiques du Moyen-Âge* (Paris: Vrin, 1934).

2. Augustine's famous phrase "da quod iubes, iube quod vis," repeated three times in book 10 of the *Confessions* (10.29, 31, 37). It also was the starting point of the Pelagian controversy.

3. Augustine, *De civitate dei*, ed. D. Dombart and A. Kalb, in Corpus christianorum, series Latina, vols. 47 and 48. I use the translation by Henry Bettenson, *Concerning the City of God Against the Pagans* (Harmondsworth, Middlesex: Penguin, 1972). I use the following abbreviations: *CC* for the Latin text; Bettenson for the English translation.

4. Janet Coleman, *A History of Political Thought: From the Middle Ages to the Renaissance* (Oxford: Blackwell, 2000), 339.

5. R. A. Markus, *Saeculum: History and Society in the in the Theology of St. Augustine* (Cambridge: Cambridge University Press, 1988). For Augustine, *saeculum* means the secular world and secular time. It is a neutral space between the two cities, comprising, for instance, political institutions. For a recent view contesting this neutral status as proposed by Markus, Ratzinger, and others, see Peter Burnell, *The Augustinian Person* (Washington, D.C.: Catholic University of America Press, 2005), 136–72.

6. Ernst H. Kantorowicz, *The King's Two Bodies: A Study in Mediaeval Political Theology* (1957; Princeton: Princeton University Press, 1997), 292.

7. Henri de Lubac, *Corpus Mysticum: L'Euchariste et l'Eglise au Moyen Âge: Étude historique* (Paris: Aubier, 1949).

8. Kantorowicz, *The King's Two Bodies*, 206.

9. Ibid., 279.

10. *De civitate dei* 1.35; *CC* 34; Bettenson 46.

11. Ibid., 5:27; *CC* 150; Bettenson 206.

12. Ibid.

13. Ibid., 5.18; *CC* 154; Bettenson 211.

14. Ibid., 1.1; *CC* 1.

15. See ibid., 14.28; *CC* 451; Bettenson 592: "Fecerunt itaque civitates duas amores duo [We see that the two cities were created by two kinds of love]."

16. Kantorowicz, following Henri de Lubac's *Corpus mysticum*, summarizes this development: "the notion of *corpus mysticum*, designating originally the Sacrament of the Altar, served after the twelfth century to describe the body politic, or *corpus iuridicum*, of the Church, which does not exclude the lingering on of some of the earlier connotations. Moreover, the classical christological distinction of the two Natures in Christ . . . has all but completely disappeared from the orbit of political discussions and theories. It has been replaced by the corporational, non-christological concept of the Two Bodies of Christ: one, a body natural, individual, and personal (*corpus naturale, verum, personale*); the other, a super-individual body politic and collective, the *corpus mysticum*,

interpreted also as a *persona mystica*. Whereas the *corpus verum*, through the agency of the dogma of transubstantiation and the institution of the feast of *Corpus Christi*, developed a life and a mysticism of its own, the *corpus mysticum* proper came to be less and less mystical as time passed on, and came to mean simpy the Church as a body politic or, by transference, any body politic of the secular world" (*The King's Two Bodies*, 206).

17. *De civitate dei*, 11.6; *CC* 326; Bettenson 435.
18. Ibid., 15.1; *CC* 454; Bettenson 596.
19. Ibid., 15.2; *CC* 455; Bettenson 597.
20. Ibid., 15.1; *CC* 453; Bettenson 595–96.
21. Ibid., 1.35; *CC* 33; Bettenson 45–46.
22. Ibid., 11.8.

Antónia Szabari, The Scandal of Religion: Luther and Public Speech in the Reformation

1. Martin Luther, "Wider den Meuchler zu Dresden" (1531), *D. Martin Luthers Werke, Kritische Gesamtausgabe*, 60 vols. (Weimar: Böhlau, 1883–1980), 30.3:470; hereafter cited as *WA*. My translation.

2. Luther, Preface to the New Testament, *Martin Luther: Selections from His Writings*, ed. and introd. John Dillenberger (New York: Doubleday, 1962), 15.

3. The Church had the right to pronounce anathemas against heretics and those who produced "scandals"—I will return to this crucial term in the second part of my essay. One prominent ritual formula was the "Judas curse"; see Archer Taylor, "The Judas Curse," *The American Journal of Philology* 43, no. 3 (1921): 234–52.

4. As Birgit Stolt has shown, Luther exaggerated the capacity of language to move, to produce affects, the *movere* of pathos, not to ignore them but in order to push rhetoric to its limits. Stolt also shows that this was not for lack of training in rhetoric, given that Luther knew well how to teach or to produce milder effects of ethos. See Birgit Stolt, *Martin Luthers Rhetorik des Herzens* (Tübingen: Mohr Siebeck, 2000), 157.

5. Cicero advises tact in his discussion of fighting in words. See his *De oratore* 2, 58, 235–32, 71, 289. Quintilian draws the lines at milder (*lenibus*) jokes and derision (*Institutio oratoria*, 6, 3, 28).

6. *D. Martin Luthers Werke: Tischreden*, 6 vols. (Weimar: Böhlau, 1912–21), 1:1649.

7. Jacob Burckhardt, *The Civilisation of the Renaissance* (New York: Oxford University Press, 1944), 87–93. See also Peter Burke's critical re-reading of Burckhardt's thesis of Renaissance individualism in *The Italian Renaissance: Culture and Society in Italy* (Princeton: Princeton University Press, 1986), 125–44.

8. Ibid., 137.

9. Notably, in his adage *Festina lente*.

10. Desiderius Erasmus, "The Tongue" (1525), *Collected Works of Erasmus* (Toronto: University of Toronto Press, 1969–), 29:367 (translation slightly modified); hereafter cited as *CWE*.

11. *CWE*, 76:11.

12. Ibid., 141.

13. Erasmus states, e.g., in a letter to the bishop Lorenzo Campegio, "I think that every man should promote and promulgate his own convictions without offensive criticism of those of others, so that on both sides this frenzy of tongue and pen [*linguae calamique rabies*] is restrained, by those

especially of whom this moderation is most to be expected [*magis decet haec moderatio*]" (letter 1062, *CWE*, 7:201; *Opus Epistolarum Des. Erasmi Roterodami*, ed. P. S. Allen [Oxford: Oxford University Press, 1992], 4:185.

14. *CWE*, 76:117.

15. In America, the 1942 Supreme Court decision about "fighting words" has fueled a great deal more debate about different forms of verbal injury (insults, racial and ethnic slurs, pornography, etc.) than Austin's reflections call for. Most recently, Judith Butler, notably in a debate with Catherine MacKinnon concerning pornography, has called into question the practicability of placing legal restrictions on verbal violence, arguing that insults and other forms of verbal violence could be "resignified" and "restaged" and their effects could be reversed. In compelling analyses, she shows that the power of words to "wound" does not depend solely on the speaker's intention but also on the situation and the interlocutor's recognition and reaction. See her *Excitable Speech: A Politics of the Performative* (New York: Routledge, 1997). In France, Didier Eribon has analyzed modern gay identity as the product of a series of literary and political acts of repeating, appropriating, restaging, and reversing the significance and effect of antigay insults. See his *Insult and the Making of the Gay Self*, trans. Michael Lucey (Durham, N.C.: Duke University Press, 2004).

16. Shoshana Felman, *The Scandal of the Speaking Body: Don Juan with J. L. Austin or Seduction in Two Languages* (rpt. Stanford: Stanford University Press, 2003), 34.

17. Judith Butler, Afterword to ibid., 117.

18. Felman analyzes this "illusion," showing that Don Juan (in Molière's play) creates belief in his promises that remain unfulfilled, and because of his seductive but unfulfilled promises he is called an atheist. Felman's interest in Don Juan stems from the fact that he deconstructs Austin's idea of continuous intentionality as an illusory effect, a seductive confusion of the merely self-referential act of promising and referential constative statements; however, Felman's analysis also reveals that Don Juan manipulates the *necessary* constative assumption of a metaphysical subject.

19. On Luther's rhetorical conception of Scripture and on the privileged relation between the heart and faith, see Stolt, *Martin Luthers Rhetorik des Herzens*, 47–57.

20. This distinction ultimately goes back to the distinction between faith and belief, central to Western religions. Persuasion can as *affective rhetoricism* (Quintilian rather than Aristotle) come very close to religious faith, especially because both operate through the affective organ of the heart. See ibid., 54–55. The distinction between faith and persuasion, being that between divine and human speech, remains essential in Luther's theology.

21. *Luther: Selections*, 15.

22. Ibid., 17.

23. Ibid.,15.

24. The myth of a clear and univocal message cultivated by Luther has been put to the test by historians who have argued that in his case the "medium was the message," i.e., that he skillfully exploited the techniques of transmission in order to disseminate his message: for example, Luther created a transparent book out of the Bible through a calculated translation, innovative chapter and verse divisions enhanced by print and typesetting, and various *parerga* such as tables and a set of prefaces, which guide the reading process toward a purportedly clear message. The processes through which Luther's other writings, sermons, devotional writings, polemical pamphlets, exegetical works, etc., were transmitted have also been analyzed. See especially Mark U. Edwards, *Print, Propaganda, and Martin Luther* (Berkeley: University of California Press, 1994). For the use of visual materials in the German Reformation, see R. W. Scribner, *For the Sake of Simple Folk: Popular Propaganda for the German Reformation* (Cambridge: Cambridge University Press, 1981). On the techniques of copying and on the transcriptions of Luther's oral sayings, see Stolt, *Martin Luthers*

Rhetorik des Herzens, 15–17. For an informed analysis of the exploitation of the new print medium in the Reformation and the parallels between Luther's innovations in sacramental theology and printing, see Manfred Schneider, "Luther with McLuhan," trans. Samuel Weber, in *Religion and Media*, ed. Hent de Vries and Samuel Weber (Stanford: Stanford University Press, 2001), 198–215.

25. "The Babylonian Captivity of the Church" in *Luther's Works*, ed. Jaroslav Pelikan, Helmut T. Lehmann, et al., 55 vols. (St Louis: Concordia Publishing House; Philadelphia: Fortress Press, 1955–1986), 36:34; hereafter cited as *LW*.

26. Compare this to Searle's analysis of the essential conditions of promising. In any "profane" act of promising, it is, of course, the speaker who is bound by obligation, but the promise is only successful if the interlocutor knows that the speaker is under obligation and recognizes, understands, the intention under the following conditions: "(6) *S* intends to do *A*; *S* intends (i-1) that the utterance of *T* will place him under an obligation to do *A*; (7) *S* intends to produce in *H* the knowledge (*K*) that the utterance of *T* is to count as placing *S* under obligation to do *A*; (8) *S* intends to produce *K* by means of the recognition of i-1, and he intends i-1 to be recognized in virtue of (by means of) *H*'s knowledge of the meaning of *T*; (9) The semantical rules of the dialect spoken by *S* and *H* are such that *T* is correctly and sincerely uttered if and only if conditions 1–8 obtain" (John R. Searle, *Speech Acts: An Essay in the Philosophy of Language* [Cambridge: Cambridge University Press, 1969], 57–61).

27. St. Thomas Aquinas, *Summa theologica* Pt. IIa-iiae q. 43.

28. Ludwig Buisson, *Potestas und Caritas: Die päpstliche Gewalt im Spätmittelalter* (Cologne: Böhlau, 1958).

29. See *Patrologia Latina*, ed. Jacques-Paul Migne (Paris: Imprimerie Catholique, 1844–55), 40, 448ff, cap. 22.

30. *Französisches etymologisches Wörterbuch: Eine Darstellung der galloromanischen Sprachsatzes*, ed. Walther von Wartburg (Bonn: F. Klopp, 1928).

31. Paul exhorts the Corinthians, a community troubled by divisions, not to offend those who still adhere to Judaic laws by eating forbidden food in their sight. He gives the opposite advice to the Galatians, however, telling them that he reproached Peter for not sitting down to eat with gentiles.

32. See Beat Hodler, *Das "Ärgernis" der Reformation: Begriffsgeschichtlicher Zugang zu einer biblisch legitimierten politischen Ethik* (Mainz: Philipp von Zabern, 1995).

33. *LW*, 31:373.

34. *WA*, 29:474.

35. See Sebastian Franck, *Paradoxa*, ed. Heinrich Ziegler (Jena: Diederichs, 1909), 178.

36. See, e.g., *WA*, 29:475.

37. Searle distinguishes between promising and warning in condition (4) of the promise: "*H* would prefer *S*'s doing *A* to his not doing *A*, and *S* believes *H* would prefer his doing *A* to his not doing *A*." If the accomplishment of the promise is not preferred by the hearer to its nonaccomplishment, we have no promise, but rather a threat or a warning. See Searle, *Speech Acts*, 58.

38. Understanding, Bakhtin argues, "assimilates the word to be understood into its own conceptual system filled with specific objects and emotional expressions, and is indissolubly merged with the response, with a motivated agreement or disagreement. . . . The speaker strives to get a reading on his own word, and on his own conceptual system that determines this word, within the alien conceptual system of the understanding receiver; he enters into dialogical relationships with certain aspects of this system. The speaker breaks through the alien conceptual horizon of the listener, constructs his own utterance on alien territory, against his, the listener's, apperceptive background" (M. M. Bakhtin, "Discourse on the Novel," *The Dialogic Imagination: Four Essays*, ed.

Michael Holquist, trans. Caryl Emerson and Michael Holquist [Austin: University of Texas Press, 1981], 282). Luther's discourse is not only dialogic in the sense that it is hybrid (he borrows from the Bible, theology, the vernacular, and the literary form of satire) but also in this sense: he "strives to get a reading" of the Catholic corpus, and his discourse lends itself to (contentious, disagreeing) appropriations.

39. Donald R. Kelley, *The Beginning of Ideology: Consciousness and Society in the French Reformation* (Cambridge: Cambridge University Press, 1981).

40. One of these poems was recorded by Nicolas Versoris, the Parisian lawyer who chronicled the reign of Francis the First in his journal. The anonymous (Catholic) author of this poem interprets the calf as a reference to Luther, who polluted the monkish state when he took his Augustinian vows. See R. Po-Chia Hsia, "A Time for Monsters: Monstrous Birth, Propaganda, and the German Reformation," in *Monstrous Bodies and Political Monstrosities in Early Modern Europe*, ed. Laura Lunger Knoppers and Joan B. Landes (Ithaca: Cornell University Press, 2004), 67–92.

41. "Deuttung der czwo grewlichen figuren, Papstesels czu Rom und Munchkalbs zu Freybergijnn Meijsszen funden. Philippus Melanchthon. D. Martinus Luther. Wittemberg M.D.xxiii" [1523], *WA*, 11:381.

42. Popular literature exploited all forms of "monstrosities" to "warn" the masses according to the ideological position of the author. See Hsia's "A Time for Monsters" for the "slipperiness" of the language of monsters in the sixteenth century.

43. *LW*, 36:107.

44. Josef Schmidt, "Luther the Satirist: Strategies and Function of His Satire," in *The Martin Luther Quincentennial* (Detroit: Wayne State University Press, 1985), 39–40.

45. This lack of a decisive program of secular amendment makes Luther, in Oberman's eyes, into a preliminary figure, a forerunner rather than a mature leader, of the Reformation; see Heiko Oberman, *The Reformation: Roots and Ramifications*, trans. Andrew Colin Gow (Edinburgh: T & T Clark, 1994), 27–28.

46. See ibid., 50.

47. See *WA*, 37:616, 9:656, 11:183, and passim. Variations on this proverb can also be found in many places in Luther's writings, such as *Je frommer . . . je erger* ("the more pious . . . the worse") and *je heiliger . . . je erger* ("the more saintly . . . the worse"). The article *arg* in the index of the *WA* contains numerous other examples.

48. *WA*, 11:381.

49. Montaigne, *Essais*, 3.13, ed. Maurice Rat (Paris: Gallimard, 1962), 1046. I am citing Michael Screech's English translation in Montaigne, *Essays* (Harmondsworth, Middlesex: Penguin, 1991), 1213.

50. J. L. Austin, *How to Do Things with Words*, ed. J. O. Urmson and Marina Sbisà (Cambridge: Harvard University Press, 1975), 101.

51. Montaigne, *Essais*, 1046.

52. Edwards, *Print, Propaganda, and Martin Luther*, 1.

Ernesto Laclau, On the Names of God

NOTE: This essay originally appeared in Susan Golding, ed., *The Eight Technologies of Otherness* (London: Routledge, 1997), 253–64. Reprinted by permission of the publisher.

1. Meister Eckhart, *Selected Writings* (London: Penguin, 1994), Sermon 28 (DW 83, W 96), 236–37.

2. Ibid., 238.

3. Ibid., Sermon 17 (DW 21, W 97), 182.

4. Ibid., Sermon 5 (DW 53, W 22), 129.

5. Pseudo-Dionysius Areopagite, "Mystical Theology," in *The Divine Names and Mystical Theology*, trans. John D. Jones (Milwaukee, Wisc.: Marquette University Press, 1980), 221.

6. Gershom Scholem, *Major Trends in Jewish Mysticism* (New York: Shocken, 1995), 64.

7. Here, of course, is where different mystical currents start to diverge. Is the experience that of the Oneness of God Himself, or that of an expression of God? For our argument in this essay, the debate about dualism, monism, and pantheism is not really relevant. Let me just say in passing that, from the viewpoint of the logic of mystical discourse, pantheism is the only ultimately coherent position.

8. Eckhart, Sermon 16 (DW 12, W 57), 177–78.

9. Ibid., Sermon 4 (DW 30, W 18), 123.

10. Jacob Korg, ed., *The Poetry of Robert Browning* (Indianapolis: Bobbs-Merrill, 1971), 286. The following are some other examples of a theme that is quite common in mystical literature. Julian of Norwich refers to a small thing that he is beholding, the size of a hazelnut. And he asserts: "In this little thing I saw three properties. The first is that God made it: the second, that God loveth it: the third that God keepth it. And what beheld I in this? Truly, the Maker, the Lover and the Keeper" (*The Revelation of Divine Love of Julian of Norwich*, trans. James Walsh, S.J. [London: Burns and Oates, 1961], 60). In his diary, George Fox sees in everything existing the "hidden unity in the Eternal Being." Commenting on that passage, Evelyn Underhill says: "'To know the hidden unity in the Eternal Being'—know it with invulnerable certainty, in the all-embracing act of consciousness with which we are aware of the personality of those we truly love—it is to live at its fullest the Illuminated Life, enjoying 'all creatures in God and God in all creatures'" (Evelyn Underhill, *Mysticism: A Study in the Nature and Development of Man's Spiritual Consciousness* [New York: Dutton, n.d.], 309).

11. Eckhart, "The Talks of Instruction," 9.

12. Ibid., 40.

13. The original formulation of this argument is to be found in Ernesto Laclau and Chantal Mouffe, *Hegemony and Socialist Strategy* (London: Verso, 1985). I have developed various dimensions of the hegemonic relationship (especially in what refers to the relationship fullness/particularity) in the essays collected in *Emancipation(s)* (London: Verso, 1996).

Claude Lefort, The Permanence of the Theologico-Political?

NOTE: This essay originally appeared in Claude Lefort, *Democracy and Political Theory*, trans. David Macey (Cambridge: Polity Press, 1988), 213–55; reprinted by permission of the publisher.

1. G. W. F. Hegel, *Philosophy of Mind*, trans. William Wallace (Oxford: Oxford University Press, 1894), 156–57.

2. This essay was first published in 1981 as "Permanence du théologico-politique?" in *Le Temps de la Réflexion* 2 (1981)—Ed.

3. Ernst Kantorowicz, *The King's Two Bodies: A Study in Medieval Political Theology* (Princeton: Princeton University Press, 1957).

4. Marc Bloch, *The Royal Touch: Sacred Monarchy and Scrofula in England and France*, trans. J. E. Anderson (London: Routledge and Kegan Paul, 1973).

5. Joseph Strayer, *Medieval Statecraft and the Perspectives of History* (Princeton: Princeton University Press, 1971).

Marc de Wilde, Violence in the State of Exception: Reflections on Theologico-Political Motifs in Benjamin and Schmitt

1. Military Order on the Detention, Treatment, and Trial of Certain Non-Citizens in the War against Terrorism, November 13, 2001.

2. Giorgio Agamben, *State of Exception*, trans. Kevin Attell (Chicago: University of Chicago Press, 2005), 3–4.

3. Walter Benjamin, "Zur Kritik der Gewalt," in Benjamin, *Gesammelte Schriften*, ed. and introd. Rolf Tiedemann and Hermann Schweppenhäuser (Frankfurt am Main: Suhrkamp, 1991), 2.1:179–203; translated as Walter Benjamin, "Critique of Violence," in Benjamin, *Selected Writings*, vol. 1, *1913–1926*, ed. Marcus Bullock and Michael W. Jennings (Cambridge: Harvard University Press, 1996), 236–52. Carl Schmitt, *Politische Theologie: Vier Kapitel zur Lehre von der Souveränität* (Berlin: Duncker & Humblot, 1996); translated as Carl Schmitt, *Political Theology: Four Chapters on the Concept of Sovereignty*, trans. and introd. George Schwab (Cambridge: MIT Press, 1985). For these texts, page references will be given to both German and English versions in following notes, with the page number of the original language preceding the English one.

4. Martin Jay, *The Dialectical Imagination: A History of the Frankfurt School and the Institute of Social Research, 1923–1950* (Berkeley: University of California Press, 1996), 197–212.

5. Jan-Werner Müller, *A Dangerous Mind: Carl Schmitt in Post-War European Thought* (New Haven: Yale University Press, 2003), 35–41.

6. In a letter to Schmitt dated December 9, 1930, Benjamin writes: "You will soon notice how much the book [Benjamin's *Ursprung des deutschen Trauerspiels*] owes to your exposition of the doctrine of sovereignty" (in Benjamin, *Gesammelte Schriften*, 1.3: 887). In a short curriculum vitae, Benjamin emphasizes the influence of Schmitt's analysis of the political and especially his "attempt to integrate phenomena . . . that only seemingly can be isolated according to fields" (in Siegfried Unseld, ed., *Zur Aktualität Walter Benjamins* [Frankfurt am Main: Suhrkamp, 1972], 46). Jacques Derrida mentions another letter, in which Schmitt expresses his gratitude to Benjamin for writing "Critique of Violence" (in Jacques Derrida, *Force de Loi: Le "Fondement Mystique de l'Autorité"* [Paris: Galilée, 1994], 81; translated as Jacques Derrida, "Force of Law: The 'Mystical Foundation of Authority,'" trans. Mary Quaintance, in *Deconstruction and the Possibility of Justice*, ed. Drucilla Cornell, Michel Rosenfeld, and David Gray Carlson [New York: Routledge, 1992], 29–30).

7. See Gérard Raulet, "Die Gemeinschaft beim jungen Marcuse," in *Intellektuellendiskurse in der Weimarer Republik: Zur politischen Kultur einer Gemengelage*, ed. Manfred Gangl and Gérard Raulet (Frankfurt am Main: Campus, 1994), 101, and Wolfgang Essbach, "Radikalismus und Modernität bei Jünger und Bloch, Lukács und Schmitt," in ibid., 149–50.

8. The argument can be found, e.g., in Karl Dietrich Bracher, *Zeit der Ideologien: Eine Geschichte politischen Denkens im 20. Jahrhundert* (Stuttgart: Deutsche Verlags-Anstalt, 1982), 154. See also Jeffrey Herf, *Reactionary Modernism: Technology, Culture and Politics in Weimar and the Third Reich* (Cambridge: Cambridge University Press, 1986).

9. See Benjamin, "Critique of Violence," 190–91 / 244, and Carl Schmitt, *Der Begriff des Politischen* (Berlin: Duncker & Humblot, 1932), 37.

10. See Hent de Vries, *Philosophy and the Turn to Religion* (Baltimore: The Johns Hopkins University Press, 1999), 2.

11. In an early text on Roman Catholicism, Schmitt claims, e.g., "in the Doctrine of the Trinity so many elements of God's immanence are added to Jewish monotheism that here [i.e., in questions of politics and law] as well mediations are possible" (Carl Schmitt, *Römischer Katholizismus und politische Form* [1923; Stuttgart: Klett-Cotta, 1984], 12; translated as *Roman Catholicism and Political Form*, trans. G. L. Ulman [Westport, Ct.: Greenwood Press, 1996], 10; the translation here is my own).

12. Lutz Koepnick, "The Spectacle, the Trauerspiel, and the Politics of Resolution: Benjamin Reading the Baroque Reading Weimar," *Critical Inquiry* 22, no 2 (1996): 282; Norbert Bolz, *Auszug aus der entzauberten Welt: Philosophischer Extremismus zwischen den Weltkriegen* (Munich: Wilhelm Fink, 1989), 93; Norbert Bolz, "Charisma und Souveränität," in *Der Fürst dieser Welt: Carl Schmitt und die Folgen*, ed. Jacob Taubes (Munich: Wilhelm Fink, 1983), 261; Michael Rumpf, "Radikale Theologie: Benjamins Beziehung zu Carl Schmitt," in *Walter Benjamin: Zeitgenosse der Moderne*, ed. Peter Gebhardt (Kronberg: Scriptor, 1976), 46; Jacob Taubes, *Ad Carl Schmitt: Gegenstrebige Fügung* (Berlin: Merve, 1987), 22.

13. Suzanne Heil, *"Gefährliche Beziehungen": Walter Benjamin und Carl Schmitt* (Stuttgart: J. B. Metzler, 1996), 160–61.

14. Wolfgang Fietkau, "Loss of Experience and Experience of Loss: Remarks on the Problem of the Lost Revolution in the Work of Walter Benjamin and His Fellow Combatants," *New German Critique* 39 (1986): 175.

15. Michael Makropoulos, "Haltlose Souveränität: Benjamin, Schmitt und die klassische Moderne in Deutschland," in *Intellektuellendiskurse*, ed. Gangl and Raulet, 206–7.

16. Schmitt, *Political Theology*, 37–38 / 31–32 (trans. modified). Highlighting this dimension of openness in Schmitt's work, Slavoj Žižek argues that the polemical nature of the political in fact involves "a tension between the structured social body, where each part has its place, and the 'part of no-part' which unsettles this order" (Slavoj Žižek, "Carl Schmitt in the Age of Post-Politics," in *The Challenge of Carl Schmitt*, ed. Chantal Mouffe (London: Verso, 1999), 27–28).

17. See Schmitt, *Roman Catholicism and Political Form*, 32 / 19.

18. See Schmitt, *Der Begriff des Politischen*, 26, 29.

19. Walter Benjamin, *Das Passagen-Werk*, ed. Rolf Tiedemann, in Benjamin, *Gesammelte Schriften*, 5.1:588; translated as Walter Benjamin, *The Arcades Project*, trans. Howard Eiland and Kevin McLaughlin (Cambridge: Harvard University Press, 1999), 471.

20. Jacques Derrida and Claude Lefort separately argue that a nontheological materialism could very well be the most consistent heritage of *"the theologico-political [du théologico-politique]."* See Jacques Derrida, *Spectres de Marx* (Paris: Galilée, 1993), 266; translated as Jacques Derrida, *Specters of Marx: The State of the Debt, the Work of Mourning, and the New International*, trans. Peggy Kamuf, introd. Bernd Magnus and Stephen Cullenberg (New York: Routledge, 1994), 211; and Claude Lefort, "Permanence du Théologico-Politique?," in Lefort, *Essais sur le politique: XIXe–XXe siècles* (Paris: Seuil/Esprit, 1986), 254; translated as "The Permanence of the Theologico-Political?" trans. David Macey, pp. 148–87 of this volume.

21. Walter Benjamin, "Theologisch-politisches Fragment," in Benjamin, *Gesammelte Schriften*, ed. and introd. Rolf Tiedemann and Hermann Schweppenhäuser (Frankfurt am Main: Suhrkamp, 1991), 2.1:203–4; translated as "Theologico-Political Fragment," trans. Edmund Jephcott, in Benjamin, *Reflections: Essays, Aphorisms, and Autobiographical Writings*, ed. and introd. Peter Demetz (New York: Schocken, 1978), 312–13.

22. Schmit, *Political Theology*, 13 / 5.

23. See Ellen Kennedy, *Constitutional Failure: Carl Schmitt in Weimar* (Durham, N.C.: Duke University Press, 2004), 173.

24. The argument can be found in Schmitt's *Die Diktatur*, which was written in the same year as *Politische Theologie* (1921) and which Schmitt understood to be its corollary (Carl Schmitt, *Die Diktatur* [Berlin: Duncker & Humblot, 1994], 133–34).

25. Schmit, *Political Theology*, 19 / 13.

26. Ibid.

27. Richard Wolin wrongly claims that "the paramount role played by the 'philosophy of life' [in Schmitt's worldview]—above all, by the concept of cultural criticism proper to *Lebensphiloso-phie*—on his political thought has escaped the attention of most critics" (Richard Wolin, "Carl Schmitt: The Conservative Revolutionary Habitus and the Aesthetics of Horror," *Political Theory* 20, no. 3 [1992]: 430). Schmitt himself argues that the most convincing philosophers of the state, Juan Donoso Cortés and Joseph de Maistre, were unable to accept the "organic world view" expressed by the "philosophy of life" (Schmit, *Political Theology*, 65 / 61).

28. Schmit, *Political Theology*, 21 / 15.

29. Taubes, *Ad Carl Schmitt*, 62.

30. Schmit, *Political Theology*, 36 / 30.

31. Ibid., 37 / 31.

32. Ibid., 67 / 63.

33. Ibid., 66 / 62.

34. Ibid., 44 / 36.

35. Ibid., 43 / 36.

36. An analysis of the difference between these theologico-political claims can be found in Jan Assmann, *Politische Theologie zwischen Ägypten und Israel* (Munich: Carl Friedrich von Siemens Stiftung, 1995), 26, 35, and in Hent de Vries, *Religion and Violence: Philosophical Perspectives from Kant to Derrida* (Baltimore: The Johns Hopkins University Press, 2003), 216.

37. Schmit, *Political Theology*, 37–38 / 31–32 (trans. modified).

38. Benjamin, "Critique of Violence," 196 / 248.

39. In line with the lawmaking function Benjamin ascribes to military violence, Schmitt, in *Der Nomos der Erde*, characterizes the military occupation of territory as a "constitutive event of international law": the occupation (*Landnahme*) is at the same time a determination of territory (*Ortung*) and a creation of legal order (*Ordnung*). See Carl Schmitt, *Der Nomos der Erde im Völker-recht des Jus Publicum Europeum* (1950; Berlin: Duncker & Humblot, 1997), 48.

40. Benjamin, "Critique of Violence," 188 / 242. In an illuminating reading of Benjamin's text, Werner Hamacher sketches the figure of an "afformative" related to the concept of this *Ent-setzung*, i.e., the (self-)deconstruction of positive law (Werner Hamacher, "Afformative, Strike," *The Cardozo Law Review* 13, no. 4 (1991): 1133–57).

41. Benjamin, "Critique of Violence," 189 / 243.

42. Ibid., 190 / 243. Observations concerning the police's lawmaking violence can also be found in Hannah Arendt's *Origins of Totalitarianism*. As she observes, on the eve of the Second World War—for the first time in the history of modern democracies—the police obtained the competence to rule directly over people's lives: "it was no longer an instrument to carry out and enforce the law, but had become a ruling authority independent of government and ministries" (Hannah Arendt, *The Origins of Totalitarianism* [1951; New York: Harcourt, 1966], 287). Referring to both Arendt and Benjamin, Derrida stresses the "ghostly apparition" of the police, which, because of a mixture of lawmaking and law-preserving violence, is not bound to any law and operates "beyond all accountability" (Jacques Derrida, *Cosmopolites de tous les pays, encore un effort!* [Paris: Galilée, 1997], 37; translated as Jacques Derrida, "On Cosmopolitanism," trans. Mark Dooley and Michael Hughes, in Derrida, *Cosmopolitanism and Forgiveness* [London: Routledge, 2003], 14). Sim-

ilar remarks on the lawmaking violence of the police can be found in the works of Giorgio Agamben and of Michael Hardt and Antonio Negri. They discuss the law-positing authority of the police explicitly in the context of an analysis of new forms of sovereignty. Hardt and Negri emphasize, in the spirit of Benjamin, that the police's lawmaking violence is related to its competence to decide the exceptional case: "here, therefore, is born, in the name of the exceptionality of the intervention, a form of right that is really *a right of the police*" (Michael Hardt and Antonio Negri, *Empire* [Cambridge: Harvard University Press, 2000], 17).

43. Benjamin, "Critique of Violence," 191 / 244.

44. Ibid., 190 / 244.

45. Walter Benjamin, "Über Sprache überhaupt und über die Sprache des Menschen," in Benjamin, *Gesammelte Schriften*, 2.1:142; translated as Walter Benjamin, "On Language as Such and on the Language of Man," in Benjamin, *Selected Writings*, vol. 1, *1913–1926*, 64.

46. Georges Sorel, *Réflexions sur la violence* (1908; Paris: Rivière, 1950). See: Manfred Gangl, "Mythos der Gewalt und Gewalt der Mythos: Georges Sorels Einfluss auf rechte und linke Intellektuelle der Weimarer Republik," in *Intellektuellendiskurse*, ed. Gangl and Raulet, 171–96; and Chryssoula Kambas, "Walter Benjamin, Lecteur des 'Réflexions sur la Violence,'" *Cahiers Georges Sorel* 2 (1984): 71–87.

47. Benjamin, "Critique of Violence," 199 / 249–50 (trans. modified).

48. Derrida, "Force de loi," 119.

49. Ibid., 134.

50. A critical analysis of metaphors suggesting a war beyond the political is urgent. We could, for example, refer to wordings like the "decisive victory for the forces of freedom" in the National Security Strategy of the United States (see http://www.whitehouse.gov/nsc/nss.pdf).

51. See Charles Lane, "Secrecy Allowed on 9/11 Detention: High Court Declines to Hear Appeal," *The Washington Post*, January 13, 2004, and Ronald Dworkin, "What the Court Really Said," *The New York Review of Books* 51 (2004): 13.

52. Judith Butler argues that the detention of "illegal enemy combatants" in Guantánamo Bay may well be in agreement with international law and, more specifically, the Geneva Conventions. International law proves to be biased toward the nation-state, offering protection only to its subjects: "The Conventions aid and abet the United States by guaranteeing prisoners not affiliated with state-centered military actions fewer rights than those who are" (Judith Butler, "Guantánamo Limbo," *The Nation* 274 [2002]: 12).

53. Under Article 5 of the Third Geneva Convention, should any doubt arise as to whether captured individuals do in fact belong to one of the hostile parties, a "competent tribunal" must ascertain their identity. According to the U.S. government, however, such an examination is not necessary in the exceptional case of "non-state enemy combatants."

54. Benjamin, "Critique of Violence," 189 / 243.

55. Ibid., 188 / 242.

56. Ibid., 186 / 240.

Judith Butler, Critique, Coercion, and Sacred Life in Benjamin's "Critique of Violence"

1. All citations in this essay are from Walter Benjamin, *Selected Writings*, vol. 1, *1913–1926*, ed. Marcus Bullock and Michael W. Jennings (Cambridge: Harvard University Press, 1996), and in

German from Walter Benjamin, *Kritik der Gewalt und andere Aufsätze*, (Frankfurt am Main: Suhrkamp, 1965). Page numbers in the text and notes refer to the English translation.

2. Benjamin's word for "fate" is *das Shicksal,* which is more aptly translated as "destiny."

3. Rosenzweig argues that the commandment is a verbal and written effort on the part of God to solicit the love of his people (*The Star of Redemption*, trans. William Hallo [Notre Dame, Ind.: University of Notre Dame Press, 1985], 267–70). His focus on love corresponds to the efforts during that time to revive the spiritual dimension of Judaism over and against rabbinic reforms that focused on the elaboration of rules and the science of their interpretation. Rosenzweig's concern with Judaism as a spiritual movement led him to argue that "the Jewish people must deny itself the satisfaction the peoples of the world constantly enjoy in the functioning of their state" (332). He argues further that "The state symbolizes the attempt to give nations eternity within the confines of time." For such an eternity to be secured, however, nations must perpetually be refounded, and they require war to perpetuate themselves. In Rosenzweig's view, life is constituted by preservation and renewal. Law emerges as antilife to the extent that law establishes an endurance and stability that works against life and becomes the basis for state coercion. He sought to understand Judaism as beyond the contradictions that afflict nations, and so to distinguish the idea of the Jewish people from the Jewish nation (329).

4. For a record of Benjamin's indecisive relation to Zionism, see the correspondence between Benjamin and Scholem in the summer of 1933, *The Correspondence of Walter Benjamin and Gershom Scholem, 1932–1940* (New York: Schocken, 1989).

5. See Jacques Derrida, *Force de loi* (Paris : Galilée, 1994), 69.

6. Hannah Arendt, "On Violence," in *Crises of the Republic* (New York: Harcourt Brace Jovanovich, 1972).

7. Benjamin associates atonement and retribution with myth both in this essay and in several other essays of the period. He also clearly opposes the operation of critique to myth, which, in his view, wars against truth. See, e.g., "Goethe's Elective Affinities," in Benjamin, *Selected Writings*, 1:297–362. This essay was written between 1919 and 1922.

8. Also in 1921, Benjamin writes of "the immeasurable significance of the Last Judgment, of that constantly postponed day which flees so determinedly into the future after the commission of every misdeed. This significance is revealed not in the world of law, where retribution rules, but only in the moral universe, where forgiveness comes out to meet it. In order to struggle against retribution, forgiveness finds its powerful ally in time. For time, in which Ate [moral blindness] pursues the evildoer, is not the lonely calm of fear but the tempestuous storm of forgiveness which precedes the onrush of the Last Judgment and against which she cannot advance. This storm is not only the voice in which the evildoer's cry of terror is drowned; it is also the hand that obliterates the traces of his misdeeds, even if it must lay waste to the world in the process" ("The Meaning of Time in a Moral Universe," Benjamin, *Selected Writings*, 1:287).

Forgiveness, which we might ordinarily understand as a capacity achieved upon reflection when passions have quieted down, is here figured as a storm, a storm with a hand and a voice, and so a divine force, but *not* one that is based on retribution. Importantly, this storm of forgiveness constitutes a radical alternative to the closed economy of atonement *and* retribution. For a further discussion of this issue of forgiveness in Benjamin, see my "Beyond Seduction and Morality: Benjamin's Early Aesthetics," in Dominic Willsdon and Diarmuid Costello, eds., *Ethics and Aesthetics* (London: Routledge, forthcoming).

9. "Theologico-Political Fragment," in Walter Benjamin, *Reflections: Essays, Aphorisms, Autobiographical Writings*, trans. Edmund Jephcott, ed. and introd. Peter Demetz (New York: Harcourt Brace Jovanovich, 1978), 312–13; originally published in Benjamin, *Kritik der Gewalt und andere Aufsätze*, 95–96.

10. The reason for the commandment, Benjamin writes, should be found "no longer in what the deed does to the victim, but what it does to God and the doer" (251).

11. See Benjamin's remarks on "critical violence" in "On Semblance" (224), written in 1919–20, and in his "Goethe's Elective Affinities" (341), both in *Selected Writings*, vol. 1.

12. Benjamin writes that "in all language and linguistic creations, there remains in addition to what can be conveyed something that cannot be communicated," which he refers to as "the nucleus of all languages" ("The Task of the Translator," *Selected Writings*, 1:261).

13. See Werner Hamacher, "Afformative, Strike," trans. Dana Hollander, in *Walter Benjamin's Philosophy: Destruction and Experience*, ed. Andrew Benjamin and Peter Osborne (London: Routledge 1993), 110–38.

Stéphane Mosès, From Rosenzweig to Levinas: Philosophy of War

NOTE: Translated from "De Rosenzweig à Levinas," in Stéphane Mosès, *Au-delà de la guerre: Trois études sur Levinas* (Paris: Éditions de l'éclat, 2004), 19–46, by permission of the publisher.

1. Emmanuel Levinas, *Totality and Infinity*, trans. Alphonso Lingis (Pittsburgh: Duquesne University Press, 1969), 28.

2. Ibid., 117–20.

3. G. W. F. Hegel, *Phenomenology of Spirit*, trans. A. V. Miller (Oxford: Oxford University Press, 1977), 272–73.

4. G. W. F. Hegel, *Philosophy of Right*, trans. T. M. Knox (London: Oxford University Press, 1967), 209 (par. 324).

5. Franz Rosenzweig, *The Star of Redemption*, trans. W. W. Hallo (Notre Dame, Ind.: University of Notre Dame Press, 1985), 5.

6. *Franz Rosenzweig: Philosophical and Theological Writings*, trans. and ed. Paul W. Franks and Michael L. Morgan (Indianapolis: Hackett, 2000), 52–53 (trans. modified).

7. Ibid., 54.

8. Immanuel Kant, *Critique of Pure Reason*, trans. F. Max Müller (Garden City, N.J.: Doubleday & Co., 1966), 371 (Second Division, Book II, chap. II, section 9, § III, "Explanation of the Cosmological Idea of Freedom in Connection with the General Necessity of Nature").

9. *Franz Rosenzweig: Philosophical and Theological Writings,* 60 (trans. modified).

10. Rosenzweig, *The Star of Redemption,* 288 (trans. modified).

11. Cf. Sigmund Freud: "Where id was, there shall ego be" (Freud, *New Introductory Lectures on Psychoanalysis,* trans. James Strachey [New York: W. W. Norton & Co., 1964], 80).

12. Levinas, *Totality and Infinity*, 21.

13. Ibid., 21.

14. Ibid., 25.

15. Ibid., 21.

16. Ibid.

17. Ibid.

18. Ibid., 26.

19. *Emmanuel Levinas: Basic Philosophical Writings*, ed. Adriaan T. Peperzak et al. (Bloomington: Indiana University Press, 1996), 155.

20. Levinas, *Totality and Infinity*, 24.

21. Ibid., 25.

Levinas, Spinoza, and the Theologico-Political Meaning of Scripture, Hent de Vries

1. Those relevant for me in this context will be his 1955 "The Case of Spinoza" ("Le Cas Spinoza") and 1966 "Have You Reread Baruch?" ("Avez-vous relu Baruch?"), plus an intervention presented during a Spinoza conference held in Jerusalem in 1977 in response to a lecture by the Chicago philosopher Richard McKeon, "L'Arrière-plan de Spinoza." Emmanuel Levinas, "The Spinoza Case" and "Have You Reread Baruch?," in Levinas, *Difficult Freedom: Essays on Judaism*, trans. Seán Hand (Baltimore: The Johns Hopkins University Press, 1990), 106–10 and 111–18; "Réponse au Professeur McKeon," in Nathan Rotenstreich and Norma Schneider, eds., *Spinoza: His Thought and Work, Entretiens in Jerusalem, 6–9 September 1977* (Jerusalem: Publications of the Israel Academy of Sciences and Humanities, 1983), 47–52, also published as "L'Arrière-plan de Spinoza," in *L'Au-delà du verset: Lectures et discours talmudiques* (Paris: Minuit, 1982), 201–6; "Spinoza's Background," in Levinas, *Beyond the Verse: Talmudic Readings and Lectures*, trans. Gary D. Mole (Bloomington: Indiana University Press, 1994), 168–73. See also the remarks Levinas devotes to Jean Lacroix's *Spinoza et le problème du salut*, "Jean Lacroix: Philosophie et Religion," *Noms propres* (Montpellier: Fata Morgana, 1976), 119–30; "Jean Lacroix: Philosophy and Religion," *Proper Names*, trans. Michael B. Smith (Stanford: Stanford University Press, 1996), 80–89.

Essays from *Difficult Freedom* will hereafter be cited by page number in the text, with the page number of the English translation preceding that of the French original. All translations have been modified where need be for purposes of the present discussion.

2. Sylvain Zac, *Spinoza et l'interprétation de l'Écriture* (Paris: Presses Universitaires de France, 1965).

3. Levinas, "Jean Lacroix: Philosophy and Religion," in *Proper Names*, 84 / 124.

4. Ibid., 83 / 123.

5. Levinas, "Have You Reread Baruch?," *Difficult Freedom*, 112 / 160. The quote is from Zac, *Spinoza et l'interprétation de l'Écriture*, 36.

6. Stuart Hampshire, *Spinoza and Spinozism* (Oxford: Oxford University Press, 2005).

7. Jean-Francois Rey, "Levinas et Spinoza," in *Spinoza au XXe siècle*, ed. Olivier Bloch (Paris: Presses Universitaires de France, 1993), 230. Rey notes further: "Levinas devotes himself to . . . an operation that consists, not in confronting Spinoza with a tradition that he did not recognize as his own, but rather in opposing Spinoza to Spinoza, that is to say, in his terms, to show the coexistence of Spinozism with an anti-Spinozism" (ibid., 227). See also Edith Wyschogrod, "Ethics as First Philosophy: Levinas Reads Spinoza," in *Journal of Eighteenth Century Studies* 40, no. 3 (Fall 1999): 195–205. For Deleuze, see his *Spinoza et le problème de l'expression* (Paris: Minuit, 1969); *Expressionism in Philosophy: Spinoza*, trans. Martin Joughin (New York: Zone Books, 1990), and *Spinoza: Philosophie pratique* (Paris: Minuit, 1981); *Spinoza: Practical Philosophy*, trans. Robert Hurley (San Francisco: City Lights, 1988), and numerous essays and scattered remarks throughout his writings.

8. The quote is from Zac, *Spinoza et l'interprétation de l'Écriture*, 99; see also 76, 97.

9. Levinas, "Spinoza's Background," in *Beyond the Verse*, 168 / 201.

10. Ibid., 168–69 / 201–2.

11. Ibid., 169 / 202.

12. Ibid., 172 / 205.

13. Ibid., 171, 173 / 204, 206.

14. Ibid.

15. For a discussion, see my *Religion and Violence: Philosophical Perspectives from Kant to Derrida* (Baltimore: The Johns Hopkins University Press, 2002), chap. 1.

16. Levinas, "Jean Lacroix: Philosophy and Religion," in *Proper Names*, 83–84 and 178–79n.5 / 123 and 191n.2.

17. Ibid., 84 and 180n.6 / 123 and 191n.3.

18. Ibid., 84 / 123–24.

19. See my "Zum Begriff der Allegorie in Schopenhauers Religionsphilosophie," in *Schopenhauer, Nietzsche und die Kunst, Schopenhauer-Studien 4*, ed. W. Schirmacher (Vienna, 1991), 187–97.

20. Levinas, "Spinoza's Background," in *Beyond the Verse*, 171 / 204.

21. Ibid., 169 / 202.

22. Ibid., 171 / 204.

23. Ibid., 172 / 205.

24. Steven B. Smith, *Spinoza's Book of Life: Freedom and Redemption in the "Ethics"* (New Haven: Yale University Press, 2003), 87–88.

25. Y. Yovel, *The Marrano of Reason* (Princeton: Princeton University Press, 1989), 1:134–35.

26. Baruch Spinoza, *Theologico-Political Treatise*, xxxviii; see also *Ethics*, IV; 35–37, 40.

27. Ibid. See also Sylvain Zac, "Thèmes spinozistes dans la philosophie de Bergson," in *Études bergsonniennes* 8 (Paris: Presses Universitaires de France, 1968), 123–58.

Jürgen Habermas, On the Relations Between the Secular Liberal State and Religion

NOTE: ©Verlag Herder, Freiburg, first edition, 2005. The essay earlier appeared in English translation by Matthias Frisch, in *The Frankfurt School on Religion: Key Writings by the Major Thinkers*, ed. Eduardo Mendieta (New York: Routledge, 2005), 339–48.

1. E. W. Böckenförde, "The Rise of the State as a Process of Secularisation," in his *State, Society and Liberty: Studies in Political Theory and Constitutional Law*, trans. J. A. Underwood (New York: Berg, 1991), 45.

2. Jürgen Habermas, *The Inclusion of the Other: Studies in Political Theory*, ed. C. Cronin and P. de Greiff (Cambridge: MIT Press, 1998).

3. The concept *materiale Wertethik* comes from Max Scheler. See his *Formalism in Ethics and Non-Formal Ethics of Values: A New Attempt Toward the Foundation of an Ethical Personalism*, trans. Manfred S. Frings and Roger L. Funk (Evanston, Ill.: Northwestern University Press, 1973)—Trans.

4. Jürgen Habermas, *Between Facts and Norms: Contributions to a Discourse Theory of Law and Democracy*, trans. W. Rehg (Cambridge: MIT Press, 1996), chap. 3.

5. H. Brunkhorst, "Der lange Schatten des Staatswillenspositivismus," *Leviathan* 31 (2003): 362–81.

6. Böckenförde, "The Rise of the State as a Process of Secularisation," 44.

7. *Theologen des 20. Jahrhunderts*, ed. P. Neuner and G. Wenz (Darmstadt: Wissenschaftliche Buchgesellschaft, 2002).

8. K. Eder, "Europäische Säkularisierung—ein Sonderweg in die postsäkulare Gesellschaft?" *Berliner Journal für Soziologie* 12 (2002): 331–43.

9. John Rawls, *Political Liberalism* (New York: Columbia University Press, 1993): 133 ff.

10. See, e.g., W. Singer, "Keiner kann anders sein, als er ist. Verschaltungen legen uns fest: Wir sollten aufhören, von Freiheit zu reden," *Frankfurter Allgemeine Zeitung*, January 8, 2004, 33.

11. Jürgen Habermas, *Glauben und Wissen* (Frankfurt am Main: Suhrkamp, 2001).

Pope Benedict XVI, Prepolitical Moral Foundations of a Free Republic

1. R. Spaemann, "Weltethos als 'Projekt,'" *Merkur* 50 (1996): 893–904.

2. The German word *Recht* means both "law," in the sense of the totality of laws or general norms, and "right," as in *Menschenrechte*, "human rights." Thus the reader should keep in mind, both in this passage and in what follows, that the word translated "law" or "rights" according to context would be the same word, *Recht*, in German—Trans.

3. Despite some minor corrections, this still-dominant philosophy of evolution is impressively carried out in J. Monod, *Chance and Necessity: An Essay on the Natural Philosophy of Modern Biology*, trans. Austryn Wainhouse (New York: Knopf, 1971). For the distinction between the actual scientific results and the philosophy that accompanies it, *Evolution: Ein kritisches Lehrbuch*, ed. R. Junker and S. Scherer (Gießen: Weyel, 1998), is useful. For a discussion of how the philosophy that accompanies the theory of evolution is critically questioned, see J. Ratzinger, *Glaube—Wahrheit—Toleranz* (Freiburg: Herder, 2003), 131–47.

4. For the three dimensions of medieval natural law (dynamics of being in general, directionality of the shared nature of man and animal [Ulpian], and specific directionality of the reasonable nature of man) see P. Delhaye, "Naturrecht," *Lexikon für Theologie und Kirche* (Freiburg: Herder, 1998), 7:821–25.

5. I have attempted to give a more detailed account of this in my book *Glaube—Wahrheit—Toleranz*. See also M. Fiedrowicz, *Apologie im frühen Christentum* (Paderborn: Schöningh, 2001).

6. K. Hübner, *Das Christentum im Wettstreit der Religionen* (Tübingen: Mohr Siebeck, 2003), 148.

Bruce Lincoln, Bush's God Talk

NOTE: Reprinted by permission from *The Christian Century*, October 5, 2004, 22–29; © 2004 *The Christian Century*. Subscriptions: $49 per year, from P.O. Box 378, Mt. Morris, IL 61054, 1-800-208-4097.

1. George W. Bush, *A Charge to Keep: My Journey to the White House* (New York: William Morrow & Co., 1999). All quotations are from the paperback edition (New York: Perennial, 2001).

2. Ibid., 136–37.

3. Doug Wead goes unmentioned in *A Charge to Keep* but is discussed in many other publications. See, e.g., David Aikman, *A Man of Faith: The Spiritual Journey of George W. Bush* (Nashville: W. Publishing Group, 2004), 80–84, or Stephen Mansfield, *The Faith of George W. Bush* (New York: Jeremy Tarcher, 2003), 83–84. Wead's motto, "Signal early and signal often," is quoted in Guy Lawson, "George W.'s Personal Jesus," *Gentleman's Quarterly* (September 2003), 394.

4. *A Charge to Keep*, 1.

5. Ibid., 8–9.

6. Ibid.

7. Ibid., 229–30.

8. Ibid., 232.

9. See the materials selected for the volume *Renewing America's Purpose: Policy Addresses of George W. Bush, July 1999–July 2000* (n.p.: Republican National Committee and Bush for President, Inc., 2000), esp. part 2, "A New Agenda for Compassion," 109–210.

10. Remarks by the president after two planes crash into the World Trade Center, Emma Booker Elementary School, Sarasota, Florida, September 11, 2001. The full text is included in *We

Will Prevail: President George Bush on War, Terrorism, and Freedom, Foreword by Peggy Noonan (New York: Continuum, 2003), 1.

11. Remarks by the president upon arrival at Barksdale Air Force Base, September 11, 2001, in ibid., 1–2.

12. Presidential address to the nation, September 11, 2001, in ibid., 3.

13. Ibid.

14. Presidential address to a joint session of Congress, September 23, 2001, in ibid., 15.

15. Responding to questions by the press on September 16, 2001, Bush said "This is a new kind of—a new kind of evil. And we understand. The American people are beginning to understand, *this crusade*, this war on terrorism is going to take a while" (my emphasis). He has never made such a statement since. Presumably, his staff made it very clear why the term was ill-chosen. A transcript is available at http://www.whitehouse.gov/news/releases/2001/09/20010916–2.html.

16. Presidential address to the nation, October 7, 2001, in *We Will Prevail*, 33.

17. Speech to the United Nations General Assembly, November 10, 2001, in ibid., 71–72.

18. State of the Union Address, January 28, 2003, in ibid., 220–21.

19. Remarks at the twentieth anniversary of the National Endowment for Democracy, available at http://www.whitehouse.gov/news/releases/2003/11/20031106-2.html.

20. Thus: "Americans, of all people, should never be surprised by the power of liberty to transform lives and nations. . . . I believe that America is called to lead the cause of freedom in a new century. . . . I believe all these things because freedom is not America's gift to the world, it is the Almighty God's gift to every man and woman in this world." Acceptance speech at the Republican National Convention, September 2, 2004. Quoted from the *New York Times*, September 3, 2004, P4.

21. Ibid. Note that the version on Bush's Web site omits the benediction.

22. Devon Largio delineates the twenty-seven rationales in "Uncovering the Rationales for the War on Iraq: The Words of the Bush Administration, Congress, and the Media from September 12, 2001, to October 11, 2002," senior honors thesis, University of Illinois at Urbana-Champaign, on which see William Raspberry, "Tracking Why We Went to War," *Washington Post*, May 31, 2004, A23, available at http://www.washingtonpost.com/wp-dyn/articles/A3523–2004May30.html.

23. Remarks by the president at Victory 2004 Dinner, August 12, 2004, Santa Monica, Calif. Available at http://www.whitehouse.gov/news/releases/2004/08/20040812–15.html.

24. It is worth noting that Michael Gerson, the president's chief speechwriter, holds a degree in theology from Wheaton College, "the Evangelical Harvard." Others, however, including Karl Rove and Karen Hughes (who ghost-wrote *A Charge to Keep*) also play a significant role in the production of Bush's texts and bring to them a slightly different religious sensibility.

25. Remarks to employees at the Federal Bureau of Investigation, September 25, 2001, in *We Will Prevail*, 22.

William E. Connolly, Pluralism and Faith

NOTE: A version of this essay appeared as "Pluralism and Relativism," chap. 2 of William E. Connolly, *Pluralism* (Durham, N.C.: Duke University Press, 2005), 38–67. Reprinted by permission of the publisher.

1. Leo Strauss, *Liberalism: Ancient and Modern* (Chicago: University of Chicago Press, 1968), 5.

2. Ibid., 36.

3. Ibid., 28.

4. Ibid.

5. Ibid., 31.

6. Ibid., 31 and 34.

7. Ibid., 40.

8. Ibid., 40–41.

9. Ibid., 56–57.

10. Ibid., 63.

11. Ibid., 254.

12. Ibid., 254–55.

13. In a thoughtful essay, "A Postmodern Return to Orthodoxy: Leo Strauss's Early Critique of Modern Liberalism," delivered at the fall 2003 convention of the American Political Science Association in Philadelphia, Miguel Vatter contends that Strauss "envisages a return to orthodoxy that is both 'postmodern' and 'democratic'" (3). He also argues that Strauss attempts to display the dependence of classical reason on faith. While impressed with Vatter's reading, I do not seek to decide whether Strauss is a believer or thinks most people must have such a belief in order to contain themselves.

14. William James, *The Will to Believe: And Other Essays in Popular Philosophy* (New York: Dover, 1956), x.

15. William J. Bennett, *Why We Fight* (New York: Doubleday), 79.

16. Reported in Nicholas Kristoff, http://forums.nytimes.com/webin/WebX?50@@.f3beae7 (August 17, 2003).

17. Bennett, *Why We Fight*, 86.

18. For a rich history of the "Radical Enlightenment" in Europe, the pivotal role Spinoza played in it, the harsh punishments meted out to those in Holland, France, Germany, and England for a hundred years who either avowed Spinozism or were accused of it, and the ways in which the political advent of Spinozism helped to create space for the "Moderate Enlightenment," see Jonathan Israel, *Radical Enlightenment: Philosophy and the Making of Modernity, 1650–1750* (Cambridge: Cambridge University Press, 2001). I review this book and probe sore spots in both the Spinozist and Kantian ideas of reason in "The Radical Enlightenment: Theory, Power, Faith," in *theory & event* (Spring 2004), http://muse.jhu.edu/journals/tae/.

19. Bennett, *Why We Fight*, 100.

20. Strauss, *Liberalism, Ancient and Modern*, 228.

21. Talal Asad, "Reading a Modern Classic: W. C. Smith's 'The Meaning and End of Religion,'" in *Religion and Media*, ed. Hent de Vries and Samuel Weber (Stanford: Stanford University Press, 2001), 216.

22. Talal Asad, *Formations of the Secular* (Stanford: Stanford University Press, 2003), 38.

23. Ibid., 38–39.

24. Ibid., 55.

25. Ibid., 169.

26. Gyanandra Pandey, in *Silencing the Present: History and the Homogenization of Contemporary India* (Cambridge, forthcoming), applies a similar analysis and prescriptive orientation to the contemporary politics of India. He shows how the partition of Pakistan and India, organized around a religio-national imperative, intensified conflicts between Muslims and Hindus. And he pursues the possibility of a post-secular India that is pluralistic in shape.

27. As Johns Rawls puts it in one formulation, "We appeal to a political conception of justice to distinguish between those questions that can be reasonably removed from the political agenda

and those that cannot. . . . To illustrate: from within a political conception of justice let us suppose we can account . . . for equal liberty of conscience, which takes the truths of religion off the agenda. . . . But by avoiding comprehensive doctrines we try to bypass religion and philosophy's profoundest controversies so as to have some hope of uncovering a stable consensus" (John Rawls, *Political Liberalism* [Cambridge: Harvard University Press, 1993], 151–52).

28. I first emphasized the signal importance of multidimensional pluralism to the health of a polity in *Identity/Difference*, first published in 1991 and republished with a new preface in 2002 (Minneapolis: University of Minnesota Press). I did not see then the effect such a process could have on amplifying the experience of difference within faith practices. Etienne Balibar, in *Politics and the Other Scene* (London: Verso, 2002), has very insightful things to say about the political effect of multiplying the types of minorities.

29. Multidimensional pluralism must be discussed in conjunction with the need to reduce the stratification of income, education, job security, and retirement prospects. I argue elsewhere that pluralism and the reduction of inequality set mutual conditions of possibility for each other. See *The Ethos of Pluralization* (Minneapolis: University of Minnesota Press, 1995), chap. 3, and "Assembling the Democratic Left," *boundary 2* (February 1999).

30. Asad comes to terms with this issue in Islam in *Genealogies of Religion: Discipline and Reasons of Power in Christianity and Islam* (Baltimore: The Johns Hopkins University Press, 1993). In a very thoughtful book edited by Fabio Petito and Pavlos Hatzpoulos, *Religion in International Relations: The Return from Exile* (New York: Palgrave Press, 2003), several essays explore the effects of the Westphalian accord in privatizing religion and address this "site" as a potential source of connection across faiths. It is where they both resist secularism and transcend the quest for formation of an ecumenical creed that the essays make their most promising innovations. In that respect, the pieces by Scott Thomas, Cecelia Lynch, Carsten Bagge and Ole Waever, and Richard Falk and Fred Dallmayr are very thoughtful. The one limit is that few, if any, of these supporters of multiple orientations to transcendence concedes the nobility that can reside in philosophy/faiths of radical immanence. A corrective to that omission, in a book that also explores the time in Spain when Christianity, Judaism, and Islam coexisted uneasily, is John Docker, *1492: The Poetics of Diaspora* (London: Continuum Books, 1999).

31. I in fact support a "double-entry orientation" to the universal. See *Pluralism* (Durham, N.C.: Duke University Press, 2005), chap. 4.

32. When secularists do focus on such practices, the tendency is to define them as modes of manipulation to be transcended by intellectual effort. My argument, however, is that practices of rationality themselves involve disciplines and enactments that become embodied in the soft tissues of life, so that it now becomes a more complex matter to sort out manipulation from self-enactment.

Wendy Brown, Subjects of Tolerance: Why We Are Civilized and They Are the Barbarians

1. Mahmood Mamdani, *Good Muslim / Bad Muslim: America, The Cold War, and the Roots of Terror* (New York: Pantheon, 2004), 18.

2. Bernard Lewis, "The Roots of Muslim Rage," *The Atlantic* (September 1990); Samuel Huntington, "The Clash of Civilizations?," *Foreign Affairs* 72, no. 3 (Summer 1993): 31; both cited in Mamdani, *Good Muslim / Bad Muslim*, 20–21.

3. Liberalism is used here in the classic sense: it is the distinctly Western body of modern political theory and practices built on the assumption of the ontologically a priori nature of the

individual, which accord primacy to private individual liberty. Liberalism in this sense is not a political position within liberal democracies but their groundwork.

4. If national "civic religion" was featured by the classic social contract theorists—Hobbes, Locke, and Rousseau—as a necessary *supplement* to the social contract, where did the contents of what was deposited in that supplement go, and what is the relationship of this loss to the rise of subnational identities requiring civic tolerance?

5. Immanuel Kant, "What Is Enlightenment?" in *Political Writings*, ed. H. S. Reiss (Cambridge: Cambridge University Press, 1970), 54. Kant, of course, also problematizes this very formulation.

6. On Bush's regular consultations with rapture Christians and the effects of these consultations on foreign policy, see Rick Perlstein, "The Jesus Landing Pad," in *The Village Voice*, May 18, 2004. See also Bob Woodward's *Plan of Attack* (New York: Simon and Schuster, 2004), in which Bush responds to the question of whether he consulted his father before deciding to launch war on Iraq: "You know he is the wrong father to appeal to in terms of strength. There is a higher father that I appeal to" (94). Bush also told Woodward, "I believe the United States is *the* beacon for freedom in the world. . . . I say that freedom is not America's gift to the world. Freedom is God's gift to everybody in the world. . . . And I believe we have a duty to free people" (88–89).

7. Chandran Kukathas is a significant exception in his argument that liberty of conscience and autonomy are not only not equivalent but may well conflict at times. He argues that liberty of conscience, not autonomy, is the basis of toleration and that liberty of conscience must trump autonomy when they do conflict. See his *The Liberal Archipelago: A Theory of Diversity and Freedom* (Oxford: Oxford University Press, 2003), esp. chap. 1, 36–37.

8. Susan Mendus, *Toleration and the Limits of Liberalism* (Atlantic Highlands, N.J.: Humanities Press, 1989), 56.

9. Will Kymlicka, "Two Models of Pluralism and Tolerance" in *Toleration: An Elusive Virtue*, ed. David Heyd (Princeton: Princeton University Press, 1996), 97.

10. Bernard Williams, "Toleration: An Impossible Virtue?" in *Toleration*, ed. Heyd, 24.

11. Michael Ignatieff, "Nationalism and Toleration," in *The Politics of Toleration*, ed. Susan Mendus (Edinburgh: Edinburgh University Press, 1999).

12. In his comments on my work at a symposium, Barry Hindess reminded me that the temporalization of difference is an insidious and pervasive trope in Western political and social thought, one that is not limited to liberalism or even to colonial discourse. Comment by Barry Hindess at the Launch of the Center on Citizenship, Identity, and Governance, Open University, Milton Keynes, England (March 2005). For an elaboration of this position, see the essay he co-authored with Christine Helliwell, "The Temporalising of Difference," *Ethnicities* 5, no. 3: 414–18.

13. See, e.g., Michael Ignatieff, *Blood and Belonging* (New York: Farrar, Straus, Giroux, 1995).

14. Sigmund Freud, *Civilization and Its Discontents*, trans. James Strachey (New York: Norton, 1962); Freud, *Totem and Taboo*, trans. James Strachey (New York: Norton, 1952).

15. Sigmund Freud, *Group Psychology and the Analysis of the Ego*, trans. James Strachey (New York: Norton, 1950).

16. The phrase "primary mutual hostility" appears in Freud, *Civilization and Its Discontents*, 69, and natural "sexual rivalry" in *Totem and Taboo*, 144.

17. Freud, *Group Psychology*, 68.

18. Ibid., 13.

19. Ibid., 12.

20. Ibid., 24.

21. Continued revelations about the deliberate development and approval of the techniques of torture and abuse practiced at Abu-Ghraib, and their continuity with those practiced both at

Guantánamo and in United States detention sites for "suspected terrorists," gives little credence to initial defenses of the Abu-Ghraib scenes as "animal house" behavior. For news on these links, see, e.g.: Josh White, "Abu Ghraib Tactics Were First Used at Guantánamo," *Washington Post*, July 14, 2005, A01; Oliver Burkerman, "Bush Team 'Knew of Abuse' at Guantánamo," *The Guardian*, September 13, 2004, http://www.guardian.co.uk/guantanamo/story/0,13743,1303105,00.html; Richard Serrano and John Daniszewski, "Dozens Have Alleged Koran's Mishandling," *LA Times*, May 22, 2005, A1.

22. Ibid., 41.

23. The latter distress is one Freud makes quite concrete in his brief discussion of panic, a feeling he describes as "feeling alone in the face of danger," which is experienced psychically whenever the emotional ties that sustain us are felt to disintegrate (Freud, *Group Psychology*, 36).

24. Ibid., 50.

25. Ibid.

26. The idealization of the beloved gratifies the demands of the ego-ideal upon the ego, demands that are always punishing and that this roundabout order of love seeks partially to relieve from such punishment and failure through this idealization. The headiness of being in love, Freud suggests, issues in part from such relief.

27. Ibid., 56.

28. Ibid.

29. Ibid., 57.

30. Rousseau's version of the social contract follows this model precisely, however. His effort to "transform each individual, who by himself is entirely complete and solitary, into a part of a much greater whole, from which the same individual will then receive, in a sense, his life and his being" parallels Freud's understanding of a group as individuals in love with something common that is also external to the group. See Rousseau, *The Social Contract*, trans. Maurice Cranston (New York: Penguin, 1968), 84. Note, too, that *commune moi* ("common me, or common ego") is Rousseau's norm for the formation (exceeding a mere tie that binds) produced by and at the heart of the social contract (*Social Contract*, 61).

31. Presumably this explains why the sexual organization of modern cults often involves injunctions to abstinence, injunctions to promiscuity, and/or the unlimited sexual access of the leader to all women in the group.

32. "Civilization . . . obtains mastery over the individual's dangerous desire for aggression by weakening and disarming it and by setting up an agency within him to watch over it, like a garrison in a conquered city" (Freud, *Civilization and Its Discontents*, 84). Cities represent the literal conquest of man, the containment of his instincts, but Freud is also analogizing the civilized psyche *to* a conquered city. Civilization thus entails a double subjection, first by the aim-inhibition required by civilization, and then by the introjection of civilization's demands into the psyche. Both of these are challenged by the psychic undoing that produces the group.

33. Freud, *Group Psychology*, 13–15.

34. This converges with Hegel's analysis of the philosophical movement from family to ethical life: "Love means in general the consciousness of my unity with another, so that I am not isolated on my own, but gain my self-consciousness only through the renunciation of my independent existence and through knowing myself as the unity of myself with another and of the other with me. But love is a feeling, that is, ethical life in its natural form. In the state, it is no longer present. There, one is conscious of unity as law; there, the content must be rational, and I must know it. The first moment in love is that I do not wish to be an independent person in my own right and that, if I were, I would feel deficient and incomplete" (*Philosophy of Right*, trans. H. B. Nisbet, ed.

Allen W. Wood [Cambridge: Cambridge University Press, 1991], Addition to Paragraph 158, 199). "The family disintegrates, in a natural manner and essentially through the principle of personality, into a *plurality* of families whose relation to one another is in general that of self-sufficient concrete persons and consequently of an external kind" (ibid., §181, 219).

35. Freud, *Group Psychology*, 15.

36. Freud, *Totem and Taboo*, 161.

37. See "President Sworn-in to Second Term," Inaugural Address, George W. Bush http://www.whitehouse.gov/news/releases/2005/01.

38. Bob Woodward, *Plan of Attack*, end of chap. 3. See also State of the Union Address, February 2, 2005: "In the long term, the peace we seek will only be achieved by eliminating the conditions that feed radicalism and ideologies of murder. If whole regimes of the world remain in despair and grow in hatred, they will be the recruiting grounds for terror, and that terror will stalk America and other free nations for decades. The only force powerful enough to stop the rise of tyranny and terror, and replace hatred with hope, is the force of human freedom. Our enemies know this, and that is why the terrorist Zarqawi recently declared war on what he called the 'evil principle' of democracy. And we've declared our own intention: America will stand with the allies of freedom to support democratic movements in the Middle East and beyond, with the ultimate goal of ending tyranny in our world" (http://www.whitehouse.gov/news/releases/2005/02).

39. For the Bush quotation, see coverage of Bush's interviews with the Al-Arabiya and Al-Hurra television networks, May 5, 2004 (CNN.com 6 May 2004 http://www.cnn.com/2004/ALL POLITICS/05/05/bush.abuse/). Regarding Blair's statement, I heard this on BBC between May 3 and 5, 2004, but have not been able to find a corresponding print version.

40. Talal Asad makes a similar argument in *Genealogies of Religion: Discipline and Reasons of Power in Christianity and Islam* (Baltimore: The Johns Hopkins University Press, 1993). See 268, 306.

41. Convergent studies that have linked liberalism's constitutive outside with its internal operations (as opposed to treating its involvement with colonial or imperial discourses as "alien intrusions," to use Barry Hindess's phrase) include: Uday Mehta, *Liberalism and Empire: A Study in Nineteenth-Century Thought* (Chicago: University of Chicago Press, 1999); Dipesh Chakrabarty, *Provincializing Europe: Postcolonial Thought and Historical Difference* (Princeton: Princeton University Press, 2000); Paul Gilroy, *The Black Atlantic: Modernity and Double Consciousness* (London: Verso, 1993); and Barry Hindess and Christine Helliwell, "The 'Empire of Uniformity' and the Government of Subject Peoples," *Cultural Values* 6, no. 1 (2002): 137–50.

42. Raymond Williams, *Keywords: A Vocabulary of Culture and Society*, rev. ed. (Oxford: Oxford University Press, 1983), 87.

43. Ibid., 88.

44. A decisive change, Williams argues, comes with Herder in the late eighteenth century, who insisted on the pluralization of culture across nations and periods, as well as among social and economic groups within any given nation (ibid., 89).

45. Ibid., 90.

46. Seyla Benhabib, *The Claims of Culture: Equality and Diversity in the Global Era* (Princeton: Princeton University Press, 2002), 106. Benhabib elaborates: "These norms expand on the principles of universal respect and egalitarian reciprocity, which are crucial to a discourse ethic. . . . voluntary self-ascription and freedom of exit and association expand on the concept of persons as self-interpreting and self-defining beings whose actions and deeds are constituted through culturally informed narratives" (132).

47. Ibid., 124–25.

48. If contemporary liberal political rationality articulates such a subject, it also stumbles over and even rejects several of the implications of this articulation. First, the idea that only nonliberal peoples are organized by a "common way of life" features so blatant a conceit about the civilizational maturity of Europe and the primitivism of others that even liberals are embarrassed by it and will quickly correct themselves when these implications of their positioning of culture as always elsewhere from liberalism are reflected back to them. Second, if liberals fully endorse the privatization of culture defined as a "way of life," this concedes a stark thinness to public life in liberal societies. Indeed, it concedes that liberal public life is no way of life at all but only a set of juridical principles combined with a set of market principles, which work independently of any actor. This condemns public life to a culturally impoverished, morally relativistic state, oriented by nothing more than legislators, lawyers, manipulated public opinion, and market forces. It confesses as well the absence of a public bond among citizens, other than that rooted in fealty to the nation-state, on the one hand, and that driven by diverse *privatized* cultural-religious attachments or economic interests, on the other. That is, it positions public life as buffeted between private desires and *raison d'état* and without any organized aim, ethos, or purpose of its own. Third, if culture is only ever something that nonliberal peoples have as a group, if it only belongs to "less mature" peoples, this cedes something of value—culture in the intellectual and artistic sense, and in the civilizational sense—to these peoples. Through a linguistic inadvertency that provides a window on the unconscious of liberalism, it admits what we already fear: rights and the market, and nothing more elevated or substantive, determines what we collectively share as well as what we value.

In short, if, in contemporary liberal democratic parlance, "culture" signifies moral and intellectual advancement and knowledge, it also signifies the absence of moral and intellectual autonomy, being ruled by something other than reason. This means that liberalism simultaneously claims and disclaims culture; culture is part of the greatness of the West and also that which liberal individuals have thrown off in their movement toward maturity and freedom, producing "cosmopolitanism" in its stead. These two crucial and opposed implications of having culture—moral elevation and the absence of moral autonomy—are not just a happenstance collision of meanings of the word but a symptomatic one. They represent a deep and fundamental bind of liberalism in modernity, a bind at the very heart of a project of freedom rooted in reason and individualism.

49. Benhabib, *The Claims of Culture*, 105 and 111.

50. Avishai Margalit and Moshe Halbertal, "Liberalism and the Right to Culture," *Social Research* 61, no. 3 (Fall 1994): 491–510.. Benhabib tries to have it both ways: culture is both something to which one has a right *and* constitutive, in the same way that persons are "self-interpreting and self-defining," while their "actions and deeds are constituted through culturally informed narratives" (*The Claims of Culture*, 132).

51. Even Will Kymlicka, who works assiduously to establish "cultures or nations [as] basic units of liberal political theory" because "cultural membership provides us with an intelligible context of choice, and a secure sense of identity and belonging," formulates the project of "liberalizing culture" as a legitimate one even for those outside the culture at issue. Liberals, he writes, should "seek to liberalize [nonliberal nations]" and "should promote the liberalization of [illiberal] cultures" (Kymlicka, *Multicultural Citizenship* [Oxford: Oxford University Press, 1996], 93, 94–95, 105). The justification for this lies in the distinction between liberal legalism and culture that we have been considering. Drawing upon Yael Tamir's *Liberal Nationalism* (Princeton: Princeton University Press, 1993), Kymlicka depicts liberal nations as having "societal cultures," which provide their "members with meaningful ways of life across the full range of human activities, including social, educational, religious, recreational, and economic life, encompassing both public and private spheres" (76). Striking in their absence from this list of what "societal culture" comprises, however,

are politics and law, the very domains liberalism treats as primary domains of power. Liberalized cultures (including the "societal cultures" of liberal society) are considered to generate and circulate meaning but not power, because liberalization is by definition the devolution of power to the morally autonomous subject theorized by Kant and Freud, and the secular state theorized by social contract theorists. Thus, while Kymlicka, more than many other liberals, acknowledges that liberal societies "are cultural too," he legitimates the imposition of liberal political values on nonliberals, i.e., he legitimates liberal imperialism.

52. George W. Bush, "State of the Union Address," U.S. Department of State, January 29, 2002, http://www.state.gov.g/wi/.

53. The language of non-negotiable demands, borrowed from the lexicon of labor and peace talks, is itself curious. Not only does it suggest that the United States is engaged in negotiation rather than war, it also positions the United States as righteous supplicant rather than superpower.

54. Asad, *Genealogies of Religion*, 257.

55. There is plenty of intellectual help here. Philosophers as diverse as Jean-Luc Nancy, Emmanuel Levinas, Michel Foucault, Luce Irigaray, and Jacques Derrida have offered critiques that figure being in terms other than autonomy versus organicism; and post-Nietzscheans such as Michel Foucault, Gilles Deleuze, Giorgio Agamben, and Judith Butler undo the grip of the autonomy-organicism binary by pressing a formulation of the subject in terms of "becoming" rather than "being." Edward Said, Talal Asad, David Scott, Lila Abu-Lughod, Saba Mahmood, William E. Connolly, Ashis Nandy, Partha Chatterjee, Rajiv Bhargava, and Dipesh Chakrabarty, among others, have contributed to deconstructing the secularism/fundamentalism opposition. And postcolonial and cultural studies scholars too numerous to name have placed pavestones for conceptualizing the extraordinary miscegenations among cultural and political forms wrought by late modernity.

56. Justification is not to be confused with motivation. The current imperial policies of the United States are wrought from power-political motivations that have little to do with the human rights and antifundamentalist discourses I have been discussing here.

Chantal Mouffe, Religion, Liberal Democracy, and Citizenship

1. Ludwig Wittgenstein, *Philosophical Investigations* (Oxford: Basil Blackwell, 1958), I, 241, p. 88.

2. Ibid., I, 242, p. 88.

3. This point is developed in my book *The Return of the Political* (London: Verso, 1993).

4. I have theorized this distinction in *The Democratic Paradox* (London: Verso, 2000).

Lars Tønder, Toleration Without Tolerance: Enlightenment and the Image of Reason

NOTE: The author would like to thank Jane Bennett, William E. Connolly, Thomas Donahue, Paulina Ochoa, Sacramento Roselló Martínez, Matthew Scherer, Helen Tartar, Lasse Thomassen, Hent de Vries, and two anonymous readers for their comments and suggestions.

1. Rainer Forst, "Toleration, Justice and Reason," in *The Culture of Toleration in Diverse Societies: Reasonable Tolerance*, ed. Catriona McKinnon and Dario Castiglione (Manchester: Manchester University Press, 2003), 78, emphasis in original. See also: Jürgen Habermas, "Intolerance and Discrimination," *International Journal of Constitutional Law* 1, no. 1 (2003): 2–12; John Rawls,

Political Liberalism (New York: Columbia University Press, 1993); Joseph Raz, "Autonomy, Toleration and the Harm Principle," in *Justifying Toleration*, ed. Susan Mendus (Cambridge: Cambridge University Press, 1988): and T. M. Scanlon, "The Difficulty of Tolerance," in *Toleration: An Elusive Virtue*, ed. David Heyd (Princeton: Princeton University Press, 1996).

2. Georg Wilhelm Friedrich Hegel, *Phenomenology of Spirit*, trans. A. V. Miller (Oxford: Oxford University Press, 1977), 159, §262. Other sources of inspiration include: William E. Connolly, *The Ethos of Pluralization* (Minneapolis: University of Minnesota Press, 1995), 16–19; Gilles Deleuze, *Difference and Repetition*, trans. Paul Patton (New York: Columbia University Press, 1994), 129–68; Hubert L. Dreyfus, *Being-in-the-World: A Commentary on Heidegger's 'Being and Time,' division I* (Cambridge: MIT Press, 1991), 108–27; and Charles Taylor, *Modern Social Imaginaries* (Durham, N.C.: Duke University Press, 2004), 23–30.

3. Apart from the *Oxford English Dictionary*, I base this distinction between *tolerance* and *toleration* on: Preston King, *The Value of Tolerance* (London: Frank Cass, 2001); Andrew R. Murphy, "Tolerance, Toleration, and the Liberal Tradition," *Polity* 29, no. 4 (1997): 593–623; and G. Schlüter and R. Grötker, "Toleranz," in *Historisches Wörterbuch der Philosophie*, ed. Joachim Ritter and Karlfried Gründer (Darmstadt: Wissenschaftliche Buchgesellschaft, 1998).

4. Ole Peter Grell and Roy Porter, "Toleration in Enlightenment Europe," in their edited volume *Toleration in Enlightenment Europe* (Cambridge: Cambridge University Press, 2000), 19. A partial list of historians and theorists who have explored the connection between the Enlightenment and the questions of tolerance and toleration includes: Martin Fitzpatrick, "Toleration and the Enlightenment Movement," in *Toleration in Enlightenment Europe*, ed. Grell and Porter; John Gray, *Enlightenment's Wake: Politics and Culture at the Close of the Modern Age* (London: Routledge, 1995), 18–30; James Schmidt, "Introduction: What Is Enlightenment? a Question, Its Context, and Some Consequences," in his edited volume *What Is Enlightenment? Eighteenth-Century Answers and Twentieth-Century Questions* (Berkeley: University of California Press, 1996), 1–45; and Richard Tuck, "Scepticism and Toleration in the Seventeenth Century," in *Justifying Toleration*, ed. Mendus.

5. See: Ian Hunter, *Rival Enlightenments: Civil and Metaphysical Philosophy in Early Modern Germany* (Cambridge: Cambridge University Press, 2001); Jonathan Israel, *Radical Enlightenment: Philosophy and the Making of Modernity 1650–1750* (Oxford: Oxford University Press, 2001); J. G. A. Pocock, "Enlightenment and the Revolution: The Case of North America," in *Seventh International Congress on the Enlightenment: Introductory Papers* (Oxford: Oxford University Press, 1987); and Quentin Skinner, *Vision of Politics*, vol. 1: *Regarding Method* (Cambridge: Cambridge University Press, 2002).

6. Hunter, *Rival Enlightenments*, 21–22.

7. James Tully, *An Approach to Political Philosophy: Locke in Contexts* (Cambridge: Cambridge University Press, 1993), 48. Other theorists and historians who attribute the same importance to Locke as Tully (but may disagree why this is so) include: John Dunn, "The Claim to Freedom of Conscience: Freedom of Speech, Freedom of Thought, Freedom of Worship?" in *From Persecution to Toleration: The Glorious Revolution and Religion in England*, ed. Ole Peter Grell et al. (Oxford: Oxford University Press, 1991); John Marshall, *John Locke: Resistance, Religion, and Responsibility* (Cambridge: Cambridge University Press, 1994), 33–72; Ian Shapiro, "John Locke's Democratic Theory," in John Locke, *Two Treatises of Government* and *A Letter Concerning Toleration* (New Haven: Yale University Press, 2003), 318–22; and Alex Tuckness, *Locke and the Legislative Point of View: Toleration, Contested Principles, and the Law* (Princeton: Princeton University Press, 2002), 17–25.

8. Henry Kamen, *The Rise of Toleration* (Toronto: McGraw-Hill, 1967), 231; and Joseph Lecler, *Toleration and the Reformation*, trans. T. L. Westow (New York: Association Press, 1960), 2:473.

9. Maurice Cranston, "John Locke and the Case for Toleration," reprinted in *John Locke: A Letter Concerning Toleration in Focus*, ed. Susan Mendus and John Horton (London: Routledge, 1991), 82–83. The majority of the contributors to this collection of essays follow Cranston in emphasizing the importance of Locke's theory of private property for the argument against the rationality of religious persecution.

10. John Locke, "A Letter Concerning Toleration," in *Two Treatises of Government* and *A Letter Concerning Toleration*, 218.

11. Ibid., 217. See also: Kim Ian Parker, *The Biblical Politics of John Locke* (Waterloo, Ontario: Wilfrid Laurier University Press, 2004), 38–68; and Jeremy Waldron, *God, Locke, and Equality: Christian Foundations of John Locke's Political Thought* (Cambridge: Cambridge University Press, 2002), 208–14.

12. Jeremy Waldron, "Locke: Toleration and the Rationality of Persecution," in *Justifying Toleration*, ed. Mendus, 63. See also: John Dunn, "What Is Living and What Is Dead in the Political Theory of John Locke," in his *Interpreting Political Responsibility: Essays 1981–1989* (Cambridge: Polity, 1990), 19; and Alex Tuckness, "Rethinking the Intolerant Locke," *American Journal of Political Science* 46, no. 2 (April 2002): 288–98.

13. John Locke, *Two Tracts on Government* (Cambridge: Cambridge University Press, 1967). See also Kirstie M. McClure, "Difference, Diversity, and the Limits of Toleration," *Political Theory* 18, no. 3 (August 1990): 361–91, esp. 375–81.

14. Locke, *A Letter Concerning Toleration*, 229.

15. John Locke, *An Essay Concerning Human Understanding* (Oxford: Oxford University Press, 1975), bk. 2I, chap. 21, §50 (p. 266); emphasis in original.

16. Charles Taylor, *Sources of the Self: The Making of Modern Identity* (Cambridge: Harvard University Press, 1989), 161.

17. François-Marie Arouet de Voltaire, *Dictionnaire philosophique*, reprinted in *Les Œuvres Complètes de Voltaire* (Oxford: Voltaire Foundation, 1994), 36:552, my trans.

18. The following is based upon Voltaire, *Traité sur la tolérance*, reprinted in *Les Œuvres Completes de Voltaire* (Oxford: Voltaire Foundation, 2000), 56C:131–33. Voltaire's account of the events is not always historically accurate, but it indicates how he theorizes the circumstances under which the issues of tolerance and toleration arise.

19. Ibid., 155, my trans.

20. Ernest Cassirer, *The Philosophy of the Enlightenment*, trans. Fritz C. A. Koelln and James P. Pettegrove (Princeton: Princeton University Press, 1951), 168.

21. Preston King, *Toleration*, new ed. (London: Frank Cass, 1998), 99–100.

22. Rainer Forst, *Toleranz im Konflikt: Geschichte, Gehalt und Gegenwart eines umstrittenen Begriffs* (Frankfurt am Main: Suhrkamp, 2003), 389; emphasis in original, my trans.

23. Onora O'Neill, *Constructions of Reason: Explorations of Kant's Practical Philosophy* (Cambridge: Cambridge University Press, 1989), 28. See also: Jürgen Habermas, "The Unity of Reason in the Diversity of Its Voices," trans. William Mark Hohengarten, reprinted in *What Is Enlightenment?* ed. Schmidt, 399–425; Christine Korsgaard, *Creating the Kingdom of Ends* (Cambridge: Cambridge University Press, 1996), 188–221; and Hans Saner, *Kant's Political Thought: Its Origins and Development*, trans. H. B. Ashton (Chicago: University of Chicago Press, 1983), 302–4.

24. Immanuel Kant, *Critique of Pure Reason*, trans. Norman Kemp Smith (Houndmills, Basingstoke: Macmillan, 1929), A708 / B736

25. Michel Foucault, "Qu'est-ce que la critique? [Critique et *Aufklärung*]," *Bulletin de la Société française de Philosophie* 84, no 2 (April-June 1990): 36.

26. Immanuel Kant, "An Answer to the Question: 'What is Enlightenment?'" trans. H. B. Nisbet, in *Kant: Political Writings*, 2d ed. (Cambridge: Cambridge University Press, 1970), 54.

27. Kant, *Critique of Pure Reason*, A738 / B766.

28. Apart from Onora O'Neill, scholars who have done the most to advance the Kantian interpretation of toleration include: Barbara Herman, "Pluralism and the Community of Moral Judgment," in *Toleration*, ed. Heyd; and Philip L. Quinn, "Religious Diversity and Religious Toleration," *International Journal for Philosophy of Religion* 50 (2001): 57–80. See also the references in notes 2 and 24, above.

29. Kant, "An Answer to the Question," 58. I base my translation of *Toleranz* as "tolerance" (and not "toleration" or "tolerant") on *Grimm Deutsches Wörterbuch* (Leipzig: S. Hirzel, 1935), which suggests that the root of *Toleranz* is Latin *tolerantia* and French *tolérance*.

30. See Howard Caygill, *A Kant Dictionary* (Oxford: Basil Blackwell, 1995), 346–50, for an overview of the different divisions within Kant's discussion of reason.

31. Immanuel Kant, *Critique of Practical Reason*, 3d ed., trans. Lewis White Beck (Upper Saddle River, N.J.: Prentice-Hall, 1993), 48, A81.

32. Ibid., 138–40, A238–39.

33. See, e.g., Kant, *Critique of Pure Reason*, A11 / B24 and A50 / B74.

34. I pursue this exploration in "Subsistent Tolerance: Merleau-Ponty and the Embodiment of Democratic Pluralism," *Culture and Politics* 1, no. 1 (forthcoming).

35. Maurice Merleau-Ponty, *Phenomenology of Perception*, trans. Colin Smith (London: Routledge, 1962), 56–57.

Matthew Scherer, Saint John: The Miracle of Secular Reason

1. Amy Gutmann, "A Tribute to John Rawls 1921–2002," posted on the Harvard University Center for Ethics and the Professions Web site, <http://www.ethics.harvard.edu/memoriam_rawls.php>.

2. Peter Laslett had put this claim quite directly, writing: "For the moment, anyway, political philosophy is dead" (*Politics, Philosophy and History* [Oxford: Basil Blackwell, 1956], vii).

3. Sheldon Wolin, "The Liberal/Democratic Divide," *Political Theory* 24, no. 1 (February 1996): 97–119.

4. For a discussion of the figure of the miracle, spanning its ancient origins and contemporary invocations, see Hent de Vries, *Of Miracles and Special Effects*, forthcoming.

5. "Miracles," in Shailer Matthews and Gerald Birney Smith, eds., *A Dictionary of Religion and Ethics* (New York: Macmillan, 1921), 285–86.

6. For a comparison of the biblical instances of these terms, see "Miracles," in James Hastings, ed., *Encyclopedia of Religion and Ethics* (New York: Charles Scribner's Sons, 1970), 676–90. For arguments concerning miracles, see: Baruch Spinoza, *Theological-Political Treatise* (Indianapolis: Hackett, 2001), chap. 6; David Hume, *An Enquiry Concerning Human Understanding* (Oxford: Oxford University Press, 2006), chap. 10; Thomas Hobbes, *Leviathan* (Indianapolis: Hackett, 1994), chap. 37; and John Locke, "A Discourse of Miracles," in *Reasonableness of Christianity and a Discourse of Miracles* (Stanford: Stanford University Press, 1958), 79–87.

7. Thomas Pogge, "Memorial for John Rawls: The Magic of the Green Book," *Kantian Review* 8 (2004): 153–55, and his "A Brief Sketch of Rawls's Life," in Henry S. Richardson and Paul J. Weithman, eds., *The Philosophy of Rawls*, 5 vols. (New York: Garland, 1999), vol. 1.

8. According to Anthony Simon Laden, "three thousand articles that discuss the work of John Rawls have been published in journals of philosophy, law, economics, political science, and related

fields" ("The House That Jack Built: Thirty Years of Reading Rawls," *Ethics* 113, [January 2003]: 367). Consider, as well, Amy Gutmann's observation that "Many students read Rawls in their philosophically formative years and grew up, as it were, with strong Rawlsian sympathies" ("The Central Role of Rawls's Theory," *Dissent* [Summer 1989], 338).

9. Alan Ryan, "How Liberalism, Politics Come to Terms," in *The Washington Times*, May 16, 1993.

10. For the former development, see Alexander Nehamas, "Recent Trends in American Philosophy," *Daedalus* 126, no. 1 (1997): 209–24, and for the latter, Amy Gutmann, "The Central Role of Rawls's Theory," 338–42.

11. Stuart Hampshire, "A New Philosophy of the Just Society," *New York Review of Books* 18, no. 3 (February 24, 1972).

12. Wolin, "The Liberal/Democratic Divide," 97.

13. Gutmann, "The Central Role of Rawls's Theory."

14. Stanley Cavell, *Conditions Handsome and Unhandsome* (Chicago: University of Chicago Press, 1990), 3.

15. H. L. A. Hart, "Rawls on Liberty and Its Priority," in *Reading Rawls*, ed. Norman Daniels (Stanford: Stanford University Press, 1989), 230–52.

16. Michael Sandel, "Political Liberalism," *Harvard Law Review* 107, no. 7 (May 1994): 1765.

17. Daniels, ed., *Reading Rawls*, xi.

18. Laden identifies the persistence of two divergent "blueprints" guiding most of the critical literature on Rawls: "The standard blueprint of the structure of Rawls's work includes four related elements: (1) Rawls is engaged in a grand philosophical project; (2) in particular, he is developing a theory in the traditional sense of that word; (3) that theory is Hobbesian in that it starts from an account of human rationality; and (4) it aims to show the rationality of justice via its centerpiece, the argument from the original position in favor of the choice of the two principles of justice," whereas, according to "an alternative blueprint . . . (1) Rawls's projects are focused and narrower than is generally thought; (2) he is engaged in philosophy as defense rather then philosophical theorizing; (3) his arguments are meant to serve as public justifications rather than as deductions from premises about human nature or rationality; and (4) the central idea and high point of his achievement is the idea of public reason and its accompanying picture of political deliberation" ("The House That Jack Built," 371, 379).

19. Rawls writes, "My aim is to present a conception of justice which generalizes and carries to a higher level of abstraction the familiar theory of the social contract as found, say, in Locke, Rousseau, and Kant." Viewing Hobbes as a difficult case, Rawls declines to associate himself with that part of the tradition, noting only that, "for all of its greatness, Hobbes's *Leviathan* raises special problems" (Rawls, *A Theory of Justice* [Cambridge: Harvard University Press, 1971], 11, 11n.4).

20. For a paradigmatic statement of this standard interpretation of the Enlightenment, see Immanuel Kant, "An Answer to the Question: 'What Is Enlightenment?,'" *Kant: Political Writings* (Cambridge: Cambridge University Press, 1991); for a concise statement of this theme, which runs throughout Nietzsche's works, see, e.g., *The Gay Science*, trans. Walter Kaufmann (New York: Random House, 1974), esp. 279–80 (section 343); for a concise statement of Schmitt's argument, see his *Political Theology* (Cambridge: MIT Press, 1985), 36.

21. Talal Asad's work is exemplary here. See esp. "What Might an Anthropology of Secularism Look Like?" in his *Formations of the Secular: Christianity, Islam, Modernity* (Stanford: Stanford University Press, 2003), 21–66.

22. Conclusions such as this, taken from an article by Jean Hampton, are all too common in the literature: "I hope to have shown that Rawls is incorrect here, that he has been more fully Kantian than he realizes" (*The Philosophy of Rawls*, ed. Richardson and Weithman, 1:132).

23. This has recently been treated by Paul Ricoeur, "The Political Paradox," in *Legitimacy and the State*, ed. William E. Connolly (New York: New York University Press, 1984), and by Connolly himself in both *Political Theory and Modernity* (Ithaca, N.Y.: Cornell University Press, 1993) and *The Ethos of Pluralization* (Minneapolis: University of Minnesota Press, 1995).

24. Jean-Jacques Rousseau, *On The Social Contract*, trans. Judith R. Masters (New York: St. Martin's, 1978), 46 (bk. 1, chap. 1).

25. Ibid.

26. Ibid., 67 (bk. 2, chap. 6).

27. Ibid., 68 (bk. 2, chap. 7).

28. Immanuel Kant, *The Critique of Practical Reason*, trans. Lewis White Beck (Upper Saddle River, N.J: Prentice Hall, 1993), 169 (conclusion; AK 161).

29. Rousseau, *On the Social Contract*, 70 (bk. 2, chap. 7).

30. Ibid., 69 (bk. 2, chap. 7).

31. Ibid.

32. Ibid.

33. Ibid., 69 (bk. 2, chap. 7).

34. Ibid., 130 (bk. 4, chap. 8).

35. Paul Ricoeur, "On John Rawls' *A Theory of Justice*: Is a Pure Procedural Theory of Justice Possible?" *International Social Science Journal* 42 (1990): 555.

36. Hampshire, "A New Philosophy of the Just Society."

37. Aristotle, "Rhetoric," *The Complete Works of Aristotle*, ed. Jonathan Barnes, 2 vols. (Princeton: Princeton University Press, 1984), 2:2155 (1356a).

38. Rawls, *A Theory of Justice*, viii.

39. John Rawls, "The Sense of Justice," *Philosophical Review* 72, no. 3 (July 1963): 305; later incorporated, with slight emendations, into sections 70–74 of *A Theory of Justice*, 462–90. Page numbers refer to the original journal article.

40. Ibid., 304–5.

41. Ibid., 305, emphasis added.

42. Rawls, *A Theory of Justice*, 485.

43. Rawls, "The Sense of Justice," 305; *A Theory of Justice*, 443.

44. John Rawls, *Political Liberalism* (New York: Columbia University Press, 1993), xv.

45. Ibid., 3.

46. Rawls, *A Theory of Justice*, 3.

47. Williams observes the translation of argumentative force from one conversation to the next with great precision: Considering a point made in Rawls's argument from the original position, he notes, "this comes perilously close to a requirement on the original choice, that it be of a system which *will be just*—which of course would be to moralise the original itself, and to put in at the beginning what we are supposed to get out at the end." Considering the unacknowledged force of a Kantian outlook on Rawls's argument for the strong preference for liberty, he notes, "the strong preference for liberty is part of the outlook in which men are in general seen as essentially autonomous beings, and Rawls is disposed to explicate it in terms of a Kantian view of human relations. This view is not supposed to be that of his contracting parties, but the choice they are pictured as making seems—to put it mildly—to make most sense when they are understood as already possessing this view of themselves"; concerning the unacknowledged influence of altruistic, hence moralized, assumptions, he notes, "the contracting parties were indeed introduced as fathers of families, with a natural concern for one generation ahead, but the way in which Rawls speaks of their commitment to not taking risks implies a heavier, and surely already moralised, onus of responsibil-

ity towards posterity"; and, in general, he notes that Rawls's conclusions "must rest both on a rather saintly view of things on the part of the contracting parties, and a quite unreasonable belief that they would retain such a saintly view if they were top dogs in . . . society"; but he concludes only that Rawls has made a rather bad argument. (Bernard Williams, "Rawls and Pascal's Wager," in his *Moral Luck* [Cambridge: Cambridge University Press, 1981], 95, 96, 97, 99.)

48. As Rawls puts it, in order to avoid misinterpretation, "it is important to distinguish three points of view: that of the parties in the original position, that of citizens in a well-ordered society, and finally, that of ourselves—of you and me who are elaborating justice as fairness and examining it as a political conception of justice" (*Political Liberalism*, 28).

49. Ibid., 45.

50. "Saints," in Adrian Hastings et al., eds., *The Oxford Companion to Christian Thought* (Oxford: Oxford University Press, 2000), 639.

51. The *Oxford Companion to Christian Thought* points out that "Saints from different periods . . . stand in sharp contrast to each other," taking as an example that "Seventeenth-century philanthropic saints such as Vincent de Paul represent a very different model of holiness from that of the founding fathers of great 12th-century monastic orders, such as Bernard of Clairvaux or Norbert of Xanten" (ibid.).

52. William James, "The Present Dilemma in Philosophy," *The Writings of William James: A Comprehensive Edition*, ed. John J. McDermott (Chicago: University of Chicago Press, 1977), 374.

53. Ibid., 364.

54. This point has been suggested by Sheldon Wolin, who notes that "Rawls is truly the virtuous philosopher whose great personal achievement is to have rejected celebrity status" ("The Liberal/Democratic Divide," 97).

55. Thomas Pogge, "A Brief Sketch of Rawls's Life," 2–3; "Memorial for John Rawls," 153.

56. Pogge, "A Brief Sketch of Rawls's Life," 4–6.

57. Bonnie Honig, *Political Theory and the Displacement of Politics* (Ithaca: Cornell University Press, 1993), 126–27.

58. See Stanley Cavell, *Conditions Handsome and Unhandsome* and *Cities of Words* (Cambridge: Harvard University Press, 2004), 82–101, 119–44, 164–89 (chaps. 5, 7, and 9).

Bhrigupati Singh, Reinhabiting Civil Disobedience

1. Slavoj Žižek, "The Ongoing 'Soft Revolution,'" *Critical Inquiry* 30, no.2 (Winter 2004): 292–323.

2. I am referring in particular to Cavell's *This New Yet Unapproachable America: Lectures after Emerson after Wittgenstein* (Albuquerque: Living Batch Press, 1989), his *The Senses of Walden* (1972; expanded edition, San Francisco: North Point Press, 1981), where this question was first posed ("Why has America never expressed itself philosophically? Or has it?"), and his *Emerson's Transcendental Etudes*, ed. David Justin Hodge (Stanford: Stanford University Press, 2003), which collects his writings on Emerson from over two decades. Cavell's books on Hollywood cinema are also linked to his conception of America: *Pursuits of Happiness: The Hollywood Comedy of Remarriage* (Cambridge: Harvard University Press, 1981) and *Contesting Tears: The Hollywood Melodrama of the Unknown Woman* (Chicago: University of Chicago Press, 1996).

3. Martin Heidegger, "Building, Dwelling, Thinking," in *Poetry, Language, Thought*, trans. Albert Hofstadter (New York: Harper & Row, 1971), 143–61.

4. See Gilles Deleuze, *Difference and Repetition*, trans. Paul Patton, (New York: Columbia University Press, 1994), 129.

5. While Deleuze is much more explicit in his attack on Hegel and dialectics, as in *Nietzsche and Philosophy*, trans. Hugh Tomlinson (New York: Columbia University Press, 1983), Cavell's mode of argumentation seeks to maintain tensions, rather than considering its end to be resolution in a "higher synthesis" or to sustain difference without turning it into contradiction or negation. See, esp., Cavell's discussion of morality in *The Claim of Reason: Wittgenstein, Skepticism, Morality, and Tragedy* (Oxford: Oxford University Press, 1979), 247–329.

6. For Deleuze on the "a-subjective" or "pre-individual," see Gilles Deleuze, *The Logic of Sense*, ed. Constantin V. Boundas, trans. Mark Lester and Charles Stivale (New York: Columbia University Press, 1990). On a related conception of philosophy, see also Gilles Deleuze / Felix Guattari, *What Is Philosophy?*, trans. Hugh Tomlinson and Graham Burchell, III (New York: Columbia University Press, 1996). For Cavell on the "achievement of the un-polemical," see his essays on Emerson, in particular "Emerson's Constitutional Amending: Reading 'Fate,'" in *Emerson's Transcendental Etudes*, 192–214.

7. *Expression* is a central problem for Deleuze, starting with his first published work, *Expressionism in Philosophy: Spinoza*, trans. Martin Joughin (New York: Zone Books, 1990), esp. in the injunction not to ask if *x* represents *y*, but how it "works" or what manner of forces it brings together. See also Deleuze, *Essays Critical and Clinical*, trans. Daniel W. Smith and Michael A. Greco (Minneapolis: University of Minnesota Press, 1997). For Cavell, the problem of expression takes the form of his repeated evocations of language as a "bodying forth" or of a "pitch" of philosophy. In this regard, see Cavell's *Philosophical Passages: Wittgenstein, Emerson, Austin, Derrida* (Oxford: Basil Blackwell, 1995) and *A Pitch of Philosophy: Autobiographical Exercises* (Cambridge: Harvard University Press, 1994).

8. "Difference internal to being" is perhaps the central proposition of Deleuze's *Difference and Repetition*, which may be read as a response to Heidegger's *Being and Time*. On this conceptual trajectory, see the sense of the "self" in Cavell's *The Claim of Reason* or *A Pitch of Philosophy*, or, in a different way, his proposition that "translation internal to a culture is as, if not more, difficult than that between cultures," in "Emerson's Constitutional Amending: Reading 'Fate,'" *Emerson's Transcendental Etudes*, 210.

9. On the internal relation of sense and non-sense, see Deleuze, *The Logic of Sense*, and Cavell's essay "Wittgenstein and Benjamin: Signals and Affinities," *Critical Inquiry* 25, no. 2. (Winter 1999): 235–46.

10. Immanence is one of the key themes throughout Deleuze's oeuvre, from his conception of Spinoza as the preeminent philosopher of immanence to his final published essay, "Immanence: A Life," in *Pure Immanence: Essays on A Life*, trans. Anne Boyman (New York: Zone Books, 2001). In Cavell, immanence expresses itself in his constant preoccupation with the "ordinary," or in his repeated assertion that Wittgenstein's task is one of "leading words back from their metaphysical to their everyday use." A synonym for Cavell's usage of the term *metaphysical*, in this case, would be *transcendence*.

11. A comparison of Cavell's and Deleuze's work on cinema would be very interesting. In conceptualizing the relation between cinema and philosophy, both arrive at strikingly similar conclusions regarding cinematic expression in the period after the Second World War. Compare, e.g., Cavell, "End of the Myths," *The World Viewed: Reflections on the Ontology of Film* (enlarged edition, Cambridge: Harvard University Press, 1979), 60–68, and Deleuze, "The Crisis of the Action-Image," *Cinema I: The Movement-Image*, trans. Hugh Tomlinson and Barbara Habberjam (Minneapolis: University of Minnesota Press, 1986), 197–215, the bridge section to his *Cinema II: The*

Time-Image, trans. Hugh Tomlinson and Robert Galeta (Minneapolis: University of Minnesota Press, 1989).

12. Stanley Cavell, *Cities of Words: Pedagogical Letters on a Register of the Moral Life* (Cambridge: Harvard University Press, 2004).

13. In their emphasis on Wittgenstein and Bergson, respectively, Cavell and Deleuze begin to move further apart, although even these series remain open for investigation, since they are not definitively separate.

14. Quoted in H. Hummel, "Emerson and Nietzsche," *The New England Quarterly* 19, no. 1 (1946): 80. See also I. Makarushka, "Emerson and Nietzsche on History: Lessons for the Next Millennium," in *Literature and Theology at Century's End*, ed. G. Salyer and R. Detweiler (Atlanta: Scholar's Press, 1995), 89–101.

15. See, e.g., Cavell's essays "Aversive Thinking: Emersonian Representations in Heidegger and Nietzsche" and "Old and New in Emerson and Nietzsche," in *Emerson's Transcendental Etudes*, 141–70 and 224–33.

16. M. K. Gandhi, *Hind Swaraj and Other Writings*, ed. Anthony J. Parel (Cambridge: Cambridge University Press, 1997). See also Gandhi, *An Autobiography; or, The Story of My Experiments with Truth*, trans. Mahadev Desai (Ahmedabad: Navajivan Publishing House, 1927).

17. Ralph Waldo Emerson, *Essays and Lectures* (New York: The Library of America, 1983).

18. Quoted in Louis Fischer, ed., *The Essential Gandhi: An Anthology*. (New York: Vintage, 1962), 303.

19. Quoted in Pierre Hadot, *Philosophy as a Way of Life*, ed. and introd. Arnold I. Davidson (Oxford: Basil Blackwell, 1995), 247.

20. Ibid., 241.

21. We may say "falteringly" for Foucault, taking into account Hadot's critique, in *Philosophy as a Way of Life*, of the treatment of the Stoics in Foucault's *History of Sexuality* volumes. In sum, Hadot believes that Foucault lacks a proper conception of the "outside" or an engagement with an infinite totality, which was crucial for the Stoics and for spiritual exercises. The question of the outside, an open totality, or a "whole" is central to the philosophical lineage we are working through from Emerson to Deleuze.

22. Stanley Cavell, "Aversive Thinking: Emersonian Representations in Nietzsche and Heidegger," *Conditions Handsome and Unhandsome: The Constitution of Emersonian Perfectionism* (Chicago: University of Chicago Press, 1990), 33–63.

23. Deleuze, *Difference and Repetition*, 130.

24. Gilles Deleuze / Felix Guattari, "1933: Micropolitics and Segmentarity," *A Thousand Plateaus: Capitalism and Schizophrenia*, trans. Brian Massumi (Minneapolis: University of Minnesota Press, 1987), 208–32.

25. In using the term *Romanticism*, I am prompted primarily by Cavell's outline of this region of thought in his *In Quest of the Ordinary: Lines Through Skepticism and Romanticism* (Chicago: University of Chicago Press, 1988).

26. For an exploration of this reading of Rousseau, see Claude Lévi-Strauss, "Jean-Jacques Rousseau, Founder of the Sciences of Man," *Structural Anthropology*, vol. 2, trans. Monique Layton (New York: Basic Books, 1976), 33–42.

27. This is one of the central questions in Veena Das's attempt to receive Cavell within anthropology. See, esp., her "Voice as Birth of Culture," *Ethnos* 3–4 (1995): 159–81

28. See Deleuze/Guattari, "10000 B.C.: The Geology of Morals (Who Does the Earth Think It Is?)," *A Thousand Plateaus*, 39–75, as well as the opening section of the book, "Introduction: Rhizome," ibid., 3–25.

29. Ibid., 21.

30. See Stanley Cavell, *Philosophy the Day after Tomorrow* (Cambridge: Harvard University Press, 2005), 131.

31. Ajay Skaria, "Gandhi's Politics: Liberalism and the Question of the Ashram," *South Atlantic Quarterly* 101, no. 4 (Fall 2002): 955–86. See also Faisal Devji, "A Practice of Prejudice: Gandhi's Politics of Friendship," in *Subaltern Studies XII*, ed. Shail Mayaram, M. S. S. Pandian, and Ajay Skaria (New Delhi: Permanent Black, 2005), 78–99. The concept of "neighborliness," central to both these essays, is a crucial term in Thoreau's lexicon, in his sharp redrawing or inversion of the Christian moral injunction "Love thy neighbor as thyself." Is Gandhi more Christian than Thoreau? The answer is probably yes. But let us leave this question open for further discussion, indicating that it is perhaps as much a matter of the soil one inhabits, and the seeds that can be, or must be, planted within it—or, in Deleuzian terms, the way in which a concept is deterritorialized from one milieu and reterritorialized in another.

32. This relationship is described by Andrew Kirk in Henry David Thoreau, *Civil Disobedience*, ed. and introd. Andrew Kirk (New York: The Ivy Press, 2004), 77.

33. See Gilles Deleuze, "The Simulacrum and Ancient Philosophy," *The Logic of Sense*, 253–80.

34. Immanuel Kant, *Perpetual Peace and Other Essays on Politics, History, and Morals*, trans. Ted Humphrey (Indianapolis: Hackett Publishing, 1983).

35. See Deleuze/Guattari, *A Thousand Plateaus*, 291.

36. Bhikhu Parekh, *Gandhi's Political Philosophy: A Critical Examination*. (Notre Dame, Ind.: University of Notre-Dame Press, 1989).

37. Thoreau, *Civil Disobedience*, 38.

38. J. Sen, A. Anand, A. Escobar, and P. Waterman, eds., *World Social Forum: Challenging Empires* (New Delhi: The Viveka Foundation, 2004), 70.

Samuel Weber, Rogue Democracy and the Hidden God

1. Jacques Derrida, *Rogues: Two Essays on Reason*, trans. Pascale-Anne Brault and Michael Naas (Stanford: Stanford University Press, 2005), 14 (all translations have been modified where necessary to reflect aspects of the text under discussion); *Voyous: Deux essais sur la raison* (Galilée: Paris, 2003), 35. Quotations from this book will be given in the body of the text, with page numbers of first the English translation, then the French original.

2. In the lead essay to a volume entitled *Deconstruction is/in America*, Derrida describes the United States as being today "the most sensitive, receptive, or responsive space . . . to the themes and effects of deconstruction." He also notes that "in the war that rages over the subject of deconstruction, there is no front; there are no fronts. But if there were, they would all pass through the United States. They would define," he adds, a certain "partition of America" (*Deconstruction is/in America*, ed. Anselm Haverkamp [New York: New York University Press, 1995], 37). The following remarks on "rogue democracy" can be read as an effort to explore one dimension of this partitioning.

3. Jacques Derrida, *Positions*, trans. Alan Bass (Chicago: University of Chicago Press, 1981). Derrida explains his misgivings with respect to the notion of "position"—political and otherwise—by asking: "If the alterity of the other is *posed*, that is, *only* posed, does it not amount to *the same* . . . ? From this point of view, I would even say that the alterity of the other *inscribes* in this

relationship that which in no case can be "posed." Inscription, as I would define it in this respect, is not a simple position: it is rather that by means of which every position is *of itself confounded*" (95–96). Derrida's discussion of democracy will continue this line of questioning by relating it to the "rule of the same"—ipseity or ipsocracy—as the principle informing all theories of "sovereignty," including that of the sovereignty of the people.

4. National Security Strategy of the United States (2002), http://www.whitehouse.gov/nsc/nss.-pdf; my emphasis.

5. A related process, although described from a very different political perspective, is at the heart of the much-discussed study of the CIA by Chandler Johnson, *Blowback: The Costs and Consequences of American Empire* (New York: Henry Holt, 2000).

6. In response to growing signs of a possible U.S. or Israeli preemptive attack on Iran, Zbigniew Brzezinski observes that "In the absence of an immanent threat (and the Iranians are at least several years away from having a nuclear arsenal), the attack would be a unilateral act of war. If undertaken without a formal congressional declaration of war, an attack would be unconstitutional and merit the impeachment of the president. Similarly, if undertaken without the sanction of the United Nations Security Council . . . it would stamp the perpetrator(s) as an international outlaw(s)" (Zbigniew Brzezinski, "Been There, Done That," *Los Angeles Times*, April 23, 2006).

7. On the relation of "terror" to violence and force, see the excellent essay by Marc Redfield, "War on Terror," in *Provocations to Reading: J. Hillis Miller and the Democracy to Come*, ed. Barbara Cohen and Dragan Kujundžić (New York: Fordham University Press, 2006), 128–58. It is of particular significance that the epitome of "terrorist" acts—so far, at least—seems associated with "suicide": as though it were *life itself*—life *as* self—that were at issue, in its relation to death, above and beyond its individual or collective embodiments.

8. Carl Schmitt, *Politische Theologie* (Berlin: Duncker & Humblot, 1985), 11.

9. Schmitt, *Roman Catholicism and Political Form*, 52.

10. Derrida's most elaborate discussion and critique of Schmitt is to be found in his *Politics of Friendship*, trans. George Collins (London: Verso, 2005), 83–170.

11. It would be revealing to contrast Derrida's deconstruction of sovereignty in terms of what he calls "ipsocracy" or "ipseity" to an earlier critique of the notion of "self" to be found in the first chapter of Adorno and Horkheimer's *Dialectic of Enlightenment*, trans. Edmund Jephcott (Stanford: Stanford University Press, 2002). One would find many of the same motifs: namely, critique of a notion of sovereignty derived from monotheistic theology and historically institutionalized in the principle of "self-preservation." But such convergences would presumably also serve to highlight the very significant divergences between the two critiques of "self." Whereas for Derrida the key relationship that entails the deconstruction of sovereignty and self involves above all *time* and *language* as media of alterity, for Adorno and Horkheimer that role is assigned to "nature," as in the following passage: "The self which, after the methodical extirpation of all natural traces as mythological, was no longer supposed to be either a body or blood or a soul or even a natural ego but was sublimated into a transcendental or logical subject, formed the reference point of reason, the legislating authority of action" (22). "Nature" here is by implication a form of self-presence, since its "traces" are "extirpated" by the self in the process of demystification.

12. Michael Naas, " 'One Nation . . . Indivisible': Jacques Derrida on the Autoimmunity of Democracy and the Sovereignty of God," *Research in Phenomenology*, 2006, p. 1.

13. I hope to explore this problem further in relation to the notions of "defense" and "danger" with reference both to Derrida and to Freud.

14. This unusual term, which sounds like an all too literal combination of the German *Heimat* with *Vaterland*, undoubtedly was chosen precisely to avoid the criticism of inconsistency: what is

being defended is not "democracy" as such but its "homeland." The traditional term, still in use, is *national security*. But the security of the "nation" is abstract compared to the security of the "homeland." "Homeland security" thus is part of a trend that can be described as the "privatization of the political." One belongs to the nation as a citizen, which is to say, as a member of a public. One belongs to the homeland, by contrast, as to an extended family. It would surely be revealing to pursue the history of this term. *The Merriam-Webster Online Dictionary* defines *homeland* as follows: "A state or area set aside to be a state for a people of a particular national, cultural, or racial origin; *especially*: BANTUSTAN." *The American Heritage Dictionary*, in its fourth edition, dated 2000, defines the term as designating "A state, region, or territory that is closely identified with a particular people or ethnic group" and also gives as sole example of usage "Any of the ten regions designated by South Africa in the 1970s as semiautonomous territorial states for the Black population. The Black homelands were dissolved."

15. Michael Naas, in the text cited, indicates the decisive significance of "auto-immunity" in rethinking this "force": "As a 'weak force,' a force that turns on and disables force or power, autoimmunity at once destroys or compromises the integrity and identity of sovereign forms and opens them up to their future—that is, to the unconditionality of the event."

16. The analysis and deconstruction of the political ramifications of "fraternity" constitutes one of the major motifs of Derrida, *Politics of Friendship*.

17. It is difficult here not to be reminded of Judge Daniel Paul Schreber's description of God in his *Memoirs of My Nervous Illness* (Cambridge: Harvard University Press, 1988)—with, of course, the hardly untrivial difference that Aristotle's Prime Mover, although erogenous, is not corporeal, in sharp contrast to Schreber's deity.

18. But, interestingly enough, never (to my knowledge) as "autocracy."

19. Prouty's first and major book, L. Fletcher Prouty, *The Secret Team: The CIA and Its Allies in Control of the United States and the World* (Prentice-Hall: New York, 1973, rpt. 1992), disappeared from most libraries and bookstores shortly after its appearance. Meanwhile, Prouty's numerous books, essays, and interviews are available in CD format as well as in print.

20. Max Weber, *The Spirit of Capitalism and the Protestant Ethic* (London: Routledge, 1992).

21. In his essay "The Work of Art in the Age of Its Mechanical Reproducibility," Benjamin uses the terms *cult* and *cult-value*, which he associates both with art in its early stages and with the fascist use of technology to produce "cult-value." Although this seems to bear little *direct* resemblance to the "cult-religion" of capitalism as described in the earlier text, it does share with it the tendency to conceal its object: "Cult-value as such tends to keep the work of art concealed [*im Verborgenen*]." The "immature" deity of the capitalist cult, by contrast, is "kept secret [*verheimlicht*]," which is more and other than just hidden or concealed. See Walter Benjamin, *Gesammelte Schriften* (Frankfurt am Main: Suhrkamp, 1980), I.2:443. (Hereafter *GS*.)

22. Walter Benjamin, "Kapitalismus als Religion," *GS* VI:100.

23. It is significant, perhaps, that as a noun the word signifies guilt in the singular, and debt(s) in the plural.

24. *GS* VI:102.

25. The banknotes of the new European currency, the euro, have replaced representations of personal "figures" with monuments and maps. This separation of ornamentality from figuration may contribute to the sense of distance and detachment that increasingly is manifest in the attitudes of Europeans to the European Union.

26. This was the brief slogan of an advertising campaign launched in the 1970s by the predecessor of Nissan Motors, which had then to be withdrawn because of protest by religious groups.

Rafael Sánchez, Intimate Publicities: Retreating the Theologico-Political in the Chávez Regime?

NOTE: Versions of this paper were presented at an "alternative" panel of the American Anthropological Association at Columbia University and in the Departments of Anthropology at the University of California, Berkeley, and the University of Chicago. Earlier versions were also given at a conference entitled Religion, Media, and the Public Sphere, and at a conference entitled Political Theologies in 2001 and at its follow-up in 2004. All these conferences were held at the University of Amsterdam. It was also the focus of a helpful, lively discussion by the members of the NWO-sponsored Pionier research program Modern Mass Media, Religion, and the Imagination of Communities, of which I am a part, also at the University of Amsterdam. I would like to thank the members of these different audiences for their comments. Edmundo Bracho, Victor Bravo, Diómedes Cordero, Luca diSanto, Marianne Ferme, Charles Hirshkind, Marilyn Ivy, Javier Lasarte, Fausto Masó, Saba Mahmood, Birgit Meyer, Peter Pels, John Pemberton, Jim Siegal, and Paula Vásquez read versions of this paper and offered valuable contributions and feedback. I am especially grateful to Rosalind Carmel Morris for her extensive, highly insightful, and helpful commentary. I would like to thank Helen Tartar for expert editorial advice. As always, Patricia Spyer has provided invaluable intellectual companionship at every stage of the writing.

1. Carl Schmitt, *The Concept of the Political* (New Brunswick, N.J.: Rutgers University Press, 1976); Schmitt, *Political Theology: Four Chapters on the Concept of Sovereignty*, trans. George Schwab (Cambridge: MIT Press, 1985). See Hent de Vries, "In Media Res: Global Religion, Public Spheres, and the Task of Contemporary Comparative Religious Studies," in *Religion and Media*, ed. Hent de Vries and Samuel Weber (Stanford: Stanford University Press, 2001), 23–29, for an illuminating discussion of the political-theological significance of miracles and the miraculous, apprehended in their relations to the vast field of technicity and special effects.

2. Lisa Trahair, "The Comedy of Philosophy: Bataille, Hegel, and Derrida," *Angelaki* 6, no. 3 (2001): 155.

3. Georges Bataille, "Un-knowing Laughter and Tears," trans. Annette Michelson, *October* 36 (1986): 102.

4. Simon Critchley, *On Humour* (London: Routledge, 2002), 1.

5. Trahair, "The Comedy of Philosophy," 157; Wilhelm S. Wurzer, "Nancy and the Political Imaginary after Nature," in *The Sense of Philosophy: On Jean-Luc Nancy*, ed. Darren Sheppard, Simon Sparks, and Colin Thomas (London: Routledge, 1999), 95

6. Pierre Clastres, *Society Against the State* (New York: Zone Books, 1987).

7. In order to prevent possible misunderstandings, it is, however, important to say that the way in which the panties incident affected the local political situation cannot be assimilated to the action of some discrete cause from which later events may then be said simply to follow as so many equally discrete consequences or effects. Things are more indirect and complicated, even if this does not in any way detract from (rather the opposite) the significance that this incident has had for later developments in Venezuela. According to my argument, if the panties incident was crucial, this is because it was the first time that the limits of the regime's political theology, the relative hollowness of its totalizing claims, became publicly exposed amid explosive laughter. Now, as Bataille and others have remarked, laughter is contagious—once it starts it is not easily stopped. Since that time, whenever in its totalizing claims the regime brushes against its limits, such deflating laughter has become customary. It is therefore inconsequential whether the panties incident still occupies local people's imagination. Indeed, for all practical purposes, they may well have forgotten it. What is important is that they laugh and, in so doing, somehow repeat the corrosive effects

which that distant episode had for the local political theology. It is in this precise sense that I say this incident, from which the regine has never quite recovered, continues to haunt the present. Even if I am not sure that I have succeeded in doing so, I am grateful to Birgit Meyer for insisting that I clarify how, precisely, the incident keeps contagiously inflecting Venezuela's present predicament.

8. Roger Santodomingo, *TalCual*, January 11, 2001.

9. Pablo Aure, "Generales en pantaletas," *El Nacional*, January 30, 2001.

10. Teodoro Petkoff, "La noche de la pantaleta," *TalCual*, January 12, 2001; Carlos Vicente Torrealba, "La noche de las pantaletas,"*Venezuela Analítica*, 2001.

11. Pablo Aure, "Generales en pantaletas."

12. Of panties in these earlier incidents, one may say what Pietz says of the fetish. For him, the fetish is "'territorialized' in material space"; likewise, panties are located in the irreducibly material domains of privacy. They are also "personalized," evoking an intensely passionate individual response that, going well beyond any collective significance that these objects may have in the culture, is largely "incommensurate" with it. (See William Pietz, "The Problem of the Fetish," pt. 1, *Res* 9 (Spring 1985):12–13). In this respect, one might say that, in their strong interpellating capacity, much like surrealist *objets trouvés*, fetishes, in this case the panties, are firmly rooted in the modern economy of the subject. Not only that, but they are indispensable to the workings of such an economy. It is a crucial argument of this essay that, unlike the earlier episodes, in the latest Venezuelan incident concerning panties, it is this economy, and in it the very status of panties as fetish, that is placed under erasure—i.e., not put behind or overcome as something once and for all relegated to the past but rather destabilized or, more precisely, deconstructed.

13. I am, of course, here loosely invoking Lacan to refer not to any actually given evolutionary stage but to the kind of retroactive hallucinations that all subjects presumably undergo after entering the "symbolic" order.

14. Philippe Lacoue-Labarthe and Jean-Luc Nancy, *Retreating the Political*, ed. and trans. Simon Sparks (London: Routledge, 1997), 3.

15. "Militares enjuician al abogado Pablo Aure," *El Nacional*, January 10, 2001.

16. "Liberado el Profesor Pablo Aure pero el juicio militar continúa," *El Nacional*, January 11, 2001.

17. *TalCual*, January 11, 2001.

18. "Pantaletas van y pantaletas vienen," *TalCual*, January 12, 2001.

19. Angel Bermudez, "Conspiración Boba," *El Universal*, January 12, 2001.

20. Antonio López Ortega, "Prendas," *El Nacional*, January 27, 2001. Although I am citing this author's text in a context that somewhat ironically brings out some unexpected possibilities, as witnessed by his many newspaper articles, essays, short stories, and novels, it is surely testimony to his many gifts as a writer that this can so fruitfully be done.

21. "Subió cotización de pantaletas," *TalCual*, January 12, 2001.

22. Jean-Luc Nancy, *Being Singular Plural*, trans. Robert D. Richardson and Anne O'Byrne (Stanford: Stanford University Press, 2000), 2.

23. Ibid., 2–3.

24. Ibid., 3.

25. Ibid., 5.

26. Jacques Derrida, *Politics of Friendship*, trans. George Collins (London: Verso, 1997), 99.

27. For Bolivar's status in Venezuela's political imaginary, see Rafael Sánchez, "Dancing Jacobins: A Genealogy of Latin American Populism (Venezuela)" (Ph.D. dissertation, University of Amsterdam, 2004), 387–438.

28. Ibid., 139–258.

29. Philippe Lacoue-Labarthe, *Typography: Mimesis, Philosophy, Politics*, ed. Christopher Fynsk, introd. Jacques Derrida (1989; rpt. Stanford: Stanford University Press, 1998), 138.

30. Jean-Luc Nancy, *Hegel: The Restlessness of the Negative*, trans. Jason Smith and Steven Miller (Minneapolis: University of Minnesota Press, 2002), 3.

31. As I argue in my dissertation, the frequent insistence, in Venezuelan and Latin American constitutionalism, on regarding a new nation's constitutional texts as tools for molding the nation or bringing it into being must be understood in light of these highly troubled circumstances. The need to mold or give shape arose so urgently precisely because, with the demise of the empire, things had so thoroughly imploded. The claim, commonly found in the literature, that because of their highly abstract, formal character these "modern" texts are radically at odds with their presumably "traditional" contexts and thus have little or no formative efficacy there is fundamentally misguided. Rather, it is largely on account of their very abstractness that these foundational texts can shape or intervene in the very modern circumstances in which they continuously emerge. It is, in other words, due to this very abstractness that they are at all capable of somehow meeting the (demiurgic) challenge that, since Independence from Spain, these modern circumstances continue to pose. See my "Dancing Jacobins," 3–32, 287–358.

32. Ibid., 139–258.

33. Jean-François Lyotard, *Des dispositifs pulsionnels* (Paris: Union Générale d'Editions, 1973), 180–81.

34. For the relevance of a theatrical paradigm of representation for understanding the Venezuelan situation after Independence from Spain, see my "Dancing Jacobins," 236–58.

35. Ibid., 259–313.

36. I am grateful to Rosalind Morris for pointing out that the crowd/audience opposition can be fruitfully addressed by analyzing the different "positions and relations" that these two different social modalities maintain vis-à-vis "speakers," here the tribunes of the republic. According to Morris, "whereas an audience is interpellated, no such "dyadic" relationship obtains for a crowd. As a result, where an audience listens, a crowd is "distracted" and "diffuse." While I fully agree with Morris, I cannot here go into the complex issues and circumstances that, in Venezuela, account for something so consequential for the nation's republican history as a breakdown of the speaker/audience relation. Such a breakdown, indeed, accounts for the (re-)emergence of crowds as a dimension endemic to this history. In *Dancing Jacobins*, I do, however, address that issue in terms of the emergence, conditions of possibility, and existential limits of a theatrical paradigm that was first installed in Venezuela as a response to the crisis of Independence from Spain.

37. Lacoue-Labarthe and Nancy, *Retreating the Political*, 122–34.

38. Michel Foucault, *"Society Must Be Defended": Lectures at the Collège de France, 1975–1976* (New York: Picador, 2003), 239–63.

39. Marshall Sahlins, in "The Strange King or, Dumézil Among the Fijians," has argued that throughout the world the notion of the king as "stranger" or foreigner amounts to an ontology of the political in which state power is necessarily extrinsic to and in excess of society, an alien element that needs to be domesticated (Marshall Sahlins, *Islands of History* [Chicago: University of Chicago Press, 1985], 73–103). See also Bonnie Honig, *Democracy and the Foreigner* (Princeton: Princeton University Press, 2001), 7, 20–22, for the pervasiveness of the "classic foreigner founder script" as a means of "managing some paradoxes of democratic founding, such as the alienness of the law." (ibid., 7). I leave for another occasion reflecting on whether such a script is relevant only to "democratic founding" or whether, as Sahlins suggests, it applies to all sorts of founding, given the irreducibly democratic element that he discerns in "society" once, for analytic purposes, the state is abstracted.

40. Geoffrey Bennington, *Dudding: Des noms de Rousseau* (Paris: Galilée, 1991),73.

41. Sánchez, "Dancing Jacobins," 387–438.

42. Michael McCaughan, *The Battle of Venezuela* (London: Latin America Bureau, 2004), 54.

43. Jacques Derrida, "Force of Law: The 'Mystical Foundation of Authority,'" in *Deconstruction and the Possibility of Justice*, ed. Drucilla Cornell, Michel Rosenfeld, and David Gray Carlson (New York: Routledge, 1992), 3–67

44. Jason Smith, "Introduction: Nancy's Hegel, the State, and Us," in Nancy, *Hegel*, ix.

45. This caricature is from a time before oil had reached the extravagant prizes that it enjoys today.

46. Oswaldo Barreto, "Soberanías menguadas," *TalCual*, April 17, 2002.

47. Ernesto Laclau, "Populismo y transformación del imaginario político en América Latina," *Boletin de Estudios Latinoamericanos y del Caribe 42* (Amsterdam: Cedla, 1987), 25–38.

48. Rafael Sánchez, "Channel Surfing: Media, Mediumship, and State Authority in the María Lionza Possession Cult (Venezuela)," in *Religion and Media*, ed. Hent de Vries and Samuel Weber (Stanford: Stanford University Press, 2001), 388–434.

49. Jean-Luc Nancy, *The Birth to Presence*, trans. Brian Holmes and others (Stanford: Stanford University Press, 1993), 111.

50. Roland Barthes, *Camera Lucida: Reflections on Photography*, trans. Richard Howard (New York: The Noonday Press, 1993), 98.

51. Claudio Nazoa, "Se me fue la media," *El Nacional*, August 8, 2001.

52. Michael Warner, *Publics and Counterpublics* (New York: Zone Books, 2002), 21–25, 62.

53. Of the subject, i.e., of that which, as I have tried to suggest in this essay, is currently undergoing strong deconstructive pressures in Venezuela.

54. Hannia Gómez, "El Coliseo," *El Nacional*, January 25, 2004; Fernando Rodríguez, "Atrapados," *TalCual*, March 02, 2004.

55. Leopoldo Tablante, "De la 's' a la 'l,'" *El Nacional*, June 26, 2002.

56. I find this transition particularly fascinating because in it panties may be seen literally shedding their status as fetishes to become something else. As the transition suggests, such a process is, moreover, laden with momentous consequences not just for the subject but also, concomitantly, for the topographical ordering of the world where such a subject had hitherto thrived.

57. Mario Perniola, *The Sex Appeal of the Inorganic: Philosophies of Desire in the Modern World* (New York: Continuum, 2004); Nancy, *Being Singular Plural*, 5–8.

58. After some thought, I decided to publish this essay basically as it was before the referendum, without making any changes in light of that event. (I have added only a few sentences at the very end about the status of the public/private divide in contemporary Venezuela, something that I had always intended to do.) Even if some of the essay's assertions betray the moment in which it was written, by and large I believe that the majority of its conclusions still hold. The decision to leave the paper as is also issued from my belief that, with all its possible insights and shortcomings, it should stand as testimony both to the moment in which it was written and to the possible virtues and—why not?—limits and limitations of the kind of analysis that I pursue.

59. I take this expression from the title of a somewhat hagiographic book on the Chávez presidency. See Richard Gott, *In the Shadow of the Liberator* (London: Verso, 2000).

60. The outcome was also helped by the government's intense efforts. Backed by skyrocketing oil prices in the international market, in the months preceding the referendum, the government successfully used all its resources to alter how it was perceived among the general population. Although a few months before the referendum a majority of opinion polls gave the government at most 30 percent of the vote, with roughly another 30 percent going to the opposition and the

remaining 40 percent undecided, in a surprisingly short period of time the government managed to change the proportions in its favor. It did several things to achieve this. For one, it repeatedly (and unilaterally) pushed back the date of the referendum, while aggressively launching a series of social programs and expanding the franchise to include sectors—e.g., foreigners long resident in the country as illegal workers or scores of the poor who lacked official documents—heretofore excluded from voting. The irony of the situation, which made it difficult for the opposition to criticize these measures effectively, is that no matter how unconstitutional some of them were in terms of timing, it was difficult to find fault with either giving citizenship to individuals to whom in the past it had been unfairly denied or documents to those deprived of them by an inefficient and unjust system. Something different might be said of such measures as altering voters' circumscription on a massive scale where the results were likely to be unfavorable to the government. But not even there was the opposition, lacking effective leadership and animated by a vapid triumphalism, capable of mounting an effective critique. So confident was this sector of its success in the referendum, regardless of what the government did, that at no point did it take to the streets in order to counter whatever it was that the government was doing to assure itself a favorable outcome.

61. The results were 60–40 in favor of the government.

62. Louis Marin, *Portrait of the King* (Minneapolis: University of Minnesota Press, 1988), 6–7.

63. Or, as government sympathizers like to say, are instantly fabricated by the media. In my view, the distinction on which such sympathizers often insist—between "virtual realities," which they claim the opposition media project, and "real realities," Venezuela as the government presents it—does not begin to address the vexed implications of the "really real" in its manifold mediations.

64. Roberto Giusti, "La (re)vuelta de los fantasmas," *El Universal*, June 14, 2001.

65. Teodoro Petkoff, "Magnicismo," *TalCual*, June 7, 2005.

66. The sources from the Venezuelan press are somewhat contradictory and confusing on this point.

67. Sánchez, "Dancing Jacobins," esp. 188–303. See also Sánchez, "Channel Surfing."

Veena Das, The Figure of the Abducted Woman: The Citizen as Sexed

NOTE: Reprinted from chap. 5 of Veena Das, *Life and Words: Violence and the Descent into the Ordinary* (Berkeley: University of California Press, 2006), with the permission of the publisher.

1. Gyanendra Pandey, "The Prose of Otherness," *Subaltern Studies*, ed. David Arnold and David Hardiman (Delhi: Oxford University Press, 1994), 8:188–221.

2. Ibid., 205.

3. It is, however, important to note that, despite the gesture toward the ordinary, what is at stake in this testimonial literature is not the history of the ordinary but rather the retelling of the story from the perspective of ordinary people in extraordinary times. Hence, the emphasis is on remembering the Partition and not on how it folds into everyday life in the present. See Gyanendra Pandey, *Remembering Partition: Violence, Nationalism and History in India* (Cambridge: Cambridge University Press, 2003). Among the most important contributions within this genre of writing are Urvashi Butalia, *The Other Side of Silence: Voices from the Partition of India* (Durham, N.C.: Duke University Press, 1998), and Ritu Menon and Kamla Bhasin, *Borders and Boundaries: Women in India's Partition* (New Brunswick, N.J.: Rutgers University Press, 1998). See also Sukeshi Kamra, *Bearing Witness: Partition, Independence and the End of the Raj* (Calgary: University Press of Calgary, 2002).

4. Rada Ivekovic has analyzed the manner in which gender hierarchies in ordinary times are further utilized in times of war and ethnic strife to create new hegemonies, although she is mindful of the way that the future can be opened up in these very times. See Rada Ivekovic, *Le Sexe de la nation* (Paris: Léo Scheer, 2003).

5. The Fact Finding Report set up by the government never saw the light of day.

6. Speaking of the Eichmann trial, Shosana Felman says, "The trial was a conscious legal effort not just to give victims a voice and a stage, to break the silence of the trauma, to divulge and to uncover secrets and taboos, but to transform these discoveries into one national, collective story, to assemble consciously, meticulously, diligently, an unprecedented public and collective legal record of mass trauma that formerly existed only in the repressed form of a series of untold, fragmented private stories and traumatic memories." See Shosana Felman, *The Juridical Unconscious: Trials and Traumas in the Twentieth Century* (Cambridge: Harvard University Press, 2002), 7. At this point I will only say that Felman's formulation does not allow for many situations in which the public telling and the attempt to create a *national* story of a wound can itself take on the character of rumor, of words gone wild, and convert justice into vengeance. A good example is the speech Felman quotes from George W. Bush after September 11 in which he said, "I will never forget the wound to our country and those who inflicted it. . . . Our grief has turned to anger and anger to resolution. Whether we bring our enemies to justice or justice to our enemies, justice will be done" (quoted in Felman, p. 3). Interestingly, Felman concludes that "the promised exercise of *legal* justice—of justice by trial and by law—has become civilization's most appropriate and most essential, most ultimately meaningful response to the violence that wounds it" (p. 3). Yet this speech was not about justice but about justice as *vengeance*, as the reference to enemy clearly implies, a fact that strangely goes unnoticed in Felman's account. Subsequent events have shown more clearly that naming the tragic events of September 11 acts of *war* rather than *crimes* shows the easy slippage between these categories. The attempt to create a national story of hurt can take the form of rumor rather more easily than Felman allows. In that sense, the Eichmann trial was exceptional rather than paradigmatic, because the line between victims and perpetrators was so clear—those lines become blurred in most situations of ongoing violence, as the experience of Truth and Reconciliation Commissions in various countries have shown. See: Fiona Ross, *Bearing Witness: Women and the Truth and Reconciliation Commission in South Africa* (London: Pluto Press, 2003); Richard Wilson, *The Politics of Truth and Reconciliation in South Africa* (Cambridge: Cambridge University Press, 2003).

7. G. D. Khosla, *Stern Reckoning: A Survey of the Events Leading Up To and Following the Partition of India* (1949; Delhi: Oxford University Press, 1989).

8. It is worth quoting Pandey in detail on this pattern: "On the basis of published and unpublished materials and oral evidence provided to him by officials and non-officials in Pakistan, Symonds declared that, 'at the lowest estimate' half a million people perished and twelve million became homeless.' . . . Nothing in the surviving records, in the calculations made at the time, or in the contentious debates that have gone on since then, gives us anything like a persuasive basis for such an inference. Is it, rather, a question of what we can live with? Yet, it is not entirely clear why it is easier to live with 500,00 dead than with larger or smaller figure. Is it the 'median' that allows one to emphasize the enormity of Partition and point to our surviving humanity at the same time? Or is it a figure that has gained credibility in academic circles simply by repetition?" (Pandey, "The Prose of Otherness," 90–91). It seems to me that the issue is not one of our surviving humanity or of arriving at some kind of an average from widely discrepant numbers, but rather one of tracking how official discourse functions as rumor and asking what this authorizes. I argue that the reference to the enormity of the numbers involved authorizes an idea of unprecedented violence that has unsettled the very possibility of the social contract because the sexual contract is not in place.

9. The form of this story is an ancient one, for instance, in the epic depictions of Sita and Draupadi in the *Ramayana* and the *Mahabharata*. The movement of this story to a new register, in which it becomes a state obligation to recover abducted women, is, however, a new way of anchoring the state to the mythological imagination. For an analysis of the movements of gift and counter-gift, marriage and abduction, in the stories, see Veena Das, "Narrativizing the Male and the Female in Tulasidas's Ramacharitamanasa," in *Social Structure and Change: Ritual and Kinship*, vol. 5, ed. A. M Shah, B. S. Baviskar, and E. Ramaswamy (Delhi: Sage Publications, 1998), 67–93.

10. All quotes involving this discussion are from *Proceedings of the Indian National Congress 1946–1947* (New Delhi: Government of India, 1947).

11. Khosla, *Stern Reckoning*, 234.

12. Rajashree Ghosh, "The Constitution of Refugee Identity," M.Phil. dissertation, University of Delhi, 1991.

13. Kamlabehn Patel, *Mula Suta Ukhledan* (Bombay: R. R. Seth & Co.,1985).

14. Later chapters in the book from which this essay has been excerpted, Veena Das, *Life and Words: Violence and the Descent into the Ordinary* (Berkeley: University of California Press, 2006), show the specific ways in which stories were framed in the first person and especially the place of silence in the "telling." Here I am interested in the logic of the state of exception with regard to how law was instituted to shape the nation as a *masculine* nation, so that the social contract became a contract between men conceived as heads of households.

15. This and the following quotations from these discussions are taken from *Constituent Assembly of India (Legislative) Debates* (New Delhi: Government of India, 1949).

16. The mythic motif of the abduction of the innocent Sita by Ravana and her subsequent banishment by Rama was evoked as a metaphor in popular literature as well as in popular Hindi films.

17. Veena Das, "Sexual Violation and the Making of the Gendered Subject," in *Discrimination and Toleration*, ed. K. Hastrup and G. Urlich (London: Kluwer Law International, 2002), 271.

18. The text of the Abducted Persons (Recovery and Restoration) Act 1949 is reproduced as Appendix 1 in Menon and Bhasir, *Borders and Boundaries.*

19. On the relative weight given to men and women in the procreative process in Punjabi kinship, see Veena Das, "Masks and Faces: An Essay on Punjabi Kinship, "*Contrib. to Ind. Soc.*, n.s. (1976 [1]): 1–30. A vast literature in anthropology shows how theories of procreation codify ideologies of kinship. Much of this was published in the late sixties and early seventies under the category of the "virgin birth debate." As an example, see Edmund Leach, "Virgin Birth," *Journal of the Royal Anthropological Institute of Great Britain and Ireland* (1996): 39–49.

20. In an astute analysis of sexual violence and the creation of public memory in the Bangladesh Liberation War of 1971, Nayanika Mookherjee shows the subtle changes in the nature of reproductive (in addition to sexual) violence against women. She points out that one of the purported reasons for violence against Bengali women by Pakistani soldiers was to improve the genes of the Bengali people and to populate Bangladesh with a race of "pure" Muslims. This eugenic ring was completely absent in the case of Hindu-Muslim violence and shows that the image of Hinduized Muslims could be mobilized for hate in the Bangladesh Liberation War. Thus creation of boundaries is part of the shifting discourses of community rather than something pregiven and held in perpetuity. See Nayanika Mookerjee, "'A Lot of History': Sexual Violence, Public Memories, and the Bangladesh Liberation War of 1971," Ph.D. Dissertation, School of Oriental and African Studies, University of London, 2002.

21. I owe this insight to the important work of P. K. Dutta and Charu Gupta.

22. See Veena Das, "Secularism and the Argument from Nature," in *The Powers of the Secular Modern: Talal Asad and His Interlocutors*, ed. David Scott and Charles Hirschkind (Stanford: Stan-

ford University Press, 2005), 93–112. Gauri Viswanathan argues that the convert was subjected to social death and thus denied all earlier forms of sociality. I see this to be a more complicated question. The notion of fatherhood was at the center of theological and political debates in eighteenth-century Europe. The core of the disagreement was on the kind of "natural" rights that the father had over the son. Thus, even with conversion the rights of the father did not automatically disappear, since conversion affected the *social* position of the convert but not necessarily the relations that were seen to derive from nature.

23. See Paola Bachetta, *La Construction des identités dans les discours nationalists hiundous (1939–1992): Le Rahstriya swayamsevak Sangh et la Rashtriya Sevika Sasaiti* (Lille: ANRT, Université de Lille III, 1996), and Charu Gupta, *Sexuality, Obscenity, Community: Women, Muslims, and the Hindu Public in Colonial India* (New York, Palgrave, 2002; rpt. of Delhi: Permanent Black, 2001). Page references are to the Palgrave edition.

24. Gupta, *Sexuality, Obscenity, Community*, 248.

25. Ibid., 267.

26. Claude Lévi-Strauss, *The Elementary Structures of Kinship*, rev. ed., trans. J. H. Bill and J. R. von Sturmore, ed. Rodney Needham (London: George Allen & Unwin, 1969).

27. Mary Laura Severance, "Sex and the Social Contract," *ELH* 67, no. 2 (2000): 453–513. In Filmer's theory, fatherly power is the basis for kingly power—hence, the father had the right to kill the son without incurring any legal penalty. See Sir Robert Filmer, *Patriarcha and Other Writings* (1680; Cambridge: Cambridge University Press, 1991). I discuss this in some detail in my "Paternity, Sovereignty and the Argument from Nature."

28. Severance, "Sex and the Social Contract," 456.

29. Jean-Jacques Rousseau, *Emile* (New York: Everyman's Library, 1974).

30. See Veena Das, "Secularism and the Argument from Nature," in *Powers of the Secular Modern*, ed. Scott and Hirschkind.

31. Rosseau, *Emile*, 448; my emphasis.

32. Ibid., 325.

33. Mario Feit has examined the implications of Rousseau's theory of the relation between sexuality and mortality for same-sex marriage in an innovative and interesting way. While I see that there are important implications of Rousseau's thesis of citizenship for non-normative forms of sexuality, I am much more interested here in the way in which the figure of the Father places Rousseau in the debate on fatherhood in Filmer, Hobbes, and Locke. I have learned much from Mario Feit's discussion concerning population. Mario Feit, "Mortality, Sexuality, and Citizenship: Reading Rousseau, Arendt, and Nietzsche," Ph.D. dissertation, The Johns Hopkins University, 2003.

34. The term *pativrata* refers to a woman who shows single-minded devotion to her husband. It has strong religious connotations in Hinduism.

35. This quote is from a Hindi vernacular tract of 1927, cited in Gupta, *Sexuality, Obscenity, Community*, 292. Gupta does not explore the similar Urdu-language popular culture, but it would have been very interesting to see what tropes were used to delegitimize popular practices of women in the attempt to purify the Muslim community of Hindu influence.

Markha G. Valenta, How to Recognize a Muslim When You See One: Western Secularism and the Politics of Conversion

NOTE: For their careful readings and critical comments, I would like especially to thank Lawrence Sullivan, Talal Asad, Peter van der Veer, and Peter van Rooden. Each in his own way played a crucial role in enabling this paper—as, indirectly but fundamentally, has the vibrant legacy of Edward Said.

1. This is a space that to a large extent remains non-Muslim. Which is to say, there are diverse, fascinating, and extended discussions taking place about the veil among Muslims that will not be addressed here because within the West these remain largely relegated to the "private" realm of homes, grassroots organizations, Internet sites, mosques, and minority media and have yet to be given full and equal access to the public realm. This essay, then, in focusing on the public realm, addresses only one part of what is actually a larger discussion—reproducing in this way the very exclusion (of Muslim arguments) that I critique. It is, of course, a lesson in how we are shaped by our objects of study. At the same time, this essay is the first step in a larger project of opening up our spaces of debate to fuller encounters between "Western" and "Muslim" arguments, as well as to the recognition that these two positions as often blend with as challenge each other, that the Muslim may be Western and the Western Muslim.

2. As Robert N. Bellah argues in "Religion and Belief: The Historical Background of 'Non-Belief,'" *Beyond Belief: Essays on Religion in a Post-Traditional World* (New York: Harper & Row, 1970), 216–29.

3. While my concern is with the nature of the debate about the veil in Western public space as a whole, the most urgent and contested discussions are in fact centered in continental Western Europe. English-speaking nations of the West share the same prejudices toward the Islamic veil as Western Europe, but this has not generated the same level of distressed debate, political posturing, and legislation. I'll come back to the reasons for this below. For now, I want to recognize that in many ways the debate about the veil is in fact more about the nature of (continental Western) Europe specifically than about the West in general. Yet precisely the historical slippage between "Europe" and the "West," and the question of the extent to which Europe still can imagine that it represents the West as a whole, is one of the most central issues here. In line with this slippage, I continue at moments to use the term *West* to refer both to the larger collection of nation-states tracing their primary descent lines to all of Europe and more specifically to the smaller collection of powerful Western European nations that continue to conceive of themselves as representing the West as a whole. Most specifically, my locale is the public space of the Netherlands—the West's first modern world power, once the world's largest "Muslim" empire, and today perhaps the Western European nation-state most torn between modernity's contradictory heritage of tolerant, pragmatic humanism and purist, idealist rationalism (a distinction Stephen Toulmin develops beautifully in his *Cosmopolis: The Hidden Agenda of Modernity* [New York: Free Press, 1990]). This is not an argument I can elaborate here, but I might note that the deep complexities and contradictions of Pim Fortuyn's intellectual legacy and political trajectory as an openly gay, reactionary populist, who was at once anti-immigration and open about his nights of pleasure with young North African men, culminating in his assassination by a radical animal-rights activist, offer one useful starting point for thinking about the Netherlands as more "representative" of the West's crisis-ridden modernist project than its tiny size today might suggest.

In the U.S. context, the veil's equivalent in terms of affective resonance and political sensitivity is perhaps the Spanish language of Latino (im)migrants, likewise read as a synechdochal index of an "alien," nonwhite, Catholic presence. Here too, in the U.S., the likes of Pat Buchanan and Samuel Huntington argue that Hispanics, specifically Mexican immigrants, resist linguistic and cultural integration and in doing so threaten both the integrity of American national identity and the future of the nation-state. Unlike in Europe, however, there exists in the U.S. a much more extensive repertoire of counter-narratives and scholarly critiques with which to engage such arguments. See Samuel Huntington's recent *Who Are We?: The Challenges to America's National Identity*

(New York: Simon & Schuster, 2004), along with the furious letters in response to an extract from this book collected by the journal *Foreign Policy* 142 (May/June 2004): 4–13, 84–91. Notably, Huntington's previous book, *The Clash of Civilizations and the Remaking of the World Order*, provided the blueprint for this one in arguing the incompatibility of Western and Islamic civilizations.

An article that offers a comparative overview of these issues from a sociological perspective is Aristide R. Zolberg and Long Litt Woon, "Why Islam Is Like Spanish: Cultural Incorporation in Europe and the United States," *Politics & Society* 27, no. 1 (March 1999): 5–38. (I thank Jan Rath for bringing this article to my attention.) The critical question of the relation between language and religion relative to the construction of the nation-state, both conceptually and practically, is unfortunately not one of the concerns of this paper.

A crucial difference between the U.S. and Europe on this point, however, is that widespread resistance to Hispanic language and culture within the U.S. is mixed with widespread response and appeal to it—whether by commercial interests seeking to benefit from new media markets or presidential candidates, such as Bush, striving to benefit electorally. Spanish is, furthermore, the most popular foreign language among high-school children. We have yet to see the equivalent development in Europe: a non-Muslim political candidate at moments donning a headscarf (or, in the case of a heterosexual man, enticing his wife to do so) in order to appeal to Muslim voters, while Turkish, Arabic, and Berber become not only widely accessible languages at school but top European languages in the number of students they draw.

4. Charles S. Maier, "Consigning the Twentieth Century to History: Alternative Narratives for the Modern Era," *The American Historical Review* 105, no. 3 (2000), www.historycooperative.org/journals/ahr/105.3/ah000807.html 3 (December 12, 2003).

5. Ibid., par. 18.

6. Ibid., par. 22.

7. Ibid., par. 25, 21. The citation is from George Lord Curzon of Kedleston, *Frontiers: The Romanes Lectures of 1907* (1908; Westport, Conn.: Greenwood Press, 1976), originally cited by Ewan W. Anderson in "Geopolitics: International Boundaries as Fighting Places," *Journal of Strategic Studies* 22 (June-September 1999): 128.

8. Maier, "Consigning the Twentieth Century to History," par. 26.

9. See on this point Henri Lefebvre, *The Production of Space*, trans. Donald Nicholson-Smith (Oxford: Basil Blackwell, 1991).

10. Ibid., 332; cited by Maier, "Consigning the Twentieth Century to History," par. 29.

11. Simon Critchley, "The Problem of Hegemony," Albert Schweizer Series on Ethics and Politics, New York University (April 22, 2004), in *Political Theory: Essays*; http://www.politicaltheory.info/essays/critchley.htm (May 14, 2004).

12. On this process and the imbrication of the territorial with the capitalist in the field of literary studies, see Edward W. Said's "Opponents, Audiences, Constituencies, and Community" (1987), *Reflections on Exile and Other Literary and Cultural Essays* (London: Granta Books, 2000), 118–47. Said traces the ways in which originally radical forms of literary criticism, ones with comprehensively liberating, democratic intentions, such as the American and French New Criticisms, Leavisite criticism in Britain, or Marxist literary theory, have become depoliticized, privatized, and self-confirming through a process of disciplinary specialization. At the same time, the university's fragmentation of knowledge not only produces particular economic constituencies—the audience/client-base of 3,000 scholars in a given literary field likely to buy a scholarly book in that field—but also specifically strives to develop the techniques necessary for "protect[ing] the coherence, the territorial integrity, the social identity of the field, its adherents and its institutional presence" (126).

13. Maier, "Consigning the Twentieth Century to History," par. 22.

14. For an interesting and useful elaboration of this argument, see Johannes Fabian's *Time and the Other: How Anthropology Makes Its Other* (New York: Columbia University Press, 1983).

15. The wonderfully evocative and telling phrase "waiting room of history" I borrow from Dipesh Chakrabarty, though Amit Chauduri notes that the German playwright Heiner Muller also used it to refer to the Third World in a 1989 interview. Amit Chauduri, "History's Waiting Room," *Australian Financial Review* (August 6, 2004), http://www.afr.com/articles/2004/08/05/1091557987 708.html (May 12, 2005).

16. See Leila Ahmed, *Women and Gender in Islam: Historical Roots of a Modern Debate* (New Haven, Conn.: Yale University Press, 1992), esp. chap. 8.

17. On the universalizing intent of particularly British colonial discourse, see Edward W. Said, *Culture and Imperialism* (London: Vintage, 1993), esp. the first three sections of chap. 2, "Consolidated Vision" (73–132). On Egypt "as mirror of the Arab world in the modern age," a common standpoint among scholars, based on Egypt's influential cultural, intellectual, political, and social role in the modern Middle East, see Ahmed, *Women and Gender in Islam*, 6. Just as important, however, has been the West's habit of selectively universalizing Egyptian discourse, when convenient. So, e.g., the fatwa of the head ulama of Al-Ahzar University fully affirming the right of the French state to prohibit headscarves within its domain has been given wide coverage by the Western press and various publicists. These like to present the ulama as embodying the highest (and implicitly universal) Islamic authority, but leave aside considering his complex local relations to the Egyptian state (his employer), along with the dose of practical cynicism with which his decision has been received by those portions of the Egyptian and broader Islamic public that do take such complex local relations into account.

18. Ahmed, *Women and Gender in Islam*, discusses these developments in chap. 2, "The Mediterranean Middle East." I should note that there has been much questioning of the historical validity and thoroughness of Ahmed's account of the ancient Middle East. My initial introduction of this section as a story, then, was in full awareness of the complex location of storytelling between fabrication and truth. Elaborating as it does on weak historical evidence, the account here is as much a narrative of what might have been as of what actually was. The point is to enable a creative rethinking of the relation between Europe and the Middle East, Christianity and Islam. To reimagine our past, so that we can reconsider the present. This is always risky. Always. But vital too. Precisely because we need new imaginations to uncover new facts.

19. Linda Kerber and Jane DeHart-Mathews, eds. *Women's America: Refocusing the Past*, 2d ed. (New York: Oxford University Press, 1987), 224.

20. The case of the Dutch, once Europe's largest "Islamic" empire, offers an intriguing and important divergence in this regard. While the Netherlands, like the rest of the West, experienced a number of strong feminist impulses in the late nineteenth and early twentieth centuries, these were effectively contained within and by the nation's "pillarized" socio-political structure. That is, the vast majority of women, including women's rights activists, continued to remain first and foremost committed to their pillar—Protestant, Catholic, Socialist, or Liberal—rather than to their gender or to an imagined (trans)national community of sisters. Correspondingly, issues such as Dutch women's underemployment relative not only to men but to other Western women rarely were raised to the level of national issues. Not only did this mean that Dutch women's nineteenth- and early-twentieth-century activism challenged reigning divisions between male and female spheres less radically than did the work of Anglo-American women activists—even when they shared specific goals such as suffragism—but, more significantly, their concerns were not able to lay claim to and reconfigure the public and political world in their own terms, as did Anglo-American women activists. The twofold result is that such feminist discourse remained largely unavailable (and unap-

pealing) to Dutch colonial administrators and writers and that the veil itself did not become an issue of contention as it did in British-occupied Egypt, even for someone as internationally versed as Snouck Hurgronje in his most imperialist phase. Only today, when the Netherlands' former religio-socio-political pillars have more or less dissolved into a larger collective national identity, and as mainstream Dutch women's self-identity has come to include an active sexuality and a secular, rationalized individualism, has the discourse of the veil as a threat to the nation and Western civilization come to exert a strong appeal.

21. Ahmed, *Women and Gender in Islam*, 152.

22. I have in mind here, among many others, the work of the Malaysian "Sisters of Islam," the growth of feminist Muslim organizations in Indonesia, the activism of female Turkish students protesting the ban on headscarves in universities, the dramatic increase in the number of female students attending Iranian universities following the Revolution, precisely because by wearing the veil they could now go out in public, and a recent march organized by French Muslim schoolgirls. Working through informal Internet networks and wearing the French flag as a headscarf, these girls protested the French (secular) state's right to prohibit the scarf and to impose the "priority" of its authority to define Muslim women's identity, relative to the authority of immigrant cultures and Islam, in the name of protecting and liberating these women.

23. Catherine A. MacKinnon's discussion of pornography comes to mind here as one of the few relevant, and radical, engagements with this issue, *Toward a Feminist Theory of the State* (Cambridge: Harvard University Press, 1989), esp. chap. 11, "Pornography: On Morality and Politics." More generally, while extant Western feminist discussions of women's construction and consumption through the male gaze under capitalist liberalism are highly developed and at moments quite powerful, they have yet to tap the rich resources (or engage the challenge) offered by the intricate dynamics of veiling. This entails, on the one hand, veiling as a dynamic response to the difficult problem of how to contend with the potency of human sexuality and, on the other hand, veiling as a practice that situates itself at the vital intersection between subjection and agency, abjection and identity, the social and the divine, the male and the female, the personal and the political, in ways as complex as they are demanding.

24. Ahmed, *Women and Gender in Islam*, 153.

25. Edward Said, *Culture and Imperialism*, 129. The essay Said references offers a particularly useful elaboration of this point: Anna Davin, "Imperialism and Motherhood," *Patriotism: The Making and Unmaking of British Identity*, ed. Raphael Samuel (London: Routledge, 1989), 1:203–35.

26. This is, in fact, precisely how Toynbee represents the British position on the eve of the First World War in his *Civilization on Trial*, written at the close of the Second World War.

27. On the human consequences—the disrupted lives, broken families, flights into exile, and forced repatriations—resulting from, for example, the U.S. security and registration acts, see the collection of articles in the *Chicago Tribune* special report "Tossed Out of America" (November 16–18, 2003) http://www.chicagotribune.com/news/nationworld/chi-031116immigration-storygallery.special (May 17, 2004).

28. Pim Fortuyn's foregrounding of this standpoint in his political campaign helped to usher in much of the current atmosphere of aggressive controlling gestures, fear, and revulsion toward Islam so frequently expressed not only in the media and government but in the everyday contacts of shopping lines, work, and on the street. For one of the few truly thoughtful and powerfully elaborated critiques of this development in the Netherlands, see Peter van der Veer, *Islam en het 'beschaafde' Westen: Essays over de 'achterlijkheid' van religies* [Islam and the "Civilized" West: Essays on the "Backwardness" of Religions] (Amsterdam: Meulenhoff, 2002).

29. Bastiaan Patermotte, "Boris Dittrich versus Theo van Gogh," *Metro* (May 26, 2004), 13; Stephan Sanders, "De stok, de hond & de wond" [The Stick, the Dog, & the Wound], *Vrij Nederland* 64, no. 39 (September 27, 2003): 51.

30. While I bracket the question of the nature and extent of active repression within Western societies, this certainly is a relevant question—particularly, at this moment, in the face of the United States' repeated gross violations of potential and suspected enemies' human rights. More generally, there is the ongoing problem of American police brutality and the state's excessive incarceration of its citizens (after Rwanda, the country with the highest proportion of its citizens in jail, accounting for one quarter of all the world's prison inmates) and dubious death sentences (such as the case of the radical black journalist Mumia Abu-Jamal), alongside the fact that the national media is owned by a small handful of conglomerates, some with close ties to the military and government. Similarly, serious concerns can be raised when it comes to the treatment of asylum seekers and immigrants in Europe and Australia.

At the same time, such violations of the West's democratic ideals are publicized and challenged by a wide range of grassroots religious, intellectual, and political interest organizations committed to confronting Western nation-states with their own failures and hypocrisies. Too infrequently remarked, however, are the ways in which this confrontation between democracy and "restricted" repression within the West parallels similar tensions in Iran, Morocco, and Indonesia, among others, between democratic and dogmatically repressive forces. The general assumption that Western democracy is a given—and most especially the assumption of the priority, superiority, and refinement of its democratic practice relative to the Rest's democratic backwardness (temporal as well as practical)—too often obscures the global nature of the tension between modern states' totalizing intentions and "true" democracy's disruptive nature. That is, even in light of Western nation-states' relative democracy, there is much to be learned and emulated from the debates and developments beyond its borders. In particular, what those in the West seem to forget is the existence of intensely layered underground intellectual and artistic cultures beyond its horizon, flowering persistently under the most repressive conditions: cultures capable of a richness, nuance, and productivity at moments far superior to the relatively simplistic images and positions (progressive as well as conservative) so stimulated by the West's saturation in market-driven media, expert opinions, books, and films. On this last point see, e.g., the Iranian Shervin Nekuee's account "Een Armeense wijsheid" [An Armenian Proverb], *De Helling* 4 (Winter 2003): 19.

31. Critchley, "The Problem of Hegemony," par. 23.

32. The most recent elections for the European Parliament, e.g., drew dramatically few voters (a bit more than 30 percent in the Netherlands), who themselves were shockingly uninformed about the issues at stake—according to international observers from Asia and Latin America.

33. In fact, so imbricated and interdependent are these discourses that one is hard put to present them as two distinct realms. Yet it is worthwhile to tease them apart in order to foreground the extent to which each of these fields of tension on the one hand invigorates and on the other hand distorts the other field.

34. Talal Asad, "Muslims as a 'Religious Minority' in Europe," in *Formations of the Secular: Christianity, Islam, Modernity* (Stanford: Stanford University Press, 2003), 159.

35. Michael Wintle, "Cultural Identity in Europe: Shared Experience," *Culture and Identity in Europe* (Aldershot: Avebury, 1996), 13; discussed in Asad, *Formations of the Secular*, 166. Crucially, Wintle himself has been influenced in his work by both Edward Said and Michel Foucault, and at times locates his contemporary project in the realm of postcolonial criticism.

36. Asad, "Muslims as a 'Religious Minority' in Europe," *Formations of the Secular*, 166.

37. See Dipesh Chakrabarty's development of this argument in *Provincializing Europe: Postcolonial Thought and Historical Difference* (Princeton: Princeton University Press, 2000).

38. T. M. Scanlon, "The Difficulty of Tolerance," *Secularism and Its Critics*, ed. Rajeev Bhargava (Delhi: Oxford University Press, 1998), 60–61.

39. Michel Rocard, "Europe's Modest Mission," http://www.project-syndicate.org (May 27, 2004).

40. On Dutch assumptions about their nation's superiority as *Gidsland* (Guiding Nation) for the world and immigrants' resistance to the Dutch national narrative and culture, see Joris Luyendijk, "Vraag niet van de ander 'ons' te willen zijn" [Don't Ask the Other to Want to Be "Us"], *NRC Handelsblad* (January 15, 2004). More generally, the scholarly literature on the Netherlands as *Gidsland* is extensive.

41. On the risks and challenges of rigorous, serious tolerance, see Scanlon, "The Difficulty of Tolerance."

42. I take this phrase from the title of Peter van der Veer's anthology *Conversion to Modernities: The Globalization of Christianity* (New York: Routledge, 1996).

43. I am in this section heavily indebted to Peter van Rooden's discussion in "Nineteenth-Century Representations of Missionary Conversion," in *Conversion to Modernities: The Globalization of Christianity*, ed. Peter van der Veer (New York: Routledge, 1996), 65–87. See also A. D. Ward, *The Counter-Reformation: Catholic Europe and the Non-Christian World* (London: Weidenfeld and Nicolson, 1982).

44. Van Rooden, "Nineteenth-Century Representations of Missionary Conversion," 78.

45. As Callum Brown points out, even the most secular and atheist of nineteenth-century socialist radicals invariably understood and narrated his life as a "conversion" from irresponsible, thoughtless pleasure-seeking to serious and responsible activity. See Callum G. Brown, *The Death of Christian Britain: Understanding Secularisation 1800–2000* (London: Routledge, 2001).

46. C. Snouck Hurgronje, *Nederland en de Islâm* [The Netherlands and Islam], 2d ed. (1911; Leiden: Brill, 1915), xiii–ix.

47. Ibid., 84.

48. Ibid., 86.

49. Charles Taylor, "Modes of Secularism," in *Secularism and Its Critics*, ed. Bhargava, 31–53.

50. Talal Asad, Introduction, *Formations of the Secular*, 6.

51. Peter van Rooden is one of the few scholars to have traced this crucial historical development. See specifically his "Nineteenth-Century Representations of Missionary Conversion and the Transformation of Western Christianity" and, more comprehensively, *Religieuze regimes: Over godsdienst en maatschappij in Nederland, 1570–1990* [Religious Regimes: On Religion and Society in the Netherlands, 1570–1990], (Amsterdam: Bert Bakker, 1996).

52. Hélène Cixous and Jacques Derrida, *Veils*, trans. Geoffrey Bennington, drawings by Ernest Pignon-Ernest (Stanford: Stanford University Press, 2001).

53. Immanuel Kant, "On a Newly Arisen Superior Tone in Philosophy," trans. Peter Fenves, in *Raising the Tone of Philosophy: Late Essays by Emmanuel Kant, Transformative Critique by Jacques Derrida*, ed. Peter Fenves (Baltimore: The Johns Hopkins University Press, 1993), 71; cited in Hent de Vries, *Philosophy and the Turn to Religion* (Baltimore: The Johns Hopkins University Press, 1999), 375. I thank Yolande Jansen for bringing this quotation to my attention.

54. Hent de Vries, *Philosophy and the Turn to Religion*, 375.

55. For an intriguing reading of this moment, see Dianna Rhyan Kardulis, "Odysseus in Ino's Veil: Feminine Headdress and the Hero in *Odyssey* 5," *Transactions of the American Philological Association* 131 (2001): 23–51.

56. Cited by Cynthia D. Schrager, "Both Sides of the Veil: Race, Science, and Mysticism in W. E. B. Du Bois," *American Quarterly* 48, no. 4 (1996): 551. My whole discussion of Du Bois here

is heavily indebted to Schrager's essay. On the historical and contemporary precedents for Du Bois's use of this trope, see also Dickson D. Bruce, Jr., "W. E. B. Du Bois and the Idea of Double Consciousness," *American Literature* 64, no. 2 (June 1992), 299–309.

57. Schrager, "Both Sides of the Veil," 554–55.

58. Ibid., 556.

59. Sam Gill, "Territory," in *Critical Terms for Religious Studies*, ed. Mark C. Taylor (Chicago: University of Chicago Press, 1998), 300.

Yolande Jansen, Laïcité, or the Politics of Republican Secularism

NOTE: Epigraphs to this chapter are from the following sources: Talal Asad, "Reflections on *Laïcité* and the Public Sphere" (2004), available at http://www.ssrc.org/publications/items/v5n3/reflections4.html, accessed on June 2, 2005, p. 4; Olivier Roy, *La Laïcité face à l'islam* (Paris: Stock, 2005), 167; Henri Pena-Ruiz, *Qu'est-ce que la laïcité?* (Paris: Gallimard, 2003), 112. Here and in all following quotations, where no published translation exists, the translation is my own.

1. The law was adopted in response to ongoing conflicts about the wearing of headscarves in public schools, but it prohibits all "conspicuous religious signs," including "large crosses" and kippas. I translate *ostensible* as "conspicuous," following Asad, "Reflections on *Laïcité* and the Public Sphere."

2. The law separating state and church, dating from December 9, 1905, has two central articles. Article 1: "The Republic ensures the freedom of conscience. It guarantees the free exercise of religions with some reservations owing to the safeguard of 'public order.'" Article 2: "The Republic does neither recognize, nor pay nor subsidize any religion." (Pena-Ruiz, *Qu'est-ce que la laïcité?*, 109; English translation Jean Baubérot, "Two Thresholds of Laïcization," in *Secularism and Its Critics*, ed. Rajeev Bhargava [Delhi: Oxford University Press, 1998], 117.) Since 1946, *laïcité* has been explicitly mentioned in the Constitution. In the latest version of the Constitution, from 1958, it is stated that "France is an indivisible, secular, democratic, and social Republic."

3. Cécile Laborde, "On Republican Toleration," *Constellations* 9, no. 2 (2002): 167–83.

4. For recent examples, see: Asad, "Reflections on *Laïcité* and the Public Sphere"; Roy, *La Laïcité face à l'islam*; Esther Benbassa, *La République face à ses minorités* (Paris: Mille et une Nuits, 2003).

5. This was especially so in the colonial context. There, the doctrine of *laïcité* was accompanied by strong state intervention in religious matters. See: Achi Raberh, "La Séparation des Églises et de l'État à l'épreuve de la situation coloniale: Les Usages de la dérogation dans l'administration du culte musulman en Algérie (1905–1959)," *Politix* 17, no. 66 (2004): 81–106; and Edward Webb, "Turkey's France, Syria's France: *La Laïcité* in Two Ottoman Successor States" (2005), available at http://histoire-sociale.univ-paris1.fr/Collo/Migrations/Webb.pdf; accessed on June 10, 2005.

6. See Pierre Birnbaum, *The Idea of France* (1988; New York: Hill and Wang, 2001).

7. Please note that the use of "nation" in this context differs significantly from the internationally most common one, in which nation and ethnic origin are closely linked. The political nation has been understood by Ernest Renan as the result of a "daily plebiscite." Both concepts of nation imply their own nationalisms.

8. Ferdinand Buisson, "Le Devoir présent de la jeunesse," *La Morale sociale*, ed. Emile Boutroux (Paris, 1899); quoted from Gérard Raulet, *Apologie de la citoyenneté* (Paris: Cerf, 1999), 30. Buisson was director of primary education from 1879 to 1896 and edited the *Dictionnaire de pédagogie et d'instruction primaire*, which Gérard Raulet calls the "bible of republican educators at all levels in the Third Republic" (ibid., 16).

9. Schooling had been discussed from the Revolution onward, most famously by Condorcet, but in the Third Republic it became one of the focal points of government, particularly in relation to the dangers produced by the (male) *suffrage universel* and by the possibility of uproars such as the Commune. See Jean Baubérot, *Histoire de la laïcité en France* (Paris: Presses Universitaires de France, 2000).

10. Cécile Laborde, "On Republican Toleration," *Constellations* 9, no. 2 (2002): 171, 170.

11. Quoted in Baubérot, *Histoire de la laïcité*, 108.

12. Claude Langlois, "Catholics and Seculars," in *Realms of Memory*, ed. Pierre Nora, trans. Arthur Goldhammer (New York: Columbia University Press, 1996), 109.

13. As is the notion of "recognition" in the text of the 1905 law.

14. Roy, *La Laïcité face à l'islam*, 42.

15. Stasi, le rapport de la commission [The Stasi Report] (2003), available at http://lesrap ports.ladocumentationfrancaise.fr/BRP/034000725/0000.pdf; accessed on June 6, 2005. All translations are mine. Stasi commission members quoted in this article are Jean Baubérot, Gilles Kepel, Alain Touraine, and Henri Pena-Ruiz. Only Baubérot spoke out against the law prohibiting "conspicuous religious signs." Together with other critics such as Émile Poulat and Pierre Tevanian, he was among those who stressed that the law in no way followed from the principle of *laïcité* but instead might even contradict it. I agree with that view, but in what follows I try to demonstrate that ritualistic references to *laïcité* and the lack of mediating concepts between "belonging" and "freedom" inherent in the opposition between religion and politics have produced a blindness to the possibility of less confrontational interpretations of the presence of Islam in the public sphere.

16. One of the signatories of the petition against the headscarf organized by the fashion magazine *Elle* (and published in *Le Monde* on December 10, 2003) was Samira Bellil, who, in "L'Enfer des tournantes," wrote a moving account of her escape from a ghetto where women are assaulted on a daily basis (Samira Bellil, *L'Enfer des tournantes* [Paris: Gallimard, 2001]).

17. Interview in *Le Monde*, December 18, 2003. The Stasi commission's interpretation of the scarf did not emerge overnight. In 1989, just after the first headscarf affair, the Conseil d'Etat ruled that the proselytizing attitudes accompanying the wearing of the scarf were prohibited but that, in principle, the scarf was no more than a private expression of religious belief. Therefore, it had to be tolerated in schools. At the time, only certain neo-republicans perceived the scarf to be a threat, while others defended it as a symbol of a modernizing Islam.

18. This is why I think the quote from Pena-Ruiz heading this article summarizes the absurdity of the law and its underlying conceptual schemes. Theorizing about participation, we could, for example, elaborate on a combination of what is called, in the international literature on multicultural questions, "real exit options" and "parity of participation,." The notion of "real exit options" is developed in Veit Bader, "Associative Democracy and Minorities Within Minorities," in *Minorities Within Minorities: Equality, Rights and Diversity*, ed. Avigail Eisenberg and Jeff Spinner-Halev (Cambridge: Cambridge University Press, 2005), 219–339). Nancy Fraser introduced the normative frame of "parity of participation" in Nancy Fraser and Axel Honneth, *Redistribution or Recognition? A Political-Philosophical Exchange* (London: Verso, 2003).

19. A more perverse proposal is to prohibit only the headscarves and not other "conspicuous" religious signs. This solution has been suggested by some Dutch and German politicians, who want to accept crosses and kippas as religious signs, while rejecting the headscarf as being a political sign of fundamentalist politics and the submission of women. This proposal does not address the real, underlying problems any more than the French law does. The advantage of dealing with the specific problem of radical Islam is outweighed by the fact that this would be a plainly discriminatory measure against a large group of citizens, which would be generally and systematically associated with terror, radicalism, and the oppression of women.

20. The opposition against an unspecified *communautarisme* that lurks behind the prohibition of religious insignia excludes concessions to religious and cultural expressions with extensions into the public realm. To my mind, this results from a generalized fear that violence hides behind public religious claims. The reasons for the actual violence probably should be localized more specifically in a heritage that merges religious claims with anticolonial ones in the period of decolonization, as well as in the incapacity of the Islamic community to find strategies for pacification in that ongoing postcolonial context. This thesis has been put forward by, among others, Roy, *Globalised Islam*.

21. These two aspects are central in the literature on multiculturalism; they have, e.g., been elaborated by Rainer Bauboeck, who understands multiculturalism to be an answer to the lives of "minorities in transition" ("Minderheiten im Uebergang," available at http://www.gfbv.it/3dossier/eu-min/20assimila.html). The committee also does not reflect on the possibility that conservative claims may be developed in an assimilationist dynamic, causing a "reactive culturalism" on the part of orthodox groups, as has been argued by Ayelet Shachar in her *Multicultural Jurisdictions* (Cambridge: Cambridge University Press, 2001).

22. John Rawls, in *The Law of Peoples* (Cambridge: Harvard University Press, 1999), rejects the universalizability of the concept of autonomy as self-reflection, calling it a form of (Western, liberal) parochialism.

23. Gilles Kepel has made similar observations several times. Already in 1993, talking about Islamism in the French banlieus, he states: "They are tribes that determine their communitarian boundaries around projects and not around what we usually think tribes do: inherited belonging, whether this be ethnic, racial or other" (Kepel, quoted in Raulet, *Apologie*, 100). I will return to this issue below. The Stasi commission forgets to mention the fact that secularist regimes in the Islamic world, particularly communist ones, had earlier prohibited the scarf. An Afghan refugee friend of mine (a secularist and liberal doctor) told me that in the 1970s his sisters were forbidden to wear scarves and forced to wear red trousers when going to school.

24. Kintzler, "La Tolérance, la laïcité et l'école," *Le Nouvel Observateur*, July 17–23, 2003, p. 63.

25. Ibid., p. 64.

26. The following analysis is inspired by Gérard Raulet's excellent discussion of Durkheim's answer to the Kantian antinomy of morality in Raulet, *Apologie*. I quote Durkheim's lessons from Raulet, 24–27. The page numbers given refer to those listed by Raulet when he quotes from Émile Durkheim, *L'Éducation morale* (Paris: Félix Alcan, 1925). All quotes from Durkheim are taken from Raulet's book; the translations are my own.

27. Durkheim, *L'Éducation morale*, 123.

28. Ibid., 8, 10.

29. Immanuel Kant, "On a Newly Arisen Superior Tone in Philosophy," in *Raising the Tone of Philosophy: Late Essays by Immanuel Kant, Transformative Critique by Jacques Derrida*, ed. Peter Fenves (Baltimore: The Johns Hopkins University Press, 1993), 51–72. For a commentary on Kant's concept of autonomy, see Hent de Vries, *Philosophy and the Turn to Religion* (Baltimore: The Johns Hopkins University Press, 1999). Commenting on the passage quoted, de Vries argues that "it is at this neurological point of the present yet absent moral law that the extremes, that is to say, critical philosophy and so-called obscurantism, touch upon each other" (ibid., 375; the quote by Kant is also from this page).

30. Olivier Roy, *Globalised Islam: The Search for a New Ummah* (London: Hurst & Co., 2004), and *La Laïcité face à l'islam*.

31. Roy, *La Laïcité face à l'islam*, 63.

32. This is why Roy criticizes the use of the term *political Islam* for globalized Islam. "Political Islam" was introduced as a better name for the movement that is often called Islamic fundamental-

ism, because the latter term is linked to Protestantism and to the reading of theological texts in purely theological and not political terms. According to some, fundamentalism is a frequently used misnomer that suggests the desire for a return to an authentic religion and neglects the fact that Islamism and other current religiously inspired movements are modern and "far from merely *retrograde* or *reactive*" (Hent de Vries, "In Media Res: Global Religion, Public Spheres, and the Task of Contemporary Comparative Religious Studies," in *Religion and Media*, ed. Hent de Vries and Samuel Weber [Stanford: Stanford University Press, 2001], 6, paraphrasing Joel Beinin and Joe Stork, *Political Islam: Essays from the Middle East Report* [Berkeley: University of California Press, 1997]). Roy, by contrast, distinguishes between political Islam, which was prevalent in the 1970s and 1980s and concentrated on the creation of an Islamic state, and what he calls "neo-fundamentalism" or "salafisme," which is not aimed at the state but at purifying Islam of all cultural or ethnic relations in order to internationalize and even globalize it.

33. Roy, *La Laïcité face à l'islam*, 132.

34. Roy's criticism of the reified use of the concept of culture within multiculturalism is familiar from the debates within multiculturalism discourse itself. Constructivists have made a critique of the reified concept of culture supposedly underlying multiculturalism into a program for redefining or even rejecting multiculturalism. See, e.g., Gerd Bauman, *The Riddle of Multiculturalism: Rethinking National, Ethnic, and Religious Identities* (New York: Routledge, 1999). Critics who have stressed the links between constructivist concepts of culture and a return to classic liberalism are, e.g.: Talal Asad, *Genealogies of Religion: Discipline and Reasons of Power in Christianity and Islam* (Baltimore: The Johns Hopkins University Press, 1993); Veit Bader, "Culture and Identity: Contesting Constructivism," *Ethnicities* 2, no. 1 (2001): 251–85 (in debate with Gerd Bauman); and Tariq Modood, "Anti-Essentialism, Multiculturalism and the 'Recognition' of Religious Groups," *The Journal of Political Philosophy* 6, no. 4 (1998): 378–99.

35. Durkheim, however, also initiated a preliminary deconstruction of his own view by "sociologizing" Kantian transcendental morality into religious collective memory. In my book *Stuck in a Revolving Door: Secularism, Assimilation, and Democratic Pluralism* (Amsterdam: Eigen Beheer, 2006), I trace how such a notion of strong secularization underpinned concepts of Jewish assimilation surrounding the Dreyfus Affair and address the ambivalences of this "assimilation" as it appears in the work of Marcel Proust.

36. Veit Bader, *Secularism or Democracy? Associational Governance of Religious Diversity* (forthcoming).

37. Such a critique of modernity's conceptualizations of religion has been developed by Charles Taylor in "Lichtung or Lebensform: Parallels between Heidegger and Wittgenstein,"in his *Philosophical Arguments* (Cambridge: Harvard University Press, 1995), 61–78.

38. Ludwig Wittgenstein, *Philosophische Untersuchungen* (Frankfurt am Main: Suhrkamp, 1984), 344.

39. Bonnie Honig, "My Culture Made Me Do It," in *Is Multiculturalism Bad for Women?*, ed. Joshua Cohen, Matthew Howard, and Martha C. Nussbaum (Princeton: Princeton University Press, 1999), 35–41.

40. See Birnbaum, *The Idea of France*.

41. Petition in *Le Monde*, December 10, 2003; my emphasis.

42. I would like to thank Veit Bader, Karin de Boer, Odile Verhaar, and Hent de Vries for their inspiring critical comments on earlier versions of this article; Murat Aydemir, Mathilde Fournier, and Irena Rosenthal for our great conversations about scarves, pedagogy, feminism, and Republican identities in general; Esther Peeren for her translations and careful corrections of the

English, and Samia Touati for our day spent together in the summer of 2003 and for her comments on an earlier version of this article.

Talal Asad, Trying to Understand French Secularism

NOTE: I am grateful to a number of friends for comments on various versions of this essay: Mustapha Alem, Jonathan Boyarin, Marcel Detienne, Baber Johansen, Mahmood Mamdani, Ruth Mas, Gyan Pandey, Nathaniel Roberts, David Scott, Markha Valenta, and Peter van der Veer. They should not, of course, be taken as endorsing my views.

1. It is important to keep in mind the distinction between what one thinks a liberal democracy *should* do and what actually happens in liberal democracies. Thus in the most modern liberal democracy, the United States, in a number of the constituent states Americans who are convicted felons have no right to vote in national elections even after they have served their sentences. This situation has many critics in the United States, but no one, to my knowledge, has argued that such inequality undermines the integrity and stability of the nation. Perhaps even more striking is the disqualification of citizens residing in the District of Columbia (in which the national capital is located) from voting for the president.

2. S. Harding and D. Phillips, *Contrasting Values in Western Europe*, cited in Grace Davie, *Religion in Modern Europe* (Oxford: Oxford University Press, 2000), 7.

3. See Henri Tincq, "Constitution européenne: La Défaite du 'parti chrétien,'" *Le Monde*, June 28, 2004.

4. "La laïcité garantit à toutes les options spirituelles ou religieuses le cadre légal propice à cette expression. Sans nier l'héritage de l'histoire, en particulier du rationalisme grec et du legs judéo-chrétien, elle leur permet de trouver leur place [Secularism guarantees to all spiritual or religious options the legal framework favorable to that expression. Without denying the heritage of history, in particular of Greek rationalism and of the Judeo-Christian legacy, it allows them to find their place]" (*Laïcité et République, Commission présidée par Bernard Stasi* [Paris: La Documentation française, 2004], 33).

5. Rodrigo de Zayas, "Le Précédent des morisques d'Espagne," in *Les Génocides dans l'histoire*, Manière de voir 76, *Le Monde diplomatique*, August-September 2004, 7.

6. Ibid., 36.

7. See John Bowen, "Muslims and Citizens, France's Headscarf Controversy," *Boston Review* (February/March 2004). This is also a useful overview of the controversy.

8. Valuable social research had even been done following the earlier headscarf crisis in 1989. In the first book-length study on the headscarf worn by women in France, two sociologists identified three classes of women who wear "the veil"—older immigrant women, adolescents, and youth between sixteen and twenty-five. The latter, they wrote, "claim the veil sometimes with their parents' agreement, sometimes against it." Such young offspring of immigrants are the most integrated into French culture and often speak excellent French. The authors went on to state, "One can understand this phenomenon only in the context of a French society undergoing a profound crisis in its values and institutions" (F. Gaspard and F. Khosrokhavar, *Le Foulard et la République* [Paris: La Découverte, 1995], 45–46).

9. It is estimated that more than half the inhabitants of French prisons are young Muslims of North African origin. (See Nicolas Simon, "Young, Male and Angry: French Muslims Know Little about the Middle East but They Are Taking Out Their Frustration on the Jews," *Jerusalem Report*, May 6, 2002.)

10. Grace Davie, *Religion in Modern Europe: A Memory Mutates* (Oxford: Oxford University Press, 2000), 19.

11. See Ernst H. Kantorowicz, *The King's Two Bodies* (Princeton: Princeton University Press, 1957).

12. See François Furet's masterly narrative *Revolutionary France, 1770–1880* (Oxford: Blackwell, 1988). Surprisingly, this account has nothing to say of France's colonial conquests—as if these could only be peripheral to the formation of the Republic. Algeria is barely mentioned. But the bond with Algeria, at once three *départements* and a colony, had fateful consequences for France. Algeria was the object of various laws, including the Crémieux Decree of 1870—issued by the National Defense Government during the Prussian War—which made Jews full citizens, endowed with all the rights enjoyed by the colons, while the Muslim majority retained their inferior status as "subjects," technically able to accede to the secular status of "citizens" if and when they gave up aspects of their religious belonging. The decree was revoked by the Vichy government and restored with its fall; Muslim Algerians were accorded citizenship unconditionally in 1946. (On some of the political controversy in France surrounding that decree at its proclamation, and on the brutally suppressed Algerian rebellion of 1871, see the first chapter of Charles Robert Ageron, *Les Algériens musulman et la France [1871–1919]*, vol. 1 [Paris: Presses Universitaires de France, 1968]).

13. C. R. Ageron, *France coloniale ou parti coloniale?* (Paris: Presses Universitaires de France, 1987), 189–234.

14. Henri Laurens, "Les Arabes et nous," *Le Nouvel Observateur*, August 19–26, 2004. See also his "La Politique musulmane de la France," *Monde Arabe: Maghreb/Machrek,* no. 152, April-June 1996.

15. Davie cites a poll conducted in 1990 in Western European countries on religious beliefs, according to which 57 percent of the French population believe in God (only Sweden has a lower score) and 50 percent believe in the soul (only Denmark has a lower score). By all other criteria France emerges as the most "irreligious" (Davie, *Religion in Modern Europe*, 10).

16. See the excellent study of religious discourse in the United States Supreme Court by Winnifred Fallers Sullivan, *Paying the Words Extra* (Cambridge: Harvard University Press, 1994). For an account of the shifting relations between church and state in the U.S. over four centuries, see Mark De Wolfe Howe, *The Garden and the Wilderness: Religion and Government in American Constitutional History* (Chicago: University of Chicago Press, 1965).

17. *Rapport au Président de la République: Commission de réflexion sur l'application du principe de laïcité dans la République*, December 11, 2003 (http://www.ladocumentationfrancaise.fr). The report has also been published in book form as *Laïcité et République, Commission présidée par Bernard Stasi* (Paris: La Documentation française, 2004). My references are to the latter.

18. The Union of Islamic Organizations of France (UOIF) ordered its youth wing, one of the organizers of the February 13 demonstration against the law, to desist from open struggle, although it did not discourage people from participating as individuals. At the annual meeting of the UOIF at Le Bourget in April 2004, its president denounced what he saw as the move from a "tolerant, open, and generous secularism, that is to say, a secularism aiming at integration [*une laïcité d'intégration*], to a secularism of exclusion [*une laïcité d'exclusion*]" signaled by the new law. See the account by Catherine Coroller, "UOIF: 'La Loi sur la laïcité est là et nous l'appliquerons,'" *Libération*, April 12, 2004.

19. French Sikhs made a special case to the president for boys to be allowed to wear the turban in schools. Their argument was that, since it is long hair that is prescribed for males by the Sikh religion and not the wearing of a turban, the latter was a *cultural* and not a *religious* sign, and that

therefore the law banning religious signs should not apply to it. In April 2004 the ministry accepted the Sikh argument: the new law did not apply to "traditional costumes which testify to the attachment of those who wear them to a culture or to a customary way of dressing"(Luc Bronner, "François Fillon propose son 'mode d'emploi' de la loi sur le voile," *Le Monde*, April 12, 2004). This apparent exception was eventually voted down in August 2004 by the National Assembly, who considered the ban to apply equally to the turban (but not to long hair) for Sikh men as an obvious religious sign. There was never any question of examining the categorical opposition of *cultural* to *religious*; what mattered was where the turban was to be placed as a sign. This ambiguity was resolved by law.

20. "Dans le cadre laïque, les choix spirituels ou religieux relévent de la liberté individuelle: cela ne signifie pas pour autant que ces questions soient confinées à l'intimité de la conscience, 'privatisées,' et que leur soient déniées tout dimension sociale ou capacité d'expression publique. La laïcité distingue la libre expression spirituelle ou religieuse dans l'espace public, légitime et essentielle au débat démocratique, de l'emprise sur celui-ci, qui est illégitime. Les représentents des différentes options spirituelles sont fondés à ce titre dans le débat public, comme toute composante de la société [In the secular framework, religious or spiritual choices are a matter of individual freedom, yet this does not mean that these questions should be confined to the privacy of conscience, 'privatized,' and that they are denied all social dimensions or the possibility of public expression. Secularism distinguishes free religious or spiritual expression in public space, which is legitimate and essential to democratic debate, from control over the latter, which is illegitimate. Representatives of the different spiritual options are thus entitled to take part in public debate, as are all who make up society]" (*Laïcité et République*, 31).

21. Ghislaine Hudson, in an interview with a group of young people published as "Laïcité: Une loi nécessaire ou dangereuse?" *Le Monde*, December 11, 2003.

22. See *Laïcité et République*, 102–3.

23. "After we heard the evidence, we concluded that we faced a difficult choice with respect to young Muslim girls wearing the headscarf in state schools. Either we left the situation as it was, and thus supported a situation that denied freedom of choice to those—the very large majority—who do not want to wear the headscarf; or we endorsed a law that removed freedom of choice from those who do want to wear it. We decided to give freedom of choice to the former during the time they were in school, while the latter retain all their freedom for their life outside school" (Patrick Weil, "A Nation in Diversity: France, Muslims and the Headscarf"; www.opendemocracy.com, March 25, 2004).

24. The Stasi report cites various international court judgments in support of its argument that the right to religious expression is always subject to certain conditions (*Laïcité et République*, 47–50). My point here is not that this right—or any other—*should* be absolute and unlimited; it is simply that a right *cannot* be inalienable if it is subject (for whatever reason) to the superior power of the state's legal institutions to define and limit. To take away a right in part or in whole on grounds of utility (including public order) or morality means that it is alienable.

25. "Le juge n'a pas cru pouvoir se prononcer sur l'interprétation du sens des signes religieux; il s'agit là d'une limite inhérente à l'intervention du juge: Il lui a semblé impossible d'entrer dans l'interprétation donnée par une religion à tel ou tel signe. Par conséquent, il n'a pu appréhender les discriminations entre l'homme et la femme, contraires à un principe fondamental de la République, que pouvait revêtir le port du voile par certaines jeunes filles [The judge did not believe he was able to pronounce on the interpretation of the meaning of the religious signs. It was a matter of an inherent limit to a judge's intervention: it seemed to him impossible to enter into the interpretation

given by a religion to such or such a sign. Consequently, he was unable to understand the discriminations between man and woman that the wearing of a veil by some young girls could assume—contrary to a basic principle of the Republic]" (*Laïcité et République*, 69–70). Insofar as school is concerned, however, the report believes that, in dealing with some religious signs (texts), pupils should *not* concern themselves with theological meanings (ibid., 34).

26. "La laïcité suppose l'indépendance du pouvoir politique et des différentes options spirituelles ou religieuses: Celles-ci n'ont pas d'emprise sur l'État et ce dernier n'en a pas sur elles. . . . La laïcité implique la neutralité de l'État [Secularism presupposes the independence of political power and of the different spiritual or religious choices: The latter do not have control over the state and the former have none over them. . . . Secularism implies the neutrality of the state]" (*Laïcité et République*, 30).

27. According to Bruno Etienne, most French Muslims are in favor of integration and consumerism. In Marseilles, where there is a large concentration of Muslims, Etienne claims that only 17 percent practice their religion. Thus integration into a secular society and immersion in consumerism are both seen—rightly, in my view—as mutually supportive. (See the interview in *Le Monde*, April 12, 2004: "Entretien avec Bruno Etienne; islamologue et professeur à l'IEP d'Aix-en-Province.")

28. "L'apprentissage de la citoyenneté dans notre société riche de cultures et d'origines diverses suppose qu'on apprenne à vivre ensemble. En articulant unité nationale, neutralité de la République et reconnaissance de la diversité, la laïcité crée, par-delà les communautés traditionelles de chacun, la communauté d'affections, cet ensemble d'images, de valeurs, de rêves et de volontés qui fondent la Republique [Learning to be a citizen in our society, rich in cultures and diverse origins, presupposes that one learn to live together. In articulating national unity, the neutrality of the Republic, and recognition of diversity, secularism creates, beyond the traditional communities of each, the community of emotions, that collection of images, of values, of dreams and wills that establishes the Republic]" (*Laïcité et République*, 41).

29. Thus *Laïcité et République*, 58. A saleswoman in a large commercial establishment was dismissed, however, for wearing a veil and refusing to remove it or wear a cap instead; in March 2001 the Paris court of appeal upheld the employer's right to dismiss her. In another case, in December 2002, the dismissal of an employee for wearing a veil in an office was annulled on the ground that she was wearing one when recruited (ibid., 61). In fact, since 1989 the judgments in particular cases on this subject have been inconsistent, not to say confused.

30. See www.education.gouv.fr/systeme_educatif/enseignment_prive.html. Of course, not all the parents of children enrolled in these schools have concerns about the spiritual education of their offspring; it is simply that they want them to have "a good education." Because they are more selective (i.e., middle class) and often better funded than public schools, religious schools tend to maintain higher educational standards. Their teachers are also less likely to go on strike than those working in public-sector schools.

31. Alsace-Moselle was reincorporated into France after the First World War, and therefore after the 1905 law whose article 2 reads: "La République ne reconnaît, ne salarie ni ne subventionne aucun culte [The Republic does not acknowledge, nor pay the salary of, nor subsidize any religion]" (cited in *Laïcité et République*, 52).

32. "La commission estime que la réaffirmation de la laïcité ne conduit pas à remettre en cause le statut particulier de l'Alsace-Moselle, auquel est particulièrement attachée la population de ces trois départements [The commission believes that the reaffirmation of secularism does not put in question the particular status of Alsace-Moselle, to which the populations of these three departments are especially attached]" (ibid., 113).

33. Nicolas Senèze, "La Régime particulier de l'Eglise catholique," *La Croix* 6 (November 2003).

34. At the very end of 2004, talks were being held between "liberal" Muslims and the interior minister with a view to establishing a more representative body for French Muslims, on the model of the Conseil Représentatif des Institutions Juives de France (CRIF). It was maintained that since the existing council, the Conseil Français du Culte Musulman (CFCM), represented practicing Muslims only, it should confine itself to religious matters, such as the training of imams, and a secular body should be set up to represent the (majority) nonpracticing Muslims in France. (See Piotr Smoler and Xavier Ternisien, "Le Ministre de l'intérieur souhaite faire émerger une instance représentative d'un 'islam laïque,'" *Le Monde*, December 7, 2004). There is also much talk of creating "a French Islam," that is, of promoting doctrinal as well as institutional reform of Islam in order to adjust it to France as a nation-state. What is notable for my argument, however, is that, despite the rejection of communitarianism, the Republic encourages the formation of "representative" bodies of Jews and Muslims.

35. See *Laïcité et République*, 52–54.

36. "La République est laïque et respecte toutes les croyances. De ce principe fondateur, découlent de nombreuses obligations, juridiques aussi bien pour les usagers que pour les services publics, à commencer par l'éducation nationale. Mais ce régime juridique est loin de constituer un bloc monolithique. Il est à la fois épars, car dispersé dans de nombreuses sources juridiques, et divers, car la laïcité n'a pas les même contours à Paris, à Strasbourg, ou à Mayotte [The Republic is secular and respects all beliefs. From this foundational principle flow many obligations, legal as much for public services as for those who use them, beginning with national education. But this legal regime is far from being a monolithic block. It is at once scattered, because dispersed in numerous legal sources, and diverse, because secularism does not have the same contours in Paris, in Strasbourg, or in Mayotte]" (ibid., 45).

37. See Emile Poulat, *Eglise contre Bourgeoisie: Introduction au devenir du catholicisme actuel* (Paris: Casterman, 1977), chap. 3.

38. The common term that I have translated here as "fundamentalist Islam" is *l'islamisme*. At an earlier time, when there were very few Muslims in France to speak of (it is estimated that there were fifty thousand in 1900), the enemy was identified quite simply as "Islam." In referring to the anticolonial movements in North Africa immediately after the Second World War, for example—with which the French Communist Party sympathized—Georges Duhamel wrote: "Morocco, Tunisia, Algeria. . . . Everything in these countries is working against France: the forces of Islam as well as those of communism" (*Le Figaro*, February 5, 1954; cited in Gérard Vincent, "Communism as a Way of Life," in *A History of Private Life*, vol. 5, ed. A. Prost and G. Vincent [Cambridge: Harvard University Press, 1991], 329). Many commentators on present French attitudes toward North African "immigrants" have insisted that they must be understood as the restructuration of racist attitudes in colonial Algeria, of the experience of a brutal war of independence, and of the French concern to keep the Islamists from coming democratically to power there. For an interesting account of the interconnection between concerns about Algerian immigration and about Islamic fundamentalism (expressed in the notorious Folembray affair of 1994), see Thomas Deltombe, "Quand l'islamisme devient spectacle," *Le Monde diplomatique*, August 2004.

39. Although the state use of torture is recorded by organizations such as Human Rights Watch and objected to by most liberals, neither the publication of evidence nor the protests have a long-term inhibiting effect on its practitioners. Witness, most recently, the U.S. employment of torture in Guantánamo Bay, Iraq, and Afghanistan—and the impunity that senior officials (government and military) enjoy with regard to it.

40. Vincent Geisser, *La Nouvelle Islamophobie* (Paris: La Découverte, 2003), 15.

41. Daniel Lindenberg, *Le Rappel à l'ordre: Enquête sur les nouveaux réactionnaires* (Paris: Seuil, 2002).

42. "Many journalists and intellectuals consider the distinction between religion and politics in this case to be specious, and give one to understand that Islam (and Muslims) ought to be subjected to surveillance. The Catholics, like Alain Besançon and Pierre Manent, who have long been hostile to 'dialogue' with the Prophet's Faithful, find in this an excellent occasion for settling accounts with what they consider to be the errors and strayings of the post-Conciliar Church, and thus approach sections of the population who are most hostile to modernity. . . . What is new is that these thinkers are now followed not only by other, publicly Catholic individuals, but also by unbelievers unhappy with the idea—even before the World Trade Center attack—that Catholicism should be the only religion to be openly attacked with impunity" (ibid., 38).

43. "Les menaces à la laïcité vont de pair avec un regain de violence à l'égard de personnes appartenant ou censées appartenir à la communauté juive [The threats to secularism go together with a rise in violence toward persons belonging to or supposed to belong to the Jewish community]." The report then adds in strong terms: "Toute injure, toute action, toute violence à caractère antisémite est répréhensible et doit être punie sévèrement, conformément à la lois. [All injury, every act of violence having an anti-Semitic character is reprehensible and must be punished severely in accordance with the law]" (*Laïcité et République*, 105).

44. "Rémy Schwartz, the *conseiller d'état* who in effect ran Stasi's commission and oversaw its hearings, told me about the first veil hearings, in 1989. 'There was one common thread,' he said. 'We were there to judge law, not souls. But this time I was reinforced in my conviction that a new law was necessary. The older laws were not applicable to the situation now. What we have now is part of a global politics of anti-Semitism, and it had to be limited.' Schwartz reminded me that in six years the majority of citizens in Holland's four biggest cities will be Muslim" (Jane Kramer, "Taking the Veil," *The New Yorker*, November 22, 2004, 70–71).

45. Some young men interviewed in Angouleme angrily claimed that "Having a political lobby that represents the interests of a particular community is perfectly acceptable for some; for others, the very idea of a community is forbidden." (In France, unlike the United States, the mere suggestion that Jews "have a political lobby" is heard with alarm by liberals because it is typically part of right-wing rhetoric.) It is the journalists—so these young men insisted—who, on the one hand, repeatedly describe a youth as "North African" or "Arab" (especially when he is in trouble) and, on the other hand, express outrage at the identification of an intellectual as a Jew. (The reference here is to the scandal caused by Tariq Ramadan, a well-known Swiss professor and activist, when he identified certain French public intellectuals as Jews.) See Phillippe Bernard, "On nous qualifie sans cesse d' 'Arabes' et on prétend nous empêcher de nous situer par rapport à l'Islam," *Le Monde*, July 5, 2004.

46. Complaints about increasing anti-Semitism in France relate largely to such things as desecration of Jewish graves, damage to synagogues and other property, and insults to Jewish children wearing kippas in school playgrounds and in the streets. Although such acts are highly offensive and disturbing, it is necessary to bear in mind that they can be perpetrated by a handful of hoodlums. There is still, to my knowledge, no comprehensive study of anti-Semitism as institutional discrimination—i.e., as the systematic prejudice promoting social, economic, and political exclusions and inequalities—something for which there is ample evidence relating to people of African and Arab origin. The assimilation of Jews into French society appears to be well advanced, despite social prejudice in some quarters against them. France has had several Jewish prime ministers since the Second World War—a record unmatched by any other liberal democracy. One wonders whether

a prime minister of West African or Arab origin is even conceivable in this secular Republic that claims to see no religious or ethnic differences among its citizens.

47. See the excellent article by Dominique Vidal, "Les Pompiers pyromanes de l'antisémitisme," *Le Monde Diplomatique*, May 2004, which recounts the mounting accusations of anti-Semitism against anyone publicly critical of Sharon's policies toward the Palestinians. Vidal argues powerfully for a *joint* campaign against anti-Semitism and Islamophobia, in spite of moves to separate the two in order to give the former priority.

48. Take, for example, "Je hais l'islam, entre autres . . . ," by the psychoanalyst and author Patrick Declerck on the Analyses et Débats page of *Le Monde*, August 12, 2004. The article explodes with rage against "Islam." (All religions are collective neuroses, as Freud said, but Islam is absolutely the worst.) The article considers itself to be presenting a daring and original view (one should reclaim the right to hate, to identify the enemy publicly, and to express one's hatred of him), but in fact it is neither. Hatred of Islam (Muslims) is common—and is more commonly expressed in *acts* than in words. Of course, Declerck's piece does not reflect the viewpoint of *Le Monde*. My point is not that the article should not have been published; it is simply that an argumentative article written by a non-Jew with the title "I hate Judaism" would be inconceivable today in any respectable daily. What does that indicate about the patterns of affect underlying the secular Republic?

49. See, e.g., Jean Daniel, "Anti-sémitisme: La Vérité en face," *Le Nouvel Observateur*, July 15–21, 2004.

50. See above, n. 25.

51. Esther Benbassa, "Juifs de France, des sionistes sans sionisme," *Le Monde*, August 31, 2004.

52. Benbassa points out that since the end of the 1950s, in the wake of the process of decolonization, most Jews from Morocco and Tunisia went to Israel, while Algerian Jews, having been French citizens since 1870, went to the hexagon. She does not note, however, the new historiography written by the latter about their assimilation into French culture since the latter part of the nineteenth century. The Crémieux Decree, which gave French citizenship to Algerian Jews, is regarded ambivalently as a moment in the imposition of metropolitan secular culture on the latter. See Pierre Birnbaum, ed., *Histoire politique des Juifs de France entre universalisme et particularisme* (Paris: Presses de la Fondation nationale des sciences politiques, 1990).

53. This is the subject of an interesting ethnography, *The Architecture of Memory: A Jewish-Muslim Household in Colonial Algeria, 1937–1962*, by Joëlle Bahloul, who reconstructs a vanished domestic life as remembered by her relatives. According to this author, relations between Jews and Muslims in Algeria were amicable. The former's sense of fearfulness arises partly from the memory of anti-Semitism directed at them by the Christian pieds-noirs—especially under the Vichy government during the Second World War—and partly from the militant hostility of all Islamists, including Algerian Islamists, toward Israel.

54. Muslims complain of bias on the part of the state in its response to incidents of racism. Thus when a Jewish school was destroyed by arson, they say, government ministers were quick to denounce anti-Semitism, even though police investigations had not yet arrived at a definite conclusion about the crime. When two mosques were fire-bombed, statements from government sources came only after much prodding ("Les Responsables Musulmans déplorent le temps de réaction des politiques après l'incendie de deux lieux de culte," *Le Monde*, March 8, 2004). In fact, throughout France far more mosques have been deliberately set on fire or vandalized than synagogues, and yet—so Muslims say—it is only the latter that are as a rule afforded police protection (see "France: Land of Phobias," *Middle East International*, March 19, 2004). Even the Interior Ministry, Muslims point out, finds it necessary to compile statistics on anti-Semitic incidents but not on Islamophobic

ones. This bias on the part of the authorities is echoed in the media, they say, where every anti-Semitic incident is highlighted and Islamophobic ones often underplayed.

55. Total war as a modern strategy was invented by French generals in their conquest of Algeria, and torture as a planned part of counterinsurgency warfare was perfected as an art by French officers in Algeria.

56. Joan Wolf, *Harnessing the Holocaust: The Politics of Memory in France* (Stanford: Stanford University Press, 2004), 23.

57. In this regard, see Henri Rousso, *The Vichy Syndrome: History and Memory in France since 1944* (Cambridge: Harvard University Press, 1991).

58. Consider the recent public statements of Nicolas Sarkozy, head of the right-of-center Union pour un Mouvement Populaire (UMP), who not only hopes to become President of the Republic but also wants to strengthen ties with America and further Americanize French society. His interventions in the matter of anti-Semitism are carefully calculated. Thus on April 28, 2004, on his return from the United States, "where he had been received with great ceremony by the influential American Jewish Committee (AJC), he accused the [previous, socialist] Jospin government of giving France the reputation of being 'an anti-Semitic country.' This statement set off a lively polemic with the left." See "Sarkozy veut convertir les juifs à sa religion élyséenne," *Libération*, December 14, 2004.

59. The phenomenon of men beating their female partners remains quite widespread in France—see, e.g.: Catherine Simon, "Hommes violents et fermés," *Le Monde*, March 24, 2004; Ignacio Ramonet, "Violences mâles," *Le Monde diplomatique*, June 2004; and Blandine Grosjean, "En France, des femmes tuées en silence," *Libération*, September 9, 2004. Ramonet's survey of violence by males toward female partners in Europe, written after the death of the actress Marie Trintignant at the hands of her lover Bertrand Cantat, gives the startling figure of six women killed every month in France alone. One wonders how many of them die because they reject the veil.

60. Islamic law treats men and women unequally, but it does give women rights. I say this because it is a popular misconception in the West that "Islam" gives women no rights, as if they were all equivalent to slaves.

61. E. Terray, "Headscarf Hysteria," in *New Left Review*, no. 26 (March/April 2004).

62. See Michelle Perrot, "The Family Triumphant," in *A History of Private Life*, vol. 4, ed. M. Perrot (Cambridge: Harvard University Press, 1990), 105.

63. At the end of June 2004, a large number of graves of colonial Muslim soldiers in a military cemetery in Alsace were vandalized by neo-Nazis. Headstones were damaged and daubed with swastikas. Reaction on the part of the government and major parties was swift and unequivocal. The president, the prime minister and the interior minister condemned the acts strongly. But it is not entirely clear what motivated them on this occasion, since there had been a stream of similar acts against Muslims in France, even in Alsace itself, without such a quick response. Was it the perception that these acts "are an insult to the memory of soldiers who gave their lives for our fatherland" (Jacques Chirac)? Was it that "respect for the dead, *whoever* they may be, *whatever* their religion, is *a respect that is required of us all*" (Jean-Pierre Raffarin)? (See "Profanation de 50 tombes musulmanes en Alsace," *Le Monde*, June, 24, 2004; my emphasis.) The outrage expressed in such cases by representatives of a rigorously secular state is intriguing. Positivism notwithstanding, the dead are not just dead, and they are readily accorded a "respect" that is less easy to give to some of the living.

64. "L'État a pour vocation de consolider les valeurs communes qui fondent le lien social dans notre pays. Parmi ces valeurs, l'égalité entre l'homme et la femme, pour être une conquête récente, n'en a pas moins pris une place importante dans notre droit. Elle est un élément du pacte républi-

cain d'aujourd'hui. L'État ne saurait rester passif face à toute atteinte à ce principe [The task of the state is to consolidate the common values that establish the social bond in our country. Among those values, the equality of man and woman does not have a less important place in our law simply because it is a recent achievement. It is an element of today's republican pact. The state cannot remain passive when confronting any attack against this principle]" (*Laïcité et République*, 35).

65. "La Crise du catholicisme vient de son immobilisme face aux changements culturels" (interview with Danièle Hervieu-Léger), *Le Monde*, August 7, 2004, 2.

66. See the fascinating "Essay on French Singularity" in Mona Ozouf's *Women's Words* (Chicago: University of Chicago Press, 1997).

67. Ibid., 272. Commenting on Ozouf's book, Elizabeth Badinter agrees that in France, as opposed to England, Germany, and America, men have changed more easily in a civilized direction by conceding women's claims. She not only makes an unsupported claim for French exceptionalism but also offers a hilarious explanation: the fact that Frenchmen do not fear their women as men do in other countries, that their relations with Frenchwomen are gentler, more interdependent, more seductive even, than are the relations of men in other nations with their women, Badinter tells us, is due to French mothers not being as possessive of their sons as Anglo-Saxon mothers are. (See E. Badinter, "L'Exception française,," *Le Débat* 87 [November-December 1995].) Thus the power of universality is made dependent on the alleged uniqueness of French mother-son relations!

68. Ozouf, *Women's Words*, 273.

69. Incidentally, not everyone in favor of gender equality employs a theological language. Thus a group of feminists have argued vigorously against the new law simply on the grounds that it penalizes women only and that its effect will be educationally disastrous because it will push young women who refuse to remove their headscarves out of state schools and into private religious schools or back into patriarchal family life. They argue against self-styled "principled feminism" and for what they call "responsible feminism," which takes seriously into account the consequences of actions in the real world. In other words, they employ fruitfully a method close to casuistry. See Communiqué de l'association *Femmes Publiques*, "Être féministe, ce n'est pas exclure!" http://sysiphe.org/).

70. Joan Wallach Scott, *Only Paradoxes to Offer* (Cambridge: Harvard University Press, 1996), 172–73.

71. The integrity of the Republic was finally achieved through the secularizing efforts of humanist politicians such as Leon Gambetta, Emile Littré, and Jules Ferry (all followers of Auguste Comte's philosophy) in the latter part of the nineteenth century. See Claude Nicolet, *L'Idée Républicaine en France (1789–1924)* (Paris: Gallimard, 1982), esp. chap. 6.

72. "Each form of civilization has its social sacred. We respect that of others, so let them respect ours. For us it is the pact of citizenship. For others it is divine revelation" (Régis Debray, "Chaque modèle de civilisation a son sacré social," *Le Figaro*, February 14, 2004; see also his *Critique de la raison politique* [Paris, 1981]).

73. http://www.laicite-republique.org/association/index.htm.

74. Henri Pena-Ruiz, "Laïcité et égalité, leviers d'émancipation," *Le Monde diplomatique*, February 2004, 9.

75. The idea that America—like France, the bearer of a revolutionary tradition—has an international role as a redeeming nation took shape at the turn of the nineteenth century. Liberal Christians, closely associated with leading politicians and businessmen, argued strongly that it was America's *Christian* duty to spread brotherhood, democracy, and perpetual peace in the world. See Richard Gamble, *The War for Righteousness: Progressive Christianity, the Great War, and the Rise of the Messianic Nation* (Wilmington, Delaware: ISI Books, 2003).

76. Ibid.

77. See, e.g., Pena-Ruiz, "Laïcité et égalité, leviers d'émancipation," and Pierre Tevanian, "Une loi antilaïque, antiféministe et antisocial," both in *Le Monde diplomatique*, February 2004.

78. Nawal al-Saadawi, "An Unholy Alliance," *Al-Ahram Weekly*, February 18, 2004.

79. Vincent Geisser, *La Nouvelle Islamophobie* (Paris: La Découverte, 2003), 31; emphasis in original. Geisser cites the *Nouvel Observateur* for the picture now favored by much of the media: "Are these young girls from the St. Etienne suburb—a sinister territory controlled by fundamentalists—manipulated? They are, at any rate, indoctrinated by an active Muslim environment. In the course of their conversation, one learns that they benefit from educational help from an association close to the UOIF, that one of the girls goes every year to Nièvre in order to follow courses of religious education given by Saudi Arabian imams, that another devotes every Sunday to religion: recitation in the morning, the study of texts in the afternoon. They often go to the Islamic bookshops and to the new Association of Emancipated French Muslim Women in Lyon, and they talk calmly of militants of the pietistic Tabligh movement" (ibid., 32).

80. "Il ne peut se contenter d'un retrait des affaires religeuses et spirituelles [It cannot limit itself to withdrawal from religious or spiritual matters]" (*Laïcité et République*, 32).

81. Tevanian, "Une loi antilaïque, antiféministe et antisocial," 8.

82. "L'avis énonce que le principe de laïcité impose que 'l'enseignement soit dispensé dans le respect, d'une part, de cette neutralité par les programmes et par les enseignants, d'autre part, de la liberté de conscience des élèves' [The decree states that the principle of secularism demands that education be provided respecting, on the one hand, by that neutrality on the part of the programs and the teachers, and on the other hand, the freedom of conscience of pupils]" (*Laïcité et République*, 66).

83. A well-known example of this is the ambivalence with which many people in rural France regard Parisians.

Peter van der Veer, Pim Fortuyn, Theo van Gogh, and the Politics of Tolerance in the Netherlands

NOTE: First published in *Public Culture* 18, no. 1 (2006): 111–25; © 2006 Duke University Press. Reprinted by permission; all rights reserved. I want to thank Claudio Lomnitz, Markha Valenta, and my audience when I presented the argument at the New School in February 2005 for incisive comments.

1. These events have been reported in the Dutch newspapers. A general description has been given in a book by the Dutch journalist Hans Wansink, *De Erfenis van Pim Fortuyn na de opstand van de kiezers* (Amsterdam: Meulenhoff, 2004).

2. I am thinking here not only of such great and classy entertainers as Wim Kan and Wim Sonneveld, but also of more low-class entertainers, such as Albert Mol and Andre van Duyn.

3. On the process of globalization and its discontents in Holland, see Peter van der Veer, "Nederland bestaat niet meer," in *Islam en het "beschaafde Westen"* (Amsterdam: Meulenhoff, 2002).

4. For a general description of these events, see Kees Schuyt and Ed Taverne, "1950: Welvaart in zwart-wit," *Nederlandse cultuur in Europese context* (The Hague: Sdu, 2004).

5. *In het zicht van de toekomst—Sociaal en Cultureel Rapport* (The Hague: Sociaal-Cultureel Planbureau, 2004).

6. Unni Wikan, *Generous Betrayal: Politics of Culture in the New Europe* (Chicago: University of Chicago Press, 2001).

7. Nancy Fraser and Axel Honneth, *Redistribution or Recognition? A Political-Philosophical Exchange* (London: Verso, 2003).

Job Cohen, Can a Minority Retain Its Identity in Law? The 2005 Multatuli Lecture

NOTE:This lecture was delivered in the Grote Kerk of Breda on October 21, 2005. The Multatuli Lecture is a joint Dutch-Flemish annual event. It has taken place since 1996, alternately in Breda in the Netherlands and in Leuven, Belgium, and is supported by the governments of the provinces of Noord-Brabant and Vlaams-Brabant, as well the cities of Breda and Leuven and several private parties. The event is organized by the Multatuli Foundation, the European Centre for Ethics, and various socio-cultural organizations.

The Multatuli Lectures concern topics related to multiculturalism, addressing such questions as: Under what circumstances will cultural confrontation lead to enrichment rather than antagonism? In what way is culture exploited for political ends? and What role can culture play in the development of democratic relations?

Multatuli, which is Latin for "I have born much," is the pseudonym of the Dutch writer and journalist Eduard Douwes Dekker (1820–87). After eighteen years of colonial civil service in the Dutch East Indies, he returned to Europe in 1856 a disillusioned man. The way indigenous peoples were treated in the Dutch East Indies, by their own people as well as by the Dutch rulers, offended him so much that he resigned after a public conflict. In his novel *Max Havelaar*, published in 1860, he recorded his experiences. The book, the first anticolonial novel written in the Netherlands, was an instant success and became a bestseller throughout Europe. Multatuli became a kind of Dutch national conscience of his time, inspiring movements such as the freethinkers, socialists, and anarchists—even though in Dutch society he remained an outsider with little popularity. He is now considered one of the greatest writers in the Dutch language.

The form of Multatuli's writings was diverse: sometimes they consisted in only one or two sharply formulated sentences; at other times he wrote novels. Many of these miscellanies were published in uniform volumes called *Ideas*, of which seven appeared between 1862 and 1877. "Idea no. 7," mentioned at the start of my lecture, is taken from the first volume of *Ideas*, published in 1862.

In the conception and writing of this lecture, I am indebted to Maria Cuartas y de Marchena, my chief of staff and principal speechwriter.

The Dutch text of the lecture can be accessed at: www.amsterdam.nl/gemeente/documenten/toespraken/cohen/2005. Its Dutch title is "Ruimte" (Space).

1. Piet de Rooij, *Republiek van rivaliteiten* (Republic of rivalries) (Amsterdam: Mets & Schilt, 2002).

2. See Job Cohen, "Cleveringarede 2002," University of Leiden, 2002.

3. Hans Boutellier, *Intermediair*, October 31, 2002.

4. Interview by Bart Top with James Kennedy in *Religie en verdraagzaamheid* (Religion and tolerance) (Ten Have: Uitgeverij, 2005), 36–47.

5. Sjoerd de Jong in *NRC Handelsblad*, November 30, 2004.

6. See Top, interview with James Kennedy, *Religie en verdraagzaamheid*, 42.

7. *Staatsblad* (Stb) 2004, 681.

8. *Tractaatblad* (Trb) 2005, 77.

9. Article 7 of the Constitution reads:

1. No one shall require prior permission to publish thoughts or opinions through the press, without prejudice to the responsibility of every person under the law.

2. Rules concerning radio and television shall be laid down by Act of Parliament. There shall be no prior supervision of the content of a radio or television broadcast.

3. No one shall be required to submit thoughts or opinions for prior approval in order to disseminate them by means other than those mentioned in the preceding paragraphs, without prejudice to the responsibility of every person under the law. The holding of performances open to persons younger than sixteen years of age may be regulated by Act of Parliament in order to protect good morals.

4. The preceding paragraphs do not apply to commercial advertising.

10. Article 6 of the Constitution reads:

1. Everyone shall have the right to profess freely his religion or belief, either individually or in community with others, without prejudice to his responsibility under the law.

2. Rules concerning the exercise of this right other than in buildings and enclosed places may be laid down by Act of Parliament for the protection of health, in the interests of traffic, and to combat or prevent disorders.

11. Article 9 of the Constitution reads:

1. The right of assembly and demonstration shall be recognized, without prejudice to the responsibility of everyone under the law.

2. Rules to protect health, and in the interests of traffic and to combat or prevent disorders may be laid down by Act of Parliament.

12. Article 23 of the Constitution reads:

1. Education shall be the constant concern of the government.

2. All persons shall be free to provide education, without prejudice to the authorities' right of supervision and, with regard to forms of education designated by law, their right to examine the competence and moral integrity of teachers, to be regulated by Act of Parliament.

3. Education provided by public authorities shall be regulated by Act of Parliament, paying due respect to everyone's religion or belief.

4. The authorities shall ensure that primary education is provided in a sufficient number of public-authority schools in every municipality. Deviations from this provision may be permitted under rules to be established by Act of Parliament on condition that there is opportunity to receive the said form of education.

5. The standards required of schools financed either in part or in full from public funds shall be regulated by Act of Parliament, with due regard, in the case of private schools, to the freedom to provide education according to religious or other belief.

6. The requirements for primary education shall be such that the standards both of private schools fully financed from public funds and of public-authority schools are fully guaranteed. The relevant provisions shall respect in particular the freedom of private schools to choose their teaching aids and to appoint teachers as they see fit.

7. Private primary schools that satisfy the conditions laid down by Act of Parliament shall be financed from public funds according to the same standards as public-authority schools. The conditions under which private secondary education and preuniversity education receive contributions from public funds shall be laid down by Act of Parliament.

13. Article 10 of the Constitution reads:

1. Everyone shall have the right to respect for his privacy, without prejudice to restrictions laid down by or pursuant to Act of Parliament.

2. Rules to protect privacy shall be laid down by Act of Parliament in connection with the recording and dissemination of personal data.

3. Rules concerning the rights of persons to be informed of data recorded concerning them and of the use that is made thereof, and to have such data corrected, shall be laid down by Act of Parliament.

14. See the judgment of the three-judge criminal chamber of The Hague Court of Appeal, November 18, 2002.

15. Judgment in interim injunction proceedings of The Hague District Court, March 15, 2005.

16. The Constitution provides the scope to deal adequately with social issues resulting in part from the increasingly plural nature of society. This concerns issues such as discrimination, wearing a headscarf and other items of clothing or jewelry that reflect religious views, honor killings, female genital mutilation, and the creation of prayer areas in public buildings, such as schools. The Constitution need not be amended for this purpose. This is the main conclusion to be drawn from the policy document "Grondrechten in een pluriforme samenleving" (Fundamental rights in a plural society), Ministry of the Interior and Kingdom Relations, May 18, 2004.

17. See *De sociale staat van Nederland 2005*, Social and Cultural Planning Office (SCP), The Hague, September 2005, chap. 2, "Demografie, vergrijzing, verdunning, verkleuring" (Demography, aging, falling birth rate, and the changing racial mix), 17–46.

18. Mérove Gijsberts and Jaco Dagevos, *Uit elkaars buurt: De invloed van etnische concentratie op integratie en beeldvorming* (Not in touch: the influence of ethnic concentration on integration and perceptions), SCP publication 2005/13, Social and Cultural Planning Office, The Hague, June 2005.

19. See Job Cohen, Abel Herzberg Lecture 2001, "Grenzen" (Boundaries), De Rode Hoed, Amsterdam, 2001, in which I submit that "Abel Herzberg argued, however, throughout his life that anti-Semitism was not a Jewish problem and that it is not therefore the attitude or behavior of the Jews that determines how they will be treated by society. On the contrary, Herzberg stated (e.g., in his essay 'On the cause and intention of the persecution of the Jews in Germany,," 1967) that 'it is a problem about which a minority never and nowhere decides, but is always decided by the majority. If it is about the status of the minority itself, it depends entirely on the will of the majority whether the minority has any say in the matter.'"

20. Remco Campert, in *De Volkskrant* of November 3, 2004.

21. See: "Staat maken op elkaar" (Counting on one another), WRR lecture by Job Cohen in The Hague on November 27, 2003; "Scheiding van kerk en staat in de 21-ste eeuw" (Separation of church and state in the twenty-first century), Willem van Oranjelezing 2004, lecture given by Job Cohen in Delft on June 1, 2004; "De zoektocht naar sociale cohesie" (The search for social cohesion), address by Job Cohen on the occasion of the celebration of the fiftieth anniversary of the establishment of the Dutch Society of Mayors in Alphen aan de Rijn on October 6, 2005.

Bettina Prato, Prophetic Justice in a Home Haunted by Strangers: Transgressive Solidarity and Trauma in the Work of an Israeli Rabbis' Group

1. This essay is based on fieldwork conducted in Jerusalem in the fall of 2002 and spring of 2004. For their generosity, patience, and kindness, I thank everybody at RHR headquarters, particularly Rabbi Michael Schwartz. Heartfelt gratitude also goes to the rabbis who took time to meet with me and talk about their involvement in the group. Among them, I am especially indebted to Rabbi Jeremy Milgrom, whose comments on my work have been challenging and precious. My gratitude also goes to Wendy Brown and Mario Nordio, who have been attentive and encouraging readers of the first draft of the paper, and to two anonymous reviewers and Helen Tartar for their suggestions about how the paper could be improved. Of course, responsibility for the interpretation of RHR's work and of various texts discussed here is mine.

2. *Al-Nakbah* is the term commonly used in Arabic to refer to the creation of the state of Israel in part of Mandate Palestine and the subsequent defeat of Arab forces in the 1948 Arab-Israeli

war, which led to the forced displacement of hundreds of thousands of Palestinians. Like the Hebrew word for the Holocaust (*Shoah*), *Nakbah* corresponds to the English term for "catastrophe."

3. Freud's analysis of trauma is perhaps most clearly formulated in *Beyond the Pleasure Principle*, ed. and trans. James Strachey (New York: Norton, 1961), where psychic trauma is defined as a wound in the protective membrane that shields the psyche from external stimuli, resulting in the failed binding of certain events to images or symbols that may be stored in memory and then elaborated and communicated through language. Psychic trauma is thus not only an experience of violent victimization or intense suffering but also the occurrence of a failure to represent and symbolize experience. As I will mention later, on an individual level this failure may lead to a compulsion to repeat traumatic events, which Freud linked to a "death principle" that drives us retroactively to attempt to "undo" trauma. Some authors (e.g., Vamik Volkan) evoke a similar process to explain mutual violence between ethnic groups whose identity narratives are marked by events passed on as "unspeakable."

4. Examples of such spaces include schools, national commemoration ceremonies (e.g., Holocaust Day), the rhetoric of political parties, public debates on questions related to security and Israeli-Palestinian relations, the media, the world of art and culture, and so forth.

5. See, e.g., Shoshana Felman and Dori Laub, *Testimony: Crises of Witnessing in Literature, Psychoanalysis, and History* (New York: Routledge, 1991).

6. Derrida develops the theme of sovereignty and of its relation to "ipseity" in several of his works, most recently *Rogues: Two Essays on Reason*, trans. Pascale-Anne Brault and Michael Naas (Stanford: Stanford University Press, 2005), esp. pt. 1.

7. Freud, *Beyond the Pleasure Principle*, 40–49.

8. See, e.g.: Judith Herman, *Trauma and Recovery* (New York: Basic Books, 1992); Ronnie Janoff-Bulman, *Shattered Assumptions: Toward a New Psychology of Trauma* (New York: The Free Press, 1992); or the standard definition of trauma and post-traumatic stress disorder given by the American Psychiatric Association, *Diagnostic and Statistical Manual of Psychiatric Disorders*, vol. 3 (DSM-III) (Washington, D.C.: American Psychiatric Association, 1980).

9. Vamik Volkan, *Bloodlines: From Ethnic Pride to Ethnic Terrorism* (Boulder, Colo.: Westview, 1997).

10. As concerns Israeli society, see, e.g., Edna Lomsky-Feder and Eyal Ben-Ari's "Trauma, Therapy and Responsibility: Psychology and War in Contemporary Israel," in *The Practice of War*, ed. Monica Boeck, Aparna Rao, and Michael Bollig (Oxford: Berghahn Books, forthcoming).

11. On the notion of "hospitality of visitation" as the "im-possible" horizon of the political in democratic contexts, see, e.g., Derrida's conversation with Giovanna Borradori in the aftermath of 9/11 in G. Borradori, *Philosophy in a Time of Terror: Dialogues with Jürgen Habermas and Jacques Derrida* (Chicago: University of Chicago Press, 2003), 128–29.

12. This is in contrast to some recent elaborations of ethical and political projects that build upon trauma theory, particularly in literary criticism, cultural studies, and political theory. An example of such literature is Kelly Oliver, *Witnessing: Beyond Recognition* (Minneapolis: University of Minnesota Press, 2001).

13. For a review of different meta-theoretical approaches to the notion of human rights (notably universalist liberalism, communitarianism, cosmopolitan pragmatism, and antifoundationalist theory), see Tim Dunne and Nicholas J. Wheeler, eds., *Human Rights in Global Politics* (Cambridge: Cambridge University Press, 1999).

14. As Levinas puts it, "If there were no order of Justice, there would be no limit to my responsibility" ("Philosophy, Justice, and Love," in *Entre Nous: Thinking of the Other*, trans. Barbara Harshav, with Michael B. Smith [New York: Columbia University Press, 1998], 105).

15. Emmanuel Levinas, *Alterity and Transcendence* (New York: Columbia University Press, 1999), 145, 146.

16. Ibid., 149.

17. Peter Jones, "Human Rights and Diverse Cultures: Continuity or Discontinuity?" *Critical Review of International Social and Political Philosophy* 3, no. 1 (Spring 2000): 38. For an example of the literature that challenges the universality of Western notions of human rights, see Daniel Bell, "The Limits of Liberal Justice," *Political Theory* 26, no. 4 (1998).

18. See, e.g., the liberal debate on tolerance and multiculturalism in contemporary Western democracies.

19. Quoted from a flier distributed by the group and entitled "Who Are Rabbis for Human Rights?"

20. This aspect of their work has become more prominent in the past couple of years (2004–5), given increasing poverty and the erosion of social security programs in Israel.

21. The notion of *tikkun olam* (or *tikkun ha olam*) derives from a mystical legend in the Lurianic Kabbalah (named after the sixteenth-century rabbi Isaac Luria), telling how God made the world by pouring a holy light into all things. The light was so intense, however, that it broke the vessels that were to contain it, filling the world with shards. The task of human beings is to put back together whatever they find "broken," so as to "repair" the divine beauty and wholeness of creation.

22. In this regard, it is important to note that RHR members have different interpretations of the meaning of the principle of justice or of any other values that are central to the group. Only recently has RHR tried to produce a detailed exposition of its textual and religious bases. In relation to specific issues and events, members are often divided among themselves. One notable exception has been the issue of Israeli demolitions of Palestinian houses built or enlarged without legal permits, which has also been at the center of Arik Ascherman's recently concluded trial in Jerusalem. In support of his position at the trial, Ascherman was able to collect the signatures of over five hundred rabbis from different strands of Judaism and different countries, notably the U.S.

23. In this regard, it is also not coincidental that most members of RHR are originally American.

24. Yeshayahu Leibowitz, *Judaism, Human Values, and the Jewish State* (Cambridge: Harvard University Press, 1992), 241.

25. Ibid., 207.

26. Ibid., 88.

27. Lenn E. Goodman, *Judaism, Human Rights, and Human Values* (New York: Oxford University Press, 1998), 55.

28. Another possible radical reading of Jewish humanism is the one offered by Levinas, for whom "the man whose rights must be defended is in the first place the other man, it is not initially myself. It is not the concept 'man' which is at the basis of this humanism, it is the other man" (Emmanuel Levinas, *Nine Talmudic Readings* [Bloomington: Indiana University Press, 1990], 98). Of course, and especially considering the empirical orientation of the present essay, we must keep in mind that Levinas explicitly denied that Palestinians and Jews or Israelis were mutual "others" linked by ethical relations of "responsibility" in the specific sense he gave to the term.

29. David Novak, "Religious Human Rights in the Judaic Tradition," available on-line at http://www.law.emory.edu/EILR/volumes/spring96/novak.html.

30. This literature includes primarily the *RHR Newsletter*, weekly biblical commentaries (Parashat haShavua), and Noam Zohar, *Life, Freedom, and Equality in the Jewish Tradition* (Jerusalem, 2003).

31. Zohar, *Life, Freedom, and Equality in the Jewish Tradition*; quoted from an unpublished English translation.

32. Ibid., 9.

33. The dynamic relationship between infinity and being, whereby the latter is expression, crystallization, contraction, and betrayal of the former (as well as its realization), is discussed in many of Levinas's texts, sometimes with rather different theoretical and ethical implications. Here I am mostly referring to Emmanuel Levinas, *Otherwise than Being or Beyond Essence* (Pittsburgh: Duquesne University Press, 1998).

34. Zohar, *Life, Freedom, and Equality*, 5.

35. Hannah Arendt, *The Human Condition* (Chicago: University of Chicago Press, 1998).

36. Haim H. Cohn, *Human Rights in the Bible and Talmud* (Tel Aviv: MOD Books, 1989).

37. Ibid.

38. Levinas, *Otherwise than Being*.

39. David Forman, "Rabbis for Human Rights," *The Jerusalem Post*, January 10, 2002.

40. Marc Ellis, *Israel and Palestine out of the Ashes* (London: Pluto Press, 2002).

41. When I wrote the first draft of this essay in spring 2004, Ascherman and a colleague were on trial for obstructing police work in 2003 during the demolition of Palestinian homes in Beit Hanina and Issawiyyah, both Palestinian neighborhoods regarded by Israel as part of East Jerusalem. During those months, the RHR Executive Director was also arrested and later released after taking part in demonstrations against the the separation wall, alongside Palestinian villagers from Biddu, just north of Jerusalem in the West Bank. After giving court testimony on September 21, 2004, and in late December 2004 that challenged the justice of Israeli laws in light of both international law and the Torah, Ascherman was finally convicted for obstructing policy in the course of duty in March 2005. Although the prosecution immediately asked to revoke the conviction (apparently in order not to set a negative precedent that would draw media attention at a time of public debate on "disengagement" from Gaza), the trial marked RHR's failure to obtain legal recognition of the injustice of the practice of demolition of homes, since it is virtually impossible for Palestinians to obtain building permits in areas claimed by Israel, particularly within greater Jerusalem.

42. These are Orthodox (in its different variants), Conservative (Masorti), and Progressive (Reform) Judaism. The first represents the majority among religious Jews (less than one-third of the population) in Israel, and it is also the strand of Judaism that has historically enjoyed exclusive recognition by the state. This has entailed privileged access to state funds and control over institutions regulating marriage, conversion, identification of who is a Jew (and thus right of citizenship), and kashrut. In recent years, there have been openings on the part of the state to non-Orthodox Jewish institutions, but the balance of power is still very much in favor of the Orthodox.

43. In an article in *The Jerusalem Post* on January 10, 2002, David Forman wrote: "RHR offsets a portrayal of Judaism in Israel that is often characterized by a chauvinistic theology, in which a national ego is projected onto God, and any act is justified as a Divine right. . . . In this world-view, anyone who opposes an extreme 'particular' version of a 'heavenly course' for the Jewish people in the Jewish state is a traitor. . . . Indeed, one would think that rabbis who oppose some of RHR's positions would do so in a way that would cling to the principle of pluralism: that is, disagreement 'for the sake of heaven.' But this is not the case with a small but vocal group within the Israeli Conservative movement. They have defied any pluralistic debate by labelling RHR members 'traitors' and 'enemies of the Jewish people.'"

44. An interesting analysis of Levinas's writings about Israel and Israeli Palestinian affairs is contained in Howard Caygill, *Levinas and the Political* (London: Routledge, 2002).

45. Leibowitz, *Judaism, Human Values, and the Jewish State*, 198.

46. Specifically, for Fackenheim "You shall not grant Hitler a posthumous victory" may be regarded as the 614th commandment of the Torah. See, e.g., Emil Fackenheim, *To Mend the World: Foundations of Post-Holocaust Thought* (New York: Schocken, 1982).

47. Butler speaks of this preoccupation, for instance, in "Violence, Mourning, Politics," where she reflects on the possibility of taking an experience of forced realization of vulnerability, such as 9/11 in the U.S., as a point of departure for imagining and practicing political community from a standpoint of mutual vulnerability among "others." The experience of RHR and of a few other groups in Israel/Palestine may speak to this possibility as prefigured or at least advocated by Butler. See her *Precarious Life: The Powers of Mourning and Violence* (London: Verso, 2004), 19–49.

48. Cathy Caruth, *Unclaimed Experience: Trauma, Narrative, and History* (Baltimore: The Johns Hopkins University Press, 1996).

49. David Forman, "Hell No, We Won't Go," *The Jerusalem Post*, February 28, 2002.

50. Samson Raphael Hirsch, *The Pentateuch*, translated and explained by Samson Raphael Hirsch, vol. 2: *Exodus*, English trans. Isaac Levy (London, 1960), 373.

51. Yehiel Grenimann, "Shomrei Mishpat: New Directions, Old Directions," *RHR Newsletter* 10 (January 2000): 3.

52. Interview with the author, Jerusalem, April 8, 2004.

53. Rabbi David Forman, "A Judaism for Our Day," *RHR Newsletter* 13 (April 2003): 3.

54. Rabbi Arik Ascherman, "Balata," message circulated through RHR mailing list.

55. Levinas, *Otherwise than Being*, 6.

56. Ascherman's speech was circulated to the RHR e-mail list on March 22 and 24, 2005.

57. One is reminded here of Arendt's linking of active togetherness to authentic power, as well as of Levinas's notion of respect as a necessary component of justice (understood as a political, rather than an ethical, category). In his words, "The respected one is not the one to whom, but with whom justice is done. Respect is a relationship between equals. Justice assumes that original equality" ("The I and the Totality," in *Entre Nous: Thinking of the Other*, trans. Barbara Harshav, with Michael B. Smith [New York: Columbia University Press, 1998], 35).

58. Abdelaziz Rantisi was a Hamas leader assassinated by the Israeli army in Gaza in April 2004.

Paola Marrati, Mysticism and the Foundation of the Open Society: Bergsonian Politics

1. Henri Bergson, *The Creative Mind* (1934; New York: Citadel Books, 1974).

2. Ibid., 101.

3. Ibid., 100–101.

4. Gilles Deleuze, *Difference and Repetition* (1968; New York: Columbia University Press, 1994), 211–12.

5. Adorno describes one of the essential aims of metaphysics in just the same terms. In his 1965 lectures published under the title *Metaphysics: Concept and Problems*, Adorno understands the key problem of Aristotle's philosophy to be bringing together the change in existing things with the Platonic demand for eternity and immutability. The concept of movement as the realization of a possibility provides the link between change and eternity that guarantees the ontological priority of immutability: "Latent in his philosophy is the contradiction between the Eleatic and Platonic element of the doctrine of Being and the unmistakable moment of change associated with Greek or Hellenic enlightenment. Thus all the construction of Aristotle's *Metaphysics* is really focused on this

one problem: how is change possible? . . . The answer to this question given by Aristotle . . . is that movement—by which he means an upward movement of change, the advancing amelioration of everything which is through its increasing determination by the absolute—is to be equated with the realization of the possible, insofar as the possible is opposed to natural causality. That is really Aristotle's central proposition. And this proposition, that movement is the realization of the possible, already implies the Hegelian thesis of history as progress in the consciousness of freedom . . . movement is the becoming real of the possible" (Theodor W. Adorno, *Metaphysics: Concept and Problems* [1998; Stanford: Stanford University Press, 2000], 81–82).

6. On the difference between the Greek and the modern way of understanding time, see Henri Bergson, *Creative Evolution* (1907; New York: Dover, 1998), 304–43.

7. Ibid., 342.

8. Apart from Deleuze, a remarkable exception is Levinas, who writes, in the preface added to the German translation of *Totality and Infinity* and included in the subsequent French editions of the book, that the Bergsonian concept of duration is one of the very few attempts to break with an ontological conception of time.

9. Bergson, *Creative Evolution*, 340.

10. Bergson, *The Creative Mind*, 90.

11. Ibid., 10.

12. The very idea of a singular concept for a singular object seems nonsensical from a philosophical perspective, as well as from the perspective of the ordinary definition of the term *concept*. This is a decisive point in Bergson's conception of philosophy, however. Against any tendencies to abstract generalization, Bergson believes in the possibility, indeed the necessity, for knowledge of the being of the singular, for respecting and adapting to the specificity of objects and events, and for the ability to recognize their novelty. In this regard, Bergson is calling for a philosophy of difference as the necessary counterpart to a philosophy committed to thinking time as the invention of the new.

13. Bergson's political activities are now well known, thanks to Philippe Soulez's remarkable *Bergson politique* (Paris: Presses Universitaires de France, 1989).

14. See Bergson, *Creative Evolution*, xiii.

15. Henri Bergson, *The Two Sources of Morality and Religion* (1932: Notre Dame, Ind.: University of Notre Dame Press, 1977), 15.

16. Ibid., 25.

17. Bergson thus openly rejects the idea of a "primitive mind," governed by its own rules, that Lévy-Bruhl had elaborated in his influential *La Mentalité primitive*, first published in 1922.

18. In this regard, Bergson anticipates the important work of scholars such as Leroi-Gourhan and Simondon on the impact of technological objects on human societies. See Gilbert Simondon, *Du mode d'existence des objets techniques* (1958; Paris: Aubier, 2001) and André Leroi-Gourhan, *Gesture and Speech* (1964; Cambridge: MIT Press, 1993).

19. Bergson thus provides an account of the "situation of exception" different from the one that Schmitt develops and Agamben further formalizes.

20. Bergson, *The Two Sources of Morality and Religion*, 33.

21. Ibid., 38.

22. Gilles Deleuze and Félix Guattari, *What Is Philosophy?* (1991; New York: Columbia University Press, 1994), 7.

23. Bergson, *The Two Sources of Morality and Religion*, 103 ff.

24. Ibid., 58.

25. Ibid., 317.

Jane Bennett, The Agency of Assemblages and the North American Blackout

NOTE:This essay first appeared in *Public Culture* 17, no. 3 (2005): 445–65; © Duke University Press. Reprinted by permission of the publisher; all rights reserved. I am grateful to Natalie Baggs, Diana Coole, William Connolly, Ben Corson, Jennifer Culbert, Ann Curthoys, John Docker, Ruby Lal, Patchen Markell, Gyanendra Pandey, Paul Saurette, Michael Shapiro, Helen Tartar, and the anonymous reviewers for Fordham University Press for their contributions to this essay.

1. See Michael Hardt and Antonio Negri, *Empire* (Cambridge: Harvard University Press, 2001) and *Multitude: War and Democracy in the Age of Empire* (New York: Penguin, 2004).

2. An assemblage is, first, an ad hoc grouping, a collectivity whose origins are historical and circumstantial, though its contingent status says nothing about its efficacy, which can be quite strong. An assemblage is, second, a living, throbbing grouping, whose coherence coexists with energies and countercultures that exceed and confound it. An assemblage is, third, a web with an uneven topography: some of the points at which the trajectories of actants cross each other are more heavily trafficked than others, and thus power is not equally distributed across the assemblage. An assemblage is, fourth, not governed by a central power: no one member has sufficient competence to fully determine the consequences of the activities of the assemblage. An assemblage, finally, is made up of many types of actants: humans and nonhumans; animals, vegetables, and minerals; nature, culture, and technology.

3. James Glanz, "When the Grid Bites Back," *International Herald Tribune*, August 18, 2003.

4. Bruno Latour defines an *actant* as something that modifies "other actors through a series of trials that can be listed thanks to some experimental protocol" (Latour, *The Politics of Nature*, trans. Catherine Porter [Cambridge: Harvard University Press, 2004], 75). "An" actant can itself be a composite entity: scientists and machines may form an actant called "the lab," which is itself a member of a larger and more diverse assemblage, e.g., the pharmaceutical industry, which under other circumstances would be the relevant actant.

5. Patrick Hayden calls these "non-totalizable sums," in "Gilles Deleuze and Naturalism: A Convergence with Ecological Theory and Politics," *Environmental Ethics* 19, no. 2 (1997): 185–204. For Henri Bergson, the universe as a whole is a nontotalizable sum, a "whole that is not given," because its evolution produces *new* members and thus an ever-changing array of effects. The world is "an indivisible process" of movement and creation, where there is "radical contingency in progress, incommensurability between what goes before and what follows—in short, duration." See Henri Bergson, *Creative Evolution* (New York: Dover, 1998), 29n1.

6. I develop this materialism in Jane Bennett, *The Enchantment of Modern Life* (Princeton: Princeton University Press, 2001) and "The Force of Things: Steps Toward an Ecology of Matter," *Political Theory* 32, no. 3 (2004): 347–72, drawing upon Henry David Thoreau's notion of the wild, Lucretius's contention of an unpredictable motility intrinsic to matter, Baruch Spinoza's claim that bodies have a natural propensity to form groups, and complexity-theory accounts of the autopoetic or self-organizing capacity of some physical systems.

7. A material body is always in the process of dissolving and reforming, albeit with periods of deceleration or relative arrest. Such bodies are alternately expressive and impressive: initially arrayed in one way, they eventually press out of one configuration and then, newly organized, can again impress upon other bodies.

8. Andrew Pickering, *The Mangle of Practice: Time, Agency, and Science* (Chicago: University of Chicago Press, 1995), 6.

9. For a subtle review of how the notion of generative negativity is differentially developed in poststructuralism, phenomenology, and critical theory, see Diana Coole, *Negativity and Politics: Dionysus and Dialectics from Kant to Poststructuralism* (New York: Routledge, 2000).

10. Romand Coles, "The Wild Patience of Radical Democracy: Beyond Žižek's Lack," in *Radical Democracy: Politics Between Abundance and Lack*, ed. Lars Tønder and Lasse Thomassen (Manchester: Manchester University Press, 2005), 68–85.

11. Baruch Spinoza, *Ethics* (New York: Hackett, 1992), 199.

12. Damir Nosovel, "System Blackout Causes and Cures," www.energypulse.net/centers/article/article_display.cfm?a_id=495.

13. U.S./Canada Power Outage Task Force, "Initial Blackout Timeline: August 14, 2003, Outage Sequence of Events," September 12, 2003, www.nrcan-rncan.gc.ca/media/documents/Blackout_Summary.pdf.

14. Ibid., 6. According to Novosel, "evaluation of disturbances shows that protection systems have been involved in 70% of the blackout events" ("System Blackout," 2).

15. Jodi Di Menna, "Grid Grief!" *Canadian Geographic*, special feature, www.canadiangeographic.ca/blackout_2003/grid.html; accessed November 20, 2003.

16. The task force was appointed by Canadian Prime Minister Jean Chrétien and U.S. President George W. Bush. The first report of the task force (issued September 12, 2003) was a description of about twenty grid "events" occurring from 2:02 P.M. until 4:11 P.M. (EST) on August 14, 2003.

17. The grid is an AC (alternating-current) system. For a fascinating historical account of the development of electrical systems, see Jill Jonnes, *Empires of Light: Edison, Tesla, Westinghouse, and the Race to Electrify the World* (New York: Random House, 2003).

18. U.S./Canada Power Outage Task Force, "Initial Blackout Timeline," 2.

19. Novosel, "System Blackout," 2.

20. Eric J. Lerner, "What's Wrong with the Electric Grid?" *The Industrial Physicist* 9, no. 5 (2003), www.aip.org/tip.

21. Garrett Hardin, "The Tragedy of the Commons," *Science* 162 (1968): 1244.

22. John A. Casazza and George C. Loehr, eds., *The Evolution of Electric Power Transmission under Deregulation: Selected Readings* (Hoboken, N.J.: Wiley, 2000), www.elucem.com/outlet/books/ieeexcerpt.html.

23. U.S./Canada Power Outage Task Force, "Initial Blackout Timeline," 7, my emphasis.

24. Matthew L. Wald, "Report on Blackout Is Said to Describe Failure to React," *New York Times*, November 12, 2003. FirstEnergy was formed from the merger of seven utilities (Toledo Edison, Cleveland Electric, Ohio Edison, Pennsylvania Power, Pennsylvania Electric, Metropolitan Edison, and Jersey Central Power & Light) and has very close ties to George W. Bush. As indicated by Tyson Slocum, "FirstEnergy President Anthony Alexander was a Bush Pioneer in 2000—meaning he raised at least $100,000—and then served on the Energy Department transition team. H. Peter Burg, the company's CEO and chairman of the board, hosted a June event that raised more than half a million dollars for Bush-Cheney '04" ("Bush Turns Blind Eye to Blackout Culprit," August 21, 2003, www.corpwatch.org/issues/PID.jsp?articleid=8131).

25. "The moral law is the sole motive of the pure will." See Immanuel Kant, *Critique of Practical Reason*, pt. 2 (Cambridge: Cambridge University Press, 1997), 115.

26. For example, Donald Davidson says that "a man is the agent of an act if what he does can be described under an aspect that makes it intentional," but what he means by this is complicated. See Davidson, *Essays on Actions and Events* (Oxford: Oxford University Press, 1980), 46.

27. Diana Coole, "Rethinking Agency: A Phenomenological Approach to Embodiment and Agentic Capacities," *Political Studies* 53, no. 1 (2005), 124–42.

28. As Maurice Merleau-Ponty describes it in *Phenomenology of Perception*, trans. Colin Smith (New York: Routledge, 1962), 110, motor intentionality is a kind of directionality inside the motion of an arm or hand that is not reducible to any subjective or self-conscious decision.

29. Bernard Stiegler contends, e.g., that conscious reflection first emerged in protohumans (millions of years ago) when they began to use stone tools. The stone tool is the first known exteriorization of memory and anticipation. Conscious interiority *emerges through* the incorporation of this nonhuman exteriority, articulated in parallel in the material evolution of the brain (corticalization). The materiality of the tool functions as an exterior "archive" of its function, recalling to consciousness its projected and recollected use, thereby producing the first interiorization, the first hollow of reflection, by way of this nonhuman outside (Stiegler, *Technics and Time 1: The Fault of Epimetheus*, trans. George Collins and Richard Beardsworth [Stanford: Stanford University Press, 1998]). I am grateful to Ben Corson for this point. See his "Speed and Technicity: A Derridean Exploration" (Ph.D. dissertation, The Johns Hopkins University, 2000).

30. This tendency to figure the efficacy of human-nonhuman groupings in passive terms is exemplified in the following quotation, which describes the consensus within archaeology: "all agree that agency refers to the intentional choices made by men and women as they take action to realize their goals . . . [But all also insist that] these actors are socially constituted beings . . . embedded in sociocultural and ecological surroundings that both define their goals and constrain their actions" (Elizabeth Brumfield, "On the Archaeology of Choice," in *Agency in Archaeology*, ed. Marcia-Anne Dobres and John E. Robb [New York: Routledge, 2000], 249). Or, as the sociologist Margaret Archer puts it, people are "both free and enchained, capable of shaping our own future and yet confronted by towering . . . constraints" (Archer, *Realist Social Theory: The Morphogenetic Approach* [Cambridge: Cambridge University Press, 1995], 65).

31. The debate over which is more potent, agency or structure, seems to have been settled with the view that agentic individuals and constraining social systems are mutually constitutive—as per Anthony Giddens's dialectical notion of structuration or Michel Foucault's idea of a disciplinary power that engenders the individual as a responsible, moral agent. But despite Foucault's insistence upon the *productive* power of collective agency, most social scientists continue to conceive of social forces as exercising only a *passive* or restraining kind of efficacy—i.e., the power to block or interrupt the more active agency of purposive individuals.

32. The extensive literature on actor network theory is usefully summarized at The Actor Network Resource, www.comp.lancs.ac.uk/sociology/ant.html.

33. See Bruno Latour, *Aramis; or, The Love of Technology* (Cambridge: Harvard University Press, 1996). See also the elegant account of *Aramis* in Eric Laurier and Chris Philo, "X-Morphising: Review Essay of Bruno Latour's *Aramis; or, The Love of Technology*," www.geog.gla.ac.uk/~elaurier/text.

34. Colin Barron, ed., "A Strong Distinction Between Humans and Non-humans Is No Longer Required for Research Purposes: A Debate Between Bruno Latour and Steve Fuller," *History of the Human Sciences* 16, no. 2 (2003): 81.

35. Adorno writes that it is simply not possible to "unseal" a concept (e.g., agency) by dividing it neatly into constituent parts; one can only "circle" around it. See Theodor W. Adorno, *Negative Dialectics*, trans. E. B. Ashton (New York: Continuum, 1999), 166.

36. Latour, *Politics of Nature*, 76.

37. Jacques Derrida, "Marx and Sons," in *Ghostly Demarcations: A Symposium on Jacques Derrida's Specters of Marx*, ed. Michael Sprinker (London: Verso, 1999), 248–51. Disappointment is absolutely essential to messianicity: the "promise is given only under the premises of the possible retraction of its offering" (Werner Hamacher, "Lingua Amissa: The Messianism of Commodity-Language and Derrida's *Specters of Marx*," in *Ghostly Demarcations*, 202).

38. Derrida, "Marx and Sons," 253–56.

39. Bergson, *Creative Evolution*, 73.

40. According to William Connolly, "emergent causality is causal . . . in that a movement at [one] . . . level has effects at another level. But it is emergent in that, first, the character of the . . . activity is not knowable in precise detail prior to effects that emerge at the second level. [Moreover,] . . . the new effects become *infused* into the very . . . organization of the second level in such a way that the cause cannot be said to be fully different from the effect engendered . . . [Third,] . . . a series of . . . feedback loops operate between first and second levels to generate the stabilized result. The new emergent is shaped not only by external forces that become infused into it but *also by its own previously under-tapped capacities for reception and self-organization.*" Connolly also says that an emergent cause is one in which the new effect is one about which we lack a clear concept before it occurs. See William Connolly, "Method, Problem, Faith," in *Problems and Methods in the Study of Politics*, ed. Ian Shapiro, Rogers Smith, and Tarek E. Masoud (Cambridge: Cambridge University Press, 2004), 342–43.

41. Hannah Arendt, "On the Nature of Totalitarianism: An Essay in Understanding," 1953, Hannah Arendt Papers of the Library of Congress, http://memory.loc.gov/cgibin/query/P?mh arendt:1:./temp/~ammem_3YUE. My thanks to John Docker for this reference. See also his "Après la Guerre: Dark Thought, Some Whimsy," *Arena Journal* 20 (2002–3): 3–16.

42. Other readings suggest that Arendt, especially given her notion of "action," may be even more amenable to a distributive notion of agency than I suggest. My thanks to Paul Saurette for this point.

43. I am grateful to George Shulman and Bonnie Honig for pointing this issue out to me.

44. Gilles Deleuze and Félix Guattari, *A Thousand Plateaus*, trans. Brian Massumi (Minneapolis: University of Minnesota Press, 1986), 313.

45. François Jullien, *The Propensity of Things: Toward a History of Efficacy in China* (New York: Zone, 1995), 13.

46. Archer, *Realist Social Theory*, 66.

47. Recall that reactive power happens when the waves of current and voltage in an electron stream are ninety degrees out of sync.

48. Hayden, "Gilles Deleuze and Naturalism," 187.

49. Latour, *Politics of Nature*, 67.

Kate Khatib, Automatic Theologies: Surrealism and the Politics of Equality

1. Karl Marx, "Contribution to the Critique of Hegel's *Philosophy of Right*" [1844], *The Marx-Engels Reader*, ed. R. Tucker (New York: Norton, 1978), 53.

2. Don LaCoss, "9–11 and the Theology of Terror" [2001], *Surrealist Subversions: Rants, Writings & Images by the Surrealist Movement in the United States*, ed. R. Sakolsky (Brooklyn: Autonomedia, 2002), 371.

3. Hent de Vries, *Philosophy and the Turn to Religion* (Baltimore: The Johns Hopkins University Press, 1999), 11.

4. Franklin Rosemont, "The Crisis of the Imagination," *Arsenal 2: Surrealist Subversions* (Chicago: Black Swan Press, 1973), 14.

5. After the death of Elisa Breton, widow of André Breton, exorbitant inheritance taxes imposed by the French government forced their daughter, Aube Elléouet, to sell her father's personal collection of art and artifacts, which had been housed for so long in the legendary flat at 42 Rue Fontaine. The announcement of the sale and the following appeals to the French government by

the "Breton committee" requesting the state to turn the collection and the apartment that housed it into a "Breton Museum," prompted outcries and protests from the surviving members of the Paris Surrealist Movement and the Surrealist Movement in the United States. See the manifestos "Surrealism Is Not for Sale!" and "Who Will Embalm the Embalmers?" online at http://www.surrealistmovement-usa.org/ for more information.

6. Penelope Rosemont, "All My Names Know Your Leap: Surrealist Women and Their Challenge," *Surrealist Women: An International Anthology* (Austin: University of Texas Press, 1998), xxix.

7. Quoted in Mike King, "Art and the Postsecular," *Journal of Visual Art Practice* 4, no. 1 (2005): 16.

8. Throughout this essay, the term *surrealism* is used to refer to the political and epistemological project that arose in France in the second decade of the twentieth century. Its use is, however, in no way limited to the praxis of the Parisian surrealists between the wars; later incarnations of this same project, in particular, the American Surrealist Movement, founded in 1966 with the explicit support of Breton and the remaining members of the Paris Surrealist Movement, are also included here not only as examples of surrealist practice but as participants and co-conspirators in exactly the same movement. I am greatly indebted to Ron Sakolsky for his incomparable discussion of Surrealism's heritage—European, American, and otherwise—in the introduction to the 2002 compendium *Surrealist Subversions*.

9. Walter Benjamin, "Surrealism: The Last Snapshot of the European Intelligentsia" [1929], trans. Edmund Jephcott, in *Walter Benjamin: Selected Writings*, vol. 2, *1927–1934*, ed. Michael W. Jennings, Howard Eiland, and Gary Smith (Cambridge: Harvard University Press, 1999), 208.

10. Walter Benjamin, "On the Program of the Coming Philosophy" [1918], trans. Rodney Livingstone, in *Walter Benjamin: Selected Writings*, vol. 1, *1913–1926*, ed. Marcus Bullock and Michael W. Jennings (Cambridge: Harvard University Press, 1996), 101.

11. Benjamin, "Surrealism," 215.

12. Benjamin had already established his unwillingness to accept any epistemological system that could not take into account the myriad experiences that the Kantian paradigm refused to accept. "A philosophy that does not include the possibility of soothsaying from *coffee grounds*," he told Gershom Scholem in 1918, "and cannot explicate it, cannot be a true philosophy" (Gershom Scholem, *Walter Benjamin: The Story of a Friendship* [1975], trans. H. Zohn [New York: Schocken Books, 1981], 59). The theory of experience that Benjamin puts forth in his early text "On the Program of the Coming Philosophy," a more or less direct response to Kant's *Prolegomena to Any Future Metaphysics*, is echoed strikingly in his essay on surrealism's critical practice, written some ten years later.

13. Benjamin, "Surrealism," 208.

14. F. Rosemont, "Crisis of the Imagination," 14. Although Chicago Surrealism would develop more than twenty years after Benjamin's death, it is, without a doubt, one of the surrealist manifestations that remains closest to what Benjamin thought of as the movement's critical and political practice. Chicago Surrealism, which grew up around the husband and wife team Franklin and Penelope Rosemont, both of whom are still vocal activists and surrealists today, is one of the most militantly political incarnations of surrealism to date. More than the Paris Surrealist Movement, whose adherents dabbled in Marxism, but could never seem to make prolonged productive use of its theories, the Chicago Surrealist Group, which was founded primarily by student activists, has a strong political background, utilizing both Marxist and anarchist theories as a springboard from which continue the development of Breton's original—if somewhat abstruse—political project. Interestingly, however, the Chicago Surrealist Group is also where surrealism begins to differ from Benjamin on a number of interesting points, among them the distinction between the unity of

concepts and the equality between concepts, which differentiates a purely messianic project from a purely political one, and the question of meaning in relation to the surrealist use of language. Both of these points of distinction are discussed at a later point in the present essay.

15. Isidore Ducasse (Comte de Lautréamont), "Poésies" [1870], *Maldoror and the Complete Works of the Comte de Lautréamont*, trans. A. Lykiard (Cambridge, Mass.: Exact Change, 1994), 244; Benjamin, "Surrealism," 208.

16. See, e.g., "On Language as Such and on the Language of Man" (in *Walter Benjamin: Selected Writings*, vol. 1), where Benjamin discusses the linguistic relationship between the divine realm and the profane world of things, some phrases from which are repeated almost explicitly in the "Surrealism" essay. See also "The Task of the Translator" in the same volume, the prefatory essay to Benjamin's translation of Charles Baudelaire's "Tableaux parisiens," in which he continues the development of the linguistic themes first discussed in "On Language as Such and On the Language of Man."

17. Benjamin, "Surrealism," 214.

18. Ibid., 210–11.

19. André Breton, "Surrealism and Painting" [1928], trans. S. W. Taylor, *Surrealism and Painting* (Boston: MFA Publications, 2002), 4.

20. P. Rosemont, *Surrealist Women*, li. Meret Oppenheim was one of the key women involved with the Surrealist Movement in France between the two world wars. She is perhaps best known as the creator of Surrealism's well-known object *Dejeuner en fourrure*, often called *Fur-Covered Cup, Saucer, and Spoon*. (See P. Rosemont, *Surrealist Women*, 74, for additional background information.)

21. Ibid.

22. Mircea Eliade, *The Sacred and the Profane: The Nature of Religion*, trans. W. Trask (New York: Harcourt Brace Jovanovich, 1959), 11.

23. Ibid.

24. Paul Ricoeur, "Manifestation and Proclamation," *Figuring the Sacred*, trans. D. Pellauer (Minneapolis: Fortress Press, 1995), 49–50.

25. Breton, "Surrealism and Painting," 46.

26. Ibid.

27. Mary Ann Caws, "Reading André Breton," *Context* 11 (2002), http://www.centerforbook culture.org/context/no11/Caws.html. "Communicating vessels" is used to describe one of the most basic examples of a system in modern physics. The experiment—or demonstration, more accurately—uses a number of vertical tubes of different heights and shapes that "communicate" by a tube that joins them together at the bottom. According to the laws of the physics of fluid, any increase or decrease of water in one tube affects the water in all of the other tubes and results in an immediate reshifting of matter to achieve an absolute equality in the water level, and thus the potential energy of the milligrams of water on the surface of each tube. In essence, the communicating vessels effectively represent a single vessel. See Ranier Radok's online discussion of this system for more information: http://kr.cs.ait.ac.th/~radok/physics/e2.htm.

28. Benjamin, "Surrealism," 209.

29. Breton, "Surrealism and Painting," 9.

30. Quoted in David Gascoyne, "Introduction to *The Magnetic Fields*," *The Automatic Message* (London: Atlas Press, 1997), 44.

31. Ibid., 41.

32. André Breton, "Manifesto of Surrealism" [1924], trans. R. Seaver and H. R. Lane, *Manifestoes of Surrealism* (Ann Arbor: University of Michigan Press, 1972), 30.

33. On the first use of "stream of consciousness," see chapter 10 of William James, *Principles of Psychology* (1890), where James outlines the concept as a collection of ever-changing inner thoughts and sensations that belong to every conscious individual. Dujardin was the first author to notably employ this technique, in his 1888 novel *Les Lauriers sont coupes*, although May Sinclair was, perhaps, the first explicitly to transfer the term from the psychological context to the literary one.

34. F. Rosemont, "Crisis of the Imagination," 15.

35. The fact that the surrealist experience of the world always has a basis in real, lived experience resonates interestingly with the historical genesis of the practice of automatism, which has its roots in the dual sense of "psychic" in Breton's "psychic automatism in its pure state" (Breton, "Manifesto of Surrealism," 26). On the one hand, *psychic* refers back to the psychoanalytic theories of Freud and to the practice of diagnostic hypnosis, from which some of the early surrealist experiments drew their inspiration. On the other hand, and in a totally different sense of *psychic*, automatism also owes much to the practice of mystics, as well as to mediums and soothsayers. See Gascoyne's introduction to *The Magnetic Fields* for more information on the development of automatism, or see Breton's own "The Automatic Message" in the same volume for a brief history of automatism from the standpoint of surrealism.

36. Maurice Blanchot, "Reflections on Surrealism" [1949], trans. Charlotte Mandell, in Blanchot *The Work of Fire* (Stanford: Stanford University Press, 1995), 86.

37. Ibid., 88.

38. Benjamin, "Surrealism," 208.

39. On the question of practical truth in poetry, see Lautréamont, "Poésies," 237, and F. Rosemont, "Crisis of the Imagination," 14.

40. André Breton, "Introduction to the Discourse on the Paucity of Reality" [1924], in Breton, *What Is Surrealism? Selected Writings* (New York: Pathfinder, 1978), 25.

41. Ibid.

42. Ibid.

43. F. Rosemont, "Crisis of the Imagination," 14.

44. Suzanne Césaire [1941], quoted in P. Rosemont, *Surrealist Women*, lii.

45. André Breton, "The Automatic Message" [1933], trans. A. Melville, *The Automatic Message* (London: Atlas Press, 1997), 26, my emphasis.

46. Anne Olsen, "The Marvelous Against the Sacred" [2001], *Surrealist Subversions*, 368.

47. Walter Benjamin, "On the Concept of History" [1940], trans. H. Zohn, *Walter Benjamin: Selected Writings*, vol. 4, *1938–1940* (Cambridge: Harvard University Press, 2003), Thesis XVII, p. 397. The translation of *die kleine Pforte* as "the strait gate" is actually from an earlier version of Zohn's translation, published in *Illuminations* (New York: Schocken Books, 1978). In his revised translation for the Harvard collection, Zohn renders the phrase "the small gateway in time through which the Messiah might enter."

Stefanos Geroulanos, Theoscopy: Transparency, Omnipotence, and Modernity

1. Thomas Pynchon, Preface to George Orwell, *Nineteen Eighty-Four* (Harmondsworth, Middlesex: Penguin, 2003).

2. Augustine, *Confessions*, trans. H. Chadwick (Oxford: Oxford University Press, 1992), 10.2, p. 179. See also 10.5, with its citation of 1 Corinthians 13:12.

3. Augustine describes this torment in part in the *Confessions*, e.g., 5.20, pp. 85–86.

4. Niklas Luhmann, "Contingency as Modern Society's Defining Attribute," *Observations on Modernity* (Stanford: Stanford University Press, 1998), 51–52.

5. See, e.g.: Jean-Jacques Rousseau, *Emile*, trans. and ed. Allan Bloom (New York: Basic Books, 1979); Jeremy Bentham, *The Panopticon Writings*, ed. Miran Bozovic (London: Verso, 1998). Foucault himself explicitly connects Rousseau to Bentham in his interview "The Eye of Power," *Power/ Knowledge* (New York: Pantheon, 1981), 152. A list of texts that redrew the maps of surveillance, regulation, and pedagogy by humanizing yet also problematizing univectoral scopic regimes should also include the early discussions in Thomas Hobbes's *Leviathan* and Etienne de la Boétie's *Discourse on Voluntary Servitude*.

6. The path of this motif can be traced from Protestantism and seventeenth-century Jansenism through Rousseau's social contract, democratic theory, utopian socialism, and Marxism (most significantly, Georg Lukács's *History and Class Consciousness*). Writing on Rousseau, Jean Starobinski has argued that the divine gaze posited the transparency and opacity of man with regard to the gaze of God and hence recreated the conception of the Fall, this time as within (recent) human history. See his *Jean-Jacques Rousseau: Transparency and Obstruction* (Chicago: University of Chicago Press, 1988), cited in Martin Jay, *Downcast Eyes: The Denigration of Vision in Twentieth-Century French Thought* (Berkeley: University of California Press, 1993), 90–91. T. J. Clark links Debord with Rousseau in his foreword to Anselm Jappe's *Guy Debord* (Berkeley: University of California Press, 1999), viii.

7. By contrast, in the recent outburst of scholarship on Western visuality this link is underexamined, and theological implications and subtexts to vision-related themes and the political regimes these facilitate are ignored. See, e.g., David Michael Levin, ed., *Modernity and the Hegemony of Vision* (Berkeley: University of California Press, 1993); Jay, *Downcast Eyes*; and Jonathan Crary, *Techniques of the Observer: Vision and Modernity in the Nineteenth Century* (Cambridge: MIT Press, 1990). But see Astrit Schmidt-Burkhardt, "The All-Seer: God's Eye as Proto-Surveillance," in Thomas Y. Levin, Ursula Frohne, and Peter Weibel, eds. *CTRL[SPACE]* (Cambridge: MIT Press, 2002), 17–31. Schmidt-Burkhardt provides a more elaborate, but far from exhaustive art-historical view of God the All-Seer. Jay does study the relationship between religion and spectatorship, though not really past the nineteenth century, and he treats it only as a metaphor in his discussion of Foucault and Debord.

8. For the purposes of the present essay, I will consider mainly the Foucault of the mid-1970s and the Debord of *Society of the Spectacle,* trans. Donald Nicholson-Smith (New York: Zone Books, 1994; with references to paragraph, not to page). In the case of Foucault, this choice does not express the range and transformation of his work but addresses his work on power, which is my main interest here.

9. Luhmann and certain other thinkers could be discussed in the same context. But Luhmann's concept of observation is much closer to cognition and intentional activity than the ones of Foucault and Debord, which center on the visual (and indeed, passive) aspects of the gaze. Foucault's concept of observation also shares a cognitive dimension (Foucault, *Birth of the Clinic* [London: Routledge, 1997], 107), but it presupposes a *gaze*—a specifically *visual* apprehension of the world.

10. The distance is suggested by, among others, Jappe, *Guy Debord*, 133. The New Left's suspicion of Foucault is described well by Cornelius Castoriadis in *World in Fragments: Writings on Politics, Society, Psychoanalysis, and the Imagination*, ed. and trans. David Ames Curtis (Stanford: Stanford University Press, 1997), 34, 51ff.

11. Foucault, *Discipline and Punish*, 217. Note Foucault's use and rejection of terms that have situationist resonance: spectacle, abstraction of exchange, surface of images, amputation of the

("beautiful"!) totality of the individual, stage, etc. Also note Foucault's revision in his attention to bodies, the formation of individuals, the training of forces, the play of signs, etc.

12. Despite their differences, Foucault and Debord share an important debt to Jean Hyppolite—whom Foucault respected immensely, and whose 1967 lectures Debord followed. See Didier Eribon, *Michel Foucault et ses contemporains* (Paris: Fayard, 1994), and Jappe, *Guy Debord*, 128n.

13. It is unfair to speak of Debord and "power." Fairly standard readings of Debord see his understanding of power as bound by the limits of classical Marxism. Nonetheless, Debord did speak of power *as such*, and he set it at once in and at the root of the spectacle (Debord, *Society of the Spectacle*, §§22–23). It is also worth wondering whether Debord and Foucault's respective conceptions of spectacle/power and power differ completely (see Debord's usage of *power* as *practical* or *specialized*; ibid.), especially in their nonempirical, transcendental aspects. While I do not wish to reduce spectacle to power, I will occasionally use the latter for purposes of simplicity.

14. "I'd like to mention only two 'pathological forms'—those two 'diseases of power'—fascism and Stalinism. One of the numerous reasons why they are so puzzling for us is that, in spite of their historical uniqueness, they are not quite original. They used and extended mechanisms already present in most other societies . . . they used, to a large extent, the ideas and devices of our political rationality" (Foucault, "The Subject and Power," in *Power: Essential Works of Foucault, 1954–1984*, vol. 3, ed. James D. Faubion [New York: The New Press, 2000], 328). The "evil" remark is in Foucault, "The Ethics of the Concern for the Self as a Practice of Freedom," in *Ethics, Subjectivity, and Truth: Essential Works of Foucault, 1954–1984*, vol. 1, ed. Paul Rabinow (New York: The New Press, 1997), 298. See also Foucault, "Body/Power" and "Truth and Power," in *Power/Knowledge*, 59 and 124–25.

15. The connection to Socialisme ou barbarie was first made in Richard Gombin, *Les Origines du gauchisme* (Paris: Seuil, 1971). Gombin's history is too linear and teleological, by contrast to the somewhat better Jappe, *Guy Debord*, 90–93. Jappe notes Debord's relative respect for *Les Origines du gauchisme* (175).

16. "The ruling class of Europe is all but . . . forgotten. . . . Television won't talk about it, and the left only talks about what television talks about" (*Internationale Situationniste*, 10:32). Debord's Situationist International celebrated the failure of the New Left journal *Arguments* and loudly rejected Lefebvre.

17. Debord, *Society of the Spectacle*, §§24–28, 54, 63, 69, 72.

18. Jay, in *Downcast Eyes* (chap. 7), provides clear and cogent analyses of Debord and Foucault, and indicates the difference in the traditions from which the two emerged. Jay does not elaborate on the specific topic I am considering here, and it is somewhat peculiar that he is hesitant to draw a closer connection between the two. Ultimately, he limits his conclusion to: "Foucault's critique of surveillance and Debord's of the spectacle provided a generation of critics with ammunition in their struggle against the hegemony of the eye" (434).

19. Foucault, *Birth of the Clinic*, 107; also 54.

20. Debord, *Society of the Spectacle*, §§4, 1.

21. Curiously, the spectacle is absent from Debord's writings between *Potlatch* and the last issues of the *Situationist International*. Among Debord's nine signed articles in the latter, only one centers on the "spectacular character of modern industrial society." This is his presentation of the opening of *Society of the Spectacle* in "La Séparation achevée," 11:43–48. Unsigned editorials also shy away from the issue. Foucault did not use the term *spectacle* extensively; on the most significant occasion, he uses it to determine the apprehensible stage of the scaffold as a political operation (*Discipline and Punish*, chap. 2, esp. 53).

22. See Thomas Y. Levin, "Dismantling the Spectacle: The Cinema of Guy Debord," in *On the Passage of a Few People Through a Rather Brief Moment in Time*, ed. Elizabeth Sussmann (Cam-

bridge: MIT Press, 1989), 73–78. Republished in Tom McDonough, ed., *Guy Debord and the Situationist International* (Cambridge: MIT Press, 2002), reference on 321–28.

23. This very excess explains, insofar as Debord's work is concerned, a popularization and even denigration of the concept of the spectacle in seventies tracts and eighties postmodernism (notably in Baudrillard). Jonathan Crary remarks on the problem in "Spectacle, Attention, Counter-Memory," in *Guy Debord and the Situationist International*, ed. McDonough, 455–66.

24. Foucault, *Discipline and Punish*, 195–228.

25. Foucault, "Governmentality," in *Power*, 201–22.

26. See the essays in Michel Foucault, *Religion and Culture*, ed. Jeremy Carrette (London: Routledge, 1999), as well as: "Afterword to *The Temptation of Saint Anthony*"; "The Thought of the Outside"; the writings on the Enlightenment in "What is Enlightenment?" and "What is Critique?"; the essays on ethics and the short pieces on Pasolini and Syderbergh, namely, "Sade: Sergeant of Sex," "The Gray Mornings of Tolerance," and "The Four Horsemen of the Apocalypse and the Everyday Worms," collected in the *Essential Works*. Many of these texts, even when not treating religious themes, take seriously the relations between philosophy and religion, questions of ethics, humanism, and non-Christian categories of theological (or para-theological) value.

27. Alexander Nehamas, *The Art of Living: Socrative Reflections from Plato to Foucault* (Berkeley: University of California Press, 2000), 170.

28. See Jeremy Carrette, "Prologue to a Confession of the Flesh," in Foucault, *Religion and Culture*, ed. Carrette, 5–6.

29. Cf. ibid., 31—Carrette completely ignores and undermines this comment. There is a deep and definitive vulnerability and uncertainty in Christian categories, highlighted perhaps most clearly in Foucault's "Afterword to the *Temptation of Saint Anthony*." It is not that Foucault is not pleased to use them, but rather that he uses them with the same excess that characterizes his use of non-Christian categories, an excess that betrays the hope of their rejuvenation in a different context.

30. Foucault, *The Order of Things: An Archaeology of the Human Sciences* (New York: Vintage, 1994), 342.

31. Foucault, *Discipline and Punish*, 194, emphasis in original; trans. modified.

32. Ibid.

33. Foucault, "Omnes et Singulatim," *Power*, 308.

34. Foucault describes this case in "Truth and Juridical Forms," in *Power*, 74–75.

35. In *Political Theology*, Schmitt couples historical development with foundation and structural analogy. See Carl Schmitt, *Political Theology: Four Chapters on the Concept of Sovereignty*, trans. G. Schwab (Cambridge: MIT Press, 1989), esp. 36–37. Blumenberg, Courtine, and de Vries have all noted the fragility of setting up the theologico-political on derivation and foundation, though it seems to me the structural element is not lost in Schmitt. See Jean-François Courtine, "Problèmes théologico-politiques," in *Nature et empire de la loi* (Paris: Vrin, 1999), 167–68, cited in de Vries, *Religion and Violence*, 218.

36. Foucault, "The Subject and Power," *Power*, 332.

37. Foucault, *Discipline and Punish*, 28–29.

38. Ibid., 29.

39. Foucault, "Omnes et Singulatim," *Power*, 325.

40. I take the term *isomorphism* from Foucault's consideration of Raymond Roussel's language as self-immobilizing and gradually regressing, as "isomorphic" to death, in "Seeing and Speaking in Raymond Roussel," *Aesthetics, Method and Epistemology: Essential Works of Foucault, 1954–1984*, vol. 2, ed. James D. Faubion (New York: The New Press, 1999), 27. Here, "isomorphic" does not suggest *perfect* analogy; instead, it retains a certain component of (perhaps asymptotic) approximation. It also retains the optical metaphor that "analogous" reduces to a certain mathematics.

41. The remark "infinite" is in Foucault, "Useless to Revolt?" in *Power*, 452.

42. Foucault, "The Subject and Power," ibid., 327.

43. Hubert Dreyfus and Paul Rabinow, *Michel Foucault: Beyond Structuralism and Hermeneutics*, 2d ed. (Berkeley: University of California Press, 1983), 241.

44. Foucault, "Omnes and Singulatim," *Power*, 307.

45. Foucault, "Useless to Revolt?" ibid., 449–53.

46. Foucault, *The Order of Things*, chap. 9, esp. 310–11.

47. Foucault, "The Order of Things," in *Aesthetics, Method, and Epistemology*, 264.

48. Foucault, *The Order of Things*, 309.

49. Foucault notes, in *The Order of Things*, that the creation of "man" in the modern era occurs at about the time of the death of God but is not recognized as such until much later, with Nietzsche and the rise of anthropology (and structuralism), to say the least (*The Order of Things*, 342). It is significant that Foucault elsewhere suggests having taken up the "end of man" directly from Nietzsche and the space that he leaves open when he declares God to be dead (Foucault, *Religion and Culture*, 85). It is not the temporal connection between Nietzsche and the "modern age" that defines modern man, but rather man's self-knowledge in its link to this opening.

50. Foucault, *The Order of Things*, 312.

51. Ibid., 313–15. Of course, the "analytic of finitude" is a Heideggerian theme, one of several I have alluded to here (e.g., the existential/epistemological, or, in Heidegger's terms, existentiell/existential distinction targeted earlier). Though references to Heidegger are largely absent from Foucault's texts, a thorough engagement with Heidegger is central not only to this motif but also to other issues throughout *The Order of Things* (esp. the section "The Analytic of Finitude," 312–18) and especially *The Archaeology of Knowledge*. To expand upon this analysis is, however, beyond the scope of the present discussion.

52. Foucault, *The Order of Things*, 314, my emphasis.

53. Ibid., 264.

54. Foucault, *Discipline and Punish*, 226.

55. Ibid., 204.

56. Ibid., 216, amended translation in brackets.

57. Ibid., 200, 202.

58. Ibid., 201.

59. Ibid., 317n.4.

60. Ibid., 206.

61. Consider, e.g., Rome's Pantheon, which was later rededicated to the Virgin Mary; or the original dome of Constantinople's Hagia Sophia, which appeared to be floating in the sky due to its separation from the main ceiling through the use of windows; or the (occasional) depiction in Orthodox churches of a decorporealized divine eye in the dome or the ceiling ("sky") of the congregation area. See also Schmidt-Burkhardt, "The All-Seer."

62. Martin Jay hints at this but never treats it as a specific analytic behind the later Foucault's theory of vision and power. See his *Downcast Eyes*, 408.

63. Jay correctly notes that Foucault "resisted exploring" the potential of *le regard* as a "reciprocal, intersubjective, communicative" exchange (*Downcast Eyes*, 414–15). I would also point out that Foucault's conception of vision is almost by definition univectoral, because of his powerful intent of founding it on scopic asymmetry and the fundamental potential absence of a determinable viewer "seeing the subject." As such, the return of a gaze is but a different gaze, having the same (vis-à-vis the first gaze, contrasting) power effects of such a singular, other gaze. In a mode that has reached considerable popularity through films like *The Conversation* and *Enemy of the State*, the

established surveillant regime is overturned by the sheer presence of an active counter-gaze. I think that, counter to de Certeau's and Jay's claim that Foucault ignored the potential of resistant micro-practices, Foucault was specifically unwilling to accept that they operate outside, or even on a different foundation from, the panoptic apparatus characteristic of "the hegemonic ocular apparatus" (*Downcast Eyes*, 415, 415n.124).

64. As Jay has written, "the Panopticon, with its hidden and invisible God, was an architectural embodiment of the most paranoid sartrean fantasies of the absolute look" (*Downcast Eyes*, 410).

65. Foucault explicitly reduces an observer to the gaze in "The Eye of Power," *Power/Knowledge*, 155.

66. Bentham, *The Panopticon Writings*.

67. Foucault suggests that the rules of the Panopticon still apply in a more complicated and less surveillant social space, though in a somewhat different manner. Scopic asymmetry breaks into dissymmetry but does not disappear: the viewers multiply, as do the viewed, and the connections between them become less absolute. The basic fact, however, does not change: you still do not know when or how you are being watched, what the other sees, and so forth. The trick to the Panopticon, to Foucault's power theory in general, follows from this premise: being seen no longer requires an actual spectator, a specific or literal observer.

68. Foucault, *Discipline and Punish*, 206.

69. Greil Marcus's remarkable *Lipstick Traces: A Secret History of the Twentieth Century* (Cambridge: Harvard University Press, 1989), treats the Anabaptists of Münster as part of the same antinomian, negationist spirit as punk and the situationists but, for obvious reasons, an extended analysis of the "affinity" cannot be substantiated. Situationist-inspired tracts on religion tend to identify religion with religious authorities ("the Church") and these with the spectacle—which is not Debord's attitude. See the pamphlet by SI translator Ken Knabb, "The Realization and Suppression of Religion" (http://library.nothingness.org/articles/SI/en/display/85; last accessed Aug. 1, 2002).

70. A good example is the line "The Cathars Were Right," from the LI journal *Potlatch*, (Guy Debord, ed. *Potlatch* [Paris: Gallimard, 1996], 33–34). See Marcus's analysis in *Lipstick Traces*, 399–406.

71. Marcus describes the incident in *Lipstick Traces*, 279–96.

72. I am not reducing Debord's spectacle to its visual dimension, but rather using his own note in *Society of the Spectacle* that "the spectacle is heir to all the weakness of the project of Western Philosophy, which was an attempt to understand activity by means of the categories of vision" (*Society of the Spectacle*, §19). This negotiation of the problematics of vision makes possible my discussion of visual themes.

73. This concerns especially the questions of time, the sacred, and the issue of potlatch. Both Debord's group and Bataille picked up on Marcel Mauss's discussion of potlatch, though their respective analyses differ fundamentally. Also compare to Debord Bataille's rejection of capitalism as destructive of intimacy and productive of a false, illusory historical mission, in *The Accursed Share*, vol. 1 (New York: Zone, 1991), 76–77, 126–27, 140–41.

74. Debord, *Society of the Spectacle*, §25.

75. Ibid., §§138, 102, emphasis in original.

76. Debord uses "seemingly" to denote the pointlessness of such choice, which he considers equivalent to the presentation of modern society with the glittering distractions of the spectacle.

77. All quotes in the above paragraph are from Debord, *Society of the Spectacle*, §59; emphasis is Debord's.

78. There is a significant reference in Jappe's *Guy Debord* to Lukács's reliance on Max Weber, though it seems to me that Jappe has ignored the profound difference between Debord's consider-

ation of religion and Lukács's usage of Weber. "In 1923, Lukács recorded the passing of all totality and implicitly adopted Max Weber's notion of the "disenchantment of the world"; Debord indeed evokes continued global domination by a "banalizing trend" (*Society of the Spectacle*, §59), but he sees this as arising from a spurious reconstruction of the totality, from a totalitarian dictatorship of the fragmentary" (Jappe, *Guy Debord*, 25). Jappe suggests an analogy between a "disenchantment of the world" (for which he offers no citation) and a "banalizing trend," which is not uncalled for. Nonetheless, I am not convinced by the analogy, which glosses over what Debord says of "the vestiges of religion" in *Society of the Spectacle*, §59.

79. Foucault, like Debord, was a major exponent of the illusive aspect of "gratification," so touted in the 1960s, and he spoke repeatedly of control via stimulation. See Foucault, "Body/Power," in *Power/Knowledge*, 59. See also his *The History of Sexuality, Volume I: An Introduction*, trans. Robert Hurley (New York: Vintage, 1995).

80. Ludwig Feuerbach, *The Essence of Christianity* (Amherst, N.Y.: Prometheus, 1989), xix, in Debord, *Society of the Spectacle*, §10; translation amended by D. Nicholson-Smith; emphasis Debord's.

81. Debord, *Society of the Spectacle*, §§3, 25 etc.

82. Ibid., §1.

83. Jappe, *Guy Debord*, 8.

84. Debord, *Society of the Spectacle*, §20.

85. For the term *situationists*, I use Debord's 1958 definition: "An international association of situationists can be considered to be a union of the workers of an advanced sector of culture, or, to be exact, to be a union of all those who reclaim the right to a labor that social conditions presently harness, and thus as a quest seeking the organized positioning of professional revolutionaries in culture" (Guy Debord, "Theses sur la Révolution Culturelle," *Internationale Situationniste* 1:21 [thesis 4], my translation).

86. My analysis of the spectacle not only owes a considerable debt to the first part of Jappe's *Guy Debord* but essentially subsumes it, in part for the sake of brevity. As regards my use of the term *power*, it is important to recall that, unlike Foucault, Debord is profoundly indebted to the Marxist tradition and presents power as a priori separated from the worker/consumer qua subject. Debord opposed the division between bourgeoisie and proletariat, preferring to posit a class of masters (which *does not* comprise subjects, only implied "system managers"), against a "proletarianised world" separated from power and dominated by the spectacle. (See Debord, *Society of the Spectacle*, §26–29, 33.)

87. Ibid., §§25, 39.

88. Ibid., §25. See also §23.

89. Read somewhat against the grain, Debord's spectacle reflects some of Foucault's thoughts, in *The Order of Things*, about the discourse of man. In a further, lesser parallel, the two thinkers set up the implications of their respective concepts very differently. But compare Debord on the spectacle's distortion of life to Foucault's "There was no longer any transparency between the order of things and the representations that one could have of them; things were folded somehow into their own thickness and onto a demand exterior to representation. It is for this reason that languages with their history, life with its organization and its autonomy, and work with its own capacity for production appeared" (*The Order of Things*, 264).

90. Debord, *Society of the Spectacle*, §§60, 72.

91. Clark, Foreword to Jappe, *Guy Debord*, ix.

92. Compare Adorno's "What the philosophers once knew as life has become the sphere of private existence and now of mere consumption, dragged along as an appendage of the process of

material production, without autonomy or substance of its own" (*Minima Moralia* [London: Verso, 1978], 15) to Debord's opening "The whole life of those societies in which modern conditions of production prevail presents itself as an immense accumulation of spectacles. All that was once directly lived has become mere representation" (*Society of the Spectacle*, §1). Both of these, of course, rest on the opening of Marx's *Capital*.

93. It is interesting that, once the *Bilderverbot* trope is introduced, resonances multiply between Debord and Adorno's essay "The Culture Industry" (in Max Horkheimer and Theodor W. Adorno, *Dialectic of Enlightenment: Philosophical Fragments*, ed. Gunzelin Schmid Noerr, trans. Edmund Jephcott [Stanford: Stanford University Press, 2002], 94–136). For the latter, see Anson Rabinbach, "The Cunning of Unreason," in *In the Shadow of Catastrophe* (Berkeley: University of California Press, 1997), chap. 5, and Gertrud Koch, "Mimesis and the Ban on Images," in *Religion and Media*, ed. Hent de Vries and Samuel Weber (Stanford: Stanford University Press, 2001), 151–62.

94. Debord, *Society of the Spectacle*, §1.

95. Ibid. §4–5.

96. See Levin, "Dismantling the Spectacle," in *On the Passage of a Few People Through a Rather Brief Moment in Time*, ed. Sussmann, 73–78, 321–28.

97. Debord, *Society of the Spectacle*, §18.

98. Ibid., §20.

99. Ibid., §§16, 22–23.

100. Ibid., §25.

101. Ibid., §12.

102. This is precisely why Debord endorses the demonstration of the spectacle's contradictions as a tactic for undermining its pretense to being a unified whole.

103. Debord, *Society of the Spectacle*, §13, my emphasis.

104. Ibid., §125.

105. Ibid., §136.

106. Ibid., §§135–38.

107. Ibid., §138, italics in original.

108. The argument regarding Debord's theory of history is not directed toward the identification of Marxism with messianism; nonetheless, several indications could be made. Most striking, here, is how explicitly Debord accepts the analogy.

109. Debord, *Society of the Spectacle*, §§148, 142.

110. Ibid., §150. Debord's irreversible time also carries with it echoes of Bataille's analysis of time, intimacy, and religion in *The Accursed Share*, esp. 131–32, 140.

111. Debord, *Society of the Spectacle*, §149.

112. Ibid., §153.

113. Ibid., §§155, 158.

114. Ibid., §105.

115. Ibid., §29.

116. "The revolutionary project of a classless society, of a generalized historical life, is also the project of a withering away of the social measurement of time in favor of an individual and collective irreversible time which is playful in character and which encompasses simultaneously present within it a variety of autonomous yet effectively federated times—the complete realization, in short, within the medium of time, of that communism which 'abolishes everything that exists independently of individuals'" (ibid., §163).

Thierry de Duve, Come On, Humans, One More Effort if You Want to be Post-Christians!

An earlier version of this essay appeared in the catalog for Heaven, an exhibition held from July 30 to October 17, 1999, at the Kunsthall Düsseldorf, and from December 11 to February 27, 2000, at the Tate Gallery, published by Hatje Cantz Verlag, Ostfildern-Ruit, Germany.

1. Marcel Gauchet, *Le Désenchantement du monde: Une histoire politique de la religion* (Paris: Gallimard, 1985), v.

2. Ibid., 12.

3. Max Weber, *The Protestant Ethic and the Spirit of Capitalism* (London: Routledge, 1992).

4. Olympe de Gouges (1755–93), French woman of letters, of revolutionary persuasion, author of the *Déclaration des droits de la femme et de la citoyenne* (1792).

5. See: Hans Jonas, *Der Gottesbegriff nach Auschwitz: Eine jüdische Stimme* (Frankfurt am Main: Suhrkamp, 1984); Emmanuel Levinas, *Ethics and Infinity: Conversations with Philippe Nemo*, trans. Richard A. Cohen (Pittsburgh: Duquesne University Press), and *Totality and Infinity: An Essay on Exteriority*, trans. Alphonso Lingis (Pittsburgh: Duquesne University Press, 1969).

6. Levinas, *Ethics and Infinity*, 99.

7. "To my mind, the Infinite comes in the signifyingness of the face. The face *signifies* the Infinite. It never appears as a theme, but in this ethical signifyingness itself; that is, in the fact that the more I am just the more I am responsible; one is never quits with regard to the Other" (ibid., 105). And also: "The face is what one cannot kill, or at least it is that whose *meaning* consists in saying: 'thou shalt not kill'" (ibid., 87).

8. See Marie-José Mondzain, *Image, Icon, Economy: The Byzantine Sources of the Contemporary Imaginary*, trans. Rico Franses (Stanford: Stanford University Press, 2005).

9. Alain Badiou, *Saint Paul: The Foundation of Universalism*, trans. Ray Brassier (Stanford: Stanford University Press, 2003), 74.

10. Ibid., 59.

11. "We are confronted here with a profound general problem: Can one conceive of the event as a function, as a mediation? We should mention in passing that this question ran through the entire epoch of revolutionary politics. For many of those faithful to it, the revolution is not what arrives, but what must arrive so that there can be something else; it is communism's mediation, the moment of the negative. . . . For Paul, by contrast, just as for those who think a revolution is a self-sufficient sequence of political truth, Christ is *a coming* [une venue]; he is what interrupts the previous regime of discourses. Christ is, in himself and for himself, *what happens to us*. And what is it that happens to us thus? We are relieved of the law. . . . This question is decisive for Paul, because it is only by being relieved of the law that one truly becomes a son. And an event is falsified if it does not give rise to a universal becoming-son. Through the event, we enter into filial equality" (ibid., 48–49).

12. Gauchet, *Le Désenchantement du monde*, 195–97.

13. "Through Christ's death, God renounces his transcendent separation, he unseparates himself through filiation and shares in a constitutive dimension of the divided human subject. In so doing he creates, not the event, but what I call its site" (Badiou, *Saint Paul*, 70).

14. Ibid., 10–11.

15. For example: "The wife does not rule over her own body, but the husband does . . . and likewise the husband does not rule over his own body, but the wife does" (1 Corinthians 7:4, quoted in ibid., 104).

16. Ibid., 105.

17. Ibid., 87.

18. "The fundamental question is that of knowing precisely what it means for there to be a single God. What does the 'mono' in 'monotheism' mean? Here Paul confronts—but also renews the terms of—the formidable question of the One. His genuinely revolutionary conviction is that *the sign of the One is the 'for all,' or the 'without exception.'* That there is but a single God must be understood not as a philosophical speculation concerning substance or the supreme being, but on the basis of a structure of address. The One is that which inscribes no difference in the subjects to which it addresses itself" (ibid., 76).

Werner Hamacher, The Right Not to Use Rights: Human Rights and the Structure of Judgments

1. See Emmanuel Levinas, *Otherwise than Being; or, Beyond Essence* (Pittsburgh: Duquesne University Press, 1998), 190 and 199.

2. Tibor Déry, *Herr G. A. in X,* trans. Eva and Stephan Vajda (Frankfurt am Main: S. Fischer, 1966), 291–93.

3. Walter Benjamin, *Selected Writings*, vol. 2, *1927–1934*, ed. Michael W. Jennings, Howard Eiland, and Gary Smith (Cambridge: Harvard University Press, 1999), 68; trans. modified.